Sociology

Sociology

Sixth Edition

John E. Farley
and
Michael W. Flota

Paradigm Publishers
Boulder • London

Paradigm Publishers is committed to preserving ancient forests and natural resources. We elected to print this title on 30% post consumer recycled paper, processed chlorine free. As a result, for this printing, we have saved:

29 Trees (40' tall and 6-8" diameter)
13,031 Gallons of Wastewater
11 Million BTU's of Total Energy
826 Pounds of Solid Waste
2,890 Pounds of Greenhouse Gases

Paradigm Publishers made this paper choice because our printer, Thomson-Shore, Inc., is a member of Green Press Initiative, a nonprofit program dedicated to supporting authors, publishers, and suppliers in their efforts to reduce their use of fiber obtained from endangered forests.

For more information, visit www.greenpressinitiative.org

Environmental impact estimates were made using the Environmental Defense Paper Calculator. For more information visit: www.papercalculator.org.

All rights reserved. No part of the publication my be transmitted or reproduced in any media or form, including electronic, mechanical, photocopy, recording, or informational storage and retrieval systems, without the express written consent of the publisher.

Copyright © 2012 by Paradigm Publishers

Published in the United States by Paradigm Publishers, 2845 Wilderness Place, Suite 200, Boulder, Colorado 80301 USA.

Paradigm Publishers is the trade name of Birkenkamp & Company, LLC, Dean Birkenkamp, President and Publisher.

Library of Congress Cataloging-in-Publication Data

Farley, John E.
  Sociology / John E. Farley and Michael Flota. — 6th ed.
      p. cm.
  Includes bibliographical references and index.
  ISBN 978-1-59451-804-1 (pbk. : alk. paper)
  1. Sociology. I. Flota, Michael. II. Title.
  HM585.F37 2011
  301—dc23

2011019107

Printed and bound in the United States of America on acid free paper that meets the standards of the American National Standard for Permanence of Paper for Printed Library Materials.

Designed and Typeset by Straight Creek Bookmakers
15 14 13 12 11   1 2 3 4 5

To Alice Farley and JoAnna Conley-Flota
With love and gratitude

Brief Contents

List of Boxes, Figures, Photographs, and Tables	*xxiii*
Preface	*xxxvii*
Acknowledgments	*xliii*
About the Authors	*xlvii*

Part I   Introduction
Chapter 1	Sociology: The Discipline	3
Chapter 2	How Sociology Is Done	25

Part II   Society and Human Interaction
Chapter 3	Perspectives on Society and Interaction	51
Chapter 4	Culture and Social Structure	79
Chapter 5	Socialization	119

Part III   Social Structure and Inequality
Chapter 6	Stratification: Structured Social Inequality	151
Chapter 7	Race and Ethnic Relations	185
Chapter 8	Sex, Gender, and Society	219
Chapter 9	Groups, Organizations, and the Workplace	261
Chapter 10	Deviance, Crime, and Social Control	291

Part IV   Social Institutions
Chapter 11	Economy and Society	325
Chapter 12	Politics, Power, and Society	365
Chapter 13	Marriages and Families	397
	Web-Based Chapter A: Education	
	Web-Based Chapter B: Religion	
	Web-Based Chapter C: Health, Population, and Aging	

Part V   Social Change
Chapter 14	Urban Society: City Life and Collective Behavior	437
Chapter 15	Social Movements and Change	479

Glossary	*G-1*
References	*R-1*
Index	*I-1*

Contents

List of Boxes   xxiii
List of Figures   xxvii
List of Photographs   xxix
List of Tables   xxxv
Preface   xxxvii
Acknowledgments   xliii
About the Authors   xlvii

Part I   Introduction

Chapter 1
Sociology: The Discipline   3

- **What Is Sociology?** 4
  - Characteristics of Sociology 4
  - Sociology and Common Sense 5
- **Sociology as a Science** 6
  - Science as a Way of Thinking 6
  - The Norms of Science 8
- **Sociology as a Social Science** 8
  - Can Human Behavior Be Studied Scientifically? 8
  - An Analogy: Meteorology 9
  - Complications in the Study of Human Behavior 9
  - The Sociological Imagination 10
- **Sociology and the Other Social Sciences** 12
  - Sociology 12
  - The Other Social Sciences 12
- **The Emergence and Development of Sociology** 13
  - The Nineteenth Century 13
  - Early Sociologists 13
- **The Development of Sociology in the United States** 17
  - The Chicago School 17
  - Symbolic-Interactionism 18
- **1940–1960: A Turn from Activism** 18
- **The 1960s: Return to Activism** 19
- **The 1970s into the New Millennium: Diversity in Sociological Perspectives** 19
- **PUTTING SOCIOLOGY TO WORK** 19
  - How Sociology Can Be Used to Solve Real-Life Problems 19

- Summary 22
- Key Terms 22
- Exercises 22

Chapter 2
How Sociology Is Done   25

- **Social Theory and Research** 26
  - Cause and Effect 27
  - Theory and Values 27
  - Theories Versus Values: Why Does It Matter? 27
  - The Relationship Between Theory and Research 28
- **Using and Measuring Variables** 31
  - Independent Variables 31
  - Dependent Variables 31
  - Operational Definitions 31
  - Validity and Reliability 32
  - Correlation 32
  - Control Variables 33
- **Key Research Methods in Sociology** 33
  - Quantitative and Qualitative Methods 33
- **Experiments** 35
  - Experimental and Control Groups 35
  - Field Experiments 36
- **Survey Research** 38
  - Questionnaires 38
  - Telephone Interviews 38
  - Personal Interviews 39
  - Survey Questions 39
  - Sampling 40
- **Field Observation** 40
  - Field Observation and Theory Generation 40
  - Participant Observation 41
  - Unobtrusive Observation 44
- **Use of Existing Data Sources** 44
  - Data Archives 44
  - The U.S. Census 45
  - Content Analysis 45
- **Reading Tables** 45
- **Summary** 47
- **Key Terms** 47
- **Exercises** 48

Part II Society and Human Interaction

Chapter 3
Perspectives on Society and Interaction   51

Perspectives in Sociology 52
Macrosociology and Microsociology 52

Macrosociology I: The Functionalist Perspective 53
The Functionalist Perspective Defined 53
Key Principles of the Functionalist Perspective 53
Functions and Dysfunctions 56

Macrosociology II: The Conflict Perspective 56
The Conflict Perspective Defined 56

Macrosociological Perspectives: Is Synthesis Possible? 60
Functional for Whom? Another Look 61
Simultaneous Forces for Cooperation and Conflict 61
Macrosociological Perspectives: A Final Note 63

Microsociology: The Symbolic-Interactionist Perspective 64
The Interactionist Perspective Defined 64
Interpreting Situations and Messages 65
The Social Construction of Reality 65
Social Roles 68
Sending Messages: The Presentation of Self 69

Micro- and Macrosociology: Is Synthesis Possible? 71
Simultaneous Effects of Function, Conflict, and Interaction 71
Exchange Theory 71
Using All Three Perspectives: An Example 74
The Three Perspectives and This Book 75

Summary 76
Key Terms 76
Exercises 76

Chapter 4
Culture and Social Structure   79

Society, Culture, and Social Structure 80
What Is Culture? 80
Shared Truths: Knowledge, Language, and Beliefs 81
Shared Values 84
Ideology 84
Social Norms 84

What Is Social Structure? 85
Social Status 86
Roles 87
Division of Labor 88
Stratification 89
Relationships Between Roles and Statuses 89
Institutions 90

Perspectives on Culture and Social Structure 90

The Functionalist Perspective: Adaptation of Culture
    and Social Structure to the Environment   90
  Cultural and Structural Variation: Do Cultural or Structural Universals Exist?   92
  Universal Social Tasks   92
  The Conflict Perspective and Culture   95
 Incompatibilities Between Culture and Social Structure   98
  Sewell's Duality of Structure Theory   98
  Culture Against Structure: The Functionalist Perspective   99
  Subcultures in Mass Society   100
  Culture Against Structure: The Conflict Perspective   103
 PUTTING SOCIOLOGY TO WORK   106
  Multiculturalism: A Pathway to Cooperation in a Diverse Society?   106
 American Culture   108
  Core American Values and Beliefs   108
  Ideal Versus Real Culture   108
  Recent Changes in American Values and Beliefs   108
 Summary   116
 Key Terms   116
 Exercises   117

Chapter 5
Socialization 119
 Becoming "Human" Through Socialization   121
  Learning About Norms and Social Roles   121
 Theories of Socialization and Development   121
  Nature Versus Nurture   121
  Interactionist Theories of Socialization: Mead and Cooley   123
  Theories About Social Expectations and Personal Dilemmas:
    Freud and Erikson   125
  Cognitive Development Theories of Socialization: Piaget and Kohlberg   127
  Overview of Theories of Socialization   133
 Agents of Socialization   133
  The Family   133
  Schools   135
  Religion   135
  Peers   135
  The Media   136
  How Socialization Works   137
  Conflicting Messages   138
 Socialization in Adulthood   140
  Life-Cycle Roles   140
  Role Change, Adult Socialization, and Stress   142
  Resocialization in Total Institutions   142
 Functionalist and Conflict Perspectives on Socialization   143
  The Functionalist Perspective   143
  The Conflict Perspective   144
 Summary   147
 Key Terms   147

Exercises 148

Part III Social Structure and Inequality

Chapter 6
Stratification: Structured Social Inequality 151

What Is Stratification? 153
Dimensions of Stratification 153
The Economic Dimension 153
The Political Dimension 153
The Social Prestige Dimension 154

The Distribution of Wealth and Income in the United States 154
The Distribution of Income 154
The Distribution of Wealth 155

Socioeconomic Mobility 156
Caste Systems 157
Estate or Feudal Systems 158
Class Systems 158
International Comparisons of Mobility 160

Social Class in U.S. Society 161
The Marxian Definition of Social Class 161
The Composite Definition of Social Class 162
The Subjective Definition of Social Class 162
Occupational Prestige 163
Class Consciousness in the United States 165

Poverty in the United States 167
How Poverty is Defined 167
Poverty in America: The Current Situation 168
Who Is Poor? 169

Causes of Poverty 170
Poor People Themselves? Work, Family Structure, and Poverty 170
Unemployment 174
Low Wages 175
Government Policy 175

Consequences of Poverty 176

Functionalist and Conflict Perspectives on Stratification 177
The Functionalist View: Davis and Moore 177
The Conflict View 177
Is Stratification Really Functional? 178
Synthesis 179

Summary 182
Key Terms 183
Exercises 183

Chapter 7
Race and Ethnic Relations 185
Racial and Ethnic Groups: What Is the Difference? 186

Majority and Minority Groups 187
Racism 187
Ideological Racism 187
Racial and Ethnic Prejudice 188
Individual Discrimination 188
Institutional Discrimination 188
Theories About the Causes of Racial and Ethnic Inequality 189
Social-Psychological Theories of Race Relations 189
The Relationship Between Prejudice and Discrimination 191
Social-Structural Theories of Race Relations 192
Racial and Ethnic Relations: An International Perspective 197
Ethnic Inequality and Conflict: How Universal? 197
Racial Caste in South Africa and the United States 197
Racial Assimilation in Latin America 198
Racial and Ethnic Groups in the United States 199
Minority Groups: African Americans, Hispanic Americans, and Native Americans 200
Economic Exploitation and the Origins of Intergroup Inequality 201
Segregation and Attacks on Culture 202
The Status of Minority Groups Today 203
Intermediate Status Groups: Asian Americans, Jewish and Muslim Americans, and "White Ethnics" 205
The Majority Group 208
Current Issues in U.S. Race Relations 209
The Significance of Race Versus Class 209
PUTTING SOCIOLOGY TO WORK 212
The Affirmative Action Debate 212
Is Affirmative Action Reverse Discrimination? 213
Is the System Fair Without Affirmative Action? 214
How Effective Is Affirmative Action? 215
The Legal and Political Status of Affirmative Action 216
Summary 217
Key Terms 217
Exercises 218

Chapter 8
Sex, Gender, and Society 219
What Are Sex and Gender Roles? 220
Sex and Gender Roles 220
Sexism 221
Traditional American Gender Roles 221
Cultural Variation in Gender Roles 223
Gender-Role Socialization: An Interactionist Analysis 225
How Gender Roles Develop 226
Teaching Gender Roles in the Home 226
Teaching Gender Roles in the School 227
Teaching Gender Roles on Television 228

Contents

    How Peers Teach Gender Roles 229
How Gender Roles Are Learned 230
    The Looking-Glass Self and Gender-Role Socialization 230
    Modeling and Gender-Role Socialization 230
Structured Sexual Inequality: Power 231
    Men, Women, and Positions of Authority 231
    Women in Politics 232
    Women in the Business World 233
    Men, Women, and Power in the Home 234
Structured Sexual Inequality: Income 235
    Some Possible Reasons for Women's Low Wages 236
PUTTING SOCIOLOGY TO WORK 240
    Understanding and Preventing Sexual Harassment 240
Functionalist and Conflict Perspectives on Gender Roles 242
    The Origins of Gender Inequality 242
    The Functionalist Perspective 243
    The Conflict Perspective 245
    Feminism: A Challenge to Male Power 245
    Feminist Social Theory 249
    Ecofeminism 250
How Are Gender Roles Changing in America? 251
    Sexual Double Standard 251
    Employment Discrimination 251
    Sexual Assault 251
    Limitations of Change 253
    Public Opinion and Future Prospects for Gender Equality 254
Intersexuality, Sexual Orientation, and the Politics of Being "Different" 256
    Sexual Orientation 256
Summary 257
Key Terms 258
Exercises 259

Chapter 9
Groups, Organizations, and the Workplace 261
Groups and Organizations: What Is the Difference? 262
Group Characteristics and Dynamics 263
    Group Size 263
    Primary and Secondary Groups 264
    Conformity Within Groups 264
    Outside Threats and Group Cohesion 264
    Dysfunctional Group Processes 266
Organizations 267
    Why Study Organizations? 267
    Characteristics of Organizations 268
Oligarchy Versus Democracy 269
    Michels's Iron Law of Oligarchy 269

Oligarchy: Iron Law or Just a Tendency?   269

Leadership in Groups and Organizations   270
Instrumental and Expressive Leadership   270
Characteristics of Leaders   271

Bureaucracy   272
Why Do Bureaucracies Develop?   273
Bureaucracy and Democracy   274
Karl Marx on Bureaucracy   274
The Pervasiveness of Bureaucracy   276
Evaluating Bureaucracy   276
Dysfunctions of Bureaucracy   277

An Interactionist View of Bureaucracy   280
Informal Structure   280
Negotiated Order   281
Roles in the Workplace: Case Studies   281

Globalization and New Trends in Work Organization   283
Globalization and Work   284
Japanese Work Organization   285
Scandinavian Workplace Innovations   287
Workplace Change in the United States   288
Alternatives to Bureaucracy   288

Summary   289

Key Terms   289

Exercises   289

Chapter 10
Deviance, Crime, and Social Control   291
How Sociologists View Deviance   293
The Sociology of Rule Making   293
Social Control   295

PUTTING SOCIOLOGY TO WORK   297
Does Capital Punishment Deter Murder?   297

Crime   298
Street Crime   298
Victimless Crime   299
Legalization or Decriminalization of Drugs: Pros and Cons   300
White-Collar and Corporate Crime   301
Organized Crime   303
Political Crime   303

Characteristics of Criminals   306
Crime Statistics: A Closer Look   306
Race, Class, and Crime Statistics   306

Explaining Deviant Behavior   307
Kinds of People: Biological and Psychological Theories of Deviant Behavior   307

Societal Explanations of Deviant Behavior   308
Anomie and Deviant Behavior   308
Subcultural Explanations of Deviance   311

Labeling Tradition 313
Functionalist and Conflict Perspectives on Deviance 315
The Functionalist View—Durkheim 315
The Dysfunctions of Deviance—Parsons 316
The Conflict View 316
Feminist Criminology 318

Summary 318
Key Terms 321
Exercises 321

Part IV Social Institutions

Chapter 11
Economy and Society   325
Economic Systems 327
Sectors of the Economy 327
Economic Change and Social Change 328
Economic Development and Society 328
Hunting-and-Gathering Economies 328
Agricultural Economies 329
Industrial Economies 329
The Shift to Postindustrial Economies 331
Effects on the Labor Force and Stratification 332
The Rise of Professions 333
The Role of Science and Education 333
Postmodernism: A Challenge to Science and Technology 334
Modern Economic Systems 335
Capitalism 335
Socialism 337
Karl Marx and Communism 338
Mixed Economies 339
Social Consequences of Modern Economic Systems 340
Does Capitalism Promote Greed? 340
Socialism, Capitalism, the Market, and Productivity 341
Is Socialism Dead? 341
The Changing Scale of Modern Economies 343
Concentration in Corporate Capitalism 343
Consequences of Concentration 345
Multinational Corporations 346
Globalization and Its Consequences 347
PUTTING SOCIOLOGY TO WORK 349
Free Trade or Protectionism? 349
Unemployment and the Economic Cycle 352
Financial Systems 353
Voice or Exit 355
Financial Crises 355
Karl Polanyi and the New Economic Sociology 358

    The Sociological Study of the Economy   358
    Karl Polanyi Enters the Dance   359
    The Embedded Economy and the Impossibility of the Self-Regulating Market   360

Summary 361

Key Terms 362

Exercises 363

Chapter 12
Politics, Power, and Society   365

Power in Modern Societies   366
    Legitimate Power and Authority   366
    Other Sources of Power   367
    Wealth, Income, and Power   367

Who Has Power in America Today?   368
    Measuring Power   368

The Distribution of Power in the United States   368
    Three Key Interest Group Coalitions   369
    Who Governs?   369
    Who Benefits?   370
    Who Wins?   371
    Overview   372

The State   373
    Types of Systems   375

PUTTING SOCIOLOGY TO WORK   375
    Welfare Reform: An Effective Tool Against Poverty?   375

Welfare Around the World   377
    Liberal Welfare States: U.S., Canada, the United Kingdom   377
    Corporatist-Statist Welfare States   378
    Social Democratic Welfare States   378
    Evaluating the Welfare States   379

Political Ideology   379

Political Parties and Special Interest Groups   380
    Lobbyists and Special Interest Groups   380

Voting Patterns of the Major Social Groups   381
    The Apathetic Voter   381

The Politics of Development in the Third World   381
    Perspectives on the Uneven Development in the Third World   382
    Modernization Theories   382
    Dependency Theories   383
    World-System Theory   383

Terrorism: A Challenge to Government   387
    Governments and Terrorism   387
    Terrorism in the Modern World   389
    Who Is Vulnerable to Insurgent Terrorism?   391
    Theories About the Causes of Terrorism   392
    Can Terrorism Be Combated?   392

Summary 393

Key Terms 395
Exercises 396

Chapter 13
Marriages and Families 397

Family and Marriage Defined 398
Extended and Nuclear Families 399
Family Memberships 400
Marriage Patterns 400
Mate Selection 401
Romantic Love and Mate Selection 402

Patterns Within Marriages 405
Power and Authority in Marriages 405
Residency Patterns 406
Inheritance and Descent Patterns 407

Functions of Families 408
Changing Functions 408
The Family as a Regulator of Sexual Behavior 409

A Conflict Analysis of the Family 411
Role Inequality Within the Family 411
Violence in the Family and in Courtship 412
The Family in the Larger Social Structure 414

Changing Patterns of Marriages and Families 414
Changing Roles Within Marriages 415
Delayed Marriage and Permanent Singlehood 415
Cohabitation 416
Gay and Lesbian Couples 417
Fewer Children, No Children 420

Marital Disruption and Divorce 421
Divorce in the United States 421
Causes of Divorce 422
Changing Divorce Laws 423

PUTTING SOCIOLOGY TO WORK 424
Should Couples Stay Together "for the Sake of the Kids"? 424
Remarriage 426

Single-Parent Families 427
Race, Poverty, and the One-Parent Family 428

The Future of Marriages and Families 431
Summary 432
Key Terms 432
Exercises 433

Web-Based Chapter A
Available at http://www.paradigmpublishers.com/Books/BookDetail
.aspx?productID=236921

Education
Education as a Social Institution

The Origins of Mass Education
Mass Education in the United States
A Global Perspective on Mass Education

The Functionalist Perspective on Education
Manifest Functions of Education
Latent Functions of Education

Race, Class, and Education: Equal Opportunity or Inequality?
Compensatory Education
Desegregation Through Busing

PUTTING SOCIOLOGY TO WORK
Does Busing Improve Minority Student Learning?

The Conflict Perspective on Education
Schools and Unequal Mobility
Unequal Funding of Schools

Symbolic-Interaction and Educational Inequality
The Effect of Teacher Expectations
Factors Affecting Teacher Expectations
Teacher Expectations: The Schoolwide Level
Tracking and Ability Grouping
Testing

The Hidden Curriculum: A Conflict Analysis
Social Class and School Orientation
Schooling and Job Status

Higher Education
Community Colleges
Recent Trends in Access to College
Higher Education for Students of Color
Does College Pay?

Is the Quality of American Education Declining?
Have Educational Changes Reduced Achievement?

Web-Based Chapter B
Available at http://www.paradigmpublishers.com/Books/BookDetail.aspx?productID=236921

Religion

What Is Religion?
Forms of Religion
Religion and Society

Religion: The Sociological Perspective
A Functionalist Analysis of Religion
Dysfunctions of Religion
A Conflict Analysis of Religion

Major World Religions
Monotheism, Polytheism, and Sacred Philosophies
History, Beliefs, and Practices of the Major Religions
Religion in the United States and the World
Types of Organized Religion
Religion and the Economy: Weber and the Protestant Ethic

Church and State in America
- Civil Religion
- Religion and Politics in America
- Fundamentalism and the New Religious Right
- Religion and Politics: The Current Scene

Two Opposing Trends: Secularization and Fundamentalist Revival
- A Trend Toward Secularization?
- Fundamentalist Revival?
- Why Secularization and Revival?

Web-Based Chapter C
Available at http://www.paradigmpublishers.com/Books/BookDetail.aspx?productID=236921

Health, Population, and Aging

Health and Society: A Functionalist View
- The Sick Role
- Criticisms of the Sick Role
- The Health Benefits of Modernization

Health and Society: A Conflict View
- Power, Environmental Quality, and Health
- Modernization and Health: The Epidemiology of Cancer
- Social Inequality and Health

Health and Society: An Interactionist View
- The Meaning of Health, Sickness, and Illness
- Gender and Health
- Personal Outlook and Health
- Mental Health
- Changing Views of Mental Disorders

The Institution of Medicine
- Traditional and Scientific Medicine
- Modern Medicine: The Medicalization of Everything?
- Roles and Stratification in the Medical Institution
- Care Based on Ability to Pay

Alternative Approaches to Health Care
- National Health Insurance
- National Health Service
- The New National Health Insurance Law

Demography: The Study of Population
- Three Basic Demographic Variables
- The Basic Demographic Equation and Population Projections
- World Population Growth
- The Demographic Transition
- The Demographic Transition in Europe and North America
- Third World Demographic Transition

Population Trends in the United States
- Decreasing Mortality
- Changing Fertility: Baby Boom, Baby Bust
- Immigration into the United States

The Changing Composition of the U.S. Population
The Aging of the Population in Industrialized Countries

Part V Social Change

Chapter 14
Urban Sociology: City Life and Collective Behavior   437

The Rise of Cities Throughout the World   438
Technology, Industrialization, and Urbanization   440
Social Change and Urbanization   440
The Demographic Transition and Urbanization   441
Urbanization in the United States   442
Economics of Urban Growth   442
Functional Specialization   443
Urban Hierarchy   444
Urbanization in the Third World   444
Urban Life   445
Differences Between Rural and Urban Life   445
Wirth on Urban Life   448
Decline of Community: Myth or Reality?   448
Urban Life and "Getting Involved"   449
Cities and Social Conflict   451
Collective Behavior   452
Causes of Collective Behavior   452
Types of Collective Behavior   453
Collective Behavior in Crowds   454
Types of Crowd Behavior   456
Mass Behavior   458
Types of Mass Behavior   459
Fashions and Fads   462
The Structure of the City   462
Human Ecology   462
Urban Social Segregation   463
The Changing City in Postindustrial America   468
The Rise of the Suburbs   468
Causes of Suburbanization   468
Life in the Suburbs   469
The Crisis of the Central Cities   471
Population Decline   471
The Urban Underclass   471
The Urban Fiscal Crisis   472
Uneven Development Among American Cities   473
Different Processes or Different Stages?   473
The Conflict Theory of Uneven Development   474
Summary   475
Key Terms   476

Exercises 476

Chapter 15
Social Movements and Change 479

Social Movements 480
Types of Social Movements 481
The Causes of Social Movements 483
Necessary Conditions for Social Movements 485
Movement Life Course: Civil Rights, Environmental and Women's Movement as Case Studies 485

Social Change 491
What Is Social Change? 491
Theories of Social Change 492
Equilibrium (Functionalist) Versus Conflict Theories of Social Change 492
Evolutionary Versus Cyclical Changes 493

Modernization: Escalating Social Change 494
Consequences of Rapid Social Change 495

New Directions in the Study of Social Change 496
Summary 497
Key Terms 500
Exercises 500

Glossary G-1
References R-1
Index I-1

Boxes

SOCIOLOGICAL INSIGHTS

Chapter 1
A Common Sense Quiz ... 5
A Common Sense Quiz: The Answers ... 6

Chapter 2
Damned Lies and Statistics:
 The Worst Statistic Ever ... 46

Chapter 3
Functionalist Theory: Some Key Thinkers ... 55
Conflict Theory: Some Key Thinkers ... 58
Eclectic Macrosociology:
 Some Key Thinkers ... 62
Doing (and Being Done by) the
 Funhouse Mirrors ... 66
Symbolic-Interactionist Theory:
 Some Key Thinkers ... 69
Micro-Macro Links: Two Key Thinkers ... 73

Chapter 4
What the Deaf Teach the Hearing About
 Language and Thought ... 86
Drift Fishing: The Norms of a Subculture ... 104

Chapter 5
Multiple Social Roles: Good for Your Health? ... 126

Chapter 6
American Social Classes Today ... 166

Chapter 7
What Makes a Fair Footrace? ... 213

Chapter 9
What Makes a Union Democratic? ... 271

Chapter 10
A Criminological Analysis
 of an Airplane Crash ... 304
A Culture of Cheating? ... 310

Chapter 11
Two Main Goals of a Financial System ... 354
Kindleberger's Simplified Model
 of Financial Crises ... 356
Shared Beliefs of Marx, Weber,
 and Durkheim ... 359

Chapter 12
Is Bin Laden's Terrorist Network
 a Case of Blowback? ... 394

Chapter 14
Metro Areas in the United States:
 Which Ones Are Growing?
 Which Ones Aren't? ... 446
The Earthquake That Wasn't ... 461

GLOBAL SOCIOLOGY

Chapter 1
Using the Sociological Imagination:
College Women Faculty and Household
Work in the United States and China — 14

Chapter 5
Language and Socialization:
Understanding "Waltzing Matilda" — 122

Chapter 6
American Poverty and Teenage Pregnancy
in Global Perspective — 173
Global Stratification — 181

Chapter 8
Treatment of Women: Comparing the
Western and Islamic Traditions — 252

Chapter 12
"Jihad" Versus "McWorld": The Battle
Between Globalism and Tribalism — 388

Chapter 13
Romance, a Novel Idea, Rocks Marriages
in China — 404

Chapter 14
A Portrait of the Preindustrial City — 439

Web-Based Chapter A
Letter to a Teacher

Web-Based Chapter B
Catholicism and Unionism:
Is There a Relationship?

Web-Based Chapter C
How Americans, British, and Canadians
View Their Health-Care Systems
Zero Population Growth: Present
and Future

SOCIOLOGICAL SURPRISES

Chapter 1
How Emigration Created a Private
School Boom — 11

Chapter 2
Doing Survey Research: Sex in America — 42

Chapter 5
Another Look at "Waltzing Matilda"—
Why Did the Words Change? — 146

Chapter 8
The Costs of the Male Gender Role
to Men (and Women?) — 246

Chapter 12
Terrorism: Not as New as We Think — 390

Web-Based Chapter A
When White Guys Can't Do Math:
The Effects of Stereotype Threat

Web-Based Chapter B
Liberal Islam

Web-Based Chapter C
Living in Cities: Bad for Your Health?

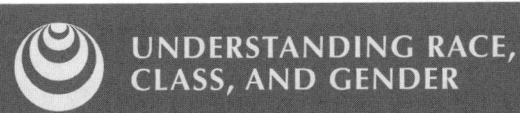

UNDERSTANDING RACE, CLASS, AND GENDER

Chapter 2
Sorting Out Cause-Effect Relationships: Single-Parent Homes and Teenage Parenthood — 34
Doing Participant Observation: Slim's Table — 43

Chapter 4
Responding to Terror: A Common Norm or Group Differences? — 101

Chapter 5
The Making of the Southern Belle — 134

Chapter 6
Herbert Gans and the Functions of Poverty — 180
Global Stratification — 181

Chapter 7
Popular Music as a Threat: The Role of Race — 194

Chapter 8
Gender and the Financial Effects of Divorce — 257

Chapter 9
Organizational Practices and Opportunities for Female Managers — 275

Chapter 10
An Argument Against Studying "Deviance" — 317

Chapter 13
Nancy and Evan — 418

Web-Based Chapter A
The Bell Curve: A Debate on Education, Intelligence, Genetics, and Achievement
Radical Equations: The Algebra Project

Web-Based Chapter B
The Black Church in America

Web-Based Chapter C
Racism and Hypertension

STUDENT LIFE

Chapter 7
Informal Segregation: The "Invisible Wall" and the "Black Table" — 206

Chapter 9
The Organization of Security — 268

Chapter 13
New Ways to Meet Partners: A Sociological Look at "The Personals" — 406

Web-Based Chapter A
College Today: More Students Than Ever Before, But Why Don't More Graduate?

PERSONAL JOURNEYS INTO SOCIOLOGY

Chapter 2
Changing Times — 36

Chapter 4
The Sociology of Sport — 112

Chapter 5
Uncoupling — 144

Chapter 7
How Societal Changes Helped Shape My Views on Race Relations and Urban Poverty — 210

Chapter 9
Work Without Bosses: Organizational Democracy as the Alternative to Bureaucracy — 286

Chapter 10
Doing Feminist Criminology — 319

Chapter 11
Sociologists Study Risks and Sometimes Take Risks — 357

Chapter 12
How I Finally Found My Way to Sociology — 372

Chapter 13
Background of "'Til Death Do Us Part": How Couples Stay Together — 424

Chapter 15
On the Way to Revolution — 498

Figures

Chapter 2
2.1 The Cycle of Scientific Inquiry ... 29

Chapter 4
4.1 Achieved and Ascribed Statuses ... 87
4.2 The Relationship Between Economic Structure and Ideational Superstructure (Ideology) in Marxian Theory ... 96

Chapter 6
6.1 Share of Income Going to Highest 5% and Lowest 20%, United States, 1967–2008 ... 155
6.2 Median Household Net Worth, 2002 ... 156
6.3 Number in Poverty and Poverty Rate: 1959–2008 ... 169
6.4 Poverty Rates by Race and Hispanic Origin: 1959–2008 ... 170
6.5 Work Status of Poor People Age 16 and Over, 2008 ... 172

Chapter 7
7.1 U.S. Hispanic Population, by Nationality, 2000 ... 200

Chapter 8
8.1 Labor Force Participation Rates of Men and Women in the United States, 1890–2001 ... 224
8.2 (a) Percentage of Women Among U.S. Senators and Representatives, 1980–2010 ... 232
(b) Percentage of Women Among Statewide Office Holders and State Legislators, 1980–2010 ... 232
8.3. Median Women's Income as a Percentage of Median Men's Income, Year-Round Full-Time Workers, 1970–2008 ... 235
8.4 Percentage of Women in the Paid Labor Force, by Marital Status and Presence and Age of Children, 2009 ... 248
8.5 Percentage of Women Among Degree Recipients, Selected Professions, 1949–2008 ... 255

Chapter 9
9.1 The Continuum from Primary to Secondary Groups ... 265
9.2 An Example of the Cards Used in Solomon Asch's Experiment ... 266

Chapter 11
11.1 Stages of Economic Evolution, According to Karl Marx ... 339
11.2 How Capital Markets Work ... 354

Chapter 13
13.1 Households by Type: Selected Years, 1970–2000 ... 399
13.2 Median Age of U.S. Men and Women at First Marriage, 1890–2009 ... 416
13.3 U.S. Divorce Rates per 1,000 Total Population, 1960–2000 ... 422

13.4	Proportion Married Couple, Female-Householder, and Male-Householder Families, 2009	428

Chapter 14
14.1	Generalizations of Internal Structures of Cities	464
14.2	Racial Composition of Census Tracts, St. Louis Metropolitan Area, 2000	466

Chapter 15
15.1	A Trend with Embedded Cycles	494

Web-Based Chapter A
- A.1 Percentage of U.S. Population Ages 25 and Over Who Have Completed High School and College, 1940–2009
- A.2 Median Earnings of Year-Round, Full-Time Workers, by Sex and Educational Level, 2008

Web-Based Chapter B
- B.1 Religious Preferences in the United States, 2008
- B.2 The Continuum from Sect to Church
- B.3 Self-Reported Church Attendance of Catholics and Protestants in the Past Week, 1955–2005

Web-Based Chapter C
- C.1 World Population Growth, 7000 B.C. to A.D. 2000
- C.2 The Demographic Transition
- C.3 Life Expectancy by Race and Sex, 1900–2003, United States
- C.4 U.S. Total Fertility Rate, 1917–2007
- C.5 Age-Sex Pyramids for the United States: 1960–2050
- C.6 Population by Age and Sex, Germany and Indonesia, 2000
- C.7 Social Security and Medicare Costs as a Percentage of GDP, Historical 1970–2008 and Projected 2009–2082

Photographs

Chapter 1
Karl Marx. (Library of Congress) — 15
Max Weber. (Hulton Archive/Getty Images) — 16
Emile Durkheim. (Bettmann/Corbis) — 16
Jane Addams pioneered the collection and mapping of data for cities and urban neighborhoods. (Library of Congress) — 17
Factors affecting immigration and immigration policy are among the recent issues that sociologists have been called upon to address. (iStockphoto) — 21

Chapter 2
An interviewer conducts a personal interview survey. Surveys are one of the most widely used research methods in sociology. (Courtesy of Michael Flota) — 39
In unobtrusive observation, the researcher observes human behavior from a position that is out of sight or relatively unnoticeable. (Courtesy of Michael Flota) — 44
When people take action such as participating in a demonstration, they are expressing value judgments—views about how things ought to be. (iStockphoto) — 47

Chapter 3
The concept of the looking-glass self points out that we use messages from others like a mirror, to form an image of ourselves. (Courtesy of Michael Flota) — 68
Small groups, such as students working on a project, can be good places to view the processes of presentation of self and impression management. (Courtesy of Michael Flota) — 70
As long as both partners' needs are being met, it doesn't matter who takes care of the house and who goes to the office. However, if a point is reached where either partner's needs are not being met, the marriage could be in trouble. (Courtesy of Michael Flota) — 74
A yard sale, like most social realities, can be analyzed from the functionalist, conflict, and interactionist perspectives. (Courtesy of John E. Farley) — 75

Chapter 4
Language both reflects and influences culture. In the past, this sign might have said "Flagman ahead"—but through the use of graphics, as on this sign, signs can be gender-neutral and understandable in any language. (©Joseph White/Dreamstime) — 82
McDonald's and western-style fashion clothing ads in Louyang, China. As contact among different cultures increases throughout the world, the potential for misunderstanding and tensions increases. (Courtesy of John E. Farley) — 83

In the classroom, there are distinct roles, student and teacher, each of which
  carries a set of expectations. In addition, stratification is attached to the roles:
  The teacher has greater prestige and power than the students.
  (Courtesy of Michael Flota) — 89

Although hip hop culture began with African American youth in central cities,
  some aspects of it have been adopted by white suburban youths. This is an example
  of how cultural diffusion can occur within a society. (iStockphoto) — 102

Many jobs that were once considered male-only are now open to women. However,
  it is still common for women and men to be segregated in separate occupations.
  In education, women predominate in the lower grades, where pay, benefits,
  and work autonomy are less generous. (iStockphoto) — 111

Chapter 5

A child has reached the game stage when he or she can interact with roles
  rather than merely with individuals. (Courtesy of John E. Farley) — 124

At the sensorimotor stage, children develop a physical understanding
  of the environment, as shown by this child's examination of and
  experimentation with a toy cell phone. (Courtesy of John E. Farley) — 129

Stage 6 moral reasoning is most often found in people with formal training in philosophy,
  such as Dr. Martin Luther King, Jr.. (AP Photo/JL) — 131

Going to school or nursery school may be a difficult transition for some children,
  because it is their first experience interacting with equals rather than
  authority figures. (iStockphoto) — 135

It matters little where this college campus is located—it is evident that
  a nationwide informal dress code for college students prevails.
  Is this a peer-group norm, something created by the media or by
  marketing, or both? (Courtesy of John E. Farley) — 140

Chapter 6

Larry Ellison and the poor family shown above illustrate the extremes
  of economic inequality in the United States. It would take the annual
  incomes of twenty-three families living at the poverty level to add up to what
  Mr. Ellison received every day in 2009. (Ellison photo: AP Photo/Paul Sakuma)
  (Family photo: AP Photo/Jae C. Hong) — 152

Heat, cold, fires, and vermin are among the risks faced by poor families that live
  in housing like this home in New Mexico. (Courtesy of John E. Farley) — 156

Under India's caste system, members of the "untouchable" class were relegated
  to jobs such as street sweeping. Although the country's caste system
  was officially ended in 1949, it continues to influence behavior,
  thereby limiting social and economic stability. (iStockphoto) — 158

Many American service industries today outsource jobs to India, where wages
  are lower. (AP Photo/Gurinder Osan, File) — 179

Chapter 7

Scottish Highlander wearing kilts and playing bagpipes. If it were not for his dress,
  could you identify the ethnic group of this person? (iStockphoto) — 186

This statue of Popay, the Native American leader of the 1680 Pueblo Revolt, is in the
  National Statuary Hall in the Capitol Building in Washington, DC. The inclusion
  of this statue reflects the influence of cultural pluralism, or multiculturalism,
  in today's society. (Chris Maddaloni/Roll Call/Getty Images) — 196

Through much of the twentieth century, whites used a variety of techniques to exclude racial and ethnic minorities from the neighborhoods where they lived. Some such techniques, such as restrictive covenants, were at one time supported by federal policy and backed by the courts. (Bettmann/Corbis) — 208

Chapter 8
Roles are transmitted through the process of gender-role socialization. Children observe their parents in roles and behavior that, depending on the parent's lifestyle, may or may not be gender typed. (iStockphoto) — 222

While the gender gap has narrowed compared to the past, women still spend more time on household work than men. When both partners work full-time, the result is that men have more leisure time than women. (Courtesy of Michael Flota) — 235

Functionalists argue that traditional gender roles contribute to family cohesiveness, while conflict theorists argue that the main beneficiaries of such gender roles are men. What do you think? (Courtesy of Michael Flota) — 242

Ideas about the role of women vary widely in Islamic countries. Here a Muslim businesswoman speaks on the phone and dresses traditionally, but wears no veil. (iStockphoto) — 253

Chapter 9
The presence of a leader is characteristic of all organizations. Even organizations that try to be leaderless usually end up with leaders. (iStockphoto) — 272

When the potter finishes his job, he can take pride in a visible product that he has designed and created. In contrast, factory workers may only participate in a process by adding one part to a larger machine or device. (iStockphoto) — 280

Chapter 10
Although tobacco kills nearly twenty times as many people every year as all illegal drugs combined, its use remains legal and brings millions in profits to large, powerful corporations. (Big Stock Photo) — 295

Police battle protestors. Functionalists view order as necessary for society to operate effectively, while conflict theorists see it as an outcome of suppression of competing interest groups. (iStockphoto) — 305

According to Merton, anomie develops when society teaches people to want or need certain things, but fails to provide legitimate opportunities to get those things. Here, favelas (shantytowns) built by the poor are located near the richer homes along the coast of Rio de Janeiro. (iStockphoto) — 309

Some people come to view themselves wholly in terms of their deviant status, for example as "nothing but a drunk." (Courtesy of Michael Flota) — 309

Chapter 11
Nowhere has the demand for services in the postindustrial economy been more evident than in the growth of fast-food and carry-out food establishments. These businesses have created many jobs, but most have low pay and limited benefits. (Courtesy of John E. Farley) — 332

The headquarters of Google. For the past century or more, most productive capability in the United States has been controlled by corporations. In recent years, corporations in information-related businesses have become particularly dominant on a global scale. (AP Photo/Paul Sakuma) — 336

This KFC near Beijing's Tiananmen Square illustrates the wide reach of multinational corporations. (Courtesy of John E. Farley) — 338

Banks are a key component of the tertiary sector of the economy, providing credit to businesses and consumers alike. In 2008, a crisis in the banking system led to one of the deepest recessions in memory. (iStockphoto) — 353

Chapter 12

Power theorists contend the system is biased toward the wealthy. When president Obama signed the financial bailout into law some saw this act as saving the national, and possibly global, economy from a Great Depression–type of downward spiral. But power theorists might point out that the same group of wealthy investors who created the financial crisis were also the ones to receive the bailout funds. Who do you think is right? Can both views be right? (Courtesy of John E. Farley) — 371

As the economy has globalized and international travel has become increasingly commonplace, the United States has become more vulnerable to international terrorism such as the September 11, 2001, attacks. (AP Photo/Jerry Torrens) — 391

Chapter 13

An engaged couple on a pre-wedding photo shoot in Beijing's Beihai Park. As marriage in China has become associated with modern concepts such as romantic love, the country's divorce rate has soared. (Courtesy of John E. Farley) — 403

Men have taken on more child-care responsibilities than in the past, but these duties tend to be those that are less routine and more "fun." (Courtesy of Michael Flota) — 413

Homosexual couples are among the many new types of marriage and family relationships that have emerged in American society. (iStockphoto) — 418

With today's high divorce and remarriage rates, a growing number of marriages result in families in which one or both of the partners bring children from previous marriages. (Courtesy of John E. Farley) — 427

Chapter 14

The pyramids and temples of Teotihuacan are typical of the religious monuments that characterized preindustrial cities. (Courtesy of John E. Farley) — 440

An "alternative" night club above a Vietnamese restaurant in Montreal. The diversity of cities leads urbanites to be somewhat more accepting of different ethnic groups and cultural lifestyles than rural populations are. (Courtesy of John E. Farley) — 451

Collectivities sometimes develop norms that give members of the group alternative guidelines for behavior. Would these people (most of whom are college professors) dress like this outside the group context? (Courtesy of John E. Farley) — 469

The construction of urban freeways has contributed to suburbanization by making it possible for people to live far from the cities in which they work. Today, one finds trends toward living nearer work, as well as telecommuting via media technology. (iStockphoto) — 470

Chapter 15

The increase in female clergy has been gradual but represents a substantial change compared to two generations ago when the role of the clergy was mostly reserved for males. (AP Photo/ Tony Avelar) — 481

Social change, in the form of urbanization and rapid population growth in the Rocky Mountain states, is transforming Utah ranch country into Salt Lake City suburbs. (Courtesy of John E. Farley) — 492

A modern car ferry loads within sight of a totem pole near Vancouver, B.C.
In the past few hundred years, there has been greater change than in all of preceding human history. This makes the study of social change one of the most central issues in sociology. (Courtesy of John E. Farley)   497

Web-Based Chapter A
An important part of becoming independent is going to school and having peers and teachers, not parents, as the main agents of socialization. (Courtesy of Michael Flota)
Teacher expectations concerning student achievement have important effects on how much students actually do achieve. (iStockphoto)
By the time today's children graduate from high school, they will likely have spent more time watching television than attending school. (Courtesy of Michael Flota)

Web-Based Chapter B
Muslim worship at the Grand Mosque in Mecca is an example of a religious ritual. (AP Photo/Hassan Ammar)
Demonstrators for and against same-sex marriage protest during a rally in front of a federal courthouse in San Francisco, Monday, Jan. 11, 2010. The first federal trial to determine if the U.S. Constitution prohibits states from outlawing same-sex marriage got under way in San Francisco that Monday, and the two gay couples on whose behalf the case was brought will be among the first witnesses. (AP Photo/Paul Sakuma)
Norms of religious ritual changed drastically with the coming of industrialization and secularization. Though religion remains a key value in the lives of most people in all countries, the ways in which those values are expressed vary greatly from those of the past. Pictured is a drive-in church where worshipers may listen to the gospel from the comforts of their own car in a converted drive-in movie theater. Does this practice blur the line between the sacred and the profane? (Courtesy of Michael Flota)

Web-Based Chapter C
The world's first double-hand transplant patient at a hospital in France.
Under the French system of national health insurance, per capita health-care expenditures is less than half that of the United States, yet top-quality care is available, and the French life expectancy exceeds that of the United States by two years. (AP Photo/Patrick Gardin)
Fertility is harder to predict than mortality, because we do not know whether women will choose to have more or fewer babies in the future. (Courtesy of John E. Farley)
Both infant and maternal mortality kept people from living to old age in the past, and populations were young because of high birth rates. But with today's lower birth rates and longer life expectancies, populations are getting older. (Courtesy of John E. Farley)
In parts of Africa, Asia, and Latin America, the standard of living has been slow to rise, and fertility has been slow to decline. (iStockphoto)
This woman has moved beyond the normal retirement age of 65 and thus is considered to have reached old age, a social category original created to open jobs for younger workers. But this does not mean she is incapable of work. Today official retirement ages are rising as government policies change. (iStockphoto)

Tables

Chapter 3
3.1 Compare and Contrast: Basic Assumptions of the Functionalist and Conflict Perspectives — 60
3.2 Compare and Contrast: Basic Assumptions of Macrosociology and Microsociology — 72

Chapter 4
4.1 American Institutions and Their Key Functions — 91
4.2 Cultural Universals Identified by George Peter Murdock — 93
4.3 Core American Values and Beliefs — 109

Chapter 5
5.1 Summary of Key Theorists on Socialization and Development — 128

Chapter 6
6.1 Income Inequality in 14 Industrialized Countries — 157
6.2 Occupational Prestige Ratings: United States Compared to 60-Country Average — 164
6.3 Number of People Living Below the Poverty Level, and Poverty Rate, Selected Groups in U.S. Population, 2008 — 171
6.4 Economic Inequality and Economic Productivity, Selected Industrial Countries, 2000 — 178

Chapter 7
7.1 Robert Merton's Typology on Prejudice and Discrimination — 191
7.2 U.S. Racial and Ethnic Group Populations, 2008 — 201
7.3 Population of Selected Asian American Groups, 2000 — 208

Chapter 8
8.1 Percentage of Bachelor's Degrees Awarded to Women by Discipline, 1966, 1981, 1989, 1998, and 2007 (Selected Fields) — 228
8.2 Median Income of Year-Round Full-Time Workers, by Sex and Level of Education, 2008 — 236
8.3 Median Income of Year-Round, Full-Time Workers, by Sex and Age, 2006 — 237

Chapter 10
10.1 Percentage of Reported Crimes Cleared by Arrest, 1999 — 305
10.2 Typology of Deviant Adaptation to Anomie — 310

Chapter 11
11.1 Concentration in the American Economy: Selected Industries, 1982, 1992, 1997, and 2002 — 345

Chapter 13
13.1 Percentage of Female-Householder Families, by Race, Hispanic Origin, Below Poverty Level, 2008 — 427

13.2	Median Family Income, by Race, Hispanic Origin, and Type of Family, 2008	431

Chapter 14

14.1	Estimated Populations of Major World Cities, A.D. 800–1600	441
14.2	World's Largest Cities (Cities with Metropolitan Population of 10 Million or Greater), 2009	442
14.3	Period of Emergence of Major Urban Centers in the United States	443
14.4	Types of Collective Behavior	454
14.5	Percent of Population in Central Cities, Suburban Areas, and Outside Metropolitan Areas, 1950–2000	469

Web-Based Chapter A

A.1 College Enrollment and Graduation Rates Among Young American Adults, by Race and Hispanic Origin

Web-Based Chapter B

B.1 Comparison of the Sect and the Denomination

Web-Based Chapter C

C.1 Number of Deaths Caused by Selected Conditions, United States, 2005
C.2 The Growth of Medicine in the United States During the Twentieth Century: Selected Indicators
C.3 Health Expense and Health Status in Industrialized Countries with Various Health-Care Systems: Selected Indicators
C.4 Current and Projected Population of the World

Preface

As this sixth edition of *Sociology* goes to press, we would like to begin by saying how gratifying it is to relaunch this successful and unique textbook. *Sociology* has enjoyed great praise over the course of its first five editions. On the way to this sixth iteration, *Sociology* has gained a second author and a new publisher. John E. Farley is joined by Michael W. Flota, a former student of Farley's and a long-time admirer and user of the book. When the opportunity came along to join Farley in the task of writing this new edition, he jumped at the chance. We now offer you this sixth and latest installment. We have incorporated many new updates and changes that bring the book up to the current moment with the latest research and important world events as well as respond to feedback from readers of earlier editions. Importantly, however, the book retains those features that readers have found useful in earlier editions. In particular, three features have made this book different from other introductory textbooks, and we have made every effort to retain and strengthen each of these features.

Three Key Features

First, from the initial edition of the book, the text has featured sociology's three major perspectives—functionalist, conflict, and symbolic interactionist—as a way of linking the very diverse topics, issues, and theories that sociology addresses. Many other introductory sociology texts briefly introduce these perspectives in a small part of an early chapter and then, at most, mention them occasionally in later parts of the book. In contrast, this book devotes a full chapter—Chapter 3—to an in-depth examination of the perspectives and how they have been used and increasingly combined to develop a better understanding of society. And throughout the rest of the book, the perspectives are used to show linkages among theories and issues throughout sociology; in every chapter in the remainder of the book, one or more of these perspectives is used to analyze and understand the subject matter. Wherever a specific sociological theory about a particular topic can be readily linked to one of the broader sociological perspectives, we have done so. The end result is a more integrated and less fragmented understanding of sociology. A second advantage of this approach is that it encourages critical thinking about how research findings in sociology support, challenge, or lead to modifications in sociological theory. Specifically, students are invited to consider how sociological research findings and data are consistent or not consistent with the claims of the broad perspectives or of more specific theories arising from these perspectives.

Second, in every edition a strong emphasis on race, class, and gender has been featured throughout the book. Reviewers of the book have noted that, while many books in effect segregate coverage of race, class, and gender to the chapters on those particular topics, this book addresses these issues in its coverage of every topic. Issues of race, class, and gender are discussed and illustrated in every chapter, thus showing their pervasive impact on every area of society from health to education to deviance and social control to urban society. In this new edition, this emphasis throughout the textual material of every chapter has been augmented by a set of boxed inserts focusing specifically on issues of race, class, and gender in the different subject areas of sociology.

Third, in the first edition, a conscious decision was made to cover slightly fewer topics than other introductory sociology texts but to cover those featured in somewhat greater depth. In addition, we place a greater emphasis than do other textbook authors on showing how one topic in sociology relates to another. In part, this is done through the theoretical linkages and the emphasis on issues of race, class, and gender. However, it is also facilitated by the decision to cover slightly fewer topics in greater depth, which provides the opportunities to make those linkages. The end result of this approach is to make the book more integrated and less disjointed than other introductory texts and to encourage students to think and reason more deeply about sociological issues, principles, and theories.

Organization: Continuity and Change in the Sixth Edition

As in earlier editions, we have divided the book into five parts. However, some organizational changes have been made in both the content of some chapters and the organization of some of the components. In this new organization, we have sought to retain organizational features that help students see key linkages among sociological topics and issues while introducing some new organizational features that may further highlight such linkages. As before, Part I introduces sociology as a discipline. Chapter 1 begins with a discussion of what sociology is all about: What insights can we gain through sociology that we may not be able to gain through other ways of knowing? What is the sociological way of knowing, and where does it fit within the broader picture of science and the social sciences? The key theories and theorists of sociology are briefly introduced, along with the social conditions that gave rise to sociology and that continue to make sociology relevant in the new millennium. Chapter 2 provides an overview of how sociology is done. The concept of the scientific method is introduced, along with an overview of the various types of methods used in sociology and key concepts such as variables. Attention is given both to the role of values in sociology and to the relationship between theory and research. Emphasis is also placed on the notion that different methods, including quantitative and qualitative methods, have tradeoffs: something is gained and something is lost in the choice of any method as opposed to another.

Part II focuses on society and interaction. Chapter 3 is devoted entirely to the three sociological perspectives—describing and presenting each one within a broader context of micro- and macro-sociology and exploring efforts to combine two or all three of the perspectives. A strength of this book has always been its focus on theory, and we have expanded our already extensive discussion of Marx, Weber, and Durkheim and their connection to the larger sociological perspectives. No other introductory text of which we are aware provides such a thorough discussion of the sociological perspectives, and this chapter lays the groundwork for all that follows. Chapter 4 provides combined coverage of culture and social structure. While this book was one of the first to treat culture and social structure together in the same chapter, it is gratifying to see that other books are now adopting this organization. We believe this to be essential, because culture and social structure are so interconnected that neither can be understood outside the context of the other. In this edition, we expand our discussion of this relationship with an examination of William Sewell's work on resources and schemas and how these concepts can help to illuminate what is an otherwise amorphous and abstract debate. To our knowledge no other major textbook takes on culture and structure in this manner, nor makes use of Sewell's important theory so that freshmen can understand it. The third chapter in Part II, Chapter 5, covers socialization, the process by which human beings become members of human societies.

As before, Part III focuses on social structure and inequality. Chapter 6 introduces the concept of stratification as structured social inequality. It provides a detailed examination of both class inequality (including wealth, income, and the problem of poverty). Chapter 6 also features an expanded discussion of global stratification and the theories used to explain its persistence. Chapter 7 provides an in-depth analysis of race, ethnicity, and racial inequality and features a new section on the historical explanations theorists have posited for the rise of racism, considerable coverage of the election of the first African American president, Barack Obama, and a discussion of the racial aspects of Hurricane Katrina and its aftermath in New Orleans and the Gulf states. We also have considerable updates of efforts to repeal, protect, or replace affirmative action policies across the United States since the book's last edition. Continuing a theme we developed in Chapter 7, Chapter 8 has an expanded discussion of the historical explanations that have been offered for the rise of gender stratification. Our discussion of these theories gives students an opportunity to wrestle with a fundamental debate in social science that is too often presented as a series of answers rather than the enduring questions that make up the heart of the discipline. Chapter 8 also expands its discussion of sexual orientation and the nature-nurture debate over what determines sexual preferences.

This section of the book also includes Chapter 9, on groups, organizations, and the workplace; and Chapter 10, on deviant behavior, crime, and social control. This organization reflects the intricate linkage of these subject areas with race, class, and gender inequality. It is impossible to study groups, organizations, or the workplace without addressing social inequality, and inequality is and always has been a major emphasis of this chapter. Similarly, inequalities along the lines of race, class, and gender are a critical element in defining, labeling, and punishing deviant behavior and crime, and many sociologists argue that a major function of social control is the preservation of such inequalities. Both work/organizations and deviance/crime are key arenas in which processes involving social inequality are played out, and such inequality has been emphasized in these chapters in each edition of the book. This emphasis provides a direct linkage of material in the stratification, race, and gender chapters to material in the work/organizations and deviance/crime chapters. Chapter 9 includes a new box on the organization of security, asking if, in the post–Patriot Act world, we have created the "surveillance society" that Michel Foucault wrote about decades ago. This chapter also examines the tragedy of Hurricane Katrina from an organizational breakdown perspective that exacerbated the natural disaster into an even more wrenching "man-made" calamity. Chapter 10 looks anew at the crimes of the rich and powerful amid the financial collapse of 2008 and the scandals that followed it, such as the Bernard Madoff affair. The chapter also examines recent events such as the shifting status of marijuana and its quasi and contested legalized status today, especially in places like California; the BP oil spill in the Gulf of Mexico; and political scandals such as those ensnaring the terms of two Illinois governors. A new box asks whether or not the culture of competitiveness in the United States has morphed into a "culture of cheating" that justifies winning at all costs.

The organization of Part IV of the book focuses on major social institutions, with chapters on economy and society and a new chapter on politics and power, a chapter on marriages and families, and three web-based chapters on education; religion; and health, population, and aging. (These three chapters may be downloaded free at http://www.paradigmpublishers.com/Books/BookDetail.aspx?productID=236921). These chapters, too, contain extensive material on race, class, and gender inequality within each of these major institutional areas. Chapter 11 offers an expanded focus on the economic sociology of financial systems in the wake of the 2008 global financial crisis and a particular focus on theorist Karl Polanyi, a fierce critic of unregulated markets. Chapter 12, the new chapter on politics and power, incorporates some material from the previous editions on power in America, terrorism, and development in the Third World with new material on the state, voting, interest groups, comparative welfare states, and political ideology just to name a few. Chapter 13 continues its focus on what's new in marriage and family trends. Web-Based Chapter A looks at education; Web-Based Chapter B is devoted to religion; and Web-Based Chapter C combines two chapters from the previous edition ("Population and Aging" and "Health and Health Care") into one new chapter called "Health, Population, and Aging." It focuses more narrowly on the changes taking place in the three main themes of the chapter as the United States undergoes a shift in its health-care system and as changing demographics strain every country's ability to care for the welfare and health of its population. In doing so, we provide a comprehensive breakdown of the new health-care law in the United States and some of the likely effects it will have based on early analyses. We also include a wide-ranging analysis of immigration, looking at the history and contemporary impact of immigration into the United States. This includes the new and controversial immigration law in Arizona and the most recent research on the controversy over crime and illegal immigration.

As before, Part V focuses on social change. Chapter 14 covers collective action in the globe's rapidly growing urban environment, and Chapter 15 focuses on social movements with an emphasis on individual social movements such as the feminist, civil rights, and environmentalist movements.

New to the Sixth Edition

Thinking Outside the Box (or Inside It . . .)

Each chapter contains several thematically linked boxed inserts aimed at bringing further analytical and expositional focus to certain issues. The boxes are focused as follows:

- *Sociological Surprises:* One common but (we believe) unjustified criticism of sociologists is that we sometimes expend a great deal of effort to prove things that are obvious. On the contrary, the reality is that what we find often goes against what people commonly believe and even sometimes against what we as sociological researchers expect to find. These boxes focus on such unexpected findings and analyze why the social reality turns out to be something different from what most people believe or would have expected to find.
- *Understanding Race, Class, and Gender:* These boxes give added emphasis to the book's focus on race, class, and gender inequality. In every issue that sociologists study, race, class, and gender play a key role—and these boxes provide students with clear and concrete examples of how this occurs.
- *Global Sociology:* One of the most pronounced social changes of the past century has been globalization—a transition from the dominance of nation-states and national economies to global interactions. Whether we realize it or not, global processes affect nearly every aspect of our lives and are a key factor in social inequality not only worldwide but also "at home," wherever "home" is. These boxes examine social change around the world and how change in one part of the world brings changes in other parts.
- *Student Life:* These boxes, which discuss student life from a sociological viewpoint, show how sociology is relevant to students in their everyday lives. They cover a range of issues that directly affect today's students, from race relations to dating and mating to paying for college, and draw out the sociological implications so students can use their own personal experiences to gain sociological understanding.
- *Sociological Insights:* These boxes focus on how sociology can help us better understand a variety of issues and how examples from everyday life can help us to understand sociological principles. They also explore the contributions of key sociologists to the development of the discipline. They are used to illustrate and elaborate on topics covered in the accompanying text material and are carefully linked to that material.
- *Personal Journeys into Sociology:* Major figures in sociology, including William Julius Wilson, Fred Block, Diane Vaughan, Harry Edwards, William Domhoff, and Charles Tilly, have written boxed inserts specifically for this book, explaining both the nature and the personal meaning of their work. In many cases, they explore how and why they became sociologists. In this edition, several of the authors have revised and updated their personal journey boxes.

Up-to-Date References and Resources

A point of pride for this book has always been the currency of each new edition. With each edition, hundreds of new sociological studies and data sources have been added to keep the book as up-to-the-minute as possible. This sixth edition is no exception. Of the more than 3,000 references in this book, nearly 200 are new to this edition. Major sociological journals from 2003 through 2010 were reviewed issue by issue to ensure the inclusion of the most current sociological research. Today, with the availability of the Internet, it is possible to present statistics that are more current than ever before, so throughout the book, national and international data have been updated using data sources on the Internet. Data released as late as the fall of 2010 are included.

Economic Sociology

In September of 2008, the economy of the United States came as close as it has ever come to repeating the tragedy of 1929. While the financial crisis that erupted in the Fall of 2008 did not devolve into another Great Depression, the economic dislocation has been the most severe the country has faced since those dark days, prompting many to call the current downturn the "Great Recession." In response, this edition of the text features expanded coverage of economic sociology and the sociological analysis of financial systems. A new "Personal Journeys" box featuring economic and political sociologist Fred Block discusses the return of economic analysis in sociology and the role he played in that return. The study of the economy was central to many of the major works of Marx, Weber, and Durkheim, so this renewed focus on the economy, now some three decades old, is really a return to tradition. In doing so, economic sociologists have borrowed from economists, and increasingly, economists borrow from us. This relationship is exhibited in the discussion of how financial crises progress in Chapter 11 using economist Charles Kindleberger's influential model. The chapter goes further, showing students how the model can be applied to and help us understand how the real estate market collapse could balloon into a general crash of the entire financial system. As families across the country and world are impacted by rising unemployment, foreclosures, and poverty, we know that many students who will read this book have themselves been touched by the crisis. We hope this expanded focus on economic sociology can help students to understand these traumatic events.

Additional Features

In addition to the above changes, the book includes a number of features designed to enhance student learning. A feature that has been carried over from earlier editions, for instance, is the inclusion of "Putting Sociology to Work" sections in selected chapters. The focus of these sections is application: how can sociology be used to solve a social problem or to make an important decision? While this feature is carried over from previous editions, most of these sections have been modified and updated, and some have been rewritten to focus on issues of current importance. For example, the "Putting Sociology to Work" section in Chapter 12 assesses the impacts of the "welfare reform" legislation that was passed in 1996: Did it achieve its goals? Did it make poor people less dependent? Did it take away their safety net? Are the people it intended to help better off or worse off because of the policy?

As in earlier editions, the book includes a variety of *pedagogical aids,* including *end-of-chapter lists of key terms,* which appear in bold print where they are first introduced and in a *glossary* at the end of the book. Each chapter begins with a *real-life vignette,* often based on actual sociological findings or data. Some have been updated for the fifth edition, and some are entirely new. Each chapter ends with a *summary,* designed to provide a succinct wrap-up of the main points of the chapter. This edition features *end-of-chapter exercises* similar to those used in the past; however, we have shifted the questions to a greater emphasis on *critical thinking and debate* that gets beyond simplistic either/or dichotomies. We often ask students to use the power of the Internet to investigate social issues and debates firsthand and to apply what they find to their own lives. Doing so, we believe, will allow them to decide for themselves about the controversies, mysteries, and marvels of today's social world using the tool of the sociological imagination.

We have strived mightily to *write clearly* in language students can readily understand, always keeping in mind the introductory sociology student as the reader. Where we have failed to do this as well as possible, skillful editors have bailed us out. Yet, while writing in as clear and direct a way as possible, we also have called upon students to *reason sociologically* and to explore the relationship between theory and research in a sophisticated way. We believe that this is something introductory-level students can and should do, but we also know they will only have the opportunity to do so if encouraged by their textbooks and instructors.

The Sociological Imagination

We now come to what we believe is the most important pedagogical feature of this book. It is not to be found in boxes, lists of key terms, or opening or closing sections of chapters, as important as all of these are. Rather, it is found throughout the book, in clearly written material with a constant emphasis on sociological thinking. In every chapter, students are encouraged to discover how ideas and concepts relate to one another. They are encouraged to reason sociologically to see whether the research evidence is consistent with the ideas advanced by one or the other of the three major perspectives. We believe that students can do this if we give them the proper tools in clear, understandable language. That is what we have tried to do, and we believe that if successful, the lives of the students who read this book will be enriched by their newfound ability to use the sociological imagination.

Web Supplements to This Text

Three web-based chapters:
 Web-Based Chapter A: Education
 Web-Based Chapter B: Religion
 Web-Based Chapter C: Health, Population, and Aging

Also on the Web: PowerPoint slides of tables and figures from the text

See all of these materials here:
http://www.paradigmpublishers.com/Books/ BookDetail.aspx?productID=236921

Additional Materials

An Instructor's Manual with Test Questions is available to professors reviewing or adopting the text. Email **examcopies@paradigmpublishers .com** for more information.

Acknowledgments

This book reflects the efforts of a very large number of people—a number that has grown with each new edition. We especially wish to thank Bill Webber for initiating the project all those years ago. Special thanks are due to the people who provided the initial drafts for the following chapters in the first edition: Larry Koch, Ball State University, for the deviance chapter; Marlene Lehtinen, University of Utah, for the marriage and family chapter; Christine M. Von Der Haar, Baruch College, for the religion chapter; and Steven Vago, St. Louis University, and Thomas D. Hall, DePauw University, for the social change chapter. We owe a deep debt of gratitude to everyone at Paradigm Publishers for bringing this new edition to life, especially Dean Birkenkamp, who first had the heart to believe in us and give this project its "rebirth" and then stuck with us even when the going got rough and deadlines got missed. Dean has been a friendly and wise voice of support throughout this process and without him this edition could not have been produced. Laura Esterman, Ashley Moore, and Jason Barry have provided a plethora of support to us, and Laura has shown more patience than we have deserved more times than we can count. We greatly appreciate their efforts on our behalf.

We would also like thank the many reviewers who offered their time and suggestions for improvements on one or more of the editions. Though some have commented on just one edition and others on more than one, all editions of the text have benefited, collectively, from their work:

Richard E. Anderson, *University of Nevada–Las Vegas*
Jeanne Ballantine, *Wright State University*
Mary Ellen Batiuk, *Wilmington College*
Joseph Behar, *Dowling College*
Casey Blanton, *Daytona State College*
Rhoda Lois Blumberg, *Rutgers University*
Jerry Bode, *Ball State University*
Dean A. Boldon, *Maryville College*
Paul B. Brezina, *County College of Morris*
Kay Broschart, *Hollins College*
Arnold S. Brown, *Northern Arizona University*
Edgar W. Butler, *University of California–Riverside*
John Cochran, *University of Oklahoma*
Ann Cordilia, *University of Massachusetts at Boston*
Larry D. Crawford, *Morehouse College*
Larry Crisler, *Millikin University*
Glenn Currier, *El Centro College*
Sandra B. Damico, *University of Florida*
Jon Darling, *University of Pittsburgh*
Lynn Davidman, *University of Pittsburgh*
Nanette J. Davis, *Portland State University*
Phyllis Davis, *Southwestern Christian College*
John DeLamater, *University of Wisconsin–Madison*
Norman K. Denzin, *University of Illinois*
D. James Dingman, *Jackson Community College*
Martin L. Dosick, *Springfield College*
Jackie Eller, *Middle Tennessee State University*
Charles F. Emmons, *Gettysburg College*
Kathryn M. Feltey, *University of Akron*
James Max Fendrich, *Florida State University*
Marvin Finkelstein, *Southern Illinois University at Edwardsville*
W. Edward Folts, *Appalachian State University*
Lee Frank, *Community College of Allegheny County*
James H. Frey, *University of Nevada–Las Vegas*
Joseph M. Garza, *Georgia State University*
Jonathan C. Gibralter, *Morrisville College*
Mahin Gosine, *New York Institute of Technology*
Linda Grant, *University of Georgia*
Paul S. Gray, *Boston College*
Richard Grego, *Daytona State College*
Frank Gunshanan, *Daytona State College*
Harry Hale, Jr., *Northeast Louisiana University*
Melissa Hardy, *Florida State University*
Charles L. Harper, *Creighton University*
Dean Harper, *University of Rochester*

Frank Hearn, *SUNY–Cortland*
Bradley Hertel, *Virginia Tech*
Douglas Horner, *Shepherd College*
James R. Hudson, *Pennsylvania State University–Harrisburg*
Craig Jenkins, *Ohio State University*
Wanda Kaluza, *Camden County College*
John Karlin, *Phillips University*
David Karp, *Boston College*
Michael A. Katovich, *Texas Christian University*
David Kauzlarich, *Southern Illinois University at Edwardsville*
Harry H. L. Kitano, *University of California at Los Angeles*
Emily E. LaBeff, *Midwestern State University*
Kurt Lang, *University of Washington*
Martin Levin, *Emory University*
Abraham Levine, *El Camino College*
Jonathan F. Lewis, *Illinois Benedictine College*
Christine Linsley, *St. John Fisher College*
Roy Lotz, *John Jay College*
William H. McBroom, *University of Montana*
Patrick McNamara, *University of New Mexico*
Linda Majka, *University of Dayton*
Christopher Marshall, *Unity College*
Joseph D. Martini, *Washington State University*
Allan Mazur, *Syracuse University*
Rodney Metzger, *Lane Community College*
James W. Michaels, *Virginia Tech*
Michael D. Miskinis, *Massasoit Community College*
Krista Moore, *Adams State College*
Peter B. Morrill, *Bronx Community College*
Jeffrey E. Nash, *Macalester College*
Donald L. Noel, *University of Wisconsin–Milwaukee*
Anthony Orum, *University of Illinois–Chicago*
Novella Perrin, *Central Missouri State University*
Joseph B. Perry, Jr., *Bowling Green State University*
Carolyn Pesackis, *Belmont Abbey College*
Cheryl Principato, *University of Wisconsin–Milwaukee*
Carl R. Redden, *University of Central Arkansas*
Wade Clark Roof, *University of Massachusetts*
Richard Ropers, *Southern Utah State University*
Susan D. Rose, *Dickinson College*
Daniel Rosenberg, *Earlham College*
Carol Schmid, *Guilford Technical Community College*
Steven Seidman, *SUNY–Albany*
Martha Shwayder-Hughes, *Metropolitan State College of Denver*
David Lewis Smith, *Georgia Southwestern College*
Robert Speyer, *College of Southern Idaho*
Steven Stack, *Wayne State University*
George F. Stine, *Millersville University*
Kenrick Thompson, *Northern Michigan University*
Melissa S. Venable, *University of Wisconsin–Milwaukee*
Theodore Wagenaar, *Miami University*
John W. Wallace, *Taylor University*
Walter L. Wallace, *Princeton University*
Kathryn Ward, *Southern Illinois University at Carbondale*
Lawrence D. Weiss, *University of Alaska–Anchorage*
Monica White, *Southern Illinois University at Edwardsville*
C. Ray Wingrove, *University of Richmond*
Michael D. Woodard, *University of Missouri*
Surendar Yadava, *University of Northern Iowa*

Acknowledgments

John Farley: As I have revised this book for each new edition, my colleagues and graduate students at SIUE have helped in a variety of ways, edition after edition. Many an idea that has gone into this book is a product of lunchtime discussions with my colleagues in the Department of Sociology at SIUE. I would particularly like to thank graduate students Xhinhe Bi, Cui-Xia Zhang, Harold Ross, John Cronin, Brenda Thomas, Karen Holtz, David Gorsage, and Craig Hughey for their helpful assistance with revisions for the second and third editions. I am also grateful to Gina Goodwin for assistance in the compilation and editing of the reference list for the third edition. In the fourth edition, sociology graduate assistant Mary Lytle performed yeoman service in merging together material carried over from the third edition with new material written for the fourth edition, as well as providing valuable proofreading assistance. Most of all, I am grateful for the love and emotional support I have received from my daughter, Megan, through all six editions, and from my wife, Alice, to whom this edition is lovingly and gratefully dedicated.

Michael Flota: It is an immense honor to have been brought on board for this sixth edition of what I have always considered the best sociology textbook on the market. When I approached John about reviving the book for a sixth edition, I knew several things would be true: a search for a new publisher, substantial revisions, and that we would have to rekindle an old relationship of teacher to student that we had lost since I left SIUE as a graduate student to pursue my Ph.D. and become a professor. What I did not anticipate was the enormous amount of respect and awe I would gain at the breadth and depth of knowledge John has of the field of sociology. As we move forward with this book into what I expect are many more editions to come, I can only hope that I can develop a token of the skill he brings to this endeavor. I thank him deeply for his patience and support in our collaboration. In this project, we have once again become John the teacher and I the student. And I have learned much more than just the craft of authorship. I have learned the heart of a great and generous friend. Thank you, John. I would also be remiss if I didn't mention the many students who assisted me with several photos in this book. Eli Blanton, Candice Cole, Mariah Dennis, Mathew Hall, and Chelsie Wehde all posed for pictures and assisted in photo shoots. Friends, colleagues, and their families can also be found in the photos on these pages. I owe a deep debt of gratitude to Richard Grego, Terry Lippelt-Grego, Cooper Barnes, Elizabeth Barnes, Michael Barnes, Wesley Barnes, Rebecca Block, Frank Gunshanan, Jason Kester, Jessica Kester, James Newell, Jennifer Veitch-Newell, Shael Newell, Gabe Newell, Azsia Thomas, Jaiden Thomas, Mikha Thomas, Harun Thomas, and Nicole Thomas. Finally, I must thank my wife, JoAnna Conley-Flota, for assisting with all of the above and for putting up with the long hours of an absent husband struggling to meet yet another deadline. This book is dedicated to her.

About the Authors
John E. Farley

John E. Farley is Professor Emeritus of Sociology at Southern Illinois University–Edwardsville, where he has taught courses ranging from introductory sociology to a course in advanced data analysis for graduate students. He conducted his undergraduate studies at Michigan State University, where he received a B.A. in political science. He continued his studies at the University of Michigan, where he received an M.A. and a Ph.D. in sociology, as well as the master of urban planning degree. He has taught at Southern Illinois University at Edwardsville since 1977.

He is the author of two other textbooks, *Majority-Minority Relations, Sixth Edition* (2010) and *American Social Problems: An Institutional Analysis, Second Edition* (1992). His articles on his sociological research have appeared in the *American Journal of Sociology*, the *American Journal of Economics and Sociology*, *Urban Affairs Quarterly*, and a number of other journals. He has also presented the results of his research at numerous professional meetings over the years and has addressed such meetings in Germany, Canada, and Sweden, as well as throughout the United States. He has provided expert testimony in a number of federal court cases pertaining to racial discrimination and segregation in housing, and he has served as a member of the editorial board of *Urban Affairs Quarterly*. He headed a research team studying public response to Iben Browning's prediction of an earthquake in the Midwest in 1990, and was editor of a special issue of the *International Journal of Mass Emergencies and Disasters* on that topic. His book *Earthquake Fears, Predictions, and Preparations in Mid-America*, which reports the results of the three-year study, was published by Southern Illinois University Press in 1998. Dr. Farley has conducted research on racial housing segregation based on each U.S. census from 1980 through 2000. He has received research grants from the National Science Foundation, the National Institute of Mental Health, and SIUE's Graduate School and Institute for Urban Research.

Professor Farley has received a number of awards for his work, including the SIUE Outstanding Scholar Award for his research on race relations and racial housing segregation, the SIUE Kimmell Community Service Award for his efforts in creating a fair housing organization in the St. Louis metropolitan area, and SIUE's Dr. Martin Luther King, Jr., University Humanitarian Award for his efforts in the community. He has served as president of the SIUE Faculty Senate and the Illinois Sociological Association. In 2000–2001, he was president of the Midwest Sociological Society, one of the largest and most active regional sociological organizations in the United States. Dr. Farley enjoys fishing, snow skiing, travel, and nature and weather photography, especially when sharing these activities with his wife, Alice, and his daughter, Megan, now grown and married with children of her own—which means that today Professor Farley has two grandchildren to spoil and to teach to ski.

About the Authors
Michael W. Flota

Michael W. Flota is Associate Professor of Sociology at Daytona State College, where he teaches Introduction to Sociology every semester. He conducted his undergraduate studies at Rend Lake College and Southern Illinois University–Edwardsville, where he was a student of John Farley. At SIUE, he received his B.A. in sociology, with minors in political science and peace studies, and later his M.A. in sociology. He continued his education at the University of California–Davis, where he received a Ph.D. in economic sociology. He has taught at Daytona State College since 2005.

Professor Flota serves as the Managing Editor for the *Journal of Florida Studies* as well as the director and cofounder of the Center for Interdisciplinary Writing and Research. He teaches in the nationally renowned interdisciplinary learning community QUANTA on the Daytona State College campus.

His research involves the study of comparative financial systems in times of crisis. His dissertation examined the policies that led up to and followed financial crises in Sweden and South Korea during the 1980s and 1990s. He is also interested in the study of policies aimed at sustainable economic development. He credits his love of teaching to his mother and his love of economics to his father. In his free time Dr. Flota enjoys writing screenplays, novels, and songs and watching his wife belly dance.

Part I
Introduction

Chapter 1
Sociology: The Discipline

What Is Sociology? — 4
    Characteristics of Sociology   4
    Sociology and Common Sense   5

Sociology as a Science — 6
    Science as a Way of Thinking   6
    The Norms of Science   8

Sociology as a Social Science — 8
    Can Human Behavior Be Studied Scientifically?   8
    An Analogy: Meteorology   9
    Complications in the Study of Human Behavior   9
    The Sociological Imagination   10

Sociology and the Other Social Sciences — 12
    Sociology   12
    The Other Social Sciences   12

The Emergence and Development of Sociology — 13
    The Nineteenth Century   13
    Early Sociologists   13

The Development of Sociology in the United States — 17
    The Chicago School   17
    Symbolic-Interactionism   18

1940–1960: A Turn from Activism — 18

The 1960s: Return to Activism — 19

The 1970s into the New Millennium:
Diversity in Sociological Perspectives — 19

PUTTING SOCIOLOGY TO WORK — 19
    How Sociology Can Be Used to Solve Real-Life Problems   19

Summary — 22
Key Terms — 22
Exercises — 22

Did education, race, and gender make any difference in how different Americans responded to the September 11, 2001, terrorist attacks?

Why did white people and black people react so differently to the arrest of Harvard professor Henry Louis Gates, an African American who was arrested after "breaking into" his own home?

Why is it that some people can't wait to use the Internet, while others hardly know what it is?

Is it true that the rich are getting richer and the poor are getting poorer?

Does capital punishment deter murder?

What can we do to make work more enjoyable and more productive? Can we do both at the same time?

Have you wondered about the answers to any of these questions, or others like them? If you have, sociology is a good place to look for the answers. What sociology does, first and foremost, is to study human groups and societal arrangements to find out the answers to questions like these. There is great diversity within sociology in terms of methods, theories, and the exact subject matter studied, but there are also two core commonalities. First, sociologists believe that questions like the ones above can be answered through systematic observation. Second, sociologists believe that in order to answer such questions adequately, we must examine the influences of human groups and societal arrangements on behavior. These two shared beliefs or viewpoints make up what sociologists often call the **sociological perspective**.

What Is Sociology?

Sociology is a systematic approach to thinking about, studying, and understanding society, human social behavior, and social groups. It is different from other approaches to understanding human behavior in two key ways. First, its major emphasis is on how social groups and the larger society influence behavior. In this regard, it is different from psychology, for example, which primarily looks within the individual for explanations of human behavior. Second, sociology does not focus on certain specific areas of human behavior (as, for example, do political science and economics), but rather seeks to explain the broad range of human behavior as it is influenced by social groups and society. The behavior studied by sociology includes the collective actions of groups and societies, not just the actions of individuals.

Characteristics of Sociology

As stated above, the sociological perspective holds that questions about human behavior can be answered through systematic observation. Because it uses systematic observation as its way of answering such questions, sociology is regarded as a *science* by most sociologists. **Science** is an approach to understanding reality that asks and answers questions based on systematic observation, generalization, and interpretation. In the next section, we shall contrast science with another way of understanding reality, common sense. But first there are two other characteristics of sociology we need to mention. One is that sociology is one of a group of sciences known as the **social sciences**. The social sciences use the methods of science in order to understand human social behavior. The other characteristic is that, as stated in our opening description of the sociological perspective, sociology focuses primarily on the influences of human groups and of the larger society on behavior. By human groups, we mean collectivities of people who share something in common, such as race, educational level, gender, or profession. Because of its interest in the influences of human groups and of society on behavior, sociology often studies human behavior on a relatively large scale. It is more interested in explaining how most people in a given situation or group will behave than in predicting how a particular individual will behave. For example, a sociologist who studies race relations would not have been at all surprised at the different reactions of black and white Americans to the arrest of Harvard professor Henry Lewis Gates: the two groups looked at it from very different sets of shared experiences, concerns, and viewpoints. These shared characteristics, which are different for whites and African Americans, led to very different patterns of reaction to the incident among the two groups. Whites saw a black man who had become belligerent and uncooperative with a police officer, whereas African Americans saw a white police officer arresting a black man in his own home. When asked if the police officer acted "stupidly" only 29 percent of whites said yes, compared with 59% of blacks (Steinhauser, 2009). The collective experiences and fears of both groups conditioned them to see the case in these different ways, and thus to come to different conclusions about who was in the wrong. Thus, while sociology could not necessarily predict with certainty how a particular white person or African American would react to the incident, the overall pattern of reactions among the two groups was quite predictable if you knew enough about the sociology of race relations.

Sociology and Common Sense

As noted previously, sociology, or any science, differs from common sense in its approach toward understanding the world. The main difference is that common sense takes things for granted, while science does not: In a science such as sociology, any assumption is up for question; nothing is taken for granted. This is not to dispute the value of common sense. Years ago, a man in Minneapolis fell off his roof trying to get a better look at a tornado passing through the city. Clearly, common sense tells us that it is stupid to stand on a roof during a tornado! But there are other things it may not be able to tell us. Try using common sense to answer the true/false questions that appear in the box "A Common Sense Quiz."

Common sense probably suggested an answer to many of these questions. But was it the right answer? Turn ahead now to the box "A Common Sense Quiz: The Answers" to find out.

How did you do? If you are like most students, you got several answers wrong. In fact, based on similar quizzes we've given in our introductory classes, we are sure that some of you got half or more of the answers wrong. The point? Common sense is great for some things (like telling you to stay off a roof during tornadoes), but in many other situations, it is totally inadequate, and we must use other means of understanding the world. Sociology is one such way.

SOCIOLOGICAL INSIGHTS
A Common Sense Quiz

Like everything else, common sense is good for some things and not for others. Try using common sense to decide whether the following statements are true or false:

1. Making contraceptives available to teenagers through school clinics will push them to be more sexually active, because they won't have to worry about pregnancy.
2. People who live in the southern part of the United States drink less alcohol than people who live in the North.
3. When exiting a "burning theater" or some similar emergency in a confined space, people are often trampled when trying to escape, because everyone thinks only of themselves in such a life or death situation and will trample others to save themselves.
4. When a disaster is forecast, the best predictor of whether people will plan and take actions to protect themselves is whether or not they believe the forecast.
5. The higher the percentage of people in a population who drink, the higher the percentage of alcoholics there will be in that population.
6. During the days immediately following the September 11, 2001, terrorist attacks, Americans were unified in their confidence that a military response to the attacks would be effective.
7. Now that we have civil rights laws, the gap between black and white family income in the United States has considerably narrowed.
8. Juvenile delinquents generally commit the same kinds of crime as adult criminals.
9. Overcrowding in American cities is an important reason for the much higher urban crime rates in the last three decades as compared with earlier decades.
10. The incidence of homosexuality in the United States today is no greater relative to the population than it was 40 or 50 years ago.

In fact, one recent president of the American Sociological Association has argued that this is the greatest benefit of sociology: it reveals the often unexpected consequences of things that we do (Portes, 2000). For example, it makes perfect sense that the 1986 immigration reforms, which penalized employers for hiring illegal aliens and increased funding for the border patrol, might reduce illegal immigration. However, actual sociological research on the consequences of the immigration law showed that this was not the case; if anything, illegal immigration increased, because both would-be immigrants and would-be employers of illegal immigrants found new, more clever ways to get around the new law (Portes, 2000).

Sociology as a Science

Science as a Way of Thinking

We have said that most sociologists view their discipline as a science. Science is one of several possible ways of understanding reality. As we have already seen, common sense is another way of understanding reality, and faith and tradition are yet others. Each of these ways is useful for understanding certain kinds of things. However, as the previous commonsense example illustrated, each also has its limitations.

Science is based on systematic observation or measurement, called **research**. While this enables us to answer questions that can't be reliably

SOCIOLOGICAL INSIGHTS
A Common Sense Quiz: The Answers

1. **False** The limited number of studies of the effects of distributing contraceptives in high school clinics have all shown that this practice either had no effect on, or slightly reduced, the amount of teenage sexual activity. The apparent reason is that students in schools with clinics became more informed about the consequences of their sexual behavior and felt more in control of their sexual behavior and thus were more willing to say no (Kirby, 1997; Moore and Caldwell, 1977; Schorr and Schorr, 1988, pp. 54–55; Zabin et al., 1986). During the 1990s teen pregnancy rates fell *both* because fewer teens were having sex and because more of those who did used contraceptives. The former accounts for about one-fourth of the decline; the latter for about three-fourths (Alan Guttmacher Institute, 1999).

2. **True** Among those who do drink, there is little regional difference in the amount of alcohol consumed. Average per-person alcohol consumption in the South, however, is lower because a significantly larger proportion of the southern population does not drink at all. The apparent reason for this is that more people in the South practice religions that forbid or discourage drinking (see Gallup, 1984; U.S. Bureau of the Census, 1988a).

3. **False** Research has shown that the majority of people exiting a burning building or some other similar emergency do so with calm urgency. The problem is that many confined public spaces do not have adequate exits for everyone to use at once. So, two things begin to occur: First, a "crush at the exit" begins as more people than can fit through try to exit at once. This leads to someone slipping and falling. Second, people in the back can't see this, so they continue to push forward, knocking down anyone in the front trying to help those who have fallen to get up. And thus, a tragic chain of events occurs in which many people are trampled. In hindsight, it appears that people simply ran over others to save themselves. But the evidence indicates that it is almost completely the opposite.

4. **False** Survey research in several instances of disaster predictions has shown that the best predictor of people's plans and actions is what they see their friends and neighbors doing. In the case of an inaccurate but widely believed prediction of a central U.S. earthquake, what friends and neighbors planned to do made even more difference than whether people believed the forecast (Farley, 1998). Similar findings were obtained in several studies of evacuation behavior during hurricane warnings (Baker, 1979).

5. **False** Some populations, such as Italians and Jews, have very high incidences of drinking

answered by common sense or faith and tradition, it has its limitations, as does any way of understanding reality. For one, it can only answer questions about things that can be observed, such as human behavior. It cannot answer questions, for example, about the existence of heaven and hell or about the meaning of life. In addition, the meaning or significance of what is observed is almost always open to some debate, particularly in the social sciences, which study human behavior. In spite of these limitations, science has become the most widely used way of understanding reality in modern industrial societies.

Through research, scientists look for regular and systematic patterns, a process called generalization. They try to find relationships in which the presence of one condition often or usually leads to some other condition. When they find such regularities, scientists try to explain them by developing a **theory**—a set of interrelated arguments that seek to describe and explain cause-effect relationships. Good theory offers new explanations for patterns that have been observed through research, or predicts findings that might be expected based upon the theory's argument. Good research may test a relationship proposed in a theory, or it may identify new patterns or relationships in need of explanation by a theory. Thus, science—including sociology—becomes an ongoing cycle of *observation,* which leads to *generalization* that describes regular patterns based upon what has been observed. The next step is *explanation* of these patterns through

---

(nearly all adults drink), but their rates of alcoholism are well below the average. Other groups, such as some fundamentalist Protestants in the United States, contain relatively few drinkers, but those who do drink exhibit very high alcoholism rates, in part because they do their drinking on the sly. Among some of these groups, the alcoholism rate is well above that of Italians and Jews (Clinard, 1974, pp. 446–71, 479–84).

6. **False** Americans were indeed unusually unified (around 90 percent) in favoring a military response, but their confidence in the effectiveness of such a response varied widely. Most confident were men, whites, Southerners, and people with less than a college education. Women, college graduates, African Americans, and people who were most worried about personally becoming a victim of terrorism were significantly less confident that a military response would be effective in preventing terrorism (Pew Research Center, 2001).

7. **False** Median family income among African Americans has consistently been around 55 to 60 percent of median white family income ever since the major civil rights laws were passed in the 1960s. The processes of discrimination that produce or perpetuate such inequalities are apparently more subtle than those addressed by the laws (Farley, 2010).

8. **False** By and large, young people and adults commit different types of crimes. Adult criminals are more likely to commit serious assaults, major thefts, and fraud and are responsible for the great majority of homicides. Juvenile delinquents are likely to commit smaller thefts, vandalism, and joy riding, as well as status offenses—things that are legal for adults to do but illegal for juveniles (for example, drinking, curfew violation, running away) (Barlow, 2000, pp. 76–77; Federal Bureau of Investigation, 1999, p. 220).

9. **False** The crime rates of American cities have been higher over the past few decades than in the past, though they have fallen since the mid-1990s. The higher rates in recent decades, however, cannot be blamed on overcrowding, because by any measure (for example, people per square mile in the city or people per room in housing units), American cities have been getting progressively *less* crowded since 1960 or earlier and are much less crowded now than they were in the past. For example, Chicago, New York, Boston, Cleveland, Detroit, and St. Louis all have far fewer people now than they had in 1950 (Macionis and Parillo, 2001, p. 78)—but their crime rates are higher than they were in 1950.

10. **True** Ever since the famous Kinsey Reports on sexual behavior were published in the late 1940s and early 1950s, survey data have found that the proportion of people with a predominantly homosexual preference has remained steady at around 3 or 4 percent for males and 2 or 3 percent for females. The proportion with some homosexual experience is considerably larger, but it, too, has remained constant.

theories, which in turn engage in *prediction* regarding relationships to be found in other situations or about new relationships that logically follow from the explanations offered by the theory. After this, the cycle begins again with a new round of research (observation) to see whether the theory's predictions can be confirmed. This basic method, used in sociology and all other sciences, is called the scientific method. Its use in sociology is more fully discussed in Chapter 2.

The Norms of Science

Organized Skepticism

The basic approach described previously—a cycle of inquiry consisting of observation, generalization, explanation, and prediction—is shared by both the **natural sciences,** such as physics, chemistry, astronomy, and biology, which study natural phenomena, and the social sciences, such as sociology, psychology, anthropology, and political science, which study human behavior. Certain norms or expectations are shared in all of the sciences (Merton, 1973). The most important of these is **organized skepticism,** which states that science accepts nothing on the basis of faith, common sense, or because someone claims it is true. Rather, it must be demonstrated by systematic observation. While science is often marked by several competing theories, each purporting to offer the true explanation for something, scientists will not believe any of the theories until the things predicted by the theory have been consistently shown by research to be true. If scientists observe patterns that are not consistent with the theory, it will be either modified or rejected.

Sociology as a Social Science

Can Human Behavior Be Studied Scientifically?

As noted earlier, sociology is one of the social sciences, which are concerned with the study of human thought and behavior and human social institutions. All of the social sciences share the common assumption that human social behavior can be studied scientifically, although there are great debates concerning how best to accomplish this. Social scientists believe that certain patterns and regularities in human behavior enable them to predict and explain human behavior to a substantial extent. Is this assumption true? Can human behavior be studied scientifically?

Many people would argue that it cannot. Because each person is an individual, capable of making free choices about an almost infinite number of things, how can we view human behavior as regular and predictable? The best answer is that every one of you experiences the regularities and predictable elements of human behavior every day. Every time you drive a car, you rely on the predictability of the other people on the road. You assume that they will go in the right direction, stop at stop signs, wait for lights to turn green, and so on. In most cases, they do. Only on the infrequent occasions when people behave **unpredictably** are accidents likely to occur. The behavior of people in other situations is similarly predictable. Imagine yourself in class, at religious services, at a football game. In each of these situations, your behavior and that of the other people present is for the most part predictable. Even less structured situations such as parties and nightclubs have fairly regular patterns of behavior. These regularities in behavior occur because there are general rules about how to behave in these situations that the participants know and for the most part follow. In each case, if you have had a reasonable amount of experience, you have a pretty good idea of how you are "supposed to" behave, and you will usually act accordingly.

Beyond such obvious cases of predictable behavior, however, social scientists have developed an impressive record of predicting behavior based on careful and systematic (scientific) measurement. In a large population of newly married couples, for example, a social scientist could predict with reasonable accuracy what kinds of couples are at the highest risk of divorce. A social scientist would predict—on the basis of findings of past research—that those couples with lower income and education levels, those who marry at a younger age, those in which the wife has a high income relative to her husband, and those with partners from sharply different social backgrounds have a higher risk of divorce than couples with the opposite characteristics. Not every couple with "high-risk" characteristics will get a divorce, but a social scientist could predict that a large group of couples with these characteristics will experience a higher divorce rate than a similar-sized group of couples without them. On this large scale, divorce is predictable, even though it is harder to predict whether a *particular* couple will get a divorce.

An Analogy: Meteorology

An analogy can be seen in the natural science of *meteorology,* the study of weather. Over a large area (such as a state), meteorologists can make fairly accurate predictions that, for example, thunderstorms will occur and will affect about one-third of the area. However, they are far less accurate at pinpointing exactly where the storms will occur. This does not mean that meteorology is not scientific or that weather is totally unpredictable. Rather, it means that the large pattern is easier to predict than the isolated experience of one location. The same is true of the social sciences: The overall behavior patterns in groups of people are frequently predictable; the exact behavior of a given individual is less so. In individual situations, predictions of behavior become much more probabilistic: Given what we know about an individual, we can state a rough level of probability that the individual will think or behave in a particular way, but we cannot predict the exact behavior with complete certainty, just as the meteorologist can predict the weather in a particular location with a probability (for example, a 30 percent chance of rain) rather than with complete certainty.

Complications in the Study of Human Behavior

Although human behavior does display considerable regularity and predictability, certain elements of complexity are present in the social sciences that are not present in the natural sciences. These complexities make human behavior somewhat more difficult to study than natural processes, and they help to explain why the predictions of social scientists are frequently less precise than those of natural scientists. These complexities also help explain why social scientists disagree sharply about the best methods for studying human behavior, even when they do agree that it can be systematically studied.

Reactivity

One problem in the social sciences is **reactivity**; that is, the tendency of people to behave differently when they are being studied than they normally would. In most social-science research, the people being studied know they are being studied, interact with the person studying them, or both. In surveys, most experiments, and some participant observation (three common methods of social-science research described in Chapter 2), the people being studied know they are the subjects of some kind of research project. Consequently, they might try to please the researcher, make themselves look good, cover up their faults, or act defensively. Thus, what the researcher observes is not normal, everyday behavior, but, in part, a reaction to the research process. Even if the subjects don't know they are being studied, their interactions with the researcher can shape the way they behave. Natural scientists generally don't have to worry about these difficulties. For example, under specified temperature and atmospheric conditions, two chemicals will react with one another the same way whether anyone is watching or not. The same is *not* true of two people. Thus, one of the great challenges of social-science research is to measure correctly what the researcher intends to measure—not the reaction of the person being studied to the research, and not the social scientist's sometimes incorrect interpretation of the meaning of that person's behavior.

Change Over Time and Place

Another complicating factor in the social sciences is that relationships can change significantly over time, and even from one place to another. This problem can be illustrated by the relationship between race and voter turnout. At one time, it was almost universally true that white voters turned out at a higher rate than black voters in the United States. In the 1980s, however, as black majorities emerged in many local electorates and black candidates became influential on the local, state, and national levels, black voter turnout surpassed white turnout in many areas. Thus, the finding that whites are more likely to vote than blacks, while once true, is no longer valid. It is still true in some situations, but the opposite is now true in others.

This complication exists to a much lesser extent, if at all, in the natural sciences. Fifty years ago, protons had a positive electrical charge and electrons had a negative charge, and they still do today and still will 50 years from now. Moreover, this will hold true whether you are in Detroit, New York, St. Louis, Houston, or San Francisco, whereas the pattern of African Americans turning out to vote at a different rate than whites will not be so stable. This adds another complication to the study of human behavior, and it underlines two important points about the social sciences:

1. Research must be kept up to date; only current research can indicate whether patterns demonstrated to be true in the past still hold true in the present.
2. Research findings generated in one locality might not hold for another locality. Thus, large-scale national research is preferable to local studies for many purposes, and caution should always be used in generalizing social-science findings to or from a particular local area.

Studying Ourselves

Compared with the natural sciences, it is harder to approach the social sciences in a detached manner, because we are, in effect, studying ourselves. Social scientists often have strong personal feelings about the material they are studying. As has been illustrated by Thomas Kuhn (1962), natural scientists also can have strong feelings about the subject matter they are studying and even set out to "prove a point." But this is probably even more true of the social sciences, where the scientist, as a human being, is often very close emotionally to what he or she is studying (Lieberson, 1992). As Kuhn points out, this does not in any way invalidate science (either natural or social), but it increases the need for social scientists to adhere to the principle of organized skepticism.

By now, some of you probably agree that human behavior can be studied scientifically, and some do not. Even sociologists disagree on the *extent* to which sociology constitutes a science (Collins, 1987; Denzin, 1987), and some have argued that the difficulties of observing and interpreting human behavior make sociology one of the liberal arts more so than a science (Denzin, 1989). Keep in mind that one limitation of science is that the *meaning* of what is observed is open to debate. This is especially true in the social sciences. Accordingly, what sociologists "observe" may not so much be behavior as it "really happens" but rather the sociologists' *understanding* of what they have observed. Thus, two sociologists observing the same behavior can and do sometimes "see" different things (Denzin, 1989, p. 67). Beyond the difficulties of observation, most social scientists do *not* accept the idea that human behavior is governed by some set of laws such that, if only we could discover all of them and measure people's social and psychological characteristics perfectly, we could totally predict human behavior. It's just too complex and spontaneous for that.

Even so, the majority of sociologists do subscribe to the view that much human behavior *can* be observed and understood through the methods of science, even though certain difficulties make the social world harder to study than the natural or physical world (Collins, 1995, 1974). Similarly, although no set of "laws" exists that totally determines human behavior, there *are* patterns and regularities to human behavior that make it largely, if far from totally, predictable.

Finally, that behavior is not always linear and predictable arguably makes sociology *more* valuable, because it is only through social research that the surprising and sometimes unpredicted consequences of our actions are revealed. For an example of this, see the box "How Emigration Created a Private School Boom."

The Sociological Imagination

One source of discomfort to nonsociologists is that sociology often tells us things that we believe are not true. For this very reason, however, sociology can be a source of very useful insights. Sociologist C. Wright Mills (1959) refers to such insights as the **sociological imagination.** By using the sociological imagination, we gain understandings that we could not achieve through other modes of reasoning. The sociological imagination helps us understand how the social situation shapes our private realities—often in ways over which we have limited control. In many societies, but especially in the United States, people usually think in terms of *individuals* and what *individuals* do. From this viewpoint, when something good happens to you, it is because of what you have accomplished or what some other person—a parent, sibling, friend, or lover—has done for you. Similarly, when something bad happens, it is because of your own failing, or perhaps because some other individual has treated you unfairly.

Divorce and the Sociological Imagination

Consider the case of divorce, mentioned earlier in this chapter. If you are ever divorced, you will likely ask yourself "Where did I go wrong?" or perhaps "Why did my spouse treat me that way?" Undoubtedly, thinking about such questions will give you some useful insights. At the same time, though, there is another part of understanding why you got a divorce that such questions can't answer. The fact is that divorce has become much more common in the United States than it was in the past, for a variety of reasons that have nothing to do with how you or your spouse treat each other. These causes of divorce, which are explored in greater detail in Chapter 13, include changes in the economic meaning of the family, longer life expectancy, changes in the roles of men and women, changes in the views of marriage, and changes in the law. Today, you are getting married in a very different social situation from that of people a couple generations ago, such as your grandparents, and in today's social conditions, far more marriages end in divorce. Thus, your divorce results only in part from your behavior or your spouse's behavior; in the past, similar behavior would not have resulted in divorce. Rather, part of the reason for your divorce has to do with social changes that have increased *everyone's* risk of divorce.

Using the sociological imagination is helpful for understanding a wide variety of events that occur in your life. The sociological imagination, for example, can be used to understand such diverse events as obtaining a college degree, losing a job, and getting sick. This can be tremendously useful to both individuals and the larger society. From the individual viewpoint, it gives us a better understanding of why things happen to us and

---

SOCIOLOGICAL SURPRISES
How Emigration Created a Private School Boom

One might expect that, with emigration (migration out of a country), private school enrollments might decline. After all, the people who move out are often young, well-educated, upwardly mobile families looking to better their situation—precisely the kind of people who often enroll their children in private schools. But when such people moved out of the Dominican Republic to the United States, just the opposite happened: There was a *boom* in private school enrollment in the Dominican Republic.

Why did this happen? The answer lies in another sociological surprise: this boom in enrollment was a response to rules against corporal punishment in U.S. schools. Unlike most Americans today, Dominicans make considerable use of corporal punishment: Few Dominican children escape spankings when they misbehave, even in school. Hence, Dominican immigrants to the United States found a school system and a society with norms contrary to their culture. Their kids would not receive what they viewed as proper discipline at school, and they quickly learned that they could reduce the frequency of spankings at home by threatening to report their parents for child abuse. This situation created a dilemma for the parents. On the one hand, they were greatly increasing their economic opportunities by leaving the Dominican Republic and moving to New York. But on the other hand, without strict discipline they risked losing control of their kids to the tough street culture of the city.

The answer, for many of the immigrant parents, was to send their kids back to the Dominican Republic to attend private schools where they would be "properly disciplined" and away from the temptations of the New York City streets. The result was that, even as more and more of these upwardly mobile families left the Dominican Republic for the United States, more and more of them sent their children to private schools in the Dominican Republic (Portes, 2000).

why others behave as they do, as illustrated in the box "Using the Sociological Imagination: College Women Faculty and Household Work in the United States and China." From a societal viewpoint, it can be a very useful tool for alleviating problems that arise from human behavior or human social arrangements.

Finally, if you are still skeptical about the usefulness of sociology, consider this: Like it or not, you live in a world where "scientific" claims about human behavior are made all the time. This is done in advertising, in politics, even in sports and entertainment. Some such claims are based on sound social research, but many are not and are merely intended to persuade (or in some cases entertain) you. The ability to distinguish valid social science from hucksterism and propaganda is a useful tool in the media and Internet age.

Sociology and the Other Social Sciences

Sociology shares some important things with the other social sciences: the use of the scientific method; the assumption that human behavior has patterns and regularities; and the belief that behavior can be studied and largely understood through systematic observation, generalization, and interpretation. Sociology also differs in certain ways from the other social sciences, which include psychology, economics, political science, and social anthropology. (Some people also include history, whereas others classify it as one of the humanities.) Several applied professions, including social work and urban planning, rely heavily on knowledge generated by the social sciences. In colleges and universities, programs in these professions are sometimes located under schools or divisions of the social sciences or of the arts and sciences, and sometimes in separate professional schools.

The various social sciences differ in the aspects of human behavior that they study, the level (individual versus group or society) at which they study human behavior, and, to a considerable extent, the methods by which they study human behavior. Although they are regarded as distinct academic disciplines, they overlap considerably. Many areas of human behavior are studied by more than one of the social sciences, sometimes with very similar methods of research. Keeping this in mind, we shall briefly describe sociology and its relationship with the other social sciences.

Sociology

Sociology is concerned with virtually all aspects of human social behavior. In this sense, it is less specialized than some of the other social sciences, particularly political science and economics. The second feature that distinguishes sociology from the other social sciences is its scale: its emphasis is on *societies* and groups within society rather than on individuals. Among the things that sociologists consider in any society they study are the major forms of organization and ways of doing things that become accepted in that society, which sociologists call institutions. Sociologists are interested in how these institutions address basic needs in society and how they relate to the interests, needs, and desires of the various groups of people within societies (ethnic groups, gender groups, religious groups, social classes). Sociologists also study such social groups to see how they develop, how they relate to one another, and how they divide (and sometimes struggle over) the society's scarce resources. In addition, they study the beliefs, values, and rules about behavior that emerge in a society, as well as how and why these things differ among the various social groups within the society. Finally, sociologists examine the ways in which both societies and social groups train and indoctrinate new members, as well as the ways in which some social groups recruit new members. As you can see, the subject matter of sociology is nearly limitless. About the only limit is that sociology generally addresses these issues at least partly on a collective level—that of the society or social group—rather than entirely on the individual level.

The Other Social Sciences

Psychology, perhaps the oldest of the social sciences, is like sociology in that it is interested in a very broad range of human thought and behavior. The main difference is that psychology studies human behavior primarily on the individual level. By doing this, psychologists seek to understand and predict (and sometimes alter) the thoughts and behavior of individuals. Psychology has one important area of overlap with sociology, known as social psychology. Social psychology concerns the interaction between the individual and society, with a particular emphasis on the influences of society and social groups on the thought and behavior of the individual. Because of its interests in both the individual and society, social psychology is an important subdiscipline within both sociology and psychology.

Economics involves the study of human behavior as it relates to the production, exchange, distribution, and consumption of wealth and income. Economics is highly quantitative, with a heavy emphasis on how markets set prices and wage rates. Attempts are made at the national and world levels to predict and explain price changes, employment levels, and trade balances. Like psychology, economics has an important area of overlap with sociology, sometimes called economic sociology or the sociology of economics. This area is concerned with societal and group processes as they relate to income, wealth, consumption of goods and services, unemployment, and other economic issues.

Political science is concerned with human behavior as it relates to government and politics. Like sociology, it tends to operate on a group or societal level, but its focus is narrower. Among the areas of interest to political scientists are the development of political institutions, such as systems of government and political parties, and how the public relates to these institutions through such means as voting, working for political parties, running for office, contacting their representatives, and participating in protest marches. The latter set of concerns is the focus of an area of overlap with sociology called political sociology.

Social anthropology is the study of human culture: attitudes, beliefs, and rules of behavior that become generalized in society. Clearly, this interest overlaps significantly with sociology, but there is a difference in emphasis. Anthropology places a somewhat greater emphasis on *describing* the cultures of various societies: its primary objective is to understand these cultures. Sociology, in contrast, tends to relate these cultures to a larger context, including the institutions, the distribution of resources, and the interactions among social groups within the societies. Some anthropologists, known as physical anthropologists, use the techniques of archaeology to understand cultures of the past and the historical and prehistorical roots of today's cultures; other anthropologists study the process of evolution, and their work overlaps heavily with that of biologists.

The Emergence and Development of Sociology

The Nineteenth Century

As was noted earlier, the term "sociology" was coined only about 150 years ago. That period—the nineteenth century—witnessed some of the most profound social change in all of human history, particularly in Europe. For the first time, cities were becoming the dominant influence in what had always been rural societies. After thousands of years of relative stability, the world's population had entered a period of rapid growth that has continued to the present (what we now call the population explosion). Tradition and religion were being displaced by science and economic rationalism as ways of understanding reality and as forces shaping people's lives. Perhaps most dramatic of all was the effect of the Industrial Revolution on the lives of ordinary people. As the urban industrial economic order replaced the rural agricultural order, thousands flocked to the cities of Europe and, later, North America. In the cities, the migrants often endured horrible working conditions, child labor, low wages, and filthy, overcrowded neighborhoods that could not begin to accommodate them. Of course, urbanization made conditions such as these more visible, and some of the great minds of the era turned their attention to trying to understand why society was changing in the ways it was. Much of their concern was focused on new social problems, such as overcrowding, poverty, crime, depersonalization, and suicide, that seemed to be outgrowths of industrialization, urbanization, and related changes.

Early Sociologists

The Frenchman Auguste Comte (1798–1857) first used the term "sociology." He set the stage for future developments within the discipline when he argued that societies contained both forces for stability and cooperation, which he called *social*

GLOBAL SOCIOLOGY

Using the Sociological Imagination: College Women Faculty and Household Work in the United States and China

Who does the housework has become an increasing source of conflict for married couples when both partners work outside the home. Looking at the problem from an individualist standpoint, it seems that many women are angry at their husbands because they don't do a larger share of the work. They may ask, "Why is he so selfish and lazy?" But if we use the sociological imagination to look at this problem, we can get a better explanation of why housework is a source of conflict between husbands and wives. It turns out that, although the gap has narrowed over the past twenty years, women still do the majority of housework among most married couples in the United States, even when both husband and wife work full time (Coltrane and Adams, 2008). But the same thing is also true in societies that are very different from the United States, if they are undergoing similar changes in the roles of men and women. The sociological imagination tells us that conflicts over who does the housework do not arise simply because one or the other individual involved "has problems or a bad attitude." Conflicts arise societywide when there is uneven change within a society—for example, both husband and wife are now working outside the house, but their roles have yet to be redefined within the home.

That's what Cui-xia Zhang, a graduate student from the People's Republic of China studying in the United States, found out when she surveyed female college faculty members in China and the United States. Zhang surveyed two samples of married women faculty, one sample teaching at a university in the United States, the other at a university in China. Despite the vast differences between the United States and China, Zhang found striking similarities in how housework was divided between the women and their husbands in both countries. In the United States, for example, the women did 65 percent of the cooking on the average, while their husbands did only 25 percent. In China, the women did 63 percent of the cooking, while their husbands did only 24 percent. In both countries, the women also did a larger share than their husbands of washing dishes, doing laundry, shopping, housecleaning, and taking care of children. The only area in which husbands did more was in making repairs, of which they did 63 percent in the United States and 56 percent in China.

In fact, there were only two areas in which there were sizable differences in the share of household work done by college faculty women in the two samples. American women did a larger share of dishwashing than Chinese women (60 percent versus 44 percent), but they did a smaller share of housecleaning (56 percent compared to 72 percent). These differences, however, had nothing to do with help they got from their husbands. American husbands did only 31 percent of the dishwashing and 19 percent of the housecleaning, and their Chinese counterparts did virtually identical shares: 34 percent of the dishwashing and 18 percent of the housecleaning. Rather, the difference in the share of these jobs done by American and Chinese women resulted from the different ways housekeepers are used in the two countries. Chinese housekeepers largely help in the kitchen, whereas American housekeepers mainly do housecleaning. Hence, it was help from housekeepers, not husbands, that reduced housecleaning for American women and dishwashing for Chinese women.

Why is the household division of labor so similar in the two countries? It turns out that, despite their otherwise great differences, China and the United States have undergone similar changes in gender roles in recent decades. Both countries had a clear history of social and legal support for male supremacy through much of their history, as is discussed further in Chapters 4 and 8. But since World War II, both countries have legislated against sex discrimination, and in both, women have shifted from a predominantly home-centered role into a full-time employment role. However, as Zhang's research shows, the notion that home responsibilities fall first and foremost upon women has survived in both countries, despite the legal changes and despite the movement of women into the paid labor force. As recent trends in the United States suggest, the gap in housework may eventually decrease the longer both men and women are mostly in full-time employment, but this shift will be, at best, a very gradual process.

Source: The preceding is based on Cui-xia Zhang, *The Relationship Between Family Life and Academic Career: A Comparison of American and Chinese College Married Women Faculty.* Master's Thesis, Southern Illinois University at Edwardsville, 1991. A summary of this research can be found in Zhang and Farley, 1995.

statics, and forces for conflict and change, which he called *social dynamics*. Even today, one of the greatest debates in sociology—and one we will consider throughout this book—concerns the relative influences upon societies of forces for change versus forces for stability.

Comte also believed strongly that society and human behavior were governed by regular laws and principles that could be understood using the scientific method—in the same way that the natural world could be understood by natural scientists and physicists. He referred to this approach as positivism, a term that is still used to describe the belief that both social and natural forces can be measured accurately and precisely through scientific observation, and *only* through scientific observation. Many sociologists today would agree that the "only" part is too extreme, so the idea of positivism is today a controversial one. Moreover, the difficulty of making purely objective measures that are not affected by the perspectives and preconceptions of the observer is better recognized among today's sociologists. Still, the basic notion that social and natural forces are patterned and subject to systematic observation remains the underpinning of sociology 150 years after Comte's lifetime. Like many subsequent sociologists, Comte was also a social reformer who believed applying the scientific method to society was the way to bring about social betterment.

Although Comte named the discipline and to a large extent set the agenda for its debates, even more lasting early influences on sociology came from three other great social thinkers: the Germans Karl Marx and Max Weber and the Frenchman Emile Durkheim. We shall briefly discuss their contributions here; more detailed discussions of their influence on sociological thought appear in Chapter 3.

Karl Marx

The earliest of the three, Karl Marx (1818–1883), was an economist and a political philosopher as much as a sociologist. His influence on world politics has probably not been exceeded by any other individual. Although Marx did not consider himself a sociologist, his theories have been as influential in sociology as in philosophy or any of the other social sciences. Marx was deeply angered by the brutal treatment of workers and their families during the Industrial Revolution. He sought to understand the causes of this situation in order to change it. Thus, as Comte had done previously, Marx combined the roles of social scientist and social activist; in fact, he saw the two as inseparable. Emphasizing what Comte called social dynamics, Marx saw virtually all societies as being shaped by a struggle between those who owned the means of production (whatever you need to own in order to produce something that can be sold) and those who did not. He then developed theories about the dynamics of this struggle in the emerging industrial capitalist societies of his time. In such societies, the owners of the means of production were those who possessed industrial capital—the bourgeoisie. The rest of the society, whom he called the proletariat, worked for this group in exchange for wages and salaries that Marx saw as being less than the value that the workers added to the goods they produced. Marx saw these two groups as having fundamentally opposing interests, as well as very unequal power. He developed theories about the ways that the bourgeoisie acted to keep its great wealth and about how the proletariat could force a fair distribution of that wealth. Marx then applied those theories to assume a position of leadership on the proletarian side of that struggle. Marx accepted Adam Smith's notion that capitalism would be extremely efficient, though it gained that efficiency through the exploitation of the proletariat. He also thought that the efficiency of the capitalist system made its adoption inevitable. And he saw how machines were replacing both human and animal labor and how much more efficient they were than either. He saw how capitalism could create more machines and technology and thought the logical conclusion was some kind of "robot economy" doing practically anything we humans wanted it to in the future. But Marx was imagining no utopia. The market's competitive nature would cause capitalists to cut workers so deeply to keep ahead of their competitors in the marketplace that, eventually, workers would be automated out of existence in the modern workplace. This would produce a surplus army of unemployed workers who would eventually rise up and realize their

Karl Marx (Library of Congress)

class interests and overthrow the system. Once the proletariat learned how to administer this highly advanced economy, equality and prosperity would be available to all and what Marx called a "classless communist society" would prevail.

Max Weber

Like Marx, Max Weber (pronounced "Vaber") (1864–1920) was highly interested in the changes brought about by the Industrial Revolution. Like Marx, too, he was aware of the forces for alienation that were being unleashed by these changes. However, Weber focused on potential benefits in these changes that Marx recognized but did not emphasize because of his concerns with the problems of the new industrial order. Weber saw a great potential for increased productivity and, as a result, an increased standard of living in what he called **rationalization**—the replacement of tradition and favoritism with a model of choice based on who and what works best in achieving a given objective. Weber saw this process of rationalization as the cornerstone of modern economic and political systems. Yet, at the same time, he recognized that such systems could only flourish within a cultural and social context favorable to their development. In particular, he developed an important theory about the role of the Protestant Reformation in bringing about a social climate favorable to the emergence of capitalism. Thus, whereas Marx saw society as largely a product of economic forces (especially economic struggle), Weber saw economic systems as being heavily influenced by the society and culture in which they developed. We can think of Weber as focusing on ideas and values, while Marx focused on material self-interest in the form of class conflict. Primarily, Weber argued that people were after prestige and status, not just money. Prestige and status are ideas and they cannot be equalized—by their very natures. No perfect socialist society like Marx envisioned was possible if the conflict was actually over status. This leaves Weber with a darker vision of the future. Because Marx and Weber offered opposite views on several important social issues, Weber has sometimes been described as carrying on a debate with the ghost of Karl Marx. Another important difference between Marx and Weber is that whereas Marx felt that social scientists should base their work on their values, Weber felt that they should attempt to be value-neutral. Even so, Weber realized that total value neutrality in the social sciences is an impossible ideal. He recognized that values inevitably influence the choice of topics chosen for study, and he also saw the usefulness of personal experiences and viewpoints for developing insights about human social behavior. Like other aspects of the disagreements between Marx and Weber, debate about the role of values in sociology continues today.

Max Weber (Hulton Archive/Getty Images)

Emile Durkheim

Emile Durkheim (1858–1917), the third great social thinker of this era, was less interested in economic change than either Marx or Weber. Perhaps Durkheim's greatest accomplishment was to do what Comte had said could be done—apply the scientific method to the study of human social behavior. In his analysis of the social factors that contribute to suicide, Durkheim was the first to carry out a study involving the large-scale collection of data to test a social theory. Durkheim, however, was important not only as the first social researcher but also as a theorist par excellence. In contrast to Marx, Durkheim focused on the forces that hold society together and bond its members in common interest. A particular interest of Durkheim's was how these forces change as a society evolves from a traditional, rural, agrarian society into a complex, interdependent, urban society. He believed the answer lies in the changing division of labor in industrial societies. Durkheim argued that society was held together by one of two fundamental forces. The first he called mechanical solidarity. In an agricultural society, everyone does the same thing like a simple machine. Solidarity is based on similarities in lifestyle, beliefs, and values. Most people were farmers who got up and did the exact same things as their neighbors, went to bed at the same times

Emile Durkheim (Bettmann/Corbis)

(sundown), attended the same churches, ate the same foods, etc. Durkheim contrasted this with what he called organic solidarity. In the Industrial Age, everyone specializes into different tasks/lifestyles—each is dependent on each other. Solidarity based on interdependency and diversity. Too much similarity would doom industrial society. So, like an organism, many different systems all work together to keep the larger organism alive. We have become interdependent on our differences and specialties. But Durkheim also argued that solidarity based on differentiation usually developed imperfectly. Society had changed too rapidly under capitalism and social rules and traditions had not kept pace with the changes in the economy. Once again, Durkheim agrees with Marx and Weber about the efficiency of the market system. That markets create change so quickly and efficiently that social regulation of norms and values can't keep up. In contrast to Weber, who taught that greed and competition would take over, Durkheim argued that many social actors would simply become confused about what societal norms really were. This created a situation that Durkheim labeled anomie. Anomie is the lack of societal consensus on the rules and values that bind the members of society together. Durkheim saw this as having intense personal costs on individual members of society, for instance, leading to an increase in suicide rates in certain instances, as well as more structural social problems, including poverty, inequality, and hopelessness among less powerful social groups. Thus, as with both Marx and Weber, important elements of Durkheim's work concentrate on the effects of modernization on society, which was one of the prime intellectual questions of his era.

The Development of Sociology in the United States

The conditions that brought sociology into being in Europe developed somewhat later in the United States. As a result, the development of sociology in the United States also lagged somewhat behind European sociology. The vast American frontier acted as a safety valve in the early industrial era by giving people a choice between moving to the cities and heading west. By the mid-nineteenth century, however, the Industrial Revolution and urban growth were well under way. In fact, the Civil War was in part a struggle between the agricultural interests of the rural South and the industrial interests of the urban North. American intellectuals, like their European counterparts, focused on the consequences of these trends: by the turn of the century, sociology had begun to find its way into the curriculum of American colleges and universities. The discipline ultimately flourished in this country to a greater extent than almost anywhere else.

The Chicago School

The first department of sociology in the United States was established at the University of Chicago in 1893, and it dominated American sociology for more than half a century thereafter. The American Sociological Association (ASA) was founded in 1905. (It was originally called the American Sociology Society, but the name was changed because of jokes about the initials.)

From the establishment of the discipline until around World War II, American sociology for the most part adopted an activist, reformist orientation (Feagin and Vera, 2001). Urban problems such as crime, overcrowding, drug abuse, and poverty were a central focus of the Chicago School of sociologists. The tone for this reformist orientation was set by the earliest major American sociologist, Lester Ward (1841–1913). Ward saw sociology as a tool for understanding and trying to solve these problems. It was also shaped by the actions and writings of Jane Addams, sociologist and founder of Hull-House, the famous Chicago settlement house. There, she and other Hull-House residents published a groundbreaking sociological text in 1893, *Hull-House Maps and Papers,* which used observation and documentation of sociological data in Chicago to make the case for social change (Deegan, 1991).

At the University of Chicago, early American sociologists such as Robert E. Park (1864–1944), Ernest W. Burgess (1886–1966), and Louis Wirth

Jane Addams pioneered the collection and mapping of data for cities and urban neighborhoods. (Library of Congress)

(1897–1952) continued this philosophy by studying such problems as juvenile delinquency and, in some cases, by setting up institutes to apply sociology to alleviating social ills. The burgeoning city of Chicago served as a natural laboratory for these sociologists by providing opportunities both to study urban problems and to try out solutions that were suggested by their research. (For an excellent overview of the work of the early Chicago School sociologists, see Faris, 1979.)

It would be a mistake, of course, to imply that early sociology in the United States was entirely a product of the Chicago School. One of the earliest uses of survey research, for example, was a study of African Americans in Philadelphia by W. E. B. Du Bois (1973 [orig. 1899]). Like his counterparts in Chicago, Du Bois (1868–1963) combined sociological research with social activism. In addition to his positions in higher education and his important research and theorizing concerning the unique situation of black people in the United States, Du Bois was also a founder and long-time leader of the National Association for the Advancement of Colored People (NAACP) and editor of its journal, *The Crisis*.

Symbolic-Interactionism

By the 1920s, another rather different branch of sociology was also blossoming at the University of Chicago. Rooted in social psychology, it asked questions about how individuals learn, fit into, interact with, and alter the *roles* that exist within the social system. This school of thought, known as symbolic-interactionism, has remained a dominant influence in social psychology (or at least the sociological branch thereof) ever since. It is discussed more fully in Chapter 3. The early leader of this school of thought was University of Chicago sociologist George Herbert Mead (1863–1931). Interestingly, Mead hated to write and therefore never wrote a book. His graduate students, however, recognizing the brilliance and importance of his work, published a book, *Mind, Self, and Society* (Mead, 1934), based on their notes from his lectures. Much of Mead's thinking constituted an elaboration of ideas that had been developed around the turn of the century by Charles Horton Cooley of the University of Michigan.

1940–1960: A Turn from Activism

By the 1940s and 1950s, sociology had become established in most major American universities. During this time, it also underwent two important changes: It began to make greater use of numbers and statistics, and it became dominated by the view that it should be value-neutral rather than activist. In part, these changes reflected the desire of sociologists to gain acceptance of their field as a legitimate science in an era when the prevailing view was that science should be value-free. In part, too, these changes reflected the economic recovery sparked by World War II that produced an era of prosperity, relative social stability, and economic growth. In the 1950s, social problems were further from the public mind than they had been in earlier decades, and sociology turned its attention away from them. This illustrates an important point: *To a large extent, the concerns and values of sociology reflect the concerns and values of the society within which it operates*. In the 1950s, public interest centered on growth, science, and technology, not on social problems—and sociology generally followed this trend.

The most influential American sociologist of this time was Talcott Parsons (1902–1979). Parsons viewed society as a stable, though complex, system of interdependent parts, each of which performed a function important to the system. He was influenced by several of the early European sociologists, particularly Durkheim, and his work in turn influenced that of other important American sociologists, such as Robert Merton. Parsons's approach was challenged by C. Wright Mills (1916–1962), one of the few major sociologists of this era who retained an activist bent. Mills, influenced by the intellectual tradition of Karl Marx, argued that the decision-making process within the U.S. government occurred largely behind the scenes and was dominated by a narrowly defined interest group composed of corporate, political, and military officials whom he called the power elite. Although Mills's influence on American sociology was limited throughout most of his life, today he is regarded as one of the more influential American sociologists, and his theories about the power elite set the stage for a good deal of important research on the American power structure. It was also Mills who wrote about the now widely recognized concept

The 1960s: Return to Activism

Sociology's retreat from social activism did not last. By the mid-1960s, the nation's attention had again turned to social problems, as exemplified by the Civil Rights movement and the Johnson administration's War on Poverty. The conflicts generated by these social changes were intensified by the sometimes violent disputes over the Vietnam War. Suddenly, it was not science and prosperity but burning cities, disrupted campuses, a "sexual revolution," and an explosive increase in the use of illegal drugs that held the attention of the public and of sociologists. Many sociologists and their students (some of whom are today's sociologists) were very much caught up in the conflict, and activism and reformism again became important forces within the profession. As had happened in the past, the sudden emergence of social change and upheaval brought a surge of interest in sociology, and in the late 1960s and early 1970s, sociology became one of the most popular majors on campus.

The 1970s into the New Millennium: Diversity in Sociological Perspectives

After the early 1970s, conflict and upheaval in American society declined for a time but appeared to be increasing again by the early 1990s. Enrollment in sociology courses also decreased for a time to its pre-1960s levels on many campuses but has been increasing again since the late 1980s. By the year 2000, the number of sociology majors on many campuses was again comparable to the peak enrollments of the 1960s. The effect of the 1960s and early 1970s on sociology has been lasting. American sociology in the past several decades has been very diverse: some sociologists have followed the activist tradition of Comte, Marx, Ward, and Mills, while others have followed the value-free science tradition of Weber, Durkheim, and Parsons. Still others have chosen the interactionist tradition of Cooley, Mead, and, more recently, Herbert Blumer. No single theoretical perspective has dominated sociology over the past two decades, nor has any one sociologist or small group of sociologists influenced the field to the extent that Marx, Durkheim, Weber, Mead, and Parsons did in the past. Important sociological voices have emerged, nonetheless. Probably nobody has had a greater influence on the field than William Julius Wilson, whose analyses of urban poverty (Wilson, 1996; 1987) have stimulated new research in sociology and helped gain greater recognition of the value of sociology among policymakers and the general public. A hallmark of Wilson's work, as well as that of contemporary sociological theorists such as Randall Collins, has been an effort to draw on insights from different sociological perspectives rather than drawing mainly on one perspective, as often was the case in the past.

This diversity of perspective has both advantages and disadvantages. On the one hand, the lack of a core body of theory and knowledge generally accepted in the discipline is seen by some as a sign of incoherence (Huber, 1995). In addition, it has sparked intense battles in the field, as in 1999 when a disagreement over the editorship of the *American Sociological Review* led to a bitter and racially charged battle within the American Sociological Association. But there is also a healthy side to current sociology's diversity of thought. No single approach has all the answers, and the challenges that the different approaches offer to one another help bring out the best in sociologists of every theoretical orientation. Indeed, the failure of the sociologists of the 1950s to predict the upheavals of the 1960s is a good illustration of what happens when one view comes to dominate the field excessively: it goes unchallenged not only when it is right but also when it is wrong, as nearly every theoretical orientation is, at least part of the time.

Putting Sociology to Work

How Sociology Can Be Used to Solve Real-Life Problems

At a time when many serious challenges face our society and societies all over the world, it seems reasonable to ask, as many new students do, "What can sociology be used for? Can it help us understand and possibly solve some of the social problems and issues that confront us today? Can it be applied in practical ways to help us solve problems?" Asking these questions is also a first step in developing critical thinking skills that will be useful to you in your academic career and beyond it, as you read the news articles describing various social crises around the world, or see the news specials on television detailing problems in various aspects of society and its institutions, or are called upon by your employer to apply your skills and knowledge to solve problems.

Consider the following examples:

- A county government is seeking federal funds for housing. One requirement for such assistance is that the county address the housing needs of its disabled population. The county officials have no idea how many people with disabilities live in their county, much less what their housing needs are. The solution is to hire a sociologist to review various sources of data and develop an estimate of the number of people with disabilities in the county, as well as to review the findings of social research on the appropriateness of various types of housing arrangements for people with various types of disabilities.
- Faced with a declining patient clientele, the administrators of a university hospital want to purchase physician practices in order to attract admissions. However, they do not know which locations are good places to purchase these practices in terms of attracting the maximum number of patients. The solution is to hire a team of sociologists to obtain and analyze data on population, physician supply, physician productivity, and the frequency of visits to the doctor, for the purpose of identifying various locations as medically overserved or underserved.
- A university campus is beset with racial problems. A racist joke is told on the campus radio station, antiblack leaflets are passed under dormitory doors, many black students at the school are dropping out, and both black and white students refuse to interact with each other. A sociologist points out that neither racial group really sees things from the perspective of the other. Whites assume that the passage of civil rights laws means that opportunities for blacks are equal when, in fact, blacks still must overcome disproportionate poverty, poor education, inadequate medical care, and high rates of unemployment. Blacks assume that whites are genuinely aware of all these things and simply don't care. The solution is a required course on race relations for all students to correct the misperceptions that each group has about the other. In this example, teaching students some of the sociology of race relations could go a long way toward easing the tensions.

As these examples illustrate, sociology is a problem-solving tool. In fact, the examples are not made up: they are all real-life situations with which we are personally familiar. Throughout the text, we will periodically illustrate ways in which sociology can be or has been applied to problems like the ones described previously. Here, we would like to begin by describing how a study on recycling might be helpful in getting more people to behave in ways that are harmonious with their environment. The study by Derksen and Gartrell (1993), entitled "The Social Context of Recycling," clearly shows that positive attitudes toward recycling and attitudes of concern for the environment are not enough to get people to recycle. In fact, if the social context is not supportive of recycling, it does not matter what people's attitudes are. The researchers found this out by surveying 1,200 people in Alberta, Canada. About one-third of them lived in Edmonton, about a third in Calgary, and about a third in the rest of the province. The survey respondents were asked a series of questions measuring their concern for the environment, and they were also asked what items were recycled in their homes. The survey showed high levels of concern for the environment: Nearly half said they were "very concerned." There was not much difference among the three geographic areas in concern for the environment, and conventional sociodemographic variables like age, sex, education, and income didn't make much difference either.

However, while geographic area was uncorrelated with environmental attitudes, it correlated strongly with recycling. People in Edmonton were more likely than people in Calgary and much more likely than people elsewhere in the province to recycle newspapers. Edmonton residents were also more likely than people in either of the other two areas to recycle plastics, milk cartons, food cans, and other paper. The reason for this difference is that of the three areas, only Edmonton had curbside recycling at the time of the study. On the one hand, it is not surprising that people with curbside recycling would recycle more than people without such a service. It is a lot easier to leave your recyclable materials at your curb on garbage collection days than to haul them off to a recycling center. However, another finding of the study is highly revealing: Among people who did not have curbside recycling, there was no relationship between concern for the environment and the number of items recycled. In other words, if it was not easy to recycle, attitudes toward the environment made no difference at all in recycling behavior. On the other hand, where curbside recycling was available, attitudes did matter: In that context, the more concerned people were about the environment, the more likely they were to recycle. Concerned people with curbside recycling recycled about twice as many items as unconcerned people with curbside recycling. On the other hand, even unconcerned Edmonton residents with curbside recycling recycled more than residents of other parts of the province that lacked curbside recycling.

The policy implications of this research are quite clear. First, people will recycle if given the opportunity to do so easily through curbside recycling, a program now available in a growing number of cities. Second, trying to change people's attitudes toward the environment has little chance of changing their behavior unless recycling is made easy and convenient. And third, when it is easy to recycle, people's attitudes toward the environment do make a difference in their behavior. So, if a community wants to encourage more recycling, it must first make it easy to do so through curbside recycling or a similar program. Then, and only then, may recycling be increased through heightened concern for the environment.

Because it is relevant to a variety of practical concerns, ranging from easing racial unrest to encouraging people to recycle, applied sociology is one of the fastest-growing areas of sociology. **Applied sociology** is the use of sociological knowledge and methods to solve problems, design

Factors affecting immigration and immigration policy are among the recent issues that sociologists have been called upon to address. (iStockphoto)

policy, and obtain information relevant to making decisions. Applied sociologists work as consultants, researchers, and managers for a wide range of organizations, such as businesses, schools, nonprofit organizations, and governmental agencies.

As important as sociology has become as a problem-solving tool, its greatest usefulness probably still lies in its use of the sociological imagination described earlier in this chapter. Sociology enables us to gain a new perspective on the forces that define our situation, thereby enabling us to see that our society sometimes acts in ways that severely limit human opportunity. It allows us to step back and look at ourselves. In so doing, it makes us aware of the presence and extent of such conditions as poverty, unemployment, crime, family conflict, racism, and sexism—conditions that, at one time or another, affect nearly all of us. It allows us to act as constructive social critics of our (or any) society, by enabling us to seek and discover, for example, the forces that throw people out of work or lead them to behave violently.

Although such discovery can be painful—we sometimes learn things about ourselves and our society that frighten or disappoint us—we cannot improve things unless we understand what is wrong. Precisely because such insight is often threatening or disappointing, people, particularly those with wealth and power, often prefer to avoid it. In Hitler's Germany, for example, university sociology departments were disbanded, and sociology has been severely restricted in a number of undemocratic countries in our own time. Even in the United States, the wealthy and powerful have often questioned the value of sociology, or at best valued it only for its practical applications. When it is allowed the freedom to do so, sociology can serve as a voice of dissent, asking important questions that otherwise would go unasked. In the long run, this is every bit as beneficial as—perhaps even more so than—the more obvious and practical social engineering applications discussed in the preceding section. The point is that, in different ways, sociology is useful both to individuals or organizations confronted with specific problems and to all of us in the larger society, by helping us to see and understand problems of which we might otherwise remain unaware.

Most of you, of course, will not become professional sociologists, even if you choose to major in sociology at the undergraduate level. However, the use of the knowledge and tools of sociology to address practical problems and issues is not limited to sociologists. Today, the tools and knowledge of sociology are increasingly being applied in a wide variety of careers and work environments to improve the quality of life. And technology is making this information available to a wider variety of people than ever before. *And, through the Internet, technology is making this information available to a greater number of people than ever before.*

Summary

Sociology operates on two basic principles. First, human social behavior has important elements of regularity and predictability. Second, this behavior is patterned and strongly influenced by group affiliations—organizations; informal groups; race, class, and gender; and society. Sociology uses scientific methods of observation and generalization to describe, explain, and predict human behavior. Sociology is useful because there are distinct limits to what common sense can tell us about human behavior: Some things that make sense turn out, on careful observation of behavior, to be wrong. Sociology is one of the social sciences, and it is distinguished from the others by the broad range of behavior with which it is concerned and by its emphasis on understanding human behavior on the group or societal level. It emerged in the nineteenth century out of a desire to understand the rapid social changes associated with urbanization and the Industrial Revolution. However, as society has changed, the concerns and emphases of sociology have changed with it. Sociology can be applied to a wide range of problems and issues of concern to government, business, education, labor, and religion. Employment opportunities for people trained in sociology exist in all of these areas, although an undergraduate degree does not prepare a student for any specific sociologist job. Nonetheless, most people who earn a bachelor's degree in sociology get a job in a field related to their training, where they frequently outperform co-workers with professional degrees.

Key Terms

sociological perspective
sociology
science
research
social sciences
theory
natural sciences
organized skepticism
reactivity
sociological imagination
social psychology
means of production
bourgeoisie
proletariat
applied sociology

Key terms in this chapter and in all succeeding chapters are defined in the glossary that begins on page G-1.

Exercises

1. Many people think that the only careers open to sociologists involve teaching and research. Many occupational specialties may be pursued with a bachelor's degree in sociology. Do an Internet search for the term "applied sociology." You will find several links to sites that describe careers for those with degrees in applied sociology. Also check out the career opportunities page for undergraduate sociology degrees from the American Sociological Association (http://www.asanet.org/employment/career_undergrad.cfm). Write a brief

report on the types of career opportunities you found.
2. The text explains how sociology is a science and the vast difference between sociology and the scientific method versus common sense. Think about a subject that you would like to know more about. How would you go about applying the scientific method to that subject?
3. In the past three decades, movies about superheroes have become increasingly popular. Starting with *Superman* in 1978, this trend has accelerated in pace in the last several years (including four major features during the summer of 2011: *Thor*; *X-Men: First Class*; *Green Lantern*; and *Captain America: The First Avenger*). What might the sociological perspective tell us about why superhero films have become more popular since 1978? Some commentators have noted that the number of such films greatly increased after the terrorist attacks of September 11, 2001. Can you think of any changes that have taken place in American society that might have produced a wave of such films?

Chapter 2
How Sociology Is Done

Social Theory and Research — 26
    Cause and Effect 27
    Theory and Values 27
    Theories Versus Values: Why Does It Matter? 27
    The Relationship Between Theory and Research 28

Using and Measuring Variables — 31
    Independent Variables 31
    Dependent Variables 31
    Operational Definitions 31
    Validity and Reliability 32
    Correlation 32
    Control Variables 33

Key Research Methods in Sociology — 33
    Quantitative and Qualitative Methods 33

Experiments — 35
    Experimental and Control Groups 35
    Field Experiments 36

Survey Research — 38
    Questionnaires 38
    Telephone Interviews 38
    Personal Interviews 39
    Survey Questions 39
    Sampling 40

Field Observation — 40
    Field Observation and Theory Generation 40
    Participant Observation 41
    Unobtrusive Observation 44

Use of Existing Data Sources — 44
    Data Archives 44
    The U.S. Census 45
    Content Analysis 45

Reading Tables — 45

Summary — 47

Key Terms — 47

Exercises — 48

Where I (Farley) used to teach, one or two blood drives occurred each semester. Chances are you have them on your campus or in your town too. Have you ever given blood? Have any of your friends given blood? If you have given blood, what motivated you to do so? If not, why did you choose not to? And if you have friends who have given blood and you have not, what do you think might explain the different choices you and they made?

Most people think about giving blood as a personal act of generosity. And in a way, sociological research supports this. Most people who give blood mention motivations of altruism when asked why they do so, and the most likely donors are relatively advantaged and healthy people. For example, in the United States, the most likely donor is a thirty-something white male with above-average income and education. However, if generosity explains blood donation, how is it that rates of donation can vary widely in two adjacent, similar countries? Survey data in France show that 44 percent of adults have given blood at some time in their lives, while in nearby Luxembourg, just 14 percent have done so (Healy, 2000). Could people in France be *that much* more generous than people in Luxembourg?

By collecting and analyzing data, sociologists such as Kieran Healy (2000) have shown that there is more to giving blood than just generosity. We are challenged by the findings of this research to go beyond generosity as an explanation of how two neighboring, culturally similar countries could have such different rates of blood donation. Fortunately, social research offers some answers to the very questions it raises through the finding of the big difference in donation rates.

It turns out that a major reason for the difference lies not in individual generosity, but in how blood is collected in the two countries. In France, blood is collected through a national health-care system run by the French government, whereas in Luxembourg it is collected by the Red Cross. The national health system of France collects more blood mainly because it is able to ask more people to give blood. (It turns out the most common reason people give when asked why they have *not* donated blood is that "nobody asked me to.") Governmental systems of blood collection such as that of France are likely to be well funded, able to reach more people, and able to link themselves to the medical benefits provided by the state. Red Cross blood-collection systems like that of Luxembourg, however, reach fewer people, so the Red Cross compensates by getting those who do give blood to do so repeatedly.

It also turns out that the individual factors that influence blood donation vary depending on the collection system. Under the Red Cross system in countries like Luxembourg, people who are more religious are more likely to give blood, while this is not true under national health-care systems like the one in France. This is true largely because the Red Cross uses churches to recruit volunteer donors, while governmental agencies do not do this. For similar reasons, knowing someone else who has given blood correlates with donation in most Red Cross countries, but not in national health-care system countries. Again, the more voluntary system must rely on personal networks (Healy, 2000).

These findings are the product of systematic research that takes into consideration both societal factors (that is, how countries like France and Luxembourg are different) and individual factors (that is, how individual people behave within each country). Through this systematic research, we are able to learn that the collection system makes a difference both in how much blood is given and who is likely to give.

In doing this kind of social research, sociologists try to explain how and why one society differs from another, as well as how societies change over time. They also identify differences in attitudes and beliefs between groups of people within a society, and seek to explain the causes of these differences. For example, in most countries men are more likely to give blood than women. The cause of this appears to be linked to the influence of traditional cultural values about gender roles. In Greece and Portugal, with more traditional gender roles, women are only about half as likely as men to give blood. In Norway and Denmark, where popular beliefs favor feminism and gender equality, men and women are equally likely to give blood. Hence, if we measure the right things, we can learn a great deal about societal, group, and individual factors that influence human behavior.

Social Theory and Research

The opening vignette illustrates the point, noted briefly in Chapter 1, that sociology is largely concerned with cause and effect. Sometimes it seeks to *explain:* Why do so many more people in France give blood than in Luxembourg? Sometimes, too, it seeks to *predict:* Under what conditions is there likely to be a larger or smaller effect of religion or of sex on the likelihood of giving blood? Of course, there are also times when sociology merely seeks to *describe:* How many people actually give blood in different countries, and what groups have higher or lower rates of blood donation? Most of the time, though, description is a step toward either explanation or prediction, both of which involve the notion of cause and effect.

Cause and Effect

By **cause and effect**, social scientists mean that the presence of one condition (the cause) makes the occurrence of some other condition (the effect) more likely than it would otherwise have been. This is a somewhat broader definition than the popular notion of cause and effect. To social scientists, the cause does not *always* have to be followed by the effect, but the effect does occur more often when the cause is present than when it is absent. Consider the example of unemployment and divorce. Social research has indicated that unemployment is a cause of divorce. By this, we mean that when one of the breadwinners in a family becomes unemployed, the family is more likely to experience a divorce than it would have been had that unemployment not occurred. It does *not* mean that a divorce will *always* follow the loss of a job, nor does it mean that the absence of unemployment guarantees that a couple will not get divorced. It simply means that, all other things being equal, divorce is more likely in the presence of unemployment than in its absence.

Theory and Values

As was explained in Chapter 1, a theory can be defined as a set of statements that describe reality. Usually, theories describe relationships of cause and effect, as discussed in the preceding paragraph. The most important characteristic of a theory is that, if you can get the right information, it can be tested. In other words, you can collect information that will help you to tell whether or not the theory is correct (Lenski, 1988). Collecting such information is what is done in sociological research. Usually such research is done either to test a theory or to get ideas for developing a new theory.

In contrast to theories are **values**: personal judgments or preferences about what is good or bad, or about what is liked or disliked. Unlike theories, values cannot be proven true or false, no matter how much information you might collect. That is because values do not try to describe a factual reality like theories do. Rather, they reflect personal preferences or judgments.

An example of the difference between theories and values can be seen in discussions of social inequality and conflict. The statement "social inequality causes conflict" is a statement of theory. If we could collect the right information through sociological research, it should be possible to show that the statement is either true or false. We would have to find a way of measuring social inequality in different places, and a way of measuring conflict. If we can agree on how to measure inequality and conflict, we can test the theory. We can see whether or not there is actually more conflict in those places that have greater inequality. If we find that there is, we would be more confident that the theory is correct. If, on the other hand, we find that there is no more conflict in places that have greater inequality, we would be less likely to believe a theory that claims that inequality causes conflict.

Now consider another statement: "Conflict is a bad thing." This statement expresses a value. There is no amount of sociological research that could prove this statement true or false. It is simply a matter of how you feel about conflict. Some people think it is bad, because it can lead to anger and violence. Others, however, think that at least some conflict is good because it can help to change society for the better. Which group of people is right? Sociology cannot answer that question, because each viewpoint simply expresses different priorities and desires. In other words, each group has different values.

Theories Versus Values: Why Does It Matter?

Why do you need to know the difference between theories and values? The answer is that, in reality, nearly all of our discussions about society and human behavior are influenced by both. This is true for sociologists as well as for ordinary people. On the one hand, the sociologist is more systematic in his or her measurement of social characteristics and human behaviors than the average person. On the other hand, sociologists are still people with values, and these values influence what subjects they study, what theories they find appealing, and so forth.

Consider the following argument: Conflict is bad because it usually leads to violence, and rarely changes anything anyway. This is a perfect example of an argument that contains both theoretical statements and value statements. The ideas that "conflict usually leads to violence" and that "conflict rarely changes anything" are statements of theory that can be tested by sociological research. Assuming we can agree on what constitutes "conflict" and on what constitutes "violence," we can conduct sociological studies to find out whether or not conflict usually leads to violence. Similarly, it is possible to determine the truth of the statement that "conflict rarely changes anything." On the other hand, we can never prove that "conflict is bad." That is a value judgment. Some people think it is bad; others think it is good. Even if sociological research proved that conflict usually leads to violence and rarely leads to change, a reasonable person might still see some good in conflict—for example, because it might lead to greater unity within a group that has been threatened by some other group.

For these reasons, you should ask yourself two questions when you encounter statements or arguments about society:

1. *What parts of the statement or argument are expressing values?* These parts cannot be proven true or false by any amount of observation or measurement.
2. *What parts of the statement or argument are statements of theory?* These are the parts that make claims about reality and are therefore subject to testing through observation or research.

Values and the Social Sciences

The above discussion holds true whether you are studying the works of social scientists, reading a newspaper, watching a television program, or having a discussion with your friends. Although social scientists place a primary emphasis on theory and research—that is, on addressing factual questions about the realities of human behavior—they, too, are human, and their work is often influenced by their values. Inevitably, the topics that social (or, for that matter, natural) scientists choose to study will be influenced by their values. In addition, scientists are not value-free concerning their theories. Science today is very competitive, and every scientist wants to gain recognition and get grant money and be published by developing a theory that works better than anyone else's. Consequently, scientists sometimes try to interpret their results to fit their theories. Finally, because social scientists study human beings, they frequently bring strong values to their research that can influence their interpretations of their findings. Both social scientists and natural scientists often have a strong interest in applying their research for some useful purpose, and they also frequently make policy recommendations. These recommendations can be influenced by both their research findings and their values. All of this is fine as long as social and natural scientists share their results and methods completely and honestly with their professional communities. The scientific community can then debate their findings, methods, interpretations, and recommendations. Such debate strengthens rather than weakens science, and therefore, few people today argue that science can or should be totally separated from values.

The Relationship Between Theory and Research

Recall from Chapter 1 that science consists of a cycle that includes observation (research), generalization, explanation, and prediction. This leads to a new round of the research cycle that may begin with new research to test the predictions generated from the previous round. This cycle is illustrated in Figure 2.1. This diagram illustrates the reciprocal relationship between research and theory. Research findings are most meaningful when considered in the context of a theory, which explains the findings by proposing cause-effect relationships that can account for them. Similarly, theory is of little use unless it can be shown by research to be correct, at least under some specified set of conditions (Lieberson, 1992, p. 4).

Explanation versus Prediction

Consider the top half of Figure 2.1, which shows research being used to *generate* theory. Here, a research finding is obtained and is found to be generally true, and a theory is then developed to *explain* it. Jiobu (1988) used this method of reasoning to develop a theory to explain the relatively high income of Japanese Americans. He began with this finding from past research studies: Compared with most other racial minority groups in the United States—even compared with much of the white majority group—Japanese Americans on the average have high levels of income and education. How did the Japanese succeed where others could not? Jiobu developed a theory that their success was based in part on their ability to gain control of certain segments of the California vegetable industry—including tomatoes, asparagus, and spinach—that required high levels of labor but little land to produce and that had wide market demand that extended far beyond the Japanese-American market.

Now, consider the bottom half of the figure. Here, research is being used to test theory. The theory predicts a particular result, and the scientist does the research to see if the predicted result can be obtained. Again, the ethnic-group success example can be used to illustrate this procedure. Jiobu's theory predicts that *any* ethnic group that gains control of an industry that produces a product for which there is a wide market should experience success to a greater extent than other ethnic groups. An obvious way to test this theory is to examine the economic history of a wide variety of ethnic groups. If we were to do such a study and find that, consistently, ethnic groups that at some point in history gained control of such an industry today have higher incomes than comparable groups that did not gain control of such an industry, we would have an important piece of evidence in support of Jiobu's theory. If, however, we found no difference in the average incomes of ethnic groups that did and did not gain control of such an industry at some time in the past, we would probably conclude that Jiobu's theory was wrong.

As shown in Figure 2.1, the relationship between theory and research works two ways. Sometimes, as in the top half of the figure, scientists do research in order to develop theories, or develop theories in order to explain a research finding. In this case, the scientists are engaging in a process of *explanation,* or *theory generation.* Other times, as in the bottom half of the figure, scientists do research in order to test a theory. In this case, the scientists are engaging in a process of *prediction,* or *theory testing.*

Research and Theory Testing

When social scientists use research to test a theory, they usually use a hypothesis. A **hypothesis** is a single statement about reality that can be tested. Usually, it is used to test a piece of a theory. When

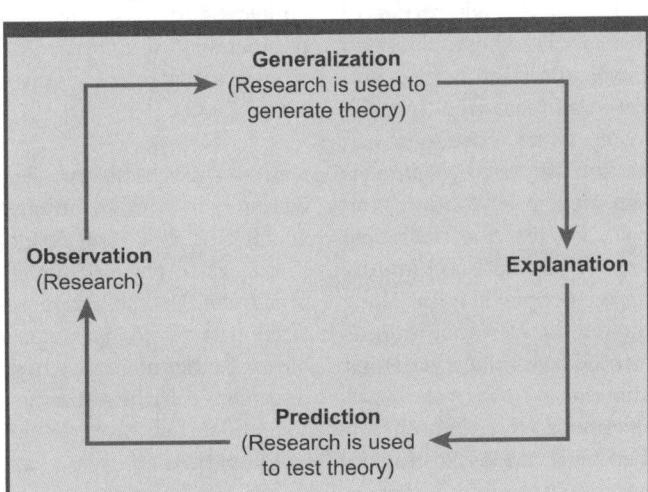

Figure 2.1 The Cycle of Scientific Inquiry

we say that a hypothesis can be tested, we mean that it is possible to observe whether or not things happen the way that the hypothesis claims they will. A hypothesis is always a statement, never a question. Usually, it describes a cause-effect relationship, such as, if condition X is present, then condition Y is more likely to follow.

The reason a hypothesis is used for testing is that a theory is usually too large and complex to test in its entirety at one time. Hence, scientists test one piece of a theory at a time by developing a hypothesis that seems to follow from that part of the theory. Thus, a hypothesis can be thought of as an educated guess about how a research project will turn out, based upon the theory the scientist is trying to test. When research is done for the purpose of theory testing, the researcher develops a hypothesis from a theory and then conducts research to see if the hypothesis can be confirmed by actual observation.

A Case Study: Durkheim on Suicide. This process can be illustrated by the first sociological study conducted according to the scientific model, Emile Durkheim's *Suicide* (1964a [orig. 1897]). Durkheim sought to explain why some people commit suicide and others don't. Although suicide is often thought of as an act by an individual, Durkheim thought that social factors could help to explain who commits suicide and who doesn't. Durkheim developed the theory that suicide is often the result of people not being well integrated into social groups. This theory suggests several hypotheses. If we can identify groups of people who are more individualistic and less integrated into some type of group life, we would expect such people to have a higher rate of suicide. Durkheim identified three such groups of people: Protestants, men, and unmarried people. Protestant religions emphasize an individual relationship with God rather than the community orientation stressed by Catholics and Jews. Men are expected to be "strong" and do things on their own, whereas the traditional female role emphasizes family and community relationships. Unmarried people may be alone much of the time and often do not have the kinds of relationships that married people have with their spouse and (usually) children.

Thus, Durkheim developed three hypotheses: Suicide rates would be higher among Protestants than among Catholics and Jews, higher among men than among women, and higher among unmarried people than among married people. He then tested the hypotheses by examining data archives on suicide cases and computing suicide rates for different categories of the population in several European countries. As he expected, he found higher suicide rates among Protestants, men, and unmarried people than among Catholics and Jews, women, and married people. These findings supported his hypotheses. Moreover, they offered an important piece of evidence in support of his larger theory.

Usually, no single study suffices to accept or reject a theory. At best, it will support or refute a few hypotheses that are derived from, or consistent with, a theory. Still, each confirmed hypothesis adds support to a theory (as in the case of Durkheim's theory about the causes of suicide), and if enough hypotheses relating to a theory are confirmed on a consistent basis, the theory will come to be widely supported. In the case of Durkheim's theory, the notion of isolation and disconnection from others as a cause of suicide has become widely accepted among sociologists. This is because (1) Durkheim and others have confirmed a number of hypotheses, all of which are consistent with the theory; and (2) many of the hypothesized relationships have held up consistently over time and in a number of different societies. Although Durkheim conducted his research in a number of European nations during the nineteenth century, similar patterns can be found in the United States today. American males today, for example, remain much more likely than American females to commit suicide. Also, church members in the United States have lower suicide rates than do nonmembers, and married people are less likely to commit suicide than are divorced people (Breault, 1986, 1988).

Research and Theory Generation

Researchers who are interested in topics about which there is no well-developed theory are likely to engage in research for the purpose of theory generation. The main purpose of such research is to develop some theory to explain some pattern of behavior. Rather than use a hypothesis to predict the research result, the researcher conducts research as a way of generating or developing hypotheses that can then be used to build a theory.

Fascism: A Case Study. An example of this can be seen in the research of Theodor Adorno, Else Frenkel-Brunswik, and others (1950) concerning fascism. Adorno, who fled Germany to escape the Nazis, was interested in why people would support a movement like Nazism. Because Nazism and fascism were very recent developments at the time, no sizable body of theory on these subjects existed. Thus, researchers had to either develop their own theories or adopt theories about related topics that might be relevant to fascism. They reasoned that some clues to the thinking of people who supported fascism might be found in the speeches and writings of Nazi leaders. Thus, they analyzed these speeches and writings for common themes. Assuming that a personality need might have contributed in some way to support for the Nazis, they particularly looked for themes that appeared regularly even though they were not directly related to fascism's political message. They found a number of such themes, including superstition, stereotyped thinking, simplistic good/bad categorization, aggression against nonconformers, and cynicism. These same themes appeared repeatedly in the speeches and writings of Nazis, fascists, Ku Klux Klan members, and other right-wing extremists. This led researchers to hypothesize that a personality test could be developed to predict intolerance of the type practiced by such extremists. They developed such a test and found that people with the personality traits measured by the test were indeed more prejudiced against racial and religious minority groups. The purpose of their initial analysis of the speeches and writings of extremists, however, was simply to generate the hypothesis, not to test it.

Using and Measuring Variables

As previously stated, social scientists are interested in identifying relationships of cause and effect. To do this, they use variables. A variable is a concept that can either take on different values or that has two or more categories. Income is an example of a variable. Your income could be $100,000 per year, or it could be $10,000. Now, there are two values that are definitely different! Religion is also a variable. It can be broken down into categories such as Protestant, Catholic, Jewish, Muslim, other, or none. It is important to know the difference between a variable and a category of a variable. "Catholic" and "Muslim," for example, are not variables. Rather, they are categories of the variable "religion."

Independent Variables

Because social science research usually involves cause-effect relationships among variables, most hypotheses describe cause-effect relationships. Hence, some variables represent causes, whereas others represent effects. In a hypothesis or research project, a variable that the researcher thinks is a cause is called an **independent variable** (or sometimes, a predictor variable). In a study involving a relationship between two variables, then, the independent variable is the one that the researcher thinks influences the other variable or precedes it in time. Keep in mind that the cause must always come before the effect: you cannot do something today that will cause something to happen yesterday!

Dependent Variables

A variable that a researcher thinks is the effect is called the **dependent variable.** This variable is thought to follow the independent variable in time or to be influenced by the independent variable. It is called the dependent variable because, if the researcher is right, its value in part depends on the value of the independent variable. If education is the independent variable and income is the dependent variable, for example, then a person's income depends, in part, on the amount of education that he or she has. In this example, education represents the cause and income the effect.

Operational Definitions

Once it has been decided which variables will be included in a study, the researcher must decide how the variables will be measured. This is done by developing operational definitions of the variables we want to measure. An **operational definition** is a precise definition developed for the purpose of measurement. It must be sufficiently precise that anyone could use it and get the same result. An operational definition of income, for example, could be the adjusted gross income that a survey respondent reported on his or her income tax return in the most recent tax year. This would work as an operational definition, because this amount should be the same no matter who is asking the questions in the survey. There is always more than one possible way to operationally define a variable. The way that is used in any given study will depend on how the researcher conceptualizes the variable and its relevance to the cause-effect relationship being studied. Any way of doing it is acceptable, as long as the following three things are true:

1. The operational definition is precise and clear enough that anyone could use it and get the same result.
2. The researcher tells you clearly how the variable was operationally defined.
3. The operational definition makes sense. In other words, its relationship to the concept the researcher is trying to measure is evident or can be explained convincingly by the researcher.

Validity and Reliability

However social researchers measure their variables, there are two criteria their measures must meet for measurement to be successful. The first, validity, is illustrated by the third condition in the preceding list. **Validity** means that a measure is correctly measuring the concept the researcher intends it to measure. Consider again the example of using the income reported on a tax return as an operational definition of income. This approach could raise problems from a standpoint of validity, because there is a sizable amount of off-the-books income that is not reported on tax returns. One obvious example is money from illegal drug sales. But a fairly large amount of legal income also goes unreported—income from odd jobs paid in cash, for example. For people with such unreported income, using the tax return figure would present a validity problem—the tax return income would be too low. One way of judging validity is illustrated by the third item in the preceding paragraph—you should be able to see some connection between a measure and what the researcher is trying to measure. This is called face validity. Other approaches to assessing validity are more complex. Should you decide to major in sociology, you will learn more about them in a course on research methods.

The other criterion a measure must meet is **reliability**, which means that a measure gives consistent results. Consider the method used by the U.S. Bureau of the Census to measure race. People are given a choice of different racial categories and asked to mark the one that best describes their race. (The 2010 Census offered fourteen choices! A respondent could check more than one of these or write in a choice not listed.) This approach to measuring race has good reliability as long as people are consistent in how they mark their race when they fill out questionnaires. As a practical matter, reliability is usually good on things people usually "know," such as their race or sex, but as the questions address more subjective issues, reliability decreases.

Finally, it is important to remember that a measure can be reliable but not valid. Using the tax return figure as a measure of income might be a good example of this. If people remember the income they reported or can look it up easily, they might answer such a question very consistently. However, their answer might be consistently too low. This can be a problem, since it is usually easier to assess the reliability of a measure than it is to assess its validity.

Correlation

When they try to determine whether or not there is a cause-effect relationship between two variables, one thing researchers look for is correlation. **Correlation** means that when one variable changes, the other also tends to change. Consider the example given in the box "Sorting Out Cause-Effect Relationships: Single-Parent Homes and Teenage Parenthood." In this example, there is a correlation between growing up in a single-parent family and having a baby while still a teenager. Girls who grow up in single-parent families are more likely to become parents as teenagers than girls who grow up in two-parent families. Correlation by itself is never enough to prove causation, for reasons we shall see in more detail shortly. On the other hand, if a study finds that there is no correlation between two variables, it is rather unlikely that one of them could be causing the other.

Control Variables

Consider again the example in the box on the next page. Two possibilities are presented. On the one hand, it could be that growing up in a single-parent family increases the likelihood of teen parenthood. In this case, there would be a cause-effect relationship. It is also possible, however, that some other variable could be influencing the likelihood both of growing up in a single-parent family and of teen parenthood. In the box, social background characteristics, including education, are presented as an example of this. In order to test for this possibility, the researchers introduced background characteristics as a control variable. A **control variable** is a third variable that is introduced to determine whether or not a correlation between two variables can be accounted for by some alternative explanation. In this example, the introduction of the control variable reduced but did not eliminate the correlation between growing up in a single-parent family and teen parenthood. This result made the researchers more confident that there is some cause-effect relationship between these two variables. However, they can never be completely sure, because it is always possible that another researcher might find some other control variable that eliminates the correlation completely.

Sociologists devote considerable effort to identifying cause-effect relationships. Most sociological research is aimed at understanding why society operates as it does. For an example of a sociological career centered around such inquiry, see the "Personal Journey into Sociology" of Joan McCord.

Key Research Methods in Sociology

The principles discussed thus far in this chapter are applicable to all of the social sciences and often to the natural sciences as well. Now, we shall narrow our focus somewhat to consider the particular research methods that are used in sociology. Once a sociologist has selected a research problem and reviewed the sociological literature to identify theories and past research that relate to the topic, the next task is to design and carry out the research. Sociologists use four major approaches to research: experiments, surveys, field observation (often combined with in-depth interviews), and analysis of existing data.

Quantitative and Qualitative Methods

Sociological research methods vary on a quantitative-qualitative dimension. At one end is **quantitative research,** which expresses results as numbers and uses statistical techniques to sort out cause-effect relationships among a number of variables. Often, this type of research is used to test hypotheses and theories. At the other end of the dimension is **qualitative research,** which uses in-depth observation and interviewing techniques to find beliefs, meanings, and social behaviors that lie beneath the easily observable surface. These two approaches have different strengths and allow us to see different pieces of social reality.

Consider, for example, the views of whites on interracial marriage. On the one hand, quantitative survey studies have shown large declines over time in the percentage of whites who object to marriages between blacks and whites (Farley, 2000, p. 61). For example, Gallup Poll data show that the percentage of whites approving of such marriages rose from 4 percent in 1958 to 79 percent in 2007 (Gallup Organization, 2007). Clearly, significant attitude change occurred over this period. But a different part of the picture can be seen by looking at qualitative data, which show such approval to be far from complete and unambiguous (Feagin, 2000, p. 110). For example, Bonilla-Silva and Forman (2000) conducted qualitative interviews with a group of white college students, of whom 90 percent had indicated acceptance of interracial marriages on a survey. In the more in-depth interviews, two-thirds of the students hedged and expressed reservations about interracial marriage.

In general, surveys and experiments tend to be more quantitative, whereas observational research techniques tend to be more qualitative, although there are exceptions to the rule with all research methods. Methods involving use of existing data can be either qualitative or quantitative, depending on the nature of the data.

UNDERSTANDING RACE, CLASS, AND GENDER
Sorting Out Cause-Effect Relationships: Single-Parent Homes and Teenage Parenthood

How sociologists sort out cause-effect relationships using control variables can be illustrated by the findings of a study of the effect of parental absence resulting from separation or divorce (the independent variable) on teenage parenthood (the dependent variable) (McLanahan and Bumpass, 1988). We know that teenage girls from single-parent homes are more likely than other girls to have babies. But is it because they are from single-parent families, or is it because of other aspects of their social background? People from low-income families, for example, have above-average divorce and separation rates, and therefore their children frequently grow up in single-parent families. At the same time, growing up poor may by itself put a person at a high risk of teenage parenthood. Thus, to determine whether growing up in a one-parent family "causes" a higher rate of teenage parenthood, we must introduce one or more control variables. And because rates of single and married parenthood vary by race, the effects of single parenthood on teen pregnancy may be different for different racial groups. Hence, it is also helpful to look at data for different racial groups separately. (We shall slightly simplify the McLanahan and Bumpass study by combining their social background and education variables into one control variable.)

The diagrams below illustrate two possibilities that could explain correlations between single parenthood and teen pregnancy. In Example 1, the relationship is *spurious:* There is no cause-effect relationship between growing up in a single-parent home and teenage parenthood. There *is* a correlation between the two variables, but this is only because people of certain social backgrounds, such as low income, are more likely to grow up in single-parent homes *and* to have babies as teenagers. This spurious correlation is represented by a dotted line, while the true cause-effect relationships are represented by solid arrows. In this example, there is *no* correlation between growing up in a single-parent home and teenage parenthood *among people whose social background is otherwise similar.*

In Example 2, there *is* a real cause-effect relationship between growing up in a single-parent home and teenage parenthood. In this example, the correlation between growing up in a single-parent home and teen parenthood remains present *even among people with similar backgrounds.* Introducing control variables

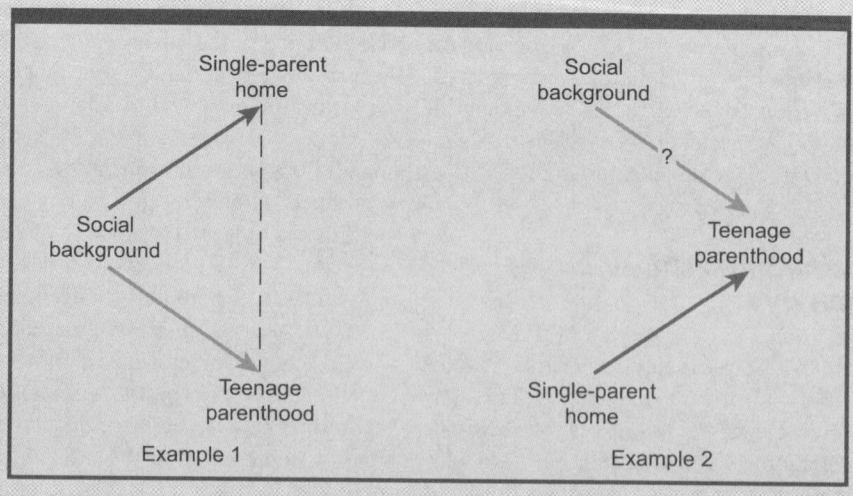

such as income does *not* eliminate the correlation between the independent variable (single-parent home) and the dependent variable (teenage parenthood). Thus, there is a solid arrow between single-parent home and teenage parenthood. The arrow between social background and teenage parenthood has a question mark, because in this case, a cause-effect relationship might or might not exist.

What did the study actually find? It found that even among people with similar backgrounds, those who grew up in single-parent families were more likely to have babies as teenagers. In the population as a whole, white teenagers who grew up in one-parent families were 111 percent more likely than other white teenagers to give birth as teens. Among those whose social background and education were similar, those from one-parent homes were 58 percent more likely to give birth as teenagers. Among black teenagers, the difference was 50 percent in the whole population and 36 percent for those with similar education and background. Thus, for both races, the control variables of education and background explained away *part* of the relationship between growing up in a one-parent home and having a baby as a teenager *but not all of it*. In this case, Example 2 was the correct choice. Note, though, that the effects of single parenthood do vary by race. Even after controlling for social background, the difference in pregnancy rates for teens from two-parent homes and one-parent homes is bigger for white teenagers than it is for African American teenagers.

Experiments

An **experiment** is research that is carried out in a situation, such as a laboratory or classroom, that is under the control of the researcher. In an experiment, the researcher changes or manipulates the independent variable, tries to keep everything else constant, and then measures the dependent variable both before and after the change in the independent variable. Suppose, for example, that a researcher wanted to find out if seeing a movie advocating tolerance would reduce people's levels of racial prejudice. The researcher could give a group of people a questionnaire measuring prejudice, then show them the movie, and then give them a questionnaire again to see if their attitudes had changed. If so, there would be evidence both of *correlation* between seeing the movie and changes in their prejudice scores, and of *correct time order*.

Experimental and Control Groups

To be really confident of their results, however, researchers must use not one but two groups of people in their experiments. One group, called the **experimental group**, goes through an experience like that described previously. They are given a "before" measure of the dependent variable (called the pretest); the independent variable is changed or manipulated (as in the showing of the movie); and the dependent variable is measured again (the posttest). The other group, the **control group**, goes through the pretest and posttest, but there is no manipulation of the independent variable. In the example above, the control group would be given the "before" and "after" prejudice questionnaire but would *not* be shown the movie. Why is this necessary? Without the control group, the scientist would have no way of knowing whether people's attitudes changed because of seeing the movie or for some other reason. It could be, for example, that their attitudes changed because answering the questionnaire made them think in ways that changed their minds. Using the control group eliminates this alternative explanation because that group also took the questionnaire twice. If the experimental group (the group that saw the movie) changed more than the control group, it was clearly influenced by something more than just taking the test—most likely by seeing the movie.

Of course, other possibilities exist. Perhaps the people in the experimental group were more easily persuaded than the people in the control group and thus were more likely to change their minds. Social researchers can minimize the likelihood of this kind of problem by *randomly assigning* each person who participates in the experiment as a subject to either the experimental group or the control group. If these two groups are large enough, such random assignment will ensure that the groups have a similar mix of social characteristics. If the groups are thus similar, differences in the experiment's results between the two groups cannot be attributed to preexisting differences between the groups.

Field Experiments

Although true experiments are conducted in situations where the researcher can control all the elements, the experimental technique is sometimes taken into situations not fully under the control of researchers in an approach called *field experiments*. This type of experiment is particularly common in sociology, which places a greater emphasis on understanding larger social patterns than on trying to predict the behavior of individuals.

Natural Experiments

Two common types of field experiments are natural experiments and social experiments. Natural experiments use pretests and posttests with naturally

PERSONAL JOURNEYS INTO SOCIOLOGY
Changing Times

Joan McCord

My high school boyfriend and I married as Stanford undergraduates and went to Harvard together. I taught elementary school in winter and attended Harvard for summer school while my husband earned his Ph.D. Classroom teaching provided an opportunity for me to learn more about children. Occasionally, I used my sixth graders to experiment with theories about learning. The students also proved useful for pretesting measures we intended to use for a book on delinquency that reflected our experiences at the Wiltwyck Reform School in New York.

The year 1956 was a beginning of sorts, for me. I had become a full-fledged graduate student and H. L. A. Hart was teaching a seminar entitled "Causation and the Law." Most of the faculty and students in the seminar maintained the Humean position that causes could not be known and beliefs about them depended on the correlation of events. Hart suddenly slid a heavy glass ashtray across the table against the stomach of Henry Aiken, a philosopher well known for his support of Hume's argument. "I caused that!" Hart announced, thereby issuing the challenge that drives my interest in research.

How can we learn that one event causes another? Despite the appeal of causal skepticism, it was impossible to reject the idea that at least sometimes, people cause things to happen. And, as Hart's gesture indicated, detection of causal relations cannot be entirely dependent on perceiving constancy of conjunction. Hart had not previously shoved anything across the conference table—much less, an ashtray. Yet it seemed clear that Hart caused his colleague's pain.

Also in 1956, I became a research assistant at Palfrey House, the study center for Child Psychology at Harvard. My first assignment introduced me to the Human Relations Area Files then being created. I coded the child-rearing section of these cross-cultural resources. We classified societies on the basis of reports for which, often, only one or two cases had been described. I could not overcome my doubts about generalizing from what might well be atypical families or erroneous reports. We rated such things as maternal warmth, use of physical punishment, and permissiveness of aggression. After classifying a culture on a particular dimension, we recorded our confidence in the rating as representing a picture of the society. My constant rating of "doubtful" led to a reassignment!

I became Eleanor Maccoby's research assistant, learning much from her about the importance of careful specification of variables. Data for the classic Sears, Maccoby, and Levin study had been collected by asking parents to evaluate their children and to respond to questions about their own child-rearing techniques. Although the authors assumed the reports were valid, the source of information both for the child's behavior and for the home environment had been the mother. I was skeptical. Mothers' reports about their children might merely reflect justifications of their own behavior. Alternatively, the reports might reflect biases about idealized parent-child relationships. Records from social workers participating in The Cambridge-Somerville Youth Study provided a means by which to overcome the problem of using mothers as informants regarding their own and their children's behavior.

occurring events to assess the effects of such events on some dependent variable. My own (Farley's) Ph.D. dissertation can serve as an example of a natural experiment. I was interested in the effect of different types of housing on children's day-to-day activities. I was permitted to use data from a survey conducted at the University of Toronto (Michelson, 1977), which had asked questions of both children and their parents about their daily activities before and after they moved into either single-family houses or high-rise apartments. By so doing, I was able to compare the activities of children both before (pretest) and after (posttest) they moved into one type of housing or the other. In this example, the naturally occurring event of the family's move substituted for the manipulation of the independent variable that would have taken place in a true experiment.

Social Experiments

In social experiments, some type of social policy is tried out in a real-life setting, and a pretest,

---

My husband and I had begun to evaluate The Cambridge-Somerville Youth Study, a program designed to prevent delinquency that had included random assignment of high-risk children to treatment and control groups. Evaluating almost a decade earlier, Edwin Powers and Helen Witmer had concluded that no beneficial effect had been demonstrated. We hoped that a delayed effect would be found. On December 10 of 1956, I put the finishing touches on our book, *Origins of Crime*. Then I went to the hospital to deliver the first of our two sons. Geoffrey's birth made understanding cause-effect relationships in personality development both more interesting and more urgent. In 1957, I obtained a grant to recode information from the social workers' records in order to use it for further investigation into personality development.

In 1957, I received the Josiah Royce Fellowship in Philosophy. Shortly after this fellowship began, my husband was invited to become Assistant Dean of Humanities and Sciences at Stanford. We moved west. I directed studies of personality development as a research associate at Stanford, where my second son, Rob, was born in 1959. The family spent most of 1961 in France. Upon our return, I resumed studies aiming toward a Ph.D. in Philosophy. At about that time, our marriage broke down. I struggled to keep food on the table. Without a Ph.D., I could not get the positions for which my experience and training had qualified me; yet employers were unwilling to hire me in assistant positions because, they said, "You will be bored." I rented rooms, tutored children, and became a consultant. Finally in 1965, the National Institute of Mental Health funded my return to graduate studies. I earned a Ph.D. in Sociology from Stanford in 1968.

By the late 1970s, boys from the Cambridge-Somerville Youth Study had become middle-aged. The coded records included detailed information about how fathers, mothers, and siblings interacted. The lure of discovering long-delayed benefits of treatment in combination with the possibility of a more adequate study of the influence of child-rearing on adult behavior drove me to apply for funds to do what was then an unpopular form of study: longitudinal research. Together with a small cadre of assistants, although thirty years had passed without contact, I retraced the 506 former members of the Youth Study. We learned that despite their descriptions of how the treatment had been beneficial, men in the treatment group actually turned out worse than those in the matched control group. We learned also that child-rearing differences predict many features of adult behavior.

I continue to analyze data from the Cambridge-Somerville Youth Study, in part because the data help to test whether investigations based on contemporary conditions should be viewed as bounded by current culture. The data also are unique for having been collected through repeated observations of many families in a variety of conditions over an extended period of time. My studies based on these data include information about the behavior of two generations.

Apart from my work with data from the Cambridge-Somerville project, my empirical studies have been based on longitudinal research of children from the Woodlawn community in Chicago and from a crime-cohort study of co-offending in Philadelphia. Many of my newer projects focus on a theory of intentional action that combines my training in philosophy with the empirical focus of work in socialization.

The late *Joan McCord*, Professor of Criminal Justice at Temple University, received a Ph.D. in sociology from Stanford University in 1968. Her contributions to research were honored with the Prix Emile Durkheim from the International Society of Criminology (1993) and the Edwin H. Sutherland Award from the American Society of Criminology (1994). She served as president of the American Society of Criminology and coeditor of the National Academy of Sciences Panel Report on juvenile crime and justice. Professor McCord passed away in 2004 at the age of seventy-three.

posttest, and control group are used to assess its effects. An example of this can be seen in the federal government's Housing Allowance Experiment of the mid-1970s (U.S. Department of Housing and Urban Development, 1979). In this study, low-income families in the experimental group were given housing allowances—money to be used for the purpose of helping them pay for their housing. In pretests and posttests, the amount of money spent on housing by the experimental and control groups was measured to see if the people in the experimental group used their housing allowances to increase what they spent on housing and thereby increase the quality of their housing. For the most part, the experiment found that they did not. Instead, by paying for their housing with the housing allowance, they freed up personal funds to cover other expenses besides housing expenses.

Survey Research

Actually, both of the housing examples above (like most field experiments) did not strictly use the experimental method of research. Rather, they combined that method with survey research, which is the most widely used type of research design in sociology. **Survey research** is any research in which a population or a sample of a population is asked a set of questions that are worked out in advance by the researcher. In survey research, the variables are constructed from individuals' responses to the survey questions. Researchers attempt to measure all of the independent and control variables that might be relevant to whatever dependent variable they are interested in. An advantage of survey research is that, with modern computer technology, it allows researchers the opportunity to study a large number of variables at once. In particular, they can introduce many independent variables at the same time and measure the relative correlation of each with the dependent variable. They can also conduct tests to see if an independent variable still correlates with a dependent variable, even while adjusting for the influence of many control variables at the same time. Survey research is conducted in three common ways: the questionnaire, the telephone interview, and the personal interview.

Questionnaires

In the questionnaire, the people answering the survey read the questions and mark or write their answers on the survey form or an answer sheet. Questionnaires are simple and inexpensive to administer. However, the researcher might not always know when people have a problem understanding questions. Also, depending on how the survey is administered, the response rate can be low. Mail-out/mail-back questionnaires frequently have low response rates, often well under 50 percent and sometimes as low as 10 percent. The response rate can be improved if the survey is handed out to a group and people fill it out on the spot. As we shall see later, however, both of these methods present problems in terms of obtaining a sample that is representative of the population of interest to the researcher.

Telephone Interviews

A second way of doing survey research is the telephone interview. This method is particularly advantageous if quick results are needed, because answers can be entered immediately into the computer by the interviewer and analyzed quickly. Telephone interviews produce a better response rate than questionnaires, though telephone answering machines have presented an increasing problem in this regard. Biases can occur because of people not owning phones or having unlisted numbers, but these problems have decreased. Random-dialing computer programs can reach unlisted numbers, and only about 3 percent of households lack phones today. For these reasons, use of telephone surveys increased sharply in the 1980s and 1990s (Babbie, 1992, p. 275) but more recently has become more challenging because of the proliferation of cell phones and unlisted home phones that make potential respondents more difficult to reach.

During the 1930s and 1940s (when more households lacked telephones than today), telephone polls occasionally made incorrect predictions of election outcomes because Democrats, with lower average incomes, were less likely to have telephones. Consequently, the polls predicted Republican victories in elections that were won by the Democrats. A classic case is the famous *Literary Digest* presidential election poll of 1936. Although it was not a telephone poll, it got into trouble by drawing much of its sample from telephone directories. Because the poll greatly overrepresented Republicans, it predicted that Alf Landon would defeat Franklin D. Roosevelt by about 15 percentage points. Roosevelt subsequently won in a landslide, carrying every state but two.

This type of problem is less common today, when nearly everyone has phones, but still can be an issue if a survey is attempted in an area with a high poverty rate, where more households are without phones. The more serious problems today are that many people are able to block phone calls using voice mail, answering machines, caller ID, and similar technologies, and cellular phones are being used in addition to or instead of home land-line phones, making valid sampling more difficult (Cox et al., 1999; Steeh et al., 1999; Oldendick and Link, 1999; Kempf and Remington, 2007). Moreover, people who have unlisted phones or who use cell phones instead of landlines may be systematically different from people who do not, creating potential biases (Pew Research Center, 2006).

An interviewer conducts a personal interview survey. Surveys are one of the most widely used research methods in sociology. (Courtesy of Michael Flota)

Personal Interviews

The third way of doing survey research is the personal interview. Unless results are needed very quickly, the personal interview is usually the most thorough and reliable method of survey research. If done properly, most of the intended sample can be reached, interviewers can recognize ambiguous questions, and visual aids can be used. The main drawback of this method of research is its expense. Each interview can take an hour, and another hour or more may be spent traveling. The researcher must pay trained interviewers for this work. Someone must also code the results and enter them into the computer for analysis. Thus, one of the biggest factors researchers must take into consideration when they decide what kind of survey research to do is what they can afford.

Survey Questions

Two general types of question are commonly used in survey research: fixed-response and open-ended. Fixed-response questions are like multiple-choice exam questions: The respondent (the person answering the survey) is asked a question and then chooses one of several possible answers listed on the questionnaire or by the interviewer. Advantages of this approach are that the results are easy to process and the respondent picks the category that his or her answer will be placed in, rather than having that done by the researcher. The disadvantage, of course, is that none of the categories may represent the respondent's true feelings about the question.

The other kind of question is the open-ended question. This type of question has no fixed choices; rather, the respondent states or writes an answer to the question in his or her own words. This offers the advantage of enabling respondents to say what they really think without limiting them to a preconceived set of categories. However, in order to analyze large numbers of such responses, researchers must usually code each response according to its meaning, so that similar responses from different people can be grouped together. This process involves a great deal of work, and there is always the risk that the coder will interpret the response differently from what the respondent intended. Thus, open-ended and fixed-response questions both have their advantages and disadvantages.

Sampling

Although some surveys include everyone in the population the researcher is interested in, most surveys are based on samples. A sample is a subset of a population that is used to represent the entire population. If a sample is properly drawn, it can produce a result that is almost as trustworthy as if the entire population had been surveyed—and at a tremendously lower cost. A poorly drawn sample can render a research project useless. In order to be trustworthy, a sample must have two key characteristics. It must be *representative* and it must be *large* enough to give reliable results.

A sample is representative of the population when everyone in the population has the same chance of being included in the sample. Thus, the mix of social characteristics in a representative sample must be similar to that of the general population. If you were interested in learning about the opinions of students at your college or university, for instance, you could not obtain a representative sample by doing the survey only in your introductory sociology class. Assuming that you are attending a four-year school, such a survey would mainly shut out juniors and seniors, and you would therefore oversample freshmen and sophomores, because they are the people who usually take introductory classes. And, regardless of whether you are in a two-year school or a four-year school, you would have too many people in your sample who are interested in sociology and not enough who are interested in other subjects. Thus, your sample would not be representative of the student body of your school. A better strategy would have been to randomly draw names (or student numbers) from a list of all students at your school. In general, representative samples are best obtained through random sampling of the population the researcher wishes to study.

Besides being representative, a sample must be *large* enough to give reliable results. What matters most is the number of people in the sample, not the percentage of the population that is sampled. Even in a small local area, a sample size of several hundred will usually be needed in order to ensure reliable results. At the same time, a sample of 2,000 to 3,000 people is adequate for a population as large as the United States. An example of such a survey can be seen in the box "Doing Survey Research: Sex in America." Keep in mind, however, that even the largest sample will not give an accurate result if it is not representative of the population that it is chosen to represent. If this is the case, the sample will be reliable, but it will not be valid. It will give misleading results, because some parts of the population are overrepresented while others are underrepresented.

Field Observation

Field observation is a method of research in which human behavior is observed by researchers as it occurs in ordinary real-life situations. It is the only method of research that permits social scientists to see directly how people actually behave in ordinary situations not under the control of the researcher. In experiments, the behavior is ordinarily observed in artificial settings such as classrooms or laboratories, so the researcher cannot assume that people will behave the same way in real-life situations. In survey research, researchers must depend upon what respondents tell them. We know that when it comes to behavior, people do not always know how they would behave in some situations, so the answers they give survey takers are not always accurate. Even accounts of what people have actually done in the past frequently contain considerable inaccuracies. Field observation gets around these problems by observing carefully and systematically how people actually behave in ordinary real-life situations.

Field Observation and Theory Generation

Field observation is especially useful for theory generation. Often, if a researcher does not have a clear theory or a body of past research findings to work with, field observation can disclose patterns that can be used to generate hypotheses. Field observation is similar in some ways to the ordinary observations of the behavior of others that we all make. The difference is that field observations are more systematic. Field observers take care to make prompt and detailed notes about their observations and to distinguish *observations* ("the woman was smiling") from *interpretations* ("the woman was happy").

Although field observation has an important advantage over other research methods in that the social scientist sees real behavior in uncontrived situations, this method also has some limitations. Most important is that the observer is never sure whether the behavior observed is representative of anyone beyond the people actually observed. In field observations, there is no way to draw a random sample of the population. The observer must, rather, observe the behavior of those with whom he or she comes into contact in the situation in which the observation is being done.

Participant Observation

The two main types of field observation are participant observation and unobtrusive observation. In **participant observation,** the researcher participates in some way in the behavior being observed. This can be accomplished by attending a meeting, participating in a group activity, or perhaps living for a time with the people being studied. A critical question here is whether the researcher should reveal his or her identity. There are arguments both for and against doing this. The main argument against it is that when people realize that they are being studied, they behave differently. Those in favor of revealing their identity argue that people may alter their behavior even more if they suspect they are secretly being studied. There is also an ethical argument in support of researchers' revealing their identities: Some social scientists feel that people have a right to know when they are being studied and a right not to be studied if they don't want to be. Others, however, argue that when people are in a public place, social scientists have the same right to observe them that anyone else has.

In most cases, participant observation is less quantitative and more qualitative than other methods of research. Whereas surveys and experiments produce numbers that can be used to test hypotheses and clarify relationships between variables, participant observation is often more subjective in nature. It offers less-precise numbers, but it allows far greater depth of knowledge. No matter what group of people a sociologist is trying to study, there are some things that he or she will not find out simply by asking questions as an "outsider." Every group of people has its informal norms and "inside information." It is not likely that the answers given to a survey taker will reveal much about this aspect of group life. To get this information, a sociologist must literally become a part of the group and often must remain so for some time. Participant observers have moved into neighborhoods, or even lived with families, for periods ranging from one year to four or five years.

Many social scientists feel that no other method can gain the degree of insight that is possible through ongoing intimate contact. Many of sociology's most important studies have been based on participant observation, and they have often produced results that have contradicted conventional wisdom—even sometimes the conventional wisdom of sociologists. Sociologists William F. Whyte (1981 [orig. 1943]) and Herbert Gans (1962) conducted long-term participant observation studies in Boston's low-income Italian neighborhoods. They found that the neighborhoods, which were generally regarded as disorganized, vice-ridden slums, were actually stable, well-organized neighborhoods where the residents worked hard and took care of one another. The residents had low incomes and were uninvolved in the city's political life, but these neighborhoods were nothing like the dens of social pathology that they were widely believed to be. Some of the things Whyte learned were surprising even to him. In his words, "As I sat and listened, I learned the answers to questions that I would not even have had the sense to ask." For another example of the things that can be learned through participant observation, see the box "Doing Participant Observation: Slim's Table."

Whyte's comments illustrate another important aspect of participant observation—it is often combined with a research technique known as

qualitative interviewing. The qualitative interview is a little like the open-ended questions used in survey research, except that there is more attention to the depth of the answers and less to standardization or to completing the interview in a fixed time frame. After having gained the trust of the people being studied, the qualitative interviewer asks questions aimed at getting certain information the researcher wants to obtain. But the possibility is always kept open of asking new questions suggested by the respondent's answer to the initial ones. Through this process, information is obtained that

SOCIOLOGICAL SURPRISES
Doing Survey Research: Sex in America

On Valentine's Day 1992, survey interviewers began work on a project that had never been done before—a survey about sexual practices and experiences among a representative sample of the U.S. population. Of course, sexual practices surveys had been done before—the famous Kinsey reports (Kinsey et al., 1948, 1953) shocked an earlier generation with their findings about sexual behavior. But Kinsey and other sex researchers before the 1990s had relied on volunteers—thus, their samples cannot be taken as representative of the U.S. population. The 1992 personal interview survey, reported in a book entitled *Sex in America: A Definitive Survey* (Michael et al., 1994), was different. It used a representative sample of 3,432 Americans obtained through random sampling processes, thus assuring a close match in social characteristics to the entire U.S. population. In addition, it obtained a response rate of about 80 percent, good for any survey on any subject. And it came up with some real surprises:

- Although Americans like to believe that love knows no bounds and can conquer all (as illustrated in the movie *Pretty Woman*), love is in fact quite predictable: The overwhelming majority fall in love with people who are very similar to themselves with regard to education, age, income, race, and other social characteristics.
- Even casual flings usually happen between people with similar social characteristics. In noncohabiting relationships lasting less than a month, the partners are just as similar with regard to education, age, and race as in marriage! Even religion is similar most of the time in short-term relationships.
- People don't have as many sex partners as one might think. The majority of adult Americans have had four or fewer sex partners in their entire adult lives. This is, incidentally, true for every major racial group in the United States and at every level of education.
- On the other hand, about one American male out of six has had more than twenty sexual partners in his adult lifetime. The percentage is about the same among whites, blacks, and Hispanics, but it is twice as high among college graduates as it is among people with a high school education or less. Only 3 percent of women have had more than twenty partners.
- Marriage does not kill sex. Married people have almost as much sex as people who are cohabiting, and both of these groups have much more sex than people who are not married and not cohabiting. People who were either married or cohabiting also reported greater enjoyment of sex than people who were not. And they enjoyed it most when they had only one partner. Married people with more than one partner enjoyed sex less, and single people who were not cohabiting enjoyed it least.
- Contrary to Kinsey's findings, most married people don't cheat on their spouses. The large majority of married men and women report having sex only with their partners, and this is true regardless of their sexual lifestyle before marriage. Some critics have argued that respondents may have been less than honest about this, but Michael et al. note that they employed far more extensive cross-checks to detect dishonesty than most surveys do, and that their respondents "passed with flying colors."
- Contrary to popular belief, people who have regular sex partners masturbate more than people who do not. In this instance, as in so many others, social research has shown us that many of the things we "just know" are wrong. And there's no area of life where there are more myths than in the area of human sexual behavior.

the researcher may not have originally thought to ask about.

In spite of its advantages, participant observation, like other methods of research, is subject to problems of reactivity. The mere presence of an observer may, for example, alter people's behavior. To lessen this problem, a researcher may try to remain as uninvolved as possible, or may try to act like most of the people being observed. There is, however, one method of field observation that entirely avoids reactivity problems—unobtrusive observation.

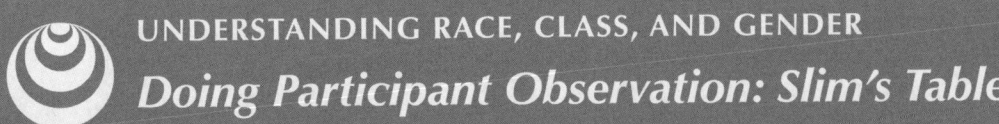

UNDERSTANDING RACE, CLASS, AND GENDER
Doing Participant Observation: Slim's Table

Mitchell Dunier (1992) conducted a participant observation study to learn about the black men you don't learn about on TV news, or even know about as much as you should from sociology books. Although the evening news, the government reports, and the sociology books often focus on problems faced by many black men—unemployment, poverty, discrimination, crime—Dunier wanted to learn about the ordinary, everyday realities of the millions of black men who don't fit this problem image. They aren't unemployed, most of them aren't poor, and they don't commit crimes. They are ordinary workers who live quiet, regular lives, just like millions of other Americans. Dunier learned about their lives by hanging out at Chicago's Valois "See Your Food" Cafeteria, observing and talking with the black men who regularly ate and chatted there at a table with Slim, a 65-year-old auto mechanic and lifelong Chicago resident.

Dunier learned rather quickly that the men who ate at Slim's table—most of whom were in their fifties or sixties—were concerned first and foremost with respectability and responsibility. This meant working hard, saving what you can, and respecting your parents and authority. In part, their attitudes reflected a generation gap that is present among both whites and blacks in American society. The men at Slim's table repeatedly expressed concern about young people spending money foolishly as soon as they get it, and about the tendency of many to be more interested in material consumption than in hard work. They expressed feelings of resentment against both young, poor blacks, whom they viewed as irresponsible and out of control, and against middle-class blacks, whom they saw as caught up in "keeping up with the Joneses." The concern about a decline of responsible and respectable behavior in American society can be seen in the following statement by Ted, one of the regulars at Slim's table. Ted contrasts his experiences with what he sees in the experience of young people today:

> We are of a completely different world. We always were. We had a paper route and would deliver papers twice a day. You got up at four o'clock in the morning, ran down to the branch, picked them up, made the run in the morning, before you went to school. Then after school you went and got your second batch for the day and threw those.... You always had a job. Sit around and wait for a check? Oh, man!

Dunier shows that there are other common perceptions of the black community that also don't fit the men at Slim's table. For example, blacks today are often seen as withdrawing from white society to socialize and interact only with other blacks. But that was not the case with the men at Slim's table. Though they often sat with other black men, the cafeteria was a means by which the men maintained contact and interaction with the larger, predominantly white society. The men did not view the white society as superior, but neither did they wish to withdraw from it totally. Strong bonds did develop between black and white patrons of the cafeteria. Slim, for example, adopted an elderly white man as a father figure and took responsibility for him as one might for an elderly parent. And in one fascinating account, Dunier describes how social bonds can form even without being apparent. One February, the cafeteria closed for remodeling. Patrons, both black and white, who had seen but never spoken with one another, began to chat and form relationships when they ran into each other in different restaurants while the Valois was closed. This provided opportunities for people in both black cliques and white cliques to reach beyond the boundaries of the groups they normally sat with—and both seized the opportunity with relish.

Unobtrusive Observation

Unobtrusive observation can be defined as field observation in which the researcher does not in any way become involved in the behavior being observed. One type of unobtrusive observation is observing human behavior from a position out of sight—through a window, across the street, and so forth. Another type is observation of physical traces—evidence that people leave behind them. A sociologist might, for example, get an idea of how safe people feel in a neighborhood by examining the proportion of cars that are locked. Frequently, such methods lead to the development of *unobtrusive measures,* which are quantifiable measures such as the percentage of males and females entering a grocery store at a certain time of day, that result from unobtrusive observation.

The great advantage of unobtrusive observation over all the methods of research discussed thus far is that, if done properly, it avoids problems of reactivity. The disadvantage is that it tends to be somewhat lacking in depth. One can obtain only so much information without any direct interaction with other people. Still, unobtrusive observation is an important social research tool, particularly in urban sociology, where researchers are interested in the characteristics of people living in and using different kinds of city neighborhoods.

In unobtrusive observation, the researcher observes human behavior from a position that is out of sight or relatively unnoticeable. (Courtesy of Michael Flota)

Use of Existing Data Sources

A final type of research that is of great importance in sociology is the use of existing data sources. Very often a social scientist need not collect original data to study an issue or a problem because the necessary data have already been collected by someone else and are available. There are three main sources of existing data: various public and private data archives, the U.S. Census and related sources, and published or broadcast media suitable for content analysis. Let us consider each further.

Data Archives

As you are probably aware, thousands of surveys have been taken in recent decades by college- and university-based researchers, private organizations and corporations, and various government agencies. Most of these surveys have resulted in computerized data archives, many of which are available to researchers. Many college professors conducting research are willing to share their data with others whose research interests are slightly different from their own. In fact, some do this on a regular basis through organizations like the Inter-University Consortium for Political and Social Research (ICPSR), a national organization in which most major universities participate. Professional organizations often conduct surveys of participants in their professions and sometimes make such data available to researchers with related interests. Many government agencies conduct surveys and other forms of research and then sell computer archives of the data at cost. The U.S. government also has a registration system that records births, deaths, marriages, and divorces as they occur, which is an important source for researchers interested in these topics. An increasing amount of material from many of these sources is being made directly available over the Internet to anyone who wants to use it.

The U.S. Census

A second major source of data, available to anyone with access to a good library or the Internet, is the U.S. Census. The Census, conducted every ten years, includes comprehensive data on population and housing characteristics for areas as small as a city block and as big as the entire country. A glance through any major sociological journal will reveal that the Census is one of the most important sources of data for sociological research. In addition to population and housing, regular censuses are also conducted on manufacturing, wholesale trade, retail trade, service industries, agriculture, mineral industries, and government. The results of all of these censuses are available through the Census Bureau's Web site, http://www.census.gov. Census data for any geographic area, along with an increasing variety of other data, are available through the Web site's American Factfinder feature. Older census data, for example, from Censuses before 1990, can be looked up at any major library.

The population Census is only conducted every ten years, however, and there is a need for more current data. This need is met, in part, by the Census Bureau's *Current Population Survey*. This survey, conducted on an ongoing basis, provides annual updates on such things as population size, age structure, racial composition, income, household and family characteristics, education, and employment and unemployment. If you need up-to-date data on any of these issues, the *Current Population Survey* is a good place to look. Finally, the Census Bureau also now conducts a detailed ongoing sample survey of communities throughout the country, as a way of providing local-level data between Censuses. This survey, known as the *American Community Survey*, replaces the Census for the data that were once collected through the "long form" administered to a sample of Census respondents. The questions once asked on the "short form," which include gender, age, race, ethnicity, relationship to the householder, and whether you own or rent your home, are now the only questions asked in the Census, beginning with the 2010 Census. This change makes the Census easier to administer and easier for citizens to respond to. At the same time, it ensures that, for local geographic areas, data no older than three years will now always be available, when in the past it was ten years between the times when comparable data were collected..

Content Analysis

A slightly different approach to using existing data sources is content analysis. We have already seen one example of this—Adorno's research on the speeches and writings of Nazis and similar extremists. **Content analysis** involves some type of systematic examination of the content of books, articles, speeches, movies, television programs, or other communications. Such analysis can look for regular patterns, as Adorno's research did, or it can examine the handling of some area of subject matter. One might, for example, compare the number and types of roles filled by male and female characters in a set of television programs. Is there any difference, for example, in the proportion of males and females who are portrayed as people in a position to make important decisions? Such portrayals can tell a good deal about how the writers of the television programs feel about the roles of men and women in society. They also say a lot about what television is teaching youngsters about men and women in society. An advantage of content analysis is that it can be either *quantitative* (for example, counting the number of words devoted to female characters as opposed to male) or *qualitative* (for example, a detailed description and analysis of how male and female characters are presented).

Reading Tables

In reports of sociological research, results are often presented in tables. Thus, being able to read tables is an essential skill for anyone who wishes to make sense of sociological research. It is also a skill of some broader usefulness, because many other kinds of information also appear in tables. In fact, in many sociological research reports, most of the actual research findings appear in the tables rather than in the text. As one of my professors in graduate school put it, "If you don't have time to read both the tables and the verbiage, skip the verbiage and read the tables."

Whether you are reading materials from tables or from the text of a journal article, it is important when working with research findings to be aware of the precise meaning of the data that were used. This means, for example, knowing the wording of the questions asked—small changes in wording can make a big difference. It also means paying attention to the circumstances under which the research was done—in interview studies concerning race and gender, for example, the race and gender of the person doing the interviewing can have significant effects on the responses that person gets in the interview. Finally, it means knowing and understanding exactly what statistics mean when they are taken from an existing data source like the Census. As is shown in the box "Damned

SOCIOLOGICAL INSIGHTS
Damned Lies and Statistics: The Worst Statistic Ever

In *Damned Lies and Statistics,* sociologist Joel Best (2001) illustrates some of the ways in which a small misunderstanding of a statistic can lead to huge errors. He begins the book by describing what he calls "the most inaccurate social statistic ever." He found it in a sociological journal after it was cited by a graduate student in a dissertation proposal. Significantly, neither the journal editor nor the graduate student noticed the error of the statement. The statement, written in 1995, read as follows: "Every year since 1950, the number of American children gunned down has doubled."

What is wrong with this statement? Well, Best asks us to imagine that the number of children gunned down in 1950 in the United States was one. (Of course, in reality it was higher than that, which would make the statement even more wrong, as we will see.) If just one child was gunned down in 1950, and the number then doubled every year, the number killed would have reached 1,024 in 1960, and 32,768 by 1965. Already, this is more than three times the total number of U.S. homicides in 1965. But continuing to double the number every year, it would have reached 1 billion by 1980 (four times the U.S. population then), and by 1987, it would have reached 137 billion—well beyond the best estimates of the total human population throughout history. And by 1995, it would have reached 35 *trillion*—about 124,000 *times* the U.S. population! (If you doubt the correctness of these numbers, get out a calculator, start with 1 in 1950, then multiply it by 2 for each year between 1950 and 1995. You will see that Professor Best's numbers are right.)

How could such a huge mistake be made and uncritically repeated? It turns out that it was made as a result of someone moving two words to the wrong place in a sentence. The statement is based on an earlier statement, published by an advocacy organization in 1994, that turns out to be correct: "The number of children killed each year by guns has doubled since 1950." While this statement is true, it is not as bad as it sounds: While the number of children killed by guns doubled, the population also nearly doubled. But what led to the really gross error was when the author of the journal article moved the words "each year" from after "killed" to the beginning of the sentence—so instead of saying the number killed each year had doubled, the statement was changed to saying that each year, the number killed doubled—something *completely different*. ("Each" was also changed to "every," but it would have been just as wrong had it been left as "each.")

How do you, as a student, avoid such errors? Best offers several suggestions. First, find out what you can about the statistic's origin—where did it come from and how was it generated? Second, be aware of some of the common ways that statistics are misunderstood and misrepresented. Third, be aware of what are appropriate and inappropriate comparisons. But most important, adopt a *critical attitude* toward statistics. Many people are awestruck by statistics and accept them blindly. Do not do that. But a critical attitude does not mean an attitude of "all statistics are damned lies." That is just as blind as the uncritical attitude. A critical attitude means looking at a statistic, asking if it makes sense, understanding where it comes from and what its flaws are, and figuring out whether the flaws are serious enough to make an important difference. For you as an introductory sociology student, it means that if you are to make sense of your social world, you must not only adopt a critical attitude, but also develop enough knowledge about social research to make sense of the statistics, findings, and reports that you will encounter in school, in the media, and in life.

Lies and Statistics," what might seem like a small editorial mistake in describing a finding can lead to monstrously incorrect conclusions.

Summary

In this chapter, we have elaborated upon the scientific method and explored the relationship between theory and research. Research generates theory, as theorists seek to explain research findings. These theories then stimulate new research by predicting what such research may be expected to find. When researchers operate in the mode of prediction and theory testing, they often use hypotheses. Hypotheses are specific statements about reality, derived from theories as a way of testing parts of those theories. A hypothesis usually contains one or more independent variables (presumed causes) and a dependent variable (presumed effect). Scientists test for such cause-effect relationships by looking for correlation between independent and dependent variables, by checking the time order (cause must precede effect), and by eliminating alternative explanations, often through the use of control variables.

In sociology, the major methods of research are experiments, survey research, field observation, and the use of existing data sources. Which of these methods a sociologist will use depends in part on that sociologist's purpose in research (for example, theory testing versus theory generation), and in part on the sociologist's judgment concerning the strengths and weaknesses of each method. Sociologists use both quantitative methods involving numbers and statistics, and qualitative methods involving less quantifiable but more in-depth observations and interviews. Each method has different strengths, and a combination of the two often presents the most complete and accurate sociological picture.

Results derived from social research are commonly expressed as numbers. Such results frequently are presented in tables; being able to read tables correctly is an essential skill for anyone trying to make sense of sociological research. And with or without numbers, the reader of sociological research reports must have a good understanding of the methods used and the meaning of the findings presented, taking a critical view that asks how the results were obtained and what they really mean. This can only be done well if the reader has some baseline of knowledge about social research methods, which is why this kind of knowledge is important for an educated and informed citizenry.

When people take action such as participating in a demonstration, they are expressing value judgments—views about how things ought to be. (iStockphoto)

Key Terms

cause and effect
values
hypothesis
variable
independent variable
dependent variable
operational definition
validity
reliability
correlation
control variable
quantitative research
qualitative research

experiment
experimental group
control group
survey research
sample
field observation
participant observation
qualitative interviewing
unobtrusive observation
content analysis

Exercises

1. Nearly everyone has heard of the *Gallup Poll,* but few people have any idea of how a social science survey, or poll, is conducted. Check out www.pollingreport.com or www.gallup.com, and look over some of the survey questions. How might slight variations in the language of the questions end up creating bias in the answers? Think of an issue that interests you greatly that is also high-profile like abortion, stem cell research, human trafficking and slavery, economic growth, global warming, evolution, or the budget deficit. Now, compile a list of questions you would like to ask others about your issue and compare it to the questions asked of the same topic on the Polling Report or Gallup Web site. How do survey makers avoid bias in their questions?

2. The U.S. Census Bureau is a fountain of information relevant to sociology and the social sciences. This exercise is designed to introduce you to the Census Bureau and to provide some experience in using its resources. Check out www.census.gov. From the opening screen, select "American FactFinder" on the left navigation bar. In the "Start with Basic Facts" window, click on "Tables." Next to "Show Me," scroll down to "Households and Families"; next to "for" scroll down to "State-County." Now, select your home state, and click "Go." When you have accessed the data for your state, scroll down to your county of residence. Examine the data for *single-parent families* by looking at the "Female Householder, No Husband Present" column. Are you in any way surprised by the prevalence of this type of family? If you have time, you may wish to explore another topic using the Census Bureau site. If your instructor has a term paper assignment, you may be able to utilize this site.

Part II
Society and Human Interaction

Chapter 3
Perspectives on Society and Interaction

Perspectives in Sociology   52
   Macrosociology and Microsociology   52
Macrosociology I: The Functionalist Perspective   53
   The Functionalist Perspective Defined   53
   Key Principles of the Functionalist Perspective   53
   Functions and Dysfunctions   56
Macrosociology II: The Conflict Perspective   56
   The Conflict Perspective Defined   56
Macrosociological Perspectives: Is Synthesis Possible?   60
   Functional for Whom? Another Look   61
   Simultaneous Forces for Cooperation and Conflict   61
   Macrosociological Perspectives: A Final Note   63
Microsociology: The Symbolic-Interactionist Perspective   64
   The Interactionist Perspective Defined   64
   Interpreting Situations and Messages   65
   The Social Construction of Reality   65
   Social Roles   68
   Sending Messages: The Presentation of Self   69
Micro- and Macrosociology: Is Synthesis Possible?   71
   Simultaneous Effects of Function, Conflict, and Interaction   71
   Exchange Theory   71
   Using All Three Perspectives: An Example   74
   The Three Perspectives and This Book   75
Summary   76
Key Terms   76
Exercises   76

In 1996, a professional basketball player, Mahmoud Abdul-Rauf of the Denver Nuggets, remained in the locker room or stood aside on the sideline while the national anthem was being played before the game. When it was finished, he quietly returned to the court to begin the game. When asked why, he said his religious and philosophical beliefs had led him to the conclusion that it was not right for him to stand at attention during the national anthem. Despite the fact that the U.S. Constitution guarantees freedom of religion and expression, Mr. Rauf was suspended from play in the NBA until he agreed to remain standing during the playing of the national anthem. *Why did this happen?*

Although the 1964 Civil Rights Act forbids discrimination on the basis of gender, it remains true that women are paid less than men for the same type of work. For each dollar that a man working year-round, full-time is paid, a woman working year-round, full-time is paid just over 75 cents. This is true even if the man and the woman have the same level of education. *Why is this the case?*

International comparisons show that Americans are more religious than people in almost all other industrialized countries. Americans are more likely than people in other industrialized countries to attend religious services on a weekly basis (although the majority do not), and Americans are more likely to say that religion is a major force influencing their day-to-day thoughts and actions. *Why are Americans more religious than people in other industrialized countries?*

Sociology is about the business of answering "why" questions like these—and each of these questions has more than one possible answer. Where sociologists will look for answers to questions like these—and what they think the answers are likely to be—depends largely upon the sociological perspectives with which the sociologists identify. In this chapter, you will learn about three perspectives that, individually or jointly, influence much of the work that modern sociologists do—including how they go about answering questions such as those posed above. In this chapter we shall also illustrate the usefulness of sociology in answering the first question above, and later chapters will use sociology to answer the second and third questions.

Perspectives in Sociology

Each of the questions posed above can be answered in different ways, reflecting the different perspectives that have been influential in sociology. A **perspective** can be defined as an overall approach or viewpoint toward a subject, including (1) a set of *questions* to be asked about the subject, (2) a general *theory* or theoretical approach to explaining the nature of the subject, and often (3) a set of *values* relating to the subject. (The difference between theories and values was explained in Chapter 2.)

Sociologists propose dozens of important theories and ask thousands of questions, but to a large extent these theories and questions can be linked to one or more of the three major perspectives in the field. These perspectives are the *functionalist perspective,* the *conflict perspective,* and the *symbolic-interactionist perspective.* Each of these perspectives offers a distinct theory concerning the key social forces that shape human behavior and society. *In other words, they offer different explanations for why people behave as they do.* Accordingly, sociologists of different perspectives disagree not only about theory, but also about what questions are important to ask.

A sociologist's preference for one or the other of these perspectives may also reflect his or her values to some extent. Here, we are referring to two kinds of values: views about what society should be like, and a personal interest in asking and answering some kinds of questions as opposed to others.

Macrosociology and Microsociology

Two of the three perspectives we shall be considering, the functionalist perspective and the conflict perspective, fall under the category of **macrosociology**. In other words, they are mainly concerned with explaining large-scale social patterns. Often they study entire societies as opposed to small groups or individuals. They may compare different societies, or they may compare different historical periods in the same society. The third perspective, the symbolic-interactionist perspective, is more interested in **microsociology**. This means that it is more concerned with processes that work at the individual level and that are concerned with interactions between individuals and the larger society. For this reason, it is largely concerned with the subfield of sociology known as social psychology, introduced in Chapter 1.

We shall begin our discussion with the two macrosociological perspectives, the functionalist and the conflict perspectives. Both of these approaches ask the same basic question: Why does a society take the form it does? For example, consider religion, a key factor in two of the questions that opened this chapter. Some societies, such as Iran and to a lesser extent Israel, are centered around religion. Others, such as the United States, are not, but religion still plays a major role in people's lives. Still others, like many European and Latin American societies, are more nominally religious: People do identify with a religion, but rarely attend church and do not see religion as a central feature in their lives. *Why do societies vary so much in the extent to which they are shaped by religious forces?* It is questions like these that the two macrosociological perspectives try to answer.

Macrosociology I: The Functionalist Perspective

The Functionalist Perspective Defined

The **functionalist perspective** (also sometimes called the *order perspective* or *systems theory*) assumes that *any society takes its particular form because that form works well for the society, or helps to preserve the society, given its particular situation*. Societies exist under a wide range of environmental situations. Some, for example, exist in harsh arctic, desert, or mountain climates, whereas others exist in temperate climates and fertile environments. Levels of technology also vary widely. Some societies have highly advanced industrial technologies, whereas others engage in subsistence farming. Societies also differ in terms of their interactions with other societies. Some have hostile neighbors; others have friendly neighbors.

All of these elements make up the total environment within which a society must exist, and each combination of these elements forces a society to adapt in a particular set of ways. Thus, what works for one society cannot necessarily be expected to work for another.

For any society, however, the functionalist theoretical perspective makes one basic argument. Whatever the characteristics of the society, *those characteristics have developed because they meet the needs of that society in its particular situation.* By so doing, they help the society to survive. The early sociologist who probably had the greatest influence on this school of thought was Emile Durkheim. Talcott Parsons and Robert Merton have been influential modern American functionalist theorists. Their work is examined in the box "Functionalist Theory: Some Key Thinkers."

Having now provided a general statement describing the functionalist perspective, let us look at several of its key principles in greater detail. These principles include *interdependency, functions of social structure and culture, consensus and cooperation,* and *equilibrium.*

Key Principles of the Functionalist Perspective

Interdependency
One of the most important principles of functionalist theory is that society is *made up of interdependent parts*. This means that every part of society is dependent to some extent on other parts of society, so that what happens at one place in society has important effects elsewhere. Early social thinkers in this tradition often likened the operation of society to that of a living organism. Auguste Comte, Herbert Spencer, and Emile Durkheim all used this analogy. Think of your own body. Your entire body depends upon your heart, brain, lungs, stomach, and liver for its survival. Each of these organs provides a vital function. A malfunction in any one of them can affect the health of your entire body. These early sociologists saw society as operating in much the same way.

If this was true a century ago when Comte and Spencer were developing their social theories, it is even more true today. Society has become more complex and more interdependent, not less so. Just think for a moment of all the people upon whom your participation in your introductory sociology course depends. Obviously, the class requires a faculty member to teach it and students to take it. However, it also depends on many other people and organizations. Someone has to provide the electricity to light the room, and in order for that electricity to be provided, someone had to build a dam, a wind farm, or solar panels, or mine some coal, oil, or uranium and get that fuel to the power plant. Someone also had to decide when the class would be held and in what room, communicate that information to you, and enroll you in that class. Someone had to write this book, and with the assistance of many other people—printers, editors, proofreaders, salespeople, and bookstore employees—it has arrived in your hands. Thus, a class that seems to involve just you, your fellow students, and your professor is in fact the product of the efforts of hundreds of people. Consider also that a failure on the part of any element of this complicated system could affect your participation in this class. Your name could be left off the instructor's class list; the book could arrive late or in insufficient numbers at the bookstore; there could be a power failure; the class could be scheduled in the same room as another class.

Functions

Closely related to interdependency is the idea that each part of the social system exists because it serves some **function**. In other words, it meets some need in society or somehow contributes to the effective operation and continuation of the society. Here again, the analogy to a living organism is apparent: Just as each organ has its function to perform, so does each part of society. Consider, for example, the *postpartum sex taboo,* a common rule in many preindustrial societies. This rule specifies that a woman may not have sex for some set period after the birth of a child. The length of time covered by the postpartum taboo has ranged from a few weeks to several years. Although few people realized it, this rule was very useful. When the mother is breast-feeding her baby and her own diet is barely adequate, becoming pregnant could so deplete the nutrients in her breast milk that her baby could become seriously malnourished. Thus, in such societies, the health of babies—and consequently, the perpetuation of the society itself—depended on the mother's not becoming pregnant again too soon after giving birth. The postpartum sex taboo prevented this. Therefore, whatever religious or mystical beliefs may have served as the basis for this rule, it turns out that the rule performed an important function for society.

Societal functions that are obvious and openly stated are referred to as **manifest functions**. A manifest function of education, for example, is to teach children about such subjects as reading, writing, and arithmetic. Sometimes, however, functions are not obvious or openly acknowledged. These are called **latent functions.** A latent function of education is baby-sitting: School relieves parents of the responsibility of taking care of their children. Thus, the parents are free to pursue other efforts or simply to take a break from child care. Latent functions are often unintentional: The school system was not set up for the purpose of baby-sitting, but it does serve that purpose. Although latent functions are less obvious than manifest functions, they can be just as important to society. For this reason, sociologists operating out of the functionalist perspective have devoted much effort to identifying the latent functions of social structure and culture.

Consensus and Cooperation

Another key principle in functionalist theory is that societies have a tendency toward *consensus;* that is, to have certain basic values that nearly everyone in the society agrees upon. Americans, for example, nearly all agree that they believe in freedom and democracy. They may not agree on exactly what they mean by either freedom or democracy, and they also may disagree on the extent to which the United States has attained these ideals. However, as ideals or principles that a society ought to strive for, the overwhelming majority of Americans express support for freedom and democracy.

According to functionalists, societies tend toward consensus in order to achieve *cooperation.* As we have already seen, the interdependency in society requires that people cooperate. If people in even one part of such an interdependent system fail to cooperate with people elsewhere in the system, the effects will be felt throughout the entire system. People are more likely to cooperate when they share similar values and goals. According to Durkheim (1947 [orig. 1893]; 1953 [orig. 1898]), they are especially likely to cooperate when they feel that they share things in common with one another; he referred to such unity as *solidarity.*

What happens when a society lacks consensus? According to functionalists, inability to cooperate will paralyze the society, and people will devote more and more effort to fighting one another rather than getting anything done. This process can be seen in the former Yugoslavia and in parts of the former Soviet Union. When the fall of

SOCIOLOGICAL INSIGHTS
Functionalist Theory: Some Key Thinkers

Emile Durkheim (1858–1917)

Much of functionalist thinking about the importance of interdependency as a force for cohesion in society can be traced to the writings of Emile Durkheim. In his first major work, *De la Division du Travail Social* (*The Division of Labor in Society*) (Durkheim, 1947 [orig. 1893]), he argued that in preindustrial societies, tradition, unquestioned belief, and forced conformity are the main forces holding society together. He referred to this as "mechanical solidarity." In modern societies, these forces are replaced by interdependency. Durkheim called this new pattern "organic solidarity" because he saw the interdependency in society as being similar to the interdependency of the organs of a living being.

Durkheim's recognition of the importance of consensus can be seen in another major concept he developed, anomie or the "state of normlessness" (Durkheim, 1964a [orig. 1897]). By this, Durkheim meant that in certain situations norms—rules of behavior—break down and become inoperative. This may occur during periods of rapid social change or intense conflict, and when it does, people are more likely to engage in behavior that is destructive to them or their society. Durkheim (1964a [orig. 1897]) illustrated this point in his pioneering study of suicide.

Talcott Parsons (1902–1979)

Functionalist theory became especially influential in the United States, where its leading proponent was Talcott Parsons. One of Parsons's major contributions to sociology was the notion that each piece of the social structure represents some underlying function. According to his theory of structural-functionalism, there are four particularly crucial functions, necessary in any society, that in turn are met by particular systems of action within society (Parsons, 1966, 1971): *integration,* holding the society together and forming a basis for cooperation, which is attained through the social system; *pattern maintenance,* the development and maintenance of common values, which is attained through the cultural system; *goal attainment,* a motivational force that creates the incentive to work and cooperate, which is attained through the personality system; and *adaptation to the environment,* which is attained through the behavioral organism, which Parsons took to include the economic system.

Robert K. Merton (1910–2003)

Although Robert Merton studied under Parsons and is generally identified with the functionalist perspective, certain elements of his thinking have been influenced by the conflict perspective as well. Unlike Durkheim and Parsons, who attempted to develop grand theories to explain the basic nature of society, Merton has often sought to develop *middle-range theories* that seek to describe and explain a narrower range of behaviors with a greater degree of precision. Merton (1967) has argued that such theories better lend themselves to testing through research than do larger-scale theories.

In keeping with his notion of middle-range theories, Merton wrote on a number of specialty areas within sociology, including the sociology of science and race and ethnic relations and especially deviant behavior (Merton, 1938, 1968). One of America's most influential scholars, he coined many of the terms now widely used both in sociology and common language, such as *role model, self-fulfilling prophecy,* and *deviant behavior.*

communism brought an end to forced conformity in the former Soviet Union and in Eastern Europe, lack of consensus led to social breakdown in several areas. Civil war erupted between Armenians and Azerbaijanis in the former Soviet republic of Azerbaijan, and between Bosnians and Serbians and between Albanians and Serbians in the former Yugoslav republics of Bosnia-Herzegovina and Kosovo respectively. Each of these cases led to many deaths and a state of virtual anarchy. From 1992 until 1996, Serbian residents of the Bosnian capital Sarajevo laid siege to the city and bombarded their own neighbors, schools, and businesses. Similar occurrences in Kosovo led to intervention by NATO, involving U.S. troops, in 1999. The critical factor in each of these cases of self-destruction was the lack of consensus between groups of different religious and nationality backgrounds who had long-standing grievances against one another. The dictatorial power of the communist regimes in the past had held these societies together by force, and kept the tensions below the surface. However, when this force was eliminated, the lack of consensus led to chaos and societal breakdown.

While they are extreme cases, these examples illustrate a key point: A society that lacks any consensus whatsoever will have a very hard time surviving as a society.

Equilibrium

A final principle of functionalist theorists is that of *equilibrium*. This view holds that, once a society has achieved the form that is best adapted to its situation, it has reached a state of balance or equilibrium, and it will remain in that condition until it is forced to change by some new condition. New technology, a change in climate, or contact with an outside society are all conditions to which a society might have to adapt. When such conditions occur, social change will take place: Society will change just enough to adapt to the new situation. However, once that adaptation has been made, the society has attained a new state of balance with its environment, and it will not change again until some new situation requires further adaptation. The picture that emerges from the functionalist perspective, then, is that of a basically stable, well-functioning system that changes only when it has to, and then only enough to adapt to changes in its situation. In short, the natural tendency of society is to be stable, because society is a smoothly operating, interdependent system.

Functions and Dysfunctions

An important refinement of the functionalist perspective has been made by Robert Merton (1968). Merton has argued that even social arrangements that are useful to society can have **dysfunctions**, or consequences that are harmful to society. No matter how useful something is, it can still have negative side effects. In general, functionalist theory argues that when the functions outweigh the dysfunctions, a social arrangement will likely continue to exist because, on balance, it is useful to society. However, because situations change, a condition that is functional today can become dysfunctional in the future. Thus, when studying any element of social structure or culture, sociologists typically raise questions about its possible functions and dysfunctions.

Macrosociology II: The Conflict Perspective

Although the conflict perspective can trace its intellectual roots to ancient Chinese, Greek, and Arabian philosophers, modern conflict theory is largely an outgrowth of the theories of Karl Marx. There are many kinds of conflict theories today, a number of which disagree in important ways with Marx's analysis. Nonetheless, the basic Marxian notion of different groups in society having conflicting self-interests remains influential in most modern conflict theories. Over the years, a number of scholars have refined conflict theory and applied it to a widening variety of issues. Among the most influential and important conflict theorists have been the German theorist Ralf Dahrendorf (1959) and the American sociologists W. E. B. Du Bois (1903), C. Wright Mills (1956), and Randall Collins (1979; 1974).

The Conflict Perspective Defined

Like the functionalist perspective, the **conflict perspective** is a macrosociological perspective that addresses the question, Why does society take the form that it does? However, the conflict perspective gives a very different answer to this question. Its answer is that *different groups in society have conflicting self-interests, and the nature of the society is determined by the outcome of the conflict among these groups.* To conflict theorists, the most important force shaping society is conflicting self-interests among different groups within society. The conflict perspective is examined in the box "Conflict Theory: Some Key Thinkers."

Conflicting Self-Interests

Why, according to conflict theorists, do different groups in society have conflicting self-interests? The reason is that every society experiences competition over **scarce resources**. A scarce resource is anything that does not exist in sufficient amounts for everyone to have all that he or she wants.

The most important scarce resources in society, those which produce the greatest competition, are money (and the things it can buy) and power. Whenever a resource is scarce, one person's gain is potentially another's loss. If you have more money or power, the result may very well be that I have less, because there is only so much to go around. It is this feature that produces conflict: Groups struggle with one another to increase their share of money and power, often by reducing the money and power of others. In this struggle, the interests of those who have a good deal of money and power conflict with the interests of those who do not. The self-interest of those who have money and power is to keep things as they are so that they can continue to enjoy an advantaged position. This group will attempt to preserve the **status quo**—the existing set of arrangements. The self-interest of those who lack money and power is just the opposite. They want to create *change* so that they can get a bigger share of wealth and power.

This point of view differs significantly from the functionalist perspective. Whereas the functionalist perspective sees the various elements of society as being interdependent, conflict theorists believe that the various human elements of society are in conflict with one another because one group's gain is potentially another group's loss.

Society: Functional for Whom?

As noted previously, the distribution of scarce resources such as money and power is usually unequal. Those who have money often have power, and vice versa. There are many debates among conflict theorists about the precise relationship between money and power, but there is one key point on which most conflict theorists agree: Those who have a great deal of money and power can use their power to hang on to their advantaged position. In other words, they have the power to shape society to their own advantage. The result of this is that a society tends to take on characteristics that work to the further advantage of the dominant groups within that society.

Here, too, there is an important parallel to functionalist theory. As we saw, functionalists argue that societies assume the characteristics they do because those characteristics are functional—useful to the society. Conflict theorists agree up to a point—but they ask the question, functional *for whom?* In other words, they believe that social arrangements exist because they are useful—but *not* to the whole society. Rather, they are useful to the dominant group in society—whatever advantaged group has the power to shape society according to its own interests. This power can be exercised in a variety of ways. The wealthy are frequently in positions to influence public opinion. Dominant groups in many societies try (often successfully) to gain control of the media, which is why freedom of the press is repressed in much of the world. Even where it is not, those with money have a better chance than others of being able to communicate through the media. The wealthy may be overrepresented in governments or may even control them directly. Other key institutions such as education and religion are often disproportionately influenced by dominant groups, or if not, they may be unwilling to challenge such groups. Finally, there is always the possibility of a dominant group using force to shape a society to its own interests.

Conflicting Values and Ideologies

Because different groups in society have conflicting self-interests, it is virtually certain, according to conflict theory, that they will have different views about social issues. In short, their values and ideologies—systems of beliefs about reality—will be based in large part on what serves their self-interests. Those who are advantaged use their power to influence the opinions of others, so that, for a time, people tend to believe in values and ideologies that support the existing order (Mannheim, 1936 [orig. 1929]; Marx, 1964). When the advantaged groups succeed, as they often do, those without power accept the beliefs promoted by the wealthy and powerful. (This condition, which Marx called false consciousness, will be explored further in Chapter 4.) Sooner or later, however, the less-advantaged groups in society come to see that their interests conflict with those of the wealthy and powerful. When this happens, they develop their own values and beliefs, which naturally conflict with those advocated by the dominant group. Thus, the inherent tendency of society is toward conflict, not consensus. Conflict comes from within society because different groups have conflicting self-interests and thus try to shape society and its values in different and conflicting ways.

Conflict Versus Violence. It is very important to stress here that *conflict does not mean the same*

SOCIOLOGICAL INSIGHTS
Conflict Theory: Some Key Thinkers

Karl Marx (1818–1883)

Karl Marx has probably had more influence over conflict theory than any other sociologist. Marx's theories concerning ownership of the means of production and concerning the bourgeoisie and the proletariat were discussed in Chapter 1. He argued that in industrial societies, the bourgeoisie uses its power to ensure that all elements of the social structure and ideology support its continued ownership of the means of production. The proletariat, in contrast, has an interest in change.

Much of Marx's social thinking can be found in *Das Kapital* (*Capital*) (1967), originally published in three volumes between 1867 and 1894.

Ralf Dahrendorf (1929–2009)

The German sociologist Ralf Dahrendorf is credited with making important modifications in conflict theory to make it more applicable to twentieth-century industrial societies. One way his theories differ from those of Marx is that he gives power a more central role than Marx did. Marx saw power as purely an outgrowth of owning the means of production, whereas Dahrendorf has identified other bases of power, including legal authority. Thus, conflicts of interest exist between those who have power and those who lack it, just as they exist between those who own wealth and those who do not. Like Marx, Dahrendorf does not believe that people are always aware of what their self-interests are. When a group of people share a common social position (such as being employed in similar types of work around the country by the same employer), they have common self-interests. When they are unaware of these self-interests, they have what Dahrendorf (1959) calls *latent interests*. At some point, however, they may become aware of their common self-interests and try to advance them. At this stage, they have developed and articulated *manifest interests*. Thus, while conflicting interests are always present in society, actual conflict only breaks out when manifest interests are articulated.

W. E. B. Du Bois (1868–1963)

The first African American with a Ph.D. degree from Harvard and cofounder of the NAACP, Du Bois has only recently received the recognition he deserves as a leading sociological theorist and researcher on race and ethnic relations in the United States. In *The Souls of Black Folk* (1903), he examined how African Americans were forced into the position of having others define their identity. Some, he observed, bought into this and sought assimilation into the larger, white society, while others withdrew and chose separatism.

---

thing as violence. Certainly conflict can be violent, as in the case of riots and revolutions. However, nonviolent conflict is more common. Conflict occurs in legislatures, as opposing interest groups seek to pass laws and policies from which they can benefit. It occurs in the courts, as different groups pursue legal strategies to get the law interpreted in their interests. Collective bargaining and civil rights panels are other mechanisms for dealing with conflict. All of these processes reflect the **institutionalization** of conflict. They reflect that society has recognized that conflict will occur and has developed ways of dealing with it. You can argue, as many conflict theorists do, that dominant groups develop institutions for dealing with conflict that favor their own interests. Even so, conflict does often occur in peaceful, institutional settings. It also sometimes occurs peacefully outside such institutional settings, as in the case of mass demonstrations and nonviolent civil disobedience. In general, when institutional means of resolving conflict exist, *and* when disadvantaged groups perceive that such institutional settings offer a fair opportunity for resolving conflict, these groups will use them. If such means do not exist, however, or if disadvantaged groups believe that these means favor the advantaged groups, conflict will occur outside institutional settings (Coser, 1956). In this situation, violence becomes more likely.

Du Bois saw that blacks had a dual identity—of being black and of being American—and claimed that true self-consciousness lay in accepting and celebrating both parts.

Another of his books, *The Philadelphia Negro* (1973 [orig. 1899]) is a classic study of early experiences of African Americans in an urban environment. In one of the earliest large-scale personal interview studies, he surveyed over 2,500 households—the entire black population of Philadelphia's seventh ward—concerning families, individuals, homes, street activity, and community institutions. Du Bois felt that racial inequality could be changed only by challenging the power structure, and he engaged in a lifelong debate with others, such as Booker T. Washington, who felt that blacks could best gain success by fitting in with the expectations of the larger white society. In addition to cofounding the NAACP, he served for many years as the first editor of its magazine *The Crisis*.

C. Wright Mills (1916–1962)

Another influential conflict theorist in American sociology was C. Wright Mills. Like Dahrendorf, Mills sought to apply conflict theory to modern industrial capitalism. He felt that one consequence of the massive scale of corporations and governments in modern society is to make the elite less visible and more removed from the people. He felt that the large scale of modern society makes those with great power largely invisible to the masses. This enhances their power even more and leads to feelings of cynicism, powerlessness, and apathy among the masses.

Mills (1956) believed that in the United States major political decisions are made by a power elite consisting of top corporate executives, high military commanders, and those in the executive branch of the federal government. This may offer a good explanation of later events such as the Vietnam War, Watergate, and the Iran-Contra scandal.

Mills also spoke and wrote often of the *sociological imagination*, and he published a book with that title in 1959. By this term, Mills meant that we should seek to distinguish personal troubles—problems affecting particular individuals as a result of something they did or didn't do—from social problems—conditions affecting many people, which, although people may think of them in personal terms, are in reality a product of larger societal processes or conditions.

The Roles of Conflict. Conflict theorists see conflict not only as natural and normal, but also as useful to society. Conflict, they argue, brings social change, which makes two things possible. First, it offers disadvantaged groups an opportunity to improve their position in society through a more equitable distribution of scarce resources. Second, it offers society an opportunity to function better, because conflict creates the possibility of eliminating social arrangements that are harmful to the society as a whole but that serve the interests of the dominant group.

Consider environmental pollution as an example of this principle. At one time in the United States and other countries, there was very little regulation of industrial activities that pollute the air or water or that indiscriminately dump hazardous wastes. Because it was cheaper to discharge hazardous materials into the environment than to dispose of them properly, many industries did so. These industries opposed any attempt to stop them from polluting and dumping by appealing to popular distrust of government, and by invoking the evils of government regulation. However, heightened public awareness of the risks to health, quality of life, and long-term survival led to strong environmental movements in the 1960s and early 1970s, and again in the late 1980s and the 1990s. In both time periods, conflicts arose between environmentalists and industrial polluters. These conflicts led to passage of environmental regulations, such as the banning of new cars using leaded gasoline in the 1970s, and the 1990 Clean Air Act. They also led to heightened public consciousness of environmental issues that forced even the industrial polluters to profess concern for the environment by the late 1980s—in contrast to Earth Day 1970, Earth Day 1990 received millions of dollars in corporate support. The new regulations and the heightened public awareness led in turn to considerable reductions in some kinds of pollution. Lead pollution, for example, decreased sharply in both the air and water as the use of leaded gasoline declined during the 1980s (Alexander and Smith,

1988; Smith, Alexander, and Wolman, 1987; U.S. Environmental Protection Agency, 1990). Similarly, the 1990 Clean Air Act was passed with the express purpose of reducing emission of pollutants that deplete the ozone layer and that cause acid rain. It, too, appears to have been successful, as rates of emission of sulfur dioxide and nitrous oxide declined sharply between 1990 and 1999 (Environmental Protection Agency, 2000).

Of course, the decreases in air and water pollution mentioned above do not mean that the environmental problems have been solved. As gains are made in some areas, we continue to discover new ways in which human activity is threatening the environment. A growing current threat is the risk of global warming resulting from both air pollution and the massive cutting of rain forests. A related problem is the extinction of growing numbers of life forms because of habitat destruction resulting from logging, farming, and urbanization. And all of these activities are driven by economic interests that rely upon or benefit from them. Consequently, conflict over environmental issues continues.

Conflict and Social Change. The environment is a good example of how conflict can result in social change. Functionalist and conflict theorists disagree, however, about the role played in social change by conflicts within society. Functionalists see social change as coming largely from outside society. They see it as a response to some new technology, some change in the environment, or some interaction with another society. Conflict theorists, however, see change as coming from within society. Different groups have opposing interests and thus engage in conflict; that conflict produces change. Therefore, to conflict theorists, it was not simply the presence of air pollution that brought about regulations to control it. Rather, change arose from people's reaction to the fact that they were threatened by pollution. They developed a social movement, engaged in conflict with those who had an economic self-interest in continuing to pollute, and helped bring about a new policy and a cleaner environment.

Macrosociological Perspectives: Is Synthesis Possible?

The differences between the functionalist and conflict schools are summarized in Table 3.1. These differences have led sociologists to ask an important question: Are the two theories incompatible, or are societies sufficiently complex so that both theories could be right at the same time?

This question has not been answered to the satisfaction of all sociologists, and debate continues concerning the compatibility or incompatibility of the two perspectives. However, we believe—and we think most sociologists believe—that although they disagree on key points, the functionalist and conflict perspectives are not totally incompatible. In the first place, certain social arrangements might be useful to society in some ways and useful to the dominant group in others. Society might also

Table 3.1 Compare and Contrast: Basic Assumptions of the Functionalist and Conflict Perspectives

	The Functionalist Perspective	*The Conflict Perspective*
Reasons for Social Arrangements	Social arrangements are useful to the society.	Social arrangements are useful to those who hold wealth and power.
Consensus and Conflict	Society tends toward consensus.	Society tends toward conflict.
Dominant Values	Shared values support cooperation.	Dominant group imposes or promotes values that justify inequality.
Equilibrium and Change	Society tends toward balance and equilibrium; change occurs gradually to adapt to changing needs or environment.	Society is an engine of change; conflict of interests within society produces constant and sometimes dramatic change.

contain forces for both consensus and conflict; under different conditions, one or the other can predominate. Let us examine each of these ideas a bit further.

Functional for Whom? Another Look

Can social arrangements be useful for the dominant group at the expense of others (as conflict theory argues), yet in other ways be useful for the society as a whole (as functionalist theory argues)? *Can both of these things be true at the same time?* Consider one of the questions that was posed at the beginning of this chapter: Why was pro basketball player Mahmoud Abdul-Rauf denied the opportunity to play when he stood aside or retreated to the locker room during the playing of the national anthem? How might a conflict theorist or a functionalist answer this question? From the standpoint of conflict theory, it could be seen as a way in which an advantaged group in society asserts its superiority and control over other groups. Abdul-Rauf is a member of a minority religion in the United States (Muslim) and a minority racial group (African American). Both groups have experienced considerable discrimination in the United States, yet they are called upon to salute a symbol representing the very society that has systematically discriminated against them. A conflict theorist might argue that if they do so, they are, in effect, honoring the society that discriminates against them. Moreover, if the dominant group in the society did not insist that they stand during the national anthem, such rebelliousness might spread. Before long, people who are discriminated against might refuse to participate in all kinds of social rituals until they get a fairer share of society's resources.

A functionalist would see it differently. From the standpoint of functionalism, a society must share a common identity in order for cooperation to occur. The flag and the national anthem are symbols of that common identity, and thus must be held sacred. At the point at which such symbols are no longer commonly accepted, the consensus necessary for cooperation breaks down, and disorder and confusion reign. Just a week after the Abdul-Rauf incident, for example, veterans and artists brawled in Arizona over an art exhibit in which the flag was placed on the floor and in a toilet. When respect for a symbol of common identity—such as a nation's flag—breaks down, functionalists argue, a society may be taking the first steps down the road toward the kind of chaos that has erupted in places like Bosnia.

Which side do you think is right in this debate? Or could it be that each side is partially correct? To a group of people that has experienced repeated discrimination, a symbol sacred to the people that are discriminating against them *could* be seen as oppressive. And to the group that is in power, the refusal of others to salute that symbol *could* be seen as threatening. Thus, there is considerable merit in the conflict theory's position that a dispute over the national anthem represents a power struggle between advantaged and disadvantaged groups. At the same time, the functionalists also have a valid point. Cases such as Bosnia make evident the dangers of a total loss of national consensus. Thus, any society has a stake in maintaining the common allegiance and support of its citizens. At the start of this chapter, we posed a question: Why was Abdul-Rauf denied the opportunity to play basketball until he stood during the national anthem? You may be better able to answer that question if you consider ideas from *both* the functionalist and conflict perspectives than if you consider only one of the perspectives.

Simultaneous Forces for Cooperation and Conflict

There is another reason why both the functionalist and conflict perspectives contribute to an understanding of society. Each of them may well be partially right in its views about whether society tends toward stability and cooperation (the functionalist perspective) or toward tension and conflict (the conflict perspective). There clearly are forces in society that lead people to cooperate: Almost any task in a large-scale modern society would be impossible without cooperation. We have already used the example of your introductory sociology course to illustrate this. At the same time, in any society where there is inequality, there will be a potential for conflict. From this point of view, there are always forces at work in society for both cooperation and conflict (Etzioni, 1996). Which one dominates depends on the circumstances of the time.

In the 1950s, for example, the U.S. economy was undergoing unprecedented growth, and optimism ruled. In such an environment, it is not surprising that a functionalist viewpoint emphasizing stability, cooperation, and growth would dominate—and it did. But the seeds of conflict were there, too: Already at the beginning of the decade, the stirrings of unrest caused by the racial discrimination and segregation in the U.S. South were evident. By the 1960s, the Civil Rights movement had revealed America's racial injustice for all to see, as police forces in the South beat and fire-hosed small children who asked only to be allowed to attend the same school as children of other races. Later in that decade, the country became embroiled in a deadly and seemingly unwinnable war in Vietnam that few understood. In that context, the forces of conflict dominated, and riots and protests swept the country. Yet, even in this context, the forces of cooperation and stability were present: The nation held together in spite of the troubles.

To a large extent, sociology itself reflects these shifting trends. The functionalist perspective enjoyed almost unchallenged dominance in American sociology in the 1950s and early 1960s, but by the end of the 1960s, a new generation of sociologists rediscovered the conflict perspective with great enthusiasm. Since that time, both American society and sociology have been more balanced. Although societal tensions and turmoil ebbed in the 1980s and surged again in the 1990s,

SOCIOLOGICAL INSIGHTS
Eclectic Macrosociology: Some Key Thinkers

Max Weber (1864–1920)

No sociologist has had a greater influence on the field than the social theorist Max Weber [pronounced "Vaber"]. Weber's thinking drew on a variety of ideas, some associated with conflict theory, some with what we now call the functionalist perspective, and some with neither. Thus, he cannot be clearly linked to any particular perspective.

Like other sociologists of his time, Weber was greatly interested in the process of modernization associated with urbanization and the Industrial Revolution. A key element of modernization, according to Weber (1962), is rationalization—a process whereby decisions are made on the basis of what is effective in helping people attain their goals rather than on the basis of tradition. This notion is similar to functionalist theory in the sense that it focuses on what works. Weber was aware of conflicts and competing interests in society, however, and rationalization included the notion of what is effective for one group in its competition or conflict with another, a concept that borrows heavily from the conflict perspective.

Gerhard Lenski (1924–)

The American sociologist Gerhard Lenski (1966) has drawn upon the functionalist and conflict theories to explain social inequality. He agrees with the functionalists—but only up to a point—that inequality creates incentives and rewards people in accordance with their skills. He also argues, however, that much inequality exists beyond what can be accounted for on this basis, and that the power arising from wealth allows the advantaged to hang on to their wealth long after their advantages serve any use to society. Lenski also notes that the degree of inequality in any society is linked to its system of production. As societies advance from the hunting-and-gathering stage to agriculture (and, usually, some form of feudalism), the degree of social inequality increases dramatically. Once society industrializes, however, this trend is reversed. Although modern industrial societies have considerable inequality, they have less than preindustrial societies. The reasons for this include the complexity of the division of labor and the presence of a large skilled and educated segment that pushes society in the direction of democratization.

Lewis Coser (1913–2003)

The American sociologist Lewis Coser has been interested in group dynamics, although he defines a group as everything from a small gathering to an entire social system. Much of his work has focused on ways that conflict—both within groups and between those two decades resembled neither the "silent generation" of the 1950s nor the rebelliousness of the 1960s. And sociology has largely reflected that: It has been marked by considerable debate between sociologists of the functionalist and conflict perspectives. At times that debate has been heated and intense, as in a bitter fight in the American Sociological Association in 1999 over who would edit the *American Sociological Review* and what theoretical and methodological directions that journal would take. Nonetheless, recent decades have also been marked by a greater willingness of sociologists to incorporate insights from both theoretical viewpoints.

This willingness is not entirely new in sociology. In fact, the early roots of this synthesis lie in the work of Max Weber, who clearly drew upon ideas from both schools of thought. In fact, Weber is not easily classified with either perspective. It is also reflected in the work of two men, the modern theorists Gerhard Lenski and Lewis Coser, and of many women in the field of sociology today, including Mary Jo Deegan. The views of these sociologists are discussed in the box "Eclectic Macrosociology: Some Key Thinkers."

Macrosociological Perspectives: A Final Note

As we finish our discussion of macrosociological perspectives, we have seen important areas of consistency and overlap between functionalist and conflict thinking. We have seen, too, that social arrangements can be useful to society in some ways, but—at the same time—useful to special interests and perhaps even dysfunctional to society in other ways. Forces for conflict and forces for cooperation are both present in society, and each may dominate under different conditions. Moreover, as Coser notes, even conflict can in some ways be useful for the larger society. Finally, society is in part shaped by relationships of exchange that involve elements of both cooperation and domination. All of these things suggest that the most useful macrosociology may be one that incorporates ideas from both theoretical perspectives.

Even so, the debate goes on between functionalist and conflict sociologists. This is not just a debate about theories; it is also a debate about values. Functionalism, because it notes society's tendencies toward stability and balance, appeals

---

groups—can improve the functioning of those groups (Coser, 1956). Thus, it could be said that Coser has conducted a functional analysis of conflict. He argues that conflict within groups can benefit the group as long as it does not challenge the group's purpose for existence. He sees the normal state as a combination of consensus on core values and conflict over specifics. Conflict offers groups ways to adapt to changing needs and can also increase long-run group cohesion by offering a way to address dissatisfactions. Conflict in general is more likely to produce breakdown in small, close-knit groups, and adaptation in large, diverse ones. Conflict over many unrelated issues is also less disruptive than sustained conflict over one issue. Conflict between groups (external conflict) can perform the functions of defining group boundaries and promoting cohesion within groups.

Mary Jo Deegan (1948–)

A prolific author who has devoted much of her career to examining how women have influenced the field of sociology, Mary Jo Deegan argues that female sociologists do not fit neatly into the largely male-created paradigms such as the functionalist and conflict perspectives. She sees such paradigms as presenting a false duality, and she calls for a "multilectic" model that "assumes that ideas, practices, and groups are sometimes complementary and supportive of one another, sometimes in conflict, and sometimes isolated or indifferent to one another" (Deegan, 1991, p. 24). In this statement, she epitomizes the emerging notion of eclectic macrosociology, drawing upon both the functionalist and conflict perspectives but at the same time pointing out that some things can be explained by neither.

Her historical research shows that often ideas and methods are developed by others than those who commonly receive credit for them, and that the contributions of women and minorities in sociology have been undervalued. For example, mapping urban population characteristics to understand urban social problems is often associated with the University of Chicago's sociology department, founded in 1893. Deegan shows, however, that Jane Addams and her colleagues at Hull-House did it first, publishing their results in *Hull-House Maps and Papers* in the same year the Chicago sociology department was founded.

to conservatives and cautious liberals. It stresses the advantages of the status quo, which appeals to those who oppose major change. Its emphasis on conformity has a similar appeal, warning of the dangers of a divided society and opposing suggestions to do things in any radically different way.

Similarly, conflict theory appeals to radicals and strong liberals who favor fundamental changes in social institutions. It stresses society's inequalities, which liberals and radicals see as society's unfairnesses. It is favorable to new ideas and to social change, which appeals to those who think society needs to change.

Although political views may well influence sociologists' preferences for one perspective or the other, it is important to distinguish such views, which represent *values,* from what the two perspectives say about social reality, which is a matter of *theory.* One can never prove that a conservative, moderate, liberal, or radical political view is "right" or "wrong," because that is a matter of values. However, sociology has gone a long way toward understanding the forces that shape society, and the evidence here suggests that both the functionalist and the conflict perspectives have important insights to offer in this regard. Thus, it would be very inaccurate to say that these perspectives are "just a matter of opinion."

Microsociology: The Symbolic-Interactionist Perspective

Almost from the time sociology emerged as an academic discipline, some people within the field felt that, to understand even large-scale patterns of human behavior, it was not enough to study only the characteristics of society. Rather, these social theorists argued that you must study the *processes by which human interaction occurs.* These processes of interaction involve social psychology or microsociology in that they often include interactions *between individuals and the larger society.* Societies do present situations, send messages, and give rules to individuals, but it is on the individual level that these situations, messages, and rules are interpreted. Moreover, how these situations, messages, and rules are interpreted is a key factor in determining how people behave. These realizations have given rise to the third major perspective in sociology, the **symbolic-interactionist perspective**. Because of its concern with the interaction between the individual and the larger society, it is also sometimes called the microinteractionist perspective (Collins, 1985c), or simply the interactionist perspective.

The Interactionist Perspective Defined

If the interactionist perspective could be summarized in one general statement, then that statement might begin with the notion that the *interpretation* of reality can often be an important factor in *determining* the ultimate reality. As previously noted, society continually presents individuals with situations, messages, and rules. Taken together, these elements, and the *meaning* given to them by the individual, define the individual's experience of social reality. Sometimes the meaning of these situations, messages, and rules is clear, and to the extent that this is the case, the individual's social reality is obvious to him or her. Usually, however, the meaning of the situations, messages, and rules is not completely clear to the individual, and the individual must *interpret* them as best he or she can (Blumer, 1969a). This interpretation occurs, of course, in the context of past messages the individual has received from society. Nonetheless, it is interpretation, and individuals with different sets of past experiences frequently interpret the same message or situation differently. Hence, the individual's understanding of social reality depends in part on the content of the messages and situations he or she encounters and in part on how he or she interprets those messages and situations. How the individual understands reality, of course, will have an important effect on how he or she will behave, which can further alter the situation. For these reasons, the interactionist perspective focuses *first* on how messages are sent and received and on how social situations are encountered by individuals, *then* on how people interpret the meanings of these messages and situations, and *finally* on how these processes shape human behavior and society. A study by sociologist Jack Katz illustrates this in an unusual way, as shown in the box "Doing (and Being Done by) the Funhouse Mirrors" on page 66.

Interpreting Situations and Messages

As noted above, one key concern of the interactionist perspective is how people interpret the messages they receive and the situations they encounter. Interactionists believe these issues are important because people's interpretations of reality are an important factor in determining how they will behave. Consider an example. You are waiting at the bus stop, and the person next to you says, "Hello. Isn't this a nice day?" Your behavior in response to this message will depend on your interpretation of the message, which in turn will be a product of past messages and experiences. If, for example, your experience has been that people at the bus stop like to chat to pass the time while waiting for the bus, you will probably respond in a friendly way and carry on a conversation with the person until the bus arrives. If, however, your experience has been different, you will probably respond differently. Suppose your experience has been that people at the bus stop usually don't talk to one another, but keep to themselves. On the few occasions when people did try to strike up a conversation with you, it turned out they were trying to sell you something, begging for money, or seeking to convert you to their religious beliefs. In this case, you would interpret the situation differently, assume the person wanted something from you, and likely try to avoid further interaction.

The Social Construction of Reality

What is significant about the above example is that *the real intentions of the person speaking to you were not important.* Even the person's behavior does not give us the entire explanation of why you experienced the reality of the situation as you did. Rather, it was your understanding of the meaning of the person's behavior, including your interpretation of his or her intentions, that determined the reality that you experienced (Charon, 1989). Sociologists refer to this process as the **social construction of reality** (Berger and Luckmann, 1966). By this, they mean that the reality that you experience is not simply determined by what goes on in an objective sense; rather, it is determined by your understanding of the meaning of what happens. Thus, depending on that understanding, the reality you experienced could have been either "This person is friendly" or "This person is trying to hit me up for something."

There are two additional important points concerning this process. First, the meaning you attribute to the person's behavior is largely a product of your past experiences in similar social situations. Thus, there is a clear social influence on your interpretation of situations you encounter. Second, how you interpret the meaning of the situation you encounter will influence how you respond to it. This principle was recognized as early as the 1920s by W. I. Thomas, in a statement today known as the **Thomas theorem:** "If men [sic] define situations as real, they are real in their consequences" (Thomas, 1966). In other words, whatever the objective reality, people behave on the basis of their *understanding* of reality, and that behavior in turn shapes subsequent realities, including objective realities of human behavior. As Collins (1985a, p. 199) put it, "If the definition of reality can be shifted, the behavior it elicits will switch, sometimes drastically."

Ethnomethodology

Symbolic-interactionist theory, then, argues that your interpretations of reality are in part socially determined, and that these interpretations in turn partly determine how you will behave. To put this a bit more broadly, human behavior is in part a product of the structure of society and in part a product of how individuals interpret that social structure. Attempting to understand the forces that influence how individuals interpret the situations and messages they encounter has developed into a major subfield within the interactionist perspective known as **ethnomethodology.** It was given this name by Harold Garfinkel, who has written extensively about it (see Garfinkel, 1967; Lauer and Handel, 1983). It is strongly influenced by a theory in philosophy known as phenomenology, generally associated with Edmund Husserl (1965; 1969).

Ethnomethodology takes the basic idea of symbolic-interactionism a step further. Symbolic-interactionism holds that what people understand about the meaning of a social situation largely determines how they behave, and that in turn alters the situation. Ethnomethodologists go further and argue that the only social reality that exists is what people create in a given situation (Antonio, 1975;

SOCIOLOGICAL INSIGHTS

Doing (and Being Done by) the Funhouse Mirrors

When people laugh, it is because something is funny, right? Possibly so, but a study by sociologist Jack Katz (1996) shows that finding something funny is a *social* process. Some "get it" and some don't, and "getting it" is a social process. Katz illustrated this by setting up a hidden camera near the "funny mirrors" in a funhouse at a Paris amusement park. The videotape clearly revealed that, while some laugh uproariously at the mirrors, others don't laugh at all. Some "experiment" with the mirrors by looking at their images from different heights and angles; some use them in more demonstrative ways (for example, kissing in front of them); and some just walk by. One key difference is that people in the company of others frequently laughed, while people walking through alone almost never did. On the rare occasions when people by themselves did laugh, it was almost always an invitation to someone nearby to join them to see whether they would share the view that the mirror was funny. By watching the tapes, Katz could observe that in order to laugh, people walking through together had to come to the shared conclusion, through interaction with one another, that the images in the mirrors were funny. For people to share a collective laugh, they had to "see what the other sees" and agree that it is funny. Moreover, when this happened, people sometimes "did" laughter and sometimes laughter "did" them. When people "did" laughter, they laughed to show someone else that they "got it." Sometimes, but not always, this was transformed into "being done by" laughter. When this happened, the laughter changed, "for example, in a shift from exhale laughter to inhale laughter or from an initial exclamatory bleat or chuckle to an ascending riff that takes off from a markedly higher octave" (Katz, 1996, p. 1198). This occurred when the person had truly come to share another's view of the mirrors as funny.

Dreitzel, 1970). To a large extent, ethnomethodology challenges the positivist view, dominant in the early twentieth century, that there is an objective reality that can be quantified and measured. In this regard, it is similar to *postmodernism,* an approach discussed in Chapter 11 that has gained influence in all of the social sciences since the late 1980s.

In contrast to positivists, ethnomethodologists hold that the only reality "out there" is what one can see, and different people looking at the same thing will "see" different things (Antonio, 1975). What they see depends on their previous perceptions and experiences, upon which they build a set of assumptions. They are largely unaware of these assumptions, but the assumptions determine how they see and define reality (Garfinkel, 1967). For example, men and women watching a video of marriage partners arguing will often offer very different descriptions of the video. Because men and women have had different life experiences, which have led them to different assumptions about the underlying patterns of relationships between men and women, they "see" the video differently. The viewer looks at the video as a documentation of underlying patterns, which are assumed or presupposed on the basis of the viewer's experiences.

Ethnomethodologists point out that even well-trained scientists are not immune to this. All of us—even scientists—will to some extent see things in ways that are influenced by our background and conditioning (Cicourel, 1974; Handel, 1993). Thus, our experiences and interpretations create our reality. And, because everyone's assumptions are subject to change as life experiences change, reality is constantly under construction and is constantly changing. Returning to the example of the video, because people's experiences have changed, their assumptions about marriage and about the roles of men and women have changed over time. In fact, this change has been quite dramatic in the years since World War II. Hence, men and women viewing the video today would "see" something quite different than men and women viewing it thirty or forty years ago.

Moreover, the changes were created by people as their experiences and their assumptions underwent constant change.

According to Garfinkel, the only way sociologists can understand the reality of a situation is by learning what assumptions about the situation are being made by the people involved. One way to do this is to upset the situation, so that the people involved give accounts that reveal the assumed rules under which they were operating. Garfinkel encouraged his students to conduct experiments aimed at doing this. For example, the experimenter might stop a person in a hallway and ask, "How do you feel?" The person might reply "very well." The experimenter would then upset the situation by asking "Why?" and relentlessly insisting upon being given more information, all the while observing the behavior of the person being questioned, whose assumptions about the situation have presumably been upset. Most often, people being interrogated in this way would display increasing anger. This showed not only that people made assumptions about how the experimenter would respond to their initial reply of "very well" but also that they viewed getting the expected response (for example, "I'm fine") as a right or expectation. One reason for this, according to Garfinkel, is that people understand that requests for more details could go on endlessly. In other words, more detail is always possible, but people protect their right to limit the amount of detail offered (Collins, 1988). Garfinkel contended that we all do this because the search for precise objective detail is endless—which is why we construct our reality based on assumptions.

In another experiment, Garfinkel had a person play the role of a therapist and recruited students to volunteer to try out a "new therapeutic technique." At Garfinkel's instructions, the "therapist" offered random "yes" and "no" responses when the students asked questions that could be answered in this manner. Nonetheless, the students had no trouble making sense out of what was in fact completely random advice. Every student was able to make thematic sense of the advice given by the "therapist," even when it was contradictory. And not one student doubted the authenticity of the "therapist." Hence, even when our expectations are upset, the assumptions we make (in this case, about the authority of the medical profession) allow us to construct a reality that makes sense to us.

Ethnomethodology has been applied to a variety of topics in sociology. It has been suggested, for example, that one factor influencing people's scores on intelligence tests is their interpretation of the meaning and importance of the test and what it will be used for (Ogbu, 1978).

The Looking-Glass Self

Another important concept that has long been used by symbolic-interactionists is the **looking-glass self.** This concept was developed by the early symbolic-interactionist theorist Charles Horton Cooley, who is discussed further in the box "Symbolic-Interactionist Theory: Some Key Thinkers" on page 69. The basic notion of the looking-glass self could be summed up as, we see ourselves as others see us. In other words, we come to develop a self-image on the basis of the messages we get from others, as we understand them. If your teachers and fellow students give you the message, in various ways, that you are "smart," you will come to think of yourself as an intelligent person. If others tell you that you are attractive, you will likely think of yourself as attractive. Conversely, if people repeatedly laugh at you and tease you about being clumsy, you will probably come to decide that you are clumsy. Over the years, you gradually develop a complex set of ideas about what kind of person you are, and to a large extent, these ideas are based on the messages you get from others (Matsueda, 1992). In Cooley's terms, you use other people as a mirror into which you look to see what you are like.

Of course, the message we get from others about ourselves is partly a product of the intended content of the message and partly a product of how we perceive the message. To Cooley, an important part of the looking-glass self was how we understand the messages we get from others. In Cooley's terms, we *imagine* what others think of us on the basis of our understanding of the messages we get from them. Thus, if we misunderstand the messages of others, we may form our self-image on the basis of a different message than what was intended. For this reason, processes of communication—the sending and receiving of messages about our personal characteristics—play a key role in the formation of self-image.

The kind of self-image this process produces, moreover, will influence many aspects of your life. Self-esteem, clearly part of this process, has been

The concept of the looking-glass self points out that we use messages from others like a mirror, to form an image of ourselves. (Courtesy of Michael Flota)

shown to be linked to success in business life and in personal life, and the lack of it has been linked to substance abuse, unemployment, suicide, and a host of other personal and social problems.

The Self-Fulfilling Prophecy

A concept closely related to the looking-glass self, but applicable to an even broader range of human behavior, is the **self-fulfilling prophecy**. The self-fulfilling prophecy is a situation in which people *expect* something to happen, and because they expect it to happen, they behave in such a way that they cause it to happen. Sociologists have discovered numerous examples of self-fulfilling prophecies. The best known concerns teacher expectations and student achievement (Brophy, 1983; Rosenthal and Jacobson, 1968). Generally speaking, students will outperform others of equal ability when teachers have higher expectations of them. (For a more detailed discussion, see Web-Based Chapter A.) Similarly, countries sometimes engage in military buildups because they expect to be attacked, which their potential enemies interpret as an aggressive move that requires a response. A cycle of this type between two polarized alliances in Europe was one of the causes of World War I (Farrar, 1978). Another example concerns the often poor relations between inner-city black and Hispanic youths and the police. The police view the youths as troublemakers who must be shown the "force of the law." The youths see the police as brutal and often racist, and they frequently respond with behavior to show them that "Nobody's going to push us around." In other words, both the police and the youth "act tough" toward each other because each expects trouble from the other. These responses virtually ensure conflict between the two groups (Kuykendall, 1970).

Social Roles

An important concept in symbolic-interactionist sociology is the notion of **social roles**: sets of expectations about how people are supposed to behave, which are attached to positions within the social system. Human interaction is defined by the relationships among various roles, such as student, teacher, parent, and school bus driver. Each day, everyone fills a variety of roles such as these, and each role carries a set of expectations about how people are supposed to behave in various situations. The exact content of these roles depends on the nature of the particular social system. Moreover, knowledge of how to behave in roles is learned through contact with others and through the messages we receive from others about (1) what expectations are attached to a particular role and (2) how well we are meeting the expectations associated with the roles we fill. The latter process, of course, is part of what Cooley meant by the looking-glass self.

A related concern of symbolic-interactionists has been determining how people learn the relationships among various roles in the social system, such as the relationship between teachers and students. As with learning the content of roles, this learning occurs largely through the messages people receive from others, as well as through observation. These learning processes have a large impact on how people behave: People usually try to behave in ways that fulfill the expectations of their roles as they understand them, and that interact in

SOCIOLOGICAL INSIGHTS

Symbolic-Interactionist Theory: Some Key Thinkers

Charles Horton Cooley (1864–1929)

Much of what later came to be known as the symbolic-interactionist perspective is based on the ideas of Charles Horton Cooley. Cooley is best known for his theories concerning self-image and the looking-glass self, which are discussed in this chapter. Cooley also proposed that the formation of self-image occurs mainly through communication with a fairly limited number of individuals, called significant others, with whom a person interacts on a regular basis. In childhood, parents, peers, teachers, relatives, neighbors, and religious leaders are most likely to be the significant others. In later life, co-workers, supervisors, spouses or lovers, and children are the most important significant others.

George Herbert Mead (1863–1931)

George Herbert Mead's thinking was similar in many ways to that of Cooley, but he added two important elements to Cooley's theories. First, he clarified the means by which the communication processes of interest to Cooley occurred. Mead (1934) pointed out that one of the features that distinguishes human beings from animals is their ability to use symbols. A symbol can be defined as anything that stands for or represents something else. This includes words, gestures, signs, and images. Most human communication uses symbols, and it is through symbols that the processes of interest to symbolic-interactionists occur. Symbols are used to communicate the expectations associated with roles, and, in response, they are used to present the image to others that an individual is attempting to fulfill the expectations of those roles. Finally, symbols are used by others to let the individual know how well or poorly he or she is doing in meeting those role expectations. Mead's other important addition to Cooley's thinking was the concept of the generalized other.

Herbert Blumer (1900–1987)

Herbert Blumer was one of Mead's many students in his famous social psychology course, which formed the basis of *Mind, Self, and Society* (Mead, 1934). Blumer went on to become the most influential symbolic-interactionist theorist of recent years, although he also made important contributions to macrosociological analysis, particularly in the area of race relations (for example, Blumer, 1965).

It was Blumer who first used the term *symbolic-interactionism*, in a 1937 article. According to Blumer (1969a), symbolic-interactionism is based on three key premises. The first is that human beings behave toward things on the basis of the meaning that those things have for them. The second is that the meanings of things for each individual are derived from social interaction with other people. This premise challenged two dominant views in the social sciences: the belief that the meaning of things is a matter of objective reality and the conviction that the meaning of things a person observes is a product of the person's psychological makeup. Blumer's third key premise is that meanings are shaped through an interpretive process used by the individual in dealing with the things he or she encounters. Thus, the actions of others are interpreted, and this interpretation is part of what defines meaning. Moreover, because of this process of interpretation, meanings of things can change as the interpretation changes.

---

the expected way with other roles. As discussed in the box entitled "Symbolic-Interactionist Theory," the contributions of George Herbert Mead have been particularly important in this area. Symbolic-interactionists have been particularly interested in the childhood socialization process, because the learning of social roles is such a critical part of that process.

Sending Messages: The Presentation of Self

The symbolic-interactionist perspective is not just concerned with how people receive and interpret social messages. It is also concerned with the messages that people send to others. We send messages both by the roles we choose to emphasize in our

Small groups, such as students working on a project, can be good places to view the processes of presentation of self and impression management. (Courtesy of Michael Flota)

lives, and by the way that we play those roles. Politicians running for office, for example, will often put out brochures or television ads showing them with their families in order to present an image of themselves as "family people" rather than "politicians." Why do they do this? Because the role of "family person" is viewed more favorably in our society than the role of "politician." Thus, politicians often seek to present themselves as supporting "family values," while portraying their opponents as "playing politics." Research has confirmed that one way people manage the self-image they project is by choosing what roles to emphasize in their lives (Backman and Secord, 1968; Kemper and Collins, 1990). People also manage their self-image by presenting to other people the image they feel is appropriate to the particular role that they are in at any given time.

The early Chicago School sociologist Robert Park (1927) put it this way: "One thing that distinguishes man from the lower animals is the fact that he has a conception of himself, and once he has defined his role, he tries to live up to it. He not only acts, but he dresses the part, assumes quite spontaneously all the manners and attitudes he conceives as proper to it." Sociologists refer to this process as the *presentation of self* or *impression management*.

The Dramaturgical Perspective

The analogy of human behavior to acting is made most explicitly by a particular interactionist theory known as the **dramaturgical perspective**. This theory, generally identified with Erving Goffman (1959, 1967, 1971), argues that in each role we fill, we try to convince people that we are filling it in a particular way, generally the way to which we think they will respond positively. Thus, the self-image a person attempts to project at work will be different, for example, from the impression he or she would likely try to project on a weekend "singles" ski excursion. In Goffman's terms, people give different performances on different occasions. These performances, however, are always shaped by what people think others expect and will respond to positively. Thus, it is only through messages from others that we develop our ideas of what is a proper image to project at work or on a ski trip.

Front-Stage and Back-Stage Behavior. An important distinction in the dramaturgical approach is that of "front-stage" and "back-stage" behavior (Goffman, 1959). "Front-stage" behavior—the performances aimed at impression management—takes place in settings where others can see us. However, there are also private settings in which we "let our guard down" and behave in ways that we would not want others to see. Goffman called this "backstage" behavior. Collins (1985c, p. 157) illustrated the distinction this way:

> [Front stage]: is the storefront where the salesperson hustles the customer, [back stage] the backroom where the employees divide up their sales territories, establish their sales line, and let their hair down after the manipulation they have gone through. In another sphere, there is an analogous distinction between the cleaned-up living room and a carefully laid table where the ritual of a dinner party is to reaffirm status membership with one's guests, and the backstage of bathroom, kitchen, and bedroom before and afterwards, where emotional as well as physical garbage is disposed of.

A fascinating aspect of the process of impression management is that we generally assist one another with our performances (Goffman, 1959).

Most of us are sufficiently insecure about our own performances that we do not make others aware of the flaws in theirs. Imagine, for example, that your professor or a classmate enters your classroom with his zipper open or her blouse unbuttoned. There may be a bit of snickering, but most people will try to spare the person involved embarrassment by pretending nothing is wrong. In fact, some people will experience discomfort or embarrassment over the situation, even though it is someone else whose performance is flawed. This embarrassment or discomfort will probably increase if anyone says anything about it in front of the class. Many people will think "That could just as easily be me." Therefore, people usually engage in what Goffman called "studied nonobservance": They go out of their way to ignore flaws in others' performances. To create or even acknowledge awareness of flaws in performances is to "create a scene": It leads to embarrassment, not only for the person whose performance is flawed, but for others as well.

The dramaturgical perspective has sometimes been criticized for attempting to reduce human behavior to a continuous process of impression management. To do this would clearly be an oversimplification, for two reasons. First, as macrosociology tells us, a person's position in the larger social structure clearly is an important force in shaping behavior. By position in the social structure, we are referring to the functions a person's roles must fill (as stressed by the functionalist perspective) and the resources attached to those roles (as stressed by the conflict perspective). Second, whatever self-image we try to project to others, we are likely to influence our own self-image in the attempt. In other words, if we "act" to impress others, we will often come to believe our own act. This will be particularly true if *others* respond positively to the act. In other words, the messages from others are once again affecting our own self-images.

Micro- and Macrosociology: Is Synthesis Possible?

Simultaneous Effects of Function, Conflict, and Interaction

Some key differences in the assumptions of macrosociology and microsociology are summarized in Table 3.2. As we saw earlier, there has been considerable effort among sociologists to combine the insights of the functionalist and conflict perspectives in order to understand social situations more fully. Is it similarly possible to combine the microsociological interactionist perspective with the two macrosociological perspectives? Increasingly, sociologists like George Homans and Randall Collins have been attempting to reconcile these differences by developing themes that combine insights of both approaches (see the box "Micro-Macro Links: Two Key Thinkers"). It is our view that most social situations can be more fully understood by using all three perspectives (or theories that combine them) rather than by using just one or two (see Emirbayer and Goodwin, 1994). We shall briefly outline the reasons why we think this is so, discuss some examples of theories combining the perspectives, and then give a concrete example of a common social situation that is best understood by using all three perspectives.

Although most sociologists operate primarily as either macrosociologists or microsociologists, We believe that there is one sense in which few would dispute the usefulness of both types of approach. To put it simply, the different approaches may be useful for understanding different aspects of the social situation. Any social arrangement may exist in part because it is useful to the society—as argued by the functionalist perspective. At the same time, it may also exist partly because it meets the needs of some particular interest group within the society—as argued by the conflict perspective. It may, in fact, even be harmful to other interest groups or, in some way, to the larger society. Despite these larger societal influences, though, the exact form of the social arrangement is likely to be shaped by the understandings of reality held by those participating in it. These understandings largely determine how people subsequently behave. Thus, as argued by the interactionist perspective, these understandings are very real in their consequences. Such understandings are partly a product of the objective reality of the larger social structure, but they are also partly a product of people's response to that reality (Handel, 1979, pp. 863–67).

Exchange Theory

One important theory that represents a linkage between macro- and microsociology is **exchange**

theory. (Blau, 1964; Homans, 1961, 1984; for examples of recent work in this tradition, see Mortensen, 1988; Molm, 1991; Uhara, 1990; Yamagishi, Gilmore, and Cook, 1988; Molm, Quist, and Wiseley, 1994; Lawler and Yoon, 1996; Molm, Peterson, and Takahashi, 1999). Exchange theory, like conflict theory, begins with the assumption that people seek to advance their self-interests. These interests sometimes conflict and sometimes coincide with those of other people. According to this theory, people enter into relationships with one another when each participant has something to offer that the other desires. Thus, each person has something to give and something to gain. Exchange theory has been applied to a wide range of relationships, from pure business relationships such as that between buyer and seller to intimate personal relationships such as that between husband and wife. In the latter case, for example, consider the personal needs of two individuals who get married. One partner may primarily have a need for companionship, whereas the other seeks status through the marriage relationship. According to Blau, people assess their needs and pick their partners accordingly, and, as long as these needs stay the same and each partner meets the other's need, the relationship is likely to remain stable. Of course, should either partner's needs change, or should one partner stop meeting the other's needs, the marriage could be in trouble.

Exchange relationships also can operate between groups and individuals. Consider the case of an individual joining a club. The club gains increased membership, dues money, and possibly someone new to work on its projects. The individual gains the personal interaction the club provides, as well as whatever activities and programs it offers members. However, if the relationship does not prove to be mutually beneficial, it will likely end.

Exchanges and Power

Ideally, social exchanges are equal. Each partner in the exchange gets a fair "return" for what he or she puts in. Many business and personal relationships in our society are governed by an expectation of reciprocity—the view that a fair exchange is one in which there is a more-or-less even trade. When this is the case, the commitment of each partner to the relationship increases (Lawler and Yoon, 1996). Similarly, studies of attractiveness show that, in the majority of cases, partners in love relationships rate fairly similarly to one another on attractiveness (Berscheid et al., 1971; Penrod, 1986, pp. 189–90; Walster and Walster, 1969). Thus, attractiveness operates as a resource for which partners in courtship make an "even" trade. Sometimes, however, people accept a lower level of attractiveness in their mate in order to get more of something else, such as money or prestige.

Exchange theorists also note that many exchange relationships are characterized by **unequal power**, in which one partner sometimes brings greater resources to the exchange than the other, as in the case of the relationship between employer and employee. When this happens, the more powerful partner usually expects and gets more (Molm, 1990). Those who lack resources—the poor, the sick, the unattractive—may have little choice but to enter relationships of unequal exchange. This concept also explains one reason why women have traditionally been more concerned about

Table 3.2 Compare and Contrast: Basic Assumptions of Macrosociology and Microsociology

	Macrosociology	Microsociology
What Drives Society and Human Behavior?	Needs and self-interests of groups and societies.	Socially generated perceptions about reality.
The Nature of Social Reality	A structure of institutions, social positions, and rewards.	An agreed-upon, negotiated understanding.
Interaction Between Society and Individual	Individuals are products of their society and social positions.	Individuals act upon society through their communications and understandings.
Key Research Interests	Social arrangements, culture, power, social inequality.	Communication, socialization, perception, self-presentation.

SOCIOLOGICAL INSIGHTS
Micro-Macro Links: Two Key Thinkers

George C. Homans (1910–1989)

The American sociologist George Homans (1961) has been one of the leading advocates in sociology of exchange theory, discussed in the text. He argues that in any human exchange, the objective is to maximize profit, which he defines broadly as reward minus cost. Because people bring unequal resources into such exchanges, they often expect and receive unequal profits.

Homans (1950) has also devoted a good deal of effort to studying group dynamics. He believes that human interaction within groups is shaped by an external system and an internal system. The external system refers to the interactions of the group with its larger environment, including other groups: an environment to which the group must adapt if it is to survive. The internal system refers to the interactions of individuals and coalitions within the group, which define group sentiment and lead to the development of a group culture. These processes involve elements of both cooperation and conflict.

Randall Collins (1941–)

Randall Collins has been one of the most prolific writers among sociological theorists over the past three decades. His early work centered around the conflict perspective, addressing a wide range of issues relating to that perspective. In *Conflict Sociology* (1974), he discusses ways in which the propositions arising from conflict theory (and other sociological theories as well) can be scientifically tested, and he assesses the contribution of the conflict perspective to the understanding of several areas of social life. He has applied the conflict perspective to religion (1974), marriage (1985b), gender inequality (1971a), and education (1971b).

More recently, however, Collins has sought to combine insights from the conflict perspective with those from microsociology. Like other sociologists in recent years, he stresses the idea that individual actions shape social structures.

His interaction ritual chain theory is one example of this thrust. This theory holds that interaction rituals, like those described by Goffman's dramaturgical perspective, are influenced by the level of resources each participant brings to the interaction. But at the same time, the process of the interaction may increase or decrease each participant's resources. Thus, both the level of resources (as conflict theory would emphasize) and the interaction ritual (as interactionist theory would emphasize) influence the outcome of the process of interaction. Collins (1986) also notes that all three sociological perspectives have common intellectual roots: All three of them were influenced by several philosophical viewpoints that were prominent in the early days of sociology.

---

appearance than men: In a sexist society, they have had fewer alternative resources like wealth and power to offer to a potential mate. Thus, although exchange theory resembles functionalism in the sense that each partner often benefits from the exchange, it resembles conflict theory in the sense that one partner can benefit much more than the other. Although it resembles the macrosociological theories in some regards, its focus is on the actions of individuals (Alexander, 1988, p. 87), which arise largely from their perceptions about what they have to gain or lose in a relationship.

Although exchange theory has been influential in both macrosociology and social psychology and acts as something of a bridge between the two, it has its critics. The strongest criticism is that it reduces all human interactions to calculated, rational exchanges. The critics argue that in reality people enter into social relationships for all kinds of reasons—some rational, some based heavily on emotion. A more balanced view, then, might be that people enter into relationships with one another partly for reasons of exchange and partly for other reasons.

We have seen, then, that there are some cases in which ideas arising from two or all three of the sociological perspectives are combined, as in exchange theory, and other cases in which different perspectives make competing claims. Through the cycle of theory and research discussed in Chapter

2, claims arising from each perspective are put to the test: Some are supported by research findings; others are not. Let us now consider an everyday example where the three perspectives combined can give us insights that go beyond those of any perspective by itself.

Using All Three Perspectives: An Example

Every Saturday morning from late spring through early fall, hundreds of thousands, perhaps even millions, of Americans participate in an event that takes place in big cities and small towns, in rural areas and suburbs, in all 50 states. We are referring to the yard sale or garage sale (also known in various areas as a "rummage sale" or "tag sale"). This is an ordinary event, not the stuff of which headline news or path-breaking sociological studies are made. Nonetheless, it is important to millions of Americans. Moreover, it is precisely for the ordinary, everyday event like the yard sale that sociology is useful for giving us special insights. Hence, we choose the yard sale, not only as an event about which sociology offers interesting insights, but also as one that illustrates the usefulness of each of the three perspectives for letting us see a part of the social reality that is occurring.

Consider how a yard sale might be analyzed from the functionalist perspective. A yard sale performs the important function of allowing things that would otherwise go to waste to be used and, for the seller, to be turned into a little extra cash. These are the functions of a yard sale that readily come to mind—in other words, its *manifest functions*. Consider, though, some *latent functions* of yard sales. For one, they offer people an enjoyable outing, an opportunity to get out of the house. In addition, they may perform the important social function of enabling people to see one another on a regular basis.

Yard sales also can be analyzed from a conflict perspective. In fact, Farley first became aware of this when he saw an article about yard sales in an "underground" newsletter published by a group of politically radical students on the campus where he teaches. The article touted yard sales as "striking a blow at capitalism through people's recycling." In a sense, it was right. Those who attend yard sales can be seen as an interest group; specifically, people with limited incomes who have a particular interest in getting things inexpensively rather than purchasing "flashy and new" merchandise. Surely this interest runs contrary to that of another set of interest groups: the manufacturers, advertisers, and retail stores, whose interests lie in persuading people to buy the "newest and best," even if something older and less flashy would work equally well. Thus, shopping at yard sales could be seen as being in the interest of those with limited incomes, and there is evidence suggesting that this is the case. In the 1970s and 1980s, as people's purchasing power failed to grow as it had in the past, the popularity of yard sales soared. Some evidence does indicate that the established business interests have come to see yard sales as a threat. In Farley's town, for example, several city council members have called for a crackdown on the posting of signs advertising yard sales, proclaiming them to be an unsightly nuisance. (Interestingly, no similar argument had been made by the city council a few months earlier when the town was flooded with political campaign signs!)

Finally, yard sales can be analyzed from a symbolic-interactionist perspective. They are often characterized by considerable bargaining between buyer and seller, and the

As long as both partners' needs are being met, it doesn't matter who takes care of the house and who goes to the office. However, if a point is reached where either partner's needs are not being met, the marriage could be in trouble. (Courtesy of Michael Flota)

course of this bargaining is certainly shaped by the perceptions the buyer and seller have of each other. If the seller is perceived as "wanting too much," the entire interaction can come to a quick end. Evidence of "wanting too much" can include not only prices that are too high, but also an unwillingness to bargain. As symbolic-interactionists point out, it is the person's perception of the meaning of the other's behavior that is critical. In other words, the reality that each of us experiences is socially constructed. It may be that the seller is having his or her first yard sale and doesn't know what prices to charge or that one is supposed to bargain. That doesn't really matter to the buyer, though, because it is the buyer's perception that determines his or her behavior. If the buyer misinterprets the seller's lack of experience as greed, the buyer experiences the seller as "wanting too much" rather than not knowing you're supposed to bargain. With this subjective understanding of reality, the buyer will likely end the interaction.

Of course, the seller's behavior is also influenced by the process of interaction. A novice seller may realize, after a few such interactions, that something is wrong. If the disgruntled buyers give the seller the right set of messages, the seller may learn from them that buyers expect the prices to be lower and to be subject to bargaining. Once the seller lowers his or her prices and begins to bargain, the entire interaction may be different. In short, the communication that occurs between buyer and seller, as well as how each interprets the other's messages, has a crucial impact on the outcomes of the yard sale. To put it in Blumer's terminology, behavior has been influenced by the meanings of the yard sale situation to the participants, which in turn is largely a product of their communication with one another.

We have seen, then, that each perspective—functionalist, conflict, and interactionist—has added something to our understanding of the yard sale. Each has helped us understand a somewhat different part of its reality. In this particular case, none of the three perspectives is in any sense "wrong," even though proponents of the three perspectives can and do debate their relative usefulness for understanding reality. Rather, as noted, each helps us understand a slightly different aspect of what is taking place. Most important, our understanding of the social meaning and significance of the yard sale is greater when we use all three perspectives than when we use any one, because each offers us part of the "big picture."

The Three Perspectives and This Book

We have provided an extensive introduction to the three sociological perspectives in this chapter because we believe that they give greater meaning to the more specific theory and research that will be discussed in the remainder of this book. The rest of the book will concern a number of major topics that make up the key subject matter of sociology. Each of these topics has a number of specific theories and lines of research pertaining to it. Many of these theories and lines of research, though specific to the topic of interest, arise in large part from one of the three perspectives introduced here. Some go further and attempt to combine insights from two or all three of the perspectives and to apply them to a particular topic. We believe that your understanding of sociology will be enhanced if you see how a theory about, for example, race relations, may relate to theories about aging, or drug use, or

A yard sale, like most social realities, can be analyzed from the functionalist, conflict, and interactionist perspectives. (Courtesy of John E. Farley)

formal organizations. The best way to do this is to try throughout the book to link specific theories to the larger sociological perspectives from which they arise. Thus, in virtually every chapter in this book, that linkage will be made. As you read this text, We hope you will see that at least one of the major perspectives, and often all three, can be used to gain important insights about every major topic discussed in the rest of this book.

Summary

In this chapter, we have examined the three theoretical perspectives that have had the greatest influence in sociology. Two of them, the functionalist and conflict perspectives, are macrosociological, focusing mainly on large-scale societal processes. The functionalist perspective holds that social arrangements exist because they meet needs in society, and it stresses interdependency, the functions of social structure and culture, consensus, cooperation, and equilibrium. The conflict perspective holds that society is made up of competing interest groups with unequal power and that social structure exists because it meets the needs of interest groups, usually those with power. It stresses conflicting interests, the relationship of culture and social structure to group interests, and the inevitability of conflict and change.

In part, these perspectives reflect competing values that cannot be judged scientifically. In larger part, though, they reflect different theories about human behavior and society, which are subject to scientific evaluation. Although the two macrosociological perspectives disagree on some key points, many sociologists believe that the two schools are not incompatible. Social structure, for example, may meet society's needs in some ways and the needs of dominant groups in other ways. Similarly, it is reasonable to argue that forces for both stability and change are always present in society, but that under different social conditions, different forces predominate.

The microsociological symbolic-interactionist perspective gives greater attention to processes involving individuals. It holds that people's understanding of reality is determined by the messages they get from others and by how they interpret these messages. This, in turn, is an important influence over how people behave. Among key concepts stressed by interactionists are social roles, the looking-glass self, the self-fulfilling prophecy, and the social construction of reality.

Attempts have been made to build links between microsociology and macrosociology. As illustrated by the example of the yard sale, each perspective—the functionalist, conflict, and interactionist—can add to our understanding of a social situation. In large part, this is true because each addresses a different piece of the reality of that situation.

Key Terms

perspective
macrosociology
microsociology
functionalist perspective
function
manifest function
latent function
dysfunction
conflict perspective
scarce resources
status quo
institutionalization
symbolic-interactionist perspective
social construction of reality
Thomas theorem
ethnomethodology
looking-glass self
self-fulfilling prophecy
social roles
dramaturgical perspective
exchange theory

Exercises

1. Consider the following questions:

   - What are the core assumptions of each major theoretical perspective: functionalist, conflict, and interactionist? What do you see as the major strengths and weaknesses of each perspective and why?
   - All of the early social theorists, such as Emile Durkheim, Karl Marx, and Max Weber, had

certain concerns in common. What are some of these common concerns and how do they relate to the perceived social problems during the time periods involved?

2. Go to one of the free major news sites on the Internet like Yahoo or Google. Find a current news story that interests you. Write a brief report on how the functionalist, conflict, and interactionist perspectives would explain the news story you chose. Are there some news stories that are better explained by one of the perspectives than by another?

Chapter 4
Culture and Social Structure

Society, Culture, and Social Structure   80
What Is Culture?   80
    Shared Truths: Knowledge, Language, and Beliefs   81
    Shared Values   84
    Ideology   84
    Social Norms   84
What Is Social Structure?   85
    Social Status   86
    Roles   87
    Division of Labor   88
    Stratification   89
    Relationships Between Roles and Statuses   89
    Institutions   90
Perspectives on Culture and Social Structure   90
    The Functionalist Perspective: Adaptation of Culture
       and Social Structure to the Environment   90
    Cultural and Structural Variation: Do Cultural
       or Structural Universals Exist?   92
    Universal Social Tasks   92
    The Conflict Perspective and Culture   95
Incompatibilities Between Culture and Social Structure   98
    Sewell's Duality of Structure Theory   98
    Culture Against Structure: The Functionalist Perspective   99
    Subcultures in Mass Society   100
    Culture Against Structure: The Conflict Perspective   103
PUTTING SOCIOLOGY TO WORK   106
    Multiculturalism: A Pathway to Cooperation in a Diverse Society?   106
American Culture   108
    Core American Values and Beliefs   108
    Ideal Versus Real Culture   108
    Recent Changes in American Values and Beliefs   108
Summary   116
Key Terms   116
Exercises   117

In the United States, women were once considered attractive only if they wore a corset—a rigid, tight-fitting garment that made the waist appear narrower and the bust larger. In ancient China, the definition of a beautiful woman included tiny, dainty feet; thus, from childhood Chinese women tightly bound their feet to keep them from growing. In the modern world, practices such as foot binding and the wearing of corsets have disappeared, but virtually every country still has standards of attractiveness for women.

Standards of attractiveness are one part of what sociologists call culture. They are a set of ideas that are shared within a society. As the above examples illustrate, culture is widely shared within a society, yet it also changes over time. If we think of standards of attractiveness only as a part of culture, however, we miss an important part of their significance. Standards of attractiveness also tell us something about the positions of men and women in society. The wearing of corsets and the practice of foot binding, for example, were both physically painful. Foot binding often led to serious physical deformity. It is highly significant that women in many societies have had to endure painful and sometimes harmful practices to make themselves attractive to men, while men in the same societies had to do no such thing to make themselves attractive to women. Thus, the wearing of corsets and the binding of feet reflect the subordinate social position of women in traditional American and Chinese societies. Such positions are a part of social structure, the system of social positions and rewards (or lack thereof) that are attached to these positions.

Just as culture changes, so does social structure. The elimination of corsets and foot binding suggests that the position of women has improved in both these societies. However, women continue to be judged more than men on the basis of physical attractiveness; for example, a number of women in America today make themselves physically and emotionally ill trying to become or stay thin. The change has been far from complete.

In this chapter, we shall explore culture and social structure in greater detail. To understand these concepts, we must first understand the concept of **society**. A society can be defined as a relatively self-contained and organized group of people interacting under some common political authority within a specific geographic area. Societies exist over an extended period of time, outliving the individual people of whom they are composed. A society can refer to a nation-state with millions of people, such as the United States, Russia, China, Nigeria, France, and Chile. It can also refer to tribal groups with a population of only a few hundred. If a group has some type of governmental system, if its members interact with one another while limiting contact with outsiders, if it exists within some reasonably well-defined territory and persists over time, that group fits the definition of a society.

Society, Culture, and Social Structure

Every society, large or small, has a culture and a social structure. **Culture** refers to the shared knowledge, beliefs, values, and rules about behavior that exist within a society. Social structure refers to the organization of society—its social positions and the ongoing relationships among these social positions; the different resources allocated to these social positions; and the social groups that make up the society (Smelser, 1988). Although culture and social structure are distinct, they are not separate. Each influences and is influenced by the other. This linkage is a major focus of this chapter.

What Is Culture?

Social scientists use the term "culture" in a somewhat different way than it is commonly used. In popular use, we often talk of people as being "cultured" or "uncultured." "Cultured" people are well read and knowledgeable, and enjoy literature, art, and classical music. In the social scientific sense, however, there are no "uncultured" people. Rather, the term refers to those things that are *shared* within a group or society: shared truths (that is, knowledge and beliefs), shared values, shared rules about behavior, and material objects that are shared in the sense that they are widely used or recognized. Sociologists generally recognize two kinds of culture: nonmaterial and material. **Nonmaterial culture** consists of abstract creations: knowledge, beliefs, values, and rules concerning behavior. **Material culture** consists of physical objects that are the product of a group or society: buildings, works of art, clothing, literary and musical works, and inventions. The two, of course, are linked: A society whose nonmaterial culture is based on scientific knowledge may, for example, produce a material culture including space shuttles and computers. In contrast, a society whose nonmaterial culture consists primarily of religious beliefs and traditions may produce elaborate temples and religious writings or music.

One final important point is that no society is without culture. For reasons explored in greater detail later in this chapter, every society requires some degree of common understanding of reality and common rules for behavior in order to function. Without this, people could not cooperate or even interact in a meaningful way, and nobody would know how to behave.

Shared Truths: Knowledge, Language, and Beliefs

The first item mentioned in our definition of nonmaterial culture is shared truths; that is, shared knowledge and beliefs. This item is mentioned first because knowledge and belief are at the core of the definition of culture. More than anything else, culture is a matter of what people in a society know or believe to be true (Goodenough, 1957). The concepts of *knowledge* and *beliefs* are very similar to each other in the sense that both refer to shared understanding of truth. Both concern what people believe to be true, and both are subject to testing, if the right information is available. However, in terms of understanding cultures, it does not really matter whether the knowledge and beliefs ever get tested, or even whether they are true in an objective sense. What matters is that people within a society *agree* on a certain reality, a certain set of knowledge and beliefs. If "everybody knows" that something is true, then it might as well be true, because people will behave as though it were.

When sociologists and anthropologists study cultures, they are interested in such social agreements about truth and reality. These social agreements are what shape people's behavior, and they are what determine how people understand their world. At one time in human history, "everybody knew" that the earth was flat. Hence, everyone behaved as though it were, and for many years nobody was so foolish as to attempt to travel around the earth. The first people who suggested that the earth might be round were treated the way you would be treated today if you said the earth was flat. Today, in modern industrial societies, "everybody knows" that the earth is round. Thus, shared knowledge and beliefs, and not reality, determine human behavior. Each society has its culture, and each culture is composed of a distinct set of knowledge and beliefs. Cultures can and do change over time, and what people "know" at one time will not necessarily be the same as what people in the same society will "know" at some other time.

Language

One particularly important area of knowledge carried by culture is **language**. Language can be defined as the set of symbols by which the people who share a common culture communicate. Language makes possible a type of communication among human beings that is unknown to animals, because of its use of **symbols**—in this case, words, which are used to represent concepts and ideas. Language also serves the function, through written records or oral traditions, of passing information from generation to generation. In this book, for example, use of the English language permits you to learn about the ideas of great social thinkers like Marx, Durkheim, and Weber, even though they have been dead for many years. Although language's main functions are to make communication possible and to preserve ideas across the generations, it also has important symbolic functions. Speaking the same language is an important symbol of cultural unity. For this reason, conquered or subordinate minority groups often cling vigorously to their language as a means of preserving their culture, and dominant groups try with equal vigor to get the minorities to speak their languages.

Language as a Cultural Symbol: An Example. An example of the cultural symbolism attached to language can be seen in Canada (Porter, 1972). Most of Canada's people belong to one of two major cultural groups, English and French. About two-thirds of the country's population is English-speaking; about one-third is French-speaking. The French-speaking group is concentrated almost entirely in one province, Quebec. In recognition of the desire of both groups to preserve their cultural heritage, Canada has proclaimed itself to be officially bilingual. Both English and French are official languages of Canada, and all activities of

Language both reflects and influences culture. In the past, this sign might have said "Flagman ahead"—but through the use of graphics, as on this sign, signs can be gender-neutral and understandable in any language. (©Joseph White/Dreamstime)

the national government are carried on in both languages. In spite of this, it is hard to describe Canada as a truly bilingual country. Although most Quebecois can speak English, the province has declared French to be its only official language. In the remainder of Canada, the overwhelming majority of the population speaks English, and nobody but the federal government makes any serious attempt to be bilingual. In fact, official attempts at bilingualism are usually treated with scorn. In the province of Ontario, for example, some stop signs have the French ARRET printed below the English STOP. More often than not, the ARRET is covered with spray paint.

The ethnic and linguistic conflict in Canada has been severe. Canada's ability to survive as a nation was threatened in the early 1990s when various provinces were unable to agree on a constitution. Negotiations to create a new constitution recognizing Quebec as a "distinct society" and giving it autonomy on matters of language broke down in 1990; and, in 1992, changes proposed to address the concerns of both Quebecois and Native Canadians (who also sought autonomy) were rejected by several provinces, including Quebec, which viewed them as insufficient, as well as others that viewed them as excessive. At the beginning of the new century, the long-term ability of Canada to remain one country continues to be uncertain.

A similar conflict has developed recently in the United States with the growth of the Hispanic population. Like the French Canadians, many Hispanic Americans have sought to preserve their native culture by speaking Spanish. Just as the English-speaking majority in Canada opposes bilingualism, the English-speaking majority in the United States has reacted strongly to the growing use of Spanish. Several cities and states, for example, have passed legislation specifying English as their only official language, and in a 1998 referendum, California voters severely restricted the use of bilingual education.

Another example can be seen in the intense debates about "Ebonics" or Black English that arose in Oakland, California, and elsewhere in 1997. Some advocates of Ebonics saw it as a way of affirming pride in African American culture. Most of its supporters, though, favored its use in the schools as a way of communicating with black youth in their own language so as to more effectively teach them to speak and write standard English (Williams, 1997; McMillen, 1997). However, even the latter idea came under attack by many, who saw any use of Ebonics as a move away from affirming the importance of learning and speaking standard English. Moreover, most of the debate ignored academic research by linguists on whether or not using Ebonics might be helpful in teaching standard English. This is not surprising, given the intensity of feeling about language as a cultural symbol. Though the academic research is not conclusive (Baron, 1997), some studies suggest that using Ebonics may lead to improved learning of standard English (McMillen, 1997; Williams, 1997).

The Linguistic Relativity Debate. Clearly, language can operate as an important symbol of a culture. Equally clearly, it can tell us a good deal about what is important in a culture. Eskimos have twelve different words to describe different types of snow; the Sami of Lapland have eighty. This reflects the fact that snow is important in the Eskimo and Sami

McDonald's and western-style fashion clothing ads in Louyang, China. As contact among different cultures increases throughout the world, the potential for misunderstanding and tensions increases. (Courtesy of John E. Farley)

experiences and that differences in snow that would be unimportant to most people are noticeable to them. Americans have a large number of words to describe different types of automobiles. Although cultures where cars are not so common have only one word, it is important for Americans—the most automobile-oriented society in the world—to distinguish among different types of cars. Thus, we speak of convertibles, station wagons, SUVs, compacts, subcompacts, sport models, sedans, coupes, four-by-fours, T-tops, and clunkers.

Having said this, it is also important to note that the extent to which language tells us what is important in a culture can be debated. While it is true that Eskimos have around twelve words for snow, it is questionable how many more words than other cultures they really have. For example, Eskimo language is structured differently than English (Martin, 1986; Pullum, 1991), and a more appropriate comparison to English would be to compare Eskimo words for snow to English words *related* to snow, such as "blizzard," "flurry," and "avalanche." When this comparison is made, the difference is greatly reduced: The Eskimo language has about a dozen words; English has about ten relating to snow.

The example of Eskimo words for snow does, however, tell us something else important about culture—the influence of oral traditions in shaping and perpetuating cultural beliefs, even among "trained experts." According to Martin (1986), the example of Eskimo words for snow began with a brief passage written by anthropologist Franz Boas in 1911 noting four Eskimo words for snow. Over the years, other anthropologists picked up the example, with the reported number of words gradually growing. By the 1950s, every anthropology student learned that Eskimos had a large number of words for snow. By the following decade, sociology and psychology students were learning the same thing, with teachers sometimes telling them that Eskimos had as many as 100 words for snow. The myth spread to the media, with *The New York Times* repeating the 100 figure and a Cleveland television station raising the number to 200. Two lessons can be learned from this: First, what is important in a culture can influence language, but the extent to which this is true varies widely. Second, oral traditions are powerful in shaping cultural beliefs, even among "experts" who are expected to be skeptical.

We know, then, that to varying degrees, the language spoken in a society may reflect that society's culture. However, does it also *influence* aspects of that culture? A group of specialists known as **linguistic-relativity** theorists (Sapir, 1921; Whorf, 1956) believe that it does. They argue that different languages categorize things differently, thus forcing people to create different categories in their own thinking. Different societies, for example, define colors differently. Where we see a spectrum of red, orange, yellow, green, blue, and purple, other societies in the world see only two or three colors. Some, for example, lump together what Americans consider the "warm" colors in one category and the "cool" colors in another category. To cite another example, we already noted the multiple words for snow among Eskimos and Laplanders. In contrast, some warm-weather cultures have only one word to cover snow, ice, frost, and cold. Finally, tenses vary. Some languages contain tenses that English lacks, and others lack tenses that we have, such as the past and future tenses. Sapir and Whorf argued that these differences affect how people think, and, thus, what they can know. How, for example, can a people conceptualize the future if their language has no tense for it?

In the sense of language *strictly* determining knowledge, however, the linguistic-relativity hypothesis is difficult to accept. Social scientists disagree over the extent to which language effects our perception of reality (Bickerton, 1995). Cognitive science critics argue that language is hard-wired into the human species (Pinker, 2002) and that some concepts exist prior to learning language. The most important might be the concept of family (Pinker, 1994). Linguistic relativists undermine their own argument to a certain extent when they can explain the meaning of different Eskimo words for snow, or of tenses in one language that do not exist in another language. Hence, language probably does not *determine* the content or organization of our knowledge and beliefs. However, language almost certainly does *influence* our knowledge and beliefs. For example, the English language often uses "black" and "dark" to represent evil and hopelessness. This usage undoubtedly has subtle influences on people's thinking about race. In fact, experiments with schoolchildren have indicated strongly that this is the case (Williams and Stabler, 1973). Thus, although a determinist notion that language defines what we *can* know and think is clearly an overstatement, there is good evidence that language can influence how we *do* think and know. This reality is powerfully illustrated by a recent study by Oliver Sacks about communications among hearing-impaired people, discussed in the box "What the Deaf Teach the Hearing About Language and Thought."

Shared Values

In addition to the shared realities represented by common knowledge and beliefs, cultures also carry common values. This is not to say that people within a society agree on everything—merely that there are certain common values in their culture that most or all people agree on. In another society with a different culture, the commonly held values will be different.

Ideology

The system of knowledge, beliefs, and values that is shared in a society is often referred to by sociologists as an **ideology;** that is, a set of ideas. In fact, the term "ideology" is very similar in meaning to the term "culture," except that culture also includes rules concerning behavior. The term "ideology" has one additional use, however. In the conflict-theory tradition of Marx (1967) and Mannheim (1936 [orig. 1929]), ideology is often taken to mean a set of knowledge, values, and beliefs that support, or give legitimacy to, the social structure. Such ideology is promoted by those in influential positions in the society, but it may be widely accepted throughout the society. Although this notion is associated with conflict-theory sociologists, the basic idea that the culture supports the social structure is something that sociologists of both the functionalist and the conflict perspectives generally acknowledge. This is one reason that functionalist theorists stress the need for consensus: They believe that society works best when people's values and beliefs are consistent with the organization of their society. In any stable society, what people believe to be true will generally support their social arrangements. If this is not the case, the society will experience pressure for change. Attempts may be made by the elite of the society to impose a new ideology, or the people in the society will attempt to change the social structure to match their ideology. Very often, both things happen.

Social Norms

Besides shared realities and shared values, culture also involves shared expectations about behavior. These expectations about behavior are called social **norms.** Sociologists commonly recognize three types of social norms. The most informal are **folkways**—informal, minor norms that usually carry only minor and informal *sanctions,* or punishments, when they are violated. Being over- or underdressed for an occasion is an example of a behavior that violates folkways. Another type of informal norm, called **mores** [pronounced "morays"], may or may not be written into law, but violations are usually taken seriously. This is so because mores are more likely than folkways to be viewed as essential to society. Reverence in church and respect for the flag are examples of mores. The flag is a symbol of the society and what it stands for; to challenge it is to challenge the very rightness of the society. Because mores are often seen as being critical to the maintenance of society, violations often evoke an emotional response. The sanctions for violating mores include ostracism, angry words, and sometimes physical violence. Finally, there are **laws**: formal, codified norms of which everyone is expected to be aware. Violations of laws carry specific sanctions, such as fines or imprisonment, that are usually stated as part of the law. Laws are usually consistent with mores.

As is the case with values and beliefs, each culture contains some social norms that are held in common by most or all of the people in the society. Moreover, the norms that are held in common in one culture are different from those in another culture. This can lead to misunderstandings when people with different cultures come into contact with one another, as in international travel. It has been frequently observed, for example, that when North Americans interact with South Americans, different norms are at work concerning the proper distance between two people speaking to each other. South Americans stand closer together when speaking than do North Americans. This leads to an interesting dynamic when a North American and a South American get into a conversation. The South American will keep approaching, and the North American will keep backing away because the South American is "too close." Thus, the two may move across the room or around in circles as the South American keeps trying to get closer and the North American farther away.

Farley had a similar experience while attending an international research conference in Sweden. At lunch one day, some Americans commented on the "rudeness" of people in Sweden. He was surprised at this statement because he had found everyone he had spoken to or done business with to be pleasant and polite. That evening, however, when a group attending the conference went out to a crowded nightclub, he realized the source of his fellow Americans' feelings. Almost immediately upon entering the nightclub, he was bumped by another person, who made no attempt to excuse himself. His reaction was, "that was rude." In fact, had the same act occurred in the United States, it easily could have caused a fight. A few minutes later, it happened again, and Farley soon noticed that it was not uncommon for people gently to push aside a person in their way without saying anything. Significantly, he also noticed that nobody (except the foreign visitors) seemed bothered by it.

As the week went on, he noticed that in any crowded situation gentle bumping and pushing without comment was common and accepted behavior among the Swedes. Not once did he see anyone get angry over it. From the American viewpoint, one could explain this behavior in two ways. One way was to conclude that "Swedes are rude." The other way was to conclude that "Swedes are exceptionally patient" because they never became upset over being bumped. Either conclusion, however, would reflect a misunderstanding of Swedish culture, as a result of looking at it only from the viewpoint of American culture. The correct explanation simply was that Swedes and Americans have different social norms about behavior in crowded places. In the United States, you are expected to avoid bumping people and to excuse yourself when you do. In Sweden, gentle bumping in crowded situations is acceptable and does not require excusing yourself. Imagine for a moment a Swede in the United States unfamiliar with American norms. If that Swede bumped someone and got yelled at, he or she would undoubtedly conclude that "Americans are impatient and belligerent." Any time people interpret the actions of people of another culture in terms of their own cultural norms, such misunderstandings can occur.

What Is Social Structure?

Recall our discussion of corsets and foot binding at the start of this chapter. This discussion showed us that culture and social structure are closely related to each other. By way of review, the concept of social structure refers to the organization of society, including its social positions, the relationships among those positions, and the different resources attached to those positions. Social structure also includes the groups of people who make up society and the relationships that exist among those groups (Smelser, 1988). We shall begin our discussion of social structure by discussing social positions.

SOCIOLOGICAL INSIGHTS

What the Deaf Teach the Hearing About Language and Thought

The relationship between language and thought is illustrated by Oliver Sacks (1989) in a fascinating book entitled *Seeing Voices*. Sacks examines the world of the deaf to gain insights about how language influences thought processes. He does this through two kinds of observations. First, he examines those (fortunately) rare cases in which deaf children are isolated from communication with others, as are the isolated feral children that will be discussed in Chapter 5. Second, he observes how the use of a visual language—Sign—influences the thought processes both of the hearing-impaired and their significant others who learn Sign in order to communicate with them.

The first kind of observation is exemplified by his observations of Joseph, an eleven-year-old boy born deaf whose deafness had not been discovered until he was four and who encountered no efforts to teach him any language until he entered a school for the deaf at the age of eleven. Joseph was an intelligent boy who could solve visual puzzles and draw diagrams of a room. That he had never learned symbolic communication, however, deprived him of many of the tools needed to carry out some of the usual human thought processes. As an example of this, Sacks points out that Joseph could not possibly communicate or even conceptualize how he had spent the weekend. First, being unable to communicate, Joseph could not conceptualize the idea of a question. Hence, he had no way to know that someone wanted him to recount what he had done. More fundamentally, though, he had not learned the concepts of time and history, so that the idea of what he had done a day ago was not something that he could understand. So while his perceptual thinking (like recognizing the layout of a room, or even becoming skilled at tic-tac-toe) was good, he could not conceptualize abstract ideas, plan, or mentally arrange the past or future. This was not because he lacked the ability to do so, but because he lacked the conceptualization schemes that come with learning a language.

In contrast, Sacks found that when people—either deaf or hearing—learn a visual language like Sign, they learn to think in ways that people who know only a written or spoken language cannot. He illustrates this with the case of Charlotte, a child of apparently well-educated parents who was diagnosed as deaf at the early age of ten months. Her parents at first tried to teach her a form of Sign language based on literal English, but eventually found that she could learn better by using the more visual forms of Sign language such as Signed English and American Sign Language. This was because the literal form was good for people who already knew written and oral English but more difficult for someone who did not. For those who did not know oral or written English, the visual types of Sign were better, because they could visualize with Sign even though they did not know English. But when Charlotte's parents switched to visual Sign, something fascinating happened. They discovered that in learning visual Sign along with their daughter, they were learning new concepts and ways of thinking themselves! Charlotte's mother reports, "It is a delight to realize that Charlotte's signing reflects visual thought patterns. We are startled into thinking differently about physical objects, and their placement and motion, because of Charlotte's expressions" (Sacks, 1989).

Social Status

Society can be thought of as being made up of a set of social positions. Sociologists refer to such a position as a **status.** Imagine that you are a single, black, twenty-year-old female who is working part-time, attending college, and majoring in physics. You are occupying a number of social positions, or statuses. You are a young single female, an employee, an African American, and a college student majoring in physics. Each of these social positions is defined, in part, by its relationship to other positions in society, which are occupied by other people. Moreover, each of these social positions, or statuses, is occupied by a number of other people besides yourself. There are other black women, other physics majors, other part-time employees. You share a common status with these people, and you are very likely to share with them some common experiences and behaviors.

Continuing with the same example, some of your statuses were ones that you were born into.

Culture and Social Structure

You were, for example, born black and female. Statuses that people are born into are called **ascribed statuses** (Linton, 1936). Besides race and sex, other ascribed statuses include characteristics of the family into which you were born, including your parents' family name, their economic level, their religion, and their national ancestry. In addition to ascribed statuses are statuses that result from something you did. You decided to go to college, to major in physics, to work part-time. Statuses that people get at least partially as a result of something that they do are called **achieved statuses** (Linton, 1936). Among the most important achieved statuses are occupations, educational levels, and incomes. Your religion (or lack of it) could also be an achieved status, if you changed at some time from the religion you were born into. Achieved statuses need not be things that are seen by society as positive. You might, for example, become a school dropout, a runaway, or a prison inmate. These, too, are achieved statuses, because they result, at least in part, from things that people do. Figure 4.1 depicts ascribed and achieved statuses.

Obviously, some statuses are more central and important in people's lives than others. For most people, one status stands above all others in terms of its influence over the person's life. Such a status is called a **master status.** For adults, the master status is most likely to be occupation, or possibly a position in the family such as parent, husband, or wife. For children, it may be the status of student or simply that of male or female.

Roles

Each social status, in turn, is attached to one or more *social roles*. As was pointed out in Chapter 3, a social role is a set of expectations for behavior that is attached to a status. Thus, a status is a social position, and a role is a set of behaviors that are expected of anyone who fills the position. As Linton (1936) put it, we *occupy* statuses, but we *play* roles. Each role in society is related to other social roles, through relationships of interdependency and cooperation (as noted by functionalist theory) and through relationships of competition, domination, and subordination (as noted by conflict theory). These roles, of course, are played by people—but the roles and the relationships between them

Figure 4.1 Achieved and Ascribed Statuses

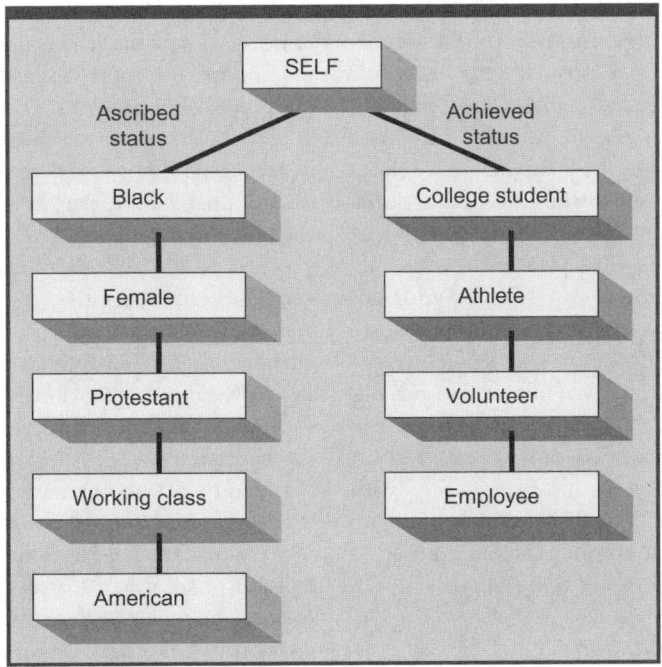

This diagram depicts the statuses occupied by a black female college undergraduate who works part-time, does volunteer work, and belongs to the track team. How many of these statuses do you share?

persist independently of which people are playing the roles. Different people may play the same role somewhat differently, but there are certain things that anyone playing a given role (such as that of a physics major) must accomplish and certain other roles with which that person must interact in socially defined ways.

Role Conflict and Role Strain

Each person must play a number of different roles, and sometimes these roles carry conflicting expectations. Returning to our example, you might experience conflicting expectations between your roles of college student, part-time worker, and single woman. These conflicting expectations are called **role conflict**. Sometimes even the same role contains conflicting expectations. This condition is called **role strain**. Thus, you are told that the expectations of you as a college student include academic achievement and enjoying what is supposed to be one of the most "fun" times of your life. Obviously, too much of one can get in the way of the other.

One reason for role strain is that any given role often calls for interaction with a variety of other statuses. Thus, what appears to be one role may in some aspects really be several roles. Consider, for example, the status of retail sales employee. At first, this status seems to give you a clear role to play: Sell things to the customers in the manner expected by your supervisor. However, this role actually involves interacting with several different statuses: supervisor, fellow employee, customer. To some extent, each of these interactions defines a different role because it carries different expectations. What pleases the boss might not please your fellow employees, and what pleases the customer might not please either your boss or your co-workers. Yet, to some extent, you must please all of them in order to succeed in your job. Thus, the status of retail sales employee in one sense carries several roles: that of subordinate (with respect to your supervisor), that of co-worker (with respect to your fellow employees), and that of seller (with respect to your customers). Merton (1968, pp. 41–45) refers to these combined roles attached to one status as the **role set** of that status.

Roles and Social Structure

In large part, the organization of society, or what we call social structure, is determined by the nature of these roles, the relationships between them, and the distribution of scarce resources among the people who play them. Different societies define, organize, and reward their activities in different ways, and thus each society has its own distinct social structure.

Although each society has its own distinct social structure, almost all social structures contain certain common elements. Any society more complex than a simple hunting-and-gathering society, for example, has some system of division of labor and some system of stratification. These differences mean, among other things, that different roles exist, they carry different expectations, and the people who play them are rewarded in different ways. Moreover, the social structure is arranged into some set of social institutions. Let us address each of these areas in somewhat more detail.

Division of Labor

One reason for the existence of diverse roles in any social structure is that any society more complicated than a simple hunting-and-gathering society requires a division of labor, or specialization. In other words, there are a variety of jobs to be done, and it is more efficient for each person to do one job than it is to try to teach everyone to do all of the jobs. The larger and more complex the society, the more essential and complex the division of labor becomes. Each job can be thought of as a social role in that it has a particular set of expectations that must be met if the job is to be done properly. Moreover, in large, interdependent societies, each of these jobs or roles relates in some way to a number of other jobs or roles. Thus, the social structure becomes, in part, a *system of roles that divides labor into specialized tasks, all of which are interdependent*. How labor is divided will vary, even among societies (and organizations within the same society) that are otherwise similar. In other words, the content of work roles and the relationships between them will not always be the same. There is no set formula for the division of labor.

One factor that has a major influence on the division of labor is the level of development of a society. As societies develop economically, their division of labor becomes more complex. Thus, modern industrial societies have far more complex divisions of labor than do preindustrial societies.

This issue, along with a number of other ways that the level of development influences society, is discussed in detail in Chapter 11. However, even at a given level of economic development, there is no one formula for the division of labor. Exactly how that division is accomplished is a key question to be answered whenever a sociologist tries to describe or understand a social structure.

Stratification

Besides carrying different expectations, different roles carry different rewards. As we shall see in much greater detail in Chapter 6, different occupations carry different levels of prestige and different economic rewards. Ascribed statuses also vary widely in prestige and in economic rewards. This system of inequality is called social stratification, and it is an important part of virtually every social structure. Social stratification is related in part to a society's division of labor. Some jobs that require detailed technical training are more difficult to learn than others. In part, such jobs are rewarded because they are harder to fill with qualified people, and some incentive is required to encourage people to get the necessary training (Davis and Moore, 1945). However, stratification exists for reasons independent of the division of labor. Even in modern societies, a good deal of economic inequality is inherited and is thus a product of an ascribed status: the family that a person was born into (Tumin, 1953).

Relationships Between Roles and Statuses

Because of social stratification, relationships of inequality exist between different roles and statuses in the social structure. Because of the division of labor, relationships of cooperation and interdependency also exist among different roles and statuses. These relationships largely define social structure. Imagine again that you are a single, black, female college student, twenty years old, majoring in physics, and employed part-time. We can see that you fit into both a stratification system and a system for the division of labor. You are in relationships of social inequality, or stratification, on the basis of both your ascribed statuses and your achieved statuses. Because of your ascribed statuses of race and sex, your society has placed you in a disadvantaged position relative to others with different ascribed statuses (whites and males). In other words, your opportunities may be restricted or you may be discriminated against because of your race and sex. The roles linked to your achieved statuses also in part define your position in the stratification system. You are in a subordinate, or lower, position relative to your professors and your supervisors. However, you are in an advantaged position relative to your peers who did not go to college, because going to college gives you a certain degree of prestige and a better chance of finding a well-paying job.

Besides fitting into a stratification system, you fit into a system of division of labor. In your part-time job, you fulfill a set of expectations (a role) that relates in some way to the work roles of others and performs some function within the larger system of division of labor. In the role of student, you are undergoing preparation for some new, and possibly more central, role within that system of division of labor.

In short, social structure is composed of systems of stratification and division of labor, each of which is an interrelated system of roles and statuses. Each person living in a society occupies a number of statuses and plays a number of roles

In the classroom, there are distinct roles, student and teacher, each of which carries a set of expectations. In addition, stratification is attached to the roles: The teacher has greater prestige and power than the students. (Courtesy of Michael Flota)

within both of those systems, which define the social structure of that society.

Institutions

Another key element of social structure is that of social **institutions.** Institutions can be defined as forms of organization that perform basic functions in a society, are strongly supported by that society's culture, and are generally accepted as essential elements of the social structure. Like the larger social structure, institutions are made up of relationships among statuses and roles that involve both division of labor and stratification. However, each institution consists of a particular set of such interrelated statuses and roles as well as specific systems of division of labor and stratification. Also, each institution is tied to a particular function or set of functions. Table 4.1 illustrates some of the key institutions in the social structure of the United States and identifies the functions those institutions perform. It also cross-references chapters in this book in which these institutions are discussed in greater detail.

As the definition indicates, a society's institutions are strongly supported by its culture. As a result, people learn to regard these institutions as essential and frequently take them for granted. Specific individuals who play roles within institutions may be criticized, but it is less common for the institution itself to be questioned. Americans might, for example, deplore the behavior of abusive parents, but their disapproval would be directed at the people involved and not at the traditional American family. Suppose, for a moment, that you heard the following argument:

> The American family is by its nature a brutal, authoritarian institution that encourages abuse by making parents all-powerful authority figures over children. Therefore, abuse is not a problem of bad individuals, but is inherent in the family. If you want to stop abuse, stop blaming the people who abuse their children and put the blame where it belongs: on an authoritarian, antiquated structure that by its very nature encourages abuse. As long as parents have authority over their children, abuse will result in a sizable number of cases.

Most of you would not accept this argument, and some of you would be angry at the person who made it. Although a well-reasoned counterargument could be developed against this argument, many of you would not respond this way but, instead, would reject the argument out of hand. Why? Because, beyond whatever logical flaws it may have, this argument attacks a cherished institution that is close—important—to most of us. In other words, the importance of the family (and other key social institutions) is strongly supported by our social norms and is something that we don't have to think about because we take it for granted.

Institutions are so strongly supported by social values and norms that when a practice or social arrangement becomes widely accepted in society, sociologists say that it has become *institutionalized*. Some sociologists even include the values and norms supporting an institution as part of the definition of an institution. At the very least, for a form of organization to qualify as an institution, it must be central to the culture of the society in which it exists.

Perspectives on Culture and Social Structure

As we have already noted, social structure and culture are closely linked, and the normal condition is for a society's culture to be compatible with, and supportive of, its social structure. There are, however, at least occasional periods when culture and social structure are not compatible, and these are the times when social change is most likely to occur. Significantly, sociologists of both the functionalist perspective and the conflict perspective have developed explanations of the conditions that produce compatibility and incompatibility between culture and social structure. Not surprisingly, these explanations are often at odds, or at least emphasize very different processes.

The Functionalist Perspective: Adaptation of Culture and Social Structure to the Environment

As we saw in Chapter 3, functionalists see society as basically a stable, interdependent system that has adopted a particular form because that form works well. To maintain this stability requires a consensus in support of the society's basic social

Table 4.1 American Institutions and Their Key Functions

Institution	Key Functions
Family (monogamous) (Chapter 13)	Replacement of generation Socialization of young/cultural transmission Status transmission Shelter; care for young and elderly Emotional support
Capitalist economic system (Chapter 11)	Economic production Provision of goods and services Means to distribute scarce resources Means to determine what is produced
Government (Chapter 12)	Provision of needed public services Representation of interest groups Protection from foreign powers Symbols of national unity Social control
Legal system (Chapter 10)	Protection of members of society from illegal actions by other members of society Orderly settlement of disputes Source of legitimacy for government Social control
Education (Web-Based Chapter A)	Socialization of young/cultural transmission Passage of knowledge between generations Creation of new knowledge through research (universities) Allocations of individuals to careers Personal development/enhancement of awareness
Health-care system (Web-Based Chapter C)	Treatment of illness Extension of life Development of new medical technology
Religion (Web-Based Chapter B)	Provision of societal belief system Socialization of young/cultural transmission Social control Personal support

arrangements. Culture performs this function. It promotes cooperation by creating solidarity and provides specific support for the social structure, which operates to meet the basic needs of the society. This basic paradigm of an interdependent and harmonious social structure and culture has been recognized by sociological functionalists dating back at least to Emile Durkheim.

It is functionalists in the tradition of social anthropology, however, who have best addressed the closely related question of cultural and structural variation. If social structure and culture exist because they are basically functional, then why is there so much variation in social structure and culture among different societies? In brief, their answer is that different societies have developed different structures and cultures as adaptations to the different environments in which they exist.

Social structure and culture, then, are seen as being in harmony with each other, and both of them are adapted to the environment of the social system (Buckley, 1967).

Much of the early insight on this issue is attributable to social anthropologist Bronislaw Malinowski, who conducted extended field observation in the Trobriand Islands in the South Pacific during the early twentieth century (Malinowski, 1922, 1926, 1948, 1967). Malinowski noted that arrangements among the people he studied existed not because they were merely functional but because *they were functional given the presence of a particular environment.* An example of this can be seen in the Trobriand Islanders' use of magic. Although they used magic extensively, they seemed to use it primarily when they were entering situations they perceived as dangerous. For example, they used magic when fishing on the treacherous open seas, but not when fishing in protected lagoons. Thus, Malinowski concluded that the function of magic was to alleviate fears and make fishing on the open seas seem less threatening.

Malinowski focused primarily on the individual, psychological function of magic in relieving anxiety in the context of a dangerous environment. However, because magic also enhanced the Trobriand Islanders' willingness to fish in the bountiful open seas, it also performed the clear function *on the social level* of helping the Trobriand Islanders deal with their environment. The idea that culture (in this case, a belief in magic) can be useful to a society in helping it adapt to its environment is generally associated with the theorist A. R. Radcliffe-Brown, who had been trained in the theories of Emile Durkheim. Radcliffe-Brown (1935, 1950, 1952), like Durkheim, saw society as being much like a biological organism, made up of many interrelated parts and having evolved in a way so as to adapt to its environment. To Radcliffe-Brown, then, the important aspect of magic was not its contribution to the individual (to alleviate anxiety), but its contribution to the larger society (to facilitate fishing on the open seas). Implicit in the work of both Malinowski and Radcliffe-Brown, as well as in that of theorists such as Walter Buckley (1967), is the idea that what is functional for a society depends on that society's environment, so that the social structure and culture that develop in any society will be in sizable part a product of that society's environment.

Aspects of the Environment

What do we mean by a society's environment? The concept includes the full range of realities to which the society must adapt. There is the *physical environment,* which includes climate, terrain, plant and animal life, and presence or absence of bodies of water. There is the *social environment,* which includes any other societies with which a society must interact. Finally, there is the *technological environment,* which is defined by the level of technology available to a society. All of these represent realities to which a society must adapt, and they interactively define the conditions to which a society must respond. It is obvious that a society in a cold, wet climate will have different needs for shelter and clothing and different ways of obtaining or producing food than one in a desert. However, it is also true that for either the desert or the cold-climate society, reality will be quite different if it is a modern society with electric heating and cooling devices than it would be if it were a hunting-and-gathering society with no technological means of indoor temperature control. Hence, it is the *combination* of the physical, social, and technological environments that defines the total environment to which a society must adapt. Functionalists see social structure and culture as reflecting adaptation to this total environment, and believe that this accounts for variation in culture and social structure from place to place and over time.

Cultural and Structural Variation: Do Cultural or Structural Universals Exist?

One question that sociologists and anthropologists have asked for many years is whether cultural or structural *universals* exist. The answer to this question probably depends on how specific something has to be in order to count as a cultural pattern or a structural arrangement. Consider the example of attempts to modify weather, cited by Murdock (1945) as a cultural universal. Are Indian rain dances really a common cultural element with modern cloud-seeding techniques? On the one hand, both are intended to induce rain. On the other hand, the assumptions and worldview behind the two are almost diametrically opposed. The Indian rain dances were based on tradition, religion, and mysticism: if one pleased the spirits, one could induce rain. Modern cloud seeding, in contrast, is based on rationalism, science, and technology.

When we speak of cultural universals, then, it makes sense to speak of broad patterns found in all societies. A list of these is shown in Table 4.2. Beyond these broad patterns, however, there are few, if any, specific cultural or structural universals. Weather is important, so people try to change it. But when we get down to *how* they try to change it, we find tremendous variation.

Universal Social Tasks

As was already noted in our discussion of social structure, there are certain issues that must be addressed in every society. We have already discussed the most critical ones: division of labor

Table 4.2 Cultural Universals Identified by George Peter Murdock

Age grading	Ethnobotany	Inheritance rules	Personal names
Athletic sports	Etiquette	Joking	Population policy
Bodily adornment	Faith healing	Kin groups	Postnatal care
Calendar	Family	Kinship nomenclature	Pregnancy usages
Cleanliness training	Feasting	Language	Property rights
Community organization	Fire making	Law	Propitiation of supernatural being
Cooking	Folklore	Luck superstitions	Puberty customs
Cooperative labor	Food taboos	Magic	Religious ritual
Cosmology	Funeral rites	Marriage	Residence rules
Courtship	Games	Mealtimes	Sexual restrictions
Dancing	Gestures	Medicine	Soul concepts
Decorative art	Gift giving	Modesty about body functions	Status differentiation
Divination	Government	Mourning	Surgery
Division of labor	Greetings	Music	Tool making
Dream interpretation	Hair styles	Mythology	Trade
Education	Hospitality	Numerals	Visiting
Eschatology	Housing	Obstetrics	Weaning
Ethics	Hygiene	Penal sanctions	Weather control
	Incest taboos		

Source: George Peter Murdock, "The Common Denominator of Culture." in *The Science of Man in the World Crisis,* edited by Ralph Linton. Copyright © 1945 by Columbia University Press. Reprinted with permission of the publisher.

and stratification. In addition, there are other key tasks that every society must accomplish. Thus, every culture must carry some knowledge about these tasks, and every social structure must provide a means for accomplishing them (Aberle et al., 1950). Among these tasks are the following:

- *Dealing with the physical environment:* Getting food and shelter, adapting to the physical terrain, and protecting oneself from weather, disease, and natural hazards
- *Governing reproduction and relations between the sexes:* Establishing some rules ensuring that the society will reproduce itself and establishing some ground rules for sexual behavior
- *Role assignment:* Deciding who will play what roles within society's system of division of labor and how the stratification system will reward those who play various roles
- *Communication:* Enabling people to communicate with one another through language and other symbols
- *Government:* Having some system through which rules are established, disputes resolved, and common goals set up
- *Norms concerning violence:* A set of rules specifying conditions under which violence is and is not acceptable
- *Socialization:* Some way of teaching children and anyone else entering the society how to function and survive within its culture

Although these issues must be addressed by all societies, the means by which they are addressed are almost limitlessly diverse. Thus, it can be said that cultural universals exist in two broad senses. First, there are regular practices or norms that occur in virtually all societies, although in different forms. Many of the items on Murdock's list fall into this category. Even the incest taboo, sometimes cited as the "only true cultural universal," is an example of this: There is no regularity among societies about what is considered incest and what is not. Second, there are issues that must be addressed by all societies, although in practice each society addresses them in different ways. Thus, cultural variation is much more the pattern than cultural or structural universals. Various aspects of cultural and structural variation, such as religion, sex roles, and marriage and family systems, will be discussed in greater detail in later chapters.

Cultural Integration

However much culture varies from one society to another, it is true that within any given culture various aspects of the culture tend to be fairly consistent with one another. This tendency is called *cultural integration*. An example can be seen in the consistencies between religious beliefs and the family system in Judeo-Christian societies. Christians and Jews believe that the law of God calls for monogamous marriage, as reflected in the Commandments "thou shalt not commit adultery" and "thou shalt not covet thy neighbor's wife." Family norms are likewise supportive of religion, as expressed in the saying "the family that prays together stays together." And, indeed, this particular saying appears to be largely true: Divorce rates are significantly lower among devoutly religious people than among the nonreligious.

As has been noted elsewhere in this chapter, there is also a tendency for the culture and the social structure to be fairly consistent with one another in any given society. A study by Frank, Meyer, and Miyahara (1995) illustrates this. They examined different societies to measure the extent to which their cultures stressed individualism, and they measured the size and influence of the profession of psychology in each society. Because psychology stresses the value and mental health of the individual, we would expect to find that the more individualistic a society's culture, the greater the institutionalization of professional psychology. And that is exactly what the researchers found, even after controlling for other relevant variables, such as a society's level of economic development.

Ethnocentrism

Recall the example of the Americans in Sweden who misinterpreted the behavior of Swedes in crowded situations as rude. This example illustrates a pattern known as **ethnocentrism**, in which people, consciously or unconsciously, view their own culture as normal and natural and judge other cultures accordingly. Throughout history, people of various cultural backgrounds have labeled those of different backgrounds as "savage," "barbaric," "hedonistic," and "primitive" because these people's behaviors differed from their own.

Ethnocentrism exists in all societies, for several reasons. First, we take much of our behavior for granted, not really thinking about why we do certain things and don't do other things. To many Americans, eating pork or beefsteak is appetizing, but the thought of eating worms or grasshoppers is repulsive. In other cultures, though, these same things are viewed very differently. Worms and grasshoppers are eaten in many societies, and in some societies, few things could be more repulsive than eating the meat of a pig or a cow. In many Middle Eastern societies, eating pork is strictly forbidden; it is against the rules of the stricter segments of both Judaism and Islam. In India, cows are considered to be sacred, and people would be horrified at the thought of killing a cow, much less eating it.

Functions of Ethnocentrism. A second reason for the universality of ethnocentrism is that it performs a function: In a society where people have a common culture, ethnocentrism in relation to other societies helps to promote solidarity (Sumner, 1906). To a certain extent, any society can promote internal unity and cooperation by comparing itself favorably to those outside. Significantly, the ever-present tendency toward ethnocentrism becomes most pronounced during wartime, as each country in the conflict emphasizes its righteousness and civility as contrasted with its evil and barbaric enemy. From a conflict perspective, ethnocentrism is also useful for justifying or rationalizing one group's exploitation of another. "After all," the colonizers tell themselves, "they're just helpless primitives whom we're actually civilizing"—in the process of making them slaves or taking their land. With this type of thinking, even the most brutal exploitation can be made to seem acceptable.

Dysfunctions of Ethnocentrism. Despite the fact that it is functional in certain ways, most sociologists see ethnocentrism as generally dysfunctional, and they try to discourage it. For one thing, it can be a major source of conflict and inequality in any society with a significant degree of cultural diversity—which, in today's world, means most societies. Second, it is a major cause of international conflict because societies that view one another ethnocentrically create international conflicts through self-fulfilling prophecies. Third, as previously noted, it is often used as an excuse for one group to treat another in a brutal and exploitative manner. Finally, ethnocentrism creates misunderstanding of social reality. In fact, one of the greatest challenges of social-science research is to avoid a tendency toward ethnocentrism when studying human behavior.

Cultural Relativism

In contrast to ethnocentrism, social scientists try to look at human behavior and culture from a viewpoint of **cultural relativism**. Cultural relativism recognizes that cultures are different but does not view difference as deficiency. Rather, it realizes that different societies develop different cultures and different social structures in response to the different environmental conditions they face. Thus, even if our ways seem natural and are best for us, they are not natural but a social product, and they certainly may not be best for someone else. Cultural relativism also means trying to understand the behavior of people in other cultures according to what the behavior means to them and not what it would mean to someone in *our* culture. Even for social scientists trained in detached observation, this is not easy to do.

It should be stressed that cultural relativism does *not* always mean value neutrality. Occasionally, cultures become despotic, as in the case of Nazi Germany. Sociologists do not carry cultural relativism to the point of accepting the values espoused by such cultures, but they do try to understand the social forces that produce them.

The Conflict Perspective and Culture

Recall from Chapter 3 that, to the conflict theorist, a society's social structure is arranged so that whatever group holds power in that society controls a disproportionate share of scarce resources. To the conflict theorist, the function of culture is to justify such social arrangements—to get people in society to accept the notion that those who have a disproportionate share of scarce resources *should* have that large share. This viewpoint is expressed most clearly in the theories of Karl Marx (1964 [orig. 1867]).

Marx on Social Structure and Culture

Marx believed strongly that any society's culture is an outgrowth of its social structure. In other words, the basic social and economic arrangements in a society largely determine what people in that society will know and believe. All societies, Marx argued, have an *economic structure* and an *ideational superstructure*. By **economic structure**, Marx was referring to those elements of social structure that relate to production, wealth, and income. It includes the economic stratification system—the distribution of income and particularly wealth—but it also is defined by the society's production system (industrial versus agricultural, for example). By **ideational superstructure,** Marx was referring to those aspects of culture that we have called ideology. Marx used the term "superstructure" because he saw ideology and culture as arising from the social structure, not having a life of their own. The true structure of a society is defined by its distribution of wealth; culture, he argued, is simply a product of that economic structure.

Social Structure. The relationship between social structure (or in Marxian terms, economic structure) and culture (or ideational superstructure) is depicted in Figure 4.2. The blocks at the top and bottom of the figure represent the social or economic structure. As the figure shows, this structure is composed of a ruling class and a subordinate class. The ruling class is the group that owns the means of production, and the subordinate class is everyone else. In general, people in the subordinate class work for people in the ruling class. Thus, as shown on the left side of Figure 4.2, the subordinate class provides labor for the ruling class. Those in the ruling class are able to sell the products of that labor for more than the cost of the labor, and this profit—or surplus value of labor, as Marx called it—enables the ruling class to enjoy a much higher standard of living than everyone else. Marx saw this as exploitation because the actual work is done by the subordinate class, who suffer a low standard of living, while the ruling class monopolizes the products of their labor, and thereby enjoys a luxurious standard of living. Thus, as shown at the right side of the figure, the ruling class exploits the subordinate class.

Ideology. Of course, because the social structure is fundamentally one of inequality and exploitation, according to Marx, the ruling class always faces the risk of an uprising by the subordinate class. The function of ideology, or ideational superstructure, is to prevent this. A culture's ideology thus explains why the ruling class should enjoy disproportionate wealth. In other words, it promotes the view that the ruling class *deserves* their great wealth. In Figure 4.2, culture or ideology is represented by the middle block. Note the arrows between the top two blocks. The ruling class creates the ideology, and the ideology justifies its exploitative relationship with the subordinate class.

How ideology justifies such exploitative relationships will depend, of course, on the broader characteristics of the society. Traditional, preindustrial societies might justify the social structure on the grounds that it is the will of God. Thus, the royalty

Figure 4.2 The Relationship Between Economic Structure and Ideational Superstructure (Ideology) in Marxian Theory

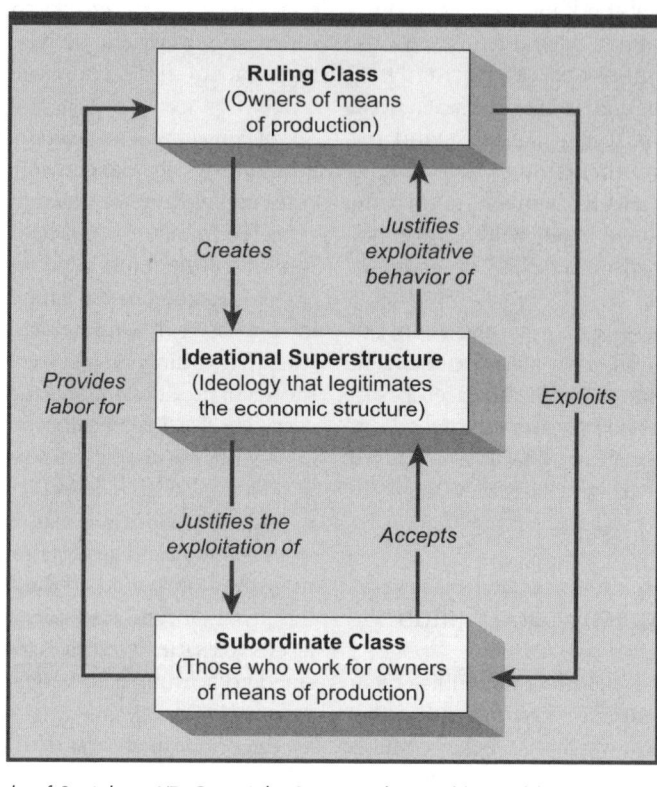

Source: From *The Study of Sociology*, I/E. Copyright © 1974, The Dushkin Publishing Group/Brown & Benchmark Publishers, a division of McGraw-Hill Higher Education Group, Guilford, CT. All rights reserved.

and nobility of preindustrial Europe—the owners of wealth in feudal society—were protected by an ideology known as the *divine right of kings*, which held that kings received their authority from God. In a modern industrial society, the concentration of wealth in the hands of a few might be justified on the grounds of productivity and incentive: Placing any limit upon the wealth that people can earn might take away their incentive to come up with innovations that improve productivity. If this sounds more persuasive to you than God's willing that the king should rule, that is not surprising. You live, after all, in a modern society that values rationality, productivity, and innovation. However, Marx and those who follow his theories would hold that this argument is merely a cultural mechanism designed to uphold the great wealth of the economic ruling class, and that society could be just as productive without so much concentration of wealth. The relationship between inequality and productivity is explored further in Chapter 6, which deals with social inequality.

False Consciousness

As the bottom half of Figure 4.2 illustrates, not only does the ruling class create and promote an ideology that justifies its exploitative behavior, but the subordinate class accepts this ideology. Marx referred to this acceptance as false consciousness. In medieval society, for example, what was critical was that people *believed* in the divine right of kings. Such a belief served the interest of the king, but it went directly against the interests of the serfs and peasants, who labored for long hours day after day, only to see the wealth that they produced taken away by a noble or king. **False consciousness,** then, can be defined as acceptance by a group of people—usually a subordinate group of people—of a belief or value that works against that group's self-interests.

False consciousness is a critical concept in conflict theories about culture and social structure because it is the key means by which the ruling class prevents protest or revolution. Why do subordinate groups so often accept ideologies that go against their own interests? According to Marx, the answer lies in the power of the ruling class over key institutions and sources of information.

False Consciousness and Social Structure. Consider again the example of medieval European society. In that time and place, the key social institution was the Church. Kings were crowned in cathedrals, and bishops were consecrated in the presence of the king. Bishops, like kings and nobles, were often major landowners. Thus, the Church and royalty shared a common position in the ruling class, and because religion was the source of truth in such traditional societies, the ruling class could promote its interests through the Church. Thus, the divine right theory was not seriously questioned until the beginnings of urbanization and industrialization created a new and powerful capitalist class whose interests often conflicted with those of the rural landowners.

In modern societies, false consciousness can be promoted through other means. Conflict theorists point out, for example, that the media are owned and controlled by large corporations, who are the wealthiest class in contemporary capitalist societies (Molotch, 1979). This does not mean that the media will speak with a unified voice, or even that they will not criticize the wealthy. However, conflict theorists do argue that there is a definite limit to how far the media will go in advocating fundamental change in the economic system, and that the media encourage people to take certain economic arrangements for granted. Often, too, the media focus heavily on entertainment rather than information, giving people largely what they want but also giving them little real information. According to some conflict theorists, this policy distracts the public from social issues that might lead to conflict that could threaten the ruling class (Gouldner, 1976, especially pp. 167–78).

False Consciousness: A Case Study. The concept of false consciousness can be illustrated by two presidential elections, in the years 1972 and 2000, during which the inheritance tax became an issue. The 1972 Democratic candidate, Senator George McGovern, proposed a major revision of the nation's inheritance laws. The McGovern plan would have taxed away any money inherited by one individual in excess of $500,000 (an amount that would be equivalent to well over $2 million in today's dollars). This proposal became so controversial that McGovern was forced to withdraw it, and many observers feel that it contributed to the candidate's landslide defeat by Richard Nixon.

As might be expected, McGovern's proposal aroused tremendous hostility among the wealthy. Significantly, however, although less than 1 percent of the population would have been affected by the plan, some of the major opposition came from the working class (Clelland and Robertson, 1974, pp. 204–5). Why did so many people who would never themselves be in a position to pass along this sum of money react this way? Apparently, most Americans still believed strongly in the "American Dream"—the belief that they *might someday* possess that kind of wealth, even though they did not possess it then. To support McGovern's proposal would be to deny this possibility, which they were unwilling to do.

A similar situation appears to have arisen during the 2000 presidential election, when the Republican candidate, George W. Bush, proposed completely *eliminating* the inheritance tax. A Gallup Poll taken that year showed that 60 percent of Americans favored the Bush proposal, while just 35 percent opposed it (Gallup Organization, 2000a). This was the case *even though* just 17 percent said they would personally benefit from such a proposal. (The actual number who would benefit was even smaller, since by 2000, the inheritance tax had already been eliminated on any amount under $1 million.)

Working-class opposition to the inheritance tax can be interpreted as an act of false consciousness because, in terms of objective interests, such people probably benefit from taxation of inheritances. In both 1972 and 2000, a sizable majority of Americans supported a position that would not have benefited them, and likely hurt them economically. In the case of McGovern's 1972 proposal, higher taxes for the wealthy could have meant lower taxes or expanded government programs (for example, college scholarships) for working people, as well as reduced deficits, which would have lowered the inflation rate. Just the opposite was true for Bush's 2000 proposal, which became law in 2001 after Bush became president. The law gradually eliminated the tax by 2010 but allows it to return in 2011 (unless Congress makes changes). If the inheritance tax is permanently eliminated, it will likely cost the average American in the form of larger deficits or reduced services due to revenue lost by eliminating the inheritance tax, particularly with the large federal deficits that have accumulated. But in both the case of the McGovern proposal to raise it and the Bush proposal to eliminate it, substantial majorities took positions against the inheritance tax and thus, against their objective self-interests. As of this writing, a bill to retain the estate (inheritance) tax from 2011 on, but with a lower rate and higher threshold before it applies, was under consideration in Congress.

Incompatibilities Between Culture and Social Structure

Maybe no two terms are more important or more difficult to define than "structure" and "culture." In this book, we have defined the two as how society is organized and what society believes, respectively. But many sociologists point out that the line between even these definitions is fuzzy. What we do know is that *culture and structure are very closely interrelated*. A classroom, for instance, is part of the social structure, but it also is a product of the culture that produced it and the ideas that motivated its construction. The fact that classrooms are set up so that the teacher stands at the front of the room, can move about freely while the students are seated below the teacher and organized in rows and are not supposed to move, is not only a reflection of the authority relationship between teacher and students but also a product of the values, beliefs, and ideologies of our society—in other words, our culture.

When only looking at the concept of culture, we acknowledge this problem by defining different kinds of culture: the idea side as nonmaterial or cognitive culture and the material side as material culture. But what about structure? Doesn't the idea of material culture encroach on the idea of social structure? Many would say yes. And this is the problem. We know the two things are different, as will be discussed later in the chapter on the conflicts between culture and structure. Yet we also recognize that the line between the two is tricky. And none of this helps us to understand how culture and structure work together!

Enter William Sewell. Sewell (1992) argues that we should, in essence, simply change the language by which we are debating these issues. By changing our language, maybe we can use Sewell's ideas to illuminate the structure/culture relationship.

Sewell's Duality of Structure Theory

According to Sewell, reality is made up of two elements: resources and schemas. *Schemas* are defined as virtual frames of reference, ideas that help us to understand and organize other ideas—sort of like mental bookshelves. The importance of schemas is that they could be anything. There are no limits to what humans might believe. We used to think the world was flat for instance (some people still do). *Resources* on the other hand are actual; they exist in the material world and can be human or nonhuman. The key thing is resources always have limits—things they can do and things they cannot do. The chair you are seated in may be able to do a lot of things if you need it to; if you had to, you could probably use it as a weapon or a shield, but it probably cannot fly you to the moon. We may never know exactly what these limits are for any given resource, but they are always there. We are simply assuming your chair could not fly you to the moon; maybe we're wrong.

When the limits of resources come up against the limitlessness of our schemas, we may see that what we believed is not true and change our minds. This is how social change takes place. This is also the importance of the structure-culture debate. In Sewell's model, resources correspond to structure and schemas correspond to culture, loosely. By changing the terms, Sewell gives us a way to see the importance of the culture-structure debate.

Both the functionalist and conflict perspectives agree that under certain circumstances culture and social structure are at odds with each other. We shall examine this issue from the viewpoints of the two schools.

Culture Against Structure: The Functionalist Perspective

Functionalist theory holds that a society's social structure and culture will help it adapt to its physical, social, and technological environment. This would seem to suggest that society could be very stable once it reached a state of equilibrium with that environment. The environment, however, is always changing. The society comes into contact with societies it did not have to deal with before, which represents a change in the social environment. New technologies are invented, which represent a change in the technological environment. Even the physical environment can change and force a society to adapt. In 1986, the Chernobyl nuclear disaster contaminated the reindeer herd of northern Sweden and Norway with radiation, which forced many people who had been herding reindeer for centuries to change their lifestyle. Although this is a particularly dramatic change in the physical environment, there are many more gradual changes that require societies to adapt. Changes in climate, environmental damage, the depletion of natural resources or the discovery of new ones, changes in the mix of animal life, and even changes in lake or ocean levels can all require substantial adaptation by human societies. Thus, they can all be important sources of social and cultural change.

Cultural Lag

When a society must change in response to its environment, its social structure and culture often do not change at the same rate. The social structure, for example, can often adapt quickly to new technology. However, the culture is usually slower to change, because people resist giving up important values and beliefs. This creates a condition sociologists call **cultural lag.** When this situation exists, a value, norm, or belief that once was functional persists even though it is no longer functional or has become dysfunctional. Cultural lag occurs any time a society's culture fails to keep up with changes in its social structure, or when one part of the culture changes and another part does not (Ogburn, 1966 [orig. 1922]). Numerous examples of cultural lag can be found in American society.

You can see an example of cultural lag every time that you eat. Americans, after they cut their meat, put down the knife and switch the fork from the left hand to the right. Only then do they put the food in their mouths. This differs from the European practice of simply raising the food to the mouth with the fork in the left hand after cutting the meat with the right. Why did Americans change this practice? Some experts conjecture that the change originated on the frontier, where people needed to keep one hand free in case they had to grab a weapon to fight off an attacker. Today, the frontier is gone, and putting down the knife and switching the fork to the other hand has no practical use. Americans continue to do it anyway, however, and to eat in the European style is considered to be "bad manners."

Cultural Diffusion

Another condition that can produce incompatibilities between culture and social structure is **cultural diffusion,** a condition that occurs when aspects of the culture of one society are gradually adopted by other societies. Examples of cultural diffusion abound. One is the worldwide popularity of American and British rock music, which is often sung in English regardless of the local language. Another can be seen in the ease with which Americans today will identify certain forms of behavior as *macho,* a concept that originated not in the United States but in Latin America. There is even evidence of diffusion of basic demographic trends, such as declines in the birth rate, which tend to spread to nearby areas once they have begun in one area (Tolnay, 1995).

Like cultural lag, cultural diffusion can produce situations where the culture and social structure are incompatible. The culture of one society may not work very well with the social structure of another. In this case, the process happens in the opposite way from cultural lag: The culture changes in some way that may make it incompatible with the social structure. In recent decades, for example, many Americans have been influenced by mystical Asian religious philosophies. Transcendental meditation, Buddhism, and other forms of Eastern mysticism, stressing inner peace and self-knowledge, have attracted sizable interest. To other Americans, however, a mode of thinking that emphasizes introspection and inner peace seems out of place in an economic system that requires achievement motivation and a certain amount of interest in material wealth. Some have even seen the spread of these new ideas as a threat to the productivity of the American economy.

When either cultural lag or cultural diffusion produces a situation where the culture and social structure are incompatible, several things can happen. The culture or the structure can change in ways that make the two more compatible. Sometimes a *subculture* will develop. In the case of cultural lag, some people will continue to hang on to the old culture, while others adopt new ways of thinking that are more consistent with the new structural realities. In the case of cultural diffusion, some people are usually quicker than others to borrow ideas from other cultures. In both of these cases, society becomes more culturally diverse as different belief systems and different sets of norms emerge among different groups of people in society. This can bring conflict if the groups confront one another, but it also can be an important source of social adaptation.

Subcultures in Mass Society

A **subculture** can be defined as a set of cultural characteristics shared among a group within a society that (1) are distinct in some ways from the larger culture within which the group exists, but (2) also have some features in common with the larger culture. Usually, a group that forms a subculture has some sense of identity, some recognition that people in the group share something among themselves that others in the larger society do not. A subculture can develop any time a group of people share some situation or experience that is different from that of others in their society. Some of the groups of people that commonly form subcultures are age groups; racial and ethnic groups; religious groups; people in a particular geographic area; and people with a common occupation, recreational interest, or economic situation. Each of these examples involves some common situation or experience among people in the group that is not shared with the larger society. It is important to stress that the preface "sub" does *not* imply that subcultures are inferior to, or less fully developed than, cultures. Rather, it is used to convey the notion that subcultures exist *within* some larger cultural context. A recent illustration of the relationship between subcultures and the common culture of the larger society can be seen in the reaction of Americans to the September 11, 2001, terrorist attacks. On the one hand, the country was unified by the attacks, as often happens. Americans of all races, religions, and cultural backgrounds died in the attacks, and to a great extent, all Americans had a common reaction of shock, disgust, and anger. When the U.S. government took military action in Afghanistan to bring to justice those responsible for the attacks, Americans initially supported it with greater unanimity than had been the case in any military action since World War II. At the same time, however, there were some ways in which cultural norms based on gender, race, class, and region still shaped the response of Americans to the attacks. This issue is explored further in the box, "Responding to Terror: A Common Norm or Group Differences?"

Case Studies: Hip Hop and "Computer Geeks"

In some cases, the values, norms, and beliefs of a subculture are in conflict with those of the larger culture, whereas in other cases, they are largely irrelevant to those of the larger culture. An example of conflict can be seen in the "hip hop" subculture that emerged among inner-city African Americans in the late 1980s and early 1990s. Through rap music and other symbols, hip hop expresses anger toward American society over racism, poverty, and lack of opportunity, and it rejects many of the values of the larger, mostly white, middle-class culture. Much of rap music's language and content seems intended to shock those who adhere to that culture. In contrast, an example of a subculture with norms largely irrelevant to the larger culture can be seen in what are commonly called "computer geeks." Like the inner-city hip hop culture, this group speaks a language different from that of most Americans. It speaks of bits, bytes, and bandwidth, as well as RAM, ROM, and FTP downloads. However, this group uses such terms not to rebel against middle-class culture, but because of its special interest in the details of computers that ordinary English doesn't describe very well. Computer geeks are not really in conflict with the larger culture. Rather, they are, at times, totally absorbed in their own subculture.

Though both the hip hop and computer subcultures share knowledge, beliefs, values, and norms that are different from those of the larger society, neither is totally apart from the larger American culture. Their members, for example, are for the most part capable of speaking ordinary,

UNDERSTANDING RACE, CLASS, AND GENDER
Responding to Terror: A Common Norm or Group Differences?

When terrorists attacked the United States on September 11, 2001, it brought an unusual degree of unity in one regard: In the days immediately following the attack, overwhelming proportions of Americans, 90 percent or more, supported a military response and supported President Bush's handling of the crisis. In fact, the president's approval rating in the weeks immediately after the attack was the highest ever recorded. Even among African Americans, a group from which Bush had previously received little support, his approval rating soared from just 32 percent in early September to 70 percent after the attacks (Pew Research Center, 2001). In such a context, reactions were in some cases quite strong against people who did not express support for the president. For example, at California State University at Chico, a professor who said that Bush administration policies may have contributed to the attack received over 70 hate-mail letters, and he was interrupted and heckled when he attempted to speak in public. The president of the university received numerous letters demanding that he fire the professor. This example shows that, in the atmosphere of anger and fear following the attacks, *support for President Bush and his policies had, to a large extent, become a norm among Americans.*

At the same time, though, social differences among Americans did not disappear, even with this broad consensus. While an overwhelming majority of Americans favored some form of military response to the terrorist attacks, their confidence in the effectiveness of such a response varied widely, often along lines of race, class, and gender. And it did so in sociologically predictable ways. For example, whites, males, people in the South, and people with lower levels of education have been the groups that have always had the highest levels of confidence in the military and in military action. This was again true in the context of the terrorist attacks. Among men, 46 percent were "very confident" that military action would be effective in stopping terrorism, compared to just 33 percent of women. Among people who had never attended college, 42 percent were very confident, compared to just 33 percent of college graduates. Among people from the South, nearly half, 47 percent, felt very confident; in all other regions, the percentage who said they were very confident was below 40 percent. And among African Americans, 39 percent were doubtful that military action would be effective, compared to just 20 percent of whites (Pew Research Foundation, 2001).

Other differences followed similar lines. For example, when asked whether military action or homeland defense should be the top priority, men chose military action over homeland defense by a two-to-one margin, while women were evenly divided on which should be the top priority. And when asked whether prevention of future terrorism or punishment of the September 11 attackers is higher priority, two thirds of college graduates said prevention should be a higher priority, compared to just half of those who had never attended college. Worry about future terrorism also varied along lines of race and gender. Generally, groups with a less advantaged or more vulnerable position in society worried more: Hispanics and African Americans were more concerned than whites and—consistent with past studies of response to natural hazards—women were more concerned than men. Significantly, the more worried people were about additional attacks, the less confident they were that military action would be effective in preventing such attacks (Pew Research Foundation, 2001).

These findings show that, even on an issue where a strong norm exists, as in how to respond to the September 11 terrorist attacks, the factors of race, class, gender, and other social characteristics still make real differences in many aspects of people's opinions about the issue.

---

standard English when the situation calls for it and they wish to do so. Despite its rebelliousness, hip hop still incorporates some basic American values, ranging from material consumption to a desire for fairness. Moreover, people in both groups watch some of the same television shows and eat at some of the same chain restaurants. Thus, computer geeks and even the hip hop culture of inner-city youth fit in to the larger culture in some ways. That is what makes them subcultures rather than totally independent cultures.

A subculture's norms may conflict with those of the larger society, or they may gradually filter into the larger society through the process of cultural diffusion, as has happened to some extent with both the hip hop and computer geek subcultures. They may also be largely irrelevant to the larger society, as is the case with some recreational subcultures. Although such recreational subcultures do not conflict with the larger culture, they do have distinct norms that are well understood by those familiar with the subculture but largely unknown to people outside it. For an example, see the box entitled "Drift Fishing: The Norms of a Subculture."

Jargon in Subcultures
We have already seen examples of language and symbol variation in our discussion of hip hop and computer geeks. When a subculture develops its own distinct terminology, this terminology is often referred to as jargon. Jargon has both manifest and latent functions. Its manifest function can be seen in the example of the computer geeks. There are areas of particular interest to people sharing the subculture, such as technical computer procedures, that ordinary language is not sufficiently detailed to describe easily. The professions—including sociology—also have extensive jargon, for much the same reason. Sociology, chemistry, law, medicine, and other professions involve detailed and specialized subject matter that requires precise terminology.

Besides this manifest function of describing specialized concepts, jargon has the important latent function of setting boundaries concerning who is "in" and who is "out of" a particular subculture. This process of *boundary maintenance* is important to the group identity of those who share a subculture. Thus, part of becoming accepted among the community of professional sociologists is the ability to use the jargon. Similarly, computer geeks and other recreational subcultures use knowledge of the jargon to distinguish novices and outsiders from "insiders."

Functions of Subcultures
We have already identified one of the functions of subcultures: permitting specialized activity. As we saw earlier in this chapter, the division of labor is essential in any society and becomes more so as society becomes larger and more complex. Because subcultures (particularly occupational subcultures) carry the knowledge necessary to perform specialized tasks, they are essential to the division of labor.

Identity in Mass Society. Subcultures also provide a source of identity in mass society, thus preventing feelings of isolation and **anomie** (see Chapter 3). In modern mass societies, where the same chain stores and restaurants are everywhere, and where your account number, student number, and social security number are often more important than your name, it is easy for anomie to occur (see, for example, Ritzer, 2008). People want to distinguish themselves from the crowd in order to feel that "I am somebody" (Riesman, 1961). Subcultures permit this by enabling people with a common interest, situation, or set of experiences to stand out from the crowd. They provide effective norms for the small group when the norms of the larger society seem meaningless.

Cultural Adaptation and Change. Another important function of subcultures is to serve as a *source of adaptation* in society. Recall our previous discussion of cultural lag and cultural diffusion. Often a subculture is the mechanism through which cultural diffusion occurs. In such cases, some group of people in the society—often the young, the well educated, or those at the forefront of developing new technologies—adopts a new set of values and beliefs that are better adjusted to the new realities. This group

Although hip hop culture began with African American youth in central cities, some aspects of it have been adopted by white suburban youths. This is an example of how cultural diffusion can occur within a society. (iStockphoto)

thus develops a subculture in response to the new conditions. Eventually, a process of cultural diffusion occurs within the society, and the values of this subculture spread to the larger society.

A process very much like this has taken place in the United States with respect to the roles of men and women. In today's highly technological and automated society, the notion of determining social roles by sex, which may once have had some basis in differences in physical strength, no longer makes much sense. The idea of more equal roles for men and women was first adopted by young, urban, well-educated people, particularly women (Yankelovich, 1981, 1974). Because the idea of different roles for men and women has been with us for centuries, there was considerable resistance to this new idea. Gradually, though, the notion that women belong in the workplace and can perform most jobs spread to the mainstream (Roper Organization, 1980; Yankelovich, 1981). Thus, what had been an adaptation to a new social and technological environment by a particular subculture gradually became accepted in mainstream American culture through a process of cultural diffusion.

Dysfunctions of Subcultures

Although subcultures perform important functions in society, they can also be dysfunctional. The most important potential dysfunction, from the point of view of the functionalist perspective, is that they can erode society's consensus. If a culture contains subcultures whose attitudes are too different from one another, or who are excessively at odds with the larger culture, cooperation can be inhibited. Each group may think of itself first and the concerns of the larger society only later. Hence, functionalists generally seek to place bounds on cultural diversity, opposing policies that encourage it, such as bilingual education (Glazer, 1981; Thernstrom, 1980), and criticizing social programs that emphasize group rights rather than individual rights or the needs of the larger society (Bolce and Gray, 1979; Glazer, 1976; Steele, 1990).

Culture Against Structure: The Conflict Perspective

Unlike functionalists, conflict theorists see incompatibility between culture and social structure as something more fundamental than adaptation to the society's environment. They see such incompatibilities as inherent in the nature of the society itself. As we saw, conflict theorists hold that social structure is shaped in the interests of the dominant group in the society and that it survives because of the *false consciousness* of other groups. Eventually, however, the people in the society may come to attain **class consciousness:** That is, they will recognize that their true interests do not lie in maintaining the social structure as it was created by the dominant group. In other words, they have now adopted beliefs, values, and norms that support their objective self-interests. This, of course, places their culture at odds with the social structure, and, as a group, the subordinate class is in conflict with the dominant group. To conflict theorists, this conflict offers the possibility of social change.

Class Consciousness and Symbolic Interaction

The process by which people's consciousness is altered involves communication within disadvantaged or oppressed groups, which leads people in those groups to redefine the meaning of their situation. Until rather recently, a shortcoming of conflict theories was their failure to focus sufficiently on the process by which such changes of consciousness occur. Several contemporary theorists who began as conflict theorists have set out to combine the insights of the symbolic-interactionist perspective with those of conflict theory in order to understand this process (Collins, 1981, 1985c; Giddens, 1978, 1985). These theorists point out that individual interpretations of meaning collectively define how groups view their situation. They argue that in order for us to understand such changes as shifts from false consciousness to class consciousness, we must understand the processes of communication and interpretation through which individual views of reality are changed.

Subculture as a Weapon in Group Conflict

Because class consciousness develops in groups that share a common interest among themselves (and an interest opposed to that of the dominant group), it is clear that subcultures play an important role in social change. Conflict theorists emphasize the idea that subcultures develop among groups that share a common self-interest. To the conflict theorists, the most important function of subcultures is to enable groups to act on behalf

SOCIOLOGICAL INSIGHTS
Drift Fishing: The Norms of a Subculture

Some years ago, on a fishing trip, I (Farley) received a good lesson in the extent to which recreational groups such as fishing people develop their own subcultures. At the lake where I was fishing, a method of fishing known as "drift fishing" is commonly used. Basically, drift fishing consists of fishing off the windward side of a boat that is allowed to drift with the wind. The boat will turn at a 90-degree angle to the wind direction and move sideways in the direction the wind is blowing, and the people fish as they sit facing into the wind. The motion extends the line away from the boat, and the moving bait is more attractive to the fish than a still bait would be. This fishing method also has the advantage that if the fish are concentrated in a small area, a number of boats can take their turns drifting over the "hot spot," and everyone gets a chance to catch fish as he or she passes over this spot. This method is shown in the diagram below.

On this particular day, with about half a dozen boatloads of people fishing this way and catching lots of fish over a small spot, another boatload of fishermen suddenly arrived. To everyone's surprise, they used their motor to position themselves motionless over the spot where the fish were biting—thus blocking everyone else's access to the spot. In addition, they caught very few fish, because their bait wasn't moving enough. Everyone else was angry, but nothing was said; people just left in search of another spot.

That night in the lodge, however, plenty was said. The offending boat was the main topic of conversation, as several boatloads of people at the lodge where I was staying had been fishing that spot. After a number of comments were made about the rudeness and selfishness of the people, the owner of our resort said, "Did you know those people are staying here? You know, what happened on the lake isn't really their fault. They come here every year, but they just sit in their cabin in the evening and never come to the lodge. They never talk to anyone while they're here. They just don't know they're not supposed to fish that way."

Later, when I thought about this, I realized I had gotten a free lesson in sociology. The people in the lodge belonged to the local fishing subculture and knew the rules so well that they took them for granted and assumed everyone else did,

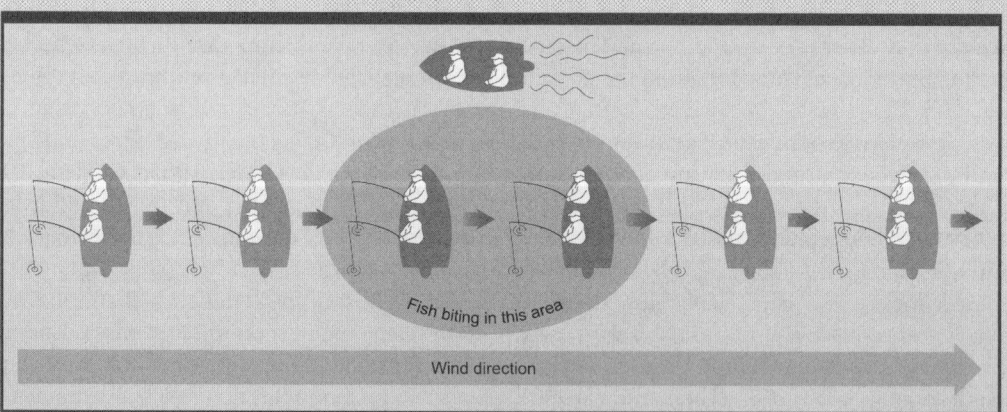

too. Hence, they (perhaps a bit ethnocentrically) defined the behavior of the other group as selfish and inconsiderate. But because the other group of people had never talked to anyone familiar with the fishing subculture, they were not part of it and had no way of knowing its norms. They probably would have been very surprised to find out that anyone was mad at them.

of a common self-interest. Consider the hip hop example again. From a functionalist perspective, this subculture would give black inner-city youth a sense of identity in a mass society. However, from a conflict perspective, hip hop does more than that. It forms a basis for people to act upon the common self-interests they share as young, poor, inner-city African Americans. Thus, hip hop becomes more than a mere source of identity in mass society; it becomes a political statement that black youth reject the dominant culture and demand the opportunity to control their own destiny. To conflict theorists, such articulation of group interests and political expression is the most important function of subcultures.

Cross-Cutting and Overlapping Cleavages

Although diversity of culture can lead to conflict in some cases, it can also help to keep conflict under control. This depends on how the various subcultures in a society divide on the basis of different issues and social characteristics. If they always divide the same way, severe conflict is likely. If they divide differently, conflict is usually more manageable. When the divisions are always the same (or very similar), a society is said to have **overlapping cleavages**: issues that divide people generally along similar lines. A good example of this is Northern Ireland. The social characteristics of ethnicity and religion divide the population almost identically, and are closely related to social class divisions. Americans think of Northern Ireland as being divided by religion: Protestants versus Catholics. However, nearly all the Protestants are of British ancestry (either Scottish or English) and nearly all the Catholics are of Irish ancestry. Moreover, the British conquered Ireland and annexed it to the United Kingdom (UK), which is the original source of the conflict. The Republic of Ireland gained its independence, but Northern Ireland remains part of the United Kingdom today. Thus, religion and nationality divide the population identically, and both divisions have their origin in force and conquest. Social class is also closely related to ethnicity, with the poorest groups being concentrated among the Irish Catholics and the wealthiest among the English-ancestry Protestants. The Scottish-ancestry Protestants fall between, and perceive themselves to be threatened by the Catholics. The result of all this is that, whether society divides along the lines of religion, ethnicity, or social class, the lines of division are much the same. Thus, Northern Ireland's subcultures were, for a long time, almost literally at war with one another.

This can be contrasted to **cross-cutting cleavages,** situations in which divisions or issues of conflict divide a society in different ways on different issues. There are ethnic differences between Catholics and Protestants in the United States, too, but here, both religions are composed of a wide diversity of ethnic groups. Irish, Italian, Polish, and Mexican American Catholics may have little in common besides their religion; in Northern Ireland, however, all Catholics share a common ethnic background. The mix of social classes is also quite similar among American Catholics and Protestants. In short, ethnicity, religion, and class all divide the American population into subcultures in *different* ways, so everyone has different loyalties, depending on the issue. This situation of cross-cutting cleavages tends to keep conflict manageable (Lipset, 1959).

Countercultures

Sometimes, particularly when cleavages are overlapping rather than cross-cutting, subcultures become so opposed to the larger culture that sociologists call them **countercultures** (Roszak, 1969; Yinger, 1982). A counterculture exists when a subculture adopts values and beliefs that are predominantly in opposition to those of the larger society. Examples of countercultures are religious cults such as the Hare Krishnas, and the Branch Davidian and Heaven's Gate cults of the 1990s. Countercultural political groups include the Ku Klux Klan and the Aryan Nations on the right and, on the left, the Weather Underground of the 1960s and 1970s and today's anarchist youth movements. The concept of counterculture also includes groups espousing radically different lifestyles, such as the Hell's Angels or the facial tattoo movement. Some groups combine lifestyle with politics, such as the hippies of the 1960s and today's "alternative" youth culture or, at the opposite end of the political spectrum, neo-Nazi skinheads. All of these groups challenge authority and the established order, and most have engaged in direct conflict with authority—sometimes with violent consequences.

At times, countercultures become widespread and influential in society, as in the 1960s when diverse groups of young people seemed to challenge nearly every social norm. Although these groups were popularly referred to as "the counterculture," it is not clear whether it was really one counterculture or many. Certainly there were some common threads that united these diverse groups—opposition to the Vietnam War; enjoyment of rock music; and new ideas concerning sexuality, the roles of minorities and women, and the recreational use of drugs. However, the diversity in this so-called counterculture was so great that it is hard to describe it as one counterculture. It is very doubtful whether middle-class college students, Black Panthers, and societal "dropouts" who used psychedelic drugs really had much in common besides challenging authority. Each of these groups had very different lifestyles, experiences, and concerns. Some, for example, were out to change society (and not always in the same ways), whereas others were simply seeking to withdraw from it (Kenniston, 1971).

It should be mentioned that some social scientists question the entire notion of countercultures. They argue that even countercultures reflect a mix of rejection and acceptance of the larger culture. Extreme rightist groups such as the Ku Klux Klan, Posse Comitatus, the Aryan Nations, and various "militia" groups may engage in violence against the police and fellow citizens, but they also carry the American flag and call themselves "true patriots." In the 1960s and early 1970s, the youth counterculture was said to be rejecting materialism and questioning technology, but you'd hardly know it by looking at the stereos and amplifiers they used to play rock music (Slater, 1970). From this perspective, these elements of acceptance and rejection of the dominant culture make it very hard to draw the line between a subculture and a counterculture. Regardless of terminology, however, the development of subcultures that at least partly oppose the larger culture is an important source of social change.

Putting Sociology to Work

Multiculturalism: A Pathway to Cooperation in a Diverse Society?

Today, more than one in three Americans is a person of color from a non-European background. This percentage will continue to grow in the coming decades for two reasons. First, the birth rate of these groups tends to be somewhat higher than that of Americans of European ancestry. Second, today's immigrants are coming mainly from Latin America, Asia, and the Caribbean, in contrast to earlier eras when most immigrants came from Europe.

It is clear that, in order to be productive, the United States must offer full opportunities to people of color to become well educated and to fill the jobs of the future, which will be more and more technically demanding. Unfortunately, patterns of discrimination and institutionalized inequality, described in greater detail in Chapter 7, have excluded many people of color—particularly African Americans, Mexican Americans, Puerto Rican Americans, and Native Americans, from such opportunities.

To combat such exclusion, many colleges and businesses have established programs in support of diversity and **multiculturalism.** Multiculturalism can be defined as a viewpoint that values and embraces cultural diversity. Such diversity is valued for several reasons. First, our society is becoming more culturally diverse, and people in all cultures value their own traditions and viewpoints. When people, in turn, feel valued by others, they are more likely to be motivated to cooperate and achieve in the school and workplace. Second, diversity frequently offers new and insightful ways of looking at a variety of subjects, which would be missed if one approached these subjects only from the viewpoint of one group.

Diversity programs are also based in part on research findings about the effects of living and working in situations dominated by a culture different from one's own. Often, this situation, along with the cultural conflicts it frequently generates, leads people of color to encounter difficulty in predominantly white workplace or school settings. They may feel unwanted and unaccepted—in some cases with good reason. These feelings have led many people of color to leave or avoid such situations, or have created tensions that have made it difficult for them to succeed. Studies have shown, for example, that social processes such as these are among the major reasons for retention problems among black college students, and that even the most successful black professionals and managers do not feel fully accepted in the places where they work (Allen et al., 1991; Zweigenhaft and Domhoff, 1991). The objective of diversity and multiculturalism programs is to encourage greater respect for people of diverse cultural backgrounds as a means of promoting both greater racial and ethnic harmony and a more hospitable workplace and school environment for people of color.

Some people—mainly social scientific functionalists and political conservatives—have criticized multiculturalism on the grounds that it encourages divisions by encouraging people to maintain their cultural differences rather than to assimilate. These critics hold that, if people would assimilate, they would have more in common with one another and would thus be more likely to cooperate. On the other hand, when people maintain greater cultural differences, the result may be conflict that divides different groups and discourages cooperation. Thus, in this view, too much cultural diversity can be dysfunctional. These critics argue that other societies with which the United States is competing, such as Japan and many European countries, are less ethnically diverse than the United States, and that this facilitates cooperation and productivity among their people. According to this view, different groups in the United States should be encouraged to assimilate into one common culture, and multiculturalism inhibits this.

There is, however, one important problem with this argument: There may be good reasons why some groups do not want to assimilate and why it may not be in their interest to do so. A variety of researchers have pointed out that groups whose original entry into a society is not voluntary nearly always resist giving up their own values and lifestyles in favor of those of the majority (Blauner, 1972; Lieberson, 1980; Zweigenhaft and Domhoff, 1991). Such groups have almost always been historically oppressed, and they do not want to accept the values of a group that has discriminated against them and economically exploited them. Moreover, conflict theorists argue that it may not be in their interests to do so; it may be a case of the false consciousness discussed earlier in this chapter. In the United States, most people of color fall into this category. African Americans, Mexican Americans, Puerto Ricans, and Native Americans all were, historically speaking, brought under American rule involuntarily and subjected to widespread discrimination and economic exploitation. Only Asian Americans originally came to the United States voluntarily, and they are indeed more culturally assimilated than other Americans of color. Hence, whatever the theoretical merits of a society with cultural consensus, it may be unrealistic to expect that to occur for many groups in the United States given its history.

In part because cultural consensus is unlikely to occur in a society as diverse as the United States, the overall society's productivity will increase if people from all groups learn to work and cooperate with others from different cultural backgrounds. In order for this to happen, research and experience suggest that workplace diversity programs must address the fears and perceptions of the dominant group, that is, of white males. All of us tend to generalize to others from the experience of our own group. White Americans, for example, often assume that the experiences of other groups are similar to their own—in other words, fairly open to opportunity and relatively free of discrimination (Kluegel, 1990; Schuman and Krysan, 1999; Gallup Organization, 2001). For this reason, they often perceive multiculturalism, affirmative action, and other diversity programs as conferring special favors for minorities. But if they are shown ways in which others do not have the same opportunities they enjoy, white Americans will often become more supportive of efforts to increase opportunity and address inequality. Accordingly, studies have found that the more that whites perceive that equal opportunity is not a reality for people of color, the more likely they are to support affirmative action and similar diversity initiatives (Kluegel, 1990; Herring et al., 2000). For this reason, making members of the majority group more aware of the different experiences of other groups may be a crucial step toward greater social harmony (Advisory Board to the President's Initiative on Race, 1998). In fact, such heightened awareness of the experiences of others has been a key aspect of successful diversity plans at Monsanto and other companies (Galagan, 1993). In addition, it makes a difference in majority workers' attitudes when employers take a strong stand in support of diversity. For example, whites who have had the greatest personal contact with affirmative action in their own workplaces are the most supportive of it (Taylor, 1995), and the same appears to be true with respect to college students and affirmative action on campus (Bowen and Bok, 1998).

The real question, then, may come down to people's ability to respect and understand cultural and experiential differences, which will help them to cooperate despite such differences. Initial successes with cultural diversity programs in such companies as Monsanto and Kodak suggest that these programs can help to bring about such cooperation if it is made clear that it is valued and expected by the organization. Research has shown that as people become more educated and as society continues to urbanize, the tendency is for people to become more accepting of diversity (Tuch, 1987). Thus, the present social context may well be creating an environment favorable to the success of programs like those at Monsanto and Kodak.

We turn now to a broader discussion of American culture, with which we shall conclude the chapter.

American Culture

Core American Values and Beliefs

What are the beliefs and values associated with American culture, and how do they differ from those of other cultures? A number of sociologists have addressed this question and have achieved a fairly broad consensus on some of the core values and beliefs that are shared by the majority of Americans. Table 4.3 lists some of the most basic American values.

Ideal Versus Real Culture

The core values contained in Table 4.3 raise certain questions and issues. Clearly, some of these values conflict with others. For example, our humanitarian belief in helping the "deserving poor" is not always compatible with our emphasis on self-sufficiency and our disdain for "welfare." To resolve this tension, our society continually distinguishes between those we consider to be victims of misfortune and those we feel are responsible for their situation, however unfortunate it might be.

In examining this list you might also have concluded that our actions, both as individuals and as a nation, frequently do not reflect these values. Although we claim to believe in equal opportunity, we have erected numerous obstacles, such as racism, sexism, and poverty, that prevent entire sections of the population from competing on equal terms (Myrdal, 1944). We consider ourselves a "freedom-loving" people, but we sometimes prevent dissenters from expressing unpopular views, and our government has supported, and in some cases helped to install, authoritarian regimes throughout the world. These examples illustrate the gap between **ideal culture**, the norms and beliefs that a people accept in principle, and **real culture**, those norms and principles that are actually practiced (Myrdal, 1944). Look again at Table 4.3. What other discrepancies between real and ideal culture can you think of?

As was previously suggested, there is evidence of some change in American core values over the past three decades. Some sociologists see the 1960s and 1970s as a time in which some key American values underwent rather fundamental change. We shall conclude our discussion of American culture by looking at some of these changes.

Recent Changes in American Values and Beliefs

Seeds of Cultural Change: The 1960s and Early 1970s

In large part, the social and political activism of the 1960s and early 1970s developed out of opposition in a large segment of the population to the Vietnam War and racism within U.S. society. This activism was most pronounced among young, well-educated children of the middle class (particularly college students) and minority-group members (Bensman and Vidich, 1984, Chap. 16). These two groups, of course, had somewhat different concerns, but they did share a sense of rebellion against the system, and they were targets of efforts by the government to restore order and repress dissent. Thus, both middle-class college youth and minority-group activists increasingly thought in terms of "us versus them," creating a situation in which it was easy to challenge a wide variety of cultural norms, values, and beliefs.

Before long, issues of conflict in American society had expanded from war and racism to include the roles of men and women; norms about sexuality, drug use, and the importance of work; the role of authority; and such cultural elements as music, style of dress, and hair length. There was a surge of political activism, both in the traditional

Table 4.3 Core American Values and Beliefs

Values	Beliefs
Freedom	Belief in personal rights, as expressed in the Bill of Rights of the U.S. Constitution, and the need to extend and defend these rights around the world.
Democracy	The belief that people should be free to choose their own government and that government decisions should be a product of the public will.
Individualism and individual responsibility	The belief that success and failure are individual, and not governmental or societal, responsibilities. People should support themselves and their families and not rely on "welfare."
Religion and morality	A concern with issues of rights and wrong, which permeates most political issues. Might reflect the fact that Americans are more religious than most industrialized peoples.
Science and technology	The belief in solving problems through the application of scientific knowledge.
Equality of opportunity	The belief that all people should have the chance to succeed according to their own abilities, rather than because of special privileges.
Competition	Strong belief in outperforming others, as expressed by current rhetoric concerning the "failure" of U.S. schools and businesses to compete with foreign nations.
Work ethic	A major emphasis on achievement through hard work. Tied to the idea that success is measured in terms of material wealth.
Humanitarianism	Belief in assisting "deserving poor" as well as the victims of serious diseases and natural disasters (flood, famines, earthquakes).
Practicality	Americans value those things they consider "useful." Business and the natural sciences are seen as more valuable than the humanities and social sciences.
Nationalism	Americans are highly patriotic and frequently label as "un-American" ideas that violate the public ethos.
Romantic love	Marriage is associated with romance and love. Differs from preindustrial societies, where marriage was often seen as an economic arrangement.
Sexual restriction	Despite changes in attitudes toward sexuality, Americans maintain more restrictive attitudes toward sex than most Western (and many non-Western) nations.

Sources: Ford and Beach, 1951; Henslin, 1975; Jones et al., 1986; Kluegel and Smith, 1986; Myrdal, 1944; Williams, 1970.

electoral arena (as young people campaigned for Eugene McCarthy, Robert Kennedy, and George McGovern) and in less traditional forms such as teach-ins, marches, sit-ins, boycotts, and, occasionally, riots.

Cultural Diffusion and Lasting Effects: The 1980s to the New Century

By the late 1970s, the counterculture appeared to have faded. Young people returned to their historic pattern of low voting rates and limited political participation. The election of Ronald Reagan in 1980 and 1984 brought an era of conservatism, and many young people were among Reagan's strongest supporters. Nonetheless, the effect of the youth and minority subcultures of the 1960s has been lasting. By the early 1970s new values in the areas of gender roles, race relations, human sexuality, and self-fulfillment had spread from college students into the larger group of noncollege youth (Yankelovich, 1974). These values continued to spread to the point that they became the dominant point of view among nonelderly adults by the beginning of the 1980s (Yankelovich, 1981), a classic example of cultural diffusion. Moreover, by the 1990s, many of the values and lifestyles of the 1960s—now popularly referred to as "alternative"—were enjoying resurgent popularity among young people, and issues such as the environment, racism, and women's rights were receiving renewed attention. This trend was evident in the 1999 "battle in Seattle," a massive and disruptive protest against the World Trade Organization over issues of environmental degradation, exploitation of labor, and world economic inequality.

In 1992 and 1996, the election of Bill Clinton and Al Gore, who stressed multicultural unity and environmental issues and played rock music at campaign rallies, occurred with strong support of younger voters. In the year 2000, youth support was split among the Democrat, Al Gore, the Republican, George W. Bush, and the Green Party candidate, Ralph Nader. Nader, whose campaign centered around issues of environmental and labor concerns and the abuse of corporate power, drew much of his support from college students. Despite receiving only a single-digit percentage of the vote, Nader drew campaign rally crowds, composed largely of college students, that were as large as those of Bush and Gore. Young people were also enthusiastic supporters of Barak Obama in the 2008 election, giving him "rock star" turnouts at his rallies. His opponents even tried to use this against him, implying that he was a "celebrity" with no substance behind his rhetoric. The extent to which these events indicate renewed political activism among young people is uncertain, since annual surveys of college freshmen continue to indicate that many are uninvolved and uninterested in politics. For example, only 15 to 30 percent of freshmen saw influencing the political structure, keeping up to date with politics, helping to promote racial understanding, or becoming involved in programs to clean up the environment as important goals (American Council on Education and Higher Education Research Institute, 2000). However, despite this, an increasing number of those under the age of thirty is voting, and the partisan advantage in this group had risen to a 2–1 Democratic advantage as of 2008 (Page, 2008). It is clear that in many areas of life, the influence of the cultural rebellion of the 1960s has been lasting. In fact, the clash between the new values of the 1960s and older, more traditional values has become a dominant theme in American political debates (Dionne, 1991), as illustrated by debates in recent presidential campaigns over issues such as "freedom of choice" and "family values."

Rights of Racial and Ethnic Groups

When Robin Williams published the third edition of his *American Society* in 1970, it still listed *group superiority* as one of the fifteen core American values. Although this idea has not disappeared from American thought, it would be hard to list it as a core value in today's America. Survey instruments of all types indicate that most Americans reject notions of one group being superior to another and in principle support racial integration and oppose deliberate acts of segregation and discrimination. Contrast these responses to 1968, when only 60 percent agreed that "white children and black children should attend the same schools." In contrast, by the 1980s, 89 percent agreed (Skolnick, 1969; National Opinion Research Center, 1983). This does not mean we have eliminated racial inequality or have developed the attitudes necessary to accomplish that goal (see Chapter 7). In fact, our attitudes remain conflicted, despite real changes. For example, by the late 1990s, the majority of white Americans responding to surveys indicated approval of marriages between blacks and whites for the first time ever (Gallup Organization, 1997a). But at the same time, in-depth interviews of people who indicate such approval on surveys show that when given the opportunity to express their views in more detail, many whites do indicate serious reservations or problems with interracial marriage (Bonilla-Silva and Forman, 2000). As shown in Harry Edwards's "Personal Journey into Sociology," on page 113, racial inequality persists even in areas such as sport that are seen as sources of opportunity for minority groups. The trendline in public opinion, however, does indicate a substantial, if less than total, shift over time in attitudes and beliefs. For instance, as we explore in Chapters 8 and 12, a significant minority of whites (and a majority in many of the Northeast, upper Midwest and Far West states) voted for president Barack Obama in the 2008 election, demonstrating the willingness to support an African American president.

Gender Roles

A similar shift has occurred in American beliefs about the roles of men and women. Most Americans today, for example, reject the notion that the woman's place is in the home, and in principle, they support equal pay for equal work. In fact, work outside the home for pay, not the housewife role, has become the norm for most American women. Some, though not all, historically male professions have witnessed a major surge in the number of women seeking and gaining entry. By the late 1990s, for example, over two-fifths of medical school graduates and law school graduates were female (Chronicle of Higher Education, 2001b). As in the case of race relations, attitudes have in many ways outstripped reality when it comes to attaining real social equality for men and women. The important point, though, is that today the norms support the idea of equal opportunity for women; as recently as three decades ago, they did not.

Moreover, despite the gaps between attitude and reality, changes in attitudes about both gender

Many jobs that were once considered male-only are now open to women. However, it is still common for women and men to be segregated in separate occupations. In education, women predominate in the lower grades, where pay, benefits, and work autonomy are less generous. (iStockphoto)

and race have made a significant difference in American political life. For example, Brooks (2000) has recently demonstrated with survey data that these attitude changes were critical to the outcome of the presidential elections in the 1990s, when Democrat Bill Clinton was twice elected to the presidency: Had there been no attitude change on race and gender after 1972, Clinton would have lost in both 1992 and 1996. In fact, had there been no change in attitudes on race and gender after 1972, Brooks's (2000) research indicates that the Democrats would have lost *every election* after 1972; in reality, they won three of the six presidential elections between 1976 and 1996, and of course, an African American was elected president for the first time in 2008.

Human Sexuality
Although the "free love" mentality of the 1960s was on its way out even before the AIDS epidemic, the "sexual revolution" has had a lasting legacy. Today, marriage is no longer a prerequisite for having sex. The majority of Americans today do not object to a sexual relationship between two unmarried people who love and care about each other. As recently as 1969, a Gallup poll showed that two-thirds of Americans viewed premarital sex as "wrong"; just five years later, 80 percent of men and 70 percent of women believed that premarital sex was permissible under at least some conditions (Hunt, 1974). The practice of unmarried men and women living together, which once brought social ostracism, is commonplace today, with perhaps the majority of couples who eventually marry cohabiting first. Another major change is the much greater acceptance of divorce and remarriage. Similarly, in 1996, an overwhelming proportion of Americans opposed gay marriage (65 percent). Today, that number has fallen to 53 percent (Pew Research Center, 2009). As recently as 2003, more Americans opposed civil unions for gays and lesbians than supported (47 percent to 45 percent), but in recent years, those numbers have moved sharply in favor with 57 percent supporting compared to just 37 percent opposed (Pew Research Center, 2009). Thus, even if American sex norms remain restrictive compared with those in other industrialized countries, they are far less restrictive than they were just thirty years ago.

Self-Fulfillment
What some people regard as the most fundamental of all the value changes is a greatly increased emphasis upon self-fulfillment (Yankelovich, 1981; Bellah et al., 1985). Self-fulfillment represents a different form of individualism than has traditionally characterized American culture. The self-fulfillment norm emphasizes attaining your potential, but not in the economic sense of maximizing wealth. Rather, you attain your potential to know yourself, to attain a higher consciousness, to perfect a skill, or to experience the world. Thus, work becomes important not as an end in itself but as a means to self-fulfillment. The goal becomes to have a fulfilling job or a job that provides income to support activities (such as travel, sports participation, or creative pursuits) that bring self-fulfillment. The growth of such activities as "adventure travel" and "extreme sports" reflects this trend, as do the massive industries that have developed around "self-help" and "personal growth."

Based on survey research, Yankelovich (1981) estimated that about 80 percent of the U.S.

population had been affected by this new norm by the beginning of the 1980s; about one in six considered it the dominant force in their lives. As you might expect, different social observers view this and other new norms differently. Many functionalists have argued that the search for self-fulfillment has caused parents to be irresponsible toward their children; husbands and wives to be irresponsible toward each other; and workers to be irresponsible toward their jobs (Etzioni, 1982; Packard, 1983; Popenoe, 1988; see also Bell, 1976). In all these cases, they argue that people place fulfilling experiences ahead of meeting responsibilities, so key social functions go unfulfilled.

Conflict theorists, in contrast, argue that the decline of racism and sexism in part reflects the fact that these discriminations are seen as barriers to people's self-fulfillment. They also argue that a deemphasis on the maximization of wealth could lessen the greed that leads people to exploitation. Finally, they note that the search for self-fulfillment is an effort to extend to everyone the opportunities that once were reserved for a small, privileged group.

PERSONAL JOURNEYS INTO SOCIOLOGY
The Sociology of Sport

Harry Edwards

From my earliest days as a graduate student in the Department of Sociology at Cornell University, I have considered myself a scholar-activist. Over the ensuing years, my career in sociology has coalesced into virtually a seamless tapestry of academic and activist pursuits and projects.

It now seems clear, in retrospect, that two principal influences propelled me along my established path of professional development. First, there were my experiences growing up Black, poor, and athletically inclined in East St. Louis, Illinois, at the dawn of both the Civil Rights movement and the age of televised, racially integrated sports. This convergence of history and biography had an enduring impact upon my perceptions of myself and what I eventually came to define as priority challenges.

Second, I was profoundly influenced by significant others. Initially, these were highly accomplished Black men and women who lived and worked in my community and who took the time and had the patience to become involved with me as informal mentors and counselors. Later the significant others in my life came to be mostly people with whom I had no personal contact at all, but who had achieved levels of excellence that gave direction to my own aspirations and goals. E. Franklin Frazier, W. E. B. Du Bois, Paul Robeson, C. Wright Mills, Malcolm X, Richard Wright, Martin Luther King, Jr., Bill Russell, Maya Angelou, and James Baldwin, along with other writers, academicians, political activists, and athletes, became my role models during my intellectually and politically formative years as an undergraduate sociology major and scholarship student-athlete at San Jose State University in California.

It was against this background that I developed my interest in relationships between sport and society in general, and between race and sport in particular. Following completion of my master's degree and a good deal of research into the role, status, and circumstances of Black people in American sport, I organized a movement among Black athletes aimed at dramatizing the widespread, deeply rooted social inequities in American domestic and international sports. In domestic sport, this effort culminated in what was popularly termed "the Revolt of the Black Athlete" during the 1960s. This "revolt" was manifested in a series of incidents occurring on more than 100 traditionally White college campuses across the nation, where Black athletes and their student supporters, threatening boycotts and disruptions of athletic events, made demands upon campus administrators for more equitable treatment and opportunities for Blacks involved in their sports programs. At the international level, the movement produced "The Olympic Project for Human Rights," which proposed a Black American boycott of the 1968 Mexico City Olympic Games. The OPHR was also the motivating force behind the demonstration atop the Olympic podium by Tommie Smith and John Carlos during the victory ceremonies for medalists in the 200-meter dash.

Following the 1968 Olympics, I returned to Cornell University to complete a Ph.D. in sociology and subsequently joined the faculty of the Department of Sociology at the University of California at Berkeley. One important product of my work is what I term "the first principle of the sociology of sport": Sport inevitably recapitulates the character, dynamics, and structure of human and institutional relationships within and between societies and the ideological sentiments and values that rationalize those relationships. In sum, a society with longstanding, ongoing traditions of discrimination and inequality inevitably exhibits powerful strains of inequity in its sports institution. In the case of the United States, then, institutional racism within professional and college sports is inextricably intertwined with the broader Black experience in America. It has been the recognition of the impact and implications of this interpenetration and interdependence that has led me to take on my late career challenge as Director of Parks and Recreation for the City of Oakland, California.

But this is by no means to suggest that sport is either static or that it functions at every turn in some mechanically reactive lock-step fashion with developments in the broader society. *Rather, sport is a dynamic institutional component of the social system that both influences and is influenced by society.* A prime example of this is the nature of the relationship between the deteriorating societal circumstances of African American youths, on the one hand, and the strong emphasis that Blacks historically have placed upon sports participation and achievement, on the other.

For decades, Black families have been far more likely than White families to push their children toward sports-career aspirations, often to the neglect and detriment of other critically important areas of personal and cultural development, largely because of: (1) a longstanding, widely held, racist, and ill-informed presumption of innate, race-linked Black athletic superiority and intellectual deficiency, (2) media propaganda about sports as a broadly accessible route to Black social and economic mobility, and (3) a lack of comparably visible, high-prestige Black role models beyond the sports arena. Indeed, this single-minded pursuit of sports fame and fortune eventually evolved into what, for more than twenty years, I adamantly claimed to be an institutionalized *triple tragedy* in Black society: the tragedy of thousands upon thousands of Black youths in obsessive pursuit of sports goals that the overwhelming majority of them will never attain; the tragedy of the personal and cultural underdevelopment that afflicts so many successful and unsuccessful Black sports aspirants; and the tragedy of cultural and institutional underdevelopment in Black society overall, partially as a consequence of the *talent drain* toward sports and away from other vital areas of career emphasis, such as medicine, law, economics, politics, education, and technical fields.

Now, in the wake of hard-won civil rights advances, some realistic, broad-spectrum Black access to legitimate means of personal and career development evolved sufficiently to generate a Black middle class estimated by some to constitute more than a third of the Black population. This segment of the Black community became increasingly more distinct not only in terms of its material success but in its values and the nature of its institutional involvement—including a diminution of its emphasis and involvement in sport. Its criticisms and admonitions warning of a Black *overemphasis* on sports participation and achievement were valid and justified so long as opportunities for socioeconomic mobility *outside* of sport were evidently viable and expanding. However, in recent years there has developed a serious decline not only in the *fact* but in the *perception* and even the *hope* of mainstream life choices and life chances for increasing numbers of Black youths in particular. A spiraling deterioration in broad sectors of Black society—encompassing the functionality of the family, education, the economy, the political infrastructure, and even the Black church—has combined with the substantial abandonment of the Black community by the Black middle class, the ongoing legacies of anti-Black racism in America, the erosion of civil rights gains such as affirmative action, and structural economic shifts in the broader society, to spawn epidemics of crime, drugs, violence, gang warfare, and a pervasive despair and hopelessness in many Black communities. In such environments, literally thousands of Black youths have institutionally, culturally, and interpersonally "disconnected": they attend school only infrequently, if at all; and seek respect from only their closest peers; they have given up hope of ever holding a legitimate job and, often, even of living beyond their teens or twenties—some even go so far as to pick out their coffins and the clothes in which they expect to be buried.

Frequently, however, owing to the pervasive overemphasis on sports achievement in the Black community, even these otherwise dispirited, disconnected youths *still like to play sports*. And this fact may be both the Black community's and the broader society's last best hope of communication and outreach to them. Without their sports involvement, there may well be no "hook" or "handle" by which society can secure a hold upon these young people in order to pull them back from the abyss of hopelessness and futurelessness.

Unfortunately, (though predictably, given that sport is a constituent institutional component of society) sports participation opportunities for these youths have also deteriorated, right along with other aspects of their institutional and cultural opportunity structure. Playgrounds, sandlots, parks, and even backyard recreational sites have been taken over by drug dealers, or they have become battlegrounds in gang disputes. Budget cutbacks and shifts in school funding from athletic to academic programs and to concerns such as classroom security have further narrowed sports participation opportunities. In the face of it all, many Black youths have opted to go with the flow, too often exchanging team colors for gang colors or simply dropping out of everything and "hanging out," "chillin'."

So while in the past I have resoundingly rejected the priority of playbooks over textbooks, today there is no option but to recognize that for increasing legions of Black youths, the issue is neither textbooks nor playbooks—*it is survival and finding a source of hope, encouragement, and support in developing their lives and building legitimate careers and futures*. Without question, the ultimate resolution to this situation lies with the overall institutional development of Black communities and with the creation of greater opportunity for Black youths in the broader society. But, in the meanwhile, if community and school sports programs can provide a means of reconnecting with at least some of those Black youths who have already lost or who are on the verge of "dropping out," then these programs deserve our strongest endorsement. Therefore, I now say that we must reconstitute and broaden access to school sports programs. Create secure and supervised playgrounds, park recreation areas, and community sports facilities. Open school sports facilities for supervised weekend community use, and bring in "midnight" basketball, volleyball, tennis, bowling, badminton, swimming, and other sports opportunities. Recruit counselors, teachers, people trained in the trades, health care professionals, and religious leaders to advise, mentor, and tutor young people at these sports sites. Network with corporate and government agencies to establish apprenticeships and job opportunities. And bring in role models who can articulate the great lessons that sports involvement offers and relate them to the life circumstances of Black youth.

The circumstances of Black males are particularly germane here. Currently, nationally at least a quarter of all Black males aged 16 to 29 are under control of the court system. One-third of all the deaths in this group nationally are homicides—usually perpetrated by other Black males. And since the age range 16 to 29 represents the prime years of self-development and career establishment, it should be no surprise that Black males are declining as a proportion of the population in virtually every institutional setting, (for example, higher education, the workforce, the church)—except the prison system. And, predictably, Black sports involvement is threatened as well. In short, we are dispiriting, jailing, and burying an increasing number of our Black potential football players, basketball players, baseball players, and other prospective athletes—right along with our Black potential lawyers, doctors, teachers, and government leaders.

Also pertinent here is the situation of Black youths who have successfully developed their athletic skills only to find themselves underdeveloped academically and unable to compete in the classroom. Despite their educational deficiencies, these athletes typically have been recruited by major Division I colleges because their talents are so critical to the success of revenue-producing sports programs, most notably basketball and football. The predictable result has been widespread Black athlete academic underdevelopment and outright failure at the Division I level. It was this tragedy along with the attention it generated from sports activists and the media that ultimately prompted the most far-reaching reform efforts in modern collegiate sports history. *But because Black athlete academic problems are in large part rooted in and intertwined with Black youths' societal circumstances more generally, there can be no effective resolution of the educational circumstances of Black athletes at any academic level except in coordination with comparable efforts in society.*

A great many Black athletes never graduate from the institutions that they represent in sport. And an unconscionable proportion of those who do manage to graduate still do so in less marketable "jock majors." Thus, principally because they ignore the societal circumstances within which Black athletes' educational problems are rooted, the recent sport-related "academic reforms" such as NCAA Propositions 48 and 92 and high school rules mandating "no pass-no play," have hurt rather than helped Black athletes because in the final analysis, these measures have diminished Black athletic *and* academic opportunities.

The diminution of Black opportunities at the high school and collegiate levels must inevitably impact the quality of sports competition at all levels in those sports in which Blacks compete in numbers. This can be seen in that collegiate and professional sports are slumping statistically, as was discussed at the beginning of this box.

And there are also other developments that individually and of themselves would seem of little significance but appear more troubling when considered within the context of emerging trends in Black sports involvement. For example, Black attendance at team sporting events other than basketball and football games is negligible or nonexistent. And as ticket prices continue to increase and more leagues and teams choose pay-per-view and cable television broadcast options, ever fewer numbers of Blacks will be watching these sports either in person or on television. With declining personal access and exposure to elite athletic performances and with school and community sports and recreation programs and opportunities also on the decline, both sports interest and involvement are likely to wane among Black youth in the lower class and working class which have traditionally produced the greater proportion of athletes in Black society.

Today it must be understood that it is no longer a simple straightforward, Black and White issue of racism obstructing Blacks' involvement in sports. Now there is a burgeoning confluence of diverse factors and developments both within and beyond the sports realm that threaten Black sports participation. And, as there is no single cause for this situation, so there is no unified opinion as to how it should be corrected. Some of the more serious thinkers continue to advocate that Blacks de-emphasize and even abandon their sports participation and instead cultivate alternative routes of personal and career development. But does anyone seriously propose to tell a developing Barry Bonds, Jerry Rice, Michael Jordan, Charles Barkley, Karl Malone, Muhammed Ali, Michael Johnson, or Kareem Abdul-Jabbar that he would be better off de-emphasizing or abandoning his sports dreams? And since these great athletes at the beginning of their sports participation were probably indistinguishable from other young aspirants to sports stardom, if the intention is to urge a change of career aspirations and focus on those who could not succeed in sport, by what calculus would one distinguish potential failures from potential stars?

In sum, I believe that reality now dictates reassessment of the unqualified perception of the Black *overemphasis* on sport as a *problem*. Rather, on balance, it constitutes more of a *virtue—and perhaps one more vital than at any time in the past*. Those who would counsel or celebrate a de-emphasis or curtailment of Black sports aspirations and involvement today are quite simply *behind the times*, seriously misreading the facts of Black life and reality, or both. Black youths' obsession with sports has been transformed from a priority problem to what for many is nothing less than a last-chance virtue.

Far from de-emphasizing or abandoning sport, Black people must *now more than ever* learn to more intelligently and constructively manage their responsibilities in the complex and convoluted realities at the interface of race, sport, and society. Here a solid beginning would be to recognize that Black sports participation need not become obsession or blind pursuit and preoccupation. Today it is desirable, even necessary, that Black youths and Black society as a whole continue to dream of achieving excellence in elite sports—there is much to be learned here from both the challenges of elite competition and the experiences of meeting those challenges. *But all involved must learn to dream with their eyes open*, always remaining fully cognizant of sports' pitfalls, of its potential as a *dead end trap* no less than its promise as a vehicle for outreach and advancement.

In the 1930s, Paul Robeson, Joe Louis, and Jesse Owens led the fight for Black *legitimacy* as athletes. In the late 1940s and into the 1950s, Jackie Robinson, Althea Gibson, Larry Doby, Roy Campenella, and others struggled to secure Black *access* to the mainstream of American sports. From the late 1950s through the 1960s and into the 1970s, Jim Brown, Bill Russell, Curt Flood, Tommie Smith and John Carlos, Muhammed Ali, Arthur Ashe, Kareem Abdul-Jabbar, Michael Warren, and Lucius Allen fought to secure *dignity* and *respect* for Blacks in sports. Even as all of these battles continued, by the 1980s we had embarked upon yet another phase of the struggle—the battle for minority access to power and decision-making authority in front-office executive-level roles in American sport.

At the onset of the twenty-first century, we are confronted with yet another dimension of the Black struggle in sport and one that might well be the most difficult, complicated, and convoluted ever to emerge at the confluence of race, sport, and society. This challenge pits the obsessive sports dreams of Black youths against the critically vital imperative that a way be found to assure that increasing numbers of young Black people will not give up on life's possibilities altogether. Ironically, it appears to be the case that these youths' obsession with achieving stardom through ever more threatened and tenuous sports opportunities is the only hook by which they can be pulled back from the abyss. It is the resolution of this conundrum that must now be a main focus of attention and concern, not the mere straightforward facts of Black overemphasis on sport or of continuing anti-Black discrimination and racism within the sport institution.

Source: By permission of the author, Harry Edwards, Ph.D., University of California, Berkeley.

Harry Edwards Because all cultures practice some sort of athletic activity, sociologists study sports to gain insights into the values, behaviors, and social structure of a people. Perhaps no individual is as closely identified with this area of study as Professor Harry Edwards. Over the years he has been hired by professional sports teams and organizations, including the San Francisco '49ers and the Office of the Commissioner of Major League Baseball as a consultant on a broad range of problems potentially having an impact on goal achievement in the sports world. He has also taught at the University of California at Berkeley since 1970, and has served as Director of Parks and Recreation in the City of Oakland, California.

Summary

In this chapter, we have seen that every society has a culture and a social structure that are closely linked to each other. Culture consists of common knowledge, beliefs, values, and norms, whereas social structure consists of a set of social arrangements. These arrangements consist of interlinked social positions organized into a set of institutions. Each social position, or status, carries behavioral expectations known as roles. Social positions also carry unequal rewards, which are a part of society's system of stratification by which scarce resources are distributed unequally.

Both functionalists and conflict theorists agree, for different reasons, that culture and social structure are usually in harmony with each other, but sometimes at odds. The functionalist perspective sees social structure and culture as meeting basic needs, the specifics of which depend largely on the society's outside environment. For this reason harmony between the culture and the social structure is important. To conflict theorists the social structure is seen as providing disproportionate wealth and reward to the dominant group, or ruling class. Culture serves the function of justifying this privileged position. Its success in doing so is illustrated by false consciousness: the tendency of disadvantaged groups to accept the dominant group's ideology, even though it is against their self-interests to do so.

According to functionalists, culture and structure can become imbalanced with respect to each other through the combination of structural change and cultural lag. Cultural diffusion resulting from contact with another society can bring a similar result. When this happens, either the culture or the structure must change to restore the balance, but must not change so much that key functions can no longer be performed. Conflict theorists, in contrast, see opportunities for society to change and improve when culture and social structure become incompatible. Often this occurs when subordinate groups attain class consciousness: They become aware of their true interests and reject the dominant group's ideology.

Both the functionalist and conflict perspectives recognize the importance of subcultures, which arise among groups in society with some shared experience that is different from that of others in the society. Through cultural diffusion, the values of subcultures can spread into the larger society; thus, subcultures are important sources of cultural change. This has been the case in the United States, as certain values that began with youth and minority subcultures have spread into the larger culture. Still, a number of enduring features distinguish American culture from the cultures even of other industrial, democratic societies.

Key Terms

social structure
society
culture
nonmaterial culture
material culture
language
symbol
linguistic relativity
ideology
norms
folkways
mores
laws
status
ascribed status
achieved status
master status
role conflict
role strain
role set
division of labor
stratification
social institution
ethnocentrism
cultural relativism
economic structure
ideational superstructure
false consciousness
schemas
resources
cultural lag
cultural diffusion
subculture
anomie
class consciousness
overlapping cleavages
cross-cutting cleavages

counterculture
multiculturalism
ideal culture
real culture

Exercises

1. *Values* are a very important ingredient of any culture. In American society over the past decade or so, there has been a resurgence of interest in "traditional values." Some religious organizations have called for a return to a more conservative and traditional way of thinking.

   - What does the phrase "traditional values" mean to you? How do you feel about "traditional values" in our society? Do you favor an emphasis on such values? Why or why not?

   - Find a copy of the short story *The Lottery* by Shirley Jackson. Read this story, keeping in mind the concept of traditional values. Why do you think the townspeople created the lottery in the first place? Why do they still use it? What, if anything, is Jackson saying about traditional values? Do you think that the value system within American culture is on shaky ground? Why or why not?

2. *Gender stereotypes* are a controversial element within our culture. The cultural messages that are sent to males and females regarding masculinity and femininity continue to be a concern for parents as they rear their children.

   - In your judgment, what are the major gender stereotypes that are present in American culture?
   - Are gender stereotypes an inherent part of culture, or can they be changed?

Chapter 5
Socialization

Becoming "Human" Through Socialization — 121
  Learning About Norms and Social Roles   121
Theories of Socialization and Development — 121
  Nature Versus Nurture   121
  Interactionist Theories of Socialization: Mead and Cooley   123
  Theories About Social Expectations and
      Personal Dilemmas: Freud and Erikson   125
  Cognitive Development Theories of Socialization:
      Piaget and Kohlberg   127
  Overview of Theories of Socialization   133
Agents of Socialization — 133
  The Family   133
  Schools   135
  Religion   135
  Peers   135
  The Media   136
  How Socialization Works   137
  Conflicting Messages   138
Socialization in Adulthood — 140
  Life-Cycle Roles   140
  Role Change, Adult Socialization, and Stress   142
  Resocialization in Total Institutions   142
Functionalist and Conflict Perspectives on Socialization — 143
  The Functionalist Perspective   143
  The Conflict Perspective   144
Summary — 147
Key Terms — 147
Exercises — 148

Human history abounds with legends of lost or deserted children who were raised by wild animals. Legend has it, for example, that Rome was founded by Romulus and Remus, who had been raised in the wild by a wolf. More recently, in the 1970s, CBS News anchor Walter Cronkite once reported that a child in Africa had been raised by monkeys. Legend and reality are quite different, however. Very few such cases have ever been authenticated. Cronkite, for example, was obliged to report the next night that news reporters had been unable to verify the story about the child raised by monkeys. However, one case that may be real involves two children, later named Amala and Kamala, who were found by Reverend J. A. L. Singh in 1920 in a jungle in India (Candland, 1995). The two girls were found living in a cave with wolf cubs, apparently being cared for by wolves. The older of the two girls, who survived for several years, was about eight when she was discovered; the younger girl was under two. Both to some degree behaved like the animals they lived with, baring their teeth at humans and making threatening sounds. About a year after they were found, both girls became ill with diarrhea and dysentery, and the younger girl died. The older girl survived and lived for eight more years, and over a period of several years, developed a very limited vocabulary of about thirty words. While they were words in the sense of referring to particular objects, they were not English words like those used by the children around her in the orphanage where she had been placed. In this regard and many others, she became somewhat socialized into human society, but only in a very limited way. And, like many isolated children, she did not survive to adulthood.

More common than children raised by animals are cases in which children are raised in isolation, locked alone in rooms by cruel, inattentive, or mentally ill parents. These isolated children are sometimes called "feral children" (wild children) because, like Amala and Kamala and the legendary Romulus and Remus, they were raised essentially without human contact. Like Amala and Kamala, but, unlike the legend of Romulus and Remus, such children usually are unable to participate in human society in a normal way.

One recent case is that of "Genie" (Curtiss, 1977; Pines, 1981). She had been kept harnessed to a potty seat until the age of thirteen in a small room in a California house, hidden away to avoid the wrath of her father, who hated children. She was fed only milk and baby food, and was never spoken to by anyone. Occasionally, in fits of rage, her father beat her, usually when she tried to speak or made noise. After her mother fled with her, following a fight with her father, she was discovered and placed in a children's hospital. At that time, Genie could not stand straight, chew, or see beyond ten feet. She blew her nose into the air and urinated and masturbated in the presence of others. Like Kamala, she was later able to learn a few words and also used a few phrases. However, she did not learn to ask questions or speak sentences. She did, however, use gestures well and was able to learn sign language. She was inquisitive, and after seven years in the hospital, her IQ score had increased from 38 to 74. When her mother eventually removed her from the hospital, she still had not come close to normality in many aspects of her behavior and development.

The cases described in the opening vignette show that, while a newborn baby has the capacity to become a member of human society, this capacity can be realized only through interaction with other human beings. In the first few years of life, a baby is completely dependent upon other human beings for survival. In the first few months, he or she can literally survive for only a matter of hours without assistance from other people. In addition to assistance with physical needs, a newborn baby requires consistent social interaction with other human beings. This need is so great that if a baby is deprived of it for an extended period, he or she may never be capable of becoming "normal." As illustrated by Amala and Kamala and "Genie," the total absence of interaction with other human beings produces personalities that cannot participate in human society or even display what would be regarded as normal behavior. Even a partial absence of interaction can be quite harmful: Babies whose parents do not isolate them but who largely ignore them over an extended time typically show poor intellectual development and high rates of personality difficulties, as do institutionalized children who have sometimes been deprived of interaction because their harried caretakers simply don't have time to provide it (Goldfarb, 1945;

Spitz, 1945). Such children typically experience ongoing developmental and emotional problems, even if they receive all the necessary physical care (Crouch and Milner, 1993; Culp et al., 1991; Steinberg et al., 1994; Kurtz et al., 1993).

Becoming "Human" Through Socialization

These effects of social isolation dramatically illustrate the human need for **socialization**. Socialization is the process whereby people learn, through interaction with others, that which they must know in order to survive and function within their society. In other words, it is the means by which people learn the roles, knowledge, beliefs, language, and values of their culture. To participate in the culture, you must be socialized. The extent to which this is true can be seen by comparing cultures that speak slightly different versions of the same language, as is done in the Global Sociology box "Language and Socialization: Understanding 'Waltzing Matilda.'"

Even among animals, studies have shown the need for interaction. The best-known example is a series of studies of monkeys by Harry Harlow and his colleagues (Harlow, 1958; Harlow and Harlow, 1970, 1962; Harlow and Zimmerman, 1959). Two key finding of these studies illustrate the importance of interaction for normal development.

First, monkeys raised in isolation from other monkeys did not develop normal behavior. Rather, they were withdrawn, responded to other monkeys with fear or aggression, and did not engage in sex. If the females were artificially impregnated, they usually neglected or abused their offspring. Among the behaviors observed were sitting on the baby monkeys, holding them upside down, and attacking them. Significantly, the effects of such isolation became harder to reverse the longer the monkeys were kept in isolation.

Second, consistent patterns were observed when monkeys in isolation were given a choice between a cloth "dummy mother" and a wire "dummy mother." Even when the wire "mother" had a feeding bottle and the cloth "mother" did not, the monkeys preferred the soft cloth "mother."

Learning About Norms and Social Roles

Studies like the ones discussed above show that primates, including human beings, have an innate need for interaction with others of their kind. Thus, we have seen that babies are dependent on others for (1) meeting basic physical needs, without which they cannot survive; and (2) meeting the need for social interaction, without which their learning capacity is lost and normal behavior is impossible. Initially, the two key functions of the socialization process, then, are to provide needed care and needed interaction. The third key function of socialization is to teach people the basic information they need in order to survive in their society. Everyone must learn the social roles that exist in his or her society and how to "play" or fulfill these roles. Furthermore, everyone must learn the norms of his or her society. (Roles and norms are discussed in Chapter 4.) As social animals, people must know how to participate in the society into which they are born.

Theories of Socialization and Development

Social scientists have developed a number of theories about how this process of learning norms and roles takes place. Although these theories disagree on some key points, many of the differences arise because different theories emphasize different aspects of the socialization and development process. Among the most important and influential theories of socialization and development are *interactionist theories, theories about social expectations and personal dilemmas,* and *cognitive-developmental theories.*

Nature Versus Nurture

In psychology and, to a lesser extent, sociology, there has been considerable debate about the relative importance of nature versus nurture in shaping human behavior. The term *nature* refers to natural or biological influences over human behavior. Those who argue on behalf of nature as the more significant force shaping human behavior

GLOBAL SOCIOLOGY

Language and Socialization: Understanding "Waltzing Matilda"

Oh, there once was a swagman camped in the billabong,
Under the shade of a coolibah tree,
And he sang as he looked at the old billy boiling,
Who'll come a-waltzing Matilda with me?
Down came the jumbuck to drink at the water-hole,
Up jumped the swagman and grabbed him with glee,
And he sang as he put him away in his tucker-bag,
You'll come a-waltzing Matilda with me.

The words above are the original words of a song some refer to as Australia's "unofficial national anthem," entitled "Waltzing Matilda." The song is in English, but do you have any idea what story it is telling? As we have seen, language learning is part of the socialization process. But even when different societies, such as England, Australia, and the United States, speak the same language, it will over time develop in different ways in each of those societies. So to understand English as spoken by Australians, you must be socialized to learn the Australian version of the language, just as you need to be socialized in the American version to understand English as spoken in the United States.

So, if you were Australian, you would know that "swagman" refers to an itinerant worker, so-called because such a worker would often carry his worldly belongings in a homemade backpack called a "swag." They were also sometimes called "bagmen." A "billabong" is what would be called an "oxbow lake" in the United States. A "billy" is a tin can with a handle, used for cooking. A "jumbuck" is a sheep, and "tucker" means food. So now you know that the song is about an itinerant worker who was cooking by a lake, when along came a sheep, which the worker grabbed and put in his food bag. But unless you were socialized in the Australian version of the English language, you almost certainly would have had no idea of the meaning of this song.

In one sense, though, even many Australians do not fully know what this song is about. That's another socialization lesson, and we will return to that later in this chapter.

---

believe that human behavior is in substantial part a product of

- the individual's genetic or hormonal makeup (Pines, 1982; Udry, 2000);
- natural instincts or drives that act as influences on the behavior of all human beings (Freud, 1970 [orig. 1920, 1962 [orig. 1930]; Lorenz, 1966; E. Wilson, 1978); and
- physiological processes of development that place limits on the range of thought and behavior of which a person is capable at any given age (Piaget, 1952, 1926; Piaget and Inhelder, 1969).

Although these theories do not all argue that human behavior is *entirely* a product of nature, they do argue that nature has extensive influence over human behavior.

The term *nurture* refers to the influence of social forces in shaping human behavior. Those who emphasize nurture as the major influence over human behavior argue that behavior is a product of interactions with other people (emphasized by symbolic-interactionists such as Mead, 1934; and Cooley, 1964 [orig. 1902]) and of the social situations in which people find themselves. These include their share of limited resources such as wealth, status, and power, and the relationship of their situations to larger societal needs.

In no area of human behavior has this debate been more intense than in childhood socialization. All schools of thought agree that what happens in childhood has important influences throughout a person's life, because it is in childhood that people first develop their patterns of thought and behavior. Although sociologists generally give greater attention to nurture than to nature, the theories we will

Socialization

be considering do disagree about the relative importance of nature versus nurture. We shall consider first interactionist theories of socialization, which weigh in heavily on the side of nurture.

Interactionist Theories of Socialization: Mead and Cooley

The symbolic-interactionist perspective has probably had more influence over the study of socialization than over any other area of sociology, and in sociology, it is probably also the most influential of the various theories about socialization. As we saw in Chapter 3, interactionists see human behavior as the result of how people understand their situations, which in turn is the result of messages they get from others and how they interpret those messages. Because a child is born without *any* understanding of his or her situation, it is clear that these processes are especially important in childhood socialization. Thus, interactionist theories of socialization focus on the ways that messages from others do the following things:

1. Provide the child with an understanding of his or her situation;
2. Teach the child about the roles that he or she will be expected to play;
3. Teach the child the norms that will govern his or her behavior and the ways that some of these norms differ from role to role; and
4. Provide the child with messages concerning how well the child is doing at playing his or her roles.

These messages, in turn, lead to the development of the child's self-image.

Mead on Socialization

One of the first sociologists to examine the socialization process from the interactionist perspective was George Herbert Mead, whose ideas were introduced briefly in Chapter 3. They continue to rank among the most influential theories about socialization. As we saw in our examples of feral children, normal human development is impossible without human interaction. Mead believed, in fact, that human behavior is almost totally a product of interaction with others. As he put it:

> The self, as that which can be an object to itself, is essentially a social structure, and it arises in social experience ... it is impossible to conceive of a self arising outside of social experience. (Mead, 1934)

Thus, to Mead, social, not biological, forces are the primary source of human behavior. To a large extent, he accepted the notion that a newborn baby is a *tabula rasa,* or a "blank slate," without predispositions to develop any particular type of personality. The personality that develops is thus a product of that person's interactions with others.

Mead referred to the spontaneous, unsocialized, unpredictable self as the *I.* In the process of socialization, others interact with the individual, developing in him or her the attitudes, behaviors, and beliefs needed to fit in to society. Mead referred to the socialized self that emerges from this process, reflecting the attitudes of others, as the *me* (Mead, 1934, pp. 175–78). Although the *me* becomes predominant with socialization, the *I* still exists, and is the source of the spontaneous and seemingly unpredictable side of a person's behavior (Mead, 1934).

The Play Stage. Social interactions begin in early childhood—a period Mead referred to as the **play stage**—with contacts with **significant others.** These are particular individuals with whom a child interacts on a regular basis early in life, including parents, teachers, and schoolmates. In the play stage, which begins with the acquisition of language, typically around the age of 1, children learn several important things through interaction with significant others. First, they learn that they exist as a separate object. Sociologists refer to the awareness of that separate identity as the **self.**

Children also learn at this stage that others, too, have separate identities, separate selves. They learn that different people behave differently, and that different people also expect children to behave in different ways. This leads to the third key role of significant others at this point: They teach children social norms. Children learn norms both through concrete messages given by significant others ("Do this, but don't do that") and by using significant others as **role models**—persons from whom children learn how to play roles. In other words, children learn what is appropriate behavior in part by observing the behavior of significant others and then trying out that behavior themselves.

Why does Mead call this the "play stage"? Essentially, the reason is that the child at this stage is capable only of play and cannot yet engage in the organized activity necessary, for example, to participate in a game such as baseball. To put it a bit differently, at the play stage children are interacting with particular *individuals* (Mommy, Daddy, Kelly, Christopher) and not *roles* (mother, father, big sister, outfielder). They do not yet really understand that, to a large extent, how they are expected to behave toward people is determined by those people's roles. Rather, they just know that different people act differently and expect them to act differently.

The Game Stage. As they get older and interact with a wider range of significant others, children move beyond thinking merely in terms of particular individuals. They begin, in effect, to learn the concept of social roles. They learn that certain positions, such as mothers, fathers, salespeople, and teachers, are each occupied by a variety of people. At the same time, they learn that there are regular patterns of behavior associated with each of these positions, regardless of who fills them. Finally, they learn that they are expected to behave in particular ways toward people in various positions such as parent, teacher, or salesperson, again regardless of who is in that position. When a child has learned these things, he or she has moved beyond interacting with particular individuals and has begun to interact with roles. In Mead's terms, the child has gone from interacting with significant others to a new and higher stage of interacting with the *generalized other*. At this stage, the child has generalized from the behavior and expectations of particular individuals to those of anyone playing various roles that relate to whatever role the child is playing at the time. He or she has, in effect, learned to respond to the expectations of his or her society.

When the child has learned to do this, he or she has reached the **game stage**—the ability to play roles and to interact with other roles, which makes organized activity, such as games, possible. Take, for example, the game of baseball. Each position in the game, such as shortstop or outfielder, has a set of expectations—a role—attached to it. If you play shortstop, you must know not only that you are expected to stop the ball if it is hit to you, but also what base you should throw to. Anybody playing shortstop needs to know this; the expectations are the same regardless of who plays the position. The same is true of any other organized activity.

A person attains this game stage through repeated messages from others. It is also through communication with others that the specific expectations of each role, such as shortstop, are learned. Through social interaction, the child learns to play different roles attached to positions that he or she occupies at various times, and to respond appropriately to the behavior of others playing various roles. People's ability to play and respond to various roles is essential in order for them to participate in society. As is shown in the box on page 126, it also turns out that playing a wide variety of roles is good for your health.

Socialization and the Looking-Glass Self

Interactionists believe that in addition to teaching us to play our own social roles and to respond appropriately to the roles of others, the socialization process helps us develop a self-image—a sense of what kind of person we are. This self-image relates closely to the various roles that we play. We normally come to think of ourselves as being very good at playing some roles and not so good at playing others. This self-image is developed through the process of the looking-glass self (Cooley, 1964

A child has reached the game stage when he or she can interact with roles rather than merely with individuals. (Courtesy of John E. Farley)

[orig. 1902]), which was introduced in Chapter 3. As children try out playing new roles, they try to imagine how they appear to others, and they pay attention to others in order to get messages about how well they are doing in these roles. Recent research has applied the concept of the looking-glass self to a wide variety of settings and issues, both in childhood and in adult life. These include judgments about the musical ability of bar bands (O'Connor, 1993) and the competence of lawyers (Stubbs, 1993); changes in self-concept (Tice, 1992); understanding eating disorders (Wax and Cassel, 1990); and family influences on teenagers' self-esteem (Margolin, Blyth, and Carbonne, 1988).

In child socialization, children try to imagine what other people think about how they are doing in their various roles and look for both clear and subtle messages from others to find out. Once they get such messages, they develop ideas about what kind of person they are based on their interpretation of these messages. This process, in turn, affects how they think of themselves. Two elements are critical to this process: the *content* of the messages a child gets from others, and the child's *interpretation* of these messages.

Self-Esteem and Significant Others

As we have indicated, a child will normally come to think of himself or herself as being good at playing some roles and not as good at playing others. In most cases, this process leads to the gradual development of a balanced self-image. Sometimes, though, children are intentionally or unintentionally given messages that are harmful to their overall self-image. Excessive criticism, for example, can lead a child to think of himself or herself as not very good at anything, which produces low self-esteem. Self-esteem refers to your judgment of yourself: Do you look upon yourself positively or negatively? This can refer to your overall judgment of yourself—called global self-esteem—or to your judgment of your performance in a particular role. How well we perform in a role affects our self-esteem, at least as it relates to that role. At the same time, however, self-esteem also affects how well we perform in a role (Rosenberg, Schooler, and Schoenbach, 1989). This suggests that if children are given negative messages that harm their self-esteem, their achievement will suffer. Poor achievement can lead to further erosion of their self-esteem.

Overly busy parents who consistently fail to take time to do things with their children and to respond to their children's concerns can unintentionally give their children such messages. To a young child, "I'm too busy" can easily sound like "I don't want anything to do with you" or "You're a pest." A child who comes to think of himself or herself in these terms might never develop good self-esteem. More children today may be getting such messages: Demographic and economic changes have led to greater social isolation of children from adults in their households (Crites, 1989). For example, Schor (1997) reports that, among dual-earner families, annual time spent at work increased by more than 600 hours between 1967 and 1989, which leaves less time to be spent with the children.

Young children develop images of themselves that, to a substantial degree, will influence how they think of themselves throughout life. Thus, poor global self-esteem at this stage can be a source of lifelong difficulties (see Clausen, 1991). This does not mean that children need to be told they are good at everything. A balanced self-image is much healthier than one that cannot accept any shortcomings. However, it is important for children to get sufficient attention and emotional support from their parents to know that they are loved and wanted, be given credit and praise when they do things well, and be reassured that it is not necessary to be good at everything.

Theories About Social Expectations and Personal Dilemmas: Freud and Erikson

Whereas symbolic-interactionists such as Mead and Cooley see human behavior and personality as almost totally the product of social interaction, their contemporary Sigmund Freud (1856–1939) saw behavior and personality as being the product of the interaction between nature and nurture. Freud believed that human beings are born with certain innate natural drives, or behavioral impulses, including some aggressive tendencies and the desire for physical (particularly sexual) pleasure (Freud, 1962 [orig. 1930]). Freud called these natural drives, which he believed to be present in some form from infancy on, the **id**. Opposing the id are the requirements of society that we control

SOCIOLOGICAL INSIGHTS
Multiple Social Roles: Good for Your Health?

At the beginning of this chapter, it was stressed that human beings have an innate need for interaction with other human beings. One of the main ways we meet this need is by learning and playing a variety of roles. A study by Phyllis Moen, Donna Dempster-McClain, and Robin Williams (1992) shows that this need is both psychological and physiological. In 1986, Moen, Dempster-McClain, and Williams sought out and interviewed a group of women who had participated in a study of their involvement in various social roles thirty years earlier, in 1956. They found and reinterviewed in 1986 more than 90 percent of the women who had participated in the 1956 study and were still alive—no small feat in itself! What they wanted to find out was whether women who had been actively involved in a greater variety of roles in 1956—such as friend, worker, church member, neighbor, relative, and club member—were healthier in 1986 than those with fewer active role involvements. The answer, it turns out, is a clear yes: The more roles in which a woman was actively involved in 1956, the healthier she turned out to be thirty years later. This was true even after adjusting for age, education and other measures of socioeconomic status, earlier health, and current family status. (All of the women were married with children in 1956, but about a third of them were divorced or widowed by 1986.)

One type of role involvement turned out to be particularly beneficial for the women's health. Women who belonged to clubs or organizations in 1956 were a good deal healthier thirty years later than women who did not. Again, this was true after adjusting for other factors that might influence health. It may be true that healthier, more affluent people are more likely to get involved in clubs, but at any given level of socioeconomic status or previous health, a person involved with clubs or organizations in 1956 turned out to be healthier in 1986. Why did a woman's involvement in a club or organization turn out to be particularly beneficial, even compared with other kinds of role involvement? Moen, Dempster-McClain, and Williams speculate that the reason may have to do with the fact that our roles are most beneficial to us when we find them rewarding. We choose club or organization involvement more voluntarily than other role involvements, and we can more freely end them and shift to other clubs or organizations if our roles are not rewarding. Thus, because of its voluntary nature, club and organizational involvement may be among the most rewarding kind of role involvement there is. Supporting this interpretation, unpaid volunteer work was also found to be quite strongly correlated with women's health. Thus, socialization into roles—particularly ones you have some choice about taking on—is not only good for you socially; it also seems to be good for you physically.

Source: Phyllis Moen, Donna Dempster-McClain, and Robin M. Williams, Jr., 1992, "Successful Aging: A Life-Course Perspective on Women's Multiple Roles and Health," *American Journal of Sociology* 97:1612–38, University of Chicago Press.

---

our aggression and our pleasure-seeking. Society's norms restricting these natural drives were referred to by Freud as the **superego**, which he saw as a socially learned *conscience* arising from messages we get from others about acceptable and unacceptable behaviors. According to Freud, everyone experiences an *inner conflict* between the id, which says "I want to do that," and the superego, which says "You can't do that." The dynamics of this conflict and the way an individual resolves them form the basis of one's personality.

Depending on the strictness of his or her home environment, and to a lesser extent the restrictiveness of other childhood environments, each person develops a somewhat different balance between the id and the superego. This balance is managed by the **ego**, the ultimate expression of the personality each person develops. The more restrictive the childhood environment is, the stronger the influence of the superego will tend to be. When the environment is too restrictive, Freud believed, natural drives are repressed but do not go away. Rather, they build up pressures that lead to increased frustration until they may eventually surface in a destructive way. Depressed people, Freud believed, felt anger and frustration because they were made to repress too much of their aggressive and sexual selves. They became depressed because they turned this anger and frustration against themselves.

Less commonly, too little restriction of the natural drives may lead a person to behave amorally—exhibiting no sense of right or wrong and no sense of guilt or remorse for anything he or she does.

Today, most social scientists would agree that how conflicts between individual drives or desires and societal expectations are resolved in childhood does have some effect on behavior later in life. At the same time, most sociologists argue that the situations people encounter in later life are important social forces in their own right, and they reject the notion that *all* behavior in adulthood is a product of childhood experiences. Recent research supports the notion that both sociological and biological influences are at work in shaping human behavior (Udry, 1988, 2000; Udry and Billy, 1987).

Erikson's Eight Stages of Life
Like Freud, Erik Erikson felt that children face dilemmas involving choices between two opposites. However, Erikson argued in *Childhood and Society* (1950) that the dilemmas people face at different stages of their lives are related more to social expectations and self-identity than to natural drives. Erikson argued that people experience a series of *psychosocial stages,* each of which contains opposing positive and negative components. At each stage, people face a dilemma or crisis as they make choices between the two components. As Mead and Cooley suggested, the choices that are made are largely a product of the social environment and messages that children receive from significant others. In the first several stages, children who receive encouragement and positive messages about themselves tend to achieve healthy modes of adaptation; children who are ignored or who get excessively negative messages tend to adapt poorly.

Erikson's eight stages are summarized in Table 5.1, which also compares Erikson's theories of socialization with other theories. We can use Erikson's second stage, autonomy versus shame, to illustrate the type of dilemma children encounter.

At this stage, which occurs between the ages of one and two or three, children are trying out their physical skills through walking, climbing, manipulating objects, and toilet training. If they master these skills—and are given the message that they have done so—they become more autonomous and self-confident. If they do not, they face shame and self-doubt. A sense of inferiority often results, and the child may either become compulsive about following fixed routines or reject all controls. Note that Erikson's approach shares something in common with interactionist theories such as those of Mead and Cooley: Whether or not a child resolves these dilemmas successfully is based in large part on the messages the child gets from significant others.

Although Erikson's stages effectively outline some of the major dilemmas that must be addressed in socialization, they should not be seen as exact descriptions of the process of development. Discrete stages have not for the most part been scientifically validated, and to the extent that they occur in a sequence, they overlap considerably. While an unresolved issue at one stage often has effects at later stages, there always remains some possibility that it can be addressed successfully later in life.

Cognitive Development Theories of Socialization: Piaget and Kohlberg

Cognitive-developmental theories resemble the theories of Freud and Erikson in two important ways. First, they rely on the idea that people move through a series of stages as they develop and experience the socialization process. Second, they include a place for the forces of nature as well as those of nurture. However, they also differ in two important ways. First, rather than dilemmas or choices, cognitive-developmental theories focus on **cognitive processes**: learning, reasoning, and the actions by which knowledge is obtained and processed. Second, they relate the role of nature to physiological development in that they acknowledge that the development of the body and brain places an upper limit on the child's capacity to learn, reason, and process knowledge at any given age.

However, although the limits on human potential may be physiologically defined, the actual

Table 5.1 Summary of Key Theorists on Socialization and Development

	Mead	Freud	Erikson	Piaget	Kohlberg
Socialization viewed as process of:	Learning roles and self-concept through interaction with others.	Struggle between natural drives and societal expectations.	Series of dilemmas to be resolved, relating to social expectations and self-identity.	Development of increasingly sophisticated interpretations of physical and social environment.	Development of increasingly sophisticated moral reasoning, through cognitive development and interaction with others.
Views on nature (natural/biological influences) versus nurture (social influences)	Emphasized nurture, little if any consideration of nature.	Socialization seen as struggle between nature and nurture.	Emphasized nurture, in context of natural development.	Emphasized natural development of reasoning ability, which allows understanding of social environment.	Reasoning seen as joint outcome of natural development and social interaction.
Stages of socialization and development, with typical age range	1. Play Stage:[1] interaction with specific persons, "I" predominates. 2. Game Stage: interaction with roles, "me" predominates.	1. Oral (0–1 yrs) 2. Anal (1–3 yrs) 3. Phallic (3–4 yrs) 4. Oedipal (4–6 yrs) 5. Latency (6–11 yrs) 6. Genital (11 yrs and up)	1. Trust vs. mistrust (0–1 yrs) 2. Autonomy vs. doubt, shame (1–2 yrs) 3. Initiative vs. guilt (3–5 yrs) 4. Industry vs. inferiority (6–11 yrs) 5. Identity vs. role confusion (12–18 yrs) 6. Intimacy vs. isolation (young adult) 7. Generativity vs. self-absorption (middle adult) 8. Integrity vs. despair (old age)	1. Sensorimotor (0–2 yrs) 2. Preoperational (2–7 yrs) 3. Concrete operations (7–11 yrs) 4. Formal operations (12 yrs and up)	Preconventional Level[1] Stage 1: punishment avoidance Stage 2: need satisfaction Conventional Level Stage 3: good boy, good girl Stage 4: law and order Postconventional Level Stage 5: social contracts Stage 6: universal ethical principles

[1]Stages are not strongly limited to age; they depend on social interaction.

level and process of learning and reasoning in any individual is mostly a function of social influences. For most of us, learning and modes of reasoning and information processing are very much influenced by the social environment. To see how this occurs, let us begin with the cognitive theories of the Swiss psychologist Jean Piaget.

Piaget: Stages of Cognitive Development
Central to Piaget's theory of development was the concept of a schema—a behavior sequence involving recognition of a stimulus (sight, sound, object, person, or message) in the environment and a motor (behavioral) response to that stimulus based on our understanding of its meaning. As new information becomes available, it is assimilated into existing schemas, and these schemas may be modified to accommodate new information that does not fit the existing schemas. Thus, cognitive reasoning becomes a process of incorporating new information into existing schemas, which become increasingly complex as new information becomes available. According to Piaget (1926), this process of cognitive reasoning develops through the following four stages:

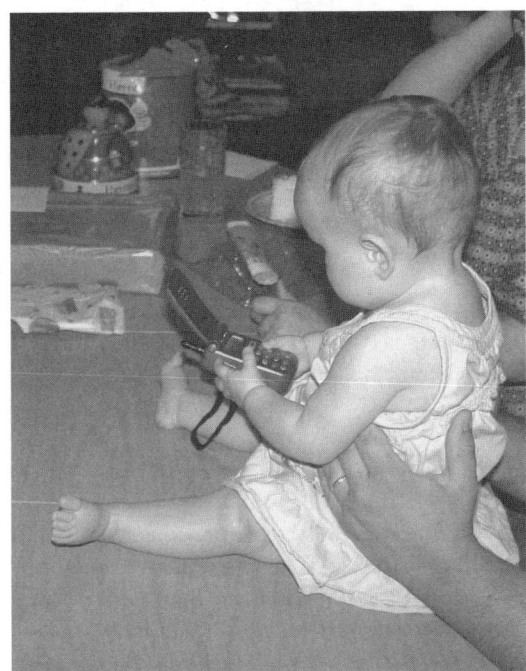

At the sensorimotor stage, children develop a physical understanding of the environment, as shown by this child's examination of and experimentation with a toy cell phone. (Courtesy of John E. Farley)

1. *Sensorimotor stage* (until age 2). This stage involves the development of a physical understanding of the environment by touching, seeing, hearing, and moving around. At this stage, schemas involve purely physical objects and properties. Children learn *object permanence*—if you show a child something and then hide it, the child will learn that it is still there and look for it.
2. *Preoperational stage* (ages 2–7). Children learn to represent schemas in their minds. They engage in symbolic play, using one object as a symbol to represent another. They may, for example, pretend that a block is a car and move it around the way a car would move. At this stage, children also develop *language*— not merely saying words, but putting them together in sentences that express increasingly complex ideas. This clearly demonstrates that they are using mental, not purely physical, schemas. They still, however, look at things from their own viewpoint, not that of someone else, and they have trouble with any task that requires them to look at themselves or their environment from someone else's viewpoint.

A boy at this stage, for example, may report having two brothers, Henry and Paul. If asked how many brothers Henry has, however, the child will mention only Paul—not himself (Foss, 1974).

3. *Stage of concrete operations* (ages 7–11). At this stage, children gain several new capabilities. Although they still think mainly in terms of concrete, readily visible objects rather than abstract concepts, they are able to think in terms of cause and effect. They can draw conclusions about the likely physical consequences of an action without always having to try it out. They also learn that quantities can remain constant even if they take different shapes and forms. They understand, for example, that if a given amount of milk is poured from a tall thin glass into a short wide one, or from a large glass into two small ones, it is still the same amount of milk. Finally, as stressed earlier in our discussion of George Herbert Mead, children at this stage can respond to the roles of others, consider things from the viewpoint of others, and play different roles themselves. Thus it is now possible for them to play games.

4. *Stage of formal operations* (ages 12 and up). When they reach this stage, children can reason not only in terms of the physical world, but also in terms of abstract concepts, such as love, happiness, wealth, intelligence, and remorse. They can think in terms of future consequences and evaluate the probable outcomes of several alternative courses of action. They can also evaluate their own thoughts and self-image. Finally, they can begin to think about major philosophical issues, such as why pain and suffering exist.

Social and Cultural Influences on Cognitive Development

As was indicated earlier, cognitive theorists believe that the *capacity* to attain these stages is defined by physiological development, but that the actual extent to which people attain them, and the ages at which they attain them, are socially determined. The ability to do these things is learned from others, and if a child is not exposed to others engaging in the type of reasoning that normally occurs at a given stage, the child may have difficulty developing that reasoning ability on his or her own. Both the larger culture in which a child grows up and the child's immediate social environment influence this process. If a culture places little value on abstract reasoning—for example, a culture in which reality is determined by tradition and not by scientific discovery—a child is much less likely to develop abstract reasoning skills. Similarly, recent studies have shown that neighborhood plays a significant role in the development of children's skills (Entwisle, Alexander, and Olson, 1994; Brooks-Gunn et al., 1993). At the more immediate level, if a child's parents do not think in terms of abstract concepts, and this skill is not emphasized in school, the child has little or no way of learning it. For this reason, a sizable part of the population—even in countries like the United States where scientific knowledge is valued—never reaches the cognitive stage of formal operations. The four stages of cognitive reasoning do appear to occur in sequence, but how far people get through that sequence seems to vary.

Piaget on Moral Reasoning

Cognitive reasoning enables people to make moral judgments—that is, to distinguish between right and wrong. Piaget (1932) offered the important insight that how children (and adults) distinguish right from wrong is greatly influenced by their process of cognitive reasoning. A child at the preoperational stage, for example, cannot and will not make judgments about right and wrong in the same way as a child at the stage of formal operations.

The Morality of Constraint. According to Piaget, children at young ages act on the basis of reward and punishment: They avoid behaviors that bring punishment and repeat ones that are rewarded. They see rules as existing for their own sake (not some larger social purpose), and they do not realize that rules are subject to change. Because it is the punishment or consequence that makes something bad, the rightness or wrongness of an act is judged purely on the basis of its consequences, not its intent. In one experiment, for example, Piaget (1932) found that children thought it was worse to break fifteen cups left behind a door where they could not be seen than to break one cup climbing to get some jam that had been placed out of reach. In other words, the *consequences* were greater in the first case. Significantly, the younger children typically paid little attention to the fact that in the second case the child's *intentions* had been worse—to get at something his mother had intended him not to have. Piaget referred to this stage of moral behavior as the morality of constraint.

The Morality of Cooperation. Piaget argued that, given the appropriate social environment, children will move from the morality of constraint to the morality of cooperation. As Piaget's theory suggests, young children will often admit that they only do the right thing because it brings reward or avoids punishment. Among older children, *intention* becomes a more important factor in determining right and wrong. In Piaget's experiments, for example, older children were more likely to say that the child climbing up to get the jam had behaved worse, because he was doing something he knew his mother didn't want him to do.

Most sociologists agree that for the majority of people moral behavior is more than a matter of reward and punishment. Most crimes—particularly, but not only, minor ones like petty theft—are not solved, and the offenders are never punished. Even so, most people most of the time do not steal. According to Piaget, the reason they don't is that they realize that stealing is wrong. If everyone stole, nobody would be secure in his or her property, and the world would be a miserable place. Thus, the recognition that stealing prevents cooperation and hurts everyone's quality of life keeps most people from stealing. This is what is meant by the morality of cooperation.

Unfortunately, many people never fully develop the morality of cooperation. Even among some adults, consequence and punishment are the main factors influencing moral behavior. At the same time, some very young children have been shown to understand intention and take it into consideration (Shultz et al., 1980). Morality of constraint always appears to precede morality of cooperation, but the age at which morality of cooperation develops, if it develops at all, is quite variable. Thus, moral reasoning, like other aspects of cognitive development, is heavily influenced by social interaction. This is clearly shown in the work of Lawrence Kohlberg, who has elaborated on Piaget's theories of moral reasoning.

Kohlberg's Stages of Moral Development

Lawrence Kohlberg (1984, 1969) expanded on Piaget's ideas by conducting research in which people were presented with moral dilemmas and asked what they would do and why they would do it. In one such dilemma, a man's wife was dying, and the druggist who had invented the only medicine that could save her was charging ten times what the medicine cost to produce—far more than the man could afford. As a result, the man stole the drug. Subjects in Kohlberg's experiments were then asked questions such as whether the man was right to steal the drug, and why. It was the "why" part that was of greater interest to Kohlberg. He found that, based on the *reasons* they gave for their responses to his moral dilemmas, his subjects could be classified into three general levels of moral reasoning (Power, Higgins, and Kohlberg, 1989), each of which could be subdivided into two more specific stages of moral reasoning. Kohlberg argues that these six stages generally occur in a set sequence: One must pass through Stage 1 before going on to Stage 2, and so forth. However, many people never develop beyond Stage 3 or 4, and some do not even get that far.

The Preconventional Level. Subjects at the preconventional level, consisting of Stages 1 and 2, are self-centered. They view the world in terms of their

Stage 6 moral reasoning is most often found in people with formal training in philosophy, such as Dr. Martin Luther King, Jr. (AP Photo/JL)

own interests, needs, and desires, without giving much consideration to the views of others. In Stage 1, *punishment avoidance,* people are concerned with avoiding that which brings punishments or bad consequences. It is very much like Piaget's morality of constraint. In the sample story, a Stage 1 subject might say "Steal the drug if you can get away with it; don't if it looks like you'll get caught." At Stage 2, *need satisfaction,* moral reasoning is a little more developed but remains very self-centered. At this stage, behavior is acceptable if it satisfies your wants or desires. A Stage 2 subject might say the man should steal the drug because his wife needs it, without addressing the druggist's behavior at all.

The Conventional Level. At the *conventional level,* which Kohlberg believes characterizes most adult behavior in industrialized countries, behavior is considered right if it is approved by others. Thus, a Stage 3, *good boy/good girl,* subject might say stealing is acceptable behavior because the druggist is a bad man, or not acceptable because stealing "isn't nice." A bit more developed is Stage 4, *law and order.* At this stage of moral reasoning, right and wrong are defined on the basis of rules and laws. By and large, such rules and laws are not thought of as changeable, and to violate any of them is nearly always seen as wrong. This group would be more likely than others to say that stealing the drug is wrong because stealing is against the law. It appears that Stage 4 is the most prevalent in the adult U.S. population (Colby et al., 1983).

The Postconventional Level. People at the postconventional level of morality realize that laws and the approval of others do not simply happen; rather, they often have some basis in people's needs and the general welfare. The stages in this level are harder to define because relatively few people—only about one in five Americans—reach this level (Kohlberg, 1975; see also Colby et al., 1983; Kohlberg, 1986, 1984). In Stage 5, people are governed by *social contracts*—agreements, implicit or explicit, that they enter into for their mutual benefit. People have an obligation, out of fairness, to live up to their end of the bargain. Stage 5 people recognize that laws exist for a reason and that there are bad laws that—even if one obeys them—can and should be changed. In Stage 6, *universal ethical principles,* people live by principles based on human rights that transcend government and laws. Stage 6 people believe that sometimes these ethical or moral principles obligate them to violate laws that work against basic human rights. Dr. Martin Luther King, Jr., is often cited as an example of a person with Stage 6 moral reasoning (Penrod, 1986, p. 74; Kohlberg, 1984, p. 270). In later formulations of his theory, Kohlberg raised questions about whether or not Stage 6 truly exists among the general population: Tests of the later, more refined versions of his theory were unable to find such people, except among those with formal training in philosophy, such as Dr. King (Kohlberg, 1984).

Like most of the other theories we have considered, Kohlberg's theory sees social interaction as highly important. Although the sequence always begins with Stage 1 and develops in order, when and how far it develops depends on the messages and examples a child gets from others. In general, urban and well-educated children attain higher levels in Kohlberg's classification system than rural and poorly educated children. Overall, people in modern industrial societies outscore those in rural and less economically developed ones. In addition, experiments reveal that even the same people will use different moral reasoning when speaking to different audiences, such as to businesspeople as opposed to philosophers (Carpendale and Krebs, 1992).

Kohlberg's work has been criticized as containing both social class and sex biases. In fact, a general problem with all developmental theories is that the stages may vary among different groups and societies (Dannefer, 1984). Middle-class people score higher on Kohlberg's scale than those of lower socioeconomic status, a difference that no doubt reflects both real differences in reasoning and social-class differences in self-expression. Men also score higher than women. This may reflect Kohlberg's system of classification. Men tend to emphasize "justice," which is closely linked to Kohlberg's Stages 5 and 6. Women, however, emphasize "caring," which also reflects a concern with the welfare of others, but is not as highly rated by Kohlberg's coding system (Gilligan, 1982; Stander and Jensen, 1993). Thus, both people's actual mode of moral reasoning and the way they express or conceptualize their reasoning are socially influenced.

Moral Reasoning and Moral Behavior

Does moral reasoning affect human behavior? In other words, do people who display different levels of moral reasoning respond differently when confronted with a real-life moral dilemma? Evidence that they do is supplied by a study of student participation in the Free Speech Movement (FSM) at the University of California at Berkeley in 1964, the first of the major student demonstrations of the 1960s.

The Free Speech Movement began when the university announced that it would no longer permit students and student organizations to set up tables in a specified area of the campus. By the time the university capitulated and permitted the tables, its administration building, Sproul Hall, had been taken over by student demonstrators, and a police car had been surrounded by a crowd of several thousand students and abandoned by the officers.

Haan, Smith, and Block (1968) interviewed a large sample of students on the campus, administering moral-reasoning tests developed by Kohlberg and asking the students what they thought of the FSM. In this college population, virtually everyone had reached at least Stage 2, and the sample included people from Stages 2 through 6. Students who supported or participated in the protest were more likely to have achieved certain stages of moral reasoning than other students. Although the majority of students at every stage expressed support of the movement, the percentage who did so was much higher among those at Stages 2, 5, and 6 than among those at Stages 3 or 4. It is not surprising that those at Stage 3 (be nice) or Stage 4 (follow rules) would be less likely to participate.

Of particular interest were the reasons for support or participation given by those at various stages of moral reasoning. The Stage 2 people participated out of self-centered motivation, as Kohlberg's theory predicts: "No university administrator is going to tell *me* what I can and can't do." Protestors in Stage 3 or 4 who supported the movement emphasized bad university administrators who violated the university's own rules or those of the U.S. Constitution concerning free speech. The Stage 5 and 6 students emphasized the basic human right to free speech. Thus, both the probability of supporting the FSM and the reasoning of those who did support it were greatly influenced by where students fell in Kohlberg's six-stage model.

These findings suggest that although moral reasoning is related to behavior, it is more closely related to the process by which people decide *how* to behave when confronted with a moral dilemma, such as fellow students requesting their support for the FSM. In fact, a review of the literature on moral development and behavior by Blasi (1980) indicates that the relationship between moral development, as defined by Kohlberg, and moral behavior is far from consistent. Although the majority of studies have found such a link, others have not (see also Kutnick, 1986). Certainly, other factors, such as peer pressures and the particular characteristics of a situation, also have important effects on behavior. However, even if people at different stages of moral development do not always *behave* differently, they do appear to *reason* differently in their decisions about how to behave—in real life as well as the laboratory.

Overview of Theories of Socialization

As is evident from the material above, theorists such as Mead, Freud, Erikson, Piaget, and Kohlberg emphasized different aspects of the socialization process, and had different ideas about the roles of nature and nurture and their relative importance in the socialization process. The ideas of these theorists are summarized in Table 5.1 on page 128. Although they do offer us very different views of the socialization process, these theories cannot be classified as "right" or "wrong." In an important sense, they are all at least partially "right," in that they emphasize different aspects of socialization and development, and seek to understand different processes that contribute to the overall course of socialization and development.

Agents of Socialization

All the theories that we have discussed agree that significant others play a prominent role in the socialization process. What we have not yet addressed is the fact that *social institutions* also play an important role. In fact, both people and institutions can act as **agents of socialization.** Agents of socialization influence the development of people's attitudes, beliefs, self-images, and behavior. In a sense, it could be said that they carry out the process of socialization, interacting with the individual in a way that permits him or her to become a participating member of human society. Agents of socialization may or may not have the primary purpose of carrying out the socialization process, but they always have that effect.

The most important agents of socialization are the family (particularly parents), the school, religion, peers, and the media. Some of these—the family, religion, the school—are institutions whose *manifest function* is, at least in part, to be agents of socialization. They exist at least partly to provide children with knowledge, values, or—most often—both. These are not the only influential agents of socialization, however. Peers and the mass media also play an important role. Neither peers nor the media exist for the *purpose* of socialization; that is, socialization is not their manifest function. However, they do have the *effect* of shaping knowledge, beliefs, and attitudes—in some cases just as much as the family, religion, or school. Thus, socialization can be described as an important *latent function* of peers and the media.

The Family

In the early years, the family is the most important agent of socialization. This is especially true of

> ## UNDERSTANDING RACE, CLASS, AND GENDER
> ### The Making of the Southern Belle
>
> A fascinating example of schools as an agent of socialization can be seen in a sociohistorical study by Christie Farnham (1994) of women's schools and colleges in the South before the Civil War. These schools played a key role in the socialization of women in the elite, land-owning class of that era. And by so doing, they helped to assure that white males would retain their dominant role in antebellum Southern society.
>
> Southern women's education was different from Northern women's education in one key way that, ironically, allowed it to flourish. In the North, women who attended college were typically seeking preparation for a period of professional work before marriage, or, less often, as an alternative to it. Though not poor, they were frequently not the daughters of the economic elite. After graduation, many worked, at least for a time, in teaching or social work. The South was different. There, it was understood that genteel women did not work, and with few exceptions, only the daughters of the elite planter class and other wealthy families attended college. The messages of college reinforced the role model of a woman educated in the classics, who would make a desirable partner for a man of the upper class. This model also reinforced the class and racial inequality of the old South—only a white woman of "good breeding" could presume to seek such a role. Because educated Southern women were not being prepared for employment, the education of women in the South was not a threat to male dominance of the professions, as it was in the North. As a result, women's colleges flourished to a greater extent in the South than in other parts of the country, but they also taught a somewhat different message to women.
>
> Farnham uses the crowning of the May Queen as an example to illustrate how Southern women's education socialized women in a way that reinforced the inequalities of the era. The May Queen's crowning was an annual ritual extremely popular among students in all Southern women's schools. She describes the crowning as "a Durkheimian collective enactment of society's definition of femininity, whereby men offered women protection in exchange for deference" (Farnham, 1994, p. 168). The May Queen was literally placed on a pedestal to be admired, while nearby stood a detachment of young men in full military regalia—there to honor her, but also to represent the notion that they were her protectors, thus teaching a message of male power and female dependency. The power these men held was noted by calling them the "lords of creation," and in Farnham's words, the May Queen always knew that "despite her magical charms, it was clear that the lords had the last word." And of course, the system of racial inequality was also reinforced, since only whites could serve in the May Queen's court or honor guard.

parents, but it is also true to a lesser extent of older siblings who are present. More than anyone else, the parents define the attitudes and beliefs of a young child. In large part, truth to preschool children is what their parents tell them. Parents remain important as agents of socialization throughout childhood and adolescence, although as children age, parents increasingly share their role with other agents of socialization.

The effects of socialization in the family are often lifelong. The family's religion usually becomes the child's, and the child's political attitudes, world view, and lifestyle are substantially influenced by those of the family. Children who encounter undesirable behaviors or attitudes in the home are more likely than other children to exhibit them in adulthood. Child and spouse abuse, alcoholism and drug abuse, and racial prejudice are all passed on through the family.

Even within the same family, however, not all children are treated the same way. Boys and girls usually experience socialization differently, as we shall see in a later chapter. First-born and only children receive greater attention and often grow up to be greater achievers. A child who is highly active from infancy on is usually treated differently than one who is less active. The child's size and health status also influence parental behavior. Thus, although certain common patterns appear in every family, even brothers or sisters in the same family do not have exactly the same socialization experience.

Social class also plays a role through what sociologists call cultural capital. Children of upper- and middle-class parents typically experience more opportunities to visit museums, foreign countries, and so on than do the children of the working class. This not only effects how children see the world but also gives them a leg up in school as well as social interaction.

Schools

As we shall see in Web-Based Chapter A, the school is an institution with a profound effect not only on children's knowledge, but also on their self-image, their understanding of reality, and their mode of reasoning. The school also plays an important role in teaching students the beliefs and values of their society. The role of the school in the socialization process has become more important in modern industrial societies, as the amount of specialized technical and scientific knowledge has expanded beyond what parents could possibly teach in the home. Some of the teaching of both knowledge and values that used to occur in the home today takes place in the school. Even more recently, as the two-career family and single-parent family have become more commonplace, school influences children at an early age in the form of day care. Although the school is more important as a socialization agent today than it was in the past, schools have engaged in socialization as long as they have been in existence, as is illustrated in the box "The Making of the Southern Belle."

Religion

The influence of religion as an agent of socialization varies widely. Although most Americans identify with some organized religion, fewer than half typically attend religious services at some time during the week. Of those who do, however, many bring their children to religion classes, and some children attend religious rather than public schools. Among

Going to school or nursery school may be a difficult transition for some children, because it is their first experience interacting with equals rather than authority figures. (iStockphoto)

people who are religious, religion is a powerful agent of socialization because it specifies what is right and what is wrong. Moreover, in religious families, religion and the family frequently (though not always) give similar messages. Religion is an important influence on the values and beliefs of the parents, who join with it to pass those values on to their children.

Peers

Peers begin to be an influence at a very young age, as children form friendships with other children (Corsaro and Rizzo, 1988, 1990). However, it is in the junior high and high school years that peer influence is the greatest, as young people seek to establish their independence by turning to influences other than the home and the school. Although peer subcultures are often at odds with those of the parents and the school, peers in another sense demand a tremendous amount of conformity. Often, little deviation from the peer-group norm in dress, speech, attitude, and behavior is tolerated. The price the peer group exacts for nonconformity is high: ridicule or ostracism precisely at a time when a young person must gain acceptance from a group outside the family in order to establish independence from it. Because of this need and because of the strong pressure for conformity, the influence of the peer group on attitudes and behaviors is, for a time during adolescence, very high—perhaps greater than that of any other agent of socialization. This effect is greatest in the areas of dress, speech, entertainment preferences, and leisure activity. Often it can extend to attitudes and behaviors in the areas of sexuality and drug and alcohol use. However, it is somewhat weaker (though often still significant) in such areas as religious and political beliefs.

The Media

In recent decades, the media, particularly television, have become very influential as agents of socialization. The average American child spends well over three hours per day watching television—in many cases, more time than he or she spends talking with parents or siblings. The spread of cable television, VCRs and now DVD and DVR players has probably enhanced the influence of the media by encouraging people to watch more television. In the past decade, the rapid growth of the Internet has also made it an important agent of socialization, and many young people now spend as much or more time on the Internet as they do watching television.

One of the more fundamental effects of the mass media on the socialization process has been to provide nearly everyone—regardless of their social status or where they live—with access to the same entertainment, information, and imagery. As a result, *place,* either geographic or social, has come to be less important (Meyerowitz, 1985). Whether you are a teenager on an Iowa farm, a New York stockbroker, or an assembly-line worker in Detroit, you can watch the same television programs, see the same movies, and access the same material over the World Wide Web. You can communicate with people far away and different from yourself by telephone, fax, or computer link. According to Meyerowitz, this has broken down boundaries and traditional status distinctions, made us in many ways more similar to one another, and weakened local influences, such as family, neighborhood, and religious congregation, on the socialization process. Another effect of the visual media, particularly television, is that we have come to expect entertaining messages and attractive personal images in everything—just like TV and the movies (Postman, 1985). Thus an unattractive politician has a more difficult time getting elected regardless of his or her message or abilities, and a teacher must be entertaining in order to keep students' attention.

The Media and Sexual and Violent Behavior. Although there is great debate over precisely how television influences attitudes and behavior, there is no doubt that television has become an important means by which young people come to understand their world. As children grow into adolescence, rock music and motion pictures also play some role in the socialization process.

One area of particular concern has been media portrayals of sexuality and violence. Most Americans have seen thousands of people killed in television dramas, and there is some evidence that this desensitizes people to violence and, at least in the short term, increases aggressive behavior (Felson, 1996; Murray, 2008; National Institute of Mental Health, 1982; Polermo, 1995; Paik and Comstock, 1994). There also appears to be a longer-term correlation between viewing media violence and engaging in violent behavior (Eron, 1995; Comstock and Strasburger, 1990; Murray, 2008). However, debate continues over whether such viewing *causes* people to be violent or whether, for example, people with a tendency toward violence also prefer watching violent shows (Wiegman, Kuttschreuter, and Baarda, 1992; Campbell, 1990; Langley, Neal, and Craig, 1992). A growing number of studies in recent years *do* suggest there is some cause and effect relationship (Zillman and Weaver, 1999; Dill and Dill, 1998; Murray, 2008; Smith and Donnerstein, 1998). It is also true, however, that other factors, such as personal exposure to violent behavior, have stronger effects on violent behavior than does exposure to violence in the media.

American children, like children in many other societies where television is widespread, also view a great deal of actual or implied sexual activity. A recent analysis of several studies suggests that the majority of all daytime and evening programs contain sexual dialogue, and one in eight depicts or implies sexual intercourse (Kunkel, Cope, and Biely, 1999). Similarly, about one in eight commercials involves some degree of undressing (Lin, 1998). In contrast to most European countries, however, in the United States television provides little information concerning how to avoid the undesired consequences of sexual activity, such as unwanted pregnancy or sexually transmitted diseases (Jones et al., 1986), and entertainment programs make little mention of risks or responsibilities associated with sex (Kunkel, Cope, and Biely, 1999). Also, in contrast to the practice in most European countries, the advertising of condoms was forbidden on American television until 1987. Even now the great majority of stations refuse to accept such advertising. This gives American youngsters a mixed message—sex is glamorized but its consequences are not discussed frankly. Significantly, survey research has found substantial and growing public support for providing information on television about condom use—even in largely rural and conservative states such as Indiana (Yarber and Torabi, 1999).

One-Way Communication. A significant difference between the media and all other agents of socialization is that the media usually communicate one way. Unlike all other agents of socialization, the people we experience through television, movies, radio, and music videos are not personal acquaintances, and we cannot really exchange ideas with them. All of the communication is in one direction—from the media to the viewer or listener. An exception to this is the Internet. Through popular social networking sites like Facebook, MySpace, and Twitter, Net users are able to communicate with each other in a manner similar to face-to-face communication. In addition, since a good deal of Internet communication is about the forms of mass media (TV shows, popular music, politics, current events, or movies), the Net may also reduce the amount of one-way communication with the other forms of mass media. The protests over the disputed Iranian presidential election in the summer of 2009 were fueled by Internet communication over a variety of platforms, such as video, social networking sites, and e-mail. A recent study also found that exposure to Internet news sources increased political participation (Tolbert and McNeal, 2003). Thus, the Internet would seem to represent a shifting terrain for the mass media, the full implications of which have yet to be seen (DiMaggio, et al., 2001).

How Socialization Works

How do agents of socialization shape the thinking and behavior of those being socialized? Social scientists have focused on these main processes: *selective exposure and modeling, reward and punishment,* and *nurturance and identification.* Let us consider each.

Selective Exposure

One of the ways that agents of socialization influence attitudes and behaviors is through selective exposure. Children are exposed to those behaviors and attitudes considered desirable and sheltered from those regarded as undesirable. Parents do this by the ways they speak and behave in front of their children and by the reading material and television shows to which they expose their children. Parents try to maximize exposure to "good influences" and protect their children from "bad influences."

It is not only parents who do this. Peer cultures, for example, expose children to certain modes of dress, speech, and behavior, and not to others. Schools attempt—through the content of classroom materials, for example—to expose children to sets of ideas and role models that are supportive of core cultural values. In the United States, such values include individual rights, hard work, and private ownership. Even the media, in the content of their entertainment, largely reinforce such values, although there may be other areas—most notably sex and violence—where their content differs from what children experience in the home.

Modeling

We know that children often exhibit behavior to which they are repeatedly and systematically exposed, through a process called **modeling** (Bandura, 1977). Modeling begins with observing the behavior of significant others and with retention of the images of such behavior in a person's memory. The next stage is imitation, or reproduction, of that behavior. Eventually, however, this goes beyond mere imitation: The behavior is repeated until it becomes a matter of habit, and it is repeated in situations beyond that in which it was originally observed (Bandura, 1977). Moreover, the child comes to develop attitudes and beliefs that are supportive of the behavior. Obviously, you cannot model behaviors to which you are not exposed, which is what makes selective exposure such a powerful tool of socialization. Of course, what agents of socialization *say* and what they *do* are not always the same, and when there is a discrepancy between the two, what they *do* seems to have a greater effect than what they say (Bryan and Walbek, 1970a,

1970b; Rushton, 1975). If, for example, a parent preaches patience but shows a child impatience, the child will likely learn impatience to a greater extent than patience.

Reward and Punishment
When children imitate and repeat behaviors they learned from significant others, these significant others respond with approval. Approval can be verbal or nonverbal, sometimes taking the form of a concrete reward, such as a cookie or a trip to the beach. Thus, the processes of reward and punishment reinforce what is already being learned through selective exposure and modeling (Sears, Maccoby, and Lewin, 1957; Skinner, 1938, 1968). Both behavior and the expression of attitudes can be rewarded or punished by agents of socialization. Because merely expressing an attitude increases the probability that we will come to believe that attitude (see Festinger and Carlsmith, 1959), the process of reward and punishment acts to shape not only behavior, but attitudes and beliefs as well (Insko and Melson, 1969).

Reward and punishment are not always as obvious as giving or denying a child a cookie. Peer groups, for example, have a variety of ways to reward conformity and punish nonconformity. A friendly slap on the back or an invitation to join a group activity may be a reward for an approved action or viewpoint. Conversely, peer groups can be very harsh in their punishment of nonconformity, through ridicule, collective expressions of anger, or—worst of all—ostracism. In fact, with the exception of the mass media, which can only communicate one way, all agents of socialization use some form of reward and punishment to shape attitudes and behavior.

Nurturance and Identification
Both of the processes discussed above—selective exposure and modeling, and reward and punishment—are more effective if the child *identifies* with the person who is acting as an agent of socialization. By **identification**, we mean positive feelings toward the individual that lead the child to want to be like that person. These feelings are built in large part by the agent of socialization's nurturant behavior toward the child. These agents love and care about the child, and, in the case of parents, are the child's main source of support. When they help the child, he or she has an obligation to cooperate. All of this leads the child to love, admire, and want to please these agents.

Besides teaching and reinforcing desired behavior and beliefs, agents of socialization also give children important messages about how well they are playing their roles, as well as about what kind of person they are overall. Several of the theories of socialization we considered earlier, such as those of Mead, Cooley, and Erikson, hold that developing a healthy self-image and making normal progress through the steps and stages of life depend upon the messages given by agents of socialization. Thus, what kind of person a child grows up to become is shaped in no small part by such messages about self and role performance received from agents of socialization.

Conflicting Messages

Agents of socialization do not always give you the same message, either about what kind of person you *are* or what kind of person you *should be*. The kind of person your parents want you to be is not always the same kind of person your teachers, your clergy, or your peers want you to be. The media, too, present you with images of the ideal person, which may vary widely depending on what you read or watch. Handling these conflicting messages and expectations is a very important part of the socialization process. How do you respond when your parents want you to go to a family gathering, your athletic coach wants you to work out, your teacher expects you to do homework, and your friends want you to party with them, *all at the same time*? More fundamentally, how do you respond when different agents of socialization want you to be a different kind of person? What happens when you have to decide whether you want to be fun-loving and carefree or serious and achievement-oriented? These choices present both opportunities and difficulties.

Conflicting Agents and Stress
Clearly, these conflicting pressures from significant others can be a real source of stress in life. For many, they are the first experience with the condition of role conflict introduced in Chapter 4. In some cases, it is simply impossible to do what all of the agents of socialization are demanding. When this happens, there are two possible responses. One is

to try to do part of what each agent of socialization wants: Go to the family event this week, party with your friends next week, work out for your sport at some other available time, and stay up late to finish your homework. If the demands are too many, you can wind up exhausted or burned out, but most people seem to manage without reaching these extremes.

One strategy people use is to cite the demands of one agent of socialization as the reason for not complying with those of another: "My parents say I can't go with you because we have to go to my family reunion," or "If I don't go to this dance when all my friends are going, people will think there's something wrong with me!" The alternative is to block out or withdraw from some agents of socialization. To please your parents, you may stop seeing your friends and classmates socially. Or, to please your friends, you may skip your homework or even drop out of school. To use this mode of adaptation with the most important agents of socialization, such as family, school, and peers, is risky and often results in problems.

Sometimes, the messages of different agents of socialization are so different that, in addition to creating stress and conflict within the individual who is being socialized, the agents of socialization come into direct conflict with one another. Take for example the many controversies in recent years over books and films used in elementary and secondary school classrooms. Frequently these conflicts have pitted teachers seeking to broaden students' viewpoints against parents seeking to protect their children from what they see as harmful influences. Another example is illustrated in a study by Curry (1993; Curry and Strauss, 1994) of the socialization of athletes to accept sports injuries as a normal part of life—a message of "No pain, no gain" that conflicts with the larger society's message of "Don't do that, you might get hurt."

Conflicting demands among agents of socialization may give children different messages about themselves. Parents value children for *who they are* and love them unconditionally, while teachers and (and in some ways, peers) value them for *what they do*; approval and liking are not automatic. This can make going to school a difficult transition for some children. In addition, one agent of socialization may give a child a positive message at the same time that another is giving that child a negative message—sometimes in relation to the same behavior. Finally, peer socialization is different from other kinds of socialization in that it is the child's first experience of interacting with equals. To be integrated successfully into peer cultures, in both childhood and later life, children must discover how to learn from equals as well as from authority figures.

Conflicting Agents and Choice

While these conflicts among agents of socialization can be stressful, they also make choices possible, and indeed help teach us how to make choices. Suppose, for example, that you find that tuition, rent, and other expenses are exceeding your limited income as a college student, so you decide to save money by buying your clothes at a secondhand store. The next time your parents see you, they ask, "What's the matter with you? Are you trying to look like some kind of bum?" In the meantime, however, a friend tells you, "I like the way you're dressing lately. It's so much less pretentious than the way you used to dress." While you are in the process of changing your appearance, your parents and friends have offered you some new ideas to consider about the meaning of how you dress.

These different messages also help us develop beliefs, values, and skills in many areas of life. Political, religious, and goal-related attitudes are largely learned in the home. Lifestyle, entertainment, and leisure preferences are more likely to be learned from peers, as are skills related to cooperation, intimacy, and interpersonal relations (Davies and Kandel, 1981; Youniss, 1980). Work habits and how to participate in organizations are largely learned in school (Bowles and Gintis, 1976; Jackson, 1968). However, in all these areas, our ultimate values and habits are usually a product of some combination of the different agents of socialization.

Conflicting Agents and Social Change

In addition to offering choices at the individual level, the messages of different agents of socialization perform an important function at the societal level: They can act as a source of social change. The college student peer group, for example, functioned as a source of opposition to the Vietnam War, offering young college students in the 1960s a contrasting viewpoint about the war from what most were getting from authority figures. During the 1950s and 1960s, the black churches in the United States offered African Americans an alternative to the dominant view of race relations, as

It matters little where this college campus is located—it is evident that a nationwide informal dress code for college students prevails. Is this a peer-group norm, something created by the media or by marketing, or both? (Courtesy of John E. Farley)

well as a forum for social change (Morris, 1984). In both cases, the media took these messages and presented them to a larger audience. The broadcast media reported and televised the brutalization of black civil rights marchers in the South, and Hollywood began to produce antiwar movies and music. Eventually, these other agents of socialization spread the values associated with the peace movement and the Civil Rights movement through much of American society (Yankelovich, 1974, 1981). Thus, the new messages from an agent of socialization that conflicted with messages from mainstream society eventually became part of the mainstream.

An important side lesson of this experience is that what appears to be nonconformity often is not. While the college student participating in a protest or the African American marching for racial equality may be seen as violating the expectation of some agents of socialization (their parents, school authorities, or the police, for example), they are in most cases conforming to the expectations of other agents of socialization (a college student peer group or an African American church group, for example).

Socialization in Adulthood

Thus far, we have spoken of the socialization process primarily with reference to how it works in childhood and adolescence. It is in childhood that we encounter the most new roles and new situations, and thus it is in childhood that the socialization process is experienced most intensely. For this reason, childhood socialization is sometimes referred to as *primary socialization*. Socialization, however, does not end when one becomes an adult. Although many attitudes, beliefs, and behavior patterns have become fairly well established by this time, the process of socialization continues throughout life. Every time we enter a new situation or learn to play a new role, we go through a socialization process.

One example of adult socialization can be seen in the parenting process. While parents are socializing their children concerning how to take care of themselves and participate in society, their children are also socializing *them*. The adults are, in effect, learning the role of parent. In part, parents learn this role from their children, as they find out what "works" and what doesn't in the rearing of their children.

Life Cycle Roles

The adult life cycle presents us with numerous new situations that require the learning of new roles. In each of these, a socialization process occurs. Among these situations are leaving home to live on your own, entering college, beginning a career, changing jobs, getting married or cohabiting, becoming a parent, getting divorced or "breaking up," adjusting when your children grow up and leave home, retiring, and losing parents or a spouse through death. Not everyone experiences all of these things, and others experience some of them more than once. Thus, these changes should not be thought of as a clearly defined cycle through which everyone passes. In fact, the life cycle has become less uniform today than it was in the past. Even so, every adult experiences *some* of these changes, and every change requires a socialization process. The nature of this process is influenced by, among other things, the type of role change. For example, role changes may be voluntary or involuntary, may occur once or repeatedly, may or may not be reversible, may be made alone or along with other people, may occur quickly or gradually, and may occur alone or along with other role changes (Glaser and Strauss, 1971).

All of these factors influence the specific kind of socialization process that occurs with any given role change. For purposes of illustration, we shall examine the socialization processes that occur when you get a new job or start a family. Other situations requiring socialization are discussed in later chapters.

Getting a Job

When you complete your college education, many of you will embark on a career. Doing so will mean entering a new phase of socialization. You will have to learn what it really means to be a teacher, police officer, salesperson, accountant, or whatever role you choose. This will require you to assess what aspects of your prior education and training apply to your new role and what aspects do not. For many people starting out in a new job, it is distressing to hear "Forget everything you learned in college" (or in law school, police academy, sales training, or wherever you have been trained).

To survive in any career or profession, you must learn the norms of that career or profession and how to play the role in an acceptable way. To do so requires learning and accepting the profession's definition of that career as opposed to the public's definition. The meaning of a "good cop" from the viewpoint of other police officers may be different from the public's meaning of that term or from the meaning learned in the police academy. Similarly, a teacher who meets only the expectations of his or her students, and not those of other teachers, is not likely to feel accepted as a teacher and may doubt his or her success in that role (See, for example, Reynolds, 1992).

This leads to a second point: Every place of employment has its own subculture, which must be learned by any new employee who wants to succeed. To be effective, even new supervisors must learn this subculture. To complicate matters further, there may be more than one subculture to which the new employee must accommodate. He or she must please not only co-workers, but also supervisors, whose norms may be quite different. For some, there are also customers, clients, voters, patients, or students to keep happy. In a very real way, all of these different groups act as agents of socialization, and their messages concerning the work role are usually different.

Marriage and Family Changes

No matter how much two people may be "in love," getting married or even cohabiting requires major adjustments that in turn require a good deal of socialization. Different ideas concerning such things as money, orderliness of the house, division of housework, and even food preferences can be major sources of conflict unless both parties can learn to compromise or find a mutually satisfactory way of doing things. Those who have lived on their own experience a loss of freedom. Those who have not, run the risk of dependency. Some young people who have lived with their parents for all their lives until getting married risk becoming dependent on their spouses the same way they were dependent on their parents. Clearly the most important agent of socialization at this stage is the partner. However, to adjust successfully to this new reality, most young people also must interact with peers who are facing the same issues. Parents (and now in-laws) continue to act as agents of socialization at this stage and can be either helpful or a source of additional problems.

Becoming a Parent. When people become parents, time management can become a critical issue, particularly if both parents are employed full time. Conflicts between spouses or with parents over child rearing can require additional adjustment. As noted, children are important agents of socialization concerning how to be a parent. Typically, parents and peers also play a major role in this socialization process, as do the media, with their abundant material on parenting techniques.

An increasing number of American women now enter the role of parent before marriage, in which case they must both support and raise the child by themselves. When teenagers become parents, this may be the first adult role to which they must become socialized, and they must learn this difficult role under highly adverse conditions.

Return to Singlehood. Another new role that large numbers of Americans now face is returning to singlehood after a divorce or the end of a "live-in" relationship. About half of all marriages in the United States now end in divorce, so this is an adjustment that a large number of people must make. This adjustment is the subject of Diane Vaughan's essay in the "Personal Journey into Sociology" box "Uncoupling" on pages 144–45. As

Professor Vaughan illustrates, an important part of this socialization process is the development of a new (uncoupled) self-image or identity.

Role Change, Adult Socialization, and Stress

Professor Vaughan's essay illustrates another important sociological principle: We undergo a socialization process whenever we *leave* a social role, as well as when we enter one (Ebaugh, 1988). Senior athletes playing their last game, students graduating from college, and workers retiring all go through a process of role exit that bears some similarities to uncoupling. So do ex-nuns, people who change careers, and people who get sex-change operations—Ebaugh's research indicates that all of these people go through a similar process. Leaving one social role usually means entering another—but part of entering a new role involves giving up the behaviors and identities associated with the old one. This involves challenges of disengagement and letting go. At the same time, the old role still retains some influence over the person's identity, as illustrated by our frequent use of terms like ex-wife, ex-nun, and ex-president.

Role change is not entirely stressful. Learning a new role can be fun and exciting, and leaving behind old roles often involves leaving behind some stress as well. Wheaton (1990) studied people who went through nine kinds of role transitions including new job, job loss, marriage, divorce, having a child, and having one's children move out, among others. For seven of the nine, the degree of stress in one's *old* role was important in determining whether learning the new role presented emotional difficulties. Similarly, marital happiness—and sometimes overall life satisfaction—improves with the arrival of the "empty nest" when the last child moves out of the home (White and Edwards, 1990). Thus, while there is a socialization process involved in learning a new role, it can lead to increased happiness.

Resocialization in Total Institutions

A less ordinary type of adult socialization, which some experience and other do not, is resocialization in **total institutions**. The term *total institution*, developed by Irving Goffman (1961), refers to any group or organization that has almost total, continuous control over the individual and that attempts to erase the effects of the individual's previous socialization and instill a new set of values, habits, and beliefs. This process is referred to as **resocialization**. There are many examples of total institutions. One is the military, which takes people who generally believe that killing is wrong and seeks to convert them into fighting machines who will kill and risk their lives on order, without asking questions. Prisons, which seek to eliminate criminal habits and tendencies and convert offenders into law-abiding citizens, are another example. Other examples are religious cults, "deprogramming" aimed at weaning people away from religious cults, prisoner-of-war camps, many boarding schools, orphanages, some residential substance-abuse programs, reform schools, some nursing homes, and the environments created by kidnappers.

The Korean War: A Case Study

How do total institutions accomplish this? It is often said that they brainwash people. Thus, American prisoners of war on occasion defected to the North Koreans and North Vietnamese; Patty Hearst joined her kidnappers in robbing a bank; peace-loving people have turned into fierce fighters after being drafted and put through boot camp. Actually, though, what goes on in total institutions—"brainwashing," if you will—bears some striking similarities to ordinary socialization processes. Consider, for example, studies of the "brainwashing" of American prisoners of war during the Korean War. It is said that the Chinese prisoner-of-war (P.O.W.) camps were especially effective at this. How did they do it?

Studies of Americans who returned from Chinese P.O.W. camps revealed several important findings (Bauer, 1957; Schein, 1957, 1961). First of all, reward and punishment were used. Those who behaved and expressed ideas consistent with the desires of their captors were given somewhat greater freedom, whereas those who rebelled were placed in solitary confinement and, in some cases, were physically punished. Second, selective exposure was used. Some P.O.W.s were allowed to spend as many hours as they wanted reading in libraries, as good a way as any to pass a very boring time. These libraries, of course, were stocked only with materials sympathetic to the Chinese and

North Korean viewpoints. Contacts with their own culture were forbidden to the prisoners. Mail, for example, was not allowed to go through. The one exception was "bad mail"—unpaid bills, repossession notices, "Dear John" letters. The effect of this program, of course, was to foster a positive image of the Chinese and North Koreans, while isolating P.O.W.s from all but the unpleasant aspects of their own background.

Most effective of all, perhaps, was the Chinese policy of "lenience" (Schein, 1961). This was intended to create an atmosphere of nurturance, a sense of obligation. Most American P.O.W.s had originally been captured in North Korea and were later taken to Chinese P.O.W. camps. Because they had been captured in the immediate war zone, conditions in Korea were harsh. Long forced marches were the rule, and they were fatal to many P.O.W.s. Scarce food and clothing went to Chinese and North Korean soldiers before it went to prisoners. In the Chinese prison camps behind the lines, however, conditions were somewhat better. Food and shelter were generally adequate, and forced marches were unnecessary. The Chinese military used this to considerable advantage. First, many P.O.W.s became grateful for being treated better in China than in Korea and wanted to cooperate for that reason alone. Second, the fear of being sent back to Korea was enough to get most of the rest to cooperate, even if they didn't really want to.

We see, then, that the prisoner-of-war camp used some of the same techniques that are used in ordinary socialization processes—selective exposure and modeling, reward and punishment, and nurturance and identification.

Ordinary Socialization Versus Total Institutions

There are, however, four very important differences between resocialization in total institutions and ordinary socialization. First, the total institution seeks to eliminate the effects of previous socialization, whereas ordinary agents of socialization do not usually do this intentionally. Second, the total institution seeks to resocialize the individual strictly in accordance with its objectives. In short, the goal is to make a "good soldier," "communist sympathizer," or "cooperative inmate" out of the person. Thus, the objectives of the total institution, as opposed to the wishes or self-interests of the individual, are the entire purpose behind the process. Third, the total institution has complete, round-the-clock control of the individual and therefore does not have to compete with other agents of socialization. Finally, some total institutions use fatigue and physical brutality as additional ways of wearing people down. Endless questions and indoctrination and sleep deprivation are common. Eventually, the individual becomes so worn down that he or she has no energy left to resist the forced socialization, at least outwardly. Despite these very important differences, it remains true that there are important parallels between resocialization in total institutions and ordinary socialization.

Functionalist and Conflict Perspectives on Socialization

While the theories of socialization discussed earlier in this chapter describe and analyze the *process* of socialization, we should also address the functions and purposes of socialization within the larger society. Let us take a closer look at two perspectives that help us understand the role and the importance of socialization. The functionalist perspective addresses ways in which the socialization process helps to preserve and meet the needs of society, while the conflict perspective sees the socialization process as a key mechanism for preserving social inequality, and ensuring that the wealthy and powerful can pass on their advantages to their children.

The Functionalist Perspective

From a functionalist standpoint, there are several ways in which socialization preserves and meets the needs of society. It provides knowledge about adaptation to a society's physical and social environment. This knowledge, passed from generation to generation, helps the society survive and meet the demands of its environment. As we discussed in Chapter 4, *culture* carries this knowledge, and socialization is the means by which culture is passed from generation to generation. Culture, of course, also includes values and norms that are widely shared in a society, and as we have seen, functionalists see such shared values and norms as being essential to solidarity and cooperation.

PERSONAL JOURNEYS INTO SOCIOLOGY
Uncoupling

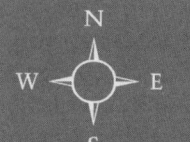

Diane Vaughan

I was married for twenty years. As I reflected on the relationship after our separation, the marriage seemed to have been coming slowly apart for the last ten. Certainly we had our good times, but I could retrospectively pick out turning points—moments when the relationship changed, times when the distance between us increased. These turning points did not hinge on arguments or the typical emotional catastrophes that beset any relationship. Instead, they appeared to be related to changes in each of our social worlds. For example, I started college because I realized I was never going to have the steady companionship of my partner and needed something of my own to do. This step, innocently taken, changed me—and us. As our marriage aged, we reacted to our difficulties by altering our relation to the world around us. Those changes, in turn, affected the relationship, changing us as individuals and our relationship to each other.

What's more, when I thought about our relationship in terms of our maneuverings in the social world, it seemed as if our marriage had eroded slowly and steadily over time in a regular, orderly way. Although we personally experienced the ending of the relationship as chaotic and disruptive, its ending took on a kind of social rhythm. That an experience could be orderly and disorderly at the same time was counterintuitive. Perhaps this orderliness was because ours was a long marriage, and thus its ending extended over a long period, giving the appearance of an orderly dissolution. Perhaps it was a natural reflection of my occupation then: a graduate student in sociology, being trained to look for order.

During the same period, I came across an article describing marriage as a process in which two individuals renegotiate who they are with respect to each other and the world around them. They restructure their lives around each other. They create common friends, belongings, memories, and a common future. They redefine themselves as a couple, in their own eyes and in the eyes of others, who respond to the coupled identity they are creating. They are invited out as a twosome; mail comes addressed to both; the IRS taxes them jointly. Single friends may hesitate to call, while the two people are readily incorporated into the social world of those who also are coupled. The coupled identity they create is constantly reaffirmed, not only by the words and deeds of others but also by the way others come to take the relationship for granted. This continual public confirmation gives them a stable location in the social world and validates their identity.

These ideas immediately captured my interest, for what appeared to have happened as my own relationship deteriorated was a reversal of this process: We slowly and over time began redefining ourselves as separate people. Rather than an abrupt ending, ours appeared to have been a gradual transition. Long before we physically separated, we had been separating socially—developing separate friends, experiences, and futures. We reacted to our changing relationship in ways that altered the definitions that we held of ourselves and that others held of us.

In order to answer the question raised by my own experience, I began interviewing people about how their relationships ended. I wanted to learn about the relationships of people who had lived together as well as those who were married. Thus, my interest was not divorce but uncoupling—how people living together

On the other hand, society must be able to change in order to adapt to new situations. The fact that there are different agents of socialization, and that these agents often give somewhat different messages, offers a means by which this can occur. Because these agents of socialization offer different messages, the individual has the opportunity to choose the message that promotes change. The youthful peer group and the media may play particularly important roles in this process (Corsaro and Rizzo, 1988, 1990; Meyerowitz, 1985).

The Conflict Perspective

From a conflict perspective, the socialization process helps the wealthy and powerful preserve and pass on their advantages. In general, the socialization process teaches people to accept, not challenge in a sexually intimate relationship (gay and straight couples as well as the married) make transitions out of their relationships. I began collecting biographies of individual relationships. In interviews, I asked people to tell me about their relationships, beginning with the moment they first sensed something was wrong. I tape recorded their narratives, interjecting questions.

As a result of my inquiry, I discovered that uncoupling occurs in a uniform way—a describable pattern that is the same regardless of sexual preference or marital status. In a reversal of coupling, the partners redefine themselves, both in their own eyes and in the eyes of others, as separate entities once again. Getting out of a relationship entails a redefinition of self at several levels: in the private thoughts of the individual, between partners, and in the larger social context in which the relationship exists. Uncoupling is complete when the partners have defined themselves and are defined by others as separate and independent of each other—when being partners is no longer a major source of identity.

Typically, uncoupling happens like this: One person, the initiator, becomes discontented with the relationship. This person begins lobbying for change and, unable to achieve it, unintentionally begins responding to his or her personal problems in a way that begins to divide the couple. The initiator begins socially and psychologically leaving the relationship. At some point, what began unintentionally becomes intentional: The initiator, though deeply affected by the possibility of the loss, wants out.

By the time the partner realizes something is seriously wrong, the initiator has already gone in many ways. The initiator has mourned the relationship, thought about living apart, begun creating a separate lifestyle, and, in many cases, experimented with it. The partner, in contrast, has done none of these things. In fact, it is often at the moment of separation that the partner first realizes the relationship is in trouble. At this point, the initiator has been in transition for some time, and the partner's efforts to save the relationship are likely to fail. The rejected partner then begins the transition that the initiator began long before: acknowledging the problems, lobbying for change, mourning the relationship, developing separate friends, seeking alternatives to the relationship, and gradually preparing for a life alone.

When relationships come apart, both people make the same transition, but it starts and ends at different times for each. Consequently, understanding the impact of uncoupling hinges upon whether one is the initiator or partner in a relationship. Initiators have the advantage of time—time to think about and, in many instances, prepare for a life without the partner. When separation occurs, the partner is thrust into an unwanted new life for which he or she is socially and psychologically unprepared. Admittedly, identifying who is the initiator and who is being left behind is not so easy in some cases. Over the course of a long relationship, these roles may be passed back and forth, with one person assuming the role of initiator at one time and the other acting to end the relationship at another. How these roles get passed back and forth is, in fact, one of the more intriguing aspects of the uncoupling process.

Diane Vaughan is Professor of Sociology and International and Public Affairs, Columbia University. Her research interests are the sociology of organizations; science, knowledge, and technology; and culture. Her work has focused on "the dark side of organizations": how organizations fail. She is the author of *Controlling Unlawful Organizational Behavior: Social Structure and Corporate Misconduct* (University of Chicago Press, 1983), *Uncoupling: Turning Points in Intimate Relationships* (Oxford University Press, 1986), and *The Challenger Launch Decision: Risky Technology, Culture, and Deviance at NASA* (University of Chicago Press, 1996). After the 2003 explosion of NASA's Space Shuttle Columbia, she worked with the Columbia Accident Investigation Board as a researcher and writer on the official accident investigation report.

---

or question, the ways of their society. Recall that conflict theorists see the values, beliefs, and practices of society as serving the interests of the dominant group in society. To ask, "Do things have to be this way?" or "Isn't there a better way?" would be to challenge a status quo that works to the advantage of the wealthy and powerful. Rather than do this, socialization generally teaches children to value the greatness of their society: "This is a great country" and "Be grateful that you live here." Significantly, virtually all societies include such content in their socialization process. As is shown in the Sociological Surprises box, "Another Look at Waltzing Matilda," even popular music and popular culture often act as socialization agents in this way.

Nonetheless, it is important to point out that opposition groups do sometimes form within and as a result of socialization processes. Black churches, for example, became organizing bases for the Civil Rights movement (Morris, 1984), and

SOCIOLOGICAL SURPRISES
Another Look at "Waltzing Matilda"— Why Did the Words Change?

As we mentioned in the earlier box on "Waltzing Matilda," this popular Australian folk song contains a second lesson about socialization. As we noted, the original first line of the song was as follows:

Oh, there once was a swagman camped in the billabong

As the song is sung today, however, the wording is slightly different:

Once a jolly swagman camped by a billabong

Why, a sociologist might ask, did the swagman become "jolly?" It turns out that when the Australian folksinger and social historian Dennis O'Keeffe (2000) researched the history of the song, he discovered a sociological surprise. O'Keefe discovered in his research that the song was based on a real event that occurred in 1894—and it turns out that the real swagman was anything but "jolly."

In the remainder of the story told by the song, three policemen arrive and demand that the swagman return the jumbuck (sheep) he has stolen. But instead, he jumps in the lake and drowns, and his ghost may be heard forevermore at the lakeshore singing the chorus of "Waltzing Matilda." In real life, however, the swagman was a union organizer for the sheep shearer's union, which was engaged in a bitter strike against the landowners who hired them to shear their sheep. In the preceding days, both the landowners and the strikers had engaged in violent conflict. The strikers had burned a boat that had been used to bring in strikebreakers and the landowners or strikebreakers had murdered a union activist. In retaliation for the murder, a group of unionists burned a shearing shed, killing over 100 sheep. One of these union activists, named Samuel "Frenchy" Hoffmeister, turns out to be the "swagman" in the song. Hoffmeister, being chased down by police the next day, apparently took his life in a final act of defiance against the police and the landowners, willing to die rather than be taken captive. Or, perhaps, he was just killed by the police, who then reported his death as a suicide.

So why did he become "jolly" in the song? Conflict theory offers us an answer. Taken in its original meaning, the song celebrates a defiant union activist willing to die rather than allow himself to be arrested by the police. Jumping in the billabong (lake) and drowning thus becomes a final act of defiance of what he viewed as an evil, corrupt, and exploitive system in the sheep-shearing industry. So telling the true story could lead people to ask questions about exploitation of labor and economic inequality. But conflict theory tells us that a function of socialization is to teach people to accept, not question, the inequalities in society. So by making the swagman "jolly," he could be presented as a harmless wanderer who just grabbed a sheep to get something to eat, rather than a union organizer challenging economic inequality and willing to die for his beliefs. In fact, one thing that popularized the song was its use beginning in 1903 (with the new words, of course) as an advertising jingle for an Australian tea. Do you think that, had the true origins and meanings of the song been known, it could have become the popular "national song" that it has become?

universities for the movement against the Vietnam War. Thus, agents of socialization *can* act as agents of social change, but that is probably not their usual or predominant effect.

Finally, conflict theory argues that socialization operates as a process of **social channeling** (Bowles and Gintis, 1976). It prepares the children of the wealthy and powerful for lives of wealth and power, by teaching them the values, beliefs, behaviors, and information they will need for such life. On the other hand, the children of the poor are channeled toward a life of poverty. We discuss this process in detail in Web-Based Chapter A. Because of the linkages between social class and race, this process also helps perpetuate racial inequality. Finally, "gender-role socialization," discussed in Chapter 8, similarly prepares women and men for different and unequal roles, thereby helping pass from generation to generation the social and economic advantages enjoyed by males. A recent study shows how long-lasting the effects of gender-role socialization can be. Women received the right to vote in the United States in 1920. But as recently as the 1980s, women who came of age before or just after women received the right to vote remained less likely to vote than women who grew up in later generations (Firebaugh and Chen, 1995).

Summary

This chapter has explained that social interaction is necessary for normal human development and that such interaction plays a central role in all theories about socialization. Besides meeting the need for interaction, socialization also teaches people the things they need to know in order to survive and develop in their physical and social environments. Particularly critical is the learning of social roles and norms.

Social scientists disagree about the roles nature and nurture play in human development. Interactionists see nurture—social interaction—as the dominant force, with personality being determined by the messages you get from others and your interpretation of those messages. As children develop, they learn the concept of roles, and they shift from interacting with individuals to playing roles and interacting with other roles played by other people. Freudian theory, in contrast, sees the expectations of society in fundamental conflict with basic drives such as aggression and sexuality. It holds that the ways in which these conflicts are resolved (or left unresolved) in childhood have a major impact on adult personality.

The cognitive-developmental approach, which focuses on reasoning processes, sees the child's physiological development as a factor limiting their cognitive development. But one's ability to reason also is affected by environmental or situational influences and experience. People develop through a series of stages with social interaction determining to a great degree how far a person proceeds and when. Closely related are theories concerning moral reasoning, such as those of Kohlberg. These theories see moral reasoning as progressing through a similar series of stages linked to reasoning ability. However, the ability to relate to the roles of others is necessary in order to move to higher stages. This, as well as a good part of the individual's reasoning ability, is gained through interaction with others.

The socialization process is carried out by agents of socialization, which include the family, schools, religion, peer groups, and the media. Although the family is probably the most influential of these agents, different agents predominate at different stages of life. To a greater or lesser extent, all of them shape behavior through processes of selective exposure and modeling, reward and punishment, and feedback and identification. Most agents of socialization also deliver messages to the individual that play a critical role in defining his or her self-image.

Socialization is a lifelong process, even though it occurs most intensively during the childhood period of primary socialization. In adulthood, people undergo a new socialization process each time they enter a new role, such as leaving their parents' home, starting college, getting a job, getting married or divorced, having children, retiring, or experiencing the death of a spouse. In extraordinary circumstances, they may experience resocialization in a total institution, such as a prison, which uses its complete control over the individual to erase old values and beliefs and instill new ones.

The functionalist and conflict theories offer different explanations of the meaning and purpose of the socialization process. To functionalists, the process helps people learn to participate in society, perpetuates social knowledge and culture, and supports consensus and solidarity. To conflict theorists, it tends to serve the interests of the dominant group by bringing about false consciousness and social channeling. Both perspectives, however, recognize that conflicting messages from different agents of socialization can act as an important source of social change. It is this social change that allows society to adapt to new conditions, and also offers a source of opportunity for disadvantaged groups to improve their position in society.

Key Terms

socialization
play stage
significant others
self
role model
game stage
id
superego

ego
cognitive-development theories
cognitive processes
agents of socialization
modeling
identification
total institution
resocialization
social channeling

Exercises

1. The text discusses the *nature vs. nurture issue*. One very interesting example of the nature-nurture debate involves the cause(s) of *alcoholism*. To what extent do people *learn* to be alcoholics, or are they biologically predisposed to become alcoholics? WebMD has medical information on alcoholism. Do a search on the causes of alcoholism on WebMD, and contrast that with a search of your library's sociological database (for example, The Sociological Abstracts). Write a short essay on where you stand on the above questions.

2. One of the best-known sociological theories of socialization is Charles H. Cooley's looking glass self (see Chapter 3). In 1902, Cooley explained this concept in his book *Human Nature and the Social Order.*

   - Try to visualize an example of your own socialization experiences involving the *looking-glass self.*
   - Can you recall a situation where you imagined how others were reacting to your behavior and you were *incorrect*? For example, you might have felt that other people were reacting *positively* to something you said or did, when, in fact, you found out later that they were reacting negatively.

Part III
Social Structure and Inequality

Chapter 6
Stratification: Structured Social Inequality

What Is Stratification?   153
    Dimensions of Stratification   153
    The Economic Dimension   153
    The Political Dimension   153
    The Social Prestige Dimension   154

The Distribution of Wealth and Income in the United States   154
    The Distribution of Income   154
    The Distribution of Wealth   155

Socioeconomic Mobility   156
    Caste Systems   157
    Estate or Feudal Systems   158
    Class Systems   158
    International Comparisons of Mobility   160

Social Class in U.S. Society   161
    The Marxian Definition of Social Class   161
    The Composite Definition of Social Class   162
    The Subjective Definition of Social Class   162
    Occupational Prestige   163
    Class Consciousness in the United States   165

Poverty in the United States   167
    How Poverty Is Defined   167
    Poverty in America: The Current Situation   168
    Who Is Poor?   169

Causes of Poverty   170
    Poor People Themselves? Work, Family Structure, and Poverty   170
    Unemployment   174
    Low Wages   175
    Government Policy   175

Consequences of Poverty   176

Functionalist and Conflict Perspectives on Stratification   177
    The Functionalist View: Davis and Moore   177
    The Conflict View   177
    Is Stratification Really Functional?   178
    Synthesis   179

Summary   182

Key Terms   183

Exercises   183

From mid-1999 through mid-2009, Larry Ellison, chief executive of Oracle, Inc., was paid a little over half a million dollars. That wasn't for ten years, though, or even his annual salary. That's how much he received *every day* over that ten-year period, making him the highest-paid American CEO of the decade. Mr. Ellison received a total of 1.8357 *billion* dollars over the ten-year period in salary, benefits, options, and long-term compensation. Although his income was the highest, others were not far behind. Barry Diller, CEO of Expedia, also received over a billion dollars for the decade, and the chief executives of Occidental Petroleum, Apple, Capital One Financial, Countrywide Financial, and Nabors Industries each were paid a half billion or more (*Wall Street Journal,* 2010). And as high as these top incomes are, they have been rising sharply over the past two decades, even as the incomes of other Americans have been at times quite stagnant. The incomes of the top 400 Americans tripled during the Clinton administration and doubled in the first seven years of the Bush administration, rising more than 30 percent in just one year between 2006 and 2007 (Johnson, 2010; Domhoff, 2010). And in 2007, the top 400 income-earners got about 1.6% of all the income in the United States—three times the share they got in the 1990s (Wessel, 2010)—even though they constitute only three ten-thousandths of one percent of the country's taxpayers. Yet these taxpayers on average paid only between 16 and 17 percent of their income in taxes (Wessel, 2010), less than the actual rate of taxes paid by Americans with annual incomes of $200,000 (MyTaxCut.us, 2010). The salary of CEOs in the United States is far higher than in other countries. According to Graef Crystal of the University of California at Berkeley, the chief executives of the largest U.S. companies were paid about six times as much as their Japanese counterparts in 1992, and U.S. CEOs are paid much more today than they were in 1992.

While executive salaries soared to stratospheric heights, the income of ordinary Americans grew

Larry Ellison, top, and the poor family shown above illustrate the extremes of economic inequality in the United States. It would take the annual incomes of twenty-three families living at the poverty level to add up to what Mr. Ellison received every day in 2009. (Ellison photo: AP Photo/Paul Sakuma; family photo: AP Photo/Jae C. Hong)

only modestly, as noted above. As recently as 1980, according to *Business Week,* the average CEO received "just" 42 times the average blue-collar worker's pay. In 2008, the average CEO received 319 times as much compensation as the average full-time worker—not as extreme a difference as in 2000, but still dramatically more than in 1980, less than three decades earlier. The immense contrast between the wealthiest CEOs and the poorest Americans is hard to imagine. The combined *annual* income of 23 four-person families living at the poverty level would be less than what Larry Ellison received *every day* for ten years! Somewhere between Larry Ellison and the family living in poverty are the great mass of middle-income Americans.

Somewhere between Sanford Weill and the family living in poverty are the great mass of middle-income Americans. Their incomes have remained stable (adjusting for inflation), but their share of the nation's income is less than it was thirty years ago. In 1967, the middle 20 percent of the population received 17.3 percent of total income. By 1999, this had fallen to 14.9 percent. Adjusted for inflation, the income of a household at the top of this middle group was almost exactly the same in 1994 as it had been in 1979; then between 1994 and 1999 it rose about 10 percent. In contrast, the much higher incomes of those in the top 5 percent of the population rose by about 16 percent between 1979 and 1994, rose by *another* 15 percent between 1994 and 1999 (U.S. Census Bureau, 2000a) and an *additional* 25 percent by 2008 (U.S. Census Bureau, 2009. World Wide Web). http://www.census.gov/hhes/www/income/histinc/ineqtoc.html.

Clearly, these figures indicate the existence of great and increasing inequality in American society. Although inequality is more extreme in the United States than in other industrialized nations, the United States has no monopoly on social inequality. In this chapter, we shall examine the nature, causes, and consequences of social stratification: structured inequality in the distribution of scarce resources. A scarce resource can be anything people want that is not abundant enough for all people to have as much as they want. Money, power, and fame are all examples of scarce resources.

What Is Stratification?

Some form of social stratification exists in all societies. These patterns of stratification can be thought of as ranking systems within societies. People can be ranked on the basis of how much of the society's scarce resources they own and control. Those with a large share of scarce resources rank high; those with a small share rank low.

Dimensions of Stratification

Different kinds of scarce resources are distributed unequally in society. A person could, for example, have a great deal of money, yet have a low status in the community—a situation humorously portrayed in the television series "Beverly Hillbillies."

These different ranking systems, based on the distribution of different scarce resources, have been referred to by sociologists as **dimensions of stratification.** A major contribution of the classic social theorist Max Weber (1968 [orig. 1922]) was his recognition that most societies have three major dimensions of stratification: an economic dimension (wealth and income), a political dimension (power), and a social prestige dimension (status). Let us consider each.

The Economic Dimension

The economic dimension of stratification concerns money and the things it can buy. It involves two key variables, *income* and *wealth*, which are related but are not the same.

Income refers to the amount of money that a person or family receives over some defined period of time, usually a calendar year. Essentially, it is what you report on your income-tax form in April. Data on income in the United States are readily available because the Census Bureau asks Americans about their incomes in annual surveys and in the decennial Census.

Wealth refers to the total value of everything that a person or family owns, minus any debts owed. It is similar in meaning to "net worth." Thus, wealth refers not to what you receive over some time period, but to what you have at a particular point in time. Data on wealth are collected less often, but are becoming more available than in the past.

The Political Dimension

Power can be defined as the ability to get people to behave as you want them to behave. Power usually is exercised through the political system, at least to some extent. Thus, voting, office holding, lobbying, contributing to campaigns, boycotting, striking, and demonstrating are all means by which people can exercise power. Because power is an abstract concept, it is hard to measure. But sociologists often study it indirectly by looking at who wins when different groups conflict, or by who occupies decision-making positions. We will examine this dimension further in Chapter 12.

The Social Prestige Dimension

The third dimension of stratification is social **prestige,** sometimes referred to as *status.* This dimension has to do with what people think of you. If people think highly of you and you are well known, you have a high level of status or prestige. If people think poorly of you, you have a low level of prestige. By definition, prestige is a scarce resource. Being "well regarded" is always a relative or comparative matter. It would be meaningless to be well regarded if everyone were equally well regarded. Then everyone would be the same, and nobody would stand out.

There are numerous ways to gain prestige or status. People can get status on the basis of their family name, if, for example, they happen to be a Rockefeller or a Kennedy, or, perhaps, a Fonda or a Jackson. They can get it on the basis of their education or occupation—as we shall see later, occupation is one of the most consistent determinants of status. Accomplishments, titles, and public exposure can be sources of status or prestige. Ultimately, however, prestige is a matter of what people think. Thus, the best way to measure it is to ask. Surveys of occupational prestige, most admired person, most recognized name, and so forth are important ways of measuring prestige.

The Distribution of Wealth and Income in the United States

The Distribution of Income

In 2008, the median family income in the United States was $50,303 (U.S. Census Bureau, 2009a). As you will recall from Chapter 2, median family income is the income level that is in the middle of the distribution: half of all families have incomes above the median; half have incomes below the median. For individual adults not married or living with their parents, the median income in 2001 was $21,314 (U.S. Census Bureau, 2004). Income is distributed quite unequally in the United States. In 2008, the top one-fifth of households received 50.0 percent of all income, nearly 15 times the share that went to the bottom fifth (3.4 percent) (U.S. Census Bureau, 2009b).

A limited number of families and individuals at the very top get an especially large share of the nation's income. For example, the richest 5 percent of American households received more than 6 times the income received by the poorest 20 percent of households in 2008, as shown in Figure 6.1. In fact, this 5 percent actually receive a much larger share of the nation's household income than the lowest 40 percent of households do.

The Trend: More or Less Equal?
Do these figures represent more or less inequality than in the past? The answer is that, over the long run, there has not been a great deal of change, but since the mid-1970s, as is illustrated in Figure 6.1, the distribution has clearly shifted in the direction of inequality (Olsen, 1990; Burtless, 1990). Over the longer term of American history, there has been some limited change in the degree of inequality. There was some shift toward greater equality between about 1929 and 1944 (Fusfeld, 1976, p. 630)—a period roughly corresponding to Franklin Roosevelt's New Deal and World War II. For the next thirty years, there was little change. Since the 1970s, there appears to be some shift back to the pre-Roosevelt pattern, as the rich have gotten richer and the poor poorer. This is a fairly significant change, given the relatively small changes across the longer term of American history (Bartlett and Steele, 1992). In fact, recent analysis of Internal Revenue Service data by Saez (2009b) shows that the share of total income going to the top 10 percent of the population in income had, by 2007, reached a higher point than in any year since 1917.

Income Inequality: A Comparative View
How does the United States compare to other countries in its distribution of income? First, it is important to point out that virtually all industrialized countries distribute income more equally than most preindustrial, less economically developed countries (Fusfeld, 1976, p. 630). As countries industrialize and modernize, their inequality tends to decrease (Lenski, 1966). The appropriate standard

Figure 6.1 Share of Income Going to Highest 5% and Lowest 20%, United States, 1967–2008

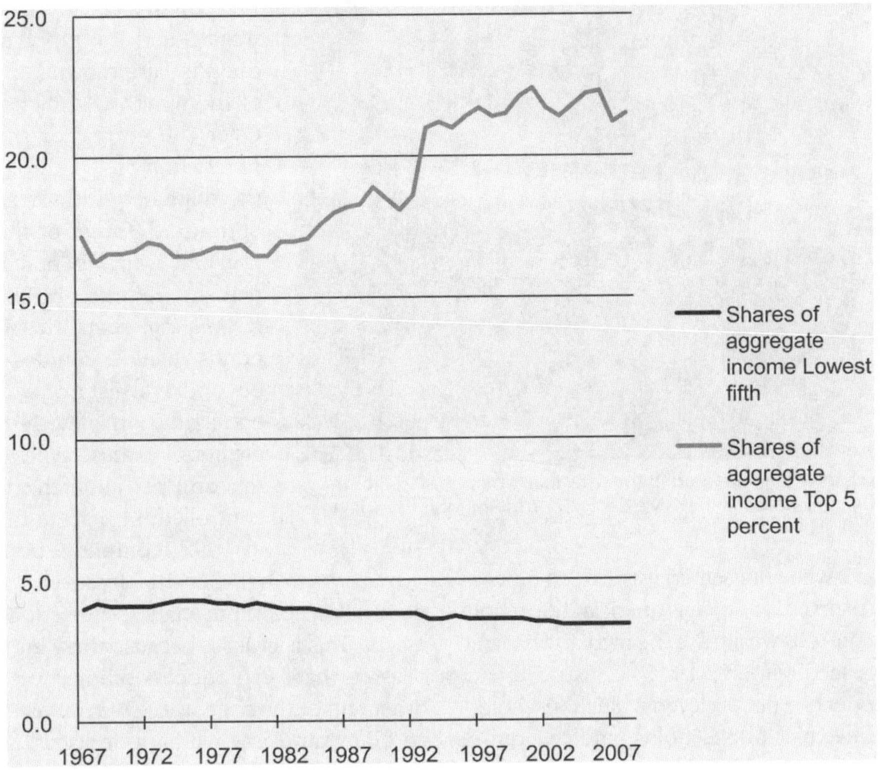

— Shares of aggregate income Lowest fifth
— Shares of aggregate income Top 5 percent

For footnotes, see www.census.gov/hhes/www/income/histinc/ftnotes.html
For suggested citations, see www.census.gov/main/www/citation.html
Source: U.S. Census Bureau, Current Population Survey, Annual Social and Economic Supplements. For information on confidentiality protection, sampling error, nonsampling error, and definitions, see www.census.gov/apsd/techdoc/cps/cpsmar09.pdf[PDF].

of comparison for the United States, then, is other countries that have already industrialized.

The United States has greater income inequality than virtually all such countries. Table 6.1 shows that income inequality in the United States is far above average for industrialized countries. The wealthiest 10 percent of Americans receive a larger share of total income than do the wealthiest 10 percent in any of the other countries, and the poorest 10 percent of Americans receive a smaller share than their counterparts in any of the other countries. Overall, the top 10 percent in the United States receive about sixteen times as much as the bottom 10 percent, more than in any other country. In the other countries, the top 10 on average receive just over eight times as much as the bottom 10 percent—half the difference that is found in the United States. Thus, in the United States, the wealthy receive more income relative to the poor than in other industrialized countries, and this gap has widened in recent years.

The Distribution of Wealth

As unequal as the distribution of income is in the United States, wealth is even more unequally distributed. A 1995 Census Bureau survey showed that, nationally, just 10 percent of the population owns half of all household wealth, and the top 30 percent of the population owns more than 80 percent of the household wealth (computed from U.S. Census Bureau, 2001b, Tables 4 and 5). Another survey in 2002 showed that the median

Heat, cold, fires, and vermin are among the risks faced by poor families that live in housing like this home in New Mexico. (Courtesy of John E. Farley)

non-Hispanic white household was sixteen times as wealthy as the median African American household and eleven times as wealthy as the median Hispanic household; see Figure 6.2 (U. S. Census Bureau, 2008b). About one out of eleven white households, one out of five black households, and one out of six Hispanic households had zero or negative net worth (U.S. Census Bureau, 2001b; see also Oliver and Shapiro, 1995).

Another survey, the Survey of Consumer Finance (SCF), is considered particularly useful because it includes an oversampling of the very wealthy, a group so small that it usually is largely missed in surveys like the Census study described above. The SCF shows that in 1998, just 0.5 percent of the population owned 26 percent of the wealth, and the top 1 percent of the population owned 34 percent of the wealth (Kennickell, 2000). Over the course of this survey series, from 1963 through 1998, the share of wealth owned by the bottom *90 percent* of the population fell from 36 percent to 31 percent (Kennickell, 2000). And for *financial assets,* that is, stocks, bonds, bank accounts—anything beyond real estate or cars—the concentration of wealth is even greater. For these types of assets, the top 1 percent of the population controlled 43 percent of all assets in 1998 (computed from Kenickell, 2000)! Moreover, the top 10 percent owned more than 75 percent of all such assets. This is crucial, because these are the kinds of assets that can produce additional wealth. At the other end of the scale, the 1993 Survey of Income and Program Participation found that, among the least wealthy one-fourth of the population, only one person out of twenty-eight owned securities (U.S. Bureau of the Census, 1995b, Table 2).

Socioeconomic Mobility

Thus far, we have described the degree of economic inequality found in the United States. A separate,

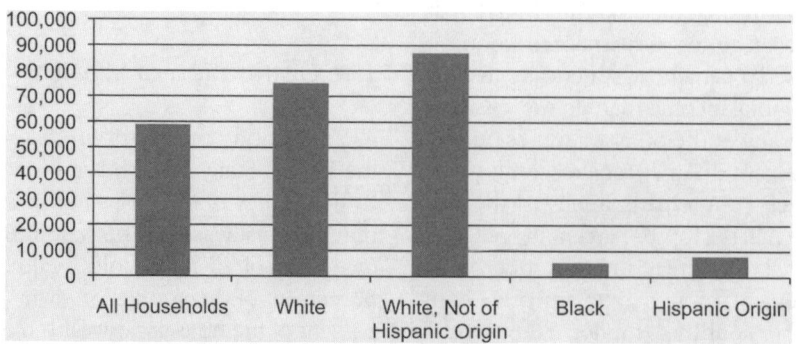

Figure 6.2 Median Household Net Worth, 2002

Source: U.S. Census Bureau, Wealth and Asset Ownership, 2002, Table 1. Median Value of Assets for Households, by Type of Asset Owned and Selected Characteristics: 2002. http://www.census.gov/hhes/www/wealth/2002/wlth02-1.html.

although related, question about the degree of inequality concerns **socioeconomic mobility**: the frequency with which people move up and down in the society's economic hierarchy. In a society with very high socioeconomic mobility, it would not be unusual for a person to be born very poor and end up very wealthy as an adult—or the other way around. In sociological terms, a society such as this would have an **open stratification system**. In this type of system, achieved statuses have substantial influence over the social status a person attains in adulthood. In a society with very low mobility, those born poor nearly always stay poor, and those born wealthy nearly always stay wealthy. This type of society is said to have a **closed stratification system**. In a closed stratification system, ascribed statuses largely determine a person's social position throughout life.

Among all societies, there is generally greater mobility in societies that have less inequality. The main reason for this is that as preindustrial societies modernize and become industrialized societies, inequality declines and mobility increases over the long run. However, among societies at any given level of industrialization, the relationship between the degree of inequality and the amount of mobility is much weaker.

Sociologists have classified societies into three types, based on their degree of mobility. The least mobility is found in *caste systems*, with only modestly greater mobility in *estate* or *feudal systems*.

Table 6.1 Income Inequality in 14 Industrialized Countries

Country	Ratio of highest 10% to lowest 10%	Gini Index
Japan	4.5	24.9
Finland	5.6	26.9
Norway	6.1	25.8
Sweden	6.2	25.0
Germany	6.9	28.3
Denmark	8.1	24.7
Belgium	8.2	33.0
Switzerland	9.0	33.7
France	9.1	32.7
Netherlands	9.2	30.9
Canada	9.4	32.6
Italy	11.6	36.0
United Kingdom	13.8	36.0
United States	15.9	40.8

Source: United Nations. 2007. *Human Development Report, 2007/2008.* New York: United Nations Development Program.

Both of these types of society are typically found in preindustrial societies. *Class systems*, usually found in industrialized societies, have greater, but far from unlimited, mobility.

Caste Systems

As noted above, the least mobility is found in a **caste system**. A caste system has formally defined and unequal groupings that are determined by birth and inheritance, and are not subject to change. A person born into a particular **caste** remains in that caste for life, can marry only other members of the same caste, and passes this caste status on to his or her children. In sociological terms, the ascribed status of the caste you are born into completely determines your position throughout life; achieved statuses make no difference.

Although caste systems have existed in some form in many societies, the two best-known examples are systems once found in India and South Africa. India's caste system was based on religion, and existed for thousands of years until it was officially abolished in 1949. South Africa's caste system was a **racial caste system**, that is, a caste system in which caste membership was determined by race. This system, known as **apartheid**, was established by law in 1948 and lasted for more than four decades until, officially speaking, it was gradually dismantled in the 1990s.

In India, different roles were assigned by caste for centuries—ranging from the priestly functions of the highest caste, the Brahmans, to a life of common labor for the lowest castes. These lowest castes were defined as "untouchable" by higher castes, meaning that all contact was forbidden—even looking at one another. In South Africa's caste system, the groups were defined on the basis of race, with whites, blacks, Asians, and "coloreds" (people of mixed race) defined as legal categories. Rules of separation were very strict: For example, it was a crime to even conspire to have sex with a person of a different race—whether or not any sex actually occurred. Voting and holding political office were initially permitted only to whites (less than 10 percent of the population), though some of these rights were later extended to Asians and coloreds.

Because such rigid systems are hard to maintain in urban, industrial societies, and because of intense external pressure for change, both India and South Africa have officially abolished their

Under India's caste system, members of the "untouchable" class were relegated to jobs such as street sweeping. Although the country's caste system was officially ended in 1949, it continues to influence behavior, thereby limiting social and economic stability. (iStockphoto)

caste systems. However, vestiges remain in both countries. In India, lower castes remain over-represented among the poor, and in many rural areas, people still pay a good deal of attention caste membership. And in South Africa, where the abolition of apartheid led to black majority rule in 1994, economic inequality is still very much tied to race. Educational levels are lower, poverty rates are much higher, and health is significantly worse in the black population than it is in the white population, with Asians and coloreds still occupying an intermediate status.

Even in the United States, a caste system once existed—the Jim Crow system of the South during much of the twentieth century. Like South Africa, where one could go and what one could do was determined by race in a strict system of legally defined segregation. Similar laws also existed in some northern areas. Today, the law forbids such discrimination, but as is discussed in Chapter 7, vestiges of the old system remain in the form of sharp socioeconomic inequalities between whites and African Americans.

Estate or Feudal Systems

The **estate system**, also called the feudal system, offers slightly more mobility than the caste system. In an estate system, status is determined on the basis of land ownership, often accompanied by some type of formal title. In general, the high-status groups are those who own land, and the rest of the population generally works for them. Some variety of the estate system has been found in most of the world at some point in history, including the feudal systems of medieval Europe and of China and Russia in the nineteenth and early twentieth centuries, and the *hacienda* systems of Latin America, some of which remain largely intact today. The American South before the Civil War, where wealth and power were concentrated in the hands of large-scale plantation owners, is often regarded as a form of feudal or estate system, although slavery also made it a type of racial caste system.

In a feudal system, your position throughout life is usually determined by the ascribed status of whether you were born into the landowning class. Occasionally, however, titles that permit entry into this elite class may be conferred. In the European feudal system, for example, a peasant could occasionally be knighted or admitted to the clergy, which gave him the privileges associated with these landowning classes. However, this was the exception to the rule. Because of their link to land ownership, estate systems are found in agricultural, preindustrial societies. When societies begin to urbanize, the feudal system almost inevitably breaks down.

Class Systems

The highest degree of mobility is found in **class systems**. In a class system, both ascribed statuses and achieved statuses have significant effects on people's income, wealth, and social position. In other words, people who are born into affluent families generally enjoy a higher status as adults than people who are born into poorer families, but what people do—the amount of schooling they attain and the success of their personal and economic decisions—also influences their status as adults. Class systems are typically found in modern industrial societies. The present-day United States, Canada, Australia, New Zealand, Israel, and most countries in Europe are examples of class systems.

Achieved and Ascribed Statuses

Many people have the misunderstanding that only achieved statuses matter in a class system. This is clearly not true. The difference between class systems and the other two systems (caste and estate) is not that ascribed statuses don't matter, but rather that achieved statuses do. This can be seen by examining studies of socioeconomic mobility in class societies. Most such studies look at **intergenerational mobility**; that is, they compare a person's status with that of his or her parents. The majority of these studies have compared the status of sons to that of their fathers, because in previous generations, mothers usually did not work outside the home and derived their social and economic status from their husbands. Recently, however, such studies have begun to include both women and men (for example, DiPrete and Grusky, 1990). What all these studies show is that mobility is quite limited in class systems. In other words, most people have statuses quite close to those of their parents (Blau and Duncan, 1967; see also Featherman and Hauser, 1978). In most cases, the status of the offspring is slightly higher than that of the parent, but this mainly reflects what sociologists call **structural mobility**—there has been growth in better-paying, more pleasant, higher-status, white-collar jobs, and a decline in the number of blue-collar jobs (Featherman, 1979).

Exchange Mobility

In contrast to structural mobility is **exchange mobility**—movement up or down *relative* to the positions of others. Consider a man who has a white-collar job in contrast to his father's blue-collar job, and whose income is higher than his father's, even controlling for inflation. Yet, as was true for his father, his income and job status remain below that of 70 percent of the population. This individual may have benefited from structural mobility, but he has *not* experienced exchange mobility—he is still in the same place relative to everyone else.

Research shows that exchange mobility is quite limited. In periods of sustained economic growth, people may, on the average, move up to better jobs than those of their parents—but most of them do not experience large changes in their status *relative* to that of others (Rytina, 1989, 1992). The most widely cited study of intergenerational mobility in the United States found that only one out of ten sons of manual laborers attains professional status—compared to *seven* out of ten sons of professional workers (Blau and Duncan, 1967). More recent research also shows that you will get a better education (and therefore in most cases a better job) if your mother has more education and

a higher job status (Kalmijn, 1994a). And your chances of getting a good job are especially low if you are born into poverty—rather, you have an above-average chance of experiencing poverty as an adult. Some studies (for example, Hout, 1988) suggest an increase in exchange mobility since the classic Blau and Duncan study, but a decrease in structural mobility due to weak economic growth between the early 1970s and the early 1990s. Moreover, in a trend that appears to be continuing, much of this exchange mobility is the result of a shrinking middle class. Research by Duncan (1996) shows that people are more likely than in the past to move either down from middle income to lower income, or up from middle income to upper income. However, they are *less* likely to move into the middle income group from either high or low income. Hence, the income distribution is becoming more polarized: more people at the top, more at the bottom, and fewer in the middle.

Race, Gender, and Class Mobility

Race and gender are closely intertwined with economic inequality, and mobility is restricted by both. Women and racial or ethnic minorities receive lower pay and work at lower-status jobs than white males do, even when their parents have similar status. Among year-round, full-time workers in 1994, for example, the median incomes of both black males and white females were about three-quarters those of white males, and the incomes of black females and Hispanic males were only about two-thirds those of white males. Hispanic females had even lower incomes (U.S. Bureau of the Census, 1996c). Thus, race and sex biases compound the influence of ascribed statuses in class societies. A final important point is that ownership of major, income-producing wealth is even more likely to be based on the luck of birth. For all these reasons, then, the status into which you are born makes a big difference, even in a class society.

A final point relates to the great inequalities in wealth noted earlier in this chapter: The overwhelming majority of income-producing wealth in the United States has, over time, remained in the hands of a small proportion of the population. Also, wealth ownership is strongly tied to race. All recent studies show that the median wealth of whites is from six to as much as sixteen times that of African Americans or Latinos, and the disparity is even greater for income-producing assets (Kennickell,

2000; U.S. Bureau of the Census, 1995b; Oliver and Shapiro, 1995).

International Comparisons of Mobility

How does the United States compare to other class societies with regard to mobility? It is often argued that the greater class inequality of the United States is offset by greater mobility. The actual findings of research suggest that this may be true, but only to a very limited extent. In general, there is little difference in the degree of mobility in different class societies (Lipset and Bendix, 1960; Tyree, Semyonov, and Hodge, 1979; Ishida, Goldthorpe, and Erikson, 1991; Grusky and Hauser, 1984; Lin and Bian, 1991; Ishida, Muller, and Ridge, 1995). All have some mobility, but in all of them, including the United States, movement from very low statuses to very high statuses is much more the exception than the rule. Movement within and out of the middle strata, in contrast, appears more common (Grusky and Hauser, 1984). Within this general observation, a case can be made that there is a little more mobility in the United States than in other industrialized countries (Krymkowski, 1991). For example, the proportion of people who move from manual labor to professional occupations—although a tiny minority everywhere—is higher in the United States than in most other countries. This may reflect high structural mobility owing to white-collar job growth rather than high exchange mobility (see Slomczynski and Krauze, 1987, p. 605; but also Hauser and Grusky, 1988).

A precise answer to the question of whether the United States has more mobility than other countries, however, depends on how you measure mobility and what countries you use for comparison. The United States does appear to have more mobility than Great Britain, for example (Yamaguchi, 1986), but that may be more a reflection of the unusually low level of mobility in Great Britain (Wong, 1990). Comparisons with Japan show conflicting results depending on the measure of mobility used (Yamaguchi, 1988), but overall the difference between the United States and Japan is not large (Wong, 1990). Wong's study found that Poland and Hungary also had levels of mobility similar to the United States and Japan; however, all of these countries had more relative mobility than countries such as Great Britain and Brazil. Slomczynski and Krauze (1987, p. 608) compared twenty-two countries on two measures of relative or exchange mobility, and found that the United States had above-average levels of mobility by one measure but average mobility according to the other measure.

Similarly, Western and Wright (1994) found that the United States and Canada had a little more mobility than Norway and Sweden in occupational status, but much less mobility in terms of the opportunity to move into a position of business ownership. At the very least, then, it would be inaccurate to say that the United States has much greater mobility than most other industrialized countries. The similarities—particularly for exchange or relative mobility—are much greater than the differences (Ishida, Goldthorpe, and Erikson, 1991), and different measures do not give highly consistent results. In a recent study, Beller and Hout (2006) find that with the slowdown in economic growth and rise of inequality in recent decades, mobility rates have also slowed in the U.S. And they find that the U.S. is in the midrange of comparable countries in occupational mobility but near the bottom in terms of income mobility.

Although the United States may have a little more mobility than most other industrialized societies, the fact remains that Americans believe we have considerable mobility. The Horatio Alger myth that anyone, no matter how poor, can succeed on a grand scale is alive and well. Seventy percent of Americans agree, for example, that "America is the land of opportunity where everyone who works hard can get ahead" (Kluegel and Smith, 1986, p. 44). Although over 80 percent agree that "people who grew up in rich families" have a better-than-average chance of getting ahead, two-thirds also think that "people who grew up in poor families" have an average or better-than-average chance of getting ahead (Kluegel and Smith, 1986, p. 49). The majority also believe the same about blacks and women, and over 90 percent feel that way about "people who grew up in working-class families." The fact is that all of these groups have a considerably poorer-than-average chance of getting ahead, yet most Americans persist in believing otherwise. In short, the reality is that there is significantly less mobility in American society than most Americans believe. The result of these beliefs is that many

Americans oppose efforts to reduce poverty, because they incorrectly place most of the blame for poverty on poor people themselves (Kluegel, 1990; Kluegel and Smith, 1986).

Social Class in U.S. Society

Sociologists refer to a group of people who are similar in terms of level of income or wealth as a social class. Inequalities in income and wealth are called class stratification, and your position within that system of inequality is called your **social class**. A term similar in meaning to social class is **socioeconomic status**. Social class and socioeconomic status are often taken to include not only your levels of income and wealth, but also the prestige of your occupation and the amount of education you have attained. Sociologists do not agree on the relative importance of these various factors in defining social class. Partly for this reason, they cannot agree on any uniform system for defining or identifying social classes. We shall focus on three common formulations of social class: the Marxian definition, the composite approach, and subjective class, recognizing at the start that none of these is accepted by all sociologists.

The Marxian Definition of Social Class

Karl Marx made the most important early contribution to thinking about social class and made the study of social class a key item on the agenda for sociology. Marx's entire analysis of society centers around social class. He believed that all aspects of a society are an outgrowth of—but also help to perpetuate in any type of society—the society's **class structure**. To Marx, there were only two classes that really mattered in any type of society—the ruling class, who owned the means of production, and the subordinate class, who did not.

In a feudal agricultural society, the landowners are the ruling class, and the subordinate class consists of peasants, serfs, tenant farmers, sharecroppers, or slaves—those who work land they do not own and turn over the products of their labor to the landowning class. When urbanization and industrialization arrive, such an economy is replaced by a new system with a new class structure. In a capitalist society—any industrial society where the means of production are privately owned—the ruling class is the bourgeoisie: the class that owns capital. By capital, we mean productive capacity—factories, mineral resources, land, or money that can be converted into these things.

Most of the population, however, belongs not to the bourgeoisie but to the proletariat: those who do not own capital but work for those who do. Much of the value of what is produced by the proletariat goes not to the proletariat, but to the bourgeoisie. The only thing that really matters in the Marxian definition of class is ownership of the means of production. No matter how much money salaried employees earn, they still do not belong to the ruling class because they do not own the means of production and hence do not gain the benefits of wealth and income produced by the labor of others. At the time Marx wrote, most people who worked for wages or salaries had very low incomes, so the exclusion of this group from the ruling class was probably more obvious than it is today. Nonetheless, modern Marxist theorists argue that this definition continues to be appropriate for two reasons. First, even today, most who work for wages or salaries have standards of living well below those few who own most of the corporate wealth. Second, even those with high salaries do not receive most of their income from the work of others, unless they use their high salaries to purchase capital on a large scale.

According to this definition of social class, even today the ruling class is very small and the subordinate class is very large. One problem with using Marx's definition is deciding how to classify what he called the *petit bourgeoisie*; people, such as "ma and pa" convenience store owners, who own small businesses that produce only marginal income. Most Marxist sociologists exclude this group from the true ruling class because their wealth produces a limited amount of income and, usually, little additional wealth. Today, most wealth that generates income and additional wealth is to be found in the **corporations**—large-scale organizations with multiple owners. Moreover, although many people own some corporate stock, the great bulk of corporate wealth is held by a small fraction of the population. In 1998, for example, the top 1 percent of the population owned 42 percent or all stock, and the top 10 percent owned 84 percent (Kennickell, 2000).

The Composite Definition of Social Class

One problem with the Marxian definition of social class is that it places a salaried person receiving $125,000 a year in the same social class with a person working for the minimum wage (whose income would be less than about $15,000 per year, based on the minimum wage in 2009). Clearly, these two people would have very different life experiences as a result of their large difference in income, although neither would live in the style of a Ford or a Rockefeller. Moreover, income is not the only thing that defines social class. For example, a highly experienced assembly-line worker with a high school diploma in a large manufacturing corporation might earn $50,000. A beginning professor with a Ph.D. at a small college might earn $45,000. Should the assembly-line worker be placed in a higher social class than the professor in this example? Many would say no, because the college professor has the advantage of a much greater education and enjoys far more freedom, autonomy, and opportunity for creativity on the job. In fact, this case illustrates the ambiguities of social class: The assembly-line worker enjoys an advantage in some areas of life, and the professor does in others.

Sociologists have attempted to deal with this problem by developing a composite approach to defining social class that considers wealth, income, prestige, education, job status, and other factors. This approach is consistent with Max Weber's view, discussed earlier in this chapter, that there are different dimensions of stratification that vary independently from one another. The composite approach does not use hard-and-fast rules for placing people into categories, and the boundaries between categories are often vague. What it does do is create groupings of people who, on the basis of a variety of considerations, are relatively similar. The first such effort, which has guided all subsequent efforts, was that of W. Lloyd Warner and colleagues (1949), in a study of a community they nicknamed "Yankee City." Warner's categories, defined on the basis of wealth, income, prestige, possessions, lifestyle, and community participation, defined six classes: upper-upper, lower-upper, upper-middle, lower-middle, upper-lower, and lower-lower. The majority of the population fell into the two lowest groups, about 40 percent into the two middle groups, and just 3 percent into the two highest groups. Since then, sociologists have used a variety of classification systems, most of which have involved five or six classes, labeled in different ways, always with unclear boundaries. Some of these studies have indicated a shrinkage of the lower categories and a growth of the middle ones, partly as a result of the decline in blue-collar employment and the growth of white-collar employment. The truly wealthy elite, however, has changed little in size since the time of Warner's study. Roughly speaking, the use of this type of classification system today would yield something like the six groupings shown in the box entitled "American Social Classes Today" on pages 166–67.

The Subjective Definition of Social Class

A third way to approach social class is to let people define their own social class. We refer to this self-defined social class as **subjective class**. In the United States, people do not like to think in terms of class distinctions and tend to place themselves and nearly everyone else in or around the middle. Thus, most studies of subjective class, including surveys we have done in our own classes many times, reveal that around 50 to 60 percent of Americans consider themselves "middle class" and about 30 to 40 percent "working class" (National Opinion Research Center, 1983; Hodge and Trieman, 1968). Very few—certainly well under 10 percent—ever admit to being "upper class" or "lower class." In our own classes, both authors have given anonymous surveys to our students, and we have had people who reported family incomes as high as $250,000 label themselves "middle class," even though such a figure at the time the students were surveyed put them in the upper 2 percent of all families. Because nearly all Americans call themselves "middle class" or "working class," this method obviously has the disadvantage of classifying people less precisely than the composite method. However, it does tell us a good deal about how Americans think about class. Although the tendency for people with wide variations in income to identify as "middle class" is particularly strong in the United States, recent research by Kelley and Evans (1995) has shown that it occurs in other modern industrialized nations as well. In countries where the working class is strong politically, however, people with lower incomes are more likely to identify as "working class" and less likely to identify as "middle class."

What factors determine how people define themselves? The answer appears to be a combination of income, education, and occupation. Those with high incomes, a college education, and a white-collar occupation nearly always answer "middle class," whereas those with a below-average income, a high school education or less, and a blue-collar job generally answer "working class." Men and women define class in somewhat different ways. Men nearly always define their social class on the basis of their own characteristics, while married women define their social class partly according to their own characteristics and partly according to those of their husbands (Simpson, Stark, and Jackson, 1988). More women today, however, define their class on the basis of their own characteristics (Davis and Robinson, 1988). This is occurring not only in the United States, but also in other industrialized countries, such as Australia, Norway, and Sweden (Baxter, 1994).

The least predictable answers come from those with status inconsistencies—people who rank high in one area but low in another. In our class surveys, for example, people from blue-collar families with incomes at or above the median family income are about as likely to call themselves "middle class" as "working class." This is because while their parents' occupations are typical of the working class, their family income is typical of the middle class.

Occupational Prestige

Closely related to subjective class is occupational prestige. In fact, we already saw that occupation is one of the key factors that determines how people see their own social class. Different occupations clearly carry different levels of prestige, and the work people do has a major effect on the entire prestige or status dimension of stratification. Significantly, the relative prestige of various jobs has remained similar over time and across different places. Surveys done over the past half-century show that jobs that had high status in the 1940s continue to have high status today. In fact, the relative status of a wide range of jobs has changed very little over the past fifty years (Davis and Smith, 1994; Rossides, 1997). About the only source of change is in the creation of new jobs or the elimination of old ones. In 1920, for example, there was no such thing as a computer programmer or a television camera operator. Similarly, technology has largely eliminated other jobs, such as keypunch and elevator operators. Even jobs that have been created by technology have later been eliminated by it, such as keypunch operators and, increasingly today, television camera operators. Rather than having each studio camera operated by a cameraperson, entire sets of cameras today are operated through remote-control robotics.

Additionally, studies comparing job status across different societies have shown that the relative status of different jobs is quite similar in a number of different industrialized societies (see Hodge, Trieman, and Rossi, 1966). Thus, a doctor, a lawyer, or an airline pilot has high status not only in the United States, but in Canada, Sweden, and Great Britain as well. A janitor or taxi driver, in contrast, has low status in all these societies. In addition, the relative status of these jobs in all these societies is about the same today as it was decades ago. Even in some less-industrialized countries, the same patterns hold. Research by Nan and Wen (1988) has revealed that the prestige of jobs in China is very similar to the prestige of jobs in other countries. There also seems to be considerable agreement among people in different countries that higher-status jobs should be paid more (Kelley and Evans, 1993).

What determines the prestige of a job? As is true of subjective class, several factors are relevant. In general, better-paid jobs have higher prestige. Prestige also depends on the educational requirements of the job and the amount of physical labor it entails. Thus, even though college professors are paid less than people in a number of other occupations that require less education, they consistently rank near the top in occupational prestige. The very highest ranked jobs, such as physician and airline pilot, are professional occupations associated with both high incomes and high levels of education. Similarly, the jobs with the lowest prestige, such as garbage collector, janitor, and shoe shiner, involve hard physical work, require little or no education, and pay poorly. A list of some jobs and their occupational prestige ratings from surveys in the United States and other countries is presented in Table 6.2.

Table 6.2 Occupational Prestige Ratings: United States Compared to 60-Country Average

Occupations	Average, 60 Countries	United States
University president or dean	86	82.4
Physician	78	81.5
University professor	78	78.3
Physicist	76	73.8
Member, board of directors	75	71.8
Lawyer	73	75.7
Architect	72	70.5
Dentist	70	73.5
Chemist	69	68.8
Sociologist	67	65.0
Airline pilot	66	70.1
High school teacher	64	63.1
Clergy member	60	70.5
Personnel director	58	57.8
Artist	57	57.0
Classical musician	56	55.0
Social worker	56	52.4
Journalist	55	51.6
Professional nurse	54	61.5
Secretary	53	45.8
Actor or actress	52	55.0
Union official	50	41.2
Real-estate agent	49	44.0
Professional athlete	48	51.4
Farmer	47	43.7
Motor-vehicle mechanic	44	35.8
Policeman or policewoman	40	47.8
Railroad conductor	39	40.9
Telephone operator	38	40.4
Jazz musician	38	37.2
Carpenter	37	42.5
Dancing teacher	36	32.3
Firefighter	35	33.2
Sales clerk	34	27.1
Truck driver	33	31.3
File clerk	31	30.3
Assembly-line worker	30	27.1
Construction worker	28	26.2
Gas-station attendant	25	21.6
Waiter	23	20.3
Janitor	21	16.1
Farm worker	20	21.4
Garbage collector	13	12.6
Shoe shiner	12	9.3

Note: In a limited number of instances, there were slight differences in job titles between Appendix A (worldwide average) and Appendix D (United States). In these instances, the closest job title was used.

Source: From *Occupational Prestige in Comparative Perspective,* by Donald J. Treiman. Copyright © 1977 by Academic Press. Reprinted by permission of Academic Press.

Class Consciousness in the United States

One important aspect of class in America is the extent to which Americans are aware of, and identify with, the social classes to which they belong. Such awareness and identification is called *class consciousness*. Americans seem to be less class-conscious than people in many other societies. We have already noted that nearly all Americans think of themselves as "middle class" or "working class." This contrasts with some other societies where, for example, the wealthy readily identify themselves as upper class. United States society was founded as a result of a rebellion against title and monarchy and was based on the principle that "all men are created equal." Although, as we have seen, the reality is that there is great social inequality in America, most Americans prefer not to acknowledge that openly. Rather, we prefer to believe that people have similar statuses and similar situations in life—that we are all pretty much alike (DeMott, 1990). America's entertainment media abet this belief as they either gloss over social-class differences, or present them as easily surmountable. The Horatio Alger myth that anyone who tries can succeed, and the assertion that love will easily overcome social-class differences between people, is still popular, as we can see in such movies as *Pretty Woman, Dirty Dancing, White Palace* (DeMott, 1991), or *The Pursuit of Happyness*.

The widespread presence of the Horatio Alger myth in the American media and popular culture illustrates another important point: It is in the class interests of the wealthy to promote the image of America as a society where class doesn't really matter and where anyone can "make it." When people perceive that there is not equal opportunity, they criticize the system and support change; when they believe that anyone can succeed, they accept the system as fair and legitimate (Kluegel and Smith, 1986; Kluegel, 1990). In other words, as long as people think the system is fair, they won't demand changes that threaten the wealthy and powerful. Thus, it is in the interests of those with wealth—who include the people who own and control newspapers, television networks, and publishing companies—to promote the idea that the system is fair.

While this undoubtedly happens to some extent in all capitalist societies, there is some evidence that people who question the accepted view that the system is fair are treated more harshly in the United States than elsewhere. For example, Sexton (1991) has amassed historical evidence that labor unions and labor organizers have been repressed more harshly in the United States than in most European countries. For example, prior to 1930 there was much use in the United States of the military, police, and private security companies to interfere with strikes, often with great violence against striking workers. Hiring of strikebreakers was commonplace before 1930, and has become so again since the 1980s. According to Sexton, these attacks have been largely successful in limiting the power of labor unions in the United States.

In many ways, U.S. laws remain hostile to labor compared with laws in others countries. Sexton (1991) contrasts the United States with Canada. In Canada, all public employees have the right to collectively organize, bargain, and strike. In the United States, public employees have only some of these rights, and only in some states. In the United States, private employers can and often do legally refuse to agree on a contract with a newly certified union. In most of Canada, this is illegal—after a period of time, either binding arbitration or a publicly mandated contract is imposed. And in Canada, unions need only submit signed cards from a majority of workers to be certified (a policy the Obama administration has pledged to support for the United States); as of 2011 in the United States, this step was followed by a long, expensive campaign and vote. Consequently, the percentage of workers represented by unions is low and has even fallen in recent decades in the United States, whereas it is much higher and has been steady or rising in Canada, Germany, and other industrialized countries. Finally, Sexton argues that the absence of a strong labor movement has inhibited class consciousness and in general weakened the political left in the United States. For example, Canada and most European countries have a major labor or "social-democratic" party; the United States does not. As a result of such differences, income inequality has been challenged less in the United States than in other industrialized countries, even though the United States is more unequal. And between 1972 and 1988, workers' wages and their standard of living fell in the United States relative to Canada, Japan, and a number of European countries (Sexton, 1991, p. 25).

SOCIOLOGICAL INSIGHTS
American Social Classes Today

At the start of the new century, Americans can be roughly classified into six social classes, each of which is briefly described below.

Corporate Elite

The corporate elite consists of two rather distinct subgroups, which together make up about 1 percent of the population. They own the bulk of the country's corporate wealth, and usually own assets well in excess of $1 million. In 2009, the net worth of each of the 400 wealthiest families and individuals in the United States ranged from $950 million to the $50 billion of Microsoft founder Bill Gates (Forbes.com, 2009). The two subgroups of the elite are the "old rich" and the "new rich." The "old rich" gain prestige from their name alone (Rockefeller, Ford, Carnegie, Danforth), and have been wealthy for generations. They tend to look down upon, and sometimes exclude, the "new rich." The "new rich" have gained corporate wealth more recently, as a result of skillful investment, foresight, or "being in the right place at the right time." They may have more money than the "old rich," but less prestige. Examples include Gates, as well as the late Sam Walton (founder of Wal-Mart), whose net worth stood at $7 billion after he lost $1 billion in one day in the 1987 stock market crash. Computer technology has created a number of "new rich" billionaires, including the founders of Hewlett-Packard, Gateway 2000, and Oracle, in addition to Microsoft's Bill Gates. Some of these new billionaires lost a lot of money in the high-tech slump of 2000–2001 and the crash of 2008 but still remained fabulously rich. Oracle chief executive Larry Ellison lost more than half his wealth in the slump but was still worth $21 billion in 2001. Investor Warren Buffet lost big in the crash of 2008 (to the tune of $10 billion for the year) but remains the second-wealthiest person in the United States (Forbes.com, 2009).

Lower-Upper Class

Amounting to about 2 to 5 percent of the population, people in this group differ from the corporate elite in that they are less wealthy and more likely to have gained their wealth as a result of a high salary or the investment of earned income than by ownership of key corporate capital. The successful rock singer and professional athlete would fall into this diverse group, as would many corporate executives and some owners of smaller-scale businesses. Although this group includes a good number of millionaires, many of them are newcomers to wealth. And unlike even the "new rich" in the corporate elite group, their income usually comes from their own labor rather than from the labor of others.

Upper-Middle Class

Accounting for perhaps 15 to 20 percent of the U.S. population, this group is made up of better-paid management and professional employees: doctors, lawyers, airline pilots, middle- and upper-corporate management, and owners of the more successful small businesses. Most people in this group are college educated, and many have graduate or professional degrees. It is taken for granted that their children will attend college and, increasingly, graduate or professional school. This group is likely to live

Two other reasons have been suggested to explain why Americans are less class-conscious than people in other industrialized countries. First, although educational attainment in the United States is in reality quite strongly tied to social class (see Web-Based Chapter A), this connection is less formalized than in other countries, such as Great Britain. This leads Americans to think of themselves as more similar to one another. Second, until the early 1970s, the United States had more structural mobility than other countries, because it experienced more economic expansion. Hence, people saw class boundaries as more permeable in the United States. However, as other countries around the world have developed and become able to compete effectively with the United States, the rate of expansion has slowed, and structural mobility has decreased.

in bigger-than-average homes in the more prestigious suburbs. Incomes run above the median family income of about $50,000, but generally not into the hundreds of thousands of dollars typical of the lower rungs of the upper class.

Lower-Middle Class

This group, which is now becoming smaller, amounts to about 25 to 30 percent of the population. Members of this group hold the lower-status white-collar jobs, which may or may not require a college degree. Some of the best-paid blue-collar workers, such as skilled building crafts workers and auto workers, could also be included in this group, largely because of their relatively high incomes. In general, the incomes in this group are fairly close to the median family income of about $50,000. People in this group tend to own their own homes and live in "good" suburbs, but not in the most prestigious areas. As in the upper-middle class, it is common for both the husband and wife to be employed full time, but here it is more likely that the wife will be working out of economic necessity and less likely that she will be "moving up" in her career. Though still diverse, this group tends to be a bit more conservative than the upper-middle class, particularly when it comes to "social issues," such as abortion, sexual freedom, and freedom of expression. The children of this group are often expected to attend college, but it is more likely to be a two-year school or the local commuter university, and fewer of them will go on to graduate or professional school.

Working Class

This group, around 30 to 35 percent of the population, works at blue-collar or clerical jobs and has incomes at or, more often, below the average level. More often than not, both the husband and wife must work to support the family. They typically have high school diplomas but no college training. They often own homes in older and less prestigious suburbs, small towns, or the nonpoor areas of the central city, although many rent. They live an adequate, though by no means extravagant, lifestyle, but they must worry more often than middle- and upper-class people about how to pay their bills. Although their attitudes may be liberal on economic issues, they tend to be conservative socially and are sometimes fearful of losing economic ground to other groups. Their children are less likely to go to college. In some families, however, where education is seen as the hope for upward mobility for the next generation, the children do attend college, particularly two-year and commuter schools in their local area. For this group, a crisis such as a divorce or the loss of a job can mean falling into poverty, and there is in general less feeling of security about life than in the middle class.

Lower Class

Amounting to 15 to 20 percent of the population, this group is always struggling just to make it. Depending on such factors as being employed, marital status, and wage level, people in this group have incomes around the poverty level or a little above it. Finding adequate food, shelter, clothing, and medical care ranges from difficult to impossible for them. Many people in this group lack even a high school education, and although their children have a better chance of completing high school than they did, many do not, and very few go on to college. Most rent rather than own their own homes, and they more frequently live in a central city, rural area, or small town than in the suburbs. Divorce and separation rates are high, as are the number of single-parent families. At the bottom of this group is the chronically poor and unemployed underclass, whose children rarely know anyone who has a stable job, a decent education, or the opportunity for upward mobility. Thus, they are psychologically prepared to be the next generation of poor and near-poor.

Poverty in the United States

The extremes of social and economic stratification are the easiest to see—and the most difficult to deny. We turn our attention now to those at the bottom of the economic stratification system: the poor. We shall begin our discussion of poverty by examining some different ways of defining poverty; then we shall see how poverty is officially defined and measured in the United States.

How Poverty Is Defined

Generally, statistics on poverty are based on the *poverty level* as defined by the federal government. To make sense of these statistics, we must understand

(1) what is meant by the term poverty and (2) how the federal poverty level is determined.

Relative Versus Absolute Concepts of Poverty

Poverty can be defined as the condition of having a very low income and standard of living. However, such a definition immediately raises a question: What do we mean by low? Low could mean "low compared with almost everyone else," or it could mean "below the level sufficient to buy necessities." For this reason, poverty can be defined in either a relative (low compared with others) or an absolute (lacking necessities) manner. In the case of relative poverty, a person's standard of living is low compared with that of others who enjoy a higher standard of living. By this definition, every society with social inequality will have some poverty. However, some societies have greater degrees of poverty than others. In the United States, where the poorest 20 percent of the population has about 5 percent of the income, poverty in a relative sense is more extreme than in Sweden, Japan, or Finland where the poorest 20 percent has about 10 percent of the income (World Bank, 2000).

Now, consider the absolute definition of poverty. By this definition, poverty exists whenever people lack some basic necessities of life. Thus, it is possible, at least in theory, for a country to have no poverty at all, even if it has considerable social inequality. If everyone gets all the basic necessities, there is no poverty.

The Official Definition of Poverty in the United States

The U.S. government's official definition of poverty is intended to delineate poverty in the absolute sense. In other words, it is meant to represent a level of income below which people are unlikely to be able to buy all of the necessities of life. The official definition of poverty in the United States originated in the 1950s, when the government estimated the cost of the minimum diet necessary to get a person or a family through a limited period of financial difficulty in good health. As a result of a 1961 government study showing that the average low-income family spent one-third of its income on food, the poverty level was set at roughly three times the cost of this minimum diet. (Because of differences in their cost of living, this multiplication factor is a little more than three for individuals and smaller families, and a little less than three for rural families.) Since 1961, the poverty level has been adjusted upward each year to take account of inflation. In 2008, the poverty level for a family of four was $21,834. For one nonelderly individual living alone, it was $11,201 (U.S. Census Bureau, 2009b). Questions have been raised about the extent to which this standard correctly measures poverty. Although some critics disagree, the dominant opinion among economists, home economists, and sociologists is that the official definition fails to include many people who are poor in the absolute sense. (See Rodgers, 1978; U.S. Bureau of the Census, 1976.)

Poverty in America: The Current Situation

In 2008, the most recent year for which data are available, 39.8 million people, or 13.2 percent of the population, were living below the poverty level (U.S. Bureau of the Census, Current Population Survey. World Wide Web. http://www.census.gov/hhes/www/cpstables/032009/pov/toc.htm). This amounts to more than one out of every eight people living in the United States today. Just how large a group is this? It is equal to more than the entire population of California, more than twice the population of Florida, or about four times the population of Michigan. Clearly, we are talking about a very large number of people.

Is the number of poor people growing? As is shown in Figure 6.3, the number of poor people has fluctuated considerably with the ups and downs of the economy, but overall, there has been an upward trend since the late 1970s, with high points during the recession of the early 1990s and the current "great recession." In fact, the nearly 40 million poor people in 2008 represented the largest number of poor people in the United States since the early 1960s, before the War on Poverty of the Johnson administration. The poverty *rate*, on the other hand—the percentage of Americans below the poverty level—fell substantially during the 1960s as a result of the War on Poverty but has fluctuated irregularly with the ups and downs of the economy since the late 1960s.

The failure of poverty to decline further since the 1970s reflects two underlying conditions—increasing economic inequality, and stagnation in

Stratification: Structured Social Inequality

Figure 6.3 Number in Poverty and Poverty Rate: 1959–2008

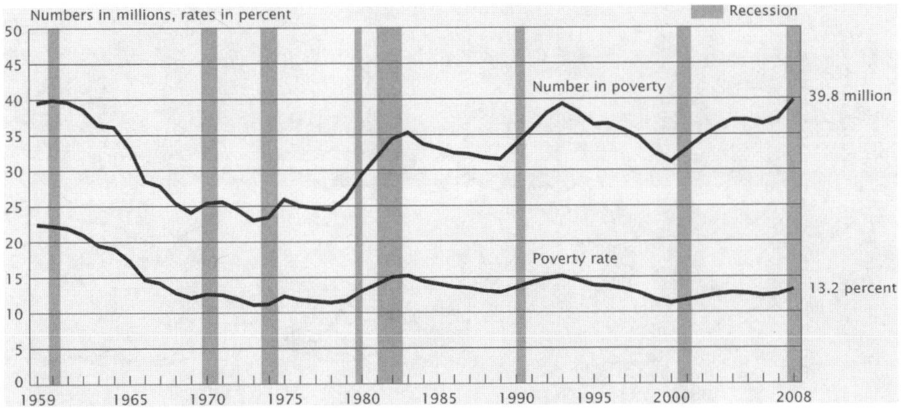

Note: The data points are placed at the midpoints of the respective years.
Source: U.S. Census Bureau, Current Population Survey, 1960 to 2009 Annual Social and Economic Supplements.

the economy. We have already discussed the fact that as middle-income jobs have disappeared, the middle class has shrunk. Some people have risen into better-paying jobs, but many others have fallen into lower-paying jobs or unemployment. Low pay is clearly a significant factor. Growing numbers of poor people—the so-called "working poor"—are poor because they have jobs, but the jobs do not pay enough to keep them above the poverty level. The number of poor people who worked year round and full time roughly doubled between 1978 and 1994 (U.S. Bureau of the Census, 1996e). As Duncan's (1996) study clearly shows, real wages fell during that period for those in the lower part of the income distribution range, and they rose for those at the top of this range. In other words, the American economic pie is being divided in a way that is more unequal today than it was in the past.

At the same time, the pie itself has not been growing for much of the past thirty-five years or so. Real wages and incomes were relatively flat between 1973 and 1993. In many cases, the only thing that prevented serious declines in family income in that time was that growing numbers of women entered the workforce, often doing so to keep their family's standard of living from falling (Olsen, 1990; Jencks, 1991). Since then, there was some growth in incomes between 1993 and 2001 and again for a few years around 2005, but there were also setbacks following the September 11, 2001, terrorist attacks and, even more so, in the severe recession that began in 2007 and worsened with the 2008 financial crash.

Because it has more economic inequality than other industrialized countries, the United States has more poverty, even by the standard of absolute poverty. Smeeding, Torrey, and Rein (1988) compared the United States to seven other industrialized countries, using the U.S. government's methods for comparing poverty rates. In five of the seven countries, the poverty rates averaged a full 5 percentage points lower than in the United States. Perhaps most disturbing is the difference in poverty among children: the United Stares had the highest child poverty rate of any of the countries and was about 10 percentage points above the child poverty rates of most of the other countries (Peterson, 1991).

Who Is Poor?

A number of social characteristics increase the risk that people will be poor. In general, the groups with disproportionate amounts of poverty are blacks, Hispanics, and American Indians; women; people living in female-headed families; children; and people who live in central cities and rural areas (as opposed to suburbs). To a large extent, this reflects the lower status accorded to these groups by society and their relative lack of power. The poverty rates of people with various characteristics is shown in detail in Figure 6.4. On the one hand, as the figure shows, poverty rates of African Americans and Hispanic Americans are about three times as high as the poverty rate of non-Hispanic whites. Hence, your chances of being poor are much greater if you

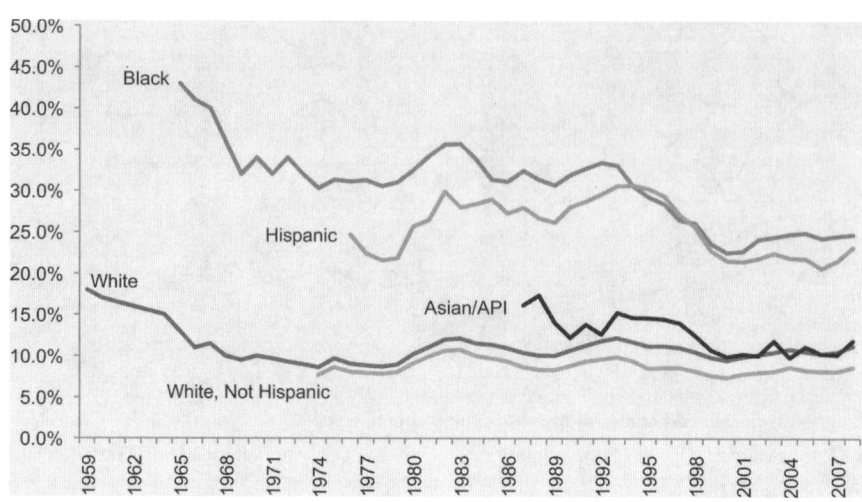

Figure 6.4 Poverty Rates by Race and Hispanic Origin: 1959–2008

Source: U.S. Bureau of the Census, *Current Population Survey,* http://www.census.gov/hhes/www/cpstables/032009/pov/toc.htm.

are African American or Latino, and this has been the case as long as poverty has been measured. Nonetheless, the *number* of non-Hispanic whites who are poor (about 17 million) is almost as great as the number of poor blacks and poor Hispanics *combined* (about 20 million). This is because nearly two-thirds of the total U.S. population is non-Hispanic white.

The single biggest risk factor for poverty is living in a family with a female householder and no husband present. Over one-third of all poor people live in such families, even though fewer than one American out of seven lives in a female householder family. It is also significant that children have a relatively high risk of poverty (Duncan and Rodgers, 1991). About one in six were poor in 2000, and more than one in three will experience poverty at some time during their childhood (U.S. Census Bureau, 2001c; Ellwood, 1987).

Causes of Poverty

Poor People Themselves? Work, Family Structure, and Poverty

It is widely believed that people often experience poverty as a result of their own actions or inactions—unwillingness to work, drunkenness, welfare dependency, and sexual promiscuity leading to out-of-wedlock births (Feagin, 1972; see also Kluegel, 1990; Kluegel and Smith, 1986; Schuman, 1975). A careful examination of the characteristics of the poor, however, indicates that these factors are relatively unimportant as causes of poverty (the poverty rate of major social groups is summarized in Table 6.3).

Work Experience of the Poor

It is true that the majority of poor people are not employed. In fact, in 2008, nearly two-thirds of poor people over age fifteen did not work. At first glance, this might appear to support the popular explanation that poor people are "unwilling to work." However, if we examine the reasons these people did not work, we get a different picture. To begin with, according to Census Bureau (data as shown in Figure 6.5), nearly three fourths of those who did not work were ill, disabled, retired, or attending school—all of which are generally regarded as legitimate reasons for being out of the workforce. In fact, these groups combined account for about 45 percent of all poor people over fifteen years old.

Another sizable group (nearly 5 percent) of the nonworking poor had looked for work but were unable to find it. Almost all of the rest of the nonworking poor—about 13 percent of all poor people—did not work because of home or family reasons. About half of these were female single parents with children, and most of the rest were nonemployed wives with children. In addition to the fact that a mother staying home to take care of

Table 6.3 Number of People Living Below the Poverty Level, and Poverty Rate, Selected Groups in U.S. Population, 2008

Population Group	Number Below Poverty Level (in millions)	Poverty Rate (percent)
Total U.S. Population	39.8	13.2
White Americans	27.9	11.3
Non-Hispanic White Americans	17.0	8.6
Black Americans	9.9	24.7
Asian Americans	1.7	11.6
Hispanic Americans	11.0	23.2
Children under 18	14.1	19.0
White children under 18	9.3	15.9
Black children under 18	4.2	33.9
Hispanic children under 18	5.0	30.6
Adults 18 to 64	22.1	11.7
Adults 65 and Over	3.7	9.7
Married-couple families	3.3	5.5
Female-householder families	4.2	28.7
Persons in female-householder families	13.8	31.4
White	6.9	34.9
Black	5.8	40.3
Hispanic	5.3	47.0
Central-city residents	17.2	17.5
Suburban residents	15.4	9.8
Nonmetropolitan residents	7.2	15.1
People living in Northeast	6.3	11.6
People living in Midwest	8.1	12.4
People living in South	15.9	14.3
People living in West	9.6	13.5

Source: U.S. Bureau of the Census, *Current Population Survey,* http://www.census.gov/hhes/www/cpstables/032009/pov/toc.htm.

her children has always been acceptable in American society (and until recently was the norm), we must consider here the cost of day care and medical care. As we shall see later, many poor people have no employment available except minimum-wage jobs, most of which include no medical benefits. By the time a poor mother pays for day care for her children (which can cost well over $600 per month per child), she may already have used up all the income from a minimum-wage job. And in many states, if she remains employed long enough, she must give up Medicaid, at least for herself, although with the Children's Health Insurance Program (CHIP), she can now at least get care for her children. In many cases, she literally can't afford to take a job—the costs of day care and medical care are simply too great.

We have now accounted for nearly all of the two-thirds of poor people who, according to the Census Bureau, did not work in 2008.

These statistics are consistent with research findings reported by Tienda and Stier (1991). In a study of Chicago's poorest neighborhoods, they found that only 6 percent of the population could be characterized as shiftless; that is, unwilling to work. The rest were either employed, caring for children, disabled, students, or looking for work.

Out-of-Wedlock Births

Single-parent, female-headed families are at a very high risk for poverty. As the percentage of such families rose in the 1970s and 1980s, the poverty rate also rose (Eggebeen and Lichter, 1991). Many female-householder families are the result of out-of-wedlock births, although many others are the result of divorces and separations. However, to say that out-of-wedlock childbearing (or, for that matter, divorce) is one of the most important causes of poverty is to ignore several key realities. First, the rate of out-of-wedlock births is far higher among people who are *already* poor or who grew up in poverty than among the general public (see Hayes, 1987b; Skolnick and Rosenkrantz, 1994; Luker, 1991; Hernandez, 1993). Wu (1996) found that both low income and declining income were associated with increased risk of giving birth outside marriage, for young women between ages fourteen and twenty-one, both black and white. Thus, poverty appears to be at least as much a cause of out-of-wedlock births as a consequence. One reason for this is that poor people are less likely to be familiar with, or have access to, birth control, which increases their nonmarital birth rates. In addition, because of high unemployment, urban minority poor women—the ones most likely to give birth out of wedlock—have a strikingly small pool of employed, marriageable men (Wilson, 1987, pp. 95–100; see also Mare and Winship, 1991; Lichter, LeClere, and McLaughlin, 1991). As a result, a larger proportion of these women never marry, and those who do marry do so later and wait longer to remarry after a divorce. This means that more of them are at risk of a nonmarital pregnancy. Like the great majority of nonmarried women of all socioeconomic levels, they are usually sexually active—but they are unmarried for a longer part of their lives, and they know less about contraception.

Research also shows that poverty affects self-image and attitudes in ways that increase the

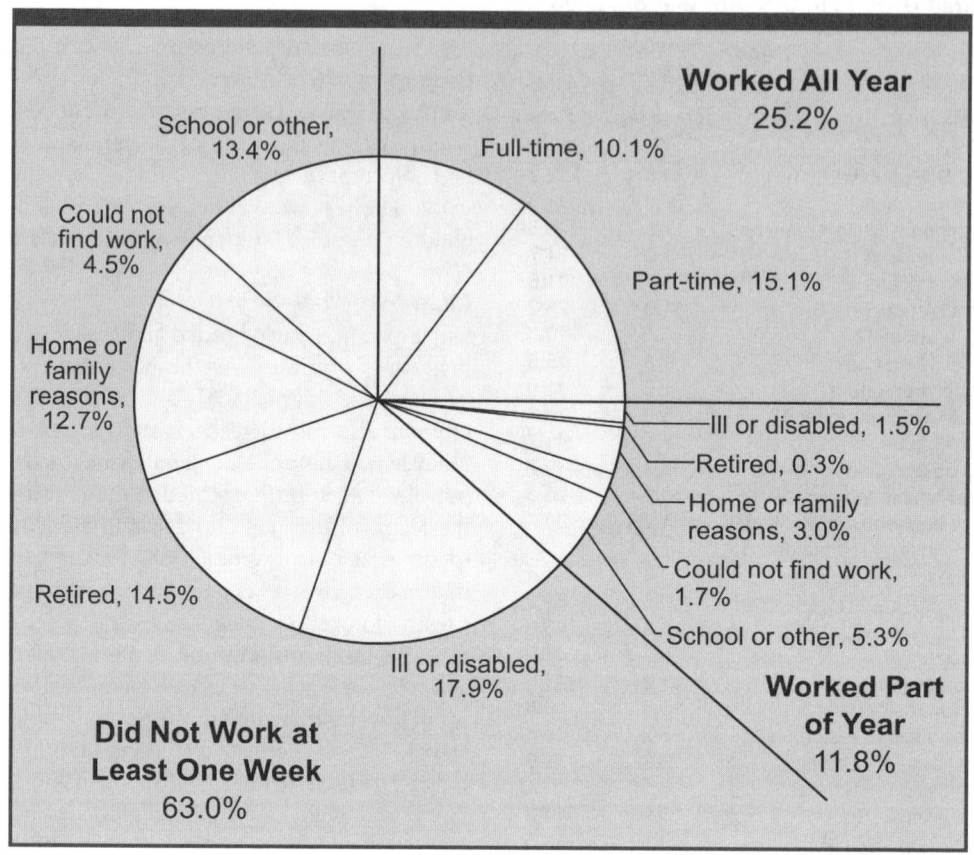

Figure 6.5 Work Status of Poor People Age 16 and Over, 2008

Source: U.S. Bureau of the Census, *Current Population Survey,* http://www.census.gov/hhes/www/cpstables/032009/pov/toc.htm.

likelihood of out-of-wedlock pregnancy, especially among teenagers (Anderson, 1991). Poor people experience less control over their lives and may feel less able to control whether they get pregnant—so they are less likely to try. To an impoverished teenage girl, a baby can sometimes be a source of self-esteem, a way of feeling grown-up. Among poor teenage boys, sexual conquest (which is valued to some extent among young males of all social classes) may be one of the few ways of feeling a sense of accomplishment, when most legitimate opportunities for achievement are blocked. Thus, however much out-of-wedlock childbirth may perpetuate poverty, it is probably more a consequence of poverty than a cause. Moreover, as shown in the box "American Poverty and Teenage Pregnancy in Global Perspective," there is much that we could do to prevent teenage pregnancy but have chosen not to do as a result of misperceptions about the likely consequences, as well as because of religious objections. Finally, as is discussed in Chapter 8, the low wages of women are a major reason for the high poverty rate among female-householder families.

These findings clearly indicate that poor people themselves are not, by and large, the cause of their own poverty. Most of them are employed, are looking for work, or have a good reason not to be working. In fact, of all people over fifteen years old who did not work in 2008, more then 90 percent were retired, ill, or disabled; in school; or caring for children (U.S. Census Bureau, 2009a). And although poor people do have high rates of divorce, separation, and nonmarital childbearing—and although a large number of poor people live in female-householder families—these characteristics

GLOBAL SOCIOLOGY

American Poverty and Teenage Pregnancy in Global Perspective

Poverty is more widespread and severe in the United States than in other industrialized countries, and children are more likely than other Americans to be poor. One contributing factor is that American teenagers are more likely to get pregnant and have a baby out of wedlock than teenagers in other industrialized countries.

When this happens, their children often experience poverty. In fact, more than 90 percent of American children who live in a single-parent home through the first ten years of life will experience poverty (Ellwood, 1987). About two-thirds of these children will be poor for the entire ten years.

The fact that American teens are more likely to become parents than their counterparts in other industrialized countries was shown in a study comparing the United States, Canada, France, Great Britain, the Netherlands, and Sweden (Jones et al., 1986). The United States had by far the highest rates of teenage pregnancies, births, and abortions of any of these countries. Although some of the difference was the product of the higher poverty rate in the United States and the relatively high incidence of teenage pregnancy among American minority groups, these factors were not by any means the whole answer. White U.S. teenagers, for example, have pregnancy rates far above those found in any of the other countries. The differences also could not be explained by differences in sexual activity: U.S. teenagers are no more likely than teenagers in the other countries (except possibly Canada) to be sexually active.

Why, then, do American teenagers get pregnant so much more often than teenagers in other countries? At least part of the answer is that they are less likely to use contraceptives (Jones et al., 1986). Part of the reason for that, in turn, is that it is harder for American teenagers to get contraceptives. Many Americans believe that making contraceptives available to teenagers will encourage them to have sex, so we have avoided doing so.

What would happen if contraceptives were more available to U.S. teenagers? We don't have all the answers, but we do have some. Experiments in certain cities, such as Baltimore, provided teenagers with contraceptives, along with information concerning human sexuality and advice that they did not have to be sexually active if they didn't want to be (Hayes, 1987b). In such a context, the provision of contraceptives did not increase teenage sexual activity; if anything, the total effect of the program was the opposite (Schorr and Schorr, 1988, p. 53). Moreover, those teenagers who did have sex were more likely to use contraception, and the pregnancy rate fell—meaning fewer teenage births and fewer teenage abortions.

Thus, the common American belief that making contraceptives more available will lead more teenagers to have sex appears not to be true, at least if school health programs are properly designed. The Jones et al. study suggests another reason for Americans' opposition to contraceptives for teenagers: Americans, more than people in other countries, may favor more sexual restrictions because of religious beliefs. However, since American teens are as sexually active as teens in other industrialized countries, the main effect of American restrictions on contraceptives seems to be a higher teenage pregnancy rate relative to other countries. Recently, contraceptives have become more available to American teenagers than they were in the past. Consequently, the use of contraception at first intercourse has increased sharply, and the incidence of teen pregnancy has begun to fall, just as one would predict based on the studies cited above (Mauldon and Luker, 1996).

---

appear to be much more a consequence than a cause of poverty. Moreover, as we shall see in Chapter 8, the economic situation of female-householder families would be far less difficult if women were simply paid at the same rate for their work as men are, and if day care and health care were publicly funded, as they are in nearly all other industrialized countries.

What, then, are the causes of poverty, and why has poverty increased since the mid-1970s? Among the explanations are unemployment and low wages, both of which have become more prevalent as socioeconomic inequality has increased in the United States since the 1970s. In addition, certain public policies have contributed to the spread of poverty or to the worsening of its impact.

Unemployment

Consider again Figure 6.5. On the one hand, only 4 percent of poor people were unemployed all or part of the year. However, 2000 was a year of record-low unemployment, and the unemployment rate since then has risen sharply, reaching approximately 10 percent by late 2009. In 1989, one out of five poor people was unemployed for part or all of the year (U.S. Census Bureau, 1990a), and with today's higher unemployment, the proportion is likely higher. In addition, many who work part-time do so because they cannot find a full-time job. Thus, unemployment still plays an important role as a cause of poverty.

Recent Unemployment Trends

Unemployment has been more prevalent since 1980 than it was in previous decades. Generally, it has fluctuated in the 5.5 to 7.5 percent range, reaching peaks of over 10 percent in the recession of the early 1980s and nearly 8 percent in the 1992 recession. From 1993 to 2000, unemployment fell, reaching around 4 percent by late 2000 before new economic troubles led to an increase in 2001. As the housing boom came to an end in 2007, unemployment again began to rise from 4.6 percent in 2006 and 2007 to 5.8 percent in 2008. Unemployment skyrocketed in 2009 to over 10 percent once again (Bureau of Labor Statistics, 2009). And of course as unemployment fell between 1993 and 2000, so did the poverty rate, as described previously. Conversely, with the rise of unemployment in the 2008–2009 period, the poverty rate, of course, also rose.

One reason unemployment rose in the 1970s and 1980s can be tied to rising numbers of people entering the labor force: baby boomers who reached working age in the 1970s and 1980s, and women who entered the labor force in many cases because their family income could not keep up with inflation without two income earners. However, other factors are more important than the growth of the labor force.

Deindustrialization

A cause of declining wages, as well as rising unemployment, is **deindustrialization** (Harrison and Bluestone, 1988; Wilson, 1987), a decline in the importance of heavy industry as a source of employment. Deindustrialization is a result of automation, international competition, and relocation of jobs—sometimes out of the United States. It is closely related to the trend of economic globalization noted earlier in this chapter. Because of more efficient operations and, in some cases, lower wages, many countries can produce cars, televisions, machine tools, and other products comparable or superior to American producers at lower cost. American companies also have contributed to deindustrialization in the United States. In search of low wages, American companies have often moved assembly operations to Third World countries, depriving Americans of jobs in the process (Harrington, 1984). Thousands of manufacturing jobs have been shifted from the United States to northern Mexico for this reason. Of the 1,400 manufacturing plants in Mexico near the border in 1988, for example, 90 percent were American-owned (Rohan, 1989). By eliminating higher-paying jobs, deindustrialization has resulted in growing inequality and rising poverty since the late 1970s.

The effects of deindustrialization have been particularly devastating for central cities, particularly manufacturing cities in the Midwest and Northeast (Kasarda, 1990; Wilson, 1987, 1991a, 1991b). The increasingly African American and Hispanic populations in these cities, devastated by the loss of jobs, also find it difficult to move into the still-segregated suburban areas, where jobs are often more readily available (Farley, 1987b; Kasarda, 1980, 1985, 1989; Massey and Eggers, 1990; Massey and Denton, 1993; Yinger, 1995; Leonard, 1987). An experiment in Chicago shows the impact of such exclusion: When poor blacks were given the opportunity to move from the city to the suburbs, their employment rose relative to others who remained behind in the city (Rosenbaum and Popkin, 1991; Popkin, Rosenbaum, and Meaden, 1993). But as a result of job losses in the inner city, the proportion of blacks and Hispanics in older cities who live in neighborhoods of highly concentrated poverty has risen. This phenomenon may further perpetuate poverty by undermining inner-city neighborhood institutions and depriving young people of successful role models (Anderson, 1991; Crane, 1991a, 1991b; Wilson, 1987, 1991a; Massey and Denton, 1993).

In some cities, manufacturing employment losses have been offset by growth of employment in the service and administrative sectors (Kasarda, 1990). However, this has been of limited benefit, for two reasons. First, these industries are highly automated and computerized and often do not employ as many people relative to their size as manufacturing did. Second, many of the jobs they do offer require a high level of education, so they are not available to displaced industrial workers or the inner-city poor (Wilson, 1987, pp. 39–42). Moreover, the service jobs that do not have high educational requirements pay much lower wages than the industrial jobs that were lost. These jobs grew rapidly during the 1990s, but because of their low wages, so did the ranks of the working poor.

Low Wages

One striking feature of Figure 6.5 is the number of people who worked but were poor anyway. In fact, nearly one poor adult out of every eight in 2000 worked full-time all year! The number of people in this situation has roughly doubled since 1978. How is it possible for these people to be poor? A little math will show you. Begin with the $7.25 minimum wage in effect in 2009. Assume that someone works at the minimum wage 40 hours a week, 52 weeks a year. Such a person would earn $10,712. If this person is the sole source of support for a family as small as two people (including the wage earner), his or her earnings will only bring the family to about $200 above the poverty level. For any family of three or larger, the earnings will leave the family below the poverty level. For a family of four, the annual pay based on the 2009 minimum wage falls more than $7,000 below the poverty level. Such poverty, even when a breadwinner is working full time, has become a critical issue since welfare reform moved thousands of Americans from welfare to work. Unfortunately, it did not at the same time move so many of them out of poverty. Hence, welfare reform, in the absence of new laws raising the minimum wage (which remained unchanged between 1997 and 2007) or mandating the provision of benefits, has led to growth in the number of Americans who work full time yet still suffer poverty.

A factor further contributing to the increasing number of working poor has been the failure of Congress to adjust the minimum wage for inflation. Despite considerable increases in the cost of living, the minimum wage was not changed between 1991 and 1997, and again remained unchanged from 1997 through 2007. Only once, in more than a decade, had any adjustment been made in the minimum wage. Not until 2007 was the minimum wage raised again. This has major consequences, given the reality of inflation. For example, the minimum wage in early 1996 had only two-thirds of the purchasing power it had in 1968 (AFL-CIO, 1995).

Low-wage jobs were among the fastest-growing areas of employment during the 1980s and 1990s. In fact, most of the job growth during that period occurred either in dead-end, low-wage jobs or in well-paid, high-tech jobs that required a high level of education. There was little job growth in between, which meant there were far fewer opportunities for a person with a limited education to get a decent-paying, stable industrial job. Hence, many displaced workers ended up working for less.

Government Policy

Both low wages and, at times, rising unemployment during recent decades have resulted partly from policies pursued by the federal government. Specifically, the government during much of this period chose to fight inflation rather than unemployment and refused for years to adjust the minimum wage for inflation. Also contributing to poverty during this period was a very substantial cutback in government antipoverty programs. Beginning in the late 1970s, and to a greater extent under the Reagan administration in the 1980s, benefits in government poverty programs were curtailed as part of an effort to reduce both federal spending and the budget deficit. (Actually, both government spending and the deficit increased because of a massive increase in military spending in the early 1980s.) Benefits in many programs were not adjusted to keep up with inflation, and standards of eligibility were tightened. Significantly, subsequent research has shown that those who were most severely hurt by these cutbacks were the working poor and the near-poor (Institute for Social Research, 1983). Many people were forced into poverty, and for many others, the impact of poverty became more severe as they were no longer able to supplement their meager incomes with government benefits such as food stamps. Further cuts were implemented in the mid-1990s, as President Clinton and congressional Republicans competed over who was more serious about balancing the federal budget and reducing the size of government. And, as noted above, the "welfare reform" legislation of the 1990s led to more growth in the ranks of the working poor, whatever other benefits it may have had.

Finally, it must be noted that the failure of the American public sector to provide certain necessities, which are taken for granted in most industrialized countries, also increases the extent and impact of poverty. Virtually all other industrialized countries, for example, use tax revenues to fund health care and day care for all who need them. As we shall see in Web-Based Chapter C, one consequence is that other industrialized countries do not have 12 to 16 percent of their population totally lacking health insurance, as is the case in the United States until the health care reforms passed in 2010 take effect several years later. And we have already addressed the role day-care expenses play in making it hard for impoverished single parents to seek employment. Thus, not only does the United States have more poverty than other modern industrialized countries, but because of lack of governmental support for health care and day care, the impact of poverty in the United States is greater than in other industrialized countries.

In summary, the relatively high level of inequality in the United States compared with other industrialized countries results in a high level of poverty. This situation worsened in the 1980s and 1990s, as deindustrialization, the growth of low-wage employment, and government policies resulted in greater inequality and more poverty. Finally, the impacts of poverty are greater in the United States than in other industrialized countries, because the United States provides far less assistance than other countries in areas such as health care, day care, and housing.

Consequences of Poverty

If the causes of poverty are complex, its consequences are clear. In virtually every way imaginable, life is more difficult for poor people. They are ill more often, receive poorer and more limited medical care, and live shorter lives. They also have a higher rate of mental illness, particularly for the more serious illnesses such as depression, schizophrenia, and personality disorders (Dohrenwend, 1975; Warheit, Holzer, and Schwab, 1973). The effects of poverty on children's mental health are particularly severe when poverty persists over time (McLeod and Shannahan, 1993). The poor also report lower levels of personal happiness than the nonpoor (Campbell, Converse, and Rogers, 1976). The children of the poor are at greater risk of dying in infancy, and if they survive, they have a greater risk than nonpoor children of getting in trouble with the law or becoming pregnant as teenagers. They will receive a much poorer education than nonpoor children, and they are far less likely to complete high school. One study showed that in Chicago's public schools, where a large proportion of the students are from poverty-stricken families, fewer than half of all 1980 ninth-graders graduated on time in 1984—and of those who did graduate, only one out of three could read at a twelfth-grade level (Wilson, 1987, p. 57).

Poor people will spend more of their income on food and housing than the nonpoor, but they still will be less adequately fed and housed. A study of housing in southern Illinois by Quinn (1984) revealed that poor people were several times as likely as the general public to live in overcrowded housing, yet 80 to 90 percent of these poor people were paying more than the government standard of 25 percent of their incomes for rent.

Poor people are more likely both to commit street crimes and to be the victims of such crimes (H. D. Barlow, 1993). Crime rates are highest in poor neighborhoods, for criminals tend to victimize those who are close by and available. As a result, a highly disproportionate number of robbery, assault, and homicide victims are poor. So high is the incidence of crime in some poor neighborhoods that poor people are afraid to venture outside their homes (Rainwater, 1966). Summer after summer in several major cities, elderly poor people have died from heat-related illnesses because they could not afford air conditioning and were afraid to open their windows because of crime.

In the winter, the risks become cold and fire. Dozens of poor people die every winter as a result of fires started by makeshift heating arrangements, some of which were attempted after their gas or electricity had been turned off because they could not pay the bill. Perhaps the greatest impacts of poverty fall on those who have no home at all. Estimates of the number of homeless in the United

States vary widely, but the 230,000 counted by the 1990 Census (Peterson, 1997) certainly represent the low end of the range. A more likely figure may the Urban Institute's 1989 estimate of 600,000 homeless. Many more—about 7 percent of the population, according to survey data—experience homelessness at some time in their lives (Link et al., 1994; Interagency Council on the Homeless, 1994). This would amount to about 18 million Americans.

Functionalist and Conflict Perspectives on Stratification

In this final section, we turn to the larger sociological issue of why economic inequality and poverty exist in society. As with other questions of this nature, the two macrosociological perspectives, functionalist and conflict theories, offer starkly different answers. Let us first consider the functionalist answer.

The Functionalist View: Davis and Moore

In one of the most widely cited and debated pieces ever to appear in a sociology journal, Kingsley Davis and Wilbert Moore presented a functionalist theory of socioeconomic inequality in their 1945 article "Some Principles of Stratification." Davis and Moore argued that economic stratification exists because it meets society's needs for productivity by motivating people. Davis and Moore started with the notions that some jobs are more critical to society's needs than others, and that some jobs—often the most critical ones—require longer and more difficult training than others. Such jobs also carry greater responsibility, are frequently very stressful, and often require people to work longer hours than other jobs. If the highly capable people needed to fill such jobs are to get the extra training and work the extra hours required, Davis and Moore argued, they must be motivated by the prospect of higher pay. Otherwise, why would people want these jobs, with all the training, stress, and extra hours they entail? More specifically, would people sacrifice current income in order to get the years of training some of these jobs require? Suppose a person could get the same money as a doctor by working seven or eight hours a day sweeping streets—with no after-hours responsibility and no long, expensive period of training, including four years of college, four years of medical school, and four years of internship/residency. Would it not be harder to get people to become doctors if they could earn just as much money doing something much easier—and earn it now, rather than twelve years from now?

The Conflict View

Although conflict theorists generally acknowledge that socioeconomic inequality occurs in nearly all societies, they do not think it exists because it meets a social need for productivity. They note, for example, that more economically developed and productive societies generally have less inequality than others, not more (see Lenski, 1966; Nielson and Alderson, 1995). In general, conflict theorists see socioeconomic inequality as existing because the wealthy and powerful—usually a small group in any society—benefit from it and have enough power to make the social system work to protect their interests.

As a result of this great inequality, conflict theorists—in the tradition of Karl Marx—see a tendency in most societies for class conflict: conflict between the wealthy and those who lack wealth. It is in the interest of the wealthy to keep things as they are, whereas those without wealth have an interest in social change. Marx predicted that this conflict of interest would eventually lead to the overthrow of most capitalist societies, as the subordinate class realized its own interest and seized the wealth from the ruling class.

In fact, this has not happened, for many reasons. One important reason is that the expansion of economies under capitalism, at least until recently, raised the standard of living of the working classes substantially, despite continued inequality. Another is that democratic reforms curtailed the more blatant excesses of the owners of wealth and afforded some protection to the rights of even those with little wealth and power. Marxists would argue that a third reason is that the wealthy use their influence over government, the media, and other key institutions to promote beliefs and ideologies that inhibit class consciousness. (The role of class conflict as a source of social change is explored in Chapter 15.) According to the conflict perspective, then, the interests of the wealthy—not the needs of the society as a whole—are served by inequality.

Is Stratification Really Functional?

In an article that is among the most widely cited in sociology, conflict theorist Melvin Tumin pointed out what he saw as several shortcomings in the logic used by Davis and Moore (Tumin, 1953; see also Tumin, 1970). First, he questioned whether some of the better-paying and more prestigious jobs are really more critical to society than others. For example, is the physician really more essential to the health of the public than the garbage collector? Without garbage collectors, the hazard of contagious disease would be tremendous. Significantly, historical demographers agree that public sanitation systems were able to increase people's life expectancies at an earlier point in history than were medical doctors. The medical treatment of illness was too unscientific to accomplish much before about 1900. Only then, for example, was the practice of washing one's hands before performing surgery becoming widespread. By around 1850, the establishment of garbage-collection systems and sanitary sewers, however, had replaced the common practice of throwing garbage and human waste in the nearest street or river in many areas, and it was certainly a key factor in the steady fall in American and European mortality rates between 1800 and 1900. (For more discussion of the effects of medicine and public sanitation on mortality, see Thomlinson, 1976, pp. 98–107.) In a similar vein, Tumin points out that if factories had all managers and engineers and no line workers, they could produce nothing. Thus, low-status, poorly paid workers can be as essential as those whose jobs carry status, power, and big paychecks.

Second, wealth is distributed more unequally than income, and a large share of wealth is inherited rather than earned (Barlow, Brazer, and Morgan, 1966; Lundberg, 1968). It is hard to see how inherited wealth could motivate people to do anything except be born into rich families—something that we have yet to figure out a way to control! About half of America's 400 wealthiest people in 1989 became wealthy through either inheritance or the investment of inherited wealth (Miller, 1997). To the extent that wealth is concentrated through inheritance, it is very difficult to see how it could serve to motivate people to enter critical jobs. A related point is that parental income has a substantial effect on a person's ability to obtain the education necessary to do the most demanding

Table 6.4 Economic Inequality and Economic Productivity, Selected Industrial Countries, 2000

Country	Inequality, 2000 Ratio of Income of Top 10% to That of Bottom 20%	Productvity, 2000. Per Capita Gross National Income (GNI) 2000	Average Annual Growth in Gross Domestic Product (GDP) 1996, 1999, 2000
Japan	2.05:1	$34,210	2.4%
Sweden	2.09:1	$26,780	3.0%
Denmark	2.14:1	$32,020	2.3%
Belgium	2.16:1	$24,630	2.4%
Finland	2.16:1	$24,900	4.6%
Norway	2.25:1	$33,650	3.0%
Italy	2.51:1	$20,010	1.8%
Germany	2.89:1	$25,050	1.8%
Canada	3.17:1	$21,150	3.6%
Netherlands	3.44:1	$25,140	3.7%
France	3.49:1	$23,670	2.4%
Switzerland	3.65:1	$38,120	1.5%
United Kingdom	4.14:1	$24,500	2.6%
United States	5.87:1	$34,260	4.1%

Source: From World Development Indicators by World Bank. Copyright © 2000 by World Bank. Reprinted by permission of Oxford University Press.

Many American service industries today outsource jobs to India, where wages are lower. (AP Photo/Gurinder Osan, File)

jobs. If stratification were really to work the way Davis and Moore argued it did, ability and motivation would have to be the main factors determining the amount of education obtained. In fact, family income plays a large role, making it easy for the wealthy to educate their children for the best jobs and hard for the poor to do so.

Third, the training required for getting better-paying jobs often is far from unpleasant; many people, for example, find college a highly rewarding time of their lives. In addition, attending college—and even more so, attending law, medical, or graduate school—gives a person a certain prestige. At the least, there is a good side as well as a bad side to the training that people must go through to get the better jobs, and that in itself can serve to motivate them.

Finally, Tumin points out that although the highest-paying jobs often require great training and long hours, they also carry considerable nonmaterial rewards, including autonomy, sense of accomplishment, prestige, and—in many cases—the ability to set your own hours. This has been confirmed by recent research by Jencks, Perman, and Rainwater (1988), who found that there are many rewards to a good job besides high pay. We do, moreover, have no shortage of people in certain occupations that require great training but pay relatively poorly—for example, social workers and college professors. There are a number of jobs people with a high school degree can get that pay as well as that of a college professor, which requires four years of college and, typically, four to six years after that to obtain a Ph.D. Even so, the supply of recent Ph.D.s has continued to outstrip the number of new college faculty positions available. Clearly, a major reason for this is that the job carries considerable nonmonetary rewards.

Synthesis

To conclude our discussion of the debate between functionalist and conflict sociologists about the causes of economic stratification, it may be useful to examine the relationship between social inequality and productivity among industrialized societies. This information is provided in Table 6.4. As a measure of inequality, the table shows the ratio of income going to the top 10 percent of the population to the share going to the bottom 20 percent. The larger this ratio, the greater the inequality of a society. The countries are ranked for inequality, with the countries with the most *equal* income distributions at the top. As a measure of productivity, the table shows gross national income (GNI) per capita for 2000. The table indicates there is little relationship between the inequality measure and the productivity measure. The two countries at the opposite ends of the scale with regard to inequality—Japan (most equal) and the United States (most unequal) had virtually identical per capita gross national income. High productivity was also found in Denmark (one of the most equal) but also Switzerland (one of the most unequal). In general, countries with both high and low productivity can be found at all levels of inequality. Overall, analysis of the data for these countries by the author showed that variation in inequality accounted for less than 3 percent of the variation in GNI per capita, and inequality was negatively correlated with productivity growth. Thus, the conclusion is unavoidable that, among these industrialized countries, the

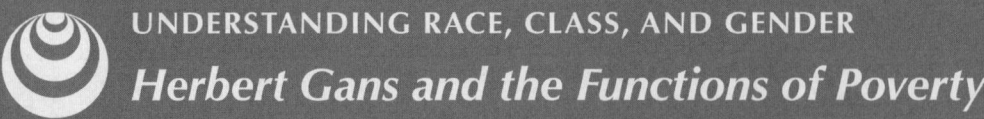

UNDERSTANDING RACE, CLASS, AND GENDER
Herbert Gans and the Functions of Poverty

A discussion of functionalist and conflict analyses of stratification could not be complete without a review of the writings of Herbert Gans (1971, 1972) concerning the functions of poverty. Gans's insights are useful not only for understanding poverty but also for seeing the similarities between functionalist and conflict theories. In an article titled "The Positive Functions of Poverty," Gans listed a number of ways in which poverty is "functional," some of which are given here:

- It provides people to do unpleasant "dirty work" that others don't want to do.
- It provides a source of employment for police and penologists, Pentecostal ministers, pawnshop owners, social workers, heroin pushers, and other legal and illegal occupations that depend upon the poor.
- It provides people to buy spoiled and damaged goods at a reduced price that otherwise would have to be thrown out.
- It provides a convenient group of people to punish in order to uphold society's rules. (In Chapter 10, we explore how the War on Drugs has victimized African Americans—even though their overall rate of drug use is no different than that of whites)
- It reassures the nonpoor of their status and worth.
- It enhances educational opportunities for the middle class by ensuring that a sizable part of the population will not compete with them.
- It is a source of popular culture that others enjoy and make money on. Jazz, blues, rock, gospel, and country music all had their origins among the poor.
- It provides people to absorb the costs of social change in the form of unemployment, cheap labor, and residential displacement—so others won't have to.

Although some people have interpreted this article as making a functionalist argument—and Gans certainly wrote it to sound that way—it has more commonly been seen as a spoof of functionalist theory written by someone who really identifies with the conflict perspective. An earlier and similar article by Gans, "The Uses of Poverty: The Poor Pay All" (1971), supports this interpretation. Whether Gans identifies with functionalist theory or conflict theory, however, his articles make a key point: A good many Americans—nonpoor and often wealthy—benefit from the continued existence of widespread poverty. Thus, the fact that influential special-interest groups benefit from poverty may be one reason that poverty persists. In essence, this is what conflict theorists have always argued: Inequality exists because some group benefits from it. It would appear that this is true to some extent, not only of overall socioeconomic inequality, but also of the widespread poverty existing amid affluence in the United States.

---

degree of economic inequality has little to do with the level of productivity.

The Dysfunctions of Inequality

From a functionalist viewpoint, we also must consider the possible dysfunctions of a condition such as social inequality along with its possible functions. Functionalists see a need for order and cooperation in society—yet economic inequality is one of the most important causes of conflict and disorder in society (Tumin, 1953). Beyond this, those who are at the bottom often become hopeless and alienated and thus "drop out" of any economically productive role. Thus, whatever benefits inequality may have, it also clearly has its costs, to the larger society as well as to those at the bottom of the stratification system.

Does all this mean that the functionalist explanation of inequality is simply wrong? Probably not. For one thing, all of the countries in Table 6.4 do have a significant amount of inequality, although the levels vary widely. In Japan, with the least inequality, the wealthiest 10 percent still receive two-and-a-half times as much income as the poorest 20 percent. The fact that economic inequality exists in all modern countries—even socialist ones—is certainly consistent with the functionalist viewpoint. What the data do suggest, though, is that although

GLOBAL SOCIOLOGY
Global Stratification

As unequal as the United States is between the rich and the poor, this gulf is dwarfed by the vast chasm between the world's poor and affluent. While about 20 percent of the world's human population lives in countries of great wealth and abundance, the other 80 percent lives in societies with far fewer material comforts. About 40 percent of humanity lives in societies in which starvation is often commonplace. In these latter countries, 50 percent of the population at any one time lives in absolute poverty, meaning they do not have enough resources, shelter, and food to meet their basic survival needs. Famine, disease, and short life expectancies are commonplace. Even among "middle-income" countries, the differences with the rich nations is striking. According to the World Bank (2010), high-income countries, less than 20 percent of the global population, earned an average of about $38,000 a year per person. Middle-income nations did much worse at about $3,000 per year, and low-income nations, making up the bottom 40 percent, came in at under $500 per year, per person.

Theories of Global Stratification

Modernization theory views cultural, institutional and political impediments to development as the cause of poverty in low-income nations. The solution it promotes is to mimic the paths taken by the high-income nations, which in this theory's view, is to transform cultural values that place science and capitalism at the top of the list; eliminate government corruption and interference in the marketplace; and promote saving and investing at levels reminiscent of the high-income nations.

Dependency theory is a conflict theory that states the poverty of the low-income nations was caused by their exploitation by the now high-income nations. The history of colonialism and resource extraction, followed by often-thoughtless division of countries after colonialism that left ancient enemies working side by side, lend credence to this theory.

World systems theory conceptualizes the world as a single economic and stratification class system, not just a group of nations. It argues that the global economy must be understood as a system with an upper class (core) set of wealthy nations, a working class (periphery) of many more poor nations, and a middle class (semi-periphery). The theory's primary architect, Immanuel Wallerstein, describes the working of this international system in much the same way as a class system within a single nation.

The Globe Emerges

In recent years a great deal of focus has fallen upon the emerging nations of India and China because of their massive populations (1.1 and 1.3 billion respectively), growing economies, and geo-strategic importance. While both nations are still very much developing, each is growing at a rapid pace and will play an increasingly important role in a world characterized by scarce resources and an exploding human population. Both countries might choose to develop massive militaries, or perhaps they will focus on knocking the United States out of its role as most important economy. No matter what road they decide to take, they are sure to shape the events of the twenty-first century and beyond in crucial ways. India, a nation known for its traditional caste system, is quickly becoming a more class-based society, especially in the urban centers of the country. Similarly, China, formally a communist state, is rapidly developing a market economy and a new set of elites seem to be gathering power: a business elite that will either compete with or find new ways to cooperate with the old political elite of the communist party (Bian, 2002).

A second issue that has gathered a lot of attention around the world, and not least in the world of sociology, is the various forms of slavery and human trafficking that take place across the globe. Human beings are routinely smuggled across national borders for profit. Many of the victims are children. Some are virtual or literal slaves. The heart of this activity takes place in the low-income nations, and while some practices can be blamed upon ancient customs of marriage or women and children traditionally being seen as property in a few societies, much of the demand and money fueling the operation of the illegal markets in human beings comes from wealthier nations.

inequality may be functional up to a point, most countries have far more of it than they need. This is especially true of the United States, which had far more economic inequality (by the measure in Table 6.4) than Japan, Norway, Denmark, or Germany, yet did no better in terms of productivity. As Lenski (1966) put it, the functionalist theory probably explains a certain amount of stratification, but it cannot count for anywhere near all of it. Undoubtedly, much of the rest exists for the reasons outlined by conflict theorists—the disproportionate power of the wealthy, and their use of that power to keep their economic advantage.

The wealthy are not the only people among the nonpoor who benefit from poverty, and therefore have a stake in the confirmation of poverty. To see how others benefit—as well as to get some enlightening insights about functionalist and conflict theories—see the box "Herbert Gans and the Functions of Poverty."

Summary

Sociologists use the term *stratification* to refer to the unequal distribution in society of scarce resources. Stratification has many dimensions. In this chapter, we looked at the economic dimension (the distribution of income and wealth) and a social prestige dimension, sometimes called *status*. In the United States, income (what a person receives annually) is distributed more unequally than in most other industrialized countries, and the distribution of wealth (the total value of everything a person owns) is even more unequal. Although the distributions of income and wealth in the United States have not changed dramatically over time, there has recently been a shift toward greater inequality.

Another area in which stratification systems vary is mobility. Open stratification systems have relatively high mobility—people can move "up" or "down"—whereas closed systems have low mobility. The most closed type of stratification system is the caste system; the estate or feudal system has slightly greater mobility. The highest level of mobility is found in class systems, but even there, ascribed statuses—those into which we are born—play an important role. The mobility that does exist is frequently structural—that is, a result of an increase in the number of better-paying jobs rather than of some people moving up while others move down. Although it is widely believed that the United States has high mobility compared with other class systems, the fact is that industrialized countries do not vary widely in their degree of mobility. The degree of mobility found in the United States is similar to that of most other industrialized societies.

Social class can be defined in a number of ways. To Karl Marx, there were only two classes: those who owned the means of production and those who did not. Many modern sociologists prefer a composite approach, which considers such factors as income, wealth, education, and occupational status. Another approach—subjective class—is to allow people to classify themselves. In the United States, most people call themselves "middle class" or "working class" because Americans don't like to divide themselves into classes, and thus tend to identify with the middle.

Poverty can be defined in either a relative sense (being poor compared with others in the same society) or an absolute sense (lacking necessities). By either definition, there are a large number of poor people in the United States, despite its relative affluence, and this number has increased since the late 1970s. Most poor people are non-Hispanic whites, but blacks and Hispanics have disproportionately high poverty rates, as do female-headed families and people who live in either central cities or rural areas. Among the key causes of poverty are unemployment, low wages, and the inability of single mothers to earn sufficient wages to pay the costs of day care and medical care and support their families. It appears that relatively few people are poor because they prefer welfare to work. Although welfare dependency does occur, it is less widespread than is commonly believed, and most of the nonworking poor have good reasons to be out of the labor force. During the late 1970s and particularly the 1980s, government policies both raised the poverty rate (by allowing unemployment to increase in order to fight inflation) and made the impact of poverty more severe (by cutting back aid to the poor). The effects of poverty are devastating in nearly every aspect of life, ranging from decreased educational opportunities to shortened life expectancy to the likelihood of being a victim of crime.

Functionalist and conflict theorists disagree about the causes of social stratification. In the view of functionalists, stratification exists because it is useful for society. It motivates people to get the training and work the long hours required for certain critical and difficult jobs. Conflict theorists, however, argue that stratification exists mainly because those with wealth and power benefit from it. At the least, it does appear that there is greater inequality in most societies than can be explained purely on the basis of the need for motivation. In the United States, with its particularly high degree of economic inequality, this seems to be especially true.

Key Terms

dimensions of stratification
income
wealth
prestige
socioeconomic mobility
open stratification system
closed stratification system
caste system
caste
racial caste system
apartheid
estate system
class system
intergenerational mobility
structural mobility
exchange mobility
social class
socioeconomic status
class structure
subjective class
corporations
poverty
deindustrialization
modernization theory
dependency theory
world systems theory

Exercises

1. In our global world, some very different ways of looking at social inequality have emerged. For example, the gap between people who have access to the Internet and those who do not has been referred to as the *digital divide*. Do an Internet search for the term "digital divide." You will find the Internet buzzing with information about the issue. What are your personal thoughts about this *new form* of social inequality? What do you believe are the potential social consequences of this socioeconomic division?

2. Social scientists have long observed that poverty is often *invisible in* American society; socioeconomically disadvantaged areas are seldom accessed by people other than the poor who live in these locations. One very visible form of social inequality is *homelessness*. Sociologists who study the homeless find that a great deal of the homeless population is composed of children and families. Do an Internet search for the National Coalition for the Homeless, and check out their fact sheet along the other links they have on the causes of homelessness. Then answer the following questions:

   - People often react to the homeless with the attitude, "Get a job!" Now that you know more about the homeless in American society, do you think the problem is this simple? Why or why not?
   - What do you think can be done to solve the problem of homelessness in our society?

Chapter 7
Race and Ethnic Relations

Racial and Ethnic Groups: What Is the Difference? — 186
   Majority and Minority Groups   187
Racism — 187
   Ideological Racism   187
   Racial and Ethnic Prejudice   188
   Individual Discrimination   188
   Institutional Discrimination   188
Theories About the Causes of Racial and Ethnic Inequality — 189
   Social-Psychological Theories of Race Relations   189
   The Relationship Between Prejudice and Discrimination   191
   Social-Structural Theories of Race Relations   192
Racial and Ethnic Relations: An International Perspective — 197
   Ethnic Inequality and Conflict: How Universal?   197
   Racial Caste in South Africa and the United States   197
   Racial Assimilation in Latin America   198
Racial and Ethnic Groups in the United States — 199
Minority Groups: African Americans, Hispanic Americans, and Native Americans — 199
   Economic Exploitation and the Origins of Intergroup Inequality   201
   Segregation and Attacks on Culture   202
   The Status of Minority Groups Today   203
Intermediate Status Groups: Asian Americans, Jewish and Muslim Americans, and "White Ethnics" — 205
The Majority Group — 208
Current Issues in U.S. Race Relations — 209
   The Significance of Race Versus Class   209
PUTTING SOCIOLOGY TO WORK — 212
   The Affirmative Action Debate   212
   Is Affirmative Action Reverse Discrimination?   213
   Is the System Fair Without Affirmative Action?   214
   How Effective Is Affirmative Action?   215
   The Legal and Political Status of Affirmative Action   216
Summary — 217
Key Terms — 217
Exercises — 218

North American black bears, like people, come in a wide variety of colors. They formed the basis of an interesting experiment about race by Lawrence Hirschfeld (1996), professor of anthropology and psychology at the University of Michigan. Hirschfeld showed Americans pictures of a light bear and a dark bear, and three bear cubs—one light, one dark, and one in-between. Most people, children and adults, correctly predicted that the intermediate-colored bear would be the most likely offspring.

Then, Hirschfeld performed the same experiment, except that instead of pictures of bears, he used pictures of people. He showed his subjects pictures of a white person, and pictures of a black person. He then showed them pictures of three babies—white, black, and an intermediate skin color. When he asked them which baby was the most likely offspring, most people from the age of nine up gave the wrong answer. Although they could correctly answer this question for bears, they could not do so for humans. Most people incorrectly said the black baby was the most likely offspring. In other words, they believed that if one of the parents is black, the baby must also be black. In fact, the right answer in the case of people is the same as it is in the case of bears: The intermediate-colored baby is the most likely offspring.

This experiment says a lot about race. First and foremost, it shows us that race is *socially constructed*: What matters when it comes to race is not so much biological fact as social agreement. And it also tells us a lot about how race is socially defined in the United States: For example, if someone has any identifiable black ancestry or characteristics, most Americans will regard that person as black or African American.

In this chapter, we shall explore some of the reasons that racial and ethnic conflicts have been so widespread throughout history. In order to address this issue we must first understand what is meant by *race* and *ethnic group*.

Racial and Ethnic Groups: What Is the Difference?

There are similarities between a racial group and an ethnic group. Both are socially defined categories of people who share a common ascribed status. Membership in both is hereditary. However, there are also differences. A **racial group** can be defined as a category of people who (1) share some socially recognized physical characteristic (such as skin color or facial features) that distinguishes them from other such categories, and (2) are recognized by themselves and others as a distinct status group (Cox, 1948, p. 402). An **ethnic group**, in contrast, is a category of people who are recognized as a distinct status group entirely on the basis of social or cultural criteria such as nationality or religion. There is no reliable way to identify a person's ethnic group by his or her physical appearance.

Although physical characteristics play a role in identifying racial groups, race is much more a social concept than a physical one, as illustrated by the opening material for this chapter. A crucial part of the definition of *both* racial and ethnic groups is that they must be *socially recognized* as distinct groups. Human societies choose to pay attention to a particular physical characteristic, which then becomes the basis for defining a racial group. In fact, there is no good scientific basis for even saying how many races there are. There is no one gene for race, and different genes affect different aspects of physical appearance (Thernstrom, Orlov, and

Scottish Highlander wearing a kilt and playing bagpipes. If it were not for his dress, could you identify the ethnic group of this person? (iStockphoto)

Handlin, 1980, p. 869). For this reason, social scientists and biologists have never been able to agree on the number of races—different schemes have identified as few as three or more than 100 races. Moreover, racial classifications vary in different societies and in different times. In the United States, until recently, you were considered black if you had any identifiable African American ancestry or physical appearance. However, many people considered African American in the United States would be placed in a mixed group, often identified as "mulatto" or "colored," in many other countries. This way of looking at race may now be becoming more common in the United States. In the 2000 Census, for the first time, Americans were able to identify themselves as belonging to more than one race.

For both racial and ethnic groups, membership is usually involuntary and lifelong; in other words, it is an ascribed status. In addition, it is usually passed from parent to child, although in some instances it may change for the offspring of marriages whose partners are of different racial or ethnic groups. The characteristics used to define races are usually ones that are consistently and reliably passed from generation to generation, which explains, for example, why skin color is commonly used to define races and eye color is not.

Majority and Minority Groups

As we have seen, many societies that have two or more racial or ethnic groups experience inequality and conflict. One or more groups are in an advantaged or dominant position with the power to discriminate, while other groups are in disadvantaged or subordinate positions and are often the victims of discrimination. Those in the advantaged or dominant positions are called **majority groups;** those in disadvantaged or subordinate positions are called **minority groups.** Often the majority group in this sociological sense is also a majority in the numerical sense, as with whites in the United States and people of British ancestry in Canada and Northern Ireland. However, a numerical minority can be a majority group in the sociological sense, and vice versa. One example is South Africa, where until recently 5 million whites dominated more than 25 million native South Africans in politics, economics, and every other aspect of life. Hence, many sociologists believe the terms *dominant group*

and *subordinate group* are more accurate, but the majority group/minority group terminology is still more commonly used.

Besides race and ethnicity, minority groups may be defined on the basis of other ascribed social characteristics such as sex, physical disability, or sexual orientation. While these minority groups are discussed in other chapters, it is significant to note that prejudice and discrimination against them is often closely linked to racial and ethnic bias.

Racism

Whenever prejudice, discrimination, or systematic social inequality occurs along the lines of race or ethnicity, we have an example of racism. Social scientists have used the term in so many ways that some have questioned its very usefulness (cf. Wilson, 1987, p. 12). Still, the reality of racial and ethnic conflict and inequality is so pervasive in the world that some powerful social processes must be responsible for it. Thus, we shall select a broad definition of racism and then specify some distinct types of racism. For our purposes, **racism** is any attitude, belief, behavior, or social arrangement that has the intent or the ultimate effect of favoring one racial or ethnic group over another. As we shall see, this definition implies that although racism is often open, conscious, and deliberate, it can also exist in subtler forms. Sometimes, in fact, people can be racist without even being aware of it.

Ideological Racism

At one time, the term *racism* referred to the belief that one race or ethnic group is naturally superior (or inferior) to another. Today, in recognition of the variety of forms that racism can take, this type of belief is referred to as **ideological racism,** or *racist ideology.* It includes such notions as Hitler's concept of a "master race," the belief of slaveholders that blacks were uncivilized and incapable of anything more than physical labor (Jordan, 1968, Chap. 2; Wilson, 1973, pp. 76–81), and the conviction among southwestern Anglos of the late nineteenth century that the partial Indian ancestry of Mexican Americans predisposed them to "savagery" and "banditry" (Mirande, 1987). It also includes repeated (though consistently unsuccessful) efforts by some scientists in the United States to prove that white people are more intelligent than other races (Feagin, 2000, pp. 82–95). Ideological racism can become institutionalized to the point where it has the status of an unquestioned "truth" that few people (in the majority group, at least) challenge. That has been the case at various points in U.S. history (Feagin, 2000).

An important function of ideological racism is to justify the exploitation of the minority group (Cox, 1948). As Davis (1966) has pointed out, to enslave a human being like yourself is a terrible thing that most people cannot accept. If you can convince yourself and others that the one you are enslaving is less than fully human, however, then you can probably convince yourself and others that slavery is not so bad. This helps to explain why, for example, racist ideologies against blacks became more extreme and were invoked more frequently *after* slavery was established in the U.S. South than *before* (Wilson, 1973, pp. 76–81).

Racial and Ethnic Prejudice

Still in the realm of racist *thinking* (as opposed to action) is racial and ethnic **prejudice:** any categorical and unfounded overgeneralization concerning a group. It can take the form of beliefs about a group, negative feelings toward a group, or the desire to discriminate against a group. In each of these cases, prejudice involves an automatic reaction to a group or to a person's group membership. If I automatically don't like you because you are white, if I want to discriminate against you because you are black, or if I think you are greedy because you are Jewish, I am prejudiced, because I am responding to you entirely on the basis of your race or ethnicity. I am choosing to ignore or disbelieve the influence of everything else about you except the fact that you are white, black, or Jewish.

One common type of prejudice is the **stereotype,** an exaggerated belief concerning a group of people. A stereotype assumes that anyone in a group is very likely to have a certain characteristic. American culture is full of stereotypes, such as the narrow-minded and authoritarian German; the greedy Jew; the lazy, musical, or sports-minded black; the hard-drinking Irish; the gang-prone Chicano; and the bigoted Southern white. Every one of these stereotypes, like all others, is a gross overgeneralization. Undoubtedly, some people in any group do fit the stereotype, but many others do not. The point is not that stereotypes do not apply to *anyone* in the group at which they are aimed, but that they are never true for *everyone* in that group. Stereotypes are commonly reinforced by the media.

Stereotypes can be positive or negative, but even the positive ones are a mixed blessing. It is, for example, undoubtedly good to be musical, athletic, or a good dancer, which are common stereotypes about African Americans. However, if whites believe that these are the only areas in which blacks can achieve, then they will probably behave in ways that close off opportunities for African Americans in professions other than sports and entertainment. Equally significant, if young African Americans internalize the message that the areas for them to get ahead in are sports and music, they can be directed away from other areas in which they could be equally or more successful.

Individual Discrimination

Although prejudices of any type concern what people think, **discrimination** concerns what they *do*. **Individual discrimination** is any behavior that treats people unequally on the basis of race, ethnicity, or some other group characteristic. Individual discrimination is usually conscious and deliberate. Examples are a restaurant owner who refuses to serve a Chinese person, or a taxi driver who passes a man by because he is black. In the United States, most discrimination on the basis of race, sex, religion, or disability is illegal. Nonetheless, some types of individual discrimination are hard to prove, and in some areas, such as housing, employment, shopping, and public accommodations, this kind of discrimination remains all too common (Carter, Hall, Carney and Rosip, 2006; Feagin, 2000; Feagin and Sikes, 1994; Kirschenman and Neckerman 1991; Yinger, 1995, Mathews, 1992).

Institutional Discrimination

The most subtle form of racism, yet perhaps the one with the most serious consequences today, is **institutional racism,** or **institutional discrimination** on the basis of race (Carmichael and Hamilton, 1967; Farley, 2010; Feagin and Feagin, 1986). This form of discrimination occurs whenever widespread practices and arrangements within social institutions have the intent or effect of favoring one race (usually the majority group) over another (usually the minority group). Institutional discrimination can be very deliberate, as in the system of school segregation and denial of voting rights to blacks that existed throughout the U.S. South until the early 1960s. A more contemporary example of deliberate institutional discrimination is the widespread practice in the real estate industry of *racial steering*—showing white customers houses in white neighborhoods and black customers houses in racially mixed or all-black neighborhoods (Lake, 1981; Pearce, 1976; Yinger, 1995).

Today, institutional discrimination is often unconscious and unintentional, though its consequences can be just as devastating as if it were deliberate. In the educational system, for example, teachers often expect less achievement from black and Hispanic students than they do from white students (Brophy, 1983; Brophy and Good, 1974; Ferguson, 1998; Hurn, 1978; Harvey and Slatin, 1975; Leacock, 1969; Moore and Pachon, 1985). In schools that are predominantly black or Hispanic, such low expectations often become generalized to the entire student body. When teachers expect less, they demand and get less, and achievement falls (Brophy, 1983). As a result, black and Hispanic students frequently learn less, are graded lower, get a poorer education, and consequently lose out on job opportunities when they grow up. Although none of this may be intentional discrimination, its consequences are every bit as serious. This issue is discussed in greater detail in Web-Based Chapter A.

Another important example of institutional discrimination is the movement of jobs out of predominantly black and Hispanic central cities and into predominantly white suburbs. This trend takes job opportunities away from the minority groups and gives them to whites (Squires, 1989; Holzer and Ihlanfeldt, 1996). Evidence shows that where jobs have become suburbanized in this manner, black and Hispanic men have higher unemployment rates than white men (Farley, 1987b; Lichter, 1988; Kain, 2004; Kasarda, 1989), and that when blacks do get opportunities to move to the suburbs, their unemployment rate declines (Rosenbaum and Popkin, 1991). To compound the problem, institutional discrimination within the real-estate industry makes it very difficult for minorities to follow the jobs to all-white suburbs. In addition, the lack of automobiles in many black and Hispanic households, combined with poor mass transit, often makes commuting to jobs next to impossible (see Alexis and Di Tomaso, 1983).

Theories About the Causes of Racial and Ethnic Inequality

We now turn to a more detailed exploration of the causes of racial and ethnic discrimination, conflict, and inequality. Social scientists offer three general explanations for these behaviors. One set of theories is based on social psychology; the other two are sociological in nature, arising, respectively, from the functionalist and conflict perspectives. We turn our attention first to social-psychological theories.

Social-Psychological Theories of Race Relations

Most social-psychological theories about race relations center around the concept of prejudice (Wilson and See, 1988, p. 226). Recall that *prejudice* refers to unfounded and inflexible overgeneralizations concerning a racial or ethnic group. Social-psychological theories argue that people's situations and social experiences influence their attitudes and beliefs. These experiences lead some people to develop prejudiced attitudes and beliefs, usually through *personality need* or *social learning*.

Personality Need
The theory of **personality need** arises largely from the work of Theodor Adorno and his colleagues (1950), discussed in Chapter 2. In his content analysis of speeches and writings of right-wing extremists such as Nazis and Ku Klux Klan members, Adorno uncovered a number of themes that were not logically related but nonetheless appeared repeatedly. Sensing that these themes might reflect a certain personality type, he developed a personality measure to rate nine distinct attitudes and beliefs, including excessive respect for authority, superstition, aggression against nonconformers, cynicism, worry about sexual "goings-on," opposition to looking inward to understand oneself, and a belief

that the world is a dangerous place. Moreover, Adorno's research found that this personality type scored a good deal higher on anti-Semitic and anti-black prejudice than did others. Over the past half-century, many additional studies have confirmed Adorno's original findings (Dru, 2007; Heaven, Organ, Supavadeeprasit, and Leeson, 2006) and extended them to other kinds of prejudice such as sexism (Case, Fishbein and Ritchey, 2008; Rigby, 1988), prejudice against homosexuals and/or people with AIDS (Cunningham et al., 1991; Laythe, Finkel, and Kirkpatrick, 2001), opposition to immigrants (Quinton, Cowan, and Watson, 1996), and hostility toward people with disabilities (Jabin, 1987). In fact, recent studies have concluded that personality types that combine Right Wing Authoritarianism (a personality measure very similar to Adorno's) with a Social Dominance Orientation (a general preference for unequal relations between groups) can be treated as a strong indicator of generalized prejudice across all groups (Altemeyer, 1998; Duckitt, Wagner, du Plessis, & Birum, 2002; Ekehammar et al., 2004; Lippa & Arad, 1999; Whitley, 1999; Zick et al., 2008). Thus, having a certain personality type—which Adorno called the **authoritarian personality**—does indeed appear to be associated with prejudice.

Scapegoats. Why are such people prejudiced? It appears that prejudice meets two kinds of personality needs in such people. The first of these needs refers back to our discussion of personality theories of socialization in Chapter 5. Recall Freud's (1962 [orig. 1930]) theory that society's expectations, the *superego,* are in conflict with the child's natural drives, the *id.* If the superego is so powerful that it represses natural drives, these drives can surface later in other forms. Adorno applied this notion to prejudice. He found, from questions he asked his subjects, that adults with authoritarian personalities usually had experienced harsh discipline as children. As a result, they built up a good deal of frustration and aggression because they did not have the necessary outlets for their natural drives. However, because respect for authority was so deeply ingrained in them, they could not take out their aggression on the true source of their anger—their parents and other authority figures. Instead, they took it out on **scapegoats**—racial, ethnic, or religious minorities, or other groups who displayed nonconformity in their dress or lifestyle. These scapegoats were not the true source of prejudiced people's anger, but they did serve as effective targets.

Projection. The second personality need met by prejudice is also related to childhood experiences. Prejudiced people had been taught that the world is made up of good and bad people, and you must always think, act, and behave as the good people do. People who adopt this good/bad worldview cannot admit any fault in themselves, because to do so would be to put themselves in the "bad" category. Using open-ended questions, Adorno and his colleagues (1950) found that prejudiced people were much less willing than nonprejudiced people to admit faults in either themselves or their parents. Moreover, their prejudices helped them to deny their faults. By exaggerating the faults of others, they could deny or minimize their own. In particular, they tended to exaggerate the faults of minority groups. Thus, they could deny or minimize their own greed by pointing to "greedy Jews" or forget about their own violent tendencies by talking about "Mexican gangs." This process is called **projection.** As with scapegoating, other researchers besides Adorno have confirmed its presence among many prejudiced people (Allport, 1954, Chaps. 21 and 24; Simpson and Yinger, 1985, pp. 73–78).

Social Learning

Although personality-need theories explain why some people are prejudiced, they do not explain all cases of prejudice. One need only look at the U.S. South during the 1950s to see this. Although the overwhelming majority of southern whites displayed relatively high levels of antiblack prejudice, the incidence of authoritarian personalities in the South was not much higher than that found in the rest of the country (Pettigrew, 1971, Chap. 5; Prothro, 1952). Clearly, something other than personality need was responsible for antiblack feelings. A large part of the answer is to be found in culture and **social learning**. The social-learning theory of prejudice is much like the subcultural theory of deviance discussed in Chapter 10. According to this view, people are prejudiced because they grow up in prejudiced environments where they learn prejudice from their significant others. This learning occurs through the processes of selective exposure and modeling, reward and punishment, and identification that were introduced in Chapter 5. When your family, neighbors, and playmates are all prejudiced, you will probably be prejudiced, too. If you are exposed only to prejudiced attitudes and beliefs, they seem like unquestioned truths. You are informally rewarded when you express such attitudes but laughed at or teased if you express contrary attitudes. Finally, if all the people you respect and love hold prejudiced beliefs, could such beliefs really be wrong?

All of these social-learning processes do tend to produce prejudice. Research has shown that those whose parents and other childhood significant others were prejudiced tend themselves to be more prejudiced as adults (Ehrlich, 1973; Garcia-Coll and Vazquez-Garcia, 1995). However, this type of prejudice is different in an important way from prejudice based on personality need in that it is easier to change. Very often, when people whose prejudices are based on social learning move to environments where their significant others are relatively unprejudiced, their prejudice levels fall. In other words, people can conform to nonprejudice as well as to prejudice (De Fleur and Westie, 1958; Ewens and Ehrlich, 1969; Fendrich, 1967). For people who have a personality need to be prejudiced, however, that need remains regardless of their social environment.

The Relationship Between Prejudice and Discrimination

The relationship between prejudice and discrimination is not always clear. As illustrated in Table 7.1, sociologist Robert Merton (1949) has shown that not everyone who is prejudiced discriminates, and some people who are *not* prejudiced do discriminate. Social pressures and the costs of discriminating or not discriminating determine whether racial attitudes will be translated into behavior. If the costs of discriminating are great (complaints, legal hearings, and penalties), prejudiced people will often not discriminate. Similarly, relatively unprejudiced people may discriminate if pressured to do so by, say, the threat of losing white customers if they welcome black customers.

Attitudes also may be changed by behavior. Prejudice, at least as measured by people's responses to questionnaires, *fell* considerably in the

Table 7.1 Robert Merton's Typology on Prejudice and Discrimination

	Does Not Discriminate	Discriminates
Unprejudiced	1. All-weather liberal	2. Fair-weather liberal
Prejudiced	3. Timid bigot	4. All-weather bigot

Source: From p. 41 in *Majority-Minority Relations*, 2nd. ed. by John E. Farley. Copyright © 1988 by John E. Farley. Reprinted by permission of Prentice Hall, Inc., Upper Saddle River, NJ.

U.S. South after desegregation was ordered by federal law. In general, it was more satisfying for southerners to say "We know now that segregation is wrong" than to say "We did what those Yankee bureaucrats in Washington told us to do." This is very consistent with a social-psychological theory called **cognitive-dissonance theory,** which states that if behavior changes, attitudes will often change to become consistent with the new behavior (Festinger, 1957; Festinger and Carlsmith, 1959).

Thus, we cannot assume that behavior is always the result of attitudes. However, this does not mean that prejudiced attitudes are unrelated to actual racial discrimination. Prejudice has decreased considerably in the United States (R. Farley, 1984, 1977; Farley and Frey, 1992; Firebaugh and Davis, 1988; National Opinion Research Center, 1983, 1991; Owen, Eisner, and McFaul, 1981), but it has not disappeared. For example, recent research shows that beliefs in stereotypes remain common among whites (Anti-defamation League, 1993; Sniderman and Piazza, 1993; Gilens, 1995). Moreover, there is evidence that these stereotypes are an important cause of discrimination against African Americans in employment (Kirschenman and Neckerman, 1991; Wilson, 1996) and in housing (Farley et al., 1994), and that they do influence public policy through their influence on political opinion (Gilens, 1995). As shown in the box "Popular Music as a Threat: The Role of Race," on page 194, stereotypes can affect behavior in ways we sometimes would not expect.

In addition, many researchers believe that modern prejudices have taken on a subtle form called **symbolic racism** (Kinder and Sears, 1981;

Kluegel and Smith, 1986, 1982; McConahay et al., 1981). Symbolic racism refers to a pattern in which people do not express overtly prejudiced or racist ideas, but oppose any social policy that would eliminate or reduce racial inequality, such as affirmative action, government spending to assist minorities, school busing to desegregated schools, and minority scholarships. Surveys show that the majority of whites do oppose most such policies (Kluegel and Smith, 1986; National Opinion Research Center, 1991; Schuman and Bobo, 1988). There has been only a slight change in these attitudes over nearly four decades (Kluegel, 1990; Valentino and Sears, 2005). Why do so many people oppose such policies?

A possible answer is that people believe that whites as well as minorities experience discrimination. For example, 42 percent of whites, according to a recent Gallup poll, believe discrimination against whites is widespread (Jones, 2008). This could mean that whites see discrimination as something not unique to racial minorities; by comparison, 51 percent of whites in the same poll said discrimination against blacks was widespread. Thirty-six percent of blacks and Hispanics (almost the same percentage as whites) also believe discrimination against whites is widespread. Because of the similarities in attitudes between whites and minorities on this issue, it seems unlikely that this accounts for the much greater opposition among whites to affirmative action and other policies designed to reduce racial inequality. This leaves us with only one plausible answer: Whites believe that the system is fair, that there is equal opportunity, and that accordingly, minorities are mainly at fault for whatever disproportionate disadvantages they suffer (Kluegel, 1990; Hoschschild, 1995). Again, these beliefs have been persistent among whites since the late 1960s or early 1970s (Schuman and Krysan, 1999). And indeed, if, as whites widely believe, minorities enjoy the same opportunities as whites, then affirmative action *would* amount to reverse discrimination.

This belief, however, is not supported by the facts. With 35 percent of black children and 29 percent of Hispanic children living below the poverty level, compared to fewer than 9 percent of non-Hispanic white children (U.S. Bureau of the Census, 2007), it is evident that large racial differences in poverty rates exist from birth. Clearly, these differences indicate that people born into different racial groups do not experience equal opportunity: Both poverty and institutional discrimination keep many of these children from enjoying the opportunities that the average non-Hispanic white child enjoys. (The effects of poverty on life opportunity are discussed in detail in Chapter 6.)

Social-Structural Theories of Race Relations

Social-structural theories see racial and ethnic inequality as arising from characteristics of societies, not individual attitudes and beliefs. Conflict theorists emphasize competition, economic motives, and unequal power, while functionalists emphasize cultural differences and ethnocentrism.

Conflict Theories

It is probably fair to say that the conflict perspective is the predominant approach today among sociologists specializing in race and ethnic relations. In fact, there are at least three important contemporary conflict theories about intergroup relations, which we shall explore shortly. These theories share certain elements. Unlike the functionalist approach, they do not see racial or ethnic inequality as resulting simply from cultural differences and ethnocentrism. Rather, they believe the critical factor is that *one group gains advantages by holding another group down.* When groups are in competition for scarce resources, or when one group has something (land, labor, wealth) that another wants, an essential condition for inequality exists. However, this by itself does not produce intergroup inequality. A second condition must also be present: unequal power, which means one group can take what it wants from another (Noel, 1968). Without this condition, inequality does not occur, and conflict may even be less likely, because groups often calculate their chances of winning before initiating a fight. However, when both competition or opportunity for gain *and* unequal power between groups exist, racial or ethnic inequality is likely to occur (Semyonov, 1988; see also Bélanger and Pinard, 1991). This is especially likely when the conditions noted by functionalists—ethnocentrism and cultural differences—are also present.

Although conflict theorists share the belief that competition and unequal power play key roles in racial and ethnic inequality, they disagree about the nature of that competition. Most societies experience competition along both racial/ethnic and economic lines, and different conflict theories offer different ideas about the precise roles of race and economics.

Internal Colonialism Theory. One conflict theory of race and ethnic relations is *internal colonialism.* Most of us are familiar with the concept of colonialism in its traditional meaning—a powerful country establishes control of a foreign area and its people. Typically, the native people of the colony are assigned a status lower than that of the colonizers. The natural resources of the colony are taken and used, often along with its people's labor, to enrich the colonizing country. In the case of internal colonialism, much the same thing happens, but within the borders of the colonizing country. In both cases, the colonized groups are placed under the colonizing country's control *involuntarily* (Blauner, 1972).

Once the colonized group takes on the status of a conquered people, certain things occur. Colonized minorities are subjected to intense attacks on their culture. Because they are defined as inferior, they are subjected either to isolation or to forced assimilation. They are also kept outside the mainstream of economic activity to ensure that they will not compete with members of the colonizing groups. Blauner (1972) points out that these experiences of colonized minorities make them different from immigrant minorities. The latter enter a society voluntarily and are not subjected to the same levels of attack on their culture or economic isolation as are colonized minorities.

The four major groups who became "American" involuntarily are African Americans, Chicanos (Mexican Americans), Puerto Ricans, and American Indians. The experiences of these groups generally fit those of colonized minorities, which helps to explain why even today they occupy the most disadvantaged positions of all American racial and ethnic groups, including immigrant groups whose arrival is much more recent (Zweigenhaft and Domhoff, 1991, Chap. 7).

Internal-colonialism theory is different from other conflict theories of race and ethnic relations in one important regard—it focuses almost exclusively upon inequalities and conflicts that occur *between* (rather than within) racial groups. Consequently, they see race as having a greater impact upon society than class: All people in colonized groups share a common experience of being discriminated against that makes their life experiences unlike those of anyone in the majority group. Two other important conflict theories of intergroup relations focus in part upon economic inequalities and conflicts *within the majority group,* pointing out that such tensions may have an important effect on majority-minority relations.

Split Labor-Market Theory. The first such theory is *split-labor-market theory,* which lists three economic interest groups: employers (owners of capital), higher-paid labor, and lower-paid labor (Bonacich, 1972). In multiethnic or multiracial societies, higher-paid labor is often made up of majority-group members, while minority-group members are concentrated in the lower-paid labor category (Bonacich, 1975, 1976; W. J. Wilson, 1978). According to this theory, the majority-group members who hold the higher-paying jobs attempt to protect their position by demanding hiring discrimination against minorities. In the United States, for example, white workers have demanded discrimination against African Americans, Chicanos, and Asian Americans. Certain jobs were defined as "white men's work," and any minority person who aspired to them encountered blatant hostility from white workers. (For a personal account of such discrimination, see Wright, 1937, pp. 5–15.)

According to split-labor-market theory, majority-group workers demand and benefit from discrimination because it protects their favored position in the labor force. Employers, on the other hand, are often hurt by discrimination, both because it drives up wages by reducing the labor pool and because it deprives them of the opportunity to hire the best worker (on this point, see Becker, 1971).

How accurate is this view? Many white workers undoubtedly *believe* that discrimination works to their advantage. However, majority-group workers can only benefit from discrimination if they (rather than their employers) control the hiring process. To a certain extent, white workers did this in the late nineteenth and early twentieth centuries by threatening to "cause trouble" if minorities were hired. However, when the costs of discrimination became high enough, employers resorted to hiring tactics that used racism to the disadvantage of both majority- and minority-group members. The reality

UNDERSTANDING RACE, CLASS, AND GENDER
Popular Music as a Threat: The Role of Race

You've probably seen it on CD cases, maybe even your own: PARENTAL ADVISORY—EXPLICIT LYRICS. For years, rock music and its various derivatives have been seen by some people as a threat to youth or to society. Even Elvis Presley (once known by his critics as "Elvis the pelvis") was seen by some as a corrupter of youth. So it's no surprise that when rap music and heavy metal music hit the scene in the 1980s, there would be some who would see them as a threat and would try to censor them. But when sociologist Amy Binder (1993) studied attacks on rap and heavy metal music, she came up with some findings that might surprise you. Although many people saw both musical styles as dangerous and sought to censor them, the nature of the threat that they saw in rap and heavy metal music was very different. Moreover, much of that difference can be tied to race.

Binder's analysis of speeches and writings about the two styles show that most of the concern about heavy metal music was either that it was a "corrupter of youth" or that it was something dangerous from which children needed to be protected. She points to an example of the corruption theme in testimony to Congress by heavy metal music critic Joe Steussy, who warned that "Its principal themes are, as you have already heard, extreme violence, extreme rebellion, substance abuse, sexual promiscuity and perversion, and Satanism." The need for protection theme can be seen in a column by William Safire arguing that "Kids get special protection in law ... and deserve protection from porn-rock profiteers" (Binder, 1993, p. 758). The message: if we don't protect our children, they will surely be corrupted by this terrible, Satanic music. In fact, many writers, like *Newsweek*'s Kathy Stroud, wrote about their own children.

The attacks on rap were different. Rather than "corruption" or "need for protection," they focused on the music as a "danger to society." But here, the danger that was emphasized was not to the people listening to the music. Rather, the concern was about what people who listened to rap music would do to others. Consider this editorial attack by columnist George Will on the rap music of 2 Live Crew, a group that was arrested over its music in Florida in 1990: "Fact: Some members of a particular age and social cohort—the one making 2 Live Crew rich—stomped and raped [a] jogger to the razor edge of death, for the fun of it." And Tipper Gore, who had testified before Congress urging restrictions on popular music, informed the public that after the attack one of the attackers had, in jail, whistled the tune of a popular rap song.

Why would people worry about what *heavy metal* music does to harm its *listeners,* but worry about what *rap* music listeners would do to *someone else*? Binder suggests it is directly tied to race, and to white America's fears and racial stereotypes. Most heavy metal performers and audiences were white. And in 1990, most rap performers and listeners were African American, though the white audience for rap became much larger in subsequent years. If it was white kids that were listening, the concern of those who wrote and testified was that the kids themselves might be harmed. But with black kids, the main fear of those who wrote and testified was that those kids might hurt someone else. This reflects white society's fears about black crime and the racial stereotypes that white people have about African Americans. And this says a lot about the state of race relations in the United States.

---

is that, except in occupations with union hiring halls, workers do not control the hiring process. Hence, most sectors of the economy operate more in accordance with a third theoretical model, to which we now turn.

Marxist Theory. The *Marxist theory of racism* holds that racism exists mainly because it benefits the ruling economic class (Cox, 1948). Today's Marxist theorists see two key economic interest groups, not three, as envisioned in split-labor-market theory. Marxist theory denies that there is any real conflict of interest between higher-paid and lower-paid labor. Rather, as wage laborers, both groups share a common interest that is in conflict with that of the owners of capital. Marxists believe that racial antagonisms are primarily a mechanism that is used by the owners of capital to divide the working class. Thus, they argue that employers encourage white workers to think that they are threatened by blacks and other minorities, because they then come to see the minority workers rather than the employer as their enemy. This divides the working class along the lines of race and ensures that employers will not have to confront a unified workforce.

The labor history of the early twentieth century in the United States offers considerable support for this viewpoint. Between 1910 and 1920, all-white labor unions conducted strikes in the railroad, meatpacking, aluminum, and steel industries. The employers played upon racial antagonisms to break these strikes. Through a combination of deception (southern blacks were offered "good jobs up North" without being told they would be strikebreakers) and skillful exploitation of black antagonism toward all-white unions, thousands of blacks were recruited to break these strikes (Bonacich, 1976; Foster, 1920; Kloss et al., 1976; Rudwick, 1964). These tactics, of course, hurt both blacks and whites over the long run: White strikers were defeated, and black workers were restricted to low-paying nonunion jobs. These incidents of strikebreaking, along with a general fear of black economic competition, led to perhaps the worst wave of race riots in American history. Between 1906 and 1921, mobs of whites in a number of cities attacked and murdered at least 125 African Americans (Farley, 2000:160). In many cities and towns, all African American residents were violently forced out of their homes and made to permanently leave town (Loewen, 2005). A study by Susan Olzak (1989) has confirmed that much of this antiblack violence was linked to labor conflict.

By the 1930s, white workers increasingly realized that their approach of demanding discrimination was hurting them more than it was helping them. Industrial workers formed the Congress of Industrial Organizations (CIO), which, especially in the North, frequently supported policies, laws, and labor contracts forbidding racial discrimination. Even today the evidence suggests that racial inequality hurts white workers more than it helps them. Comparisons of states and metropolitan areas by Reich (1981, 1986b) and Szymanski (1976) in 1970 and 1980 showed that those with greater racial inequality were also characterized by lower wages for white workers, higher corporate profits, and weaker unions. From the mid-1970s through the mid-1990s, as the minority poor and working class lost ground, inequality also grew within the white population. Both the white working class and much of the middle class lost income even as the wealthiest whites gained. Although the boom economy of the late 1990s slowed these trends somewhat, the gap between rich and poor today is much greater both in the overall society and within each racial group than was the case twenty-five years ago. While white workers worried about the perceived threat of affirmative action, their real incomes shrank—but it wasn't minorities who gained. Rather, there was a considerable shift of wealth and income to the wealthiest segment of the white population (Kennickell, 2000).

Functionalist/Assimilationist Theories About Race and Ethnic Relations

Although conflict theories predominate in the sociology of racial and ethnic relations today, the functionalist viewpoint also has some influence on thinking about racial and ethnic relations in sociology, and considerable influence in popular opinion. Generally, this viewpoint attributes racial and ethnic conflict and inequality largely to *cultural differences* among groups. These differences are usually accompanied by **ethnocentrism,** an attitude in which each group considers its own values and ways of doing things to be the natural, right, and superior way. According to functionalists, ethnocentrism contributes to racial and ethnic inequalities, because each group thinks it is better than the others. Hence, many functionalists favor **assimilation**—a process whereby differences between groups are reduced so that the different groups share a common set of values and a common social structure (Gordon, 1964).

Assimilationists believe that as societies modernize, assimilation occurs and racial inequality tends to decrease because interdependency in society increases as society becomes more complex. There is evidence from a variety of countries, including the United States, Brazil (Telles, 1994), and South Africa, that prejudice and discrimination do, sooner or later, decline (but not disappear) when modernization occurs. However, several cautionary notes are in order.

First, it can take a very long time for this to happen and it may happen only after a period of escalating conflict and, sometimes, violence (Blumer, 1965). The United States and South Africa clearly illustrate this; both had formal systems of segregation that only broke down after long and sometimes violent struggles. In addition, discrimination sometimes becomes subtler and less open, but continues to occur (Feagin and Sikes, 1994). Second, many conflict theorists have criticized assimilation on the grounds that, as a practical matter, it is the minority groups that are expected to do most of the changing to fit into the majority group's way of doing things (Carmichael and Hamilton, 1967; Ryan, 1971). In the United States, this tendency has been referred to as *Anglo-conformity*. The idea of assimilation has been popular with white Americans, and they have exerted strong pressures on minorities and immigrants to "fit in."

Third, sociohistorical studies show that cultural differences alone do not cause great racial inequality; economic motivations also play an important role in the creation of systems of racial inequality such as slavery in the United States (Noel, 1968, 1972). Finally, a variety of studies have shown that assimilation occurs more readily among immigrant minorities, who have chosen to enter a society, than it does among colonized minorities, who have no choice in the matter (Lieberson, 1980; Zweigenhaft and Domhoff, 1991).

For all these reasons, increasing numbers of sociologists have seen **pluralism** or **multiculturalism** as a better societal model than assimilation. Under this model, some social and cultural characteristics are shared in common throughout a society, but differences among groups also exist and are accepted. Such differences are seen as a basis of unity and pride for groups that have experienced discrimination, and as a source of adaptability in society (Watson, Kumar, and Michealsen, 1993). In fact, many racial and ethnic minority groups over the past several decades have moved in the direction of pluralism or multiculturalism, emphasizing the unique histories, cultures, and accomplishments of their groups over integration or assimilation with the majority group. Concepts such as Black Power and Afrocentrism among African Americans, Chicanismo and Brown Power among Latinos/Latinas, and the rediscovery of tribal traditions and the preservation of native languages and religion among American Indians have all been a part of this trend, as has increased ethnic consciousness among white ethnic groups such as Irish, Italian, and Polish Americans, among many others. In general, the idea of a cultural *mosaic,* in which society is composed of many different groups with different culture and traditions, has gained favor over the idea of mass assimilation, in which all groups become culturally similar.

Historical Explanations

Although tales of contact between alien peoples have long been filled with ethnocentric qualities and things we would today label as racist, some argue that the nature of the language in journals and public records dating back thousands of years made an important qualitative change around the time that more powerful countries began to colonize the peoples of Africa and South America. This point is disputed to be sure, but there does appear to at least be an up-tick in the "we are superior; they are inferior" quality of discussion after this period (Loewen, 1996). Before that the description of encounters between peoples seems to have been characterized more by an "exotic" quality. That is, "those other people are very exotic!" A Marxist would argue that the draw of material resources

This statue of Popay, the Native American leader of the 1680 Pueblo Revolt, is in the National Statuary Hall in the Capitol Building in Washington, DC. The inclusion of this statue reflects the influence of cultural pluralism, or multiculturalism, in today's society. (Chris Maddaloni/Roll Call/Getty Images)

located in these nations led to the idea that these "exotic people" needed to be subjugated and exploited. Therefore, an ideology of their being inferior was created to justify stealing their resources.

Loewen (1995) further explains that the concepts of good and evil had already been associated with white and black or light and dark long before more fair-skinned peoples encountered darker-skinned people and began to desire their resources. In this interpretation, it is the preexisting symbols of good and evil that helped shape and justify the imperialist designs of the lighter-skinned invaders. How might a symbolic interactionist approach this issue? Could we hypothesize that the concept of good being associated with light and evil associated with dark may be a very ancient idea, stemming possibly from early humans' vulnerability at night?

Racial and Ethnic Relations: An International Perspective

Most societies with racial and ethnic diversity experience some degree of racial conflict and inequality. Discrimination and social inequality are encountered by Chinese in Vietnam; Aborigines in Australia; Catholics in Northern Ireland; Arabs in Israel; Jews in much of Eastern Europe; blacks, Pakistanis, and East Indians in Great Britain; Asians in several African countries; French-speaking people in Canada; native Indians in several Latin American countries; and a variety of immigrant groups in Germany. In many places, violence has erupted between racial or ethnic groups.

Ethnic Inequality and Conflict: How Universal?

Does this mean that ethnic inequality and conflict are inevitable whenever different groups come into contact? It does not. In Switzerland, a variety of ethnic and language groups have gotten along in relative harmony for years. In Hawaii, racial diversity is greater than anywhere else in the United States—no race is a majority there—and interracial relations, though far from perfect, are in general more harmonious than elsewhere in the United States. British Protestants and Irish Catholics, who hate one another in Northern Ireland, get along in the United States. Ethnic and racial conflict, then, are not inevitable; rather, they are the product of certain social conditions. We have already identified some of them. One is colonization, which is as evident in other societies as it is in the United States. Other examples of societies that must cope with racial and ethnic diversity arising from a history of colonization are South Africa and Latin America.

Racial Caste in South Africa and the United States

Until very recently, South African law spelled out where people could live, whom they could marry, what jobs they could have, even where they could travel—on the basis of legally codified racial categories. In many regards, this system— called apartheid—resembled the U.S. South prior to the Civil Rights movement. There, too, elaborate rules of segregation and denial of the vote were used to keep blacks in a separate and subordinate position.

In both the U.S. South prior to the 1950s and South Africa prior to the 1990s, long periods of social upheaval were the result of legally mandated segregation and inequality. Such upheavals demonstrate that caste systems are very difficult to maintain without great conflict in modern urban societies. The greater diversity and weaker social control of the city, along with mass communications, make it more likely that people will rise up in protest against oppression (Blumer, 1965; Morris, 1984; Tilly, 1974; Williams, 1977). If the system continues to resist change, the conflict can become quite violent, as illustrated by the 2,100 deaths that resulted in South Africa between the summers of 1984 and 1986 (Cowell, 1986). Similarly, many African Americans were murdered by whites in the U.S. South from the late nineteenth to the mid-twentieth centuries. In the last sixteen years of the nineteenth century, there were more than 2,500 lynchings in the United States—mostly in the South and mostly with black victims (Franklin, 1969, p. 439). Lynchings were seen by whites as a way to keep African Americans who challenged the system of racial inequality "in their place." As Blumer (1965) has pointed out, in such periods upheaval does not always lead to the same outcome. Sometimes, stiffening resistance by the majority group leads to great violence, but keeps the caste system in place. This occurred in the U.S. South in the late nineteenth and early twentieth centuries, and in South Africa in the mid-twentieth century. In other cases, change comes and the caste system is altered, as later happened in the U.S. South in the 1950s and 1960s and in South Africa in the 1990s. Sociologists have sought to explain both why formal systems of segregation persisted so long in South Africa and the U.S. South, and why they finally collapsed.

A major reason the caste systems persisted so long is because the black population is a large majority in South Africa, and also a much larger proportion of the population in the U.S. South than elsewhere. In general, the larger the minority population is, the more threatening it seems, and the more the dominant group will perceive it has to gain through discrimination (Glenn, 1966; Dowdall, 1974). South African whites, who controlled the country for many decades, knew that majority rule meant black rule and a loss of power for whites. This made the one-person, one-vote principle highly threatening to the white minority that controlled South Africa for so long (Sparks, 1995). Similarly, keeping blacks from voting through a variety of illegal means was a cornerstone of Jim Crow segregation in the U.S. South, and efforts to keep blacks from voting persisted even after legal segregation ended, as illustrated by discrimination against African Americans seeking to vote in the 2000 presidential election (NAACP, 2000). And it is clearly established from a variety of sociological studies that fear and perceived threat are major causes of prejudice and discrimination: When people perceive a group as threatening, they tend to discriminate against it (Blalock, 1967; Quillian, 1995), and they are even more likely to engage in violence against its members (Jacobs and Wood, 1999).

In both the U.S. South and South Africa, both strong outside pressures and internal upheaval eventually led to the changes. In the United States, the massive Civil Rights movement forced this issue to the forefront. In Montgomery, Alabama, for example, thousands of African Americans walked to work or carpooled for eleven months to force the city's bus system to desegregate. Although the bus systems there and elsewhere were threatened with bankruptcy because of the boycotts, it also took a Supreme Court ruling (one of many such rulings against racial segregation laws in the 1950s and 1960s) to put an end to segregated public transit. In South Africa, pressure from a worldwide economic boycott and continuing upheaval at home similarly forced change. The South African economy was suffering under a worldwide economic boycott that, despite some leakage, was effective enough to have serious economic consequences. In addition, the violence in the country had continued unrelentingly from the late 1960s into the 1990s, and by the early 1990s it was, if anything, getting worse. Consequently, the white South African government first ended the segregation rules, then in 1993 agreed to end racial restrictions on voting. As a result, Nelson Mandela, who had been imprisoned for many years, was elected South Africa's first black president, and a black majority was also elected to the country's parliament. In both South Africa and the U.S. South, change in the racial caste system came not because people were persuaded that it was evil, but rather because internal upheaval and external pressure (the worldwide boycott of South Africa and the rulings by the U.S. Supreme Court, which in two cases had to be backed up with federal troops) forced changes to occur.

In South Africa, once apartheid was ended and majority rule came about, the violence gradually subsided. The country now appears to work in a fairly orderly manner. According to a largely functionalist analysis by Edmonds and Sparks (1995), this is because both racial groups are dependent upon one another. Over 80 percent of the population is black, which means that blacks are the country's main supply of workers—the economy could not function without them. At the same time, the history of apartheid left capital and expertise mostly in the hands of whites, so that Mandela and his colleagues and successors in the ruling African National Congress party also understood that they needed the whites. This spurred both sides to cooperate, despite their long history of conflict (Sparks, 1995). It must be recognized, though, that while legal segregation was abolished and cooperation increased, informal segregation and considerable racial inequality persist today in both the United States and South Africa.

Racial Assimilation in Latin America

A number of Latin American countries present a striking contrast to race relations in the United

States. Like the United States, they were colonized by Europeans who imported blacks from Africa to serve as slave labor and who took land from the Indians (Van den Berghe, 1978, pp. 63–65). Yet, the outcome has been ultimately very different. Both culturally and racially, such countries as Mexico and Brazil experienced a two-way assimilation that produced new cultures and ethnic groups that are neither European, African, nor Indian. A key element of this process was **amalgamation**—repeated intermarriage and interbreeding between racial groups to the point that the various groups became largely indistinguishable. In both Mexico and Brazil, a large portion of the population is of mixed European, Indian, or African ancestry. As a result, relatively few people can be identified as strictly European, black, or Indian. The great majority belong to a mixed group that is often thought of as simply "Brazilian" or "Mexican."

Why did this happen in Mexico and Brazil and not in the United States? One factor is population composition. The overwhelming majority of the Portuguese who came to the colony of Brazil were male. This led to widespread intermarriage early on, which became sufficiently accepted to continue when more European women did arrive. In the United States, by contrast, more English colonists came as families, which discouraged intermarriage. Whites in North America did, of course, have sexual contacts with Indians and black slaves—often highly sexist and exploitative ones. However, the children that resulted from these contacts were designated as part of the minority group, whereas in Brazil, they became part of the majority group.

Religious differences further contributed to these patterns (Kinloch, 1974). The Catholic religion of the Spanish and Portuguese emphasized conversion and the winning of souls (M. Harris, 1964). Thus, black slaves and especially Indians were incorporated into the dominant culture. In the United States, the Protestant religion of the early colonists placed a greater emphasis on predestination, the belief that people were either chosen to be saved or not, and not too much could be done for those who were not among the chosen. Thus, efforts to convert and integrate were less common, particularly in the case of Indians.

Other cultural attributes of both the dominant and minority groups also made a difference. In Brazil, many Portuguese of Moorish (North African) ancestry were dark-complexioned and viewed such a complexion as a standard of beauty (Pierson, 1942). This further encouraged intermarriage with Indians and Africans. In Mexico, the native Aztec Indians had a highly developed urban culture. Their largest city, with a population of 300,000, was one of the biggest in the world. Thus, in some ways, the Mexican Indians were culturally more similar to the Europeans, and therefore could more easily adjust to European ways. In Mexico, the blend of European (Hispano) and native (Indio) culture became a symbol of national unity.

Although assimilation and amalgamation have been the rule in Mexico and Brazil, neither country is a racial paradise. Brazil not only had slavery at one time, but, relative to its population, had twice as many slaves as the United States (Andrews, 1991). In both Brazil and Mexico, having a lighter skin is associated with a higher social and economic status (Bastide, 1965; Mason, 1971; Telles, 1994). In Brazil, there has been a subtle but systematic exclusion of blacks from professional and white-collar employment in recent decades. This has been even more pronounced than in the United States, at least since affirmative action was established in the United States (Andrews, 1991). Even so, the different cultural and demographic histories have produced very different patterns of race relations in Mexico and Brazil than in the United States.

The differences among the United States, South Africa, and Latin America show the myriad ways in which cultural, demographic, and historical factors interact to bring about very different patterns of race and ethnic relations in different times and places.

Racial and Ethnic Groups in the United States

Because the United States is a nation of immigrants, it is one of the most diverse nations of the world in terms of race and ethnicity. No ethnic group in the United States accounts for more than about a quarter of the population, and—depending on how you count them—there are between fifteen and thirty nationalities that are claimed by at least half a million Americans (see U.S. Bureau of the Census, 2004). About two-thirds of the U.S. population is of European ancestry; about one-third is of African, Asian, Latin American, or Native American ancestry. Although many of these groups entered American society voluntarily through immigration, some did not (Blauner, 1972). Africans were brought here as slaves, and the Mexican American group was created by the conquest of a large area of northern Mexico (now California, Texas, Nevada, Colorado, New Mexico, and Arizona). Puerto Rico became a U.S. colony after the Spanish-American War of 1898, and the entire United States was Indian territory before the arrival of the Europeans. Because we have such great racial and ethnic diversity, and because a number of groups became "American" involuntarily, the United States has experienced greater racial and ethnic inequality and conflict than many other countries.

Minority Groups: African Americans, Hispanic Americans, and Native Americans

The groups that have experienced and continue to experience the greatest systematic disadvantage in the United States are the ones we would consider *colonized minorities* according to Robert Blauner's (1972) theory, discussed earlier in this chapter. These groups include African Americans, most Hispanic or Latino Americans, and Native Americans or American Indians. As can be seen in Table 7.2, these three groups account for nearly 33 percent of the U.S. population at the beginning of the twenty-first century, a percentage that has been increasing in recent years and will continue to do so.

Historically, the largest of these groups has been African Americans, but today there are more Latino Americans than African Americans, and the former group is growing more rapidly. The great majority of African Americans live in urban areas, and over half of all African Americans still live in the South. Within the urban areas, African Americans are more likely than any other group to live in the central cities rather than in the suburbs; a major reason for this is a long-time pattern of discrimination in the sale and rental of housing that has limited access to many suburban areas. The African American population continues to grow more rapidly than the white population, but not as rapidly as that of other minority groups.

The most rapidly growing of these minority groups is Hispanic or Latino Americans, whose population increased by about 58 percent (an increase of almost 13 million people) just between 1990 and 2000. The Latino population is now larger than the African American population, and it is growing faster. However, Hispanic Americans are not really one group, but many. They include Mexican Americans, Puerto Ricans, Cuban Americans, and others. As shown in Figure 7.1, however, the majority are Mexican American, and about two-thirds of Hispanics are either Mexican American or Puerto Rican American.

These groups are distributed differently, with most Mexican Americans living in the Southwest, Puerto Ricans in the Northeast, and Cuban Americans in Florida. Like African Americans, most Hispanic Americans live in large metropolitan areas, particularly in central cities.

It is also true that Native Americans are made up of a number of distinct groups—hundreds, in fact. The total shown in Table 7.2 includes Alaskan

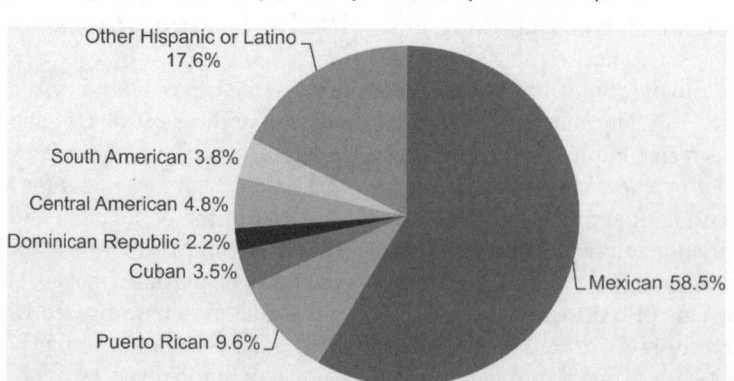

Figure 7.1 U.S. Hispanic Population, by Nationality, 2000

U.S. Census Bureau, 2001, American Fact Finder, Census 2000 Summary File 1, http://factfinder.census.gov/servlet/DTTable?-ts=25623370480.

Natives (Eskimos and Aleuts) as well as American Indians, but the 3.0 million American Indians in fact comprise hundreds of different nationalities (commonly referred to as tribes). The largest of these, the Cherokee tribe, makes up less than 20 percent of the total. Only five tribes, the Cherokee, Navajo (Diné), Choctaw, Sioux (Lakota), and Chippewa (Ojibwa), had populations over 100,000 in 2000 (U.S. Bureau of the Census, 2000, Table No. 35. American Indian and Alaska Native Population by Tribe: 2000). Almost half of all Native Americans live in rural areas, more than almost any other racial or ethnic group. Many of these live on reservations. Even so, the number of American Indians living in urban areas is at an all-time high, and is continuing to increase.

Census Bureau figures indicate that the Indian population grew rapidly between 1970 and 1990 and significantly between 1990 and 2000, but part of the apparent growth between 1970 and 1990 occurred because people of mixed Indian and white ancestry have become more likely to identify themselves as American Indian. It should also be noted that the number of Americans with significant Indian ancestry is much higher than the 2.5 million who identified themselves as Indian alone in response to the race question on the 2000 Census questionnaire. For example, on a separate question on ancestry, 7.9 million Americans identified American Indian as one of their two primary ancestry groups in 1990 (U.S. Bureau of the Census, 2004). Also, about 1.6 million people classified themselves as combinations of American Indian and one or more other races on the 2000 Census, representing nearly a quarter of all people who chose two or more races in the 2000 Census (U.S. Census Bureau 2001e).

As Blauner points out in his definition of a colonized minority, African Americans, Mexican Americans, Puerto Ricans, and American Indians all became part of American society involuntarily through conquest or forced immigration. All of them were systematically exploited for their labor, their land, or both. As a result of that history and of continuing institutionalized discrimination, these groups today remain at a collective disadvantage compared with all others. These facts distinguish them from other groups in American society that have experienced discrimination but not the same conquest, systematic economic exploitation, and continuing experience of disadvantage to the present day.

Economic Exploitation and the Origins of Intergroup Inequality

Economic motivations played a key role in the creation of the systems of racial and ethnic inequality that placed all three of these groups in disadvantaged positions in American society. In the case of African Americans, it is important to understand that the slavery that was imposed on them was a creation of the wealthy, landowning elite of the South, which sought a cheap and reliable source of labor to maximize profits in a highly labor-intensive plantation system. As Noel (1968), Boskin (1965), and Jordan (1968) have pointed out, blacks did not become slaves simply because the British colonists in America were prejudiced against them. Rather, Africans were one of many groups against whom the colonists were prejudiced, and antiblack prejudices became much stronger after slavery became institutionalized (Cox, 1948; Noel, 1972). Black slavery was a product of economic motivations and of the fact that blacks were in a weaker position to resist it than were other groups (Noel, 1968; see also Stinchcomb, 1994). The role of the economic interests and the power advantage of the southern "planter class" can be clearly seen by looking at what happened in the North. Slavery was, for a time, legal there too—but it never became

Table 7.2 U.S. Racial and Ethnic Group Populations, 2008

	Population (in millions)	Percent of Total
White, not Hispanic[1]	199.5	65.6
African American	39.1	12.8
Hispanic[1]	44.3	15.4
Asian	13.5	4.5
Pacific Islander	0.6	0.2
Native American	3.0	1.0
2 or more races	5.2	1.7
Total U.S. population	304.1	101.2

[1]Hispanic persons may be of any race (for example, white or African American). Total exceeds 100 percent because black, Asian, Native American, and Pacific Islander individuals who are Hispanic are included in both the race count and the Hispanic count.

Source: U.S. Census Bureau. 2009. Population Estimates, National – Characteristics, National Sex, Race, and Hispanic Origin, http://www.census.gov/popest/national/asrh/NC-EST2008/NC-EST2008-03.xls (Downloaded October 19, 2009).

widespread because no economic elite depended upon it for their wealth. Between 1780 and 1804, the northern states that had once allowed slavery outlawed it, but it took the Civil War to get rid of slavery in the South. This is a rather clear example of the conflict theorists' argument that social inequality occurs because it benefits the wealthy and powerful.

Both Mexican Americans and Puerto Ricans also came under U.S. rule involuntarily, through military conquest. Approximately the northern third of what was once Mexico became part of the United States as a result of the Mexican-American War in the 1840s. At that time, many Mexicans in what became the Southwestern United States were ranchers who owned large tracts of land, and most of them eventually lost their land after the war. This occurred despite a protocol accompanying the treaty that ended the war which said that Mexican landowners would keep their land. The economic motivation behind this displacement can be seen in the close correspondence between the influxes of whites into an area and the loss of land by the Mexican Americans (Farley, 2010). After they lost their land, Mexican Americans came to be treated as a cheap source of labor in western agriculture and other enterprises, and they have been among the lowest-paid American workers.

Like the Southwestern United States, Puerto Rico became part of the United States as a result of war. The Spanish-American War began when Cuba and Puerto Rico rebelled against their Spanish rulers in the 1890s. The United States joined the war against Spain in 1898. The end result was that Cuba became independent, but Puerto Rico became a U.S. territory. Thus, military outcomes, not voluntary immigration, account for both Mexican Americans and Puerto Ricans coming under U.S. rule. Many Mexicans have since emigrated to the United States and many Puerto Ricans have migrated to the mainland, but the history of both groups has been strongly shaped by their colonial history.

American Indians were not only attacked and displaced from their land; they were also subjected to genocidal attacks that wiped out at least three-quarters of their population. There is a lot of debate about how many native people were present in North America when the Europeans arrived; most estimates indicate at least a million, with 2 or 3 million a common figure (Collier, 1947; Garbarino, 1976; Josephy, 1968; Spicer, 1980a).

By 1900, that number had been reduced to about 240,000 (Spicer, 1980a, p. 59). This occurred due to wars with whites, massacres of Indians by whites, and the exposure of Indians (often accidental but sometimes deliberate) to European diseases against which Indians had no immunity. Some Indian tribes were completely wiped out, and others lost up to 90 percent of their population. In the early to mid-1700s, colonial governments sometimes offered bounties for Indian scalps, including those of women and children. In a number of instances, whites who were victorious in battles with Indians killed them rather than taking them prisoner. Thousands of other Indian people died as a result of forced moves, such as the Trail of Tears forced march of the Cherokees from Georgia to Oklahoma in 1838.

The major reason for these attacks against Indian people was whites' desire for their land. As long as only limited numbers of whites were present in any given area, they usually coexisted peacefully with the Indians. However, when larger influxes of whites increased the demand for land, Native Americans were repeatedly attacked and pushed aside. Treaties were made specifying certain areas as "Indian territory," but whenever farmland was in short supply or precious metals were discovered on those lands, the whites violated the treaties (Lurie, 1985; Spicer, 1980b). In 1871, Congress abolished the concept of treaties altogether. Official U.S. practice became one of placing Indian reservations on remote tracts of undesirable land that bore little ecological resemblance to the Indians' original homeland. As a result, farming, fishing, hunting, or gathering methods that worked in the original homeland often became useless.

Segregation and Attacks on Culture

Because the dominant group viewed any expression of independent thought by colonized minorities as a threat, the minority cultures came under systematic attack (Blauner, 1972). African American families were deliberately broken up in the slavery era, and groups that spoke different languages were mixed to prevent communication. American Indian children on reservations around the turn of the century were forcibly taken from their homes and families and placed in boarding schools where they were forbidden to speak their language or practice their religion. Both African American slaves and Native Americans on the reservations were forbidden to leave or travel by themselves. Mexican American schoolchildren in Texas and California were, for a time, punished if they spoke Spanish, even on the playground. Even well-intended policies, such as allotment, a program begun in 1887 to provide land to Indians, failed because of assumptions about the inferiority of non-European cultures. The idea of allotment was to make Indians into farmers, "just like the American family farmer." This policy was a miserable failure, because it attempted to impose white concepts of landownership and gender roles, and because it was applied even to tribes with little history or knowledge of agricultural practices. Its main effect was that American Indians lost about two-thirds of their land due to indebtedness (Guillemin, 1978; Lurie, 1985; Spicer, 1980b, p. 117).

At one time or another, African Americans, Hispanic Americans, and Native Americans all encountered systems of segregation that kept them separated from the white, Anglo majority group. The Jim Crow system, which segregated blacks and whites, lasted from shortly after the Civil War until the period following World War II. Although it was the dominant social, and in some cases legislated, pattern in the North even before the Civil War, it became a legalized system throughout the South after the Civil War. Under segregation, forced separation of the races and social isolation of African Americans was the rule. Segregation existed in both the North and the South, although it broke down somewhat sooner in the North and was stricter and more formal in the South. Segregation meant separation of the races in everything from bathrooms, bus and theater seats, lunch counters, and waiting rooms to—in some places—fishing lakes and public baseball diamonds. By law, black and white children attended separate schools in many states, and housing segregation was enforced by federal policy and by deed covenants forbidding the sale of property to blacks (and in many cases, Jews, Asians, Hispanics, and other "unwanted" groups). The races actually became more separated from one another in the South after the end of slavery. Though the master-slave relationship disappeared with the Thirteenth Amendment, whites sought to preserve the role of a master race by excluding blacks entirely from their social and economic world.

In fact, segregation most typically occurs in periods of early urbanization, such as in the U.S. South in the decades after the Civil War. In these situations, majority groups have used segregation as a new way to keep their advantages as the old systems of inequality, such as slavery, break down, and as the majority and minority groups compete in new settings. Thus, formal, legally mandated segregation emerged in the United States about twenty years after the end of the Civil War, and in South Africa around 1910, as that society also began to urbanize and industrialize (Cell, 1982).

Of course, the Indian reservation was by its very nature an attempt to separate Indians from whites, to get them "out of the way" so that white agricultural, mining, and railroad interests could grow and profit unimpeded. Latino Americans, too, encountered formal systems of segregation. Even in "liberal" San Francisco, it was at one time illegal for Mexican American, Asian American, or African American children to attend school with white children. When the rules of segregation were violated, whites retaliated violently. Thousands of blacks were lynched in the South, as were many Mexican Americans in the West. And from the Civil War through the World War II era, blacks, Mexican Americans, and Asian Americans were all the targets of mob attacks by whites in "race riots" in cities large and small. In the East St. Louis riot of 1917, forty-eight people were killed; all but a few of them were African Americans killed by white mobs (Rudwick, 1964).

The Status of Minority Groups Today

Although deliberate racial discrimination is no longer legal, African Americans, Hispanic Americans, and Native Americans remain in a disadvantaged position in American society today. All three groups, for example, receive lower wages and are more likely to be unemployed than whites. During the 2007–2008 period, the median family income of Hispanics was 68 percent of the income of non-Hispanic whites; for blacks it was 62 percent of the income of non-Hispanic whites (U.S. Bureau of the Census, 2009a). Though recent family income data are not available for American Indians, their median household income over a three-year period between 1997 and 1999 was about 69 percent that of whites (U.S. Census Bureau, 2000a). The poverty rate of all three groups—African Americans, Hispanics, and Native Americans—is around three times that of non-Hispanic whites (U.S. Census Bureau, 2000b). And in 1999, the unemployment rate of African Americans was 2.2 times that of whites, while the Latino unemployment rate was 1.6 times the white rate (U.S. Bureau of Labor Statistics, 2001). The differences in wealth—the total value of all that people own—between these racial groups and non-Hispanic whites are even larger than differences in income (Oliver and Shapiro, 1995). Members of all three minority groups remain less likely to enter and graduate from college than people in the non-Hispanic white group. In 2000, about one out of three whites between twenty-five and twenty-nine years old was a college graduate, compared to about one out of six among blacks and fewer than one out of ten among Hispanics (U.S. Bureau of the Census, 2001g). And in 1990, American Indians were only half as likely to be college graduates as were non-Hispanic whites.

For many people in these groups, conditions have gotten worse, not better, in recent years. During the 1980s, poor blacks became poorer relative to the rest of the population, and they have become increasingly isolated in inner cities, where jobs have become virtually nonexistent (Waquant and Wilson, 1989; Massey and Eggers, 1990; Massey and Denton, 1993; Wilson, 1987, 1996). Automation, globalization, and movement of jobs to suburban and rural areas have combined to eliminate thousands of industrial jobs from the inner cities, where most African Americans and many Hispanic Americans live. Among Hispanics, median income fell and poverty rose relative to non-Hispanic whites in the early 1990s, though the gap narrowed again later in that decade. For African Americans, one factor that perpetuates their economic disadvantages is a wall of housing segregation that goes beyond anything encountered by any other minority group (Massey and Denton, 1993; Yinger, 1995). This restricts black access to good jobs and good schools, which are increasingly to be found in suburban locations (Mouw, 2000; Yinger, 1995; Kasarda, 1989; Farley, 1987b). Black-white housing segregation has declined only modestly in recent decades; most blacks and most whites continue to live in separate neighborhoods where opportunities are highly unequal (Farley and Frey, 1994; Massey, Gross, and Shibuya, 1994). The practice of steering black and white home purchasers to different neighborhoods, and the discrimination found in mortgage lending, continue to perpetuate segregation and create barriers to black home ownership. In addition, many whites avoid moving into neighborhoods that have even small numbers of African Americans (Farley et al., 1994; Quillian, 1999).

Today, federal and state civil rights laws make racial discrimination in housing, lending, public accommodations, and employment illegal. Many employers and businesses have responded to these laws by establishing procedures to protect minorities from discrimination (Dobbin et al., 1993). This has resulted in some real improvements in the treatment of minorities. In states with the strongest civil rights protections, for example, minority employees do fare better than elsewhere relative to white males (Beggs, 1995). And changes in attitudes and beliefs about race in recent decades are making some real differences, as evidenced by the election of Barack Obama to the presidency in 2008, discussed later in this chapter.

Nonetheless, testing studies show that significant amounts of racial and ethnic discrimination still do occur. In these testing studies, two people who are similar except for their race or ethnicity seek housing or employment, or they may shop or try to get a loan. Careful observation is done to determine whether they are treated similarly or differently. If testing studies show that people who are similar in all regards except their race are consistently treated in different ways, there is strong evidence that discrimination is taking place. In recent years, testing studies have found evidence of discrimination in employment (Mathews, 1992; Kennedy, 1992; Bertrand and Mullainathan, 2002; Pager, 2003a, 2003b; Pager, 2007; Pager and Shepard, 2008), housing (U.S. Department of Housing and Urban Development, 1991; Galster, 1990a, 1990b; Yinger, 1995; Feagin, 2000, pp. 155–156), lending (Canner, Gabriel, and Woolley, 1991; Goering and Wienk, 1996), insurance (Smith and Clous, 1997), and auto sales (ABC News, 1991; Ayres, 1990). These and other studies indicate that African Americans, Hispanic Americans, and American Indians still encounter discrimination frequently, even though it is illegal. In fact, there is as much discrimination against black jobseekers as against people with prison records, and people discriminate on the basis of what race a voice sounds like, as well as on the basis of a "common black name" versus a "common white name" (Bertrand and Mullainathan, 2002; Pager, 2007).

Even in voting, racial discrimination continues to be quite common. In the 2000 presidential election, testimony at public hearings revealed widespread discrimination in Florida and several other states. African Americans attempting to vote in Florida were asked for multiple forms of identification while whites were asked for none, and blacks with no criminal record were told that they could not vote because they were felons. Also, in predominantly black precincts, voters were told they could not vote because they had already voted by absentee ballot when they had not. Numerous black voters were removed from the rolls (including some who had voted a month earlier in the primary), and police roadblocks were set up near some polling places (NAACP public hearing, November 11, 2000). Today's discrimination has gone underground, however, because of the legal consequences—which makes such discrimination harder to detect than the blatant discrimination of the past. When discrimination occurs today, nobody says, for example, that "you can't vote because you are black"; rather, they quietly act in ways that systematically treat blacks differently from whites, all the while denying that they are discriminating.

As noted earlier in this chapter, institutional practices also perpetuate racial and ethnic inequality. For example, the U.S. health-care system is the only one in the industrialized world that does not provide universal health insurance coverage. The health reforms of 2010 will substantially broaden coverage, but the provisions extending care to the uninsured do not go into effect for a few years—assuming that efforts by opponents of the reform law to repeal it or overturn it in court are unsuccessful. Because those without insurance tend to be people with low-paying jobs or people who are unemployed, minorities are overrepresented among people without health insurance. On average, from 2006–2008, for example, 19.7 percent of African Americans and 32.3 percent of Hispanic Americans had no health insurance of any type—compared to just 10.7 percent of non-Hispanic whites (U.S. Census Bureau, 2009b). Thus, while American race relations have improved over the past in some regards, serious inequalities remain. This has led whites and minorities to have very different perceptions about race and ethnic relations, because their experiences are so different (Kluegel, 1990; Hoschschild, 1995; Blauner, 1989). These differences became highly visible in 1995 in the very different reactions of white and black Americans to the O. J. Simpson trial and, more recently, to the arrest of African American scholar Henry Louis Gates for allegedly breaking into his own house. Another consequence of such differences in perceptions is a significant amount of self-segregation by both majority and minority group members, as illustrated by the box "Informal Segregation: The 'Invisible Wall' and the 'Black Table.'"

Intermediate Status Groups: Asian Americans, Jewish and Muslim Americans, and "White Ethnics"

Although African Americans, Hispanic Americans, and Native Americans most clearly fit the sociological definition of a minority group, there are a number of other American racial and ethnic groups that occupy an intermediate status between a minority group and a majority group. Most of these groups can be gathered together under two broad groupings—Asian Americans and "white ethnics" from Eastern and Southern Europe. Jewish and Muslim Americans are also examples of groups with intermediate status.

The most rapidly growing of these groups is the Asian American community. Asians numbered over 10 million, or 3.6 percent of the U.S. population in 2000, as shown in Table 7.2 on page 201. There are more than seven times as many Asian Americans today as there were in 1970, with growth occurring due to high immigration rates and, to a lesser extent, relatively high birthrates. Like Hispanic Americans, Asian Americans are not really one group, but several. The populations of the six largest Asian American groups according to the 2000 Census are shown in Table 7.3 on page 208.

People of Jewish heritage have been present in the United States since 1654. The largest Jewish immigration to the United States occurred from 1880 to 1924, and again in the World War II period (Goren, 1980). Today, there are about 6 million Jewish Americans, representing about 40 percent of the world's Jewish population. Like Asian Americans, Jewish Americans are highly urban, with over 95 percent of the total population living in cities or

STUDENT LIFE

Informal Segregation: The "Invisible Wall" and the "Black Table"

Informal racial segregation remains pervasive in American society today. At the university where I (Farley) taught for many years, a recent university president spoke of the "invisible wall" in the cafeteria, separating the tables occupied by white students and black students. In the following article from *The New York Times*, New York attorney Lawrence Otis Graham explores this issue. He describes how he realized that, while African Americans and other minorities are often seen as choosing such informal segregation, the reality is that both majority and minority groups choose such segregation, and that people segregate themselves on the basis of all kinds of social characteristics. In fact, such informal segregation is an almost inevitable outgrowth of a society in which our neighborhoods, our schools, our social clubs, and our churches are made up mostly of people who are "our kind"—no matter who we are. Unless this societal segregation is reduced, the "black table" will continue to be a part of our social reality.

The "Black Table" Is Still There

By Lawrence Otis Graham

During a recent visit to my old junior high school in Westchester County, I came upon something that I never expected to see again, something that was a source of fear and dread for three hours each school morning of my early adolescence: the all-black lunch table in the cafeteria of my predominantly white suburban junior high school.

As I look back on 27 years of often being the first and only black person integrating such activities and institutions as the college newspaper, the high school tennis team, summer music camps, our all-white suburban neighborhood, my eating club at Princeton, or my private social club at Harvard Law School, the one scenario that puzzled me the most then and now is the all-black lunch table.

Why was it there? Why did the black kids separate themselves? What did the table say about the integration that was supposedly going on in home rooms and gym classes? What did it say about the black kids? The white kids? What did it say about me when I refused to sit there, day after day, for three years?

Each afternoon, at 12:03 p.m., after the fourth period ended, I found myself among 600 12-, 13-, and 14-year-olds who marched into the brightly lit cafeteria and dashed for a seat at one of the 27 blue formica lunch tables.

No matter who I walked in with—usually a white friend—no matter what mood I was in, there was one

---

suburbs. Muslim presence in substantial numbers has occurred more recently in the United States. Muslims are diverse: Some are Asian, some are African Americans or African immigrants, some are from the Middle East, and some European Americans have also converted to Islam. Contrary to common belief, only a small minority of the 5 to 7 million Muslims in the United States are of Arab ethnicity.

Another set of groups to immigrate from Europe were the so-called white ethnics. Generally, this term refers to Americans of southern and eastern European ancestry. It includes Italian, Polish, Czech, Hungarian, Greek, and Ukranian Americans. Like Jewish Americans, but unlike immigrants from northern and western Europe, these groups generally immigrated in the largest numbers between the late nineteenth century and the imposition of immigration quotas in 1924. To a large extent, these groups were employed in manufacturing in the early twentieth century, settling in the industrial Northeast and Great Lakes regions. The largest of these groups today are Italian Americans and Polish Americans. Nearly 15 million Americans reported Italian ancestry in the 1990 Census, and over 9 million reported Polish ancestry (U.S. Bureau of the Census, 1996f, p. 63). Also numbering over a million each were Americans of Russian, Czech, Hungarian, Portuguese, Greek, and Slovak ancestry.

Certain features distinguish all of these groups from the minority groups discussed in the previous section. First, all of them immigrated to the United States voluntarily. In other words, they chose to be Americans. Although all were discriminated against, they were not subjected to systematic economic exploitation comparable with slavery or the displacement of American Indians and Mexican Americans from their land. The one exception to thing that was certain: I would not sit at the black table.

I would never consider sitting at the black table. What was wrong with me? What was I afraid of?

I would like to think that my decision was a heroic one, made in order to express my solidarity with the theories of integration that my community was espousing. But I was just 12 at the time, and there was nothing heroic in my actions.

I avoided the black table for a very simple reason: I was afraid that by sitting at the black table I'd lose all my white friends. I thought that by sitting there I'd be making a racist, antiwhite statement.

Is that what the all-black table means? Is it a rejection of white people? I no longer think so.

At the time, I was angry that there was a black lunch table. I believed that the black kids were the reason why other kids didn't mix more. I was ready to believe that their self-segregation was the cause of white bigotry.

Ironically, I even believed this after my best friend (who was white) told me I probably shouldn't come to his bar mitzvah because I'd be the only black and people would feel uncomfortable. I even believed this after my Saturday afternoon visit, at age 10, to a private country club pool prompted incensed white parents to pull their kids from the pool in terror.

In the face of this blatantly racist (antiblack) behavior, I still somehow managed to blame only the black kids for being the barrier to integration in my school and my little world. What was I thinking?

I realize now how wrong I was. During that same time, there were at least two tables of athletes, an Italian table, a Jewish girls' table, a Jewish boys' table (where I usually sat), a table of kids who were into heavy metal music and smoking pot, a table of middle-class Irish kids. Weren't these tables just as segregationist as the black table? At the time, no one thought so. At the time, no one even acknowledged the segregated nature of these other tables.

Maybe it's the color difference that makes all-black tables or all-black groups attract the scrutiny and wrath of so many people. It scares and angers people; it exasperates. It did those things to me, and I'm black.

As an integrating black person, I know that my decision not to join the black lunch table attracted its own kind of scrutiny and wrath from my classmates. At the same time that I heard angry words like "Oreo" and "white boy" being hurled at me from the black table, I was also dodging impatient questions from white classmates: "Why do all those black kids sit together?" or "Why don't you ever sit with the other blacks?"

The black lunch table, like those other segregated tables, is a comment on the superficial inroads that integration has made in society. Perhaps I should be happy that even this is a long way from where we started. Yet, I can't get over the fact that the 27th table in my junior high school cafeteria is still known as the "black table"—14 years after my adolescence.

Source: "Informal Segregation: The 'Invisible Wall' and the 'Black Table'. The 'Black Table' is Still There," by Lawrence Otis Graham, February 3, 1991, Op-Ed. Copyright © 1991 by The New York Times Company. Reprinted by permission.

---

this is the imprisonment of Japanese Americans during World War II. Many Japanese Americans did permanently lose their homes and businesses as a result of that experience. A total of 110,000 Americans were imprisoned for up to two years during World War II for no reason other than their Japanese ancestry. Clearly the motivation for this was at least partly racial: Although the United States was also at war with Germany, there was no such imprisonment of German Americans.

In general, however, discrimination against Jewish Americans, Muslim Americans, Asian Americans, and "white ethnics"—though very real at various times in the past and present—has been less systematic and less persistent than discrimination against African Americans, Hispanic Americans, and American Indians. Much of the discrimination the former groups have encountered over the years has been aimed at preventing them from competing economically with the more established populations of western and northern European whites. Some discrimination, too, has been related to international conflicts—the imprisonment of Japanese Americans during World War II, and attacks against Muslim Americans during the Iran hostage crisis, the Gulf War, and following the September 11, 2001, terrorist attacks on New York and Washington. This, of course, is still discrimination, and it is misguided: The great majority of Japanese Americans during World War II and the great majority of Americans who practice Islam today are loyal Americans, who are appalled as anyone else by attacks on the United States.

Still, as noted, Asian, Jewish, and Muslim Americans and "white ethnics" have no history of conquest or colonization in the United States. Consequently, all of these groups today are in a much less disadvantaged position than black and

Table 7.3 Population of Selected Asian American Groups, 2000

Chinese Americans	2,432,585
Filipino Americans	1,850,314
Japanese Americans	796,700
Asian Indian Americans	1,678,765
Korean Americans	1,076,872
Vietnamese Americans	1,122,528
Other Asian Americans	1,285,234

Source: U.S. Census Bureau, 2001, 2000 Census of Population and Housing, Profiles of General Demographic Characteristics, p. 1, http://www2.census.gov/census_2000/datasets/demographic_profile/0_National_Summary/.

Hispanic Americans and American Indians. In fact, due to their high levels of education, Jewish and Asian Americans today have somewhat above-average incomes. And the income and education distribution of "white ethnics" today is not greatly different from that of the population as a whole. For these reasons, these groups have, in part, moved away from ethnic communities and intermarried at a relatively high rate with other ethnic groups. Recent studies show that this is continuing to occur with Asian immigrants, the most recently arrived of these groups (Nee, Sanders, and Sernau, 1994).

Nonetheless, stereotypes and prejudices against all of these groups do persist. In the 1992 riots in Los Angeles, black and Hispanic rioters targeted Korean-owned stores because of cultural clashes and anger over Korean ownership of ghetto and barrio stores. Attacks on Jewish synagogues and community centers occurred repeatedly in the 1990s, and extremist elements in the right-wing militia movement in the 1990s railed against what they call the Z.O.G. ("Zionist Occupation Government"). During the week after the terrorist attacks on the World Trade Center and Pentagon, there were over 300 incidents in which Muslim or Middle Eastern Americans were attacked or harassed, including two fatal attacks. In recent decades, "white ethnics" have frequently complained that they are portrayed as "rednecks" by the white intellectual elite, and as "racists" by that group and by minority groups. They are quick to point out that they do not have the power to determine how American institutions are run, so they should not be blamed for America's problems (Novak, 1971). In this regard, they have something of a point: Although as groups they are all doing reasonably well economically, Asian Americans, Jewish Americans, Muslims, and "white ethnics" are not well represented among the owners and managers of great corporate wealth, nor have top elected U.S. officials such as the president and vice president been chosen from these groups. (Senator Joseph Lieberman, the Democratic nominee for vice president in 2000, came the closest. He was the first Jewish American ever nominated for president or vice president.)

The Majority Group

In the United States, the most advantaged societal position has always been occupied by whites from northern and western Europe. These groups include Americans of British, German, Irish, Scandinavian, French, and Dutch ancestry. They are predominantly Protestant, except for the Irish and French, most of whom are Catholic. Although virtually all of these groups except the British met with at least some prejudice and discrimination, it was less intense than that encountered by more recent immigrants, with the exception of Irish Catholics. Even they, however, are

Through much of the twentieth century, whites used a variety of techniques to exclude racial and ethnic minorities from the neighborhoods where they lived. Some such techniques, such as restrictive covenants, were at one time supported by federal policy and backed by the courts. (Bettmann/Corbis)

no longer the object of significant prejudice or discrimination, and they are thoroughly integrated into the population and culture of the United States. Northern and western European groups have intermixed and intermarried so much that today most of them are of mixed ancestry and no longer identify exclusively with any one country of origin (U.S. Bureau of the Census, 1983a, pp. 12–14).

Besides enjoying high educational levels and desirable managerial and professional occupations, the majority group to a large extent controls the politics and business of the United States. Most corporate executives are males of western and northern European ancestry, as has been every president of the United States from George Washington to George W. Bush.

There is very little growth in the majority group because of a low birth rate and because few people today emigrate from that part of the world. Thus, in the future, the numerically dominant position of this group in American society will fade.

Current Issues in U.S. Race Relations

It was an unlikely occurrence. On the night of November 4th, 2008—a multitude of seasoned television commentators—many with tears in their eyes—remarked on an event many had doubted they would ever see come to pass. Forty years after the assassination of Martin Luther King, Jr., the United States elected Barack Hussein Obama its first African American president. In an election season that saw a white woman take on a black man for the Democratic nomination in the longest, most drawn-out primary season in history, this conclusion might have been anticlimactic. Obama led his rival Senator John McCain for much of the contest and, after the financial meltdown in mid-September, never trailed him in the polls. But as the returns came in on the night of the general election, the reality began to sink in. After such a long and difficult history of race relations, an African American was being elected president. Obama's election is a watershed event in race relations in the United States, but it is still far too early to tell its full significance. Yet, despite such apparent progress, racial inequality persists in contemporary America. While some argued the United States had entered a post-racial period with Obama's election, the vast economic gulf between the races still exists. The very real change indicated by the willingness of Americans to elect an African American to the presidency does not undo the simultaneous reality of large racial inequalities in wealth, income, poverty, education, access to health care, or even the probability of surviving the first year of life.

We shall conclude this chapter by examining two current issues concerning U.S. race and ethnic relations. The first is the growing debate over the relative importance of race versus class as causes of the disadvantaged position of many African Americans and Hispanic Americans. The second is the appropriateness of affirmative action as a means of improving opportunities for minority group members.

The Significance of Race Versus Class

In 1978, William Julius Wilson published one of the most influential and controversial sociology books written in recent years, *The Declining Significance of Race*. Since then, he has elaborated on his ideas in two more books (Wilson, 1996, 1987). Wilson (1978) argued that current racial discrimination has become relatively unimportant as a cause of the economic disadvantages experienced by many blacks (and Hispanics). Rather, these groups are disadvantaged by their disproportionate presence in the **underclass,** a chronically impoverished group whose position has been worsened by recent changes in the American economy. Many blacks and Hispanics are part of this underclass largely because of disadvantages resulting from *past* racial discrimination. However, Wilson argues, their continued presence in this class results not so much from current racial discrimination as from aspects of the American economy that make it hard for members of this class to escape (see Wilson's Personal Journeys Box).

Changes in the Job Market
One of the key reasons that escape from the underclass is so difficult today is because well-paying jobs that do not require an advanced education are disappearing from the American economy, especially from the inner cities of the Midwest and Northeast where blacks are most concentrated (Wilson, 1996; 1987, p. 148). At one time, heavy industry

PERSONAL JOURNEYS INTO SOCIOLOGY

How Societal Changes Helped Shape My Views on Race Relations and Urban Poverty

William Julius Wilson

Unlike many who enter a field of specialization on the basis of graduate training, I did not pursue race and ethnic relations and urban poverty as major fields of study in graduate school at Washington State University. My graduate study focused mainly on sociological theory and the philosophy of the social sciences. However, my concentration on these fields of study could not be sustained in a period dominated by events in the black protest movement.

In my last two years as a graduate student in the mid-1960s I, like most blacks, was caught up in the spirit of the Civil Rights revolution and was encouraged by the changes in social structure that led to increasing opportunities for black Americans. I also followed with intense interest the ghetto riots in Watts, Newark, and Detroit. And although at this point I had not developed a serious academic interest in the field of race and ethnic relations, my intellectual curiosity for the subject, fed by the escalating racial protest and my sense of the changing social structure for blacks in America, was rising so rapidly that by the time I accepted my first full-time academic job as an assistant professor of sociology at the University of Massachusetts, Amherst, in the fall of 1965, I had firmly decided to develop a field of specialization in that area.

It was not until later, after I moved to Chicago and joined the sociology faculty at the University of Chicago in 1972, that my views on the intersection of class with race in the United States sufficiently crystallized. My thinking about intraracial divisions in America during the 1970s was in no small measure shaped by my perception of the changing social environments in Chicago's variegated ethnic neighborhoods. At one extreme were the upper middle-class black professional neighborhoods in parts of the South Side; at the other extreme were the communities of the ghetto poor, plagued by long-term joblessness, in other parts of the South Side and on the West Side. The widening gap between the haves and have-nots among African Americans would have been obvious to any student of urban life who cared to take the time to drive around the Chicago neighborhoods at different points in time, as I did in the early to mid-1970s.

It is one thing to recognize and describe these intragroup differences; it is quite another thing to account for their evolution and relate them not only to the problems of intergroup relations, but, more importantly, to the broader problems of societal organization in America.

To study problems of race in terms of societal organization entails an investigation of not only the political, economic, and other institutional dimensions of societal organization that affect intra- and intergroup experiences but the technological dimensions as well. This approach guided my writing of *The Declining Significance of Race*. The basic theoretical argument presented in *The Declining Significance of Race* is that different systems of production in combination with different policies of the state impose different constraints on racial group relations by producing dissimilar contexts, not only for the manifestation of racial antagonisms but also for racial-group access to rewards and privileges.

I had hoped that my major academic contribution would be to explain racial change by applying this framework to historical developments of race relations in the United States. But there was another contribution I had wished to make—I wanted to highlight the worsening condition of the black underclass, in both absolute and relative terms, by relating it to the improving position of the black middle class.

The Declining Significance of Race generated an even greater controversy than I had originally anticipated. In the initial months following the book's publication, it seemed that critics were so preoccupied with what I had to say about the improving conditions of the black middle class that they virtually ignored my more important arguments about the deteriorating position of the black urban poor. The view was often expressed that since all blacks from all socioeconomic class backgrounds are suffering there is no need to single out the black poor.

During the controversy over *The Declining Significance of Race*, I committed myself to doing two things: (1) I would address the problems of the ghetto poor in a comprehensive analysis, and (2) I would spell out, in considerable detail, the policy implications of my work. These two commitments provided direction for the writing of *The Truly Disadvantaged: The Inner City, The Underclass, and Public Policy*, published in 1987 by the University of Chicago Press.

The first commitment grew out of my personal and academic reaction to the early critics' almost total preoccupation with my arguments concerning the black middle class. It was only after I began writing *The Truly Disadvantaged* that serious scholars began to focus on my previous analysis of the underclass in *The Declining Significance of Race* (1978), particularly those scholars who are working in fields such as urban poverty, social welfare, and public policy.

The second commitment stemmed from my reaction to those critics who either labeled me a neo-conservative or directly or indirectly tried to associate *The Declining Significance of Race* with the neo-conservative movement. Although I am a social democrat, and probably to the left politically of the overwhelming majority of these critics, and although some of the most positive reviews and discussions of *The Declining Significance of Race* have come from those of the democratic left, the title of my book readily lends itself to an assumption that I am a black conservative. Nonetheless, because I did not spell out the policy implications of *The Declining Significance of Race* in the first edition, it was possible for people to read selectively my arguments and draw policy implications significantly different from those that I would personally espouse. In the second edition of *The Declining Significance of Race*, published in 1980, I wrote an epilogue in which the policy implications of my work were underlined in sharp relief, but by then, the views of many readers of the first edition had already solidified.

If the idea for *The Truly Disadvantaged* grew out of the controversy over *The Declining Significance of Race*, the former also generated controversy. *The Truly Disadvantaged* challenges liberal orthodoxy in analyzing inner-city problems; discusses in candid terms social dislocations of the inner city; establishes a case for moving beyond race-specific policies to ameliorate inner-city social conditions to policies that address the broader problems of societal organization, including economic organization; and advances a social democratic public-policy agenda designed to improve the life chances of truly disadvantaged groups such as the ghetto underclass by emphasizing programs to which the more advantaged groups of all races can positively relate.

The Truly Disadvantaged enjoys the unique distinction of generating a lot of attention both within and outside academia. And in contrast to *The Declining Significance of Race*, the scholarly attention it has attracted is not focused mainly on controversy but on the theoretical and substantive arguments raised in the book. Indeed, *The Truly Disadvantaged* has generated a new research paradigm that has stimulated studies not only in sociology, but in economics, psychology, anthropology, education, social work, history, philosophy, and political science as well.

Arguments in *The Truly Disadvantaged* also guided the research for a later book, *When Work Disappears: The World of the New Urban Poor*, published in 1996. This book focuses on the growing joblessness in the inner city and its effect on individuals, families, and neighborhoods. Discussions in the book, including those dealing with public policy, highlight the following point: The unprecedented level of inner-city joblessness represents a severe form of the broader economic and social dislocations that cut across racial and ethnic groups in the United States.

William Julius Wilson was a member of the faculty at the University of Chicago for twenty-four years and is currently the Lewis P. and Linda L. Geyser University Professor at Harvard University. A MacArthur Prize Fellow, he is past president of the American Sociological Association and has been elected to the National Academy of Sciences, the American Academy of Arts and Sciences, and the American Philosophical Society. He has written many influential books in sociology including The Declining Significance of Race: Blacks and Changing American Institutions in 1978 and The Truly Disadvantaged: The Inner City, the Underclass, and Public Policy in 1987. His latest book is More Than Just Race: Being Black and Poor in the Inner City, published in 2009. In 1998, he was awarded the National Medal of Science, the highest scientific honor in the United States.

provided many such jobs and was an important source of mobility, first for immigrant groups, and more recently for blacks and Hispanics. However, in the 1970s, American industry began to lose jobs, and thus a promising opportunity for blacks and Hispanics with limited education was lost (Kasarda, 1989). This trend, known as *deindustrialization,* is discussed at greater length in Chapter 6.

Such processes first create an underclass and then work to sustain it. As unemployment in the ghettoes and barrios rises, so does street crime, and many young males are arrested and imprisoned. Many more, of course, are not arrested, but are unemployed. Wilson (1987, pp. 83–92) points out that this situation raises the incidence of separation and divorce and reduces the pool of appropriate marriage partners in the black community (see also Anderson, 1991; Bennett, Bloom, and Craig, 1989; Lichter, LeClere, and McLaughlin, 1991; Mare and Winship, 1991; Schoen and Kluegel, 1988). This pattern has become much more pronounced over the past twenty years, and as a result, black women have far less opportunity to get married than white women. Moreover, because over 90 percent of unmarried adult women of either race are sexually active, many black children are born outside of marriage. This, of course, produces more female-householder black families, which have a very high risk of poverty for the reasons discussed in Chapter 6.

Finally, Wilson (1987, pp. 46–62) points out that black and Hispanic poor people are much more likely to live in neighborhoods with large concentrations of poor people than are poor whites (see also Massey and Eggers, 1990; Quillian, 1999). Thus, they are less exposed to successful role models, and more prone to see illegal activities as their only hope for upward mobility (see, for example, Anderson, 1991; Crane, 1991a, 1991b; Greenstone, 1991). This perception is reinforced by the fact that most sources of stable employment have left such neighborhoods, so job opportunities are few and far between (Wilson, 1996). Once a sizable number of people in a neighborhood have turned to illegal sources of income, strong pressures are created for "decent" people trying to do the right thing to join the tough "street" culture surrounding these illegal activities (Anderson, 1999). Finally, at the opposite end of the scale, there are advantages of living in areas of concentrated affluence, and just as minorities are overrepresented in areas of concentrated poverty, they are underrepresented in areas of concentrated affluence, which further limits their opportunities (Sampson, Morenoff, and Earls, 1999).

For all these reasons, Wilson sees the growing disadvantage of poor blacks and Hispanics as a product of the lack of stable, well-paying job opportunities in their neighborhoods. He argues that we must create large numbers of decent-paying jobs and provide the support poor people need to get and keep such jobs. He also sees a need for job training and for providing day care and medical insurance to employed low-income workers.

Although Wilson has made a major contribution to our understanding of the forces that have perpetuated and worsened the conditions of poor blacks and Hispanics, some critics have questioned his claim that race is declining in significance as a cause of poverty among inner-city blacks (Hill, 1978; Willie, 1979; Feagin, 2000). In more recent work, Wilson has placed greater emphasis on the problem of hiring discrimination against blacks that results from stereotypes about poor, inner-city blacks (Wilson, 1996). As noted earlier, several studies have documented the continuing effect of prejudice and discrimination (Feagin, 1991; Kirschenman and Neckerman, 1991; National Opinion Research Center, 1991; Feagin and Sikes, 1994; Yinger, 1995). In his recent work, Wilson also places greater emphasis on the concentration of blacks and Hispanics in areas that are losing jobs, whereas whites are more likely to be in areas of job growth. This pattern, arising in large part from racial housing segregation and discrimination, tends to elevate the unemployment rates of blacks and Hispanics (Farley, 1987b; Kasarda, 1989; Lichter, 1988; Mouw, 2000; see also Rosenbaum and Popkin, 1991; Massey and Denton, 1993). Finally, it is important to recognize that African Americans of all social classes experience discrimination on a frequent and regular basis. This has been documented both by discrimination-testing studies and by a variety of studies in which African Americans have been interviewed about their experiences of discrimination (Feagin, 2000; Feagin and Sikes, 1994).

Putting Sociology to Work

The Affirmative Action Debate

No issue has generated more controversy in recent years than affirmative action. **Affirmative action** can be defined as special efforts by employers to increase the number of minority or female employees, or by colleges to increase the number of minority or female students. It may include special recruitment efforts, or the more controversial practice of considering the race or gender of applicants along with other factors, as a way of increasing opportunity for underrepresented groups. It is the latter type of affirmative action that has generated the most controversy, because some see it as merely reverse discrimination against white males.

Is Affirmative Action Reverse Discrimination?

Those who oppose the use of affirmative action argue that preferences given to minority and female candidates constitute discrimination that gets in the way of choosing the most qualified person. They cite statistics showing that in many instances white male law or medical school applicants have been turned down in favor of minority or female applicants who had lower test scores (Sindler, 1978). They also argue that white males who had nothing to do with past discrimination should not be singled out to pay for discrimination caused by others, and that such policies hurt overall societal achievement by considering factors other than who is the most qualified person (Glazer, 1976). Public opinion polls indicate that such views are quite common among white Americans, the majority of whom feel that the system is basically fair as it is without affirmative action (Kluegel, 1990; Hoschschild, 1995). However, it is significant that the whites who have had the greatest personal contact with affirmative action in their workplaces are the most supportive of it (M. C. Taylor, 1995)—a fact discussed in this chapter's "Sociological Insights" box. From a minority group viewpoint, some have criticized affirmative action on the grounds that it devalues minority achievement: Whites will believe that the only reason a minority person "got in" was because of affirmative action preferences, not because of the minority person's own achievements (Steele, 1990; Sowell, 1990). A particular concern of affirmative action opponents is that it can sometimes amount to a quota system, in which a

SOCIOLOGICAL INSIGHTS
What Makes a Fair Footrace?

Imagine two runners in a twenty-mile race. One of the runners must start with a ten-pound weight on each of her feet. As a result, she cannot run as fast, tires more quickly, and falls far behind. Almost anyone would agree that this is not a fair race. So, halfway through the race, the judges decide that she can take off the weights. Is this enough to make the race fair? Does she have any realistic chance to win from her present position? Would it not be fairer to allow her to move ahead to the position of the other runner to compensate for the disadvantage of wearing the weights for the first half of the race?

This analogy has been used to illustrate the reasoning behind affirmative action (Farley, 2010, pp. 387, 468). The runner represents a member of a group that has experienced discrimination, now seeking a good job or entry into graduate or professional school. The weights represent the effects both of disadvantages resulting from past discrimination against her group, and the institutional discrimination she personally has encountered in her elementary and secondary education. Examples of such institutional discrimination, which may or may not be intentional, include low teacher expectations, tracking, biased tests and classroom materials, lack of minority and female role models, limited availability of college-preparatory or advanced-placement courses, and underfunded and segregated schools. Just as the other runner was not encumbered by weights in the first half of the race, the white male applicant was not burdened by these disadvantages in early life. Most people would agree that it would not be fair to expect the runner to catch up after having to run half the race with weights. Could the same argument be made in the case of the minority applicant who often has to run the first half of the "race" of life with the "weights" of poverty and educational disadvantage? Is it fair, when that minority person applies for college or employment, to say "Now the weights are gone, so it's a fair race"?

specified number or percentage of minorities must be hired or admitted. The reality, however, is that this happens infrequently—most affirmative action programs involve monitoring, outreach efforts, or consideration of race or gender along with many other factors (Crosby, 1995).

Is the System Fair Without Affirmative Action?

Supporters of affirmative action believe equally strongly that it is unfair *not* to have affirmative action, because without it, minorities do not really have equal opportunities. They cite two reasons. The first is the lingering effects of past discrimination, which have left minorities at a disadvantage. For example, the overrepresentation of African Americans among the nation's poor is linked to past discrimination, even by those who think present-day discrimination is not a major cause of this poverty (W. J. Wilson, 1978, 1987). A second reason given as to why equal opportunity is not possible without affirmative action is *current* discrimination. As noted earlier, recent testing studies show that deliberate discrimination continues to occur on a regular basis. In addition, more subtle and less conscious forms of institutional discrimination abound. Supporters of affirmative action particularly point to a variety of processes that create unequal opportunities in education. These include segregation, unequal school funding, low expectations of minority students by teachers, tracking, and, in many cases, a curriculum that values and emphasizes the views and accomplishments of Euro-Americans over others. As is discussed further in Web-Based Chapter A, so long as these deeply institutionalized practices remain in place, it will be very difficult for black, Hispanic, and American Indian students to obtain the same educational opportunities that most white students do. The argument for affirmative action is explored further in the box "What Makes a Fair Footrace?"

Some opponents of affirmative action say that reforming the schools so that they come closer to the ideal of creating equal opportunity is a better approach than affirmative action. In Web-Based Chapter A, some approaches to doing this, including desegregation of schools through busing, will be discussed. However, those who support affirmative action point out that school reform is a long-term effort that will not help the current generation of disadvantaged adults.

It has also been suggested by some that affirmative action might be implemented on the basis of social class rather than race. This would help to address the criticism that affirmative action does nothing to make the system more fair for working-class and poor whites, who are clearly also impacted by some of the educational practices noted in the preceding paragraph. However, studies have shown that the number of minority students admitted would fall significantly using such an approach (Lively et al., 1995).

Another alternative in undergraduate colleges has been to admit all students who are in a certain percentage of their high school class, such as the top 10 percent. Because many high schools are racially segregated, such a policy will increase the number of minority students who are eligible for admission. At the University of Texas, where affirmative action was dropped temporarily after a 1997 court order (which was later reversed by the Supreme Court), such a policy kept undergraduate minority enrollments at the University of Texas fairly close to what they were before affirmative action was suspended (Carnevale, 1999). Such policies have been criticized, however, because they depend upon schools being racially segregated (Berry, 2000). And in California and Florida, where they only guarantee admission to *some* public institution, not the top schools, they have failed to bring minority enrollment at top schools to what it was before affirmative action was ended in those states (Celingo, 2000).

Supporters of affirmative action also contend that some of the tests used to assess people's qualifications contain racial or sexual biases. Moreover, these tests are not very accurate predictors of future success. Law school admission criteria, for example, typically explain only about 25 percent of the variation in first-year academic performance of law students (Sindler, 1978, pp. 115–16), and college admissions tests are only about half that accurate (Owen, 1985; Slack and Porter, 1980). Thus, determining who is "best qualified" is a haphazard process subject to great error. In fact, the National Academy of Sciences concluded that testing that is unadjusted for possible racial biases was a poor predictor of employment performance, and that it excluded capable black and Hispanic applicants (Kilborn, 1991). In general, research shows that high school class rank or GPA is a much better predictor of college success than scores on standardized tests like the SAT and ACT (Geiser and Santelices, 2007; Lavergne and Walker, 2002), and these indicators also do not vary by race or class to the same extent as the standardized test scores. Yet many colleges and universities continue to give considerable weight to the SAT or ACT in admissions decisions. One study suggests that an important cause of such differences in test scores is that minorities may internalize widespread negative stereotypes about their academic ability (Steele, 1995). This makes affirmative action something of a double-edged sword: On the one hand, it may reinforce such stereotypes; but on the other hand, how can admissions be fair without it if test scores are artificially lowered by such stereotypes?

How Effective Is Affirmative Action?

Has the policy of affirmative action actually changed things to the point that minority group members and women enjoy an advantage over white males? Examination of income figures does *not* support this. Among young adults, white males continue to enjoy higher incomes than black and Hispanic males and women of any race, and black and Hispanic unemployment rates remain well above those of whites. Moreover, whites continue to graduate from college and enter medical, law, and graduate schools at a substantially higher rates than blacks and Hispanics. Women also remain underrepresented in law and medical schools, although their presence there has increased significantly. All these things suggest strongly that the effects of past and institutional discrimination outweigh any advantage affirmative action may bring to minorities or women. Even when we consider only those who complete college, minorities and women *still* do not appear to enjoy any overall advantage owing to affirmative action. Among recent college graduates working full time in 1999, black and Hispanic males as well as females of all races still earned less than white males. In all cases except that of Hispanic males, the income gap as compared with white males was at least $15,000 annually, and for the Hispanic males, the gap was nearly $14,000 (U.S. Census Bureau, 2000a, Table 10).

Even so, it does appear that affirmative action has helped certain segments of the minority and female populations a good deal. A definite narrowing of the income gap between blacks and whites has occurred among people who do have jobs, particularly those with relatively high education levels. Law and medical schools are enrolling significantly more blacks, Hispanics, and women than they did before affirmative action, even though most of their students are still white males. Firms with government contracts, which are covered by federal affirmative action requirements, have nearly twice the percentage of minority employees as firms without government contracts (Pear, 1983). Finally, the effectiveness of affirmative action can be seen in what has happened in three states where it was eliminated, either by court rulings or public referenda—California, Texas, and Washington. In California, it took four years for the number of minority freshmen admitted to the University of California system to get back up to what it was when affirmative action was abolished in 1997, and the number who actually enrolled remained lower in the fall of 2000 than in 1997 (Celingo, 2000). And the impact of eliminating affirmative action has been even bigger in professional schools. For example, the percentage of black students in the University of Texas at Austin's law school fell from 6.8 to 2.9, and the percentage of Hispanic students fell from 10.8 to 8.9 after affirmative action was abolished (Berry, 2000).

Still, it is mainly the more educated segments of the minority and female populations that have truly benefited from affirmative action (Wilson, 1978). This may benefit the next generation as middle-class minority youth enjoy the educational benefits of middle-class status. So far, affirmative action has done little for the chronically impoverished underclass, many of whom are lucky to get a high school diploma. Affirmative action has probably contributed to a trend that was already under way in the black and Hispanic populations: The middle class is rising in status, while the situation of the poor is worsening (Wilson, 1978, 1987). For this reason, Wilson (1978, 1987) has argued that to achieve racial equality we must implement policies to improve the situation of the chronically poor, which affirmative action does not do.

Another highly practical reason for having affirmative action is that our future productivity as a nation may depend upon it. The vast majority of new entrants into the labor force in coming decades will be people of color and women (U.S. Department of Labor, 1987). If these new employees do not get the opportunity to develop their skills and make important contributions in the workplace, the entire economy will likely suffer, becoming less able to keep up with international competitors. Some companies, such as Corning and Monsanto, have responded to this reality—with striking success—by combining affirmative action programs with programs to make the workplace more hospitable to minorities and women. At Corning, for example, nearly two-thirds of newly hired salaried employees were minorities and/or women, as were well over a third of all salaried employees (Kilborn, 1990). According to the company's chairman, this was not only the right thing to do, but it served the company's interest by giving it new sources of managers when the pool of white males, the traditional group from which such employees were drawn, was shrinking.

The Legal and Political Status of Affirmative Action

The legal and political status of affirmative action seems to be ever changing. Since it was first instituted in the 1960s by President Lyndon Johnson, it had the support of every administration, Democrat and Republican, until Ronald Reagan became president. In a series of decisions from 1978 to 1987, the Supreme Court consistently supported the notion that race and (in later rulings) gender can be considered as a way of increasing diversity or increasing representation of underrepresented groups. Recently, however, the situation has been in a state of flux. The Reagan and George H. W. Bush administrations opposed affirmative action preferences and tried, mostly without success, to reverse earlier Supreme Court rulings. The Clinton administration, in contrast, supported affirmative action, while the administration of George W. Bush largely continued the efforts of his father to reverse earlier court actions, but again with little success. The latter Bush was a strong proponent of the so-called "10 percent solution" (admitting the top 10 percent of every high school class to top universities) after affirmative action in Texas public college admissions was overturned by a court ruling (discussed below).

With the Obama administration, the federal government again became more supportive of affirmative action.

However, significant challenges to affirmative action in the states, the courts, and the Congress make its future highly uncertain. Beginning in 1989, the Supreme Court began to take a more ambivalent approach to affirmative action. In 1995, it ruled that some types of affirmative action designed to help minority firms get contracts with the government were illegal. And, in 1996, it refused on a technicality to review the anti-affirmative action *Hopwood* ruling—a lower court decision reversing the 1978 Supreme Court decision of *Regents of the University of California v. Bakke*, which had upheld minority preferences in higher education admissions. While the lower court decision was only binding in three states (Texas, Louisiana, and Mississippi), it raised questions about the future of affirmative action everywhere until it was reversed by the Supreme Court in 2003 in a case involving the University of Michigan, discussed below. Through initiative and referendum, California, Washington, Michigan, and Nebraska have eliminated all forms of affirmative action that involve taking race into consideration in public college admissions or public hiring, and the Florida legislature eliminated affirmative action in public college admissions. These efforts have taken a toll on minority enrollment. At Berkeley for instance, minority enrollment is down to 17 percent, while nearby Stanford, a private school that is not affected by propositions disallowing race to be used as a criterion for admissions, is at 26 percent (Asimov, 2010). In 2003, the University of Michigan was challenged on its affirmative action policies by a white woman who argued that, while only 9 percent of white applicants with similar test scores as herself were admitted to the law school, 100 percent of African Americans were admitted. The issue here was not that unqualified applicants got into the program, but that race was a determining factor for equally qualified applicants. The U.S. Supreme Court ruled against the woman, saying the university had an interest in increasing student diversity and supported individualized review of each applicant. However, in the same ruling, the Court also struck down the school's undergraduate admission policy that was based on a point system where race was given a point-based handicap. These decisions declared yet again the

Court's tendency to support measures to increase racial diversity but oppose strict quota-like systems and schemes that do not consider each individual as a separate case. In most other states, affirmative action remains legal, but in light of these developments and mixed signals from the courts, the future of affirmative action in the United States appears highly uncertain. For example, in 2006, Michigan voters approved an initiative to ban any consideration of race as a means of making college classes or the state's public workforce more diverse, and in 2008, Nebraska voters did the same. On the other hand, Colorado voters rejected a similar initiative in 2008, and efforts to get the issue on the ballot in a couple of other states were unsuccessful.

Summary

Races are defined according to a combination of physical appearance and social criteria, whereas ethnic groups are defined on a purely cultural basis. Some of these groups occupy a dominant position in society and are called majority groups, while others occupy a subordinate position and are called minority groups. Racism takes a number of forms, including racist thought (racial prejudice) and racist behavior (racial discrimination). Ideological racism refers to the belief that one group is in some way naturally superior to another. The most subtle, but often the most important, form of racism is institutional racism, which occurs when social institutions operate in ways that favor one group (usually the majority group) over another. This process is also called institutional discrimination.

Social psychologists emphasize prejudice in their studies of race and ethnic relations. For some people, prejudice meets personality needs that may date to childhood experiences, while other people are prejudiced largely out of conformity to the attitudes of significant others in their past or present social environment. The functionalist and conflict perspectives see prejudice and discrimination as arising from society rather than from the experiences of individuals. Functionalists view prejudice as largely the outgrowth of cultural differences and ethnocentrism. They see assimilation as the solution because it eliminates the cultural differences that form the basis of prejudice and discrimination. Conflict theorists see racial inequality as an outgrowth of economic conflict, both within and between racial groups.

Much can be learned about the conditions that produce and alter patterns of racial and ethnic relations by examining other societies such as the former Soviet Union, South Africa, the former Yugoslavia, and various Latin American countries. Each of these areas has its own set of social conditions that shape its pattern of intergroup relations.

The United States is one of the most diverse nations of the world in terms of race and ethnicity. The largest minority group in the United States is African Americans, but the rapidly growing Hispanic population may soon catch up. Hispanics are not really one group but several, of which Mexican Americans, or Chicanos, are the largest group. African Americans, Chicanos, and Puerto Ricans, along with Native Americans, have each in their own way endured conquest and internal colonization. As a result, they have experienced prejudice and discrimination far beyond that encountered by most American groups.

Groups whose status falls between that of the majority and minority groups include Asian Americans, Jewish Americans, and "white ethnics" from eastern and southern Europe. All have experienced discrimination, yet all are largely middle class today. The educational and professional achievement of Asian and Jewish Americans is particularly notable. Even so, most of America's political and economic elite continues to be drawn from the long-standing American majority group, whites from northern and western Europe.

In the United States, current sociological debates on race relations concern the relative importance of racial discrimination and social-class inequality, and the use of affirmative action as a means of bringing about racial equality.

Key Terms

racial group
ethnic group
majority group
minority group
racism
ideological racism (or, racist ideology)
prejudice
stereotype
discrimination

individual discrimination
institutional racism
institutional discrimination
personality need
authoritarian personality
scapegoat
projection
social learning
cognitive-dissonance theory
symbolic racism
ethnocentrism
assimilation
pluralism
multiculturalism
amalgamation
underclass
affirmative action

Exercises

1. Social critics charge that it is very difficult for the affluent to appreciate the plight of the *underclass* in America. Read the section on the underclass again (page 209), then answer the following questions:

   - Do people who are part of the underclass have the same "life chances" in comparison with their more socioeconomically fortunate counterparts?
   - Do you think the underclass can be eliminated in American society? Why or why not?

2. The practice of *racial profiling* by law-enforcement agencies continues to be extremely controversial. Some African Americans have referred to their plight as "DWB" (Driving While Black).

   - Do you agree or disagree with the practice of racial profiling and why? What about racial profiling to catch potential terrorists? Are such practices likely to be successful?
   - What do you think will be the long-term implications of this practice? How does racial profiling potentially come into play in efforts to enforce immigration laws?

Chapter 8
Sex, Gender, and Society

What Are Sex and Gender Roles? — 220
    Sex and Gender Roles 220
    Sexism 221
    Traditional American Gender Roles 221
    Cultural Variation in Gender Roles 223

Gender-Role Socialization: An Interactionist Analysis — 225
    How Gender Roles Develop 226
    Teaching Gender Roles in the Home 226
    Teaching Gender Roles in the School 227
    Teaching Gender Roles on Television 228
    How Peers Teach Gender Roles 229

How Gender Roles Are Learned — 230
    The Looking-Glass Self and Gender-Role Socialization 230
    Modeling and Gender-Role Socialization 230

Structured Sexual Inequality: Power — 231
    Men, Women, and Positions of Authority 231
    Women in Politics 232
    Women in the Business World 233
    Men, Women, and Power in the Home 234

Structured Sexual Inequality: Income — 235
    Some Possible Reasons for Women's Low Wages 236

PUTTING SOCIOLOGY TO WORK — 240
    Understanding and Preventing Sexual Harassment 240

Functionalist and Conflict Perspectives on Gender Roles — 242
    The Origins of Gender Inequality 242
    The Functionalist Perspective 243
    The Conflict Perspective 245
    Feminism: A Challenge to Male Power 245
    Feminist Social Theory 249
    Ecofeminism 250

How Are Gender Roles Changing in America? — 251
    Sexual Double Standard 251
    Employment Discrimination 251
    Sexual Assault 251
    Limitations of Change 253
    Public Opinion and Future Prospects for Gender Equality 254

Intersexuality, Sexual Orientation, and the Politics of Being "Different" — 256
    Sexual Orientation 256

Summary — 257

Key Terms — 258

Exercises — 259

Imagine two people, both born in 1970. Both are from upper middle-class backgrounds, and both graduated in 1992 from a well-known state university. Both obtained full-time employment when they graduated, got married in 1994, and had two children between then and 1998. Both got divorced in early 2002. Both still work today for the employer that hired them when they graduated from college. So far, they seem alike in every regard. But there are important differences. Although both have the same education level and have been working full-time, one has an annual salary of $56,000, while the other makes only $39,000. The person with the higher salary also enjoys more autonomy and opportunity for creativity at work, while the one with the lower salary works in a more structured situation and is more closely supervised.

There are also differences in the amount of time these two people spend working and at leisure. For most of the time since college graduation, the one with the higher income had *more* leisure time than the one with the lower income. Despite the higher income, this person's total work week—employment and household work combined—was 63 hours per week, compared with 67 hours for the person with the lower income. When both people got divorced, another big difference in their situations developed. After the divorce, the standard of living of the person with the higher income stayed about the same, while the standard of living of the other person *fell* by about 30 percent.

How could two people with such similar backgrounds and education have such different experiences in life? All of it can be explained by one thing: One of them is male and one of them is female. All of the differences described above are based on average statistical differences between the situations of men and women in the United States. In other words, what happened to these two individuals reflects what happens to men and women in the United States *on average*. Even when their education and social background is identical, women on average are paid less, have less autonomy at work, spend more time working and less at leisure, and suffer financially from divorce (while men may experience either gains or losses, but on average, do not experience much change in their standards of living).

In this chapter, we shall explore how and why society defines the roles of men and women as being different and unequal, and we shall consider in greater detail the socialization processes that prepare men and women for these different roles. At the same time, we shall see that society's expectations concerning the roles of men and women have in some ways changed dramatically over the past forty years. Indeed, this is one of the more profound social changes of our age. Nonetheless, we shall also see that a good deal has not changed, and that we cannot yet say that equality of the sexes has been attained in the United States or in most other industrialized countries.

What Are Sex and Gender Roles?

To begin our discussion, we should define several important terms. The chapter title mentions *sex* and *gender*, but precisely what is the difference between the two? Basically, sex is biologically defined, whereas gender is socially defined. Thus, **sex** refers to the biological fact that a person is either a man or a woman. **Gender** refers to socially learned traits associated with, and expected of, men or women (Giele, 1988, p. 294). Therefore, to be *male* or *female* is a matter of sex, but to be *masculine* or *feminine* is a matter of gender. Gender, in short, refers to socially learned behaviors and attitudes, such as mannerisms, styles of dress, and activity preferences.

Sex and Gender Roles

These socially learned behaviors often are specified by **gender roles**. Gender roles can be defined as roles society expects people to play on account of their sex. Like all roles, gender roles are made up of sets of expectations, so they can be thought of as sets of expectations that are attached to sex. One example of gender roles can be seen in the world of work (Spence, Deaux, and Helmreich, 1985). Society expects women to fill certain occupations and men to fill others. Thus, male nurses and female firefighters are still the exception to the rule. Men wishing to be nurses and women wishing to be firefighters will discover that their wishes go against the expectations of many people, and that they can become the objects of ridicule or hostility.

Gender roles also exist with respect to interpersonal behavior (it is still more common for men to ask women for dates than vice versa), the family (the wife and mother is still expected to take primary responsibility for matters pertaining to the home, even if she is employed), and recreational activities (how many women are on your college football team, and how many men do you know who sew because they enjoy it?). In fact, men and women are expected to fill different roles in virtually every area of life. Even if these roles are less rigidly defined than in the past, they are still influential. In 2001, for example, a Gallup Poll asked a national sample about ten traits—did people think the traits were generally more true of men or of women? Of the ten, five (emotional, affectionate, talkative, patient, and creative) were clearly associated with women by most respondents, and two (aggressive, courageous) with men. Only three traits (intelligent, ambitious, easygoing) were about equally likely to be associated with men or women (Newport, 2001).

Sexism

Gender roles are not only *different*, they are often *unequal*. Structured inequality between men and women, and the norms, roles, and beliefs that support such inequality, are called **sexism**. Sexism takes a variety of forms. One form is ideological sexism, the belief that one sex is inferior to another. Ideological sexism is often used to justify sexual discrimination, unequal treatment on the basis of sex. Some men believe incorrectly that women are "too emotional" for certain jobs that require high levels of responsibility—an example of ideological sexism. They then use that belief as an excuse or justification for sexual discrimination—refusal to hire or promote women into jobs with high levels of responsibility. Today, however, the most important form of sexism is probably **institutional sexism**. This term refers to systematic practices and patterns within social institutions that lead to inequality between men and women. One such pattern, which will be discussed later in this chapter, is the relatively low pay of occupations in which most workers are women—even compared to predominantly male occupations with similar educational requirements and levels of responsibility.

Traditional American Gender Roles

Different and unequal gender roles have long been a part of Western culture. In the United States and most other Western societies, social positions involving leadership, power, decision-making, and interacting with the larger world have traditionally gone to men. Positions centering around dependency, family concerns, child care, and self-adornment have traditionally gone to women.

The Male Role

These unequal gender roles mean that men and women are expected to behave differently in a number of situations (Broverman et al., 1972; Deaux and Lewis, 1983, 1984). Men are expected to be leaders, to take control, to make decisions, and to be active, worldly, unemotional, and aggressive. Through his actions, a man is said to determine his own status. At the same time, men are not expected to talk about (or even necessarily understand) their inner feelings. They are permitted to be blunt, loud, and a bit sloppy. In their relationships with women, men are expected to take the initiative, and sexual gratification is often a higher priority than interpersonal intimacy.

However, the most important characteristic of the male role in the United States is probably that it carries disproportionate power. It is this feature of the male role that allows men to be paid more for the work they do, while simultaneously enjoying more leisure time. As Barbara Reskin (1988) puts it, "Dominant groups remain privileged because they write the rules." She points out that as circumstances change, powerful groups such as men find new reasons to justify their advantage. When most breadwinners were male, men argued that their higher pay was justified because they had to support families. Today, with the large number of single female heads of households, the justification is different: Men's higher wages are justified on the basis that men are typically in different occupations than women (Reskin, 1988).

The male role carries power in a variety of ways—elected public offices and corporate boards and management positions are occupied mostly by males, while the higher income that most husbands receive often relegates wives to a position of economic dependency in the home. This was particularly true in the past when most middle-class women did not work outside the home, but women's lower pay still keeps many of them financially dependent on their husband's income. Even the emotional inexpressiveness of men has been seen by some sociologists as a source of power, because it is a mechanism many men use to withhold their true feelings from their partners (Sattel, 1989). In fact, such use of power is so much a part of the male role and the male subculture that men similarly withhold feelings from one another. They do this because they believe that to do otherwise would make them vulnerable and let other men gain advantage over them (Sattel, 1989).

The Female Role

Women have traditionally been expected to be dependent, emotional, and unable to exercise leadership, excel at math, or make decisions. As a result, their status in life was often seen as a product not of their own actions but of the actions of the man to whom they were married. Women have also been expected to be neater and more considerate than men, to have a better understanding of their own feelings and those of others, to have a higher standard of morality, and to be more appreciative of art, religion, and literature (Beutel and Marini, 1995). In relationships, they have been expected to view intimacy as more important than sexual gratification. Women who take the initiative have traditionally been regarded as "pushy."

Although a perception of basic differences in gender roles is deeply embedded in U.S. culture, some changes have occurred. In early American history, for example, property ownership and the right to vote were reserved for males. Even in the area of child rearing—where the day-to-day work was done by women—ultimate authority lay with males. Today, women, in theory, enjoy the same rights of voting and property ownership as men, although, in reality, both politics and material wealth remain disproportionately controlled by males. Our view of the female role has evolved greatly over the past two or three decades. As we shall see in much of the discussion in the rest of the chapter, though women may not have succeeded yet in ridding themselves of all aspects of the traditional female role (nor would they necessarily want to), they have expanded it to include behaviors that are much more self-determining.

Gender Role Variations in the United States

While gender roles have always been unequal, there has been considerable variation in the specific nature of gender roles, both over time and among different groups within the United States. In early America, for example, both men and women were involved in producing salable goods—and both worked at home, farming or making products that could be sold (Degler, 1980). Although both men and women were involved in child rearing and home care, the majority of this work fell to women. The authority over children, however, as well as property rights, belonged to men.

Later, for middle-class women, the housewife role became predominant. As work moved outside the home, it was the men who moved with it—which preserved their economic control. The role of housewife was justified on the basis that it protected women from the harsh realities of the workplace, and many women saw it as a gain in that they no longer had responsibility for both taking care of the home and children and producing goods to be sold. In reality, however, it limited what women could become, by prohibiting them from taking on careers.

For working-class women and most African American women, the situation was different. Economic realities forced them to work outside

Roles are transmitted through the process of gender-role socialization. Children observe their parents in roles and behavior that, depending on the parent's lifestyle, may or may not be gender typed. (iStockphoto)

the home, so most of them never experienced an exclusive housewife role (Glenn, 1980; Jones, 1985; Seifer, 1973). Many of them worked at hard, low-paying jobs in textile mills and other industries, and many others cleaned the houses and cared for the children of the more affluent.

Today, the situation has changed somewhat, with far fewer women in the housewife role. The change has been most notable for middle-class women, many of whom are moving into more challenging and lucrative careers. However, as we shall soon see in greater detail, women continue to be paid less than men with comparable education. In 2008, women employed full time were still paid only about 78 percent as much as men employed full time (U.S. Census Bureau, 2009f, p. 4). Women in the workplace often encounter a "glass ceiling" that limits their chances to move up in the organization; thus the jobs with the greatest status and power are usually occupied by males (De Prete and Soule, 1988). Moreover, there has been less change for women who lack a college education: They continue to be concentrated in low-paying clerical, household, and fast-food and other service jobs. Finally, women continue to shoulder most of the responsibility for household work and child rearing, which is the main reason men enjoy more leisure time.

Cultural Variation in Gender Roles

Gender Roles: A Cultural Universal?

As we have seen, gender roles have always existed in the United States, and, although they have changed over time, they have always been marked by inequality. Is this the case throughout the world? The answer appears to be that nearly all societies have gender roles, though the nature of those roles varies widely. In most societies, gender roles are unequal; nevertheless, there are clear examples of societies in which this is not the case.

In a classic study, Murdock (1935) found that the overwhelming majority of societies do divide at least some tasks by sex. However, the *content* of those gender roles—that is, precisely what men and women are expected to do and to be—varies widely. Murdock found only a few tasks that are nearly always done by men or by women. In over 80 percent of the societies he studied, hunting, fishing, and trapping were predominantly or exclusively the jobs of males, whereas cooking, carrying water, grinding grain, and gathering roots and seeds were primarily female chores. However, most tasks were done by males in some societies, by females in others, and by both sexes in yet others. Examples of such tasks are various farming activities, constructing shelter, starting and maintaining care of fires, carrying objects, and preparing drinks and medicine.

The housewife role, once so engrained in American society, is far from universal, even among modern industrial societies. In the former Soviet Union, both men and women have long been expected to contribute to the financial support of the household through employment. In Japan, Thailand, and the Philippines, the majority of adult women are employed outside the home, and in China, virtually all women are. Similarly, patterns of occupational segregation vary considerably. In the former Soviet Union, for example, over two-thirds of all medical doctors are women. As we shall see shortly, however, all of the aforementioned societies still have sexual inequality, despite the absence of the housewife role.

Androgynous Societies

There are at least a few societies where the roles of men and women differ little, if at all. Social scientist refer to such societies as androgynous societies. Margaret Mead's (1935) famous studies of three societies in New Guinea present two such examples. In one of them, the Arapesh, both men and women play what in America would be considered a feminine role. Both are gentle, strongly child-oriented, and giving. In the second, the Mundugumor, both men and women play a role we would consider masculine. They are loud and aggressive, fight a great deal, and are very uninterested in children. In the third society she studied, the Tchambuli, sex roles exist, but they are the opposite of what we are familiar with in industrialized countries. Economic production is the role of women, whereas men concern themselves with self-adornment and trying to gain favors and approval from women. In fact, this society could be defined as female-dominant.

At least as common as androgynous societies, however, are societies in which gender roles are different but relatively equal. One example of this can be seen in Native American groups that were primarily horticulturalist, including several Southeastern tribes. Among these groups, women were often responsible for raising crops and often provided the majority of the group's food—giving them power and status comparable to that of men in their societies. Studies of Native American societies reveal that the more women's roles involve the production of the essentials of life, the higher their status has tended to be (Nordstrom, 1992).

Are Societies Becoming More Androgynous?
There is evidence that many societies are becoming more androgynous than they were in the past. The proportion of women in the paid labor force has risen across much of the world over the past few decades. China today proclaims the legal equality of men and women, yet just a few generations ago women were virtually the property of men and were expected to live for the purpose of serving their husbands. Although China is a dramatic case that undoubtedly changed more than most countries because of the communist revolution that occurred there after World War II, its direction of change parallels that of much of the world. In most countries, including the United States, modernization eventually has been accompanied by the large-scale entry of women into the paid labor force (see Figure 8.1) and by increased legal recognition of the rights of women. Dozens of countries today have laws forbidding sex discrimination in at least some areas of life. As recently as a century ago, such laws were unheard of in many of these countries.

While modernization usually leads toward greater gender equality, the influence of modern societies on less-developed ones sometimes has the opposite effect. In the Third World, colonialism in its various forms, including the influence of multinational corporations, has often led to *increased inequality* between men and women (Boserup, 1970). When private property systems were introduced in land ownership, for example, women more often than men lost traditional land-use rights (Sen and Grown, 1987). Investment by multinationals has tended to displace women from

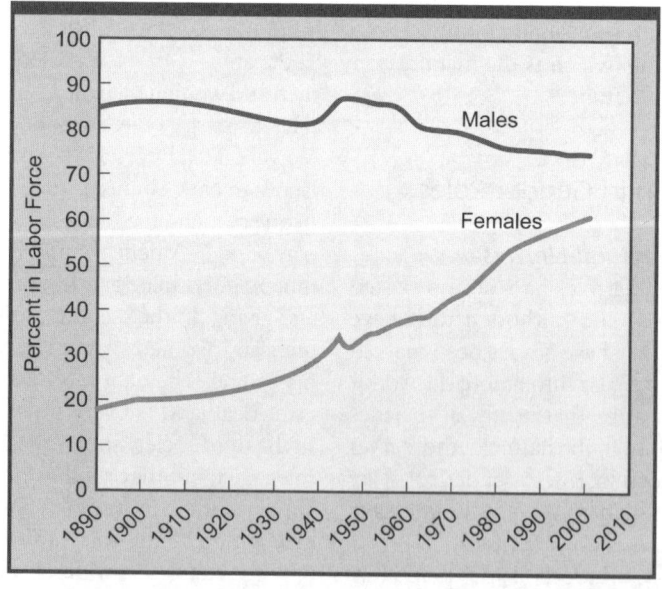

Figure 8.1 Labor Force Participation Rates of Men and Women in the United States, 1890–2001

Note that, although rates for men still substantially exceed those for women, the gap has closed significantly. What implications does this hold for the U.S. economy in the twenty-first century?

Source: Adapted from Francine D. Blau and Marianne A. Ferber, *The Economics of Women, Men, and Work*, 1986 (Englewood Cliffs, NJ: Prentice Hall), p. 70, and *Statistical Abstract of the United States*, 1988, Table 608. U.S. Bureau of the Census: 1991. *Statistical Abstract of the United States*, 1991. Washington: U.S. Government Printing Office, Table 635; U.S. Bureau of Labor Statistics, "Most Frequently Requested Series," http://stats.bls.gov/cgi-bin/surveymost U.S. Bureau of Labor Statistics. 2001. Labor Statistics from the Current Population Survey. Table A-1. Employment Status of the Civilian Population by Sex and Age, http://www.bls.gov/webapps/legacy/cpsatab1.htm.

their traditional occupations, while most of the new jobs created have gone to men (Ward, 1984).

Male Dominance: A Cross-Cultural View

The vast majority of the world's societies have historically been *male-dominant* and remain so. Although many societies are becoming more androgynous, they have yet to eliminate either distinct gender roles or gender inequality. In Russia, for example, where most doctors are women, that profession enjoys neither the prestige nor the high pay that it does in the United States. In Russian society, the leadership of both the national government and the republics have remained male domains. Women have been almost totally absent from important Soviet and Russian government posts. In China, which unlike Russia remains communist, women are not much better represented. In parts of the world, especially Africa, women are subject to surgical removal of their clitoris, referred to as female genital mutilation, simply to make them more desirable to men. The surgery is painful, often leads to medical complications, and, of course, alters a woman's sexual functioning for life. Well over one hundred million women are estimated to have undergone genital mutilation across the globe. The Scandinavian countries have long been regarded as leaders in the effort to bring about equality between the sexes, yet significant inequalities exist even there. Their parliaments are three-quarters male, except in Norway, where the percentage of women is higher. Swedish and Norwegian women earn around 85 percent of what men in those countries earn—better than women in the United States or Canada, but still not equality (Swedish Institute, 2000; Statistics Norway, 2000).

In virtually all societies studied by Murdock (1935) and others, political structures are controlled more by males than by females. This remains true today even though women such as Indira Gandhi, Margaret Thatcher, and Golda Meir have been prominent world leaders, and even though the proportion of women in government has risen in a number of countries. The significance of these findings is that, in most societies, *power* is predominantly in the hands of males. In many societies, too, economic activities performed away from the home are largely a male domain, whereas the home and family are more the domain of women. Until the past few decades, whenever women did engage in economic production, it was usually in the home. Even today, when women are active in the labor force in many societies, they nearly always earn less on average than men. Taking all this into consideration, it is hard to avoid the conclusion that male dominance, though not universal, is much more the rule than the exception among the world's societies. (Example of recent studies illustrating this include Wright and Baxter, 1995; Sorensen and Trappe, 1995; Casper, McLanahan, and Garfinkel, 1994; Zhang and Farley, 1995).

Gender-Role Socialization: An Interactionist Analysis

Gender roles, like all social roles, are learned through socialization (Bem, 1993). There are probably some behavioral differences between the sexes that reflect biological influences. Males may, for example, have a slight natural tendency to be more aggressive than females (Frieze et al., 1978; Gove, 1985). This tendency is almost a cultural universal (Whiting and Edwards, 1976), and even newborn males tend to be slightly more active than females. Part of the reason may be hormonal (Maccoby and Jacklin, 1974). For example, Udry (2000) found that hormonal variations, both prenatal and in adulthood, could explain around 16 percent of the variation in the femininity/masculinity of young adult women's behavior, and that high exposure to male hormones prior to birth made the women less sensitive to variations in how their mothers raised them. Udry suggests that an implication of this is that female behavior may more easily change to become more like traditional male behavior than the reverse. This is because nearly all males have as much in the way of male hormones as did the females in his study who had the highest levels of male hormones. Still, it is important to keep in mind that most variation in female adult behavior was left unexplained by Udry's measurements of hormonal differences. In addition, there are wide variations among societies in the levels of aggressiveness of both men and women; and male-female differences in aggression are highly situation-specific (Maccoby, 1980). These facts indicate the importance of social factors in shaping gendered human behavior.

There may also be a slight biological basis for the development of different skills in men and women (Rossi, 1985). Girls usually develop somewhat earlier than boys, while boys have slightly better visual-spatial perception (Stockard and Johnson, 1992). These small differences may be the product of either hormonal differences or differences in brain hemisphere dominance (D. Halpern, 1992). Differences in verbal and mathematical achievement, on the other hand, seem to be socially induced and are not the product of innate differences in ability. Such differences are not consistent across cultures (Tobias, 1978), and in the United States, they have been decreasing to the point that, on many tasks, there is no longer a demonstrable gender difference (Hyde and Linn, 1988; Hyde, Fennema, and Lamon, 1990; Linn and Hyde, 1989).

Although the evidence conflicts concerning moral development, there is no evidence of innate differences between males and females in such areas as conformity, social orientation, and overall achievement. Thus, social experiences are a major factor, and perhaps the dominant factor, in explaining sexual differences in how we think and behave.

How Gender Roles Develop

Given the limits to what biological differences can explain, how do males and females learn such different roles? As we saw in Chapter 5, the values and expectations of society are transmitted through the socialization process. From infancy through adulthood, male and female human beings are treated differently and given different messages. The result is that small natural differences in behavioral predisposition become greatly exaggerated, and men and women come to think of themselves in different ways and to play different roles in life. The process by which different and, in many cultures, unequal, gender roles are transmitted is called **gender-role socialization.** In this part of the chapter, we shall examine how gender roles are taught by four key agents of socialization: the family, the school, the media, and the peer group.

Teaching Gender Roles in the Home

For the most part, parents in the United States today do not try to teach boys to be aggressive or girls to be submissive or dependent (Lytton and Romney, 1991; Johnson, 1988). However, there is gender-typing in how children are expected to play, in what chores they are expected to do around the house, and in the toys that are chosen for them. Significantly (since men are the group that stands to gain from gender inequality), these differences in gender-typing are greater among fathers than among mothers (Blackmore and Hill, 2008: Bradley and Gobbart, 1989; Holub, Tisak and Mullins, 2008; Lytton and Romney, 1991; Roest, Dubas and Gerris, 2010). There are also differences in how rooms are decorated (Rheingold and Cook, 1975) and in the amount of freedom given (boys get more, particularly in father-dominant families) (Hagan, Simpson, and Gilles, 1987). Parents today are probably less likely than in the past to consciously socialize their boys and girls in different ways, but they still sometimes do so unconsciously. Campbell and Beaudry (1998) illustrate this in a study of socialization and math achievement. They found that, even among high achievers, girls had less confidence in their math ability and received a greater amount of dysfunctional help from their parents. They suggest that the parents meant well and tried to help their daughters, but in doing so conveyed an unintentional message that, no matter how good they actually were, they still "needed help." Such messages were not conveyed to boys of comparable ability.

Some gender-role socialization also occurs through modeling—children see their parents in gender-typed roles and behavior. Fathers, for example, have less contact with their children on average than mothers do, and the contact they have is more likely to involve play activities rather than directing mundane activities such as brushing teeth or getting ready for school (Stockard and Johnson, 1992). Some research suggests that modeling of peers and media images may be a more significant factor than modeling of parents, since not much correlation has been found between the degree of gender-typing in parents and their children (Whiting and Edwards, 1988). Even so, gender roles observed in the home do tell children a good deal about how men and women are expected to behave, and thus may contribute to the long-term development of gender roles.

Some effects of gender-role socialization develop quite early. By the age of five, boys and girls prefer different toys and can identify different occupations as being "men's jobs" and "women's jobs" (Garrett et al., 1977; Masters and Wilkinson, 1976). They can identify stereotypical male and female traits even earlier—sometimes as young as three (Reis and Wright, 1982). In large part, this is because of what their parents teach them, sometimes unconsciously (Witt, 1997). Even recent studies show that parents still buy action-oriented toys for boys, but home- and family-oriented toys like dolls and dishes for girls (Doskoch and Jones, 1996).

Teaching Gender Roles in the School

Gender-role socialization continues when children reach school. The tendency to prefer different kinds of toys—which symbolize different roles in life—continues. One study, for example, showed that in kindergarten, girls are encouraged to play with dolls, and boys are encouraged to play with wheeled toys and building blocks (Best, 1983). Girls' toys thus come to represent a domestic, child-oriented role, whereas boys' toys represent going out into the world, doing and building. Children also often see different images of males and females in their school books and materials, although there has been some improvement in recent years. Studies of these materials indicate a number of ways they teach gender inequality. The main characters, for example, are more likely to be male than female, particularly in older books that remain in use in some schools (Grauerholz and Pescosolido, 1989; Women on Words and Images, 1974). Male characters display creativity, bravery, achievement, and similar themes, while female characters display emotion, fear, and dependency (Key, 1975; Kolbe and LaVoie, 1981; Williams et al., 1987). Good things that happen to male characters result from their own efforts, while good things that happen to female characters result from luck or the actions of others (Penrod, 1986, p. 88). Sex stereotypes have been found in books ranging from math books (Federbush, 1974) to introductory sociology textbooks (Feree and Hall, 1990).

Stereotyping did decrease during the 1970s and 1980s, as women's groups and social researchers pointed out the stereotypes that appeared in many books and school materials. Still, recent studies show that stereotyping has not been eliminated (Feree and Hall, 1990; Vaughn-Roberson et al., 1989; Williams et al., 1987). One study found male lead characters still two to three times as common as female lead characters in the 1980s (Grauerholz and Pescosolido, 1989), while another study found gender equity in lead characters but still an overrepresentation of males in subsidiary characters (Paterson and Lach, 1990). Yet another recent study found gender equity in lead characters, slight and declining male predominance (compared to earlier studies) in all human characters, but a persistence of a strong male predominance among personified animal characters (Oskamp, Kaufman, and Wolterbeek, 1996).

Children also get a message about gender from what they see firsthand in their schools. Although the teaching profession has historically been a largely female occupation, the proportion of women in the profession falls as the importance and status of the job increases. As you move from kindergarten through grade school, junior high school, high school, and on to college, there are progressively fewer female teachers and more male teachers. At every level of education, the proportion of women among principals and administrators is lower than it is among teachers. Nationally, for example, 75 percent of elementary and secondary teachers are women, but only 35 percent of principals are women (National Center for Educational Statistics, 2001a). The message children get from this is clear: The most important and highest-status jobs are for men.

Another process that takes place in schools is subject channeling. Boys are expected to excel in math, science, and logic; girls are expected to excel in reading, art, and music. These expectations occur in the home and in school. Parents frequently believe that learning math and science is more important for boys than for girls (Parsons et al., 1982) and thus do more to encourage boys to learn these subjects. In the school, teachers and counselors have similar beliefs. They sometimes encourage boys to take more math and science than girls, and they often expect higher achievement from boys than from girls in these subjects (Coakley, 1972; Curran, 1980; Entwisle, Alexander, and Olson, 1994; Campbell, 1992; Oakes and Rand Corporation, 1990; Shroyer et al., 1994). One study found that, when boys do well in math, teachers attribute it to ability, whereas when girls do well, teachers attribute it to effort (Fennema et al., 1990). In recent years, differences in mathematics grades between boys and girls have decreased, but there has been very little change in the tendency for girls to take less high school math than boys, and the same pattern holds for men and women in college (Callas, 1993). An important consequence of such channeling is that young men and women choose different college majors, which prepare them for different occupations (Table 8.1).

Such different treatment of children on the basis of gender sometimes combines with unequal treatment based on race, creating special problems for African American girls. Observations of a first-grade classroom revealed that black female students, more than any other group, received attention based on their social skills rather than their academic skills. Similarly, they were the most likely to act as "go-betweens" in negotiations among teachers and students—particularly when the negotiators were of different race or gender. This may direct black females toward maintaining peace among others rather than developing their own skills—a stereotypical role of black women (Grant, 1984).

Teaching Gender Roles on Television

Most children in the United States today spend more time watching television than they spend either in school or talking to their parents. What kinds of messages do they get from television about the roles of men and women? Whether we consider television entertainment or television advertising, the evidence is that they often get stereotyped messages.

Table 8.1 Percentage of Bachelor's Degrees Awarded to Women by Discipline, 1966, 1981, 1989, 1998, and 2007 (Selected Fields)

Discipline	1966[1]	1981	1989	1998	2007[2]
Agriculture	2.7%	30.8%	31.1%	41.7%	46.8%
Architecture	4.0%	18.3%	39.3%	35.1%	44.5%
Biological sciences	28.2%	44.1%	50.2%	55.1%	60.2%
Business	8.5%	36.7%	46.7%	48.5%	49.2%
Computer and information science	13.01%	32.5%	30.7%	26.7%	18.6%
Education	75.3%	75.0%	77.7%	75.2%	78.7%
Engineering	0.4%	10.3%	13.6%	16.9%	18.4%
English and English literature	66.2%	66.5%	—	66.9%	68.3%
Foreign languages	70.7%	75.6%	73.3%	70.0%	69.6%
Health	76.9%	83.5%	84.9%	82.9%	85.9%
Home economics	97.5%	95.5%	90.6%	87.6%	—
Mathematics	33.3%	42.8%	46.0%	46.5%	44.1%
Physical sciences	13.6%	24.6%	29.7%	39.4%	40.9%
Psychology	41.0%	65.0%	70.8%	74.4%	77.4%
Social sciences	35.0%	44.2%	44.4%	49.2%	49.8%
Economics	9.8%	30.5%	—	31.7%	—
History	34.6%	37.9%	—	39.1%	41.3%
Sociology	59.6%	69.6%	—	68.8%	—

1 Data are for 1969, the earliest year available.
2 Data are for 2006–2007 period.
— Not available.

Note that women are most highly represented in home economics and health, which reflect the traditional female role, and are most underrepresented in such "technical" areas as engineering and architecture. However, note also the rapid changes in such areas as architecture, biology, and business, particularly in the 1966–1989 period.

Sources: U.S. Department of Health, Education and Welfare, Office of Education, "Earned Degrees Conferred: 1965–66"; U.S. Department of Education, National Center for Education Statistics, "Earned Degrees Conferred, 1980–81"; U.S. Department of Education, National Center for Education Statistics, "Trends in Bachelor's and Higher Degrees, 1975–1985"; U.S. Bureau of the Census, *Statistical Abstract of the United States,* 1992; National Center for Education Statistics. 2001. *Digest of Education Statistics,* 2000, table 257. Washington, DC: U.S. Department of Education, http://nces.ed.gov/pubsearch/pubsinfo.asp?pubid=2001034. National Center for Education Statistics. 2008, table 285, http://nces.ed.gov/programs/digest/d08/tables/dt08—285.asp.

Television entertainment, for example, often gives messages that reinforce the segregation of men and women into separate occupations. Between 1950 and 1980, 95 percent of doctors on television were men, and 99 percent of nurses were women (Kalisch and Kalisch, 1984). In general, television roles that involve leadership and decision making have historically been played by men, whereas women's roles have been either to be home-centered or, if at work, to be in a following rather than leading role. There has been some change in these stereotypes over the past few decades. Women have appeared on television in recent years as tough cops, savvy lawyers, and private investigators, but some who have researched these trends argue that new stereotypes have appeared. Although women are now portrayed more often in roles involving accomplishment or "toughness," they are playing such roles differently than men play them (Roman, 1986). Female police officers, for example, may be portrayed as either more caring than male officers or more devious and conniving; male officers are shown as more aggressive and quicker to use force—thus perpetuating gender stereotypes. Rapping (2000) points out that, while strong, successful women appear more often on TV today, their lives often center around traditional male-female relationships or family obligations. She cites as examples shows such as *Providence* where successful professional women return to their hometowns to meet family obligations (thereby subtly conveying the message that such obligations are the responsibility of women). The shift in recent years to "reality" shows has also brought renewed stereotyping. A recent study of *America's Most Wanted,* for example, showed that women were portrayed as victims in need of assistance, while men were portrayed either as brutal attackers or as "protectors" who used their expertise to protect female victims (Cavender, Bond-Maupin, and Jurik, 1999). Two other patterns are worth noting. First, women are consistently portrayed on television as younger than men (Elasmar, Hasegawa, and Brain, 1999; Milner and Collins, 2000). This reinforces the notion that youthful good looks are important for women, while experience and accomplishment may be more valued in men. Finally, despite some improvement, women remain underrepresented on prime-time TV. In the early 1990s, fewer than 40 percent of prime-time TV characters were female—up from less than 20 percent in the early 1970s, but still an underrepresentation (Elasmar, Hasegawa, and Brain, 1999).

Although sex stereotyping may have become more subtle in television entertainment, it is hardly subtle in television advertising. Very attractive and often thinly clad females are used to sell everything from cars to shaving products to electronic gadgets. Sometimes the message is more about sex than about the product. When a woman is the lead in a commercial, the message is much more likely to be based on attractiveness than when a man is the lead (Downs and Harrison, 1985). In contrast, the voice of authority on most commercials is male (Klemesrud, 1981). Significantly, male voice-overs are most common when the actors on the commercial are attractive women (Downs and Harrison, 1985). The hidden message is that women are pretty and men are knowledgeable and authoritative. Besides being attractive, women are also portrayed as engaging in rather mindless behaviors, usually in the home. They frequently become excited about a small improvement in a detergent or floor cleaner or about the softness of facial tissues or toilet paper.

Under these circumstances, it is hardly surprising that social scientists have found that children who watch more television are more stereotyped in their own thinking than children who watch less (Beuf, 1974; Frueh and McGhee, 1975; see also Tan, 1979). Moreover, those who are exposed to stereotypical television become more stereotyped in their own thinking, whereas those who see counter-stereotypical television become less stereotyped (Geis et al., 1984; Johnson et al., 1980; Johnson and Davidson, 1981; McArthur and Eisen, 1976; Miller and Reeves, 1976). Taking all this into consideration, there is no doubt that television has been and remains an important means by which gender roles are taught.

How Peers Teach Gender Roles

Some of the strongest pressures for gender-role conformity come from peers. The peer group enforces the principle that boys and girls are supposed to enjoy different activities and play different roles. The reward for conforming to such norms is approval and inclusion; the costs of violating them include rejection, ridicule, and social isolation. In general, peer pressures for gender role conformity are stronger among boys than among girls (Hartley, 1974). It is worse for a boy to be labeled a "sissy" than for a girl to be labeled a "tomboy." The "tomboy," after all, is only seeking to move from what society has defined as an inferior role into one that society views more favorably; the "sissy" is doing the reverse. In fact, boys are sometimes so negative toward the traditional female role that as a result even girls look down upon it. Best (1983), for example, has noted cases in which girls became reluctant to be seen playing with dolls by the third grade. Why? Because boys made fun of them. The message here, of course, is that the traditional female role of domesticity is inferior and is therefore to be avoided.

Pressures for conformity to "boys' play" and "girls' play" start young; they have even been found among preschoolers as young as three (Lamb et al., 1980). However, these pressures increase as children move through their education, and by the third or fourth grade they are reinforced by a strong system of sex segregation in play: Boys play with boys and girls play with girls. Within each group, strong pressures exist for "sex-appropriate" behavior. Peer pressures for boys to be masculine and for girls to be attractive appear to be strongest in adolescence (Bernard, 1981, p. 137; Coleman, 1961). In addition, on the "borders" of sex segregation, when boys and girls do interact at school or day care, it is often in the form of chasing, "pollution rituals" (such as giving "cooties"), and invasions, in which interactions between boys and girls establish male dominance and aggressiveness and female submission and victimization (Thorne, 1993; Voss, 1997).

How Gender Roles Are Learned

We have seen that the family, the school, the media, and the peer group all send children messages about the different roles of men and women. We shall now explore further the process by which these sex roles are learned, and we will see evidence that if the socialization process were different, girls and boys would not be channeled toward different roles in life in the ways that they are now.

The Looking-Glass Self and Gender-Role Socialization

Recall from Chapters 3 and 5 Charles Horton Cooley's (1929 [orig. 1909]) concept of the *looking-glass self*.

According to Cooley, our self-image is a product of the messages we receive from others and the ways we understand and interpret those messages. When the messages are different and unequal, as messages given to boys and girls often are, it is hardly surprising that boys and girls come to see themselves differently. Girls are often told that they are understanding, attractive, well-behaved, and good in art and reading, while boys are told that they are hardy, mischievous, and good at math, science, and building things. On the other hand, girls are told that they are delicate and not so good at math and science, and boys are not expected to be understanding or good at art or creative writing. These messages create a self-fulfilling prophecy: Very often, boys and girls do become different kinds of people. Thus, for example, boys *become* better than girls at math and science. Although there is no difference in their ability test scores in the early grades, boys do score higher than girls by seventh or eighth grade, with the difference increasing until high school graduation (see Benbow and Stanley, 1980; Curran, 1980; Fairweather, 1976). However, these differences are smaller today than in the past (Stockard and Johnson, 1992).

Moreover, a variety of evidence suggests that when boys and girls are exposed to similar expectations and messages, such differences either do not develop or can be largely reversed (Coser, 1986; Newcombe et al., 1983; Tobias, 1978). For example, such differences do not develop in societies that do not channel girls away from jobs involving math, science, and reasoning, even if other types of sexual inequality exist. The Soviet Union has been cited as one example of such a society (Tobias, 1978). In addition, such differences do not develop in some schools even in the United States, quite possibly because these schools make efforts not to channel boys and girls toward separate occupations. Finally, girls who, for whatever reason, resist the message and develop a sufficiently strong interest in math and science to take advanced courses do just as well as the boys in these courses (College Entrance Examination Board, 1974).

Modeling and Gender-Role Socialization

As we saw in Chapter 5, repeated and selective exposure to a particular behavior pattern leads to modeling of that behavior pattern. This is particularly true when children identify with the model, as they do with their parents. It is clear from the foregoing discussion that in nearly every aspect of their lives, children are exposed to images of men and women in very different roles. Does this selective exposure lead to modeling, as we would expect? Evidence suggests that it does.

Modeling and Occupations
One example of modeling can be seen in the occupational aspirations of boys and girls. Despite all the recent changes in the roles of men and women, most boys and girls still plan on seeking jobs that have traditionally been held by people of their sex (Sellers, Satcher, and Comas, 1999). A study of eighth-graders shows, for example, that boys are twice as likely as girls to plan on science, engineering, and technical careers, and seven times as likely to expect a skilled craft occupation. Girls, on the other hand, were three times as likely to expect clerical or sales work, service jobs, or work in the home (U.S. Department of Education, 1989, p. 30). Gender effects on job expectations interact with effects of race and class. Ladner and Gourdine (1984), for example, report a decline since around 1970 in expectations for success in any occupation among poor black teenage girls. At the same time, it is true among all social classes that boys and girls aspire to different kinds of jobs (Sellers, Satcher, and Comas, 1999). In general, the more that children are exposed to sexual stereotypes at home or through the media, the more stereotyped their thinking is (Hoyenga and Hoyenga, 1979, pp. 214–18). Robb and Raven (1982), for example, found that children of mothers who are employed full time see fewer sex-stereotyped roles in the home than other children, and that these children in fact become less stereotypical in their own thinking. And these stereotypes do matter: Recent research confirms that the different occupational goals and expectations of young men and women do frequently lead them into different lines of work (Okamoto and England, 1999).

Structured Sexual Inequality: Power

As was stated earlier, gender roles, as they exist in the United States, are not just *different;* they are also *unequal*. Whether you consider power, income, or occupational status, men in the United States are an advantaged group compared to women. Let us consider each of these areas in greater detail.

Although we have examined the concept of *power* in Chapter 6 in considerable detail, and we shall look at it again in Chapters 9, 10, and 12, we shall briefly introduce and define it here, because it is an important area in which men and women experience social inequality. Power can be defined as the ability to get other people to behave in ways that you desire. Power is often exercised through the political system. It frequently rises from authority—the right to make certain decisions that is attached to a certain social position. We shall focus on power as it relates to men and women in two key areas: positions of authority, and power within the family.

Men, Women, and Positions of Authority

One way to judge the power of a social group is to gauge whether that group is well represented among people known to hold power. Clearly, power in the form of authority is held by people in certain positions in business and government. Chief executive officers (CEOs) of businesses, political officials, and certain public administrators, such as city managers and school administrators, have considerable power.

How well represented are women in these positions of power? Part of the answer can be found in Figure 8.2. Even today, women are almost completely absent from the most important positions of power. Although more than one in five elected officials overall is female, the percentage is smaller though growing when we look at the most important positions such as governors and U.S. senators and representatives. When we consider the top political levels, we find that no woman has ever even been nominated for president by a major party, and the only women ever nominated for vice president were Representative Geraldine Ferraro, the Democratic candidate in 1984, and former Alaska governor Sarah Palin, the Republican candidate in 2008 (both of their tickets lost in the general election).

Despite some improvement in recent years, women remain severely underrepresented in top corporate executive positions and boards, and

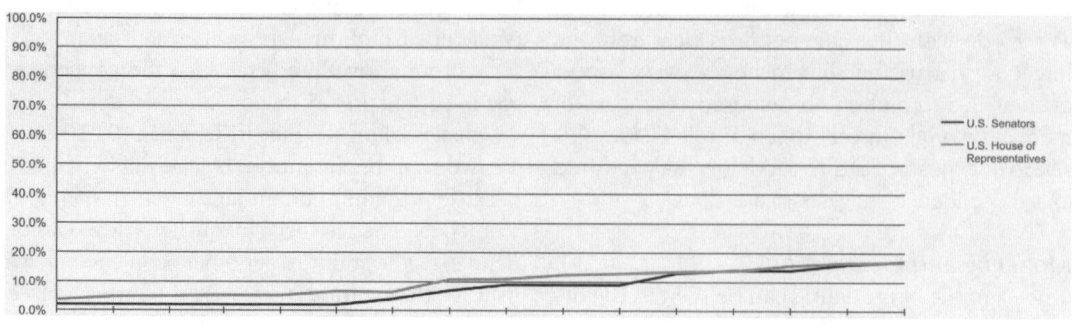

Figure 8.2(a) Percentage of Women Among U.S. Senators and Representatives, 1980–2010

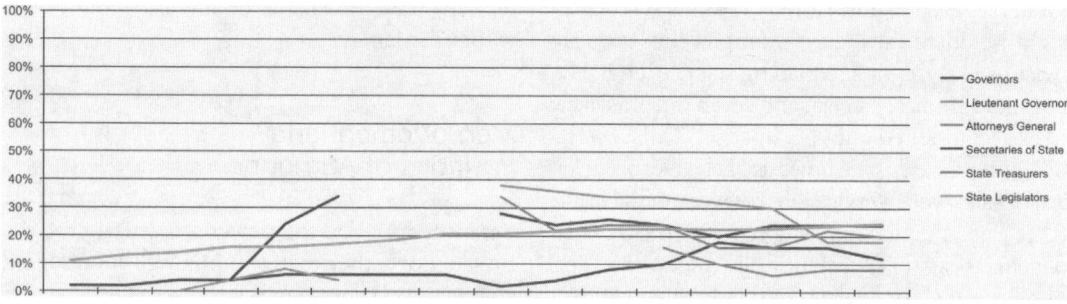

Figure 8.2(b) Percentage of Women Among Statewide Office Holders and State Legislators, 1980–2010

Source: Data for 2002–2010 and Data for some earlier years are from Center for American Women in Politics, Facts on Women Officeholders, Candidates, and Voters, http://www.cawp.rutgers.edu/fast_facts/index.php (Accessed August 6, 2010). Data for earlier years are from Taylor's World of Politics; *New York Times*; U.S. Bureau of the Census, Statistical Abstract of the United States; World Almanac and Book of Facts, 1991; *St. Louis Post-Dispatch*; 1993 Information Please Almanac; Center for the American Woman and Politics, Rutgers University, 1996 and 2001, http://www.rci.rutgers.edu/~cawp/; University of Maryland, Women's Studies, Government and Politics, 1996, http://www.inform.umd.edu:8080/Educational_Resources/AcademicResourcesByTopic/WomensStudies/GovernmentPolitics/PoliticalProgress/1995; Center for American Women in Politics, Rutgers University, 2001, Women in Elected Office, 2001: Fact Sheet Summaries, http://www.rci.rutgers.edu/~cawp/facts/cawpfs.html.

among the biggest companies, women are almost totally missing from top positions. Overall, just 6 percent of U.S. commercial organizations have women in their highest leadership positions (Guthrie and Roth, 1999). In 2008, just thirteen of the 500 largest U.S. companies had female CEOs—fewer than 3 percent of the companies but still more than six times as many as in 2001 (USA Today, 2009; Catalyst, 2001). Also, female CEOs are paid less on average than male CEOs (USA Today, 2009; Lowen, 2009). In 2008, 15.2 percent of the members of the boards of directors of the 500 largest companies were women—a small proportion but still a 50 percent increase since 1984 (Catalyst, 2008).

Women in Politics

No longer can it be said that women are underrepresented in positions of power because few women seek out such positions. Women may still be somewhat less likely than men to run for political office, but more and more have done so in recent years. More have been elected, too, and a majority of Americans say that it would be good for the country to have more women in political office (Simmons, 2001). However, women still have a hard time getting elected to the highest offices. For example, more than a third of the states had women serving as lieutenant governor throughout the past decade, but far fewer have had women as governors. The eight women governors serving in 2009 matches a record high first set in 2001—yet it still represents less than one-sixth of the states. In the U.S. Congress, the number of women also rose to a record high—seventeen senators and seventy-four representatives in 2009—but these numbers amount to only 17 percent of the seats in either chamber. Some Americans remain reluctant to vote for women, especially for the higher offices such as governor or president. As recently as 1987, a poll showed one voter in four unwilling to vote for any woman for president of the United States (ABC News, 1987). However, by 1999, a Gallup Poll found that 92 percent of Americans said they would support a qualified woman supported by their party—reflecting a steady increase since 1945, when just 33 percent said they would vote for a woman (Newport, Moore, and Saad, 1999). Additionally, there is evidence of change in actual voting behavior as well: In 2008, nearly half the voters in the Democratic primaries supported Hilary Clinton in her candidacy for the presidency.

Women in the Business World

In the business world, the absence of women in part reflects the reluctance of male boards of directors to appoint women to top executive positions. And the boards do remain male-dominated. As recently as a decade ago, a census of 1,000 of the largest U.S. companies showed that nearly half of them had no women at all on their boards of directors (Directors and Boards, 1992). By 1998, however, over 85 percent of the largest 500 companies did have at least one female board member—but by 2008, this percentage remained less than 87 percent, and fewer than one company in five had more than two female directors (Catalyst, 1998, 2008).

Over 60 percent of U.S. women were in the labor force in 2007 (Bureau of the Census, 2008: 375). In 1999, about 18 percent of full-time female workers were in executive, administrative, or managerial work, compared to 17 percent of male workers (U.S. Census Bureau, 2000a, pp. 30–31). This represents progress, since in the past, men were more likely to have these jobs than women. Today, there are many women in lower- and middle-level management, but as noted above, women still have difficulty rising to the highest levels of management that have real organizational decision-making power. Too often, their opportunities to move into such positions have been blocked by an informal "glass ceiling" that limits how high women can move in the organization.

Women in the corporate world encounter barriers that inhibit their opportunities to gain real power. In corporations with relatively few women managers, women in management are often responded to more as women than as managers, thus being deprived of the full opportunity to be evaluated and responded to on the basis of the work they do (Kanter, 1977). As the number of women increases, male managers become more accustomed to women and treat them more as they would any other employee—up to a point. However, when the number of women begins to approach a majority, male workers often feel threatened, which may inhibit opportunities for the women workers (Harlan and Weiss, 1981). Until such attitudes change, women are not likely to fill many positions of real power.

What ultimately may lead to the placement of more women in such positions is the evident economic rationality of doing so. Increasing evidence suggests that women may be particularly effective as managers in today's changing workplace, because they may be more likely than men to break down hierarchy and involve workers in decision making (Helgesen, 1990; Holusha, 1991; Rosener, 1990). As is discussed further in Chapter 9, this style of management generally leads to increased productivity.

While well-educated, middle-class women are limited by the "glass ceiling," it is economic survival, not career, that is the main concern of working-class and poor women. Virtually all of these women are employed out of sheer economic necessity; this is particularly the case for the lowest-income segment among women of color. The concentration of low-income black and Hispanic women in industries such as fast-food service and hotel housekeeping has resulted in steadier employment than what has been available to inner-city men in recent years, but it is difficult and very low-paying work (Collins, 2000). In an earlier era, when divorce and single parenthood were much less common than today, such women could combine their incomes with the somewhat higher incomes of their husbands to provide somewhat adequate support for their families. Today, when many women are the sole breadwinners for their families, however, the wages paid for such work—which remain well below the pay of men with comparably low levels of education—are woefully inadequate.

Men, Women, and Power in the Home

The relative powerlessness of women in the worlds of government and business is largely mirrored in the home. Even in homes where both the husband and wife are employed full time, several realities give greater power to the husband. For one thing, even when both partners work full time, the husband typically provides 60 percent or more of the family's income, because men's wages substantially exceed those of women. Where the wife works only part time or not at all, this discrepancy is even greater (Sorensen and McLanahan, 1987). The power of the purse within the family, then, is disproportionately in the hands of the male. Even today, women must often seek money from their husbands for various types of purchases. Until recently, married women usually could not borrow money unless they applied jointly for credit with their husbands. Today, the law has changed, but women's incomes are often too low for them to get substantial credit lines on their own, so they must still sometimes depend on their husbands.

Also limiting the power of women in the home is the continuing influence of the norm that providing income through employment is the first responsibility of the husband, while taking care of the household is the first responsibility of the wife. For one thing, even women who have good jobs must often put their husbands' jobs first when questions of relocation arise (Bielby and Bielby, 1992). Families are far more likely to move for the husband's career opportunities than for the wife's. In addition, the wife, not the husband, is expected to miss work for such household emergencies as taking care of sick children and letting in repairpersons. (For a discussion of both of these issues, see Duncan et al., 1984, pp. 156–61.)

Finally, the primacy of the woman's responsibility for the home means that women employed full time have a longer work week than men employed full time. A review of over 200 studies between 1989 and 1999 showed that, although the gender gap in housework has narrowed a little, women still spend twice as many hours a week on household work as men do (Coltrane, 2000). According to one study (Peskin, 1982), the total (employment and home) work week of a typical female full-time employee was 67 hours, compared with 63 hours for the typical male full-time employee. The difference: Women put in considerably more hours working around the house than men did. The gap may have narrowed a little since then, but studies still show that full-time working women have less leisure time and experience more stress than full-time working men.

Men have increased their work around the house, and such tasks as cooking, washing dishes, grocery shopping, and laundry are shared in far more households today than in the past. Thus, as women have entered the labor force, men have increased their share of household work to a certain extent. For many men, this is a dramatic role change from what they saw their fathers doing when they were children. In most households, however, men have still not increased their share of the household work to anywhere near an equal share, even when both husband and wife are employed full time (Coltrane, 2000). Husbands also tend not to take the initiative to do various household tasks—their wives usually have to ask them. They tend not to be concerned with matters such as doctors' appointments, household tasks, clothing purchases, or scheduling their children's engagements, for instance, unless their wives direct them to do so (Stockard and Johnson, 1992, p. 63). Studies disagree on whether this is because men are uninterested in these tasks, or because women view themselves as household "managers" and are unwilling to give up this role; perhaps it is some of both (Coltrane, 2000).

Gender inequality in the home is starkly illustrated by a recent study comparing the household work of men and women in a variety of marital statuses and living arrangements. Of the various possible living arrangements, women do the most household work when they are married or cohabiting, while men in these situations do the least (South and Spitze, 1994). Men, in contrast, do the most work if they are divorced or widowed—which may help to explain why men are quicker to remarry than women. Similarly, having an adult son living in the household increases his mother's household work, while having an adult daughter at home decreases it.

Structured Sexual Inequality: Income

Today, the average woman employed full time receives just over three-quarters of the income of her male counterpart. As shown in Figure 8.3, this represents some narrowing of the gap since the early 1970s, when women received only 57 percent of the income of men when both worked full time—although the narrowing of the gap ended after the mid-1990s.

While the gender gap has narrowed compared to the past, women still spend more time on household work than men. When both partners work full-time, the result is that men have more leisure time than women. (Courtesy of Michael Flota)

The difference between men's and women's incomes is not the result of educational differences between men and women: As shown in Table 8.2, the difference in men's and women's wages is substantial at all levels of education. It is true, as shown in Table 8.3, that gender differences in income are smaller among younger workers and greater among older workers. This fact

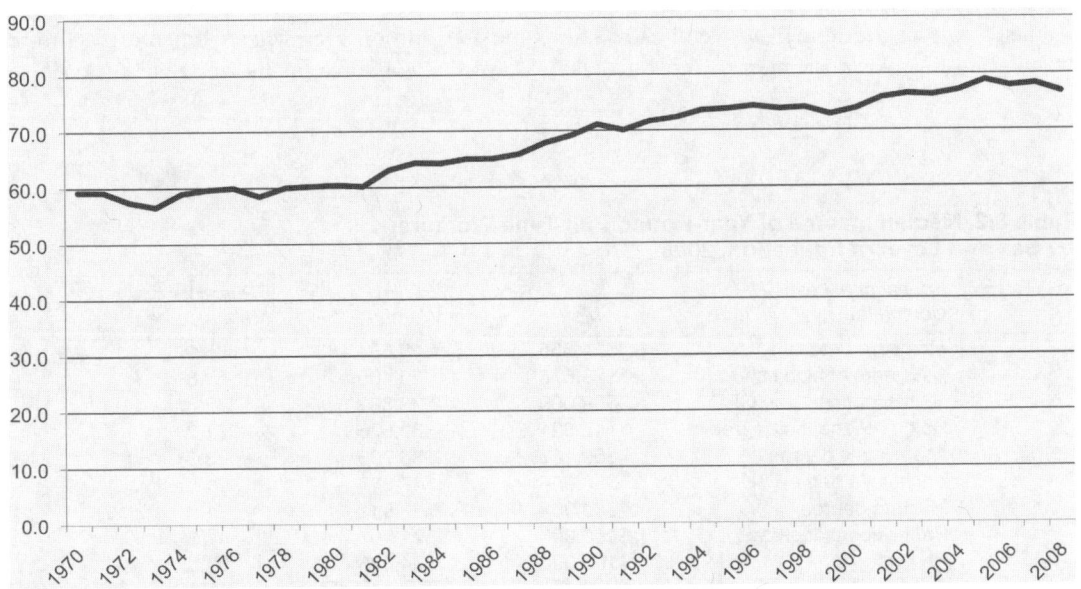

Figure 8.3 Median Women's Income as a Percentage of Median Men's Income, Year-Round Full-Time Workers, 1970–2008

Source: Calculated from U.S. Census Bureau, 2010, Income, People, Table P-36, Full-time, Year Round Workers by Median Income and Sex, http://www.census.gov/hhes/www/income/data/historical/people/p36AR.xls (Accessed August 8, 2010).

could be interpreted in two ways. The optimistic interpretation is that sexual wage inequality is decreasing, and that young women now entering the labor market are receiving fairer treatment. A less optimistic interpretation is that women do not get advanced to higher-paying jobs as quickly as men do. We have already seen that women are often excluded from the top managerial jobs. Even more important, many women work in clerical and service occupations that offer little chance for promotion to substantially higher-paying jobs. Finally, even though younger women do better relative to men than older women in terms of income, they still earn considerably less than men in their age group.

Some Possible Reasons for Women's Low Wages

Why do women continue to be paid so much less than men? A number of possibilities have been suggested, including the competing role of women in the home, wage inequality in the same job, hiring patterns, and occupational segregation. Let us consider each.

Competing Expectations of Working Women
Certainly, part of the answer is to be found in women's role in the home. As we already saw, women are less able than men to move to take a job and are more likely to miss work because of household emergencies. Both of these things impede their ability to move up to better-paying positions. Moreover, women are more likely than men to leave the job market temporarily, especially to take care of young children. (Again, if anyone quits work for this reason in a family, it is usually the wife.)

How important are these factors as a cause of low income? They are part of the reason, but not most of it, and may be declining in importance. National studies have shown that differences in work experience, work continuity, self-imposed limits on work hours and location, and absenteeism combined explain less than half the difference between men's and women's salaries (Duncan et al., 1984; Wellington, 1994). More recent research shows that women are not more likely than men to have jobs that allow them flexibility to meet family needs (Glass and Camarigg, 1992; see also Desai and Waite, 1991). With the passage of the Family Leave Act in 1993, however, both men and women may now find it possible to give up their jobs temporarily to care for their families in crisis situations. The practice of leaving the labor force to care for young children has also become less common, as (1) fewer and fewer families can afford to give up the income, (2) growing numbers of mothers are single parents and the only source of their family's income, and (3) even when women can afford to leave the workforce, many are reluctant to do so

Table 8.2 Median Income of Year-Round Full-Time Workers, by Sex and Level of Education, 2008

Educational Level Completed	Men	Women	Percent of Male Income
8th grade or less	$24,555	$18,634	75.9
1–3 years of high school	$29,678	$20,405	68.8
High school grad or GED	$39,009	$28,382	72.8
Some college, no degree	$45,821	$32,626	71.2
Associate's degree	$50,147	$36,760	73.3
Bachelor's degree	$65,800	$47,026	71.5
Masters degree	$80,962	$57,512	71.0
Professional degree	$100,000	$71,297	71.3
Ph.D.	$100,000	$74,025	74.0

Source: U.S. Bureau of the Census. 2009. Current Population Survey, Annual Social and Economic Supplement. Table PINC-03. Educational Attainment--People 25 Years Old and Over, by Total Money Earnings in 2008, Work Experience in 2008, Age, Race, Hispanic Origin, and Sex, http://www.census.gov/hhes/www/cpstables/032009/perinc/new03_000.htm.

Table 8.3 Median Income of Year-Round, Full-Time Workers, by Sex and Age, 2006

Age	Men	Women	Percent of Male Income
All ages	$57,791	$41,518	71.8
15–24	$26,170	$23,462	89.7
25–34	$46,181	$38,581	83.5
35–44	$63,247	$44,183	69.9
45–54	$67,635	$45,332	67.0
55–64	$65,956	$43,870	66.5
65 and over	$58,565	$38,629	66.0

Source: U.S. Bureau of the Census, 2009.

out of fear that they will compromise their chances of career advancement (Blair-Loy, 1999). In fact, research has revealed that women devote more effort, not less, to their jobs than similarly situated men (Bielby and Bielby, 1989).

Wage Inequality Within Occupations

Even when they work in the same occupation, women are paid less than men (Bergmann, 1986; Huffman and Cohen, 2004; Jarrell and Stanley, 2004; Kemp and Beck, 1986; Stockard and Johnson, 1992). There are a number of reasons for this. Because of employer stereotypes about women's commitment to the labor force, a woman is less likely to be offered on-the-job training—even when she has been with the firm for the same amount of time as a man (Duncan et al., 1984). Also, men are more likely to be given supervisory and/or hiring and firing authority than are women—and are paid better as a result (Cohen and Huffman, 2007; Hill and Morgan, 1979; Duncan et al., 1984). Women are also promoted less often, which also contributes to their lower pay. Within occupations, women are frequently channeled into lower-paying specialties. Female physicians are more likely to specialize in pediatrics or public health while male physicians more often specialize in cardiology or gastroenterology; female lawyers more often specialize in domestic relations and males in corporate or criminal law; and in construction, women are less likely than men to get on-site jobs such as operation of heavy equipment (Stockard and Johnson, 1992). In each case, the disproportionately "male" specialization is paid more, even though the occupation is the same (see Bellas, 1994). Such differences often reflect discrimination and gender channeling by mentors, employers, and, in some occupations, unions.

Hiring Patterns

It appears that another reason for wage inequality reflects the relative powerlessness of women: They are often tied to a locality by their husband's occupational choice. As noted earlier, if a family relocates on the basis of job availability, it is usually the husband's job that determines where they will live (Bielby and Bielby, 1992). This means that women must take what is available in the locality of the husband's job. In the case of a town with one university, for instance, wives of faculty and administrators may be forced to take whatever is available if they want a job. Because their job choices are limited, women must work for less (Blau and Ferber, 1986). Some firms take advantage of this, by hiring mostly women and paying them less than they would pay men in the same occupation. Currie and Skolnick (1984, p. 219), for example, have pointed out that accounting firms that hire mainly female accountants pay less than firms that hire mainly male accountants.

Finally, recent research shows that the trend toward greater use of part-time and temporary employees had a particular impact on working-class women. The gap between the incomes of college graduates and non-college graduates has widened for both men and women, but the causes are different. Men without college degrees have suffered because technology and industrial restructuring have forced them into lower-paying jobs, while women without college degrees have suffered because permanent and full-time jobs have gotten harder to get (McCall, 2000). This has impacted even women still working in full-time jobs, because the low cost of part-time labor has held wages down even on full-time jobs at lower skill levels. It has also reduced the job security of less-educated women, which further depresses their wages.

Occupational Segregation

Although women typically receive lower wages than men even in the same occupation, a major cause of income inequality is **occupational segregation**. This term refers to the concentration of men and women into different occupations, even when they have similar levels of skill and training. Occupational segregation has significant impacts, in terms of both the incomes and the occupational choices and opportunities for men and women (Petersen and Morgan, 1995).

Considerable occupational segregation is evident even if we look at broad categories of jobs that the Census Bureau and other statistical agencies use to classify occupations. Women are more likely than men to work in clerical and service jobs. This affects women's earnings, since clerical workers receive relatively low pay on the average, while service workers are near the bottom in terms of wages (U.S. Census Bureau, 2000a, pp. 30–31).

However, even when men and women are evenly represented in one of these broad categories, they often work at different specific jobs within the category (Bielby and Baron, 1986). Women are slightly more likely than men to be employed in the "professional specialty" category, but within this category, they often work at lower-paying jobs than men. Most physicians, lawyers, engineers, dentists, and architects are men. These men are better paid than are nurses, teachers, and social workers—professional employees who are mostly women.

Such differences can exist even within the same industry. Currie and Skolnick (1984, pp. 222–23) illustrated this point using the food and beverage industry. The highest-paid employees are brewery workers, who are 85 percent male. Their average pay in 1981 was $497 per week. At the opposite end are poultry workers, the majority of whom are women, many of them women of color. Their average pay in 1981 was only $169 per week. In general, it has been shown that the greater the number of women in an occupation, the lower the pay of that occupation (England et al., 1988, 1994; Mellor, 1984; Kilbourne et al., 1994).

Why do jobs typically held by men so often pay better than jobs typically held by women? There seem to be several reasons. First, unequal pay is probably a carry-over from the days when it was widely believed that men should be paid more because they were more likely to be supporting a family. Although this is no longer true today and deliberate sexual pay discrimination by an employer within the same occupation is illegal, there is nothing to stop unequal pay in different occupations. Custom and bureaucratic inertia also seem to play a role in perpetuating such inequalities (Bridges and Nelson, 1989). When pressures for change are exerted on such organizations, they are more likely to change than when there is no such pressure (Baron, Mittman, and Newman, 1991).

Second, predominantly male occupations are more highly unionized than predominantly female occupations. As a result, their pay tends to be better. In part, these differences may reflect different attitudes among men and women toward unionization, but they probably also reflect that, until recently, most unions were more interested in organizing predominantly male occupations.

Finally, Reskin (1988) has argued that predominantly male jobs are paid more than predominantly female jobs for the same reason that occupational segregation exists in the first place: Men—the more powerful group in society—benefit from both arrangements. She points out that in the past, when men were the main source of support for most families, that fact was used to justify their higher income. But today, when that is no longer the case, occupation has become the basis for assigning wages.

Comparable Worth

Clearly, occupational segregation is an important cause of male-female income inequality. Even when they require similar levels of skill and training, "men's jobs" usually pay better than "women's jobs." England (1999) cites several examples: secretaries (mostly female) being paid less than car-washers (mostly male) by the city of San Jose; Denver nurses being paid less than tree trimmers, even though nurses have to be better educated; and Philadelphia practical nurses being paid less than gardeners. One short-term measure that has been proposed to address this income inequality is comparable worth legislation. *Comparable worth* states that men and women who work in different occupations that require similar skills and education should receive similar wages. To implement such a policy, an employer must first conduct a comparable worth study to evaluate the relative education, skill, knowledge, and responsibility required for different occupations. This study establishes sets of occupations that are similar in these regards. The employer must then adjust the pay scale so that people in occupations that fall within the same category receive similar or equal wages.

Most of the employers that have instituted such policies are state and local governments. Most of the states have conducted comparable worth studies, but only a minority of the states and a few municipalities have actually adjusted wages on the basis of these studies. Moreover, the adjustments that have taken place as a result have been smaller than anticipated, and the overall effect on wage differences between men and women has not been large (Bridges and Nelson, 1989; Acker, 1989). The policy encountered opposition from the Reagan and Bush administrations in the 1980s, and the federal courts ruled that comparable worth was not required by civil rights laws (England, 1999). Hence, it has had an effect on only a limited number of public employees, and virtually none in the private sector. U. S. policy even seemed to take a step back in 2007 as the Supreme Court handed down a decision that appeared to greatly limit the ability of workers to sue for pay discrimination. However, President Obama's first piece of legislation signed into law was the so-called Lilly Ledbetter Fair Pay Act of 2009 (named for the woman who had brought the discrimination case that the Court had ruled against), which restored the previous rights. One reason comparable worth policy has not been more effectively implemented may be that men continue to have power over the bureaucratic structures responsible for implementing comparable worth laws (Stockard and Johnson, 1992). Of course, the political institutions that would have to legislate it are similarly male-dominated, which may be one reason why federal comparable worth legislation has languished in the Congress since 1994. In this regard, the U.S. policy is different from that of other countries. Ontario province in Canada, for example, has required pay to be based on comparable worth in both public and private employment (England, 1999).

Causes of Occupational Segregation

This leads to the question, of course, of why women are so absent from many jobs. One reason turns out to be the effect of gender-role socialization—men and women are taught to aspire to different jobs and thus end up in different jobs. Another answer is that, until recently, open discrimination was common against women seeking to enter historically male occupations. This was true both of employers and of educational programs required for entry to an occupation. Although illegal today, such discrimination has lingering effects. An occupation composed primarily of members of one sex can be quite uncomfortable for a person of the opposite sex to enter. Thus, male nurses and secretaries and female firefighters and auto mechanics may face reactions ranging from ridicule to resistance to ostracism. A more serious problem, dramatically illustrated during the confirmation hearings for Supreme Court justice Clarence Thomas, is sexual harassment of women in predominantly male occupations and workplaces. This includes both unwanted sexual advances and creation of a hostile environment through sexual jokes and comments, the display of nude pictures, and so forth (Ollenburger and Moore, 1992; Lewin, 1992). These attitudes alone tend to perpetuate occupational segregation, particularly when they operate in combination with the effects of gender-role socialization. Also, as previously discussed, many young people still aspire to sex-typed occupations (Bain and Fottler, 1980; Barrett, 1979; Sellers, Satcher, and Comas, 1999; Okamoto and England, 1999), although the extent to which this is true is declining, especially among women (Jacobs, 1989). As we would expect, occupational segregation appears to be most intense in the kinds of places where attitudes about gender roles are most traditional (Abrahamson and Sigelman, 1987). And recent research by Okamato and England (1999) shows that the different occupational aspirations of young boys and girls do contribute to occupational segregation in adulthood, though other factors are probably more important.

Finally, there is evidence that occupational segregation may exist in part because it does perpetuate gender wage inequality (Reskin, 1988). From this view, it is a means by which men maintain their pay advantage. Several studies support this view (Bielby and Baron, 1986; Bielby and Bielby, 1988, Tables 29 and 30). Strang and Baron (1990), for example, found that in a state civil service system, the more women there were in an area of similar job content such as civil engineering or legal counsel, the more job titles there were—which permitted more occupational segregation and thereby greater wage inequality. Reskin (1988) has argued that so long as men retain disproportionate power, wage inequality will persist. She points out that in occupations that have become gender-integrated, men have retained the more desirable and lucrative specializations. Also, changes in work content, autonomy, and/or pay had often taken place, which made these occupations less desirable prior to the time at which more women entered them. These jobs then opened up to women as men looked elsewhere for work (Reskin and Roos, 1990).

As noted above, one thing that sometimes discourages women from entering predominantly male, high-status occupations is the increased risk of sexual harassment in such male-dominated work settings. This issue is explored further in this chapter's "Putting Sociology to Work" section.

Putting Sociology to Work

Understanding and Preventing Sexual Harassment

The arrival of women in the workforce, notably in fields previously dominated by men, and the collapse of the old code of manners between men and women, have led to a situation where the acceptable rules of behavior in an office, in the field, or on campus are not always clear and are frequently violated. As occupational segregation has lessened, awareness of sexual harassment has increased.

Sexual harassment is defined as deliberate or repeated unsolicited verbal comments, gestures, or physical contacts of a sexual nature that are unwelcome by the recipient and create an intimidating or hostile work environment. An employer or supervisor may threaten an employee with getting fired if he or she doesn't comply to his or her sexual request. Most often, however, there is not an explicit threat. Rather, harassment consists of repeated requests for dates or sexual favors, explicit sexual language, or fondling.

Three out of four victims of sexual harassment are women. Several studies suggest that, over the course of a year or two, around half of women and 15 percent of men experience some form of sexual harassment at work (Crocker and Kalemba, 1999; Wallis, 2000). Reports of sexual harassment have increased over the past decade or so, probably because when it occurs, it is more likely to be reported today than in the past. Reports of sexual harassment to the Equal Employment Opportunity Commission more than doubled between 1990 and 1996, to more than 15,000 per year (Fisher, 1998).

Harassment is most common when women enter traditionally all-male environments, like the military, medicine, or engineering. For example, a 1995 survey showed that 78 percent of women in the U.S. military had experienced "unwanted or uninvited sexual attention" during the past year, and 55 percent had experienced behavior that they regarded as sexual harassment (U.S. Department of Defense, 1996). By 2006, the incidence of self-reported sexual harassment was lower than a decade earlier, but more than one third of women still reported experiencing sexual harassment at some time during the year (Lipari et al., 2008). In one of the military's worst sexual harassment cases, sixty women aviators were sexually assaulted in a Las Vegas hotel in 1991 at the annual Tailhook Convention, a gathering of Navy fliers. Harassment is probably experienced more frequently by rank-and-file workers and middle management than by higher-ranking executives; one study, for example, found that among chief executive officers, chief operating officers, vice presidents, and department heads in health care, 29 percent of women and 5 percent of men reported having experienced sexual harassment within the past five years (Burda, 1996). While this still amounts to a large number of people, it is a lower rate than has been found among broader samples of workers.

Victims of sexual harassment report feelings ranging from embarrassment and humiliation to depression, anxiety, and powerlessness, and they also report psychosomatic illnesses.

The issue of sexual harassment was first brought up in 1979 by the Working Women's Institute, a nonprofit organization established to support education and lobbying efforts on women's behalf. In 1980, the U.S. Equal Employment

Opportunity Commission issued guidelines on sexual harassment, defining it as a form of sex discrimination and a violation of Title VII of the 1964 Civil Rights Act.

Ironically, it was while working at the Equal Employment Opportunity Commission (EEOC) that Anita Hill claims she was harassed by her then supervisor, Clarence Thomas. At Judge Thomas's Supreme Court confirmation hearings, Hill accused Thomas of having repeatedly made sexual comments to her. Hill said she had not come forward while working at the EEOC for fear of losing her job. Thomas denied these allegations and was ultimately confirmed as a Supreme Court Justice. Another case, less publicized, involves fifty-one-year-old neurosurgeon Frances Conley. As professor of medicine at Stanford University, she allegedly endured sexual harassment from male colleagues—lewd jokes and inappropriate touching. Like Anita Hill, Dr. Conley didn't report the sexual harassment when it was going on for fear of jeopardizing her career.

Why didn't these women stand up to the men sexually harassing them at the time of the harassment, even at the risk of losing their jobs? Isn't it a weaker stance to wait ten years to invoke a feminist principle instead of fighting back on the spot?

One difficulty with this issue is the subjective nature of the offense: What one person calls sexual harassment may be considered flattery or harmless banter by another. In other words, it's only harassment if the victim (usually a woman) feels the behavior is inappropriate, and that might depend on her ethnic, religious, and/or cultural background and tolerance for outspoken sexual innuendos. Some men, on the other hand, may be unable or unwilling to understand where to draw the line between harmless sexual banter and grossly inappropriate or threatening behavior in a work environment. One young doctor at the University of California medical school complained of harassment when she was asked on dates by two doctors who were supposed to write letters of recommendation for her. Another woman might have felt flattered, or might have wanted to go out with the doctors. Some physical contact, like hugging or putting an arm around a colleague, can be viewed as harassment by women of a certain ethnic background or in certain circumstances, but may be considered a warm gesture or harmless flirting by other women. If a woman feels a colleague's behavior is inappropriate, then it is her obligation to say so, verbally or in writing. Once she has done so, the colleague is obligated to stop the behavior. However, in the atmosphere of intimidation that often accompanies sexual harassment, speaking out can be difficult to do. This is particularly the case because the person doing the harassing is usually more powerful than the person who is harassed. In such a situation, victims often fear that if they object to the harassment, they will be penalized.

Because of the ambiguities sometimes involved, it can be difficult for a court to determine if sexual harassment has actually taken place. Courts have generally determined that it is not necessarily the advances themselves that violate the Civil Rights Act, but the continuation of such advances once it is known that they are unwanted. The loss of tangible job benefits or the existence of an intimidating, hostile, or offensive work environment also have been recognized by courts as illegal sexual harassment.

Some analysts contend that sexual harassment is a way for some men who feel threatened by the emergence of women in the workplace to tell them, "You don't belong here. You're not welcome here." According to that theory, harassment isn't about sex, but about power and intimidation of women—making them feel unwelcome and undermining their job competence by treating them as sex objects. In fact, the most serious cases of harassment, involving threats of job loss or repeated sexual overtures, usually involve advances by a supervisor.

Many of the same issues also apply to student-faculty relationships in colleges and universities. Just as is the case between supervisors and workers, an unequal power relationship exists between professors and their students that can easily be abused. Is accepting a date truly voluntary when a student is asked out by a professor (or teaching assistant), knowing that the professor or teaching assistant controls the grade the student will get? Most researchers on sexual harassment argue that it is not, and cite many cases where students felt they had little choice but to say yes. For this reason, growing numbers of colleges and universities have adopted sexual harassment policies that forbid or discourage relationships between instructors and students for whom they have grading responsibility.

Functionalist and Conflict Perspectives on Gender Roles

Thus far, our discussion of sexism has focused on the forces that maintain sexual inequality. Another fundamental question is this: *Why does sexism exist in the first place?* To understand the fundamental causes of sexism, it is useful to consider the functionalist and conflict perspectives. These perspectives address such questions as what purpose or purposes are served by sexism, why societies establish social roles and social inequality along the lines of gender, and why societies teach these unequal roles to succeeding generations.

The Origins of Gender Inequality

No one has the answer of how gender stratification began in human societies, but there are a few theories (Blumberg, 1984; Chafetz, 1990; Collins, 1986; Huber and Spitze, 1983). The most common theory goes something like this: When humans were in hunter and gatherer societies, women had a great deal of power and influence. Stratification was nearly nonexistent in general, and while there was some inequality based on sex, it was not as great as what would come later in agricultural and industrial societies. Evidence suggests that in a few tribes, women may have been nearly equal to the men. There seems to have been a good deal of gender variance in terms of power and status. Women played a central role in the two most important functions of hunter and gatherer life. They gave birth to and cared for the children, and they did the majority of the gathering, which was what sustained the bands. This put them at the heart of economic production in these societies.

But as societies developed agriculture something happened. The work got more physical, further from the domestic sphere (out into the fields), and more dangerous. It was not the kind of labor that could be done while also caring for the children or while pregnant as was the case with gathering. Warfare became necessary to defend families and communities from outsiders. It is during the agricultural ages that surplus, wealth, and power are developed in human societies for the first time. Thus, women are separated from the means of production just at the time that wealth, power, and inequality rear their heads in human societies. This leaves men with nearly complete control over these crucial resources. And thus, the theory goes, the stage is set for gender inequality.

In many ways women began to gain more equality back during the industrial age, but not initially. At first, they lost even more ground as jobs became further removed from the home and women's secondary status increased. Only later did this begin to recede as women fought for their rights during the Suffragette movements and other struggles. Yet this process of male dominance is not inevitable, as the societies discovered by Margaret Mead prove (discussed earlier). There is no denying, however, that such societies remain very much the exception not the rule. Mead's research has also been challenged by some, and it seems clear that the societies she discovered have now been changed by contact with the outside world, but her main point remains solid. Gender is socially constructed. It does not have to look like it does in our society. A few ancient societies like the Minoan Crete had very peaceful, wealthy, more feminine societies that might have created very different gender stratification patterns had their cultures survived to evolve across time to the present day. We will never know. Natural disaster or more militarized societies eventually wiped them out. We now take a look at what the modern sociological perspectives

Functionalists argue that traditional gender roles contribute to family cohesiveness, while conflict theorists argue that the main beneficiaries of such gender roles are men. What do you think? (Courtesy of Michael Flota)

have to say about the development of modern gender roles that stemmed from the mysterious origins of stratification.

The Functionalist Perspective

One common school of thought among functionalist sociologists is that, whether or not gender roles perform any important functions for society today, they certainly did in the past. These sociologists note that until about a century ago, most women spent much of their young adult lives either pregnant or taking care of infants. Infant and child mortality was very high, and in order to have two or three children survive to adulthood, a woman often had to give birth to five or six. In those days, of course, there was no baby formula, so having babies meant breast-feeding. For these reasons, women had to remain in the home with the children a large part of the time, which probably explains, among other things, why hunting has been consistently performed by males across different societies.

A second consideration is physical strength. Because of their larger physical size, men are—on average—more capable of tasks that involve heavy lifting or moving large objects. At a time when most work was physical in nature, this difference probably led to some gender-role specialization. Thus, frequent pregnancy and long periods of breast-feeding, together with differences in physical strength, explain why gender-role specialization was functional in the past. But what of today?

Gender Roles as Cultural Lag

Some sociologists believe that gender roles exist today mainly as a result of *cultural lag*. Gender roles were functional in the past, but have no use to society today, according to this view. Nonetheless, they persist because society is slow to change. Gender roles, and the norms that support them, have become engrained in our culture, which is passed from generation to generation through the socialization process. Thus, they disappear only gradually. This viewpoint suggests that if gender roles are no longer functional, they will persist for some time but will become weaker with each new generation, because they have no use in today's society. A case can be made that this is in fact happening. As we shall see in more detail later, there have been major changes in the gender-role attitudes of Americans and people in many other modern societies. Nonetheless, many sociologists disagree with this interpretation. Some argue that gender roles are beneficial to society in other ways; others explain their existence from the conflict perspective. Let us consider the former group first.

Are Gender Roles Still Functional?

Most functionalists who argue that gender roles are still useful focus on the family. Some argue that gender roles permit a desirable form of specialization within the family, and others argue that traditional gender roles are conducive to family cohesiveness.

Gender Roles and Family Specialization. The notion that gender roles facilitate specialization within the family is largely associated with the writings of Talcott Parsons and Robert Bales (1955). They based their arguments on research showing that in organizations and groups performing tasks, two types of leaders typically emerge: instrumental leaders, whose main concern is getting the job done, and expressive leaders, whose role is to address the feelings of people in the group and the relations among those people. (This issue is addressed in greater detail in Chapter 9.) Parsons and Bales argued that, as a small group, the family needs both instrumental and expressive leadership. They saw the traditional male role as filling the family's need for instrumental leadership and the traditional female role as providing expressive leadership. Thus, a role division that emphasizes the man's getting the jobs done and providing income and the woman's taking care of social and emotional needs is seen as functional for the family.

Parsons's and Bales's functionalist explanation of gender roles has been strongly criticized by other sociologists for two reasons. First, even though the family might need both instrumental and expressive leadership, there is no clear reason why the instrumental leadership must come from the male and the expressive leadership from the female. It could just as well happen the other way around. Second, this functionalist explanation does not consider the possible dysfunctions of restricting women to the expressive role, which will be addressed shortly.

Gender Roles and Family Cohesion. A more contemporary functionalist argument centers around the cohesiveness of the family. This argument holds that traditional, male-dominated families experienced less divisiveness because women did not think and act independently of their husbands. Thus, as women have become more free and independent, family conflict has increased. Those who support this view often cite statistics showing that as women obtain work outside the home, the likelihood of their marriages ending through divorce rises. Finally, some people argue that when mothers work outside the home, their children suffer. These people claim that when children are in day care or must come home from school to an empty house, their mental health suffers, and they become at high risk for juvenile delinquency, drug and alcohol abuse, and teenage pregnancy.

Although some of these issues will be addressed in later chapters, several important facts relevant to these arguments can be noted here. First, time-budget studies indicate that full-time working mothers interact with their children about as much as do full-time housewives (Farley, 1977, pp. 197–202; Goldberg, cited in Hodgson, 1979; Robinson, 1977; Nock and Kingston, 1988; Benokraitis, 1993, pp. 318–19), although housewives may spend more time on care-related tasks (Hodgson, 1979; Vanek, 1973, pp. 138, 172). Women's satisfaction with their roles, whether in the home or at work, seems to be a much better predictor: Women who are more satisfied spend more time interacting with their children (Hodgson, 1979). Sometimes there are problems of supervision of children, but as we shall see in greater detail in Web-Based Chapter A, these are largely the product of the limited availability of quality day care. In general, children in properly planned and supervised day-care centers do as well as children raised at home (Hayes and Kamerman, 1983; Hoffmann, 1989; Phillips, McCartney, and Scarr, 1987; Berg, 1986). There may be an increasing tendency among adults to put their own concerns ahead of the welfare of their children (Popenoe, 1988). This tendency exists among both men and women, however, and cannot simply be attributed to changing gender roles.

With respect to family cohesion, it is true that women who work outside the home are at greater risk of divorce than housewives. This might be because dual-earner couples have less time to spend together (see Kingston and Nock, 1987). However, a more important reason is that working women are financially more able to leave an unhappy marriage. According to Thornton and Freedman (1984, pp. 27–28), social science research provides no clear evidence that families with the wife in the labor force are any less happy than families where the wife remains at home. Thus, changing gender roles may have altered how women *respond* when they find themselves in an unhappy or troubled home situation, but there is no evidence that the actual incidence of such situations has increased.

Dysfunctions of Gender Roles

Any functionalist analysis of gender roles must also consider their dysfunctions. In what ways do they *inhibit* the effectiveness of society, the family, or the individual? One area in which there is evidence of such dysfunctions is psychological well-being. Among both men and women, people with a *mix* of masculine and feminine personality traits have higher self-esteem and better mental health than those in whom traditional gender traits predominate (Deutsch and Gilbert, 1976; Lamke, 1982; Major et al., 1981; Orlovsky, 1977; Spence et al., 1975). Moreover, *androgynous* individuals—those with some of the traditional traits of each sex—display greater flexibility in various aspects of behavior (Ickes and Barnes, 1978; LaFrance and Carmen, 1980). These findings suggest that in terms of personal adjustment, self-esteem, and flexibility, adherence to a traditional gender role can be dysfunctional. These researchers conclude that women show better self-esteem, flexibility, and role performance when they have both masculine and feminine traits. Specifically in terms of roles, there is also evidence that women who are employed outside the home either part time or full time are happier on average and less at risk for depression than those who are full-time homemakers (National Center for Health Statistics, 1980; Hoffmann, 1989; Baruch, Barnett, and Rivers, 1983; Gallup, 1989, pp. 164–65, Hoyenga and Hoyenga, 1979).

From a broader functionalist perspective, one might raise serious questions about the benefits to society of denying half of its adult population the opportunity to develop fully their creativity, productive capacity, and freedom of choice. From a purely economic standpoint, the only thing that saved the typical American family from a substantial decline in its standard of living during the economically difficult 1970s and 1980s was the massive entry of women into the labor force (Olsen, 1990). Productivity growth and real hourly wages (hourly pay adjusted for the effects of inflation) generally lagged from the mid-1970s until several years into the 1990s. Millions of wives and mothers entered the labor force in part to compensate for the resultant loss of income. Had this not occurred, the standard of living of many Americans would have declined substantially between about 1973 and 1993. For many American families, the standard of living would still be lower today than forty years ago, had women not entered the labor force and thereby provided a substantial part of their families' incomes.

The Conflict Perspective

Conflict theorists ask: Who benefits from gender roles as they exist in America? The answer, they believe, is that men benefit from them. (For comprehensive statements of this view, see Collins, 1971a; Reskin, 1988.) Conflict theorists also ask: Does the group that benefits have disproportionate power, so that it can arrange society to its advantage? With respect to gender roles, they note the great power of men, something we have already discussed in reference to the political system, the family, and the world of work. Thus, gender roles persist because men use their power to maintain a system from which they benefit.

How do men benefit from traditional gender roles? We have already seen many ways in this chapter. Men receive higher wages than women and have a better chance of getting jobs that offer status, autonomy, and authority. Men enjoy greater mobility and freedom in choosing how to spend their time—their jobs take them outside the home, and if the family owns just one automobile, it is likely to be the husband's. Even in today's typical two-worker, two-car family, men still enjoy advantages. For example, when both husband and wife are employed full time, the total work week of men—on the job and in the home—is shorter than that of women. In terms of income, wealth, status, power, and free time, all indications are that traditional gender roles work to the advantage of men. As shown in the box entitled "The Costs of the Male Gender Role to Men (and Women?)," there are other areas in which men pay a price for these benefits. Even so, the material benefits of gender roles to men are real. Thus, it is hardly surprising that men would use their power to maintain such gender roles.

Sources of Male Power

One question that conflict theorists ask is this: How did males achieve unequal power in the first place? One explanation, which involves a combination of functionalist and conflict theory, is that male power is the outgrowth of a role specialization that was once useful to society. Although assigning roles to men that took them outside the home was originally useful, it also gave men certain power that women didn't have. It gave them greater freedom of movement and more contact with the outside world, and it made women dependent upon them for basic food supplies obtained through hunting or through agricultural labor in the fields. All this translated into male power, and once males had this power, they began to use it to their advantage, setting up a society that became increasingly male-dominated.

Some conflict theorists add a second line of reasoning to this. They argue that size and physical strength were sources of power that males used to get what they wanted from women. In the United States, China, and many other societies, wives used to be seen largely as their husbands' property. Certainly, the use or threat of violence is an important source of power, and it probably played a major role in the establishment of male dominance.

Today, of course, the law forbids violence by men against women, although even now the courts and police are often reluctant to intervene if such violence occurs within the family. Physical strength is largely irrelevant to most jobs, so occupational specialization by sex is far less functional than it once was. Yet today, there are other mechanisms by which men retain disproportionate power. To a large extent, we have already seen what these are—disproportionate political power and control of money within the family.

Feminism: A Challenge to Male Power

In the United States and many other societies throughout the world (particularly those with

SOCIOLOGICAL SURPRISES
The Costs of the Male Gender Role to Men (and Women?)

Although men benefit from sexism in terms of income, wealth, and power, sexism exacts some high costs in other areas of their lives. Men as well as women are denied certain freedoms by sexism. In fact, the pressure to "be a man" that males experience from early childhood probably exceeds anything that women encounter, and it takes a toll on men in a variety of ways, including their health. And similarly, as women slowly gain ground on men in terms of wealth, income, and power, they may also be suffering consequences from some of the harmful aspects of the expectations tied to what once were male roles.

The traditional expectation has been that men are supposed to be in control of every situation (which, of course, is not always possible) and to avoid any public display of emotion. Neither expressions of tenderness nor emotional breakdowns or outbursts have traditionally been seen as acceptable male behavior. Such pressures on men exact a high cost in terms of mental and physical health. In all likelihood, they are at least part of the reason why men are more likely than women to abuse alcohol and other drugs and are far more inclined to commit violence—the overwhelming majority of assaults and murders are committed by males, usually against other males. Many stress-related illnesses are also more common among men than among women, including heart disease, high blood pressure, and ulcers. Although men are often under less stress than women, they are expected to handle stress differently, always maintaining outward calm and control. Women, in contrast, have traditionally had more opportunities to release the tension by expressing their emotions. Compared to men, women also receive much more encouragement to talk with their friends about feelings, emotions, and personal concerns and problems. Men, in contrast, are usually encouraged to keep such feelings inside, in order to appear "in control." Rather than viewing their friends as confidants, they are more likely to see them as "playmates"—for example, golfing, bowling, or fishing buddies. These are among the reasons that women outlive men by more than five years on average.

Thus, a move toward a more androgynous society may offer opportunities for men and risks for women, depending on how it occurs. Men today undoubtedly feel more free to express their emotions than they did in the past. There is a growing recognition of the role of emotional expression in the mental health of both men and women. Conversely, as women move into traditionally male roles, they may experience some of the same pressures men feel, especially if they simply adopt those roles rather than defining them in new ways. In fact, there is startling evidence already of the harm that may occur if women merely adopt male gender roles "as is." While women do still live longer than men, the gap has narrowed significantly over the past two decades as the roles and expectations of women and men have become more similar. Between about 1980 and 1999, the life expectancy of men in the United States increased by about 3.9 years; in the same period the life expectancy of women increased only about 2.0 years (U.S. Census Bureau, 2000c; National Center for Health Statistics, 2001b). Thus, the life-expectancy gap between women and men was narrowed by nearly two years. Today average life expectancy for a woman is 80.7 years, and for men, it is 75.4 years (Brown, 2008). In 1980, the average woman outlived the average man in the United States by about seven and a half years; today, the gap is down to less than five and a half years.

---

higher levels of industrialization), one of the major social changes of recent decades has been the emergence of **feminism** on a large scale. Essentially, the governing principles of feminism as an ideology and social movement are that women should enjoy the same rights in society as men and that they should share equally in society's opportunities and in its scarce resources, such as income, power, status, and personal freedom.

Origins of Feminism in America

In the United States feminism can be traced back more than 150 years. The movement is generally regarded as having begun with an 1848 meeting in Seneca Falls, New York, which set forth a statement of women's rights modeled after the Declaration of Independence. For the next seventy years, the major objective of this movement was to obtain the vote for women (only men were allowed to vote in the national elections in the United States until 1920). The early feminist movement didn't succeed in changing other aspects of sex discrimination in America, however, for several reasons (Degler, 1980). First, women in that era saw some advantages in the housewife role, which was then something new. As income-producing work shifted from the home to separate workplaces, men pursued it. Their wives often remained at home, feeling protected from the dangers of the workplace, which at that time were very real. Second, just getting women the vote was a tremendous battle because opponents (as well as many supporters) of women's suffrage believed that if women got the vote, they would overturn the political order by voting in ways radically different from men. (They didn't.) After the suffrage battle was won, feminism as an issue faded for a time, only to resurface in the 1960s and 1970s in a form that amounted to a much wider and more fundamental challenge to traditional gender roles.

Contemporary Feminism

By the 1970s, U.S. feminists were challenging the housewife role in a way the earlier movement never did, and they had some real successes. For example, women have moved out of the home and into the paid labor force in unprecedented numbers over the past four decades. As shown in Figure 8.4, a clear majority of married women are in the paid labor force, and by 2009, half of the U.S. labor force was composed of women. Even among women with young children, a sizable majority work outside the home for pay. In large part, this trend reflects economic necessity, as well as changed views about the role of women. For working-class and poor women, economic necessity is the main force behind the trend, while for wealthier, more educated women, the desire to have a career is more important. Among all classes, however, the notion that women should remain in the home has lost favor, particularly among younger women.

As more and more women left the role of housewife for that of paid worker, the feminist movement increasingly addressed other issues. The right to equal pay for equal (or comparable) work has been a major issue, as has been the right to be free from sexual harassment at work and at school. Issues outside the workplace have also taken on increased importance, as feminists have increasingly objected to the fact that women do a disproportionate share of housework. Feminists have also placed a high priority on reproductive freedom, emphasizing issues such as the right to choose whether to have an abortion and opposition to any restrictions on the availability of birth control.

Some feminist issues have been of particular concern among women of color and working-class women. For example, the issue of sexual harassment has had special importance for African American women, because in addition to the risk of sexual harassment that all women face, African American women have often been expected to submit to white males because of *racial* inequality as well as gender inequality. This, in turn, "contributed to images of black women as fair game for all men" (Collins, 1991, p. 54).

African American and Hispanic women must also face low-wage work—often in service occupations—that results from a lack of opportunity arising from both racial and gender inequality. The loss of jobs in many black and Hispanic neighborhoods has also resulted in a shortage of potential mates for inner-city black and Hispanic women (Wilson, 1987, 1996). The reason for this is that as manufacturing jobs have left inner cities, black and Hispanic men have experienced rising joblessness, rendering growing numbers of them unable to provide support for a family. In an era in which most unmarried adults are sexually active, in a context of poverty that limits access to and knowledge of contraceptives, and in a society where birth outside marriage has become increasingly accepted, the result of this gender imbalance in inner cities has been predictable: a rise in the number of single-parent, female-householder families. At the same time, as low-paying service jobs have replaced the old manufacturing jobs, black and Hispanic women have often been hired for these low-paying jobs (Wilson, 1996). One consequence is that those women are more likely to be the sole support of their families—and the low-wage work available to them is often inadequate for this purpose. This trend, already in place, has likely been worsened by welfare reform, which has increased the supply of service workers with limited education (and thereby holds down their wages).

The result of these different experiences has been the emergence of different modes of feminist thought among women of color and working-class women. While they emphasize some of the same

Figure 8.4 Percentage of Women in the Paid Labor Force, by Marital Status and Presence and Age of Children, 2009

	Total			With Children 17 or Younger							
				Total			Children 6 to 17 Years Only			Children Under 6 Years		
	Single	Married	Widowed, Divorced, Separated	Single	Married	Widowed, Divorced, Separated	Single	Married	Widowed, Divorced, Separated	Single	Married	Widowed, Divorced, Separated
Percent	64.7	61.6	49.5	71.4	69.3	80.0	78.0	76.2	82.9	67.4	61.5	72.2

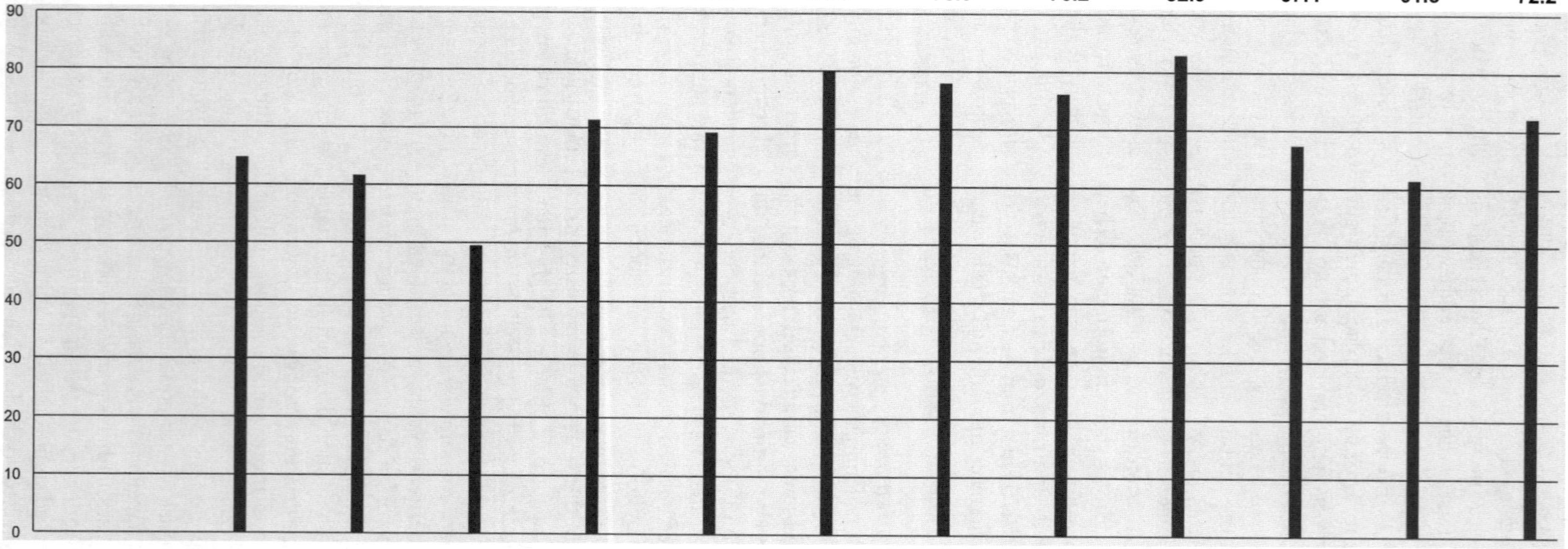

Source: U.S. Census Bureau, 2010, Labor Force, Employment, and Earnings: Labor Force Status, http://www.census.gov/compendia/statab/cats/labor_force_employment_earnings/labor_force_status.html (Accessed July 23, 2010).

issues that feminism has always stressed, these varieties of feminism also raise issues of particular concern to working-class women and women of color (Collins, 2000; hooks, 1981, 1991; Davis, 1981; Lorde, 1992; Higginbotham, 1992).

The growing influence of feminism has not been limited to the United States. Other countries had suffrage movements during the nineteenth century parallel to that of the United States (Flexner, 1975). Since the 1960s (and in some cases earlier), resurgent feminist movements have been important social forces throughout the industrialized world, and feminism has been a growing influence in the Third World as well (Ward, 1984, pp. 36–37).

Social Origins of the New Feminism

Why has feminism become so influential? Although the reasons vary somewhat from country to country, certain conditions have appeared in a number of countries. First, traditional gender roles have become less functional in modern societies, for reasons noted earlier in this chapter. Conditions also developed in many countries that made women less satisfied with their traditional roles. Women were becoming more educated but were not getting the opportunity to use that education. During World War II, women were pressed into nontraditional roles in many countries, including performing manual labor in defense plants, and they found that they could be effective in those roles. They also found that under the right conditions, they could be well rewarded for work outside the home. Although many women were happy to return to their traditional roles after the war, they realized that they could succeed in other roles, and this may have had the long-term effect of making them more interested in nontraditional roles. Also during this time, the growth of mass media throughout the world enhanced communication, which made it easier for feminist leaders to transmit their message to other dissatisfied women.

Finally, the 1960s was a period of worldwide social upheaval that witnessed the antiwar and Civil Rights movements in the United States, the student and labor upheavals in France, the Cultural Revolution in China, the struggle for political freedom in Czechoslovakia, and the beginning or reemergence of several ongoing struggles: the separatist movement in Quebec, the religious conflict in Northern Ireland, and movements that led to majority rule in South Africa and Zimbabwe (then Rhodesia).

Women were involved in all of these struggles, but they often found themselves relegated to such nonleadership roles as preparing meals, stuffing envelopes, and running errands. This had three effects. First, involvement in these movements made women realize that they, too, could create a movement. Second, the limited role allowed to women in many of these social movements heightened their dissatisfaction. Third, these movements brought dissatisfied women together, so they could communicate with each other and organize a movement of their own (Freeman, 1973). Together, these conditions greatly accelerated the development of feminist movements in many countries.

Feminist Social Theory

While feminism has been an influential social movement, it has also been a major influence on theory in sociology and the other social sciences in recent decades. **Feminist theory** can in many ways be linked to the conflict perspective, but it is different from other conflict theories in that it places greater emphasis on understanding the causes and consequences of gender inequality. In so doing, it offers us a fuller understanding of social processes than other theories—even other conflict theories—that have often left gender out. The ways in which feminist theory adds to our understanding of society can be seen throughout this book. For example, Meda Chesney-Lind (see the box "Doing Feminist Criminology," Chapter 10) shows us that theories about the causes of juvenile delinquency—based on studies of male delinquents—cannot explain female delinquency. One reason for this is that the processes by which youth are labeled delinquent are very different for boys and girls. In Chapter 14, we explore the important contributions of feminist theory to the development of conflict theories about urbanization and urban life. In fact, the physical character of the modern city can be tied to the division of labor by gender: Downtown financial districts became largely a male domain, whereas residential areas became a female domain. This could not have happened had modernization not led to a gendered division of labor, when work was taken outside the home. But this change in the location and gender division of work in turn had profound effects on the form and activities of the city.

Ecofeminism

A relatively new feminist theory that gained influence during the 1990s is ecofeminism. This holistic theory is an excellent example of how feminist theory has been helpful in understanding a broader array of social arrangements. Ecofeminism makes important linkages between the subordination of women and other destructive processes. These include harm to the natural environment, colonization, and exploitation of indigenous peoples around the world (Merchant, 1992, 1989; Adams, 1993; Gaard, 1993; Mies and Shiva, 1993; Seager, 1993). The theory of ecofeminism holds that there has been a linkage throughout the development of Western civilization between male domination of women and an ideology of the dominance of man over nature. These twin themes can be tracked to the early history of Western civilization, through analysis of sources ranging from biblical authors to writers describing the dominant beliefs of classical Greek city-states (Merchant, 1996). The basic ideology that is revealed in these sources is the belief that it is naturally ordained that men should be in control—of women, of the political system, and of land and nature (Shiva, 1990). This ideology of male control becomes both a cause of and a justifying argument in support of a wide range of destructive activity, including exploitation of the environment for profit, the subordination of women and their exclusion from positions of power, and the conquest and colonization of the Third World (Shiva, 1990; Merchant, 1996; 1989). It has been linked, for example, to the once-popular American notion of Manifest Destiny—the belief that God had destined European Americans to rule the North American continent from coast to coast. This ideology was used to justify the forcible removal of Native Americans from their homeland and the subjugation of Mexican Americans in the Southwest. It also contributed to the wholesale exploitation and destruction of natural resources in the American West, such as slaughter of the buffalo of the Great Plains and the destruction of over 90 percent of all old-growth forest in the United States (Deloria, 1994; Merchant, 1996).

Of course, this attitude of male dominance and control has also led to limits being placed on the roles and power of women throughout European and American history. What is new and important about ecofeminism is that it shows that the forces that have led to male domination of women over the centuries are much the same forces that have led to worldwide damage to the environment over the past century. The development of technology combined with an ideology of dominance and control has made possible great damage to the environment (Seager, 1993). As our ability to manufacture, produce energy, and extract even trace amounts of valued minerals from the earth has increased, so has our ability to create irreversible damage. Ecofeminism holds that the male ideology of dominance and control has often led Western societies to go ahead and do exactly that. Usually this has occurred at the expense of both the environment and non-Western peoples around the world. In these regions, resources are often extracted for the enrichment of Western interests or the wealthy elite of Third World countries. Rarely, however, has the general indigenous population benefited. Thus, the male ideology of dominance and control becomes as great a threat to the environment as it is to women, and it has also led to considerable exploitation and conquest of non-European populations around the world.

Some varieties of ecofeminism have also argued that the historical linkage of women to roles associated with food production and nurturance has led them to adopt a caretaker role with respect to the environment. Those who hold this view point out that women have played a prominent role in many environmental movements (Salleh, 1991). A case in point is northern India's Chipko movement. There, indigenous women, who for centuries have engaged in gathering activities in the forests of the Himalayan foothills, formed a movement to stop logging companies from cutting the forests that are the source of their livelihood (Dasgupta, 1995; Jain, 1984; Khator, 1989). The movement's name, Chipko, is similar in meaning to the expression "tree-hugger" that has been used to describe participants in similar movements in the United States. The Chipko movement has been successful in thwarting many attempts to log northern India's forests. Significantly, the movement has been mostly a women's movement, and in some instances has encountered opposition from local male populations who are less tied to gathering activities in the forests and who see the logging companies as a potential source of jobs (Dasgupta, 1995). Ecofeminists see such examples as illustrating the point that women are often in roles that lead them to protect the environment, whereas men are more likely to be in roles that may tempt them to damage it.

It should be noted, however, that this aspect of ecofeminism is not without its critics. Some feminists see it as a subtle justification of the distinct traditional roles of women (Rose, 1993). Others, however, counter that feminism is not about the idea that women should simply adopt male roles (Warren, 1993). Ecofeminists stress that, if this should happen, the forces that lead to destruction of the environment would continue unabated. A better approach would be for male roles to be adjusted to incorporate valuable aspects of traditional female roles. This would include rejecting the "dominate and control" ideology, which has been so much a part of the male role in Western society, in favor of greater emphasis on living in harmony with one's environment and one's fellow humans (Seager, 1993; Merchant, 1996).

Finally, ecofeminism cautions us against ethnocentrism in our thinking about gender roles in non-Western societies, given the strong tradition in Western societies of male dominance of both women and the environment. In no instance has such ethnocentrism been more widespread than in Western portrayals of gender roles in Islamic societies. In this chapter's Global Sociology box on pages 252–53, it is shown how far from reality such portrayals sometimes fall.

How Are Gender Roles Changing in America?

In this final section, we shall assess the meaning of recent changes in sex and gender roles in America and address some information that may give us an idea where our society is headed. We shall begin by noting areas in which norms concerning relations between men and women have changed.

Sexual Double Standard

Society's views concerning the sexual freedom of men and women have changed dramatically over the past few decades. The Victorian sexual double standard assumed that sex was to be enjoyed by men and that it was normal for unmarried men to want to "fool around." Women, however, were expected to remain pure and were considered "too good" to enjoy sex. As a result, sexual activity among unmarried males was largely taken for granted (even if somewhat disapproved of). For unmarried women, though, it was much more seriously forbidden, and a good deal less common. By the late 1960s, however, that system had changed (Christiansen and Gregg, 1970). Since then, norms about sexual behavior have been more similar for men and women than in the past, as have the behaviors themselves (Hunt, 1974).

Employment Discrimination

Another area in which there has been major change is the law. The Civil Rights Act of 1964 forbade deliberate discrimination against women in hiring and wages. Since then, it has been illegal to refuse to hire a person because of sex, unless the employer can prove that sex is a bona fide factor in a person's ability to perform a particular job, which is rarely the case. Similarly, you cannot pay an employee less (or, for that matter, more) than other employees in the same job with similar qualifications simply on the basis of that person's sex. Moreover, the government has often interpreted this law as requiring employers to take affirmative action to ensure that women have the same opportunities as men to get the more desirable jobs. Since 1980, this policy has been reversed several times, with Republican administrations generally rejecting the notion that employers should take such affirmative action, while Democratic administrations, including the Obama administration, have supported it. Its future remains in doubt, as it is being challenged in both the legal and political arenas.

Sexual Assault

At the level of state law, there have been important changes in the rules of evidence concerning sexual assault. In the past, a rape victim practically had to prove to the court that she did not bring on the rape by her own behavior. She was asked questions about her past sexual behavior, as well as her past relationship with the person charged with raping her. Often, if a woman indicated that she had been sexually active in the past or had previously been involved with the accused, it was assumed that she really had

GLOBAL SOCIOLOGY

Treatment of Women: Comparing the Western and Islamic Traditions

As Merchant and other ecofeminists point out, the belief that it is natural for men to dominate women is deeply rooted in Western religion and philosophy. In Athens, in ancient Greece, for example, arranged marriages were common, and daughters had to accept the husbands chosen for them by their parents. And in Rome, when a woman married, her property passed to her husband, and women were forbidden from having any role in government or law. Among the Jews in the era of the Old Testament, a common arrangement was "betrothal," under which a woman was purchased from her parents to become a man's wife. Men, but not women, could divorce their spouses. And among early Christians, women were seen as evil, because the Bible portrays Eve as tempting Adam to eat the forbidden fruit. For example, in the Catholic version of the Bible, the following verse is found: "No wickedness comes anywhere near the wickedness of a woman.... Sin began with a woman and thanks to her we all must die" (Ecclesiasticus 25:19,24). Both the Christians and the Jews had the same inheritance rule as the Romans: Women could inherit nothing. Although Western nations, Judaism, and Christianity all, to varying degrees, view women in a more positive light today, their historical roots are full of unabashed sexism.

Despite this history, today it is not the West but rather Islam that is often portrayed as subjugating women. Perhaps this is the case because of the harsh treatment of women under the Taliban regime in Afghanistan, or perhaps it is a reaction to the wearing of veils by some Muslim women. But how well does this portrayal fit reality? Not well at all, historically, and very unevenly today. Ironically in light of Islam's image, Islam was the first of today's major world religion to take the view that marriage should be a choice between a man and a woman, not imposed on women by men (Azeem, 1995). And unlike the Christian and Jewish scriptures, the Qu'ran's version of the Adam and Eve story portrays their sin as a decision of both, not something that Eve did first, then convinced Adam to do. And it was Islam that broke from the long-standing tradition (true also among Arabs before Islam) of male-only inheritance: Thirteen hundred years before Europe recognized female inheritance, the Qu'ran proclaimed that both male and female children should receive a share of all inheritances.

One might, of course, point out that the above comparisons of Christianity, Judaism, and Islam come from the past. What of today? The answer is that, among peoples of all religions, actual treatment of women varies widely from place to place. Certainly that is true of Islam. The roles and statuses of Muslim women in such far-flung places as Afghanistan, Egypt, several of the countries that emerged out of the Soviet Union, Bosnia, and the United States (which has around 6 million Muslims) vary widely, as the status of women varies widely among these different societies. In some traditional societies, such as Saudi Arabia and Afghanistan under the Taliban, Muslim women have been severely restricted and subjugated. In others, such as the republics south of Russia, they are well educated and career-oriented. And in yet others, such as some Western nations, they have become caught up in the same consumerism and "looking good to please men" pattern as is found among women of many religious and ethnic

engaged in sex voluntarily, or at least had misled the accused person into thinking she really wanted to have sex. In some cases, assumptions were made about the victim's sexual availability simply on the basis of how she dressed. In a sense, the victim was on trial, and if her past or present behavior was found wanting, judges and juries rejected the possibility that a crime might have taken place. Most states, however, have recently passed laws restricting the kinds of questions that can be asked of rape victims. It can no longer be assumed in most states that if a woman once wanted to have sex, she always will in the future, which is what the old patterns of questioning tended to assume. Still, rape victims are often subjected to personal and embarrassing questioning, and as a result many rapes still go unreported and thus unprosecuted.

Sex, Gender, and Society

backgrounds in those societies. However, these various cultural characteristics reflect differences among these larger societies, not rules of Islam. And there are similar variations in views about the role of women within other religions, including Christianity. Just among Protestants in the United States, the range of views runs from fundamentalist Christian groups who believe that the place for the woman is in the home and that abortion is murder, to liberal sects that ordain women as bishops and oppose any legal restrictions upon abortion. So what, exactly, is the "Christian" position today?

Finally, even the veil, today associated with Muslims, turns out to be Judeo-Christian in origin. According to Rabbi Dr. Menachem M. Brayer of Yeshiva University, ancient Jewish women were required to wear veils whenever in public, sometimes exposing only one eye. Brayer (1986) quotes ancient Rabbis as saying, "It is not like the daughters of Israel to walk out with heads uncovered." As for Christianity, St. Paul had this to say, "If a woman does not cover her head, she should have her hair cut off; and if it is a disgrace for a woman to have her hair cut off or shaved off, she should cover her head" (I Corinthians 11:3–10). In addition, one should not equate the veil with subjugation of women. Among Muslim women who choose to wear it, many report that they do so because it frees them from being treated as a sexual object by men (Nichols, 2001). A non-Islamic reporter for the BBC found much the same when she filed this report about her interview with two women from the household of an Islamic cleric in Nigeria: "The women talked and in their answers I saw the seeds of my own reevaluations. They argued that the veil signified their rejection of an unacceptable system of values, which debased women, while Islam elevated women to a position of honour and respect. It is not liberation where you say women should go naked. It is just oppression, because men want to see them naked" (Walker, 2001).

Ideas about the role of women vary widely in Islamic countries. Here a Muslim woman works in a business occupation and uses a cell phone, but dresses in a relatively traditional manner. (iStockphoto)

Limitations of Change

Despite some changes, women's efforts to improve their status have met with only limited success. The effect of civil rights legislation on the actual pay received by men and women, for example, has been limited. We have seen that there have been changes, but only modest ones, in the wages of women relative to those of men and in the prevalence of occupational segregation. Thus, the biggest actual change in the status of women, so far, has been the movement of many women out of the housewife role and into the labor force. Although this movement has given women a measure of freedom and independence they did not enjoy in the past, the low pay of employed women remains a major barrier to full sexual equality. In fact, when combined with the increased divorce rate, changes in divorce law, and increased childbearing outside marriage, this low pay has led to a new problem: Being a woman has increasingly become associated with being poor in the United States. As is discussed in the box "Gender and the Financial Effects of Divorce," a major reason for this is that the consequences of divorce differ sharply for men and women.

Public Opinion and Future Prospects for Gender Equality

What are the prospects for a move toward greater equality between American men and women in the future? There are a number of ways we can look for answers to this question. We can start with the attitudes of Americans. It does appear that, in many ways, American attitudes are supportive of gender equality. For example, a national survey in 2000 found the majority of both men and women agreeing that American society must go further in establishing equal rights and equal wages for women (RISMEDIA, 2000). In what Faludi (1991) referred to as a backlash against the women's movement, it was suggested that many women were frustrated that their jobs took them away from their families. However, she points out that the polls for the most part did not support such a view: Women were no more likely than men to express such frustrations, and by a margin of more than 70 percent, women from the mid-1980s to 1990 indicated a preference for high-pressure jobs with advancement opportunities over low-pressure jobs with less opportunity, and rejected the so-called mommy track—less demanding work with shorter hours—because they saw it as a way of paying women less (Faludi, 1991, p. 91).

Since that time, there has been some increased acceptance of the viewpoint that work hours have gotten too long and family and personal life have suffered as a result. However, it is significant that these concerns have arisen among both men and women, and may represent more of a backlash against the increased length of the work week than against the changed roles of women. For example, a 1998 Gallup Poll on how satisfied Americans were with thirteen aspects of quality of life found that the item with the second-lowest level of satisfaction was "the amount of leisure time you have." Moreover, of eight items tracked over time, this one was one of only two that went down rather than up over time. The other one was satisfaction with "your job, or the work you do" (Gallup Organization, 1998). Both of these items suggest a backlash against long, hard work hours, but they are evident among both men and women, so the new trend appears to represent a quality-of-life issue, not primarily a gender issue. Interestingly, satisfaction with leisure time was the only kind of satisfaction that was lower among people of higher socioeconomic status, suggesting some dissatisfaction with the levels of personal sacrifice required of today's professional and managerial workers. This suggests that the work situation, not gender, is the main factor driving this dissatisfaction—though women may well suffer more from long work hours because of the additional hours they put in on household work when they get home from their jobs. In a similar vein, a 2001 Gallup Poll showed that most Americans did not think it was good for both parents to work full-time outside the home—but when asked who, if anyone, should stay home, more than two-thirds said it did not matter whether the mother or father stayed at home (McComb, 2001). This is a dramatic change from the past, when many more said the father should work full time and the mother should stay home.

Of course, generalized support for equal opportunity does not always translate into the reality of equal opportunity. In the economic arena, for example, true equality of opportunity for men and women would require fundamental social changes. One such change would be a major change in current patterns of occupational segregation. Is there any sign that this is happening? In keeping with the finding noted earlier that gifted girls are most likely to aspire to traditionally male occupations, there has been a sharp rise in the number of women training for certain prestigious fields such as law and medicine (see Figure 8.5). However, overall occupational segregation has declined only modestly, and many occupations remain overwhelmingly male or female. As late as 1980, for example, over 95 percent of nurses, secretaries, receptionists, and kindergarten teachers were female, but less than 5 percent of construction workers, engineers, firefighters, and airplane pilots were (Blau and Ferber, 1986, p. 167). Public opinion suggests, though, that occupational segregation will likely continue to decline: In 2001, a Gallup Poll indicated that most Americans would advise young men and women to choose the same careers: Medicine, computers, technology, business or self-employment, or "whatever he or she likes" were the top five choices for both genders—much different from fifty years ago, when most said young women should choose careers in teaching or nursing (Carlson, 2001).

Although full workplace equality probably cannot occur as long as occupational segregation

Figure 8.5 Percentage of Women Among Degree Recipients, Selected Professions, 1949–2008

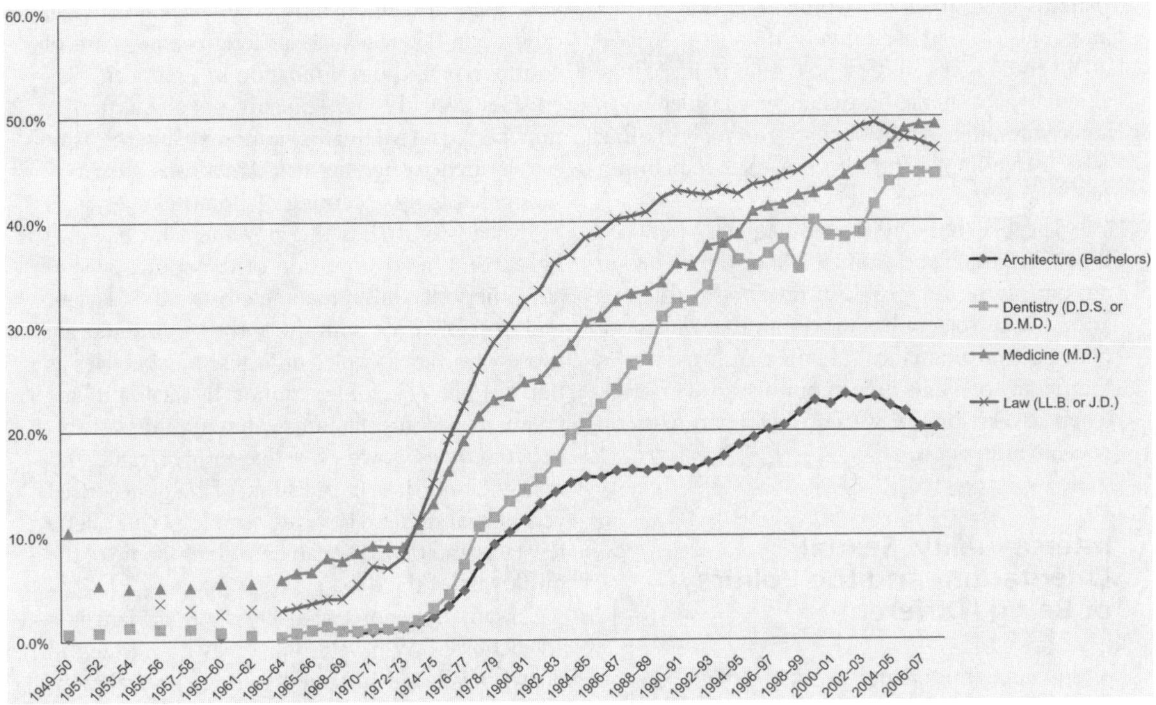

- Architecture (Bachelors)
- Dentistry (D.D.S. or D.M.D.)
- Medicine (M.D.)
- Law (LL.B. or J.D.)

Source: National Center for Education Statistics, 2009 Digest of Education Statistics, Chapter 3, Postsecondary Education, Table 279, http://nces.ed.gov/programs/digest/d09/tables/dt09_279.asp (Accessed July 23, 2010).

persists, major reductions of income inequality could occur even without a change in occupational segregation. For this to happen, however, something similar to comparable worth legislation would have to be implemented. In other words, men and women with comparable skills, education, and experience would have to be paid equal wages, even when they work at different jobs. Significantly, a 2000 Gallup Poll showed that four out of five Americans favored an initiative proposed by the Clinton administration to reduce gender-wage inequality, and 30 percent of women in the poll reported that they believed they were being paid less than they would be if they were male (Saad, 2000).

Comparable worth is unlikely to happen voluntarily in the private sector, however, because any company that decided to pay women the same as comparably skilled and educated men would experience an increase in labor costs, and therefore would be at a disadvantage vis-à-vis companies that had no such policy. In this sense, a conflict theorist could argue that our economic system, with its profit orientation, is inhibiting the move toward economic equality of the sexes.

In noneconomic areas the prospects for change also remain uncertain. Although men have changed their thinking concerning their role in the home, it is not clear that they are willing to share fully in domestic chores. Moreover, different patterns of communication continue to both reflect and reinforce inequalities between men and women.

Although there are serious questions about the adequacy of her sample, Hite's (1987) survey of American women does strongly suggest that lack of communication is one of the biggest complaints women have about their husbands. In general, men interrupt far more than women (Kollock et al., 1985; Zimmerman and West, 1975), and women are expected to spend more time listening while men talk (Kollock et al., 1985). Women are also more likely than men to use gestures associated with low status, such as nodding, smiling, and holding their arms close to their bodies (see

McKenna and Denmark, 1978). So long as these patterns exist, men and women will not interact as equals, and it is unlikely that women will attain equal access to desirable roles in life. Thus, although gender roles have changed considerably in some ways, they have not changed much in other ways. More importantly, gender roles remain not only different, but also unequal.

The likelihood that this inequality between the roles of men and women will be eliminated at any time in the foreseeable future appears dubious at best. Our society has moved in that direction, perhaps more dramatically in the past two decades than at any previous time in our history. However, it has a very long way to go before true sexual equality is attained.

Intersexuality, Sexual Orientation, and the Politics of Being "Different"

At the start of this chapter, we stated that sex refers to whether you are either a male or a female. But what if you are clearly neither? *Intersexual* people is the current term used for those born with both male and female genitalia. In the past, the term "hermaphrodite" was often used. A recent distinction is that the latter term is being reserved for the very rare cases in which the full male testes and female ovaries are present in the same individual, while intersexuality refers to the much more common occurrence of being born with some aspects, but not all, of both genitalia. This can vary greatly across individuals and does not appear to have any set pattern. A growing consensus among medical and other professionals is that while intersexuality is a rare phenomenon, it is a natural part of human sexual diversity. In societies in which the dominant social definition of sex is either male or female, living as an intersexual person can be confusing and complicated. However, not all cultures see intersexual people in this way. The Navajo tribe, for instance, view intersexuality as a higher status than either male or female.

Sexual Orientation

While the bulk of this chapter has discussed heterosexual relationships, a growing and important field of gender studies has to do with homosexual and bisexual relationships. Any *sexual orientation* other than heterosexual has long been a point of controversy and discrimination in American society. However, like intersexuality, not all cultures or time periods have treated homosexuality this way. And evidence suggests that Americans are growing increasingly accepting of homosexuality and bisexuality as well as the movement for gay civil rights. Still, a large portion of the country views any other orientation than heterosexual as deviant and possibly even sinful. On the other hand are those who view people with these perspectives as homophobic. Sociology cannot, by itself, provide an answer to this dilemma. After all, most of this debate comes down to a question of values for many. Often, it is a question of religious belief versus civil rights. However, sociology can offer a few facts and data that can help clarify some of the murkiness of the debate.

Many cast homosexuality as a "deviant lifestyle choice." While this label may have much to do with cultural judgments about gay relationships, it implies that being gay is a choice. While firm scientific proof remains, to this date, illusive, the weight of scientific evidence seems to be pointing to a biological cause for homosexual orientation (Hamer and Copeland, 1994, Wheeler, 1992; Suplee, 1991). This should hardly be surprising. First, most gay and bisexual individuals will report that they have felt their orientation for most, if not all, of their lives (Lever, 1994). Second, one must consider what is being proposed by the idea that sexual orientation is a "choice." Many times when this rhetorical device of choice is deployed, it is done so without considering that if homosexual orientation is a choice—meaning one could simply choose not to be homosexual—then it must be true that heterosexual orientation is also a choice. There is an easy way to test this proposition for yourself, if you are a heterosexual. Imagine that tomorrow the government decrees that starting at noon the next day, all sexual activity performed with another person must be homosexual. Would heterosexuality feel like a choice then? This is essentially the reverse of the situation gays and lesbians have faced every day of their lives in the United States since birth. And while this little thought experiment cannot prove sexual orientation is hard-wired into each of us, it may provide enough evidence for many of us.

UNDERSTANDING RACE, CLASS, AND GENDER
Gender and the Financial Effects of Divorce

More than in the past, being a woman has become associated with being poor. In 2008, the overall female poverty rate in the United States was 14.4 percent, compared to 12.0 percent among males (U.S. Bureau of the Census, 2009). Among adults, where virtually all the difference occurs, the poverty rate for women was 13.2 percent, compared to just 10.1 percent for men (computed from U.S. Census Bureau, 2009). The difference in poverty rates is particularly stark if we look at data for families with female householders: Their poverty rate is five times that of married-couple families. In fact, over half of all poor families in 1999 had a female householder (U.S. Census Bureau, 2000b, pp. x–xi). There are several reasons for this, but one of the biggest has to do with the different financial experiences of men and women when a divorce occurs.

With our high divorce rate—about one marriage out of two ends in divorce—far more women today than in the past must support themselves and one or more children solely on their own incomes. In the great majority of divorces, custody is awarded to the woman. For several reasons, women clearly fare worse after divorce than men. First, alimony is rarely awarded today. Many judges assume that women are employed and therefore can support their families, an assumption that is incorrect because of women's low wages. Second, although child-support decrees are often awarded in divorce cases, they are poorly enforced. Thus, a large percentage of fathers stop paying child support rather quickly, and some never pay at all, despite court orders.

All of these things might not make such a great difference if women's wages were as high as men's, and if quality, low-cost day care were as available in the United States as it is in most other industrialized countries. With women's wages so low, however, and with affordable day care so hard to find, the conditions described in the preceding paragraphs make a huge difference. The reality is that when a divorce occurs, the wife and children experience a large decline in their standard of living. Although this difference is not as large as was once believed (see, for example, Weitzman, 1985), it is nonetheless substantial (Peterson, 1996; Smock, Manning, and Gupta, 1999). The picture for men is more complicated, and not so long ago, the research indicated that men actually experienced a *gain* in their standard of living as a result of a divorce (Weitzman, 1985; Peterson, 1996). More recent research shows that this is less common today. The average effect for men is small, but some men gain and others lose. Men with high incomes whose wives provided little or none of the family income are better off, whereas men whose wives provided a large share of the family income are worse off (McManus and DiPrete, 2001). Race also makes a difference: White men tend to fare better than black men, particularly in cases where the husband and wife had provided fairly equal shares of the overall income.

Despite some variation among men, gender still makes a big difference in what happens to men, women, and children after a divorce. While the effects on men are variable and usually small, the effects on women and children are substantial and consistent: Their standard of living nearly always falls significantly. The same pattern holds in the nearly 40 percent of all births that occur outside marriage: Rarely is child support ever paid, so that the mother must support her children on her pay alone, which is less than that of a comparably educated man. The net result of all this is what sociologists call the *feminization of poverty*—an increased tendency for being poor to be associated with being female.

Still, even if alternative sexual orientations are natural, it does not mean that society must accept them. There are many apparently naturally occurring human behaviors that society does not tolerate, murder for one. The difference would seem to be, however, that no one is hurt by alternative sexual orientations. In fact, to the contrary, the bulk of violence that takes place between couples is heterosexual violence against women.

Summary

Sex refers to the biological characteristic of being male or female, whereas *gender* refers to socially learned traits that are attached to sex in society. Most societies have a system of gender roles, in which men and women are expected to play different parts. In most societies, including the United States, these roles are unequal, and male dominance is the rule. Some societies, however, are androgynous, and a few are even female-dominant. Moreover, even though male dominance is widespread, its form varies from one society to another, and it changes over time. In the United States and other Western societies, for example, the housewife role that emerged with the Industrial Revolution faded in importance after World War II.

In the United States and other industrial societies, women are increasingly entering the paid labor force. However, women work at different jobs than men, usually for lower pay. Despite some improvements, the typical American woman still receives only about three-fourths the wages of the typical man. Differences in the wages and salaries of men and women cannot be explained by differences in education or skills, or even by the greater tendency of women to work part-time and to leave the labor force temporarily. Rather, they are a product of the different jobs of women, their lesser opportunity to be promoted into jobs with supervisory authority, and their frequent need to subordinate their own careers to those of their husbands.

Some of this inequality is also the result of gender-role socialization, the process by which men and women are taught to expect and seek different and unequal roles in life. Achievement, strength, and independence are stressed for boys, while girls are taught to be nice and to look attractive. Clothes, games, children's books, television, parents, and teachers all give these messages. Through the process of the looking-glass self, boys and girls are taught different self-images. They come to believe that their skills lie in different subjects, and by high school, this process has become a self-fulfilling prophecy. Children also see men and women in different jobs (in the media, in school materials, and in their own experiences), and as a result boys and girls aspire to different jobs themselves. Recent research suggests that these differences are decreasing, but they have not disappeared.

Some functionalists see gender roles as a case of cultural lag—something that was useful in the past but no longer is today. They predict that society will gradually move toward androgyny. Other functionalists, however, see gender roles as essential to the cohesiveness of the family and blame such problems as the soaring divorce rate on the declining influence of traditional gender roles. Conflict theorists argue that gender roles exist because men benefit from them. According to conflict theories, men use their disproportionate power to maintain a system of unequal gender roles. Feminism offers the possibility of changing this system of inequality. Conflict theorists also argue that families with traditional gender roles are no happier or more functional than are more androgynous families, and that the ability of working women to afford divorce may not be all bad.

Increasingly since World War II, women in a number of countries, including the United States, have challenged unequal gender roles through powerful feminist movements. These recent movements have been more broad-based and influential than earlier women's movements. They have been facilitated by the increased education of women, improved mass communication, and the participation of women in a number of other social movements. Feminism has not eliminated gender roles or sexual inequality, but it has brought significant legal changes in many countries, as well as some important changes in public opinion concerning the appropriate roles of men and women.

Intersexuality refers to the rare instance in which one is born with some combination of both male and female genitalia. While such individuals have had difficulty living a normal life in American culture, not all societies have treated them this way. The Navajo, for instance, considered them the ultimate expression of sexuality. Sexual orientation is a growing and important field of gender studies in sociology. Though still a point of debate and controversy, gay, bisexual and lesbian orientations are meeting with increasing acceptance among Americans. While no firm scientific evidence exists to suggest that one's sexual orientation is biologically determined, much circumstantial evidence suggests it. This contradicts the widespread idea that one's sexual orientation is a choice.

Key Terms

sex
gender
gender roles
sexism
institutional sexism
androgynous societies
gender-role socialization
occupational segregation

feminism
feminist theory
intersexual
sexual orientation

Exercises

1. One very interesting dimension of studying gender roles is the relationship between *gender and language*. Deborah Tannen is a well-known authority on communication differences between men and women and her *genderlect styles* have become widely quoted in the gender studies literature.

    - Tannen refers to male-female conversation as cross-cultural communication. Do you agree with her that males and females are *that* far apart from one another in the use of language and communication?
    - Explain how the classic film *When Harry Met Sally* is an illustration of gender communication differences. Check it out if you haven't seen it.

2. Sexual harassment, particularly in the workplace, continues to be a very controversial topic in American society.

    - Do you believe you have ever been victimized by sexual harassment, or do you know someone who has? If you have experienced sexual harassment, how did it make you feel? If you know someone who has had this experience, make a point of asking them how they felt. Be sure to approach the issue in a sensitive manner and respect their wishes if they prefer not to discuss it.
    - Your college or university should have a sexual harassment policy, and it is probably stated in the institution's catalog or handbook. Access this document, and read it carefully. Do you think enough is being done in our society to combat sexual harassment? If not, what more can be done?

Chapter 9
Groups, Organizations, and the Workplace

Groups and Organizations: What Is the Difference?   **262**

Group Characteristics and Dynamics   **263**
    Group Size   263
    Primary and Secondary Groups   264
    Conformity Within Groups   264
    Outside Threats and Group Cohesion   264
    Dysfunctional Group Processes   266

Organizations   **267**
    Why Study Organizations?   267
    Characteristics of Organizations   268

Oligarchy Versus Democracy   **269**
    Michels's Iron Law of Oligarchy   269
    Oligarchy: Iron Law or Just a Tendency?   269

Leadership in Groups and Organizations   **270**
    Instrumental and Expressive Leadership   270
    Characteristics of Leaders   271

Bureaucracy   **272**
    Why Do Bureaucracies Develop?   273
    Bureaucracy and Democracy   274
    Karl Marx on Bureaucracy   274
    The Pervasiveness of Bureaucracy   276
    Evaluating Bureaucracy   276
    Dysfunctions of Bureaucracy   277

An Interactionist View of Bureaucracy   **280**
    Informal Structure   280
    Negotiated Order   281
    Roles in the Workplace: Case Studies   281

Globalization and New Trends in Work Organization   **283**
    Globalization and Work   284
    Japanese Work Organization   285
    Scandinavian Workplace Innovations   287
    Workplace Change in the United States   288
    Alternatives to Bureaucracy   288

Summary   **289**

Key Terms   **289**

Exercises   **289**

More years ago than I (Farley) would like to admit, when I was in graduate school, I participated in an exercise called "Sub-Arctic Survival." In the exercise, a group of people had become stranded in late fall just below the Arctic Circle. Faced with a cold, wet environment and a limited food supply, they had to do two things: survive until rescued, and increase their chance of being rescued. The people had fifteen items among them. The exercise was to rank the fifteen items in terms of their importance to survival and rescue. Each participant in the exercise first developed his or her own ranking of the fifteen items. Then, everyone discussed the rankings, and collectively the entire group developed a ranking based on this discussion. The group's rankings and the individual rankings were then compared with a ranking developed by experts on rescue and survival. What happened in our group was what happens in most groups: The group's rankings came closer to the experts' recommendations than did the rankings we did individually. In short, what the group accomplished collectively was better than any of the solutions its individual participants had come up with on their own.

Of course, we know that group decision making does not always work this way. Sometimes, groups undertake risky and dangerous behaviors that their individual members would never choose on their own. You have all heard of cases in which a group of teenagers has broken into a museum or trophy room, stolen something, and put it somewhere—perhaps at their school—for people to see. Sometimes, group actions take a deadly turn, as in fraternity initiations or student drinking contests that have led to accidental deaths. Group dynamics sometimes lead to bad decisions being made under pressure, as happened when the U.S. warship *Vincennes* mistakenly shot down an Iranian airliner. And pressures to meet deadlines or cost targets can create dynamics within organizations that lead to deadly results, as occurred in the ValuJet crash in 1996 (Matthews and Kauzlarich, 2000).

From these examples and similar ones, we can see that group processes have important effects on human behavior. Groups can empower us to accomplish things we cannot do as individuals, and we depend on the cooperative efforts of groups of people to provide everything from our food and shelter to our entertainment. Yet, at the same time, groups also have the power to shape our behavior in various ways that can lead to bad decisions and destructive actions. In this chapter, we shall examine how and why people group together, along with the various kinds of human groups and their impacts on our lives.

Sociologists use the term *group* in a number of ways. Sometimes it is used to refer to a *status group,* a category of people who share some common, socially important status, such as race, ancestry, sex, or social class. When sociologists use the term *social group,* however, they usually mean something a bit more specific. A **social group** can be defined as a set of two or more people who interact regularly and in a manner that is defined by (1) some common purpose, (2) a set of norms, and (3) a structure of statuses and roles within the group. By this definition, a college class, a family, a softball team, and a workplace all qualify as social groups. In contrast, people standing on a corner waiting for a stoplight do not qualify, even if they do interact. There is no regularity to these people's interaction, nor any division of roles and statuses. They share a common purpose only to the extent that they all want to cross the street, but once across, they will all go their separate ways. Sociologists refer to such a cluster of people as an *aggregate.*

Groups and Organizations: What Is the Difference?

A particular kind of group that is of great importance in modern society is the **formal organization,** which is defined as a relatively large-scale group having a name, some official purpose or goals, and a structure of statuses and roles and a set of rules designed to promote these goals. What distinguishes formal organizations from other kinds of groups is the official—and usually written—nature of the goals, rules, and statuses. The structure of a formal organization is sufficiently clear that it can be put on paper in the form of an organizational chart; in contrast, other kinds of groups are much less formal. Imagine, for example, making an organizational chart of your family or of a group of friends who meet once a week to bowl or swim.

Formal organizations can be grouped into three broad types, according to Etzioni (1975). Some organizations are normative or voluntary organizations—people choose to join them because they are interested in the group's purpose or activities. Examples are recreational clubs, political groups, and professional associations. Another type, overlapping somewhat with voluntary organizations, is the utilitarian organization—an organization designed to accomplish some task. Businesses and neighborhood improvement associations are examples of this type, as are large-scale organizations such as corporations, governments, and labor unions. Finally, there are coercive organizations—organizations that people are compelled to participate in. This category includes the total institutions discussed in Chapter 5—prisons, the military, and mental hospitals, for example. For children, however, a wider range of organizations are experienced as coercive organizations, most notably schools and religious institutions. We now turn to a more detailed examination of groups and organizations, beginning with groups.

Group Characteristics and Dynamics

Group Size

One of the most important characteristics of a group is its size. You can, for example, interact much more intensively with one other person than with fifty others. The smallest possible group is a **dyad**, which consists of two people. In a dyad, only one interpersonal relationship exists in the group—that between the two members. If either member withdraws from interaction in a dyad—by daydreaming, for example—the group's interaction stops. Moreover, the group itself comes to an end if either member chooses to depart. The effects of group size on group dynamics can be seen by comparing the dyad with the **triad**, a group consisting of three people. In a triad, three relationships exist. In a group consisting of Bill, Mary, and Sue, for example, there is one relationship between Bill and Mary, one between Bill and Sue, and one between Mary and Sue.

The presence of three relationships as opposed to one makes an important difference in several ways. First, one person can withdraw without stopping the group's interaction. Bill might daydream, but that would not stop interaction between Mary and Sue. Second, coalitions can be formed when disagreements arise within the group. Bill and Mary might, for example, form a coalition against Sue.

They want to see on[e movie, and Sue wants to] see another. In this si[tuation, Bill and Mary may] cooperate with each othe[r and pressure Sue] to go to the movie they wan[t to see. In many] cases, Sue will give in, in ord[er to remain an ac]cepted member of the group.

A third characteristic of triad[s is that they] can be balanced or unbalanced (He[ider,] 1958; Zajonc, 1960). As long as Mary, [Sue, and] Bill remain friendly, the group is balanced[:] its relationships are positive. But suppose that [one] day Mary and Bill have a terrible fight and come [to] hate each other. The triad has now become unbalanced. Consider Sue's position: She likes both Bill and Mary, who hate each other. If she chooses to do something with Bill, Mary will likely respond, "Why do you want to spend time with that jerk instead of me?" If she goes somewhere with Mary, she will likely get a similar response from Bill. Both Bill and Mary may try to get her to take "their side" in their conflicts. Sue is thus placed in an impossible position, and the likely result is that she will back away from her relationship with either Mary or Bill, thereby ending the triad.

Complexity and Group Size

Obviously, the complexity of relationships in a triad is far beyond that of a dyad. This complexity continues to increase as small groups become larger, until eventually a size is reached where, rather than one small group, there is a large group with several smaller subgroups within it. At this point, which is reached at a group size of somewhere between about seven and twelve, several important changes occur. One is that it becomes commonplace to have two or more coalitions rather than one, as in a triad. (This dynamic can be readily seen on "reality" TV shows, such as "Survivor.") The possibilities for the group to become unbalanced increase in larger groups, although the pressures on individuals may decrease because they have more potential relationships to choose from. Another important difference is the need for a system of formal recognition of speakers—deciding who "has the floor." Often, one or more side conversations go on while one person attempts to address the group. (You can probably observe this dynamic in your next sociology class.) Also, in this more formal situation, people speak differently: Rather than talking to others, they address the group, using a different vocabulary and style of speech. At this point, the group has case in the past. Even in modern urban society, friends and families remain important to most people, and primary-group relationships still play an important role in people's lives (Fischer, 1982, 1984; Reiss, 1959).

Conformity Within Groups

Pressures for conformity are present in any group. Observations of small groups show that if a clear majority holds a certain position at the start, the group generally will move toward consensus. Pressures on a dissenting individual are particularly strong, as was demonstrated by a fascinating experiment by Solomon Asch (1956). In this experiment, a group of eight people were asked, one by one, to choose which of three lines on a card matched the length of a line on another card. Actually, only one person in the group—the last to answer—was a subject of the experiment; the rest were confederates; that is, part of the experiment. After a few examples in which the confederates made the correct choice, they all gave an obviously wrong answer—such as choosing line A as the matching line in Figure 9.2. When it came time for the subject to answer, about one in three conformed to the obviously wrong opinion of the others and picked the incorrect line. (In a control group without a confederate, only 1 percent answered incorrectly.) In most cases, the conformity was only outward, but for some, it was more than that. When debriefed afterward, the majority said they knew better but went along to avoid ridicule or ostracism from the rest of the group. However, some actually disbelieved what they were seeing, and they offered such explanations as "I guess I just couldn't see it right."

Outside Threats and Group Cohesion

Conflicts of values, personality, or interest can lead to divisions within any group. Often, however, these divisions can be overlooked because of some greater outside threat or conflict with another group. In such situations, sociologists refer to the group to which a person belongs as the **ingroup** and to other groups as **outgroups.** Outgroups are often seen as threatening to the ingroup. They

groups intimate relationships throughout a large network of people. In large group and formal organizations, relationships between members are less personal. This type of group is called a **secondary group.** Examples of secondary groups are businesses, schools, and political organizations. In these groups, interpersonal contacts occur for the purpose of conducting business, gaining an education, or influencing politics—not for the sake of the contacts themselves. A secondary group may be either large or small.

As is illustrated by Figure 9.1, the line between primary groups and secondary groups is not always clear, and real-life groups can be placed along a range or continuum from clear-cut primary groups through ambiguous cases to clear-cut secondary groups. Also, primary groups can and do form within a larger secondary group. In fact, a large secondary group typically includes many primary groups. Most formal organizations are secondary groups, but within them, primary groups often develop among members or co-workers.

Historically, secondary groups have proliferated as society has modernized. Prior to industrialization, people spent most of their time in small, informal primary groups centered around family, kin, neighborhood, and religious affiliation. Today we come into contact with far more people, and most of this contact is impersonal and centers around business, education, government, or some other large formal organization.

Although secondary groups have become much more important in modern society, they have not replaced primary groups. Rather, they have been added on, so that we come into contact with a far greater diversity of people than was the

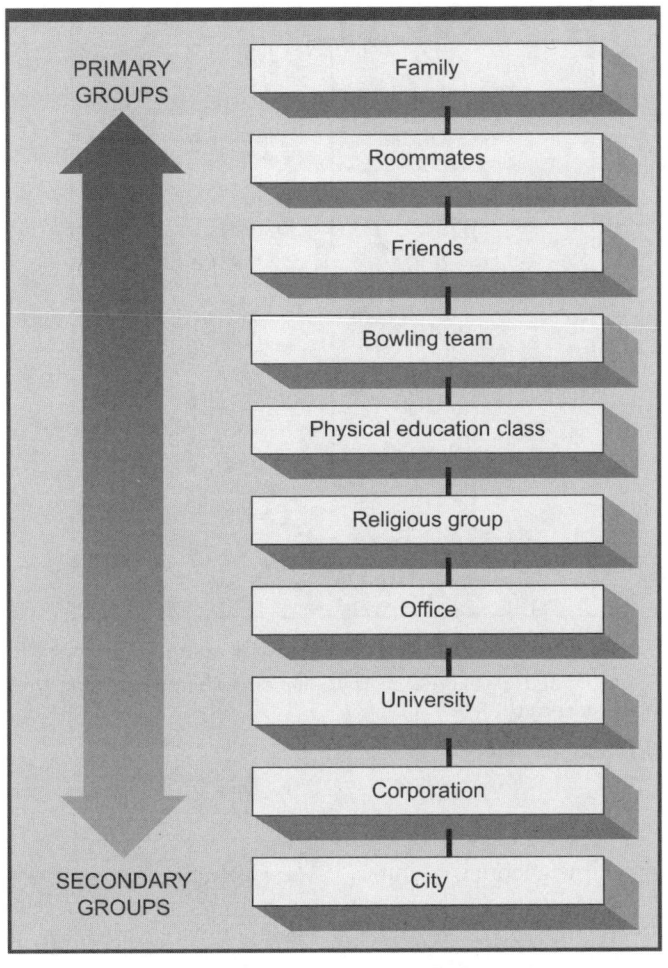

Figure 9.1 The Continuum from Primary to Secondary Groups

may be potential competitors, or they may simply do things differently. Because of the widespread tendency toward ethnocentrism discussed in Chapter 4, an outgroup that does things differently will often be seen as inferior. To acknowledge that an outgroup's way could be just as good would threaten the solidarity of the ingroup, so usually the opposite happens: The extent to which the outgroup is actually threatening or different is often exaggerated to promote ingroup unity.

The extent to which an outside threat can serve as a unifying force can be seen in the response of people to natural disasters and wars. The usual tendency is to pull together to combat the threat or deal with the emergency. An example of this can be seen in the cooperative efforts of people from many backgrounds and ethnic groups in the response to the September 11, 2001, terrorist attacks in New York, Washington, and Pennsylvania. (Unfortunately, people who in the public mind are associated with the threat can also be mindlessly targeted, as occurred in the hundreds of attacks and incidents of harassment against Arab and Muslim Americans after the terrorist attacks.)

The tendency to pull together in the face of a threat is so strong that leaders sometimes take advantage of it to strengthen their own positions. On the societal level, national leaders sometimes encourage conflicts that lead to warfare in order to make people forget about divisive internal issues or about mistakes made by the leadership (Burrowes and Spector, 1973, p. 295; Lang, 1972). This process appears to have been part of the dynamic that led to World War I, as various national leaders

Figure 9.2 An Example of the Cards Used in Solomon Asch's Experiment

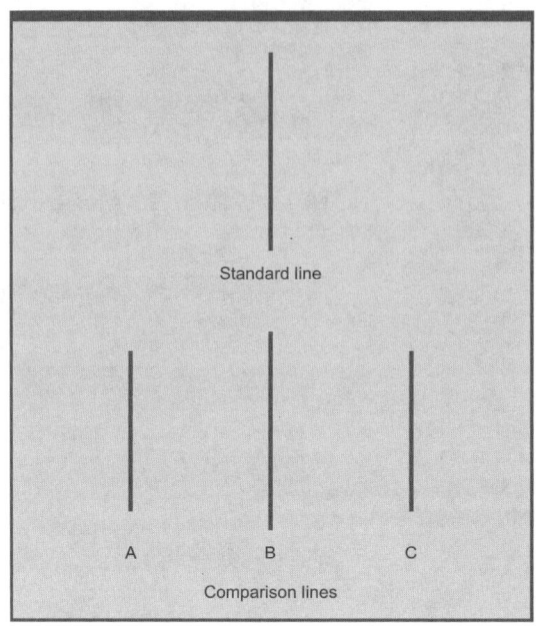

Although the standard line clearly corresponds to line B, many subjects were pressured into selecting the wrong choice.
Source: Adapted from "Opinions and Social Pressure," by Solomon Asch from *Scientific American,* November 1955. Copyright © 1995 *Scientific American.*

whipped up fervor against neighboring countries to distract people from problems in their own countries (Farrar, 1978, p. 169).

Despite this general tendency, sometimes divisions within the group are too deep to be put aside, even in the face of an outside threat. In such cases, the outside threat may even deepen the conflict. The response of families to a crisis such as a major illness or a breadwinner's loss of employment serves as an example. If a family is relatively strong, a crisis of this type will usually bring it closer together. However, the crisis may be too much for a weak or deeply divided family, in which case it often leads to a divorce.

Dysfunctional Group Processes

Groupthink

Certain processes and dynamics that occur in groups often result in dangerous or inappropriate decisions. Two such processes are groupthink and group polarization.

Groupthink is a process whereby a group collectively arrives at a decision that individual members privately oppose but do not challenge. This usually happens in small, cohesive groups with powerful leaders. Although individual members of the group believe the decision to be unwise, they do not speak out against it because they do not want to break the group consensus or challenge the leader. The result is that the group makes an unwise decision with little debate, which it might not have made had there been more discussion.

A commonly cited example of groupthink is the 1962 Bay of Pigs invasion of Cuba, in which the United States sponsored an unsuccessful attempt by a group of Cuban exiles to overthrow Premier Fidel Castro. Social psychologist Irving Janis (1972; see also Janis and Mann, 1977) examined the decision-making process that led to the Kennedy administration's support of the Bay of Pigs invasion. It turns out that many of Kennedy's advisers privately saw the foolishness of what was being contemplated but did not speak up. The result was a resounding military defeat and a diplomatic embarrassment. A more recent example may be the 2003 invasion of Iraq in which members of the Bush administration seem to have convinced themselves, despite a preponderance of disconfirming evidence, that Iraq contained an arsenal of weapons of mass destruction. In the coming years, this case may prove as fruitful as the famous cases of groupthink from the past. For instance, were officials so convinced that they would find the weapons that they knowingly used unreliable evidence to make the case for war? Or was some other agenda at work? Future researchers will be looking into these questions to determine if groupthink was the culprit.

Group Polarization

Closely related to groupthink is a process known as group polarization, in which a group moves toward a stronger position or more extreme course of action than its members individually favor. This process can lead to either excessively risky or excessively cautious courses of action.

The Risky Shift. The effects of group polarizations were first discovered in the form of the risky shift (Stoner, 1961; Wallach, Kogan, and Bem, 1962). The risky shift can be illustrated by an incident that occurred in an organization to which I (Farley) belong. Some years ago, I served for a year on the governing board of a ski club. One of the jobs of the board was to plan the club's ski trips for the coming year. Each trip has a group leader, and it so happens that one of these leaders (I'll call him "Wayne") was so popular that his trips filled quickly no matter where they went. Late in the meeting, someone suggested that we could fill a "mystery trip" with Wayne as the leader, listing on the brochure a price for the trip but not telling people the destination. After some further discussion, it was decided that it would be a clever idea to make this a trip to Florida, ending with a one-day stop at a very small local ski area a few miles outside of our town, so we could legitimately call it a ski trip. People would have so much fun, we concluded, that they wouldn't really mind spending hundreds of dollars and their precious vacation time to go to Florida when they wanted, and had paid for, a ski vacation. After loading up their ski equipment, and lots of winter sweaters and coats, we thought, they would react cheerfully to finding themselves in Florida without warm-weather clothes, and finally coming back to a place near home where they could ski any time they want for $20. We actually believed at the time that this was a good idea! Fortunately, we left the meeting without finalizing our plans, and once apart from the group, we individually realized the folly of our thinking.

Why does a group move toward such risky decisions that individuals would probably never make? Often there is a feeling that "we need to do something bold and different." The group wants to think it is being dynamic and creative, rather than doing the same old thing. In addition, there is frequently a tendency to rally around an idea that seems clever and adventurous, without considering what could go wrong. I know that both of these things happened in the ski trip example. Finally, people may try to enhance their status in the group by going along with what others suggest, which tends to move the group toward whatever idea someone suggests first (Laughlin and Early, 1982). This process may be particularly likely if the person suggesting the action has high status in the group, and research shows that such shifts are often products of inequalities of influence within the group (Friedkin, 1999).

Not all group shifts are risky, however. Some groups shift toward an overly cautious approach, shunning even moderate actions that the individual members of the group would take (Moscovici and Zavalloni, 1969). Thus, group polarization may lead a group toward a position that is either riskier or more cautious than individual members would take. Group polarization has been shown to occur in a wide variety of groups, including such diverse examples as bargaining and negotiation groups (Lamm and Sauer, 1974), groups of gamblers (Blascovich, Ginsburg, and Howe, 1975), juries (Myers and Kaplan, 1976), and school discussion groups (Myers and Bishop, 1970).

Organizations

Why Study Organizations?

A sociologist who gave suggestions on this chapter for an earlier edition of this book commented that a chapter on organizations is hard to write. He described organizations as "stodgy and boring"—certainly not as inherently interesting as other

STUDENT LIFE
The Organization of Security

In the wake of the 2001 terrorist attacks, the US government stepped up its efforts to monitor potentially threatening behavior within its own borders. The passage of legislation such as the USA Patriot Act greatly expanded the powers of the federal government to snoop into the lives of its citizens. More than one commentator has remarked on the irony of eroding the freedoms of citizens to protect freedom. But our society has long been permeated by technologies and practices that limit our privacy. Every time you use your credit card, swipe a discount card, or withdraw money from an ATM, your movements and actions are being monitored. Social theorist Michel Foucault predicted that society was evolving into a "surveillance society." The image he evoked was of a Panopticon, a round prison in which the guards could see all of the prisoners all of the time without being seen themselves. Has society reached such a level? In 2006, it was revealed that nearly all of the e-mail traffic in the United States is going through a secret room in California where it is scanned by a program looking for certain "red flag" words that would presumably warrant further examination by officials. College students routinely post the photographic record of their social activities on the Internet through various social networking sites such as Facebook or MySpace, and occasionally, such photos are used to fire or refuse to hire prospective employees. In many ways, we are more visible to each other than ever before. One might think this would make us safer. But Foucault argues that visibility is a trap; it makes us all easier to track and follow.

topics covered in this book, such as sexual behavior, racial conflict, or why people get divorced. Why, then, do virtually all introductory sociology books devote so much to organizations? Sociologist Richard Hall (1996) provides the answer in the opening of his book on organizations: They surround and influence us every day of our lives, with the certainty of death and taxes. Hall points out that most of us are born and die in organizational settings (hospitals). Almost all of the time between is spent under their influence. You might be alone in your room reading this book right now—surely something that appears to be away from the influence of organizations. But you are still under their influence. An organization (Paradigm Publishers) produced this book. And most likely, someone in an organization (your college or university) told you to read it, so the organization could give you course credit for introductory sociology. Even our recreation involves organizations. Richard Hall enjoys downhill skiing. And he points out that this activity would be very hard to do without an organization (a ski area) to make it available. Thus, it is important to understand organizations because their influences on us are so all-encompassing.

Characteristics of Organizations

Although their purposes vary widely, all formal organizations share certain characteristics. First, they have some purpose or goal, which just about any member of the organization can recognize. The purpose may be nothing more than to have fun (a social club, for example), but it is a recognized purpose. Sociologists describe this characteristic of formal organizations by saying that they are instrumental. Because organizations have a purpose, they usually involve some process of coordination to ensure that the various people in the organization are to at least some degree working toward that common purpose (Hall, 1996). In addition to these characteristics, organizations are self-perpetuating. This means they have a life above and beyond that of individual members. Old members may leave and new members may join, but the organization continues. Both of these characteristics distinguish formal organizations from other kinds of groups. Many informal groups do not have a formally defined purpose (though they usually do have some informal purpose), and many informal groups continue to exist only as long as a given set of individuals continues to participate. A group of four people who meet to play cards on Saturday night, for example, may stop meeting if two of its members move out of town.

A third characteristic of organizations, which is shared with other kinds of groups, is the presence of a leader or leaders. Often organizations try to institutionalize the presence of leaders by creating an authority structure: a set of positions, each of which carries some recognized function and decision-making power. A formal authority structure, however, is not necessary for leadership to develop: It turns out that even organizations that attempt to be leaderless usually end up with leaders.

A final characteristic of organizations is that they have boundaries (Hall, 1996). In other words, they have ways of delineating who is in the organization and who is not. Sometimes boundaries are highly visible, as in the case of a police force. Police wear uniforms to identify themselves as police officers, and it is against the law for someone who is not a police officer to wear such a uniform. In other cases, the boundaries may be fuzzier. A counselor employed by a hospital may provide counseling services at a high school. In this case, the counselor may to some extent be part of both organizations. However, even in this case the counselor is quite different from someone with no ongoing work relationship to either organization.

Oligarchy Versus Democracy

The tendency for leadership to develop in organizations is so strong that it often results in oligarchy, or rule by a small group of leaders, with little or no effective influence on the part of the members. Even in organizations that try to be democratic, certain members often end up making the important decisions.

Michels's Iron Law of Oligarchy

This insight arises from the work of political sociologist Robert Michels (1967 [orig. 1911]). Early in his life Michels was a member of political organizations that were strongly committed to democracy and social equality. He noticed that no matter what the organizations preached, they in fact were run by their leaders and not by the ordinary members. Michels became convinced that this tendency to be run by the leadership was a characteristic of all formal organizations, a principle that he called the **iron law of oligarchy.**

According to Michels, there are clear reasons why all organizations exhibit this tendency. All organizations have certain tasks that members must *delegate* to their leaders. This delegation of work helps concentrate power in the hands of leaders for several reasons. First, leaders gain access to information that others don't have, and information is a source of power. Second, leaders benefit from a sense of obligation on the part of the organization's members. Because the leaders have spared the membership the burden of doing the work, most members feel obligated to cooperate with whatever policies the leaders suggest. As the leaders accumulate power, they frequently use it to advance or protect their own interests, sometimes even at the expense of the interests of the membership. Frequently, even in political organizations committed to social change, leaders become more conservative over time, more oriented to maintaining their own power, and thus more supportive of the status quo. As a result, when revolutions or new political movements succeed, they often have the ultimate result of merely replacing one group of powerful leaders with another because their original democratic ideals are lost or forgotten.

Oligarchy: Iron Law or Just a Tendency?

If Michels were entirely correct, his discovery would be depressing for anyone who favors democracy because it leads to the inevitable conclusion that democracy is an impossible ideal. Fortunately, Michels seems to have overstated his argument. Although leaders in all organizations do have disproportionate power, that power is not unlimited. Many organizations have challenged and even removed their leaders. Moreover, as shown in the box entitled "What Makes a Union Democratic?" we do know that certain elements can make organizations less oligarchic and more democratic.

A self-conscious effort to keep an organization democratic can sometimes succeed if the organization does not become too large. An example can be found in *cooperatives* and *collectives,* small organizations that provide goods or services and that are strongly committed to a democratic ideal. Rothschild and Whitt (1986) conducted field observations of five such organizations in California in the 1970s, all of which were made up of well-educated, middle-class people committed to liberal and democratic political principles. Among the features that kept these organizations democratic were avoidance of the written rules characteristic of most modern organizations, small size, and shunning of specialization. In effect, one way they prevented the leadership from gaining too much power was by eliminating formal positions of authority. Such organizations required a great deal of time for decision making because every decision had to be discussed and debated among the entire membership. They had to keep to a narrow path between failure on the one side and "too much success" on the other. Organizations that failed often did so because of disorganization or conflict, which easily became personalized because every member was by definition deeply involved in it. Organizations that became "too successful" grew to the point that work had to be delegated and rules formalized, and at this point, oligarchic tendencies took over. Some organizations, though, were able to remain democratic and to continue to function effectively. We shall return to this issue later in this chapter.

Leadership in Groups and Organizations

Instrumental and Expressive Leadership

Although all groups and organizations have leaders, not all leaders have the same role and function within the group. Research on small groups by Bales (1953) and Slater (1955) uncovered two kinds of leaders, who play different roles within the group. One type is the **instrumental leader,** also known as the task leader. This type of leader helps the group define its job and determine how best to do it. The other kind of leader is the **expressive leader,** also known as the socioemotional leader, or inspirational leader. This leader helps maintain the cohesiveness of the group and looks out for the emotional well-being of its members. He or she may tell a joke to relieve tension or help soothe the feelings of a member who was criticized.

A successful group needs both instrumental and expressive leaders. Groups that have only instrumental leaders are likely to bog down in dissension and lose their common identity. The members may feel that their leaders are insensitive to their concerns and cease to cooperate with the group (or, in extreme cases, cease to participate). Groups having only expressive leaders may get along very well but get nothing done. Even routine tasks essential to the maintenance of the group may go undone, thus threatening the group's very existence. A recent study found that while organizations need both styles of leadership, how effective that leadership ultimately is may depend on the personalities of the followers, with some responding better to one kind of leader than the other (Moss and Ngu, 2006).

Although a group needs both types of leadership to be effective, it is rare to find both types in the same individual. Some groups initially rate the same person high on both qualities, but this estimation seldom lasts for long (Slater, 1955). Because instrumental leaders tend to upset people in the process of promoting their ideas, someone else must step forward to provide expressive leadership. Some societies have implicitly recognized this problem by institutionalizing separate roles for instrumental and expressive leadership. In constitutional monarchies such as Great Britain, Norway, and Sweden, the king or queen plays the expressive role, while the prime minister plays the instrumental role. The king or queen acts as a symbol of national pride and unity and performs a ceremonial function, while the parliament and the prime minister make the day-to-day political decisions.

Some sociologists believe that one of the characteristics of people who gain the reputation of being "great leaders" is their ability to offer both instrumental and expressive leadership. Franklin Roosevelt is sometimes cited as an example. As an instrumental leader, he developed a plan to get the country out of the Great Depression, and he got more legislation through Congress in his first 100 days in office than any of his predecessors. As an expressive leader, he soothed people with his "fireside chats," assuring them that "The only thing we have to fear is fear itself." Most leaders, though, are clearly either instrumental or expressive. Ronald Reagan, the "Great Communicator" who often couldn't keep his facts straight and left important decisions to subordinates, was clearly an expressive leader. Jimmy Carter and Richard

SOCIOLOGICAL INSIGHTS
What Makes a Union Democratic?

The general membership of a group has more influence relative to the leaders in some organizations than in others. A classic study by Lipset, Trow, and Coleman (1956) of the International Typographical Union shows some of the characteristics associated with democratic rather than oligarchic decision making. Lipset and his colleagues discovered that workers had distinctly more power relative to union leaders in the typographers' union than was the case in large-scale industrial unions such as the United Auto Workers. In other words, the typographers had much more influence over major decisions and day-to-day operations than did the autoworkers. Lipset accounted for this difference on the basis of the following characteristics of the typographers' union that made it different from many other unions:

- The small size of the typographers' union and its locals. This meant that most workers knew one another and their leaders fairly well, rather than just as faces at union meetings.
- The specialized nature of the typographers' work. This created a sense of community among the workers, a feeling that they constituted a distinct group of people.
- The tendency among typographers to socialize outside the job setting, so that the union members and leaders interacted in situations where their job and union status were irrelevant. This reduced the social distance between leaders and members.
- Limits on terms of office, especially on officers' serving successive terms. This institutionalized a rotation of leadership, which kept any one person from becoming too powerful.
- The development of organized political groupings, which became institutionalized within the union. Therefore, whoever was in office always faced an organized opposition.

These observations can be extended to other groups and organizations besides labor unions, including political systems. They partly explain why a two-party or multiparty system is usually more democratic than either a one-party or a nonpartisan system. The strong inference is that any group wanting to stay democratic should place strict limits on the amount of time its officers can serve and should encourage real elections, using an internal system of political parties if possible. The influence of this view on the American political scene can be seen in the term limits that have been established for elected officials in many states. Another inference is that the larger and more geographically dispersed a group or organization becomes, the harder it will be for that organization to remain truly democratic. In large organizations, the need for delegation is so great that the forces that led Michels to proclaim that "whoever says organization says oligarchy" are simply too strong to overcome.

Nixon, who planned and analyzed everything but ultimately failed during their presidencies to inspire much besides public distrust and ridicule, were examples of instrumental leaders.

Characteristics of Leaders

What are the personal characteristics of people who become leaders? The surprising answer is that it is not always easy to predict who will become a leader. Personality differences between people who become leaders and people who don't are rather small (Yukl, 1981). Leaders tend to be more intelligent, more extroverted, more psychologically balanced, more dominant, more self-confident, and more liberal than other group members (the last is true even in conservative groups), but the differences are minor, and many nonleaders have similar qualities (Hare, 1976; Mann, 1959; Stogdill, 1974; Yukl, 1981). Leaders also tend to be somewhat taller (Keyes, 1980) and more physically attractive than nonleaders. Becoming a leader, however, may be as much a product of a situation as of any individual characteristics, and different kinds of people emerge as leaders in different situations (Cooper and McGaugh, 1969). To some extent, becoming a leader is probably a product of being in the right place at the right time. For example, research by Friedkin (1993) suggests that a person's position in the social networks within an organization makes a big difference. When a key issue arises, the person's position in these networks strongly shapes the amount of influence that person is able to exercise. Such influence is a product of (1) being part of a cohesive group within the organization, (2) being in a position similar to others in the organization, and (3) being in a central position that offers contacts with many members in the organization.

The presence of a leader is characteristic of all organizations. Even organizations that try to be leaderless usually end up with leaders. (iStockphoto)

Styles of Leadership

There are also important differences of style among leaders (Lewin, Lippitt, and White, 1939; White and Lippitt, 1960). Some leaders are democratic; they attempt to get the group to move on its own toward their ideas, but they do not force things. Ultimately, the decision is left to the group. Others are authoritarian; they tell the group what to do. Still others are laissez-faire; they leave things up to the group, without providing any particular direction. Under ordinary circumstances, the democratic style of leadership seems to work best, at least in industrialized countries with democratic governments. Group members are happier, more group-oriented, and feel more involved, and consequently they are more cooperative and productive (Lewin, 1943; White and Lippitt, 1960). Some research has suggested that women are more likely than men to use a democratic style of leadership, and as a result they are often highly effective managers (Rosener, 1990; Helgesen, 1990).

In some situations, however, such as emergencies and wartime, decisions must be made quickly. Then authoritarian decision making may be preferable, which may explain the authoritarian structure of such organizations as the military, police, prisons, and hospitals. In societies with a strong tradition of authoritarian government, such as dictatorships and traditional monarchies, the authoritarian style of leadership may also be more effective (Bass, 1960) because people may be unaccustomed to making decisions and may prefer to let someone else do so. The laissez-faire style, in contrast, is rarely effective because it leaves the group without any form of instrumental leadership.

Bureaucracy

The dominant type of formal organization in modern society is the **bureaucracy**. Although the term as commonly used often has negative connotations, sociologists employ it purely as a descriptive term. The best definition of bureaucracy is probably still to be found in Max Weber's (1968 [orig. 1922]) ideal-type bureaucracy. An **ideal type** is an abstract description that actual entities will fit to a greater or lesser extent. It lists a set of characteristics; the greater the extent to which something has those characteristics, the better it fits the ideal type. Weber's ideal-type definition of a bureaucracy includes six characteristics:

1. *Division of labor:* Different people specialize in different jobs. Each person has responsibility for a given area of activity.
2. *Hierarchy:* Authority is specified according to a top-down chain of command. Each supervisor has specific authority, limited to specific people and areas of activity. A specific person is responsible for performance in each area of the organization.

3. *Formal rules and regulations:* Rules and policies are specific, official, and written rather than informal or oral. Records are kept in writing.
4. *Impersonality and universalism:* People are evaluated and rewarded on the basis of what they do, not who they are. Authority is linked to positions, not to individuals. Everyone in a given type of position is evaluated on the basis of a specified set of rules or performance factors; there are no special favors.
5. *Managerial or administrative staff:* There is a group of workers whose job is entirely to keep the organization operating. They are not involved in producing whatever it is that the organization produces.
6. *Lifelong careers:* It is assumed that people will continue throughout life in the same general type of career. Although the reality is that people often switch employers (especially in the United States), the ideal is that people "work their way up" in a career within an organization.

Most large-scale organizations in industrialized countries fit this definition reasonably well. Corporations, universities, government agencies, labor unions, and large religious denominations are all examples of bureaucracies. Large organizations will not have every one of the six traits to an equal extent and may be without one or more of them entirely (Hall, 1963–1964; Udy, 1959). In particular, there has been a shift away from lifelong careers. In recent years, people have switched jobs and even changed the kind of work they do with increasing frequency. This appears to reflect a declining commitment of worker and employer to one another; a major cause of this has been corporate "downsizing" that has led to the elimination of many jobs. In recent years, large corporations have eliminated jobs in some kinds of work while creating them in others. Overall, smaller firms have created more jobs in recent decades than big corporations (Ritzer, 1989), though often at lower wages and with fewer benefits (Kalle and Van Buren, 1996). As a result, many people have lost their old jobs and had to find new ones, and workers have probably also become more willing to change jobs when they find something better. Although lifelong careers appear to be on the wane, most of the traits of a bureaucracy will still be present in most large-scale formal organizations.

Why Do Bureaucracies Develop?

Rationalization

Three-quarters of a century ago, Max Weber correctly predicted that bureaucracy would become the dominant form of organization in modern society. How did he know this, and why has it happened as he predicted? The answer is to be found in what Weber called **rationalization.** By rationalization, he meant a shift toward making all decisions purely on the basis of what will accomplish organizational goals. Weber saw rationalization as one of the most significant trends in modern society, and bureaucracy as the means by which it occurs. Bureaucracy facilitates rationalization in several ways. First, it eliminates tradition and personal favoritism as influences in decision making. As is discussed in the box "Organizational Practices and Opportunities for Female Managers," research shows that, by eliminating such favoritism, rationalization can be an effective way of opening opportunities for groups that have been excluded, such as women in management. Second, it identifies the tasks that need to be done, assigns someone to do them, and provides a way of monitoring how well they get done. Third, it provides a way to coordinate the activities of a large number of people working on different tasks, so that each person's efforts contribute to some common task, goal, or product, rather than working at cross-purposes.

Bureaucracy and Large-Scale Tasks

The larger the scale of an organization and its tasks, the more crucial these tasks become. Many tasks are of such a large scale that there is no other way to do them except through a bureaucracy. Consider the steps that are involved in manufacturing and selling an automobile. Natural materials must be obtained and shipped to some central location. Thousands of parts must be manufactured and then assembled to make the car. Market research must be conducted to determine what people want so that the company doesn't produce a car nobody will buy. Thousands of workers must be hired, evaluated, and provided with benefits. Cars of various colors and design must be manufactured and shipped in accordance with customer orders, which in turn requires a large system of dealerships throughout the country. An extremely complex division of labor is necessary for any such task, and once a system of division of labor is devised, it becomes crucial to make sure that every part of the operation is working in a way that ultimately meets the organization's goals. Bureaucracy makes this possible, which is an important reason why it is so widespread. This is illustrated in a study of developing countries by Evans and Rauch (1999). They found that when the core economic development agencies of these countries use meritocratic criteria and offer rewarding lifelong careers—two of the key characteristics of bureaucracy, according to Weber—the economies of these countries fared better.

Weber's thinking on the topic of bureaucracy reflects the functionalist perspective, though he never used that term. To Weber, bureaucracy would inevitably spread because it had to. Large-scale tasks required rationalization, and bureaucracy made rationalization possible. Weber even went a step further, arguing that bureaucracy was essential to democracy itself.

Bureaucracy and Democracy

How does bureaucracy make democracy possible? Consider a presidential election in the United States. Such an election requires decisions concerning who is to be on the ballot in fifty states and the District of Columbia and who is eligible to vote. As was shown dramatically in the 2000 election, there must be a way to resolve disputes about the eligibility of voters and the validity of votes. Someone has to operate hundreds of thousands of voting places throughout the country and enforce the voting laws. After the election, millions of votes must be reported to central locations to be counted. Someone must determine who has won in every state and, ultimately, who has the most electoral votes. Can you imagine performing all these tasks without a division of labor? Can you imagine conducting an election without career officials who know how to run elections? Can you imagine doing it without a written set of rules concerning who is eligible to vote and how elections are to be run? Even the lack of uniformity in such rules caused serious problems in the 2000 election, in part because different states and even different counties in the same state used different methods of counting ballots. In Florida, where the worst problems happened, a law was passed in 2001 mandating one statewide method of voting, using optical-scanning ballots like the forms you use to take standardized tests. Doing this means more standardized statewide rules for conducting elections, and more hierarchical state control over the election process—basic characteristics of bureaucracy. And some have called for similar reforms on the national level.

The need for bureaucracy to ensure democracy goes further than elections, however. According to Weber, every political and economic right requires a bureaucracy to enforce it. If people have the right of free speech, we need a court system to determine when that right has been violated. If workers have the right to join labor unions, we need a labor relations board to conduct elections or verify card signatures to see if workers want a union. If we declare that financial security in old age is a right, we need a social security administration (or something like it) to collect taxes and distribute benefits according to a set of rules.

All of this might lead you to think that Max Weber considered bureaucracy to be a wonderful invention that would lead to the improvement of everyday life. He didn't. He actually looked upon it as a necessary evil. He perceived it as essential to accomplish tasks of any size and to protect democratic rights. At the same time, though, he saw it as depersonalizing. People would come to be treated as positions or numbers rather than as people. Many jobs would be repetitious and boring. People and their individual needs and concerns would become secondary to the goals of large, uncaring organizations. Weber did see some possibilities, such as charismatic movements (see Web-Based Chapter A and Chapter 15), for humanizing bureaucracy somewhat. In the end, though, he saw no way for modern societies to avoid bureaucracy.

Karl Marx on Bureaucracy

Unlike Weber, Karl Marx saw bureaucracy as an *unnecessary* evil. Marx analyzed bureaucracy from a conflict perspective, arguing that it does not meet a societal need, only the needs of the rich and powerful. According to Marx, bureaucracy enables the owners of the means of production to maintain *control* of organizations. Through hierarchy, the ruling class ensures that everyone in the organization works in a way that maximizes the owners' profits. If anyone in the organization fails to do this, the top-down chain of command ensures that that

> ## UNDERSTANDING RACE, CLASS, AND GENDER
> ### Organizational Practices and Opportunities for Female Managers
>
> Some companies have a lot of women working in management positions, and others have few or none. Sociologists Barbara Reskin and Debra Branch McBrier (2000) were interested in finding out why. Specifically, they were interested in what characteristics of the companies might explain the difference. One thing they looked for was *bureaucratic organization*—specifically, the use of formal rules and procedures in recruitment, hiring, and promotion. Weberian theory about bureaucracy holds that such formal procedures prevent favoritism through *rationalization:* making the choice purely on the basis of factors that make a difference in an individual's usefulness to an organization. This is supposed to eliminate favoritism, and—given that the majority of managers in most organizations are male—eliminating favoritism should work to the advantage of women seeking jobs in management. Thus, Weberian theory would predict that firms that use formal rules and procedures in hiring and promotion would have a higher proportion of women among their managers.
>
> Did it turn out this way? In short, yes, it did. Using a national sample of work organizations, Reskin and McBrier looked at the effects of formal versus informal recruitment methods, and the extent to which the firms use formal personnel rules and procedures. The proportion of managers who were women did indeed vary widely among the firms. One in four had fewer than 10 percent women among their managers, while at the other end of the scale, nearly 45 percent of the employers had at least 40 percent women among their managers. And nearly half of this variation could be explained by differences in the personnel practices of the firms. To begin with, those employers that used informal means of recruitment, such as asking current employees for referrals or contacting people they knew about and asking them to apply, had fewer women in management. Those who used more formal and open methods, such as advertisements or recruiting through employment agencies, had more women in management. Those who used formal personnel rules and procedures also had more women in management, though this difference was most evident toward the upper end of the range, that is, those who had average or above-average numbers of female managers. Among firms in this range, the more formal the procedures, the more female managers they had. Finally, those who recruit outside the organization have more women in management than those who recruit only from within. Thus, organizational practice *does* make a difference in managerial employment opportunities for women, and those firms that follow formal and open procedures, along the lines of Weber's bureaucratic model, do employ more women in management.

person will be corrected or eliminated from the organization.

To the extent that maximizing efficiency maximizes profits, you could argue that Marx and Weber are saying much the same thing: Bureaucratic organization exists because it works. You could argue further that efficient work organizations are in the interests of both the larger society and the ruling class. Indeed, very much like Weber, Marx (1967 [orig. 1867]) did emphasize the ruling class's need for efficient, low-cost labor that could mass produce a variety of products with a minimum of training. However, modern Marxist social scientists have added a very important insight: What is most profitable to the owners of the means of production is *not* always what maximizes efficiency (Blumberg, 1973; Gintis, 1974; Melman, 1983). In fact, productivity studies consistently find that giving workers more control of their work situation usually *increases* productivity (Bernstein, 1976; Blumberg, 1973; Le Boeuf, 1982, Chap. 6; Melman, 1983, Chap. 13; Schooler and Naoi, 1988; Zwerdling, 1978). This implies that reducing or eliminating the hierarchical features of bureaucratic organizations should raise an organization's productivity, not lower it. However, this does not mean that the business or factory will thereby become more profitable *for its owners*. If workers are made more powerful by eliminating hierarchical control, they may use that power to bring about higher pay, more fringe benefits, better working conditions, and other workers' benefits. In short, because the most efficient organization is not always the most profitable one for the owners, owners often sacrifice efficiency in order to maintain control (Edwards, 1979; Gintis, 1974; Hecksher, 1980; Melman, 1983). From this perspective, then, bureaucracy is functional for a specific interest group (owners of the means of production) but dysfunctional for the larger society.

Work by Wright (2000), however, suggests that once workers reach a certain level of power, it may be in the interests of both workers and employers to cooperate. In other words, once workers are powerful enough to be able to disrupt a work organization, it may well be in the interests of their employers to move toward cooperation rather than bureaucratic control. Not only will disruption be reduced, but both workers and employers may enjoy benefits from the increased productivity that results from a less top-down, more cooperative way of organizing the workplace. In other words, the work organization may be more profitable for its owners *even with* higher levels of worker pay and benefits.

Because they believed that the main purpose of bureaucracies was to enable the ruling class to maintain control, Marx and his coauthor Friedrich Engels believed that bureaucracies would "wither away" once class inequalities were eliminated through common ownership of the means of production. They wrote this explicitly about government bureaucracies, but Marx appears to have believed much the same about private bureaucracies, because he saw them, too, as a tool by which the ruling class controls and dominates the masses. In fact, Marx even questioned the need for specialization, viewing it as a means by which the masses of workers were deprived of knowledge that could make them too threatening to the ruling class.

The Pervasiveness of Bureaucracy

It appears that functionalist and conflict viewpoints both have useful insights as to the reasons bureaucracy has become so pervasive in the modern world. Every society that has industrialized has experienced the dramatic growth in organizations that fit Weber's definition of a bureaucracy. It is, in fact, very hard to see how any large-scale task could be accomplished without the coordination that bureaucracy makes possible. Factories using division of labor and mass-production assembly lines (impossible without bureaucratic organization) are far more efficient than ones where each worker makes the whole product. In every task from manufacturing to governing to waging war, organizations that fit Weber's general model appear more efficient than organizations that don't. Consequently, industrialized countries have turned to bureaucratic organizations to perform all of these tasks.

It therefore appears that the Marxian claim that bureaucracies will "wither away" is an impossible dream. Modern technology has made the need for specialization far greater today than it was over a century ago when Marx wrote. Moreover, attempts to level out socioeconomic inequalities and guarantee equal political and economic rights nearly always require more complex organization, not less. Thus, bureaucracies seem to be a growing feature of modern societies regardless of whether they are capitalist, socialist, or something in between.

Evaluating Bureaucracy

This having been said, it must be acknowledged that some features of bureaucracy seem to have developed well beyond the point where they could be considered functional. Again, this is a feature of both capitalist and socialist societies, as those in charge seek to hold on to their power and economic advantage through hierarchical control. In the Soviet Union, a policy of centralized control for years stifled the economy because of insistence that decisions be made or approved in Moscow, without regard for market forces or local needs. The resulting economic stagnation was a major cause of the collapse of the Soviet Union. In capitalist countries, a similar problem can occur when the owners of capital retain hierarchical control, even though granting their workers more autonomy would increase productivity. In these countries, too, the need for change is beginning to be recognized. In the United States, which has lost considerable ground economically to international competition, more and more companies have experimented with less centralized forms of work organization developed in Japan, Sweden, and elsewhere. These will be discussed later in this chapter.

The extent to which bureaucracy is an efficient form of organization also depends on the task being performed. In general, bureaucracy works better for complex yet routine and repetitious tasks (such as manufacturing and distributing automobiles), and less well for tasks that are nonroutine and require imagination (such as designing and building a space shuttle).

Dysfunctions of Bureaucracy

While bureaucracies tend to be more functional for routine tasks than others, there are some potential dysfunctions in bureaucracy, regardless of the task.

A bureaucracy, by definition, is a group. Therefore, it is subject to the same problems and dysfunctions as other groups, such as groupthink and group polarization. Bureaucracies also are subject to additional dysfunctions arising from their size, formality, complexity, and hierarchical organization.

Decision Avoidance
One problem of bureaucracies is that sometimes they have a hard time making decisions. Most bureaucratic organizations are designed to handle routine matters according to a known set of guidelines. When they encounter a situation that falls outside the guidelines, often they have a hard time handling it. One reason is the tendency for each person in the organization to pass such decisions along to someone else because nobody wants to be responsible for a decision that might "go wrong" or be questioned later. If you have ever encountered a billing error, a lost file, or a "mistake on the computer," you probably experienced this problem.

Trained Incapacity
In those instances when they are faced with an unfamiliar situation, people in bureaucracies may try to make the situation fit into one for which they do have guidelines. The result is a failure to adapt to the new situation, a condition sociologists sometimes call *trained incapacity* (Veblen, 1921). This tendency to "force" situations to fit the guidelines results in part from the tendency toward conformity in groups and organizations. For an individual to make a bold or innovative decision in such situations would implicitly challenge "the way we do things," a risk many people in organizations are unwilling to take. A result is that organizations that may be very good at handling *familiar* situations often cannot handle change, because the old ways of doing things tend to be self-perpetuating (Kanter, 1983, Chaps. 3, 4). An example of this may be seen in the slow initial response of federal disaster agencies to Hurricane Andrew in 1992: The agencies were experienced in handling localized disasters that were severe but limited in scope and had effective procedures for handling such disasters. However, these procedures were inadequate for the widespread devastation over hundreds of square miles that Andrew caused in Florida. This pattern was tragically repeated in the aftermath of Hurricane Katrina in 2005. As levees broke in New Orleans and residents watched helplessly as flood waters drowned the city, aid from local, state, and federal levels failed to adequately respond to the emergency. A major roadblock in this incident was the recent reorganization of the Federal Emergency Management Agency (FEMA) under the authority of the newly created Office of Homeland Security. The reorganization created a new layer of bureaucracy that slowed down response time (Tierney, 2006). In addition, in-fighting between the new agency, competitor agencies, and old agencies that had fallen under Homeland Security's purview, such as FEMA, seems to have contributed to the slow response. Homeland Security's focus was squarely on terrorism, not natural disasters. Add to that the many political appointees that had little to no disaster experience running FEMA, and a recipe for a disaster within a disaster was created (Dyson, 2006; Tierney, 2006). As more than one commentator put it, the hurricane was a natural disaster, but the real tragedy was entirely man-made and occurred after the hurricane had passed. From the levees that were not designed to withstand the water surge to the failure to respond after their breech, human factors, as much as the hurricane itself, contributed to the massive loss of life and the slow and inadequate response. The sociologist Harvey Molotch (2006) points out that people in government agencies normally follow bureaucratic rules, but in times of emergency or other urgent need for action, there is a need to set the rules aside

to act as quickly as possible, and in other cases, officials have done so. In such situations, they do what is necessary to get the job done. According to Molotch, however, there was very little of this in the case of Katrina: No person in a position of high authority pushed the panic button and ordered that things just get done. Molotch suggests that an additional factor contributing to this may have been race: most of the victims were black, whereas most of the government officials with the ability to set the rules aside were white, and this may have reduced their sense of urgency.

Normalization of Deviance

In recent years, a number of sociologists have examined how misconduct, often with deadly consequences, can frequently become the norm within organizations (Vaughan, 1996; Kauzlarich and Kramer, 1998; Matthews and Kauzlaruch, 2000). The 1986 *Challenger* space shuttle disaster is a good example of this. Sociologist Diane Vaughan spent nearly ten years examining public and private documents and interviewing people involved in the Space Shuttle program to find the underlying causes of the disaster. Her work indicates strongly that the organization, not the individuals involved, was the main cause of the disaster, *because potentially dangerous violations of procedure had become routine in the shuttle program.* This occurred for three reasons: (1) the environment within which the program operated, which generated pressures to break rules in order to meet goals; (2) organizational structures and processes that made it possible to break the rules, and (3) a regulatory environment in which the relationship between regulators and the organizations they regulate made control and deterrence of violations unlikely. The shuttle program was under strong pressure to cut delays, and NASA wanted the first teacher in space to be orbiting during President Reagan's State of the Union Address. NASA had identified many conditions that could be serious enough to stop a launch, but they had launched in spite of such conditions in the past without problems, and the professional judgment of NASA personnel had long been relied upon to decide whether a condition was serious enough to cancel a launch. This made it both possible and tempting to launch despite a known problem with the shuttle's rubber joint seals, especially at low temperatures. Add to this two truths about those who were supposed to regulate NASA, and you have a recipe for disaster: First, the autonomy of NASA and secrecy associated with the space program made it hard for regulators to know what was going on, and second, as in most cases of regulation, regulators and the people they were supposed to regulate were interdependent, so that incentives ran more to cooperation than to regulators "policing" the agency. Similar forces have been at work in many other cases of deadly organizational deviance, such as the ValuJet crash in Florida in 1996 (Matthews and Kauzlarich, 2000), nuclear experimentation by the U.S. government (Kauzlarich and Kramer, 1998), and the continued sale of dangerous sport utility vehicles by Ford even after deaths associated with their Bridgestone-Firestone tires had been brought to the company's attention (Healey and Woodyard, 2000). They may also have been at work in the 2010 BP oil disaster in the Gulf of Mexico.

Self-Perpetuation and Goal Displacement

A U.S. senator once remarked that if he believed in reincarnation, he would pray to come back as a temporary Senate subcommittee because he could then enjoy eternal life. Modern organizations do tend to persist, for several reasons. First, within any organization that has employees, a primary goal quickly becomes the preservation of the organization, which in turn preserves people's jobs (Selznick, 1957, p. 21). Sociologists refer to this process as goal displacement—whatever the original goals of the organization, its primary goal quickly becomes to preserve the organization. Consider the temporary Senate subcommittee. It has a staff whose jobs depend on the continued existence of the committee. Moreover, the senators who serve on the committee may gain status with other senators as a result of their role as committee members. They also may appear to constituents back home to be "doing something about the problem" the subcommittee was created to deal with.

The incentives for self-preservation are so strong that organizations often continue even when the problem that originally brought them into existence is gone. The American Lung Association, formerly the American Tuberculosis and Respiratory Association, was formed to reduce the incidence of tuberculosis in American society.

It was successful in these efforts, to the point that very few Americans get tuberculosis today. Did the organization declare itself a success and disband? Not at all. It turned its attention to a new set of problems and works today to combat lung cancer.

Tendency to Expand

Organizations tend not only to survive but also to grow. In a bureaucracy, a supervisor's prestige is largely determined by the number of people that he or she supervises. Thus, the manager of a large department has more prestige than the manager of a small department. It therefore becomes in every manager's interest to think of more things that "need" to be done and to get authorization to hire more employees to do them. Once more workers are hired, more supervisors must be hired to supervise them, and more secretaries must be hired to keep track of their files. A principle called "Parkinson's Law" reveals why it is never any problem to keep them busy (Parkinson, 1957). According to Parkinson's Law, work expands to use the time or personnel available. If people are available, something will be found for them to do. A job can always be done in greater detail if more time is available.

Nowhere is this principle clearer than in the case of computerization. Because computers are far more efficient than older methods of doing things, it would seem that computers could reduce the need for administrators and record keepers. Studies of organizations that have used computers to "automate their offices," however, have disproved this idea (Heskiaoff, 1977). What actually happens is that new information is collected and processed. As one study of the American Broadcasting Company (ABC) revealed, computerization actually can lead to an increase in the number of administrators, as new people are hired to work with the additional information that is generated (Melman, 1983, p. 76).

Ritualism

Another dysfunction of bureaucracies is the tendency of some workers to engage in ritualism—placing the procedures of the organization ahead of the purposes for which the procedures were designed (Merton, 1968). The main objective of such workers becomes following the correct rules and procedures rather than getting the job done properly. Workers who think and behave in this manner are sometimes said to have a bureaucratic personality. Supervisors sometimes encourage such behavior because following procedures is the "safe" thing to do. Fortunately, though, it appears that only a minority of workers in organizations develop such behavior (Kohn, 1978). Rather than devoting themselves to the rules, most workers develop an informal structure that bends the rules—a pattern that we shall explore in more detail shortly.

Alienation of Workers

Worker **alienation** is a dysfunction that was recognized in different ways by both Marx and Weber. Marx was more explicit, defining alienation as the result of separating the worker from the product of his or her labor. In large, specialized organizations, each worker does only a small part of the job, and the finished product is not the product of any one worker's efforts. Contrast the auto assembly-line worker with the cabinet maker. When a car rolls off the assembly line, the autoworker cannot look at it and say "I made that" in the same sense that the cabinet maker can when he or she finishes handcrafting a piece of furniture. Modern workers in bureaucracies cannot see that they have produced an item of value, and as a result, they may come to doubt their own value (see Schooler and Naoi, 1988).

Weber also recognized this problem. He saw bureaucracy as an "iron cage," necessary yet inevitably trapping workers in a depersonalized situation. Both Marx and Weber recognized that lack of control over their work situation would be a key source of frustration to modern workers. Bureaucracy has similar effects in higher education. In addition, education also plays a role in worker alienation. To well-educated people who value the chance to use their creative talents, jobs over which they have little control can be especially frustrating. As the average educational level of even assembly-line workers has risen, alienation among such workers seems to have increased since around 1970, leading to greater effects on productivity (Ritzer and Walczak, 1986, pp. 355–57). At the same time, we know that some workers are in far more alienating situations than others, and that women, people of color, and

When the potter finishes his job, he can take pride in a visible product that he has designed and created. In contrast, factory workers may only participate in a process by adding one part to a larger machine or device. (iStockphoto)

people with lower-than-average education levels are particularly likely to end up in alienating jobs. Fortunately, though, people in organizations have some ability to shape informally what really goes on in the organization, which partially offsets the alienating features of bureaucracy. We now turn to some of the ways they do this.

An Interactionist View of Bureaucracy

Informal Structure

We have seen, in Weber's ideal-type definition of bureaucracy, what the formal structure of complex organizations looks like. However, the symbolic-interactionist perspective reminds us that organizations also have an **informal structure**—the things people actually do on a day-to-day basis, in contrast to what the official rules say they are supposed to do (Blau and Meyer, 1971, Chap. 3). Although the formal structure of a bureaucracy consists of a complex set of positions with norms about how they are supposed to interact, these positions are filled by people, each of whom has his or her own personality, objectives, and understanding of the organization and his or her position within it. Each person acts on the basis of these factors (Blumer, 1969a). Moreover, each person has a particular reaction to the other people with whom he or she works. Any two individuals will play a particular role in the organization differently and will thus evoke different reactions from co-workers. One boss might be identified as supportive and democratic, whereas another in the same position might be seen as authoritarian and critical. The former is more likely to inspire hard work from his or her subordinates, whereas the latter may get only loafing, avoidance, and "bitching" (Filley and House, 1969; Hall, 1996, p. 145). The degree to which a supervisor appears to know his or her job will also affect employee output and cooperativeness.

Whatever the official rules of the organization, workers have their own ideas and will collectively develop informal norms (Fine, 1992). Productivity, for example, is usually governed by such norms, as Roethlisberger and Dickson (1939) discovered in their famous study of production workers at the Hawthorne plant of Western Electric. Workers who either exceed or fall below their co-workers' productivity norms will likely be made to feel uncomfortable. Those who work too hard relative to the group norm will be labeled as "rate-busters," and those who do not work hard enough will be labeled "lazy" or "goof-offs."

Flexibility

Another reason for informal structure is that the formal rules don't always work. If everyone engaged in ritualism—following all the rules all the time—most organizations would grind to a halt. In fact, a familiar tactic of labor unions that want to pressure an employer without going so far as to strike is "working to rule"—following every regulation literally and exactly. Almost inevitably, this practice leads to a big drop in productivity as workers spend most of their time filling out forms and following procedures. Usually, though, workers follow informal norms rather than strictly obeying the official rules because that works best. Because no policy can cover every possibility, in order for the organization to work, employees must use their judgment and creativity in unusual situations. They often do so, deciding how to handle any given situation as it comes up, and the decision is not always "by the rules."

Similarly, the official channels of communication can be very slow and inefficient. The "official" way for a person in an organization to consult with someone in another department is to send a memo through his or her supervisor to the other person's supervisor, who then passes on the message to the person for whom it is intended. A simple phone call or e-mail is much quicker. Similarly, you may know that you are "supposed to" communicate with one person concerning a given problem, but past experience tells you that someone else will be more helpful. Chances are, you will communicate with that "someone else."

Primary Groups and Informal Structure
Finally, we have noted that primary groups frequently develop within large organizations, even though the organizations themselves are secondary groups. Friendship networks, "buddies," and cliques form within every organization, and whether any given worker is "in" or "out" of another worker's informal group will influence how the two workers relate to one another. Workers often protect and exchange favors with co-workers they consider friends, when they would treat someone else in the same situation differently.

Negotiated Order

These examples illustrate a key point: Regardless of the formal structure, people ultimately make the organization (Scott, 1992, p. 54). These people, with their needs, objectives, and experiences of others in the organization, create a **negotiated order.** They push to get what they want, try things out, test the limits of the rules. This reality was illustrated in a now-classic study of mental hospitals by Anselm Strauss and his colleagues (1964). Strauss found that the nature of the hospital at any given time was the outcome of pressures, actions, and reactions of the many people who made the organization: doctors, attendants, nurses, administrators, and patients. Each person in each of these groups had his or her own objectives, understanding of reality, and ideas about mental illness, which governed his or her behavior and relationships to others. Compromises, "looking the other way," and "agreements to disagree" were abundant, but they were always subject to change as the characters changed and new negotiations took place. Thus, "the hospital" today is not exactly the same as "the hospital" last month, even if the formal structure remains unchanged, because the process of negotiating order continues as long as the organization does. Although Strauss et al. used the mental hospital to illustrate this process, the evidence indicates that such negotiation occurs in most kinds of organizations (Lauer and Handel, 1983). The interaction of this process with the formal and informal structures of the organization and with the goals and objectives of organizational leaders produces an *organizational culture.* This culture is unique to each organization and cannot be understood merely by examining the organization's formal structure (Fine, 1984; Ouchi and Wilkins, 1985). As with any culture, new members must be socialized into organizational cultures, and new employees who do not become appropriately socialized usually experience a very difficult time.

Roles in the Workplace: Case Studies

Because each worker occupies a particular position within the work organization, each worker experiences the organization differently. This is in part a product of the worker's personality and desires, but it also reflects the worker's situation within the organization. According to Millman and Kanter (1975), an organization can be seen as an interrelated set of groups, each with its own style, culture, norms, political allegiances, and internal hierarchy. As illustrated by the following case studies, portions of which draw largely on the research of Rosabeth Moss Kanter, different classes of workers experience and respond to the organization in different ways.

The Professional
Professionals, such as doctors, scientists, professors, and engineers, generally enjoy a good deal more autonomy on the job than most workers. This is because their jobs require extensive, specialized training, and it is assumed that nobody else in the organization knows their work as well as they do (Parsons, 1947, 1951). Professionals tend to be supervised less closely than other workers. Unlike many other workers, they are not usually evaluated to any great extent on how well they follow established procedures. Rather, the evaluation is based mainly on the outcome: Has a professional been successful in accomplishing what he or she was hired to do? Frequently, this judgment is arrived at

through a process of peer evaluation, as when college professors judge their colleagues' worthiness for tenure or promotion (Blau and Meyer, 1971, pp. 76–77; Scott, 1992, p. 254).

Professionals not only enjoy more autonomy than other workers, they expect it. When subjected to extensive bureaucratic rules and regulations, they are often the first to rebel. Moreover, they seek to secure their autonomy through the process of professionalization, in which they establish accepted procedures to obtain credentials and accreditation. These procedures serve to certify their expertise and justify both their autonomy (Collins, 1979; Wilensky, 1964) and the power they often enjoy over related occupations (Halpern, 1992). The growing importance of professionals in our economy may be having the effect of reducing the influence of formal bureaucratic hierarchy in modern organizations. Similarly, research suggests that as technology-based enterprises have become more dominant in the economy, the power of the professionals who carry out research and development has grown (Harpaz and Meshoulam, 1997).

Even with professionals, though, the organization makes a difference. Perrow (1979, pp. 50–55) points out that professionals in private corporations are more tolerant of hierarchy and regulations than are those in universities or research organizations. But even the latter institutions have broad rules and regulations within which professionals must operate. Perrow also notes that professionals with aspirations to move into management—where the best salaries frequently are—are often willing to sacrifice autonomy in exchange for upward mobility, money, and organizational prestige.

The Secretary

The role of the secretary stands in sharp contrast to that of the professional (Kanter, 1977; Millman and Kanter, 1975). Typically, secretaries enjoy very little autonomy unless they work for a top executive. However, interaction with the boss, and not bureaucratic rules, determines the secretary's working conditions. This interaction is still more often than not a male-female relationship and is shaped heavily by societal gender inequality and its supporting norms (Mills, 1951; Mesmer, 1998; Sotirin and Gottfried, 1999). A male managerial worker may be judged on the attractiveness, educational level, and personality of his secretary, and having a private secretary is an important status symbol in many organizations (Burger, 1964). In a sense, secretaries are often treated as the personal property of their bosses, expected to do personal favors and to move within the organization when the boss moves, and evaluated on the basis of the boss's personal judgment rather than bureaucratic or procedural criteria. In many organizations, a promotion for a secretary does not mean new job responsibilities, but rather, a higher-status boss. In such cases, a secretary's job status is not defined by anything the secretary does, but rather by what the boss does. This practice, sometimes known as "rug-ranking," was challenged in a 1993 lawsuit against ESPN by secretary Elaine Truskoski (Hirsh, 1993; Soukhanov, 1994). In general, research also shows that it is difficult for secretaries to move into management positions, even when other types of employees do get hired into management (Phalen, 2000; Mesmer, 1998). This is true even though long-time secretaries of top managers often know more about how the organization works than most people in the firm.

The Middle Manager

The middle manager, moving up in the organization, is probably the type of worker who conforms best to the formal bureaucratic model. Such workers seek to prove their worth by upholding the company's ways of doing things and by demonstrating their loyalty to their supervisors. This behavior is frequently successful because top managers—who actually deal with unpredictable market conditions outside the organization—are often uncertain about their decisions. To reduce their own uncertainty and to free them to deal with the external environment, these top managers need loyal, predictable subordinates (Kanter, 1977). For the most part, middle managers with upward aspirations recognize this need, comply, and seek compliance from their employees.

What is good for individuals, however, is not always good for the organization. This tendency toward compliance in management can be so strong that it can prevent the company from adapting to changing conditions. In this sense, hierarchical command can be dysfunctional rather than serving the function of rationalization claimed by Weber. If blind obedience leads people to follow the unwise policies of an organization's leader, everyone can be led down a path of failure. As Blau and Meyer (1971) put it, "To overcome bureaucratic inertia seems to require new organizations or new managers, unencumbered by traditions and personal loyalties, and not enmeshed in the social processes that characterize the interpersonal relations in the organization."

On the other hand, some recent research has suggested that hierarchical control over middle-management personnel can be useful to the organization (Prechel, 1994). Because middle-management employees act as a link between the top leadership and the front-line management and production workers in various departments, they are the one means that top management has to assure that the various departments are working in a coordinated manner. Thus, to assure such coordination, the work of middle managers may be highly controlled even when other workers experience greater autonomy.

This and other realities have made the lives of many middle-management workers difficult in recent years. They often remain tightly controlled by top management, while at the same time they have lost authority over workers lower in the hierarchy. This has happened as the workers over whom they used to have authority have gained greater autonomy as a part of workplace reforms, which we will discuss in the next section. In addition to this, middle-management workers have been among the hardest hit as companies have downsized to cut costs in the face of global competition.

The Lone Minority

Yet another distinct role in the organization is that of the lone or token minority: the only woman on a board of directors; the only black professor in a university department. This individual will face issues that others entering the same job will not. In part, co-workers will react to this person as a woman or as a black person—a role they may not be used to seeing in combination with the role of executive or professor (Kanter, 1977, Chap. 8). In their attempt to deal with this combination, colleagues may insist on fitting the lone minority into a role they associate with the person's group. They may treat a female colleague, for example, as they would their mother, or as a sex object, or as something akin to a mascot (Millman and Kanter, 1975). Or, they may expect that a female university professor will be more nurturing and caring toward her students than a male professor (Acker and Feuerverger, 1996). At the other extreme, some may view her as an "iron maiden," concluding that only a woman who fits the toughest male stereotype could rise to such heights (Kanter, 1977). Others may mistake the person's role entirely, as when female executives or professors are mistaken for secretaries (Lynch, 1973). Finally, they may put such individuals on display as tokens, rewarding them for their positions ("our woman manager" or "our black vice president") but not for what they accomplish (Kanter, 1977, pp. 213–14). When interviewed, people who are the first or only person from their group in a work situation often report that they experience extreme pressures to succeed because they are perceived by others as indicators of what people in their group can or cannot do (Phalen, 2000). Finally, several studies indicate that it is not unusual for lone minorities to be excluded from informal interactions and networking, and sometimes from opportunities for training and advancement (Yoder and Aniakudo, 1997; Burke and McKeen, 1995).

All of this means that the lone minority must spend time working to define her or his role to colleagues in a way that others do not have to (Epstein, 1970). This burden diminishes the lone minority's ability to "take charge" of the job, makes interaction with colleagues clumsy, and leads to feelings of frustration and isolation. Ultimately, it means that until they become a substantial proportion of the workforce in any given work setting, women and minorities may take longer than others to establish secure working relationships with colleagues based on their competence. This probably reduces the rate at which even the most capable women and minority-group members can move up the corporate ladder. It is also an important reason why it is better both for the work organization and for women and people of color when their presence in the workplace goes well beyond the kind of tokenism that produces lone minorities (see, for example, Watson, Kumar, and Michaelsen, 1993; Livingston, 1991).

Globalization and New Trends in Work Organization

We have seen that the bureaucratic form of organization has become pervasive in modern society because of its efficiency in handling large-scale tasks, but that bureaucracy has also tended to be more formal and hierarchical than what is required for such efficiency. Especially, but not only, in democratic societies, the informal structure is often as influential as the official, formal structure, and studies show that less hierarchy and more worker autonomy usually lead to better productivity. As more countries have modernized and industrialized in recent years, pressures to be efficient have increased. **Globalization** of the economy—a transition to a worldwide economy that transcends national boundaries—has occurred at an increasing rate. Efficient mass production of some products is possible virtually anywhere in the world, so that today rather than operating on a local, regional, or national scale, economic competition is on a global scale. This means that companies and their workforces must compete not only with their traditional domestic rivals, but also with growing numbers of competitors worldwide.

Globalization and Work

Globalization has led to both positive and destructive tendencies in work organizations. Among the more destructive have been the closely related trends of *downsizing* and *outsourcing,* which together have shrunk the supply of good-paying jobs, particularly for people with less than a college-level education. This has occurred during some recent periods of overall job growth when lower-paying jobs have grown at a rate equal to or greater than the shrinkage of higher-paying jobs. Some higher-paying jobs, especially in larger corporations, have fallen victim to "downsizing," a process whereby employers have reduced the size of their workforce through (1) automation; (2) relocation of jobs to areas with cheaper labor, often overseas; and (3) outsourcing. *Outsourcing* is a process whereby work that had been done by employees of a company is contracted out to some external company. This has led to reductions in workers' pay, because the jobs that are eliminated are usually full-time jobs with benefits and, often, the protections of a union contract. In contrast, the jobs that are outsourced are usually contracted out to employers who pay lower wages, offer fewer benefits, and often use part-time and/or nonunion labor (Henson, 1996). In the public sector, much the same has happened through "privatization," in which jobs that had been done by public employees are contracted out to private employers, who typically offer less in the way of wages, benefits, and union representation.

In part for these reasons, real (inflation-adjusted) wages have been relatively flat since around 1973. From then until the mid-1990s, the three-fourths of U.S. workers without college degrees lost ground, and those with college degrees have had, on the average, no wage growth. (Bluestone, 1995). Only those with masters degrees or more education gained ground between 1973 and 1993. By early 1995, American workers had the lowest compensation growth in two decades (Mishel, 1995). Beginning in the mid-1990s, there was some rebound in wage growth due to the overall growth of the economy, but wage growth was less than in previous boom periods and was concentrated among the best-educated employees. Even in the boom of the 1990s, workers with low levels of education, who became increasingly concentrated in service industries, experienced wage stagnation or decline. In 1995, about one U.S. worker in seven worked in a low-wage job with no health insurance and no retirement benefits (Kalleberg, Reskin, and Hudson, 2000). This was most likely to occur in nonstandard (part-time, temporary, outsourced) jobs as opposed to regular full-time employment. Women without a college education are especially likely to suffer as a result of such employment (McCall, 2000). When the boom of the 1990s ended and was replaced by recessions following the September 11, 2001, terrorist attacks and the 2008 economic crisis, wage stagnation similar to that of the 1970s and 1980s returned. As a result of all these trends, economic inequality has risen steadily over the past four decades (Duncan, 1996; Saez, 2009a, 2009b).

According to Mishel, two-thirds of this increase in inequality can be attributed to two factors: globalization and declining union representation. The latter, with the resultant loss of wages and benefits, is closely tied to outsourcing. Between 1978 and 1985, part-time employment grew eight times as fast as overall employment, and it grew by another 50 percent by 1989 (Howell, 1994). The growth in part-time and temporary work, closely tied to the practice of contracting out, continued through the mid-1990s and beyond. Conflict over outsourcing has been an increasing source of workplace tension. In the mid-1990s, bitter strikes over the issue occurred at General Motors, McDonnell Douglas, Boeing, and other large industrial companies. Because globalization has created similar pressures in all industrialized countries, outsourcing, privatization, and the weakening of unions have occurred not only in the United States but in other nations as well. One study of eighteen industrialized countries showed that unions were weakened in all of them during the 1980s (Western, 1995). Since the late 1990s, however, workers and their supporters have responded to these trends with increasing protest against the economic effects of globalization and unrestrained free trade, and this activism may be reversing the trend of unions weakening. Particularly notable have been protests against the World Trade Organization (WTO) in Seattle in 1999 and in Quebec City in 2001, as well as growing student protests against the production of college athletic wear in sweatshops around the world and in support of college-campus workers.

On the positive side, increasing numbers of employers have responded to the pressures of global competition by experimenting with new forms of work organization that offer greater efficiency than the traditional hierarchical model. These efforts have gone the furthest in Japan and the Scandinavian countries but they are becoming increasingly influential in the United States as well. The common features of these efforts are to change the structure of work organization so that they (1) shift some decision-making authority from management to workers, and (2) organize workers into groups or teams that make or recommend those decisions.

Japanese Work Organization

From the 1970s through the 1990s, Japanese products gained a worldwide reputation for high quality and reasonable cost. In the 1970s and 1980s, productivity of the Japanese economy grew faster than that of most other industrialized countries, and the result was a rapid improvement of the economic standard of living of the Japanese worker. A major reason for this is that in Japan, more than in most other industrialized nations, a cooperative relationship between workers and management developed that involved workers in shaping decisions about the work process. One way this has been done is through the quality control circle (QC circle), a small group of usually about five to ten workers who meet regularly to assess the group's performance. This serves three purposes. It contributes to the improvement of the product or enterprise, improves human relations and worker satisfaction, and allows workers the opportunity to express their full potential (Ishikawa, 1984). QC circles are based on the idea that involving workers in shaping the work process on the basis of their experiences and knowledge will lead to higher productivity. This stands in contrast to the traditional American view that the route to improved productivity is hierarchical control and automation that simplifies the worker's job and speeds the work process. Obviously, Japan has extensively automated as well, but the objective has not been to make the job simpler so much as to make the overall process more efficient, using the problem-solving skills of the workers.

Part of the principle of QC circles is to reward workers directly for their commitment to productivity. When a worker comes up with ideas that save the company money, the benefits are often passed on to the worker. As a result, Japanese workers enjoyed wage growth well above that of American workers over an extended time from the early 1970s to the mid-1990s (Karatsu, 1984, pp. 10–11; Kmitch, Laboy, and Van Damme, 1995; Taira and Levine, 1996). Japanese wages were hurt after 1995 by the general slump in the Asian economy, and Japan, like other industrialized countries, has been impacted by globalization in the form of competition from low-wage countries such as South Korea and China. Nonetheless, Japanese workers experienced lasting gains in their standards of living as a result of their large wage increases in the 1970s and 1980s.

Some Japanese workers are also rewarded for their commitment to their employer through lifetime employment: In many Japanese firms, once workers complete a probationary period, they are guaranteed that their job will not be eliminated, even if the company has to cut costs. In some cases, top management employees in Japan have taken large pay cuts in order to avoid laying off workers (Le Boeuf, 1982). This, however, carries a reciprocal responsibility for the worker: He or she must not jump ship to another employer. Just as the employer commits to the worker, so must the worker commit to the employer. A case such as that of Lee Iacocca, who served as chief executive of both the Chrysler Corporation and Ford Motors at different times in his career, would be unheard of in Japan. It should be noted, however, that the lifetime employment system has been threatened

PERSONAL JOURNEYS INTO SOCIOLOGY
Work Without Bosses: Organizational Democracy as the Alternative to Bureaucracy

Joyce Rothschild

My investigation into worker cooperatives was born, I suppose, out of my personal frustration with bureaucracy. Who has not encountered, in the daily course of events, some functionary telling us what can or cannot be done? If we respond that this makes little sense, that the proscribed or prescribed action runs contrary even to the stated goals of the organization, the bureaucrat remains undaunted: "I'm sorry; it is our rule; it is our policy."

There may be tremendous costs associated with running everything bureaucratically—for example, millions of employees, surveys tell us, hold back their best energies and ideas because they feel they have no real voice in the workplace decisions that affect their lives. Several social movements have shed new light on this issue. During my undergraduate years, antiwar activists defended the right of the Vietnamese people to decide their own fate. The women's movement was asserting the right of women to redefine their rights and roles in modern society. The Civil Rights movement, too, was about self-determination. Everywhere people seemed to be demanding the opportunity to decide for themselves the fundamental conditions of their lives.

The heated debates of the day, however, seemed to present a choice between the Soviet model of state-owned industry and the American model of private investor-owned industry. I reasoned that a socialist bureaucracy was not likely to be any more satisfying for the average working person than capitalist bureaucracy had been. Both models located the centers of power way up in the hierarchy of the organization, far removed from the input of the average individual. If people wanted a voice in the decisions that affected their lives, I concluded that it was in their workplaces that they most needed to be heard. Any institution that absorbs this much of our time and energy as adults and that so shapes our sense of ourselves simply cannot be forfeited to hierarchical control.

In short, it seemed to me that a third path would have to be found in the world. Both socialist and capitalist economies would need to find a way to go beyond bureaucracy, or to dismantle bureaucracy if necessary, in order to include the voice of working people in crucial workplace decisions. This was a requirement if work organizations were to provide the sort of self-managed or autonomous work that people said they wanted, and if organizations were to remain responsive to their customer base and therefore competitive.

These observations led me to read about bureaucracy and to wonder whether a cooperative form of organization—one that was owned and run by its workers—might be a practical alternative. In my reading I discovered that bureaucracy and centralized control over organizations were accepted as a necessity, if not an inevitability, in social science. Weber had argued convincingly that bureaucratic authority would become a permanent and indispensable characteristic of modern society. Once firmly established, bureaucracy would be revolution-proof: Modern societies might undergo changes in who controls the bureaucratic apparatus, but the structure of bureaucratic control would remain intact. Domination (*herrschaft*), in Weber's view, would always require an administrative apparatus to execute commands, and conversely, all administration would require domination. Robert Michels took Weber's philosophy one step further. His "iron law of oligarchy" asserted that organizational democracy would inevitably yield to oligarchy. Michels's

by hard economic times, as some Japanese firms reconsidered this policy during the chronic recession of the 1990s. As a result, the percentage of long-tenure employees in the Japanese workforce does seem to be declining. While some firms went to great lengths during the 1990s to avoid layoffs of regular employees who were covered by lifetime employment guarantees (Taira and Levine, 1996), others are ending the system. Today, just one in five Japanese workers—mainly male employees with large employers—still enjoy lifetime employment (Hirakubo, 1999; Ono, 2006).

law became a cornerstone of twentieth-century social science, which subsequently dismissed the possibility of democracy in large organizations.

As I became immersed in the literature and traditions in organizational studies, I could not help but notice that right outside my window worker co-ops—or "collectives," as they were called—were appearing all over. These collectives were organized to do what the social science literature said was impossible: to throw out accepted notions about bureaucracy with its chain of command, its written rules, and its strict separation of labor and management. In its place they wanted to create organizations where everyone had an opportunity to participate in decisions, where those who did the work of the organization also did the managing.

In their experimentation, the cooperatives offered a glimpse into how real-life functioning democracies would operate. I chose to examine a number of these organizations from different domains in order to identify the key organizational structures and processes that are essential to democratic organizations. Just as Weber had identified the key characteristics of bureaucracy, we needed to learn if there were key characteristics of democracy. From my study, it became evident that the characteristic practices of democracies were made cohesive by the basic values of their participants (what Weber had called "substantive rationality"), just as the practices of bureaucracies are unified by their formal rules and procedures (which Weber calls "formal rationality"). In other words, to the three bases of authority put forward by Max Weber (traditional, charismatic, and legal-rational) would have to be added a fourth basis of authority: value-rationality or substantive-rationality. In the bureaucratic model, authority resides in office incumbency that ideally is based in expertise; but in the collectivist-democratic model authority rests in the collectivity as a whole whose decisions are based on allegiance to their values or substantive purposes, and it requires a consensus-based decision system to ascertain the collective will.

Beyond allowing me to see that a fourth basis of organization was possible, the very existence of the co-ops as participatory-democratic entities permitted me to search for the specific conditions that appeared to favor organizational democracy. I ended up identifying ten conditions that support democracy within an organization. There are inherent trade-offs, however, that go with the pursuit of democracy. For each condition I identify as supporting democracy, I show the problems that it raises for the organization in terms of productivity and efficiency. Cooperative enterprises must get a job done while retaining a democratic form. Although they do not always succeed, my study showed that, contrary to the iron law of oligarchy, they do not always fail.

Thus, my research both specified the key characteristics of a whole new model of organization and identified some of the conditions that facilitate or undermine this model. Since this original research, many other worker-owned and worker-run enterprises have been developing around the United States and around the globe. As a result of this research, any viable social science must now consider democratic forms of organization as legitimate alternatives to bureaucracy.

Years after my study of the grass roots collectives and co-ops, I asked myself what people who were equally values-driven would do if they found themselves working in a bureaucracy, be it public or private. I concluded that these employees would become the "whistleblowers," exposing wrongful or illegal corporate conduct. I set out to discover what drives these people and what happens to them. I learned that many employees (about a third) witness some things that trouble them in the workplace, but not all of these people blow the whistle. What distinguishes the whistleblowers is that they are stirred by strongly held substantive values like the desire to protect the public from health or environmental dangers or the desire for a discrimination-free workplace. For their trouble, they usually encounter a management campaign to discredit and fire them. I found that this is what happens in two-thirds of these cases. I conclude that our standard bureaucracies have a long way to go in learning how to tolerate, much less to constructively change, on the basis of internal criticism and dissent.

Source: Excerpted from *The Cooperative Workplace: Conditions and Dilemmas of Organizational Democracy* by Joyce Rothschild and J. Allen Whitt. Reprinted by permission of Cambridge University Press.

Scandinavian Workplace Innovations

Japanese workplace innovations are limited in one sense: While they empower workers in certain ways, that is not their main objective (the main purpose is to improve efficiency). Furthermore, there is a definite limit: Management typically sets production goals, and QC groups plan ways to meet those goals (Cole, 1979). In Sweden and Norway, however, empowering workers was part of the reason that decision making was shifted from management to groups of workers. To a large extent, workplace changes in Scandinavia were the outgrowth of national policies, and they involved a joint effort of government, management, and labor unions (Ritzer and Walczak, 1986, p. 357; Cole, 1979, 1989). In the late 1970s, an innovation known as the cooperative work agreement was widely adopted. It arranged workers into small groups, called "work teams" or "autonomous work groups," which made decisions about work conditions and assignments that had once been reserved to management. As with QC circles (which were also widely adopted in the Scandinavian countries in the 1980s), workers received some of the benefits when their ideas saved companies money.

Workplace Change in the United States

Both QC circles and work teams have been increasingly used in the United States, but not on the scale of Japan or the Scandinavian countries. There are a variety of reasons for this. One is that, in different ways, both the Japanese and Scandinavian cultures are more collective and less individualistic than that of the United States. The Scandinavian countries have long emphasized the notion that society should meet certain basic needs of its citizens, as reflected in their comprehensive network of social services. In Japan, the notion that individuals should commit to the organization—and only by so doing will their needs be met—has long been an important belief. This is reflected in a variety of ways, such as company songs and uniforms and group exercises, as well as company-sponsored recreation and housing, that would seem quite unfamiliar to Americans. Similar practices are common in other Asian countries such as South Korea, Taiwan, and China. In several of these countries, QC circles were quickly and widely adopted.

The United States, by contrast, places great emphasis on individual rights and responsibilities, so there is less willingness on the part of both organizations and individuals to commit to one another. Would you agree to stick with the same employer for the rest of your life, for example? Would you enjoy singing the company song every morning? One result of this difference is that in both Japan and Sweden, the driving force behind workplace change has been corporate (and to some extent government) commitment. In contrast, the main advocates of group work in the United States have been individual efficiency consultants trying to sell the idea to corporations (Cole, 1989). The result is that, compared with Japan and Sweden, the United States has "tried less and accomplished less" (Cole, 1989, p. 308).

Nonetheless, American workplaces have increasingly emphasized work teams and decentralization of the workplace because, to some extent, they have been forced to do so by international competition. QC circles were tried with mixed results in some American companies in the 1980s. Today, work teams have become commonplace in American work organizations, though their power to make decisions varies widely. These teams seem to have one advantage over QC circles: Entire organizations can be organized into teams, whereas QC circles have typically involved only a fraction of the workforce, even in Japan (Townsend, 1990). The case seems strong that the autonomous, cooperative work group can improve organizational efficiency (Pugh, Hickson, and Hinings, 1985, p. 89; Scott, 1992, p. 251; Shonk, 1992). The question is whether the United States, with its strong traditions of hierarchy and individualism and its highly concentrated wealth, is prepared to empower workers in this manner (Baron, Jennings, and Dobbin, 1988). There has also been some resistance by labor leaders, who fear that work teams and worker autonomy are sometimes established to co-opt workers and reduce worker solidarity. However, recent research by Hodson et al. (1993) suggests that this is not the usual result, and that participation in work groups may even enhance worker solidarity, and work by Wright (2000) suggests that under some circumstances, both workers and employers may benefit from cooperation (on this point, see also Finkelstein, 2004).

Alternatives to Bureaucracy

As was mentioned earlier in this chapter, some people have sought to develop forms of organization completely different from bureaucracy, in the form of cooperatives and collectives. Although such organizations risk either failing for lack of decision making or evolving into bureaucracies, some of them do neither. These forms are probably not suitable for all types of tasks, but for some kinds of economic production they have been effective. In the "Personal Journeys into Sociology" box on page

286, sociologist Joyce Rothschild discusses how a democratic belief system can form the basis of a successful, nonbureaucratic organization.

Summary

We began this chapter by contrasting social groups and formal organizations. Formal organizations are different from other kinds of groups in that they have a stated purpose and an official role structure and set of rules. They are self-perpetuating; that is, they have a life beyond that of their individual members. Formal organizations are but one example of secondary groups—groups that exist for some purpose beyond the group itself or the individuals that constitute the group. A primary group, in contrast, is a close-knit group of people who interact for the sake of the interaction itself—for example, families and friends. Secondary groups and formal organizations have grown tremendously in importance as a result of modernization, but primary groups—once the main form of group life—remain important.

Groups and organizations usually have leaders, whether or not they are so designated. Some are instrumental leaders, who focus on the job to be done, others are expressive leaders, who focus on the social and emotional needs of the group and its members. Groups and organizations usually tend to be oligarchic; that is, ruled largely by their leaders. Groups can do certain things to minimize this tendency, but as a group becomes larger, the tendency toward oligarchy increases. Groups also create strong pressures on their members to conform. Pressure to conform increases when the group comes into conflict with another group, referred to by social scientists as an outgroup.

The form of organization that has become most common in modern society is bureaucracy—a large, formal organization characterized by specialization, hierarchy, formal rules, impersonality, lifelong careers, and a specialized administrative staff. Max Weber developed what amounted to a functionalist analysis of bureaucracy, arguing that it has spread because it permits rationalization, making decisions on the basis of what best gets the job done. Conflict theorists, however, argue that bureaucracy also concentrates control over the organization in the hands of those at the top, which is one reason it is so widespread. Bureaucratic organization apparently is necessary for large-scale tasks, but most organizations are more formal and more hierarchical than is necessary in order to maximize efficiency. Bureaucratic organization also has many undesirable side effects, a reality that even Weber recognized.

Whatever the formal structure, there is always an informal structure—what people "really do"—that differs in significant ways from "official policy." In any organization, the reality of the situation is always the product of social negotiation among the people in the organization, each of whom has a different understanding of the organization and a different set of concerns and interests. A person's position and function in the organization, individual personality, and social characteristics such as sex, class, and race all influence the response to the organization. As a result, organizations are best understood as changing, rather than static, entities.

Key Terms

social group
formal organization
dyad
triad
primary group
secondary group
ingroup
outgroup
iron law of oligarchy
instrumental leaders
expressive leaders
bureaucracy
ideal type
rationalization
alienation
informal structure
negotiated order
globalization

Exercises

1. One very important component of formal organizations in today's society is *bureaucracy*. Sociologist Max Weber identified a number of key features of bureaucracy. After you have

read the material on bureaucracy in this chapter, respond to these questions:

- Why do bureaucracies develop? What are the primary functions of bureaucracies?
- What are the primary dysfunctions of bureaucracies?

2. Think of the place that you or a loved one is employed or the college or university that you attend. How is the workplace organized? Do see elements of bureaucracy? What about organizational democracy? An interesting exercise is to create an "organization chart" of your workplace. Do an image search for the term *organization chart* in an Internet search engine. based on the models you find, chart out the workplace you have chosen. Based on your chart would you say it is overly bureaucratic? Or is it "lean," with only a few layers?

Chapter 10
Deviance, Crime, and Social Control

How Sociologists View Deviance — 293
  The Sociology of Rule Making 293
  Social Control 295
PUTTING SOCIOLOGY TO WORK — 297
  Does Capital Punishment Deter Murder? 297
Crime — 298
  Street Crime 298
  Victimless Crime 299
  Legalization or Decriminalization of Drugs:
     Pros and Cons 300
  White-Collar and Corporate Crime 301
  Organized Crime 303
  Political Crime 303
Characteristics of Criminals — 306
  Crime Statistics: A Closer Look 306
  Race, Class, and Crime Statistics 306
Explaining Deviant Behavior — 307
  Kinds of People: Biological and Psychological
     Theories of Deviant Behavior 307
Societal Explanations of Deviant Behavior — 308
  Anomie and Deviant Behavior 308
  Subcultural Explanations of Deviance 311
  Labeling Tradition 313
Functionalist and Conflict Perspectives on Deviance — 315
  The Functionalist View—Durkheim 315
  The Dysfunctions of Deviance—Parsons 316
  The Conflict View 316
  Feminist Criminology 318
Summary — 318
Key Terms — 321
Exercises — 321

Prison. It is now home to well over 2 million Americans—a number that has risen dramatically in recent years. In 1973, 98 of every 100,000 Americans were serving a prison sentence. This number rose to 325 per 100,000 by 1992, 468 per 100,000 by 1998, and 509 per 100,000 by 2008—more than five times as many as in 1973! This reflects the dramatic increase in crime over the past few decades—right? No, wrong! In fact, both police reports and victim surveys indicate that crime rates fell between the 1970s and 2008 (Barlow, 2000; Bureau of Justice Statistics, 2009). Now, consider this. In Germany between 1970 and 1984, there was a 75 percent increase in the crime rate, but the imprisonment rate rose only 50 percent—and then it fell after 1984. In 1968, the U.S. imprisonment rate was only slightly higher than Germany's—but by 1991, it was five times as high as Germany's. And, as we've seen, these differences can't be explained by differences in crime trends in the two countries.

These findings come, in part, from a comparative study by sociologist Joachim Savelsberg (1994). They illustrate a key point in this chapter: The definition, creation, labeling, and punishment of crime—as well as other types of deviant behavior—are socially defined. Differences in institutions in the United States and Germany, not differences in crime trends, are what explain the dramatically different trends in imprisonment in the two countries. For example, public opinion plays a greater role in policy in the United States, whereas the bureaucracy of Germany's stronger political parties influences policy there. This meant that in the United States public perceptions about a "crime wave," which have often been tied to racial fears and stereotypical attitudes held by the majority white population, have easily led to harsher treatment of crime. In Germany, public opinion plays a smaller role in the punishment of crime (Savelsberg, 1994). Even within the United States, such differences can be seen. The imprisonment rate for drugs is six times as high in California as it is in Oregon, and five times as high in Illinois as in Oregon. This is true even though Oregon and California have similar rates of illegal drug use, and Illinois has much *less* illegal drug use than Oregon (Fellner, 2000). Again, racial fears and stereotypes seem to play a role: Both Illinois and California are much more racially diverse than Oregon. As we shall see later, drug use is seen and treated differently when it occurs in minority populations than when it occurs among whites, and this has become increasingly true since the "War on Drugs" began in the 1980s.

On the other hand, some crimes can go unnoticed for years, even decades, because they are committed by the most powerful members of our society. These perpetrators are often shielded from detection by the cover of the resources they possess and the legitimacy of their positions in society. For instance, in 2008, it was discovered that investor Bernard Madoff had been running a fraudulent Ponzi scheme in which he paid off old investors with the money from new investors. The size of the Ponzi scheme is truly mind-boggling: nearly $65 billion lost from 4,800 clients. Madoff was able to get away with this fraud for nearly thirty years because he was able to hide his activities behind a veil of complex accounting rules and the wall of legitimacy that his billionaire status accorded him. The socially constructed category of criminal is not supposed to include billionaires like Bernie Madoff.

Crime and illegal drug use are forms of **deviance**, which is any behavior disapproved by a large or influential portion of society. Deviance is *socially defined*: It is behavior that does not conform to the expectations or norms in a group or society. For example, Peter Conrad and Joseph Schneider (1980, p. 3) define deviance as "behavior that is negatively defined or condemned in our society." Kai T. Erikson (1987 [orig. 1962], p. 21) argues, "Deviance is not a property *inherent* in certain forms of behavior; it is a property *conferred* upon these forms by the audiences which directly or indirectly witness them."

As discussed in Chapter 4, social norms are rules that govern behavior. Sociologists recognize three major categories of norms: folkways, mores, and laws. Laws, which are defined and enforced by the state, are the most serious and formal. Failure to conform to a law constitutes a **crime.**

In this chapter, we shall examine how and why some behaviors come to be defined as deviant. We shall examine why and to what extent people engage in deviant behaviors, and how and why society attempts to control such nonconformity. We shall also examine the role of deviance in the larger society.

How Sociologists View Deviance

Sociologists view deviance as defined by society rather than as a violation of absolute norms for several reasons. First, cross-cultural analysis demonstrates that notions of right and wrong change from culture to culture. Among some preindustrial societies in warm climates, for example, wearing clothing, except perhaps for ornamental dress, was considered deviant. *Not* wearing clothing is deviant in the United States.

Second, historical analysis demonstrates that notions of deviance change over time. For example, women's rights advocate Susan B. Anthony was arrested and convicted for casting a ballot in the presidential election of 1872. Today, female voting is considered normal, if not a patriotic duty. In precapitalist Christian societies, lending money for interest (usury) was considered sinful. Modern societies consider such behavior not only moral, but necessary.

Third, observations of social interaction reveal that definitions of deviance tend to vary according to who performs the act. In other words, actions performed by one person may be condemned as deviant, but when performed by another they are acceptable. For example, violent international behaviors such as bombings, invasions, assassinations, and espionage are often described as "heroic" when conducted by "our side," while similar activities by "the enemy" constitute "terrorism."

Finally, behavior is evaluated according to the context in which it appears. Few people in the United States recognize competitive boxing as assault or killing by military personnel or the execution of a convicted criminal as murder. Under certain circumstances, assault, theft, and killing are not considered deviant.

Thus, whether a given behavior is considered deviant depends on the situation. For this reason, sociologists view deviance as a violation of socially defined rules rather than a violation of absolute moral standards. As Kai T. Erikson (1966, pp. 5–6) put it:

> Behavior which qualifies one man for prison may qualify another for sainthood, since the quality of the act itself depends so much on the circumstances under which it was performed and the temper of the audience which witnessed it.

The Sociology of Rule Making

Because rule breaking requires rule making, sociologists have studied history to learn how definitions of deviance develop. These studies suggest that what is defined as deviant is often the outcome of political processes. In other words, notions of deviance are the consequence of struggle between competing ideas and interests. Political struggles occur in the form of moral crusades or interest-group politics. Whenever individuals or groups attempt to define a behavior as deviant for the "moral" good of the community, a moral crusade is under way.

In addition to moral crusades, group interests play an important role in defining what behaviors are considered deviant. As stressed by the conflict perspective, individuals and groups often seek to define behaviors of others as deviant so as to enhance their own political, social, or economic position. Interest groups can do this to the extent that they control significant political or economic resources.

Studies on the origins of law tend to focus on public order statutes and abuse of political (law-defining) power. Howard Becker (1963), in a study of the 1937 Marijuana Tax Act, discovered that the Bureau of Narcotics conducted a moral crusade to criminalize marijuana. The crusade used pseudoscientific language and assertions to argue that marijuana caused everything from madness to murder. These assertions were treated as fact by the popular press. Articles warning of death, insanity, and murder helped move the U.S. Congress to pass the 1937 act.

A study by Handel (1997) suggests that ethnic prejudice also played a key role in the passage of the act. At that time, marijuana smokers came largely from three groups—African Americans, Mexican Americans, and the intellectual-bohemian subculture. Antagonism toward the two former groups appears to have contributed to passage of the law: The push for the law in Congress came from representatives of urban areas like Detroit and Denver that were experiencing large increases in their African American and Mexican American population. As Becker (1973, p. 145) has pointed out, marijuana smokers were an unorganized and therefore relatively powerless group. They sent no representatives to the congressional hearings. As a result, their viewpoint was not heard, and the legislation that was passed created a new group of deviant people—marijuana users (Becker, 1973, p. 145).

Power, Rule Making, and the Definition of Deviance

Note Becker's emphasis on the relative powerlessness of marijuana smokers. This illustrates two important points about the sociology of rule making. First, power plays a major role in determining what behavior gets defined as deviant and what does not (Goode, 1990, p. 20). Second, by defining behaviors or people as deviant, powerful people try to protect their advantaged status—sometimes successfully, sometimes not.

Joseph Gusfield's (1986 [orig. 1963]) study of alcohol Prohibition illustrates the sociology of rule making. Gusfield concluded that the temperance movement of the early twentieth century was backed mainly by the influential rural middle class, who believed its power was threatened by the new urban immigrant class. As cities gained economically and rural areas declined, the rural middle class viewed urban populations as a threat and as the cause of all that was wrong in American society. The middle class moved to prohibit alcohol consumption—a fairly common practice among the immigrants—to restrain a group it labeled threatening and immoral. With its political power the rural middle class was able to pass the Prohibition Amendment, which reinforced its sense of moral security and superiority.

The temperance movement was not an isolated incident. Earlier in American history, urban elites campaigned against obscenity, gambling, and other vices in cities such as New York and Boston. During the nineteenth century these campaigns were directed by wealthy elites who had lived in America for generations against the newly arrived immigrant working class. Nicola Beisel (1990) conducted historical research to explain the curious fact that in Philadelphia, unlike elsewhere, the upper class did not support these movements. The reason, according to Beisel: Philadelphia had fewer immigrants and a less organized working class. Therefore, its elite felt less threat and had less reason to suppress its working class or its immigrants. Thus, we see again that power and class interests play a key role in the definition and punishment of deviance.

Elite interests also can cause behavior that was once considered deviant to be redefined as socially acceptable. In the 1970s, when the practice of marijuana smoking had become widespread among middle-class youth, a movement backed by the middle class was successful in reducing penalties for first-time marijuana possession in a number of states (Galliher and Cross, 1983). Recently, as a number of states have partially legalized the drug for medical treatment, Americans' opinions in favor of legalization have been steadily on the rise. Yet, Milhorn et al. (2009) find that Americans are also increasingly favoring harsher penalties for those in possession of small amounts. Trevino and Richard (2002) find that support for legalization is strong among drug users themselves, which leads to the possibility that as the generation of the 1960s has entered into the elite themselves, they are leading the way toward eventual legalization.

Vagrancy laws also illustrate the sociology of rule-making. When rural landowners were the dominant group in medieval England, vagrancy laws were widely used to maintain a cheap supply of agricultural labor (Chambliss, 1964). As England urbanized and the rural elite lost influence, the vagrancy laws were no longer enforced. However, when regional commerce grew later on, the vagrancy laws were enforced again, in order to allow the arrest of people who had not committed a crime but who were considered capable of crimes that might interfere with transportation of goods.

Power, Race, Gender, and the "War on Drugs"

A prime example of the role that power plays in defining deviance can be seen in the treatment of drugs in America today. The two deadliest drugs used in the United States are tobacco, which kills over 435,000 people a year (one out of every five deaths), and alcohol, which causes about 85,000 deaths a year (Mokdad et al., 2004). While both of these drugs are legal (and the main source of income for some of the nation's largest corporations), we wage a "War on Drugs" aimed at illegal drugs, none of which kills even one-tenth the number who die from alcohol abuse. In fact, all illegal drugs combined kill about 17,000 people per year—only one-fifth the number who die as a result of alcohol abuse (Mokdad et al., 2004).

Moreover, the illegal drugs that are most targeted by the "War on Drugs" are the ones used by

Although tobacco kills nearly twenty times as many people every year as all illegal drugs combined, its use remains legal and brings millions in profits to large, powerful corporations. (Big Stock Photo)

the least powerful. For example, penalties—and arrest rates—are much higher for crack cocaine (used largely by the poor and people of color) than for powder cocaine (used more often by the upper classes). Hence, as the rate of imprisonment soared in the United States due to the "War on Drugs," so did the proportion of prisoners who are black or Hispanic. During the 1980s—the peak years of the "War on Drugs," the number of African Americans admitted to state and federal prisons per year rose by 190 percent, while the number of whites rose by 81 percent (Fellner, 2000). In fact, by the end of the decade, more blacks than whites were being admitted to prison even though just 12 percent of the population was black and about 75 percent was white! Drug imprisonments account for much of this increase: The rate of commitment to state prison per drug arrest was five times as high at the end of the decade as it was at the beginning (Fellner, 2000). And the percentage of federal inmates imprisoned for drug offenses rose from 25 percent in 1980 to 59 percent by 1998 (Bureau of Justice Statistics, 1998). This increase in drug imprisonment has fallen very heavily on African Americans, even though there are only small racial differences in the percentage who use illegal drugs. By 1996, over 62 percent of people admitted to state prisons for drug offenses were black (Fellner, 2000), even though less than 13 percent of the population was black! The "War on Drugs" has also had a disproportionate impact on women, whose rate of imprisonment rose twice as fast as that of men during the early 1990s. Drug cases accounted for nearly all of this growth: Between 1986 and 1996, the number of women imprisoned on drug charges rose by 888 percent, compared to a 129 percent increase for all other offenses. Clearly, the main casualties in the "War on Drugs" have been African Americans and women. This is true even though the rate of illegal drug use varies little by race (9.2 percent of blacks, 8.1 percent of non-Hispanic whites, and 7.4 percent of Hispanic Americans reported illegal drug use during the past month in 2004 and 2005) and even though men are nearly twice as likely as women to use illegal drugs (Substance Abuse and Mental Health Services Administration, 2008; National Institute on Drug Abuse, 1999).

Social Control

Social control refers to all social processes used to minimize deviance from social norms (see Black, 1984, pp. 4–5). These processes can be divided into indirect and direct social control. Indirect control is regulation through ideological or cultural influences. It is the most pervasive and effective means of social control, and because it is accomplished through *socialization,* people generally do not view it as repressive. The institutions of family, religion, education, and government present people with a largely, if not totally, consistent definition of morality. People then come to judge themselves in terms of how well they conform to these expectations. We gain psychological pleasure when we do things "right," and we often experience guilt when we violate social norms. Thus social control becomes self-control (Gottfredson and Hirschi, 1990). In most circumstances, people conform to social expectations because they perceive them as legitimate constraints on their behavior, not because they are physically coerced. For example, it is not merely fear of getting caught that keeps people from stealing. Most people don't steal because they believe stealing is wrong.

Formal and Informal Sanctions

Socialization can never entirely eliminate deviance, however. Therefore, direct control, or **sanctions,** are also necessary to ensure social conformity. Sanctions consist of rewards for conforming behavior and punishments for nonconforming behavior. They fall into four categories: informal-positive, informal-negative, formal-positive, and formal-negative.

Informal sanctions take the form of gestures, frowns, and smiles; locution (gossip and praise); companionship; avoidance; and, occasionally, violence. They are frequent, spontaneous reactions to behaviors that anyone can administer, and are applied to violations of folkways and, sometimes, mores. Informal-negative sanctions include the gossip and condemnation traditionally associated with unwed teenage motherhood, whereas the praise and attention connected with "legitimate births" constitute informal-positive sanctions.

Formal sanctions, in contrast, are well defined and can be applied only by people with proper institutional credentials, such as priests, police, and judges. Formal sanctions are far less frequently applied than informal sanctions. Receiving a diploma or winning a gold medal at a track meet are examples of formal-positive sanctions. Excommunication from a religious organization, expulsion from high school, and criminal punishment are types of formal-negative sanctions. Criminal sanctions constitute the most powerful negative sanctions a society can apply.

Just as it affects what is defined as deviant, power also affects the type of sanctions that are used in response to deviance. Formal sanctions, particularly law, are used most often by the powerful against the relatively powerless (Black, 1984). Historically, many societies have identified groups with limited or nonexistent legal rights: children and slaves, for example. On the other hand, in some societies wealthy and powerful groups such as the landowning nobility in feudal societies are essentially above the law. Even in modern democracies formal and legal sanctions are most often applied against the poor and powerless (Black, 1976, 1984, p. 3). In contrast, relatively powerless people rarely use the law to apply social control to the deviant acts of the wealthy (Baumgartner, 1984). In fact, formal and especially legal sanctions are rarely used except when the powerful seek to control the behavior of the powerless (Black, 1984).

The United States uses formal and legal sanctions more than most countries, and that use is increasing. On a per capita basis, the United States now imprisons more people than any other country in the world. Moreover, as was noted at the beginning of this chapter, the use of imprisonment has grown rapidly in the United States, with the prison population doubling during the 1980s. Today, the U.S. imprisonment rate surpasses those of Russia and South Africa, which until a decade or so ago had the highest rates of imprisonment (*The New York Times,* 1991a; British Broadcasting Corporation, 2009).

Do Formal Sanctions Deter Deviant Behavior?

Although formal sanctions are less widely used than informal sanctions, it is clear that they are more widely used in the United States than in other societies. One of the main purposes for having formal negative sanctions is **deterrence.** The belief that formal negative sanctions deter deviant behavior comes from the classical criminology school of thought. Dating back to the late eighteenth century, classical criminology held that deviant behavior represents rational decisions made by free-willed individuals who calculate the potential gains and risks of engaging in such behavior (Vold and Bernard, 1986). This school of thought also held that if the costs of deviant and criminal behavior could be made high enough, through formal and legal sanctions, people would avoid such behavior.

In classical criminology, the *certainty* of punishment was seen as a more likely deterrent to deviant behavior than the *severity* of punishment. If, for example, potential criminals know that they will be caught and punished, they will avoid criminal behavior, even if the punishment is not too severe. On the other hand, a severe penalty will not deter deviant behavior if potential deviants know that they are not very likely to be caught and punished. This belief led even the earliest classical criminologists, such as Cesare Beccaria, to oppose capital punishment. Whether or not capital punishment in fact does deter homicide rates has been the subject of many sociological studies, which are discussed in this chapter's "Putting Sociology to Work" section.

Putting Sociology to Work

Does Capital Punishment Deter Murder?

Over the years, many studies have attempted to determine whether capital punishment, as opposed to life imprisonment, deters people from committing murder. Some studies have compared states with the death penalty to adjacent states without it; most such studies find little or no difference in homicide rates. One of the most thorough of these studies, by Sellin (1980; 1959), compared "matched groups" of adjacent states with similar economic and population characteristics across various periods between 1920 and 1955. Consistently, little difference in murder rates was found. For example, in the 1940–1955 period, Iowa had the death penalty. Its homicide rate was 1.4 per 100,000. In nearby Minnesota and Wisconsin, which did not have the death penalty, the homicide rates were 1.4 and 1.2 respectively (Sellin, 1959, pp. 25, 28). One difference Sellin did find is that states with the death penalty had somewhat *more* killings of police officers than states without it (Sellin, 1980). Studies of more recent periods have also found little difference in homicide rates in states with and without the death penalty (Peterson and Bailey, 1988). If anything, recent studies suggest *higher* rates of homicide in states *with* capital punishment (Fessenden, 2000; Bonner and Fessenden, 2000).

In the mid-1970s, a study using multivariate statistical techniques examined the relationship over time in the United States between execution rates and homicide rates (Ehrlich, 1975). This study caused quite a stir, because unlike earlier studies, it appeared to show a relationship between capital punishment and murder rates. However, this study has been widely criticized as methodologically flawed. It used national rates rather than state rates; thus, it involved the questionable assumption that executions in states with capital punishment could influence the homicide rate in states without it. It also did not control for policy changes. In the 1960s, the execution rate fell as capital punishment was increasingly challenged in the courts. At the same time, crime rates were rising for all types of crimes. Importantly, the deterrence effect showed up only if years after 1962 were included in the analysis—there was no correlation before that year (Paternoster, 1991). Moreover, the homicide trend after 1962 was the same in states with and without the death penalty, so it is hardly likely that it was caused by the declining use of the death penalty (Zeisel, 1976; Zimring and Hawkins, 1986; Nathanson, 1991). Finally, most other crimes, for which there had been no death penalty, rose faster than homicide.

Other studies have compared the rates of homicide before and after executions. A nationwide study showed no relationship in either direction between publicized executions and homicides in the United States from 1976 to 1987 (Bailey, 1990). This further supports the view that capital punishment does not deter murder. (Some regional studies have shown brutalization effects according to Paternoster [1991], but Bailey's national study did not.) There is also no evidence that abolition, institution, or reinstatement of the death penalty by states is associated with changes in homicide rate (Paternoster, 1991). All this has led two researchers to conclude that "there is room for debate only about whether the marginal deterrent effect is nil or very small in relation to total homicide volume" (Zimring and Hawkins, 1986, pp. 180–81; see also Fagan, 2006).

While research does suggest that certain punishment is more likely to deter crime than severe punishment (Blumstein, Cohen, and Nagin, 1978; Barlow, 1990, p. 520), there are limits on the ability of even certain punishment to deter crime. For one thing, violent crimes are often crimes of passion that involve little or no calculation of costs and benefits (Chambliss, 1967; Minor, 1978). This is probably another reason why capital punishment does not deter homicide. Even for property crimes, however, deterrence does not always work, for two reasons. First, some property crimes are undoubtedly committed on impulse. Second, some are committed by career criminals. People who have chosen crime as a way of life are not usually deterred by the threat of punishment—it is merely something they have learned to live with (Chambliss, 1967; Piliavin et al., 1986; Barlow, 1993). For more casual criminals, who are not as committed to crime as a way of life, deterrence may be more effective.

Looking at crime as a whole, studies on the effect of deterrence are inconsistent at best. Although certain punishment may deter casual property crime, there are many kinds of crime for which even certain punishment is not a very effective deterrent (Chiricos and Waldo, 1970; Gibbs 1981). In general, informal sanctions seem to be more effective than formal sanctions in deterring crime. According to research by Paternoster et al. (1983), it is fear of the disapproval of significant others, rather than fear of legal punishment, that keeps people from engaging in deviant and criminal behavior.

These findings, combined with high crime rates despite a high and rapidly rising rate of imprisonment in the United States, call into serious question the "common sense" notion that formal sanctions deter crime. According to criminologist Elliott Currie (1985, pp. 28–29), the high crime rates of the United States are hard for deterrence theorists to explain.

Crime

As previously explained, crime is any deviant act that violates a law. When the media, politicians, and citizens speak of "the crime problem," however, they are usually referring to street crime—illegal acts generally carried out by members of the lower classes. Nonetheless, white-collar crimes account for much larger economic losses and, in some instances, greater human misery (Kramer, 1984; Barlow, 1990, pp. 289–92).

Street Crime

The Federal Bureau of Investigation (FBI) divides **street crime,** or predatory crime, into two categories: violent offenses and property offenses. Violent offenses include murder, forcible rape, assault, and robbery; property crime includes burglary, larceny-theft, and motor vehicle theft.

Patterns in Street Crime
In a typical year, up to 25 percent of U.S. households are touched by some form of street crime. Property crime is at least six times as common as violent crime, but the rates of violent crime are nonetheless staggering. About 275 people are murdered, 1,700 women raped, and 16,000 people assaulted every week in the United States (computed from FBI statistics for 2008)—and these totals include only those crimes reported to police. The majority of both violent and property crimes go unreported (National Criminal Justice Reference Service, 1996). FBI statistics show peaks in crimes reported to police in 1980 and again in 1991. Between these two years, crime reports fell and then rose again; since 1991, overall crime rates have been declining modestly, according to both police reports and victim surveys. However, the number of violent crimes committed by juveniles rose sharply between the mid-1980s and the mid-1990s. This continued even after overall crime rates began to decline in the early 1990s, but after about the mid-1990s, violent crime among juveniles also declined, as did overall crime (Federal Bureau of Investigation, quoted in *U.S. News* Online, 1996; Federal Bureau of Investigation, 2000).

Compared with other industrialized countries, the United States has a very high rate of violent crime. In 2005, for example, the homicide rates per 100,000 in Japan, England, Germany, Denmark, and Canada ranged from 0.64 in Japan to 2.04 in Canada (computed from Canadian Centre for Justice Statistics, 2006). The U.S. rate of 5.63 in 2005 was 175 percent higher than Canada's rate and nearly nine times as high as Japan's. Rapes, robberies, and serious assaults are also much more common in the United States than in other industrialized countries. Differences in property offenses (burglary, theft, and auto theft) are less pronounced. Burglaries are about equally common in the United States and Europe, though the numbers vary widely in European countries. U.S. rates of theft and auto theft, however, are about double those of European nations (National Institute of Justice, 1988a, p. 2).

Murder, the rarest of criminal offenses, and assault, the most common violent offense, are most often unplanned and impulsive. Nonetheless, both crimes arise from similar circumstances. They tend to evolve out of spontaneous quarrels between neighbors, drinking partners, and family members. Roughly 60 percent of assaulters and murderers are relatives or acquaintances of their victims (National Institute of Justice, 1987, pp. 170, 262). One factor that contributes to the high rate of interpersonal violence in the United States is the availability of handguns. When a gun is present, a dispute that would otherwise lead to only minor violence can quickly become deadly (R. Farley,

1980; Newton and Zimring, 1969; Fisher, 1976; Sloan et al., 1988).

Victims of Street Crime

Some Americans are much more likely to be victims of street crime than others. While white females and the elderly express great fear of crime, their victimization rates are relatively low. In 1994, only one person out of 196 over the age of 65 was a victim of violent crime—compared to one out of nine between the ages of twelve and fifteen. One out of sixteen blacks was victimized, compared to one out of twenty whites. And one out of seventeen men was victimized, compared to one out of twenty-four women (National Criminal Justice Reference Service, 1996). The poor are also more likely to be victimized. In 1994, women in households with incomes under $15,000 were three times as likely to be raped as women in households with higher incomes. And low-income people were twice as likely to be robbed and one and a half times as likely to be assaulted (National Criminal Justice Reference Service, 1996).

While males remain more likely to be attacked than females, the gap is narrowing. And women are about six times as likely as men to be attacked by their domestic partners or former partners (Lewin, 1991). In 1994, 28 percent of women who were murdered were killed by their husbands or boyfriends; just 3 percent of men who were murdered were killed by their wives or girlfriends. When women do commit violent crime, they are far more likely than men to be doing so in response to violence committed against them by their domestic partner (Browne, 1987; Browne and Williams, 1987). The problems of courtship violence and spouse abuse are discussed further in Chapter 13.

Victimless Crime

Victimless crime refers to illegal acts in which all direct participants are consenting adults. In other words, they are engaging in legally forbidden personal conduct, such as drug use, illegal sexual acts between consenting adults, and use of illegal sexually explicit materials. The term "victimless crime" does not mean that these crimes never have victims, simply that they do not require a victim. In some cases, there are indeed victims, such as the young men or women whose poverty or sexual abuse is manipulated to recruit them into prostitution, or the family members of a person dependent upon drugs. On the other hand, there are instances in which no one except possibly the person doing the behavior is harmed, as in the case of someone smoking one marijuana cigarette, viewing a sexually explicit film, or engaging in an illegal sex act with another consenting adult.

To be sure, some "victimless" crimes do harm people, and it is in some ways functional for society to define and punish deviance. (This issue is discussed in greater detail later in the chapter.) On the other hand, victimless crime laws are often largely a product of what group has power, as we saw earlier in our discussion of Prohibition and other legislation. The same is often true of the enforcement of these laws, as illustrated by the fact that prostitutes are arrested more often than the men who patronize them. Moreover, victimless crime laws can be dysfunctional. They can, for example, divert considerable resources of the criminal justice system away from crimes with clear victims. Between 25 and 30 percent of all arrests are for victimless crimes, and more than *four times* as many people are arrested each year for drunkenness and drug violations than for burglary, robbery, and auto theft combined (Federal Bureau of Investigation, 2000, Section IV). Also, because there are no victims to report these crimes, police often must use intrusive measures to detect them, which may represent a threat to privacy and freedom of expression. Examples of intrusive measures are decoys, buggings, and "working the bus"—a practice, approved by the Supreme Court in 1991, in which police enter buses and ask permission to search the possessions of everyone on the bus, without telling the passengers that they have the right to say no.

Finally, some argue that victimless-crime laws can increase crime and lawlessness, by creating a lucrative market for that which is illegal. According to Handel (1988), making drugs illegal makes them profitable and thereby breeds organized crime, with annual drug revenues of $100 billion to $150 billion. Finally, drug laws may also lead to street crime, as addicts steal to support their habits, which are much more expensive because drugs are illegal. The debate over whether or not drugs should be legalized is explored further in the following section.

Legalization or Decriminalization of Drugs: Pros and Cons

Although the vast majority of Americans support tough law enforcement, more and more dissenting voices are calling for decriminalization and legalization of drugs. A small step in this direction may have occurred in 1996 when voters in California and Arizona voted to legalize medical use of marijuana—an idea strongly opposed by those who favor continued drug prohibition. Voters in several other states have done the same since, though the Supreme Court ruled in 2001 that such state laws do not supercede federal laws against marijuana, which forbid its use even for such medical purposes. However, in October, 2009, U.S. attorney general Eric Holder announced that the federal government would not prosecute medical marijuana suppliers or users in states where medical marijuana is legal.

The leaders of the decriminalization movement compare the present situation to that during the Prohibition of alcohol in the United States in the 1920s. They assert that (1) the need for mind-altering substances, such as alcohol and drugs, is ingrained in human nature and won't go away, and (2) the drug war doesn't work. Just as Prohibition financed the rise of organized crime and miserably failed as legal and social policy, they argue, drug prohibition creates a huge black market, drives up prices, and gives an economic incentive for drug dealers to promote the use of narcotics, while it enhances the appeal of certain chemicals because they are forbidden.

Decriminalization would take the profits out of illegal drugs, eliminate a major reason for gang violence and killings, and remove drug dealers from the market, just as the repeal of Prohibition ended bootlegging and its related crimes. Proponents of decriminalization go as far as blaming drug prohibition for the increased potency and danger of the new drugs (heroin led to cocaine, to crack, and now to the synthetic drug "ice") because drug dealers make more profits from more potent drugs.

What abolitionists propose as an alternative to the drug war is to shift the billions of dollars that are presently poured into law enforcement to a social policy of education, job assistance, child care, health care, housing, and economic development. Addicts would be treated and, if not cured of their addiction, provided with pure drugs and clean needles—which would also control the spread of AIDS. Some revolutionary programs even propose the sale of drugs to the general population of adults in government-controlled stores.

Proponents of drug decriminalization are willing to take a gamble that the number of addicts wouldn't skyrocket, and that drug use would be controlled thanks to education and prevention programs. Just as Americans have learned to consume less tobacco and less fatty food, they could learn to take responsibility and moderate their use of drugs. As evidence that this can be done, abolitionists cite London, Liverpool, and Amsterdam, where addicts are tolerated and treated in health clinics. The rates of crime and AIDS in those cities are very low compared with equivalent U.S. cities.

The argument for keeping drugs illegal is that laws send a message from society to its citizens about what behaviors will or will not be tolerated. Opponents of drug legalization point out that alcohol consumption, though still widespread, did fall during Prohibition and rise afterward. They argue that if drugs are legalized, more people will use them. They firmly believe that enforcing strict laws is an essential element in discouraging drug use. They contend that the permissiveness of the middle classes during the 1960s contributed to the drug epidemic. Equating permissiveness with social indifference, they argue that refusing to penalize drug use or easing the penalties encourages the use and abuse of drugs.

Decriminalization of drugs could be a trade-off between lowering crime associated with drug use and contributing to increased drug use. Both the potential benefits and the potential costs of this trade-off are greatest among the inner-city poor. Although the middle class and whites are at least as likely as people of color in the inner city to use drugs, the illegal drugs used in the inner city are more potent and dangerous. Using drugs can be an escape from the hopelessness of living in areas of concentrated poverty and joblessness, so rates of addiction and drug-induced health problems (such as babies born addicted to crack or heroin) are high. Those who oppose decriminalization believe that if such drugs were cheaper and more available, "state-sponsored" addiction could turn the poor into an underclass of addicts condemned to self-destruction.

On the other hand, many feel the drug laws themselves victimize African Americans. Though both are dangerous and addictive drugs, the federal penalties for powder cocaine (used mostly by whites) are much less severe than the penalties for crack cocaine (used largely by African Americans). The advent of mandatory sentencing in federal drug laws has consequently led to a rapid growth in the number of African Americans in the prison system. Also contributing to high imprisonment rates are the facts that (1) blacks are more likely than whites to use drugs in a public rather than private setting—thus increasing their risk of getting caught, and that (2) dealing drugs can bring a better income than any available legal work in the inner city. The end result of all this is that, while illegal drug use is common among all racial and ethnic groups, it is African Americans (and to a lesser extent Latinos) who are usually the ones punished for drug use.

White-Collar and Corporate Crime

The term **white-collar crime** was coined by the criminologist Edwin Sutherland (1940) to refer to illegal acts carried out by "respectable" members of the community. Sutherland's work exposed an inherent class bias in traditional explanations of criminality. The notion of "white-collar crime" brought the middle and upper classes into the "crime problem."

Sutherland's (1983 [orig. 1949, p. 7]) original conception of white-collar crime as an act "committed by a person of respectability and high status in the course of his occupation" has been modified to include almost any crime committed by high-status people. Thus, it is useful to distinguish between white-collar crimes motivated by individual interests and those motivated by organizational or corporate interests (corporate crime and state crime).

White-Collar Crime: Individual Offenders
Individually motivated white-collar crimes are nonviolent offenses carried out by people of relatively high social status who attempt to gain money, property, or personal benefit through deceit (Sykes, 1978, p. 86). Employers, organizations, and the general public are victimized by these activities. White-collar crimes directed toward employers include larcenies of time (getting paid and not working), embezzlement (stealing money from employers), and padding expense accounts. Income-tax evasion, insurance fraud, credit-card fraud, and computer theft victimize organizations such as government and businesses. Consumer fraud in health care, real estate, and automotive sales victimizes the general public (Bloch and Geis, 1970, p. 301). The economic losses from white-collar offenses are far greater than those from street crimes. For example, conservative estimates of the cost of consumer fraud alone are five times higher than the combined economic costs of all street crimes (Hagan, 1985, p. 103). Recent estimates of the cost of white-collar crime have ranged from $300 to 660 billion per year (Kane and Wall, 2006, p. 5). In human terms, a California director of public health stated that medical quackery causes more deaths in the United States than all crimes of violence (in Geis, 1974, p. 125). Nevertheless, the media, politicians, and enforcement agencies express little concern over white-collar offenses. Most go unnoticed or unreported, and when white-collar offenders are apprehended, they tend to avoid significant punishment (Eitzen and Timmer, 1985, pp. 196–99). Even so, one national survey found that more than one third of individuals, and someone in nearly half of U.S. households, was aware of being victimized within the past year (Kane and Wall, 2006, p. 2).

Corporate Crime
Corporate crimes are unique in that offenders are large organizations—corporations rather than individuals. Such crimes result from deliberate decisions made by corporate personnel to increase or maintain organizational resources or profits. The general public, employees, and organizations are victimized by corporate crime. Crimes against the general public include multinational bribery (paying foreign officials to obtain business), price-fixing, the sale of unsafe products, and polluting the environment. Requiring people to work in an unhealthy or life-threatening environment and illegal or violent suppression of union activities are examples of corporate crimes against employees. Tax evasion and industrial espionage are examples of corporate offenses against other organizations.

Even though the FBI does not collect data on corporate crimes, several studies suggest that corporate deviance is common (Clinard and Yeager, 1980; Sutherland, 1983 [orig. 1949]). According to Marshall Clinard and Peter Yeager (1980, pp. 116–19), during 1976 and 1977 three-fifths of the largest U.S. manufacturing firms had at least one administrative, civil, or criminal action initiated against them. Forty-two percent faced multiple actions. A small percentage of corporations, however, committed a disproportionately high number of offenses. Large corporations accounted for nearly three-fourths of all serious corporate offenses. The annual economic impact of corporate crime likely exceeds $200 billion (Simon and Eitzen, 1993, p. 290), over fourteen times the cost of street crime. Human misery associated with corporate crime is no less dramatic.

Examples of serious corporate crimes abound. On April 20, 2010, the BP-owned Deepwater Horizon oil rig exploded, killing eleven workers and ultimately spilling hundreds of millions of gallons of oil into the Gulf of Mexico. The spill is sure to cause untold damage to marine and wildlife habitats up and down the south Atlantic coastline. Early estimates of the total economic impact of the spill are difficult to calculate. However, estimates of damage to the region's fishing industry alone are $2.5 billion, while far away Florida's Paradise Coast could see as much as a $3 billion loss in tourism (Walsh, 2010). On June 1, 2010, the FBI announced it was opening a civil and criminal investigation of BP actions leading up to the disaster. The A. H. Robins Company, in the production of an intrauterine contraceptive device called the Dalkon Shield that was marketed during the 1970s, knowingly substituted less-expensive bacteria-conducive multifilament string for bacteria-resistant monofilament string. The cheaper component reduced the cost of production by 5 cents per unit. In the United States alone, this substitution, in conjunction with subsequent cover-up attempts, caused at least twenty deaths and almost 200,000 serious injuries (Eagan, 1988, pp. 23–30). Another deadly example of corporate crime can be found in the 1996 ValuJet crash in Florida, which took 110 lives. The box "A Criminological Analysis of an Airplane Crash" shows how this event might better be thought of as a crime rather than an accident.

During the 1980s, widespread fraud in the savings-and-loan industry contributed to the failure of hundreds of lending institutions. Fraud contributed to between 35 and 60 percent of savings-and-loan failures (Hayes, 1990; Lohr, 1992). The fraudulent activities included using savings-and-loan assets for personal purposes, illegally making loans for projects from which savings-and-loan officers personally benefited, paying savings-and-loan officers high salaries while the institution was insolvent (and lying about it), and making illegal and unsafe investments that resulted in large losses (*The New York Times*, 1992; Lohr, 1992). Up to 360 savings and loans are believed to have been involved in 21,000 cases of criminal wrongdoing; by July 1990, 237 cases had gone to trial, resulting in 200 guilty verdicts and just three not-guilty verdicts (Johnston, 1990). The trials continued into the mid-1990s, leading to the conviction in 1996 of Arkansas governor Jim Guy Tucker and two business associates of President Clinton. The cost of savings-and-loan failures to U.S. taxpayers ultimately came to about $124 billion, with an additional cost of about $29 billion to private entities (Curry and Shibut, 2000, p. 31). In contrast, the annual cost of property crimes such as larceny and burglary runs around $5 billion (Michalowski, 1985). One thing that made it easy for savings and loans to make risky and sometimes illegal investments was federal deposit insurance. Savings-and-loan officials knew that if they made bad loans that resulted in losses, the government would bail out their depositors (Kane, 1992). It is still far too early to tell how much fraud and other similar crimes were committed during the run-up to the 2008 financial crash, but judging from past episodes, the total will likely be counted in billions. As mentioned at the start of this chapter, one person alone (Bernie Madoff) has already been responsible for $65 billion.

Punishment for corporate crimes is generally limited to fines. It is, after all, impossible to put a corporation in prison. Moreover, because offenses generally involve large numbers of corporate officials over extended periods of time, it is difficult to attach individual blame (Shapiro, 1990). Finally, because corporate offenders are usually white, middle-class, and highly educated, they generally are not viewed as "criminal types." That label is reserved for street criminals. Thus, corporate lawbreakers, like other types of white-collar offenders, often tend to go unpunished (Clinard and Yeager, 1980, pp. 272–98).

Organized Crime

Organized crime is similar to corporate crime in that it involves large-scale organizations rather than individuals, but differs in that these organizations exist mainly for the purpose of conducting illegal activity. Often, groups involved in organized crime also are involved in legitimate businesses, but these activities are incidental to their large-scale illegal activities or serve as a cover or protection for them. Organized crime usually provides some type of illegal service for which there is a market, including the importation and distribution of illegal drugs, prostitution, gambling, and loansharking (making loans at illegally high interest rates) (Cressey, 1969).

Organized crime gains control of these activities by a combination of threats and promises. People engaged in drug-running or prostitution, for example, may be threatened with violence if they try to compete with organized crime or fail to make the required payoffs. On the other hand, organized crime provides protection from the law in exchange for the right to control such illegal activities. Such protection can be offered because of organized crime's substantial penetration of state and local governments, as well as elements of the federal government. So crucial is this political influence that organized crime probably could not exist without it (Barlow, 1993).

Historically, organized crime has been dominated by immigrant and working-class ethnic groups for whom more traditional means of upward mobility have been less available (Ianni, 1974, 1975). Through much of the mid-twentieth century it was dominated by Italian Americans (mainly of Sicilian origin), largely because that group happened to be the dominant group in organized crime when Prohibition was enacted after World War I. By creating a situation in which there was a huge market for an illegal commodity (alcohol), Prohibition led to a massive increase in organized crime activity and allowed the groups then in control to consolidate their power and amass tremendous illegal wealth. In earlier periods, when they were new immigrants, Irish Americans and Jewish Americans similarly had substantial involvement in organized crime.

As immigrant and economically disadvantaged groups have changed, so has the face of organized crime. In more recent years, black, Hispanic, and Asian involvement has grown. Today, drug prohibition creates similar markets for illegal goods to those once created by alcohol prohibition. Some Cuban Americans and immigrants from Central and South America, as well as new Russian and Asian immigrants, have been involved in the lucrative illegal drug trade. It is important to stress, however, that among all the ethnic groups mentioned above, only a small minority of each group has been involved in organized crime.

Political Crime

Related to both corporate and organized crime is political crime—the abuse of a government or political office or position, or crime carried out to gain office or political influence. Political crime includes a wide variety of activities. Some, such as bribery and influence peddling, are directed toward personal gain. This type of political crime is sometimes referred to as political white-collar crime. After being accused of engaging in this type of activity as governor of Maryland, Spiro Agnew had to resign the vice presidency in 1973. In 1990 and 1991, five U.S. senators were investigated for accepting contributions from indicted savings-and-loan official Charles Keating in exchange for protecting him from investigation for fraud. And, of course, in 1998 President Clinton was impeached by the House of Representatives (but acquitted by the U.S. Senate) on charges that he committed perjury and interfered with an investigation in order to cover up his sexual relationship with a White House intern. In 2006, former Illinois governor George Ryan was convicted of selling trucking licenses, steering contracts to friends and accepting payments in return, and illegally directing campaign funds to family members, and he was sentenced to six and a half years in prison. Two years later, Ryan's successor, Rod Blagojevich, was arrested for similar offenses, including trying to sell Barack Obama's Senate seat after Obama was elected president. In early 2009, Blagojevich was impeached and removed as Illinois's governor.

When political crime is committed by governmental organizations for organizational gain, it is often called state crime (Kauzlarich and Kramer, 1998). Some state crime is ideological in nature: Illegal attempts are made to support some cause that officials favor. One example is the Iran-Contra case,

SOCIOLOGICAL INSIGHTS
A Criminological Analysis of an Airplane Crash

On May 11, 1996, ValuJet flight 592 caught fire and crashed in the Everglades 17 miles northwest of Miami International Airport, killing all 110 people on board. The cause of the crash was a fire triggered by explosions of oxygen generators being shipped in boxes in the plane's cargo hold. The oxygen generators, which are used to produce oxygen in emergencies on airplanes, were old ones that had been replaced on ValuJet planes and were being shipped for disposal. When an oxygen generator is set off, it creates great heat capable of starting a fire—that's why they are behind heat barriers when used. When one or more of the generators activated in the cargo bin, it started the fire that brought down the plane. While we commonly use the word "accident" to describe events like this, sociologists Rick Matthews and David Kauzlarich (2000) argue that "crime" is a more appropriate description in this case, and probably others.

In their study, Matthews and Kauzlarich discuss several acts of organizational deviance that were revealed to have contributed to the crash. First, the contractor, SabreTech, did not follow proper procedures in shipping the oxygen generators. Before shipping, the generators must be expended or capped in order to prevent them from starting fires, and neither procedure was done. This is clearly stated in the McDonnell Douglas maintenance manual, and several SabreTech mechanics asked if the generators had been or would be capped. But, under pressure from a contract specifying a $2,500 daily penalty for missing the deadline for replacing the generators, SabreTech ended up packing them for shipping without either expending or capping them. Federal aviation law also states clearly that any airline that uses a contractor like SabreTech is legally responsible for ensuring that proper procedures are followed. No one from ValuJet, however, paid enough attention to how SabreTech was doing its job to know that the generators were packed without proper preparation. Hence, both SabreTech and ValuJet violated aviation safety laws. But that is not all. Matthews and Kauzlarich point out that, had the Federal Aviation Administration (FAA) done the job it is mandated by law to do, the crash could have been prevented. This agency is mandated to ensure that the nation's airlines are safe. For example, the FAA knew that the rate of emergency landings on ValuJet was doubling every year, to the point that in 1996 up to the date of the crash, there was an emergency landing nearly every other day. It also was aware, or should have been, that a review by the Department of Defense had concluded that ValuJet was so unsafe that the Department could not safely use it to transport government employees. Furthermore, the FAA also knew from two previous incidents that if flammable materials are stored in the D cargo hold (as was done with the oxygen generators), fires could spread from the cargo hold to other parts of the plane. This had caused the crash of a Saudi airliner in 1981 and caused a fire on an American Airlines plane in 1988 (which did not cause a crash because it started minutes before the plane landed and there was time to evacuate the passengers). Yet in spite of these circumstances, the FAA ordered no changes in the cargo holds and continued to certify ValuJet as safe.

Because the FAA, ValuJet, and SabreTech all failed to live up to their obligations under the law, Matthews and Kauzlarich argue that this case is an example of *state-corporate crime*—crime that is committed, for reasons of organizational goals, with the involvement and interaction of both public and private organizations. In this case, they argue, the crime was committed because organizational goals were placed ahead of safety laws and obligations. Both SabreTech and ValuJet acted in response to pressures to make a profit, and the FAA acted in response to pressures to make its deregulation program look successful. Specifically, ValuJet *outsourced*—hired contractors like SabreTech to do its maintenance rather than doing its own work—because it was cheaper, and then did not spend the necessary money and resources to properly supervise them. SabreTech wanted to avoid the $2,500 daily penalty for lateness, so it rushed to complete the job, causing the improper shipping of the generators. And the FAA ignored warning signs about ValuJet's safety record, because it wanted to make its deregulation program look successful in creating low-cost start-up airlines like ValuJet. In all three cases, pressures to meet organizational goals took precedence over legal obligations and safety concerns. Kauzlarich and Kramer compare this case to that of the *Challenger* disaster, discussed in Chapter 9. As Diane Vaughan (1996) found in her study of the *Challenger* disaster, *normalization of deviance* occurred in the ValuJet case. In their pursuit of organizational goals, ValuJet, SaberTech, and the FAA had all gotten in the habit of cutting corners and being careless about safety rules and laws. In the end, this organizational deviance had disastrous results, just as was the case with the *Challenger*.

which involved unlawful diversion of government funds to the Nicaraguan contras under the Reagan administration—a use of tax money that was explicitly banned by a law passed by Congress.

A great deal of state crime is aimed at preventing or controlling dissent. Activities of this type range from wiretapping, opening mail, and other forms of illegal spying to the use of provocateurs to induce opponents to violate the law so that they can be discredited. Often, illegal attempts to suppress dissent are more direct: Protestors are beaten, illegally arrested, or even shot. One instance occurred in 1969, when police attacked the Black Panthers' headquarters in Chicago, apparently while the people inside were sleeping; this action led to two deaths (Farley, 2010, pp. 195–196). Ultimately, those who survived the attack and relatives of those who were killed sued and received over $2 million in damages (Simpson and Yinger, 1985, p. 424). In a case that has attracted great attention more recently, FBI agents shot and killed the fourteen-year-old son and unarmed wife of white supremacist Randy Weaver in 1992 at Ruby Ridge, Idaho. Subsequent investigations revealed that the agents had been given unusual rules of engagement that they interpreted to mean "shoot on sight." At a later Senate hearing, FBI director Louis Freeh described the rules of engagement as "contrary to law and FBI policy."

Another common type of state crime involves governmental sponsorship of activities harmful to the public, for research or political purposes. There have been numerous cases in which unknowing citizens have been exposed to diseases or to substances known to be dangerous, either for purposes of medical experimentation or weapons development (Kauzlarich and Kramer, 1998). And in 2000, an investigation by the newspaper *USA Today* revealed that hundreds of private contractors were hired by the government to process nuclear materials in the 1940s and 1950s, knowingly exposing thousands of workers, without telling them, to radiation levels the government recognized as dangerous (Eisler, 2000). The government even produced classified reports detailing radiation levels hundreds of times above the upper limit regarded as safe.

Other political crimes, such as illegal wiretapping and political "dirty tricks," may contain elements of both political white collar crime and state crime, because they are intended for both individual and organizational gain. These crimes are usually aimed at gaining political office or influence. The Watergate burglary, which eventually led to the resignation of President Richard Nixon in 1974, is an example of this. In this case, burglars who were hired by people in Nixon's campaign broke into his opponent's campaign headquarters, and Nixon, along with many of his aides, later participated in an illegal cover-up to prevent the facts from becoming public.

Table 10.1 Percentage of Reported Crimes Cleared by Arrest, 1999

Violent Crimes	50
Murder	69
Aggravated Assault	59
Forcible Rape	50
Robbery	28
Property Crimes	18
Larceny/Theft	19
Motor Vehicle Theft	15
Burglary	14

Source: Bureau of Justice Statistics, *Sourcebook of Criminal Justice Statistics Online—Characteristics and Distribution of People Arrested,* http://www.albany.edu/sourcebook/1995/tost_4.html#4_1.

Police battle protestors. Functionalists view order as necessary for society to operate effectively, while conflict theorists see it as an outcome of suppression of competing interest groups. (iStockphoto)

Characteristics of Criminals

Describing the "typical" criminal is an impossible task. Most people, regardless of their criminal record, conform to most norms. They tend to stop at traffic signals, get married, love their families, believe in private property, and respect human life. It is rare indeed to find an offender with no redeeming human qualities. The evil criminals portrayed on television and movie screens are intended to entertain, not to describe reality. Further, most people with no arrest record do violate laws at one time or another in their lives. Thus, human beings do not fit into distinct criminal versus noncriminal categories. Differences, where they exist, are of degree.

Only one-sixth of approximately 9 million arrests made in the United States each year are for street crimes (Bureau of Justice Statistics, 2001a). Thus, the vast majority of people processed by the U.S. criminal justice system are not accused of predatory crimes (National Institute of Justice, 1988b, p. 67). The people described in arrest, jail, and prison statistics tend to be predominantly male and disproportionately young and black. About 43 percent of all people arrested for street crime in 1999 were less than twenty-one years old, 73 percent were male, and 64 percent were white. For violent crimes, 29 percent were under eighteen, 83 percent were male, and 59 percent were white. However, 39 percent were black, even though only about 12 percent of the population is black. The latter statistic supports studies showing that blacks are arrested in numbers that are out of proportion to the amount of crime they commit: In victim surveys, just 24 percent of the offenders in violent crimes were reported to be black (Bureau of Justice Statistics, 2001b).

Crime Statistics: A Closer Look

There are additional problems with assuming that official statistics describe the majority of offenders (see Table 10.1). Only 44 percent of violent crimes and about one-third of property crimes are even reported to the police (Bureau of Justice Statistics, 2001b). Additionally, most crimes that are reported to the police are never solved. Only 50 percent of violent crimes and 18 percent of property crimes are cleared by arrest (Bureau of Justice Statistics, 2001a). Of those arrested, many never face a judge or jury because charges are dropped. And of those who do go to court, many are not convicted. Data from large urban counties suggest that about 60 percent of those charged with violent offenses and 72 percent of those charged with property crimes are convicted (Bureau of Justice Statistics, 2001a). Since the characteristics of the offenders are unknown if the offender is not caught, prosecuted, and convicted, we are left with the conclusion that offender characteristics are unknown in over 95 percent of all property crimes!

Race, Class, and Crime Statistics

Official statistics also reflect widespread class and racial biases. Chambliss (1969, p. 86) summarized findings of research on such bias as follows:

> The lower-class person is (1) more likely to be scrutinized and therefore be observed in any violation of the law, (2) more likely to be arrested if discovered under suspicious circumstances, (3) more likely to spend the time between arrest and trial in jail, (4) more likely to come to trial, (5) more likely to be found guilty, (6) if found guilty, more likely to receive harsh punishment than his middle- or upper-class counterpart.

Later studies suggest that these biases continue to exist in many, if not all, geographic areas (Farley, 2010). For example, a study of Wing County, Washington, felony cases (Lotz and Hewitt, 1976) found that people with "unsteady" work histories were five times more likely to be imprisoned as those with "steady" work histories. Blacks and people with little formal education were most likely to be sentenced to prison. Studies of juvenile processing have produced similar findings. Barry Krisberg and colleagues (1987, p. 200) reported that minority youths were several times more liable to be arrested than white youths for the same delinquent behaviors. A study of juvenile offenders found that minority youths received harsher prison sentences than white youths (Fagan et al., 1987, p. 250). And as noted above, the "War on Drugs" has widened racial discrepancies in imprisonment in recent years.

Finally, relatively few white-collar or corporate criminals are arrested, despite the high costs of corporate and white-collar crime. This is the case both because of the difficulty of detecting and identifying the persons responsible for this type of crime (Shapiro, 1990) and because white-collar criminals possess greater resources for avoiding punishment. As respected "pillars of the community," white-collar criminals are able to gain the sympathy of police, prosecutors, judges, and juries (Galanter, 1974; Mann, 1985; Wheeler, Mann, and Sarat, 1988). Since those who have the opportunity to commit white-collar and corporate crimes are disproportionately upper-class and white, these people are, overall, less likely to be arrested or imprisoned than poor and minority criminals.

Explaining Deviant Behavior

We can offer many explanations of why people do not conform to social norms. Early thinkers tended to blame deviant behavior on the influence of evil spirits. Modern theories about deviant behavior and crime emphasize biological, psychological, and sociological causes. Biological and psychological theories are described as "kinds of people" theories, because they locate the causes of deviant behavior in characteristics of the individual. Sociological theories, in contrast, emphasize social situations as the main cause of deviant behavior.

Kinds of People: Biological and Psychological Theories of Deviant Behavior

Biological theories of crime and deviant behavior became influential during the late nineteenth century. These theories have argued that physical abnormalities (Lombroso, 1972 [orig. 1911]), body type (Sheldon, 1949), or genetic makeup (Jacobs et al., 1965) are associated with crime and deviant behavior. Often, these theories have been based on crude or uncontrolled examinations of prison populations. Usually, once more carefully controlled studies have been done, these theories have turned out to be groundless (Goring, 1913; Katz and Chambliss, 1991, p. 257).

Consider, for example, Sheldon's body-type theory. Sheldon held that *mesomorphs*—people with stocky, muscular build—were more inclined to commit crimes, and both his research and a later study by Glueck and Glueck (1956) seemed to show higher proportions of mesomorphs among convicted male juvenile delinquents than among other young males. However, this does not prove that body type causes crime. Research has shown that this relationship does not hold for all populations. For example, body type seems to be correlated with delinquency among whites, but not among blacks (Harris, 1991; McCandless et al., 1972). Also, there is no evidence of correct time order between the presumed cause (body type) and the presumed effect (crime). It might be, for example, that a culture of "toughness" encourages people to engage in body-building, resulting in muscular, "mesomorphic" builds, and that the same culture also encourages aggressive behavior. Finally, nearly all the studies addressing this issue have been limited to juvenile males (Harris, 1991).

Overall, these and other biological theories share certain shortcomings, and are not generally relied upon by sociologists today (Gould, 1981). In addition to problems mentioned above, they fail to recognize that all crime and deviance is socially constructed: In other words, human decisions define what is deviant and what is not (Katz and Chambliss, 1991). In addition, the biological theories often are used for the political purpose of blaming the powerless for crime—rarely are they applied to, nor do they appear useful for explaining, deviance and crime committed by the wealthy and powerful (Katz and Chambliss, 1991; Lewontin, Rose, and Kamin, 1984).

Although it is widely believed that people "would have to be sick" to commit many of the heinous crimes we hear about, psychological theories about crime and other deviant behavior also do not stand up well to empirical testing. Criminals as a group do not have more mental illness than other social groups (Monahan and Steadman, 1983; Lunde, 1970), nor have psychological categories been very useful in identifying violent people before they act (Morris and Hawkins, 1970; Kozol et al., 1972). Similarly, research seeking to identify an "addictive personality" that leads people to become dependent on drugs or alcohol has not been fruitful: Substance abusers, like others, are diverse with respect to personality type (Institute of Medicine, 1990, p. 258), and whatever differences do exist may develop after rather than before dependency (Clinard, 1974). A technique known as profiling, used by the FBI in recent decades, is based in part on the notion that people who commit a particular crime may leave patterns that allow them to be identified on the basis of distinct psychological characteristics (although social characteristics are also used) (Barlow, 2000, pp. 177–78). However, this technique, too, has its limits and has not yet shown convincingly that personality makeup has much to do with crime. An FBI survey of 192 cases in which profiling had been used found that the offender had not been caught in the majority of cases, and in fewer than one out of five cases could it be said that the profiles had led directly to identification of the offender (Levin and Fox, 1985, p. 176).

Societal Explanations of Deviant Behavior

Societal theories of deviance differ from biological and psychological explanations in that they locate the causes of crime in the social order rather than in individual psychologies or anatomies.

Anomie and Deviant Behavior

The term **anomie**, coined by Emile Durkheim, refers to a condition in society of normlessness—a lack of effective norms governing people's behavior. When social norms are ineffective—in other words, when there is a situation of anomie—there is nothing to restrain people from taking whatever they want (Durkheim, 1964a [orig. 1897]). Because society does not contain enough resources to satisfy all of the desires of its members, criminality increases in anomic situations.

According to Durkheim, conditions of anomie are most likely to occur during periods of rapid social change. Old rules break down or are rejected, and behaviors once considered deviant spread. At the same time, new rules often have not yet become widely accepted. Thus, it is predicted that during periods of rapid social change, nonconforming behaviors will increase.

Merton and Anomie
Although Durkheim coined the term anomie, it is Robert Merton whose work focuses most directly on the relationship between anomie and deviant behavior. According to Merton (1968), anomie develops when society teaches people to want or need certain things, but fails to provide legitimate opportunities to get those things. In effect, society creates appetites that cannot be satisfied by complying with its norms. For example, television programs and advertisements often portray and glorify an affluent lifestyle that most viewers cannot attain, at least through any legal means. According to Merton, this situation is anomic because when following society's rules does not lead to society's rewards, people may disregard or disobey the rules in a variety of ways.

According to Merton's reasoning, deviance is prevalent in the United States because all social participants are taught to desire and strive for economic success, while individual variation and class structure prevent many from achieving that goal. Socially approved means of achieving the "American Dream"—an education, a good job, homeownership, inherited wealth—are systematically denied to low-income and minority people. Assets of the lower classes, especially the ability and willingness to do hard physical labor, count for little.

Confronted with this anomic situation, excluded people often respond with deviant behavior (Farnsworth and Leiber, 1989). An important implication of Merton's theory is that it is not poverty itself that generates deviant behavior, but poverty surrounded by wealth, in a society where wealth is the norm.

Merton identified four deviant adaptations people make to the anxiety and frustration of anomic situations: innovation, ritualism, retreatism, and rebellion.

Innovation. Innovation occurs when people remain committed to economic success but reject legitimate methods. Innovators use alternative methods, including criminal ones, to achieve legitimate ends. Thus, innovation often leads to crimes such as theft, burglary, and embezzlement, as well as such activities as drug dealing, illegal gambling, and prostitution. Although the ringleaders of these activities do not always come from disadvantaged backgrounds, those who directly provide them very often do. To those who cannot find a job or whose wages fall below the poverty level, the promise of "big money fast" that is frequently offered by such criminal activities can be very alluring.

According to Merton, anomie develops when society teaches people to want or need certain things, but fails to provide legitimate opportunities to get those things. Here, favelas (shantytowns) built by the poor are located near the richer homes along the coast of Rio de Janeiro. (iStockphoto)

Ritualism. Ritualism occurs when people reject or give up on the goal of economic success, but continue to follow the rules—often in a very compulsive way. This reaction is exemplified by the middle-level bureaucrat, unable to rise further in the hierarchy, who mindlessly follows organizational rules. Such people are concerned with neither the purpose of the rules nor personal advancement. Ritualists simply want to put in their time, receive their pay, and "punch out" (go home). They follow every small detail of the rules but are uncommitted to the process. Ritualism illustrates the point that deviance is not always a matter of people *breaking rules;* sometimes it is a matter of people *overconforming* to rules.

Retreatism. People who practice retreatism reject and withdraw from both the goals and the means of society. In this category Merton places hobos, alcoholics, and drug addicts, among others. They are the "dropouts" of society. They are criminal only to the degree that society criminalizes victimless behaviors.

Rebellion. The final adaptation, rebellion, is exhibited by people who, like retreatists, turn away from accepted goals and means of achieving them. However, unlike retreatists, rebels seek to substitute a different set of goals and means. They may use illegal tactics, either nonviolent (civil disobedience) or violent (rioting, sabotage, vandalism). Unlike innovators, their purpose is not to attain society's goals; they seek to change society, or at least to express a complaint about the unfairness of society. (The various adaptations to anomie are summarized in Table 10.2.)

Anomie and Gang Behavior

Albert Cohen (1955) modified Merton's notion of rebellion to account for the often violent behavior of lower-class youth. Cohen argued that these young people react to their shared frustration and resentment of the dominant society by forming subcultures that turn middle-class values upside down. For example, the middle-class value of delayed gratification is replaced by a commitment to short-term pleasure seeking. Deviant value systems allow socially disadvantaged youth to strike out at middle-class society and satisfy their status needs. Through violence, drug use, and theft, gang members earn the respect of their

Some people come to view themselves wholly in terms of their deviant status, for example as "nothing but a drunk." (Courtesy of Michael Flota)

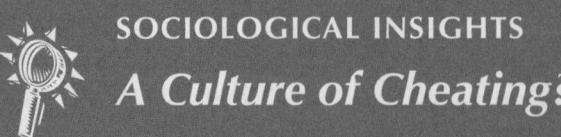

SOCIOLOGICAL INSIGHTS
A Culture of Cheating?

The United States has long been known for its competitive culture. With a spate of high-profile instances of official wrongdoing in recent years, some cultural critics are beginning to ask if a "culture of cheating" has developed in its place. Just search "culture of cheating" on the Web, and you'll see what we mean. A decade ago, the marital indiscretions of a sitting president and the subsequent legal and political maneuvering that behavior created fostered claims from both sides of the political aisle about a loss of national morals. Enron and other companies followed with financial scandals that would impact the lives of thousands of employees. Martha Stewart became the poster-girl for insider trading of financial information and spent time in prison. The Catholic church found itself under scrutiny for covering up sexual abuse among its clergy for decades. Soon, an initially popular war in Iraq was rocked by charges that the administration lied about the reasons for starting hostilities in the first place. Finally, with the collapse of the global financial system in 2008, the largest pyramid scheme in history was discovered to have been perpetrated for decades by millionaire Bernie Madoff, one of the most powerful players on Wall Street. The world of professional sports has been rocked by scandals involving performance-enhancing drugs. Has our competitive culture given way to a cheating culture? Does competition always lead to cheating? What do you think?

---

peers, even though such behaviors are considered deviant by the dominant society.

As poverty rates have risen and poverty has become more concentrated since the 1970s, delinquent youth gangs have become an increasing problem in American cities. These gangs have become more violent than in the past, with gun-related youth homicide rates much higher than in the past in inner cities (Froehlke, 1990). They also are more seriously involved in drug-dealing, a behavior clearly related to Merton's concept of innovation. As large, quick profits from dealing crack came to far exceed anything inner-city youth could earn from available "straight" jobs, the lure became almost irresistible. The increased involvement of youth gangs in drug-dealing clearly illustrates Richard Cloward and Lloyd Ohlin's (1960) argument that opportunity structure is a major determinant of delinquent gang behavior: When environmental conditions make delinquent activities profitable, delinquent youths tend to form profit-oriented criminal gangs. As poverty rose in the 1980s, legitimate opportunities for employment declined (Wilson, 1987; Anderson, 1990), and illegal opportunities such as crack dealing increased.

During the 1980s the concentration of poverty increased along with the rate of poverty.

In urban areas more and more of the poor lived in neighborhoods where other people were also poor (Wilson, 1987; Massey and Eggers, 1990; Jargowsky and Bane, 1991). This further reduced the legitimate opportunities for employment and probably enhanced young poor people's exposure to illegal activities. Crane (1991a, 1991b) found that as poverty becomes more concentrated and high-status workers scarcer in urban neighborhoods, youths in those neighborhoods become increasingly likely to drop out of school, placing them at greatly increased risk for becoming involved

Table 10.2 Typology of Deviant Adaptation to Anomie

	Acceptance of Goals	Acceptance of Institutionalized Means
Innovation	Accepts	Rejects
Ritualism	Rejects	Accepts
Retreatism	Rejects	Rejects
Rebellion	Rejects and substitutes	Rejects and substitutes

Adapted from *Social Theory and Social Structure, Revised and Enlarged Edition*, by Robert K. Merton. Copyright © 1968, 1967 by Robert K. Merton. Reprinted by permission of The Free Press, a Division of Simon & Schuster, Inc.

in delinquent gangs. These factors help to explain why violent crime by juveniles, much of it linked to gang activity, continued to rise until the mid-1990s, even after violent crime by adults had leveled off.

Evaluating Anomie Theory

Although the anomie theory presents a plausible explanation for a good deal of deviance in the United States, its implicit assumption that deviance is fundamentally a lower-class phenomenon is inconsistent with empirical facts. Accordingly, although Merton's anomie theory is useful for understanding deviant behavior by people whose opportunities for advancement have been blocked, it may be less applicable to much deviant behavior among those who have "made it" in our society, and who account for the majority of deviant behavior (Goode, 1990, p. 43). However, research on state crime by Kauzlarich and Kramer (1998) does suggest that when organizations are unable to attain their goals by legitimate means, they do often substitute illegitimate means if such means are readily available to them.

To the extent that anomie theory is correct, its social-policy implications are quite clear, at least with regards to crimes committed by the poor: If we continue to block the aspirations of certain groups to share in our wealth, we will continue to have high levels of crime and deviant behavior. In this regard, the current trend of increasing economic inequality is a cause for concern.

Subcultural Explanations of Deviance

Subcultural explanations of deviance contend that deviance arises from membership in one or more "deviant" groups. In other words, people are not deviant because they have antisocial or unsocialized personalities; rather, they are deviant because they learn and conform to the expectations of deviant or criminal subcultures instead of the norms and values of the dominant society.

Differential Association

The subcultural approach to deviance is indebted to the notion of **differential association** developed by Edwin Sutherland. Central to this notion is the assumption that deviance, like any behavior, is learned. Primarily, people learn attitudes within the context of intimate personal groups. One reason is that such groups reward behavior of which they approve and punish behavior of which they disapprove. If a group approves behavior defined as deviant by the larger society, it will reward that behavior (Akers, 1985). The effect of contact with criminal behavior is determined by the intensity and duration of exposure of that contact. People are more likely to be influenced by deviant attitudes of close friends or relatives than of strangers. Exposures occurring in childhood and adolescence have greater influence than those occurring later in life. Long-term associations with attitudes that condone lawbreaking have more influence than do brief exposures. If intimate contacts with criminal and noncriminal behaviors are equal in intensity and duration, people are less likely to participate in criminal behavior (Sutherland, 1947, pp. 5–9).

Lower-Class Culture and Crime

Walter B. Miller (1958) contended that lower-class people in the United States constitute a unique subculture. He argued that the disproportionate number of female heads of households among poor families forces lower-class males to develop masculine identities through peer-group association in gangs. These gangs promote "machismo," an exaggerated sense of maleness that encourages delinquent behavior. Whereas middle-class socialization encourages and rewards such values as achievement, lower-class youth culture encourages and rewards toughness, thrill-seeking, being able to trick others, and being able to avoid being tricked or bossed around. One possible flaw of Miller's theory is that, when asked whether they have participated in delinquent behaviors, nonpoor youth are just as likely to reply in the affirmative as poor youth (Goode, 1990, p. 48). However, it also appears that delinquency among poor youth is more serious and more frequent than among nonpoor youth (Elliott and Ageton, 1980; Goode, 1990, p. 49; O'Brien, 1985, pp. 63–69). Thus, the evidence is fairly consistent with the concept of a delinquent subculture among some low-income youths, although it is important to keep in mind that the majority of low-income youths do not become involved in serious delinquent behavior (Goode, 1990). Nonetheless, the influence of delinquent subcultures has probably increased as urban poverty became more concentrated in the latter half of the twentieth century (Wilson, 1996,

1987; Massey and Denton, 1993). In areas of concentrated poverty and joblessness, opportunities to get ahead through legitimate activities have become less and less, so people have turned to the illegitimate, as predicted by Merton's theories. And when the illegitimate "street" culture becomes dominant, its effect is powerful, because even those who try to be "decent" must show toughness and "heart" to avoid getting hassled or even physically threatened (Anderson, 1999).

Subculture of Violence

The notion of a violent subculture also has been used to explain high rates of unplanned murder among low-income males (Wolfgang and Ferracuti, 1981). This view holds that values placed on "toughness" and masculinity lead—indeed may require—these men to respond violently to remarks and actions that most people in other groups would ignore (Anderson, 1999). Similarly, some argue that a violent subculture, including an emphasis on gun ownership, in the southern United States can explain that region's higher rates of violent crime (Reed, 1972). However, such theories are hard to confirm, because there are always alternative explanations for why a group may have high rates of violence. Hence, the notion that subcultures of violence lead to high rates of homicide remains a hotly debated theory, and it is important for research to measure both cultural attitudes and actual rates of violence (see Corzine and Huff-Corzine, 1989; Dixon and Lizotte, 1987, 1989; Ellison and McCall, 1989).

Corporate Culture and Crime

Although the notion of criminal or deviant subcultures has most often been applied to the poor, it is equally applicable to some forms of corporate crime. Often, norms within corporate organizations are at odds with the larger society's norms about acceptable behavior (Clinard and Yeager, 1980; Ermann and Lundman, 1978). In such cases, the attitude of corporate officials toward such crimes is "everybody does it" or "you have to do it to make a profit." When a General Electric official was convicted of violating the antitrust laws, his response was "sure collusion was illegal, but it wasn't unethical" (Nader and Green, 1972). Similarly, in the late 1990s, when defective Firestone-Bridgestone tires on Ford sport utility vehicles were causing fatal accidents, eighteen months passed between the time when Ford employees first warned of a problem and any action was taken. In January 1999, a Ford employee wrote, "Is it possible that Firestone is not telling us the whole story to protect them from a recall or lawsuit? I feel it is possible, and we owe it to our customers and our shareholders to investigate this for our own (peace) of mind." Yet, in corporate cultures that valued public image over safety, neither company's officials took any action to warn the public about the tires until July 2000. In the meantime, over a hundred people in the United States and forty-seven in Venezuela had died in accidents believed to be linked to the tires (Healey and Woodyard, 2000). Cost cutting also seems to have led to the worst environmental disaster in U.S. history when the BP oil rig Deepwater Horizon exploded and sank off Louisiana's Gulf Coast in 2010. In the wake of the spill many critics charged BP was more concerned with repairing its damaged public image than the oil well. In general, in organizational cultures where attainment of goals is emphasized more than the means by which the goals are obtained, the risk for such deviance is high (Kauzlarich and Kramer, 1998, Chap. 7).

Evaluating Subcultural Explanations

A fundamental problem with subcultural theory is its failure to explain why some groups share deviant subcultures and others do not. A deviant subculture may perpetuate deviant behavior through differential association, but how did that subculture develop in the first place? Consider the case of the poor. A growing body of research suggests that criminal subcultures among the poor, to the extent that they are real, are a response to social conditions such as unemployment, poverty, and inequality. Thus, the ultimate cause of deviant behavior is to be found in these conditions (see Braithwaite, 1979; Loftin and Hill, 1974; Anderson, 1999). Sometimes, too, cultural characteristics believed to cause crime are misinterpreted. A cultural value is not always what it appears to be on the surface. This is illustrated by a classic study by Elliot Liebow in which, over time, he observed and gained the trust of a group of poor, inner-city black males. Liebow found that characteristics identified by social scientists as components of black or lower-class culture—for example, an exaggerated sense of masculinity—are actually "public fictions" offered by people to protect their self-concepts against failures at work, marriage, and life in general. Similarly, Anderson (1999) found that even those who are not part of a violent street culture in neighborhoods of concentrated poverty have to dress and act "street" in order to avoid harassment and attack—with the result that "outsiders" like police and school teachers often cannot tell who is "street" and who is "decent." Significantly, both Liebow and Anderson point out the the ultimate reason people must put on such displays relates to the limited opportunity for legitimate success in inner-city neighborhoods where all but unskilled and often temporary jobs have departed. They do so either to cover their lack of success in life, or to protect themselves from those who have turned to the violent "street" culture. Thus, the ultimate cause lies not in the cultural heritage of African Americans, but in the restricted opportunity structure of the neighborhoods where many African Americans live.

Labeling Tradition

The labeling tradition represents a major shift in scientific explanations of human behavior. It arises largely from the symbolic-interactionist perspective (Heimer and Matsueda, 1994; Matsueda, 1992), but it also uses important ideas from conflict perspective. Earlier explanations of deviant behavior had accepted law as a reflection of a natural moral order or of social consensus. Deviants were seen as people who violate norms, and nondeviants as those who conform. **Labeling theory** has challenged these assumptions by arguing that deviance is defined by societal reaction to certain groups, individuals, and behaviors, and not by the behaviors themselves. Furthermore, messages given to deviant people—including punishment—enhance rather than decrease deviant behavior. Labeling theory is based strongly on *relativism*, the contention, introduced in our discussion of the sociology of rule-making, that what is deviant in any society is the consequence of social or political processes. Social agreement, rather than objective moral reality, defines what is identified and punished as deviant in a society.

It is at this point that the conflict perspective influences labeling theory. Although there is some agreement on what is deviant, this agreement usually is not complete, partly because different interest groups define reality differently and in ways consistent with their own interests (Goode, 1990, p. 24). The Eighteenth Amendment, for example, which prohibited the manufacture and sale of alcoholic beverages, reflected the values and interests of the Women's Christian Temperance Union and other reformist groups, but contradicted the interests of many European immigrants. Currently, a number of illegal acts, such as drug use, gambling, antitrust violations, and the sale of sexually explicit materials, are not considered immoral by a significant proportion of the U.S. population. The same principle applies to homosexual behavior, which was illegal in a number of states until 2003, when in the *Lawrence v. Texas* ruling, the U.S. Supreme Court overturned state sodomy laws. Thus, the labeling tradition argues that definitions of deviance reflect the ability of certain groups to legitimize and enforce their interests over those of other groups (Schrag, 1984, pp. 1–2). Not surprisingly, those groups with the largest membership, greatest financial resources, and best internal organization will be able to enforce their definitions (Spector and Kitsuse, 1977).

Similarities Between Deviants and Nondeviants

Labeling theory also contends that deviants are not fundamentally different from nondeviants—they are just *treated* differently. For example, although few people are arrested and processed as criminals, self-report surveys (studies that measure crime by asking people how many and what types of offenses they have committed) reveal that most people violate rules. In most such studies, more than 75 percent admit committing at least one illegal act (Barlow, 1993). In a sample of several hundred Texas college students, Porterfield (1946) found that although all of them had engaged in delinquency, few had ever been involved with the police or courts. Short and Nye's (1958) self-report study of noninstitutionalized youth (midwestern and western high school students) and institutionalized youth (delinquents in western training schools) found high rates of deviance among the high school sample, and similarities in delinquency rates between the delinquent and the high school population. Although self-report methods have been legitimately critiqued for several methodological weaknesses (see Wilson and Herrnstein, 1985; Currie, 1985), the weight of the evidence continues to indicate that people cannot be divided into criminal and noncriminal categories. The vast majority of people engage in deviant behavior, but only a minority are labeled by society as deviant (Kitsuse and Cicourel, 1963; Becker, 1963).

The Consequences of Labeling

To understand the argument that social reaction creates deviants and increases the likelihood of future deviance, we must review the concepts of primary and secondary deviance (Lemert, 1978). **Primary deviance** is related to unique social, cultural, or psychological situations. It is not the result of labeling, nor is it associated with the basic psychological makeup of the offender. Taking money left unattended, shoplifting for a thrill, drinking alcohol before the age of twenty-one, and smoking marijuana with college peers are examples of this type of behavior. Such behaviors are seldom repeated or cease with adult status, and they are only marginally related to the offender's self-concept. **Secondary deviance**, on the other hand, evolves out of an offender's self-concept. People engage in secondary deviance because they have come to see themselves as deviant as a result of labeling by others. An occasional marijuana smoker may come to be identified by his acquaintances as a "doper," or a woman who is known to have had multiple sexual partners may be labeled "promiscuous." (The fact that this label is applied more often to women than to men is a clear reminder that power plays a key role in determining which people and behaviors are labeled as deviant.) When people are told that they are "dopers" or "promiscuous," they often come to believe that they are, and they are rejected or ridiculed by others. Once this has happened, they are more likely to move into further deviant behavior, such as using crack or cocaine or engaging in prostitution. This process was illustrated in a study by Matsueda (1992). He found that when people perceive that other people think of them as "rule-violators" or as people who "get in trouble," they are in fact more likely to violate rules. When people reach this point, they are engaging in *secondary deviance:* They are stealing because they think of themselves as thieves, or bartering their sexuality because they think of themselves as prostitutes. Because such self-images have become internalized, secondary deviance often continues throughout adulthood.

Deviance and the Self-Fulfilling Prophecy

Increasing involvement in deviant behavior follows the principles of the Thomas theorem (discussed in Chapter 3): If society defines a situation as real, it is real in its consequences. Thus, labeling theory holds that deviant behavior often is the result of a self-fulfilling prophecy. If society treats a person like a criminal, he or she will become a criminal. Being caught in an act of primary deviance sets in motion a process that develops its own momentum. Although the majority of identified offenders, through personal and class resources, can avoid being labeled as deviant, some cannot. For the latter group, a deviant label overrides all other personal characteristics and functions as a *master status*. The label "ex-con," for example tends to overshadow all other personal traits in the eyes of potential employers. Thus, systematic exclusion can force the labeled person to resort to crime in order to survive. Moreover, if the labeling becomes pervasive, it will be nearly impossible for the person to retain a positive self-image. At the extreme, some people come to view themselves wholly in terms of their deviant status—as nothing but thieves, prostitutes, or drug addicts. Then the self-fulfilling prophecy is complete. People have become what they were defined as being, thereby increasing the likelihood of deviance or crime (Schur, 1980, pp. 12–17).

Assigning Deviant Labels

Labeling theorists further argue that this process is neither random nor haphazard. Access to power is critical in distinguishing between those who are labeled deviant and eventually take on deviant careers, and those who avoid deviant identities. In addition to having a better chance of avoiding arrest in the first place, people with greater resources who are arrested can obtain bail and secure private legal counsel, two factors that greatly reduce chances of conviction (Lizotte, 1978). Race plays a role, as it has been well documented that police often engage in racial profiling: stopping people for no reason other than their race (Barovick, 1998; Feagin, 1991; 2000). Additionally, middle- and upper-class offenders are less likely to receive harsh punishments. They are less likely to go to prison, and if they are imprisoned, they serve less time (Sheldon, 1982, p. 295).

William J. Chambliss (1984, p. 135) succinctly described the dynamics and outcome of labeling in his study "The Saints and the Roughnecks," which compared two delinquent youth gangs: the Saints and the Roughnecks. The Saints were a middle-class gang; the Roughnecks came from low-income backgrounds. Both groups engaged in a variety of illegal activities, but only the Roughnecks were labeled as deviant. In the two years during which Chambliss carried out his observations, not one Saint was arrested, despite the fact that this group engaged in a number of dangerous and destructive activities, including vandalism, drunken driving, and removing barricades from street-repair sites. The Roughnecks, in contrast, were constantly in trouble with the police, in part because their deviant activities were more public and more visible to the police.

The effects of these differences in labeling did not end in adolescence. Because the Saints were not labeled deviant, their deviant behavior ended when they outgrew the need to "sow their wild oats." The Roughnecks, in contrast, were steered toward careers of deviant behavior as a result of being labeled deviant.

Critique of the Labeling Tradition
A number of criticisms have been directed at the labeling tradition. First, labeling theory cannot account for primary deviance; that is, deviant behaviors that occur before any labeling. Labeling does not account for first-time serious offenders—murderers, rapists, robbers. In addition, critics point to research that shows labeling that occurs as a result of some behavior of the person labeled, not because of that person's social characteristics (Tittle, 1980; Hirschi, 1980). In other words, most labeling follows primary deviance, and therefore cannot cause people to begin deviant behavior. Second, researchers in the labeling tradition have concentrated on less-serious offenses, even noncriminal behaviors, including mental illness. Findings in these studies may not be applicable to violent or serious property crimes or to white-collar crime. Third, although the labeling tradition has historically been concerned with humanizing the deviant, labeling researchers, like other deviance researchers, may have actually helped label the powerless as deviant. This criticism is developed in the box "An Argument Against Studying 'Deviance'." Finally, critics argue that rather than acting as a self-fulfilling prophecy, deviant labels can discourage deviant behavior, as people conform in order to avoid the many bad consequences of being labeled deviant. Thus, while the labeling tradition offers many useful insights about the nature of deviance, how it occurs, and the consequences of society's response to it, labeling, like other approaches, has its limitations and can offer only part of the answers to the questions it asks about deviant behavior.

Functionalist and Conflict Perspectives on Deviance

Within the discipline of sociology the functionalist and conflict schools provide different ways of understanding deviance and social control. Functionalist views are best represented by the works of Emile Durkheim and Talcott Parsons. Conflict views are heavily influenced by the works of Karl Marx and Ralf Dahrendorf.

The Functionalist View—Durkheim

Although Durkheim regretted the negative consequences of deviant behavior, he considered a limited amount of crime to be a normal and necessary characteristic of all societies. He argued that deviance was so crucial to social order that societies lacking a given amount of it would redefine acceptable behavior to create deviance, as was noted earlier in our discussion of victimless crimes.

Without deviance, Durkheim contended, societies are unable to adjust to the demands of changing environments. Rigid societies with an unyielding commitment to outdated rules deteriorate and perish. By providing alternative ways of thinking, organizing, and behaving, deviance enables societies to adapt to new situations. To Durkheim, what is condemned as deviance today can become the norm of tomorrow. The civil rights activism of the 1960s offers a good example of this reasoning. The initial violators of Jim Crow laws were treated as criminals. Activists were physically abused, even murdered, and subjected to legal sanctions. Today, few people consider civil rights organizers and participants as criminal. In fact, their demands for social, economic, and political equality are, at least nominally, supported by most major politicians and some of them have been incorporated into law.

Durkheim also identified boundary maintenance and increased solidarity as positive consequences of deviance and social control. Identifying and punishing deviants clarifies the rules that society expects its members to obey. By making clear what a society rejects, the definition of deviance helps a society define what it is and what it approves (Durkheim, 1947 [orig. 1893]; 1964b [orig. 1893]). Defining and punishing deviance also demonstrates the consequences of breaking society's rules. Further, the use of social control reinforces a sense of righteousness and superiority among conformists and thereby strengthens social cohesion. Conformists are pushed together as they battle a shared threat, the deviants—be they criminals, witches, homosexuals, dope addicts, or communists (see Vold and Bernard, 1986, pp. 144–52). The "War on Drugs" of the late 1980s and early 1990s can be cited as another example of this process.

The Dysfunctions of Deviance—Parsons

Although Durkheim recognized the positive consequences of deviance, he also warned that deviance beyond a certain level threatens social order and is dysfunctional. This point of view was echoed by Talcott Parsons. According to Parsons, the primary function of social control is to reduce tensions between different elements of the social system in order to ensure the cooperation necessary for a society to function reasonably well (Parsons, 1962, p. 58). Accordingly, all social participants benefit when society operates in a stable and harmonious fashion. Thus, deviance is counterproductive and reflects failure to understand the common social interests that bind all members of a society. Social control enables a society to move people into the different social roles required for its functioning. When socialization, rewards, and persuasion fail to accomplish this task, some form of coercion is required. Functional reasoning argues that this use of coercive social control is legitimate because laws are enacted by representatives of the people in the interest of the people. Moreover, these laws are in theory applied equally to all members of society (Chambliss and Mankoff, 1976, pp. 7–9), though, as we have seen, this often is not the case in reality.

The Conflict View

Conflict theorists deny the existence of a harmony of interests or value consensus in modern society. Rather, diverse groups, with varying degrees of social, economic, and political power, compete to have their interests and values protected and preserved in law. Rather than reflecting harmony and cooperation, social order reflects the suppression of competing interests (Vago, 1988, pp. 16–17). Definitions of deviance and the enforcement of those definitions perpetuate the dominance of elites over the less powerful or powerless. To support this contention, conflict analysts point to the relative absence of legal restrictions against socially destructive elite behaviors. As mentioned earlier in this chapter, for example, alcohol and tobacco together kill hundreds of thousands of Americans a year. The annual cost of the abuse of these substances to the U.S. economy is over $200 billion. These human and dollar costs are far beyond those of all illegal drugs (marijuana, cocaine, heroin, and others) combined, yet enterprises that produce alcohol and tobacco are allowed to advertise and market their goods. In the case of tobacco, the enterprise is supported with federal subsidies. Further, although the economic and human costs of corporate crime are greater than those of all other types of crime combined, few enforcement resources are directed against this problem (Simon and Eitzen, 1986, pp. 228–30). People almost never go to jail for violating antitrust laws, endangering their employees, damaging the environment, or selling products known to be dangerous. Thus, for the conflict perspective, the laws that exist, the laws that are enforced, the methods, targets, and harshness of enforcement all function to protect the interests of the ruling classes.

According to conflict theorists in criminology, the laws and the ways they are enforced do this in several ways. Not only does overattention to crimes committed by the poor deflect the wealthy from criticism; it also leads the public to view the poor—and especially the minority poor—as a dangerous class. Hence, the worries of the middle class are deflected from economic concerns that might threaten the owners of real wealth, and

UNDERSTANDING RACE, CLASS, AND GENDER
An Argument Against Studying "Deviance"

In 1972, sociologist Alexander Liazos published what was destined to become one of the more widely cited journal articles in the sociology of deviance—a paper in which he questioned whether sociology should even study "deviance." The unusual title of his paper was "The Poverty of the Sociology of Deviance: Nuts, Sluts, and Preverts." That's right—"preverts." The title came from the nicknames his students had given to the deviance course—nicknames that underscored the idea that the study of deviance actually tends to further stigmatize those it seeks to understand.

Liazos's point was that, even when they emphasize ways in which society defines, creates, and stigmatizes deviance, most courses and books about deviance end up emphasizing not society but "deviant" people and the problems they present for themselves and others. He studied sixteen textbooks on deviance, half of which emphasized the labeling perspective. He found that they contained three major biases. First, even when they tried to humanize the "deviant," the courses led to stigmatization of people who do not conform by focusing on the "deviant" rather than on society's role in establishing what is thought to be deviant. Liazos argued that the term deviant itself is stigmatizing—it underscores the idea that we think there is something "different" about those who do not conform.

Second, although the books talked about the role of power in defining deviance, their discussions of deviant behaviors tended to focus on deviance by the powerless and ignore deviance by the powerful. Thus, topics such as robbery, rape, prostitution, mental illness, drug use/abuse, and homosexuality were covered in all of the books, and some books also covered political radicals and religious dissenters. On the other hand, the books paid little if any attention to unethical, illegal, and destructive behaviors of the wealthy and powerful. The subtle message was that violence was committed by the ghetto poor, youth gangs and motorcycle gangs, and other powerless groups, not by the wealthy and powerful.

The third bias, related to the second, was that the books tended to focus on the dramatic—murders, muggings, prostitution, juvenile delinquency, and so forth. They did not focus on what Liazos saw as more subtle but deadly forms of violence committed by everyday operations of social institutions—for instance, that a black baby is twice as likely to die in the first year of life as a white baby. The black infant mortality rate is a reflection of racism and inequality in American society, resulting from a black poverty rate that is three times the white poverty rate and a health-care system in which blacks are twice as likely as whites to be uninsured. As Liazos points out, "This is surely much worse violence than anything committed by the Hell's Angels or street gangs." Yet, because of the way most sociology textbooks and college courses teach about deviance—even those that emphasize the labeling perspective—we associate deviance with Hell's Angels and street gangs, not the health-care or economic system. According to Liazos, the people who control and benefit from these systems are presented not as deviants, but as "pillars of the community."

Source: From "The Poverty of the Sociology of Deviance: Nuts, Sluts, and Perverts" by Alex Liazos, *Social Problems* 20, 1 (Summer, 1972). Copyright © 1972 by the Society for the Study of Social Problems. Reprinted by permission of University of California Press Journals.

against the ghetto poor that the middle class has come to define as a threat (Gordon, 1971; 1973). In fact, when the economy worsens—and when such worries among the middle class might be heightened—researchers have shown that punitiveness toward the poor increases (Michalowski and Carlson, 1999). This underlines the elite's message that the poor are the real threat to the middle class, making the poor the scapegoat for middle-class economic frustrations. At the same time, of course, blame is deflected from the truly wealthy.

Another theme in conflict theories of crime and deviance is that capitalism and inequality do actually lead to higher rates of crime in society. Societies characterized by extreme capitalism and a high degree of inequality tend to overemphasize economic gain, so that such material gain is valued over human relationships and social and cultural solidarity. Consequently, families and neighborhoods are weakened because more hours of work are demanded at the expense of parental leave, family vacations, and leisure time (Currie, 1997).

Contrast the United States—where even long-time employees get only two weeks of vacation, minimal family leave, and a few holidays a year—with European countries where five or six weeks of vacation a year, generous family leaves, and a holiday every month are the standard. In the United States, the rates of divorce, juvenile delinquency, and family violence are far higher than in any European country. In addition, the American emphasis on material gain often leads people in all social classes to seek gain through illegal means—so rates of theft, embezzlement, burglary, and other crimes for material gain exceed those of other industrialized countries. Similarly, corporations and government agencies often press their employees to meet the goal and make the bottom line come out good, regardless of the means, leading to corporate and state crime. Hence, conflict theorists stress that societal and organizational situations, as well as individual ones, are important causes of crime and deviance (Kauzlarich and Kramer, 1998).

Feminist Criminology

An increasingly influential variant of conflict theory is *feminist criminology,* an approach illustrated by the work of Meda Chesney-Lind, featured in this chapter's Personal Journeys into Sociology box. Feminist criminology stresses that the unequal roles and resources of men and women lead them to commit different kinds of deviant acts, to do so under different social conditions, and to be labeled as deviant as a result of different behaviors (Morris, 1987). For example, women who commit violent crime are more likely than male criminals to be married, and much less likely to have prior criminal records (Barlow, 1993). This may reflect recruitment into criminal activity by their spouses, or perhaps a reaction to violence against them by their partners, which happens to women much more often than to men. The relationship between unemployment and crime among men also appears not to be true for women (Alder, 1986), perhaps reflecting the different meanings of employment for men and women. We also know that women commit much less crime than men; Messerschmidt (1986) suggests that one reason for this is that the more restricted roles of women give them less opportunity to commit crimes. Another difference is that female juvenile delinquents are more likely than male delinquents to be in trouble because of running away (Chesney-Lind, 1996). This happens partly because girls often run away to escape sexual abuse, but also because girls are more likely than boys to be arrested for running away (Chesney-Lind, 1996).

Feminist approaches to criminology have emphasized also the differences in why and how men and women commit crimes (Barlow and Kauzlarich, 2002). Crime by males, for example, is often done to reaffirm their masculinity—either to show themselves to be "tough" or in response to challenges to their masculinity (Messerschmidt, 2000; see also Anderson, 1999). Females, on the other hand, may turn to crime due to their greater economic marginalization, or commit violence to defend themselves from males (Maher, 1997). They may also commit crimes in different ways, such as targeting other women rather than men, or using feigned vulnerability or sexual availability to trick males into becoming crime victims (Miller, 1998). Because traditional theories of crime and deviant behavior often "don't work" for women, the influence of feminist criminology has grown in recent years. This change in the study of crime and deviance is discussed by criminologist Meda Chesney-Lind in her Personal Journeys into Sociology box. Among other issues, feminist criminologists have explored how boys and girls are subjected to different kinds of social control as children, as well as the consequences of this different treatment.

Summary

Deviance refers to behavior that violates social norms. Social norms can be categorized as folkways, mores, and laws. Although common sense frequently condemns deviant behavior as inappropriate or immoral, sociologists treat deviance as a label attached to certain behaviors by certain groups within society. They are aware that the behaviors that are labeled deviant vary both within a culture and among different cultures.

A behavior that violates a law is referred to as a crime. Punishments of crime are formally specified and are carried out by state apparatuses. Crime is a broad term that can include the following categories: street crime, which refers to attacks against people and property; victimless crime, in which all participants are consenting adults; and

PERSONAL JOURNEYS INTO SOCIOLOGY
Doing Feminist Criminology

Meda Chesney-Lind

I can still vividly recall hearing a male researcher who, reporting on birth rates at a population meeting in Seattle, referred to his subjects using male pronouns throughout his presentation. Since his subjects were female (we are, after all, the only ones who can give birth), I was puzzled. As a graduate student attending my first national meeting and rather daunted by the setting, I waited until the break to ask him about his word choice. Without any embarrassment, he informed me that "I say 'he' or 'him' because to say 'she' or 'her' would trivialize my research." For many years, criminology was not haunted by this problem. Unlike demography, it was seen as an incontrovertibly male, even "macho" field. Crime has, in fact, sometimes been described as an ultimate form of masculinity. In Albert Cohen's words, "the delinquent is a rogue male" whose behavior, no matter how much it is condemned on moral grounds, "has at least one virtue: It incontestably confirms, in the eyes of all concerned, his essential masculinity."

The criminological fascination with male deviance and crime is not simply a reflection of the American crime problem. I suspect that it also is explained by Margaret Mead's observation that whatever men do, even if it is dressing dolls for religious ceremonies, has higher status and is more highly rewarded than whatever women do. For this reason, fields focus on male activities and attributes wherever possible: Studying them confers higher status on the researcher. Hence, the academic rush to understand boys and men and the disinterest, until relatively recently, in all things female.

The question now is whether theories of delinquency and crime, which were admittedly developed to explain male behavior, can be used to understand female crime, delinquency, and victimization. My research experience convinces me that they cannot. About twenty-five years ago, when I was reading files compiled on youth who had been referred to Honolulu's family court during the first half of the twentieth century, I ran across what I considered to be a bizarre pattern. Over half of the girls had been referred to court for "immorality," and another one-third were charged with being "wayward." In reading the files, I discovered that this meant that the young women were suspected of being sexually active. Evidence of this "exposure" was vigorously pursued in all cases—and this was not subtle. Virtually all girls' files contained gynecological examinations (sometimes there were stacks of these forms). Doctors, who understood the purpose of such examinations, would routinely note the condition of the hymen on the form: "Admits intercourse, hymen ruptured," "Hymen ruptured," and "No laceration," as well as comments about whether the "laceration" looked new or old, were typical notations.

Later analysis of the data revealed the harsh sanctions imposed on those girls found guilty of these offenses. Thus, despite widespread repetitions about the chivalrous treatment of female offenders, I was finding in the then-skimpy literature on women's crime that girls referred to court in Honolulu in the 1930s were twice as likely as boys to be detained. They spent, on the average, five times as long as males in detention facilities, and they were three times as likely to be sent to training schools. Later research would confirm that this pattern also was found in other parts of the country and that similar, though less extreme, bias against girls existed well into the 1960s.

Reflecting on this pattern recently, it occurred to me that girls were being treated in this fashion as the field of criminology was developing. So while criminologists—mostly male—were paying a lot of attention to the male delinquent, large numbers of girls were being processed, punished, and incarcerated. Indeed, one of the classic excuses for neglecting female offenders—their relatively small numbers—did not hold during these years. I found, for example, that girls made up half of those committed to Hawaii training schools well into the 1950s.

---

white-collar and corporate crime, which involves illegal activities by "respectable" members of society. In general, people from lower-income backgrounds are more likely to commit street crimes, whereas higher-status people tend to commit white-collar crimes. Although our society generally focuses on the problems associated with street crime, the costs of white-collar and corporate crime in this country are enormous.

Theories of criminal behavior have changed over the centuries. Biological theories that prevailed in the nineteenth century portrayed criminals as

One reason for this neglect of girls may have been the inability of researchers to identify with their problems or situations. By contrast, I was not able to distance myself from their lives. At that time, the women's movement was a major part of my life. For the first time, I was seeing the connections between my life and the lives of other women. I knew, firsthand, about physical examinations, and I knew that even under the best circumstances they were stressful. I imagined what it would have been like to be a thirteen- or fourteen-year-old arrested on my family's orders, taken to a detention center, and forcibly examined by a doctor I didn't know. Later, I also would read of legal cases where girls in other states were held in solitary confinement for refusing such examinations, and I would talk to women who had undergone this experience as girls. Their comments and experiences confirmed the degradation and personal horror of this experience.

I bring up this particular point simply to demonstrate that the administration of a medical examination, the larger meaning of that medical examination in the girl's delinquent "career," and the harsh response to the girl so identified had no place in the delinquency theories I had studied.

Certainly, one can patch together, as I did, notions of stigma, degradation rituals, and labeling, but the job was incomplete and the picture imperfect. I have come increasingly to the conclusion that my own research results, in conjunction with the work of other feminist researchers, argue for a feminist revision of delinquency, crime, and criminal victimization—a feminist criminology.

Though I see the need for this, I am keenly aware that professional rewards for such an undertaking may be slow in coming. The work I just described on female delinquency was completed for my master's thesis. The sociology department where I did this research failed to perceive its import. In order to complete my work for the Ph.D., I was forced to abandon the topic of women and crime and venture into population research—that's how I got to Seattle to hear that even a woman's ability to give birth can be obfuscated.

Despite the professional liabilities, I would argue that an overhaul of criminological theory is essential. The extensive focus on disadvantaged males in public settings has meant that girls' victimization, the relationship between that experience and girls' crime, and the relationship between girls' problems and women's crime have been systematically ignored. Feminist research has established that many young women who run away from home, for example, are running from sexual and physical abuse in those homes. These backgrounds often lead to a street life, also rigidly stratified by gender, that frequently pushes girls further into the criminal world and, for some, into adult crime.

Also missed has been the central role played by the juvenile justice system then and now in the criminalization of girls' survival strategies. In a very direct way, the family court's traditional insistence that girls "obey" their parents has forced young women, on the run from brutal or negligent families, into the lives of escaped convicts.

More recently, girls account for an increasing number of those arrested for delinquency, and they are being brought into the system for a wider variety of offenses (though they are still far more likely than boys to bring the trauma of abuse with them). Now, one in four of all juvenile arrests are of girls, and because we still have woefully few programs for girls, the nation's detention centers are filling up with young women who do not belong there.

We need to rethink our responses to "delinquency" in ways that put the lives of girls at the center, rather than the periphery, of delinquency prevention and intervention strategies. Gender matters, in short, in both the problems that bring girls into the juvenile justice system and in the ways in which the system should respond. So, finally, a plea, no more studies of "delinquency" that only include boys, and no more "girls watching boy's play sports" approaches to youth programming.

Meda Chesney-Lind is professor of women's studies at the University of Hawaii at Manoa. Author of *Fighting for Girls*; *Girls, Delinquency and Juvenile Justice* (with Randy Shelden); *The Female Offender*; and *Female Gangs in America* (with John Hagedorn). She has been named a fellow of the American Society in Criminology and received the Bruce Smith Sr. Award for "Outstanding Contributions to Criminal Justice" by the Academy of Criminal Justice Sciences.

suffering from pathological defects and therefore unable to control their behavior. Various psychological theories have focused on the mental processes of criminals, attributing crime to such phenomena as an imbalance between id and ego or an inability to experience guilt. All of these explanations assumed that criminals are different from the rest of society. More recent theories have defined crime in terms of social conditions, such as anomie or violent subcultures. Prominent among these is the labeling theory, which denies that deviants are inherently different from other people. Rather, deviance is defined as a label that powerful groups can impose on less-powerful groups and individuals. Labeling people as deviant often creates a self-fulfilling prophecy in which those people accept the deviant label and come to define themselves—and behave—accordingly. At the organizational level, theories of corporate crime examine ways in which organizational goals create pressures to commit illegal and/or dangerous actions. Although some of these various theories are more legitimate than others, none offers a complete explanation for all types of crime.

The functionalist and conflict theories differ over the nature and role of deviance. Functionalists like Durkheim argue that a limited amount of deviance performs the positive role of providing a society with alternative ways of thinking, organizing, and behaving, thus facilitating adaptation to changing conditions. When deviance becomes excessive, however, it threatens social cohesion and must be repressed. The conflict view, in contrast, argues that powerful groups use definitions of deviance to repress groups they perceive as threatening, thus enabling them to maintain their privileged position. Conflict theorists point to the relative lack of enforcement of laws against white-collar and corporate crimes as opposed to the national preoccupation with street crime as evidence that enforcement of social norms tends to protect the interests of the ruling classes. Similarly, feminist criminologists have shown that the labeling and punishment of crime are different for males than for females.

Key Terms

deviance
crime
social control
sanctions
deterrence
street crime
victimless crime
white-collar crime
anomie
differential association
labeling theory
primary deviance
secondary deviance

Exercises

1. Students sometimes have difficulty understanding the sociological approach to deviant behavior. Review the section "How Sociologists View Deviance" (on pages 293–296) if you need a refresher and then answer the following questions: What might be some strong arguments *against* the sociological approach? How would a sociologist counter them?

2. This chapter includes an interesting discussion of whether capital punishment deters murder. Predictably, the position of the American Civil Liberties Union (ACLU) on the death penalty brings polarized reactions: in favor or opposed. Check out their site for the issue at http://www.aclu.org/capital-punishment, and then answer the following questions:

   - Do you think that the death penalty deters capital crime? Why or why not?
   - Would American society benefit from eliminating the death penalty? If put to a vote, would you favor *life imprisonment without possibility of parole* in lieu of capital punishment? Why or why not?

3. In a box in this chapter, the 1996 ValuJet crash is analyzed as an example of state-corporate crime, in which multiple companies and the federal government all disregarded safety laws to meet deadlines and keep costs down. The box also discusses the *normalization of deviance*. To what extent do you think the forces at work in the ValueJet case were similar to or different from ones at work in the 2010 BP oil spill in the Gulf of Mexico? Explain your reasoning.

Part IV
Social Institutions

Chapter 11
Economy and Society

Economic Systems   327
    Sectors of the Economy   327
    Economic Change and Social Change   328

Economic Development and Society   328
    Hunting-and-Gathering Economies   328
    Agricultural Economies   329
    Industrial Economies   329

The Shift to Postindustrial Economies   331
    Effects on the Labor Force and Stratification   332
    The Rise of Professions   333
    The Role of Science and Education   333
    Postmodernism: A Challenge to Science and Technology   334

Modern Economic Systems   335
    Capitalism   335
    Socialism   337
    Karl Marx and Communism   338
    Mixed Economies   339

Social Consequences of Modern Economic Systems   340
    Does Capitalism Promote Greed?   340
    Socialism, Capitalism, the Market, and Productivity   341
    Is Socialism Dead?   341

The Changing Scale of Modern Economies   343
    Concentration in Corporate Capitalism   343
    Consequences of Concentration   345
    Multinational Corporations   346
    Globalization and Its Consequences   347

PUTTING SOCIOLOGY TO WORK   349
    Free Trade or Protectionism?   349
    Unemployment and the Economic Cycle   353

Financial Systems   353
    Voice or Exit   355
    Financial Crises   355

Karl Polanyi and the New Economic Sociology   358
    The Sociological Study of the Economy   358
    Karl Polanyi Enters the Dance   359
    The Embedded Economy and the Impossibility
       of the Self-Regulating Market   360

Summary   361
Key Terms   362
Exercises   363

You've probably seen Korean cars on the road—Kias, Daewoos, Hyundais. Although, until recently, these cars had the highest rates of problems of any new cars, they have enabled Korea to become the fifth-largest exporter of cars in the world because they are cheap. On the other hand, you probably haven't seen many Taiwanese cars lately—can you even think of the name of a car made in Taiwan? Even so, there is a good chance that the car you are driving contains some *parts* made in Taiwan. Many of the auto parts sold at Sears and Wal-Mart, for example, come from Taiwan. In contrast, very few parts are manufactured in Korea. Even if you need a part for a Kia or Hyundai, chances are it will come from somewhere other than Korea.

Why is it that one Asian country, South Korea, has been successful at developing an auto manufacturing industry but cannot produce parts, while another, Taiwan, is a big parts producer but cannot develop an auto manufacturing industry? Sociologists Nicole Biggart and Mauro Guillen (1999) studied the two countries to find out, and came up with some interesting answers. In Korea, large-scale, family-based organizations exist that gain help by gaining favor with the government, but never cooperate with one another. All three auto companies are examples of this. In Taiwan, on the other hand, business organizations are much smaller, and they cooperate with one another much more than in Korea. This allows the two countries to tap into different parts of the global *economy*. Korea, with its large organizations getting government help, is able to engage in large-scale manufacturing. However, the hierarchical, family-controlled manufacturing companies are very oppressive toward their labor. This lets them produce cars cheaply, but, with their alienated workers, the quality has traditionally been low (though in recent years at least Hyundai has turned this around). Still, there is enough of a market for cheap cars in the world that they can make good money selling inexpensive, second-quality cars. On the other hand, these large, top-down organizations that do not cooperate with one another cannot produce standardized or high-quality parts or respond quickly to market changes, so Korea has never been successful at selling auto parts.

Taiwan, on the other hand, with its small organizations that readily cooperate with one another, has become quite dominant in the parts market. But its companies are too small to be serious players in auto manufacturing. One reason for this is that, unlike Korea, Taiwanese inheritance laws (reflecting the country's Chinese culture) split inheritances among all family members. Korea, in contrast, concentrated on passing intact enterprises from generation to generation. These differences favored large firms in Korea and small ones in Taiwan (Biggart and Guillen, 1999). In addition, Taiwan's government offered less help (and less effective help) to the auto industry than Korea's government, in part because Taiwan was more focused on military matters.

Korea and Taiwan show how differences in social arrangements interact with global economic forces to produce different outcomes. The two countries had different kinds of economic organizations, which related to one another and to government in different ways. These differences, in turn, arose from different social and cultural traditions involving inheritance rules, cooperation, and the role of government. These differences allowed the two countries to fit into different niches in the global economy. Korea's social patterns allowed it to find a niche selling cheap but second-rate cars, while Taiwan's allowed it to develop a major car-parts export economy, but kept it from being able to manufacture cars on a significant scale. In this chapter, we shall examine such relationships between social patterns and economic systems, and how they affect all our lives.

Such relationships work both ways. As the opening example shows, social arrangements affect economic systems. But economic systems affect social arrangements, too, as illustrated by patterns of urban development in the United States. As the economic systems of the United States and the world have changed, some urban areas have benefited and others have been hurt. The story of Detroit illustrates this change. Detroit's economy, based on heavy industry, suffered greatly when heavy industry became less important as a source of employment in the economies of the United States and most other industrialized countries. As world economic systems change, fewer people work in heavy industry, and more are involved in the production and transfer of information. As a result industrial areas, such as Detroit, have rapidly declined, while areas specializing in "high tech," such as California's Silicon Valley, have grown.

Some industrial areas, such as Pittsburgh, have been able to develop major new economic bases in service, information, and financial industries. This has kept such areas economically viable and largely staved off population loss, though the economic base of these areas is dramatically different from what it was in the past. Collectively, economic changes like the decline of industry and the growth of information technology have created new patterns of regional growth and decline, both within countries like the United States and worldwide.

We can see the effects these changes have on both national economies and regional growth and decline, but what about the impact on individuals? Some people have been displaced not only from their jobs but also from their homes, like thousands of workers from Detroit who headed south and west to places like Houston, as manufacturing declined in the 1970s and 1980s. Even in areas like Pittsburgh that have managed to adapt, change has come at a cost to individuals. Many of the new jobs that have been created pay substantially less than the old jobs that have disappeared, especially for people with anything less than a college education (Duncan, 1996).

Economic Systems

Economic systems are the means by which scarce resources are produced and allocated within and between societies. Economic systems can be classified in three ways. The first is based on the level of economic development—how are goods and services produced, and how much of them can the system produce? The second classification is based on who owns the means of production. Third, economic systems may be classified on the basis of their scale, ranging from local to national to global. We shall examine all three of these issues in this chapter.

Sectors of the Economy

At different levels of development, different sectors of the economy predominate. Economies contain up to three basic sectors: primary, secondary, and tertiary. The primary sector consists of the direct extraction of natural resources from the environment. The primary sector includes farming, fishing, mining, woodcutting, oil drilling, and generating solar or hydroelectric power. The economic viability of the primary sector depends on the availability of natural resources and the market for products derived from natural resources, so it can be subject to severe fluctuations, both short- and long-term. Though still important, the primary sector has generally become a smaller proportion of the overall economy over time and with technological advancement.

The secondary sector consists of making or manufacturing products, such as cars, airplanes, televisions, dishes, and computers. It includes not only mass production but also the handcrafting of such items as furniture, carriages, and building fixtures. Generally, if a product is made by machines or human hands rather than taken directly from the environment, it is part of the secondary sector. This sector, too, has experienced considerable fluctuation, and seems to be declining in importance today. In the 1950s and early 1960s, when the secondary sector of the American economy was a major and growing source of employment, industrial workers prospered. However, by the 1970s, the secondary sector was declining in importance as a source of employment for a variety of reasons that will be discussed in this chapter. As a result, employment in heavy industry declined in the United States and in other technologically developed countries.

The tertiary sector consists of producing and processing information and providing services. The products of the tertiary sector are less tangible than physical products such as cars or houses. Examples of activities in the tertiary sector include teaching, research, data analysis, Web page design, management and investment consulting, broadcasting, entertaining, and writing. This sector also includes personal services, such as washing and repairing cars, cleaning houses, and providing medical care and legal assistance. The tertiary sector is growing most rapidly in today's economy. This is why places like Silicon Valley have the advantage over places like Detroit. People who have the technical and specialized training required for the better jobs in the tertiary sector will also have the advantage over those who do not. This is an important reason why the income of college graduates has been rising while the income of people with low levels of education has been falling (after adjustment for inflation) over much of the past three decades.

Economic Change and Social Change

Over time, as the economy has evolved from one level of development to another, different types of economic activity have taken place, different sectors of the economy have predominated, and different regions of the country have benefited. This process is but a small part of a much larger process of economic development going back to the origins of humankind. This process has led to great increases in the standard of living for much of the world's population, but it has also led to great upheavals and displacements. Today, there are strong indications that economic change is affecting economies like the United States in two ways. First, it has led to stiff international competition, as other economies, such as Korea and Taiwan, are able to develop their own highly efficient manufacturing and information industries. Second, it is leading to growing socioeconomic inequalities between those with the training to take advantage of the new opportunities and those who lack such training and have been displaced by the decline of the secondary sector in the United States.

Economic Development and Society

Changes in levels of economic development have also had tremendous impact on the world, leaving different parts of the world at dramatically different levels of economic development. As we shall see in Web-Based Chapter C, such changes have also increased both world population and world consumption of natural resources—so much so that human survival may be threatened. Let us take a closer look at these different levels of economic development, including hunting-and-gathering economies and agricultural economies, in which the primary sector predominates; industrial economies, in which the secondary sector predominates; and postindustrial economies, in which the tertiary sector becomes increasingly important.

Hunting-and-Gathering Economies

The most basic level of economic development, with the simplest division of labor, is the hunting-and-gathering economy. This type of economy has no cultivation and no manufacturing. People live on what they can obtain directly from the natural environment by gathering wild fruit and vegetables, fishing, and hunting—the primary sector predominates in such economies. Societies with hunting-and-gathering economies are usually small (often fifty or fewer people) and are usually organized as a tribe or as a clan, a group in which everyone is related. Thus, the entire society could be characterized as a primary group. The small size of such societies is a product of their economy and environment: In most places, hunting and gathering can support only a limited number of people. Most of these societies operate at or near a **subsistence level,** producing just enough food, clothing, and shelter to survive. They produce little or no **surplus.** In other words, they produce little or no wealth beyond what is necessary to meet basic needs for food, clothing, and shelter.

Hunting-and-gathering societies are often **nomadic**—they move to another place, within a limited geographic range, when they use up the food available. They have relatively little division of labor; work distribution is based on gender and on physical capabilities. Occasionally the society assigns a group of people to a military role, but usually this is not needed, as the sparse population that hunting and gathering can support tends to keep groups separated from one another.

Because of this limited specialization and relative isolation from other societies, hunting and gathering societies tend to have high levels of consensus. Also, ownership is usually communal since the meager level of production dictates that everything be shared (Lee, 1984). People in such societies usually have a fair amount of time to spend interacting with one another and participating in group rituals because once they have collected enough food to meet group needs, they have little reason to collect more (Lee, 1984). Therefore, people in such societies frequently spend less time working than people in societies with more complex economic systems (Gowlett, 1984; Lee, 1984; Lee and DeVore, 1968).

From the origin of human societies several million years ago until around 10,000 B.C., all societies had hunting-and-gathering economies. Today, a limited number of such societies still exist, mostly in thinly populated tropical, arctic, and desert areas remote from modern societies.

Agricultural Economies

The evolution of economic systems began with the transition from hunting-and-gathering economies to **agricultural economies**. This transition occurred gradually, along with the development of intermediate forms known as horticultural economies and pastoral, or herding, economies. Horticulture consisted of slashing and burning a small plot of forest, working the soil with a hoe or digging stick, and raising a crop. After a few years, when the soil was no longer fertile, horticulturalists moved on to another nearby location. Pastoral societies raised small herds of domesticated animals, also moving from place to place as forage was used up. Eventually, true **agriculture** developed. True agriculture is different from horticulture: those who practice it are permanently attached to the same location. This change occurred because of changes in the environment and advances in technology. Recent evidence suggests that while climate changes made hunting and herding more difficult, repeated raising of grain crops on the same site became easier (Hole and McCorriston, 1991). This may have led to the first true agriculture, as early as 10,000 years ago. By 3,000 to 6,000 years ago, the plow had come into use. Through the invention of the plow harnessed to animals such as oxen or horses, societies were able to raise crops on the same land year after year, because the plow could bring up nutrients from the subsoil and work weeds and leaves into the ground to act as fertilizers. Thus, people were no longer compelled to move from place to place to survive. Also, a much larger plot of land could be worked by one person, making the creation of a surplus possible for the first time (Lenski and Nolan, 1984).

The production of surplus food enabled societies to exist on a larger scale and in one location. It also freed some people to perform tasks other than food production. Towns and small cities became possible, and greater effort could be devoted to such secondary-sector activities as the construction of temples and public buildings. The production of a surplus also added a critical new element to the economic system: inequality, or economic stratification. In a subsistence economy, everybody lived at a bare survival level, but in an agricultural economy, those with power and prestige accumulated more than the rest of the population—usually much more.

In agricultural societies, the means of production is land, and those who own the land obtain most of the wealth and power. Some agricultural societies are based on family farms, but more often a small elite—usually deriving its position from religious tradition or military power—owns the land, while the rest of the population works for them. The system is usually headed by a monarch, and those who own land often have some formal political or religious title that is passed on between generations (along with land ownership). This type of system is referred to as a feudal system or an estate system (see Chapter 6), or sometimes simply as feudalism.

In various forms, feudal systems existed until a few hundred years ago in Europe, and even more recently in Asia, Africa, and Latin America. The southern U.S. plantation system bore an important resemblance to this system as well. As agriculture became more efficient, very large-scale governments occasionally emerged, as in the Roman and Chinese empires. More often, though, infighting among regional elites made warfare a constant reality. Such systems, though warlike and dramatically unequal, created enough surplus to allow the development of increasingly complex philosophy, art, religious institutions, architecture, and governments. Although the secondary and tertiary sectors were both larger than in less-developed economies, the primary sector still predominated in agricultural economies.

Industrial Economies

During the eighteenth and early nineteenth centuries, a new system of economic production based on manufacturing took hold in England and spread through the rest of western and northern Europe, as well as to North America. Since that time, it has spread in varying degrees to virtually every part of the world. This new system, the **industrial economy,** was based on the use of machines to produce a variety of products ranging from military hardware to consumer goods to new machines that could produce more new products. Thus, the secondary sector became the sector of greatest economic importance. Beginning with the steam engine, a series of inventions made possible more and more efficient manufacturing. These inventions grew out of *technology*—the application of scientific knowledge to practical tasks. This new economic system so dramatically transformed society that we refer to its development as the Industrial Revolution.

The industrial mode of production was made possible not only by new technology but also by the changes in social organization discussed in Chapter 9, including the rise of bureaucracy and the accompanying trend of rationalization. Tradition became less influential, and science, technology, and education more so. As we shall see later in this chapter, large-scale governments, based on legal-rational authority (see Chapter 12), replaced the traditional authority of monarchies.

Increased Standard of Living. With industrialization, the economy's ability to produce a surplus increased dramatically. This had a number of important consequences. One was a dramatic long-term rise in the standard of living, because the application of technology meant that far more could be manufactured per person (Rostow, 1965). In its early stages, however, industrialization did make life harder for many because of the long hours, low wages, and brutal working conditions it created. Over the long run, though, the increased productivity of industrial economies meant that people could have better diets, more adequate shelter, better health care, and more luxury goods. Life expectancy increased dramatically.

Greater Social Equality. Second, industrialization has been associated over the long run with greater social equality, at least with respect to income and standard of living (Lenski, 1966; Simpson, 1990). At first, industrialization often does increase inequality, because the new industrial sector creates so much more wealth for its owners than the old agricultural sector (Nielson and Alderson, 1995). But once industrialization begins to have an effect upon most of the population, the trend turns toward greater equality. Although the huge surplus created by industrialization has allowed the wealthiest people, usually the owners of factories, to amass previously unheard-of fortunes (Bobbio, 1987), it has improved the standard of living of the masses more than that of the wealthy. The surplus produced by industrial economies is so great that the wealthy can have their wealth and still allow much more income to go to the bulk of the population, thereby avoiding a revolution that might deprive them of their wealth. This tendency toward greater equality is also reinforced by declining birth rates (which reduce scarcity) and by democratization, both of which usually occur sooner or later along with industrialization (Nielson and Alderson, 1995). One note of caution is in order, however: The trend toward greater equality may well be reversed when societies move from the industrial stage to the postindustrial stage, discussed in the next section.

War and Revolution. Because of their high standard of living, industrialized societies seldom experience revolutions. The transition from an agricultural to an industrial economy has often been accompanied by a revolution, but once a society becomes industrialized, it is not likely to experience revolution. Industrialized societies also seem to go to war less often than preindustrial ones. One reason, hotly debated among political scientists, may be related to the previously mentioned correlation between industrialization and democracy. Some evidence suggests that democracies are reluctant to go to war with other democracies, though they still do attack nondemocracies, as in U.S. actions against Iraq and Vietnam, and the British war with Argentina over the Falkland Islands in 1982 (Lynn-Jones and Miller, 1995; Shea, 1996). However, the infrequent wars that do occur among industrial countries can be catastrophic, because the populations of industrialized societies are larger and because such societies have the technology to develop deadlier weapons (Beer, 1981; Singer and Small, 1972; Sorokin, 1937). In World War II, for example, over 40 million people died (Beer, 1981). Nuclear weapons can destroy all the world's industrialized societies in one war, and for several decades the United States and the Soviet Union spent vast sums on such armaments, though such expenditures decreased dramatically with the demise of the Soviet Union.

In today's world, many societies have fully developed industrial economies, while others remain predominantly agricultural or even horticultural (Lenski and Nolan, 1984, 1986). Many Third World societies are at intermediate stages between agricultural and industrial economies. The most industrialized areas of the world are Europe, North America, Russia, Israel, Australia, New Zealand, and parts of Asia. Some of these areas are now shifting to the *postindustrial* stage, discussed next.

The Shift to Postindustrial Economies

In the United States, in many European countries, and in other societies that have experienced industrialization, the role of manufacturing as a source of employment has declined recently. Instead, more and more people in these societies are employed in the provision of services and the generation and dissemination of information. In such an economy, there are more lawyers, accountants, researchers, computer designers and operators, and advertising and public relations specialists. Note that, in some way, each of these occupations involves obtaining, processing, presenting, or disseminating knowledge or information. There are also more waiters, auto repair persons, entertainers, travel agents, and household and business maintenance workers and cleaners. All of these occupations in some way involve providing a service. Such an economy, in which fewer people are employed in manufacturing and more are employed in information, knowledge, and service activities, is referred to as a **postindustrial economy**.

The idea that a postindustrial economy represents a new stage of economic development was first raised around 1970 by a group of sociologists including Alain Touraine (1971 [orig. 1969]) and Daniel Bell (1973). According to Bell, the main characteristics of a postindustrial economy include the transition from an industrial to a service economy, the growth of professional and technical occupations, a key role for theoretical knowledge as the main source of innovation and policy formation, and a shift to decision making on the basis of problem-solving rules rather than intuitive judgment.

In such economies, the tertiary sector has taken on greater importance than either of the other two sectors. Ownership of capital may become less important than control of information, the capability to develop new technologies, and the ability to provide services. More important, the ability to do these things may enable people to quickly amass great amounts of capital, as illustrated by the "instant billionaire" status of Microsoft founder Bill Gates, the world's wealthiest person at the start of the new millennium.

Many of the changes predicted by Bell, Touraine, and others in the early 1970s have indeed taken place in the most technologically developed societies. In the United States and Western Europe, heavy industry has declined as a source of employment. This is the process of deindustrialization introduced in Chapter 6. This happened partly because new technologies automated these industries, and partly because the core of economic growth shifted from manufacturing to services. It also happened in part because of globalization, a trend whereby competition and economic exchange occurs on a worldwide scale. In recent years, the United States, Europe, and even to some extent Japan have lost manufacturing jobs because of international competition. Such competition has reduced the number of manufacturing jobs in these countries in two ways. First, international competition has taken away some of the market for goods produced in these countries. Korean cars compete with Japanese cars, and Taiwanese auto parts compete with parts made in the United States. Second, it has led to increased *automation* (the replacement of people with machines, computers, and robots) as manufacturers have sought to cut costs to meet the competition, which sometimes comes from countries where wages are very low (Rohan, 1989). Globalization has also increased the tendency of manufacturers in the United States and other high-wage countries to move jobs to other countries where they can pay lower wages. Globalization and its effects are described in greater detail later in this chapter.

Between 1950 and 1980, the proportion of American workers employed in industries that produce goods fell from 49 percent to 33 percent, while the share in service-producing industries rose from 51 percent to 66 percent (Clark, 1985, p. 22). Banking and investment, entertainment, accounting, health care, engineering, hotels and restaurants, and the electronics industry have been the growth areas—and all of these either are in the service sector or involve generating and processing information. This shift has generally hurt the industrial Midwest and Northeast and helped the South and West (Sternleib and Hughes, 1975; Weinstein,

Gross, and Rees, 1985). Unlike heavy industry, these businesses can locate to areas with a desirable climate and recreational amenities (see Morgan, 1976), rather than being tied to areas that have natural resources or transportation waterways.

Effects on the Labor Force and Stratification

The transition to a postindustrial economy has resulted in the loss of hundreds of thousands of jobs in manufacturing, with job growth occurring in the professional and managerial sectors (as Bell predicted), but also in the service and clerical sectors. One consequence of this shift has been an increasing division of the labor force into two distinct and highly unequal segments. One segment, including doctors, lawyers, research workers, financial specialists, technicians, and engineers, is technologically educated, is relatively well paid, and enjoys high prestige. The other segment, bigger and faster growing, is made up of service, clerical, and retail sales workers (Reich, 1986a). These workers are usually poorly educated and often work for very low wages.

Thus, in the United States at least, the development of the postindustrial economy appears to have contributed to greater socioeconomic inequality (Eitzen and Zinn, 1989; Harrison and Bluestone, 1988; Olsen, 1990; Duncan, 1996). The more advantaged segment of the population creates demand for increasingly diverse services. In part, the advantaged segment of the population creates this demand by spending its time and money in search of self-fulfillment, good health, and fun. It also creates demand for services in the process of making its money, through expenditures for child care and help in the home, and through such activities as business travel. One example of this is the rapid growth in eating out, a time-saver for those who work long hours. The percentage of meals eaten out roughly doubled between 1977 and 1995, by which time 27 percent of U.S. meals were purchased from restaurants (Stenson, 2001). By 2009, this percentage was 48 percent, despite a slight decline from 2008 due to the severe recession (Zagat, 2009). This, of course, has led to rapid growth of employment in the restaurant and fast-food businesses, often with low wages and limited benefits.

The high educational level of professional, technical, and managerial workers, along with the mobility and diversity that are typical of the postindustrial society, strengthens some of the forces for democratization already present in industrial society. More people demand to be informed, refuse to follow rules blindly, and object to discrimination based on race, sex, and religion. In such a society, women tend to be as educated as men and to work outside the home.

Although the less-advantaged segment of society is also affected by these trends, its members have been hurt economically as lower-paying service jobs have replaced higher-paying manufacturing jobs. This group provides the services the higher-status group demands, but its members often cannot afford to purchase many of them for themselves. In particular, they cannot afford the education necessary to gain access to professional and managerial employment. They also cannot afford the travel and the wide variety of entertainment enjoyed by more affluent classes, nor do they have the money to take advantage of investment and financial services. On the other hand, electronic entertainment media such as televisions, radios, and stereos have become affordable to nearly everyone, so even the less affluent have been touched to some extent by the burgeoning entertainment and information businesses that are typical of postindustrial economies. In

Nowhere has the demand for services in the postindustrial economy been more evident than in the growth of fast-food and carry-out food establishments. These businesses have created many jobs, but most have low pay and limited benefits. (Courtesy of John E. Farley)

addition, the disadvantaged, like everyone else, have access to the "instant information" the media make available.

The collective result of these changes since the early 1970s is quite clear. The share of income going to people who are relatively low in the income distribution has fallen quite sharply, whereas the share going to those near the top has risen quite sharply (Duncan, 1996). With the arrival of postindustrial society, the rich have gotten richer and the poor, poorer. It appears that this pattern is not limited to the United States. Nielson and Alderson's (1995) international study of the relationship between development and income inequality supports such a notion. Their graph clearly shows that the tendency for inequality to decline as development increases levels off and ends at the highest levels of development—in other words, in the postindustrial economies.

The people who have been most directly hurt by the transition from an industrial to a postindustrial economy have been the workers (and their families) who once had high-paying manufacturing jobs, but have since become unemployed or moved to low-paying service jobs. The Detroiters displaced to Houston are a prime example. In recent decades, blacks and Hispanics in large cities in the Midwest and Northeast have especially had great difficulty finding employment, as the manufacturing jobs they were once dependent upon disappeared (Wilson, 1987, 1991a, 1991b; Anderson, 1990; Kasarda, 1989; Farley, 1987b).

The Rise of Professions

In postindustrial economies, the role of professions in both economy and society is enhanced. The basic characteristics of professionals—people who work in professions—were outlined in Chapter 9. Compared with other occupations, professions enjoy greater autonomy, status, and often pay, and require extensive and specialized training to enter. Doctors, lawyers, nurses, accountants, social workers, and teachers are examples of professionals. Note that to a large extent, professionals are involved in providing services. With the service-oriented economy of postindustrial society, growth in the tertiary sector has led to increased demand for professionals. Thus, the proportion of workers in the professions has risen steadily. The percentage of workers in what the Census Bureau considers professional occupations rose from 11 percent in 1960 to 14 percent in 1990 (U.S. Bureau of the Census, 1992g, 1963) to 20.2 percent in 2000 (U.S. Census Bureau, Census 2000, Summary File 3).

While some occupations like those outlined above are quite clearly professions, others are more ambiguous. It takes some specialized training to become a police officer or firefighter, but not as much as it takes to be a doctor or lawyer. So is a police officer or firefighter a professional? While there is no clear answer to such a question, it is clear that increasing numbers of occupations are seeking to define themselves as professions. This trend, called professionalization, involves establishing credentials and qualifications to enter the occupation, such as increased educational requirements for police officers. As is noted in Chapter 9, an occupation that succeeds in defining itself as a profession may enjoy greater autonomy and authority. It may also receive greater pay.

The Role of Science and Education

Because of the role of information in the postindustrial society, science and technology play a central role. Education is a key institution, for it is through the educational system that information is generated (in research universities) and taught. In some postindustrial societies such as the United States, however, privately funded and controlled research and development rival university research, as companies compete to discover for themselves the new technology that brings wealth.

Science is influential in postindustrial societies because it is widely understood that technology arising from scientific knowledge has made possible the high standard of living and relatively good health that the majority of people in such societies enjoy. Because science has made these gains possible, it is valued because it is seen as the most likely source of further gains. It is also valued because it can lead to the invention of products—such as the computer, video game machine, and various electronic medical scanners—that have been highly profitable to their developers.

The danger is that our ability to create risks—nuclear war, air pollution, hazardous chemicals, the "greenhouse effect"—may outstrip our ability to create knowledge to deal with those risks.

Yet, our society persists in creating risks, in large part because it is profitable in the short run for those who own wealth to do so. This new role of science and education has its dangers. There is a tendency to believe that technology can solve all problems, including those that are created by the new technologies themselves. To the extent that we miscalculate on this point, the very survival of humanity could be jeopardized.

Postmodernism: A Challenge to Science and Technology

For a variety of reasons, increasing numbers of people in postindustrial societies have begun to ask whether science and technology have been given too great a role. This has led to a broad but rather ill-defined intellectual movement called postmodernism (Doherty, Malek, and Graham, 1992). People who identify with this movement generally believe that the science, technology, and rational thinking that characterize industrial and postindustrial societies are harmful to society in various ways. More broadly, they not only question the influence of science and rationality, but also question the view that any one kind of knowledge can tell us what we need to know. Postmodernism rejects the idea that there is any one way of knowing things, whether it be science, religion, or an ideology such as Marxism (Jencks, 1992; Lyotard, 1984). With respect to science, it argues that knowledge consists of more than what can be tested scientifically—it also includes cultural, artistic, and ethical elements that science cannot address. Lyotard (1984) points out that knowledge includes such elements as justice, happiness, and beauty. Similarly, Postman (1992) argues that modern societies have become technopolies—that is, societies in which technology has come to define the meaning of religion, art, family, politics, history, truth, privacy, and intelligence. He argues that this tendency has robbed us of our souls and deprived us of opportunities to see alternative ways of living and believing.

In general, postmodernists reject the notion of anything having only one possible meaning (Olsen, 1992; Jencks, 1992). Thus, neither science nor anything else can tell us the meaning of things like religion, art, or family: These meanings are different to different people. In fact, the postmodernist notion that meaning is subjective can be tied closely to the theoretical viewpoint in sociology known as ethnomethodology, discussed in Chapter 3. Postmodernism has developed as a school of thought in most academic fields in the humanities and social sciences. In all of these fields, it has rejected the notion of any dominant paradigm that can tell us "how things are."

Postmodernism also rejects the notion of "high" and "low" culture. For example, for many years jazz, a highly complex and sophisticated type of music, was not taken seriously by academics because it was not classical music (and, some say, because its origins were African American, not European). But with the influence of postmodernism on the field of music, jazz has been given the recognition it deserves. Today, you may well be able to take classes on jazz at your college or university; in the past, you would not have been able to. Thus, postmodernism has challenged not only science, but the notion of singular ways of thinking in many other disciplines as well. In addition, postmodernism has had significant influence in popular culture, especially in the more avant-garde circles. It has been tied, for example, to the rise in popularity of various forms of punk and alternative rock music, as well as to new movements in art and filmmaking.

From a sociological standpoint postmodernism represents two important developments. First, it is a challenge to established ways of thinking such as functionalism, Marxism, and Weberian sociology, all of which developed in the early days of industrialization and may be less relevant in a postindustrial society (Pescosolido and Rubin, 2000). For example, postmodernist sociologists identify with the nineteenth-century writings of Friedrich Nietzsche (Antonio, 1995). Nietzsche was not taken very seriously by earlier sociologists because he challenged their dominant paradigm, Max Weber's view on bureaucracy and rationalization (discussed in Chapter 9). What Weberian sociology saw as rationalization, Nietzsche saw as regimentation and cultural domination. Second, postmodernism is an outgrowth of the movement toward a postindustrial society. Its viewpoint is not particularly new (Olsen, 1992), but it is highly appealing in postindustrial society. According to Lash (1990), the people who find postmodernism most appealing are precisely the groups who are ascendant in the postindustrial era: the "new class" of information specialists, and people who have "expressive occupations" (writers, researchers, entertainers) in the tertiary or service sector. Thus, theoreticians like Nietzsche are viewed differently today than in the past. They were rejected when sociology, like much the rest of society, saw industrialization as the hope of the future, but their words are appealing today when deindustrialization has made that seem like a false promise. And they are especially appealing to the growing number who do not rely on industrial work for a living.

More specifically, postmodernists point out that science and technology, while useful, cannot by themselves solve problems. A society such as the United States, for example, can have the most advanced medical technology in the world, but that technology cannot and does not guarantee a healthy population. Rather, ethical, political, and philosophical choices determine whether our population has access to the benefits of that technology. Global warming and catastrophic oil spills, like the Deepwater Horizon spill off the Gulf of Mexico in 2010, are all examples postmodernist might cite to question the very notion of "progress" that was taken for granted during most of the industrial age. Thus far, postmodernism has not been a sufficiently strong influence to move postindustrial societies away from their great emphasis on science and technology. But its influence is visible nonetheless in the questioning attitudes of people in postindustrial economies. People in these societies have increasingly come to question not only tradition, as science calls upon them to do, but also the influence of science itself, as postmodernism calls upon them to do.

Perhaps the most significant change associated with postmodernism is that what once was a great confidence in science has been replaced with the same skepticism that science has always displayed toward tradition and unproven assumptions. Ironically, then, postmodernism is in some ways a victory of modern thinking (that is, critical, skeptical, unsatisfied thinking) that is now turned against the science and technology that characterizes modern society (Bauman, 1992, pp. viii–ix). However, one criticism of postmodernism is that, while it shows the limitations of science and rationalism in understanding postindustrial society, it does not really offer an alternative that does offer such understanding (Pescosolido and Rubin, 2000). In other words, it is better at deconstructing theories that are flawed in explaining postindustrial society than it is at constructing new theories that do a better job.

Modern Economic Systems

Modern economic systems—industrial and postindustrial—vary in several important regards. One of the most important is the question of who owns capital, or productive capacity. In some modern economies, capital is for the most part privately owned; in a few others it is mainly publicly owned; and in yet others there is a mixture of public and private ownership.

Capitalism

An economy in which most of the productive capacity is privately owned is called a **capitalist economy.** This system of ownership is called capitalism or private enterprise. **Capital,** or productive capacity, includes manufacturing plants, distribution systems, land, raw materials, and money that can be converted into such things. Capital can be thought of as income-producing wealth: If you own something that produces income, you own capital. The larger the share of capital that is owned privately, the more capitalist an economy is said to be. In a purely capitalist economy—an *ideal type* that does not exist in real life—*all* productive capacity would be privately owned. The United States is one of the most highly capitalistic nations in the industrialized world. More of its productive capacity is privately owned than is the case in most European countries—but it is not completely capitalist. Certain important economic functions (highway construction, mail delivery, education) are performed predominantly by government-owned organizations. Moreover, even economic activities that are *usually* privately owned are not always so: The United States has publicly owned electric power companies, bookstores (on college campuses), campgrounds, marinas, and ski areas. In addition, even highly capitalist countries, such as the United States, have some government involvement in the economy in the form of social security and welfare programs, though such involvement is more limited than in mixed economies. In addition, the extent of such programs varies over time, growing during periods when the working class is politically organized and mobilized (Hicks, Misra, and Tang, 1995; Hicks and Misra, 1994), but also shrinking during times like the 1980s when it is less influential (Western, 1995).

Although capitalism is primarily found in industrialized economies, its basic characteristics have been adopted by countries in various stages of industrializing, such as South Korea, Taiwan, and Brazil.

Individual and Corporate Capitalism

Capitalist economies can be further subdivided into two types: individual capitalism and corporate capitalism. In individual capitalism, income-producing wealth is owned by individuals or families. In the past, the U.S. economic system was primarily one of individual capitalism. Productive capacity was largely owned by a limited number of very wealthy families, such as the Carnegies, Fords, and Rockefellers. In contrast to individual capitalism is corporate capitalism, in which most income-producing wealth is owned by **corporations**. These are large organizations whose ownership is shared by a number of people, called stockholders. A share of ownership in a corporation is called corporate stock. Corporations exist as separate legal entities. The corporation itself, and not any individual, assumes responsibility for the consequences of corporate decisions. Corporations enjoy various legal rights and must meet certain legal responsibilities; they can be sued and penalized if they fail to do so.

As industrial societies grow and modernize, the tendency is for individual capitalism to be replaced by corporate capitalism. In the United States, this happened quite rapidly, between about 1890 and 1905 (Roy, 1983). By 1905, corporations accounted for 74 percent of domestic production (Roy, 1983). The amount of capital required to produce, market, distribute, and sell products in today's large national and international markets is so great that even the wealthiest individuals lack sufficient means to own or finance the entire operation. Therefore, large numbers of individuals pool their wealth and jointly own the corporation. Corporate stock is usually bought and sold on public markets. Although a good many people own some stock, *most* stock is owned by a very small, wealthy segment of the population (see Chapter 6). In fact, because a corporation's rights include ownership of stock in other corporations, a large share of corporate stock in the United States is owned by corporations rather than by individuals.

Corporate Management

Rather than being run directly by their owners, corporations are run by boards of directors elected by the owners, and by managers hired by these boards of directors. Whereas in individual capitalism the owner actually operates the business, in corporate capitalism the owners hire someone else to do so. As a practical matter, the control of the corporation lies with its board of directors and managers, not its owners (Mintz and Schwartz, 1985). Boards of directors are effectively self-perpetuating: Although their members are elected by stockholders, most stockholders vote by proxy; that is, they allow someone else to vote for them. The board of directors makes recommendations to the stockholders concerning its membership, and the proxies ratify these recommendations. The only major exception to this rule is a "hostile takeover," in which

The headquarters of Google. For the past century or more, most productive capability in the United States has been controlled by corporations. In recent years, corporations in information-related businesses have become particularly dominant on a global scale. (AP Photo/Paul Sakuma)

a group of investors (which may include other corporations) buys the majority of the stock over the objection of the board of directors.

The American economy in the twenty-first century is best classified as a corporate capitalist system. Although many individual enterprises remain, the bulk of wealth is owned, produced, and sold by corporations. The 500 largest manufacturing corporations—a tiny percentage of all businesses—account for 42 percent of the U.S. gross national product and two-thirds of after-tax profits (Guzzardi, 1988). Even retailing, once dominated by small, family-owned stores, is today dominated by big corporations such as J. C. Penney, Sears, Wal-Mart, and Target.

Socialism

A system in which capital is publicly owned is called a **socialist economy**. Sometimes, to emphasize the major role of government, the system is referred to as state socialism (Edwards, Reich, and Weisskopf, 1986). The clearest examples of socialism today are Cuba, Vietnam, and North Korea. China remains officially socialist but, in fact, has moved sharply in the direction of becoming a mixed economy. For many years, the Soviet Union and its satellite countries in Eastern Europe also had socialist economies. However, this changed dramatically in the 1980s and 1990s. During the latter half of the 1980s, under the leadership of President Mikhail Gorbachev, elements of capitalism were gradually introduced into the Soviet economy, and the Eastern European countries were given greater freedom to choose their own direction. By the late 1980s, several of them, led by Poland, had shifted sharply toward capitalism. And in 1991, after an attempted coup against Gorbachev, Boris Yeltsin took over as president and a democratic government was established. The Soviet Union was subsequently abolished and the former Soviet republics became independent countries, loosely federated in a Commonwealth of Independent States. The largest of the new nations, Russia, began to move sharply toward capitalism under Yeltsin's leadership. However, both political conflict and economic difficulties have slowed this transition. Today, an increased share of productive capacity in Russia is privately owned, but a number of functions—such as health care, transportation, and some industries—remain state-owned. In many cases, ownership is a complicated mix of public and private. For example, defense industries are owned about one-third by labor, one-quarter by government, and most of the rest by private investors and directors (Kosals, Ryvkina, and Intriligator, 2000). While most newspapers are privately owned, some TV stations are publicly owned, some are private, and some have a mix of public and private owners (CNN, 2001). In the late 1990s, the state owned some proportion of almost 3,000 enterprises (Fortescue, 1999).

It is hard to tell just how much has really been privatized. On the one hand, the efforts to privatize agriculture have proceeded slowly despite a public policy aimed at doing so; only 6 percent of Russian agriculture had been privatized at the end of 1994 (Central Intelligence Agency, 1995). On the other hand, private interests—often former Communist Party officials with inside knowledge—have gained control of some of what is still officially public. The transmission of energy (that is, gas pipelines, the electric power grid, and so on), for example, officially remains a public enterprise, but 60 percent of the stakes in large companies were in fact in the hand of ex-bureaucrats and company insiders in the mid-1990s (Frydman, Murphy, and Rapaczynski, 1996), and more recent estimates still indicate that half of the investments of the state-owned gasline company are lost through corruption (Larson, 2006). Such insiders and former government officials also control much of what is officially private. Although their precise mix of public and private ownership varies and is hard to discern, Russia, the other former Soviet republics, and the countries of Eastern Europe today are probably best classified as mixed economies, a type of economic system we shall discuss in greater detail shortly.

The corruption associated with "insider" owership and control, along with Russia's inability to replace its past socialist economic system with a viable alternative, led to a 45 percent decline in its gross domestic product during the 1990s, according to the U.S. Central Intelligence Agency (2001). Kogut and Zander (2000) note that a similar drop in industrial output occurred in former East Germany in just one year between 1989 and 1990, when it was merged with West Germany and abruptly became capitalist. They argue that such a radical economic change as a transition from socialism to capitalism simply cannot be implemented in a very short time—a period of adjustment is required.

The largest and most important officially socialist country today is the People's Republic of China. But even China, though it remains staunchly socialist in its ideology, has large and growing elements of private ownership in its economy. Even as it has sought to centralize and tighten political control since the 1989 student uprising in Beijing, the Chinese government has continued in recent years to try to decentralize economic decision making. It has done this in several ways—allowing small business and private production of goods and services, recruiting multinational corporations to establish manufacturing enterprises in China, and making increased use of market influences in economic decision making, even in publicly owned industries. In many cases, it is easy for China's publicly owned industries to act on the basis of market forces, because they are owned locally (Walder, 1995). Until recently, enterprises owned by local governments have been the leaders in China's economic growth, but in the past decade, private entities have also accounted for a great deal of China's dramatic growth. Thus, it is fair to say that the Chinese economy, though still officially socialist, has become increasingly influenced by private ownership and market forces. Even when the Communist Party was in full control in the Soviet Union, that country's economy was never completely socialist. For example, black markets—illegal private sales of goods and services—always existed in the Soviet Union. Thus, all economies in the real world, whether mainly capitalist or mainly socialist, include some elements of each system.

Karl Marx and Communism

In part because it was ruled by the Communist Party, the Soviet Union was considered by most Americans to be communist. It is true that its ideology was communist, but its economy was not—at least as defined by Karl Marx, on whose theories virtually all twentieth-century socialist economies have been based. As Marx saw it, **communism**—or what he called the "classless communist society"—could come only after the long historical process illustrated in Figure 11.1, which Marx believed would end with the "withering away" of the state. The top bar of the figure represents changes over time in levels of economic development, as discussed earlier in this chapter. The bottom bar represents what Marx believed would be the dominant system of ownership at different points in time under each level of development.

The historical process envisioned by Marx began with hunting-and-gathering economies, which produced no surplus and tended to produce and share essentials on a communal basis. For this reason, Marx called such societies "primitive communism." When these societies gave way to agriculture, the dominant economic system became either feudalism or a plantation system, often with slavery. In both of these systems, a small, wealthy elite owned land and a large, impoverished segment of the population worked for that elite, which enjoyed the benefits of whatever surplus was produced. Marx believed that industrialization would be dominated by capitalism in its early stages, but that the inequalities of capitalism would lead to revolutions establishing socialism. (The extent to which this

This KFC near Beijing's Tiananmen Square illustrates the wide reach of multinational corporations. (Courtesy of John E. Farley)

Figure 11.1 Stages of Economic Evolution, According to Karl Marx

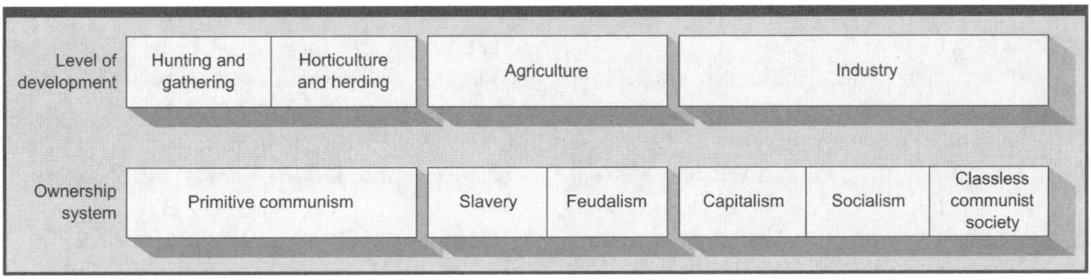

Level of development	Hunting and gathering	Horticulture and herding	Agriculture		Industry	
Ownership system	Primitive communism		Slavery	Feudalism	Capitalism	Socialism	Classless communist society

actually happened is explored in Chapter 15.) Marx saw socialism, however, as only an intermediate step toward the development of communism—a step that would be needed only temporarily to ensure that capitalists overthrown by revolution would not regain their wealth and power. He believed that eventually socialist countries would evolve into communism. Under communism as envisioned by Marx, government would be unnecessary because decisions would be made by collectives of workers who would run the places where they work. Individuals would contribute according to their abilities, and receive according to their needs. In reality, however, Marx's ideal has never been achieved—all of the countries that have been ruled by communist parties have in reality been socialist. In fact, it is doubtful that Marx's ideal could ever be achieved, given the tendencies toward bureaucracy in complex societies and toward oligarchy in organizations (both discussed in Chapter 9).

More generally, history has not unfolded in the ways Marx predicted. Major socialist economies did appear, but they did not develop out of capitalism. Rather, they typically emerged as societies, such as Russia and China, underwent the transition from an agricultural economy to an industrial one. Thus, these societies went directly from feudalism to socialism, without a period of capitalism in between, as Marx had predicted. And the majority of socialist economies have in turn been replaced with capitalism or mixed economies—not the classless communist society into which Marx predicted socialism would evolve.

One reason for this is that Marx did not foresee the transition to a postindustrial economy. In such economies, based largely on information and technology, economic success depends on the ability to respond quickly to changes in technology, markets, and society—and bureaucracies associated with the kind of top-down governmental control found in socialist societies cannot respond this way. Neither can some large private-sector bureaucracies, which explains why new startups, international competition, and less hierarchical organizations have taken business away from old, established, hierarchical business organizations like General Motors and IBM.

Mixed Economies

The final modern economic system that we shall discuss is the **mixed economy**. In this system, characteristic of most of Western Europe, some means of production are privately owned and some are publicly owned. Great Britain, France, and Sweden are prime examples of this system. In the developing world Zimbabwe can be cited as an example. China has also taken on some, but not all, of the characteristics of a mixed economy.

Railroads, airlines, and utilities such as gas and electricity are nearly always publicly owned in a mixed economy, although there may be private competition. Day care for children, which is mainly a private industry in the United States, is run by government on a nonprofit basis in virtually all mixed economies. Health care is publicly financed, although doctors may or may not be government employees. Certain manufacturing industries are state-owned. Shipbuilding, mining, and petroleum are also frequently public enterprises. At the same time, there is a great deal of for-profit private economic activity, and even government-operated firms often try to maximize profits. Private firms compete with government-owned ones, and some industries are entirely private, although they are typically more regulated than in more capitalist countries such as the United States.

The prevailing political trends can and do influence the precise mix of public and private control. Especially in Great Britain and France, there was a trend toward privatization in mixed economies in the 1980s, reflecting in part the election of more conservative governments. This trend primarily took the form of selling off part or all of the stock in some government-owned industries. Even so, the role of the public sector in these economies remains far greater than in the United States. The key difference is that most European public-service functions, such as health care, utilities, child care, and domestic transportation, remain in the public sector, whereas they are usually in the private sector in the United States.

Social Consequences of Modern Economic Systems

Sociologists are interested in the social consequences of living under various economic systems. What does it matter for the nature of society and the experiences of ordinary people whether an economic system is capitalistic, socialistic, or mixed? Since its inception, a common criticism of capitalism has been that it promotes greed and inevitably produces extreme inequalities between the wealthy and the poor. On the other hand, the recent collapse of the Soviet Union and many other socialist economies raises serious questions about the social and economic viability of socialism. Does socialism inevitably lead to poor productivity and authoritarian, hierarchical forms of government—the conditions that brought down the Soviet Union and its satellites?

Does Capitalism Promote Greed?

As noted, a long-standing criticism of capitalism is that it promotes greed. In fact, some critics have argued that capitalism could not work without greed. In 1972, Richard Edwards and colleagues wrote, "Capitalism would collapse if capitalists followed Christ's command, 'If you would be perfect, go sell what you possess and give it to the poor.'" Why do these critics think it would collapse? Because, they argue, capitalism depends on a **norm of maximization** that assumes people will want to get as much as they can. A review of capitalist economists will reveal that economically rational behavior is defined as that which brings the maximum possible return in income, wealth, or profits (see, for example, Riddell, Ramos, and Shackelford, 1979, Chap. 11). Early capitalist economists such as Adam Smith (1910 [orig. 1776]) believed that such a norm of maximization would benefit everyone in society, because it would reward efficiency with higher profits. Because people want to get as much money as possible and efficiency is the route to profits, they will become as efficient as possible. However, critics point out, wealth is still limited, and when one person maximizes his or her wealth, it often occurs at the expense of someone else. For this reason, they point out, capitalism promotes inequality. The highly capitalistic United States is often cited as an example of this: As was shown in Chapter 6, the United States has greater economic inequality and more severe poverty than most other industrialized countries, nearly all of which are less capitalistic than the United States.

By now, some of you may be thinking that wanting to maximize one's wealth and income is simply human nature, not the product of any particular economic system. However, sociohistorical analysis strongly suggests that maximization is *not* simply human nature, because it has not existed in many past societies. Max Weber (1958b [orig. 1920]) studied cultural values, particularly as they related to religion, in a wide variety of past societies. He found that through most of human history, people did *not* value maximizing personal wealth and comfort. Rather, values in most preindustrial societies centered on spiritual life, interpersonal relations, community, and tradition. As we shall see in greater detail in Web-Based Chapter B, Weber links the spread of a norm of maximization with the more individualistic values of Protestantism, and argues that by promoting individualism, Protestantism created a cultural atmosphere in which capitalism could flourish. In this classic study, Weber made two points that are relevant to our present discussion. First, the norm of maximization is not universal—it has existed only in *some* societies through history. Second, the culture and values of a society may make it more or less conducive to capitalism—a view that is consistent with the notion that capitalism needs the norm of maximization in order to fully develop.

One important counterargument could be made. It could be argued that the norm of maximization is a product of modernization and industrialization, not capitalism *per se*. In fact, Weber saw Protestantism, capitalism, and industrialism as all contributing to the set of values that includes maximization. Also, it appears that the norm of maximization has arisen in socialist societies as well as capitalist ones, and may have even contributed to the downfall of many of the socialist economies that collapsed in 1989 and the early 1990s. In many cases, people in these economies were angry because they learned through news media and, in some cases, through travel that people in capitalist economies were enjoying a higher standard of living than they were. And there is no question that even former communist party officials have quickly adopted—or perhaps already believed in—the norm of maximization: Many of them have made considerable fortunes by gaining ownership of formerly public enterprises (Frydman, Murphy, and Rapaczynski, 1996).

Socialism, Capitalism, the Market, and Productivity

The anger in communist countries over reports of higher standards of living elsewhere brings us to the key criticism of socialism: It cannot produce a good standard of living, because it does *not* provide the incentives necessary to get people to be as efficient as they can. The strength of capitalism is often seen in the *market:* If it is left free from interference, the laws of supply and demand will bring rewards to those who supply what people want and can buy, particularly to those who do it the most efficiently. In fact, the extent to which capitalism actually works this way varies, because the market can only function when there is free competition—that is, a number of suppliers competing with one another to offer the best product at the lowest price. Today, capitalism in many cases has become *oligopolistic*—markets for any given product are controlled by only small groups of producers, who collude rather than compete—or even *monopolistic*—there is only one producer of a given product. To the extent that this is true in any given economy, there cannot be competition so the market cannot encourage efficiency, unless there is international competition. Thus, the market does not always exert great influence under capitalism.

Critics of socialism, however, point out that it is almost impossible for the market to function under state socialism, because it is almost by definition monopolistic: The only producer is the state. Moreover, in part because of the state's monopoly power and in part because of a philosophy that emphasizes taking care of people rather than doing what is most efficient, economic decisions are made on the basis of government decision or social policy rather than market factors such as supply and demand. As a result, these critics argue, socialist economies cannot possibly be as efficient as capitalist ones (Clark and Wildavsky, 1992). The consequence is a low standard of living for everyone, even though nobody may go without very basic essentials.

Is Socialism Dead?

In the modern era of mass communications, such a low standard of living can make socialist societies highly unstable. In fact, it has led many to question whether state socialism is pretty much a thing of the past, even though as of this writing state socialist societies still existed in North Korea, Vietnam, Cuba, and, to some degree, China. During the 1980s, in the Soviet Union and its satellites, media images of the higher standard of living of Western countries with their capitalist or mixed economies led to great dissatisfaction with socialism. And once they were given the choice of free, multiparty elections, people in formerly socialist countries have for the most part voted for politicians favoring capitalist or mixed economies based primarily on market forces, although in some of these countries, more socialist-leaning parties have won some elections more recently.

It may be, for reasons suggested earlier in this chapter, that as economies move from early industrialization toward the information-based postindustrial economy, socialism becomes less and less viable (Berman, 1993). We have noted above that, contrary to Marx's predictions, the socialist economies that have existed have not been the result of an overthrow of capitalism. Rather, the socialist economies of both the Soviet Union and China resulted from the overthrow of feudalism.

To a large extent, the same is true of Cuba and Vietnam. Thus, socialism has been an alternative to capitalism as a route from an agricultural to an industrial economy. It is an open question whether Russia and China could have industrialized to a greater or lesser extent with a capitalist system, but it is clear that they succeeded in substantially industrializing under socialism (Brus and Laski, 1989, Chap. 3). China has adapted to these changes more successfully, but in part, it has done so by becoming more capitalist.

As the economy became more based on information, computers, and free world trade, however, socialism became more and more of an impediment because it was not as effective as the market in adapting to these rapid changes (Berman, 1993). As one might expect from this, the economic growth of the Soviet Union and its satellites from the 1960s through the 1980s was vastly poorer than in the earlier era of industrialization (Brus and Laski, 1989, p. 31). All of this suggests that while a state socialist economy may be a viable means of industrialization, it does not function well in an advanced industrial or postindustrial economy or under conditions of globalization.

In addition to this, globalization and the information economy have another effect. They make people more and more dissatisfied with the poor productivity of state socialism. When state socialism collapsed, it was in no small part because Russians, Poles, and East Germans were well aware of the vastly higher standard of living in West Germany, the United States, the Scandinavian countries, and other capitalist or mixed economies.

On the other hand, it appears that some formerly state socialist countries, while moving to a market economy, could develop forms of worker ownership that are in fact closer to Marx's ideal communist society than state socialism ever was. Before it was abolished in 1991, the Soviet Union was developing worker-owned industries that functioned in an increasingly market-oriented economy. Many of these employee-owned industries continued to function thereafter, and the Russian government developed a policy of awarding 25 percent of the ownership of enterprises to the workers in those enterprises. An additional 15 percent was available for sale at reduced rates to workers and managers (Logue and Bell, 1992). This is why, as noted above, significant portions of some Russian industries are owned by labor—that is, by the workers in those industries.

The future of this remains uncertain, however. Research has shown that, although workers did get the majority of stock when Russian companies were privatized, most of the ownership of some companies eventually ended up in the hands of managers and former Communist Party officials, who were in many cases one and the same (Frydman, Murphy, and Rapaczynski, 1996). This has occurred both because these groups had important power advantages, and because, to a large extent, they were the only people around with management skills and experience (Rona-Tas, 1994). Still, as of the mid-1990s, more than half of Russian enterprises had majority employee-ownership, though in some cases the employees who owned the companies were the managers (Fortescue, 1998). More recently, however, many of these employee-owners have sold their stock, so few Russian companies remain employee owned today (Australian Employee Ownership Association, 2008) Thus, while Russia has tried to encourage worker ownership as firms have been privatized, it has been only partly successful in doing so. In China, on the other hand, employee ownership has been fairly common as the country has moved to a less socialist and more capitalist economy (Australian Employee Ownership Association, 2008). Such worker ownership is an alternative type of economic system that incorporates some important elements of socialism, but retains a market economy rather than attempting to plan and manage the economy centrally, as was done under state socialism. The main challenge facing these employee-owned companies is the challenge facing such companies everywhere: To what extent to the workers think in terms of the long-term welfare of the organization (and thus their own long-term welfare) versus short-term maximization of wages?

As was noted earlier in this chapter, another socialist alternative that seems to be producing improved economic growth in China is locally owned enterprises. Like the enterprises of the old Soviet Union, these organizations are governmentally owned. Unlike in the Soviet Union, however, many of China's public enterprises are locally owned, and compete with other businesses (public and private) in a market economy. This competition, which the Chinese government calls "market socialism," creates many of the same market incentives as would be found in a competitive capitalist economy. With this and other changes from its previous centrally controlled socialist system, the Chinese gross domestic product has increased by a factor of nearly thirty since 1978, reaching $4.33 trillion in 2008 and making China today the world's second-largest economy. However, its per capita gross domestic product remains far below that of industrial capitalist and mixed economies. One limitation of market socialism can be seen in the former East Germany. On the one hand, East Germany used a system of market socialism to become the most productive of the old Soviet satellites. A study that compared two similar companies in socialist East Germany and capitalist West Germany found the East German company every bit as technologically competent as the West German company. However, there was a problem: The East German company was less able to innovate, despite its competence, because it was constrained by pressures from the government to meet central planning goals. So even though it was independent and competent (much like today's locally owned Chinese companies), pressures from central planners kept it from adapting as well as it could have (Kogut and Zander, 2000).

While state socialism has largely failed because of its inability to be productive, particularly with the development of globalization and postindustrial economies, mixed economies do not seem to be subject to such problems. Mixed economies such as Sweden, Germany, and Norway are among the most productive in the world (Pontusson, 2005; World Bank, 1992, p. 219). In mixed economies, the market continues to exercise great influence, but government ownership of some industries and regulation of others act as a counterforce to the tendencies of capitalism to produce socioeconomic inequality. The mixed economy model has also drawn substantial support from the growing environmentalist "green" movement (Hill, 2010; Rae, 1991), and it appears that mixed economies such as Sweden may provide stronger environmental protection than either capitalist ones like the United States or socialist ones like the old Soviet Union. Through strong but flexible environmental regulation, Japan between 1970 and 1990 was able to attain rapid economic growth and substantially improve its air quality at the same time (World Bank, 1992, p. 92). Although social democratic parties have suffered setbacks in some countries such as Sweden and Great Britain during the 1990s, some of these setbacks have been only temporary, as these parties regained power in the mid-1990s. Moreover, such parties have gained ground in other countries such as Canada, where the democratic socialist New Democratic Party won a majority in the Ontario parliament in 1990. And even in Sweden and Great Britain, moves to reduce the role of government and increase the role of the private sector were limited in scope: The role of the public sector in these countries remains far greater than it is, for example, in the United States.

The Changing Scale of Modern Economies

Today, goods and services are produced on a larger scale than ever before. When you purchase a good or service, there is a good chance that its producer or provider is a massive international corporation. This is true whether you buy a car, rent a hotel room, eat a meal out, or go shopping: You will likely be dealing with international giants such as General Motors, Holiday Inn, McDonalds, or K-Mart. We have already noted that the *corporation* rather than the individual or family business has come to dominate modern capitalist economies. We shall now examine an additional reality: In many cases, the number of corporations producing any given product has become very small.

Concentration in Corporate Capitalism

An economy in which the number of producers of any given product is small is referred to as a **concentrated economy.** Because only a very few producers control almost all the market for any given product, there is little or no competition. An economy in which there are many producers is referred to as a deconcentrated economy. As is shown in Table 11.1, the American economy is highly concentrated. The table shows the share of the market for various products that is controlled by the four largest producers of the product. Note that for most of the products shown in the table, the top four producers control a clear majority of the market, and for some products, they control nearly all the market—as much as 90 percent. In cases such as this, **oligopoly**—control of virtually all of the market by just a few producers—clearly exists.

The origins of the current high levels of concentration in the American economy can be traced to around the beginning of the twentieth century. In the late nineteenth century, large American producers began to combine into a few giant corporations known as *trusts,* thereby eliminating competition and creating oligopoly in various industries including railroads, steel, oil, banking, and others (Herman, 1981). In some cases, this concentration went so far as to create **monopoly**—control of all or nearly all of a product market by just one producer. In the early twentieth century, growing concern about the effects of concentration in the U.S. economy led to the passage of antitrust laws. However, these laws have rarely been strictly enforced, and current statistics reveal that the American economy has remained concentrated throughout this century. Indeed, some industries have become *more* concentrated over time. There were, for example, over 2,200 breweries in 1880 and there were still 750 in 1935—but by 1979, there were only about 40 (Currie and Skolnick, 1988, p. 31). With the advent of "microbreweries"—many of which sell their beers only on-premises—the number of brewers had grown again to 160 in 1992 and nearly 500 by 1997. But by 1992, the top four producers controlled 90 percent of the market, up 13 percentage points from a decade earlier. Despite an increase of more than 300 breweries between 1992 and 1997, the four biggest producers still controlled 90 percent of the market in 1997 and still did in 2002. The popularity of microbrews in the 1990s has not significantly reduced the market share of large brewers; indeed they have capitalized on it by developing their own specialty brands. This pattern is not limited to beer: Table 11.1 reveals that in a number of industries, the number of producers increased between 1992 and 1997, but the market share controlled by the four biggest producers remained the same or grew. Between 1997 and 2002, the number of producers rose in some industries and fell in others, but concentration again did not change much. Examples include industries that produce pet food, chocolate, soap, tires, telephones, and aircraft.

For a period of time, economic concentration extended beyond any one product or industry: In the 1960s and 1970s, the dominant corporate form was the *conglomerate:* a huge company that owned large producers in a number of industries. However, during the corporate takeovers of the 1980s, many conglomerates were dismantled, as companies financed their purchase of other companies by later selling off parts of their acquisitions that were unrelated to the main product (Davis, Diekmann, and Tinsley, 1994). This, ironically, produced even bigger companies, but ones that were more specialized in one industry, such as publishing. Retrospective analyses of the conglomerate era suggest that the conglomerate was not an effective form of corporate organization, because the disparate industries were too hard to manage. In fact, it appears to have contributed significantly to U.S. difficulties in competing in a global market (*Economist,* 1991b).

Interlocking Directorates

A feature closely related to concentration, which has also reduced the degree of competition in modern capitalism, is the **interlocking directorate.** This occurs when the same individual serves on the board of directors of more than one corporation. In effect, it means that the same people may have a hand in the operation of numerous legally autonomous corporations. The overwhelming majority of major U.S. corporations have interlocking directorates with other corporations. In fact, interlocking directorships have been widespread ever since the U.S. economy shifted from individual to corporate capitalism around the beginning of the twentieth century (Roy, 1983). Of 1,131 corporations studied by Mintz and Schwartz (1985, p. 145), 998 were part of a continuous network of interlocking directorates. At the center of the network, and connected directly to nearly all of the largest corporations, are banks and insurance companies. Thus, a relatively small group of people has vast power over the economy, and great opportunities and pressures exist for producers who are supposed to compete to collude instead (Burt, 1983; Mintz and Schwartz, 1981a, b). Another very important effect of interlocking directorates is that they help large corporations act on behalf of their political self-interests by enabling them to operate

Table 11.1 Concentration in the American Economy: Selected Industries, 1982, 1992, 1997, and 2002

Industry	Number of Firms in Industry				Domestic Market Share of Four Largest Producers			
	1982	1992	1997	2002	1982	1992	1997	2002
Breakfast cereal	32	42	48	45	86%	85%	83%	78%
Pet food	222	102	129	176	52%	58%	58%	64%
Cookies and crackers	296	374	322	296	59%	56%	60%	67%
Chocolate products	77	146	152	138	75%	75%	80%	69%
Beer	67	160	494	349	77%	90%	90%	91%
Soap and detergents	642	635	738	699	60%	63%	66%	61%
Tires	108	104	110	112	66%	70%	72%	77%
Guns (small arms)	138	177	189	179	51%	43%	42%	43%
Household cooking equipment	71	80	77	69	52%	60%	58%	56%
Home refrigerators and freezers	39	52	21	18	94%	82%	82%	85%
Home laundry equipment	15	10	10	13	91%	94%	90%	93%
Household vacuum cleaners	29	35	25	29	79%	59%	68%	78%
Electric lamps	113	76	54	57	91%	86%	90%	89%
Radio and TV equipment (1982)	432				49%			
Records and tapes (1982)	548				61%			
Audio-visual equipment (1992/97)		391	521	544		39%	52%	43%
Telephones	259	479	548	456	76%	51%	54%	56%
Motor vehicles	284	398	325	308	92%	84%	82%	81%
Aircraft	139	151	172	184	64%	79%	85%	81%
Motorcycles and bicycles	269	244	373	348	59%	65%	68%	72%
Watches and clocks	227	179	145	123	51%	40%	52%	47%
Burial caskets	270	195	161	148	52%	64%	80%	73%

Source: Concentration data for 1982 are from U.S. Bureau of the Census, 1986c. Table 5; Data for 1992 are from U.S. Bureau of the Census, 1996i. Data for 1997 are from U.S. Census Bureau, 2001j. Data for 2002 are from U.S. Census Bureau, 2008#.

Source for 2002 data: U.S. Census Bureau. 2008#. Economic Census: Concentration Ratios. 2002 Economic Census, Manufacturing, Value of Shipments, http://www.census.gov/epcd/www/concentration.html (Downloaded October 28, 2009).

as a relatively unified political force (Useem, 1984; Zeitlin, 1974).

Consequences of Concentration

When industries are so concentrated that oligopolies form, several problems can result. First, there may be some of the same efficiency problems that exist under state socialism: If there is no competition, the market cannot reward the most efficient producer. Poor productivity, low-quality products, overpricing, and failure to respond to changes in demand can all result from the lack of competition when there is too much concentration. The U.S. automobile industry is often cited as an example of this. In the 1960s and early 1970s, the three major U.S. automakers—General Motors, Ford, and Chrysler—controlled the overwhelming share of the domestic market. During this time, car prices soared, and those companies continued to produce large, gas-guzzling cars even when looming energy shortages and environmental concerns militated the production of smaller, more efficient automobiles. Only through the return of competition, in the form of Japanese and European automakers capturing a growing share of the market, were American automakers forced to produce more efficient and reliable products. In the process, however, American automakers lost a substantial part of their market; this might have been avoidable had they produced more efficient and reliable cars without being forced to do so by international competition. This example also shows that excessively concentrated capitalism is subject to some of the same vulnerabilities as socialism in today's globalized economy. In this situation, any domestic economic system that does not include effective competition is highly vulnerable to international competition, as will be explored in greater detail in a later section of this chapter.

Another problem is that concentration can be a source of great power. At the national level, this power is exercised through the lobbying, PAC contributions, and policy institutes discussed in Chapter 6. However, power is also exercised on the local level. Large firms can use the local need for jobs to create policy favorable to the firm. For example, a large firm might encourage several localities to compete for their new plants. The firm is able to extract subsidies from local governments in the form of property tax abatements, public services, road construction, and sometimes even land. Many state laws allow the use of property tax abatements as an enticement to plant construction, and most of the time, the maximum legal abatement is routinely given (Wolkoff, 1983). This amounts to a massive subsidy of big business, paid for by taxpayers.

Bigness is also a source of power in the marketplace that can be used to eliminate potential sources of future competition. This is often done through a process known as predatory price cutting: Producers in a monopoly or oligopoly keep new competitors out by temporarily cutting their prices below that of the new producer, often by using money earned in one activity to temporarily subsidize another (Burgess, 1989, pp. 172–79).

Finally, concentration often contributes to inequality in society. To some extent it does so by its very nature, by placing great wealth and power in the hands of a few people. The effects of concentration on wages and prices, however, are more complicated than the foregoing suggests. Concentration may actually lead to *higher* wages, because it eliminates the competition that creates pressures to keep wages low. In the nineteenth century, when the U.S. economy was characterized by individual capitalism and intense competition, wages were very low. The reason was that producers tried to outsell the competition by keeping prices—and hence wages—low. To a large extent, concentration eliminated this incentive to pay low wages by reducing the incentive to cut prices—monopolies and oligopolies involve little or no price competition. More recently, competition was introduced into the airline industry through deregulation in the 1980s, and again the result was declining wages. Unions were broken or suffered serious damage at TWA, Eastern, and Continental, and wages fell throughout the industry (Salpukas, 1988). (Eventually, severe economic difficulties put Eastern out of business and led TWA to be absorbed by American, and at the time of this writing, a deal to merge Continental with United Airlines was nearing completion.) Competition from lower airfares also put pressures on the bus industry. Following the examples of the airlines, Greyhound hired strikebreakers when its drivers struck to oppose wage and benefit cuts. It was three years before the resultant conflict was finally resolved in 1993. As these examples show, intense competition can lead to increased inequality by reducing workers' wages and benefits.

While concentration may reduce pressures to cut wages, it can still lead to inequality through prices, profits, and other mechanisms. For example, producers without competition can raise their prices more than enough to cover the costs of the higher wages they may pay, so profit margins may actually increase to a greater extent than wages. In addition, monopolistic producers may become highly vulnerable to international competition as the economy globalizes—an issue that will be discussed in greater detail shortly. When this happens, job loss and displacement, such as that of Detroit's autoworkers, is often the result. Typically, the workers suffer more than their bosses when this happens. In the auto industry, as in the other industries, executive salaries soared in the 1980s and 1990s. This occurred even as some workers were laid off and others who remained were told they would have to sacrifice wages and benefits in order to save their jobs and their companies.

Multinational Corporations

A particular feature of concentrated corporate capitalism is the **multinational corporation,** a giant business that is headquartered in one country but operates in many. Multinational corporations engage in production, resource extraction, and marketing in different parts of the world, locating each operation wherever it will best contribute to the corporation's profitability. Such corporations may dominate markets not just in their home country, but in many other countries as well. To some extent, multinational operations may be necessary in today's world economy. In dollar value, about one-fifth of what is manufactured in the United States today is sold elsewhere, and more than one-fifth of what is sold here is manufactured elsewhere. Both markets and sources of essential natural resources are often located far from a company's home country. For example, American Levi's are partially manufactured in Mexico; Toyota, Honda, and Volkswagen have manufacturing operations in the United States. Another common pattern is for a corporation based in one country to be absorbed into one based in another; RCA televisions are today the product of a French government–owned corporation, Thomson SA.

Although multinational corporations often do pay higher wages than Third World workers might otherwise receive, their activities in the developing world are in many ways detrimental. For one thing, they take the profits from what they produce out of the Third World country, depriving it of the opportunity to invest and grow. This issue, which is addressed by world system theory, is discussed further in Chapter 15.

Multinational corporations are also often involved in bribery and coercion. Their great wealth and power makes it easy to do this in poor countries that often depend upon them for jobs. Additionally, preindustrial societies tend to have great inequality of wealth and power, and may be ruled by monarchs or dictators who have their own interests at heart to a greater extent than those of the people. Such leaders are often easily swayed by the great wealth of the multinationals, and in some cases may even demand bribes as a cost of doing business. Since congressional investigations of business and political corruption began in 1976, hundreds of American corporations have admitted making payments to foreign government officials to gain favors. Payments totaling hundreds of millions of dollars were made by various American corporations (particularly in the aerospace industry) to government officials in South Korea, Bolivia, Japan, the Netherlands, Turkey, Italy, Pakistan, and Colombia, among others (Barlow, 1987, p. 261). Since World War II, corporations have been involved—with the assistance of the American government—in overthrowing the governments of Chile, Guatemala, and Iran.

Multinational operations are by their very nature exceedingly difficult to regulate. Every country has different rules, and the corporation can simply move around until it finds either rules it likes or officials willing to bend or ignore the rules. The very threat to move usually discourages enforcement of the rules, for fear that the country will lose jobs. Thus, to a large extent, multinational corporations can operate outside the law.

Globalization and Its Consequences

In Chapter 9, we introduced the concept of **globalization**—a trend whereby production, competition, and economic exchange increasingly occur on a worldwide scale. The growth and development of multinational corporations is both a cause and an effect of globalization. Production and trade occur in worldwide markets today more than ever before. This can be seen in several ways. First, it can be seen in the growth of international trade: Today, 70 percent of all goods produced in the United States compete with imports, and imports to the United States increased by 80 percent just between 1982 and 1986 (Pattison, 1990), and more than doubled between 1990 and 2000 (U.S. Bureau of the Census, 1996f; 2001h). At the same time, American-made products and services are distributed worldwide, and compete in many countries with products and services produced there. There are, for example, over 3,000 7-11 stores in Japan. In virtually all industrialized countries the share of product markets taken by imports has risen; in fact, the increase has been faster in a number of other countries than in the United States (Vernon, Spar, and Tobin, 1991).

With globalization, the line between domestic products and imports becomes increasingly unclear: 85 percent of all U.S. manufacturers use foreign materials in their domestic manufacturing process, and U.S. materials are similarly used by foreign producers. U.S. firms have many production plants in other countries, and foreign firms have many production plants in the United States. During the 1980s, Japanese companies created over 10,000 jobs in Tennessee (Pattison, 1990), and U.S. firms employed thousands of people in Mexico. Today, even Korean auto manufacturers have plants in the United States.

Globalization also affects capital markets—that is, the buying and selling of stocks and bonds and the lending and borrowing of money. In part because of computer technologies, these activities have become so worldwide that international borders have almost ceased to have any meaning (Aho and Levinson, 1988). Currency trading has also grown dramatically. Between 1973 and 1993 the amount of money changed from one currency to another every day soared from $10 billion to $1.3 trillion—130 times as much (Menshikov, 1997) and by 2007, the figure had reached a mind-boggling $3.2 trillion (Bank for International Settlements, 2007). That figure represents the entire U.S. economy for 2007 ($13.8 trillion) being traded every five days. One consequence of this was that as U.S. public and private debt increased during the last three decades, more and more of what was borrowed came from overseas investors.

Globalization has been going on for a long time, but we are now in a period of unprecedented acceleration of this process. Chase-Dunn, Kawano, and Brewer (2000) studied world trade in relation to domestic production over a 160-year period in the nineteenth and twentieth centuries. They found a long-term trend of globalization, along with three distinct surges of globalization: in the mid-to-late nineteenth century (about 1845–1880), in the first quarter of the twentieth century, and in the last half of the twentieth century. However, the third surge took globalization to a level beyond what was attained in any previous time period, so that the level of globalization today is unprecedented in human history.

Consequences of Globalization for the United States

The trend toward globalization has had a number of social and economic consequences for the United States. First and foremost, it has meant a loss of economic dominance (Vernon, Spar, and Tobin, 1991; Aho and Levinson, 1988). In the past, the United States was the world's largest manufacturer. American products were sold not only in the United States, but throughout the world. With globalization, however, more and more countries around the world have developed the capacity to produce the same products that are made in the United States, and they compete with American producers in world markets. Today, for example, Japan and Korea account for a substantial share of worldwide automobile production; forty years ago, their share was much smaller and the American share much larger. In the early 1950s, the United States produced about 60 percent of the world's manufactures; by the early 1980s, it produced less than 30 percent (Gill and Law, 1988, p. 340). Today, the combined gross national product of the European Community exceeds that of the United States. Japan, with less than half the population of the United States, had two-thirds the gross national product of the United States in 1993 (U.S. Bureau of the Census, 1996f, p. 853; Krugman, 1990). However, after the difficulties of the Asian economy during the 1990s, this had fallen to barely more than half that of the United States by 1998—but still higher on a per capita basis than that of the United States (U.S. Bureau of the Census, 2001i, p. 831).

In some cases, international competitors have prospered in the world market in part because they pay lower wages. Korean Hyundai cars, for example, can be produced and sold at a lower price than American, European, or Japanese cars largely because Korean autoworkers are paid less than those in other countries. However, globalization's contribution to low-wage employment cannot be blamed purely on international competition. As companies in industrialized countries such as the United States have sought to cut costs, they have exported jobs to Third World countries where wages are lower. The most visible example of this is the large-scale shifting of jobs to Mexico by American companies. The number of foreign-owned (mostly U.S.) manufacturing plants in Mexico near the border reached 1,250 by 1988, and 3,600 by 2001 (Rohan, 1989; Lindquist, 2001). And by 1996, three-quarters of a million Mexican workers were employed in *maquiladoras*—mostly foreign-owned plants located in Mexico to take advantage of Mexico's low wages (Brouthers, McCray, and Wilkinson, 1999). Most of these plants are owned by American or (to a lesser extent) Japanese interests. Mexico is highly attractive to American businesses, because workers there can be paid as little as 15 to 20 percent of what they would have to be paid in the United States. Another reason companies can operate more cheaply in Mexico is that, for the most part, there has been little enforcement there of environmental protection requirements. In some cases, hazardous wastes are simply allowed to run into the streets in border towns dominated by American-owned plants. This movement of jobs across international borders has sparked an intense debate in the United States, which is examined

Economy and Society

further in this chapter's "Putting Sociology to Work" section.

Putting Sociology to Work

Free Trade or Protectionism?

As the economy has continued to globalize, debate has intensified over issues surrounding the global economy and international commerce. During the 1990s and into the new century, harsh debates have occurred in the United States over the North American Free Trade Agreement (NAFTA) and on the extent of and rules governing trade between the United States and the People's Republic of China. Similarly, Seattle, Quebec, and several European cities have been snarled by massive protests during recent meetings of the World Trade Organization (WTO), World Bank, International Monetary Fund (IMF), and similar organizations. One view in this growing debate, free trade, holds that countries like the United States ultimately benefit from globalization, because they can sell more of their products abroad. The opposite view, protectionism, holds that because many less-developed countries lack the wage, benefit, and environmental standards of the industrialized countries, the latter countries need protection against price competition from products that are produced cheaply in countries without these standards. As we shall see shortly, the advocates of protectionism have proposed various ways to make it harder for such products to be sold cheaply in countries like the United States.

A third model that has gained attention in recent years has been fair trade. This position, somewhat an intermediate between free trade and protectionism, suggests that rather than imposing high tariffs or restricting imports, free trade should be permitted subject to rules about the labor and environmental practices of nations and companies involved in international trade. This model holds that free trade should be permitted, but not at the expense of workers being denied a living wage and safe working conditions, and not at the expense of environmental damage due to lack of environmental protection in many low-wage countries. Some free trade supporters, though, argue that fair trade is really nothing but protectionism in disguise.

The advocates of free trade won a major victory when Congress ratified the North American Free Trade Agreement (NAFTA). Moves such as relocation of plants to Mexico by U.S. corporations have been made easier by NAFTA, which became effective at the start of 1994. However, NAFTA supporters argue that such movement was happening anyway, and that NAFTA would create other jobs in the United States by opening up Mexican and Canadian markets for U.S. products. It was also argued that provisions negotiated by the Clinton administration prior to NAFTA implementation would bring improved environmental protection in Mexico. (In a sense, the Clinton administration began from a free-trade position, but in response to criticism from NAFTA opponents, incorporated elements of the fair trade model into the agreement. However, opponents argued that the environmental controls in the agreement were weak and ineffective.) The overall argument made by NAFTA supporters was that the United States, Mexico, and Canada would all benefit from increased trade and larger markets in which to sell their products.

There has been considerable and inconclusive debate about NAFTA's actual effects both on U.S. jobs and wages and on the environment in Mexico. NAFTA did not create as many U.S. jobs as its backers promised (Public Citizen, 1995), and the U.S. trade surplus with Mexico narrowed in 1994 because the surge in U.S. imports from Mexico outpaced the increase in exports to Mexico (International Economic Review, 1995). This is probably one reason why NAFTA did not create as many jobs in the United States as was predicted, although the exact number of jobs created and lost due to NAFTA is very hard to measure. The Clinton administration estimated that NAFTA created around 320,000 U.S. jobs due to increased exports to Mexico, while the U.S. Department of Labor certified that NAFTA caused the loss of 215,000 U.S. jobs due to job relocation to Mexico. In general, NAFTA supporters claim it created more jobs than these figures indicate, while opponents claim it eliminated more. Probably the net effect in the United States is rather small—it has been neither the disaster its opponents predicted nor the boon its supporters claimed.

Another reason for the failure of NAFTA to create as many U.S. jobs as hoped lies in the Mexican peso. The peso lost much of its value in 1994 for reasons largely unrelated to NAFTA.

This made it hard for Mexicans to buy American products. It also reduced Mexican investment in environmental protection, which prevented many of the promised environmental improvements from occurring. Finally, by lowering Mexican wages further, it increased the incentive for U.S. employers in search of cheap labor to relocate to Mexico (Brouthers, McCray, and Wilkinson, 1999). For all these reasons, NAFTA did not bring the predicted benefits, but so many factors are at work that it is hard to tell whether American workers are better or worse off than they would have been without it.

There appears to be some validity to the argument that NAFTA's environmental protections were weak and ineffective. Environmental pollution has become a serious problem around the border plants, and there is some research suggesting that this has had significant health effects on the Mexican population of these areas. One study, for example, found an increase in birth defects near the plants in the Matamoros, Mexico–Brownsville, Texas, area, and the lack of proper water and sewer treatment in housing surrounding some of the plants has led to increases in hepatitis (Wallach and Sforza, 1999).

Regardless of NAFTA's specific effects, international competition and the exportation of American jobs have had effects on the U.S. standard of living. There are now many countries in which workers are as well or better trained than American workers, and where production equipment is more modern (Aho and Levinson, 1988, pp. 125–30). And not all of these countries pay low wages or lack environmental protection standards. Some are more efficient because they are more innovative. The result of this competition has been reduced growth in the American standard of living. In the 1950s and 1960s when the United States dominated world production more than it does today, the standard of living of Americans rose rapidly. But since the early 1970s, that has not been the case (Aho and Levinson, 1988; Gill and Law, 1988). Since the early 1970s, the average wages of American workers, after adjustment for inflation, have grown much more slowly, and the wages of younger workers and workers without a college education have actually shrunk after adjustment for inflation. As noted in Chapter 6, these tendencies have been exacerbated by increased income inequality since around 1980.

Some Americans have suggested trying to fight the trend toward a global economy by engaging in protectionism: restricting imports or charging high import tariffs. This could actually have harmful effects, for two reasons. First, it could lead to retaliatory restrictions on U.S. exports to other countries, thus depriving U.S. manufacturers of the opportunity to sell their products (Vernon, Spar, and Tobin, 1991). Second, it could lead to reduced productivity and higher prices in the United States, particularly in oligopolistic industries, by eliminating the incentives created by competition. The highly concentrated U.S. auto industry is an example of this: As protectionist measures added about $1,000 to the cost of imported cars in the 1980s, American producers were, in effect, allowed to be $1,000 less cost-efficient than producers of imported cars (Farley, 1992b, p. 432). This may help American producers sell more cars or ask a higher price for cars in the short run, but it may have also made them less competitive and efficient in the long run. Hence, it may have contributed to the crisis that, in 2009, resulted in bankruptcy, massive government bailouts, and, for a time at least, partial government ownership of Chrysler and General Motors.

On the other hand, free trade means one thing when competitors, like Japan and the European nations, pay their workers living wages and have environmental protection requirements such as those in the United States, but quite another when U.S. workers must compete with places where wages are much lower and no environmental protection is required. Many Americans argue that when overseas workers are paid less than a living wage and when those who move jobs overseas are subject to no environmental regulation, everyone loses except the owners of capital. According to this view, the overseas worker is not helped (Mexican wages have actually fallen since NAFTA was implemented, for example), U.S. workers lose jobs or must work at a lower wage, and the environment is harmed—all while corporate profits soar due to the lower wages and lower environmental-protection costs. On the other hand, a common viewpoint in developing countries is that efforts to restrict free trade amount to an effort by developed countries to maintain a monopoly over world economic production. For all these reasons, there is no easy answer to the ongoing debate over free trade, fair trade, and protectionism.

Consequences of Globalization for the World

It has been suggested that as economic activities continue to globalize, nations as entities become less influential and less important. In an economic sense, at least, boundaries are rendered increasingly meaningless. An "American" car today may be made of parts assembled in Canada, Mexico, France, and Japan as well as the United States. The same may be true of a "Japanese" car. The corporations that produce these cars are not only multinational in the sense that they sell their products worldwide: They also *produce* them worldwide. The growth of such international modes of production makes these producers more powerful relative to governments than corporations were in the past (Gill and Law, 1988, p. 365). Not only can multinationals move jobs around in search of cheap labor, as when they shift jobs from the United States or Japan to Mexico or Korea; they can also use the *threat* of such moves to extort or pressure governments to pursue policies that serve their interests.

Several writers on globalization have suggested another way in which individual nations may become less important. They point to regional economic coalitions of countries that may cooperate within each coalition and compete with other coalitions (Gilpin, 1979; Krugman, 1990). There is already evidence that this is happening in Europe, as a free trade zone has been created and economic and political cooperation has increased among the nations of the European Union, including the creation of a common currency, the euro. To a lesser degree, similar trends are happening in North America with the North American Free Trade Agreement between Canada, the United States, and Mexico. Gilpin and others foresee a similar trend among Pacific Rim countries such as Japan, Taiwan, South Korea, and possibly China.

As nation-states weaken, some analysts argue that democracy is threatened (Barber, 1996). For one thing, democracy has always operated in the form of the nation-state (for example, through election of the president and the Congress), so as the nation-state is weakened, what can be influenced through its democratic decision-making process becomes more limited. Closely related, the power of global market forces takes more and more decisions out of the hands of democratically elected representatives. This may be efficient, but it can also be undemocratic. Finally, as is explored in the box "'Jihad' vs. 'McWorld': The Battle Between Globalism and Tribalism" (see Chapter 12), globalization is likely a key factor contributing to the type of fundamentalist tribalism that lies beneath both domestic and international terrorism.

Finally, the greater power of the multinational corporations in a globalized economy creates increased risk of ecological crisis. Deforestation is occurring rapidly worldwide, and along with increased fossil fuel use creates the threat of global warming. Ozone depletion owing to use of aerosol sprays and air conditioning and the spread of several of the world's deserts because of depleted water supplies and other environmental alterations are also growing threats. Environmental disasters such as the BP oil spill in the Gulf of Mexico can create destruction far from the country where the company that caused the disaster is based. The potential for social conflict over such issues is great. On the one hand, everyone in both advanced industrial countries and developing countries is threatened by these environmental problems. At the same time, however, developing countries have clearly stated that they do not want to be deprived of the economic development that has led to the growth of the industrialized countries, even though such growth incurred substantial costs. Often, they see the concerns raised by labor and environmental groups in developed countries as thinly disguised efforts to block competition by preventing them from developing.

These debates often surround the issue of sustainable development: How can we encourage economic growth in developing countries in a way that will benefit those countries (not just the multinational corporations that operate there), and in a way that can be sustained over the long run without further damaging the environment? A closely related issue is the question of who really benefits when international corporations build plants or extract natural resources in developing countries. One view, modernization theory, argues that both the corporations and those who live in developing countries benefit because of the jobs and new markets that are created by the investment that the corporations bring (de Soysa and Oneal, 1999). But others, following dependency theory and world-system theory, argue that the corporations take wealth out of the developing countries, and gain control of resources that could otherwise have been developed and benefited from by the people living in the countries (Bornschier and Chase-Dunn, 1985). This question, which has become a major debate among sociologists who study globalization and social change, will be examined in detail in Chapter 15. Among the general publics of many countries, as well as among sociologists, debates about globalization and its effects on workers, the environment, and sustainable development intensified around the turn of the new millennium. These issues dominated the 1992 environmental summit in Rio de Janeiro, and since then they have been at the center of debates—and at times loud protests—over NAFTA, the World Trade Organization, international trade policies, and the extent and causes of global warming as well as efforts to control it.

Unemployment and the Economic Cycle

Two closely related problems in modern economies are unemployment and the economic cycle. Unemployment occurs when people who want to work are unable to find jobs. Unemployment rises and falls along with an economic cycle, a periodic movement of the economy between "boom" and "bust." During boom periods, jobs are plentiful, wages rise, businesses grow, and unemployment is low. During bust periods—called recessions or depressions, depending on their severity—unemployment rises, wages fall, and businesses shrink in size. As the economy has globalized, periods of boom and bust have become worldwide in scale. For example, in the early 1990s and again in 2007–2009, economic slowdowns occurred not only in the United States but throughout the industrialized world, including Japan and virtually all of Europe. This occurs because producers of goods increasingly rely on a worldwide market, rather than only on buyers in the country where the goods are produced.

The functionalist and conflict perspectives offer different interpretations concerning the meaning of the economic cycle. The functionalist perspective sees the economic cycle as a means by which the economy corrects itself. When demand outstrips supply, a boom period occurs, until prices rise high enough that people cannot pay them, or people borrow so much that they have trouble handling the debt. At that point, people stop buying, loans are not paid back, and the economy goes into a "bust" period. Eventually, prices fall or stop rising, people learn to live within their means, and a new upturn occurs.

Conflict theorists view the economic cycle and unemployment as means by which some people gain at the expense of others. In most capitalist countries, if it is profitable to lay workers off, it will be done. In mixed and socialist economies, workers' welfare is more likely to be considered in decisions regarding layoffs. This clearly makes the employer less profitable in hard times, and it is one reason that government-owned companies in Western Europe have sometimes been less profitable than private ones. In these countries, an additional consideration is that laid-off workers may vote against the government.

Some conflict theorists believe that the economic cycle itself is useful to the owners of capital. The idea dates to Marx (1967 [orig. 1867–1894]) and a concept he called the *reserve army of the unemployed*. According to Marx, this reserve army serves an important function for the owners of capital: It reminds workers that they can easily be replaced and keeps them from demanding too much in the way of higher wages and benefits. Modern conflict economists and sociologists have applied this argument to the economic cycle. They argue that when a boom economy creates pressures for increased wages, a recession is actually useful to employers because it raises the unemployment rate and this allows employers to threaten their workers with replacement if they demand too much (Lekachman, 1982). Sometimes they deliver on this threat, as happened with increasing frequency in meatpacking, the airline industry, and other industries in which striking workers were replaced during the 1980s. One reason that the strategy succeeded was the presence of large numbers of unemployed workers—there were over 11.5 million at one point. In fact, recessions can be very profitable. During the twentieth century, the share of American corporate income going to profits, as opposed to wages, was generally higher after recessions than before. (For further discussion of these and related issues, see Gordon, 1975, and Heilbroner, 1978.) During the 1991–1992 recession, for example, many workers suffered wage freezes, and in some cases even cuts. Reductions in employee health insurance coverage (or sharp premium increases) were widespread, with increased numbers of workers left without coverage at all. Conversely, during the boom of the mid- and late 1990s, wages and benefits recovered somewhat, though more so for well-educated workers than for those lacking skills demanded by the information economy. Still, employers such as fast-food outlets did have to raise wages and improve benefits somewhat in the late 1990s, in order to be able to attract workers in an economy where jobs were less difficult to find than in the early 1990s.

Financial Systems

The 2008 financial crisis and recession highlighted the importance of finance to the health and functioning of the overall economy. Investors (banks included) had put their money into risky investments tied to the booming U.S. housing market. As this market collapsed in the wake of the late 2007 economic downturn, heavy losses began to be suffered by these investors. In September of 2008, with banks seeing their investments spiraling downward, they simply stopped lending to one another—or anyone else. Without a massive government infusion of cash, policymakers were afraid the crisis would have plunged the world economy back into another Great Depression. Financial systems are mysterious, because they are crucial to how an economy operates. In this section, we will examine how finance can affect the character of an economy and why it sometimes plunges them into crisis as it did in the fall of 2008.

A *financial system* can be defined as the set of institutions that funnel money from savers to competing investors (Zysman, 1983, page 57). Primarily this system consists of banks and stock markets (sometimes referred to as equity markets or capital markets). The character of the financial system will largely determine the character of the entire national economy. An economy can be more dynamic, but volatile, or it can be more stable, but rigid. We will examine this trade-off as well as the basics of financial systems and their impact on overall economic performance. Essentially, financial systems try to accomplish two main goals, as illustrated in the following box.

The financial system is an intermediary between the households, businesses, and public agencies that wish to save money (savers) and the households, businesses, and public agencies (users) that wish to invest those savings for productive uses. Figure 11.2 shows this relationship between savers and users of financial capital. Money is funneled from savers (households, businesses, and public agencies) through the major institutions of the financial system (stock markets, bond markets, banks, etc.) to those who use that money (other households, businesses, and public agencies) to invest in the economy. But this activity also has a social class element to it that is not widely known. Financial markets are split between primary markets and secondary markets. Primary markets are the face-to-face transactions between elite market players of the upper class who actually set the stock, bond, or other prices. Secondary markets are those that all others participate in after the prices have already been set and the best deals already taken.

The two goals of facilitating the flow of resources and information are tightly linked to one another. Without proper information about firm performance, investors will not know where to invest in the first place. Without an efficient

Banks are a key component of the tertiary sector of the economy, providing credit to businesses and consumers alike. In 2008, a crisis in the banking system led to one of the deepest recessions in memory. (iStockphoto)

> **SOCIOLOGICAL INSIGHTS**
> # Two Main Goals of a Financial System
>
> 1. **Facilitate the Flow of Resources**: especially money from savers to productive uses (investors such as banks or stock markets).
>
> 2. **Facilitate the Flow of Information**: Monitor where funds should go, to whom they should go; as well as where and to whom they should not go.

flow of resources, the best information in the world will not be useful. In order to achieve these two interrelated goals, national economies tend to build their financial systems either around debt (banks) or equity (stock) markets. The choice of *debt* from banks or *equity* from stock markets is very important for the monitoring and ultimate character of a national economy.

In some countries like Germany or Japan, the national economy is organized around debt. Banks fund most economic activity, as firms borrow the money they use to invest in new projects. This often takes two main forms. First are loans from a bank. The downside to this is that the borrower must pay interest on the loan, which can be difficult in bad times when the business is not making much money. Second are bonds. Bonds pay out interest to investors on a regular schedule. These payments must be made regardless of the financial health of the business. Thus, both of these options can be very tough on new businesses that are struggling to make a profit. In stock market systems like the

Figure 11.2 How Capital Markets Work

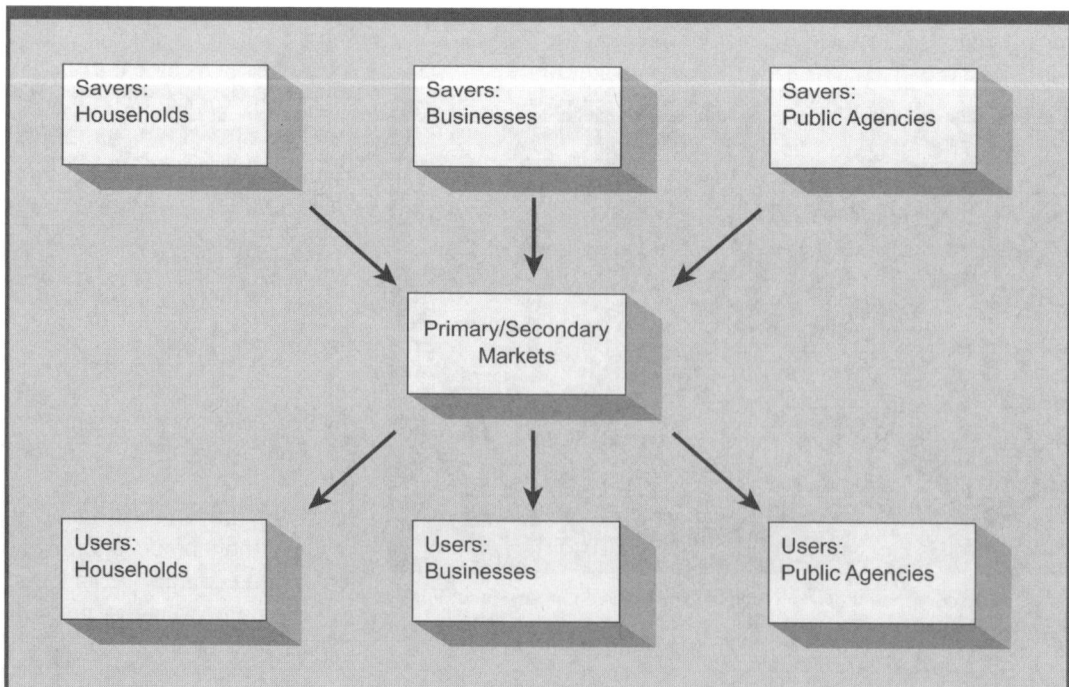

United States, the national economy is organized around equity. Investors purchase shares of ownership in a company (equity) and are then paid only for a percentage of the profit, once profit is made. This puts off payment until the business is ready and able to pay out cash. The downside is that it also represents a loss of control in ownership.

Now it is important to note that debt/bank-based systems like Japan also have stock markets and equity/stock market–based systems like the U.S. also have big influential banks. But the role of banks in the U.S. or stock markets in Japan is of less importance. The different forms of financing have important and powerful effects on the subsequent behavior of the businesses they fund. Social scientists have developed the concepts of Voice and Exit to illuminate this effect (Hirschman, 1970; Zysman, 1983).

Voice or Exit

Equity markets monitor economic performance through the threat of *exit*. If investors are unhappy with the economic performance of a firm, they can exit from their relationship with it by pulling out their funds. Equity financing is attractive because investors only have to be paid *after* the business is already making a profit. Until then, no payments have to be made. A downside is that the relationship between investor and firm may not be very close and may not generate very detailed or robust information about the firm. Without reliable information, the monitoring function of the financial system may not be very effective. Bank or debt-centered systems rely more on *voice*—taking an active role or "voice" in the decisions that are made at the firm, because relationships are based on loans between the bank and its client firms, and if things start to go wrong, the bank will know about it (as the firm fails to make their payments). The bank is more likely to profit if the firm succeeds, so it is in the bank's interest to monitor the behavior of its firms by ensuring the bank has a voice in what goes on. This may include specifying the terms of the loan from the outset to avoid trouble proactively, or sending out teams of experts from the bank to look over a firm's operations when times are tough. Thus voice-based monitoring is a "hands-on approach," while exit is an "arm's length" approach.

Thus, banks/voice tend to produce better information and longer term relationships, but are somewhat slow and rigid. They tend to be slow to respond to sudden changes in economic fundamentals, because the terms of their loans are locked-in for longer periods of time than the "easy breezy" relationships equity market investors have with the firms they own. Equity markets/Exits tend to produce less reliable information and shorter-term relationships, but they are fluid, flexible, and respond better to sudden changes in economic conditions. In general then, we can say that Equity markets probably do a better job of facilitating the flow of resources, while debt systems do a better job of facilitating the flow of information. The financial systems of the United States, Canada, and the United Kingdom are largely equity markets; Japan, Germany, South Korea, and Sweden are largely bank-centered. Equity markets also appear to be better at bouncing back from crises; however critics of equity markets will claim that they are also more likely to cause a crisis because they feed financial speculation, a term we will investigate below. Finally, it should be noted that in 1999 the United States significantly complicated the distinction between debt and equity by allowing commercial banks to essentially merge with investment banks. In essence, it became possible for banks to invest in equity. Banks subsequently invested in the highly profitable subprime mortgage market of the 2000s but found their entire operations threatened when those markets crashed in the latter years of the decade. This seems to point out the need for financial systems to be generally characterized by either debt/voice or equity/exit, but not both (Flota, 2010).

Financial Crises

In September of 2008, a global recession became a global financial crisis. It was the latest of many that have occurred across the globe since the early 1970s, when such crises became more common after the collapse of the Bretton Woods system. Bretton Woods was a system aimed at regulating the flow of money around the world and the value of currencies in relation to one another. As a result, very little of it actually flowed across national borders. That which did, did so mainly to facilitate trade between two parties in two different nations.

SOCIOLOGICAL INSIGHTS
Kindleberger's Simplified Model of Financial Crises

1. **Mania:** New opportunities for profit result in an irrationally rapid rise in prices.
2. **Distress:** Investors begin to fear that values may be getting too high.
3. **Panic:** A general sell-off begins as values crash.
4. **Contagion:** refers to any case in which the above process also begins to affect other markets.

When the system collapsed in the 1970s money began to fly around the world in increasingly large numbers as investors began to speculate in markets across the globe. *Speculation* is when investors invest in something purely to make money from the sale of the investment, not to produce a good or service with that investment. As this occurred, many global investors became very rich, but a spate of financial crises also began to occur. Financial crashes like the one that started the Great Depression in 1929 or the crisis of 2008 are part of a phenomenon that has been ongoing since markets were formed. In this section, we examine briefly how and why the crises occur.

Economic historian Charles Kindleberger (1989) studied financial crises. He elaborated a model of how such crises proceed, presented in the accompanying box. As the model makes clear, a great deal of what makes markets work and what makes them fail is social and psychological. The stages of distress and panic are periods in which market participants begin to fear the actions of others. They literally begin to fear others' fears. This was likely not far from his mind when President Franklin Roosevelt reminded Americans in the depths of the Great Depression that "the only thing we have to fear is fear itself."

In the recent financial crisis of 2008, the mania stage can be seen in the astronomical rise of real estate prices across the United States after 2001. As prices continued to rise, many commentators began to worry that a financial "bubble" was forming. The implication being that this bubble was getting too big and could "burst," meaning a rapid decline in prices. The term bubble is common slang for a market that is rising too high too fast, beyond any rational reason. The implication is that the prices were being driven up by speculators who simply wanted to make a quick buck. The term "flipping" became a common term for someone who buys a home and then very quickly resells it (flips it) as the value of the home rises. Commonly, the buyer would only hold the property for a few weeks or months before flipping it, thereby making a quick profit. Often, several thousand dollars could be made in a short period of time at the height of the mania. But the fact that some people began to question the rationality of the market's meteoric rise was a telltale sign that a period of distress was about to set in. Many began to worry that the prices were going to reach their peak. Speculators began to wonder if the time was soon approaching that they should pull their money out, so they would not be left holding properties with falling values. Slowly, buyers began to shift into selling and the prices began to fall, slowly at first. As prices fell, however, the final stage, panic, eventually set in. Investors began to sell off the properties as fast as they could, causing the real estate prices to fall just as fast as they had risen. Businesses and individuals that had invested in real estate and had not sold in time were left with massive losses. The economy began to crash as these losses rippled across the economy. Thus concluded the latest financial crisis to beset the American economy. But this crisis was the worst since the Great Depression of the 1920s and 30s. Commentators would later label it "the Great Recession."

PERSONAL JOURNEYS INTO SOCIOLOGY
Sociologists Study Risks and Sometimes Take Risks

Fred Block

My claim to fame is that I started doing economic sociology as a graduate student in the late 1960s about fifteen years before this field started to re-emerge as a legitimate area of inquiry for sociologists in the U.S. My interest in the intersection of the economy, government, and society was shaped by the radical student movement of the 1960s. I had been radicalized as an undergraduate fighting against the Vietnam War, and like many others, I was trying to understand the structures of power in the United States that generated wars abroad and racial inequality at home.

While I considered pursuing a Ph.D. in economics or political science, I chose sociology, because I thought it would give me the most freedom to pursue my own intellectual agenda. As it happens, I started graduate school at U.C. Berkeley in the fall of 1968, and for the first two years of my studies, the campus was dominated by protests against war and racism. By the time things had settled down, some of the faculty were happy to support students' doing work that was intellectually serious, even if it had no precedents in recent sociology.

In 1971, Richard Nixon ended the long established commitment of the United States to sell gold to other central banks for $35 an ounce. That commitment had been one of the pillars of the Bretton Woods international monetary order that was negotiated in 1944 and implemented during the 1950s. The crisis of the Bretton Woods system raised big questions about how the global economy would be organized in the years ahead. I took advantage of the intellectual freedom in the Berkeley sociology department to propose a dissertation on the rise and fall of the Bretton Woods international financial order. I was hard pressed to find any recent sociological precedents for this kind of study, but I was able to put together a committee that gave me a green light.

When I finished this project and entered the academic job market, I suddenly realized the risks of my chosen topic. Describing my dissertation to prospective employers was often intimidating; some of them looked blank and others suggested that it wasn't sociology. But miraculously, I did get hired by a department that was looking for young scholars doing off-beat or unconventional work and I was relatively safe.

One key intellectual development also helped make me considerably safer. Immanuel Wallerstein, who had been my teacher when I was an undergraduate, published the first volume of his history of the Modern World System in 1974. While his focus was on European and global developments in the sixteenth century, the positive reception his work received helped to establish that the organization of the global economy was a legitimate subject for sociological investigation. By the time I published my dissertation as a book in 1977, it no longer seemed like a preposterous project for a sociologist.

By the 1980s, I started to have company as more and more sociologists began working on issues that had previously been monopolized by economists. A Swedish-based sociologist named Richard Swedberg made frequent trips to the United States in that period and he started to suggest to people, myself included, that a whole group of us were doing economic sociology without calling it that. Swedberg went further; he explained that the revered classical figures in the sociological tradition, especially Marx, Weber, and Durkheim, had all focused on the intersection between society and economy. Economic sociology, in short, had initially been central to the sociological tradition and it should be once again.

It didn't take much persuasion to get me to jump on this bandwagon. Rather than feeling marginal and barely tolerated by the mainstream of the discipline, I was now part of a group reclaiming the core of the sociological tradition. I have been doing economic sociology ever since, and I am grateful that I started down that path when I was young, radical, and impulsive.

Fred Block is professor of sociology at University of California–Davis. He received his B.A. at Columbia University and his Ph.D. at University of California, Berkley. His books include: The Vampire State and Other Myths and Fallacies About the U.S. Economy (1996), Postindustrial Possibilities: A Critique of Economic Discourse (1990), The Mean Season: The Attack on the Welfare State (co-authored with Richard A. Cloward, Barbara Ehrenreich, and Frances Fox Piven) (1987), Revising State Theory: Essays In Politics and Postindustrialism (1987), and The Origins of International Economic Disorder: A Study of United States International Monetary Policy from World War II to the Present (1977).

Karl Polanyi and the New Economic Sociology

In this final section, we look at the field of economic sociology and its classical founder Karl Polanyi. Sociologists refer to the sociological study of the economy as "new" to differentiate the "old" study of the economy that Marx, Weber, and Durkheim devoted a great deal of their time to. With Polanyi, who we will learn about below, sociologists broke not only with many of the assumptions of Marx, Weber, and Durkheim but also with those of professional economists, creating a tension between the fields of economics and economic sociology that survives to this day.

The Sociological Study of the Economy

Sociologists study the economy in almost exactly the opposite manner in which economists study it. That is, economists look at numbers, self-interest of the individual and numerical relationships and hold all other "social" factors to the side (saying that, although "social" factors make a difference, they do not change fundamental economic realities). For them, everything can be reduced to numbers.

The reason for this is simple: economics wants to be a predictive science. The easiest way to do this is to create a model of human behavior that is easy to predict. So, economists traditionally accomplished this by assuming that humans are always maximizing good things and minimizing bad things, the norm of maximization mentioned earlier in the chapter (economists define this as an actor's individual self-interest). While contemporary economists have significantly complicated this simple model, this did allow them to reduce everything to numbers. One does not need to know exactly what a person's wants and desires are to be able to predict behavior. (Remember algebra? We don't have to know the values of X and Y to be able to create a formula.) Thus, human behavior is actually quite simple to understand in economics and because of that, easy to predict.

Economic sociologists tend to say exactly the opposite. Although self-interest is important, numerical relationships can be held aside, because it is the social influences that really matter. Of course, as with all other topics, a variety of sociologists take a variety of approaches to studying the economy. But in general, sociologists see economic activity generated by the same forces that generate all other forms of social activity: group identity, socialization, love, passion, hate, status, revenge, sex, and so on. Competition and self-interest certainly play a role in these, but it is not simply about what is best for "me," it is also what is best for "we." Sometimes, "me" and "we" even conflict with one another, for instance, in the form of self-sacrificial behavior in support of a group.

Let's imagine that it is a sunny day, and you are strolling to class on your college's campus. There is likely place on campus, possibly near the student union, where people and organizations attempt to sell things like t-shirts, credit cards, posters, or snacks to students as they pass by. Let's imagine that one day you are surprised to find a vendor offering raw meat. But not just any raw meat. This vendor is selling dog and cat meat. What do you think you and your fellow students' reaction would be to such a situation? Would you be angry, disgusted, or both? Or would you become a willing customer? Based on my experience (Flota) of offering up a similar hypothetical situation to my students over the years, I would say that you would not be happy. In fact, a similar story usually results in audible groans and shocked looks from my students. Not only would this person be engaging in behavior that is not appropriate for a college campus (selling raw meat) but they are violating the cultural values of their "customers" by killing and trying to sell animals that Americans define as "pets" not "food." The person would never be granted a permit to sell such items at a college and would likely be charged with animal cruelty. Yet, in many parts of the world, dogs and cats are indeed defined as food, and the act of selling such meat in a street market in parts of Asia, for example, would not be considered deviant.

So, the point of this ridiculous example is that what is considered efficient economic activity is completely wrapped up in the cultural and social context in which that activity takes place. So is, sociologists contend, all economic behavior. The goal of most economic sociologists is to rescue the study of the economy from the mathematicians. Ironically, the first step in doing this is not to examine economics, but to revisit the guiding lights of sociological theory Marx, Weber, and Durkheim.

For all of their differences, one thing they shared in common was a belief in the efficiency of

> ### SOCIOLOGICAL INSIGHTS
> ## Shared Beliefs of Marx, Weber, and Durkeim
>
>
> 1. The efficiency of the market.
> 2. Separate logics for the economy and society.

the market. A second idea they shared was a notion that "society" and the "economy" ran on different "tracks" or with separate logics. The economy was thought to follow one set of rules, while society followed quite another. Marx thought that the economy would eventually self-destruct and be overthrown by revolutionary socialism because of the amount of social destruction it would bring.

Weber saw society inevitably seduced into a more and more meaningless, materialistic, and narcissistic existence. Society would be helpless to reverse the decline. Durkheim saw a growing gap between rapid technical/economic change on the one hand and the much slower cultural/social change on the other (we discuss this further in Chapter 15). Durkheim was concerned that this growing gap could create greater levels of anomie in the future.

Karl Polanyi Enters the Dance

These assumptions were famously challenged by a social scientist by the name of Karl Polanyi. Today, Polanyi is a leading classical influence in economic sociology. Polanyi represents the transition to a "new economic sociology" from the classical economic sociology of Marx, Weber, and Durkhiem (Block, 1990; Granovetter, 1985). Polanyi's work directly challenged the notion that the economy and society were two separate spheres. In fact, Polanyi challenged the economists' notion that the market was a universal or natural part of human society ([1944] 2001). To fully understand what Polanyi was criticizing we have to learn a little economics. Just a little—we promise!

Economics is built on the notion of the *invisible hand* of supply and demand. Adam Smith, the "father of capitalism," is credited with this idea ([1776] 1910). Basically, the idea is that if we produce something and decide we are going to gouge you, the consumer, with really high prices, a competitor can come along and charge a lower price for the same goods and steal you, our customers, away from us. It's all good though, because we were trying to screw you anyway! Our competitor comes in and offers a lower price to you, which helps you out, and of course, it helps our competitor out because they get your money and your business. The only person who loses is us, and we are the one who was trying to cheat you anyway. So, in Smith's famous phrase:

> "It is not from the benevolence of the butcher, the brewer, or the baker, that we expect our dinner, but from their regard to their own interest.
>
> Every individual ... generally, indeed, neither intends to promote the public interest, nor knows how much he is promoting it ... he intends only his own gain, and he is in this, as in many other cases, led by an invisible hand to promote an end which was no part of his intention." (Adam Smith, *The Wealth of Nations*)

So, the market itself is said to *self-regulate*. No need to interfere with the market; the invisible hand will protect us all. In fact, the more we interfere the less effective and efficient the market becomes and the less protected we will all be by the invisible hand.

But Smith and his followers also went further. The market became thought to be part of human nature. We *naturally* know how to interact in a market, they thought. Markets have since been seen by these theorists to be everywhere: marriage markets, friendship markets, and so on. The idea is that human beings are always engaged in market-like behavior, maximizing good things and minimizing bad things. This is called Rational Choice theory. So economists will say that human beings are Rational Maximizers. That is, we are *rational*: we make conscious, deliberate decisions based on weighing alternatives and the choices we have. And, we *maximize* the things that bring us good things and go for those things that will best satisfy our desires (Hodgson, 1988).

Empirical research has not been too kind to this theoretical assumption. Today, we know that most of human behavior is "reflexive" (Hodgson, 1988; Massey 2005). That is, it happens more or less without us really thinking about it, like a reflex or habit. Humans certainly do engage in rational behavior and most social scientists agree that in Western societies like the United States, most of us want to be rational (intentionally rational). But most human behaviors still occur out of reflex, emotion, or habit. Add the many addictive behaviors we have, self-sacrificial behavior, and mental disturbance and you have a very small amount of the time that we are actually being stone-cold rational. Finally, we humans never have complete information about the world around us (Hodgson, 1988). For us to really maximize anything, we need to have complete information and we almost never do. Add in the fact that we are constrained by the tastes of our culture and we have a process that is very far from rational maximization. On the minority of occasions when we do consciously choose, we do so within the constraints of culture. Polanyi would have been very comfortable with these subsequent findings had he lived to see them verified.

Another assumption of the classical economists like Adam Smith is that humans are more or less naturally greedy or self-interested. Markets are such a magnificent invention because they take that natural greediness and turn it into something that benefits all humankind. Polanyi questioned this. Who is to say humans are naturally greedy? What evidence is there for that? Instead Polanyi found evidence for a variety of human behaviors. We are greedy and selfless, kind and cruel. It is more complicated than Smith imagined.

Polanyi questioned whether these assumptions about human nature would really stand up to empirical investigation ([1944] 2001). What he found was that this kind of market behavior was an ancient human practice just as Smith and his followers had said. But he also found something else. If we go back to the hunters and gatherers we will find no real market in the activities they engaged in.

In fact, even in the Agrarian Ages, the market was a very small part of economic behavior for thousands of years ([1944] 2001). Instead, Polanyi found that there were other more important *modes of economic production and distribution* ([1944] 2001; 1963).

Rather than a universal reliance on market *exchange*, Polanyi demonstrated that throughout most of human history, human livelihood was structured by kinship, religion, or other cultural practices all of which had little or nothing to do with exchange on a market (1963). He argued that economic activity had been based on a set of principles of which market-like exchange was only one. Others included *reciprocity* and *redistribution*. These represented the most important forms of economic activity for most of human history (97–98%). *Reciprocity* was found in the hunter-gatherer (and is still found in some) societies that used gift giving, dowries, or kinship obligations as main engines of economic activity (Polanyi, [1944] 2001; 1963). Mutual obligation or a shared sense of identity drives economic activity. *Redistribution* takes place when resources are collected by a central authority and then given back to everyone more or less equally (Polanyi, [1944] 2001; 1963). The authority to do this is usually organized around religious and political authority. This was common in early agricultural societies and like reciprocity is still practiced in different ways today across the globe.

This led Polanyi to argue that prior to Adam Smith the economy had always been seen as secondary to the rules of society. But starting with Smith, and his argument for the *self-regulating* nature of the invisible hand, all of this changed. Now, society was being told to change itself according to the rules of the market.

The Embedded Economy and the Impossibility of the Self-Regulating Market

But to Polanyi, the economists' notion of a self-regulating market was a fiction. Instead, it was only social regulation that allowed markets to function properly. Without these social regulations, markets would spiral into destruction and social chaos. Any attempt to create a true self-regulating market was doomed to failure and thus impossible. Even just the effort to create one would inevitably lead to human suffering.

Polanyi described this as the economy being *embedded* in society (Polanyi, [1944] 2001; 1963). Society and the economy are not on separate paths; they are one and the same. Indeed, the economy is a subsector of society. Any attempt to disembed the market from society would result in devastation and destruction (Polanyi, [1944] 2001). Not only would people begin to treat each other as commodities to be bought and sold; so would they treat things like the truth, life and death, children, and morality. All of these are things that are supposed to be "outside" of economic activity according to most economists, but Polanyi argues they are simply things that economists have defined as "not economic." But in reality, they are critical to an economy actually being able to function. Imagine the chaos that would follow if I knew that the only way you would ever tell me the truth was if there was money in it for you! How confident would you be in giving out your credit card number over the phone, the Internet, or even at the counter at a pizzeria? What if you determined you could get more money out of me by cheating, lying, stealing? Who would trust anyone, who *could* trust anyone? Economies simply could not function without the social and cultural rules they are embedded in.

Polanyi proved this point by drawing on the three **fictitious commodities**: land, labor, and money. Smith and his followers treat these three as if they are commodities, but Polanyi argues that they are not. And, if they are treated like commodities, the end result will be a disaster: economic and social destruction (probably a war or revolution). Here is why.

A true commodity must have at least one main principle in order for it to be a commodity and work in the normal rules of supply and demand. One must be able to reduce one's inventory of that commodity to zero (Polanyi, [1944] 2001). On a normal market the hope is that the market will "clear"—that is, the number of products supplied for sale on the market is equal to the number of products demanded by consumers—through the shifting of prices—and all products are purchased. But Polanyi argues society cannot tolerate allowing these three markets to "clear" in the same way as other commodities ([1944] 2001; 1963).

Think about it. An abundant supply of any other good results in a falling price for that good which restores "equilibrium" or balance to the market by encouraging increased consumption and discouraging further production (lower profits from lower prices drives producers to produce other products that can make them more money). But markets do not control the supply of land, labor, or capital. The money supply is the only one of the three that could be controlled by the market even in theory, but in reality, money has to be controlled by the government to ensure a stable economy. Allowing a national economy to run out of money or "clear" would be disastrous. Modern economists have long recognized this but have not realized the deeper implications, according to Polanyi. Those implications being a steep decline into economic and social chaos not unlike the Great Depression ([1944] 2001). In fact, Polanyi's work was heavily influenced by the depression and the wars that followed it (Block, 2003). From his perspective, the world nearly destroyed itself because it had tried to create the self-regulating market in the 1920s. Fred Block, who is featured in this chapter's "Personal Journeys into Sociology" section, has made the argument that society nearly repeated this process by deregulating markets for twenty years, leading to the economic crisis of 2008 (Block, 2009). Would Polanyi agree with this assessment?

Summary

The economic system of any society is partly a product of that society's level of economic development and partly a result of who owns the means of production. The simplest level of economic development is the hunting-and-gathering society—a small nomadic tribe or clan. Its economy produces no surplus, and property is usually communally owned. People in such societies live at a bare subsistence level, yet they enjoy considerable leisure time and engage in common activities that hold the group together. Eventually, the group may learn to cultivate crops or raise animals. Such horticultural and pastoral societies are an intermediate between hunting-and-gathering and agricultural economies. Agricultural economies farm larger plots of land using plows and draft animals, which enables them to produce a surplus. This surplus allows a certain portion of the population to live in permanent towns and engage in activities other than food production; it also creates socioeconomic inequality.

In agricultural societies, the means of production is land, and the wealthy are those who own land. Typically, they develop a feudal system, which is characterized by a landowning gentry and a large peasant class who work for the landowners. When society reaches the industrial stage, the means of production becomes capital, or productive capacity. In industrial societies, manufacturing—made possible by new technologies and by bureaucratic organization—is the most important economic activity and a key source of employment. Industrial societies tend over the long run to produce a large increase in the standard of living and some leveling of inequalities.

A new form emerging in some of the most highly developed countries is the postindustrial economy. In this system, the provision of services becomes the predominant activity, as industry becomes more automated and a relatively affluent population demands more services. Application and control of new technology become the route to economic growth, and possession of information may become almost as important as ownership of capital for the accumulation of wealth.

Whereas agricultural economies were generally organized on feudalist lines, new systems of ownership emerged in industrial societies. Most such systems are either capitalist, with private ownership of the means of production; socialist, with public ownership of the means of production; or some mix of the two. Capitalist economies are highly efficient but produce greater inequality than socialist ones. Socialist economies place a high priority on meeting everyone's basic needs, but they are less efficient and productive than capitalist ones, especially in today's postindustrial economies. An intermediate type is the mixed economy, where part of the means of production is publicly owned and part is privately owned. Some analysts feel that mixed economies combine the best features of capitalist and socialist economies: They are more efficient than socialism and do a better job of meeting everyone's basic needs than capitalism.

Another dimension along which modern economies vary is the degree of concentration. In a concentrated economy, ownership and power are in the hands of a few, with little competition. A deconcentrated economy, in contrast, has many competing producers. As economies have modernized, they have become more concentrated, which has reduced incentives for efficiency. Their scale has also increased. More and more of today's economic activity is worldwide in scope. This trend, known as globalization, has had a variety of effects and has posed a challenge to formerly dominant economic powers such as the United States. It has also weakened the nation-state as an institution, and some see it both as a force increasing economic inequality at home and abroad, and as a threat to democratic decision making. As globalization has made the world smaller and more standardized, it has also given rise to opposition movements, which are both political and religious/tribal in nature. Financial systems are designed to facilitate the flow of both resources and information. They can be organized around equity markets that use a threat of exit to monitor economic actors, or they can use debt and employ voice to make sure firms are staying profitable. Financial systems are susceptible to periodic crises in which a manic bubble can develop by a panicked sell-off that results in a crash.

Finally, Karl Polanyi is the leading classical influence for contemporary economic sociology. Polanyi argued that the economy was not able to self-regulate but instead depended on social, cultural, and political regulations to function effectively. Sociologists take issue with economists' use of rational maximization to explain human behavior and use Polanyi's theories as a basis by which to show that culture, emotion, and habit form important bases of economic action as well.

Key Terms

economic systems
primary sector
secondary sector
tertiary sector
hunting-and-gathering economy
subsistence level
surplus
nomadic
agricultural economy
agriculture
industrial economy
postindustrial economy
capitalist economy
capital
corporation
socialist economy

communism
mixed economy
norm of maximization
concentrated economy
oligopoly
monopoly
interlocking directorate
multinational corporation
globalization
financial system
debt or equity
exit or voice
speculation
contagion
invisible hand
self-regulating market
embeddedness
rational maximization
exchange, reciprocity, and redistribution
fictitious commodities

Exercises

1. This chapter queries, "Is Socialism Dead?" Many people feel that with the demise of the Soviet Union, any favorable view of socialism was lost in the process. Others disagree. With the 2008 collapse of the global financial system, global warming, and the 2010 oil spill in the Gulf of Mexico more people are also questioning the sustainability of capitalism.

   - Do you think that socialism is an inferior economic system in comparison with capitalism? Try to be as objective as you can in answering. Why or why not?
   - How do you feel about the text's query, "Is Socialism Dead?" What is your rationale as you answer this question?

2. The 2008 financial crash has been blamed in part on the rise and fall of the American housing market. Some popular explanations for the "great recession," as it is often called, blame home buyers for taking out mortgages they should have known they could not afford. Others blame lenders that talked people into taking out loans they could not pay back, who then sold the mortgages to other financial institutions, thereby avoiding the risk. Yet others say that the removal by Congress of financial protections and regulations that were established after the Great Depression is the primary culprit. And there are some who say the "American Dream" of everyone owning their own homes is simply unrealistic and led all sides to bad decisions. Do an Internet search for the "causes of the Great Recession." Which of these explanations, if any, are supported by the "experts"? What do you think was the cause?

Chapter 12
Politics, Power, and Society

Power in Modern Societies — 366
  Legitimate Power and Authority 366
  Other Sources of Power 367
  Wealth, Income, and Power 367

Who Has Power in America Today? — 368
  Measuring Power 368

The Distribution of Power in the United States — 368
  Three Key Interest Group Coalitions 369
  Who Governs? 369
  Who Benefits? 370
  Who Wins? 371
  Overview 372

The State — 373
  Types of Systems 375

PUTTING SOCIOLOGY TO WORK — 375
  Welfare Reform: An Effective Tool Against Poverty? 375

Welfare Around the World — 377
  Liberal Welfare States: U.S., Canada, the United Kingdom 377
  Corporatist-Statist Welfare States 378
  Social Democratic Welfare States 378
  Evaluating the Welfare States 379

Political Ideology — 379

Political Parties and Special Interest Groups — 380
  Lobbyists and Special Interest Groups 380

Voting Patterns of the Major Social Groups — 381
  The Apathetic Voter 381

The Politics of Development in the Third World — 381
  Perspectives on the Uneven Development
    in the Third World 382
  Modernization Theories 382
  Dependency Theories 383
  World-System Theory 383

Terrorism: A Challenge to Government — 387
  Governments and Terrorism 387
  Terrorism in the Modern World 389
  Who Is Vulnerable to Insurgent Terrorism? 391
  Theories About the Causes of Terrorism 392
  Can Terrorism Be Combated? 392

Summary — 393
Key Terms — 395
Exercises — 396

Power in Modern Societies

In our discussion of class consciousness in the United States, we saw that the relatively harsh treatment of labor unions is one factor in the relative lack of class consciousness. When the military or police are used to control strikes, or when the law says that strikebreaking is acceptable, owners and employers are exercising power. That is, they are getting the government to act on their behalf and against groups that threaten their wealth. **Power,** then, *can be defined as the ability to affect the actions of others.* If you can get others to behave as you want, or if you can affect the outcome of a struggle or conflict, you are exercising power.

Power is largely exercised through the political system. For that reason, when Max Weber identified power as one of three key dimensions of stratification, he referred to it as "party." But power can be exercised any time people interact with one another. Exchange theorists point out, for example, that power is exercised even in intimate relationships (Blau, 1964; Emerson, 1972; Molm, 1991, 1987). Partners offer one another something that allows each partner to gain from the relationship, but the partner who has more resources (beauty, wealth, popularity) to offer gets his or her way more often.

Legitimate Power and Authority

In many cases, power is **legitimate power,** that is, people agree that the person exercising power has the right to do so. Often, legitimate power is attached to a position that a person holds. At about this point in my introductory classes, I (Farley) generally ask my students to stand up. They always do. This is because, as the professor, I have **authority**—legitimate power attached to the position that I hold. Because I am the professor, my students will do as I ask, so long as I remain within the bounds of reason.

There are several sources of legitimate authority. Three of them—*traditional authority, legal-rational authority,* and *charismatic authority*—were identified by Max Weber in his writings on power and authority. The fourth, *expertise,* is a more modern phenomenon.

Traditional authority is based on long-standing, institutional, and largely unquestioned practices. The authority of a king or queen, or, within the Catholic Church, of the pope, are good examples of traditional authority. In a monarchy, it is obtained by birth, and in the case of religious leaders like the pope, is believed to lie in part in divine inspiration. The role carrying traditional authority is generally attached to a person for life, so that a king or pope reigns until he dies.

Legal-rational authority is also attached to a position, but it is done so for the purpose of carrying out some assigned task, and it is usually limited in both time and scope. Unlike the queen, the British prime minister belongs to a political party that must be reelected to a majority in Parliament if he is to continue in office. Similarly, because I am a professor, not a king, I have no authority outside the specific context of the classroom, my classes, and my students.

Somewhat different is **charismatic authority.** It is more attached to the person—and to a particular person's qualities—than any other form of authority. Charismatic leaders have authority because they excite and inspire people. Examples of charismatic authority can be seen in Minister Louis Farrakhan of the Nation of Islam and in the Rev. Jesse Jackson. Although both occupy positions of authority, it is their personal ability to inspire and mobilize people that has made them successful. In 1995, under Farrakhan's leadership, the Million Man March drew the biggest crowd ever to attend a Washington march. Similarly, the Rev. Jesse Jackson has generated a big turnout for any cause to which he has lent his support. Although others could hold their official titles, it is their personal charisma that has enabled them to mobilize large numbers of people. Others could fill the role of leader of the Nation of Islam, but it is not clear that others could mobilize the massive numbers of people as well as Farrakhan did.

A final form of authority, not included in Weber's original typology, is **expertise.** This refers to specialized knowledge that others value. In postindustrial societies, which place a premium on information and scientific knowledge, such specialized knowledge is highly valued. One widely used way of determining whether or not people have expertise is **credentials**—academic degrees, professional memberships, scientific publications that they have written, and similar indicators. One characteristic of credentials is that they are subject-specific. Hence, as Ph.D. sociologists and authors of sociology books and articles, at conference presentations we are often asked for expert opinions on social issues. Our credentials would not allow us, however, to claim expertise in some other area, such as medicine or weather forecasting.

Other Sources of Power

Besides authority, there are many other sources of power. Some are generally regarded as legitimate, others as not legitimate, and some may be either legitimate or illegitimate. In a democratic system, for example, people exercise power by voting. On the one hand, voting is often based more on candidate personalities than the issues, particularly in the United States where political parties exercise relatively little control over their candidates. However, even in the United States, large interest groups do sometimes vote together and influence the outcome of elections. In 2008, for example, women and minorities who had become dissatisfied with the policies of the George W. Bush administration played a crucial role in the election of Democrat Barack Obama to the presidency.

Power is also frequently exercised through force and coercion. Such use of power may be either legitimate or illegitimate. When police arrest people, that is generally accepted as a legitimate use of force. When protestors block highways, that is often seen as illegitimate, because such protests are illegal and the ability of others to go where they want is impeded. However, in democracies, such protests can succeed—and therefore exercise power—if they draw attention to a grievance that others see as real. Hence, such protests against the Vietnam War probably did force changes in the war policies of the Johnson and Nixon administrations. More recently, a 1999 protest in which demonstrators blocked a highway in St. Louis has been widely credited with getting the local business community and the State of Missouri to address a lack of minority participation in highway construction projects (Kee and Leiser, 2000).

A very important source of power is control of information. If you can control information, you can strongly influence how people perceive events. An example can be seen in medical experimentation in which the U.S. government allowed populations of U.S. cities to be exposed to hazardous substances in order to determine what might happen in cases of germ, chemical, or nuclear warfare (Kauzlarich and Kramer, 1998). These experiments were kept secret, and false information was provided to the public. Hence, the ability of the government to carry on these experiments was unimpeded. Only later did the true nature of these experiments become public. Imagine what would have happened if an army general had announced, "We are going to spray toxic chemicals over Minneapolis to see what will happen," or "We will inject hospital patients with radioactive plutonium without telling them so we can learn the effects of exposure to radiation." (Both of these examples are based on real cases described by *The New York Times* [1994] and by Kauzlarich and Kramer [1998].)

Wealth, Income, and Power

Finally, there is a definite link between wealth and high income and political power. Money can be translated into power in many ways: access to the mass media (advertising, publishing books, making movies and television programs); running for political office (around two-thirds of U.S. senators are millionaires [New York Times, 2009]); making campaign contributions (directly or through political action committees [PACs]); and through funding foundations, public policy institutes, and think tanks.

In fact, one of the great debates of sociology is about how closely power is related to wealth and income. The classic theorists Karl Marx and Max Weber offer different viewpoints on this issue. According to Marx, wealth—in the form of owning the means of production—is the key to all political power. Marx believed that all aspects of a society, including its political system and power structure, are determined by and serve the interests of whoever owns the means of production. Marx's colleague, Friedrich Engels, believed this so strongly that he predicted that, once economic inequality was eliminated through common ownership of the means of production, the state would "wither away."

Weber, on the other hand, saw class (economic income and wealth), status, and power as three separate dimensions of inequality. He recognized that wealth influences power, but he believed that wealth *does not determine* power. In other words, it is possible to be wealthy but not powerful or powerful but not wealthy.

In its modern form, this debate often places *pluralists* against *power elite* theorists. The **pluralist model** of power distribution holds that the wealthy cannot monopolize power because power is in fact divided among many competing groups (Dahl, 1961; 1981; 1982; Riesman, 1961; Pampel and Williamson, 1988). These groups include business, labor, ethnic, racial, regional, and religious interests. Often, they operate as **veto groups**—that is, they are not strong enough to get their way on everything, but they can block political actions that would seriously threaten their interests. The pluralist model is primarily derived from the functionalist perspective. It does reflect some influence of conflict theory because it clearly recognizes that different groups have competing interests. But it sees the system as functional in that it accommodates those interests so no group is downtrodden and no group consistently dominates. One final important point: this does *not* necessarily mean that the average citizen has much control over politics. Rather, people belong to groups like labor unions, churches, professions, and ethnic groups whose leaders watch out for their collective interests.

The *power elite model,* best exemplified by the work of C. Wright Mills (1956) and G. William Domhoff (1967; 1978; 1983), sees things differently. The **power elite model** holds that real political power is held by a small group made up almost entirely of those who own corporate wealth. It points out that much of the decision making is done behind the scenes, involving nonelected political appointees and administrators who are often influenced by foundations and public policy institutes funded by the wealthy. It also points out that a small number of people have overlapping positions of power on corporate boards, in the executive branch of the federal government, and in the top echelons of the military (Mills, 1956).

Ideas about the power elite are in some ways similar to theories about group dynamics, which hold that groups always tend to be dominated by a small leadership group. These theories include Michels' "iron law of oligarchy" (1967 [orig. 1911]) and related theories developed by Pareto (1935 [orig. 1915–1919] and Mosca (1939 [orig. 1896]). These theories—discussed in greater length in Chapter 9—argue that it is the nature of organizations to be controlled by a small elite. The power elite model, however, sees such concentration of power not so much as an inevitable characteristic of organization. Rather, it is the result of a great concentration of wealth, which leads to a concentration of power.

Who Has Power in America Today?

Measuring Power

To determine who has power, we must have some way of measuring power. This is not easy to do, because power is an abstract concept, or *construct,* that cannot be measured directly. Domhoff (1983) has proposed three questions to help sociologists determine who has power. One way is to ask "*Who governs?*" In other words, what social groups seem to be well represented among people who hold elective and appointive office? A second question is "*Who benefits?*" from governmental decisions. The assumption is that, if a group of people consistently gets governmental actions that favor their interests, they are exercising power. Finally, we can learn about power by asking "*Who wins?*" when controversial issues arise. If an interest group wins consistently, we can conclude that it has power. If one group wins nearly all the time, that group likely constitutes a *power elite.* If, however, different groups win on different issues, and/or if real compromises are common, power is probably dispersed among a number of groups, as suggested by the *pluralist model* (Banfield, 1962; Banfield and Wilson, 1963).

Besides Domhoff's three ways of measuring power, there is the *reputational approach.* This approach assumes that when someone repeatedly exercises power, others know about it. Thus, this approach seeks to measure power by asking people in politics who is powerful (Hunter, 1955, 1980). This method has two shortcomings: (1) People do not always know who has power, and (2) asking people "Who is powerful?" may lead them to assume that *someone* must have great power, thus biasing their answer (Cousins and Nagpaul, 1979; Polsby, 1980; Walton, 1966; 1977).

The Distribution of Power in the United States

Domhoff and others have used the methods described above to assess the power of different groups in the United States. In 2009, there were more than 12,500 official congressional lobbying groups in the United States (Reuters, 2009), and many others that seek in less direct ways to influence policy. However, most of them tend to represent certain groupings of interests.

Three Key Interest Group Coalitions

According to Domhoff (1983, 2009), there are three main interest groups that try to influence policy at the national level: multinational corporations, a small business coalition, and a labor/liberal coalition. The **multinational corporations** include companies, many but not all of which are based in the United States, that conduct business on a global scale. This group includes a number of policy foundations and research institutes that do not call themselves lobbyists, but rather claim to operate on the behalf of "good government" or "national interest." Examples include the Ford, Rockefeller, and Carnegie Foundations, the Committee for Economic Development (CED), the Council on Foreign Relations (CFR), the Trilateral Commission, and the Business Roundtable. Although they present themselves as "public interest" or "good government" groups, these groups in fact lobby for policies that promote free trade and other policies that allow the multinationals to operate in the world economy with a minimum of restrictions. The North American Free Trade Act (NAFTA), General Agreement on Trade and Tariffs (GATT), and U.S. government's support for Mexico's Maquiladora program are all outgrowths of the efforts of this group. (The Maquiladora program provides U.S. corporations with cheap labor in Mexican plants near the border; it has employed over a half million workers at wages sharply lower than those paid in the United States [Bartlett and Steele, 1992, p. 35].)

The second interest group identified by Domhoff is a small business coalition. It is represented by the Chamber of Commerce and by national organizations of professions that operate as small businesses—the American Medical Association (AMA), the American Dental Association (ADA), and the Farm Bureau. This group is more conservative and concentrates on opposition to governmental regulation of business. It is less involved in foundations and research institutes than the corporate group, but does support some, most notably the American Enterprise Institute and the Hoover Institute. This group may also be less cohesive than it once was; for example, the American Medical Association endorsed the health reforms passed in 2010, which groups like the Chamber of Commerce staunchly opposed.

The third group—and the most diverse—is a loose coalition of liberal, labor, ethnic, feminist, and environmental groups. It includes organized labor (the AFL-CIO) and such organizations as the National Association for the Advancement of Colored People (NAACP), Urban League, National Organization for Women (NOW), National Education Association (NEA), and the Ralph Nader–based organizations. It is less unified than the other groups, though on certain issues such as free trade and affirmative action, it has been able to exert a forceful and unified presence.

By examining who governs, who benefits, and who wins, we can assess the relative power of these three interest groups. If the power elite model were correct, we would expect power to lie almost totally in the hands of the wealthiest of these groups, the multinational corporations. If the pluralist model were correct, we would expect power to be scattered among the three groups, with different ones winning on different issues, lots of compromises, and all three groups well represented among decision makers. Research shows that the truth lies between the two models, but reality may be closer to the power elite model, since the corporate group does in fact exert disproportionally great power.

Who Governs?

An examination of the characteristics of national elected officials shows that corporate wealth is very well represented. About two thirds of the 100 U.S. senators are millionaires, compared to about 2 percent of the U.S. population. Wealthy families with names like Rockefeller, Danforth, and Kennedy have been well represented over the years. On the other hand, groups such as women, African Americans, and Latinos are very underrepresented in both the House and the Senate. In 2008, just 17 (out of 100) U.S. Senators and 77 (out of 435) U.S. House Representatives were women (Congressional Quarterly, 2008). There are no African Americans in the U.S. Senate (former senator Barack Obama, at the time the only African American senator, was elected president in 2008) and only three Hispanics in the U.S. Senate. Only two blacks were elected to the Senate in the entire twentieth century. In 2008, just 9.7 percent of the U.S. House (forty-two representatives) were African American, while about 5.8 percent of House members (twenty-five representatives) were Hispanic (Congressional Quarterly, 2008). And as low as they are, all of these percentages are at or near record highs for U.S. history.

The executive branch and the advisory groups who govern "behind the scenes" also show great overrepresentation of the wealthy. For example, the majority of professors who served on the President's Science Advisory Commission over a sixteen-year period had also been on the board of directors of large corporations. If you add consultants to large corporations and board members of smaller ones, the proportion rises to two-thirds (Schwartz, 1975). And Stryker's (1990) study of social scientists' roles in two government agencies found that when such experts support the interests of the wealthy their involvement becomes institutionalized—but when they oppose such interests, their role is usually eliminated. All this is consistent with the findings of C. Wright Mills's classic study *The Power Elite,* in which Mills found a small group of wealthy individuals who moved freely among positions in the executive branch of government, the military, and corporate boards of directors.

One critique of the "who governs" approach is that millionaires do not always agree on social policy, as illustrated by Ted Kennedy and George Bush. Hence, the critics argue, they cannot be a true power elite if they lack a common agenda (Dahl, 1982). In addition, the politicians must pay some attention to their constituents if they are to be elected, which may limit their power to promote their own self-interests (Riesman, 1969). Still, there is little doubt that the wealthy are greatly overrepresented and that poor people, women, and minorities are very underrepresented among our government's decision makers.

Who Benefits?

Measuring who benefits from governmental policies is probably the most difficult and subjective of Domhoff's three questions. One way is to look at distributions of wealth and income, which might to some degree indicate how favorable a government's policies are toward the wealthy. As we have already seen in Chapter 6, wealth and income are distributed more unequally in the United States than in most other industrialized countries. A more direct indicator is how the government spends its money. In the United States, for example, a larger share of the budget goes to defense than in most industrialized countries. Clearly there are beneficiaries of this, considering that (1) 10 of the 50 biggest U.S. corporations rely *primarily* on sales to the military, and at the peak of U.S. military spending in the 1980s, eight Pentagon contractors had sales greater than the entire gross national product of Norway (Currie and Skolnick, 1984). Critics argue that much of this spending is driven by the interests of the companies involved rather than national need. For example, in 2000, fifty U.S. Nobel laureates signed a statement arguing that a missile defense system being tested by the Pentagon could never work in combat conditions, was wastefully expensive, and was likely to trigger dangerous worldwide arms races. Nonetheless, Congress voted to continue funding the program, with a total projected cost of $60 billion if the full system is implemented. Ninety-seven of the 100 U.S. senators supported it—and corporations such as Raytheon and Boeing will clearly benefit from it.

The question "Who benefits?" can also be asked about tax legislation in the United States. As noted earlier in this chapter, wealth and income became more unequally distributed in the second half of the twentieth century. Did tax changes play a role in this? There is little question that effective rates of taxation for those in the higher income brackets have fallen, and research shows that this did contribute to the rising inequality (Auten and Carroll, 1999). For example, tax reform legislation in the 1980s effectively cut taxes 7 percent for middle-income taxpayers, but 31 percent for upper-income taxpayers. Consequently, the average household in the $100,000–2 million range got a cut of $7,203, while for households with incomes below $10,000, the cut was $37 (Bartlett and Steele, 1992). The tax reform also shifted the effective tax burden from corporations to individuals: The share of taxes paid by corporations fell from 21 percent to 17 percent of taxes between 1982 and 1992. Since then, Congress has reduced the capital gains tax (paid on investment income) to a lower rate than that paid on wages, and it has eliminated the so-called "marriage penalty." While both of these moves sound appealing, they mainly benefit upper-income taxpayers. Low-income taxpayers gained little from the capital gains cut, because they had no money to invest. And an analysis of the marriage penalty elimination showed that 78 percent of the tax savings would go to those taxpayers in the top 20 percent income bracket (Institute for Taxation and Public Policy, 2000). Again in 2001, Congress passed a tax cut bill, proposed by President Bush, that disproportionately benefits the wealthy. Under this tax cut, for example, a family of four with an income of $1 million got a tax cut of nearly $48,000, or 13.3 percent. A family the same size with an income of $400,000 got $14,000, or 11 percent (CNN 2001a). In contrast, a family of four with an income of $50,000 only got $1,825 in tax cuts, and the average single mother just $772 (CNN, 2001b). At the time of this writing, Congress was beginning a debate on whether these cuts should be extended for everyone beyond their expiration date at the end of 2010, or whether they should only be extended for people with incomes below $250,000 per year. (Fewer than 4 percent receive incomes of more than $200,000, so the vast majority of Americans will keep their tax cuts either way.)

Power theorists contend the system is biased toward the wealthy. When president Obama signed the financial bailout into law some saw this act as saving the national, and possibly global, economy from a Great Depression–type of downward spiral. But power theorists might point out that the same group of wealthy investors who created the financial crisis were also the ones to receive the bailout funds. Who do you think is right? Can both views be right? (Courtesy of John E. Farley)

Who Wins?

Finally, we can learn about who has power by examining who wins when conflicts, debates, and controversies arise over public policy. Domhoff (1983) reviewed much of the literature on this question, focusing on the relative influence of the three coalitions he identified: multinational corporate, small business, and labor/liberal. His review showed that when there is substantial disagreement among these three groups, the corporate group nearly always gets what it wants (see also Neustadtl and Clawson, 1998). One example can be seen in the inability of doctors and hospitals to block health-care cost controls desired by corporations in the 1980s (Imershein, Rond, and Mathis, 1992). Over about five decades, the corporate group's only clear defeat was the passage of the National Labor Relations Act in 1935. And even this law was later modified to make it more acceptable to the corporations. More recent research by Domhoff (2009) has shown that the corporate group continues to get its way the great majority of the time.

Among the other two groups, the small business group appears to have a fair amount of veto power: It could usually stop something that threatened it. It regularly defeated initiatives of the labor/liberal group, and in some cases it could modify, though not block, initiatives of the corporate group. However, it fared less well with its own initiatives, winning only when it had the backing of the corporate group (Domhoff, 1983).

Least powerful was the labor/liberal group. It could veto initiatives of the small business group only if it could get the support of the corporate group. It rarely passed its own initiatives, and when it did, it was usually with the support of the corporate group. Significantly, its power did increase during times of social conflict and upheaval, as the corporate group sought to maintain order by making concessions (see, for example, Gilbert and Howe, 1991, pp. 215–16; Jenkins and Brents, 1989, 1991). Why, according to Domhoff, did this group have the least ability to win? First, as noted above, it was a looser and more diverse coalition, which made it less unified. Second, it had fewer economic resources than either of the other groups. Third, it had less access to governmental officials. As Domhoff mentions in his "Personal Journey into Sociology" box, it is possible that recent political realignments may increase the influence of this group, but it is too early to tell whether any long-term power shift is occurring.

Overview

We have seen that, whether the question is "Who governs?" or "Who benefits?" or "Who wins?" the answer supplied by research evidence is much the same. Though neither model has the whole answer, the political system operates more in the way predicted by the power elite model than by the pluralist model. In the latter part of the twentieth century, the rich got richer and the small share of income and wealth that went to the poor got even smaller—and research shows that, while government action is not the only reason for this, it did definitely contribute to it.

Much of what we know about the U.S. power structure has been influenced by the research of G. William Domhoff. In the "Personal Journeys into Sociology" box, he tells us how he started out as a researcher on dreams and became a student of power structure.

PERSONAL JOURNEYS INTO SOCIOLOGY
How I Finally Found My Way to Sociology

G. William Domhoff

I write these words with the hope that they may be of use to students who are not sure why they are in college, or who worry about what educational and career path they should follow in the future. That's because nothing about my background or youthful interests predisposed me to become a political sociologist interested in analyzing the distribution of power in the United States, and it took me a long while to arrive there.

My family was average in every way and took no interest in politics, and only much later did I learn that my parents had voted for the person who became president, whether a Democrat or Republican, from 1932 through 1980. While growing up I played sports and wrote for the high school newspaper, and I thought I might be a journalist when I left the Midwest to go to college in the South. When I started college, I had never heard of sociology.

Still, I always had a strong dislike for injustice and unfairness. The poverty and segregation I saw as a child when we drove through some areas of the city always puzzled and upset me. But my inclination to question unfairness manifested itself only in crusading articles about school issues in my high school and college newspapers. Then, too, one of my early college term papers concerned the famous muckraking journalists of the Progressive Era. Their investigations into the rise of the "money trusts" and giant corporations, and the heat they took for these efforts, were fascinating to me.

In college my interest in journalism slowly gave way to a liking for the mysteries of human psychology. I became interested in why people do what they do, reading case histories of mental patients, studies of the unconscious, and interpretations of myths and rituals. After much hesitation, I decided to go to graduate school in psychology, although many aspects of psychology bored me, and especially those areas that had to do with vision and hearing, or with experiments on rats and pigeons. I had to steel myself for the fact that some of what I would study would not be enjoyable to me, and that I would have to suffer through this material to attain my goal. That problem may sound familiar to some of you.

In graduate school I gradually became involved in the systematic studies of dreams, the revealing picture stories of the night. This was mainly because I had a chance to work with one of the few well-known psychologists who studied that almost-taboo topic, but since dreams were thought of at the time as the "royal road to the unconscious," studying dreams also fit with my interest in human motivation. I did a dissertation comparing dream reports collected in the

The State

Max Weber argued that the *state* is the institution that holds a legitimate monopoly over physical violence in a given territory. Although often debated, this definition has become the cornerstone of how we think about the concept of the state. Yet, this kind of power is most effective if never used. Once a state resorts to violence it shows weakness. Resorting to violence means a state has no other way to enforce its will and this often leads to a loss of legitimacy. This paradox is at the heart of the power states wield. In practice it means that states rarely use such power. Instead they resort to numerous other means to enforce their will, including prohibiting others in a society from using force. Modern states like the U.S. have taken on a much larger role than the early states that emerged some 5,000 years ago. Today they engage in activities along a very diverse a range of areas such as education, medical, family services, workplace safety, food and drug safety, technology, and many others. As we will see later, Western states have become the primary institution in guaranteeing a minimum level of welfare of citizens. States that do this are referred to as *welfare states*.

Sociologists see the state differently depending upon their theoretical orientation. Functionalists tend to see the state as a necessary evil in modern societies. The state is the only institution with enough power to control and unite large diverse

---

sleep laboratory with those written down at home by the same participants, and in the first few years after I finished my Ph.D., I coauthored a few articles on the typical content of dreams from everyday people.

But questions of power were creeping up on me, too, sometimes in very roundabout ways. Traveling in Europe the summer after my second year of graduate school, I met a woman from California. I had never been west of the Mississippi at the time, but the next summer we were married, and I have lived in California ever since. It was her family that started me reading and thinking about power: They were all political activists of varying stripes who disagreed on many issues, and they were avid readers besides. When I read a now-classic book by C. Wright Mills called *The Power Elite*, first published in 1956, I decided I wanted to do research on the topic. It was a whole new world I knew nothing about, a world of wealth and power that was just as new and surprising to me as the private motives underneath our individual behavior.

Even so, I might not have switched my research interest from dreams to power if it had not been for the excitement and hopefulness of the Civil Rights movement. That movement started to gain national attention just as I was finishing graduate school in Florida and taking my first teaching job at a state college in Los Angeles. I was also intrigued by the way the Civil Rights activists used research on local and national power to help their cause.

I still wouldn't have made the transition to political sociology and power-structure research if I hadn't come across another sociology book, this one by E. Digby Baltzell, *Philadelphia Gentlemen: The Making of a National Upper Class* (1958). Although dry and descriptive, Baltzell's book was crucial to me because it made it possible to construct a list of "indicators" of upper-class standing, meaning that we could tell who was part of the social elite by attendance at expensive private schools, membership in exclusive social clubs, and listings in in-group telephone and address books, usually called "blue books" or "social registers." His book enabled me to think in terms of systematic research that traced networks of power from the social upper class to the corporations, and then to foundations, elite policy-discussion groups, and the government.

In other words, I immediately saw ways that I could use Baltzell's upper-class indicators to test Mills's ideas as well as those of various Marxists and pluralists. It made it possible for me to see for myself with new research. It has always been my tendency to try to test the most exciting ideas with the best methods available. I also like to synthesize the ideas of different people, so my first book, *Who Rules America?*, began by saying it would build on the work of four people with different perspectives: Mills, Baltzell, the Marxist Paul Sweezy, and the pluralist Robert Dahl. It was written in a direct and graphic way, thanks to all that journalism experience in my background, and it was loaded with what we like to call empirical information.

When I finished the book, I thought that I would probably go back to dream research, although I had lost much of my interest in it. I was not prepared for the book's success. It had hit at just the right time, the late 1960s, when Civil Rights activism had been combined with antiwar and other movements to create tremendous ferment in the country. My book made sense to people because they were watching the power structure I described continue to fight the war in Vietnam despite the fact that growing numbers of people opposed it.

Academic reviewers were not totally negative toward my book, which was surprising in an era when just about everyone in academia denied the existence of a power elite. Some tried to say it was mere muckraking, but I was able to point out it was network analysis. Pluralists tried to claim that I had confused wealth with power, but I was able to answer that wealth is just an indicator of power, not power itself, and that I had used other indicators besides. As for their other criticisms, by then I realized I could do more research to answer them, so I plunged back into research on power.

But I was still in a psychology department, by this time at the small, new, and experimental University of California, Santa Cruz, that did not worry as much about disciplinary boundaries as established universities. It was thus easier for me to be welcomed by the sociology group than it would have been elsewhere. That was the final piece of good luck for me. I was caught up in an exciting dialogue in my new discipline, and the result has been many authored and coauthored books.

Some of the fun went out of it for me in the late 1970s, however, as the social movements disappeared and interest in the study of power structures declined. Moreover, a new breed of young Marxists began to claim that my books were part of the problem because they supposedly discouraged potential activists by making change seem hopeless. Thus, after being seen as useful in the 1960s, helping people to focus their actions and formulate their perspectives, I was now viewed by purists as a hindrance. This change from one decade to the next reinforced what I already knew, that research such as mine has only a limited effect on political action, and that it is often interpreted in terms of the atmosphere within which it is being read. In that sense, a book can take on a life of its own, whatever the author may have intended.

But events in the United States in the 1980s, and then the implosion of the Soviet Union in the early 1990s, discredited the theories and political strategies put forth by Marxists, who all but disappeared from the academic scene. They were replaced by high-level theorists who claimed that the American government is quite independent of big business—"autonomous" was their catchword—but they didn't last long either. These failures opened space for new thinking and research that builds on sounder premises. I hope some of the revived energy in political sociology is reflected in the sixth edition of *Who Rules America?*, which came out in 2010.

My research is first and foremost an attempt to describe and understand, letting the chips fall where they may. However, my books have been useful to democratic activists interested in loosening up the power structure, because they show where new cracks and openings develop. For example, it turns out that the Civil Rights movement reshaped American politics by making it possible for African Americans in the South to vote, and thereby to push the most conservative and antiblack Southern Democrats into the Republican Party. This change makes it possible for a nationwide liberal-labor coalition to have its own political party, the Democratic Party, for the first time in American history. The transformation of the Democrats by liberals, women activists, strong environmentalists, minority-group leaders, and labor is still a work in progress, but the election of an African American president in 2008 and the increasingly liberal nature of Democrats in the House of Representatives shows what is possible. The final and most difficult hurdle is the Senate, where the party still lacks the ten to fifteen Senate seats that would be needed to transform the social support system into something resembling Canada or Germany. At the same time, I also know from letters and conversations that my books have been used by social climbers to find the "right" schools or summer resorts, and by young members of the upper class to gain an overview of the complex power structure they are destined to enter. My books end up as guides to how power operates in the United States that turn out to be of potential use to anyone, which once again demonstrates that books can take on lives of their own and have uses never thought of by the author.

As the years go by, I have less and less interest in the abstract theories that capture attention for a few years and then fade away. They usually make the problems seem more complicated than they really are, and they are often based on false premises. Most often, they make claims about alleged changes in the past decade or two—changes for which there is no real evidence. Or else they make big predictions about the near future, which are soon proven wrong by events. Sociology tells us that societies do change, and often in unexpected ways, but no one can predict the future. There is no substitute for the gradual development of knowledge through good sociological research. My ongoing efforts in this regard can be found on my Web site, www.whorulesamerica.net.

G. William (Bill) Domhoff is a Research Professor in Sociology at the University of California, Santa Cruz. He received his B.A. at Duke University and his Ph.D. at the University of Miami. His books include *Who Rules America?* (1967), *The Higher Circles* (1970), *The Powers That Be* (1979), and *State Autonomy or Class Dominance?* (1996). He also coauthored *Blacks in the White Elite* (1991), *Diversity in the Power Elite* (2006), and *The Leftmost City: Power and Progressive Politics in Santa Cruz* (2009).

groups of people around common goals, values, and norms. For the functionalists, we enter into the state to control the potential chaos that would ensue were their no overriding authority. The state also serves the function of defending us from other groups of people or states that may threaten us for various reasons. For conflict theorists, the state represents an institution that imposes the rule of the powerful over the weak. So, in capitalist societies, conflict theorists tend to see the state as promoting the interests of capitalism and capitalists over the working and middle classes.

Many sociologists take a middle view. The state is autonomous from capitalism and does create unity among citizens; however it is also true that the state is, in normal times, controlled by those with the most power. But this rule is far from complete. In a crisis their control can be broken in important ways. This was evident during the Great Depression when New Deal legislation curtailed the powers of capitalists and extended social protections to the working and middle classes that were not there before. Further, many capitalists actually supported the creation of welfare states (Swenson, 2002). Nor is it the case that capitalists and business interest in general always oppose the welfare state. Many businesses find they derive benefits from welfare state programs (Flota, 2003). A good example is not having to pay for their employees' health insurance costs. This has traditionally been one of the greatest expenditures for American businesses, for instance, that do have to provide this coverage. During the 1980s and 1990s when Sweden debated cutbacks in welfare state activity some of the same kinds of firms and business sectors that favored the creation of the welfare state (primarily small businesses and industries tied to domestic production, such as forestry) also opposed the dismantling of the welfare state (Flota, 2008, 2003). Further, the state itself has interests as an organization and bureaucracy. Once a program is put into place, vested interests form to keep the program, not the least of which are the incomes and livelihoods that are derived from such programs. Capitalist opposition is not enough to guarantee such programs will not survive, though as a group they are the most likely to get their way, as we discussed earlier in the section on *Who Wins*. Finally, it should be recalled that capitalists themselves are in competition with each other and are from all the various sectors of the economy. They do not always speak with one voice.

Types of Systems

There are three main kinds of states: democracies, dictatorships, and monarchies. **Democracy** is defined as a political system in which there is civic control over the state. The idea is that the ultimate authority for the society rests with its citizenry. In a **dictatorship**, the people as a whole are not allowed to participate in the governance of their society. The classic form of this is derived from the title where a dictator, one person, rules with impunity. In actual practice even dictators have limits. They must, after all, get other people to do their bidding. They cannot do it all. But the fact that they do get others to do their bidding speaks to the power they have in society. Oligarchy, rule by the few (which we talked about in Chapter 9), would also fit into this category, although it is sometimes considered a system of its own. China would be a contemporary example. We make a distinction between an authoritarian state in which democracy is denied and a totalitarian state in which all aspects of life are controlled more or less by the state. Totalitarian states are rare in actual practice. Nazi Germany was one example. Today, many point to North Korea as a contemporary example. **Monarchies** are the final type of state and they are ruled by a family through hereditary succession. These states were common during agrarian stages of development and the legacy of these states is very much with us today. Sweden, Norway, and the other Scandinavian states are often held up as the most democratic societies in the world. However, in a technical sense they are also monarchies in that they have retained their monarchical leader as formal head of state. The United Kingdom also has this structure. We call these states constitutional monarchies, as all important functions of government have been transferred to the democratic representatives of those states. Saudi Arabia is an example of a modern state that retains a powerful ruling monarchy.

Putting Sociology to Work

Welfare Reform: An Effective Tool Against Poverty?

In 1996, legislation providing for major "reforms" in welfare was passed. A lifetime limit of five years was placed on how long people could receive welfare, based in part on the belief that welfare actually causes people to stay poor. Mandates that people with certain needs be covered by welfare were eliminated, leaving the five-year time limit as the key federal welfare mandate (states could impose shorter, but not longer, limits). The name of the main welfare program was changed from Aid to Families with Dependent Children (AFDC) to Temporary Assistance to Needy Families (TANF) to emphasize the notion that welfare should be only temporary.

These changes reflect a widespread belief that welfare encourages people to be dependent on aid rather than to find jobs and support themselves. Many also believe that welfare acts as an enabler that encourages teenage pregnancy and single parenthood, which further perpetuate poverty. The strongest sociological statements of this viewpoint have been made by Charles Murray (1984, 1993). In part because of such concerns, the two political parties competed in the 1990s to present themselves as wanting to "end welfare as we know it," and the 1996 legislation was the result. In addition to the five-year lifetime time limit on welfare, the 1996 law also included a requirement that people receiving welfare must accept employment, reduced to one year the amount of time that education could be substituted for employment, and excluded all types of education (including college) other than vocational education. The law also limited the time that unemployed adults could receive food stamps. At the same time, it increased federal funding for day care and provided some expanded access to Medicaid for the working poor.

Sociological research, however, raises serious doubts about some of the assumptions that underlie welfare reform. William Julius Wilson, for example, researched the actual correlation over time between the level of welfare benefits and the poverty and unemployment rates. If welfare really causes poverty by discouraging people from working, we ought to find that when welfare benefits are high, more people are poor and unemployed. But Wilson's research shows just the opposite! The time period when poverty grew most rapidly was between 1978 and 1983. (You can see this by reviewing Figure 6.3.) But real (adjusted for inflation) welfare benefits fell steadily and substantially from 1972 into the mid-1980s. In fact, the inflation-adjusted value of welfare and food stamps was 22 percent lower in 1984 than it was in 1972 (Wilson, 1987, p. 94). In other words, the correlation is just the opposite of what Murray predicted: Poverty increased when welfare was reduced. Wilson is not the only one to obtain such findings: Jencks (1991, pp. 56–62) found that availability and levels of welfare benefits had little effect on the proportion of single mothers who were employed.

Similarly, Robert Moffit (1992) examined the correlation over time between levels of welfare and rates of single parenthood. His conclusion: "The evidence does not support the conclusion that the welfare system has been responsible for time-series growth in female headship and illegitimacy." He found little or no correlation over time between welfare benefits and either illegitimate births or the percentage of female-householder families. Similar findings have been obtained in other research by Ellwood and Bane (1984), Rank (1989), and Wilson (1987, pp. 77–81).

Nothing in any of this research argues against the view that it would be better for most welfare recipients if they were stably employed rather than receiving welfare. But there is little reason to believe that welfare reform by itself will significantly reduce poverty, and now that it has been more than ten years since welfare reform went into effect, there is a growing amount of research that can help us assess the actual effects of welfare reform on poverty. The research, as well as numbers showing large declines in the number of people receiving welfare, do confirm that welfare reform moved many people from welfare to work, as it was intended to do. For example, Loprest (1999) reports that about 70 percent of those who had left welfare were still off welfare in 1997, and of these, 60 percent were employed. (This was actually a higher percentage than for poor mothers who had *not* been on welfare in the past.) However, most are working in low-pay service or clerical jobs. The median pay was $6.61 an hour, and three-quarters of their jobs provided no health insurance. Significantly, only about a third received Medicaid, suggesting that nearly half had no health insurance. One-quarter received an income of $5.29 per hour or less—not enough to get even a two-person household above the poverty level, even if the person worked year-round full-time, which many do not. In 1999, 41 percent of recent welfare leavers had incomes below the poverty level—a little lower than in 1997, but still high (Urban Institute, 2001).

Overall, the total annual household earnings of former welfare recipients (which includes spouses' incomes when present) were, on average, only high enough to provide a poverty-level income for a family of three. Loprest also examined reasons why some who left welfare were not working (about 40 percent of those who left welfare). The most common reason, accounting for more than one-fourth of those not working, was medical disability. About another one-fourth did not work because they were taking care of someone at home. About 15 percent had looked but could not find a job, and 12 percent mentioned transportation problems or inability to get child care.

Several additional findings from Loprest's (1999) study show how great are the economic difficulties of those who have made the transition from welfare to work. One-third of former welfare recipients reported that they had to skip meals or eat smaller meals because they did not have enough money for food. Nearly 40 percent had missed paying rent, mortgage, or utility bills in the past year, and one out of every fourteen had to move in with someone else because they could not pay their bills.

Research also shows that even when eligible and in need, many who moved from welfare to work are not receiving food stamps (Zedlewski and Brauner, 1999; Urban Institute, 2001), which aggravates problems like those described in the preceding paragraph. Perhaps for this reason, the U.S. Conference of Mayors reported a 17 percent increase in requests for emergency food assistance in 2000, and one-third of the adults requesting assistance were working (American Friends Service Committee, 2001). As was true for food stamp programs, Medicaid enrollment fell in 1998, and studies indicate that the declines in enrollment were biggest where the most people were moved off welfare (Bruen and Holahan, 2001). This further supports the view, noted above, that many who moved from welfare to work lost medical coverage in the process. Finally, research suggests that, like much else in America, race makes a difference in the effects of welfare reform. The American Friends Service Committee (2001) reports that blacks leaving welfare have received less assistance from caseworkers in finding jobs, have been more often required to take a test in order to get a job, and—even at the same levels of education—have been less likely to find jobs than whites leaving welfare.

All of this suggests that if we are serious about welfare reform and combating poverty, issues such as job training, child care, medical coverage, low wages, and racial discrimination cannot be ignored,

as they largely were in the federal welfare reform legislation in 1996. In addition, starting in 2001, a serious crisis emerged for two reasons. First, this was the year in which the first welfare recipients ran up against the five-year limit. Second, the economy entered a recession after eight years of prosperity and growth. This meant that large numbers of former welfare recipients were forced into the labor pool precisely at the time when the economy was least able to accommodate them. One reason that so many did move off welfare in the first few years after welfare reform is that the economy was enjoying healthy growth. Social scientists had long warned that the true test of welfare reform would come when the economy entered a slowdown (Dervarics, 1998), and unfortunately, that occurred precisely at the time when the five-year time limits were being reached. As a result, poverty, homelessness, and income insecurity have all increased for the poor (Burnham, 2001; Griffen 1999; Hennessy, 2005). In addition, Hao and Cherlin (2004) find that teenage pregnancy and school dropout rates have increased for welfare families during the post-reform period. Thus, while welfare reform was successful in moving people from welfare to work in strong economic times, it has not been successful in getting them out of poverty. Nor is it able to provide stable employment during weaker economic periods. Clearly, many former welfare recipients are unable to find work when the overall unemployment rate rises to 10 percent, as it did early in 2010.

Welfare Around the World

As we have seen, a major responsibility modern states have is to provide for the welfare of their citizens. The United States is no exception to this. In this sense, though it is the smallest of them all, the United States can be said to be a welfare state. Yet a variety of welfare states exist across the globe. In this section we will look at the broad outline of the variety of welfare states that can be found among the wealthy nations of the world.

Liberal Welfare States: U.S., Canada, the United Kingdom

The first set of nations we will call the Liberal Welfare States. These include all the predominantly English-speaking countries of the wealthy nations:

the U.S. of course, along with Australia, Canada, Ireland, New Zealand, and the United Kingdom. In general, these countries are characterized by having smaller welfare states in terms of the money they spend as a percentage of their entire economies. The focus here is on efficiency: spending as little as possible to help those in need. They are also more "liberal" in the sense that they rely more on market forces than the other sets of nations (Esping-Anderson, 1990). Adam Smith, the father of economics, used to be called a "liberal" economist to distinguish him from the "conservative" economists he was arguing against who wanted to conserve the authoritarian powers of the monarchs to control the economy. Smith and his contemporaries wanted to liberate the market, workers, and businesspeople from these controls. The system Smith sought to replace was called Mercantilism. Mercantilism dominated the sixteenth and seventeenth centuries. The philosophy behind the system was to maximize the wealth of the aristocracy by increasing a country's exports abroad by selling cheap goods to trading partners. These exports would then bring in gold to the nation's treasury and enrich the ruling aristocracy or royalty. Workers were organized into guilds, which in turn controlled the workers and pledged loyalty and cooperation to the aristocracy in exchange for protection from competition, high-cost suppliers and other threats to making cheap products that would sell abroad. Smith criticized this system for being corrupt and inefficient. He felt that the market could provide liberation to society from the power of the royalty at the same time that society became wealthier. So, while the label might seem to make little sense in our political debate today, calling these welfare states liberal, as did an influential study by researcher Gosta Esping-Anderson, makes sense historically. He pointed out that liberal welfare states are not just small in terms of the amounts of money they spend compared to other types of welfare states. They are also more likely to using *means tested* welfare programs. That is, programs that test whether or not you have the means to get by on your own or whether you need some kind of assistance from the government. Traditional American welfare programs, now workfare, are organized around this principle. So are subsidized student loans! The belief at work here is that the market tends to be a fair and just arbiter of economic outcomes, and while society has a responsibility to limit any pain or suffering of the poor, the market should be left to do most of this. Possibly as a result, there is less reduction of inequality and poverty in these types of system than in the others. However it should be noted that even in this category the United States stands out. The United States has a smaller public sector, more poverty and inequality, and more means tested programs than any other nation in this category by a wide margin. No wealthy industrialized nation produces as wide a gulf between its rich and its poor and no nation other than Japan among the wealthy nations spends less on its welfare state.

Corporatist-Statist Welfare States

These countries have larger welfare states and have fewer qualms about intervening in the market if need be. Prominent countries in this category include Germany and France. The imagery Esping-Anderson (1990) uses to describe these welfare states is that of the strong-father family. The rich have a responsibility to look after the poor, but it is recognized that the status differences between the two are there for a reason. A father does not give his child equal rights in the family because children are not equal. A parent knows better than a child what is safe and proper and thus they have greater rights. At the same time, the father does not simply force the children to fend for themselves; he makes sure the children are safe and comfortable and grow to adulthood in the proper manner— the father has greater responsibilities because of his greater rights. The same is true for welfare in these nations. Welfare is used to soften the blow of market outcomes to a much greater degree than in the Liberal states, but by no means is the point to try and make everyone equal or even have equal benefits from the welfare state. The family, the church, and the state have levels of power and hierarchy that are there for a reason and they should be respected. As a result these states tend to have a medium level of inequality when compared to the other two types of states.

Social Democratic Welfare States

The Scandinavian welfare states are what populate this category. Here the strategy of the state is to provide *universal benefits* that ensure a decent standard of living to all citizens, regardless of what happens to them in the marketplace. The philosophy behind this is that human welfare should not be for sale. No one should be allowed to suffer in a rich nation simply because they have had misfortune in the labor market. In Sweden, the political imagery that has been used for decades is that of the "People's Home." Everyone has a responsibility to take care of each other. The state is seen as best equipped to take primary responsibility for this. Although citizens in these countries typically complain about the high taxes (they pay the some of the highest in the world) they lavish praise on the comprehensive set of welfare benefits they get from cradle to grave. Unlike the means tested benefits one must qualify for in the Liberal welfare states, benefits in Social Democratic countries tend to be *universal*; that is, they are received by all people no matter of income. The philosophy behind this system is to "de-commodify" the citizen. That is, remove the market from being the primary vehicle in which people's prosperity is achieved. Citizens in these states enjoy the most comprehensive set of social benefits in the world. Poverty has been all but eliminated in many of these countries, health care is very cheap, and yet they have some of the healthiest, longest-living people on Earth and many of these states give their citizens two-week government-paid holidays. A fact that has been a nuisance to more than one sociologist wishing to use their summer to study a country like Sweden. Sweden virtually shuts down during the summertime as nearly everyone seems to be on holiday! As a result these nations have the lowest levels of poverty and inequality of the bunch.

Evaluating the Welfare States

So which is best? The answer to this likely lies in one's ideological appeal. For many in Liberal welfare states, the goal may not be to eliminate poverty as it is in the Social Democratic states. The Liberal states tend to take the Davis-Moore perspective talked about in Chapter 6 to heart and argue that a certain level of inequality and poverty is useful for motivation, although in fact their overall productivity is not much different from the social democratic states. If we assume that the welfare state's goal really is to create as much welfare for the citizens as possible, then Liberal welfare states should have two distinct advantages when trying to reduce problems such as poverty. One, they target the money they spend directly at the most vulnerable populations. Two, they spend less because they are only helping those who actually need the help. So why are they less effective in reducing poverty and inequality? One major reason is that with means tested programs aimed at the poor it is easier for a stigma to gain hold in people's minds about those programs. This does not happen when a program is universal and aimed at everyone. The American programs Social Security and Medicare (both of which cover virtually all elder people in the United States) are universal programs and are both wildly popular and successful. In fact, Social Security and Medicare have been shown to have a greater effect on reducing poverty than either the very means tested programs designed to do so, or the lower tax rates and various tax cuts that are all aimed at the poor (Marmor, et al., 1990). When a program gains a stigma people are less likely to favor funding it. As the descriptions above indicate, all else equal, you get what you pay for when it comes to reducing inequality through social welfare programs.

Political Ideology

At a very basic level political ideology breaks down between *liberals, conservatives,* and *moderates.* We have all heard these terms but what do they mean? Liberals are said to lean to the left of the political spectrum and support more government intervention in the marketplace on behalf of the working and middle classes. They also favor a more lenient stance when it comes to regulating moral behavior—what social scientists often refer to as "social issues." So, on economic and social issues, conservatives and the right wing of the political spectrum tend to favor less government intervention in the economy on behalf of the working and middle classes and a more restrictive/traditional stance toward moral or social issues. Notice we said less intervention on behalf of the working and middle classes. Most sociologists who study the economy make the argument that government always intervenes in the economy, it's just a matter of how and on whose behalf. In this case conservatives often intervene on the side of the upper class or business interests. While liberals tend to argue that government should help those who are less fortunate, conservatives tend to argue that government should make it as easy as possible for the folks who create jobs and wealth to do so. Conservatives found themselves in awkward ideological territory after both a Republican and a Democratic administration spent hundreds of billions of dollars in 2008 and 2009 to bail out some of the largest banks in the U.S. financial system. Both the George W. Bush and Obama administrations have sharply increased government spending and thus the size of the state. Voices from the right and the left have criticized both parties for supporting the very wealthy, and the Tea Party movement of conservative activists rose up in the summer of 2009 to challenge both the Obama administration and the elements of the Republican establishment that oversaw the run-up of government spending during the Bush years. In the middle of all of this, moderates tend to try to take the best of both the right and the left, but this is not always an easy task. Many people who report to be moderates are found to be less interested in, knowledgeable about, and involved in politics than liberals or conservatives. In the United States, this means that many politicians make great efforts in general elections to court the elusive moderate swing vote, which is populated largely by people who have very limited political or policy knowledge and who tend to make their minds up about candidates and issues at the last minute. A rough picture of how people self-report their ideological leanings finds that about a quarter of people consider themselves liberal; four in ten say they are moderates; and a third conservative.

Political Parties and Special Interest Groups

The two-party system in the United States reflects this ideological split. Democrats tend to represent liberals and the Republicans tend to represent the conservatives with moderates vacillating between the two. The outcomes of elections tend to rely on the mobilization of the liberal or conservative base of the two parties during the low-turnout elections (like off-year congressional elections, where a third of those eligible typically vote); and wining the moderate middle during high-turnout elections (like presidential elections where roughly half of those eligible typically vote). Sometimes moderate voters become so connected to their identity as neither a Democrat nor a Republican that they declare themselves Independents. But not all independents are moderates. They also come from the liberal or conservative fringes and are not satisfied with center-right or center-left positions of the major parties.

Lobbyists and Special Interest Groups

For a host of reasons, not the least of which is that representatives in Congress are elected as individuals from specific districts, U.S. political parties tend to be fairly weak. That is, party unity is weak. The interests of a northeastern Democrat from an urban district are going to be very different than those of a southern democrat from a mostly rural district. In fact southern Democrats have historically had as much in common with the Republicans as they have with the members of their own party or its platform. The same can be said for northeastern Republicans, who tend to be rather liberal and have often voted with Democrats, especially those from New England. As Domhoff points out, these differences have decreased somewhat in recent years, but they have not entirely disappeared.

With all of this incoherency at the party level, lobbyists and special interest groups have gained a great deal of power and influence in Washington, D.C. *Special interest groups* are just what they sound like, groups of people who come together to support particular issues or interests. Interest groups use their financial resources to hire lobbyists. *Lobbyists* go to the capitol to attempt to influence legislation. *Political action committees,* called PACs, are creations of these groups to raise money for their causes. PACs typically funnel money to political candidates who support their positions. PACs have many critics who charge that they amount to little more than legalized bribery (Cook, 1993). On the other hand, PACs make no secret about what they are doing: trying to influence politics in the direction that they favor. PACs were created in the 1970s, though some trace the first PAC back to 1944. They exploded in number during the 1980s and have continued that explosive growth to this day. Critics blame PACs for being a major contributor to the rising costs of political campaigns in the US. Ironically, it is probably the high costs of running a national campaign that contributes to political candidates' accepting money from PACs in the first place. And this vicious cycle looks to have no end unless specific legislation is passed to curtail it. Either way, the influence of special interest groups, the lobbyists, and their PACs is now well entrenched in the workings of government. Well-funded groups like the National Rifle Association (NRA) can block gun control legislation year after year despite the fact that a majority of Americans support moderate gun control legislation and have for decades. The same can be said for a multitude of major issues. And while critics charge this amounts to a small minority of voices drowning out the majority, supporters of the system counter that interest groups allow the passion of an organized minority to counterbalance the passivity of a larger opposition. In other words, isn't it appropriate, supporters ask, if a smaller group of people who really care about an issue (likely because they are going to be heavily affected by the outcome) get their way over a larger group who do not feel as passionately about their side (and likely won't be as affected by the outcome)? Is majority rule always appropriate, especially when the minority may be disproportionately affected?

Voting Patterns of the Major Social Groups

The dominant social locations that we have looked at in this book are very evident when one examines voting patterns in American elections. Class, race, and gender along with other social forces play important roles in shaping how people vote. White, rural voters tend to vote Republican. More men vote Republican than women. But that gender gap is dwarfed by the race gap. African Americans and Latinos vote Democratic in very large numbers: 90 percent and 75 percent in most elections. White women tend to support the winner in presidential contests, but white men vote overwhelmingly Republican. Class also plays a role, with working-class voters supporting Democrats and upper-class voters supporting Republicans. The middle class is split and often votes with the winner.

The Apathetic Voter

What is distinctive about American elections is how many people *don't vote at all*. With the lowest voting rates of any advanced industrial society, the reasons for this low turnout are complex. But chief among the culprits would appear to be a belief that politics do not matter in the lives of those who do not vote. Many nonvoters report a cynicism about being able to impact meaningful change. They feel they have little stake in the system. Others have argued however that those who do not vote do so because they are basically satisfied with their situation (Jackman, 1994).

By looking at which groups participate and which groups do not, most sociologists believe the first view. In general, as we will see, those with more power in American society tend to vote in greater numbers while those with less power vote less. One area where this does not hold true, however, is sex. Men and women vote in roughly the same numbers. But race shows the trend quite clearly. Overall, whites vote the most followed by African Americans and then Hispanics. However, the race and ethnicity of the candidates and the nature of the issues in the election sometimes lead to exceptions to this pattern. Home owners, parents, the highly educated, and the wealthy are all more likely to vote than renters, singles, those with less education, or the poor.

The Politics of Development in the Third World

The term "development" is used both narrowly and broadly in the sociological literature. The narrow sense refers to economic development, the economic changes associated with the Industrial Revolution. In the broad sense, development refers to *all* the changes that have occurred in the last 200 to 300 years. In this sense the term is used interchangeably with the term *modernization*. In this chapter we will use the term *development* for this broad meaning and the term *economic development* for the narrow meaning.

Sociologists frequently place different countries in categories that reflect different degrees of economic development. Developed countries are those that have modern political institutions, industrial economies, high standards of living, high literacy rates, and good medical care. Examples are the United States, Japan, and the Scandinavian countries. The less-developed or developing countries lack some or all of these things and have low standards of living. Many countries in Africa, Asia, and South America fall into this category. Another common term, referring to a group of countries that roughly corresponds to the developing countries, is *Third World* countries. This term was originally coined to refer to countries not clearly aligned with either of the two major groups of developed countries in the mid-twentieth century, the capitalist/democratic bloc and the communist bloc (Worsley, 1984). Although this distinction is less meaningful today, the "Third World" terminology continues to be widely used, and is preferred by some who see negative connotations in the term "less-developed."

Perspectives on Uneven Development in the Third World

One issue of great interest to sociologists who study social change in the Third World is that of uneven development between First World and Third World countries, as well as within Third World countries. The term *uneven development* refers to differences in growth and economic development among different geographic areas. Theories concerning social change and uneven development in the Third World fall into two broad categories that generally correspond to the functionalist and conflict theories.

Modernization Theories

The major functionalist approach to uneven development is **modernization theory,** which holds that as Third World countries modernize and industrialize, uneven development will gradually decrease. Functionalists believe that, as the process of modernization spreads to the developing countries, they will benefit from it much as the industrialized countries have. Modernization theorists see the development of Third World societies as linked to a process of diffusion, both cultural and technological (Rostow, 1960). On the technological side, economic development is seen as an outgrowth of technologies that were first developed in Europe or North America. These technologies allowed dramatic increases in productivity in Europe and North America, particularly from the mid-nineteenth century to the mid-twentieth century. Modernization theory holds that similar gains in productivity can be realized in Third World countries through the importation of modern technology and modern forms of organization, along with infusions of the capital necessary to build factories that use these technologies. Modernization theorists would point to economic booms in Third World countries such as South Korea, Hong Kong, Singapore, and Taiwan as examples of this, noting that all of these countries have received substantial investment from corporations and other organizations based in more developed countries. More recently, such investment and growth has also been occurring in mainland China.

Modernization theorists give equal importance to cultural diffusion. Theorists such as David McClelland (1961) point to the need for such values as individualism and self-reliance, the ability to defer gratification, and the desire to achieve. He argues that countries with such values will experience economic growth, while countries without them will not. In a sense, McClelland's view is a modern version of Max Weber's theories about the Protestant work ethic, discussed in Web-Based Chapter B. According to this view, countries that have these values to begin with will be better able to take advantage of imported technologies. In countries that do not have them, it may be necessary for the values to be introduced and accepted through the process of cultural diffusion discussed earlier in Chapter 4. We will also return to the topic in our last chapter.

A comparison of the opposite trends in economic growth in Russia and China in the early 1990s has been used to illustrate this point (Klein, 1993). Although Russia is not a Third World country, its standard of living remains low compared with other Western countries, and it has not thus far received major economic benefits from its transition from socialism to capitalism. Klein points out that, when China made moves to privatize its economy in the late 1980s and early 1990s, the entrepreneurial aspects of China's culture created an atmosphere favorable to economic development.

For example, Chinese farmers jumped at the chance to make a profit, and when the Shenzhen stock exchange opened in 1992, so many Chinese wanted to buy stock that a riot ensued. In addition, the 55 million Chinese living abroad include many successful businesspeople, eager to bring what they have learned to their homeland in the form of investment. According to Klein, 80 percent of foreign investment in China in the early 1990s came from ethnic Chinese living abroad. Russia has neither of these advantages. In contrast to China, Russians appear to lack values of entrepreneurship and distrust potential investors as speculators. One Russian manager in 1993 lamented that, "there's a philosophy here that if it's good for business, it must be bad for the country" (Watson, 1993). In Russia, foreign investment that could provide needed capital is distrusted. Undoubtedly, one reason is that it is truly "foreign": Unlike China's situation, there are not masses of ethnic Russians around the world waiting with money to invest in Russia.

Modernization theorists would hold that, despite Russia's possession of advanced technology, it will not experience a real economic takeoff until it adopts values more supportive of investment and growth. Many of them make the same point about other less-developed countries, most of which, unlike Russia, can be classified as Third World countries. This may occur through cultural diffusion, though countries such as China that have favorable values already may be better able to take advantage of the importation of technology and infusions of capital.

Despite examples such as Russia and China, modernization theory does have its critics. Certain of its arguments have not held up when researched. For example, in many countries with low levels of economic development, research has not demonstrated that people's need to achieve is any less than in more-developed countries. Moreover, there is also some evidence indicating that international investment can harm the development of Third World countries. Whatever the benefits of the diffusion of technology and cultural attributes favorable to development, there may be other effects that offset these benefits. For these reasons and others, sociological criticisms of modernization theory have increased (Chirot, 1981; Wallerstein, 1976). A major alternative to modernization theory is dependency theory, to which we now turn.

Dependency Theories

Some conflict theories argue that First World countries have developed at the expense of less-developed countries and have even pushed these countries backward. This process is called the development of underdevelopment, a name popularized in North America by Andre Gunder Frank (1969). These theories are called dependency theories because they claim that the activities of the industrialized countries keep the Third World countries in a dependent position, rather than enabling them to develop on their own. Some dependency theories argue that the "help" provided by the First World to the Third World is either disguised benefits for its own international corporations or political blackmail used to force Third World countries to support First World political goals.

World-System Theory

In North America, the most widely accepted version of dependency theory is **world-system theory,** associated with the work of Immanuel Wallerstein (1974a, 1974b, 1979, 1980, 1989; Chirot, 1981; Chirot and Hall, 1982). Wallerstein defined *world-system* as a worldwide economic and political system that includes a division of labor among different countries, as well as a stratification system among these countries. The world-system is an outgrowth of the process of *globalization* discussed in Chapter 11. As more and more economic activity occurs on an international scale, international boundaries become less important. Social inequality, economic exchange, and political and economic domination once occurred within the boundaries of particular countries. But in the world-system, they occur on a worldwide scale. Thus, for example, it makes as much sense today to talk about inequality between two different countries as it does to talk about inequality between two different groups within the same country. Wallerstein argued that the "modern world-system" began in what he called the "long sixteenth century," which ran from about 1450 to 1650 in Western Europe. During the last few centuries, this world-system expanded to encompass the entire planet. The appearance and growth of this world-system is the fundamental context for the spread of capitalism, the Industrial Revolution, and modernization.

As the modern world-system grew, it produced a division of labor among the different countries of the world. This division of labor divided the countries of the world into three major, interrelated groups. At the center are core countries, characterized by industrialization, economic diversification in secondary and tertiary production, heavy investment in foreign areas, and considerable political and economic autonomy in pursuing their own interests. Currently, the leading core countries are the United States, Germany, and Japan. Peripheral countries, in contrast, have little or no industrialization, specialize in primary production, are heavily invested in by foreign countries, and experience frequent outside interference in their political and economic affairs. Core countries use the resources of peripheral countries to enhance their own development and consequently retard the development of peripheral countries. Examples of peripheral countries are Sri Lanka, El Salvador, and Zimbabwe. In between core and periphery are semiperipheral countries that are more developed than peripheral countries but less developed than core countries. Because semiperipheral countries exploit peripheral countries even as they are exploited by core countries, they (or at least their economic elites) have a vested interest in keeping the entire system stable. Brazil, Spain, and Greece are semiperipheral countries.

It is only within this world-system that the rise and fall of states, relative rates of development, and social relations in general can be fully understood. Although the system has always had core countries, the countries in the core have varied through time. In the same way, world-system theory sees the origin of the modern nation-state as a result of the expansion of the international system. Semiperipheral countries are especially volatile, because they are typically declining former core countries or rising former peripheral countries.

Relationships Within the World-System

The basic arguments of world-system theory are that relations between core countries and peripheral countries are imperialistic and that core development and continued economic growth occur at the expense of the underdevelopment of peripheral and semiperipheral countries. Core countries use peripheral countries as sources of cheap raw materials and, increasingly, cheap labor. Thus, the objective of investment by core countries in peripheral countries is to increase profits in core countries and not to assist peripheral countries. Specifically, a large proportion of the profits generated in peripheral countries are taken out of those countries by the multinational corporations of the core countries, as discussed in Chapter 11.

World-system theory is in some regards an outgrowth of imperialism theory, first advanced by the Russian revolutionary V. I. Lenin (1916). **Imperialism** can be defined as a system in which one country uses the resources of another to its own advantage, while not giving the other country a fair return for its contribution. Lenin saw imperialism as a product of saturated markets and depleted natural resources in industrialized countries. When this occurs, banks and corporations use their influence to encourage their governments to engage in colonial expansion to secure new sources of natural resources and new markets for their products, which include not only goods but also capital investments.

In today's world, we might add two modifications to Lenin's theory. First, as multinational corporations have grown stronger, they have become less reliant on governments to engage in colonial expansion—in a sense, they do it themselves, though often still with the backing of their governments. American and European corporations, for example, have invested heavily in the oil resources of the Middle East; American companies are shifting jobs from the United States to Mexico, where wages are much lower, and Japanese companies are similarly shifting jobs to Korea, Taiwan, and other low-wage Asian countries. All of this is occurring without any actions by government to establish colonies in the Third World—indeed, most of the old colonies have gained independence. However, Western governments will still act to protect their business interests or those of their corporations. This is illustrated by the Persian Gulf War, which was fought largely to protect Western oil interests in Kuwait and Saudi Arabia.

Second, cheap labor is increasingly what multinational corporations seek in their international activities, as is illustrated by the American and Japanese job shifts described above. According to world-system theory, these kinds of investments and economic relations distort class stratification in peripheral countries. They lead to the development of a small, wealthy class that owes its position to the economic relations with core countries. In order to maintain their position, members of the wealthy class must continue to support core investment and related policies. It might be added that these patterns of economic relations also distort class stratification in core countries: A key consequence of globalization in the United States, discussed in Chapters 9 and 11, has been increased economic inequality and a shrinking middle class. Similarly, working-class institutions, such as labor unions, appear to have weakened during the era of globalization (Western, 1995).

In addition, investment in primary production (that is, the extraction of natural resources) does not lead to economic development in peripheral countries. Primary production creates relatively few jobs, and those it does create are unskilled and low-paying. Thus a large, poor working class or, in the case of agricultural production, a large class of peasants, develops. In either case the gap between rich and poor in peripheral countries increases with development—just the opposite of what happened in core countries, until recently.

Peripheral Countries and Socialist Revolution
The world-system described above helps to explain why socialist revolutions have happened mainly in peripheral or semiperipheral countries, rather than in core industrialized countries, as had been predicted by Marx. Peripheral and semiperipheral countries have vast gaps between the wealthy and the poor. Their people are aware of the internal gaps as well as the gap between their countries and the core countries. Moreover, they often trace their problems to the actions of the core countries. For these reasons, these countries are often attracted to socialist and communist philosophies. Since the Russian Revolution of 1917, nearly all socialist revolutions have occurred in Third World, peripheral countries, such as China, Cuba, Vietnam, Zimbabwe, and Nicaragua. Many other peripheral countries are leftist and sympathetic to the ideals of socialism, even though they may not have experienced socialist revolutions. Still, it should not be forgotten that part of the objective of these countries is to modernize, and that they view socialism as an alternate route to modernization.

The core countries have tended to oppose virtually all Third World socialist revolutions. In Chile in 1973, socialists who had been freely elected to lead the government were ousted by a CIA-backed coup. Ostensibly, the core countries have opposed socialist revolutions out of a desire to support democracy, but two realities suggest strongly that other motivations play an equal or greater role. In the case of Chile, Socialist president Salvador Allende was ousted and killed with American backing, and his successor, Augusto Pinochet, was a brutal dictator who ruled with an iron fist for more than a decade. Second, the response of core countries to governments of peripheral countries has in many cases depended more upon whether they were capitalist or socialist than on how democratic they were. For years the United States opposed Nicaragua's socialist Sandinista government, while supporting a capitalist government in nearby El Salvador, despite a worse record on human rights and a more repressive regime in El Salvador than could be found in Nicaragua. This suggests that, in large part, core countries oppose socialist revolutions because they threaten the assets of multinational companies based in the core countries.

Ironically, in light of Marx's theories, socialist revolutions that occur in peripheral or semiperipheral countries may be reversed by capitalist revolutions once those countries reach a certain level of modernization and industrialization. This has happened in the Soviet Union, and nearly happened in the Tiananmen Square uprising in China in 1989. Moreover, China's economy has become increasingly capitalist, despite its continued authoritarian government and Marxist ideology. Investment by multinational corporations has been encouraged in recent years; much of its farming has been privatized; and, as noted earlier, a stock exchange was opened in 1992. Also, the country's system of stratification has become increasingly tied to market forces, according to recent sociological research (Nee, 1996). Vietnam, too, has become increasingly capitalistic, particularly in the southern part of the country, which had been capitalist prior to the departure of U.S. troops in 1975. These examples make an important point: In some cases, economic systems established by socialist revolutions may become quite capitalist without capitalist revolutions such as Russia's in 1991. Eastern Europe experienced a particularly swift series of capitalist revolutions in 1989 and 1990. But there, socialism had been imposed by the Soviet Union, not established by revolution—and hence never had the constituency it had elsewhere.

Foreign Aid and International Loans

From the standpoint of world-system theory, foreign aid, loans from the International Monetary Fund (IMF), and development loans from private banks are all forms of imperialism because they require the recipient to buy goods and supplies from the lending country and to follow certain economic and political policies. Thus, foreign aid ensures large markets for firms in core countries. To some extent, it is also designed to ensure large profits for banks in the form of interest on development loans. This is one cause of the current debt crisis. So much money has been loaned to developing countries that their failure to repay the loans could lead to the collapse of major core banks. The lack of development in these countries, on the other hand, has made many of them unable to pay their loans. Ironically, this crisis gives some control to debtor countries and forces core countries to take some interest in peripheral development in order to protect their money.

World-System Theory: An Analysis

A good deal of empirical research supports some aspects of world-system theory. Snyder and Kick (1979) analyzed international networks of trade, military intervention, diplomatic ties, and treaty memberships to see if they could verify the existence of the global division of labor postulated by world-system theory. They found that countries did fall into three groups, and that each of the three groups of countries had development patterns described by world-system theory.

Heavy foreign investment, presence of international corporations, and concentration on raw material production (especially in agriculture) do seem to slow development in Third World countries (Bornschier and Chase-Dunn, 1985). Core countries are developing faster than peripheral countries. Thus, the gap between rich and poor countries continues to widen (Breedlove and Nolan, 1988). This is consistent with the view that international relations work to the advantage of the First and Second Worlds and to the disadvantage of the Third World. Also as predicted by world-system theory, modernization and industrialization have had opposite effects on internal inequality in core and peripheral countries. In core countries, as we saw in Chapter 11, industrialization has led to a *decrease* in inequality. In peripheral countries, however, inequality has *increased* (Chirot, 1986; Nolan, 1987). But even though this is true, there is also evidence that (1) growth benefits everyone to some extent, by leading to improvements in the overall national welfare (Firebaugh and Beck, 1994), and (2) even core countries may experience increased inequality as they move beyond industrialization into the postindustrial stage.

Finally, Wimberley (1990) has shown—using mortality level as his indicator of well-being—that in peripheral countries with higher levels of involvement by multinational corporations from the core countries, the people of the peripheral countries are worse off. This supports the view of world-system theory that involvement by multinational corporations inhibits the development of a higher standard of living in Third World countries. It also challenges the view of modernization theory that the importation of technology and capital will improve the standard of living in these countries.

Critiques of World-System Theory

Dependency theories are not without criticism. Bairoch (1986) and O'Brien (1982) challenge the argument that imperialism was necessary for the origin of the capitalist world-system. They find that, at most, the raw materials taken from early colonies sped up the development of the core countries but were not crucial to it. They do not, however, dispute the contention that colonization may have had some harmful effects on the development of colonial areas. This suggests that Lenin's theory, and hence a major portion of world-system theory, may describe *what* happened but not *why* it happened.

World-system theory has also been criticized for an overemphasis on economic factors and a relative neglect of class, politics, culture, and gender (Brenner, 1977; Evans et al., 1985; Denemark, 1992; Ward, 1984, 1988; M. Zeitlin, 1984). Some recent research also suggests that the size of a country's economy has a more significant effect than its level of development on how it fits into the world-system (Van Rossem, 1996). Despite these criticisms, a major contribution of this theory has been to prompt sociologists to look carefully at historical and international aspects of social change. It has also raised important questions about the assumption that the importation of capital and technology leads to economic development, even if many of these questions remain less than fully answered.

Terrorism: A Challenge to Government

Occasionally, either social movements (which we will discuss at length in Chapter 15) or their opponents turn to **terrorism**: the use of violence, usually against civilian targets, as a means of intimidation through fear. Terrorism can be committed either by clandestine organizations or by governments, or by the two in cooperation. Clandestine organizations that commit terrorism are usually associated with insurgent groups, militant and highly ideological protest groups that are generally, but not always, revolutionary in nature. Significantly, these groups tend to be made up of—or at least led by—relatively well-educated rebels, not the very poor (Radu, 1987, p. 300). Usually, they are acting on behalf of an ideology, and they tend to be both "true believers" and "ideological purists" who see their own views as "correct" and see those who disagree with them as being "in need of education." In many cases, terrorist groups form among ethnic or religious separatists or nationalists who seek to create their own state apart from the larger society in which they live. Examples of separatist or nationalist movements that have led to terrorism are Osama bin Laden's Al-Qaeda network, based on fundamentalist Islamic nationalism; French-speaking separatists in Quebec, Canada; Basque separatists in Spain; and some elements among Palestinians seeking to create a homeland in the Middle East. Countermovement groups such as the Ku Klux Klan, various neo-Nazi and "skinhead" organizations, and some segments of the antigovernment militia movement have also used terrorism. In fact, groups of this type have been an important source of terrorist actions within the United States (Oakley, 1987), as illustrated by the 1995 Oklahoma City bombing. In contrast to insurgent groups, members of these groups tend to be poor and relatively uneducated, although their leaders might have somewhat higher levels of education. An example of countermovement terrorism in the United States is the 1993 murder by an antiabortion activist of Dr. David Gunn, a physician who performed abortions at a Florida clinic.

Terrorist groups tend to be limited in the types of violence in which they engage. The most common forms of terrorism by insurgent groups are bombings, assassinations, armed assaults, kidnappings, hostage taking, and hijackings (Jenkins, 1982).

Recently, terrorism, particularly in the form of bombings and other large-scale attacks, has increased in the United States and become much more deadly. These attacks have been carried out by both international and domestic terrorists. The most obvious example is the September 11, 2001, attack on the World Trade Center and the Pentagon using hijacked airliners, which caused over 3,000 fatalities. Other examples include the 1995 bombing of the Murrah Federal Building in Oklahoma City, which killed 168 people; the 1993 World Trade Center bombing; and the bombings at the Atlanta Olympics and at an Atlanta abortion clinic in 1996. While all of these attacks occurred on U.S. soil, there have also been attacks against U.S. interests overseas, including bombings of the U.S.S. *Cole* in the port of Yemen in 2000 and bombings of two U.S. embassies in Kenya and Tanzania, in Africa, in 1998. The embassy bombings took 224 lives. In addition, a number of terrorism plots, both domestic and international, were discovered and foiled in the 1990s, around the date of the millennium, and since the attacks on September 11, including a failed attempt to blow up a passenger airliner over Detroit on Christmas day 2009. It appears that international terrorist networks like Al-Qaeda became better funded and better organized in the 1990s, and domestic terrorism also increased during this period. Since then, their operations have been greatly disrupted, but they have also spread to essentially every country on the globe. Both antigovernment militia groups and racist youth "skinhead" groups gained strength in the late 1980s and early 1990s, and both kinds of groups accounted for a growing number of violent attacks. (For information on "skinheads," see Hamm, 1993.)

Governments and Terrorism

Terrorism is also committed by governments. Often, government terrorism takes the form of countermovement terrorism: an attempt to intimidate its opponents or critics. Countermovement terrorism

GLOBAL SOCIOLOGY

"Jihad" Versus "McWorld": The Battle Between Globalism and Tribalism

Political scientist Benjamin Barber (1996) sees grave threats to democracy in both economic globalization (which he calls "McWorld") and fundamentalist tribalism (which he calls "Jihad"). He calls globalization "McWorld" because of the worldwide standardization and control it brings, linking it to the "McDonaldization" process discussed by Ritzer. And he uses "Jihad" *not* in the traditional Islamic meaning of "struggle for justice" but rather in the more warlike sense of the word that has been expropriated by extremist and terrorist organizations. However, it refers not to Islam or to any other religion, but rather to narrow, tribal, and warlike tendencies associated with religious fundamentalism and tribal nationalism in all parts of the world. In this sense, it applies equally to the terrorists behind the September 11 attacks, the right-wing extremists who bombed the Murrah Building in Oklahoma City, and groups like the "Army of God" who bomb abortion clinics and gay bars.

Writing *before* the Seattle protests against globalization and *before* the September 11, 2001, attacks, Barber warned that the twenty-first century would likely be a century of battle between the forces of "McWorld" and the forces of "Jihad." He sees both as threats to democracy, because both undermine democracy by undermining the nation-state. "McWorld" (globalization) does so by taking power away from any individual country and giving it to worldwide economic forces. Thus, the impersonal force of the global market erodes every nation's ability to democratically determine its future. "Jihad," on the other hand, undermines democracy by taking power away from nation-states, as they are fragmented into warring ethnic and religious factions. Thus, the Soviet Union was split into dozens of ethnically based countries, many of which still fail to function because they are torn apart by internal ethnic conflict. French Canadians demand that Quebec become independent, and Canadian Indians demand that if it does, they have the right to become independent from it. Former Yugoslavia is torn apart by conflict among Serbs, Albanians, Croatians, and Bosnian Muslims. And conflict in Rawanda between Hutus and Tutsis led to the genocidal murder of hundreds of thousands. Regarding the threat to democracy posed by both "Jihad" and "McWorld," Barber states the following:

---

is most common in authoritarian and totalitarian governments. Sometimes, however, democratic countries contribute to it, through their support of "friendly" authoritarian governments, as in the case of United States support of El Salvador, discussed below. The most common kinds of terrorism by governments are political executions, death squads, torture, imprisonment without trial, and military attacks against civilian targets. In El Salvador, for example, 37,000 political murders were documented by human rights organizations affiliated with the Archdiocese of San Salvador during the period from 1979 to 1984 (Neier, 1985). These murders were committed by government security forces and by paramilitary organizations working with them. Despite this terrorism, the Salvadoran government received strong political and economic support from the U.S. government.

Governments can also assist insurgent groups in other countries as, for example, Iran has in Lebanon, and Libya and probably the Taliban regime in Afghanistan have done in the United States. However, governments do not usually engage directly in insurgent terrorism; rather, they assist underground terrorist organizations who carry out the actual attacks. Governments also engage in terrorism when they attempt to intimidate their military opponents by bombing entirely civilian targets. This has been done by both democratic and authoritarian governments. Significantly, this type of terrorism rarely has the intended effect. For example, Germany's saturation bombing of London appears only to have intensified British resolve and hatred of the Nazis; much the same appears to have been true in the case of Allied saturation bombing of German

> Jihad forges communities...that slight democracy in favor of tyrannical paternalism or consensual tribalism. McWorld forges global markets rooted in consumption and profit, leaving to an untrustworthy...invisible hand issues of public interest and common good that once might have been nurtured by democratic citizenries and their watchful governments.
>
> Perhaps most disturbing, Barber argues that McWorld and Jihad are each to some degree a product of the other. In Barber's words, "Jihad not only revolts against but abets McWorld, while McWorld not only imperils but recreates and reinforces Jihad. They produce their contraries and need one another." Although Barber wrote before the September 11 attacks, what happened after the attacks illustrates his argument well. Americans rallied around their economic and political system, and protests against globalization consequently fizzled. Massive aid was given by Congress to the very companies at the center of globalization. Seen as an attack on the modern way of life, the terrorism not only stopped criticism of globalization, but created an international coalition of all "global powers"—the United States, United Kingdom, France, Canada, Russia, and Japan. With the global economy so based in these countries, globalization could not help but benefit. At the same time, however, Jihad was strengthened by the same chain of events. The attempts by the West to incapacitate the terrorists and the Taliban in Afghanistan were seen by the extremist, fundamentalist wing of Islam as yet another attempt by the godless West to destroy Islam and impose its way of life on Muslims. The subsequent Iraq War further reinforced this viewpoint. Hence, it became easier for them to recruit more moderate Muslims to their extremist points of view. This, of course, was merely an extension of what was already happening before the attacks: Islamic fundamentalists needed an enemy in order to rally people to their cause, and they found it in the godless economic forces of the global economy that threatened to overwhelm their traditional way of life. In this regard, they are not so different from extreme Christian fundamentalists or right-wing patriot groups in the United States, who draw recruits by warning that the godless New World Order threatens their traditional way of life.
>
> Finally, even though McWorld and Jihad need each other as mortal enemies, they also each borrow from and partake of one another when it suits their purposes to do so. For example, both Muslim and Christian fundamentalists use the Internet and worldwide mass media to communicate and promote their message, and Internet service providers (ISPs) are happy to provide them Web sites to do so, for a monthly fee. And California businessmen formed a joint venture with the Russian Orthodox Church, known as Saint Springs Water Company, to produce and sell bottled water with a religious marketing theme.
>
> This box is based on Benjamin R. Barber, 1996, *Jihad vs. McWorld: How Globalism and Tribalism Are Reshaping the World*. New York: Ballantine Books.

cities such as Dresden (U.S. Strategic Bombing Survey, 1947). Critics of the United States war in Iraq characterized the 2003 campaign of "shock and awe" at the start of the war as nothing more than state terrorism.

A final point is that the word "terrorism" is an emotionally charged term. For this reason, both governments and advocacy groups tend to characterize their opponents as "terrorists" and their supporters as "freedom fighters" or "defenders of the nation." Yet, according to experts on terrorism, it is the *behavior, not the cause,* that defines terrorism (Jenkins, 1980). Attacks on civilian rather than military targets are terrorism, no matter who commits them. Thus, for example, both Palestinian bombing attacks on Israeli civilians and Israeli attacks on Palestinian refugee camps are properly classified as terrorism (Jenkins, 1980, p. 2).

Terrorism in the Modern World

Although—as shown in this chapter's "Sociological Surprises" box—terrorism has a long history, it has become more common and deadly since about 1970. Not only has the number of terrorist incidents risen dramatically, but the attacks are increasingly directed against people rather than property. In the 1980s, about half of all terrorist attacks were directed against people, far more than in the early 1970s. Moreover, the number of attacks indiscriminately aimed at innocent bystanders, such as large bombs in cars, trucks, and airport lockers, has increased (Jenkins, 1987) for several reasons. First, today's international economy requires world travel and world trade on a massive scale. This makes it virtually impossible to screen out every potential terrorist. Second, the

SOCIOLOGICAL SURPRISES
Terrorism: Not as New as We Think

The building lay in a smoldering pile of rubble, as emergency workers frantically dug to find survivors inside. Although a few badly injured survivors were found, hope faded as the rescuers mainly found dead bodies, many charred by the flames that accompanied the building's collapse. In reading this, you may be reminded of the World Trade Center in 2001 or perhaps the Murrah Federal Building in Oklahoma City in 1995. But the description also fits the offices of the *Los Angeles Times* on October 1, 1910. On that day, a dynamite bomb had been planted next to the building, causing a wall to collapse. This, in turn, caused the second floor, laden with heavy printing machinery, to collapse on the workers on the first floor. Twenty-one people were killed, and others were maimed for life. Apparently, the bombing was related to citywide labor strife occurring at the time; two union activists later pled guilty. This case, from 1910, shows that, while terrorism is considered a plague of the present era, it is in fact nothing new. In fact, while terrorism today may be deadlier than in the past because of the vulnerability of our massive urban populations, it has been used in many forms for many purposes throughout human history.

In the days after the September 11, 2001, terrorist attacks, many Americans were again terrified when anthrax spores were sent through the mail, causing several deaths. But again, there is nothing new about germ warfare. Earlier in American history, the American Indian population was decimated by epidemics of European diseases such as smallpox to which Indian people were highly vulnerable. Because they had not previously encountered these diseases, their populations had not built up immunity over time in the ways that the Europeans had. In most cases, the exposure was accidental. But in some cases, it was intentional—what today we would call bioterrorism. For example, British soldiers in the French and Indian War gave Indians blankets that they knew were contaminated with smallpox, with the deliberate intention of giving them the disease (Thornton, 1987). While this appears to have been the action of individuals and did not represent British army policy, it nonetheless constitutes an action strikingly similar to mailing people envelopes with anthrax. In fact, anthrax itself may have been used as a biological weapon as long as two thousand years ago: ancient Greek, Assyrian, and Roman soldiers used carcasses of animals that had died of anthrax to poison wells (Hampel, 2001).

The use of bioterrorism against American Indians illustrates another point: Terrorism is not always committed by insurgent groups trying to upend society. Sometimes, it is used by members of dominant groups in society to terrify and intimidate minority groups. Besides the exposure of Indians to smallpox, another example can be seen in the use of lynching by white Americans to intimidate African Americans at various points in U.S. history. In the last sixteen years of the nineteenth century, for example, over 2,500 lynchings occurred in the United States. The great majority of these occurred in the South, and the victims were usually black. Although the frequency of lynchings decreased over time, there were cases as recently as sixty years ago in which African American males, sometimes as young as fourteen, were kidnapped and murdered for offenses as minor as "talking fresh" to a white woman. Certainly, by any reasonable judgment, this fits our definition of terrorism presented earlier in the chapter: "the use of violence, usually against civilian targets, as a means of intimidation through fear." It is the act, not the purpose or the technology used to perpetrate the act, that defines terrorism. And by that definition, terrorism has been around for a long time, has occurred in a variety of forms, and has been used for a variety of purposes, both in the United States and elsewhere.

development of modern mass media gives terrorists a way to get attention and instill fear—much of what they do is done for the benefit of the television cameras. The effectiveness of terrorism in instilling fear can be seen, for example, in the massive drop in U.S. tourism to Europe during the summer of 1986 after terrorist attacks on U.S. military personnel in Europe and the retaliatory raids on Libya; and again in the sharp drop in travel within the United States in the fall of 2001 after the World Trade Center and Pentagon attacks. Finally, the relative openness of today's industrial democracies makes them especially vulnerable to terrorism. You cannot prevent people from committing terrorism without curtailing personal freedom. For example, we now accept more extensive personal searches than ever before, as part of the cost of making air travel safer.

In spite of all this, terrorism must be kept in perspective. At least four out of five terrorist incidents involve no deaths (Jenkins, 1987, p. 353), and the number of incidents that result in many deaths is surprisingly small. Between 1900 and 1985, only seven incidents involved 100 or more deaths, and only a dozen or so involved 50 to 99 deaths (Jenkins, 1987, p. 353). The consequences of terrorism have been substantial in two regards, however. First, many public officials have been killed by political assassins, including the prime ministers or presidents of India, Sweden, Egypt, Israel, and Pakistan, in just the past three decades. Thus, an individual or a small group of terrorists can and often does overrule established law in the choice of government leaders. Second, terrorism invokes fear, which does influence people's behavior. And there is no doubt that the massive fatalities that occurred in a few recent terrorist attacks, particularly on September 11, 2001, have provoked considerable fear and changed behavior, particularly travel routines, in significant ways.

As the economy has globalized and international travel has become increasingly commonplace, the United States has become more vulnerable to international terrorism such as the September 11, 2001, attacks. (AP Photo/Jerry Torrens)

Who Is Vulnerable to Insurgent Terrorism?

In general, the countries that have been most vulnerable to insurgent terrorism are those that are either relatively democratic (Western European nations, the United States, and Japan) or that lack effective central governments (in different periods of time, Lebanon and several countries in eastern Europe). Countries that routinely have a large number of foreign visitors are particularly vulnerable to international terrorism.

It is true that the incidence of terrorism may now be on the increase in the United States. Certainly, there have been more dramatic and deadly incidents in recent years, such as the 2001 attack on the World Trade Center and Pentagon, and the earlier bombings of the World Trade Center (1993), the Murrah Federal Building in Oklahoma City (1995), and Atlanta's Olympic Centennial Park (1996). Despite the massive casualties in the 2001 attack, there have been fewer incidents of terrorism in the United States than in many other countries, including France, Great Britain, Russia, and Israel, where such attacks occur with great regularity. The United States has been the target of many terrorist acts, but most of them have occurred elsewhere, mainly in Europe and in the Middle East (Jenkins, 1982). The attack on the U.S.S. *Cole* in Yemen in 2000 is typical of this pattern. The United States is relatively isolated, sharing borders with only two foreign countries. European countries have far more foreign visitors relative to their population and are thus more frequently infiltrated by international terrorists. However, the relative safety of the United States may be decreasing for two reasons. First, there has been an increase in domestic terrorism in the past couple decades. Second, the volume of international travel to the United States has grown dramatically as the economy has globalized.

The countries that have been most free of insurgent terrorism have been authoritarian and totalitarian countries that systematically and effectively repress dissent. In countries where individual rights are disregarded, terrorism is more easily detected and suppressed. As authoritarian regimes such as the former Soviet Union have broken down, terrorism has increased—indeed it has become commonplace in Russia since the collapse of the Soviet Union. In a sense, it could be said that the risk of terrorism is one of the prices of freedom.

Theories About the Causes of Terrorism

The previous section suggests one possible reason for the increase in terrorism in recent years: As more societies have become more free, and the economy has become more global, terrorism has become more common (Johnson, 1987). Thus, terrorism could be explained from a functionalist standpoint as a predictable dysfunction of modern democratic societies and of a global economy. In recent years, sociologists have devoted increasing effort to developing more specific theories that account for the spread of terrorism. One problem with this effort is that different kinds of terrorism—insurgent terrorism verses countermovement terrorism, for example—may have different causes. Two things that are generally agreed upon: (1) terrorism is influenced by some of the same principles that influence other forms of collective action (a topic that will be examined in detail in our final chapter), and (2) terrorists generally have grievances. However, most collective action does not involve terrorism, and people do not usually resort to terrorism when they have grievances. Moreover, both grievances and collective action have been commonplace throughout human history, but terrorism, though it has been around for a long time, has become common and more deadly in recent decades (Johnson, 1987). Social scientists attribute this in part to the opportunities presented by modern democratic societies, but other explanations have been suggested as well.

One theory of terrorism proposed by Vester (1990) is based on various theories of *postmodernism*, which are also discussed in other chapters. He argues that as social movements have become less coherent and structured, they have become more fragmented and more expressive as opposed to instrumental. He sees this as reflective of the postmodern condition, in which no one system of knowing is generally accepted. Just as fragmentation has occurred in the larger society, it has occurred among social movements. In this context, it is significant to note that terrorism is often committed by small groups that have broken off from the larger movements with which they are associated. Examples of these groups are the smaller, more violence-prone elements of the larger militia movement in the United States, or the offshoot groups of the Palestine Liberation Organization (PLO) that reject its negotiated agreements with Israel.

One common thread of all these theories is that terrorism is in part a product of contemporary social conditions. If democracy, technology, and the postmodern condition all contribute, in their own ways, to the spread of terrorism, it may well be that terrorism is to some extent an inevitable feature of contemporary life.

Can Terrorism Be Combated?

Can anything be done about terrorism? Briefly, the answer is yes, but at a cost. Effective dictatorships do not usually have problems with terrorism, as we already noted. But a free government, unwilling to engage in terrorism itself, probably cannot entirely prevent terrorism. Arresting terrorists reduces the incidence of terrorism (Laqueur, 1987), at least in the short term. This is particularly true if arrests come swiftly as they did after the 1993 World Trade Center bombing and the Oklahoma City bombing. Yet, if only some of the terrorists are arrested, the result may be reprisals by their collaborators. Acts of retaliation against terrorists may convince them that the costs of their actions are too great, as may well have happened when the United States made raids against Libya's Ghadafi in reprisal for his support of anti-American terrorists. Still, reprisals can lead to new incidents of terrorism, as is illustrated by the cycle of violence between Israelis and Palestinians. Experts do agree on one thing: It is clearly unwise to threaten acts of reprisal and then fail to carry them out (Whitaker, 1985).

According to Brophy-Bearmann and Conybeare (1994), rational expectations theory predicts that retaliations that are unexpected are the most effective in deterring future terrorism, since terrorists take into account the expected actions of authorities in making their plans. And their research suggests that unexpected retaliations, such as the unexpectedly large Israeli retaliation for the massacre at the 1972 Munich Olympics, do temporarily deter further terrorism. However, such retaliations do not seem to have much long-term effect (Brophy-Bearmann and Conybeare, 1994).

There is an expert consensus on two other points. First, the opportunities for terrorism should be decreased, by instituting better security at airports and potential targets such as embassies, and by improving intelligence gathering (Whitaker, 1985). There is no doubt that improved intelligence-gathering has prevented a number of terrorist attacks since September 11, 2001. Second, although negotiations with terrorists are essential in many cases, it is unwise to give in to their demands because this only gives them an incentive to commit more terrorism. However, when government leaders are genuinely concerned about freeing hostages, the temptation to make concessions to terrorists can be great, as even President Reagan came to discover when he sold arms to Iran in an effort to free American hostages held by pro-Iranian groups in Lebanon.

Although terrorism can be reduced, the reality is that in democratic societies operating in a worldwide economy, it cannot be eliminated entirely. Moreover, attempts to eliminate it can threaten the freedoms that are valued in democratic societies. In the United States, for example, many provisions of a congressional terrorism bill proposed after the 1995 Oklahoma City bombing provoked intense debate, with critics arguing that such provisions would infringe on the constitutional rights and freedoms of Americans. Furthermore, additional antiterrorism measures have been enacted since the September 11, 2001, attacks, and some of these have been seen by a rather wide spectrum of political-opinion holders as threatening to civil liberties. Among the most controversial were changes that ease legal limits on telephone wiretaps and intercepts of e-mail and that allow noncitizens to be held without charges for extended periods of time. Concerns were also raised over the government's plans to use secret military tribunals to try some international terrorists—the first use of such tribunals in the United States since World War II—and action by the Justice Department calling in thousands of immigrants and international students in the United States for "voluntary questioning." Some saw the questioning of Middle Eastern immigrants and students, many of whom had done nothing to raise suspicion, as a form of racial profiling.

In Great Britain, where terrorism has been more frequent than in the United States and where there is no absolute constitutional guarantee of free speech, strong concerns have been raised about actions taken to prevent terrorism. For example, a 1988 government policy banned media coverage of terrorists and terrorism in the United Kingdom, an action that clearly limited the free exchange of information and, in the eyes of some, the public's right to know what was occurring (Kenney, 1992).

A final concern is to avoid actions in international relations that may lead to more terrorism. Clearly, much resentment was generated against the United States in the Arab and Muslim worlds because of sanctions against Iraq in the 1990s that harmed civilians by limiting the availability of food and medicine but did nothing to weaken the government of Saddam Hussein, which was the real target of the sanctions. These feelings were obviously reinforced in 2003 by the U.S. decision to invade Iraq despite the absence of any authorization from the United Nations for such an attack. Resentment was also generated by the failure of the United States to speak forcefully against Israeli attacks on Palestinian refugee camps in Lebanon, and because the weapons used in these and other Israeli actions against Arabs were U.S. made. Importantly, resentment is different from terrorism, and most who oppose a policy do not resort to terrorism. However, the resentments do make it easier for extremists, like bin Laden, to recruit new members into the terrorist networks.

A final concern is *blowback*—the unintentional side effects of policies and actions overseas that can occur years later. As is discussed in the box "Is bin Laden's Terrorist Network a Case of Blowback?" many of the military and organizational resources that the Tailban and Al Quaeda network are today using against the United States were originally provided by the United States because in the 1980s, their predecessors were waging war against America's then-enemy, the Soviet Union.

Summary

Political power and authority in the United States are not divided equally among the population. There are various forms of power. Legitimate power is power the others accept, and in the United States, a good deal of power channels through the political system by way of voting, lobbying, campaigning, and so on. But power is an abstract concept and difficult to measure. It is often executed through positions of authority, expertise, charisma, or long-standing practices. Power may also be exercised through (sometimes) less legitimate forms of power such as force, coercion, or the control of information. Wealth and income are also closely related to power; sociologists debate to what extent America is a pluralistic society, made up of a

SOCIOLOGICAL INSIGHTS
Is bin Laden's Terrorist Network a Case of Blowback?

UCLA cultural studies specialist Douglas Kellner (2001) argues that a useful concept for understanding the September 11, 2001, terrorist attacks is the concept of *blowback*. The term "blowback" was first used by agents of the Central Intelligence Agency (CIA) to describe the unintended (and sometimes delayed) effects of covert operations. Although invented by CIA agents, the concept of blowback has received increased attention in recent years from social researchers who study international relations (Johnson, 2000). The basic idea is that actions set in motion events that can often have long-term effects quite different from what was intended at the time the actions were taken.

In the case of the September 11 terrorism, Kellner sees a case of blowback dating from U.S. support of the Afghan Mujahedeen, a largely religious-based guerilla movement that sought to throw the Soviet Union out of Afghanistan during the 1980s. In fact, the roots of the Mujahedeen went back to at least 1979, when a socialist (but not Soviet-created) government gained power in Afghanistan. The Mujahedeen opposed that government, largely because of the government's modernist tendencies, which went against the Mujahedeen's fundamentalist beliefs. At that time, the Mujahedeen was receiving money from both the CIA (which also opposed the socialist government) and Libya's Muammar Ghadafi, labeled by the U.S. government as a state sponsor of terrorism.

When the socialist government was overturned in late 1979 by a military coup, the Soviet Union invaded to keep a socialist government in place, and to prevent a government that might favor either the United States or Muslim fundamentalists from forming. After this happened, the CIA increased its support of the Mujahedeen, in order to oppose the Soviet invasion and to entrap the Soviet Union in a difficult, no-win war. Up to $40 billion was funneled by the United States and Saudi Arabia to the rebels, who included Osama bin Laden and many of the others who later would become the Al-Qaeda terrorist network. The funding included "training and arming radical Islamic groups who would emerge with a desire to fight other great wars for Islam" (Kellner, 2001).

After a ten-year war, the Soviet Union was ousted from Afghanistan in 1989. The costs of this war, and the internal dissent it created, are credited by some as major factors in the eventual demise of communism in the Soviet Union. So in this sense, the support of the Mujahedeen could be seen as successful. However, this success came at a terrible price: the support, training, and arming of what would become the terrorist network that would kill over 3,000 Americans on September 11, 2001. And today in Afghanistan, U.S. troops are fighting some of the same guerrilla fighters that they were training two decades ago.

In addition, this situation was compounded by one further major error, according to Kellner. Distracted by other concerns, including the Persian Gulf War, the United States and other Western countries simply left Afghanistan to fare on its own after the Soviets were expelled in 1989. In Kellner's words, the administration of George H. W. Bush "decided to completely pull out of Afghanistan, rather than working to build democracy and a viable government in that country." Civil war resulted, and with the backing of Pakistan, the Taliban—composed of the most extremist elements of the Mujahedeen and apparently including non-Afghan terrorists, such as Osama bin Laden (a Saudi Arabian)—won the civil war and gained control of the government. Thus, the Taliban and Al-Qaeda were helped to come into power both by the support and training they received from the United States to throw out the Soviets and by the power vacuum that was created when the Western countries left Afghanistan to fend for itself with no outside help after the Soviets withdrew.

None of this, of course, is to say that anyone but the terrorists are responsible for what happened on September 11. But the history of Afghanistan does present a sobering lesson on *blowback*—how unintended effects of actions taken can contribute to tragic events many years later. Had the religious extremists not been backed in their efforts to throw out the Soviets, or had help been provided to create a more representative government after the Soviets were thrown out, the Taliban, bin Laden, and Al-Qaeda would not have been as likely to be in a position to be able to commit the terrible acts of September 11.

competing group of varied interests, as opposed to an elite-dominated society in which the interests of a wealthy few predominate over the rest of society through their use of power.

Political systems start with the state, the one institution that holds a monopoly on the use of legitimate violence in society. There are three main kinds of states: democracies, dictatorships, and monarchies. States have also greatly expanded their scopes of activity in the last two centuries, including increased focus on improving the welfare of citizens. Thus, contemporary nation-states, especially wealthy nations, are often referred to as welfare states. Three types of welfare states are often identified: liberal, like the United States or Canada; corporatist-statist, like Japan or Germany; or social democratic, like Sweden and Norway.

Political systems are shaped by ideologies. In the United States, the most common breakdown of political ideologies consists of conservatives, moderates, and liberals. Political parties often spring up around ideologies as their basis of support, or possibly around special interests that are linked to one ideology or another. In the United States, liberals tend to be Democrats and conservatives tend to be Republicans, but both parties have some representation of the other ideological extreme and moderate wings as well. The most powerful special interest groups are those tied to the wealthy or to large segments of the population like the elderly, gun owners, and the Chamber of Commerce. Through lobbyists, these groups wield an enormous, some would say inordinate, amount of power in our political system. Possibly due to that unequal distribution of power in our society, major social groups along class, race, and gender lines vote in varying degrees of regularity. In general, the more powerful and privileged the group, the more often its members participate in political life, and the more influence they exercise. Some say this reflects the power of the groups involved, while others argue it simply reflects the fact that powerful groups have more at stake. Whatever the reason, voters in the United States vote in much lower percentages than in most other democracies.

Despite the rapid rate of change in societies in the past century, different states remain at different levels of development. Sociologists have developed systems for classifying countries according to a variety of factors related to economic development, as well as diverse theories to account for differences among countries. Modernization theories, which draw heavily from the functionalist perspective, argue that the less-developed nations will pursue a path similar to that of the developed nations and will enjoy similar benefits. Dependency theories, which reflect the conflict perspective, maintain that the imperialistic policies of the developed nations keep the less-developed nations in a dependent state in which they serve as markets and sources of raw materials for the developed nations. One form of dependency theory, the world-system theory, sees all the world's economies as part of a worldwide system dominated by the developed, or core, nations. Dependency theories help to explain the preponderance of socialist revolutions in the Third World, and they argue that traditional foreign policies such as investment and foreign aid to less-developed countries will increase rather than solve their problems.

One of the most pressing concerns for nations such as the United States is terrorism, made all the more critical since the attacks on New York and Washington, D.C., in 2001. Although terrorism has been around for centuries, it has become more deadly in recent decades. One deadly form of terrorism is government terrorism against its own citizens. Insurgent terrorism has taken growing numbers of lives in recent decades and has had significant effects in terms of changing people's routines and creating fear. Terrorism has also led to the loss of a number of important world leaders through assassination. Short of creating dictatorships that lead to government terrorism, insurgent terrorism probably cannot be entirely prevented, although certain actions can be taken to reduce its impact and frequency.

Key Terms

power
legitimate power
authority
traditional authority
legal-rational authority
charismatic authority
expertise
credentials

pluralist model
veto group
power elite model
multinational corporations
the state
welfare state
democracy
dictatorship
monarchy
means tested benefits
universal benefits
liberal
conservative
moderate
special interest groups
lobbyists
political action committee (PAC)
modernization theory
dependency theories
world-system theory
imperialism
terrorism

Exercises

1. Considering the discussion of power in the early part of this chapter and the unusual way in which American elections work, would you say that the United States is a democracy? How would you define democracy? What would have to change in the United States for the country to not be a democracy (if you think it is) or for it to become one (if you think it is not)?

2. Typically, Democrats are labeled as being in favor of "big government," and Republicans are labeled as being in favor of "small government." Can you think of any instances in which Democrats are typically in favor of smaller government than Republicans? Can you think of examples in which Republicans are typically in favor of bigger government than Democrats? What are the underlying social values that lead the parties to take the views that they take in the examples you chose?

Chapter 13
Marriages and Families

Family and Marriage Defined — 398
- Extended and Nuclear Families   399
- Family Memberships   400
- Marriage Patterns   400
- Mate Selection   401
- Romantic Love and Mate Selection   402

Patterns Within Marriages — 405
- Power and Authority in Marriages   405
- Residency Patterns   406
- Inheritance and Descent Patterns   407

Functions of Families — 408
- Changing Functions   408
- The Family as a Regulator of Sexual Behavior   409

A Conflict Analysis of the Family — 411
- Role Inequality Within the Family   411
- Violence in the Family and in Courtship   412
- The Family in the Larger Social Structure   414

Changing Patterns of Marriages and Families — 414
- Changing Roles Within Marriages   415
- Delayed Marriage and Permanent Singlehood   415
- Cohabitation   416
- Gay and Lesbian Couples   417
- Fewer Children, No Children   420

Marital Disruption and Divorce — 421
- Divorce in the United States   421
- Causes of Divorce   422
- Changing Divorce Laws   423

PUTTING SOCIOLOGY TO WORK — 424
- Should Couples Stay Together "for the Sake of the Kids"?   424
- Remarriage   426

Single-Parent Families — 427
- Race, Poverty, and the One-Parent Family   428

The Future of Marriages and Families — 431

Summary — 432

Key Terms — 432

Exercises — 433

"Surrogate Mother Refuses to Give Up Baby"
"One-Quarter of Conceptions End in Abortion"
"Working Moms Lobby Legislature for Day-Care Assistance"
"More than Half of All Marriages End in Divorce"
"Researchers Find Higher Cancer Risk with More Sexual Partners"
"Fewer than One-Fourth of Households Are Married Couples with Children"
"Iowa Supreme Court Rules Gay Marriage Ban Unconstitutional"
"Four in Ten Babies Born Outside Marriage"

Headlines such as these reflect our growing concern, disagreement, and, sometimes, anger over changes in the family. Only forty years ago, things were quite different. Surrogate mothers and AIDS were unknown, abortion was illegal in most states, and openness about sexuality still made many people uncomfortable. Fewer women worked outside the home, and more couples stayed married for a lifetime. The changes that have affected marriage and families over the past forty years are almost overwhelming.

Despite this rapid social change, the family is one subject students often believe they already know all about. After all, the vast majority of people have had firsthand experience of at least one family. But in fact, most people have only limited knowledge of families precisely because their beliefs about the family are formed largely from their own experiences. Their personal background does little to prepare them for the wide diversity of families, even within their own society.

Try, for example, to answer the following questions. Do marriages in which the bride is pregnant have a higher risk of divorce? Has love always been the main reason for marriage? Do the majority of American children today live with stepparents? In the past, did the majority of adult Americans live with other relatives besides their spouse and children? When it comes to marriage, do "opposites attract"? Although common beliefs could lead a person to answer yes to each of these questions, the correct answer to all of them is no. Thus, much of what many people think they know about families is not true.

Many people still cling to the nostalgic image of the American family composed of a breadwinner father, a stay-at-home mother, and one or more children. In reality, however, only 9 percent of all American families fit this picture (U.S. Census Bureau, 1998b, pp. 1, 133). The other 91 percent are made up of many other types: dual-earner families in which both spouses provide financial support, single-parent families, married couples who have chosen not to have children, and countless other variations. Moreover, these figures do not even include the increasing number of unmarried couples, both heterosexual and homosexual, living as a family. Some of the changes in American family structure over the past quarter century can be seen in Figure 13.1. Note that the number of married couples with children has declined from about 40 percent to just over 23 percent of households. One thing the figure does not show is that whether they have children or not, the majority of wives in married-couple families are now in the paid labor force. Furthermore, as shown in the figure, about 32 percent of American households—nearly twice as many as three decades ago—are not family households, consisting instead of one or more unrelated persons. More than one out of four households consists of one person living alone (U.S. Bureau of the Census, 2009).

The family has never been a "golden" institution that fulfilled the needs of all its members while providing them with security and love. In fact, many marriages in past eras were little more than economic arrangements in which men were the primary beneficiaries. Although some families were characterized by considerable warmth and emotional support, the socioemotional functions of marriage were generally seen as secondary to its economic functions until fairly recently.

Family and Marriage Defined

Although the exact meaning of *family* and *marriage* can vary from one society to another, these institutions do share certain key features that can be found in all societies. The **family** is a social group of people related by ancestry, marriage or other committed sexual relationship, or adoption, who live together, form an economic unit, and rear their children, if they have any. Of course, this definition says nothing about the psychological bonds between family members, which, to some people, is what the meaning of family is all about. **Kinship** also refers to people related by ancestry, marriage,

Figure 13.1 Households by Type: Selected Years, 1970–2000

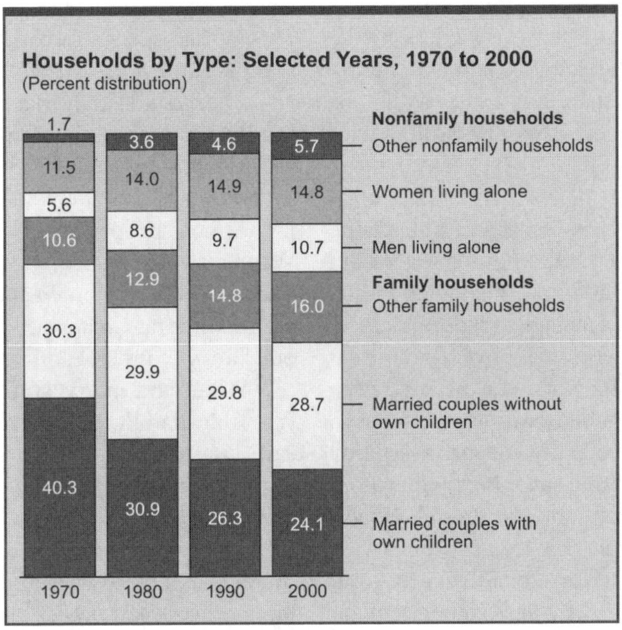

	1970	1980	1990	2000	
Other nonfamily households	1.7	3.6	4.6	5.7	Nonfamily households
Women living alone	11.5	14.0	14.9	14.8	
Men living alone	5.6	8.6	9.7	10.7	
Other family households	10.6	12.9	14.8	16.0	Family households
Married couples without own children	30.3	29.9	29.8	28.7	
Married couples with own children	40.3	30.9	26.3	24.1	

Source: U.S. Census Bureau. 2001. Current Population Reports, P20–537: America's Families and Living Arrangements. http://www.census.gov/prod/2001pubs/p20-537.pdf (downloaded December 21, 2010).

or adoption, but kin can, and often do, live independently from one another. Societies around the world exhibit tremendous diversity in determining who are considered to be kin.

Marriage is a socially approved arrangement, usually between a male and a female, that involves an economic and a sexual relationship. Although historically marriage has usually been between a male and a female, today, a number of countries and several states in the United States allow same-sex marriage for gay or lesbian couples. Society has generally disapproved of births outside of marriage, in part because such children are more likely to need support from the larger society. Nonetheless, the proportion of births occurring outside marriage in the United States has been rising, reaching 38.5 percent by 2006 (Martin et al., 2009).

Extended and Nuclear Families

All family systems can be divided into one of two basic types: extended and nuclear families. The **extended family** is made up of more than two generations who generally live together, contribute to the economic well-being of the household, and share housekeeping and child-rearing responsibilities. Extended families can include a large number of people, such as grandparents, aunts, uncles, and cousins. The **nuclear family** is made up of two or fewer generations who live together, and it most often includes a husband, a wife, and their dependent children.

Although in many other cultures extended families have been and continue to be common, the most common form of the family is and probably always has been the nuclear family. Relatively few families in modern societies consist of more than two generations living together in the same residence. When this does occur, it most often involves either an aging parent living with a grown child and his or her family or a single mother and her child living with one or both of her parents.

Even though relatively few Americans live in extended families, extended family members (called *extended kin* when they do not live under the same roof) may interact frequently, and they are often important in terms of providing assistance of various types, such as child care and financial help. Holidays and other social occasions are often spent with extended kin.

Growth of Nuclear Families in the United States

Although nuclear families have always been the primary family form, the extended family was more common in the past than it is today. With the spread of industrialization, extended families have become less common. Although "many hands" are economic assets in preindustrial societies in which agriculture and cottage industries shape the economy, they become "more mouths to feed" in industrial societies. In addition, highly industrialized economies require a trained, mobile workforce. Because it has fewer people to move, the nuclear family makes it easier for workers to go where the jobs are. Also, social mobility was less frequent in the past; today, social mobility has made required contact with extended family members, with whom there may be little in common, less useful. Finally, nuclear families today are able to get services from other institutions, such as social security and schools, which makes them less dependent on extended family members.

In spite of all these conditions, there are many in the United States for whom extended family remains important. We have already noted that many extended family living situations involve either elderly parents or unmarried mothers—both groups who frequently need assistance and seek it from family members. To some extent, the use of extended families for help and support occurs among all ethnic groups in the United States (Uttal, 1999). However, the extended family and extended kin contacts are more common, and probably more valued, among African Americans (Uttal, 1999; Higginbotham and Weber, 1992, Farley and Allen, 1987; Stack, 1974; Martin and Martin, 1978) and among Mexican Americans (Uttal, 1999) than among white Anglo Americans. These relationships have developed in part as a survival strategy, and may reflect a greater value placed upon blood ties relative to marital ties in the African American and Mexican American communities (Benokraitis, 1993, p. 337).

Family Memberships

Most Americans will belong to at least three different families in the course of their lifetime. When you are born, you become a member of your **family of orientation**, which consists of your father and/or mother, and any brothers or sisters. It also includes stepparents and stepsiblings when they are present. This is the only family membership about which you have no choice.

The second family that most people have is the **family of procreation**. Formed when you marry, it includes your spouse and children. Because nearly 90 percent of people in our society marry at some point, most people have a family of procreation. When a divorced person remarries, he or she forms a second family of procreation. Given the current high divorce rate, many people will have more than one family of procreation.

When you marry, you become a member of yet a third family, the in-law family. As discussed earlier, even though most people in our culture reside in a nuclear family, they often have frequent contact with members of their extended families. In American culture, we have terms to refer to these relationships with a spouse's family, including mother-in-law, father-in-law, sister-in-law, and brother-in-law. Beyond this, however, we have only fairly awkward means of referring to in-law family members, such as "my wife's grandmother" or "my husband's uncle." Although technically we choose our in-law families, many people feel they have little choice in the matter. They choose a spouse, and the in-law family comes with that choice. Perhaps this forced relationship explains the existence of "mother-in-law jokes." There are no clear-cut rules as to what happens to the in-law family when a couple divorces. Although marriage creates the tie, divorce does not necessarily terminate it, especially when strong feelings of attachment exist between a divorced person and an ex-spouse's family, or when there are children who create a grandparent-grandchild relationship.

Marriage Patterns

Forms of marriage have varied among different societies and historical periods. The main form of marriage today in the United States and other industrialized societies is **monogamy,** the marriage of one husband to one wife. In many cases, monogamy in the United States has become **serial monogamy** because many people will have more than one spouse in their lifetime, although only one at a time.

In some societies, marriage practices have allowed, or even required, people to have more than one spouse at a time. This system is referred to as **polygamy**. When males have more than one wife, the arrangement is called **polygyny**. Although this practice is most common in preindustrial societies, it has been practiced in the United States. For example, Mormons practiced polygyny until 1890, when the Utah territory sought acceptance into the Union. The federal government made the outlawing of polygyny a condition of statehood. However, as was illustrated by a highly publicized legal case in 2001, there are still a few traditionalists who continue to practice polygyny. In some instances of polygyny, males may be required to have the first wife's approval before marrying another wife; in others, a man may marry sisters. Both patterns are thought to reduce jealousy between wives. **Polyandry** is the pattern of women having more than one husband. Although numerous societies have condoned polygyny, few have allowed polyandry.

Although many—perhaps most—societies permit polygamy for at least some people (often high-status males), the reality is that most marriages have been monogamous. There are several reasons for this. To begin with, the number of males and females in most populations is roughly equal. Whenever a male takes more than one wife, he effectively deprives another male from having any wife. Beyond this is the issue of cost. The financial costs of supporting multiple wives and the large number of children that might be born would be great. Traditionally, only the wealthiest, most powerful males have had more than one wife.

Mate Selection

Although there are few legal restrictions on who can marry whom, most people in fact choose marriage partners who are relatively similar to themselves. In the United States, there are only three restrictions on selection of marriage partners. The first involves age: Most states have laws specifying a minimum age at which people can marry. Often, there are two ages specified: one for marriage with parental consent, another for marriage without such consent. The second restriction is the **incest taboo**, which exists in some form in nearly all societies. The incest taboo forbids marriage between people who are related to one another. Societies vary in defining which relationships violate the incest taboo. In the United States, no state permits marriage between parent and child, brother and sister, uncle or aunt and niece or nephew, or grandparent and grandchild. Marriages between first cousins are illegal in many states. The incest taboo reduces potential jealousy between family members, fosters alliances with other families, and may keep the gene pool healthier. Historically, only a few societies have made exceptions to their incest taboos. Marriages between brothers and sisters from royal families, such as in ancient Egypt and early Hawaii, have been the most common exception to this rule. Third, all but a few states limit marriage to members of the opposite sex.

Exogamy Versus Endogamy

Until 1967, when the United States Supreme Court ruled them unconstitutional, miscegenation laws existed in some states, especially in the South, to prohibit marriage between people of different races. These laws represented an attempt to prohibit **exogamy:** marriage between people from different groups, such as racial, religious, or ethnic groups. On the other hand, exogamy may be required in some societies that desire to cement relations between certain groups, such as between two potentially hostile tribes.

Endogamy is the pattern followed when marriage partners are required or expected to be from the same groups. For example, a particular religious faith might prohibit its members from marrying members of other religions. Many societies attempt to prohibit marriages between partners from different social groups. Sometimes this is done by law, as in the case of South Africa, where interracial marriages were forbidden until fairly recently. Sometimes the prohibition is informal; in Northern Ireland, for example, there is a strong norm against Catholics marrying Protestants.

The United States has no legal prohibitions to mixed marriages. In practice, however, most American marriages tend to be between people of the same race, ethnic background, religion, and social class, and are therefore *endogamous* (Pagnini and Morgan, 1990). Interracial marriages—particularly between blacks and whites—remain rare in the United States, though they are becoming less so. Of all American married couples in 2007, about eight out of 1,000 were composed of a black person and a white person. There were nearly three times as many such couples in 2007 as there were in 1980 (U.S. Bureau of the Census, 2009).

Spouses: How Similar? How Different?
Researchers have found that similarities between marital partners go beyond race, religion, and ethnic background. Most husbands and wives tend to be similar in terms of social-class background, educational attainment, intelligence, physical characteristics such as attractiveness and age (although husbands tend to be slightly older than wives), personality traits, and values (Mare, 1991; Hout, 1982; Epstein and Guttman, 1984; Kalmijn, 1994b). This pattern is referred to as **homogamy**, or the idea of "like marrying like." Homogamy occurs partially because people often marry on the basis of propinquity, or geographical nearness. The people we live near and associate with are often similar to us in social background. These people serve as a pool of potential marriage partners: People usually marry someone they live near, work with, go to school with, or otherwise have associated with (Kalmijn and Flap, 2001). At the same time, homogamy also reflects the greater ease with which people with similar values and interests interact. Though homogamy remains the norm, there is some evidence of a move away from it since the 1980s (Mare, 1991; Rytina et al., 1988; Smits and Ultee, 1999). With the greater variety of opportunities to meet others—singles clubs and sports clubs, computer and video dating services, personals columns, social networking sites on the Internet, and singles bars—people are not limited in their choices of mates. Research also shows that, while both married couples and cohabiting couples tend to be homogamous, married couples are more so (Blackwell and Lichter, 2000; Forste and Tanfer, 1996).

People who marry and stay married are nonetheless likely to be similar to one another, creating a compatible relationship based on shared values, habits, and lifestyles. At the same time, each partner must feel that he or she is both giving something to the relationship and receiving something from it. This is consistent with the principles of *exchange theory,* introduced in Chapter 3: People enter into and maintain relationships because each offers something of value to or needed by the other. They maintain the relationship as long as this continues, but when one partner's needs change or are no longer met by the other partner, the relationship is in trouble (Walster et al., 1973). Similarly, if one partner is doing all the giving and the other all the getting, the giving partner is likely to feel angry, and the receiving partner may feel guilty or question his or her value as a person.

Romantic Love and Mate Selection

Love, in the sense of our selection of a mate, is clearly multifaceted, and has been defined in a variety of ways. One definition holds that love involves a series of stages—rapport (a feeling of sharing something in common), self-revelation, mutual dependency, and, finally, personality need fulfillment: joint decision making and helping one another to be successful in life (Reiss, 1960; Reiss and Lee, 1988). Other definitions focus on different components of love—intimacy (feelings of closeness), passion (romance and sexual excitement), and decision/commitment: deciding to be and remaining committed to loving one another (Sternberg, 1988). Bergner (2000) adds four other components: investment in the other person's well-being, appreciation or admiration, exclusivity, and understanding. For love to be real, most or all of these elements must not only be present, but also relatively balanced between partners.

A distinctive type of love—much idealized in American society but fraught with risks—is *romantic love*. It involves physical and emotional attraction, as well as idealization, which means seeing the person in an entirely positive light and failing to recognize any negative qualities or traits (Benokraitis, 1993). If you were to ask most Americans on their wedding day why they were marrying their soon-to-be wife or husband, they would likely answer that they are "in love." In fact, if they said they were marrying for money, power, or some equally unromantic reason, many people would view the marriage as a sham. In fact, a key characteristic of love is that it goes beyond self-interest, often involving self-sacrifice on behalf of the partner (Bahr and Bahr, 2001; Bergner, 2000).

Limits of Romantic Love
In our culture, movies, television plots, and novels support romantic love as the basis for marriage. Infrequent attention is given to the fact that this type

of love, at least in its initial, intense phase, does not last more than a few years, at most. In long-term marriages, romantic love develops into a different type of love based on other factors such as companionship and shared goals. Unfortunately, many people believe that marriage without the intense type of romantic love depicted in the movies lacks a critical element. As a result, they may become disenchanted with their relationship. The belief in romantic love is particularly strong in the United States, and is often cited as one reason the U.S. divorce rate is among the world's highest. However, the notion of romantic love seems to be spreading to other societies. This interest in romantic love has developed in part through the influence of American and European movies, music, and books, and in part through an improved standard of living allowing people the luxury of choosing a mate for love. Will the divorce rates rise in these societies? A look at the box "Romance, a Novel Idea, Rocks Marriages in China" shows what happens in one society as couples choose love matches over marriages of convenience.

Romantic Love: A Cross-Cultural View

Love, at least as we understand it, has not always played such an important role in the selection of a spouse or in marriage. In the past, marriages were often arranged by parents or others, and love either developed later or was not seen as an essential part of marriage. Even today in many other, especially non-Western, cultures, the selection of a marriage partner is considered too important to be based on love. People in love are considered too emotional to make such a critical decision. Love is often viewed with suspicion, and attempts may be made to prevent its occurrence. For example, young males and females may be isolated from one another, and chaperones may monitor the activities of their charges to ensure that no inappropriate relationships develop. In such societies, an unmarried woman's virginity is a valuable commodity, and a sexually experienced young woman is not considered a desirable marriage partner. In some cultures, girl and boy babies may be betrothed to one another at birth, or even before. In such societies, love is not a prerequisite for marriage. Community elders or parents decide who should marry whom, basing their decisions on such issues as cementing ties between two families, maintaining power, or increasing wealth. The young couple may eventually grow to love each other, but the failure to do so is not considered important. In our culture, because many necessary services are performed by institutions other than the family, love may be required to hold the family unit together.

Courtship

How do people meet and select mates? The process by which people meet and become familiar with potential mates is sometimes called *courtship*.

Historically, people have met most often at work, in school, in their neighborhood, and in churches and other organizations. Today, however, the ways in which people meet potential partners have become more diverse and varied, as illustrated by the box "New Ways to Meet Partners: A Sociological Look at 'The Personals'."

The early stages of courtship involve dating or informally "getting together" in groups, practices that take different forms in different cultures. Sometimes, relationships of this type develop into exclusive relationships, which, in turn, sometimes lead to living together or getting married.

An engaged couple on a pre-wedding photo shoot in Beijing's Beihai Park. As marriage in China has become associated with modern concepts such as romantic love, the country's divorce rate has soared. (Courtesy of John E. Farley)

GLOBAL SOCIOLOGY

Romance, a Novel Idea, Rocks Marriages in China

Centuries ago, a wife in China could divorce her husband only if he had denounced her ancestors or killed someone in her family. Love never entered the picture.

For more than a thousand years customs did not change much, and the family remained a sacrosanct institution and the nucleus of the entire Chinese society. But these days divorce is beginning to change all that, particularly in China's large cities, where divorce is occurring because young people are taking a second look at what it means to love the person they marry.

More Chinese couples are getting divorced than ever, with one divorce for nearly every dozen marriages nationwide in 1990, and one in eight marriages in Beijing. Most of the nation's 800,000 divorces in 1990—up from 341,000 in 1980—occurred in large cities, and some people in Beijing are divorcing a second or third time. China's divorce rate continues to rise, and by 2004 the number of divorces in China had exceeded 1.6 million—nearly one-fifth the number of marriages that year (China Daily, 2005).

The rise in divorce is linked not to a cynicism about love or marriage but to a starry-eyed faith in true love that many people believe they are missing in their present relationships.

Some Chinese say they have learned about romance partly from foreign movies and music and now want to experience it instead of just dreaming about it. And so they are reappraising their marriages, particularly those that were made in the 1970s and earlier, when many couples formed for reasons of security or status rather than love.

A Stress on True Love

"Divorces have been increasing steadily because as the standard of living improves, people are beginning to seek spiritual emancipation, which was not possible when China was a more closed society," said Gong Sha, a lawyer who manages divorce cases in Beijing. "Now, people are stressing true love."

Divorce procedures are often complicated by social problems, like the desperate shortage of housing in

---

Dating. The processes of dating or informal "getting together" in groups allow people to become acquainted and to determine whether they want to spend more time together. Today, as noted above, personals columns and computer and video dating services enable dating partners to meet one another in ways more diverse than ever before. These modern techniques have somewhat reduced the tendency of people to date others with similar social characteristics to themselves, though this tendency is far from having been eliminated.

Dating serves a number of other functions besides mate selection. For younger adolescents and those with no immediate interest in marriage, dating can be an enjoyable recreational activity involving the companionship of another person. Dating also allows young people an opportunity to learn more about the opposite sex and about themselves. It can also provide an opportunity for sexual experience and satisfaction. Finally, dating can help some people improve their status or prestige by being seen with someone who is popular, attractive, or wealthy.

Exclusive Relationships. Sometimes, people who date or meet through informal groups develop a closer relationship that becomes exclusive. Such relationships involve at least one element of love—exclusivity—and may lead to cohabitation or marriage. At least as often, though, they end when the partners find themselves to be incompatible or when one partner is more committed to the relationship than the other. At one time, exclusive relationships were quite formal, often referred to as "going steady" and accompanied by rituals such as "getting pinned" or wearing a ring. Today, they are less formal, and commonly referred to as "going out" or "seeing someone."

Chinese cities. Song Minghui, an art book editor from the southern city of Changsha, waited 20 years before she finally got the nerve to divorce her husband in 1986. But then she could not get new housing and was forced to continue to live in the same tiny apartment with her former husband for two more years.

Ms. Song retained custody of the couple's teenage daughter and the two slept in one room, sharing a bed, while Ms. Song's former husband slept in the second room. She cooked for herself and her daughter while he took his meals at his parents' home nearby. The former couple hardly uttered a word to one another during those two years.

"There was no harmony in our relationship and we had talked about divorce a long time ago, but my husband didn't agree," said Ms. Song, as she talked freely of her feelings during the 1970s, when the relationship went sour. "Also, I didn't dare divorce. At that time, if you divorced, you were considered a bad woman."

Ground for Divorce

In 1980, an amendment to the Chinese marriage law was approved saying that love is the most important element in marriage and stipulating that the deterioration of love is ground for divorce. This helped bring a wave of divorces that resulted from mismatched marriages during the Cultural Revolution. At that time, intellectuals, branded with a low social position, often sought to marry more socially respectable peasants and workers to improve their status.

When the policies of the Cultural Revolution were forsaken for an opening to the outside world, couples who realized they had nothing in common obtained divorces. "I married someone who had never gone to college," said a Chinese scholar, who divorced a few years ago. "At the time, she fit my standard, when workers and intellectuals were thrown together. We never expected the society to turn upside down again."

Divorce can still hurt career prospects for those people working in the government or the Communist Party, especially if an affair is involved. But these days in the cities there is much less social discrimination against divorcees, and in some circles it is almost fashionable to be divorced. The property—a television set, washing machine, refrigerator, and other large consumer possessions—is divided and the two people part ways, after a brief procedure at the local district office.

"In the group I hang out with, there's only one guy who's still married," said a divorced entrepreneur. "He often complains about being embarrassed that he's still married."

Source: From "Romance, A Novel Idea, Rocks Marriage in China" by Sheryl WuDunn, *The New York Times,* April 17, 1991. Copyright © 1991 by The New York Times Co. Reprinted by permission.

Relationships of this type offer a level of intimacy and commitment that goes beyond that of dating or "getting together," but they require neither long-term commitment nor the accommodation to one another's habits and idiosyncrasies necessary in marriage or cohabitation.

Patterns Within Marriages

When courtship does lead to marriage, the nature of that marriage will reflect the culture and social structure of the larger society within which it occurs. Thus, while all societies have some kind of marriage system, the nature of marriage varies widely from one society to another. It also can vary widely across different time periods within the same society, and among different social and cultural groups within one society. While each individual couple to some extent creates its own marriage, their choices are often determined by these larger societal patterns.

Power and Authority in Marriages

In the majority of societies throughout history, men have dominated the decision making in marriage, a pattern called **patriarchy**. In patriarchal societies, husbands have the right to control their wives and children and are expected to do so. In a **matriarchy**, women have the power and right of decision making. There are no known cultures that could be described as being matriarchal by preference. In the United States, some family systems have been classified as matriarchal, but such patterns typically occur when the husband is not present because of death, divorce, separation, or desertion. In an increasing number of cases today, however, matriarchal families are set up when a child is born outside marriage, since it is the mother who raises such children in the large majority of cases. The sociological debate over the effects of living in female-headed families will be discussed later in this chapter.

The United States is in the process of moving from a primarily patriarchal pattern to an egalitarian one, in which neither males nor females necessarily control or dominate one another. This transformation is largely the result of changing gender roles. Later in this chapter we will discuss the changes that have occurred in male-female relationships.

Residency Patterns

Most newly married couples in industrialized societies prefer to establish their own residence away from the control and scrutiny of their parents. Sociologists use the term **neolocality** to refer to a residency pattern in which married couples form a separate household and live in their own residence. For most young people, getting married and moving out on their own represents independence from parental control. A couple who marries but continues to live with one spouse's parents continues to be dependent to some extent, and their decisions must take the parents into account. In other societies, usually preindustrial, a newly married couple might be expected to take up residence with the

STUDENT LIFE

New Ways to Meet Partners: A Sociological Look at "The Personals"

Over the past couple of decades, formal systems for meeting potential mates—ads in "the personals" columns of newspapers, Internet "personals" sites, computerized and video dating services, and the like, have proliferated in the United States. Increasing numbers of people, from college age on up, are using these services as a way to meet people. Sociologists are interested both in the causes of this trend and in its consequences for how people meet dating partners and potential marriage partners. College students are particularly likely to use Internet personals, with thousands of students now using the Internet every day to meet people. As with many other things in life, research shows us that gender and life-cycle stage are key factors in the extent to which college students use Internet personals. A study by Hatala, Milewski, and Baack (1999) shows, for example, that twice as many ads are placed by male students as by female students, and freshmen, seniors, and graduate students—people who are undergoing or about to undergo changes in life circumstances—are twice as likely as sophomores or juniors to place ads. On the other hand, the mix of racial groups and sexual orientations represented in personal ads seems to be fairly typical of college students in general. One difference does stand out between Internet and newspaper ads, however: Hatala, Milewski, and Baack found that college students who place Internet personals disclose much less about themselves than people who place newspaper personal ads. For example, 9 percent did not even state their gender, and a third did not reveal their sexual orientation—characteristics that are nearly always revealed in newspaper ads. One out of four did not reveal their age, nearly half did not tell their race or ethnicity, and over half did not reveal their year in school. The researchers suggest that a reason for this may be that responses to Internet ads are instantaneous, so it may be easier for Internet advertisers to figure that they can give out more information when they get a response.

Several reasons for the popularity of systems such as newspaper and Internet personals have been pointed out by Ahuvia and Adelman (1992). For one thing, there are more single people today, because people are waiting longer to marry and more people are getting divorced. The number of unmarried adults soared from 47 million in 1975 to 68 million in 1985 (Bennet, 1989); by 2007 it had reached 92 million (U.S. Census Bureau, 2001, 2009). In addition, these single people are more individualistic. They feel more free to have sex outside marriage, and women are more economically independent (Bellah husband's family, called **patrilocality,** or with the wife's family, called **matrilocality.**

The relative wealth of a society and the availability of affordable housing can affect residency patterns. Historically, couples in the United States often delayed marriage until they could afford a home of their own. In the early twentieth century and before, unmarried adults had to choose between delaying marriage until they were in their mid-twenties or older, or living with one partner's parents after marriage. It is a major reason why the typical age at first marriage was fairly high. By the 1950s, most couples could afford to live on their own at an earlier age. The age of marriage fell, and few couples lived with parents. More recently, however, costs of housing have risen faster than young couples' purchasing power. This has forced some couples to share their parents' residence or rent apartments, though they would prefer their own home. This rise in the cost of housing has also contributed to the recent rise in the age at first marriage.

Inheritance and Descent Patterns

Societies differ in their practices that determine how property is inherited and how descent is traced. In a **patrilineal system,** wealth is handed down to males but not to females. This system has contributed to the high birthrates of many developing countries, including India, Korea, Pakistan, and Egypt: No matter how many daughters they

---

et al., 1985). All these things make people choosier about potential marriage partners, and more willing to go to a fair amount of trouble to find the right partner. This is partly because they see marriage less as a necessity and more as a source of emotional gratification—without which marriage or even a serious relationship seems pointless. In addition, the trend toward using ads in "the personals" and dating services may be seen as one more extension of the service economy, as discussed in Chapter 11. Such services are often targeted toward professionals and young people already accustomed to using a variety of services. Getting help meeting "Mr. or Ms. Right" is now presented as just one more service (Ahuvia and Adelman, 1992).

Who uses dating services and personals? At one time, such people were stigmatized as "losers" in the dating market. They were seen as less attractive and socially skilled than people who meet partners through informal means such as parties and mutual friends. However, most of the recent studies show that this is no longer true; the main difference is that people using the formal services are choosier than others. They are less shy and have higher self-esteem, but they also have higher standards for the personality and appearance of potential partners (Bernard et al., 1991).

As for the process itself, it seems that men and women offer somewhat different attributes and also seek different attributes in potential partners. There is mixed evidence on whether or not men are more likely than women to mention attractiveness in their ads, but women do seem more likely to mention interest in marriage and a financially secure partner (Ahuvia and Adelman, 1992). Research comparing heterosexual and homosexual ads shows that lesbians are the most likely group to mention wanting a permanent relationship whereas heterosexual women were the group most interested in financial and occupational information about possible partners (Deaux and Hanna, 1984). To some extent, however, what people offer and seek in "the personals" varies with the publications in which the ads are placed: In magazines appealing to professionals, for example, more women mention their education or job, and fewer emphasize their appearance.

The notion of gender differences is supported by research on what kinds of ads get the most responses. Men get the most responses if they mention being older and taller, if they mention educational or professional success, if they convey masculinity, and if they avoid sexual references. Women get the most responses if they mention youth and activity (which may signal attractiveness), if they make positive or neutral self-descriptions that mention intelligence, and if they mention sex (Ahuvia and Adelman, 1992; Goode, 1996). More generally, most studies show that more men than women reply to personal ads (Ahuvia and Adelman, 1992; Goode, 1996).

While formal services may be changing how people meet, they may not be changing how people ultimately pick marriage partners. One study compared a computer dating service's clients who dated but did not marry each other with other clients who ultimately married, and found in the marrying partners the same characteristic that has always been linked to marriage: similarity. The most likely to marry were couples who were similar to each other, particularly with respect to pessimism versus optimism and concrete versus abstract thinking.

have, couples continue trying to have children until they have a son (Weeks, 1986, pp. 113–14). Furthermore, kinship is traced through male kin, not female. In other words, a child would be considered related to his father's extended family, but not to his mother's. In a **matrilineal system,** the reverse is true; wealth and descent are passed through female family members. This system is much less common than the patrilineal system.

Like other industrialized societies, the United States has, with one exception, a **bilineal system.** Americans consider themselves to be related to both their father's and their mother's families, and wealth is generally passed down to the children regardless of their sex. This pattern increases the independence of the nuclear family by reducing deference to either the husband or the wife's family. The exception to this bilineal system is the usual practice of giving children their father's last name. Some pioneering couples have decided not to follow this pattern and have given their children a combination of both parents' last names. However, the majority continue to give their children the father's last name.

Functions of Families

Since all societies have some type of family system, it is reasonable to ask what the family does for society. After all, if the family did not serve some function that could not be performed equally well elsewhere, it might well cease to exist. In the 1930s and 1940s, some sociologists predicted the disappearance of the family, precisely because many of its functions, such as economic production and the education of children, had been taken over by institutions such as the factory and the school (Ogburn, 1933). The family *has* changed, but it has not disappeared. The same might be said of the family's functions: They have changed, but they have not necessarily decreased. We now examine some of those changes.

Changing Functions

Economic
As noted earlier, families in the past were economically more independent than they are today. A higher proportion of the population lived on family farms where they grew their own food and produced much else of what they needed. Home-based businesses and cottage industries also allowed families to be economically productive. Industrialization transformed the economic function of the family from production to consumption. Most families became dependent on outside employers for their income, which allowed them to purchase, rather than produce, the things that they needed. Grocery stores replaced the garden plot and barn, and department stores replaced the sewing rooms. The family's economic function did not cease to exist, it just changed.

Status Transferral
Status transferral refers to the way in which a person acquires his or her social status or social class. The family used to be the primary source of a person's social position. People inherited social status just as they inherited material goods. Today, however, social status is partly inherited and partly a product of market forces. Although many personal characteristics are still determined by family background, and predictions about a person's future based upon family factors are still fairly accurate, modern societies frequently place as much or more emphasis on people's achieved statuses as on their ascribed statuses. In traditional societies such as India, however, a person's entire lifestyle is often still dictated by the social status of his or her family.

Religious, Educational, Protective, and Recreational
Although the family used to be the primary source of religious training, much of this responsibility has been turned over to churches, synagogues, Sunday schools, and other organizations supported by religious institutions. Nevertheless, people generally adopt the same religion as their family, and many families still give their children religious training.

Before schools were available on a widespread basis, the family often taught its children to read and write at home. Fathers also taught their sons the work skills they would need to provide for their families. Education now is the responsibility of school systems, colleges, and universities, and relatively few people follow in the occupational footsteps of their parents. Still, the family is critical in supporting and encouraging the education of children. Parents send their young children to preschools and summer camps to provide them with lessons in certain subjects. Whether a teenager graduates from high school is largely determined by parental attitudes toward the importance of education. Furthermore, many parents sacrifice financially so that they can send their children to college. Recently, a small but growing number of families have chosen to *home school* their children. For these families, concerns about the social institutions that have taken over the education of children have led to the family seeking to reclaim this function. About 3 percent of children are currently home-schooled, and the number continues to increase (Lloyd, 2009).

Protection refers to the provision of food, shelter, and care. It used to be entirely the responsibility of nuclear or extended family members or neighbors. Although the family still cares for children, the sick, the elderly, and others in need of help or care, it is greatly supported by hospitals, pension plans, police and fire departments, nursing and retirement homes, and day-care centers. Nonetheless, the family still appears to serve some protective function: The mortality rates for both men and women are lower for those who are married (Lillard and Waite, 1995).

With respect to the recreational function, the common belief is that families in the past often spent their limited leisure time together. Recreation today often takes family members in different directions—to movie houses, golf courses, and video arcades. On the other hand, this has been partially offset by other trends, such as growth in family vacations (Nye, 1974). It is also important to consider what time period we are comparing today's family to. Families may have spent more time together in the 1950s than now, but that time period was something of an anomaly: Through much of history, parents spent very limited time, recreational or otherwise, with children. They were too busy working (both for financial support and on household tasks), and children often worked too. In many cases, too, children in early America did not even live at home most of the time: They were sent out as household workers, apprentices, or to be cared for by kin (Coontz, 2000).

Socialization and Emotional Support

Talcott Parsons and R. F. Bales (1955) identified two "basic and irreducible functions" of the family. The family provides children with the necessary socialization to allow them to become functioning, contributing members of society, and it gives adults the emotional support they need to function in a depersonalizing world.

As discussed in Chapter 5, socialization means that family members provide children with the training that equips them to exist as members of a particular society. Families teach children the behaviors, beliefs, and customs necessary to function within their culture.

Perhaps the emotional value of the family can best be appreciated by considering to whom most people turn in times of sickness, sorrow, joy, or financial setback. Although most people have close friendships that give them emotional support, family members generally play a larger role in this area. Most people feel a particular bond with family members that is unlike that felt in any other social relationship.

Affectional

For all the functions discussed so far, the family's role still exists, though sometimes in an altered fashion. One function that has become *more* the domain of the family than in the past is the affectional function. The family has been referred to as the "shock absorber of society" in that it offers support for the individual who must cope in a difficult world (Toffler, 1970). As the family has become less important as a unit of economic production and the notion of romantic love has become more influential, the affectional function of the family has received greater emphasis. The importance of both the affectional and emotional functions of the family is demonstrated in a recent study by Yabiku, Axinn, and Thornton (1999). They examined a study of mothers who had children in 1962, and a later survey of the children twenty-three years later. They found that the more closely integrated the mothers' families were in 1962, the higher the children's self-esteem was twenty-three years later.

The Family as a Regulator of Sexual Behavior

In the words of Malinowski (1962, pp. 98–99), "the sexual impulse is never entirely free, nor can it ever be completely enslaved by social imperatives." Human sexual norms and practices are primarily learned through the process of socialization. All societies control sexual behavior in some manner. In fact, three cultural universals or patterns relating to the family are found in all societies. The first is the incest taboo, discussed earlier in this chapter. The next universal is marriage. Societies have typically encouraged sex within marriage and discouraged or regulated it outside of marriage to provide a stable environment for the nurturance of children. Thus, the family in most societies performs a function of, in some way, regulating sexual behavior. The final cultural universal is an expectation of heterosexuality for at least part of the population, which is necessary for the perpetuation of the species. The functionalist perspective is helpful in understanding these patterns (Malinowski, 1939, 1962). Note that each of the three general patterns outlined above is in some way related to a societal need.

Outside of these expectations, however, a great deal of variety exists in what practices different societies require, encourage, permit, ignore, discourage, or condemn. Some cultures encourage premarital sex; others discourage it. Some societies condemn homosexuality, others ignore it or are neutral toward it, and some approve of it for certain groups. These values can change over time. Although a sexual relationship is expected of couples when they marry, the details of that relationship can vary significantly between cultures, social classes, or religions, and from one couple to another. Unlike in other species, human sexuality is quite diverse.

Nonmarital Sex

Nonmarital sex refers to any sexual activity outside of a marital relationship. Within this category, premarital sex is sexual activity prior to marriage and *extramarital sex* refers to a married person's sexual relations with anyone other than his or her spouse. Although sex outside of marriage has never been socially supported in the United States, premarital sex has become increasingly common and acceptable over the past century.

Sex outside of marriage has been discouraged for various reasons, including disease, pregnancy, and social and religious disapproval. When effective means of treating most sexually transmitted diseases were found and contraception became widely available, much of the resistance to premarital sex broke down. Extramarital sex, however, is still frowned upon by most people (Scott and Sprecher, 2000).

The Sexual Revolutions. Before World War I, approximately three-quarters of all new brides and half of grooms were virgins. During World War I and the 1920s, however, a little-recognized sexual revolution occurred that involved significant changes in sexual behavior. By the mid-1920s, only half of brides and one-third of grooms were sexually inexperienced on their wedding day. Because of the lack of social support for sex outside of marriage, however, these new behavior patterns were not discussed. When Alfred Kinsey et al. (1948, 1953) conducted their monumental studies of sexual behavior in the late 1940s and early 1950s, they noted that 85 percent of males had engaged in premarital sex, as had about half of all women. Furthermore, half of males and one-quarter of females had engaged in extramarital sex. (Recent studies, with more representative samples, however, suggest that this number may be too high. As noted in the box, the large majority of both married men and married women in the more recent "Sex in America" survey [and in other recent surveys with representative samples] report having sex only with their partner during the time they have been married [Laumann et al., 1994; Greeley, 1991].)

It was not until the second sexual revolution, from the mid-1960s to mid-1970s, though, that people openly espoused the sexual values that had, to a great extent, already taken hold. Although the figures are somewhat lower for college students, studies now consistently find that on their wedding days more than 80 percent of brides and 90 percent of grooms are nonvirginal. Among all unmarried adults in their twenties, similar percentages, around 90 percent of men and 80 percent of women, are sexually experienced (Scott and Sprecher, 2000). Attitude surveys suggest that despite some disagreement, overall attitudes toward premarital sex have moved in the direction of moral neutrality. Close to 40 percent in recent years see premarital sex as not wrong at all, and nearly another quarter view it as only sometimes wrong (Scott and Sprecher, 2000). Using two differently worded questions, a Gallup Poll in 2001 reported that 53 percent agreed that premarital sex is "acceptable" and 60 percent disagreed with a statement that it is "wrong." Only 38 to 42 percent, depending on wording, saw premarital sex as wrong (Saad, 2001). Nearly identical results were obtained in 2003 (Gallup Jr., 2003). In general, approval of premarital sex is higher when it is tied to some form of emotional commitment, and those who are less religious, younger, more liberal, urban, and single are more accepting, as are people who do *not* have teenage children.

The increase in premarital sexual activity has been greater for women than for men. Male rates have been less affected because men in the past often had sex with prostitutes. There has been a move away from the double standard in which premarital sex was condoned for men but condemned for women. Although promiscuous sexual behavior—that is, having sex with a number of different partners—is still particularly frowned upon among females, society today is much more tolerant of a woman having sex with a partner with whom she is emotionally involved. The changing role of women is partially responsible for this shift, as is the availability of effective contraception. The availability of birth-control pills beginning in the mid-1960s enabled women to control their reproductive behavior.

We have moved away from another double standard that required people to say that they believed in abstinence before marriage when, in fact, most of them were behaving differently. Christensen (1960) found that when people valued chastity and yet engaged in premarital sex, they were more likely to feel guilty about their behavior. If they saw nothing inappropriate in engaging in sexual relations before marriage, however, their behavior provoked no guilt.

AIDS

Fear of contracting AIDS (acquired immune deficiency syndrome) has caused many people to alter their sexual behavior. Both homosexuals and heterosexuals are limiting the number of their sexual partners, a trend that was already under way before AIDS became widespread but has been accelerated by the fear of AIDS. In addition, more people today are engaging in safer sex practices, such as the use of condoms. However, these trends are modest among heterosexuals, more evident in men than in women (DeBuono et al., 1990; Ishii-Kuntz, 1988), and practically nonexistent among younger people. In recent surveys, for example, about 45 percent of never-married men in their twenties and 30 percent of never-married women between fifteen and forty-four have reported having sex with more than one partner over the time period of a year to a year and a half (Scott and Sprecher, 2000). Teenagers have hardly changed their sexual practices at all (Wattleton, 1988), perhaps because they mistakenly think they are not at risk. As a result, they may be more likely to contract the disease. Generally, however, some people believe that AIDS has contributed to a swing of the pendulum back toward traditional sexual values.

Marital Sex

Sexuality within marriage has also been undergoing change. Years ago women were not expected to enjoy sex. In fact, a woman who did was considered to be highly unusual and undesirable. Sex was viewed as a "wifely duty." This is no longer the case. Today sexual pleasure is considered to be equally important and desirable for males and females. A woman's sexual role is no longer defined as simply to satisfy her husband's sexual needs. As sexual relations within marriage have moved toward equality with greater emphasis on mutual fulfillment, studies have reported increased enjoyment of marital sex. In addition, married partners report somewhat greater enjoyment of sex than do unmarried partners (Laumann et al., 1994). At the same time, many dual-career couples find that between their jobs, children, and household responsibilities, they don't have much time or energy for sex. Women, especially, state that fatigue reduces their interest in sex. On the average, several studies during the 1990s suggested that the typical married couple has sex about six to seven times a month. The rates are higher for younger couples, new marriages, and recent remarriages (Scott and Sprecher, 2000). These most recent studies show little change in the frequency of sex in the 1990s from the previous decade or two.

A Conflict Analysis of the Family

Role Inequality Within the Family

Whereas functionalists view the family as a cooperative arrangement meeting the needs of its members and the larger society, conflict theorists see the family as a microcosm of the larger society in which groups who possess wealth and power exploit those who do not. In the family, conflict theorists believe that men dominate women and exploit them both economically and sexually (Marx and Engels, 1969 [orig. 1848]).

In even the fairly recent past, women were considered the property of their fathers and husbands. Many traditions and rituals remind us of this: the bride's father "giving her away" at the wedding; the promise to "love, honor, and obey"; and the practice of a woman taking her husband's last name. Today, fewer women promise to "obey," and more keep their maiden name or use hyphenated names. However, the majority still take their husband's name.

When a couple marries, the agreement is more than a two-party arrangement. The couple is bound by the rights and responsibilities dictated by the state in which they reside. In the United States, this has meant, until recently, that when a woman married, she lost control of her property, both inherited and earned. She also could not sign a contract without her husband's permission and, until 1970, could not get a credit rating in her own name. Until 1985, there had never been a provision in the law that would allow the prosecution of a husband for raping his wife, though nearly all states do have such a provision now. The presumption was that a husband has the legal right of sexual access to his wife. There are still some states in which a husband can only be prosecuted for rape under specified conditions. In addition, in many jurisdictions, it is much more difficult to prosecute a husband for assaulting his wife than if a stranger were the offender. This is of particular concern because research has found that the family is one of the most violent institutions, surpassed only by the police and the military (and then only in times of war) (Gelles and Straus, 1979).

Violence in the Family and in Courtship

Although violence in the family was not recognized as a social problem in the academic literature until 1970 (O'Brien, 1971), violence between family members has always been a feature of family life. The closeness and dependency created in the family unit can breed anger, hostility, and physical abuse. Family violence ranges from the physical punishment of a child to physical assault, and it frequently results in serious injury. The fact that the abuse takes place in the privacy of the family makes it especially difficult to prevent, detect, and control.

Conflict theorists point out that the overwhelming majority of serious family violence reflects inequalities of power. Husbands engage in serious violence against their wives far more often than vice versa (Straus, 1980), and serious violence in courtship is also usually committed by men (Makepeace, 1981). Similarly, children are abused by adults or, sometimes, older children.

Child Abuse

Physical violence against children has traditionally been viewed as a necessary part of child rearing, as indicated by the expression "Spare the rod and spoil the child." Extreme physical violence against children is one form of **child abuse**. Although child abuse has always existed, it has only received serious recognition during the last few decades. Today it is unfortunately all too common for news stories to report the death of a child as a result of abuse, often at the hands of a parent, or the arrest of an adult, again often the parent, for sexual abuse of a child. In 2005, about 885,000 cases of child abuse or neglect were substantiated by state family service agencies—a decline from the mid-1990s, when annual reports topped 1 million (U.S. Department of Health and Human Services, 2001a; U.S. Bureau of the Census, 2009). A national study in 1995 estimated the total number of abused or neglected children at around 2.8 million (*Nation's Health*, 1997). Of these, nearly 1 million involved physical or sexual abuse (Sharp, 1996). National surveys conducted in the mid-1970s and again in the mid-1980s indicated that a little more than 2 percent of U.S. parents had engaged in serious violence—such as kicking, punching, beating, or burning a child, or threatening a child with a weapon (Gelles and Straus, 1987, 1988; Straus and Gelles, 1986; Gelles and Cornell, 1985). These surveys may understate the actual amount of violence, since some people will not admit to it in a survey (Gelles, 1995).

Parents who are under a great deal of stress are more likely to abuse their children (Emery, 1989; Berkowitz, 1983), as are those with limited knowledge of child development. Children who cause family stress, such as the physically or mentally disabled, are likely targets of abuse, as are babies and very young children, who are too young to tell anyone. Although the cases that most frequently come to public attention are from lower-class families, child abuse occurs among all social classes.

Middle-class families may be more successful at keeping violence hidden. There is some evidence, however, that lower-class people may not be as aware of child development or of more appropriate ways of dealing with stress, and may therefore resort to violence more readily than middle-class people. Also, because stress increases the risk of abuse, and poverty itself is a major stressor, there may be a relationship between social class and increased risk of abuse. The "cycle of violence" refers to the fact that abused children often grow up to be abusing parents, modeling their child-rearing practices after those of their own parents (Egeland, Jacovitz, and Sroufe, 1989). This fact underscores the need to break the cycle through education, counseling, and training. Women are a little more likely than men to engage in violence against children, but this is because they bear more of the responsibility for child rearing than men (Wolfner and Gelles, 1993; Gelles, 1995). When researchers compare men and women who have similar levels of child care responsibility, males are more likely to be abusive (Margolin, 1992).

In recent years we have become increasingly aware of another form of child abuse—sexual abuse of children. Such abuse is most often committed by family members (including parents and stepparents) or their friends. There has also been increased awareness in recent years of abuse by priests, teachers, and other adults who interact with children in institutional settings. Overall, girls are victimized more often than boys. While the precise amount of abuse is impossible to estimate because people are so reluctant to talk about it, the best studies indicate that 30 percent or more of American girls are sexually abused in some manner by age eighteen (Finkelhor et al., 1986, Chap. 1; Bolen and Scannapieco, 2001). The factors associated with sexual abuse of children are much the same as those associated with other forms of violence against children: Authoritarian males, substance abusers, the unemployed, and people who were themselves abused as children are disproportionately likely to be sexual abusers (Finkelhor et al., 1986; Gebhard et al., 1965; Rubin, 1966).

Men have taken on more child-care responsibilities than in the past, but these duties tend to be those that are less routine and more "fun." (Courtesy of Michael Flota)

Spouse Abuse

Some studies suggest that men and women are about equally likely to engage in violence against their spouses (Straus and Gelles, 1986), whereas other studies show that men engage in violence more often (Dobash et al., 1992). But studies agree that *serious* violence resulting in injuries is more commonly committed by males, and that males are more likely to initiate the violence against their spouses.

Researchers estimate that about 2 million cases of spouse abuse occur each year and that one out of every twenty couples will experience severe abuse. The 1985 National Family Violence Survey found that 16 percent of couples had experienced some form of violence in the past year, and 28 percent had experienced violence at some time in their marriage (Gelles, 1995, p. 460). A statewide survey in Washington state in 1998 showed that 21.6 percent of women and 7.5 percent of men had experienced injury from violence by their spouse or partner sometime in their lives (*Morbidity and Mortality Weekly Report,* 2000). Again, there is a cycle of violence—males who were abused as children or whose fathers beat their mothers are more likely to become abusers than other men. Although some social scientists have predicted that as women's status improves, the incidence of wife-beating will decline, one study found that high-status wives may actually be perceived as a threat by insecure males, thus resulting in *greater* levels of abuse.

Abused children are usually too immature to escape the situation, but battered adult women also often stay in abusive situations. The reasons range from economic dependency and an inability to see alternatives, to low self-esteem that results in perceived helplessness. Some wives are committed to their husbands and their marriage regardless of the situation; others blame themselves for bringing on the abuse.

Courtship Violence

Violence also occurs between many dating couples. Most cases involve slapping, punching, and hitting, but some involve sexual attacks. In one study, three out of four college women reported that they had been the victims of sexual aggression at some time in their lives, with 15 percent actually being raped (Muehlenhard and Linton, 1987). Many of these cases involved what is called acquaintance rape, or sometimes "date rape."

Most acquaintance rapes do not occur on the first date, but after the people involved have known each other for a while (Muehlenhard and Linton, 1987). Some acquaintance rapes apparently occur because of incorrect assumptions by male partners about consent. The male may assume that because he has not been explicitly told no or encountered physical resistance, his partner has consented to sex—yet that partner may be submitting out of fear, not because she is truly willing (Celis, 1991). Studies consistently show that the percentage of women who report being raped by their dates is higher than the proportion of men who believe that they have committed rape. Clearly, better education about what constitutes rape would prevent some acquaintance rapes. Many college campuses, where a sizable proportion of date rapes occur, have started education programs on this topic. In some cases, of course, men who rape their dates understand exactly what they are doing. Violence that begins in courtship generally continues into marriage (Roscoe and Bernaske, 1985). In fact, one study of battered wives seeking shelter found that more than half had also been physically abused in a dating relationship (Roscoe and Bernaske, 1985).

Physical as well as sexual violence is common in courtship. Studies of college students suggest that 20 to 40 percent have experienced courtship violence (Benokraitis, 1993, p. 208). As with family violence, most victims of serious courtship violence are female (Makepeace, 1981). At least half the time, such violence occurs more than once between the same man and woman. Like battered wives, many of the women who are victimized feel too powerless to leave the people who are abusing them: Half the women in the Makepeace study remained with the men who had attacked them. Males who engage in courtship violence tend to be traditionally "masculine" males, and the women most likely to be victimized are less traditionally "feminine" women (Bernard et al., 1985). Their assertiveness is likely to be seen as threatening by authoritarian males, and such men often use violence to control their partners.

The Family in the Larger Social Structure

The conflict perspective is also relevant to the role and position of the family within the larger society. Specifically, when the needs of other institutions conflict with those of the family or its members, the family must generally conform or adapt. For example, in order to compete for jobs, families often must be prepared to go where the work is. To pull up roots and move to a distant location for a breadwinner's job can be an unpleasant experience. Social ties may be difficult to break, and if the other spouse is employed, he or she might not want to quit a good job with no firm prospects in the new location. Significantly, women give up their jobs when their husbands get better offers out of town much more often than the reverse (Bielby and Bielby, 1992).

There are many other situations of potential conflict between the family and other institutions. Parents often experience conflict between the need to provide child care and the demands of work; school schedules fail to conform to work vacations; ill family members must get treatment when medical personnel are available, regardless of the inconvenience; and even religious services may conflict with family schedules.

Changing Patterns of Marriages and Families

During the 1960s, social movements such as women's liberation, the sexual revolution, and the gay rights movement transformed many of our traditional concepts concerning marriages and families. Since the 1990s, additional trends have emerged.

Changing Roles Within Marriages

Undoubtedly, the most fundamental change in American marriage and family life revolves around the changing roles of men and women. Women have entered the labor force in record numbers, a trend that is expected to continue. In fact, a 1986 Gallup Poll found that more than 70 percent of full-time housewives and mothers would like to be employed outside the home. In addition, three-quarters of working mothers claimed that they would continue to work even if they did not need the money (Kantrowitz, 1986). In a 1989 Gallup Poll, Americans preferred marriages in which both partners have jobs and share in child rearing over ones where the husband has a job and the wife takes care of the children by a margin of 57 percent to 37 percent (Gallup, 1990, p. 14). As discussed in Chapter 8, there has been some concern in years since then with the effects of both mothers and fathers working long hours away from home. But this is not much linked to who should be doing what in the home: While many think it is better if one parent stays home, few think it matters whether it is the mother or father (McComb, 2001). And despite these concerns, the actual labor force participation of women with children is very high and has changed little in the past decade. In 2007, 78 percent of married women with children between six and seventeen years of age worked, as did 67.4 percent of those with children under six (U.S. Bureau of the Census, 2009).

Both women and families have benefited economically from this movement of wives and mothers into the workforce. The additional revenue helps meet family expenses, provides for the children's education, and avoids poverty in old age. No longer entirely dependent on their husbands for financial support, working wives exercise increased power within the marriage, which helps to create a more equal relationship (Sorensen and McLanahan, 1987; see also Plutzer, 1988). Even young children can benefit when their mothers enter the labor force, because of the greater resources this brings to their families (Parcel and Menaghan, 1994).

Men's Contributions to Housekeeping and Child Care

Although in many ways the movement of women into the labor force has been positive, some studies have shown that women have had new responsibilities thrust upon them but have not been relieved of many of their traditional duties. Despite significant changes in the roles women play outside the home, there have been only modest shifts in the allocation of tasks within the home between males and females over the past thirty years, and women still do about twice as much household work as men (Coltrane, 2000). This issue is discussed in detail in Chapter 8, pp. 234–35.

Because women continue to assume the bulk of child-care and housekeeping responsibilities, even when both spouses work full time, men have more time to devote to their careers than do working mothers. For instance, a survey of executives in the 1980s found that women who become financially successful frequently are unmarried or married without children, which is not true of men. Fifty-one percent of top female executives were unmarried and 61 percent are childless, compared with 4 percent and 3 percent, respectively, for men (Fraker, 1984). In general, women with children earn about 20 percent less than those who remain childless (Bloom, 1986). Unlike men, women often must choose between home and career.

The division of work in the home has become an increasing source of marital conflict in recent years (Townsend and Walker, 1990). This aspect of the issue, along with some of the reasons for the uneven distribution of housework, is explored in the box "Nancy and Evan," excerpted from Arlie Hochschild's *The Second Shift* (1989).

Delayed Marriage and Permanent Singlehood

About one in four households in the United States today is made up of one person living alone (U.S. Bureau of the Census, 2009). In comparison, just thirty years ago only about one in ten households was made up of a single person. These households come about in a number of ways.

First, some people are unmarried; of these, some may never marry—an increasingly common and socially acceptable pattern. Currently, at least

10 percent of the population never marries, and this percentage has increased a little, but may be leveling off as more people over forty are now marrying for the first time.

There has also been a trend to delay marriage. The average age at first marriage for women has risen from 20.4 in 1960 to 25 in 1998, the highest in the twentieth century (Coontz, 2000 [see Figure 13.2]). Today, the trend can clearly be seen in the latest Census data: the age was 25.5 in 2005, 25.9 in 2006, 26.0 in 2007, and 26.2 in 2008 (U.S. Census Bureau 2009). For men, the average age at first marriage is a couple of years older. Women today are delaying marriage to complete academic degrees and establish careers. In addition, because premarital sex has become more acceptable, people no longer need to marry in order to enter into a sexual relationship.

Single-person households are also created when a married person becomes widowed or divorced. Although younger people in this category often remarry, older people frequently do not. Because women significantly outnumber men by age sixty, widowed women are especially unlikely to find another partner.

Finally, there are more single-person households because it is somewhat more common today than in the past for young unmarried adults to live independently rather than with their parents (Goldscheider and Goldscheider, 1987). Economic difficulties caused a modest reversal of this trend beginning in the late 1980s (Bouvier and DeVita, 1991), and subsequent recessions have forced more young adults to live with their parents. In some cases, this is contrary to the preferences of the young adults, the parents, or both.

Cohabitation

According to U.S. Census data, the incidence of **cohabitation,** an unmarried couple living together, has increased rapidly since 1970. As of 2006, 5.4 percent of all U.S. households fell into this category. Just over 6 million households were composed of unmarried partners in 2006. Previous studies have found that 60 percent of cohabiters are under thirty-five years of age (U.S. Bureau of the Census, 1991a), but the incidence of cohabitation is rising among people in their thirties, forties, and

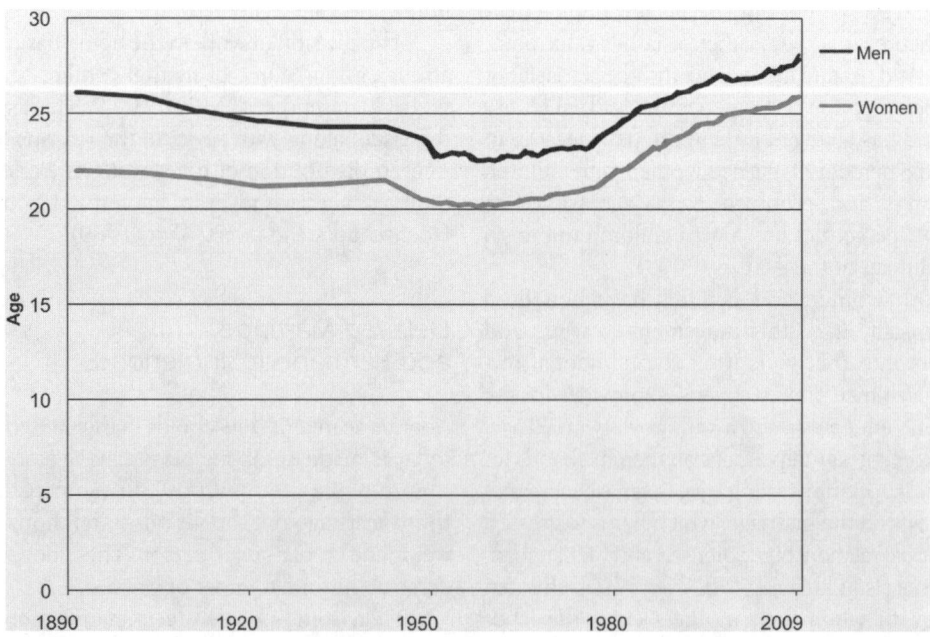

Figure 13.2 Median Age of U.S. Men and Women at First Marriage, 1890–2009

Sources: U.S. Census Bureau, Current Population Survey, March; Annual Social and Economic Supplements, 2009 and earlier.

older, particularly people who have been divorced. Nearly half of people who cohabit have been previously married, and 30 percent have children in the household.

Cohabitation and Marriage

For many but not all, cohabitation is a step toward marriage. One study found that the proportion of applicants for marriage licenses who listed the same address rose from 13 percent in 1970 to 53 percent in 1980 (Gwartney-Gibbs, 1986). Other research during the first half of the 1980s found that 44 percent of all couples who ultimately married had lived together (Bumpass and Sweet, 1988). Some see living together as a way to test the relationship under more realistic conditions than dating allows. In fact, cohabitation is similar in some respects to marriage, and the lives of couples who live together are not much different from those of married couples. Cohabiters generally are committed to an exclusive sexual relationship, although they may be less committed to a long-term relationship with the person they live with. For example, some studies do indicate higher rates of unfaithfulness among cohabiting couples than among married couples (Forste and Tanfer, 1996). As in marriage, women perform a disproportionate share of the housework, and men make more of the decisions.

Living together, however, does not always lead to marriage. The couple can enter the relationship with this understanding, or they can arrive at this decision after living together for a while. Misunderstandings can occur, however, when partners have different expectations about whether the arrangement will lead to marriage.

Sociologists have conducted research to find out whether couples who live together before marriage have better or worse marriages, or a greater or lesser risk of divorce, as compared to couples who do not live together before marriage. At first, such studies found little or no difference (Newcomb and Bentler, 1980; Olday, 1981). However, more recent studies in the United States, Canada, and Sweden have found that couples who live together before marriage appear to experience a higher rate of divorce and report lower levels of marital happiness (De Maris and Leslie, 1984; Balakrishnan et al., 1987; Bennett, Blanc, and Bloom, 1988; Dush, Cohan and Amato, 2003). A possible reason for such differences is that those who cohabit before marriage are less committed to the institution of marriage and are more hesitant to make the long-term commitment of marriage. This suggests that it may not be cohabitation itself that leads to later divorce, but rather that people who are willing to cohabit are also more willing to divorce. For example, people who are less religious are both more likely to divorce (Colasanto and Shriver, 1989) and more likely to cohabit (Thornton, Axinn, and Hill, 1992).

Gay and Lesbian Couples

The 2000 Census, for the first time, offered a national count of the number of same-sex unmarried partners. About one out of ten unmarried-partner households was composed of two men or two women, according to preliminary census data (U.S. Census Bureau, 2001m). This is about 0.5 percent of all households, amounting to over half a million households and over a million people. In most respects, homosexual couples are quite similar to heterosexual couples. One significant difference, however, is that homosexual relationships frequently do not receive the social recognition extended to heterosexual relationships, including legal recognition, support from family and community, and rituals such as a marriage ceremony. (Only five states—Massachusetts, Connecticut, Iowa, New Hampshire, Vermont, and the District of Columbia—legally recognized homosexual marriages in 2011, while other states have passed legislation specifically rejecting gay marriages as illegal no matter where they were initiated.) For these reasons, and because homosexual couples face most of the same problems as heterosexual couples, homosexual relationships may have a higher rate of instability than heterosexual relationships. Nevertheless, many homosexuals remain with the same partner for a number of years. Compared with heterosexuals, homosexual relationships tend to be more egalitarian (Harry, 1982). There is also less gender-based role playing in homosexual relationships (Maracek et al., 1982).

Whether in heterosexual or homosexual couples, however, women and men do tend to exhibit some of the same gender differences. For example, both heterosexual and lesbian women show more interest in emotional, lasting relationships, and tie sex more strongly with emotional intimacy, than do men of either sexual orientation

Homosexual couples are among the many new types of marriage and family relationships that have emerged in American society. (iStockphoto)

(Kurdek and Schmitt, 1986). Lesbian couples are also less likely to fight over money and are more home-centered as opposed to work-centered than either gay male or heterosexual couples (Blumstein and Schwartz, 1983). Male homosexuals are also more likely than lesbians to have sex with someone other than their partner (Peplau, 1981; Blumstein and Schwartz, 1983), though concern about the risk of AIDS has probably reduced the incidence of such behavior.

The AIDS epidemic led to an upturn in prejudice against homosexuals during the mid-1980s, but

UNDERSTANDING RACE, CLASS, AND GENDER
Nancy and Evan

Why has the division of work in the home become an increasing source of conflict in recent years? And what are some of the reasons for the unequal distribution of housework? These questions are dealt with in the following excerpt from Arlie Hochschild's *The Second Shift*.

Between 8:05 a.m. and 6:05 p.m., both Nancy and Evan are away from home, working a "first shift" at full-time jobs. The rest of the time they deal with the varied tasks of the second shift: shopping, cooking, paying bills; taking care of the car, the garden, and yard; keeping harmony with Evan's mother who drops over quite a bit, "concerned" about Joey, with neighbors, their voluble babysitter, and each other. And Nancy's talk reflects a series of second-shift thoughts: "We're out of barbecue sauce.... Joey needs a Halloween costume.... The car needs a wash...." and so on. She reflects a certain "second-shift sensibility," a continual attunement to the task of striking and restriking the right emotional balance between child, spouse, home, and outside job.

When I first met the Holts, Nancy was absorbing far more of the second shift than Evan. She said she was doing 80 percent of the housework and 90 percent of the child care. Evan said she did 60 percent of the housework, 70 percent of the child care. Joey said, "I vacuum the rug, and fold the dinner napkins," finally concluding, "Mom and I do it all." A neighbor agreed with Joey. Clearly, between Nancy and Evan, there was a "leisure gap": Evan had more than Nancy. I asked both of them, in separate interviews, to explain to me how they had dealt with housework and child care since their marriage began.

One evening in the fifth year of their marriage, Nancy told me, when Joey was two months old and almost four years before I met the Holts, she first seriously raised the issue with Evan. "I told him: 'Look, Evan, it's not working. I do the housework, I take the major care of Joey, and I work a full-time job. I get pissed. This is your house too. Joey is your child too. It's not all my job to care for them.' When I cooled down I put to him, 'Look, how about this: I'll cook Mondays, Wednesdays, and Fridays. You cook Tuesdays, Thursdays, and Saturdays. And we'll share or go out Sundays.'"

According to Nancy, Evan said he didn't like "rigid schedules." He said he didn't necessarily agree with her standards of housekeeping, and didn't like that standard "imposed" on him, especially if she was "sluffing off" tasks on him, which from time to time he felt she was. But he went along with the idea in principle. Nancy said the first week of the new plan went as follows. On Monday, she cooked. For Tuesday, Evan planned a meal that required shopping by the end of the decade, support for the rights of homosexuals to enjoy equal opportunity and freedom from discrimination was at an all-time high in the United States—and it continued to rise through the 1990s (Gallup, 1990; Gallup Organization, 2001b). By 2001, Americans favored equal rights for homosexuals by a margin of 85 percent to 11 percent, with majorities also agreeing that homosexuality should be considered "an acceptable alternative lifestyle" and supporting the hiring of gay and lesbian people for every occupation they were asked about, including teachers and clergy (Gallup Organization, 2001b). At least twelve states, the District of Columbia, and 110 municipalities have outlawed discrimination by private employers on the basis of sexual orientation, and some additional states and cities forbid it in public employment (Human Rights Campaign, 2001). In Denmark, homosexual marriages gained legal recognition in 1990 (Benokraitis, 1993), but formal recognition of gay marriages has been slower to develop in the United States, owing in part to strong opposition from traditional Christian religions. Hawaii was ordered by a state court in 1996 to recognize gay marriages, but the court order was subsequently nullified by a state constitutional amendment. Besides Hawaii, a handful of other states, including California, have passed referenda banning same-sex marriages. Gay marriage remains a controversial issue in the United States today. Both sides in the issue have won some recent battles. In 1996, Congress passed and President Clinton signed the Defense of Marriage Act, which states that marriage in the United States could only be between a man

---

for a few ingredients, but on his way home he forgot to shop for them. He came home, saw nothing he could use in the refrigerator or in the cupboard, and suggested to Nancy that they go out for Chinese food. On Wednesday, Nancy cooked. On Thursday morning, Nancy reminded Evan, "Tonight it's your turn." That night Evan fixed hamburgers and french fries and Nancy was quick to praise him. On Friday, Nancy cooked. On Saturday, Evan forgot again.

About two years after I first began visiting the Holts, I began to see their problem in a certain light: as a conflict between their two gender ideologies. Nancy wanted to be the sort of woman who was needed and appreciated both at home and at work—like Lacey, she told me, on the television show "Cagney and Lacey." She wanted Evan to appreciate her for being a caring social worker, a committed wife, and a wonderful mother. But she cared just as much that she be able to appreciate Evan for what he contributed at home, not just for how he supported the family. She would feel proud to explain to women friends that she was married to one of these rare "new men."

For his own reasons, Evan imagined things very differently. He loved Nancy and if Nancy loved being a social worker, he was happy and proud to support her in it. He knew that because she took her caseload so seriously, it was draining work. But at the same time, he did not see why, just because she chose this demanding career, he had to change his own life. Why should her personal decision to work outside the home require him to do more inside it? Nancy earned about two-thirds as much as Evan, and her salary was a big help, but as Nancy confided, "If push came to shove, we could do without it."

Nancy was a social worker because she loved it. Doing daily chores at home was thankless work, and certainly not something Evan needed her to appreciate about him. Equality in the second shift meant a loss in his standard of living, and despite all the high-flown talk, he felt he hadn't really bargained for it. He was happy to help Nancy at home if she needed help; that was fine. That was only decent. But it was too sticky a matter "committing" himself to sharing.

After seven years of loving marriage, Nancy and Evan had finally come to a terrible impasse. Their emotional standard of living had drastically declined: They began to snap at each other, to criticize, to carp. Each felt taken advantage of: Evan, because his offering of a good arrangement was deemed unacceptable, and Nancy, because Evan wouldn't do what she deeply felt was "fair."

Not long after this crisis in the Holts' marriage, there was a dramatic lessening of tension over the issue of the second shift. It was as if the issue was closed. Evan had won. Nancy would do the second shift. Evan expressed vague guilt but beyond that he had nothing to say. Nancy had wearied of continually raising the topic, wearied of the lack of resolution. Now in the exhaustion of defeat, she wanted the struggle to be over too. Evan was "so good" in other ways, why debilitate their marriage by continual quarreling? Besides, she told me, "Women always adjust more, don't they?"

Source: From *The Second Shift* by Arlie Hochschild and Ann Machung. Copyright © 1989 by Arlie Hochschild. Used by permission of Viking Penguin, a division of Penguin Books USA Inc.

and a woman. In 2004, the state Supreme Court of Massachusetts ruled in favor of gay marriage, and in 2009, the State Supreme Court of Iowa did the same. Several other states maintained limited marital rights for gays and lesbians. California, for instance, now acknowledges any homosexual unions granted during the five months the practice was legal in the state or any other state during that time period. Across the globe, Belgium, Canada, Denmark, the Netherlands, Norway, Spain, South Africa, and Sweden allow homosexual marriage. Most of these rights of marriage were gained since 2008. Additionally, some cities, including Minneapolis and San Francisco, have passed domestic partnership ordinances, giving legal recognition to both homosexual couples and unmarried heterosexual couples who wish such recognition.

The growing support for protecting the legal rights of homosexuals in the United States has been met with a backlash from those who want to discriminate against homosexuals. Violence against homosexuals has grown, and more hate crimes are directed against homosexuals than any other group. However, in 2009, Congress passed, and President Obama signed, national legislation against hate crimes that for the first time included hate crimes based on sexual orientation. Several attempts were made in the 1990s through referenda to pass laws discriminating against homosexuals or to repeal ordinances forbidding discrimination against them. Most such attempts failed, except for efforts to prevent gay marriages. However, a Colorado initiative repealing local antidiscrimination laws was approved by a majority of voters in 1992. It never went into effect, though, because it was overturned by the courts on the grounds that it denied gay and lesbian citizens equal protection under the law because it singled them out as one group who could not be protected from discrimination. Another example of backlash against laws designed to protect gays and lesbians came in 1996, after a Hawaii state court ruled that in Hawaii the right to be married could not be denied to gay and lesbian couples. The U.S. Congress quickly passed legislation, which President Clinton signed, allowing other states not to recognize gay and lesbian marriages performed in states that do allow them. An effort to repeal this legislation was under way in 2010, but its prospects appeared uncertain at best. It is important to note that people do not "choose" to be homosexual. Rather, people discover that they are homosexual; growing evidence suggests a genetic factor in sexual orientation (Wheeler, 1992; Suplee, 1991).

Fewer Children, No Children

Large families are no longer considered ideal. In a poll taken in 1941, about 70 percent of the respondents thought that three or more children would make an ideal-size family. Today, just 41 percent hold this view (Gallup Organization, 1997b).

In addition to the economic changes discussed previously, one reason for the trend toward smaller families is the rejection of the belief that an only child will grow up lonely and spoiled. In fact, recent research has found that only children are happy, mentally healthy, and tend to be high achievers (McCoy, 1986), although children raised in larger families do tend to be more outgoing and sociable.

Until recently, childless couples were pitied because it was assumed that they could not have children. A *decision* not to have children, on the other hand, was considered selfish because communities and countries wanted to see their populations grow. Today there is more concern about the problems of overpopulation, and many couples admit that they are voluntarily childless. Recent evidence estimates that up to one in five married women might ultimately remain childless. Couples who voluntarily remain childless are often highly educated and career-oriented. They may have been previously married or have married later in life, and their relationships are more egalitarian. Women who are heavily involved in demanding careers often believe that advancement on the job will be slowed if they have children. Couples sometimes argue that their lives are fulfilling without children. With the skyrocketing costs of child rearing, financial considerations may also play a part in the decision to remain childless. Research has shown that couples without children are happier than couples with children; paradoxically, they also have a modestly greater risk of divorce (Morgan, Lye, and Condran, 1988; Waite and Lillard, 1991), perhaps because couples with children often try to stay together for the sake of the children.

Some couples "drift" into childlessness. They keep delaying having children until they are entrenched in an enjoyable lifestyle or until the wife is too old to become a mother.

There are some couples who are not childless by choice. However, couples with fertility problems who want to have children now have options that were not available even a few years ago. Medical technology has developed various innovative means of allowing couples to produce a child, including in vitro fertilization and artificial insemination. Surrogate mothers are bearing children for couples with fertility problems, provoking intense debate. Some people perceive surrogate motherhood as "selling babies." In addition, because surrogate mothers sometimes act out of economic need, the practice raises questions of lower-income women serving as "breeders" for the wealthier classes. Adoption has always been a possibility, but with the legalization of abortion and with more single mothers choosing to keep their babies, there are fewer children available for adoption.

Marital Disruption and Divorce

Americans depend heavily on marriage for their psychological well-being (Glenn and Weaver, 1981). If the choice of a spouse is a good one, the result can be a happy, satisfying future. If the choice is poor, however, the unhappiness of the marriage can penetrate other areas and reduce the overall quality of a person's life.

Divorce in the United States

The United States has one of the highest marriage rates in the world, but it also has the highest level of divorce (Stack, 1994). In the year ending with November, 1998 (the last year for which official national statistics were kept), there were 1,135,000 divorces, meaning that 2,270,000 people ended their marriages (U.S. Census Bureau, 2000d, p. 101). According to Bumpass (1990), more than half of all recent first marriages will end in divorce, and the divorce rate for remarriages is even higher (Becker, 1981). The divorce rate has been fairly steady since the mid-1970s, as shown in Figure 13.3. However, the incidence of divorce in the United States rose substantially over the period between 1900 and the present time (Huber and Spitze, 1988). Just over 100 years ago, about one divorce would occur for every twenty-one marriages. During World War I, there was one divorce for every nine marriages. In the 1960s, the divorce rate increased again to one divorce for every 3.5 marriages.

Today, there is about one divorce for every two new marriages performed and over the long term, more than half of current marriages will end in divorce if current rates prevail (Stack, 1994; National Center for Health Statistics, 1996a). Although the divorce rate of the United States is well above those of other countries (and has been for a long time), divorce rates have been rising in all modern industrialized countries (Gelles, 1995, p. 396).

Who Gets Divorced?

The risks of divorce are highest in the early years of marriage, with the average divorce occurring in the seventh year. The longer a marriage has been intact, the lower the chance of divorce. There is also an increased risk for divorce when a person has previously been divorced or comes from a family with a history of divorce. A couple is also more likely to divorce if they married very young. Because those who marry younger have a higher probability of divorce (Bramlett and Mosher, 2001), the recent increase in the age at first marriage should help reduce this risk. Couples who knew each other less than six months before they married have higher rates of divorce, as do those in which the wife had a child prior to marriage (Bumpass and Sweet, 1972; Teachman, 1983). On the other hand, research shows that the incidence of divorce is no longer elevated by premarital pregnancy, except when the child is born before the parents get married (Teachman, 1983; Waite and Lillard, 1991). Couples with low income, limited educational attainment, and unemployment tend to have a higher risk of divorce. This probably explains most of the racial difference in divorce (African American rates are slightly higher than those of whites), except for the low rates of divorce for Asian Americans, who are less likely to divorce than any other racial group. Money problems are a major cause of stress in marriage, and when problems such as unemployment make it impossible for breadwinners to support their families, divorce or separation is often the result. For similar reasons, divorce rates in general tend to be slightly lower during periods of economic prosperity (Stack, 1994).

Divorce rates are also higher among couples with dissimilar social characteristics. This is particularly true for religious preference, but to a lesser extent holds true for age, education, and race.

Figure 13.3 U.S. Divorce Rates per 1,000 Total Population, 1960–2000

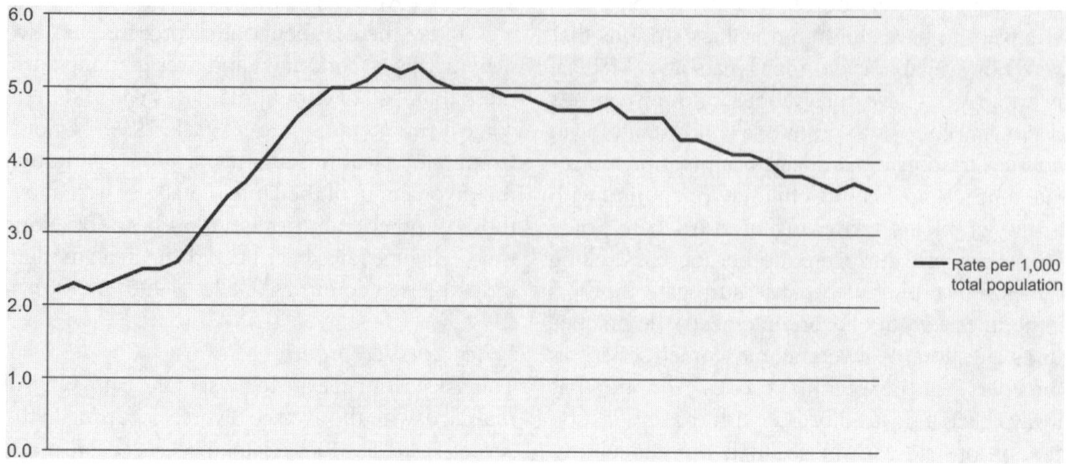

Sources: *Statistical Abstract of the United States, 1989,* Table 126; *Statistical Abstract of the United States, 1996,* Table 142; National Center for Health Statistics, 2001, National Vital Statistics Report 49, 6, Births, Marriages, Divorces, and Deaths: Provisional Data for January–December 2000, http://www.cdc.gov/nchs/data/nvsr49/nvsr49_06.pdf.

Divorce rates are also higher among people who have friends or relatives who are divorced, people who live in cities, and people who are less religious (Stack, 1994). These three factors probably reduce inhibitions against getting divorced, making it more likely that when a marriage encounters problems, people will choose to divorce. Finally, some recent research suggests that people may be more willing to get divorced when they have "spousal alternatives," that is, when they have access to other potential partners for relationships after a divorce (South and Lloyd, 1995).

Not all bad marriages end in divorce. Many of the same factors that contribute to high divorce rates also create stress in marriage, producing unhappy, unsatisfying marriages that remain outwardly intact but are internally broken. Sometimes these relationships have been termed "empty-shell" marriages.

People may remain in unhappy marriages for reasons unrelated to the quality of the relationship, such as fear of being alone, unwillingness to break the "until death do us part" vow, or a (usually misguided) desire to stay together "for the sake of the kids." People in such marriages may quietly coexist without emotional attachment, or they may engage in constant conflict with one another. They may convince themselves to accept the devitalized quality of their marriage, or be so dependent upon the conflictual relationship that they do not view divorce as a realistic option.

Causes of Divorce

Longevity

Some people interpret today's high divorce rate as evidence that many people are making poor decisions regarding their choice of a mate. Others believe that greater life expectancy almost inevitably leads to more divorces. In the past, when people had much shorter life expectancies, couples who married until "death do us part" frequently didn't have to wait very long to be parted. The *combined* risk of marital disruption from either death or divorce was only modestly lower then than now (Cherlin, 1981; Sweetser, 1985). However, marriages were more likely to be ended by death and less likely to be ended by divorce. Today, with average life expectancy exceeding seventy years, a couple who marries in their early twenties could, in the absence of divorce, expect their marriage to last fifty or more years. It may be unrealistic to expect that the right mate for a person of twenty will still be the best choice twenty, forty, or sixty years later. People continue to change throughout life, and spouses often find that they are not changing in parallel ways.

Economic Independence of Women

Today, when women are more independent economically, such changes are more likely to lead to divorce. As women have become better educated and have entered the labor force, they have become less economically dependent upon their husbands. As a result, a woman in an unhappy marriage has the option of leaving the marriage because she is, or can become, economically self-sufficient (Stack, 1994). This trend may have run its course by the end of the twentieth century, however: Some recent research shows no correlation between a wife's income and the risk of divorce (Rogers and DeBoer, 2001).

Unrealistic Expectations
Another factor in divorce is the high level of expectations people have for marriage. With the decline of the extended family, husbands and wives increasingly look to each other for needs that had previously been met by other family members. It may be unrealistic to expect any marital relationship to be able to meet all the diverse needs of both partners at all times.

Of course, many marriages are happy and remain so throughout life. What is it that distinguishes successful and rewarding marriages from ones that end in divorce or drag on unhappily? Sociologists Jeanette and Robert Lauer conducted research on this question, and they tell us what they discovered in their "Personal Journey into Sociology."

Changing Divorce Laws

Until recent decades, divorce was a cause of public censure and personal humiliation. Today, however, the emphasis is on reducing the negative impacts on the divorcing spouses and especially on the children. Social and legal accommodations have been made to ease the trauma.

No longer do spouses have to accuse each other of adultery, alcoholism, or physical cruelty to get a divorce. In New York State, adultery was the only legal grounds for divorce until 1973. In 1970, California became the first state to eliminate any requirement of fault in cases of divorce in its much-copied no-fault divorce law. The majority of states now have statutes allowing no-fault divorce. Just as no-fault automobile insurance seeks to save court expenses by eliminating the need to determine responsibility, so no-fault divorce seeks to allow divorce without requiring that one spouse prove the other was at fault. In no-fault divorce, marital partners agree that the marriage has broken down and that they have irreconcilable differences. This reduces potential hostility between spouses and saves children much trauma.

Although many people hail this trend as humane and farsighted, others fear that it has made divorce too easy. They argue that such laws have contributed to the increase in the divorce rate in the United States, and social research backs this argument to some extent. Divorce rates did increase after states introduced no-fault divorce laws, although it was also found that sociodemographic variables explained divorce rates better than divorce laws did (Stack, 1994, p. 155). Critics of such divorce laws argue that more people would stay married if divorces were harder to get. Of course, there is no guarantee that the marriages would be any happier.

There have been other legal changes regarding divorce. Although fathers most often got custody of children in the nineteenth century, this pattern reversed in the twentieth century and by the 1940s, mothers nearly always got custody (Stack, 1994). Recently, it has become less automatic to give custody to the mother in disputed cases. Data from the 2000 census indicate that among all one-parent families (not just ones resulting from divorce), about 20 percent were composed of an adult male living with one or more children (computed from U.S. Census Bureau, 2001k). Typically in divorces involving children, the noncustodial parent has visitation rights. Joint custody, in which children are with each parent a roughly equal portion of the time, has become increasingly common.

Effects of Divorce on Women and Children
Some evidence indicates that liberalized divorce laws may actually harm many women economically. Although this effect is not as large as was once believed (for example, Weitzman, 1985), it is still substantial (Smock, Manning, and Gupta, 1999). Following a divorce, a woman's standard of living declines by about 27 percent on the average, whereas her ex-husband's rises by about 10 percent (Peterson, 1996). The effects of taxes and social benefits reduce this gap somewhat, but men still fare better than women after a divorce, even adjusting for taxes and social benefits (DiPrete and McManus, 2000). When a woman who has been a full-time homemaker and has not been on the job market in years is divorced, she may have a difficult time supporting herself. At the same time, she is less likely to receive alimony. Now

PERSONAL JOURNEYS INTO SOCIOLOGY

Background of "'Til Death Do Us Part": How Couples Stay Together

Jeanette C. Lauer and Robert H. Lauer

Ideas for research come in various ways. Some of the research we have done has been stimulated by unanswered questions or ambiguous findings or suggestions made in the literature. Our study of long-term marriages, however, grew out of a technique that we urge our own students to use—introspection. Think about your own experiences. What questions are raised? In reflecting on and questioning your experiences, you may find a rich source of research ideas.

The idea for long-term marriages came to us as we were running together one day. We were concerned that so many of our friends' marriages seemed to be breaking apart. In each case, we knew the reasons they gave. Then the conversation took a different turn. We jokingly said that we were going to be one of the last married couples in our group of friends. Then we seriously asked the question why. What keeps a marriage going? Why do some marriages not fail? What is the cement that makes some relationships not only lasting but thriving?

At that moment we agreed to research the topic. We had a personal as well as a professional interest in the outcome. Our first step was to research the literature. We were stunned. At the time, there were no books and only a handful of articles that addressed the question of what keeps a marriage together. At least, they didn't address it by looking directly at marriages that had succeeded. We immediately went to work to design an instrument. We decided to use the Dyadic Adjustment Scale, a widely used measure of marital satisfaction. But again using introspection, we thought about our own relationship and decided that the scale did not capture all of the important ingredients. We added six items that reflected our own experience. We also used some open-ended questions to probe such things as our subjects' perceptions of why their marriages had lasted, their methods of dealing with conflict, and how they maintained vitality in their relationships.

Using doctoral students and friends, we eventually made contact with 351 couples in various parts of the country who had been married for fifteen years or more. We chose fifteen as a reasonable number of years for "long-term" because the median number of years of marriage among those who eventually break up is seven. Thus, our couples had been married slightly more than twice as long as the median.

Initially, we assumed that anyone married so long would be happy. We were wrong. In fifty-one of the couples, one or both spouses was unhappy with the relationship. This unexpected finding gave us useful data for comparisons. Not only could we now say what factors seemed to be involved in stable marriages, but we could also determine how stable and satisfying marriages differ from those that are stable but unsatisfying.

---

that women are more often able to take care of themselves financially, courts are awarding alimony much less frequently, in less than 17 percent of divorces. Even when awarded, alimony is paid only three-quarters of the time, and the average alimony payment is only about $4,000 per year. Child support is awarded more often—about 57 percent of custodial parents had some type of child support agreement or order as of 2006. But nearly one in four parents (usually fathers) who are supposed to pay child support paid nothing, and only 53 percent of the total amount due in 2005 was paid. The average amount of child support actually paid is only $3,640 per year (U.S. Bureau of the Census, 2007, p. 2). Overall in 2005, more than half of all custodial mothers received *no* child support.

Putting Sociology to Work

Should Couples Stay Together "for the Sake of the Kids"?

Many parents in unhappy marriages wonder whether they should try to stay together even though they are unhappy, in order to prevent their children from suffering the damaging effects of divorce. Social research has provided some

We asked each individual to look at thirty-eight factors (thirty-two on the Dyadic Adjustment Scale and the six we added) and identify those most responsible for the stability of their marriage. We also asked them to volunteer any other factors that they perceived as important. For couples where one or both partners was unhappy, the most frequent reasons for staying together were commitment (for religious reasons or family tradition) and children. In a sense, they said that they were determined to keep the marriage intact no matter how dissatisfied they were. The marriage itself, and not their personal happiness, had priority.

For those in happy marriages, an interesting thing happened. First, although men and women were interviewed and filled out the questionnaires separately, the first seven factors most frequently listed were identical for husbands and wives. Four of the seven were items from the six that we had added to the scale, underscoring our conviction that introspection can frequently be an important part of the research process. The seven factors identified by people as important to long-term, happy marriages are listed below:

1. Their spouse is their best friend.
2. They like the spouse as a person.
3. They are committed both to the spouse and to the institution of marriage.
4. They believe in the sanctity of marriage.
5. They agree with the spouse on aims and goals.
6. They believe that the spouse has grown more interesting over the years.
7. They strongly want the relationship to succeed.

Perhaps the central factor was captured well by one wife who said of her husband: "I like him. I like the kind of person he is. Even if he weren't my husband, I would want to have him as a friend." Like those in unhappy unions, the happy spouses were committed. But there was a difference. Whereas the unhappy people were committed to the marriage no matter how miserable they were personally, the happy people were committed in the sense of being determined to confront any problems and work through them. Unhappy spouses may ignore or avoid or simply endure problems. Happy spouses are not willing either for themselves or their mates to be unhappy in the relationship.

Although not in the top seven, humor was also one of the factors frequently mentioned. Respondents often said that humor is very important in maintaining a vital relationship. Some people consciously work at maintaining humor in the relationship. For example, one woman said that she saves cartoons and shares them with her husband so that they can laugh together.

Finally, we are pleased to report that a follow-up study was done by a doctoral student who used our questionnaire to interview 200 couples married forty-five years or more. Her results were virtually identical to ours. We feel some confidence, therefore, in saying that we have been able to identify the factors that are necessary for a marriage to be both long-term and satisfying to both husband and wife.

Jeanette C. Lauer and Robert H. Lauer are coauthors of Watershed: Master Life's Unpredictable Crises, *chosen as the main selection of the Psychology Today Book Club. Each has written numerous other books dealing with human behavior. Both received doctorates from Washington University in St. Louis, and both are Professors Emeritus at Alliant International University in San Diego.*

---

information that may be helpful in answering this question. In part, whether or not divorce is bad for children may depend on the level of conflict in the marriage. If the level of conflict in a marriage is high, the children are probably better off on average if the parents divorce (Amato, 2000; Amato and Booth, 1997). However this is only the case in a minority of marriages. In the rest, studies show consistent though relatively small (on average) disadvantages for children of divorced parents in a number of areas (Amato, 2000).

To begin with, divorce is usually very stressful to children when it occurs, and many children of divorced parents still have strong feelings about the divorce years or even decades later (Wallerstein and Blakeslee, 1989). They also experience increased risks of psychological maladjustment and low self-esteem (Amato, 1993). They are at a higher risk of criminal behavior, in part because their one custodial parent has less time to supervise them (Stack, 1994). They also experience somewhat less academic success and greater behavioral problems in school, and less economic success over the course of their lives. Children of divorced parents are not necessarily more likely to have unhappy marriages or to get divorced, though they may be more likely to divorce if they do have a bad marriage (Webster, Orbuch, and House, 1995; Thornton, 1991). They are also more likely to cohabit as adults, perhaps reflecting a fear that their own marriages will fail (Thornton, 1991).

None of this, however, means that if a marriage goes bad, the children will benefit if the parents stay together. First of all, it is open to question whether these problems result from divorce, or were there anyway, perhaps as a result of family problems that contributed to the divorce. Several studies show that, *even before a divorce,* children in families that end up divorcing fare less well—and this pattern continues after the divorce (Amato, 2000; Amato and Booth, 1996; Aseltine, 1996; Hetherington, 1999; Doherty and Needle, 1991). It is also clear that how well children do after a divorce varies widely from case to case. Not surprisingly, research has shown that children of divorced parents are less prone to problem behavior when they receive adequate economic support from their noncustodial fathers (Furstenberg, Morgan, and Allison, 1987). In addition, there can be some *positive* effects of divorce, as well as any negative ones. For example, many children actually experience *closer* relationships with their custodial mothers after a divorce (Arditti, 1999; Amato and Booth, 1997).

Three things discussed above call into question the wisdom of "staying together for the sake of the children." First, average differences between children from divorced and married families, though consistent, are small. Second, it is not clear whether they reflect effects of divorce or differences already there before the divorce. And third, children may benefit in some ways from divorces, especially in marriages where there was severe tension or conflict.

Because of the wide variation in outcomes of divorce for children, more recent social research has focused on the sources of this variation. The most important factor is conflict: If divorced parents engage in conflict, especially in front of their children, the children tend to do poorly. In fact, this is bad for children whether the parents are divorced or married (Amato, 1993, p. 31). If divorced parents can avoid such conflict, the children do much better—sometimes even better than children in intact families. Research also supports the idea that if the custodial parent is better adjusted psychologically, the children generally do better (Amato, 1993). The effects of conflict and adjustment are hard to sort out, however, because conflict and poor adjustment often occur in the same parents. The overall research picture suggests that the welfare of children whose parents have marital problems is not so much a product of whether or not their parents get divorced, but rather of how they do it and how they behave toward each other and their children after the divorce. It is also clear that if parents have marital problems, there are potential consequences for children whether the parents divorce or remain married. One final point is worthy of mention: Divorce is a major cause of one-parent families, and there is considerable debate about the possible effects of living in such families regardless of their cause. This debate will be addressed later in this chapter.

Remarriage

Although divorce rates are high, remarriage rates are also high. Three-fourths of all divorced women remarry within ten years of the divorce (Bramlett and Mosher, 2001). Americans may be disenchanted with their current marital partners, but they do not seem to be disenchanted with the institution of marriage. Males tend to have even higher rates of remarriage than females. As women grow older, the number of males in their age range diminishes rapidly, reducing their chances of finding a second husband. Also, divorced men often marry women considerably younger than they are, further reducing the pool of potential partners for divorced women, who less frequently marry younger males. Women with higher educational attainment levels also remarry less frequently (Glick and Sung-Ling, 1986), demonstrating the marriage gradient; that is, the pattern of women marrying "up" (men with more education and higher incomes) and men marrying "down." Although most divorced people do remarry, the percentage who do so has been falling, and people have been waiting longer after a divorce before they remarry. Between 1970 and 1987, for example, the median amount of time between divorce and remarriage more than doubled for both men and women in the United States (National Center for Health Statistics, 1988), reaching four and a half years for women by 1995 (Bramlett and Mosher, 2001). To a large extent, however, these changes have been offset by an increase

With today's high divorce and remarriage rates, a growing number of marriages result in families in which one or both of the partners bring children from previous marriages. (Courtesy of John E. Farley)

in cohabitation. About half of these cohabitants eventually marry their partner (Bumpass, Sweet, and Cherlin, 1991; Wilson and Clarke, 1992).

Second marriages have only a slightly higher risk of divorce than first marriages, except that those with children tend to have somewhat higher rates (White and Booth, 1985). Overall, about 39 percent of second marriages end in divorce within ten years, compared to 33 percent of first marriages (Bramlett and Mosher, 2001). The highest rates of divorce occur when both partners have children (Booth, 1991). When children are involved and a "blended" family is created, the remarriage experience is considerably different from a first marriage. Today, about one child in nine lives with a stepparent (Popenoe, 1996). Two-thirds of these have stepsiblings, half-siblings, or both (Huber and Spitze, 1988, p. 434). There are few established norms or rules to guide relationships between stepparents and stepchildren, stepbrothers and stepsisters. This often results in uncertainty, confusion—and a higher divorce rate.

Women who are widowed later in life have low rates of remarriage because of the lack of eligible males. Only 7.7 percent of males between the ages of sixty-five and seventy-four are widowed, whereas 26.2 percent of females are. For those seventy-five and older, the difference is even greater, with 20 percent of males and 58.2 percent of females widowed (U.S. Bureau of the Census, 2009).

Single-Parent Families

According to the most recent figures, at any given time, more than one of four children in this country are living in one-parent households. This compares to fewer than one of ten in 1960. Forty-two percent of white children and 86 percent of black children will live in a single-parent household at some point before reaching the age of eighteen (Bumpass, 1984). About 74 percent of single-parent households are headed by a female (U.S. Bureau of the Census, 2009), a slightly lower proportion than a decade ago. About two-thirds of children in single-parent households have parents who are divorced or separated. The remainder have parents who never married (U.S. Bureau of the Census, 1992c). An increasing share of single-parent households are the result of out-of-wedlock births, which now account for more than 38 percent of births in the United States (U.S. Census Bureau, 2010, Tables 78 and 85).

The number of single-parent, female-headed households has increased for several reasons. One is the rising rates of divorce and separation, discussed above. Another is the rapid increase in the birth rate among unmarried people, and an increasing tendency for unmarried mothers to keep and raise their children rather than putting them up for adoption. Today only 10 percent of single mothers choose not to keep their babies.

About 42 percent of all children in families with no father present live in poverty (U.S. Census Bureau, 2000b). Children from single-parent households exhibit rates of delinquency double those for children from two-parent homes, but this may be related to poverty as much as to living

Table 13.1 Percentage of Female-Householder Families, by Race, Hispanic Origin, Below Poverty Level, 2008

	White Families	Black Families	Hispanic Families
Families below poverty level	28.5%	47.4%	46.3%

Source: U.S. Bureau of the Census, 2009.

arrangements. Often having lower educational and economic levels to begin with, single parents must then cope with living on only one income while playing both mother and father to their children.

Race, Poverty, and the One-Parent Family

For more than two decades, sociologists and policymakers have debated the importance of the growing number of one-parent families as a cause of poverty. Since there are racial differences in the proportion of one-parent families, this debate has often taken on racial overtones. The statistics concerning race, poverty, and family type are clear, but their meanings are not. The incidence of one-parent, female-headed families is much higher among the poor than among the nonpoor population for all races (U.S. Census Bureau, 2000b). This is illustrated in Table 13.1. However, the incidence of such families is lowest among whites, higher among Hispanics, and highest of all among African Americans, as shown in Figure 13.4. Nonetheless, there have been substantial increases in the proportion of one-parent families among all racial and income groups since the late 1960s.

Single-Parenthood and Black Families

The high incidence of single-parent families among African Americans and poor people has led some sociologists to argue that the structure of the black family is an important cause of disproportionate black poverty. These sociologists, operating largely from a functionalist perspective, see danger in any group having a family structure too different from the standard nuclear family. The best-known proponent of this viewpoint is former U.S. senator Daniel Patrick Moynihan, who in 1965 published a very controversial report on the subject (U.S. Department of Labor, 1965). Moynihan's report was controversial not because of the statistics it cited, but because of the interpretation of those statistics (Rainwater and Yancey, 1967). Moynihan argued, in effect, that the disproportionate number of single-parent, female-headed families among African Americans was the most important cause of high black poverty rates. Although the debate today is much less centered around the Moynihan Report than it once was, the controversy over the

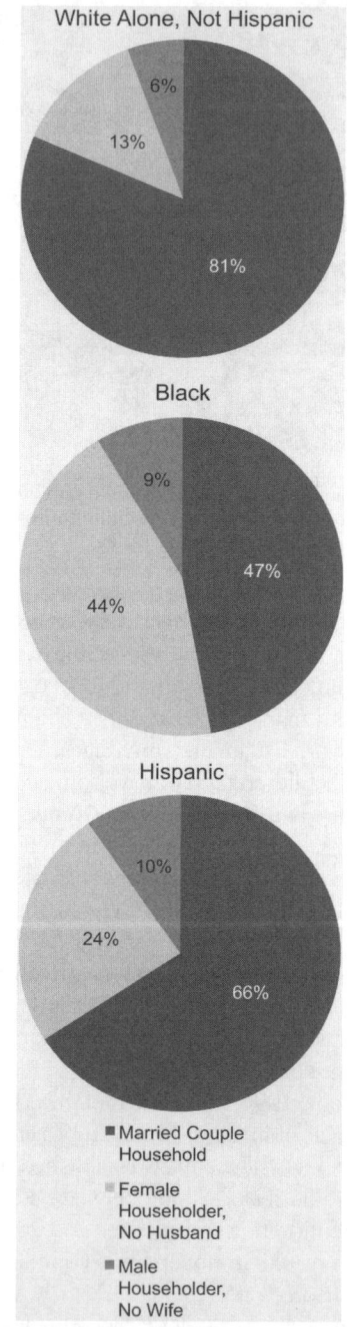

Figure 13.4 Proportion Married Couple, Female-Householder, and Male-Householder Families, 2009

Source: U.S. Census Bureau, 2010, America's Families and Living Arrangements, 2009, Table F1. Family Households by Type, Age of Own Children, Age of Family Members, and Age, Race and Hispanic Origin of Householder, 2009, http://www.census.gov/population/www/socdemo/hh-fam/cps2009.html, Tables F-1 and H-1.

importance of the single-parent family as a cause of minority inner-city poverty continues (Jencks and Peterson, 1991). The view that single-parenthood is a major cause of poverty has been criticized on several points.

First and foremost, the single-parent family is at least as much a product of poverty as a cause of it. Poverty both breaks up existing families and prevents the formation of new married-couple families. Our society continues to expect men to support their families (or at least be the main source of support), but poverty makes that impossible. Thus, these men avoid marriage (Mare and Winship, 1991). If they are married, they may leave the family when they become poor or unemployed. The stresses of poverty also increase the risk of conflict, violence, and substance abuse within the family. For these reasons, low socioeconomic status is associated with higher divorce rates (Waite and Lillard, 1991) and much higher separation rates than occur among middle- and upper-class families.

Low socioeconomic status is even more strongly associated with births outside marriage (Jencks, 1991). For reasons discussed in Chapter 6, poor teenage girls are much more likely than nonpoor ones to become pregnant. Poor inner-city women—particularly among African Americans—experience a severe shortage of marriageable men, because many of the men in their community are unemployed, imprisoned, or prematurely dead (Wilson, 1987; Lichter, LeClere, and McLaughlin, 1991). Yet, like their middle-class counterparts, most of these single women are sexually active. This fact, combined with the higher percentage of unmarried women among the inner-city poor, results in a higher percentage of children born to single mothers (Stokes and Chevan, 1996; Seeborg and Jaeger, 1993). Inadequate access to and knowledge about contraceptives—owing to the general inadequacy of health care in poor areas—exacerbates this pattern further, and plays an even bigger role in teenage pregnancy. All of this points strongly to poverty being a major cause of one-parent families. If this is the case, the logical policy direction is to address the direct causes of poverty, discussed in Chapter 6, rather than to try to reduce poverty by changing families.

With respect to black families, several other issues have been raised in this debate. It is commonly argued that matriarchy is part of African American culture, and that the disproportionate number of female-headed families has roots that can be traced at least to slavery. At and before the beginning of the twentieth century, female-headed families were indeed more common among blacks than whites (Morgan et al., 1993; Ruggles, 1994). However, most evidence suggests that the vast majority of black families were two-parent families until the mid-twentieth century, and that female-headed families became much more common among African Americans only when the black population began to urbanize on a large scale (Furstenberg, Hershberg, and Modell, 1975; Gutman, 1976; Lammermeier, 1973; Wilson, 1987). This further suggests that the urban poverty experienced by African Americans is an important factor in shaping black family structure. Still further support for this interpretation can be seen in recent research showing that the sexual behavior of black and white teenage girls is much the same under similar economic and neighborhood conditions (Brewster, 1994).

It is also important to remember that there is no one black family pattern, just as there is no one white family pattern or Hispanic family pattern. At the time of the Moynihan Report, only 23 percent of black families were headed by women, so "the black family" then could hardly be characterized as "female-headed." Even today there are nearly as many husband-wife families (about 42 percent in 2007) among African Americans as there are female-headed families (about 53 percent). Finally, it is important to point out that a father who does not live with his children is not necessarily uninvolved. Hamer (2001) found that most noncustodial African American fathers saw their children regularly and were quite involved with their child rearing. However, their financial support was usually limited because their incomes were meager, and in some cases, conflict between the fathers and their children's mother was a significant impediment to their interaction with their children.

Family Structure: A Cause of Poverty?
An important criticism of the Moynihan Report was that it made no real attempt to test its assumption that single-parent families are an important cause of poverty (Gans, 1967b; Ryan, 1967). Over the past three decades, research has indicated that the rising incidence of female-headed households has

been accompanied by increases in poverty and a worsening of the position of the urban "underclass" (Bianchi, 1981; Wilson, 1987; Reimers, 1984; Mare and Winship, 1991). In one sense, single-parent families would seem to be at greater risk of poverty. They have only one potential earner and thus cannot take advantage of the trend in the American family toward having two sources of income. For never-married poor women who have children, this disadvantage is heightened, because they have a lower probability than other women—even divorced women with children—of eventually getting married. As mentioned previously, they often face a shortage of employed men in their neighborhoods. Furthermore, they may be seen as undesirable partners: Their incomes are low, their education and job skills are often limited, and their children present additional economic costs and parental responsibilities to any potential partner.

This disadvantage may be further heightened by the "welfare reform" legislation passed in 1996. This legislation placed strict time limits on how long a mother may receive welfare, in order to encourage women to enter the workforce rather than rely on welfare. Since welfare has often worked in ways that keep poor mothers dependent rather than allowing them to become self-supporting and independent, the goal of the legislation is to address a genuine problem. And in the short term, many did move from welfare to work, since the legislation occurred at the height of the 1990s economic boom. There are at least two reasons, however, that this legislation may, over the longer term, create more problems than it solves. First, it does not address situations where jobs are unavailable—and this situation clearly exists in many areas of concentrated poverty, in both inner-city neighborhoods and in underdeveloped rural areas. This condition was alleviated somewhat by the economic growth of the 1990s, but with the recessions of the following decade, jobs have become much more scarce, especially in places where poverty and unemployment were already common. Second, even if jobs are available, the legislation does little to address the need for affordable day care. If single mothers are to enter the labor force, they must have some way to ensure that their children are cared for while they work. At least initially, many who leave welfare work at or near the minimum wage, and a mother with two children working at the minimum wage could easily spend half or more of her income on day care alone—thus leaving her without nearly enough to feed, shelter, and clothe her children. So, while the "welfare reform" legislation did succeed in moving many from welfare to work, in a good number of cases it meant nothing more than a shift from being unemployed and poor to being a member of the working poor (Greenberg, 2001). As Greenberg put it, "But welfare caseloads have fallen far more rapidly than child poverty, many families have lost benefits without finding work, and many who have found work have had little or no increase in economic well-being." Because their jobs lack benefits, many also have limited access to health care. Children of people leaving welfare for work were supposed to continue to be eligible for Medicaid, but the percentage of children covered by Medicaid actually fell after 1996 (Smith et al., 2000). However, the creation of the Children's Health Insurance Program (CHIP) in 1997 reversed this trend and provided coverage for more children. By 2008, 9.9 percent of U.S. children had no health insurance, representing a substantial decline since 1987. But this still amounts to more than 7 million children (U.S. Census Bureau, 2009h). The health reforms enacted in 2010 should further lower this number, however, once they are fully in effect by 2014.

However much single parenthood may elevate the risk of poverty, it is also clear that a major cause of poverty among single mothers and their children is gender-related inequality in pay. As shown in Table 13.2, the median income of one-parent, male-headed families is quite close to that of the "traditional" family where the husband is employed and the wife is a homemaker. Thus, the low wages of women, rather than single parenthood per se, are a major cause of whatever economic disadvantages female-headed families suffer. Among black and Hispanic women, this condition is worsened by relatively low levels of education, which further depress wages.

Of course, what many social scientists and others have argued is that other disadvantages of growing up in a female-headed family can lead to the perpetuation of poverty into successive generations, even though single-parenthood is itself often the result of poverty (Wilson, 1996). Until recently, research findings provided limited support for this viewpoint. Lieberson (1980, pp. 183–93), for example, found that very little of the black-white gap in educational attainment could be explained by differences in family structure. More recent research, though, indicates that growing up in single-parent families can have long-term effects for both blacks and whites (McLanahan and Bumpass, 1988; McLanahan, 1988; Upchurch et al., 1999), including a greater risk of early and premarital childbearing, a greater risk of divorce, and lower education and income. Research by Sampson (1987) also found that black family disruption led to increased rates of juvenile crime. Undoubtedly, some of these effects are the result of teenage pregnancy rather than single-parent families per se. In addition, a number of studies suggest that it is mainly the lower income of single-mother families, not the family type itself, that leads to many of the longer-term effects (Biblarz and Raferty, 1999). Also, recent research suggests that the negative effects of one-parent families are partially mitigated by their smaller size. Children with more brothers and sisters do less well on average, perhaps because their parents, like single parents, are busier (Featherman and Hauser, 1978; Jencks, 1991, p. 87). Since one-parent families are smaller than other families (particularly among the poor), the disadvantages of a one-parent family are in large part offset by the advantages of a smaller family (Jencks, 1991; Biblarz and Raferty, 1999).

Although growing up in single-parent families does appear to be detrimental in some ways, it also appears that one-parent families are here to stay in the United States. Moreover, virtually all studies agree on certain points. First, people with low incomes—black, Hispanic, and white—are more likely than others to form one-parent families either by premarital childbearing or by divorce and separation. Second, an important source of problems among people in female-headed families is the low income of their wage earners (Reimers, 1984), not the mere fact that there is a single female parent. Therefore, dealing with such causes of poverty as low wages and high unemployment will likely reduce the number of urban single-parent families, and taking steps to eliminate wage inequalities based on sex and to enforce payment of child support by absent fathers would alleviate many of the disadvantages of female-headed families.

Finally, it is important to stress that the disadvantages associated with growing up in a single-parent family in and of itself appear to be relatively small, and frequently are offset by the smaller number of children in such families. Many who grow up in single-parent families are highly successful. For example, Michelangelo, John Lennon, Tom Cruise, Madonna, Nathaniel Hawthorne, Jodie Foster, Johnny Depp, and Presidents Bill Clinton and Barack Obama have something else in common besides success and fame—all of them grew up in single-parent families.

The Future of Marriages and Families

The changes that have affected marriages and families over the past few decades are dramatic. What will families be like twenty-five years from now, and what problems will they face?

Just as sociologists fifty years ago feared the disintegration of the family because it was losing its traditional functions, today some social observers point to sexual permissiveness, smaller families, higher divorce rates, single-parent households, teenage pregnancy, family violence, increasing number of people not marrying at all, and the prevalence of alternative family structures as evidence that the family is a decaying institution

Table 13.2 Median Family Income, by Race, Hispanic Origin, and Type of Family, 2008

| | Married-Couple Families | | | | |
	All Families	Wife in Paid Labor Force	Wife Not in Paid Labor Force	Male Householder, No Wife	Female Householder, No Husband
White	$70,070	$90,632	$52,359	$47,815	$35,883
Black	$39,936	$75,266	$39,835	$35,563	$25,011
Hispanic	$40,466	$62,255	$33,483	$39,368	$23,866
U.S. Total	$61,521	$86,621	$48,502	$43,571	$30,129

Source: U.S. Census Bureau, Historical Income Tables—Families, 2009, http://www.census.gov/hhes/www/income/histinc/incfamdet.html.

(Popenoe, 1988; 1996). Others look at these same developments and proclaim that the family is a resilient institution that is "here to stay" (Bane, 1976). Most people still ultimately marry and, if they divorce, later remarry.

Ideally, the changes we are undergoing in the family and in gender roles will allow people to choose what is right for them individually rather than conform to predetermined roles. However, the new options available today, especially to women, make it difficult to know what to do or whether to be content with our choices. This can produce a lack of effective norms that can lead to confusion and alienation. At the same time, people are less likely to be stigmatized for the personal choices they make. American society has become increasingly tolerant of alternative forms of marital and family life. People are choosing family systems to complement their social and economic situations. As these institutions have changed, so has the family.

Summary

The family is the most basic and universal of all human social institutions. A family can be defined as a group of related people who live together as a unit. The precise form and functions of families vary from culture to culture. The most basic family types are the nuclear family and the extended family; the former is the predominant type in the United States. The family you are born into is called your family of orientation; the family you create when you marry and have children is called your family of procreation. Although monogamy is the only legally recognized form of marriage in Western societies, many cultures have practiced different forms of polygamy.

Because the family is a cultural universal, functionalists assume that it must perform certain roles that other institutions cannot. The key functions of families can be divided into general categories, including economic, status transferral, religious and educational, affectional, socialization, and emotional support. In modern societies, families must share these functions with outside institutions, but they continue to play a critical role in all of them.

Conflict theorists argue that the family reflects the inequalities of the larger society. They point to such social realities as role inequality and violence within the family to argue that family structure and behavior are designed to promote the well-being of the dominant group in the society—males.

As with most institutions, families have changed in response to larger societal and cultural changes. As women have increasingly entered the workforce, many have chosen to delay marriage and childbirth. More women and men than in the past do not marry, and among those who do, the percentage of couples who choose to remain childless has increased. Cohabitation has become acceptable. Married and cohabiting couples divide household responsibilities more equally than in the past, although the woman still assumes a disproportionate share of such responsibilities in most relationships.

As a result of women's increased economic independence and related legal and ideological changes, divorce has become more common and acceptable in U.S. society. On the one hand, this change has benefited people, especially women, by allowing them to escape from unhappy marriages. On the other hand, increased divorce rates have created many one-parent families and placed severe economic hardships on many women. One consequence of this trend has been the feminization of poverty.

Despite all these changes, the family remains a viable unit, and warnings of the "demise of the family" are probably exaggerated. Most people still marry and have families. If divorce rates are high, so are remarriage rates, although the latter are falling. Although families must change to adapt to changes in other social institutions, they will continue to play a crucial role in modern societies.

Key Terms

family
kinship
marriage
extended family
nuclear family
family of orientation
family of procreation
monogamy
serial monogamy
polygamy

polygyny
polyandry
incest taboo
exogamy
endogamy
homogamy
patriarchy
matriarchy
neolocality
patrilocality
matrilocality
patrilineal system
matrilineal system
bilineal system
child abuse
cohabitation

Exercises

1. Not that long ago, "family violence" was more-or-less synonymous with "spousal violence" or "child abuse." More recently, family violence also focuses on youth violence. Tragedies like those that have taken place in Littleton, Colorado and Virginia Tech have piqued the nation's interest in violence among America's young people. Predictably, one of the most commonly heard questions regarding these incidents is "What was wrong with the families these youngsters came from?"

   - Do you think there is a crisis of youth violence in our society or is this perception fueled by what might be called an "adult panic"?
   - If you were a policymaker, what approach would you recommend in reaction to episodes of youth violence?

2. This chapter poses the question: "Should couples stay together 'for the sake of the kids'?" Sociological research has demonstrated that more harm can come from maintaining an unhappy marriage than from dissolving that marriage. In addition, research demonstrates that how much a divorce hurts children can depend upon how the adults handle the dissolution.

   - How does adversarial divorce affect the children involved?
   - How can divorce mediation and collaborative law assist in relieving the harmful impact of divorce on dependent children?
   - If you were married and decided to divorce, would you consider divorce mediation? Why or why not?

Part V
Social Change

Chapter 14
Urban Society: City Life and Collective Behavior

The Rise of Cities Throughout the World — 438

Technology, Industrialization, and Urbanization — 440
- Social Change and Urbanization 440
- The Demographic Transition and Urbanization 441

Urbanization in the United States — 442
- Economics of Urban Growth 442
- Functional Specialization 443
- Urban Hierarchy 444

Urbanization in the Third World — 444

Urban Life — 445
- Differences Between Rural and Urban Life 445
- Wirth on Urban Life 448
- Decline of Community: Myth or Reality? 448
- Urban Life and "Getting Involved" 449
- Cities and Social Conflict 451

Collective Behavior — 452
- Causes of Collective Behavior 452
- Types of Collective Behavior 453
- Collective Behavior in Crowds 454
- Types of Crowd Behavior 456
- Mass Behavior 458
- Types of Mass Behavior 459
- Fashions and Fads 462

The Structure of the City — 462
- Human Ecology 462
- Urban Social Segregation 463

The Changing City in Postindustrial America — 468

The Rise of the Suburbs — 468
- Causes of Suburbanization 468
- Life in the Suburbs 469

The Crisis of the Central Cities — 471
- Population Decline 471
- The Urban Underclass 471
- The Urban Fiscal Crisis 472

Uneven Development Among American Cities — 473
- Different Processes or Different Stages? 473
- The Conflict Theory of Uneven Development 474

Summary — 475

Key Terms — 476

Exercises — 476

You know it well. It's where you go to learn, to have fun, to be uplifted. The zoo, the symphony, theatre, opera, the best museums and libraries—they're all there. So are the liveliest nightclub districts—where you can hear the best of the blues, jazz, rock, funk, alternative, soul, or even country—sometimes all within a block or two of each other! It's where you go to see the ball game, hear U2 in concert, or try some kind of food you've never eaten before. And it is the place that has those offbeat little shops where you can buy things you can't find anywhere else. It's also where you see those spectacular works of public art and architecture—the Gateway Arch, the Statue of Liberty, the Eiffel Tower, the Parthenon. Or is it?

Some of you know it quite differently. To you, it may be that scary place you see on the news every night—the place where there has just been a murder even bloodier and more shocking than the one you heard about last week. The place where you hear about people complaining that they can't get to sleep because of the gunfire every night, or where a two-year-old is abducted and murdered by two ten-year-olds. Maybe you think of it as the place where people loot stores and burn buildings when their home team wins the World Series, Super Bowl, or NBA Championship, or where terrorists create mayhem by blowing up crowded buildings or setting off bombs in shopping districts. Also, perhaps, you know it as the place where corrupt politicians keep finding new ways to divert public money to their own personal use, or where corporate moguls hatch new plots to dodge antitrust laws and get more of your money.

Of course, in both cases I'm talking about the city. In fact, both images of it are prominent in contemporary culture, and each contains a piece—but only a piece—of the truth. Those who see the city as described in the first paragraph may see it as "the only place to live"; if they don't live there, they visit it as often as they can. Those who see the city as described in the second paragraph look upon it as a frightening place to be avoided whenever possible. Why do people have such different images of the city? And why are so many activities, both good and bad, concentrated there?

In this chapter, we shall explore why the city has become such a dominant force in modern societies—why so much of what goes on in the world happens there, and why societies like the United States have undergone an abrupt (in historical terms) transition from rural societies to urban societies. As the opening vignette illustrates, our new urban life has been both glorified and vilified. Though both the glorification and vilification contain elements of truth, both are also great oversimplifications.

To truly understand the city, we must first define it. The most widely used definition of the city probably is that of Louis Wirth (1938), who defined it as "a relatively large, dense, permanent settlement of socially heterogeneous individuals." This definition encompasses four characteristics of cities: the large size of population, the high density of population (in other words, a large number of people per square mile), the permanence of the settlement, and the heterogeneity or diversity of the population. This definition is relative: A city has these characteristics as compared with other settlements. Thus, what was considered a city in the past might not be today. In past eras, a settlement of 10,000 people would have qualified as a city; today it would not because such a population is relatively small. Moreover, a settlement of 10,000 people during certain past eras would certainly have been a highly specialized and complex place; more so than a town of that size today, and certainly more so than most human settlements at the time. Finally, it would have had a much higher population density (people per square mile) than a town of 10,000 today.

Wirth's definition leaves room for debate as to whether a given settlement is or is not a city, but it continues to be widely used because it makes two important points. First, what is or is not a city is relative and must be considered in the context of any given society. Second, a city is defined not merely on the basis of size, but also on the basis of the diversity of its inhabitants and the complexity of their activities. This point was later elaborated upon by Childe (1950), who pointed out that cities are associated with such things as specialization, monumental public buildings, trade, and the development of writing and the arts and sciences.

The Rise of Cities Throughout the World

Large-scale urbanization is a recent phenomenon. **Urbanization** can be defined as the process by which an increasing share of a population lives in

GLOBAL SOCIOLOGY
A Portrait of the Preindustrial City

Most of the earliest cities around the world would be almost unrecognizable to anyone living in a modern city. Certain features appeared independently in the earliest cities in Mesopotamia, China, and Central America, and, with minor variations, these features characterized most preindustrial cities throughout history.

One major way preindustrial cities differed from modern ones was in the nature of the city center. Rather than centering on a downtown commercial district, early cities were built around a religious center: a temple, tower, or pyramid in the earliest cities; a cathedral in medieval cities. This layout can be readily seen in the photo on the next page, showing the well-preserved remains of Teotihuacan. This city, built over 1,000 years ago by an indigenous population near what is now Mexico City, was centered on two large pyramids. The photo was taken from one; the other can be seen on the left side of the photo.

In the earliest cities, the temple was more than just a religious center. It also served as "a place for meditation and research, a warehouse, an accounting and distributing agency" (Comhaire and Cahnman, 1959, p. 2). Records of animal herds and crop yields were kept there; grain and treasures were stored there; loans were made there—all, of course, under the supervision and control of a high priest or a king who was often believed to be divine. In medieval cities, the economic function of the religious center itself declined, but it was taken over by open-air markets that typically located close to the cathedral.

Another difference between preindustrial and modern cities had to do with who lived where. The wealthiest and most powerful people in virtually all preindustrial cities lived near the center. In the photo of Teotihuacan, for example, the buildings nearest the central mall and pyramids were residences of the high priests; more ordinary people lived toward the outside of the city. This pattern was common for two reasons.

First, it was desirable to live near the religious center, and such a privilege was reserved for priests, military leaders, kings, and their courts. Second, it was safer to live near the center. City-states were frequently at war with one another, and living near the city wall was riskier than living near the center. Thus, the further from the center, the lower the social and economic status of the population—just the opposite of what we find in the modern American city. Walled cities sometimes outgrew the area enclosed by their walls, so that some people had to live outside the walls, at least until new ones could be built. As you might expect, this unhappy fate befell those with the lowest social status.

Early cities were denser and more compact than today's cities. When the main mode of transportation is walking, nobody wants to be too far from anything. The ancient city of Uruk, for example, may have had a population of about 29,000 per square mile (computed from Spates and Macionis, 1987, p. 37), and Ur's population density may have been as great as 125,000 per square mile (Thomlinson, 1976, p. 403). Teotihuacan likely had a population density of around 25,000 per square mile. These figures compare to about 12,000 per square mile in modern Boston and under 10,000 in Washington, D.C., (U.S. Bureau of the Census, 1986b, pp. 42, 418). When early cities grew, their density usually increased, as more and more people crammed into the space inside the city walls.

Closely related to high density was the absence of a distinction between work and home (Sjoberg, 1955, 1960). People worked at home, and they often sold their products on the street outside their homes or through a window in their houses. Both people and businesses were frequently segregated by occupation. In medieval London, for example, streets and neighborhoods were named for the occupational group that resided there. There was a Beer Street, where the breweries were located, and a Baker Street, where the city's bakeries were located.

---

cities (Choldin, 1985, pp. 150–52). Urbanization does not mean merely that cities are growing; that is urban growth. We say that urbanization occurs when cities not only grow, but grow to a greater extent than rural areas or grow when rural areas do not. Although sociologists usually speak of urbanization as a process, they also sometimes refer to the level of urbanization. Generally, this refers to the percentage or proportion of the population that lives in cities and their suburbs.

It is only within the past two centuries that any sizable proportion of the human population has lived in cities. Only the Roman Empire and the Inca, Aztec, and Mayan Indians of Central and South America were able to attain urbanization levels of as much as 10 or 20 percent

(Childe, 1946; Davis, 1955; Hawley, 1981; Kornberg, 1975; Rivet, 1960). Most early cities had small populations, usually under 40,000 and often well under 10,000. The largest early cities were ancient Rome, which probably had a population of 350,000 to 600,000, and the Central and South American Indian cities, the largest of which had populations of around 200,000—hardly large cities by today's standards (Chandler and Fox, 1974; Rivet, 1960; Russell, 1958; Kornberg, 1975). As shown in the box "A Portrait of the Preindustrial City," these early cities differed from cities in today's industrialized societies in a number of ways besides size.

After around A.D. 500, cities grew somewhat larger, but truly large cities remained rare for another thousand years or more. As shown in Table 14.1, only a handful of cities in the world had populations exceeding 150,000 at any time between A.D. 800 and 1600, and none had populations that came even close to 1 million. Today, in contrast, the industrialized societies have become overwhelmingly urban, and the rest of the world is urbanizing rapidly. By the year 2000, there were more than 380 cities or metropolitan areas worldwide with populations of more than 1 million people, and there will be more than 500 by the year 2015 (Brinkhoff, 2001; World Resources Institute, 1996). (The term "metropolitan area" refers to a city and its suburbs.) The twenty-one largest cities in the world, all with metropolitan populations of more than 10 million, are shown in Table 14.2. The United States alone had fifty metropolitan areas with populations of more than 1 million as of the 2000 Census. The majority of all Americans live in these large metropolitan areas (Fiske, 1991; Haub, 1991). At least fifty-seven metropolitan areas in Europe have populations of 1 million or more (Brinkhoff, 2001). Today, the population is about 75 percent urban in North America and 73 percent urban in Europe (Population Reference Bureau, 2001).

Technology, Industrialization, and Urbanization

This rapid urbanization was the result of both technological and social innovations. When inventions such as the steam engine, the spinning jenny, and the automatic weaving machine made mass production possible, the place of work shifted from the home to the factory. Industrialization also created a demand for a substantial labor force. Outside the cities, better roads and inland canals made the movement of both people and food from the countryside to the city far more feasible. Agriculture, too, was transformed by technological changes associated with the Industrial Revolution. In the eighteenth and nineteenth centuries, such innovations as crop rotation, selective breeding of animals, and new tools led to dramatic improvements in productivity (Mumford, 1938; Wrigley, 1969). This meant that a larger *agricultural surplus* could be produced, and therefore a larger urban population supported.

Social Change and Urbanization

At the same time, important social changes that encouraged urban growth were emerging. One was the development of effective national governments. In contrast to the feudal era, when violent

The pyramids and temples of Teotihuacan are typical of the religious monuments that characterized preindustrial cities. (Courtesy of John E. Farley)

Table 14.1 Estimated Populations of Major World Cities, A.D. 800–1600

Population	Year				
	800	1000	1200	1400	1600
900,000					
800,000	Sian, China				
700,000	Baghdad, Persia				Peking, China
					Istanbul, Turkey
600,000					
500,000		Cordoba, Spain		Cairo, Egypt	
		Istanbul, Turkey			
400,000		Kaifeng, China			Cairo, Egypt
					Osaka, Japan
					Tokyo, Japan
					Kyoto, Japan
				Peking, China	
300,000	Istanbul, Turkey	Sian, China			
				Paris, France	Naples, Italy
			Istanbul, Turkey		Paris, France
			Fez, Morocco		
200,000	Alexandria, Egypt	Kyoto, Japan	Cairo, Egypt	Kyoto, Japan	
	Kyoto, Japan				London, England
			Kamakura, Japan	Sian, China	
	Cordoba, Spain	Cairo, Egypt	4 cities[1]	Fez, Morocco	3 cities[2]

Sources: Bardo and Hartman, 1982; Chandler and Fox, 1974.
[1] Palermo, Italy; Peking, China; Kaifeng, China; Sian, China.
[2] Venice, Italy; Potasi, Mexico; Sian, China.

disputes among nobles discouraged travel and trade, national governments created an environment in which national and international trade flourished. National governments also brought about a common monetary system, greater consistency of laws, and uniform systems of weights and measures—all of which are vital to trade. Increased trade led to a growth in manufacturing, which in turn further stimulated urbanization. These trends were reinforced by world exploration, trade, and colonization, which created new demand and supplied new raw materials.

Gradually during the seventeenth and eighteenth centuries, the urban business-owning class, called the bourgeoisie, replaced the rural lords and barons as the dominant group in European society. In the city, craftsmen who formerly had owned their own businesses began to work in factories for the bourgeoisie. This change created a new form of social stratification in the city, and power became more concentrated in the hands of the bourgeoisie, who used it to institute national policies that favored urban growth.

The Demographic Transition and Urbanization

The demographic transition, described in Web-Based Chapter C, also contributed dramatically to urbanization. As death rates fell, more children survived to adulthood and rural areas became overpopulated. To avoid the splitting of farmland into ever-smaller pieces, many societies enacted laws dictating that parents had to pass on a plot of land only to one child. Most children, therefore, were left with no source of economic support in the rural areas at a time when the demand for industrial workers in the cities was increasing. Thus, the *push* of overpopulation in rural areas and the *pull* of employment opportunities in cities led increasing numbers of young people in Europe and North America to leave the countryside and head for the city.

Urban life was hard for most people in the early stages of industrialization. Industrial laborers, who in many cases were only ten years old, worked thirteen hours per day, seven days per week (Choldin, 1985, pp. 100–02). They had no health insurance, workers' compensation, or government-mandated safety rules. In many cities sanitation remained deplorable through much of the nineteenth century. As a result, death rates in cities were higher than in rural areas (Thomlinson, 1976). In fact, urban death rates were so high during the earlier stages of the Industrial Revolution that some of the fastest-growing cities would actually have lost population had it not been for in-migration.

Urbanization in the United States

As in Europe, industrialization was a major source of urban growth in the United States. When the first U.S. Census was taken in 1790, the American population was only 5 percent urban, despite the fact that any town with a population of 2,500 or more was regarded as urban. By 1840, the urban population had risen to about 10 percent. The Civil War was a major stimulus to industrialization in the United States, and it accelerated an already rapid urbanization. By 1870, the U.S. population was one-quarter urban; by 1900, it was 40 percent urban. By 1920, the majority of the American population lived in cities, and the percentage continued to increase rapidly (except during the Great Depression) until 1960, when it reached about 70 percent. After that, it rose only slowly to about 74 percent in 1980 (U.S. Bureau of the Census, 1983c), and has remained near that level since.

Economics of Urban Growth

The growth of different cities at different points in U.S. history reflects the various stages in the development of the U.S. economy (Duncan and Lieberson, 1970; Glaab and Brown, 1967; Glaab, 1963; Hawley, 1981). As Table 14.3 shows, the most rapidly growing cities in early American history were seaports. During the nineteenth century, New York became the preeminent American city because it had a great natural harbor, water access to the interior, and a central location relative to early America's population. A key to its development was the construction of transportation systems: first the Erie Canal in 1825, which connected the city to the Great Lakes shipping routes, and later the railroads (Palen, 1987, p. 67).

Table 14.2 World's Largest Cities (Cities with Metropolitan Population of 10 Million or Greater), 2009

	Urban agglomeration	Population in Millions
1	Tokyo, Japan	36.5
2	Delhi, India	21.7
3	São Paulo, Brazil	20.0
4	Mumbai (Bombay), India	19.7
5	Ciudad de México (Mexico City), Mexico	19.3
6	New York-Newark, United States	19.3
7	Shanghai, China	16.3
8	Kolkata (Calcutta), India	15.3
9	Dhaka, Bangladesh	14.3
10	Buenos Aires, Argentina	13.0
11	Karachi, Pakistan	12.8
12	Los Angeles–Long Beach–Santa Ana, United States	12.7
13	Beijing, China	12.2
14	Rio de Janeiro, Brazil	11.8
15	Manila, Philippines	11.4
16	Osaka–Kobe, Japan	11.3
17	Al-Qahirah (Cairo), Egypt	10.9
18	Moskva (Moscow), Russian Federation	10.5
19	Paris, France	10.4
20	Istanbul, Turkey	10.4
21	Lagos, Nigeria	10.2

Source: United Nations, Department of Economic and Social Affairs, Population Division. 2010. *World Urbanization Prospects,* The 2009 Revision. New York: United Nations.

The next surge of growth, before and during the Civil War, took place in the "inland ports"—cities located at transshipment points; that is, at the junction of two rivers, or where water routes ended and land transportation took over. Chicago is the leading example: Between 1850 and 1890, its population doubled every ten years, at least. From 1880 to 1900, the most rapid growth occurred in cities whose economies were based almost entirely on manufacturing. Most of these cities, like Cleveland, Buffalo, and Detroit, were located on the Great Lakes. To the west, new port and transshipment cities were also growing, like Minneapolis–St. Paul and San Francisco. From 1900 until the beginning of World War II, the automobile was the dominant force shaping the growth of American cities. Rapid growth continued in Detroit and other auto-manufacturing cities in Michigan and Ohio, as well as in cities near oil fields, such as Los Angeles and Houston. Since World War II, the fastest-growing American cities have been in the Sun Belt—the South and the West. These cities have had diversified economies that benefited from tourism, energy extraction, military spending, and service industries.

Functional Specialization

Note the references above to auto-manufacturing cities and cities near oil fields. This illustrates the concept of **functional specialization:** Different cities specialize in different kinds of economic activity. Historically, Detroit has specialized in auto manufacturing, Pittsburgh in steel making, Seattle in aircraft manufacturing, and Hartford and Des Moines in finance and insurance services (Duncan and Lieberson, 1970; Getis, Getis, and Fellman, 1981). Houston's economy is based mainly on oil; New Orleans is a major seaport; Minneapolis and San Francisco are regional trade and commerce centers. The Minneapolis–St. Paul area, for example, has major livestock and grain markets as well as regional distribution centers for a variety of national companies. Some cities, of course, are more diversified. Examples include Boston, Dallas, Atlanta, Indianapolis, and Miami (Noyelle and Stanback, 1983). Often, diversified cities are more protected from economic fluctuations than cities highly specialized in one industry. Sharp "busts" hit Detroit when imports hurt domestic car sales, Seattle during declines in the aircraft industry, and Houston when the price of oil fell. Much of California struggled with harder economic times in the early 1990s, as a result of cutbacks in military spending and base closings. Military spending had been a major stimulus to California's rapid growth during and after World War II (Hooks, 1994), but the same forces that contributed to California's growth during military buildups have made it vulnerable to hard times during military scale backs.

A few cities, including Washington, Los Angeles, Chicago, and, above all, New York, are national metropolises. In other words, they are the centers of economic activities that are national or international in scope. Many national and multinational corporations have their headquarters in or near these cities; national organizations are headquartered in these places; network television originates from these locations (Hawley, 1981, pp. 244–48). Washington, of course, is virtually guaranteed such a status by its position as the nation's capital. With the rise of the Sun Belt cities, Atlanta also appears to be developing some of the characteristics of a national metropolis. The functional specialization of cities, along with other factors, helps to determine which areas grow and which ones do not under a given set of circumstances. Metropolitan growth in the first decade of the new century is discussed in the box "Metro Areas in the United States: Which Ones Are Growing? Which Ones Aren't?".

A new trend in the past two decades has been the emergence of greater functional specialization within the larger metropolitan areas. During the 1970s and 1980s, the suburbs increasingly became centers of highly specialized employment. Some, for example, specialized in high-tech electronic and computer-related industries; others developed economies based on major medical centers or sports complexes; yet others developed retail economies centered around shopping malls and related commercial development. In the

Table 14.3 Period of Emergence of Major Urban Centers in the United States

Before 1850	1850 to 1880	1880 to 1900	1900 to 1940	1940 to Present
New York	Chicago	Buffalo	Los Angeles	Dallas
Charleston, SC[1]	St. Louis	Cleveland	Houston	Atlanta
Boston	Cincinnati	Detroit		Miami
Philadelphia	San Francisco	Milwaukee		Seattle
Baltimore	Washington	Minneapolis–St Paul		Denver
New Orleans	Pittsburgh	Kansas City		San Diego
				San Antonio
				Phoenix

[1] Failed to grow rapidly after 1850, and no longer regarded as major urban center.

Sources: James E. Vance. 1976. "Cities in the Shaping of the American Nation," *Journal of Geography* (January): 41–52; Beverly Duncan and Stanley Lieberson. 1970. *Metropolis and Region in Transition* (Beverly Hills, CA: Sage); and U.S. Bureau of the Census. 1913. Thirteenth Census of the United States: 1910.

meantime, downtown areas became more specialized in banking, government, law, and investment (Suro, 1991).

Urban Hierarchy

The United States, like other industrialized countries, has developed a system called an urban hierarchy within which different cities, depending on their size and level of economic activity, may supply goods and services to less populated areas on the one hand, and be dependent on larger cities for goods and services on the other hand (Golden, 1981; Hawley, 1981; Simmons, 1978). Those products and services for which a nationwide market is required tend to be concentrated in the national metropolises. For other goods and services, the market is regional. Cities such as Minneapolis, Kansas City, and San Francisco do not provide goods and services just for the people who live in them, but also for the **hinterland**: a surrounding area that is dependent on the city for goods, services, and markets. Another step down the scale are smaller cities like Peoria, Illinois; Bakersfield, California; Knoxville, Tennessee; and Springfield, Massachusetts. These cities are part of the hinterland of larger cities and rely on those larger cities for certain specialized goods and services. Yet, these cities provide other products and services (local television stations, regional shopping malls, smaller-scale wholesaling) for hinterlands of their own (Bourne and Simmons, 1978). This hierarchy continues until you reach the level of the very smallest towns that can support only a gas station, a convenience store, and perhaps a grain elevator.

Urbanization in the Third World

Since World War II, many Third World countries have experienced rapid urbanization. This process results from some of the same social forces that produced urbanization in Europe and North America, although the *push* factors forcing people out of rural areas have been more important than the *pull* factors attracting them to the cities. As discussed in Web-Based Chapter C, the decrease in mortality rates that accompanies the demographic transition has happened much more quickly in the Third World than it did in the Western industrialized nations and Japan. As a result, rural overpopulation has been more sudden and severe, and millions of people around the world have left their rural homes for the city.

Unfortunately, many Third World countries have not industrialized to the extent that Europe had when the demographic transition took place there, so millions of people in Third World cities have no useful economic role to play. Lacking any real means of support, they live by the thousands—sometimes by the millions—in shantytowns, or squatter settlements, on the fringes of major cities. The squatter population of Mexico City, for example, has been estimated at 4 million, and estimates for Calcutta, India, reach 2 million (Palen, 1987, p. 342). The squatters live crowded together in makeshift structures built from cardboard, scrap wood, or metal, without running water, flush toilets, or electricity.

Although the deplorable conditions of today's Third World shantytowns may not be any worse than those of nineteenth-century European working-class neighborhoods, there are some important differences. First, today's Third World urbanization is occurring on a far larger scale. São Paulo, Brazil, for example, has a population of 18.8 million, over five times the population of Paris in 1900. Second, urbanization in many Third World countries is running ahead of industrialization, whereas in Europe it tended to follow or accompany industrialization. Thus, urban populations in these countries have grown far beyond what the economy can support. This condition is known as **overurbanization.** The term does not mean that the population in these countries is "too urban"—usually the urban standard of living exceeds that of rural areas, even in the poorest nations—but rather that the economy has not developed enough to employ the urban population (Gugler, 1982; Palen, 1987; Sovani, 1964; Wellisz, 1971).

This problem is especially severe in the least industrialized countries, such as Mexico, India, Peru, Indonesia, and Thailand. Many of these countries lack the urban hierarchy of industrialized countries. Instead, they are characterized by primate cities (Portes, 1977). A primate city is one large city into which the great share of the country's population and economic growth is channeled. The extreme example is probably Bangkok, Thailand, which has thirty-three times the population of the country's next-largest city, and more than half of the entire urban population of Thailand (Spates and Macionis, 1987, p. 272). Many theorists argue that primate cities hinder economic development in two ways. First, they are said to retard economic growth in the rest of the country because the perception develops that the only place where there is opportunity is "the big city" (Bradshaw, 1987; London and Smith, 1988). Second, they are especially subject to overurbanization because people flock to the primate city in hopes of bettering their lives.

We must, however, be careful in generalizing about Third World cities. Some countries have primate cities (especially those with long histories of colonial domination), but others do not. The concept of overurbanization is far more applicable to some countries than to others. A number of Third World nations are rapidly industrializing, and for them overurbanization is not such a problem. Several of the "Pacific Rim" countries, such as Taiwan, South Korea, and Hong Kong (now part of The People's Republic of China), have industrialized to such an extent that they are able to employ most of their urban populations. In China overurbanization was largely prevented by governmental controls on migration to the city, a solution that would probably only work under China's centralized economic and political system. Today, those controls have been relaxed, but the rapid growth of the Chinese economy has thus far been able for the most part to absorb the growing number of migrants to the cities. Nonetheless, there has been an increase in crowded, substandard housing on the fringes of China's largest cities, as more people have fled the rural areas for urban opportunities.

Despite the problems in many Third World cities, the urban population continues to soar. In general, over three-quarters of the population of Latin America is urban, as is nearly 43 percent in Asia and more than one-third in Africa (Population Reference Bureau, 2001). These figures represent a sharp increase since World War II. In fact, there are more than fifty *times* as many people living in Third World cities of over 1 million today as there were in 1950. In 1950, seven of the world's ten largest cities were in industrialized countries. Today, only two of the world's ten largest cities (Tokyo and New York) are in industrialized countries. The population of some cities in developing countries is very large and growing rapidly. As Table 14.2 shows, fourteen of the top twenty most populous cities are in developing countries.

Urban Life

The large-scale growth of cities has generated intense debates about the relative merits of urban and rural life. As was previously noted, the city has been both praised as the cradle of civilization, and condemned as impersonal, brutal, and corrupt. Early sociological theories about the city reflected both views. Sociologists sought to identify what it was about city living that seemed, for example, to spur both creativity and deviance. As noted in Chapter 1, urban problems associated with industrialization were a major focus of early sociology in both Europe and the United States. More recently, sociologists have used empirical research to test systematically the accuracy of popular and sociological perceptions about the city. This research has shown such perceptions to be right in some ways and wrong in others.

Differences Between Rural and Urban Life

Probably the earliest systematic sociological comparison of urban and rural life was that of the German sociologist Ferdinand Toennies (1963 [orig. 1887]). Toennies's theory, like others that followed it, was not simply a comparison of rural and urban life, but rather a comparison of traditional, preindustrial society—which is rural in nature—and modern industrial society—which is urban. It is, therefore, difficult to sort out the effects of modernization, industrialization, and urbanization in this and other theories.

Toennies referred to the traditional rural society as *gemeinschaft*, a German word that, roughly translated, means "community." In this society, relations between people were close and personal, behavior was governed by widely accepted traditions, and contact with strangers was rare. People were closely bound together by kinship, friendship, and neighborliness. They recognized "common goods—common evils; common friends—common enemies" (Toennies, 1963 [orig. 1887]). They trusted one another and were careful to fulfill their mutual obligations. Modern, industrial, urban

SOCIOLOGICAL INSIGHTS

Metro Areas in the United States: Which Ones Are Growing? Which Ones Aren't?

Which metropolitan areas are growing fastest as we enter the new millennium? Which ones, by contrast, are losing population? The answers to these questions can be found in the tables in this box. Look first at the unnumbered table below, which shows the twenty-five metropolitan areas in the United States that had the highest percentage growth rates between 2000 and 2007. Can you make any generalizations about these areas?

Most of the areas that experienced rapid growth are relatively new areas located in the South and the West. Note that Texas, Florida, and the Rocky Mountain states are especially well represented. As modern communication techniques (fax, the Internet, express mail) and air travel have given people a wider variety of places to live, the amenities offered by different locales have become more important. And many of these places do have amenities, such as mountains or warm climates, that make them attractive to people seeking a particular lifestyle. Note, too, that several of them are the homes of major universities where a good deal of the research and expertise so important to the postindustrial economy takes place.

25 Metropolitan Areas Showing the Largest Population Growth Rate of Top 50 MSAs, 2000-2007

Rank	Metropolitan Area Name	Change, 2000 to 2007 (Percent)
1	Fort Myers–Cape Coral, FL MSA	33.9
2	Las Vegas, NV MSA	33.5
3	Raleigh, NC MSA	31.4
4	Provo-Orem, UT MSA	30.9
5	Phoenix-Mesa-Scottsdale, AZ MSA	28.5
6	Austin–Round Rock, TX MSA	27.9
7	Boise City–Nampa, ID MSA	46.1
8	Naples–Marco Island, FL MSA	45.3
9	Fayetteville-Springdale-Rogers, AR MSA	44.9
10	Ocala, FL MSA	39.8
11	Riverside–San Bernardino–Ontario, CA MSA	38.9
12	Port St. Lucie, FL MSA	38.9
13	MaCellen, TX MSA	36.5
14	Atlanta, GA MSA	36.3
15	Charlotte, NC MSA	35.1
16	Wilmington, NC MSA	34.3
17	Orlando, FL MSA	33.3
18	Reno, NV MSA	32.9
19	Bakersfield, CA MSA	32.1
20	Houston, TX MSA	31.6
21	Dallas, TX MSA	31.0
22	Stockton, CA MSA	30.5
23	Lakeland, FL CMSA	30.4
24	Hagerstown-Martinsburg, MD-WV MSA	30.2
25	Ogden, UT MSA	29.3

Now, take a look at the table below, which shows the fifteen metropolitan areas that experienced the lowest population growth rates between 2000 and 2007. Are you able to make any generalizations about these areas?

Most of these metropolitan areas that have been losing population since the 1990s are older metropolitan areas in the Northeast, with some also in the Midwest and just a handful in the South. In fact, the majority of these areas are in just three states: New York, Pennsylvania, and Ohio. These metropolitan areas have economics based on industrial manufacturing or on getting and shipping raw materials, such as iron and steel, for manufacturing. Many of them are also located in cold climates with fewer recreational amenities than many of the fast-growing areas enjoy. Only three are in the warm regions of the South (including the large exodus of population from New Orleans in the aftermath of 2005's hurricane Katrina), and only one is in the West. The large population loss from New Orleans is clearly anomalous as the MSA grew 4.1 percent between 1990 and 2000 and would likely have grown again had the hurricane not struck.

15 Metropolitan Areas Showing the Greatest Population Loss of Top 50 MSAs, 2000–2007

Rank	Metropolitan Area Name	Change, 2000 to 2007 (Percent)
1	New Orleans–Metarie–Kenner, LA MSA	−21.7
2	Youngstown-Warren-Boardman, OH, PA MSA	−5.4
3	Buffalo–Niagara Falls, NY MSA	−3.6
4	Pittsburgh, PA MSA	−3.1
5	Bangor, ME MSA	−2.4
6	Beaumont–Port Arthur, TX MSA	−2.3
7	Scranton–Wilkes-Barre, PA MSA	−2.0
8	Charleston, WV MSA	−1.8
9	Utica, NY MSA	−1.7
10	Huntington-Ashland, WV-KY-OH MSA	−1.6
11	Dayton, OH MSA	−1.5
12	Santa Cruz–Watsonville, CA MSA	−1.5
13	Toledo, OH MSA	−1.2
14	Rochester, NY MSA	−0.7
15	Syracuse, NY MSA	−0.7

Source: U.S. Bureau of the Census, 2009.

society, or *gesellschaft*, presented a sharp contrast, according to Toennies. *Gesellschaft*, roughly translated, means "association," a term that captures the more formal, instrumental nature of this society. According to Toennies, people in modern urban societies follow their own individualistic agendas, which are often driven by economic self-interest. As a result, they are less likely to know and care about one another. The city becomes an impersonal arena where everyone looks out only for himself or herself. Common identity and consensus based on tradition disappear, and people become isolated and alienated.

As another German sociologist, Georg Simmel (1964 [orig. 1905]), pointed out, part of the reason for these differences is that the city simply contains more people and more situations than any one person can possibly become familiar with. As a result, Simmel believed, urbanites protect themselves from overstimulation by withdrawing and developing what he called a "blasé attitude," which involves tuning out most of what is going on and paying attention only to that small part that is interesting or useful in terms of personal concerns and goals. According to Simmel, this is why urbanites so often "don't want to get involved."

(For a modern elaboration of Simmel's viewpoint, see Milgram, 1970.)

Wirth on Urban Life

In the United States, the most influential sociological theory about urban life has been Louis Wirth's, presented in his 1938 article entitled "Urbanism as a Way of Life." Wirth was a product of the "Chicago School" that was so influential in early American sociology (see Chapter 1), and like his colleagues at the University of Chicago, he had a strong interest in understanding the social problems that were evident in American cities in the early twentieth century. The large population size of cities, Wirth argued, produces a need for specialization. When this happens, people begin to interact in terms of their particular roles in a situation, rather than with one another as people. In the terminology introduced in Chapter 9 of this book, *primary-group* relations are replaced by *secondary-group* relations. As a result, relationships become "impersonal, superficial, transitory, and segmental" (Wirth, 1964, p. 71).

The high population density of urban areas leads to the type of overstimulation discussed by Simmel, and people respond to it not only by "tuning out" but also by simplifying and stereotyping. Thus, people's images of the city are organized (but simplified) into "Little Italy," "the Gold Coast," "the ghetto," and so forth, and the residents of these areas are psychologically lumped into categories: "immigrants," "Yuppies," "the underclass." According to Wirth, this process leads to a greater tolerance of differences in the city, but it also leads to depersonalization, stereotyping, and withdrawal in order to avoid contact with those who are "not like us." A common variation on Wirth's arguments is the notion that high population densities are stressful and lead to pathological behaviors such as violence, crime, conflict, and withdrawal from normal human interaction (Hall, 1966). Evidence for this line of reasoning is provided in part by studies of animals showing that they behave abnormally when crowded beyond some limit (Calhoun, 1962).

Perhaps the most important of all the characteristics of the city, to Wirth, is heterogeneity. It is easy for urbanites to stereotype and avoid one another because they are, in fact, far more diverse than people who came into contact with one another in preindustrial rural societies. Different professions; different racial, ethnic, and religious groups; different social classes; and different personality types are all mixed together in a relatively confined space. The city also enhances physical and social mobility, so that people interact with different sets of neighbors and co-workers at different times in their lives—an experience far different from that of traditional villagers. As a result, people resist the tendency to "get too close," knowing that soon they will be associating with a new set of people. (How many of your current classmates will you be close to five years from now?) Consequently, Wirth saw urbanites as isolated and alienated, using one another to advance their own personal interests, and largely devoid of close, meaningful primary-group relationships.

Decline of Community: Myth or Reality?

There is one common theme in the writings of Toennies, Simmel, Wirth, and others: the idea that urbanization, modernization, and industrialization lead to a decline of community. To understand this, we must understand the meaning of "community," a term that even sociologists have used in a wide variety of ways (Schwab, 1992; Hillery, 1955). In general, though the term **community** refers to a group of people who share three things: They live in a geographically distinct area (such as a city or town); they share cultural characteristics, attitudes, and lifestyles; and they interact with one another on a sustained basis (Schwab, 1992). It is the latter two elements of community that writers such as Simmel and Wirth argue are on the decline in modern urban societies: People share less and less in common, and interact with one another less and less. This situation leads to the alienation that decline of community theorists see as a characteristic of modern urban life.

The decline of community hypothesis has stimulated a great deal of research. On the basis of this research, we know today that important points Toennies, Simmel, and Wirth made about the city are true, but we also know that some of their views were overly pessimistic. It is true that urbanites spend much more of their time in secondary-group relationships than the rural people or villagers of the past, or even the farm population of today (Reiss, 1959). It is also true that city residents do not and cannot interact with most of the people they encounter, and that they engage in a variety of mechanisms to avoid unwanted interaction (Milgram, 1970). They also think in a stereotyped manner, as Wirth argued, but urbanites have no monopoly on this type of thinking.

Urban Life and Interpersonal Relationships
Nonetheless, certain aspects of the Toennies-Simmel-Wirth viewpoint have been disproved. First, most urbanites are not lacking in close, interpersonal relationships. Rather, they typically have family and friends with whom they share relationships that are as close and personal as anything found in the traditional gemeinschaft-type society (Bell, 1968; Fischer, 1982; Wellman, 1979). Often, though, the friends of urbanites are not neighbors; they may live miles away, but they interact regularly on the basis of common interests, work, or family background (Wellman, 1979). Second, there is no evidence that people living in cities are more alienated or suffer more mental illness than people living in rural areas (Srole, 1972, 1980; Srole et al., 1962; Fischer, 1984). If anything, mental illness is slightly more common in rural areas than in urban areas (Fischer, 1973; Srole, 1972). It is hard to judge accurately just how much mental illness existed in preindustrial rural societies, but there is good reason to believe that there was a significant amount. Today, in the societies that most closely resemble preindustrial societies, mental illness is not unusual. Eaton and Weil (1955), for example, studied the Hutterites, a very traditional religious organization whose members live in rural communities in the northern plains, in a manner that closely approximates Toennies's concept of gemeinschaft. The researchers found their rates of mental illness to be just as high as those in highly urban New York State. The only difference was that the Hutterites cared for their own members when they were mentally ill, rather than hospitalizing them or sending them to a mental-health professional.

Population Density and Crowding
Although Wirth and others saw the high population density of cities as alienating and destructive of community, research has also found no substantial relationship between population density and mental illness or other pathologies, after controlling for other factors such as poverty (Baldassare, 1979; Booth, Johnson, and Edwards, 1980; Choldin, 1978; Farley, 1982). Some urban lifestyles even thrive on density, such as that of ethnic neighborhoods where interaction is based on kinship (Gans, 1962; Jacobs, 1961). There are some studies showing that feeling crowded is associated with problems, but feeling crowded is not always associated with real crowding, and it may even be a consequence of family conflict (Booth, 1976). Although crowded cities have been blamed by some observers for riots and rising crime rates, there is a serious flaw in this reasoning. Urban population densities have fallen throughout most of the twentieth century; they were lower in the 1960s than they had ever been before; and they are even lower now. There is one qualification to the general conclusion that population density does not by itself cause problems. Crowding within houses or apartments may cause some adverse effects, especially if it is combined with poverty and the presence of small children (Baldassare, 1981; Gove, Hughes, and Galle, 1979). However, no such effect has been shown for population density in the sense of persons per square mile.

Urban Life and "Getting Involved"

Sociologists also question whether urbanites are as uncaring as they are portrayed to be. To be sure, certain dramatic incidents appear to support this portrayal. In New York City in 1964, for example, a woman was attacked and repeatedly stabbed in the view of dozens of people. Nobody intervened; indeed, nobody even called the police until after she had died. In 1984, a virtually identical incident occurred in Brooklyn, and in St. Louis a woman was attacked in front of a crowd of people filing out of Busch Stadium after a baseball game (Spates and Macionis, 1987, p. 107). Again, nobody intervened or even notified the police—they just kept walking by. Certainly such incidents are very disturbing, and they have often been used as evidence that urbanites don't care about one another.

Diffused Responsibility. There are, however, alternative explanations. For one thing, direct intervention can be dangerous. Around the time of the St. Louis incident, an off-duty fireman in nearby

Alton, Illinois, was killed when he saw a man beating a woman in the front yard of a house and tried to stop him. Of course, this doesn't explain why people do not even call the police in such situations. Here sociologists refer to the concept of diffused responsibility. It is significant that the fireman in this example was the only person who witnessed the event, and he did try to do something about it. In the other three instances a large crowd of people saw the event, and no one person felt individually responsible for doing something about it. Instead, everyone who correctly recognized the situation as an emergency assumed that someone else had called the police, but tragically, nobody had.

Pluralistic Ignorance. Besides the fact that nobody felt responsible, it also appears that many people misidentified the situations as nonemergencies, such as lovers' quarrels. This, too, happens more often when a number of people witness an event, because each person interprets the nonparticipation of others as a cue that the situation is not really an emergency. This phenomenon has been referred to as pluralistic ignorance (Latane and Darley, 1970; Penrod, 1986, p. 395). Dozens of studies have demonstrated that as the number of people who witness an emergency increases, the chances that anyone will help decrease (Latane, Nida, and Wilson, 1981). These studies suggest that, rather than not caring, urban crowds either do not realize that the situation is an emergency or they assume that someone else is already taking care of it.

When people do recognize a situation as an emergency and understand that others are not likely to intervene, they often do step in, even in the most urban of environments, and sometimes in the face of danger. This can be seen in the case of Reginald Denny, the white truck driver who was dragged from his truck and beaten during the 1992 riots that followed the acquittals of the police in the Rodney King beating case in Los Angeles. Denny's life was saved by four African Americans who understood that if they did not intervene, he would be beaten to death. Despite the danger that Denny's attackers would turn on them, these individuals stepped in, chased away the people attacking Denny, and summoned medical assistance.

Variations in the Urban Experience

One other important consideration that was underemphasized by Wirth and his intellectual predecessors is that, because cities are highly diverse, the experiences of one group of urban residents can be very different from those of others. Herbert Gans (1972), for example, has identified several distinct groups of people who live in central cities and at least one distinct group in the suburbs. These groups are summarized below.

Cosmopolites. These are well-educated and affluent people who like the cultural and entertainment opportunities of the city. Though they may be unmarried or childless if married, they typically have a number of friends with whom they share interests. Often, these friends are not neighbors; common interest, not proximity, draws them together. Cities facilitate this process by providing a critical mass of people with similar interests (Choldin, 1985, pp. 50–52).

Unmarried. These residents live in the city for some of the same reasons as the cosmopolites, but often reside there only during certain parts of their lives, such as during young adulthood before marriage, or after a divorce. Also included in this group is the substantial gay population that lives in some central cities. The unmarried, too, often have citywide rather than neighborhood-based friendship networks. Though many prefer the city, some also live in today's large suburban apartment complexes.

Ethnic Villagers. These are families with children who live in ethnically segregated neighborhoods, often near their relatives (Gans, 1962). They are working class, but not poor. Gans called their neighborhoods "urban villages" because they have many of the characteristics of a traditional rural village. Extended family relationships are important, relatives often live near one another, and neighborhood interaction is strong. This group is probably the most removed from the urbanites portrayed by Wirth. Many Italian, Puerto Rican, Jewish, and Mexican neighborhoods fit this description, as do some of the newer communities of Asian immigrants and some black and Irish working-class neighborhoods. These neighborhoods are communities in all three senses of our definition of community. Frequently, their residents are strongly attached to the neighborhood and wouldn't move to a "better" one even if they could (Terkel, 1967, p. 198).

The Deprived, the Trapped, and the Downwardly Mobile. These groups (which Gans treated as several distinct, though similar, groups) are made up of the poor and the unemployed. The chronically poor constitute what has come to be called the underclass (Jencks and Peterson, 1991; Wilson, 1987). This group—which probably best fits Wirth's pessimistic view of urban life—is described in greater detail in a later section of this chapter. However, it should be stressed that its difficult situation is the result of extreme poverty, not of urban life per se.

Suburbanites. The final group identified by Gans was suburbanites. This group has become increasingly diverse since Gans wrote his article, and it will also be discussed at some length later in this chapter.

The City and Tolerance
Despite the growth of the urban population and the homogenizing effects of the mass media, important differences between cities and rural areas continue to exist. One difference that has been confirmed by research is that people in cities are more tolerant of diversity and of nonconforming lifestyles, including alcohol use, nonconforming sexual behaviors, and marijuana use (Fischer, 1975, 1971; Tuch, 1987), than people in rural areas. They are also more tolerant toward different racial, ethnic, religious, and cultural groups (Tuch, 1987) and toward unpopular political views (T. Wilson, 1991). These differences have long been recognized by urban theorists. Simmel, though pessimistic about other aspects of city life, saw this as a great advantage. He argued (1964 [orig. 1905]) that the metropolis "assures the individual of a degree and type of personal freedom to which there is no analogy in other circumstances." Importantly, though, there are wide differences in tolerance within both cities and rural areas: In each kind of area, some people are far more tolerant than others.

Cities and Social Conflict

Think of the last time you heard about a riot, strike, terrorist attack, or political assassination. Whether it took place in the United States or in another country, chances are it happened in an urban area. Most outbreaks of conflict do. The United States, for example, has a long history of urban rioting, going back at least to violent antiblack rioting in New York City nearly 150 years ago during the Civil War. We associate terrorism in our cities with recent decades (the World Trade Center attacks, the Oklahoma City bombing), but its history is much longer than that. For example, in 1910 the headquarters of the *Los Angeles Times* was destroyed by a terrorist bomb, which killed twenty-one employees. This reality has often led to speculation that city living *causes* conflict, that is, urban living is so stressful and difficult that people can't handle it and respond by engaging in conflict, which is sometimes violent.

An Arena of Conflict
The reality, however, is quite different. Rather than causing conflict, the city acts as an arena of conflict. In other words, it serves as the place where societal

An "alternative" night club above a Vietnamese restaurant in Montreal. The diversity of cities leads urbanites to be somewhat more accepting of different ethnic groups and cultural lifestyles than rural populations are. (Courtesy of John E. Farley)

conflicts are fought out. As conflict theorists point out, social inequality and the existence of competing interest groups work to create conflict in all societies. Notably, the riots and bombings described above involved groups who felt threatened or were relatively powerless. These conflicts are fought out in the cities for several reasons.

First, the most important political and corporate decisions are made in the cities because that is where governments, corporations, and organizations are headquartered. Thus, the conflicts that affect cities are often national or international in character, but the city is where they are fought out. *Second,* a critical mass of the disaffected is more easily attained in cities. When people with deep grievances are scattered, it is harder for them to get together and act collectively (though mass communications and the Internet have somewhat changed that in recent years). In cities, though, there are enough disaffected people in one place to come together and take action. *Third,* important national and international symbols, such as the World Trade Center and federal office buildings, are usually located in cities. For these reasons, even when dissenters are based in rural areas or distant lands, they often attack symbols of government and commerce located in cities: the World Trade Center; the Pentagon; the Murrah Federal Building in Oklahoma City. A *fourth* factor is relative deprivation, which is discussed in greater detail later in this chapter. The basic idea of relative deprivation is that people are more likely to engage in conflict when they feel they have been disadvantaged or mistreated relative to someone else. Obviously, such feelings can develop more easily in a big, diverse city, where the wealthy and poor regularly come into contact with each other, than in a homogeneous rural area or village, where even if you are poor, most of the people you see and associate with are equally poor (see Williams, 1977, p. 28). *Fifth,* and finally, the costs and benefits of dissent are different in urban and rural areas. The greater freedom of the city, where you can be anonymous if you choose, makes you less likely to "get in trouble" for dissenting than you would in a small town. Thus, it is less costly to you to engage in conflict in the urban setting, and the benefits of conflict may also be greater because there is a better chance of finding the critical mass necessary for an effective movement.

Collective Behavior

Not only violence and conflict, but many other forms of collective behavior occur more often in cities for the reasons stated above. Again, these forms of collective behavior *do not* occur because of any alienating feature of the city, but rather because, for many of the reasons noted above, people come together in crowds and masses more readily in cities than they do in rural areas.

Collective behavior can be defined as large numbers of people acting together in an extraordinary situation, in which usual norms governing behavior do not apply. In some instances, people make up new norms as they go along. Collective behavior occurs in a great variety of forms, including crowds, rumors, panics, riots, "urban legends," fashions and fads, mass hysteria, and mass suicide. As different as these things are, they all involve behaviors or shared beliefs by sizable numbers of people that deviate from normal patterns or from past norms (Lofland, 1985, p. 37).

Causes of Collective Behavior

One way in which collective behavior differs from other social behavior is that it does not normally occur in ongoing social groups; that is, groups that interact regularly and share a common purpose (see Chapter 9). Rather, it occurs among aggregates or collectivities: sets of people, often large in number, who interact only in a temporary or superficial way. These sets of people may be localized in one place, in which case they are called **crowds**, or they may be dispersed, as in the case of rumors, urban legends, and fashions (Turner and Killian, 1987). Dispersed collectivities are called **masses**. Obviously, today's highly urbanized society and its extensive networks of "instant communications" are highly conducive to both the localized and dispersed varieties of collective behavior.

There are two important characteristics of aggregates or collectivities that lead to behavior that does not occur in ordinary, ongoing social groups. First, as the distinction implies, collectivities themselves interact only temporarily, even though they often include many small clusters of friends and acquaintances. Second, unlike groups, collectivities do not have clear boundaries: In other words, it is not clear who belongs to a collectivity and who doesn't. Consider an outdoor rally on a college campus. Some people are clearly participating; others are "just watching"; still others are "passing through" on their way to somewhere else. Are all of these people part of the crowd? Or does the crowd consist only of those who are actively participating? There is no obvious answer.

Because of these differences, some of the usual norms that govern human behavior can break down in collectivities, and people in collectivities therefore frequently behave in different ways than they otherwise would. Neil Smelser (1963) developed what he called a value-added theory to identify conditions that increase the likelihood of such collective behavior. Among the key elements of his theory are the breakdown of social control, structural conduciveness and structural strain, and precipitating incidents.

Breakdown of Social Control

Clearly, social control (Chapter 10) is often weaker in collectivities than in groups, because the individual has no ongoing relationship with the collectivity to be concerned about. At the same time, the collectivity frequently develops norms of its own, often on the spot, which may not conform with the usual norms of society. For example, in a crowd it may be acceptable, or even expected, to sing loudly, engage in bawdy or controversial chants, or rush madly toward some common goal or away from some perceived threat. Thus, when interacting with a collectivity, people sometimes do things they would never do either when alone or when part of their everyday, ongoing social groups.

Structural Conduciveness

Although there must be a crowd or a mass in order for collective behavior to occur, crowds and masses do not always result in collective behavior.

Rather, collective behavior occurs when there is **structural conduciveness**—that is, when the situation in some way encourages collective behavior. Just what this means depends on the type of behavior. For example, people spread rumors concerning things they are afraid of or suspect but about which they lack direct information (Rosnow and Fine, 1976). And in the case of a riot, some collective grievance is often (though not always) present (Smelser, 1963). Smelser referred to the conflicts of interest that produce such grievances as structural strain. While structural strain is a type of structural conduciveness, it is *people's response* to that situation that leads to action. In other words, a generalized belief must exist among a sizable segment of the population, arising from the situation, in order for collective behavior to occur. That belief could be a grievance, or the belief that something unusual, such as a natural disaster, is under way or about to happen.

Precipitating Incident

Finally, there is usually a precipitating incident that triggers some type of collective behavior (Smelser, 1963). In the case of fashion, it could be a particular style of clothes or hair worn by a famous person: Figure skater Dorothy Hamill, Princess Diana of Great Britain, and former U.S. first lady Jacqueline Kennedy Onassis each triggered a major fashion trend in hairstyle when each was at the peak of popularity. In the case of riots, a fight or an arrest often acts as a precipitating incident; the 1992 Los Angeles riots, which were precipitated by the acquittal of police officers in the videotaped beating of Rodney King, illustrate this process.

Types of Collective Behavior

As has already been noted, one way to classify the various types of collective behavior is by the type of collectivity involved: crowd or mass. Another is by the predominant type of emotion expressed. According to Lofland (1985), three emotions are commonly expressed by collective behavior: fear, hostility, and joy. Other emotions, such as grief, may also drive collective behavior (Plutchik, 1962). Table 14.4 classifies various types of collective behavior according to the type of collectivity involved and the dominant emotion expressed. Our discussion of collective behavior is organized around this classification system. It should be stressed that the types of collective behavior described in Table 14.4 are not always distinct. Rather, they are ideal types that are only approximated in social reality. It is quite common, for example, for a crowd to represent something of a mixture of two or more of the types of crowd behavior shown in the table.

Collective Behavior in Crowds

When the situation is conducive, there are at least three distinct dynamics that can lead to the spread of collective behavior. One, which has been known to sociologists for over a century, is contagion (Le Bon, 1960 [orig. 1895]). An individual or small group of people in a crowd urges a course of action, or begins to move, chant, sing, or behave in some other visible way, and the behavior rapidly spreads through the crowd (Turner and Killian, 1987, p. 21). It is this aspect of crowd behavior that renders it capable of sudden changes and often leads to the appearance that crowd behavior is unpredictable.

Although it can change quickly, crowd behavior is not necessarily irrational. Crowds do not do everything that is urged upon them, they do not imitate everything that some people in the crowd do, and they do not respond to every incident that occurs in their midst or near them (Rose, 1982, pp. 7–8). Rather, they are selective. Moreover, not everyone in the crowd adopts the most visible crowd behaviors (McPhail and Wohlstein, 1983, p. 581). In virtually every crowd action, some people are merely spectators.

Even participants do not always behave in the same way. In crowd situations where violence occurs, for example, usually only a minority of those present participate in the violence. Others cheer them on, and still others just watch (Lewis, 1972; Turner and Killian, 1987). Hence, the crowd is not a mindless collectivity. Behaviors are suggested to the crowd through verbal and nonverbal communication (Wright, 1978). Sometimes the crowd follows these suggestions, sometimes it does not; even when it does, not everyone in the crowd participates.

The second important crowd dynamic is convergence (Berk, 1974; Turner and Killian, 1987). This concept refers to the sharing and consequent amplification of emotions, goals, or beliefs by many people in a crowd. As Allport (1924) expressed it, "The individual in the crowd behaves just as he would alone, only more so." In other words, people in the crowd are influenced by common emotions or desires, as we have already seen. When they get in the crowd situation, they act upon these common emotions in a way they might not otherwise, because usual norms do not apply, and because speakers or actions of people in the crowd may intensify these emotions. More important, though, the behavior of the crowd is not irrational and would not be unpredictable to someone who understood the emotions of the people in the crowd.

One problem with this viewpoint is that the attitudes of those who participate in crowd behavior are not always distinguishable from those of nonparticipants. McPhail (1971), for example, was able to find little attitudinal difference between participants and nonparticipants in urban riots. One answer to this issue may be found in Rose's (1982, p. 97) notion of "protesters as representative." He argues that certain groups among whom protest occurs (he cites inner-city blacks and college students in the 1960s as examples) do share attitudes conducive to collective behavior, and these attitudes are different from those of others in their society. From this viewpoint, convergence may explain why collective behavior occurred among blacks and college students much more than among other groups in the 1960s. It may not be of much use, however, in explaining why some people in these groups participate in protest and others do not.

Table 14.4 Types of Collective Behavior

Type of Collectivity	Dominant Emotion			
	Fear	Hostility	Joy	Mixed or Other
Localized (crowd behavior)	Panics	Mobs Riots Protest Crowds	Expressive Crowds Public Grief	Mass Suicides
Dispersed (mass behavior)	Mass hysteria	Vilification	Fads Fashions	Rumors

Source: Adapted from John Lofland, 1985, *Protest: Studies of Collective Behavior and Social Movements*. Reprinted with permission from Transaction, Rutgers, The State University of New Jersey. The "fear," "joy," and "hostility" categories were formulated by Lofland; the "mixed or other" category was added by the authors of this book.

The third important crowd dynamic is *emergent norms,* the process whereby the crowd collectively and interactively develops its own definition of the situation and norms about how to behave. If the crowd comes to some agreement on such definitions and norms, they then come to dominate the behavior of people in the crowd. If it does not, collective behavior will not occur. Turner and Killian (1987, p. 27) argue that the more unfamiliar and uncertain the situation, the more easily members of a crowd mutually influence one another, which increases the likelihood that the crowd will come to such agreement.

Crowd Dynamics: Two Examples
Contagion, convergence, and emergent norms are each dynamics that have been offered as explanations of why people in crowds often behave differently than they usually would. When they were originally developed, these crowd behavior theories were seen as mutually exclusive (Wright, 1978, p. 133). In reality, however, all three theories can tell us something about the processes that influence crowd behavior. This can be illustrated by crowd dynamics in two protests observed by one of the authors of this book (Farley). One of these was a 1992 student protest at the campus where I teach. Although the main target was a large tuition increase, the broader theme was that the administration did not care very much about what students thought.

The protest began with an outdoor rally that lasted about an hour. Then, one of the leaders of the protest turned toward the administration building and shouted, "Mr. President, are you listening to your students?" Turning back to the crowd, she added, "I don't think so. Maybe we should go up there, peacefully and nonviolently, and let him know what we think. In fact, I think I will. Anyone want to go with me?"

At that point, the student started walking toward the building, followed by several other protest leaders carrying an effigy of the president. Nearly everyone in the crowd immediately followed, and the result was a sit-in in the president's office that caught campus security authorities completely by surprise.

This example illustrates some important points about crowd dynamics. The speaker's rhetoric and example had been followed quickly by the rapid spread through the crowd of the idea of marching to the president's office and sitting in. This happened even though no march had been advertised and most people had no intention of taking such an action when they arrived at the rally. Thus, there was a process of contagion. The crowd did not blindly follow the speaker's exhortation in some irrational manner, however, nor was it inevitable that a march and sit-in would occur just because a speaker urged it. Rather, the speaker was able to successfully tap a common emotion in the crowd—a frustration with what nearly everyone in the crowd perceived as unresponsiveness on the part of the university's administration. Thus, contagion did not *cause* the march and sit-in to occur; more generally, it does not cause collective behavior to occur. Instead, contagion is a process by which the idea of taking an action—in this case, marching and sitting in—spreads through a crowd. The underlying condition that made the rapid spread of the idea possible was convergence: Nearly everyone in the crowd was unhappy with the university's administration and wanted to "do something about it." These attitudes had existed all along; when the speaker tapped into these attitudes, the norm she advocated—that the crowd should march—emerged and the crowd quickly took that action.

Another demonstration I observed more than two decades earlier at the campus where I attended graduate school illustrates that it is not inevitable that a crowd will take an action urged upon it. This protest, against the Vietnam War, had drawn a particularly angry crowd, frustrated by a sudden escalation of the war—the bombing of Hanoi—at a time when there was increasing talk of peace and of winding down the war. Despite the anger of the crowd, its behavior changed abruptly when a small group behaved in a way that violated the norms of most people in the crowd. This group broke into a building and began throwing chairs and typewriters through the windows. Within minutes, almost the entire crowd of about 2,000 had turned its back on those vandalizing the building and had instead walked over to a nearby street and sat down. Dramatically, the crowd had rejected the behavior of the vandals and said "Civil disobedience yes, violence no." In this case, there was no contagion leading to imitation, and neither convergence nor an emergent norm in support of the violent behavior of would-be leaders. Rather, the emergent norm was to reject that behavior, and substitute the more acceptable behavior of peacefully blocking traffic in a street. Thus, although crowds often follow, they do not necessarily do so blindly.

Types of Crowd Behavior

Although collective behavior in crowds usually spreads as a result of one or more of the three dynamics discussed above, the emotions that lead to that behavior vary widely among different types of crowds. Again referring to Table 14.4, the two examples presented above can best be classified as cases where the dominant emotion expressed by the crowd is hostility. This emotion typically produces either protest crowds like the ones in the above examples (McPhail and Wohlstein, 1983), or the more violent acting crowds, as seen in the case of mobs and riots (Blumer, 1969b). If the dominant emotion is fear, the likely result is a panic. Joy leads to expressive crowds, illustrated by the example of a World Series celebration (Blumer, 1969b). Various other emotions or mixtures of emotions can produce other types of crowd behavior, of which public grief and mass suicide are examples. As noted earlier, these crowd types are ideal types; real crowds may only roughly approximate them, or may show characteristics reflecting two or more of these types.

Protest Crowds

We have already seen examples of protest crowds: crowds whose purpose is to achieve political goals (McPhail and Wohlstein, 1983) and whose dominant emotion is often hostility or anger (Lofland, 1985). The two student demonstrations previously discussed were excellent examples of protest crowds. Some recent examples of protest crowds include the massive mobilization of environmentalists, labor unionists, and young people outside the meeting of the World Trade Organization in Seattle in 1999, and the protests at the Republican and Democratic conventions in 2000. In large part, the Million Man March in 1995 also was a protest crowd, though its celebration of black manhood and its call for responsible actions by the marchers themselves also gave it some of the characteristics of an expressive crowd (discussed in the next section). More recently the Tea Party protests of summer 2009 were aimed at opposing the return of "big government," the increase in the national debt following the financial industry bailouts, and the Obama administration's economic stimulus package. Large protest crowds also occurred in 2010, as opposing sides dueled over Arizona legislation requiring police to check papers of suspected illegal immigrants and requiring legal immigrants to carry their papers at all times.

The activities of protest crowds include rallies, marches, picket lines, and sometimes **civil disobedience**—actions such as sit-ins, blocking traffic, and mass trespassing that violate the law but are nonviolent. Although the vast majority of protest crowds remain nonviolent (Eisinger, 1973; Gamson, 1975), they do occasionally turn violent, at which point the protest crowd has been converted into an *acting crowd*.

Expressive Crowds

Expressive crowds are crowds whose predominant action is to express some emotion, usually joy, excitement, or ecstasy. Examples of expressive crowds are audiences at sports events and at rock concerts, and people attending religious revivals. In each of these examples, people collectively express their emotions in ways that they would not in other situations. Such behaviors include cheering, booing, and throwing streamers at sports events; moving with the music, clapping, and holding up lighted matches at rock concerts; and shouting, singing, arm waving, and "speaking in tongues" at religious revivals.

Although expressive crowds are most often moved by joy or exuberance, they can also express other emotions, such as grief. The thousands of people who lined the streets for the funeral of Princess Diana were expressing a common emotion. Public grief, however, can be either a crowd behavior or a mass behavior. Although the crowds were feeling and expressing grief over the death of Princess Diana, so were millions of others worldwide who were watching the funeral on television. A more recent example would be the public outpouring of grief over the death of singer Michael Jackson in June 2009. Large crowds formed outside of the hospital where he was pronounced dead as well as his funeral several days later. Though many in these crowds were indeed grieving, press reports at the time also described many in the crowds as simply there to celebrate his life and career. The same phenomena played out across the world as people watched on television, blogged online, or shared memories on social networking sites like Facebook, MySpace, or Twitter.

Acting Crowds: Mobs, Riots, and Panics

Protest crowds, expressive crowds, and even casual or conventional crowds can, under the right circumstances, be transformed into *acting crowds*. Acting crowds are crowds that engage in violent or destructive behavior. There are three main types of acting crowds, all of which overlap somewhat: mobs, riots, and panics.

Mobs. A **mob** is an extremely emotional acting crowd that directs its violence against a specific target. This target can be a person, a group of people, or a physical object. Mob violence is often of short duration, because once the mob has vented its anger against its target, it often views its work as finished and breaks up.

A type of mob behavior that has been particularly common in the history of the United States (much more so than elsewhere) is the lynch mob, which captures and kills, often by hanging, a person suspected or accused of a crime or other social transgression. In the United States, lynching has frequently been a form of racial violence. It was particularly common in the South between the end of the Civil War and about 1930 (Franklin, 1969, p. 439). Some reports estimate that 2,500 lynchings occurred during the last sixteen years of the nineteenth century. The majority of the victims were black males. Although many of them were accused of murder or rape (often without evidence), many others were killed for real or imagined violations of Jim Crow segregation practices (Raper, 1933). These "violations" included such things as being in an area reserved for whites, "talking smart" to whites (especially white women), or simply being too prosperous or well educated.

Lynchings were also fairly common in the West, particularly in the nineteenth century. There, more of the victims were white, although a disproportionate number were of Mexican or Asian ancestry (Mirande, 1987). The nature of these mob actions is captured in the following excerpt from Pitt (1966, p. 77) concerning one mob during the Gold Rush days in California:

> Miners gathered at nearby Devil Springs and vowed to "exterminate the Mexican race from the country." Thereupon, some Yankees seized one Mexican each at Yaqui's Camp and at Cherokee Ranch for extraneous reasons and strung them up immediately. Hundreds of miners thrust guns and knives into their belts, roamed angrily over the 5-mile region from San Andreas to Calaveras Forks, and methodically drove out the entire Mexican population—as prospectors had done in previous seasons—and confiscated all property.

Riots. The main difference between a mob and a riot is that a riot is less focused on a particular target. A **riot** can be defined as violent crowd behavior aimed against people, property, or both, which is not directed at one specific target. As with mobs, the emotions that most often underlie riots are anger and hostility. Sometimes these emotions are the result of competition between two groups, each of which feels it is being treated unfairly. When this occurs, rioting often takes the form of mass street fighting between opposing groups, or of attacks by crowds of one group against people in another group. Earlier chapters described the frequent history of this type of violence in the United States; similar violence has occurred between Chinese and Malays in Malaysia, Sikhs and Hindus in India, and Armenians and Azerbaijanis in the former Soviet Union.

On other occasions, underlying resentment and feelings of unfair treatment among one group lead that group to rise in violent rebellion. This is often triggered by a precipitating incident, such as an arrest (U.S. National Advisory Commission on Civil Disorders, 1968). In this type of riot, most of the crowd violence is directed against property rather than people, except for violence between the crowd and police or troops. This pattern of violence, marked by rebellion rather than street fighting, was the typical form of violence in the so-called ghetto riots of the 1960s. In riots in which the dominant pattern is rebellion, studies have indicated that when deaths occur, they are usually the result of police action, not actions by rioters (Conot, 1967). In some cases, riots involve combinations of rebellion and attacks on people, as occurred in the 1992 Rodney King riots in Los Angeles (McPhail, 1993).

In some instances, riots occur when protest crowds get out of hand, as occurred in Seattle in 1999. They can also occur when agents of the state seeking to control a protest crowd themselves get out of order, as also appears to have happened in Seattle. Two other prime examples of this are the "police riot" outside the Democratic National Convention in Chicago in 1968 (U.S. National Commission on the Causes and Prevention of Violence, 1968) and the beatings of civil rights demonstrators in 1963 by the Birmingham, Alabama, police.

In all of the preceding examples, hostility or anger was the dominant emotion of the crowd. In other cases, however, joy, exuberance, or the desire to have fun may either lead to or sustain a riot. Sometimes, expressive crowds like those celebrating a sports team victory or students on spring break turn into acting crowds that break windows, loot stores, or fight with police. In some cases, the situation is exacerbated by excessive alcohol consumption by much of the crowd.

Panics. Another type of crowd action is the **panic**. Panics occur when crowds react suddenly to perceived entrapment or exclusion, resulting in spontaneous and often self-destructive behavior. Thus, panics differ from riots and mobs in that fear, rather than anger, is the dominant emotion. There are two common types of panic. In the most common type, people seek to escape some perceived danger, such as a fire, an earthquake, or a military attack. They perceive themselves as entrapped and react accordingly. This reaction is especially likely when the danger is sudden and unexpected and the escape routes are limited. The other type of panic occurs when a crowd is seeking to gain access to an event or a location and perceives itself to be in danger of being excluded. In both types of panic, surging and pushing occur, and deaths often result from suffocation and trampling. Examples of the first type of panic are fires at the Iroquois Theater in Chicago (1902; 602 deaths), the Coconut Grove Nightclub in Boston (1942; 491 deaths), the Beverly Hills Supper Club in Southgate, Kentucky (1980; 164 deaths), and a nightclub in Manila in the Philippines (1996; 150 deaths). Examples of the second type of panic are stampedes at the entrance to a concert by the rock band The Who in Cincinnati (1979; 11 deaths) and soccer matches in Sheffield, England (1989; 95 deaths) and in Guatemala (1996; 84 deaths) Although the exact circumstances remain under investigation, this is also most likely what happened at the Love Parade music festival in Duisburg, Germany in July, 2010, resulting in 21 deaths.

Turner and Killian (1987) list four main factors characteristic of panic situations. The first is *partial entrapment*—limited escape routes in escape panics, and limited entrance routes in panics directed toward entry. Second is *perceived threat*—a generalized belief, usually sudden, that there is danger of exclusion or entrapment. This leads to an emergent norm that the crowd must act immediately. For example, in the case of both the rock band The Who concert and the Sheffield soccer match, the crowd suddenly surged forward when people believed that the event they were waiting for had started. Next comes *breakdown of escape route*—the path the crowd is trying to take becomes jammed, so nobody can move through. Finally, there is *failure of front-to-rear communications*—people in back keep pressing forward because they do not know that people in front have blocked their escape routes. In fact, the reverse appears to be true: The rear of the crowd moves forward because people in front are being jammed ever more tightly together.

In addition, Mintz (1951) has noted that once panic behavior begins, it becomes a model and a threat: If you see others pushing in a theater fire situation, you may push back to protect your own position. The disturbance spreads as people press their personal advantage at the group's expense, ultimately to everyone's detriment. At this point, panic behavior has become the norm of the crowd—a situation Smelser (1963) calls the *derived phase* of the panic.

Mass Behavior

As noted above, mass behavior is collective behavior that takes place among dispersed collectivities—people who are separated from one another yet share some common sources of information or communication and respond with similar forms of collective behavior. The most important types of mass behavior are rumors, urban legends, mass hysteria, fashions, and fads. It is important to stress that although these behaviors are treated as mass behaviors, some of them can also occur in crowds. Rumors and the 1974 "streaking" fad (running naked through public places) are two examples. Rumors can and do sweep through crowds, although they can also travel in the absence of crowds. Streaking was usually a crowd behavior, but it spread quickly from place to place by means of communication that did not involve crowds. In fact, the peak of the behavior occurred the day after all three television networks reported it on the evening news (Aguirre, Quarantelli, and Mendoza, 1988).

Types of Mass Behavior

Rumors

Rumors are unconfirmed items of information that are spread by word of mouth and, in some cases, by unconfirmed media reports. Today, many rumors are spread rapidly via the Internet. Rumors can be partially based on fact; however, in all cases, they tend to change as they are spread.

Rumors often begin in a context where something unusual is happening. For example, numerous rumors spread rapidly following the attacks on the World Trade Center and Pentagon on September 11, 2001. Rumors are also common when some other form of collective behavior has taken place or is expected to take place. Thus, for example, whites fearful of black violence in cities during the 1960s often believed rumors such as the one that blacks had decided to meet at some specified time and march into the downtown area to attack whites and burn stores. At the same time, many African Americans believed rumors that white gangs or police had beaten, raped, or castrated innocent blacks.

Few of these rumors were true. However, all the conditions conducive to rumors were present. Rumors, like other collective behavior, occur when the situation is structurally conducive. Generally, this means that complete, unambiguous, and confirmed information is unavailable; that people are distrustful of sources of information; and that people either want to believe something is true or fear that something is true. In the example above, whites and blacks knew very little about each other's actions, but believed rumors that confirmed their worst fears: the fear by whites that they or their businesses would be attacked by angry blacks; the fear by blacks of being brutalized by whites, particularly the police. In the absence of such fears, these rumors would have been far less believable.

Rumors have also circulated nationwide concerning certain products and companies. One such rumor that circulated for years was that the corporate logo of Procter and Gamble was a symbol of devil worship. Actually, the logo, which had been used in various versions since 1882, represented something very different. The man in the moon was a popular design in the early days of the company in the late nineteenth century, and the thirteen stars on the logo represented the original American states. Despite great efforts over the years by Procter and Gamble to dispel the rumors, they persisted, and in 1991 Procter and Gamble replaced the logo it had used for over a century.

Urban Legends

Consider the following story. Perhaps you've heard it, or something like it:

> A Bergen citizen who several days a week drives a ready-mix cement truck as a second job the other day came by his own residence and saw a friend's car with a sun roof parked there. He stopped the cement truck and went in the apartment building to say hello. But sounds from the bedroom gave him to understand it wasn't him but rather his wife that the fellow had come to visit. Without disturbing the couple in the bedroom, the man went back out of the building and over to his friend's car. He pulled the sun roof back, and backed the cement truck alongside it. Then he switched on the delivery system and filled the parked car with about two cubic meters of cement. When the lover came back for his car, the cement was completely hard.

Though this story appeared in a Norwegian newspaper in 1973, local versions of it circulated throughout all the Scandinavian countries, as well as Germany, England, and Kenya. Its origin, however, was in the United States, not Norway, and it dates back at least to 1960. By 1961, forty-three distinct versions had circulated in various parts of the United States, most of which claimed that the event had taken place in the local area where the story was being circulated (Brunvand, 1981, pp. 126–32). This story is an example of an **urban legend**: an unsubstantiated story containing a plot that is widely circulated and believed. Urban legends are very similar to rumors, except that they are more complex. Like rumors, they are based on fears and concerns that people have—such as what your partner is up to when you aren't around. Like rumors, they change as they are circulated. The Norwegian version of the concrete car story involved a Volkswagen, whereas the American version usually involved a Cadillac. Like rumors, they may be partially based in fact. This story, for example, may have been partially based on a 1960 publicity stunt by a Denver concrete company, in which a car (a fourteen-year-old De Soto) was filled with concrete and publicly displayed (Brunvand, 1981). The story was already in circulation before that incident, however, and most versions of the legend bore little resemblance to the real incident.

In some cases, the themes of urban legends are very similar to the themes of rumors. Unexpected problems with fast-food or mass-produced food are a common theme, as are stories about mice in soft-drink bottles or about people eating fast-food fried chicken in the dark, deciding that it "tastes funny," and turning on the light to discover they are really eating a batter-fried rat that somehow "went through the process." Such stories carry a moral: If you shirk your responsibilities by opting for fast-food, you will be at risk. A particular aspect that highlights this is the fact that it is usually a woman who supposedly eats the rat, suggesting that if she had attended to the traditional female role and cooked dinner, she would have avoided her awful fate (Fine, 1979).

The key point about urban legends (which are not limited to cities) is that they are not only told but believed. We have heard convincing versions of all the stories mentioned above, in some cases recounted by fellow sociologists who believed every word of them. Typically, they happened to a "friend of a friend," and some of them (like the cement car) even get reported in newspapers. They can never be fully verified, however, or if they are verified, it turns out that what actually happened is quite different from what is reported in the story (Brunvand, 1981, 1984, 1986). They are believed because they call up fears or concerns that are real; because they describe embarrassing situations that we could imagine happening to ourselves; or because they relate to some aspect of modern life that we accept yet find at least mildly disturbing. Often, like true fictional stories, they contain a moral: Don't become involved with your friend's wife; don't eat too much fast-food.

Mass Hysteria

Mass hysteria occurs when many people in a sizable geographic area perceive and respond frantically to some danger. Often the danger is not real or, if real, is not as great as people believe. The Y2K computer bug scare in 1999 is an excellent example of the latter. As is discussed in Web-Based Chapter C, contagious diseases often lead to mass hysteria. The plagues of medieval Europe, the worldwide influenza epidemic of the early twentieth century, and the current AIDS epidemic have all provoked mass hysteria. Although the danger of disease is real, the hysteria leads people to behave in ways that either heighten the danger or create other problems, while doing nothing to curtail the spread of the disease. This happened in the case of the plagues: People spread the disease by fleeing from the cities where it broke out, and doctors refused to treat sick people for fear of contracting the disease themselves. Scapegoats were common: Such diverse groups as Jews, deformed people, and nobles were persecuted for creating this suffering (Thomlinson, 1976, p. 90). Similar reactions occurred in 1999, when a variety of extremist groups predicted doom because of the Y2K computer bug (Southern Poverty Law Center, 1998). Some, for example, argued that the government was understating the Y2K threat because conspirators who secretly controlled the government wanted to create a disaster that would trigger a race war.

Mass hysteria resembles panics, except that it does not take place in crowds, but rather among dispersed masses who often become agitated as a result of rumors or media broadcasts. The best-known example occurred on the night before Halloween in 1938, when Orson Welles broadcast the radio play "The War of the Worlds," based on the book by H. G. Wells. Made to sound like a news report about an invasion by Martians, Welles's program was believed by many people who—despite a disclaimer at the midway point that it was only a play—flooded police switchboards with frightened calls. Others gathered in groups to discuss the frightening invasion, and still others jumped in their cars to flee, which created massive traffic jams in some areas. Just how many people really believed the report is a disputed point: It may have been only a tiny percentage (Rosengren et al., 1975), or it may have been as many as a quarter of those who heard it (Cantril, 1940).

Part of the reason that this radio play about an invasion by hostile Martians led to mass hysteria was that the world was on the brink of World War II. People felt insecure and afraid; events seemed to be out of control. Fears of war may have also played a role in a more recent, and highly studied, incident of mass hysteria: a 1990 Midwest earthquake scare,

SOCIOLOGICAL INSIGHTS
The Earthquake That Wasn't

Scientists agree that it is not possible to predict when and where an earthquake will occur. But that didn't stop self-proclaimed climatologist Iben Browning from predicting a 50–50 chance of a major earthquake on Missouri's New Madrid Fault around December 3, 1990. It also didn't stop thousands of people in a half-dozen states from Arkansas to Indiana from believing his forecast. A dozen or so studies of this outbreak of collective behavior were conducted (including a study one of the authors participated in) which revealed a number of fascinating findings. Surveys revealed that 10 to 25 percent of the population in the area for which the earthquake was predicted clearly believed the forecast, and another 20 to 35 percent gave it some credibility. This was despite scientific disclaimers that Browning's method had been disproven and that, contrary to widely circulated news reports, there was no evidence he had ever successfully predicted an earthquake. Belief in the forecast decreased with level of education, and younger people and women were somewhat more likely to believe it than older people and men. Yet, in all groups, a significant minority believed Browning's forecast.

People also planned and (less often) took a variety of actions to protect themselves from the feared earthquake. Some actions were useful preparation for the earthquake that is indeed likely someday to occur on the New Madrid Fault—storing food and water, securing objects that could fall, learning to turn off utilities. Thus, the scare had the useful effect of increasing earthquake preparedness in the New Madrid seismic zone. But other responses are better described as hysteria, based on unfounded concern about a quake on a particular date. These responses included planning to keep children home from school, to stay home from work, to avoid crossing bridges, and even to leave town. Interestingly, such plans were not particularly related to whether or not people believed the forecast: Rather, they seemed to be a product of communication between significant others. Those whose friends and neighbors planned such actions were also likely to plan them themselves, whether or not they believed in the forecast. This illustrates what Turner, Nigg, and Paz (1986) called the *two-step flow of communications:* People get their information from the media, such as television reports about earthquake forecasts, and may use these sources to decide what to believe. But when it comes to deciding what to do, they look to their friends for guidance.

Follow-up surveys after the predicted December earthquake failed to materialize showed that the number who actually took such actions was smaller than the number who planned to—but some did so, nonetheless. Around 1 percent of those surveyed in eastern and southeast Missouri, for example, acknowledged leaving the area because of the forecast. About one out of six made some schedule changes. But the majority of these people did so because their children's schools closed as a result of the forecast. Nearly all schools in southeast Missouri, and some in neighboring areas, closed December 2 and 3.

Why did this event happen? For one, people in the Midwest have little experience with earthquakes, yet have been warned that they are in an earthquake-prone area. Their awareness of the risk was heightened by the dramatic videos of damage in San Francisco and Oakland from the 1989 Loma Prieta earthquake. In such an atmosphere, Browning offered an easy answer, and many people turned to it. In addition, the media had been quite uncritical in reporting—incorrectly, it turns out—that Browning had predicted previous earthquakes, including the one in San Francisco–Oakland. Finally, public apprehension surrounding the impending Persian Gulf War may have played a role: One survey showed that people who expected war with Iraq were also more likely to expect a December earthquake.

Sources: Findings from the survey by the author's research group, reported in Farley et al., 1991a and 1991b; and from other surveys reported at a research conference held at Southern Illinois University at Edwardsville in May 1991. These findings are summarized in Farley et al., 1991c. Many of these studies are reported in the November 1993 issue of the *International Journal of Mass Emergencies and Disasters*. A complete account of the event, along with detailed analysis of the surveys and two later ones assessing long-term consequences of the prediction, may be found in Farley, 1998.

precipitated by a pseudoscientific prediction that a damaging earthquake would occur on December 2 or 3. Though scientists discredited the idea that the date of an earthquake could be predicted, it was widely believed nonetheless. In part, this was because the idea that the region was at risk for a damaging earthquake (which, in the long term, it is) was a new idea that was scary and poorly understood, because earthquakes in that area are infrequent enough that most people have had little experience with them. However, fears relating to the buildup to the Gulf War probably also played a part, since people who expected a war were more likely to believe the prediction of an earthquake than those who did not foresee a war (Farley, 1998). This earthquake prediction and public reaction to it are discussed further in the box "The Earthquake That Wasn't."

Fashions and Fads

Fashions

Two closely related types of collective behavior among masses are fashions and fads. A fashion is a style of appearance or behavior that is favored by a large number of people for a limited amount of time. The most common fashions concern dress and hair style (Lofland, 1985, p. 67), although there are also fashions in automobiles, home decoration, landscaping, and city neighborhoods. Even activities are sometimes governed by fashion; for example, surfing, tennis, Transcendental Meditation, and stamp collecting (Irwin, 1977). Language, too, is the subject of fashion. Lofland (1985, p. 67) illustrates this point with the changing terms used by young people to show approval: "Swell!" in the 1930s, "Neat!" in the 1950s, "Right on!" in the 1960s, and "Really!" in the 1970s. By definition, fashions change over time. In this regard, fashions are a product of modern industrialized society. In preindustrial societies, dress and behavior are governed by long-standing traditions that do not change as long as the same society persists (Lofland, 1973). Popular dress in Morocco today, for example, is the same as it was 200 years ago. Contrast this to the United States, where styles of dress today bear little resemblance to those at the time of the American Revolution.

Like other aspects of collective behavior, fashions reflect people's values. During the 1960s, when sexual freedom and new experiences were valued, the miniskirt was popular. In the 1970s, however, that style changed, reflecting two shifts in values: the rise of feminism and a more conservative sexual climate.

Fads

Fads are amusing mass involvements or activities, usually somewhat unconventional, that are temporary in nature. They are similar to fashions, except that they are of shorter duration and are typically adopted by a smaller number of people. The short duration of fads is illustrated by streaking, which came and went in 1974 within a period of about two months, with a peak of intensity that lasted only one week (Aguirre, Quarantelli, and Mendoza, 1988). Fads typically are less serious and more frivolous than fashions, and are much less likely to be linked to core values or lifestyles. Besides being more frivolous, fads are often limited to one item or behavior. According to Lofland (1985, p.69), there are four common types of fads: object fads, such as Hula-Hoops, beanie babies, pet rocks, and trolls; idea fads, such as the practice of astrology; activity fads, such as streaking and bungee jumping; and fads centered around personalities, such as Britney Spears or Leonardo DeCaprio.

The Structure of the City

Human Ecology

In addition to studying human behavior in the city, urban sociologists are very interested in how and why different groups are distributed across the physical space of the city. One of the most influential approaches among sociologists who study the city has been **human ecology,** also sometimes called urban social ecology. Human ecology is concerned with the interrelationships between people and territory (see Park and Burgess, 1921), including how people adjust and adapt to their environment (Hawley, 1981, pp. 9–10; 1950). Specifically, it is concerned with the growth and decline of cities and city neighborhoods and with the distribution within the city of people with different social characteristics, such as race, social class, and marital and family status. It is also concerned with the economic processes that shape population distributions and with the distribution of different land uses within urban areas. Duncan (1959) has described human ecology as the study of relationships among population, organization, environment, and technology—a combination sometimes referred to as the P.O.E.T. complex. Because the patterns of interest to human ecologists largely concern population characteristics and are an outgrowth of migration, the ecological orientation is closely related to the sociological specialization of demography, discussed in Web-Based Chapter C.

Three Models of City Population Distribution
One of the most important contributions of human ecology has been to improve our understanding of how different land uses and different groups of people are distributed within urban areas, and why they are so distributed. Human ecologists have developed three distinct theories concerning these questions: the concentric-zones model, the sectoral model, and the multiple-nuclei model. And even in the same city, one model may do a good job of describing one social characteristic (such as marital status), whereas another works better for another social characteristic (such as ethnicity).

The **concentric-zones** model (Burgess, 1925) holds that, as one moves away from the center of the city to the fringe—and from older to newer parts of the city—the characteristics of the population and land-use change. As people become more affluent, they move from the center to the fringe, where more space and newer homes are available, and congestion and pollution from nonresidential land-uses are less. Families also prefer the fringe because of its bigger yards, quieter neighborhoods, and newer and often better schools. This produces a pattern of rings, as shown in Figure 14.1. Although the boundaries between rings are not as sharply defined as the model suggests, it is generally the case that industry and commercial areas are near the center, and that as one moves out there is a gradual shift from poor or working-class to middle-class and then to affluent neighborhoods. There are also fewer single people and more married people and families.

The **sectoral model** (Hoyt, 1939) is also based on the notion that people move outward from the center of the city. However, because different groups initially settle in different neighborhoods and move outward, they create sectors with different population characteristics on different sides of town as they move outward. This creates a distribution much like slices of a pie, as shown in the second part of Figure 14.1.

Both the concentric zones and sectoral model have been criticized on the grounds that they work better for some types of cities than for others. They were developed in Chicago, and both seem to work best for cities like Chicago: ones that have one main center, that are industrially based, and that are not divided by sharp geographical features like mountains or deep river valleys. Cities with the opposite characteristics often develop a **multiple nuclei pattern** (Harris and Ullman, 1945), in which development occurs around not just one main center, but a number of distinct centers. This pattern is shown in the third diagram in Figure 14.1. This is especially likely when a number of nearby cities grow together into one major urban area, or when an urban area is divided by mountains, ridges, or gorges. It also occurs when suburbs develop into "edge cities," separate centers of commerce that come to rival the main downtown area, such as Clayton, Missouri, near St. Louis. Many of the fastest-growing cities in recent decades have fit this pattern (Suro, 1991), which has probably led to a shift toward the multiple nuclei pattern in many areas.

It should, finally, be kept in mind that these models were developed based on studies of industrialized capitalist countries like the United States, which have large-scale transportation systems that have, over time, become increasingly based on auto transportation. Different land-use patterns are found in preindustrial cities and in cities in countries with a history of socialism (Sjoberg, 1955; Shibutani, 1986). And even in industrial capitalist societies, most cities do not neatly fit any one of these models, but represent combinations of the three. Also, different social characteristics can be distributed differently even within the same urban area, as has been discovered by sociologists who study urban social segregation.

Urban Social Segregation

The models discussed above are all partly based on a pattern sociologists call **social segregation,** in which people with similar social characteristics live together in the same neighborhoods. Social segregation occurs largely because people with similar lifestyles prefer to live together, and some neighborhoods are better suited to a given lifestyle

Figure 14.1 Generalizations of Internal Structures of Cities

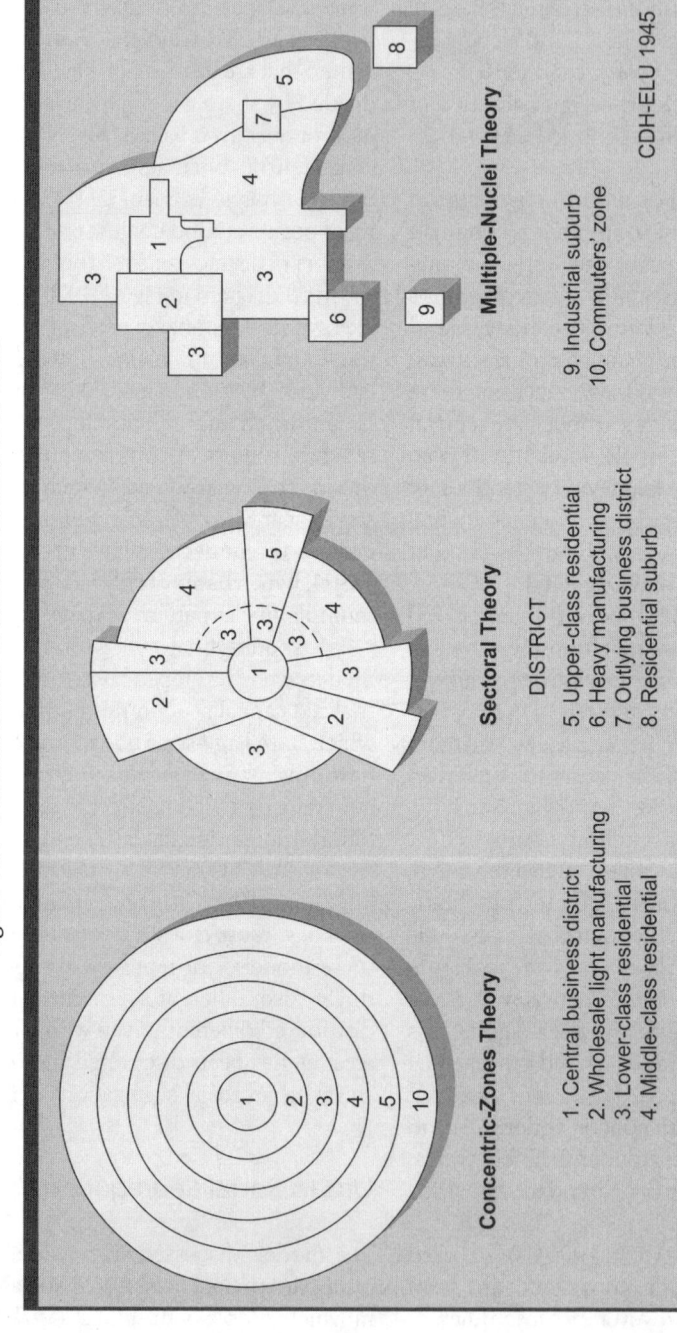

The concentric-zones theory is a generalization for all cities. The arrangement of the sectors in the sectoral theory varies from city to city. The diagram for multiple nuclei represents one possible pattern among innumerable variations.

Source: Chauncy D. Harris and Edward L. Ullman, 1945, "The Nature of Cities," *The Annals of the American Academy of Political and Social Science* 242: 7–17.

than others (Michelson, 1976, 1977). However, it also develops because people in one group try to keep people in other groups out of their neighborhoods, particularly different racial groups. Sociologists who study urban social segregation ask two main questions about the city: "What are the characteristics on which people are segregated in cities?" and "How are people with a given set of characteristics distributed in urban areas?" Sociologists interested in the second question have drawn heavily upon the concentric-zones, sectoral, and multiple-nuclei models, and they have developed sophisticated techniques using computers and census data to test the accuracy of these models for particular social characteristics. One factor that has made such studies possible is the availability of a wide range of data for census tracts—small neighborhood areas within cities, each of which has a population of about 3,000 to 6,000. An example is shown in Figure 14.2.

Social-Area Analysis and Factorial Ecology

Using a technique they call social-area analysis, sociologists Ehsref Shevky and Wendell Bell (1955) argued that urban social segregation occurs on the basis of three fundamental social characteristics: socioeconomic status, family status, and race or ethnicity. They then identified specific variables from the 1940 and 1950 Censuses that they thought captured each of these concepts. In general, they also found that people were indeed segregated on the basis of each of the three fundamental characteristics (Shevky and Bell, 1955; Shevky and Williams, 1949; Anderson and Bean, 1961; Van Arsdol, Camilleri, and Schmid, 1958).

Around the time Shevky and Bell were introducing social-area analysis, researchers began to use computers to study human ecology. Through a technique known as factorial ecology, researchers were able to take large data sets of 100 or more census variables and identify clusters of similar variables that represent underlying dimensions or concepts. This method shows that a broad range of census variables can be reduced to three basic dimensions: socioeconomic status, family status, and race or ethnicity (Rees, 1979; see also Elgie and Clark, 1980; Perle, 1981)—the same three bases of segregation that were identified by Shevky and Bell. In many of these studies, up to 75 percent of the geographic variation in as many as 100 variables can be reduced to these three underlying concepts (Farley, 1985).

Factorial ecology can also be used to map the three dimensions to see whether each better fits the concentric-zones, sectoral, or multiple-nuclei patterns (Boal, 1976; Murdie, 1976). In general, family status fits the concentric-zones model, with unmarried people, childless couples, and renters living near the city's center, and families, children, and homeowners living farther away (Berry and Rees, 1969), though apartment complexes recently have led more singles to live in the suburbs (Farley, 1985). Socioeconomic status is often distributed according to both the concentric-zones and sectoral models: It is higher going in some directions from the center than others (in other words, sectoral), but it also increases as you move from the center (concentric).

Racial Segregation

The most pervasive form of urban social segregation in the United States is racial segregation, particularly between blacks and whites. Levels of segregation in American cities have declined since 1960, but not much. Most African Americans still live in neighborhoods that are mostly African American, and most whites live in neighborhoods that are overwhelmingly white (Logan, 2001; Farley, 2002, 2001b; 1987a; Jakubs, 1986; Massey and Denton, 1987, 1988, 1993; and Farley and Frey, 1994). Findings from the 2000 Census indicate that, despite modest decline in segregation between 1980 and 1990 and again between 1990 and 2000, many cities remain quite highly segregated (Logan, 2001). Older cities in the Midwest and Northeast, with their long-established patterns of segregation, are the most rigidly segregated (Logan, 2001; Jakubs, 1986; Massey and Denton, 1987; Farley and Frey, 1992).

Unlike some other forms of urban social segregation, racial segregation is mainly the product of discrimination. It is not the product of black preferences, because study after study has shown that most blacks prefer to live in racially mixed rather than all-black neighborhoods (Farley et al., 1994, 1979, 1978; Lake, 1981; Pettigrew, 1971). Neither is it a product of affordability. Although most blacks cannot afford to live in the wealthiest white neighborhoods, a large portion of the black population can afford to live in many white neighborhoods—but they don't. Studies based on every

Figure 14.2 Racial Composition of Census Tracts, St. Louis Metropolitan Area, 2000

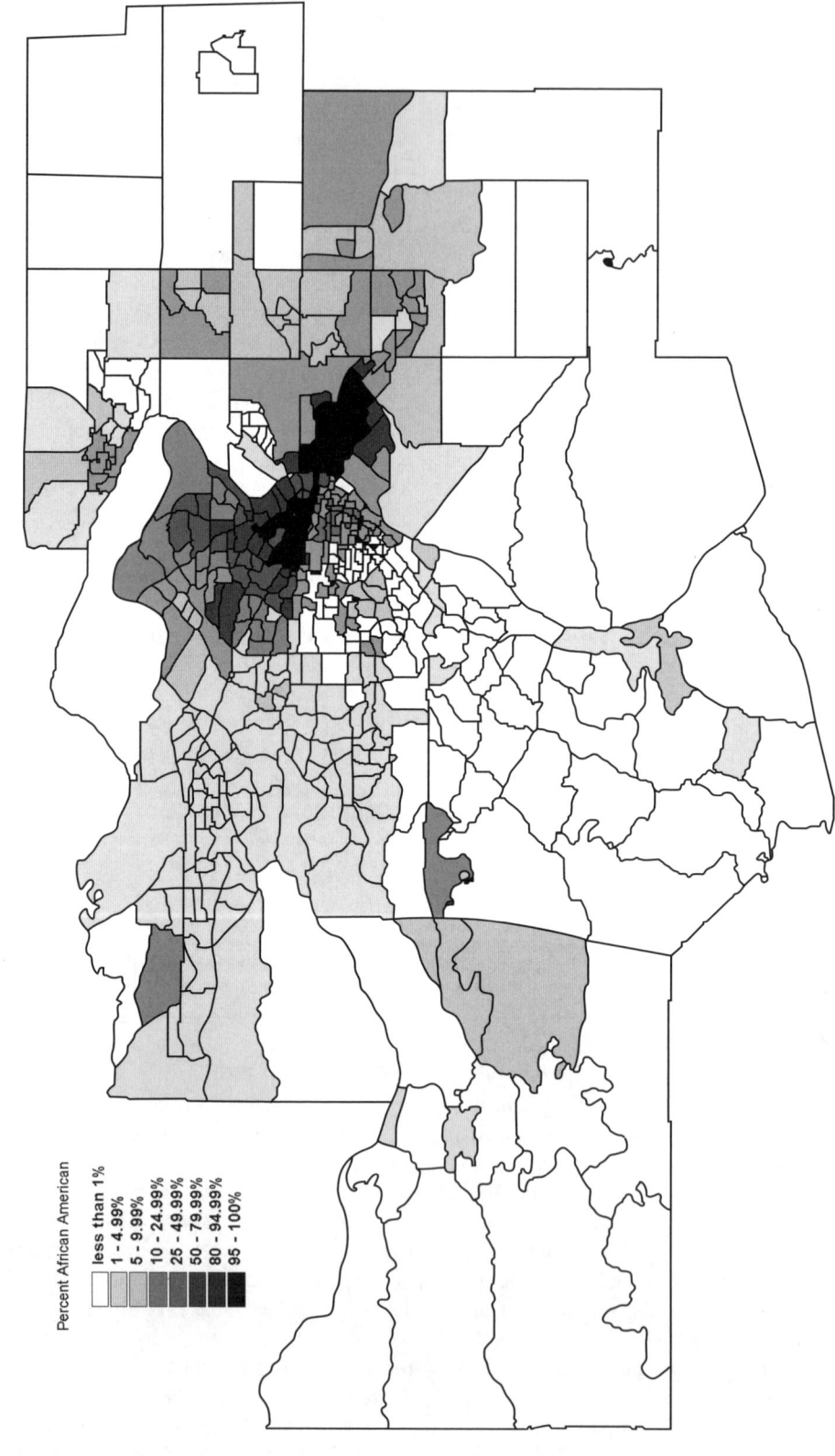

Source: John E. Farley, "Racial Housing Segregation in the St. Louis Metropolitan Area, 2000." *Edwardsville Journal of Sociology* 2 (2002), http://www.siue.edu/sociology/EJS/FARLEYV2.HTM.

census from 1960 through 1990 have found that if affordability were the only consideration, our urban areas would be, at most, only about one-quarter as segregated as they actually are (Darden, 1987; Farley, 1995, 1987b; Kain, 1987; see also Denton and Massey, 1988; Hermalin and Farley, 1973; Taeuber and Taeuber, 1965).

Racial Steering. Today, common forms of racial housing discrimination include racial steering and redlining. Racial steering is a practice whereby real estate agents direct whites toward housing in all-white neighborhoods and blacks toward housing in all-black or racially mixed neighborhoods (Lake, 1981; Pearce, 1976; Yinger, 1995). This perpetuates segregation, because in order for integrated neighborhoods to remain integrated, both races must move into them.

Recent studies show that racial steering continues to be widespread. There were at least 36 studies of racial steering conducted between 1974 and 1987, and the great majority of them found evidence of steering (Yinger, 1995). Nationwide studies in 1989 and 2000 showed that steering and other forms of racial discrimination remained common (Turner et al., 2002; U.S. Department of Housing and Urban Development, 1991; 2005; Yinger, 1995). The average white person lives in a neighborhood that is 80 percent white. For blacks the number is 51 percent African American in their neighborhoods; for Latinos, it is 46 percent Latino; and for Asians, only 18 percent Asian, though this number is on the rise for this group (Charles, 2003; Iceland and Wilkes, 2006; Lewis Mumford Center, 2001; Logan et. al. 2004; Wilkes and Iceland, 2004).

Discrimination-testing in 1996 by a St. Louis fair-housing organization with which I (Farley) work closely has confirmed that racial steering continues to occur. The testing illustrates how it often happens. We tested for racial steering in a suburban municipality in the St. Louis area by sending white and African American prospective home buyers, with similar incomes and family situations, to real estate offices. Although white and black testers went to the same real estate offices and expressed interest in the same type of housing, we found that they were shown houses according to their race in different parts of the town, which was split about in half by a major thoroughfare. Nearly all the white testers were shown housing in the predominantly white half of town on one side of this road, whereas nearly all the black testers were shown houses on the opposite side where the neighborhoods are racially mixed.

Redlining. Another important form of racial discrimination is redlining: a practice whereby lenders and insurance companies refuse to make loans or sell insurance in certain neighborhoods, usually ones that are racially mixed or predominantly black. Redlining, along with general discrimination in the approval of individual mortgages, makes it a good deal harder for African Americans to purchase homes. In part, for this reason, African Americans are a good deal less likely than whites to be homeowners. Because owning a home is the main source of wealth for all but the wealthiest Americans, this translates into a big difference in net worth: The average net worth of white Americans is about ten times that of African Americans (Oliver and Shapiro, 1995). Recent studies have shown that minority-group mortgage applicants are much more likely to be rejected for loans than white applicants, even when their incomes are the same. For example, a study by the Boston Federal Reserve found that black and Hispanic loan applicants were 56 percent more likely to be rejected than white applicants with similar risk, income, property, and credit backgrounds (Munnel et al., 1992). A recent study also found that neighborhoods of historical redlining linked up remarkably well with the areas hardest hit by subprime mortgages that have now plunged minority homeowners into foreclosure in disproportionate numbers (Hernandez, 2009). Redlining also occurs in insurance: In 1998, a jury assessed $100 million in damages against Nationwide Insurance Company after tests found that that the company discriminated against African American homeowners and inner-city neighborhoods (Squires, 1998).

In addition to denying housing opportunities to minorities, redlining has other damaging consequences: It transforms housing in racially mixed or largely minority neighborhoods from owner-occupied to renter-occupied; prevents upkeep of buildings; and contributes to the abandonment of homes, apartment buildings, and businesses whose owners cannot obtain loans or insurance. Moreover, by setting these processes in motion, redlining makes whites more reluctant to buy in mixed neighborhoods. In spite of redlining and racial steering, survey data indicate that a sizable segment of the white population is willing to (and in some cases actively desires to) buy homes in racially mixed neighborhoods (Farley et al., 1978, 1979; Lake, 1981). The problem is that racial steering and redlining make it nearly impossible for them to do so.

The Changing City in Postindustrial America

As the United States has gradually undergone the transition from an industrial economy to a postindustrial economy (see Chapter 11), America's urban areas have been profoundly affected. The declining role of industry, the shift toward a service economy, the changing distribution of wealth and income, and the pervasiveness of the automobile have all brought dramatic changes to American cities since World War II. These changes include the rise of the suburbs; the decline of the central city; the increasing concentration of urban poverty, joblessness, and homelessness; and the shift of urban growth from the "Frost Belt" (or "Rust Belt") of the Midwest and Northeast to the "Sun Belt" of the South and West. We shall begin our examination of these changes with a discussion of suburbanization.

The Rise of the Suburbs

As illustrated by Table 14.5, the percentage of Americans living in the suburbs has risen dramatically since World War II. The statistics in the table are based on a concept known as the **metropolitan statistical area (MSA)**. This concept was developed by the Census Bureau to reflect the fact that by the end of World War II, the population of urban areas was beginning to expand beyond the legal boundaries of the city. Using counties as building blocks, metropolitan statistical areas are intended to include the full extent of the metropolitan area, both city and suburbs. Each MSA consists of one or more central cities, which must have a combined population of 50,000 or more, and a suburban ring, which consists of the rest of the county or counties containing the central cities plus any adjoining counties that are largely urban in character and economically linked to the central cities. As an example, the Memphis MSA consists of Shelby County, Tennessee (which contains the city of Memphis), and adjoining Tipton and Fayette Counties, Tennessee; Crittendon County, Arkansas; and DeSoto County, Mississippi. As this example shows, MSAs can cross state lines. As of 2008, there were 363 metropolitan areas in the United States.

Over the past half-century, the proportion of people who live in metropolitan areas has risen steadily, and of these, more and more live in the suburbs rather than the central city. Today, more people—half of all Americans—live in the suburbs than anywhere else, a complete reversal of the situation that existed just fifty years ago. As more people have moved to the suburbs, jobs, retail businesses, office complexes, warehouses, and factories have all followed (Choldin, 1985, pp. 363–69). In most metropolitan areas, the majority of the population is suburban (the average is about 60 percent), and in some areas the majority of economic activity is also suburban. Moreover, despite much talk about a "return to the city" in the 1970s and 1980s (discussed below), the movement of people and economic activity from central cities to the suburbs continues. In part, this is because people or businesses who move to a new urban area tend to locate in the suburbs rather than the central city.

Causes of Suburbanization

There are a number of reasons for the tremendous surge of people and economic activity into the suburbs. One is human preference. People want the open space, peace, and quiet of rural areas, but they depend on cities for jobs, services, and a variety of amenities. The suburbs offer the best compromise between these two competing sets of needs and desires (see Glaab, 1963, pp. 233–34). Moreover, for those who want and can afford a large house and a big yard, the open space of the urban fringe is the obvious choice of location. The generally healthy growth of the economy after World War II made the suburbs affordable to growing numbers of Americans.

Suburbanization is not entirely the product of people's choices, however. Government policy, technology, demographic trends, and economic interests all contributed to the growth of the

Table 14.5 Percent of Population in Central Cities, Suburban Areas, and Outside Metropolitan Areas, 1950–2000

Year	1950	1960	1970	1980	1990	2000
Total in metropolitan areas	62.4	66.7	68.6	74.8	77.7	80.3
In central cities	35.4	33.4	31.4	30.0	30.5	30.3
In suburban areas	27.0	33.3	37.2	44.8	47.2	50.0
Outside metropolitan areas	37.5	33.3	31.4	25.2	22.3	19.7

Note: Data are based on metropolitan area boundaries as they were defined in each census year. New areas were added to metropolitan areas in each census, both because new areas grew large enough to be defined as metropolitan, and because new counties were added to existing areas to reflect the expansion of these areas.

Sources: 2000 data are from U.S. Census Bureau, 2000 Census of Population and Housing, Profiles of General Demographic Characteristics, http://www.census.gov/Press-Release/www/2001/2khus.pdf. 1990 data are from U.S. Bureau of the Census (1990), Current Population Reports, Series P-60, No. 168. 1980 data are from U.S. Bureau of the Census (1983), Statistical Abstract of the United States, 1982–83, p. 15. Data for earlier years are from U.S. Bureau of the Census (1972), Statistical Abstract of the United States, 1972, p. 16.

suburbs (Palen, 1987, pp. 182–87). The U.S. government encouraged and subsidized homeownership through such mechanisms as the home mortgage tax deduction and, after World War II, substantial subsidies of mortgage interest through loan programs administered by the Federal Housing Administration (FHA) and Veterans Administration (VA). These subsidies enabled millions of middle- and lower middle-income Americans to purchase their own homes. Although these policies were undoubtedly popular because people wanted to buy homes in the suburbs, it should be stressed that they also served the interests of large-scale real-estate developers, who were able to amass great fortunes by mass-producing standardized, relatively low-cost suburban housing.

Another government policy that contributed to suburbanization was the construction of the interstate highway system. The freeways enabled people to commute up to fifty miles within an hour. Finally, the 1950s were the years of the baby boom, which meant a massive surge in families with children—the group with the lifestyle best suited to the suburbs. In short, a number of factors worked together to produce the suburban transformation of the United States after World War II.

Life in the Suburbs

Like cities, suburbs have been both praised and condemned. On the one hand, they are praised as the ideal place to raise children—quieter, safer, and roomier than the city, but with all the urban amenities close by. On the other hand, suburbs are condemned as uninteresting places of conformity where "they all live in little boxes, and all look just the same." As usual, both the praisers and the condemners overstate their case. On the whole, suburbanites are somewhat more affluent and less heterogeneous than central-city residents, and there are fewer African Americans and Hispanics in the suburbs than

Collectivities sometimes develop norms that give members of the group alternative guidelines for behavior. Would these people (most of whom are college professors) dress like this outside the group context? (Courtesy of John E. Farley)

in the city. However, the socioeconomic differences are not great, and neither are some lifestyle differences. Research published in the early 1960s showed little difference between city and suburban residents of similar socioeconomic status with respect to organizational participation and cultural and recreational interests (Berger, 1960; Cohen and Hodges, 1963), but more recent research has uncovered some differences. Choldin (1980), for example, found that suburban women are more involved in neighborhood and community organizations than are city women of the same race and socioeconomic status.

There are other ways in which suburbanites differ on the average from city residents. Partly because they more often own their homes and thus have a greater investment in their neighborhoods, suburbanites interact more with their neighbors and are in general more involved with their neighborhoods (Choldin, 1980; Fava, 1959; Fischer and Jackson, 1976; Gans, 1967a). Another reason for this interaction is that suburbanites are more likely than city residents to have children, and adult neighbors often become better acquainted because their children are playmates. On the other hand, research results conflict on the question of whether suburbanites' lives are more centered around their children (Berger, 1960; Gans, 1967a). Gans has characterized suburban neighbors as "quasi-primary groups" because their relationships are typically closer than the secondary-group relationships of the business and commercial world but not as close as the bond between close friends and family members. To a large extent, the suburban neighbor relationship seems to be one of mutual assistance, which is one of the characteristics Toennies associated with the rural gemeinschaft. In general, suburbanites like their place of residence better than city dwellers do, but this partly reflects their higher average socioeconomic status.

Although suburbanites do have some differences from central-city residents in certain ways on average, suburbs and suburbanites are themselves very diverse, and becoming more so (Schwab, 1992, p. 319). There are wealthy, middle-class, working-class, and poor suburbs. There are predominantly white, black, and Hispanic suburbs, even though African Americans and Hispanics are underrepresented in the suburbs. And there are not only family-oriented suburbs, but also suburbs where apartment complexes occupied mostly by unmarried adults and childless couples predominate.

The claim that the suburbs produce a certain type of lifestyle appears to be an overstatement. Michelson's (1977) study of people moving into city and suburban neighborhoods in Toronto offers a better analysis. Michelson found that people largely choose a neighborhood and housing type that fits their lifestyle at a given point in their lives. The city fits the lifestyle of unmarried people and childless couples, especially those who are cosmopolitan in outlook, whereas the suburbs fit the lifestyle of families with children. The only people who are likely to feel real dissatisfaction with their environment are those who for some reason—such as cost—cannot get the kind of housing that fits their lifestyle or aspirations.

Finally, we should note that in a variety of ways, some suburbs are becoming more like central cities.

The construction of urban freeways has contributed to suburbanization by making it possible for people to live far from the cities in which they work. Today, one finds trends toward living nearer work, as well as telecommuting via media technology. (iStockphoto)

We have already mentioned the growing number of single and divorced people in the suburbs, making them less the domain of family life than they once were. We have also noted the growth of employment and specialized economic activity in the suburbs: More people now commute into some suburbs than out of them. Finally, some suburbs, especially older ones, are developing the problems that have plagued the central cities: job loss, housing abandonment, racial conflict, poverty, and population decline. However, it is still in the central cities where these problems have been most severe, a pattern to which we now turn our attention.

The Crisis of the Central Cities

While the suburbs have experienced booming growth, the central cities have experienced decline since World War II. Despite a few bright spots, such as the rejuvenation of the downtown area in many cities, the dominant condition of the larger, older central cities has been deepening crisis. This has been manifested in a number of ways.

Population Decline

The majority of large cities have lost a substantial portion of their population through out-migration. This trend has been particularly pronounced in the Midwest and Northeast: Between 1950 and 1980, St. Louis lost nearly half of its population; Detroit, Cleveland, Boston, Minneapolis, and Cincinnati all lost between one-quarter and one-third; and New York, Chicago, Baltimore, and San Francisco lost between 10 and 20 percent. Most who have left have moved to the suburbs, but in the Midwest and Northeast, many have also moved to other parts of the country.

During the 1980s and 1990s, population decline slowed or reversed in a number of large cities (Haub, 1991; U.S. Census Bureau, 2001t). New York gained population in the 1980s and 1990s after decades of loss, and St. Louis lost less population in the 1980s than in any decade since the 1940s. And in the 1990s, several additional large cities that had been losing population, including Chicago, posted gains. Still, most large cities in the Midwest and Northeast still had much lower populations in 2000 than they did four or five decades earlier. And several, including St. Louis, Detroit, Cleveland, Cincinnati, and Baltimore, continued to lose population through the 1980s and 1990s. In some cases, the losses have been devastating—St. Louis lost nearly 60 percent of its population—half a million people—between 1950 and 2000. Detroit lost about a million people. Another pattern that emerged in the 1980s is that a number of smaller cities—particularly small industrial cities in the Midwest—suffered pronounced population losses. For some of these cities, like Peoria, Lansing, Evansville, and Flint, this trend continued in the 1990s.

The Urban Underclass

As those who could afford to relocate to the suburbs did so, an increasing concentration of the minority poor was left behind in the central cities. Sociologists sometimes refer to the poorest of these poor people, who are often chronically unemployed, as the underclass (see Chapter 11). Wilson (1987, p. 50) uses a study of Chicago to illustrate the growing concentration of poverty in the cities. Between 1970 and 1980, the population of the Chicago fell by 11 percent, but the number of poor people living in the city grew by 24 percent. The major reason a number of people living in Chicago (and other central cities) became poor during the 1970s was increased joblessness (Wilson, 1996; 1987). This rise in joblessness occurred for several reasons that are discussed elsewhere in this book: loss of jobs from the central city (Chapter 6), housing segregation that excludes minorities from areas with the greatest job growth (Chapter 7), and limited educational opportunities combined with rising educational requirements for many jobs (Web-Based Chapter A). Another factor is the increasing proportion of female-headed households in the central cities; these women literally cannot afford to work in the absence of subsidized day care and health care (Chapter 8 and Web-Based Chapter C). Finally, one other cause of concentrated poverty is that racial housing segregation concentrates minority groups with high poverty rates into certain neighborhoods (Massey, Gross, and Shibuya, 1994; Massey and Denton, 1993). The segregation problem is discussed further in Chapter 7.

Growing Up in the Underclass

The growth of the urban underclass has major implications for the future of the United States. Historically, the cities have served as a launching ground for upward mobility and assimilation for both the native poor and immigrants (Bradbury, Downs, and Small, 1982). With today's unprecedented concentration of poverty, cities may be losing that function. Poor urban dwellers are more likely than ever to live in neighborhoods where nearly everyone is poor or near-poor. Millions of children today are growing up in neighborhoods where jobs are scarce, in families where nobody can find a job, and in areas where key institutions have left along with the middle class (Wilson, 1987, pp. 140–46). In such an environment, the traditional work ethic doesn't pay, but a "fast buck" can be made through drug dealing, theft, or prostitution. The result has been rapid growth of youth gangs, and in the future, there could be an entire generation of inner-city residents outside the legitimate workforce. Research has confirmed that in such neighborhoods, adolescents are more likely to drop out of school than poor kids in other neighborhoods, and that teenage pregnancy rates are higher (Anderson, 1991; Crane, 1991a,b; McLeod and Shannahan, 1993; Brewster, 1994; Brooks-Gunn et al., 1993).

Homelessness

One effect of the increasing amount and concentration of poverty has been an increase in homelessness. Major increases in homelessness occurred in the 1980s and again with the recent economic crisis. The precise number of homeless people is difficult to determine, because people with no permanent place to live are hard to locate and count. The best estimates are that, in the late 1980s, the number of homeless people in the United States at any one time was somewhere between 400,000 (Jencks, 1994) and 600,000 (Burt and Cohen, 1989). More recently, an effort by the Department of Housing and Urban Development to count the homeless in January 2007, resulted in an estimate of about 672,000 homeless people nationwide (U.S. Department of Housing and Urban Development, 2008). But homeless people are not just found in shelters and on the streets. They are also in subway stations, "welfare hotels," and even campgrounds. Also included in many estimates of the homeless are people who have no residence of their own but seek temporary shelter with relatives or friends.

Just when the poverty rate soared in the early 1980s, major cutbacks were made in federal low-income housing programs. This, coupled with the deinstitutionalization of many mentally ill people, contributed to a big surge in the number of homeless, most of whom end up in urban areas. Many people drift in and out of homelessness, and some are homeless for only relatively short periods of time. For this reason, the number of people who experience homelessness at one time or another over a period of five or ten years is much greater than the number homeless at any one time. For example, the Urban Institute estimates that at least 3.5 million Americans have been homeless at some point in time. Homelessness rates had been falling in the first few years of the new century, but the severe economic recession in 2007–2009 led to large increases in the number of homeless people. For example, there were large increases in 2008 in the number of homeless families seeking shelter in cities across the United States, including New York, Minneapolis, Phoenix, Atlanta, Boston, Seattle, and many others (Koch, 2008).

The Urban Fiscal Crisis

The combination of an overall population decline and a rise in the number of poor residents is affecting cities in a number of ways. First and foremost, it means a sharp increase in the proportion of the city's population that is poor. Poor populations require more services, particularly in the areas of health, welfare, and police protection; however, they pay less in taxes. The consequence is that city governments have had to do more with less, a reality further aggravated by cutbacks in federal aid to cities in the 1980s. City after city has had to curtail needed services; in the worst cases, cities such as New York, Cleveland, and East St. Louis have experienced financial emergencies. Besides cutting back on services, cities have been unable to maintain their aging and overused infrastructures: roads, sewers, mass transit, water systems, and bridges. Thus, the collapse of bridges and sewers has become an increasingly common event in American cities. Any American who lives in or near a major city has experienced the frustrations and delays that result from inadequate transportation systems.

Uneven Development Among American Cities

Although suburbanization and urban decline have occurred to some extent in all parts of the United States, these trends have been far more pronounced in the Midwest and Northeast (the "Frost Belt") than in the South and West (the "Sun Belt"). In general, Sun Belt metropolitan areas are growing; Frost Belt metropolitan areas are not. Sociologists refer to such regional differences in urban growth as **uneven development** (Frisbie and Kasarda, 1988, pp. 657–58; Watkins and Perry, 1977). This term is also sometimes used to describe the differences in growth between cities and suburbs, or between downtown and residential neighborhoods. Sociologists have two fundamental disagreements over the meaning of uneven development among cities in different regions. The first concerns whether Frost Belt and Sun Belt cities are simply at different stages of a similar process of growth and decline or whether they are following fundamentally different courses of development (Frey, 1987). The second concerns whether regional differences in urban development reflect differences in the efficiency and effectiveness of different kinds of cities (the functionalist view) or whether they are the product of fundamental societal inequalities in power and wealth (the conflict view).

Different Processes or Different Stages?

One view about the uneven development of American cities is that Frost Belt and Sun Belt cities are in different stages of a similar process of growth and decline. According to this view, Frost Belt cities such as New York, Philadelphia, Pittsburgh, Chicago, Detroit, St. Louis, and Cleveland have lost population and become increasingly poor because they are older cities. The quality of housing is deteriorating, and people are moving out. City governments cannot do much about it, because they are surrounded by established suburbs and cannot expand their boundaries by annexing these growing areas. Sun Belt cities such as Houston, Phoenix, San Diego, Los Angeles, Tampa, San Antonio, and San Jose are at an earlier stage of development. They are still growing, they have considerable new housing within their boundaries, and they can expand those boundaries outward to accommodate new growth (Fleischman, 1977). In all these ways, they are similar to the Frost Belt cities in the early twentieth century. At that time, the major cities of the Midwest and Northeast were all experiencing rapid growth.

This view that Sun Belt and Frost Belt cities are in different stages of the same process of growth and decline predicts that the now-growing cities of the West and South will eventually age, become surrounded by suburbs, and begin to lose population. It appeared that this was starting to happen in the 1970s, when Denver, San Francisco, Atlanta, Fort Worth, and Portland, Oregon, all lost population, and Los Angeles barely grew. However, between 1980 and 1990, all of these cities except Denver and Atlanta again grew significantly, and all of them grew between 1990 and 2000.

An opposing view, which predicts continued growth for these cities, emphasizes the transition from an industrial to a postindustrial economy in the United States. As was discussed in Chapter 11, the postindustrial economy is based largely on services, such as commerce, finance, tourism, and real estate, as well as on high-technology industries, such as electronics, aircraft, and energy (see Sale, 1975). From this standpoint, the South and West, with their warmer climates, greater recreational amenities, and abundant energy supplies, are the natural locations of new growth. Proponents of this viewpoint note that even though some Sun Belt cities have lost population recently, the overall growth of MSAs has been far greater in the South and West than in the Northeast and Midwest. In the latter two regions, even some inner suburbs have lost population; in the former two regions, the majority of central cities have gained population, and suburban growth has been even more dramatic.

Metropolitan statistical areas such as New York, Chicago, Detroit, Philadelphia, and St. Louis barely grew, or even lost population, between 1970 and 1990 because suburban growth was at best just sufficient to offset central-city decline. Most of them grew again in the 1990s, but much more slowly than metropolitan areas in other parts of the country. In contrast, the growth rates of the Dallas, Houston, Atlanta, and San Diego MSAs averaged about 45 percent in the 1970s, and, except for Houston, these areas grew by another 33 percent during the 1980s. In the 1990s, their growth averaged 27 percent. Thus, over three decades, these areas grew at a much faster pace than the older manufacturing areas in the Midwest and Northeast. Accordingly, uneven development does not involve just the situation of the central city, but also the overall rate of metropolitan growth reflecting the various economic specializations of different areas (Watkins and Perry, 1977).

The Conflict Theory of Uneven Development

Conflict theorists argue that uneven development reflects inequalities of wealth and power (Sawers and Tabb, 1984). More-powerful interest groups and more-powerful cities erect barriers to ensure their own growth and to prevent growth elsewhere that might threaten their interests (Gordon, 1977b; Squires, 1989b; Watkins and Perry, 1977, p. 26; see also Molotch, 1976). Many examples can be used to illustrate this process. Federal taxing and spending policies for a number of years generally favored the South and West over the Northeast and Midwest. In other words, Frost Belt cities paid more in taxes and got less back in federal expenditures than cities in the South and West (Watkins and Perry, 1977, p. 50).

Another example concerns uneven development within cities. Large real-estate companies, banks, and corporations use their influence with city officials to get such benefits as abatement of property taxes on new developments, or local tax money to upgrade streets, sidewalks, and lighting in neighborhoods where new businesses or expensive housing are being located. In more and more instances businesses secure the land for their projects free or at very low prices through government use of the right of *eminent domain*. This right allows government to take land from its owners "for the greater good" and "at a fair market price" even when owners don't want to sell it. In Detroit, this right was used to force over 1,000 families out of the Poletown neighborhood, at a cost to the government of $200 million—after which the land was sold to General Motors for $8 million (Palen, 1987, p. 281; see also Wylie, 1989). Finally, although substantial public money was used to stimulate downtown development in Baltimore, the poor and unemployed did not share in the benefits (Levine, 1987). The project contributed to the development of the downtown area and aided the financial interests of downtown businesses, but it did little for anyone living in the neighborhoods. Thus, uneven development in Baltimore was clearly the product of government policies, and benefited certain interest groups who had disproportionate power over the decision-making process. In general, conflict theorists see uneven development as resulting from cooperative actions between governments and wealthy private interests that have disproportionate influence over government (Jaret, 1983).

More generally, conflict theorists point out that cities, just like the societies in which they exist, are greatly shaped by the interests of dominant social groups. Feminists, for example, point out that the structure of the city has traditionally reflected male interests (Wekerle, 1980). The industrial city was built around the notion of males leaving the home for the workplace and women staying behind to tend the home and children. Thus, for the workday at least, the downtown business and financial center became a male domain, the home and neighborhood a female domain. In fact, Boserup (1970) has argued that the separate domains of men and women are a product of urbanization and modernization, and would not have occurred without them. The process began in the early stages of urbanization, when men went from rural areas to cities to take advantage of the economic opportunities there, while women were left behind in rural areas to take care of the home (Boserup, 1970, pp. 139–40). This pattern still persists in some Third World countries. With industrialization, this separation typically intensifies, as illustrated by the emergence of the housewife role in industrial society (Degler, 1980), as was discussed in Chapter 8. This separation contributes to a situation in which power, authority, and control of wealth become mainly a male domain.

Today, with two-car and two-worker families more common, this has changed to some extent. However, Lopata (1980) and Wekerle (1980) have found that the city still imposes difficulties upon women that it does not on men. The most serious is the limited availability of child care, discussed in Chapters 8 and 13.

Marxist urban sociologists argue that the structure of the city has always reflected the needs of the capital-owning class (Castells, 1977, 1985; Gottdiener, 1985; Harvey, 1973; Tabb and Sawers,

1978). They point out, for example, that urban land use is in large part determined by what is profitable for banks, corporations, and real-estate interests (Feagin, 1983, 1985; Logan and Molotch, 1987; Whitt, 1982). These interests favor growth regardless of its consequences, because they benefit from it (Molotch, 1979). Though the consequences often include urban sprawl that creates pollution, congestion, and racial and class segregation, the growth interests have enough power and influence to nearly always get their way. This can be illustrated by a recent event in the town where I (Farley) live. A national grocery chain and a shopping center developer requested a subsidy in the form of lower taxes to build a new grocery store. There was widespread opposition expressed at public hearings, in part because the chain planned to close the only grocery store downtown, and the new store would be next door to an existing grocery store. However, the city council approved the subsidy anyway because of fear that the company would close the downtown store anyway and build the new one in another nearby town.

It is not just through politics, however, that the owners of capital shape the city. Such decisions as the opening or closing of a factory, for example, have tremendous impact on a city. Capitalists determine urban growth patterns largely through their decisions about where to locate. The way this process works is illustrated by historical analyses by Gordon (1978, 1977a, 1977b). Gordon's basic premise is that capitalists put their plants where they can make the most money, which in part involves locating wherever workers' wages can be kept low. In today's global economy, this often means anywhere in the world, as is discussed in greater detail in Chapter 11. The impacts of such moves on areas left behind are often devastating, and they have been especially severe in the industrial urban areas of the Midwest and Northeast. The booming service economy did create new jobs in these areas in the 1990s, but the standard of living these new jobs could support was far below that provided by the now lost manufacturing jobs of the past.

Summary

Cities are defined on the basis of population size, density, and heterogeneity. They were made possible by production of an agricultural surplus, the development of regional transportation systems, and growth in demand for urban products.

However, through much of history these factors allowed only limited urbanization, and cities accounted for only a small share of the population in virtually all societies until the Industrial Revolution. The demographic transition added another impetus to urbanization: As rural populations grew beyond the numbers that rural areas could support, people migrated to the city. And as urban economies grew with industrialization and could support more people, growing numbers were drawn to cities. The populations of cities today have reached levels unimagined in the past, and, in a very recent development, there are many countries where most people now live in cities.

In the United States, rapid urbanization began in the mid-nineteenth century and continued until around 1960. In the developing world, urbanization has been more recent, and in some countries, the majority of the population is still rural. In some developing countries, urbanization has exceeded the ability of the economy to support an urban population, resulting in massive urban poverty and shantytowns. Even so, the fastest-growing cities in the world today are in the less economically developed countries.

Since the surge of urbanization that accompanied industrialization, sociologists have been interested in the effects of urban living on society and human behavior. Early theorists such as Toennies, Simmel, and Wirth were generally pessimistic, arguing that urban life resulted in social isolation, impersonal relations, and other problems. Actual research, however, has cast doubt on most of these arguments. Although urbanites may have a greater number of impersonal contacts and client relationships than people in rural areas, they generally do not lack friends and close family relationships, and their mental health is as good as that of people in rural areas. In addition, there is no such thing as the "typical urbanite": There are many different groups of people in urban areas, with many different lifestyles. Some groups have very close relationships with neighbors and kin; others have relationships that are more wide-ranging and are based on common activities and interests rather than neighborhood or kinship. Because of this diversity, urbanites tend to be somewhat more tolerant and enjoy greater personal freedom than people in rural societies.

Collective behavior occurs when large numbers of people act together in extraordinary situations, where usual norms do not apply. Because of the numbers of people available and the ease of communication, it occurs more easily in modern urban settings. It can take place in either crowds or masses; in both cases, the temporary norms of the collectivity permit or encourage behavior that would not normally occur. Collective behavior emerges when the situation is structurally conducive—in other words, the situation generates feelings of fear, anger, happiness, excitement, sorrow, or some other strong emotion. But even when the situation is conducive, collective behavior does not occur until some precipitating incident triggers it.

The main kinds of crowd behavior are panics, mobs, riots, protest crowds, expressive crowds, and public grief. Obviously, different kinds of conditions generate these various types of collective behavior. A most extreme type of crowd behavior, fortunately very rare, is mass suicide. This behavior illustrates the extent to which the collectivity's norms can replace society's usual norms when conditions are conducive.

The main forms of mass behavior are rumors, urban legends, mass hysteria, fads, and fashions. As with crowd behavior, these different forms of mass behavior reflect different predominant emotions and are generated under different social conditions. Here, too, a precipitating incident, such as a radio broadcast of a rumor, can often trigger widespread collective behavior, but, again, only when the conditions are otherwise conducive.

A key area of urban sociology is human ecology, the study of relationships between population and territory. Social segregation, a pattern whereby people with similar characteristics live together, is found in all cities. Depending on its history, a particular city can exhibit various combinations of three common patterns of population distribution and land use: concentric-zones, sectors, and multiple nuclei. The most important factors influencing where people live and how they group together are social class, family status, and race or ethnicity. Racial and ethnic segregation have been especially persistent in American cities, and racial segregation has often been the product of deliberate discrimination. In part because of segregation, the poor have become concentrated in central city neighborhoods in some cities, and uneven development between different cities and between different parts of urban areas has widened the economic gaps among these areas.

Since World War II, the bulk of the urban population of the United States, and a good deal of economic activity, have shifted from the central cities to the suburbs. Transportation innovations, preferences for more space, government policy, and economic trends have all contributed to this development. The suburbs tend to have higher-income populations than cities, a higher percentage of families with children, and a higher percentage of whites. However, as the suburbs are becoming more diverse, some of these differences are gradually decreasing.

Key Terms

urbanization
functional specialization
hinterland
overurbanization
gemeinschaft
gesellschaft
community
collective behavior
crowds
masses
structural conduciveness
civil disobedience
mob
riot
panic
rumors
urban legend
human ecology
concentric-zones model
sectoral model
multiple nuclei model
social segregation
metropolitan statistical area (MSA)
uneven development

Exercises

1. A major social problem created by the spread of urbanization is called *urban sprawl*. This is where an urban area spreads across open

land as low-density living spaces proliferate and are separated from the areas people work and shop. Large roadways must be devised to join these separated areas, eating up even more open space and leading to increased pollution and consumption of fossil fuels. Research the phenomenon online and investigate why this sprawl might be such a common occurrence in urban environments. Then try to answer the following questions:

- Do you live in a community where this phenomenon is a problem, or do you know someone who lives in such a community?
- Even if you have no practical or indirect experience with urban sprawl, *imagine* that where you live has this problem. What if the area you now live in grew rapidly and developed sprawl? What do you think your reactions would be? What would you want to do about it?

2. The aftermath of Hurricane Katrina in New Orleans showed the difficulty of organizing a mass rescue operation in a large urban area. However, it also showed another reality of urban life in the United States. Imagine that Hurricane Katrina had hit area code 90210. Would the residents of that wealthy urban area have to face the same problems of coordination and mobilization as those in New Orleans? Why or why not?

Chapter 15
Social Movements and Change

Social Movements	**480**
Types of Social Movements 481	
The Causes of Social Movements 483	
Necessary Conditions for Social Movements 485	
Movement Life Course: Civil Rights, Environmental, and Women's Movement as Case Studies 485	
Social Change	**491**
What Is Social Change?	**491**
Theories of Social Change	**492**
Equilibrium (Functionalist) Versus Conflict Theories of Social Change 492	
Evolutionary Versus Cyclical Changes 493	
Modernization: Escalating Social Change	**494**
Consequences of Rapid Social Change 495	
New Directions in the Study of Social Change	**496**
Summary	**497**
Key Terms	**500**
Exercises	**500**

Imagine yourself on vacation. Your family has worked hard for this trip—your dad put in many hours of overtime on the assembly line, and at home—in addition to cleaning the house, taking care of your four younger siblings, and cooking all the meals—your mother has spent many hours growing a garden and canning fruits and vegetables so you can eat less expensively and save for this vacation. It will be your first trip to the Gulf Coast, and you are excited. But when you stop at a gas station along the way, you are startled and taken aback to see that the gas station has three restrooms, marked "men," "women," and "colored." When you ask about this, you are even more surprised to find out that, in the areas you will be visiting, it is illegal for whites and "Negroes" to swim in the same pools, eat lunch at the same lunch counters, sit together in a theater, or, in some places, even play baseball on the same diamond.

Did the description above seem odd to you? Did it anger you? Did it seem unreal? In fact, it could have described a typical experience of an American less than sixty years ago—a time when much of the country was strictly and legally segregated by race, and when social roles were sharply defined by sex. For example, it was generally unacceptable for a married woman—especially with children—to have a career. Female doctors, lawyers, or police officers were so rare as to be considered major oddities. And the idea of black and white children attending school together was considered so radical that the majority of Americans opposed it (Hyman and Sheatsley, 1964).

The description above, when compared to the realities of today, offers a vivid illustration of social change. Everywhere in today's world there are examples of social change. Some, like the abolition of Jim Crow segregation and public acceptance of women having careers, are the results in large part of social movements. In other words, an important reason that conditions like those above seem odd today is that people struggled collectively to change them. Hundreds of thousands of people demonstrated against racial segregation, thousands were arrested, hundreds of lawsuits were filed, and dozens of people died in the struggle. As a result, laws mandating separation of the races were abolished, and seem odd to us today (though subtler forms of racial inequality remain commonplace). Similarly, years of public protests and private challenges to sexism gradually undid the notion that the place for women is in the home. (Though, again, big inequalities in the wages of women and men still persist.) Race and gender relations, then, are two key areas in which the United States has experienced significant social changes, in no small part because millions of Americans joined together in social movements demanding change.

While some instances of social change have resulted from collective action such as social movements, others may be totally unplanned, and seem at first glance to be unrelated to any conscious human action. Similarly, some social change is very gradual, such as the gradual transition of the United States over 200 years from an overwhelmingly rural society to one where most people live in large metropolitan areas. But social change can also be as abrupt as the sudden collapse of the Soviet Union in the early 1990s.

In this chapter, we explore social movements and social change—how do they happen, what is their relationship to one another, and how do they relate to the various aspects of society we have examined in preceding chapters?

Social Movements

The examples of change in race and gender relations illustrate a key point about social movements and social change: The two interact, and each can arise from the other. The baby boom and the growth of higher education helped to spawn student activism, but that activism in turn contributed to the changes in race relations and gender roles described in the opening vignette. Because social movements are mutually related to social change in these ways, we begin this chapter with a discussion of social movements.

A **social movement** can be defined as a large number of people acting together on behalf of some objective or idea. Usually, it involves the use of noninstitutionalized means, such as marches and protests, to support or oppose social change. Social movements involve substantial numbers of people and usually continue for an extended length of time (Blumer, 1974). Typically, a social movement will have an ideology—a set of beliefs and values that it seeks to promote. To a large extent, the success of a movement depends on its ability to convince potential participants, as well as the larger public, of the merits of its ideology (McAdam, McCarthy, and Zald, 1988, pp. 724–25; Snow et al., 1986; Gerhards and Rucht, 1992). Social movements are more common in industrialized countries than in preindustrial countries, and they are more common in relatively democratic societies than in authoritarian ones. With industrialization, interest groups become far more diverse, and social control weaker, which makes it easier for people to organize against conditions or ideas they oppose. Democracy has similar effects, whereas authoritarian regimes view social movements as a threat and use such techniques as surveillance and imprisonment to immobilize them before they can achieve a popular following. Industrialization makes this more difficult to do, however, and countries such as the former Soviet Union and communist Poland powerfully illustrate this. By 1991, the Solidarity movement, begun as a protest movement, had become the governing force in Poland. In 1991, the Soviet democracy movement, its hand greatly strengthened by successful resistance to the attempted coup against Mikhail Gorbachev, brought an end to communism and ultimately to the Soviet Union itself. Once the former Soviet Union and Eastern European countries democratized, a bewildering variety of ethnic, religious, and nationalist movements arose, and struggles among these movements continue today.

Types of Social Movements

There are five common types of social movements: protest movements, regressive movements, religious movements, communal movements, and personal cults. Although these are classified as different kinds of movements, they do overlap, and a particular movement may contain elements of more than one of the five types. Let us consider each in some detail.

Protest Movements

Protest movements are movements whose objective is to change or oppose some current social condition. This is the most common type of social movement in most industrialized countries; examples in the United States are the Civil Rights movement, the feminist movement, the gay rights movement, the antinuclear movement, the environmental movement, and the peace movement. Most protest movements are reform movements—they are aimed at achieving certain limited reforms, not remaking the entire society. They urge a new policy toward the environment, foreign affairs, or a particular racial or ethnic group—but not a wholesale elimination or remaking of basic social institutions. Occasionally, however, protest movements take the form of *revolutionary movements,* which seek to remake an entire society through eliminating old institutions and establishing new ones. Revolutionary movements are rare, and when they do happen it is often only after a series of related reform movements have failed to achieve the objectives they seek. Although rare, successful revolutions do occasionally happen. Countries as diverse as the United States, Russia, France, China, Iran, Mexico, Zimbabwe, and the Philippines have this in common: In every one of these countries, the current system of government is directly or indirectly the product of a revolution at some time in the past.

Regressive Movements

Regressive movements are social movements whose objective is to undo social change or to oppose a protest movement. An example of a regressive movement would be the antifeminist movement,

The increase in female clergy has been gradual but represents a substantial change compared to two generations ago when the role of the clergy was mostly reserved for males. (AP Photo/Tony Avelar)

which opposes recent changes in the role and status of women and urges them to remain at home and take care of their children rather than seek outside employment. In some regards, the Tea Party movement of 2009 and 2010 also has characteristics of a regressive movement, since it has been driven in part by opposition to the health care reforms enacted in 2010. More extreme forms of regressive movements include the Ku Klux Klan and various neo-Nazi and racist "skinhead" groups, which believe in white supremacy and favor a return to strict racial segregation.

Sometimes a regressive movement forms directly in response to a protest movement. This type of regressive movement is called a countermovement. A current example is the anti–gay rights movement, which opposes legislation banning discrimination based on sexual orientation and efforts to legalize same-sex marriage. In the 1990s, this movement succeeded in passing a ballot initiative overturning such antidiscrimination laws in Colorado, though the measure was later ruled unconstitutional by the courts. It also blocked a 1992 proposal to end the ban on homosexuals in the military, supported a federal law that allows states to refuse to recognize same-sex marriages performed in other states, and used referenda to reverse laws permitting same-sex marriage in California and Maine.

Almost any protest movement that becomes large and influential can generate a countermovement (McAdam, McCarthy, and Zald, 1988, pp. 721–22). Countermovements develop among groups whose interests, values, or ways of life are challenged by the original protest movements. Once they have emerged, protest movements and their countermovements often engage in efforts to capture the support of public opinion (McAdam, 1983). Such interaction between opposing movements can become a long-term, sustained process, in which each movement reacts and responds to the actions of the opposing movement (Meyer and Staggenborg, 1996). An example of this can be seen in the efforts of opposing sides in the abortion debate to label themselves "pro-choice" and "pro-life" and to label their opponents as oppressors of women or killers of babies.

Religious Movements

Religious movements can be defined as social movements relating to spiritual or supernatural issues, which oppose or propose alternatives to some aspect of the dominant religious or cultural order (see Lofland, 1985, p. 180; Zald and Ash, 1966; Zald and McCarthy, 1979). This broad category includes many sects, and even some relatively institutionalized churches, that nonetheless oppose some element of the dominant religion or culture. Examples are the Jehovah's Witnesses, Christian Scientists, and Mormons. This category includes movements that combine a religious message with political protest, such as the Nation of Islam (once popularly called the "Black Muslims") in the United States and "liberation theology" among Latin American Catholics. Also included in the category of religious movements are cults, such as the Unification Church (the Moonies), the Hare Krishnas, and the Scientologists, as well as movements within major religious organizations, such as the Pentecostal movement within several Protestant denominations and the Catholic Church. Because these types of movement are discussed in Web-Based Chapter B they will not be further explored here

Communal Movements

Communal movements attempt to bring about change through example by building a model society among a small group. They seek not to challenge conventional society directly, but rather to build alternatives to it. This is done in various ways. Some seek to create household collectives, popularly known as communes, in which people live together, share resources and work equally, and base their lives on principles of equality (Kanter, 1972, 1979). Others develop work collectives, in which people often live separately but jointly own, govern, and operate an organization that produces and sells some product (Rothschild-Whitt, 1979). They prefer this approach to the hierarchy and inequality that characterize more typical work organizations.

Personal Cults

A final type of movement, which usually occurs in combination with one of the others, is the personal cult. This kind of social movement centers around a person as much as around an idea, and that charismatic individual is revered by the people in the movement and elevated to a godlike status. Personal cults seem particularly common among religious and revolutionary political movements. Examples of religious personal cults can be seen in Jim Jones and his People's Temple, and in David Koresh and the Branch Davidians—both instances that led to mass suicide. In many ways the Heaven's Gate group was also a personal cult, with its members following the directives of its leader "Do" to the point of castration and, ultimately, death. An example of a personal cult in a political movement is the cult centered around Chinese Communist leader Mao Zedong in the 1960s.

The Causes of Social Movements

It was once thought that social movements were largely the outgrowth of the personality characteristics of their participants, or of their psychological response to social conditions. For example, it was believed that people participate in movements to satisfy a personality need rather than to address a real grievance (Adorno et al., 1950; Carden, 1978; Feuer, 1969), or that they join social movements because they feel isolated and alienated in today's large-scale and often impersonal society. The problem with both theories, however, is that, according to most studies, movement participants are not very different from the rest of the population in terms of personality or psychological makeup. They are no more "alienated" than other people; rather, they are often drawn into these movements by their friends and family (McAdam, 1986; McAdam, McCarthy, and Zald, 1988; Snow, Zurcher, and Ekland-Olson, 1980; Hedstrom, 1994; McAdam and Paulsen, 1994; Opp and Gern, 1993). Today, sociologists look at movement participation in the context of the larger social environment, and are more likely to view collective action as a rational response to the constraints, restrictions, and opportunities of that environment.

Smelser (1963), for example, emphasizes the notion of structural strain: conflicts or inequalities in society that are the source of feelings of dissatisfaction, such things as gaps between what leaders preach and what they do. A prime example can be seen in the behavior of former Soviet Communist Party officials, who talked about a government of workers but enjoyed luxuries no Soviet worker could get. In addition, social conditions must be conducive to the formation of a social movement. People seeking to organize movements must have resources available with which to organize, and people must see some usefulness in forming a social movement. Relative deprivation theory, resource-mobilization theory, and political-process theory are among the theories sociologists use to understand how and when social movements arise.

Relative-Deprivation Theory

Relative-deprivation theory holds that social movements emerge when people feel deprived or mistreated *relative to* either (1) how others are treated or (2) how people feel they *should be* treated (Geschwender, 1964; Gurney and Tierney, 1982). Although this theory also refers to a psychological state or feeling, that state is clearly the product of certain kinds of social conditions. The important point here is that *absolute* deprivation does *not* cause social movements. In a country where everyone is poor, there is great absolute deprivation, but no relative deprivation. Nobody knows anything but poverty, so nobody feels unfairly treated (de Tocqueville, 1955 [orig. 1856]).

In a society where wealth and poverty exist side by side, however, the poor are very conscious of their different situation and may well come to feel deprived. Similarly, when people are led to believe that their lot is going to improve and it does not, they are more likely to feel deprived. This is sometimes called the revolution of rising expectations (Davies, 1962). Social movements and revolutions often occur when conditions have improved but then either stop improving or don't improve as fast as people expect. This fact, along with the fact that more affluent societies have more social movements (McAdam, McCarthy, and Zald, 1988), provides some evidence in support of the relative-deprivation theory. It is hard to measure precisely how people feel, however, and studies that have correlated feelings of deprivation with participation in social movements have not generally revealed strong relationships (Mueller, 1980; Wilson and Orum, 1976). People who participate in movements often feel quite discontented with the status quo (Opp and Gern, 1993), but many of those who do not participate also feel considerable discontent. These individuals don't become involved because they face barriers to taking action, or because they do not get support from others around them (Oegema and Klandermans, 1994). Among those who do become involved, development of a collective identity is a crucial step, so that they not only share a sense of dissatisfaction, but identify as individuals with the movement's viewpoint (Gamson, 1990, 1991).

Resource-Mobilization Theory

Resource-mobilization theory argues that social movements emerge when people have access to resources that enable them to organize a movement. This theory assumes that some discontent is always present in a society, but that the resources necessary to form social movements are not always available (McCarthy and Zald, 1973, 1977). Money, communication **technology**, and intellectual elites (from which leaders emerge) are all resources that can be used to organize a social movement (Zald and McCarthy, 1975). Because these resources are more available in a prosperous economy, growing prosperity is often associated with growing protest. How well a movement taps these resources also influences its chances of success (Morris, 1993; Ganz, 2000). The black Civil Rights movement of the 1960s was able to gain strength, for example, by tapping significant resources offered by sympathetic whites, including money, legal representation, and direct participation. The mobilization of these resources did not generate the Civil Rights movement, but it did help to sustain and strengthen the movement once it had become large and influential (Jenkins and Eckert, 1986; McAdam, 1982; Morris, 1984). One of the most important resources any movement can mobilize is interpersonal contacts (Macy, 1991; Opp and Gern, 1993; Hedstrom, 1994). These contacts are the major source of new recruits, as well as of money and other kinds of assistance (Bolton, 1972; Snow et al., 1986; Gerhards and Rucht, 1992). Clearly, such activities as recruitment and fundraising are also facilitated by modern communication technology (McAdam, McCarthy, and Zald, 1988, pp. 722–23). They are also helped by a concentration of like-minded people in the same place and by other situations, such as networks from organizations or past movements, that bring like-minded people into contact with one another (Freeman, 1973, 1979; D'Emillio, 1983; Lofland, 1985, Chapter 3; Morris, 1984, pp. 4–12; Wilson, 1973, pp. 140–51; McAdam and Paulsen, 1994). Finally, characteristics of the organization itself influence its ability to successfully mobilize resources. As shown by the experience of two farm worker movements—one successful, one not—organizations with diverse leadership teams including "insiders" and "outsiders" are more likely to succeed than ones with more homogeneous leadership teams (Ganz, 2000).

Political-Process Theory

Closely related to resource-mobilization theory is **political-process theory.** This approach stresses opportunities for movements that are created by larger social and political processes (Tilly, 1978). The absence of repression that is associated with democratic societies, industrialization, and urbanization, for example, makes it easier for social movements to emerge. When people realize that the system is vulnerable to protest, movements are much more likely to develop (Jenkins and Perrow, 1977). People often make cost-benefit assessments of their potential participation in a social movement: Will the movement, or their participation in it, make any difference? One comparative study demonstrates how social movements are more likely to develop in the proper political environment (Nelkin and Pollak, 1981). It compared the development of the antinuclear power movement in Germany and France. The movement started similarly in both countries, but it grew and prospered in Germany, while it atrophied in France. The reason: The German governmental review procedures provided opportunities for intervention by those opposed to nuclear power plants; the French procedures did not. In at least one case, the mere perception that the system was vulnerable to change led to a successful social movement even when the reality may have been otherwise. A recent study of the 1979 Iranian revolution by Kurzman (1996) shows that a key factor in the revolution was that people believed the monarchy was weak and vulnerable—even though by objective measures it was not. Because they acted on their beliefs, they created a powerful social movement that unexpectedly (to nearly everyone except the people in the movement itself) succeeded in toppling the monarchy.

Political processes, including interactions between the state and the movement participants, can also influence what courses the movement takes and what symbols it uses. The student movement in China in 1989 illustrates this. On the one hand, China's earlier Maoist government, which based its legitimacy on ideology, had been replaced with a government in which its effectiveness and performance had become a more important basis of legitimacy. This enhanced the likelihood that corruption in the government, which was common, would lead to protests like the student movement. But at the same time, the government still had something close to a monopoly on political organizations—there was no opposition party. Hence, protestors had to worry about the ease with which the government could repress them. It responded to this by using more traditional arguments and symbols than past Chinese student movements, in order to make the movement seem less threatening and harder to repress (Zhao, 2000). In the end, of course, it was repressed anyway, with the death of hundreds of protestors in Tiananmen Square.

Necessary Conditions for Social Movements

Taken together, these theories identify a number of important social conditions that must be present in order for a social movement to emerge. First, as pointed out by the relative-deprivation and structural-strain approaches, people must be dissatisfied. Second, as the resource-mobilization approach emphasizes, people who are dissatisfied must be able to communicate with one another. Third, as the political-process model suggests, the movement must be able to survive any attempts at repression, and it must be seen by potential participants as having a reasonable chance for success. This condition is a product both of its actual chances and of people's sense of their ability to make a difference. Finally, the movement must have adequate resources, including leadership, money, and supporters, to grow and develop. Any one of these by itself is not sufficient to generate a social movement, but when all of them occur together, the likelihood of a movement is greatly increased.

Movement Life Course: Civil Rights, Environmental, and Women's Movement as Case Studies

Thus far, we have focused largely on social conditions that lead to the emergence of social movements. This is only the first in a series of stages that movements pass through over time (Blumer, 1969b, 1974; Tilly, 1978; Zald and Ash, 1966). Social movements also go through a phase of organization, followed by bureaucratization or institutionalization. Finally, many movements sooner or later reach a period of decline. To illustrate this process, we shall use the Civil Rights movement as a main case study and follow it up with two shorter case studies of the environmental and women's movements.

Emergence

Movements emerge when conditions are structurally conducive, as outlined above. An important part of movement emergence is having leaders who recognize that conditions are favorable for a movement and who can successfully tap into people's dissatisfaction and desire to do something about the situation.

The origins of the Civil Rights movement illustrate this. By the 1950s, urbanization had heightened blacks' sense of relative deprivation, as had the experience of many African American soldiers who had fought for their country in World War II, only to return to a society that did not regard them as full citizens. The concentration of African Americans in urban ghettos facilitated communication and organization. A key event in the emergence of the Civil Rights movement occurred in 1955 in racially segregated Montgomery, Alabama, when a black woman named Rosa Parks refused to give up her bus seat to a white person. Though this act has commonly been portrayed as spontaneous, Parks had carefully thought out her plans and discussed them with church and civil rights leaders. Through Montgomery's black churches, a massive citywide bus boycott was organized to desegregate the buses; in a short time, thousands of supporters were mobilized. The boycott helped bring about a legal ruling forcing the bus system to desegregate. It also projected its leader, Dr. Martin Luther King, Jr., to national prominence, and it marked the beginning of the protest phase of the Civil Rights movement.

Organization

During the organizational phase, the emphasis is on mobilizing people, recruiting new participants, and attracting media attention. At this stage, events such as protest marches, picket lines, petition campaigns, boycotts, and efforts to pass legislation are common. Frequently, there are attempts to build coalitions with other groups with related or similar goals. Building a viable organization is crucial at this stage. A large-scale social movement requires both national and local organization (McAdam, McCarthy, and Zald, 1988). The local organization in Montgomery was provided through a citywide boycott masterminded by black religious leaders under Dr. King's leadership. At the national level, the Southern Christian Leadership Conference (SCLC) emerged, also under Dr. King's leadership, to coordinate activities in various locales.

In the organizational stage, movement leaders must adapt their goals, tactics, and public stances to the changing strategies of their opponents (Zald and Useem, 1987; Steinberg, 1999). When television images of police turning fire hoses on small children shocked the nation, civil rights activists were able to mobilize new support among Americans who had been angered by what they saw. When Dr. King was jailed, he used the resultant media attention as an opportunity to present his message to a wider audience.

In the organizational stage of social movements, there can be a great deal of interaction of this type between social movements and the media. The movement and the media each influence one another when this occurs. How favorably movements are portrayed by the media depends in part on the organization of the movement, its division of labor, and its ability to focus on one key issue (Gamson and Wolfsfeld, 1993). In turn, the degree to which the media emphasizes visual material and entertainment value influences the movement's use of dramatic tactics and confrontation.

As movements grow, new organizations using new tactics often appear. The Student Nonviolent Coordinating Committee (SNCC), for example, emerged using the effective new tactic of sit-ins at segregated lunch counters. In addition, organizations sometimes used multiple tactics, a strategy that appears to have contributed to the success of the Civil Rights movement (Morris, 1993). As diverse organizations evolved with different mixes of strategies and tactics, many of them cooperated in various ways, yet competed for supporters' acceptance. A high point of the organizational phase came in 1963, when 250,000 people marched on Washington and were inspired by Dr. King's famous "I Have a Dream" speech. (For more on the emergence and organization phases of the Civil Rights movement, see Morris, 1984; Jenkins and Eckert, 1986; Killian, 1984; McAdam, 1982; Geschwender, 1964; Orum, 1972.)

Institutionalization

When a social movement has reached the stage of bureaucratization or institutionalization, it has begun to cross the boundary from something "out of the ordinary" to an accepted part of the political, religious, or cultural patterns of society. Offices and bureaucratic structures are created to complete the tasks of the movement, and if the movement's goals are widely accepted in a society, the movement becomes an ordinary part of the society's social structure. By 1964, the influence of the Civil Rights movement had become sufficient to lead to the passage of major civil rights laws. The most important of these were the Civil Rights Act of 1964, the Voting Rights Act of 1965, and the Fair Housing Act of 1968. These laws, along with a series of Supreme Court rulings, effectively forbade virtually all forms of formal and deliberate racial discrimination and segregation. The courts and civil rights commissions took responsibility for enforcement, and a number of former civil rights leaders such as Andrew Young were elected or appointed to public office. The SCLC, NAACP, and other civil rights organizations became an accepted part of the political landscape, coming to be viewed more as political lobbies than as protest organizations.

These changes did not come easily. Before this stage could be reached, fierce opposition had to be overcome. A number of civil rights workers were killed, and on two occasions reluctant presidents sent federal troops to southern states to enforce the law in the face of local defiance. President Eisenhower sent troops to Little Rock, Arkansas, when Governor Orval Faubus used the state's national guard to block integration of the city's high school. President Kennedy did the same in Mississippi after rioters attacked federal marshals sent to desegregate the University of Mississippi when Governor Ross Barnett refused to do so. Two people had been killed by the mob before the troops arrived. One hundred sixty of the marshals were injured, twenty-eight by gunfire.

A risk for every movement is that once the movement reaches the institutionalization stage, it will become a part of the social structure that it originally opposed and take on some of the characteristics of this structure. In fact, it is a common tactic of institutions challenged by social movements to offer leaders of the movements positions within the institution they are challenging. In so doing, they give protest leaders "a stake in the system" and often succeed in getting them to moderate their criticisms. This process is called *co-optation*. For example, many corporations and governments have hired civil rights activists as community relations or human relations specialists, including in some cases people who had been among their critics.

Decline

Eventually, a movement may decline. This may happen for a number of reasons: the loss of a charismatic leader, loss of support, or perhaps because the movement achieved its goals and did not succeed in developing new ones. Research by Frey, Deitz, and Kalof (1992) suggests that social movements more frequently fail because of factionalism than for any other reason. Although decline is listed last, it may occur at any point in the development of a social movement. Unless it is later reversed, it usually signals the end of a social movement. In a fair number of cases, however, the decline is eventually reversed, as social conditions become conducive to a new round of movement activity.

In the 1970s, civil rights activity temporarily declined, probably for two main reasons. First, the assassination of Martin Luther King, Jr. in 1968 created the type of confusion and power vacuum that often follows the loss of a charismatic leader. Second, the movement had succeeded in removing the visible villains of segregation laws and police attacks on nonviolent demonstrators. At that point, the villain was an abstract set of processes, not well understood and not even recognized by most whites (Kluegel and Smith, 1982, 1986; Schuman, 1975), that continued to keep blacks disproportionately poor and unemployed. From a recruitment standpoint, blacks saw less point in getting involved, because their previous successes had made so little difference in their everyday lives.

By the mid-1980s, however, the Civil Rights movement enjoyed a resurgence of support, which has since continued. This resurgence was galvanized by the presidential candidacies in 1984 and 1988 of the Reverend Jesse Jackson; by racist attacks, such as a 1987 Ku Klux Klan attack on civil rights marchers in Forsythe County, Georgia; and by growing resentment of the policies of the Ronald Reagan and George H. W. Bush administrations, which opposed affirmative action and gave urban problems a low priority. Thousands came out to vote for Jackson and other black candidates; 20,000 Americans from nearly every state marched on Forsythe County just a week after the Klan incident; and by 1992, a movement at the University of North Carolina demanding a black cultural center drew the biggest protest crowds since the Vietnam War. The latter incident also marked another notable pattern: a resurgence of college student activism in the early 1990s. And, of course, African Americans and younger voters turned out in massive numbers to support the candidacy of Barack Obama in 2008, both at the polls and in the form of a large grass-roots organization of volunteers.

The Environmental Movement

Emergence. Water is not supposed to burn. Let alone an entire river. But that is precisely what happened to one river in Ohio, the Cuyahoga, in 1969. The burning river seemed to be the symbol of a social movement whose time had come. Dykstra (2008) gives a compelling account of the movement's major events. It had all started with a book. *Silent Spring,* written by scientist Rachel Carson in 1962, had started a revolution in how people thought about industrialization, chemicals, and possibly even progress itself (Sale, 1993:4). Her book was primarily an attack on the chemical pesticide DDT and its wide-ranging and devastating impact on a multitude of bird species (it would take ten years, but eventually the pesticide was banned). Just as Carson had hoped, the book sparked fears and concerns that went beyond the immediate topics under study in its pages. Soon a whole host of environmental topics began to pierce the nation's consciousness. In an era defined by social protest, the movement for the environment found voice against the smog of America's cities and factories after eighty people perished in heavy air pollution in New York City on Thanksgiving day in 1966; three years later, a massive oil spill along the Santa Barbara coast created more outrage.

Organization. The more one looked for problems, the easier they became to find. When compared with both the women's movement and the civil rights movement, the speed at which the environmental movement progressed is breathtaking. By April 1970, the movement had won Earth Day as a kind of American holiday, complete with parades and student activities at the nation's schools. From 1969 to 1971, a spate of new organizations supporting the movement (Friends of the Earth in 1969, Natural Resources Defense Council in 1970, Greenpeace in 1971) and books expounding its virtues burst on the scene (Dykstra, 2008). As awareness grew, some decided to "return to nature." This coincided with a general malaise on the part of many for modern society. The Vietnam War, racial injustice, and other modern ailments helped to create the modern counterculture that rebelled at "the establishment."

Institutionalization. Political pressure was building all across society, culminating in President Nixon's embrace of the environment as an issue. The Nixon administration created the Environmental Protection Agency and signed into law the Endangered Species Act, the Clean Air Act, and the Clean Water Act. Following these initial successes, the movement slowed down. Many social movements end up being institutionalized at some point in their history. If they institutionalize too fast, they fail to achieve all they can. If they institutionalize too late, or fail to institutionalize, they risk being seen as too out of the mainstream of society to enable lasting political reform.

Decline. Then the movement stalled. It is hard to say exactly why; possibly because of the movement's success fears about the environment abated. This was quickly followed the by the election of Ronald Reagan and the turn to the right in American politics. Environmental issues took a distinct back seat in this atmosphere and several regulations were rolled back through selective nonenforcement. But, starting in the mid-1980s, three disastrous incidents served to move environmental concerns back into the public eye. The first was a horrific explosion at a Union Carbide chemical plant in Bhopal, India in 1984 that resulted in the deaths of thousands of people and the release of tons of toxic chemicals into the atmosphere. The second incident was the nuclear meltdown and explosion at the Chernobyl plant in the Soviet Union. Some fifty deaths resulted from the explosion and an indeterminable number of victims from radiation exposure have or will die from the incident. Finally, the discovery of the hole in the ozone layer over Antarctica became widespread public knowledge in the late 1980s, adding to further concerns.

In 1988, Reagan's vice president, George H. W. Bush, ran on the platform of environmental support as part of his being a kinder, gentler Republican. This included being the "environmental president" (along with the "education president"—two important Democratic issues he hoped to co-opt). Within just a few years the environment was once again trendy. Membership in environmental groups began to grow steadily in the early 1990s. In 1992, the United Nations held the Earth Summit, which garnered a great deal of attention and featured U.S. vice president Al Gore as a key speaker. Gore's book *Earth in the Balance* was being celebrated at the time as an important environmental statement. Yet, the high expectations associated with the Clinton administration were soon dashed, as the administration was slow to address the movement's concerns, and then in 1994, congress was taken over by the GOP with a platform of reducing regulations, including environmental regulations that they viewed as alarmist at best and simply liberal power-brokering at worst. Some argued that liberals were simply creating a growth field for themselves and that the solution to environmental problems lies in markets. If consumers thought the environment was threatened, they would stop purchasing environmentally damaging products, and businesses would be forced to change. Others argued that the private ownership of all natural resources was the way to "marketize" the interest in the environment. As property, people would care for the Earth, just like they cared for their other investments. Though these Republicans would lose their influence over the course of the decade, the weakened and scandal-ridden Clinton administration would never make a serious return to the issue of the environment. But this did not mean that the most committed members of the movement stopped their work. In 1997, a twenty-three-year-old woman named Julia "Butterfly" Hill climbed a redwood tree to stop the Pacific Lumber Co. from clear cutting the redwood forest in the area. Hill spent just over two years living in the tree. In the end, the company agreed not to cut in the area.

In 2001, with the new administration of George W. Bush and the terrorist attacks of that same year, environmental concerns again faced a steep fall from priorities. The new Bush administration made no pretenses toward being friends of the environment. Instead, it put political pressure on EPA reports to water down evidence of global warming, cut the budget for enforcement of existing law, and relaxed actual enforcement and regulation. Bush also pushed for new drilling of oil in protected federal lands.

Resurgence. However, the scientific evidence for global warming began to break through, despite the official resistance. Scientific and photographic evidence of the melting of the ice caps and bizarre weather patterns put the issue front and center in the lives of many Americans. Florida suffered four major hurricanes in succession in 2004, and the devastation of Katrina in Louisiana and Mississippi in 2005 seemed to confirm for many that the environment was out of control. Al Gore's film *An Inconvenient Truth* won an Oscar and renewed respect for both himself and his favorite issue. Forty years after Earth Day began, it continued, but in a much more institutionalized form, with the sponsorship and participation of big corporations such as F.A.O. Schwartz Toys, Pepsico, and Gray Line Tours (Kaufman, 2010). With the collapse of the global financial system in 2008 and the election of Barack Obama, the new president has committed to tying economic recovery to environmental sustainability by creating new "green jobs," a longtime goal of the environmental movement. Time will tell if this effort proves to be successful, but what is clear is that any effort to reduce dependency on oil faces strong opposition, as illustrated by the inability of Congress to pass "cap and trade" legislation to limit use of the carbon fuels that contribute to global warming. And despite near-unanimous agreement among climate scientists about the presence of global warming and evidence that it is at least in part the product of human activities (Doran and Zimmerman, 2009), denial of global warming became a cottage industry in 2009 and 2010. President Obama pointed to the BP oil disaster in the Gulf of Mexico as another reason to move away from oil and toward development of renewable energy, but questions about the effectiveness of the federal response to the spill may limit public support for his position.

The Women's Movement

Emergence. It all started with a tea party. On July 13, 1848, Elizabeth Cady Stanton attended a party with four of her close friends. Stanton expressed her frustration with status of women in American society and her friends agreed. They realized that many women felt this way, but no one seemed to know what to do about it. Stanton had been active in the abolitionist movement to outlaw slavery and yet she had also seen how, even in a movement like the abolitionists' that was dedicated to human rights, women were accorded second-class status. She resolved to do something about it. With her friends, she helped to organize the Seneca Falls women's rights convention, which was held only a few days after the tea party. The convention, often referred to simply as Seneca Falls for the small upstate New York city it was held in, produced an iconic document of the movement: the Declaration of Sentiments, cowritten by Stanton herself. Stanton and her friend and fellow activist Lucretia Mott based their own declaration off of the Declaration of Independence. The message of the statement was clear: America, live up to your promise of equal rights for all by making women full citizens.

Organization. The passage of the Declaration at the convention had a wide-ranging impact. Newspapers across the country carried the full text of the document, and many named the names of signatories. Much of the press attacked both the ideas and the women involved and a minor moral panic broke out about the movement. Only a matter of days after the little tea party among friends, the entire nation was talking about women's rights. Although the initial tenor of the discussion was strident and, more often than not, ridiculed the movement, this national discussion had put the movement in the foreground of the national debate. From then on, women's conventions were held across the country right up until the dawn of the Civil War. The era of the Suffragettes was born.

Early on, a cadre of great leaders emerged, such as Susan B. Anthony, Lucy Stone, and the freed slave Sojourner Truth. Truth spoke with passion at an 1851 meeting, in what has come to be known as the "Ain't I a Woman" speech, about the need for the movement to embrace concerns beyond white middle-class women—a concern the modern feminist movement is still grappling with. Powerful leaders, thinkers, and orators such as Stanton, Anthony, and Truth gave great vitality to the movement and swelled its membership. Although originally one of the most controversial of platform planks from the 1848 Declaration, the movement settled on the right to vote as its main objective. All other goals could be possible if women could vote their interests at the polling booth. An interesting split took place during this historic struggle as Stanton, Anthony, and others diverged from their abolitionist allies during the debate over the Fourteenth and Fifteenth Amendments ensuring voting rights for freed male slaves after the war. Stanton and Anthony's faction opposed the amendments on the grounds that women should be included in them as well. Stanton and Anthony supported many racist and nativist politicians in hopes that they would support the suffrage cause, while Lucy Stone would lead a faction that would remain steadfast in its support of the abolitionists and later Reconstruction (MacLean, 2009, p. 4).

Institutionalization. The women's movement would remain split for twenty years over this issue. When the two factions came back together, Stanton was their chosen leader. Stanton, Anthony, Stone, and Truth would not see the victory they worked so hard for, but their efforts and those of millions of less-well-known women and men eventually paid off. In 1920, women won the right to vote as the First Wave of the women's movement came to an end.

Decline. A Second Wave started in the early 1960s. But that is not to say that nothing happened in the intervening forty years. First, the National American Woman Suffrage Association reconstituted itself into the League of Women Voters. Having won the vote, women now recognized that they needed to stay organized to fight for women's rights through the ballot box and by leveraging their new-found power. In this sense, the First Wave institutionalized the social movement into the fabric of the American system itself. In 1923, the Equal Rights Amendment (ERA) was drafted by Alice Paul; it would, among other things, ensure equal treatment of women in the workplace. Second, a nurse by the name of Margaret Sanger took up the cause of birth control for women, a cause that would boldly propose the notion that women were in control of their own bodies. Despite any religious or moral interests society might have in the decisions women choose to make about their bodies, women had the right, Sanger and her allies argued, to decide whether or not they wanted to become mothers, workers, housewives, or something else. Women should make those choices, not men on their behalf, not the church, not government. The fight was a difficult one. Until 1936, even discussing birth control issues in a public forum was considered criminal indecency, and Sanger and her supporters were arrested and jailed for such "offenses" more than once. It was an important expansion of the movement that continues to this day. We see the underlying contours of this debate still raging in issues like abortion.

Resurgence. The women's movement would not take up an oppositional, grassroots identity again until the 1960s. Inspired most prominently by a 1963 book called *The Feminine Mystique* written by Betty Freidan, the Second Wave of the movement was very different than the first. Feminists replaced the Suffragettes. The book challenged the role of the middle-class housewife as the ideal for women. Women's experiences in the civil rights and antiwar movements, not all of which were positive, also helped to motivate their resurgence as a movement (Freeman, 1973, 1979; Robnett, 2000). If the First Wave challenged the official inequality of women in American society, the Second Wave also took on the unofficial inequalities that take place in the homes, at the workplaces, or in the bedrooms of America (Schnittker, Freese, and Powell, 2003). In many ways, its goals were considerably more radical than those of the First Wave. Feminists argued that men enjoyed unearned privileges on the backs of the women in their lives. We can point to at least three main reasons for the rise of this Second Wave. First, the United States was undergoing an unprecedented postwar economic boom. This new wealth and prosperity made it easier for women to pursue endeavors outside of the home, yet considerable cultural pressure was being placed on women to stay in the home. This was a direct result of the events that occurred during the war when women and minorities were brought in to "man" the industrial factories while so many white men were drafted to become soldiers in the war effort. Women more than proved they were capable of doing these jobs (and for less money than the men had done them), but when the war ended, the work went back to the white male soldiers (Milkman, 1987). This experience during and after the war constitutes a second reason for the rise of the Second Wave. Third, the movement for civil rights for racial minorities (reviewed as a case study earlier in this chapter) inspired many other movements of the time to follow suit. In many ways, the struggle of African Americans and others can be credited with helping to change the landscape of America in ways that would be too numerous to effectively quantify. Additionally (and not unlike what happened in the earlier abolitionist movement), women in the civil rights and peace movements often encountered male dominance (for example; women were often expected to stuff envelopes and run off leaflets, while men gave speeches at rallies). Women increasingly came to see this as a violation of the very principles of the civil rights and peace movements, and thus the seeds of a new feminist movement were sown (Freeman, 1973, 1979).

Organization. A very concrete illustration of how the Civil Rights movement led to changes in gender roles came in 1964 when, in an attempt to scuttle the landmark Civil Rights Act of that year, language adding "sex" to the protected categories of race, religion, and national origin was inserted into the legislation by Southern legislators opposed to the Civil Rights Act, in hopes that legislators would vote against the law as a result of that addition. But the addition of sex as a protected category for civil rights did not kill the bill, and in the years to come, the Civil Rights Act of 1964 would become an important tool in the effort to achieve equal rights for women in American society.

Institutionalization. Discrimination claims could now be legally filed for a host of work-related abuses. However, early enforcement of the sex provision was thin at best. In response, a new organization was formed by Betty Freidan and other activists. The National Organization for Women (NOW) opened its doors in 1966. In 1972, another significant legal victory came with the inclusion of Title IX in the Education Codes. This law guaranteed equal access to higher education for women and has resulted over the years in an exploding number of women in professional occupations and sports.

Decline. Possibly the greatest defeat for the Second Wave, however, was the failure to ratify the ERA. Reintroduced after nearly five decades, the amendment started off as a phenomenal success. But as it inched closer to passage, the opponents of the ERA stepped up their campaigns against it. In the end, the amendment fell just three states short of passage. A Third Wave of the women's movement is often said to now be under way, emphasizing the diversity of women and a broad range of issues from the rights of women in less-developed countries to the challenge of feminists who openly embrace sex work and pornography.

Social Change

In the remainder of this chapter, we shall examine the major sources of social change and the processes by which social change takes place, and some key theoretical perspectives on social change and their relationship to the larger sociological perspectives. We shall also examine long-term social change and how it has occurred in different ways in industrialized Western societies.

What Is Social Change?

We define **social change** as any alteration of behavior patterns, social relationships, or social structure over time. As noted above, social change can occur *rapidly and unexpectedly* or it can occur *gradually,* often going unnoticed by most for quite some time. It can also be *planned,* as occurred in the 1970s when Canada decided as a nation to guarantee health care to all and established a national health insurance system and, in the present time, as the United States moves forward with implementation of health care reforms passed in 2010 and intended to move the United States toward universal health insurance coverage. More often, however, it is *unplanned,* as illustrated by recent dramatic increases in population in the Rocky Mountain states—currently the fastest-growing region of the United States. Unplanned change occurs because of basic social forces that shape people's lives. For example, one reason for the growth of the Rocky Mountain states is that technologies such as fax machines and the Internet have made where people live less important from an economic standpoint. If, for example, hand delivery were the main way to transfer information, the two authors of this book would need to live near each other and near the company that publishes our book. But in fact, neither is the case; today such things as faxes, the Internet, and overnight express mail have long since made that unnecessary. In such an environment, many people who have "always wanted to live in the mountains" can now do so, and still make a living. Hence, Utah, Wyoming, Colorado, Montana, and other Rocky Mountain states have experienced a population boom since the early 1990s.

Every case of social change is somewhat different, with distinct causes and consequences. Each case of social change also has consequences for other aspects of society. For example, higher education, the real estate market, and the workplace have all been affected by changes in the roles of men and women in the family. Such consequences make the study of social change both fascinating and difficult. Part of the task is to synthesize (see connections between) effects of changes in various aspects of society that have been analyzed (taken apart) separately in earlier chapters of this book.

Social change often has an unsettling effect. For example, ranching families in the Rocky Mountain region are finding their lives dramatically changed by the region's growth: Old ways of life are becoming virtually impossible to maintain as, for example, yesterday's ranch becomes today's sprawling suburb. Often, these unsettling effects lead to conflict. In many places in the Rocky Mountain states, for example, fierce battles have broken out between growth advocates and people who want to maintain a traditional or natural environment. Social movements have arisen among ranchers who want to preserve ranching against suburbanization, tourism, and environmental restoration efforts, such as the reintroduction of wolves. Similarly, environmental movements have sought to protect environmentally sensitive areas from logging, mining, and ranching. Thus, social change feeds social movements and conflicts, just as the reverse is true.

Theories of Social Change

Theories of social change may be compared along a couple dimensions. For one, social change can be examined through the functionalist or conflict perspectives. For another, various theories argue that social change may be either *evolutionary* or *cyclical*.

Equilibrium (Functionalist) Versus Conflict Theories of Social Change

When the functionalist perspective is applied to social change, equilibrium is usually a key concept. **Equilibrium** is a state of balance in society, in which the components of society—institutions, social classes, political parties, families—interact with one another in a way that helps the society to function effectively. Equilibrium theory holds that once these various components attain such a balance, the society maintains a stable state until something happens to upset that balance. What could upset the balance? Any change in the social or physical environment of the society could do so. Among the possibilities are external changes, such as shifts in the world price or supply of fuel; technological changes, such as the invention of the automobile, the television, or

Social change, in the form of urbanization and rapid population growth in the Rocky Mountain states, is transforming Utah ranch country into Salt Lake City suburbs. (Courtesy of John E. Farley)

the Internet; and demographic changes, such as a shift in immigration patterns or birth rates, leading to changes in a society's ethnic composition.

Any of these environmental changes could require a society to change, because the society needs to adapt to the new situation. However, because of the effective balance that was in place in society before the environmental change, the society will change *only* enough to adapt to its new environment. Any change beyond what is needed to adapt would alter the basically effective workings of the society, so the change that occurs is the minimum amount needed to adapt. For example, a sudden increase in world fuel prices might lead to reduced driving or more fuel-efficient cars in the United States. However, it would not likely lead to abandonment of the automobile as the main means of transport, because too much of the society is built around an automobile-based transportation system—over 90 percent of U.S. workers depend on the auto as their main means of transportation to work (U.S. Census Bureau, 2001a).

In contrast, conflict theories see social change coming not so much from the need to adapt to environmental changes as from basic conflicts that are rooted in the society. Karl Marx, the classic conflict theorist, saw conflicts of interest among different social classes as the main driving force of social change. Most conflict theories today use parts of Marx's ideas, but add other elements as well.

The basic idea of conflict theories of social change is that, over history, some groups have dominated other groups and by so doing have obtained more than their proportionate share of scarce resources. This brings about a fundamental conflict of interest between the dominant groups who hold the resources, and the exploited groups who are denied resources. When the groups in society act upon these conflicting interests, conflict and social change occur.

An example of this can be seen in race relations. Today, race relations are in some ways quite different from what they were in the past. Although racial discrimination still occurs frequently, it is today illegal and is frowned upon to the extent that those who discriminate usually will not admit to it. Those who are caught in acts of discrimination may face large fines and civil penalties. As noted in Chapter 14, a jury fined Nationwide Insurance Company $100 million after they were found to have violated fair-housing law (Squires, 1998). A half-century ago, in contrast, discrimination was so entrenched that schools, public transportation, theaters, and even ball fields were segregated by law in much of the country. Why did the pattern change? A major reason is that social conflict erupted in the 1950s and early 1960s. African Americans and their supporters engaged in mass civil disobedience, economic boycotts, numerous lawsuits, and massive national protests. White supporters of segregation responded with mob attacks by civilians, beatings by police, mass arrests of civil rights demonstrators, and violations of federal court orders by many Southern governors. But the outcome of this change is that racial discrimination was banned by law, and public opinion turned against deliberate racial discrimination and against open expression of prejudice. Hence, social change occurred because of conflicts that arose within society.

Evolutionary Versus Cyclical Changes

Some theories of social change hold that social change is evolutionary, while others hold that it is cyclical. Evolutionary change is unidirectional; in other words, social change proceeds in a predictable direction over time. Usually, this direction involves increased complexity or an improved quality of life; hence **modernization theory**, discussed later in this chapter, is an important example of an evolutionary theory. Karl Marx's theory of social change is also an evolutionary theory, because Marx predicted that societies proceed through a fixed set of stages, beginning with hunting and gathering societies and ending with what Marx called the "classless communist society." Yet another example of evolutionary theory is demographic transition theory, discussed in Web-Based Chapter C. This theory is evolutionary because it sees all societies over time as moving from high birth and death rates to low birth and death rates. In fact, it is closely related to modernization theory, because it sees the demographic transition as tied to industrialization and urbanization.

Other theories see social change as cyclical. They posit that, over time, societies shift back and forth between opposite patterns. Some time periods, for example, are characterized by innovation and challenges to established ways, while others emphasize a return to traditional values. One example of a cyclical theory can be seen in the work of Pitirim Sorokin (1941), who sees society as shifting between two major forms: ideational culture and sensate culture. Ideational culture emphasizes faith as the key to knowledge and values spirituality. Sensate culture sees empirical, scientific evidence as the path to knowledge and emphasizes a more hedonistic way of life. Sorokin argues that societies tend to shift back and forth over time between ideational and sensate cultures.

Evolutionary and cyclical forms of social change can be hard to sort out, because often both are occurring at the same time. This is illustrated in Figure 15.1. The figure shows a long-term, evolutionary trend upward in a particular social characteristic, but it also shows short-term, cyclical fluctuations. One of the challenges of studying social change is to be able to measure social variables regularly and repeatedly over time. With too short a time span or with unrepresentative points in time, a trend can be badly misread. For example, a sociologist could draw many wrong conclusions by taking measurements only at certain times: Points A and C suggest no change over time; points B and D suggest a rapid increase; points A, B, C, D, and E suggest a totally cyclic pattern.

Only by measuring points A, B, C, D, E, F, and G do we see the true pattern: a cyclic pattern embedded within a long-term increase.

Modernization: Escalating Social Change

As noted above, **modernization**—the transition from rural, traditional, agricultural societies to urban, industrial, rationalistic societies—has brought both a degree of social change and a rate of social change unprecedented in human history. For this reason, modernization has been a major topic of study among sociologists interested in social change. There is considerable controversy among these sociologists concerning the nature and social consequences of modernization. In fact, social scientists even disagree on what this process should be called.

But before exploring these controversies, let's summarize the changes that have occurred in the last 200 to 300 years. According to economic historian Phyllis Deane (1969), the Industrial Revolution included:

- the widespread application of modern science to the processes of production for the market (that is, technology);
- the specialization of the economic activity that is directed toward production for the market;
- the movement of population from rural to urban communities;
- the shift in production toward corporate or public enterprise and away from the family;

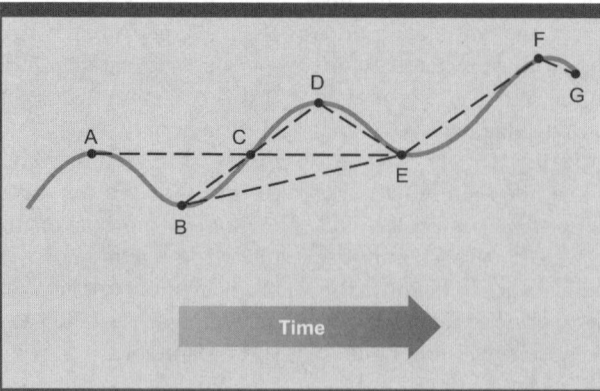

Figure 15.1 A Trend with Embedded Cycles

This stylized diagram shows how the choice of points for comparison could lead to different estimations of the average change over a long period.

- the movement of labor from production of raw materials (primary production) to manufacturing (secondary) and eventually to services (tertiary);
- the use of capital resources as a substitute for human labor; and
- the emergence of new classes determined by ownership of, or relationship to, the means of production, especially capital as opposed to land.

Other changes discussed in earlier chapters of this book include:

- a 600 percent increase in global population, with a decline in birth rates and an even faster decline in death rates;
- major increases in literacy rates and in per capita production and consumption of goods;
- changes in the economic and social roles of women, children, and the family;
- the appearance of new economic and political ideologies, including capitalism, socialism, and representative democracy;
- the emergence of sociology and other social sciences as ways of understanding these changes, and as major disciplines in colleges and universities.

While the above changes have occurred over the past 200 to 300 years, the pace of change quickened considerably in the last half of the twentieth century. Among the changes in that short time period were the following:

- the widespread adoption of televisions, computers, and VCRs, and the use of cable, wireless, and Internet communications;
- the movement toward *globalization*—a transition from local or national to worldwide economic exchange and competition;
- a bigger increase in world population (3.5 billion more people in fifty years) than had occurred in all previous history;
- a shift, in industrialized countries, from an economy based on manufacturing to one based on information and services;
- a renewed skepticism about worldviews based on science and rationalism and the emergence of a viewpoint sometimes called *postmodernism* (discussed in Chapter 11).

Because of the accelerating pace of social change, the study of social change represents both a huge challenge and a major growth area for sociology. While there is much that we do not yet understand about the changes occurring today, there are some general principles about the consequences of rapid social change that we do understand.

Consequences of Rapid Social Change

Rapid social change gives a distinct advantage to young people over older people. In an era of rapid change, older people must constantly learn new things and "unlearn" old ones. This is one reason for the decreasing respect for the elderly. Living a long time no longer means you are especially capable, and experience is not all that valuable when it occurred in a different setting. Young people, moreover, are primarily interested in learning current information that can be used in present-day situations. Of course, what they learn as current soon becomes obsolete. This is especially true in technical areas, such as in computer technology and engineering, where change is especially fast. For these reasons, many people now long for older, simpler times. Of course, the "good old days" were not typically all that good. People lived shorter lives and were sicker; there was often great discrimination against women, ethnic minorities, and religious dissenters; and child labor and the physical and emotional abuse of children were rampant. Because the "good old days" were familiar, however, people tend to look back upon them in a selective way, remembering the positive and forgetting the negative.

The longing for simpler times is one source of religious fundamentalism in both Iran and the United States. In Iran, the Shah's program of rapid modernization disturbed old patterns and produced a high level of anomie. In the United States, the many changes that occurred during the 1960s also disturbed many people's sense of security by undermining prevailing norms. In both places, people sought security and reduction of anomie by returning to rules of behavior with which they were more familiar. In Web-Based Chapter B, we examined in greater detail some of the ways in which the forces of modernization feed the tendency toward fundamentalism, noting a complex relationship between the forces of modernization and secularization on the one hand and fundamentalism on the other. In the new century, this clash remains a key social force affecting events in both the United States and Iran, as well as in many other societies.

Rapid social change also increases the general level of anomie in society. Things are changing so fast that people do not know what to do or how to behave. They literally do not know what the norms are. For example, rapid changes in the roles of men and women, discussed in Chapters 8 and 13, have led to a certain amount of anomie, which in turn has contributed to increased divorce rates. As more women work outside the home the household division of labor is changing. For many young couples this is a major source of stress. We learn how to behave as marriage partners largely by observing our own parents, but for many of us our parents had a different type of marriage than we will or do have. Consequently, we have not learned how to be marriage partners in a dual-career marriage. Contrary to the arguments of those who long for a simpler past, it is not that the new system is "bad," but that we do not understand it (yet) and have not yet developed a workable set of norms to guide our behavior (see, for example, Hochschild, 1989). It is in this sense that the speed of change is a source of social problems and further change. It is important to understand, though, that anomie as a result of social change is not a permanent condition; new norms will sooner or later be developed to address the new social situation. This often occurs through processes of conflict and negotiation among different interest groups and between those tied to older and newer ways of doing things.

New Directions in the Study of Social Change

There are many new directions in the study of social change. As you read about these topics, think about how new knowledge in these areas would affect your view of social change and the world.

The causes of modernization and development remain an important research topic. Some researchers are tracing the origins of the Industrial Revolution further back in history (Chase-Dunn, 1989; Abu-Lughod, 1989). Others are looking at the role of technology, education, and population (Meyer and Hannan, 1979; Chirot, 1986). Studies of the micro and macro processes of social change converge in the analysis of the revolutions and social movements, as depicted in Charles Tilly's personal journey box in this chapter. An important theme of Tilly's work on social change was that, no matter how rapid social change may be occurring, it is necessary, in order to understand social relations in any time period, to understand the social history that brought society to that point. A fascinating related area of research is the study of various long cycles of change (Bergesen, 1983; Boswell, 1989; Goldstein, 1988).

How can we use the sociological imagination in the study of social change? First, we can note that the effect of individual activities on long-term social change is usually very limited: They may be able to alter such trends, but they cannot create or reverse them. An insightful leader like Mikhail Gorbachev can take steps to institute democracy in the Soviet Union but democracy cannot take hold unless conditions favorable to it exist: industrialization and modern communications technology, for example. Nonetheless, deep ethnic and nationality conflicts could yet torpedo the move toward democracy in parts of the former Soviet Union. Russia in 2011, under the leadership of President Dmitry Medvedev and Prime Minister Vladimir Putin, is less democratic than it was under Yeltsin, with considerable restrictions placed on independent media and opposition political parties. Both in Russia and elsewhere in the former communist world, long-standing ethnic conflicts are one factor that may limit movement toward democracy. The growth of democracy in former Yugoslavia was impeded by bloody ethnic conflicts in the 1990s, and similar conflicts continue today in parts of the former Soviet Union, leading to sometimes-brutal efforts to control them and the terrorism they sometimes bring. Hence, individuals like Gorbachev and Yeltsin could take actions that made democracy more possible, but the long-term outcome is likely subject to larger social forces. While the influence of individuals is limited, collective action on the part of large groups of people, for example, ethnic groups or public elements longing for democracy or for a higher standard of living, often does serve as an important engine of social change.

The long-term ability of powerful individuals to block a trend toward democracy is just as uncertain as their ability to bring it about. China's Deng Xiaoping could temporarily stop democracy through the bloody crackdown in Tiananmen Square—but over the long run, the possibility remains that democracy will eventually prevail. Thus far, the Chinese people have seemingly accepted political restrictions in exchange for a rapid improvement in their standard of living, particularly in the cities. However, such practices as restriction of access to certain Web sites are controversial, even in China, and any interruption in the trend toward a higher standard of living could rapidly destabilize society. For example, in 2010, as hundreds of thousands of young workers who had moved from rural areas to cities in hope of a better life encountered the reality of low wages and hard working conditions in factories, a wave of strikes spread across China (BBC, 2010). Hence, the future course of social change remains uncertain, despite the sometimes-dramatic actions taken by individual leaders to either promote or impede democracy. A key issue in the sociological study of social change is to figure out what can be affected by individual efforts and /or by collective action, and what is determined by larger societal processes.

Of course, we must remember, as Charles Tilly's box shows us, every one of us plays a part in these larger societal changes, both contributing to and being affected by them. Today, for example, you and I typically make quite different decisions regarding family relations and structures, relations between men and women, racial and ethnic relations, and sexual behavior than were made two, three, or four generations ago in our own society. In so doing, we are heavily influenced by the rapid social change that has taken place in our society in the recent past. At the same time, we are in a small way contributing to the social change of today and tomorrow. The value of sociology is to help us understand how and why these things are happening, and, hopefully, to give us insights that will help us to promote useful and desirable forms of social change.

Summary

Social change and social movements are closely related. Social change often is the result of social

A modern car ferry loads within sight of a totem pole near Vancouver, B.C. In the past few hundred years, there has been greater change than in all of preceding human history. This makes the study of social change one of the most central issues in sociology. (Courtesy of John E. Farley)

movements, and social change can also cause social movements. Although social movements often lead to situations of collective behavior like those discussed in Chapter 14 (protest marches, for example), social movements differ from collective behavior in important ways. In particular, social movements are more planned and goal-oriented than collective behavior. In addition, they require sustained and often complex organization. Collective behavior does not; in fact, it is typically characterized by a lack of such organization. The main kinds of social movements are protest movements (which may seek either reform or revolutionary change), regressive movements (including countermovements), religious movements, communal movements, and personal cults. Movements tend to develop when people experience relative deprivation, when they have the necessary resources to organize themselves, and when the situation creates opportunities to alter the conditions that led to dissatisfaction. Dissatisfaction, the ability of

PERSONAL JOURNEYS INTO SOCIOLOGY
On the Way to Revolution

Charles Tilly

At Harvard in the 1940s and 1950s, four remarkable teachers guided me to historical studies of conflict, collective action, state formation, and revolution. Pitirim Sorokin, veteran and victim of the Russian Revolution, was a hard taskmaster, but he showed his students the value of confronting large theories of social change with systematic evidence. Samuel Beer, a specialist in British politics, taught generations of undergraduates (not to mention the graduate assistants, myself among them, who worked in his famous lecture course on "Western Thought and Institutions") how and why to confront political thought, social-scientific analysis, and major historical crises such as the English Revolution. George Homans combined sociology, history, and poetry in his own work, and he demonstrated the possibility of addressing pressing problems of sociological theory by means of analyses that would stand up to the scrutiny of professional historians. Barrington Moore, Jr., exemplified the restless, committed, independent scholar who undertakes large comparisons in order to seek answers to urgent contemporary questions such as the social foundations of tyranny. All four of them did me the enormous favor of letting me make my own mistakes and stumble toward my own definitions of the problems worth pursuing.

Over many years, those problems came to be these: How and why do large processes of structural change such as urbanization, industrialization, and the formation of national states occur, and what impact do they have on the lives of ordinary people? Under what conditions, and with what outcomes, do ordinary people act together on behalf of common interests? How do large structural changes alter the conditions for collective action? As a result of my own experiences and the influence of my teachers, I was skeptical from the beginning about prevailing functionalist theories, in which social order was normal, deviations from social order the result of system breakdowns and excessively rapid social change, and intense collective action a symptom of system overload. Much of my work has combated those theories and attempted to develop valid alternatives.

Early in my career, I approached these problems in two different ways: through studies of migration and population change in contemporary American cities such as Wilmington, Delaware, and through an examination of rural conflicts during the French Revolution. The two studies converged in a series of empirically based attacks on the common notion that rapid social change disorganizes people and therefore produces both individual disorders and collective protests. It took me a long time to work out positive alternatives to these negative ideas. Eventually, I constructed a series of models of class formation, state formation, collective action, and relative social processes. In attempting to test these models and make them empirically workable, my collaborators (mostly advanced graduate students at the University of Toronto, the University of Michigan, and the New School for Social Research) and I developed methods for standardizing tangled historical evidence into comparable events, especially strikes, violent conflicts, and "contentious gatherings": occasions on which a number of people gathered publicly and made claims bearing on someone else's interests.

dissatisfied people to communicate, and a belief that "something can be done" are all critical to the emergence of a social movement. In order to grow, a movement must avoid or survive attempts at repression. Often, unsuccessful attempts at repression become an important organizing tool, as was the case with the African American Civil Rights movement.

Social change can be defined as any alteration of behavior patterns, social relationships, or social structure over time. Certain cultural patterns, like fads and fashions, change very quickly; others, like political and social institutions, usually change very slowly. According to the functionalist perspective, societies tend toward equilibrium, a condition in which the various components of the culture function together. Change, therefore, is usually a response to exogenous forces, those originating outside the society. Conflict theorists, in contrast, view change as the norm. Change arises from endogenous factors, especially internal conflicts over the unequal distribution of scarce resources. Early theories of social change were either evolutionary, which often stressed a unilinear progression from a traditional to an industrial society, or cyclical,

Our painstaking definitions and procedures made it possible to create large computerized files of events such as our descriptions of about 6,000 contentious gatherings that occurred somewhere in Great Britain between 1828 and 1834, the period of the first successful popular mobilization for reform of Parliament and expansion of suffrage. This work involved me in organizing sizable research teams and inventing techniques for transcribing bulky, complicated historical material. A number of other researchers have since improved these methods in studying such subjects as ethnic conflicts in the United States, coffee growers' politics in Brazil, and industrial conflicts in postwar Italy.

As my research groups worked on models and methods, the nation entered a period of intense social conflict over civil rights, the Vietnam War, educational reform, and other salient issues of the 1960s and 1970s. That wave of struggle undoubtedly helped inspire my effort and probably made its results more credible to students, other researchers, and the general public. On the whole, analyses of collective action were moving away from ideas of breakdown, disorder, and protest toward ideas of organized claim making. It is hard to know how much my work merely reflected the temper of the times and how much it actually made an independent difference to shared understanding of collective action. Some of each, no doubt.

In recent years, my collaborators and I have continued to analyze violent encounters and routine contention, but have also spent more time examining transformations of state power, political identities, and political institutions. I am now, for example, comparing paths toward and away from democracy in different parts of Europe since 1650. All this work echoes a theme that has reverberated in my research and writing for 40 years: relations, in both directions, between large structural changes and the experiences of ordinary people.

I have yielded to an ever-present temptation. Looking back on our complicated lives, most of us feel an urge to make them tell coherent stories, as if they spelled out a plan that worked from the beginning. Someone else could easily make the same events tell a much more contingent story. When I was writing my book on the Vendée's counterrevolution, for example, Harry Eckstein was starting a project on "internal war" at Princeton. Harry's invitation to submit a fellowship proposal led me to lay out a research program on "urbanization and political upheaval" in France that now seems naive, but that started me on a series of studies I have never abandoned. What if no invitation to spend a year at Princeton had come along? I might easily have ended up much more heavily involved in the study of contemporary cities and urbanization, the other main topic on which I was working at the time. All I can honestly claim is that my great teachers taught me to watch for theoretical problems and research opportunities in which systematic evidence spread over considerable blocks of time and space could help narrow our uncertainty about the connections between large structural changes such as state formation, revolution, and urbanization, on the one hand, and alterations in the experiences—especially the collective experiences—of ordinary people, on the other.

Charles Tilly received a Ph.D. in Social Relations from Harvard University in 1958. At the time of his death in 2008, he was the Joseph L. Buttenwieser Professor of Social Science at Columbia University in New York City. He previously taught at the Universities of Delaware, Toronto, and Michigan; Harvard University; and the New School in New York City. He was the author, coauthor, or editor of more than 35 books, many published in multiple editions and languages, and authored or coauthored more than 275 journal articles and book chapters. His honors include honorary doctorates from the universities of Rotterdam, Paris, Strasbourg, Geneva, and Toronto.

---

which sometimes referred to the life cycle of a civilization. These theories are no longer accepted by most sociologists. More widely accepted is the theory of sociocultural evolution, which examines how hunting and gathering societies changed into other types of societies. Sociocultural evolution focuses on general patterns, within which there are many individual variations.

Although we live in a period of rapid social change, a long-term perspective teaches us that throughout most of human history, change occurred very slowly. Rapid social change is basically the product of the Industrial Revolution, which began only a few centuries ago. Within that period, traditional agricultural societies have been transformed into technologically advanced industrial (and postindustrial) societies. Sociologists refer to this process and the accompanying political and social changes as modernization. Although many of these changes have increased life expectancy and raised the overall standard of living, the rate of change has led to increased anomie and other social problems as skills and norms quickly become obsolete.

Key Terms

social movement
relative-deprivation theory
resource-mobilization theory
political-process theory
terrorism
social change
technology
revolution
equilibrium
modernization
modernization theory

Exercises

1. Since the September 11th attack on the World Trade Center in New York City, terrorism has become one of the hottest topics within American media. On May 10, 2001, the director of the Federal Bureau of Investigation, Louis J. Freeh, gave an address before the U.S. Senate Appropriations Committee entitled "The Threat of Terrorism to the United States." This address was delivered just four months prior to the attack on the Twin Towers of the WTC. Read the statement in its entirety at http://www.fbi.gov/congress/congress01/freeh051001.html, and respond to the following questions:

   - Do you think the FBI was expecting an attack like the one on the WTC? Why or why not?
   - Do you think anything could have been done to more accurately track the activities of terrorist cells within the United States so that the incident could possibly have been prevented?
   - What steps do you think should be taken to prevent similar acts of terrorism in the future?

2. The September 11th WTC tragedy has punctuated social concerns about *Internet terrorism*. Such concerns threaten cyberspace freedom and raise questions about future government-imposed controls on the Internet. Some in Congress have even called for the president to have the power to stop virtually all traffic on the Internet.

   - Do you think that certain controls on the Internet are necessary? For example, imagine that the perpetrators of the World Trade Center tragedy had a Web site that encouraged people to engage in terrorist acts. Should such a site be banned? If so, how might this be accomplished? How should this kind of behavior be addressed?
   - Do you think that censorship of the Internet is a problem? If so, how could reasonable controls on terrorist activities on the Internet be imposed, without sacrificing freedom of speech? If controls are needed, how should the government go about imposing them?

3. Interview an older relative or friend about changes in technology, families, race relations, or gender relations, and ask that person to think about ways in which those changes have been both for the better and for the worse. Are you surprised by what that person said? Do you agree or disagree with his or her assessments? How might generational differences relate to how you and your interviewee see the world? Do people really change their minds about social issues or is "social change" really just "generational change"?

Glossary

acculturation A process in which immigrant minority groups are expected to adopt the dominant culture of the host country.

achieved status Any status that a person has attained at least in part as a result of something that the person has done.

acting crowd A crowd that engages in violent or destructive behavior.

activity theory A theory arguing that activity is beneficial to the health and self-esteem of older people, and that there is no social need for them to give up socially valued roles and activities.

acute disorder A medical disorder of limited duration, which is followed either by rapid recovery or death.

affirmative action Any effort designed to overcome past or institutional discrimination by increasing the number of minorities or females in schools, jobs, or job-training programs.

age groups Socially defined categories of people based on age; for example, childhood, adolescence, old age.

age roles Roles that are associated with age and carry the expectation that people of different ages should behave differently.

age stratification Social inequality among age groups.

ageism Prejudice and discrimination based on age.

agents of socialization People and institutions that carry out the process of socialization; they act as important influences on the individual's attitudes, beliefs, self-image, and behavior.

agricultural economy A system of production based primarily on raising crops through the use of plows and draft animals.

agriculture The growing and harvesting of crops in one permanent location; usually facilitated through implements such as the plow.

alienation As defined by Marx, the separation or isolation of workers from the products of their labor; more broadly, feelings or the experience of isolation, powerlessness, or loss of control.

amalgamation A process whereby different racial or ethnic groups in a society gradually lose their identities and become one group as a result of intermarriage.

androgynous societies Societies in which the roles of men and women differ little, if at all.

anomie A condition in society of normlessness—a lack of effective norms governing people's behavior.

apartheid The official name for the racial caste system in South Africa, where political and economic rights were historically defined according to which of four official racial groupings—white, black, coloured, and Asian—a person belonged to.

applied sociology The use of sociological knowledge and methods to solve problems, design policy, and obtain information relevant to making decisions.

ascribed status Any status that a person receives through birth, including race, sex, and family of origin.

assimilation A process by which different ethnic or cultural groups in a society come to share a common culture and social structure.

authoritarian government A government in which the leaders have virtually unrestricted power and the people have little or no freedom of expression.

authoritarian personality A personality pattern believed by social psychologists to be associated with a psychological need to be prejudiced.

authority A right to make decisions and exercise power that is attached to a social position or to an individual and is accepted because people recognize and acknowledge its legitimacy.

bilineal system A system in which wealth and kinship are passed on through both males and females.

birth cohort The set of all people who were born during a given time period.

bourgeoisie In a capitalist economy, those who own capital, who constitute the dominant group or ruling class.

bureaucracy A form of organization characterized by specialization, hierarchy, formal rules, impersonality, lifelong careers, and a specialized administrative staff.

capital Productive capacity in an industrialized economy, including manufacturing and distribution capacity, raw materials, and money.

capitalist economy An economic system, found mainly in industrialized countries, in which the means of production are privately owned.

caste A grouping into which a person is born that determines that person's status in a caste system.

caste system A very closed stratification system in which the group or caste into which a person is born determines that person's social status on a lifelong basis.

cause and effect A relationship in which some condition (the effect) is more likely to occur when some other condition (the cause) is present than it otherwise would be.

central tendency A measure of where the center of a distribution lies, or where the middle, average, or typical person falls in some distribution of scores or characteristics.

charismatic authority Authority that is based on the personal qualities of an individual, such as the ability to excite, inspire, and lead other people.

child abuse Extreme or sustained physical or psychological violence directed against children.

chronic disorder An extended or ongoing medical disorder from which a patient cannot expect to recover.

church A religion with a formalized hierarchy and set of rules that accommodates itself to the larger society.

civil disobedience Nonviolent protest actions that violate the law.

civil religion A series of beliefs, not associated with any single denomination, that portray a society's institutions and structure as consistent with the will of God.

civil war An armed conflict among different groups or factions within the same nation.

class A grouping of people with similar socioeconomic status in an industrialized society.

class consciousness A situation in which a group of people with a common self-interest correctly perceive that interest, and develop beliefs, values, and norms consistent with advancing that interest.

class structure The distribution of wealth and other scarce resources in society.

class system A system of social inequality, usually found in modern, industrial societies, in which a person's position in life is influenced by both achieved and ascribed statuses.

clergy Religious officials with special authority to conduct ceremonies, establish rules, and administer sacraments.

cliques Relatively close and exclusive informal groups with distinct boundaries, usually consisting of about three to nine people.

closed stratification system A system of inequality in which opportunities for mobility are relatively limited.

coercion An exercise of power that forces people to recognize and obey a group or an individual whose legitimacy they do not accept.

cognitive-developmental theories Theories of socialization that emphasize the development of reasoning ability.

cognitive-dissonance theory A social-psychological theory that claims that people often adjust their attitudes to make them consistent with their behavior to eliminate the stress that results when their attitudes and behaviors are inconsistent.

cognitive processes Mental processes involved in learning and reasoning.

cohabitation An arrangement in which an unmarried couple forms a household.

collective behavior Large numbers of people acting together in an extraordinary situation, in which usual norms governing behavior do not apply.

communism As used by Karl Marx, a utopian society, to date not attained in the real world, in which all wealth is collectively owned, workers control the workplace, and government is unnecessary.

community A group of people who live in a geographically distinct area such as a city or town, share cultural characteristics, attitudes, and lifestyles, and interact with one another on a sustained basis.

concentrated economy An economy in which competition is limited or absent because there are very few producers of any given product.

concentric-zones model A theory in urban sociology holding that population characteristics and land use change systematically as you move away from the center of the city, such that they are arranged roughly as a series of rings around the center of the city.

conflict perspective A macrosociological perspective based on the key premise that society is made up of groups that compete, usually with unequal power, for scarce resources; conflict and change are seen as the natural order of things.

contagion A process through which a proposed or initiated action is rapidly adopted or imitated by a crowd or mass.

content analysis A research method based on the systematic examination of the content of some message or communication.

continuity theory A theory about aging which holds that people adapt best to age role changes when they are able to continue roles and activities that they have experienced and found rewarding earlier in life.

control group In experimental research, a group that experiences no manipulation of the independent variable; it is used for purposes of comparison to the experimental group.

control variable A variable that is introduced into an experiment to determine whether correlation between an independent and a dependent variable is the product of some other influence operating on both of them.

convergence A dynamic in which a crowd acts as one because many people in the crowd share emotions, goals, or beliefs.

cooptation A process whereby leaders of social movements are led to adopt more moderate positions by being given positions of status or authority in institutions.

corporation A large-scale private company with multiple owners (called stockholders) that is legally independent and has legal rights and responsibilities separate from either its owners or managers.

correlation A relationship between two variables in which a change in one is accompanied by a change in the other.

counterculture A subculture that has developed beliefs, values, symbols, and norms that stand in opposition to those of the larger culture.

credentials Items of information used to document or support the claim that an individual has certain capabilities, or expertise.

crime A deviant act that violates a law.

cross-cutting cleavages Situations in which divisions or issues of conflict divide a society in different ways on different issues.

crowd A large set of people who are localized in one place and whose interaction is only temporary.

crude birth rate The number of births occurring in a year per 1,000 population.

crude death rate The number of deaths occurring in a year per 1,000 population.

cult A religious group that is withdrawn from, and often at odds with, the religious traditions of a society.

cultural deprivation A condition that functionalist theorists believe commonly exists among lower-income groups, whereby such groups suffer disadvantages in education and economics because they lack cultural characteristics associated with success.

cultural diffusion A process whereby a belief, value, norm, symbol, or practice spreads from one culture into another, or from a subculture into the larger culture.

cultural lag A pattern whereby some aspect of culture that was once functional persists after social or technological change has eliminated its usefulness.

cultural relativism A view that recognizes cultures other than one's own as different, but not odd or inferior; other cultures are not judged by the standards of one's own.

culture A set of knowledge, beliefs, attitudes, and rules for behavior that are held commonly within a society.

deconcentrated economy An economy characterized by competition resulting from a large number of producers.

de facto segregation Racial school segregation that is brought about as a result of housing and neighborhood segregation patterns.

deindustrialization A decline in the importance of heavy industry as a source of employment in the United States and other modern economies. Automation, job decentralization, and the transition to a postindustrial economy all play a role in this process.

democratic government A system in which government is chosen by the people, who enjoy freedom of expression and the right to vote for their leaders.

demographic transition A historic process whereby declines in mortality are not immediately followed by declines in fertility, thereby creating a period of rapid population growth.

demography The scientific study of human populations.

denomination One of several major religions in a society that usually tolerates other religions.

dependency theories A group of theories holding that industrialized nations keep Third-World nations in a dependent position to maintain the advantages of the industrialized nations.

dependent variable A variable that is assumed by the researcher to be the effect of some other variable, called the independent variable.

deterrence The prevention of crime or deviant behavior through punishment, whereby fear of the punishment prevents people from engaging in the deviant behavior.

deviance Behavior that does not conform to the prevailing norms of a society.

dictatorship A modern form of authoritarian government in which one person rules by absolute power.

differential association A theory that explains criminal behavior as a product of long-term exposure to criminal activities.

dimensions of stratification The different bases on which people in a society are unequally ranked, including economic (wealth and income), political (power), and prestige (status).

discrimination Behavior that treats people unequally on the basis of an ascribed status such as race or sex.

disease A condition defined by a medical practitioner as the cause of an illness.

disengagement theory A theory, drawing largely on the functionalist perspective, that supports older people's giving up their role obligations to create opportunities for younger people.

division of labor A characteristic of most societies in which different individuals or groups specialize in different tasks.

dramaturgical perspective A theory arising from the symbolic-interactionist perspective that holds that human behavior is often an attempt to present a particular self-image to others.

dyad A social group that consists of only two people.

dying A process of physical deterioration and preparation for death.

dysfunction A consequence of a social arrangement that is in some way damaging or problematic to the social system.

economic structure In Marxian terminology, those aspects of social structure that relate to production, wealth, and income.

economic systems Systems that determine the production and distribution of scarce resources.

ego In Freudian theory, that part of the personality that mediates between the id and the superego.

emergent norms A process whereby a crowd collectively and interactively develops its own norms about how to behave.

endogamy Marriage between people from the same racial, religious, and ethnic groups.

epidemiology The measurement of the extent of medical disorders in a population, and the social, demographic, and geographic characteristics of those with such disorders.

equilibrium A condition in which the components of a society function together in a state of balance.

estate system A relatively closed stratification system, also called a feudal system, that is found in agricultural economies, in which a person's status is determined on the basis of landownership and, frequently, formal title.

ethnic group A group of people who are recognized as a distinct group on the basis of cultural characteristics such as common ancestry or religion.

ethnocentrism An attitude commonly found among human groups in which members of the group consider their ways of doing things to be normal, natural, and superior to the ways of other groups.

ethnomethodology A theory arising from the symbolic-interactionist perspective that argues that human behavior is a product of how people understand the situations they encounter.

exchange mobility A type of socioeconomic mobility that occurs when some people move to higher positions in the stratification system, while others move to lower positions.

exchange theory A theory holding that people enter a relationship of any kind because each participant expects to gain something from it.

exogamy Marriage between people from different racial, ethnic, or religious groups.

experiment A research method in which the researcher manipulates the independent variable while keeping everything else constant in order to measure the effect on the dependent variable.

experimental group In experimental research, the group that experiences some manipulation or change of the independent variable.

expertise An individual's specialized knowledge concerning some specific topic, issue, or scientific discipline.

exponential growth Growth based on a percentage rate of increase that results in larger numerical growth in each successive year.

expressive leaders People who exercise leadership by taking care of the social and emotional needs of people in their group.

extended family A family consisting of more than two generations who live together and share responsibilities for the maintenance of the family.

fad An amusing mass involvement or activity, usually somewhat unconventional, that is temporary in nature.

false consciousness A condition in which people, usually in groups that are relatively powerless, accept beliefs that work against their self-interests.

family A group of people related by ancestry, marriage, or adoption who live together, form an economic unit, and cooperatively rear their young.

family of orientation The family into which a person is born.

family of procreation The family a person forms by marrying and having children.

fashion A style of appearance or behavior that is favored by a large number of people for a limited amount of time.

fee-for-service payment A method of payment for health care in which providers receive a set amount of money (fee) for each service that they provide.

feminism An ideology or a related social movement advocating the ideas that an equal share of scarce resources should go to women and men and that social roles should not be assigned on the basis of sex.

feminist theory A theoretical approach emphasizing efforts to understand the causes and societal consequences of gender inequality, and often applying such knowledge to correct this inequality.

fertility The number of births occurring in a population.

field observation A research method in which the researcher observes human behavior as it occurs in natural, "real-life" situations.

folkways Relatively minor informal norms that carry only informal sanctions such as mild joking or ridicule, when they are violated.

forced assimilation A type of assimilation in which a minority group is required to adopt the culture of the majority group.

formal organization A relatively large self-perpetuating social group with a name, an established purpose, a role structure, and a set of rules.

function A consequence of a social arrangement that is in some way useful for the social system.

functional illiteracy The inability to read, write, add, or subtract well enough to perform everyday tasks.

functionalist perspective A macrosociological perspective stressing the basic notion that society is made up of interdependent parts that work together to produce consensus and stability.

functional specialization The tendency of different cities or metropolitan areas to specialize in different types of economic activity.

fundamentalism A form of religion characterized by strict rules and by literal and unquestioning acceptance of sacred writings and teachings.

game stage According to George Herbert Mead, a stage of socialization at which organized activity becomes possible.

gemeinschaft According to Toennies, a traditional community in which relations between people are close and personal, behavior is governed by tradition, and contacts with strangers are rare.

gender Socially learned traits or characteristics that are associated with men or women.

gender roles Social roles that people are expected to play because they are male or female, which often carry unequal status, rewards, and opportunities. Also called sex roles.

gender-role socialization The process by which sex roles are taught and learned.

generalized other Classes of people with whom a person inter-acts on the basis of generalized roles rather than on individual characteristics.

gentrification The movement of the upper class into older central-city neighborhoods, leading to renovation of buildings and a turnover in neighborhood population.

gesellschaft According to Toennies, an urban society in which personal goals come before community objectives, relations are impersonal, and tradition is weak.

globalization A transition to a worldwide economy that transcends national boundaries.

group See social group.

health A condition in which a person can function effectively on the physical, mental, and social levels.

health maintenance organization (HMO) A medical coverage plan in which members prepay their health care and receive services as needed without a fee.

hidden curriculum The values, beliefs, and habits that are taught in the schools in addition to factual content and skills.

hinterland The area around a city that is dependent upon the city for goods, services, and markets.

homogamy "Like marrying like"; marriage between people of similar backgrounds and social characteristics.

human capital The pool of trained workers necessary for productivity in modern industrial and postindustrial economies.

human ecology An area of sociology that is concerned with the relationships of people and their activity to territory and the physical environment.

hunting and gathering economy A level of economic development in which people live on what they can collect, catch, or kill in their natural environment.

hypothesis A testable statement about reality, usually derived from a theory and developed for purposes of testing some part of that theory.

id In Freudian theory, that part of the human personality that is a product of natural drives such as hunger, aggression, and sexual desire.

ideal culture The norms and beliefs that people in a society accept in principle.

ideal type An abstract definition based on a set of characteristics.

ideational superstructure A Marxian term for ideology; so named because Marx considered ideology an outgrowth of the economic structure.

identification A process whereby an individual develops strong positive feelings toward a person acting as an agent of socialization.

ideological racism The belief that one racial or ethnic group is inherently superior or inferior to another.

ideology A system of beliefs about reality that often serves to justify a society's social arrangements.

illness The condition that occurs when an individual believes that he or she has a medical disorder.

imperialism A system in which a more-powerful country uses the resources of a less-powerful country to its own advantage, often by controlling that country's economic or political system.

incest taboo Societal rules that prohibit marriage or sexual relationships between people defined as being related to each other.

income The dollar value of that which a person or family receives during a specified time period, including wages and returns on investment.

independent variable A variable that is presumed by the researcher to be the cause of some other variable, called the dependent variable.

individual discrimination Behavior by an individual that treats others unequally on the basis of an ascribed status such as race or sex.

industrial economy A level of economic development in which machines are used to manufacture things of value.

infant mortality rate The number of deaths in a year of people under 1 year of age per 1,000 births.

informal structure The actual day-to-day norms, roles, statuses, and behaviors that exist within an organization, which differ from the official and formal structure of the organization.

ingroup A social group that a person belongs to or identifies with.

institution A form of organization, with supporting sets of norms, that performs basic functions in a society, is strongly supported by that society's culture, and is generally accepted as an essential element of the society's social structure.

institutional discrimination Behaviors or arrangements in social institutions that intentionally or unintentionally favor one race, sex or ethnic group—usually the majority group—over another.

institutional racism Institutional discrimination on the basis of race.

institutional sexism Systematic practices and patterns within social institutions that lead to inequality between men and women.

institutionalization A process whereby a condition or social arrangement becomes accepted as a normal and necessary part of a society.

instrumental leaders People who exercise leadership in a group by focusing attention on the task to be done and by suggesting effective ways of completing that task.

intergenerational mobility Attainment by people of a socioeconomic status higher or lower than that of their parents.

interlocking directorate The presence of some of the same people on boards of directors of different corporations.

iron law of oligarchy A principle stated by Robert Michels that argues that in any organization, power will become concentrated in the hands of the leaders, who may then use that power to protect their own interests.

kinship A pattern in which people are related by ancestry, marriage, or adoption but can live independently from one another.

labeling theory A theory holding that deviance is defined by societal reactions to certain behaviors, not by the behaviors themselves.

laity The general membership of a religion, who play a limited, and often passive, role in religious activities.

language A set of symbols through which the people in a society communicate with one another.

latent function A function of a social arrangement that is not evident and is often unintended.

laws Officially stated social norms that carry formal, specific, and publicized sanctions when violated, and which are enforced through formal agencies of social control.

legal-rational authority Authority that is tied to a position rather than to an individual, and which is based on principles of law or on an individual's proper appointment to a position.

legitimate power Power that others accept as proper.

life expectancy The number of years that the average person in a society can be expected to live, based on current patterns of mortality.

linguistic relativity A theory holding that language not only reflects, but also helps to shape, people's perceptions of reality.

looking-glass self A self-image based on an individual's understanding of messages from others about what kind of person that individual is.

macrosociology Those areas of sociology that are concerned with large-scale patterns operating at the level of the group or society.

majority group A group of people who are in an advantaged social position relative to other groups, often having the power to discriminate against those other groups.

manifest function A function of a social arrangement that is evident and, often, intended.

marriage A socially approved arrangement between a male and a female that involves an economic and a sexual relationship.

mass A large number of people who are physically separated yet interact and are subject to common social influences.

mass hysteria A behavior in which people dispersed over a sizable geographic area perceive and respond to a threat, either real or imagined.

mass media Popular published and broadcast means of communication, including television, radio, newspapers, magazines, and motion pictures, that reach a substantial segment of the public.

master status A status that has a dominant influence in shaping a person's life and identity.

material culture Physical objects that are the product of a group or society.

matriarchy A form of society in which females possess power and the right of decision making.

matrilineal system A system in which wealth and kinship are passed on through females.

matrilocality A residency pattern in which married couples live with the wife's family.

maturation theory A theory about aging which holds that developmental processes lead most people to become better-adjusted and more accepting of themselves as their adult life progresses. This theory, based on Erikson's developmental theories, powerfully rejects ageist stereotypes.

mean The arithmetic average of a set of numbers or scores, dividing the sum of the scores by the number of scores.

means of production Those goods or services, including land in an agricultural society and capital in an industrial society, that a person must own to produce things of value.

median The middle score or number in a distribution of scores or numbers.

medically indigent The condition of lacking health insurance and not having sufficient resources to pay for one's own health care.

medicalization A trend whereby an increasing number of conditions and problems are defined as diseases and treated by the institution of medicine.

medicine An institution found in some form in all societies, whose purpose is to treat illness.

meritocracy A reward system based on ability and achievement rather than social background.

metropolitan statistical area (MSA) An area consisting of a central city or cluster of up to three central cities, the remainder of the county containing the central cities, and any adjacent counties that are urban in character and linked to those cities.

microsociology An area of sociology that is concerned with interaction of individual with larger societal influences.

migration Large-scale movement of people to different neighborhoods, areas, or countries.

military-industrial complex A grouping of powerful individuals and organizations who share a common interest in large military expenditures.

minority group A group of people who are in a disadvantaged position relative to one or more groups in their society, and who are often the victims of discrimination.

mixed economy An economic system in which the government provides extensive social services and performs some major economic functions while manufacturing and other industries are at least in part privately owned. Also called democratic socialism.

mob An extremely emotional acting crowd that directs its violence against a specific target.

mode The most frequently occurring number or score in a distribution of numbers or scores.

modeling A process whereby the behavior of a significant other is observed and imitated.

modernization The process of development of industrial societies from agricultural societies, and the accompanying social, economic, and cultural changes.

modernization theory A theory holding that developing countries will follow the same general pattern of development as industrial nations.

monarchy A form of authoritarian government with a hereditary ruler whose absolute power is based on traditional authority.

monogamy The marriage of one husband to one wife.

monopoly A condition in which there is only one producer of a given product, thereby eliminating competition.

monotheism A religion that teaches the existence of one God.

mores Informal but serious social norms, violations of which result in strong sanctions.

mortality The number of deaths occurring in a society.

multiculturalism A viewpoint that values and embraces cultural diversity, viewing different experiences and viewpoints as a source of strength and adaptability rather than division.

multinational corporation A large corporation that produces or sells its products, and usually owns property, in a large number of countries.

multiple-nuclei model A theory holding that population groups and land use in urban areas tend to concentrate in distinct and scattered clusters, often around a number of distinct centers of activity scattered around an urban area.

national health insurance A governmentally mandated system of health insurance for the entire population, based on fee-for-service payment, that is funded through taxes or through a combination of taxes and employer-paid insurance.

national health service A system of health care operated by the government, in which doctors become salaried employees of the government or are paid a fixed amount per patient.

nation-state A legally recognized government that effectively rules a relatively large geographic area and provides services, including military protection, law enforcement, and the regulation of commerce.

natural sciences Those sciences that are concerned with the natural or physical world, including chemistry, biology, physics, astronomy, geology, oceanography, and meteorology.

negotiated order The character of an organization that is the product of fluid agreements arising from the ongoing interaction of its members.

neolocality A residency pattern in which married couples form a separate household and live in their own residence.

nomadic A society in which members move from place to place rather than living permanently in one place.

nonmaterial culture Abstract creations, such as knowledge or values, that are produced by a society.

norm of maximization A value in capitalist countries of trying to derive maximum benefits from scarce resources.

norms Socially defined rules and expectations concerning behavior.

nuclear family A family that is restricted to a parent or parents and their unmarried children.

occupational segregation A pattern whereby two groups—most often men and women—hold different kinds of jobs.

oligarchy A form of authoritarian government in which a small group rules with absolute power. Also sometimes refers to the tendency of large-scale organizations to be ruled by their leaders, even if they are formally democratic.

oligopoly A condition in which there are only a few producers of a given product, so that competition is limited or nonexistent.

open stratification system A system of inequality in which opportunities to move to a higher or lower status are relatively great.

operational definition A precise statement of the meaning of a variable or categories of a variable for the purpose of measurement.

organized skepticism A norm or principle specifying that scientists will be required to support their claims about reality through observed evidence.

outgroup A group that a person does not belong to or identify with.

overlapping cleavages Divisions or issues of conflict in society that divide people along generally similar lines on different issues.

overurbanization A situation, common among less-developed countries, in which the population of cities expands beyond what can be supported by the economy of these cities.

panic An acting crowd that is suddenly swept by fear and responds with spontaneous and often self-destructive behavior.

participant observation A form of field observation in which the researcher participates in some way in the behavior that is being studied.

patriarchy A form of society in which males possess power and the right of decision making.

patrilineal system A system in which wealth and kinship are passed on through males.

patrilocality A residency pattern in which married couples live with the husband's family.

personality need A psychological need for a particular attitude, belief, or behavior that arises from the particular personality type of an individual.

perspective A general approach to a subject, including a set of questions to be addressed, a theoretical framework, and, often, a set of values.

placebo A nonmedicated substance that can provide relief against an illness because patients believe that their condition is being treated.

play stage According to George Herbert Mead, a stage of socialization in which the child acquires language, recognizes the self as a separate entity, and learns norms from significant others.

pluralism A process whereby different racial, ethnic, or cultural groups in a society retain some of their own cultural characteristics while sharing others with the larger society.

pluralist model A theory holding that power is dispersed among a number of competing power centers, each representing a different interest group.

political parties Organizations, usually with different viewpoints or ideologies, that run slates of candidates for elective office.

political-process theory A theory arguing that social movements arise in response to opportunities created by political and social processes, such as modernization, democratization, and economic growth.

political socialization A process through which political beliefs and values are learned through interactions with others and from messages received from the media.

polyandry A form of marriage in which a woman has more than one husband.

polygamy Any form of marriage that involves more than two partners.

polygyny A form of marriage in which a man has more than one wife.

polytheism A religion that teaches the existence of two or more gods.

population projections Estimates of the future size and composition of populations, based on specific assumptions about future fertility, mortality, and migration.

postindustrial economy A modern economy dominated by services, technical knowledge, and information, rather than industry.

poverty The condition of having an extremely low income and standard of living, either in comparison with other members of society (relative poverty), or in terms of the ability to acquire basic necessities (absolute poverty).

power The ability of a person or group to get people to behave in particular ways.

power elite A relatively small group that holds a disproportionate share of power in a society or a political system.

precipitating incident An event, often dramatic, unexpected, or highly publicized, that acts as a trigger for collective behavior under conditions of structural conduciveness.

prejudice A categorical and unfounded attitude or belief concerning a group.

prestige The degree to which a person is respected and well regarded by others.

primary deviance Deviant behaviors that are short-term or cease with adult status.

primary group A small, close-knit group whose members interact because they value or enjoy one another as people.

primary sector That part of an economy consisting of the direct extraction of natural resources from the environment.

profane Aspects of everyday life, which are not usually associated with religion.

progressive tax A tax that requires those with higher incomes to pay a greater percentage of their income in taxes.

projection A process by which a person denies or minimizes personal shortcomings by exaggerating the extent to which these same shortcomings occur in others.

proletariat In a capitalist economy, the class who work for wages or salaries and who are employed by the owners of capital.

Protestant Ethic A belief in hard work, frugality, and material success that Max Weber associated with the emergence of Protestantism in Europe.

qualitative interviewing An open-ended interview technique involving greater attention to the depth of the answers and less to standardization. Questions are aimed at getting general information the researcher wants to obtain, keeping open the possibility of asking new questions suggested by the respondent's answer to the initial ones.

qualitative research An approach to sociological research that uses in-depth observation and interviewing techniques to find beliefs, meanings, and social behaviors that lie beneath the easily observable surface.

quantitative research An approach to sociological research that expresses results as numbers and uses statistical techniques to sort out cause-effect relationships among a number of variables.

racial caste system A closed stratification system in which castes are established on the basis of race.

racial group A category of people who (1) share some socially recognized physical characteristic (such as skin color or facial features) and (2) are recognized by themselves and others as a distinct status group.

racism Any attitude, belief, behavior, or institutional arrangement that has the intent or effect of favoring one race over another.

rationalization In Weberian sociology, the process by which tradition, faith, and personal relationships are set aside in the conduct of business, with decisions being made on the basis of what is expected to work best.

reactivity The tendency of people being studied by social scientists to react to the researcher or to the fact that they are being studied.

real culture The norms and principles that people in a society actually practice.

real wages Wage and salary levels expressed in terms of purchasing power to adjust for the effects of inflation.

rebellion A movement to express disapproval of or to change policies or specific officeholders, often using force, but without changing the structure of the government.

relative-deprivation theory A theory holding that social movements emerge when people feel deprived or mistreated relative to others, or relative to what they feel they should be receiving.

reliability The ability of a measurement process to produce consistent results when the same variable is measured several times.

religion Formalized beliefs and practices that are directed toward the sacred elements in a culture.

research The process of systematic observation used in all sciences.

resocialization A process occuring in total institutions designed to undo the effects of previous socialization and teach an individual new and different beliefs, attitudes, and behavior patterns.

resource-mobilization theory A theory arguing that social movements grow when they are able to obtain and use available resources successfully.

revolution A rapid fundamental change in the basic institutions, relationships, and ideologies within a society.

riot An outbreak of violent crowd behavior, aimed against people, property, or both, that is not focused on one specific target.

rites of passage Formal or informal rituals marking the passage from one age group or age role to another.

ritual A system of established rites and ceremonies that is often religious in nature.

role See social role.

role conflict Conflicting or opposing expectations attached to different roles played by the same person.

role model A significant other from whom a child learns to play a role.

role set A set of related roles attached to one social position or status.

role strain A condition in which one role contains conflicting expectations.

ruling class In Marxist terminology, the class that owns the means of production and therefore enjoys a dominant economic and political position in society.

rumor An unconfirmed item of information spread by word of mouth and sometimes by unconfirmed media reports.

sacred That which inspires awe, reverence, fear, or deep respect in people.

sacred philosophy A form of religion that does not revolve around a deity but does have a concept of the sacred from which moral and philosophical principles and behavioral norms are derived.

sample A subset of some larger population that is studied for the purposes of drawing conclusions about that larger population.

sanctions A form of direct social control that uses rewards and punishments to encourage conformity to social norms.

scapegoat A person or group against whom an individual displaces feelings of anger or frustration that cannot be expressed toward the true source of the individual's feelings.

scarce resources Material goods, statuses, and other things that people want, but that do not exist in sufficient quantities to satisfy everybody's needs or desires.

science An approach to understanding the world based on systematic observation and generalization, which is used to generate theories to explain what is observed and to predict future results under similar conditions.

secondary deviance Chronic deviant behavior by people who come to identify themselves as deviants.

secondary group A social group, large or small, that exists for some purpose beyond the relationships among the group's members.

secondary sector That part of an economy consisting of the making or manufacturing of tangible physical products.

sect A religious group, often created through a schism with an established church, that is not well integrated into the larger society.

sectoral model A theory holding that urban population groups and land use are arranged in pie-shaped segments extending outward in different directions from the center of the city.

secularization A process in which the influence of religion in a society declines.

self A distinct identity attached to a person; an awareness of that person's existence as a separate entity.

self-fulfilling prophecy A process in which people's belief that a certain event will occur leads people to behave in such a way that they cause the expected event to happen.

self-image The totality of the type of person that one perceives oneself to be.

serial monogamy A system in which people engage in a series of monogamous relationships; it usually occurs as a result of divorce and remarriage.

sex The physical or biological characteristic of being male or female. See also gender.

sexism Structured inequality between men and women, and the norms and beliefs that support such inequality.

sex roles See gender roles.

sickness A condition in which a person is recognized by others as having a medical problem or disorder.

sick role A social role played by people who are recognized by others as having a sickness, which exempts them from normal role obligations.

significant others Specific individuals with whom a person interacts and who are important in that person's life.

social change The alteration of behavior patterns, social relationships, institutions, and social structure over time.

social channeling A process whereby socialization prepares an individual for a particular role in life.

social class See class.

social construction of reality A process in which people's experience of reality is largely determined by the meanings they attach to that reality.

social control Those processes that minimize deviance from social norms.

social evolution A gradual process of social change whereby a society develops, increases in complexity, and offers its members a better quality of life.

social group A set of two or more people who interact regularly, share some common purpose, and have some structure of roles and statuses.

social learning A process by which attitudes, beliefs, and behaviors are learned from significant others in a person's social environment or subculture.

social movement A large number of people acting together on behalf of a shared objective or idea.

social psychology An important subspecialty of both sociology and psychology that is concerned with the interaction of the individual with larger societal forces.

social role A set of behavioral expectations that are attached to a social position or status.

social sciences Those sciences that are concerned with the study of human behavior, including sociology, anthropology, psychology, economics, political science, and, by some definitions, history.

social segregation The tendency for people with similar social characteristics to live together in the same neighborhoods.

social structure The organization of society, including institutions, social positions, the relationships among social positions, the groups that make up the society, and the distribution of scarce resources within the society.

socialist economy An economic system, normally found in industrialized countries, in which the means of production are publicly owned.

socialization The process by which new members of a society are taught to participate in that society, learn their roles, and develop a self-image.

society A relatively self-contained and organized group of people who interact under some shared political authority within some reasonably well-defined geographic area.

sociocultural evolution The process whereby hunting and gathering societies develop into more technologically advanced societies.

socioeconomic mobility The movement of people to higher or lower positions within the stratification system.

socioeconomic status (SES) A person's overall position within the stratification system, reflecting such things as income, wealth, educational level, and occupational prestige.

sociological imagination A series of insights or perspectives toward society that is achieved through the study of sociology.

sociological perspective A belief that questions about human social behavior can be answered through systematic observation of the influences of human groups and societal arrangements on behavior.

sociology The systematic study of society, human social behavior, and social groups.

sociopath A personality type characterized by a poorly developed sense of right and wrong and the absence of guilt for harm caused to others.

status Any position within a social system. The term status is also sometimes used to refer to prestige.

status quo The existing set of arrangements within a society.

stereotype An exaggerated belief concerning a group of people that assumes that nearly everyone in the group possesses a certain characteristic.

stratification A pattern whereby scarce resources, such as wealth, income, power, and prestige, are distributed unequally among the members of a society.

street crime Illegal acts directed against people or property, including murder, robbery, and rape.

structural conduciveness A condition in which the social situation is favorable for the emergence of a particular behavior, such as collective behavior or a social movement.

structural mobility A type of socioeconomic mobility that occurs because of an increasing proportion of jobs in the higher-status, white-collar categories.

subculture A set of knowledge, beliefs, attitudes, symbols, and norms held by a group sharing some common experience or situation within a larger society.

subjective class The class to which people perceive that they belong.

subsistence level A level of economic production that meets a population's minimum needs but produces no surplus.

superego In Freudian psychology, that part of the personality that internalizes the norms and expectations of society and of significant others.

surplus Whatever an economy produces in excess of the minimum needed to keep everyone alive.

survey research Any research in which a population is asked a set of questions by a researcher, who then analyzes the responses.

symbol Anything including words, signs, and gestures, that is used to represent something else.

symbolic-interactionist perspective A major microsociological perspective stressing the importance of messages from others and from society, how people understand and interpret these messages, and how this process affects people's behaviors.

symbolic racism A modern type of racial prejudice that does not express overtly prejudiced attitudes but does blame minority groups for any disadvantages that they experience.

technology The application of scientific knowledge to a practical task.

terrorism The use of violence, usually against civilian targets, as a means of intimidation or social control.

tertiary sector That part of an economy consisting of producing and processing information and providing services.

theory A set of interrelated statements about reality, usually involving one or more cause-and-effect relationships.

third-party payment A system of health-care payment in which providers of health care are paid by someone other than the patient, usually government or an insurance company.

Thomas theorem A sociological principle that states that situations defined by people as real, are real in their consequences.

total institution An organization or group that has complete control over an individual and that usually engages in a process of resocialization.

totalitarian government An extreme form of authoritarian government that takes total control over all aspects of life.

tracking An educational practice in which students are grouped according to their teachers' judgments of their ability.

traditional authority Authority based on long-standing custom, often reinforced by a sacred element.

triad A social group that consists of three people.

underclass Poor people who are chronically unemployed or underemployed and who lack the necessary skills to obtain stable, quality employment.

uneven development The tendency of some cities or

neighborhoods to grow and prosper while others stagnate or decline.

unobtrusive observation A type of field observation in which the researcher does not interact with the people being studied, participate in the behavior being studied, or reveal his or her identity as a researcher.

urbanization The process whereby an increasing share of a population lives in cities.

urban legend An unsubstantiated story containing a plot, which is widely circulated and believed.

validity The ability of measurement process to measure correctly that which it is intended to measure.

values Personal preferences, likes and dislikes, or judgments about what is good and desirable or bad and undesirable.

variable Any concept that can take on different values or be classified into different categories.

veto groups Interest groups that possess the power to block policy changes or proposed laws that threaten their interests.

victimless crime Illegal acts in which the only victims are the offenders.

war Armed conflict among different nations.

wealth The total value of everything that a person or family owns, less any debts.

white-collar crime Illegal acts committed by members of high-status groups.

world-system theory A form of dependency theory that divides all countries into core, peripheral, and semiperipheral nations, in which the more-developed nations keep the less-developed ones in a weak and dependent position.

References

ABC News. 1991. "True Colors." *Prime Time Live*.
———. 1987. World News Tonight. September 17.
Aberle, D. F. et al. 1950. "The Functional Prerequisites of a Society." *Ethics* 60: 100–01.
Abrahamson, Mark, and Lee Sigelman. 1987. "Occupational Sex Segregation in Metropolitan Areas." *American Sociological Review* 52: 588–97.
Abramson, Harold. 1980. "Religion." Pp. 871–75 in Stephan Thernstrom, Ann Orlov, and Oscar Handlin (eds.), *Harvard Encyclopedia of American Ethnic Groups*. Cambridge, MA: Belknap Press of Harvard University Press.
Abu-Lughod, Janet. 1989. *Before European Hegemony: The World System A.D. 1250–1350*. New York: Oxford University Press.
Acker, Joan R. 1989. *Doing Comparable Worth: Gender, Class, and Pay Equity*. Philadelphia: Temple University Press.
Acker, Sandra, and Grace Feuerverger. 1996. "Doing Good and Feeling Bad: The Work of Women University Teachers." *Cambridge Journal of Education* 26, 3: 401–23.
Adams, Carol. 1993. *Ecofeminism and the Sacred*. New York: Continuum.
Aday, Lu Ann. 1976. "The Impact of Health Policy on Access to Medical Care." *Milbank Memorial Fund Quarterly* 54: 215–33.
Addams, Jane, and the residents of Hull-House. 1893. *Hull-House Maps and Papers, by Residents of Hull-House, a Social Settlement, a Presentation of Nationalities and Wages in a Congested District of Chicago, Together with Comments and Essays on Problems Growing Out of the Social Conditions*. New York: Crowell.
Adler, Jerry, with Niko Price. 1991. "The Melting of a Mighty Myth: Eskimos Don't Really Have 23 Words for Snow." *Newsweek* (July 22): 63.
Adorno, Theodor W., Else Frenkel-Brunswik, D. J. Levinson, and R. N. Sanford. 1950. *The Authoritarian Personality*. New York: Harper & Row.
Advisory Board to the President's Initiative on Race. 1998. *One America in the 21st Century: Forging a New Future. The Advisory Board's Report to the President*. Washington, DC: U.S. Government Printing Office.
Advisory Committee on Student Financial Assistance. 2001. "Access Denied: Restoring the Nation's Commitment to Equal Educational Opportunity." http://www.ed.gov/offices/AC/ACSF/access denied.pdf.
AFL-CIO. 2009. "2008 Trends in CEO Pay." http://www.aflcio.org/corporatewatch/paywatch/pay/index.cfm (Downloaded October 13, 2009).
———. 2001. "Runaway CEO Pay: What's Happening and What You Can Do About It." http://www.aflcio.org/paywatch/ceopay.htm.
———. 1995. "AFL-CIO Fact Sheet—The Needs of Working America: MINIMUM WAGE." http://www.aflcio.org/estatements/feb95/attack/fsminwag.txt.
Aguirre, Benigno E., Ernest L. Quarantelli, and Jorge L. Mendoza. 1988. "The Collective Behavior of Fads: The Characteristics, Effects and Career of Streaking." *American Sociological Review* 53 (August): 569–84.
Ahmad, S. 1977. "Population Myths and Realities." *Race and Class* 19(1): 19–29.
Aho, C. Michael, and Marc Levinson. 1988. *After Reagan: Confronting the Changed World Economy*. New York: Council on Foreign Relations.
Ahuvia, Aaron C., and Mara B. Adelman. 1992. "Formal Intermediaries in the Marriage Market: A Typology and Review." *Journal of Marriage and the Family* 54: 452–63.

Aiken, Michael. 1970. "Distribution of Community Power: Structural Bases and Social Consequences." Pp. 487–25 in Michael Aiken and Paul E. Mott (eds.), *The Structure of Community Power*. New York: Random House.
Akers, Ronald L. 1985. *Deviant Behavior: A Social Learning Approach*, 3rd ed. Belmont, CA: Wadsworth.
Alan Guttmacher Institute. 1999. "Why is Teenage Pregnancy Declining? The Roles of Abstinence, Sexual Activity and Contraceptive Use." http://www.agi-usa.org/pubs/or_teen_preg_decline.html.
Alder, Christine. 1986. "Unemployed Women Have Got It Heaps Worse: Exploring the Implications of Female Youth Unemployment." *Australian and New Zealand Journal of Criminology* 19: 210–24.
Aldrich, Mark, and Robert Buchele. 1986. *The Economics of Comparable Worth*. Cambridge, MA: Ballinger.
Alexander, Jeffrey C. 1988. "The New Theoretical Movement." Pp. 77–101 in Neil J. Smelser (ed.), *Handbook of Sociology*. Newbury Park, CA: Sage.
———. 1985. *Neofunctionalism*. Beverly Hills, CA: Sage.
Alexander, Karl L., Martha Cook, and Edward L. McDill. 1978. "Curriculum Tracking and Educational Stratification: Some Further Evidence." *American Sociological Review* 43: 47–66.
Alexander, Karl, Doris R. Entwisle, and Maxine S. Thompson. 1987. "School Performance Status Relations, and the Structure of Sentiment: Bringing the Teachers Back In." *American Sociological Review* 52: 665–82.
Alexander, Karl L., and Aaron M. Pallas. 1987. "School Sector and Cognitive Performance: When Is a Little a Little?" Pp. 89–112 in Edward H. Haertel, Thomas James, and Henry M. Levin (eds.), *Comparing Public and Private Schools*. Vol. 2: School Achievement. New York: Falmer Press.
Alexander, Richard A., and Richard B. Smith. 1988. "Trends in Lead Concentration in Major U.S. Rivers and Their Relation to Historical Changes in Gasoline-Lead Consumption." *Water Resources Bulletin* 24: 557–69.
Alexis, M., and Nancy Di Tomaso. 1983. "Transportation, Race, and Employment: In Search of the Elusive Triad." *Journal of Urban Affairs* 5: 81–94.
Alford, Robert R. 1969. *Bureaucracy and Participation: Political Culture in Four Wisconsin Cities*. Chicago: Rand McNally.
Allen, Walter R., Edgar G. Epps, and Nesha Z. Haniff (eds.). 1991. *College in Black and White: African American Students in Predominantly White and Historically Black Public Universities*. Albany: State University of New York Press.
Allied Health Services. 2001. Nursing Salaries Surveys. http://www.alliedhealthservices.com/nurse salaries.html.
Allport, Floyd H. 1924. *Social Psychology*. Boston: Houghton-Mifflin.
Allport, Gordon W. 1954. *The Nature of Prejudice*. New York: Addison-Wesley.
Alston, Jon. 1975. "Review of the Polls." *Journal for the Scientific Study of Religion* 14: 165–68.
Altbach, P. G., R. F. Arnove, and G. P. Kelly (eds.). 1982. *Comparative Education*. New York: Macmillan.
Altemeyer, B. 1998. "The Other 'Authoritarian Personality.'" *Advances in Experimental Social Psychology* 30: 47–92.
Altman, Dennis. 1982. *The Homosexualization of America: The Americanization of the Homosexual*. New York: St. Martin's Press.
Altman, Lawrence K. 1991. "W.H.O. Says 40 Million Will Be Infected with AIDS Virus by 2000." *The New York Times* (June 18): C3.

Alwin, Duane F., and Arland Thornton. 1984. "Family Origins and Schooling Process: Early Versus Late Influence of Parental Characteristics." *American Sociological Review* 49: 784–02.

Amato, Paul R. 2000. "The Consequences of Divorce for Adults and Children." *Journal of Marriage and the Family* 62: 1269–87.

———. 1993. "Children's Adjustment to Divorce: Theories, Hypotheses, and Empirical Support." *Journal of Marriage and the Family* 55: 23–38.

Amato, Paul R., and Alan Booth. 1996. "A Prospective Study of Parental Divorce and Parent-Child Relationships." *Journal of Marriage and the Family* 58: 356–65.

———. 1997. *A Generation at Risk: Growing Up in an Era of Family Upheaval*. Cambridge, MA: Harvard University Press.

Amelan, Roni. 1995. "Paris University Won't Replace Grants with Loans." *Chronicle of Higher Education* (February 3): A47.

American Council on Education and Higher Education Research Institute (UCLA). 2000. *The American Freshman: National Norms for Fall 1999*. Los Angeles: University of California at Los Angeles, Higher Education Research Institute.

American Friends Service Committee. 2001. "Five Years and Counting: Welfare Reform's Failure: National Welfare Reform Findings Reflect Disturbing Trend." News Release, June 1. http://www.afsc.org/news/2001/nrwelf.htm.

American Sociological Association. 2009. Section Counts 2008 Final. http://www.asanet.org/cs/root/leftnav/sections/section_counts_2008_final (Downloaded November 30, 2009).

Ames, Van Meter. 1973. "No Separate Self." Pp. 43–58 in Walter Robert Corti (ed.), *The Philosophy of George Herbert Mead*. Winterthur, Switzerland: Amriswiler Bucherei.

Ammerman, Nancy Tatom. 1987. *Bible Believers: Fundamentalists in the Modern World*. New Brunswick, NJ: Rutgers University Press.

Anastasi, A. 1988. *Psychological Testing*, 6th ed. New York: Macmillan.

Anderson, Elijah. 1999. *Code of the Street: Decency, Violence, and the Moral Life of the Inner City*. New York: Norton.

———. 1991. "Neighborhood Effects on Teenage Pregnancy." Pp. 375–98 in Christopher Jencks and Paul E. Peterson (eds.), *The Urban Underclass*. Washington, DC: Brookings Institution.

———. 1990. *Streetwise: Race, Class, and Change in an Urban Community*. Chicago: University of Chicago Press.

Anderson, Perry. 1974. *Passages from Antiquity to Feudalism*. London: New Left Books.

Anderson, Robert, John Farley, and Janet McReynolds. 1986. "Southern Illinois University at Edwardsville." Pp. 35–43 in American Association of State Colleges and Universities (ed.), *Defining and Assessing Baccalaureate Skills: Ten Case Studies*. Washington, DC: American Association of State Colleges and Universities.

Anderson, Ronald, and Odin W. Anderson. 1979. "Trends in the Use of Health Services." Pp. 371–91 in Howard E. Freeman, Sol Levine, and Leo G. Reeder (eds.), *Handbook of Medical Sociology*, 3rd ed. Englewood Cliffs, NJ: Prentice Hall.

Anderson, Theodore R., and Lee L. Bean. 1961. "The Shevky-Bell Social Areas: Confirmation of Results and a Reinterpretation." *Social Forces* 40: 119–124.

Andreasen, Nancy C. 1987. "Creativity and Mental Illness: Prevalence Rates in Writers and Their First-Degree Relatives." *American Journal of Psychiatry* 144: 10.

Andrews, George Reid. 1991. *Blacks and Whites in Sao Paulo, Brazil: 1888–1988*. Madison: University of Wisconsin Press.

Anti-Defamation League. 1993. *Highlights from an Anti-Defamation League Survey on Racial Attitudes in America*. New York: Anti-Defamation League.

Antonio, Robert. 1995. "Nietzsche's Antisociology: Subjectified Culture and the End of History." *American Journal of Sociology* 101: 1–43.

———. 1975. "Phenomenological Sociology." Pp. 108–24 in George Ritzer (ed.), *Sociology: A Multiple Paradigm Science*. Boston: Allyn and Bacon.

Apple, Michael. 1982. *Education and Power: Reproduction and Contradiction in Education*. London: Routledge and Kegan Paul.

Arditti, J. A. 1999. "Rethinking Relationships Between Divorced Mothers and Their Children: Capitalizing on Family Strengths." *Family Relations* 48: 109–19.

Arendt, Hannah. 1951. *The Origins of Totalitarianism*. New York: Harcourt Brace.

Argyle, M., and M. Cook. 1976. *Gaze and Mutual Gaze*. Cambridge, England: Cambridge University Press.

Aries, Philippe. 1981. *The Hour of Our Death*. New York: Alfred A. Knopf.

———. 1962. *Centuries of Childhood: A Social History of Family Life*. New York: Alfred A. Knopf.

Arluke, Arnold, and Jack Levin. 1985. "'Second Childhood.' Old Age in Popular Culture." Pp. 151–58 in Beth B. Hess and Elizabeth Markson (eds.), *Growing Old in America: New Perspectives on Old Age*. New Brunswick, NJ: Transaction Books.

Aronowitz, Stanley, and Henry Giroux. 1993. *Education Still Under Siege*, 2nd ed. Toronto, Ontario: OISE Press.

———. 1985. *Education Under Siege: The Conservative, Liberal, and Radical Debate over Schooling*. South Hadley, MA: Bergin and Garvey.

Aronson, Joshua, Michael J. Lustina, Catherine Good, Kelli Keough, Claude M. Steele, and Joseph Brown. 1999. "When White Men Can't Do Math: Necessary and Sufficient Factors in Stereotype Threat." *Journal of Experimental Social Psychology* 35: 29–46.

Asch, Solomon E. 1956. "Studies of Independence and Conformity: A Minority of One Against a Unanimous Majority." *Psychological Monographs* 70, 9 (Whole No. 416).

Aseltine, R. H. 1996. "Pathways Linking Parental Divorce with Adolescent Depression." *Journal of Health and Social Behavior*, 37: 133–48.

Asimov, Nanette. 2010. "UC Minority Enrollment Among Lowest in Nation." SF Gate, January 14, 2010. http://articles.sfgate.com/2010-01-14/bay-area/17828191_1_uc-berkeley-flagship-schools-latino-students.

Astin, Alexander W. 1990. *The Black Undergraduate: Current Status and Trends in Freshmen*. Los Angeles: University of California.

———. 1977. *Four Critical Years*. San Francisco: Jossey-Bass.

Atchley, Robert. 1989. "A Continuity Theory of Normal Aging." *Gerontologist* 29(2): 183–90.

Australian Employee Ownership Association. 2008. Employee Ownership Around the Globe. http://www.aeoa.org.au/docs/0024/Employee%20Ownership%20Around%20The%20Globe.pdf.

Auten, Gerald, and Robert Carroll. 1999. "The Effect of Income Taxes on Household Income." *Review of Economics & Statistics* 81, 4: 681–93.

Auter, Philip J., and Ray Lane, Jr. 1998. "Locus of Control, Parasocial Interaction and Usage of Radio or TV Ministry Programs." Paper presented at Research Division of the 1998 Broadcast Education Association conference, Las Vegas. http://www.uwf.edu/pauter/Auter/papers/MediaMinistry/mediamin1.html.

Ayres, Ian. 1990. Fair Driving: Tests of Race and Gender Discrimination in Retail Car Negotiations, Working Paper 8903. Chicago: American Bar Foundation.

Azeem, Sherif Abdel. 1995. "Women in Islam Versus Women in the Judaeo-Christian Tradition." http://twf.org/Library/WomenICJ.html. Originally published by by the World Assembly of Muslim Youth in 1995.

Babbie, Earl. 2001. *The Practice of Social Research*, 9th ed. Belmont, CA: Wadsworth.

———. 1992. *The Practice of Social Research*, 6th ed. Belmont, CA: Wadsworth.

Backman, Carl W., and Paul F. Secord. 1968. "The Self and Role Selection." In Chad Gordon and Kenneth J. Gergen (eds.), *The Self in Social Interaction*. New York: Wiley.

Bahr, Howard M., and Kathleen S. Bahr. 2001. "Families and Self-Sacrifice: Alternative Models and Meanings for Family Theory." *Social Forces* 79: 1231–59.

Bailey, Lucy. 1995. "The Correspondence Principle and the 1988 Education Reform." *British Journal of the Sociology of Education* 16: 479–94.

Bailey, William C. 1990. "Murder, Capital Punishment, and Television: Execution Publicity and Homicide Rates." *American Sociological Review* 55: 628–33.

Bain, David. 1982. *The Productivity Prescription: The Manager's Guide to Improving Productivity and Profits*. New York: McGraw-Hill.

Bain, Trevor, and David Fottler. 1980. "Male-Female Professionals: A Model of Career Choice." *Industrial Relations* 19 (3): 366–70.

Baird, Jim. 2006. "Black Employment Opportunities: The Role of Immigrant Job Concentrations." Paper presented at annual meeting of the American Sociological Association, Montreal.

Bairoch, Paul. 1986. "Historical Roots of Economic Underdevelopment: Myths and Realities." Pp. 191–216 in Wolfgang Mommsen and Jurgen Osterhammel (eds.), *Imperialism After Empire: Continuities and Discontinuities*. London: Allen and Unwin.

Baker, Earl. 1979. "Predicting Response to Hurricane Warnings: A Reanalysis of Data from Four Studies." *Mass Emergencies* 4: 9–24.

Balakrishnan, T. R., R. V. Rao, Evelyne Lapierre-Adamcyk, and Karol J. Krotki. 1987. "A Hazard Model of the Covariates of Marital Dissolution in Canada." *Demography* 24: 395–406.

Baldassare, Mark. 1981. "The Effects of Household Density on Subgroups." *American Sociological Review* 46: 110–18.

———. 1979. Residential Crowding in Urban America. Berkeley: University of California Press.

Bales, Robert F. 1953. "The Equilibrium Problem in Small Groups." Pp. 111–62 in Talcott Parsons et al. (eds.), *Working Papers in the Theory of Action*. Glencoe, IL: Free Press.

Bales, Robert F., and P. E. Slater. 1955. "Role Differentiation in Small Decision-making Groups." Pp. 259–306 in Talcott Parsons, Robert Bales et al. (eds.), *Family, Socialization, and Interaction Process*. Glencoe, IL: Free Press.

Ball, Robert M. 1996. "A Secure System." *The American Prospect* 29: 34–35, also available on http://epn.org/prospect/29/29ball.html.

Balmer, Randall. 1989. *Mine Eyes Have Seen the Glory: A Journey into the Evangelical Subculture in America*. New York: Oxford University Press.

Balz, Dan, and Jon Cohen. 2009. "Public option gains support." *Washington Post*. October 20. http://www.washingtonpost.com/wp-dyn/content/article/2009/10/19/AR2009101902451.html.

Bandura, Albert. 1977. *Social Learning Theory*. Englewood Cliffs, NJ: Prentice Hall.

Bane, Mary Jo. 1976. *Here to Stay: American Families in the Twentieth Century*. New York: Basic Books.

Bane, Mary Jo, and David T. Ellwood. 1983. "The Dynamics of Dependency: Routes to Self-Sufficiency." Unpublished paper supported by U.S. Department of Health and Human Services Grant, Contract No. HHS-100-82-0038.

Banerjee, Neela. 2008. "Taking Their Faith, but Not Their Politics, to the People." *New York Times* (June 1). http://www.nytimes.com/2008/06/01/us/01evangelical.html (Downloaded July 30, 2010).

Banfield, Edward C. 1962. *Political Influence*. New York: Free Press.

Banfield, Edward C., and James Q. Wilson. 1963. *City Politics*. Cambridge. MA: Harvard University and MIT Press.

Bank for International Settlements. 2007. *Foreign Exchange and Market Activity 2007*. Basel, Switzerland: BIS Press.

Banta, David, and Stephen B. Thacker. 1979. *Costs and Benefits of Electronic Fetal Monitoring: A Review of the Literature*. DHEW Publication No. (PHS) 79-3245. Washington, DC: National Center for Health Services Research.

Baquet, Claudia R., John W. Horm, Tyson Gibbs, and Peter Greenwald. 1991. "Socioeconomic Factors and Cancer-Incidence Among Blacks and Whites." *Journal of the National Cancer Institute* (April), pp. 551–57.

Baratz, Steven S., and Joan C. Baratz. 1970. "Early Childhood Education: The Social Science Base of Institutional Racism." *Harvard Educational Review* 40: 29–50.

Barber, Benjamin R. 1996. *Jihad vs. McWorld: How Globalism and Tribalism Are Reshaping the World*. New York: Ballantine Books.

Bardo, John W., and John J. Hartmann. 1982. *Urban Sociology*. Itasca, IL: F. E. Peacock.

Baris, Dalsu, Linda Morris Brown, Debra T. Silverman, Richard Hayes, Robert N. Hoover, G. Marie Swanson, Mustafa Dosemeci, Ann G. Schwartz, Jonathan M. Liff, Janet B. Schoenberg, Linda M. Pottern, Jay Lubin, Raymond S. Greenberg, and Joseph F. Fraumeni Jr. 2000. "Socioeconomic Status and Multiple Myeloma Among U.S. Blacks and Whites." *American Journal of Public Health* 90: 1277–81.

Barkan, Steven E. 1986. "Interorganizational Conflict in the Southern Civil Rights Movement." *Sociological Inquiry* 56: 190–209.

Barlow, Hugh D. 2000. *Criminal Justice in America*. Upper Saddle River, NJ: Prentice Hall.

———. 1993. *Introduction to Criminology*, 6th ed. New York: Harper Collins.

———. 1991. "Explaining Crimes and Analogous Acts, or The Unrestrained Will Grab at Pleasure Whenever They Can." *Journal of Criminal Law and Criminology* 78: 229–42.

———. 1990. *Introduction to Criminology*, 5th ed. Boston: Little, Brown.

———. 1987. *Introduction to Criminology*, 4th ed. Boston: Little, Brown.

Barlow, Hugh D., and David Kauzlarich. 2002. *Introduction to Criminology*, 8th ed. Upper Saddle River, NJ: Prentice Hall.

Barlow, Robin, Harvey E. Barzer, and James M. Morgan. 1966. *Economic Behavior of the Affluent*. Washington, DC: Brookings Institution.

Barnes, Fred. 1990. "The Zillionaires' Club." *New Republic* 202(5) (January 29): 23–25.

Baron, Dennis. 1997. "Ebonics is Not a Panacea for Students at Risk." *Chronicle of Higher Education* (January 24): B4.

Baron, James N., P. Devereaux Jennings, and Frank R. Dobbin. 1988. "Mission Control? The Development of Personnel Systems in U.S. Industry." *American Journal of Sociology* 53: 497–514.

Baron, James N., Brian S. Mittman, and Andrew F. Newman. 1991. "Targets of Opportunity: Organizational and Environmental Determinants of Gender Integration Within the California Civil Service, 1979–1985." *American Journal of Sociology* 96: 1362–1401.

Barovick, Harriett. 1998. "DWB: Driving While Black: Incidents in New Jersey and Maryland Heat Up the Issue of Racial Profiling by State Highway Patrols." *Time* 151, 23 (June 15). Also available on http://cgi.pathfinder.com/time/magazine/1998/dom/980615/nation_driving while.html.

Barrett, Nancy. 1979. "Women in the Job Market: Occupations, Earnings, and Career Opportunities." In Ralph Smith (ed.), *The Subtle Revolution*. Washington, DC: Urban Institute.

Barron, James. 1989. "Unnecessary Surgery." *The New York Times* (April 16): Sect 6, Part 2, 25.

Bart, Pauline. 1973. "Portnoy's Mother's Complaint." Pp. 222–28 in Helena Z. Lopata (ed.), *Marriages and Families*. New York: Van Nostrand.

Bartlett, Donald L., and James B. Steele. 1992. *America: What Went Wrong?* Kansas City, MO: Andrews and McMeel.

Baruch, Grace, Rosalind Barnett, and Caryl Rivers. 1983. *Lifeprints: New Patterns of Love and Work for Today's Women*. New York: Signet.

Bass, Bernard. 1960. *Leadership, Psychology, and Organizational Behavior*. New York: Harper & Row.

Bastian, Ann, Norm Fruchier, Marilyn Gittell, Cohn Greer, and Kenneth Haskins. 1985. *Choosing Equality: The Case for Democratic Schooling*. Philadelphia: Temple University Press.

Bastide, Roger. 1965. "The Development of Race Relations in Brazil." Pp. 9–29 in Guy Hunter (ed.), *Industrialization and Race Relations*. London: Oxford University Press.

Bauer, Raymond A. 1957. "Brainwashing: Psychology or Demonology?" *Journal of Social Issues* 13(3): 41–47.

Bauman, Zygmunt. 1992. *Intimations of Postmodernity*. New York and London: Routledge.

Baumgartner, M. P. 1984. "Social Control from Below." Pp. 303–45 in Donald Black (ed.), *Toward a General Theory of Social Control*. Vol. I: *Fundamentals*. Orlando, FL: Academic Press.

Baxter, Janeen. 1994. "Is Husband's Class Enough? Class Location and Class Identity in the United States, Sweden, Norway, and Australia." *American Sociological Review* 59: 220–35.

Bayer, Ernest L. 1987. *College—The Undergraduate Experience in America*. New York: Harper & Row.

BBC. 2010. "China's Factories Hit by Wave of Strikes." (June 28). http://www.bbc.co.uk/news/10434079 (Downloaded August 4, 2010).

Beck, E. M., and E. Tolnay Stewart. 1990. "The Killing Fields of the Deep South: The Market for Cotton and the Lynching of Blacks, 1882–1930." *American Sociological Review* 55: 526–39.

Beck, Paul Allen. 1986. "Choice, Context, and Consequence: Beaten and Unbeaten Paths Toward a Science of Electoral Behavior." Pp. 241–83 in Herbert F. Weisberg (ed.), *Political Science: The Science of Politics*. New York: Agathon.

Becker, Gary. 1981. *A Treatise on the Family.* Cambridge, MA: Harvard University Press.

Becker, Gary S. 1971. *The Economics of Discrimination,* rev. ed. Chicago: University of Chicago Press. (Originally published in 1957.).

———. 1964. *Human Capital.* New York: Columbia University Press.

Becker, Howard S. 1973. *Outsiders.* New York: Free Press.

———. 1963. *Outsiders: Studies in the Sociology of Deviance.* New York: Free Press.

Bedau, Hugo Adam, and Chester M. Pierce (eds.). 1976. *Capital Punishment in the United States.* New York: AMS Press.

Beer, Francis A. 1981. *Peace Against War: The Ecology of International Violence.* San Francisco: Freeman.

Beez, W. V. 1968. "Influence of Biased Psychological Reports on Teacher Behavior and Pupil Performance." *Proceedings of the 76th Annual Convention of the American Psychological Association* 3: 605–06.

Beggs, John J. 1995. "The Institutional Environment: Implications for Race and Gender Inequality in the U.S. Labor Market." *American Sociological Review* 60: 612–33.

Beisel, Nicola. 1990. "Class, Culture, and Campaigns Against Vice in Three American Cities, 1872–1892." *American Sociological Review* 55: 44–62.

Bélanger, Sarah, and Maurice Pinard. 1991. "Ethnic Movements and the Competition Model: Some Missing Links." *American Sociological Review* 56: 446–57.

Bell, Alison. 2000. Some HMOs Return to Fee for Service Model. National Underwriter, http://www.nunews.com/archives/pc_archive/2000/p12-18/p200051somehmos.asp.

Bell, Daniel. 1976. *The Cultural Contradiction of Capitalism.* New York: Basic Books.

———. 1973. *The Coming of Post-Industrial Society: A Venture into Social Forecasting.* New York: Basic Books.

Bell, Wendell. 1968. "The City, the Suburb, and a Theory of Social Choice." Pp. 137–43 in Scott Greer et al. (eds.), *The New Urbanization.* New York: St. Martin's Press.

Bellah, Robert N. 1970. *Beyond Belief.* New York: Harper & Row.

———. 1964. "Religious Evolution." *American Sociological Review* 29(3) (June): 358–74.

Bellah, Robert N., R. Madsen, W. M. Sullivan, Ann Swidler, and S. M. Tipton. 1985. *Habits of the Heart: Individualism and Commitment in American Life.* Berkeley: University of California Press.

Bellas, Marcia L. 1994. "Comparable Worth in Academia: The Effects on Faculty Salaries of the Sex Composition and Labor-Market Conditions of Academic Disciplines." *American Sociological Review* 59: 807–21.

Beller, Emily, and Michael Hout. 2006. "Intergenerational Social Mobility: The United States in Comparative Perspective." *Future of Children* 16(2): 19–36.

Bem, Sandra L. 1993. *The Lenses of Gender.* New Haven, CT: Yale University Press.

Benbow, Camilla, and Julian Stanley. 1980. "Sex Differences in Mathematical Ability: Fact or Artifact?" *Science* 210: 1262–64.

Bendix, Reinhard. 1967. "Tradition and Modernity Reconsidered." *Comparative Studies in Society and History* 9(3): 292–46.

Bennet, J. 1989. "The Data Game." *The New Republic* (February 13): 20–22.

Bennett, Neil G., Ann Klimas Blanc, and David E. Bloom. 1988. "Commitment and the Modern Union: Assessing the Link Between Premarital Cohabitation and Subsequent Marital Stability." *American Sociological Review* 53: 127–38.

Bennett, Neil G., David E. Bloom, and Patricia H. Craig. 1989. "The Divergence of Black and White Marriage Patterns." *American Journal of Sociology* 95: 692–722.

Benokraitis, Nijole V. 1999. *Feuds About Families: Conservative, Centrist, Liberal, and Feminist Perspectives.* Upper Saddle River, NJ: Prentice Hall.

———. 1993. *Marriages and Families: Changes, Choices, and Constraints.* Englewood Cliffs, NJ: Prentice Hall.

Benovat, Aaron, Yun-Kyung Cha, David Kamens, John W. Meyer, and Suk-Ying Wong. 1991. "Knowledge for the Masses: World Models and National Curricula, 1920–1986." *American Sociological Review* 56: 85–100.

Bensman, Joseph, and Arthur J. Vidich. 1984. *American Society, the Welfare State and Beyond,* rev. ed. South Hadley, MA: Bergin and Garvey.

Berardo, Felix M. 1968. "Widowhood Status in the United States: Perspectives on a Neglected Aspect of the Family Life Cycle." *Family Coordinator* 17: 191–203.

Berg, Barbara J. 1986. *The Crisis of the Working Mother.* New York: Summit Books.

Berger, Bennett. 1960. *Working-Class Suburb.* Berkeley: University of California Press.

Berger, Peter. 1986. *The Capitalist Revolution.* New York: Basic Books.

Berger, Peter, and Thomas Luckmann. 1966. *The Social Construction of Reality: A Treatise in the Sociology of Knowledge.* Garden City, NY: Doubleday.

Bergesen, Albert. 1983. "Modeling Long Waves of Crisis in the World-System." Pp. 73–92 in A. Bergesen (ed.), *Crises in the World-System.* Vol. 6: *Political Economy of the World-System Annuals.* Beverly Hills, CA: Sage.

Bergin, A. E., R. D. Stinchfield, T. A. Gaskin, K. S. Masters, and C. E. Sullivan. 1988. "Religiousness and Mental Health Reconsidered: A Study of an Intrinsically Religious Sample." *Journal of Counseling Psychology* 34: 91–98.

Bergmann, Barbara R. 1986. *The Economic Emergence of Women.* New York: Basic Books.

Bergner, Raymond M. 2000. "Love and Barriers to Love." *American Journal of Psychotherapy* 54(1): 1–18.

Berk, Richard A. 1974. *Collective Behavior.* Dubuque, IA: William C. Brown.

Berkowitz, L. 1983. "Aversively Stimulated Aggression: Some Parallels and Differences in Research with Animals and Humans." *American Psychologist* 38: 1135–44.

Berman, Paul. 1993. "The Future of the American Left." *Dissent* 40(1) (Winter): 97–104.

Bernard, A. C., Mara B. Adelman, and J. E. Schroeder. 1991. "Two Models of Consumption in Mating and Dating." Pp. 18, 532–37 in R. H. Holman and M. R. Solomon (eds.), *Advances in Consumer Research.* Provo, UT: Association for Consumer Research.

Bernard, J. L., S. L. Bernard, and M. L. Bernard. 1985. "Courtship Violence and Sex-Typing." *Family Relations* 34: 573–76.

Bernard, Jesse. 1981. *The Female World.* New York: Free Press.

Berndt, Harry. 1979. "Displacement and Relocation Practices in Five Midwestern Cities." Paper presented at the annual meeting of the Society for the Study of Social Problems.

Bernstein, Paul. 1976. *Workplace Democratization: Its Internal Dynamics.* Kent, OH: Kent State University Press.

Berrueta-Clement, J. R., C. J. Schweinhart, W. S. Barnett, A. S. Epstein, and D. P. Weikart. 1984. "Changed Lives: The Effects of the Perry Preschool Program on Youths Through Age 19." *Monographs of the High/Scope Educational Research Foundation* 8.

Berry, Brian J. L., and Philip H. Rees. 1969. "The Factorial Ecology of Calcutta." *American Journal of Sociology* 74: 445–91.

Berry, Mary Frances. 2000. "How Percentage Plans Keep Minority Students Out of College." *Chronicle of Higher Education.* August 4.

Berscheid, E., K. Dion, E. Walster, and G. W. Walster. 1971. "Physical Attractiveness and Dating Choice: A Test of the Matching Hypothesis." *Journal of Experimental Social Psychology* 7:173–89.

Bertrand, Marianne, and Sendhil Mullainathan, 2002. "Are Emily and Greg More Employable than Lakisha and Jamal? A Field Experiment on Labor Discrimination." Paper presented at Yale University Seminar on Microeconomics, November 18. http://www.economics.harvard.edu/faculty/mullainathan/files/emilygreg.pdf (Downloaded October 19, 2009).

Best, Joel. 2009. "The Stupidity Epidemic." Keynote address, Midwest Sociological Society Annual Meetings, Des Moines, IA, April 4.

———. 2001. *Damned Lies and Statistics: Untangling Numbers from the Media, Politicians, and Activists.* Berkeley: University of California Press.

Best, Kathleen. 1993. "Poverty Programs Cut Second Consecutive Year." *St. Louis Post-Dispatch* (February 12): 1, 12.

Best, Raphaela. 1983. *We've All Got Scars: What Boys and Girls Learn in Elementary School.* Bloomington: Indiana University Press.

Best, Steven, and Douglas Kellner. 2001. *The Postmodern Adventure:*

Science, Technology, and Cultural Studies at the Third Millennium. New York: Gilford.

Bettelheim, Bruno. 1959. "Feral Children and Autistic Children." *American Journal of Sociology* 54: 455–67.

Beuf, A. 1974. "Doctor, Lawyer, Household Drudge." *Journal of Communication* 24(2): 142–45.

Beutel, Ann M., and Margaret Mooney Marini. 1995. "Gender and Values." *American Sociological Review* 60: 436–48.

Bian, Yanjie. 2002. "Chinese Social Stratification and Social Mobility." *Annual Review of Sociology* 28: 91–116.

Bianchi, Suzanne. 1981. *Household Composition and Racial Inequality.* New Brunswick, NJ: Rutgers University Press.

Bianchi, Suzanne M., and Daphne Spain. 1986. *American Women in Transition.* Report for the National Committee for Research on the 1980 Census. New York: Russell Sage Foundation.

Biblarz, Timothy J., and Adrian E. Raftery. 1999. "Family Structure, Educational Attainment, and Socioeconomic Success: Rethinking the 'Pathology of Martriarchy.'" *American Journal of Sociology* 105: 321–65.

Bickerton, Derek. 1995. *Language and Human Behavior.* Seattle: University of Washington Press.

Bidwell, Charles E., and Noah E. Friedkin. 1988. "The Sociology of Education." Pp. 449–71 in Neil J. Smelser (ed.), *Handbook of Sociology.* Newbury Park, CA: Sage.

Bielby, Denise D., and William T. Bielby. 1988. "She Works Hard for the Money: Household Responsibilities and the Allocation of Work Effort." *American Journal of Sociology* 93: 1031–59.

Bielby, William T., and James N. Baron. 1986. "Men and Women at Work: Sex Segregation and Statistical Discrimination." *American Journal of Sociology* 91: 759–99.

Bielby, William T., and Denise D. Bielby. 1992. "I Will Follow Him: Family Ties, Gender-Role Beliefs, and Reluctance to Relocate for a Better Job." *American Journal of Sociology* 97: 1241–67.

———. 1989. "Hollywood Writers Report, 1989 Update." West Hollywood, CA: Writers' Guild of America, West.

Biggar, Jeanne C. 1979. "The Sunning of America: Migration to the Sunbelt." *Population Bulletin* 34(1).

Biggart, Nicole Woolsey, and Mauro F. Guillen. 1999. "Developing Difference: Social Organization and the Rise of the Auto Industries of South Korea, Taiwan, Spain, and Argentina." *American Sociological Review* 64: 722–47.

Binder, Amy. 1993. "Constructing Racial Rhetoric: Media Depictions of Harm in Heavy Metal and Rap Music." *American Sociological Review* 58: 753–67.

Binstock, Jeanne. 1970. "Survival in the American College Industry." Unpublished Ph.D. dissertation, Brandeis University, Waltham, MA.

Bishop, J. 1987. "Information Externalities and the Social Payoff to Academic Achievement" (Working Paper). Ithaca, NY: School of Industrial and Labor Relations, Cornell University.

Black, Donald. 1984. "Social Control as a Dependent Variable." Pp. 1–36 in Donald Black (ed.), *Toward a General Theory of Social Control.* Vol. 1: *Fundamentals.* Orlando, FL: Academic Press.

———. 1976. *The Behavior of Law.* New York: Academic Press.

Blackmore, Judith E. Owen, and Craig A. Hill. 2008. "The Child Gender Socialization Scale: A Measure to Compare Traditional and Feminist Parents." *Sex Roles* 58:192–207.

Blackwell, Debra L., and Daniel T. Lichter. 2000. "Mate Selection Among Married and Cohabiting Couples." *Journal of Family Issues* 21: 275–303.

Blair-Loy, Mary. 1999. "Career Patterns of Executive Women in Finance: An Optimal Matching Analysis." *American Journal of Sociology* 104, 5: 1346–97.

Blalock, Hubert M. 1967. *Toward a Theory of Minority Group Relations.* New York: Wiley.

Blank, Grant, James L. McCartney, and Edward Brent. 1989. *New Technology in Sociology: Practical Applications in Research and Work.* New Brunswick, NJ: Transaction Books.

Blascovich, Jim, Gerald P. Ginsberg, and Rene C. Howe. 1975. "Blackjack and the Risky Shift. II: Monetary Stakes." *Journal of Experimental Social Psychology* 11: 224–32.

Blasi, Augusto. 1980. "Bridging Moral Cognition and Moral Action: A Critical Review of the Literature." *Psychological Bulletin* 88:1–45.

Blau, Francine D., and Marianne A. Ferber. 1986. *The Economics of Women, Men, and Work.* Englewood Cliffs, NJ: Prentice Hall.

Blau, Peter M. 1964. *Exchange and Power in Social Life.* New York: Wiley.

Blau, Peter M., and Otis Dudley Duncan. 1967. *The American Occupational Structure.* New York: Wiley.

Blau, Peter M., and Marshall W. Meyer. 1971. *Bureaucracy in Modern Society,* 2nd ed. New York: Random House.

Blauner, Bob. 1989. *Black Lives, White Lives: Three Decades of Race Relations in America.* Berkeley: University of California Press.

Blauner, Robert. 1972. *Racial Oppression in America.* New York: Harper & Row.

———. 1966. "Death and Social Structure." *Psychiatry* 29: 378–94.

Bloch, Herbert A., and Gilbert Geis. 1970. *Man, Crime and Society,* 2nd ed. New York: Random House.

Block, Fred. 2009. "Is the United States in Decline: Critical Choices and Possible Futures." Talk presented at Daytona State College, November 6th.

———. 2003. "Karl Polanyi and the Writing of 'The Great Transformation.'" *Theory and Society* 32 (3): 275–306.

———. 1990. *Postindustrial Possibilities: A Critique of Economic Discourse.* Berkeley: University of California Press.

Bloom, Allan. 1987. *The Closing of the American Mind.* New York: Simon and Schuster.

Bloom, D. F. 1986. "Women and Work." *American Demographics* 8: 25–30.

Blot, William, L. A. Brinton, J. F. Fraumeni, and B. J. Stone. 1977. "Cancer Mortality in U.S. Counties with Petroleum Industries." *Science* 198: 51–53.

Bluestone, Barry. 1995. *The Polarization of American Society: Victims, Suspects, and Mysteries to Unravel.* New York: Twentieth Century Fund Press, also http://epn.org/tcf/xxblue.html.

Blumberg, Paul. 1973. *Industrial Democracy: The Sociology of Participation.* New York: Schocken.

Blumberg, Rae Lesser. 1984. "A General Theory of Gender Stratification." *Sociological Theory* 2: 23–101.

Blume, Marshall F. 1974. "Stock Ownership in the United States: Characteristics and Trends." *Survey of Current Business* (U.S. Department of Commerce) 54: 16–40.

Blumer, Herbert G. 1974. "Social Movements." In R. Serge Denisoff (ed.), *The Sociology of Dissent.* New York: Harcourt Brace Jovanovich.

———. 1969a. *Symbolic Interactionism: Perspective and Method.* Englewood Cliffs, NJ: Prentice Hall.

———. 1969b. "Collective Behavior." Pp. 65–121 in Alfred McClung Lee (ed.), *Principles of Sociology,* 3rd ed. New York: Barnes and Noble.

———. 1966. "Sociological Implications of the Thought of George Herbert Mead." *American Journal of Sociology* 71: 535–44.

———. 1965. "Industrialization and Race Relations." Pp. 220–553 in Guy Hunter (ed.), *Industrialization and Race Relations: A Symposium.* London: Oxford University Press.

———. 1955. "Social Movements." Pp. 99–220 in Alfred McClung Lee (ed.), *Principles of Sociology.* New York: Barnes and Noble.

———. 1946. "Collective Behavior." Pp. 167–219 in Alfred McClung Lee (ed.), *A New Outline of the Principles of Sociology.* New York: Barnes and Noble.

Blumstein, Alfred, Jacqueline Cohen, and Daniel Nagin (eds.). 1978. *Deterrences and Incapacitation.* Washington, DC: National Academy of Sciences.

Blumstein, Philip, and Pepper Schwartz. 1983. *American Couples.* New York: William Morrow.

Boal, F. W. 1976. "Ethnic Residential Segregation." Pp. 41–79 in D. T. Herbert and R. J. Johnson (eds.), *Social Areas in Cities.* Vol. 1: *Spatial Processes and Form.* London: Wiley.

Bobbio, Norberto. 1987. *The Future of Democracy: A Defence of the Rules of the Game.* Roger Griffin (trans.). Minneapolis: University of Minnesota Press. (Originally published in Italian in 1984).

Boëldieu Julien, and Catherine Borrel. 2000. 1999 Population

Census: The proportion of immigrants remains stable for 25 years. No. 748, November 2000. http://www.insee.fr/en/ffc/ficdoc_frame.asp?doc_id=538&analyse=1&path=/fr/ffc/docs_ffc/IP748.pdf.

Boer, J. Tom, Manuel Pastor, Jr., James L. Sadd, and Lori D. Snyder. 1997. "Is There Environmental Racism? The Demographics of Hazardous Waste in Los Angeles County." *Social Science Quarterly* 78: 793–810.

Boffey, Philip M. 1987. "Physicists Express Star Wars Doubt: Long Delay Seen." *The New York Times* (April 23): 1, 6.

Bogdanor, Vernon. 1987. *The Blackwell Encyclopedia of Political Institutions.* New York: Basil Blackwell.

Boger, John Charles, and Gary Orfield. 2005. *School Segregation: Must the South Turn Back?* Chapel Hill: University of North Carolina Press.

Bolce, Louis Henri, III, and Susan Gray. 1979. "Blacks, Whites, and Race Policies." *The Public Interest* 54: 61–75.

Bolen, Rebecca M., and Maria Scannapieco. 2001. "Can Valid Estimates Be High Estimates?" *Social Service Review* 75: 159–66.

Bolton, Charles D. 1972. "Alienation and Action: A Study of Peace Group Members." *American Journal of Sociology* 78: 537–61.

Bonacich, Edna. 1976. "Advanced Capitalism and Black/White Relations in the United States: A Split Labor Market Interpretation." *American Sociological Review* 41: 34–51.

———. 1975. "Abolition, the Extension of Slavery, and the Position of Free Blacks: A Study of Split Labor Markets in the United States, 1830–1863." *American Journal of Sociology* 81: 601–28.

———. 1972. "A Theory of Ethnic Antagonism: The Split Labor Market." *American Sociological Review* 37: 547–59.

Bonilla-Silva, Eduardo, and Tyrone A. Forman. 2000. "'I'm Not a Racist, But…': Mapping White Students' Racial Ideology in the U.S.A." *Discourse and Society* 11: 51–86.

Bonner, Raymond, and Ford Fessenden. 2000. "States with No Death Penalty Share Lower Homicide Rates." *The New York Times* (September 22). Also available on http://www.nytimes.com/2000/09/22/national/22DEAT.html.

Boocock, Sarene Spence. 1978. "The Social Organization of the Classroom." Pp. 1–28 in Ralph H. Turner, James Coleman, and Renee C. Fox (eds.), *Annual Review of Sociology.* 1978. Palo Alto, CA: Annual Reviews.

Booth, Alan. 1991. Presidential Address at annual meetings of the Midwest Sociological Society, Des Moines, IA, April 11–14.

———. 1976. *Urban Crowding and Its Consequences.* New York: Praeger.

Booth, Alan, David R. Johnson, and John N. Edwards. 1980. "In Pursuit of Pathology: The Effects of Human Crowding." *American Sociological Review* 45: 873–78.

Borjas, George J., Jeffrey Grogger, and Gordon H. Hanson. 2006. "Immigration and African American Employment Opportunities: The Responses of Wages, Employment, and Incarceration to Labor Supply Shocks." *National Bureau of Economic Research Working Paper 12518.* http://www.nber.org/papers/w12518.

Bornschier, Volker, and Christopher Chase-Dunn. 1985. *Transnational Corporations and Underdevelopment.* New York: Praeger.

Boserup, Ester. 1970. *Woman's Role in Economic Development.* London: Allen and Unwin.

Boskin, Joseph. 1965. "Race Relations in Seventeenth-Century America: The Problem of the Origin of Negro Slavery." *Sociology and Social Research* 49: 446–55.

Boswell, Terry. 1989. "Colonial Empires and the Capitalist World-System. A Time Series Analysis of Colonization, 1640–1960." *American Sociological Review* 54(2): 180–96.

Bourdieu, Pierre. 1966. "L'école Conservatrice: Les Inegalités Devant L'école et Devant la Culture." *Revue Francaise de Sociologie* 7: 325–47.

Bourdieu, Pierre, and Jean Claude Passeron. 1977. *Reproduction in Education, Society, and Culture.* Beverly Hills, CA: Sage Publications. (Originally published in French in 1970.).

Bourne, Larry S., and James W. Simmons (eds.). 1978. *Systems of Cities.* New York: Oxford University Press.

Bouvier, Leon F. 1980. "America's Baby Boom Generation: The Fateful Bulge." *Population Bulletin* 35(1).

Bouvier, Leon F., and Carol J. DeVita. 1991. "The Baby Boom—Entering Midlife." *Population Bulletin* 46(3).

Bouvier, Leon F., and Robert W. Gardner. 1986. "Immigration to the United States: The Unfinished Story." *Population Bulletin* 41(4).

Bowen, Howard R. 1977. *Investment in Learning: The Individual and Social Value of American Higher Education.* San Francisco: Jossey-Bass.

Bowen, William G., and Derk Curtis Bok. 1998. *The Shape of the River: Long-Term Consequences of Considering Race in College and University Admissions.* Princeton, NJ: Princeton University Press.

Bowers, William J., and Glenn L. Pierce. 1975. "The Illusion of Deterrence in Isaac Ehrlich's Research on Capital Punishment." *Yale Law Journal* 85: 187–207.

Bowles, Samuel, and Herbert Gintis. 1976. *Schooling in Capitalist America.* New York: Basic Books.

Bowles, Samuel, David M. Gordon, and Thomas E. Weisskopf. 1983. *Beyond the Waste Land: A Democratic Alternative to Economic Decline.* Garden City, NY: Anchor-Doubleday.

Boyer, Ernest L. 1987. *The College Experience in America.* New York: Harper & Row.

Bowman, Lee, and Guido H. Stempel, III. 1999. Americans in HMO Plan Less Satisfied with Health Coverage, Poll Finds. Nando Media, http://www.calnurse.org/cna/new2/ndt111599.html.

Bradbury, Katherine L., Anthony Downs, and Kenneth A. Small. 1982. *Urban Decline and the Future of American Cities.* Washington, DC: Brookings Institution.

Braddock, Jomills Henry, II. 1987. "Segregated High School Experiences and Black Students' College and Major Field Choices." Paper presented at the National Conference on School Desegregation, Chicago.

———. 1985. "School Desegregation and Black Assimilation." *Journal of Social Issues* 11(3): 8–22.

Braddock, Jomills Henry, II, Marvin P. Dawkins, and W. Trent. 1994. "Why Desegregate? The Effect of School Composition on Adult Occupational Desegregation of African Americans, Whites, and Hispanics." *International Journal of Contemporary Sociology* 31: 109–19.

Bradley, Ben S., and Susan K. Gobbart. 1989. "Determinants of Gender-Typed Play in Toddlers." *Journal of Genetic Psychology* 150: 453–55.

Bradley, Bill. 1990. "Corporations Pay More of Profits in Taxes." *The New York Times* (March 26): A16.

Bradshaw, Del, and Richard B. McKenzie. 1989. "Tax Reform Misses Most Taxpayers." *Christian Science Monitor* (January 31): 9.

Bradshaw, York. 1987. "Urbanization and Underdevelopment: A Global Study of Modernization, Urban Bias, and Economic Dependency." *American Sociological Review* 52: 224–39.

Braithwaite, John. 1979. *Inequality, Crime and Public Policy.* London: Routledge and Kegan Paul.

Bramlett, Matthew D., and William D. Mosher. 2001. "First Marriage Dissolution, Divorce, and Remarriage: United States." *Advance Data* 323 (May 31). Centers for Disease Control.

Brayer, Menachem M. 1986. *The Jewish Woman in Rabbinic Literature: A Psychosocial Perspective.* Hoboken, NJ: Ktav Publishing House.

Breault, K. D. 1988. "Beyond the Quick and Dirty: Problems Associated with Analyses Based on Small Samples of Large Aggregates: Reply to Girard." *American Journal of Sociology* 93(6): 1479–86.

———. 1986. "Suicide in America: A Test of Durkheim's Theory of Religion and Family Integration." *American Journal of Sociology* 92(3): 628–56.

Breedlove, William L., and Patrick D. Nolan. 1988. "International Stratification and Inequality 1960–1980." *International Journal of Contemporary Sociology* 25(3–4): 1005–1123.

Brenner, Robert. 1977. "The Origins of Capitalist Development: A Critique of Neo-Smithian Marxism." *New Left Review* 104: 25–93.

Brescia, William, and Jim C. Fortune. 1989. "Standardized Testing of American Indian Students." *College Student Journal* 23(2): 98–104.

Brewster, Karin I. 1994. "Race Differences in Sexual Activity Among Adolescent Women: The Role of Neighborhood Social Characteristics." *American Sociological Review* 59: 408–24.

Bridges, William P., and Robert L. Nelson. 1989. "Markets in Hierarchies: Organizational and Market Influences on Gender Inequality in a State Pay System." *American Journal of Sociology* 95: 616–58.

Brinkhoff, Thomas. 2001. *City Population.* http://www.citypopulation.de/.

Brischetto, Robert, and Tomas Arciniega. 1973. "Examining the Examiner: A Look at Educators' Perspectives on the Chicano Student." In Rudolph O. de la Garza, Z. Anthony Kruzezewski, and Tomas A. Arciniega (eds.), *Chicanos and Native Americans: The Territorial Minorities.* Englewood Cliffs, NJ: Prentice Hall.

British Broadcasting Corporation (BBC). 2009. "World Prison Populations: UK and Rest of World." http://news.bbc.co.uk/2/shared/spl/hi/uk/06/prisons/html/nn2page1.stm (Downloaded October 26, 2009).

Brooks, Clem. 2000. "Civil Rights Liberalism and the Suppression of a Republican Political Realignment in the United States, 1972 to 1996." *American Sociological Review* 65: 483–505.

Brooks-Gunn, Jeanne, Greg J. Duncan, Pamela Kato Klebanov, and Naomi Sealand. 1993. "Do Neighborhoods Influence Child and Adolescent Development?" *American Journal of Sociology* 99: 353–95.

Broom, Leonard, and Norval D. Glenn. 1969. "The Occupations and Income of Black Americans." In Norval D. Glenn and Charles M. Bonjean (eds.), *Blacks in the United States.* San Francisco: Chandler.

Brophy, Jere E. 1983. "Research on the Self-Fulfilling Prophecy and Teacher Expectations." *Journal of Educational Psychology* 75: 631–61.

Brophy, Jere E., and Thomas Good. 1974. *Teacher-Student Relationships.* New York: Holt, Rinehart and Winston.

Brophy-Bearmann, Brian, and John Conybeare. 1994. "Retaliating Against Terrorism: Rational Expectations and the Optimality of Rules Versus Discretion." *American Journal of Political Science* 38: 196–210.

Brouthers, Lance Eliot, John P. McCray, and Timothy J. Wilkinson. 1999. "Maquiladoras: Entrepreneurial Experimentation to Global Competitiveness." *Business Horizons* (March–April). Also available on http://www.findarticles.com/cf_0/m1038/2_42/54370814/print.jhtml.

Broverman, Inge K., S. R. Vogel, D. M. Broverman, F. E. Clarkson, and P. S. Rosenkrantz. 1972. "Sex-Role Stereotypes: A Current Appraisal." *Journal of Social Issues* 28: 59–78.

Brown, Bernard. 1985. "Head Start: How Research Changed Public Policy." *Young Children* 40: 9–13.

———. 1978. *Found: Long-Term Gains from Early Intervention.* Boulder, CO: Westview.

Brown, David. 2008. "Life Expectancy Hits Record High in U.S." *Washington Post,* Thursday June 12. http://www.washingtonpost.com/wp-dyn/content/article/2008/06/11/AR2008061101570.html.

Brown, Lawrence L., Alan L. Ginsberg, J. Neil Killalea, and Esther O. Tron. 1978. "School Finance Reform in the Seventies: Achievements and Failures." Pp. 57–110 in Esther O. Tron (ed.), *Selected Papers in School Finance.* Washington, DC: U.S. Department of Health, Education, and Welfare.

Brown, P., and H. Lauder. 1991. "Education, Economy, and Social Change." *International Studies in Sociology of Education* 1: 3–23.

Brownstein, Ronald. 1990. "On Election Day Only a Little over One-third of the 186 Million Americans Eligible to Vote Bothered to Do So." *Los Angeles Times* (November 21): Part A.

Browne, Angela. 1987. *When Battered Women Kill.* New York: Macmillan.

Browne, Angela, and Kirk R. Williams. 1987. "Gender-Specific Effects on Patterns of Homicide Perpetration." Paper presented at the annual meeting of the American Psychological Association.

Brozan, Nadine. 1980. "The Sandwich Generation." In Eleanor Goldstein (ed.), *Aging. Social Issues Series,* Article 52.

Bruce, Steve. 2001. *Fundamentalism,* Oxford, England: Polity Press.

———. 1988. *The Rise and Fall of the New Christian Right: Conservative Protestant Politics in America, 1978–1988.* Oxford, England: Clarendon Press/Oxford University Press.

Bruce-Briggs, B. 1979. "An Introduction to the Idea of the New Class." Pp. 1–18 in B. Bruce-Briggs (ed.), *The New Class?* New Brunswick, NJ: Transaction Books.

Bruen, Brian, and John Holahan. 2001. "Medicaid Spending Growth Remained Modest in 1998, But Likely Headed Upward." Kaiser Commission Medicaid and the Uninsured, Issue Papers. Washington, DC: Kaiser Commission. http://newfederalism.urban.org/pdf/medicaid-spending.pdf.

Brunvand, Jan Harold. 1986. *The Study of American Folklore.* New York: Norton.

———. 1984. *The Choking Doberman and Other "New" Urban Legends.* New York: Norton.

———. 1981. *The Vanishing Hitchhiker: American Urban Legends and Their Meanings.* New York: Norton.

Brus, Wlodzimierz, and Kazimierz Laski. 1989. *From Marx to Market: Socialism in Search of an Economic System.* New York: Oxford University Press.

Bryan, James H., and Nancy H. Walbek. 1970a. "Preaching and Practicing Self-Sacrifice: Children's Actions and Reactions." *Child Development* 41: 329–53.

———. 1970b. "The Impact of Words and Deeds Concerning Altruism Upon Children." *Child Development* 41: 747–57.

Buckley, Walter. 1967. *Sociology and Modern Systems Theory.* Englewood Cliffs, NJ: Prentice Hall.

Buggle, Franz, Dorothee Bister, Gisela Nohe, Wolfgang Schnieder, and Karl Uhmann. 2000. "Are Atheists More Depressed than Religious People?" *Free Inquiry* 20: 50–54.

Bumpass, Larry L. 1990. "What's Happening to the Family?" *Demography* 27: 483–98.

Bumpass, Larry, and James Sweet. 1988. "Preliminary Evidence on Cohabitation." Paper presented to the Population Association, New Orleans, LA.

———. 1984. "Some Characteristics of Children's Second Families." *American Journal of Sociology* 90: 608–23.

———. 1972. "Differentials in Marital Instability: 1970." *American Sociological Review* 37: 754–66.

Bumpass, Larry L., James A. Sweet, and Andrew Cherlin. 1991. "The Role of Cohabitation in Declining Rates of Marriage." *Journal of Marriage and the Family* 53: 913–27.

Burch, Philip, Jr. 1980–1981. *Elites in American History,* Vols. 1–3. New York: Holmes and Meier.

Burd, Stephen. 2001. "Students Don't Realize the Extent of Their Debt, Report Warns." *Chronicle of Higher Education* (April 6).

———. 2001b. "Lack of Need-Based Financial Aid Still Impedes Access to College for Low Income Students, Report Finds." *Chronicle of Higher Education* (March 2).

Burda, David. 1996. "ACHE Survey Response Spurs Expedited Sexual Harassment." *Modern Healthcare* 26, 42: 2–5.

Bureau of Justice Statistics. 2009. *Crime and Victims Statistics.* http://www.ojp.usdoj.gov/bjs/cvict.htm (Downloaded October 26, 2009).

———. 2001a. *Sourcebook of Criminal Justice Statistics* online—Characteristics and Distribution of People Arrested. http://www.albany.edu/sourcebook/1995/toc_4.html.

———. 2001b. Criminal Victimization in the United States—Statistical Tables. http://www.ojp.usdoj.gov/bjs/abstract/cvusst.htm.

———. 1998. "Prisoners in 1998." *Justice Research and Statistics Associates, Crime and Justice Atlas.* Office of Justice Programs, National Institute of Justice, U.S. Department of Justice (June), p. 134.

Bureau of the Census. 2009. *Statistical Abstract, 2009.* Washington, DC: US Government Printing Office.

———. 2008. *Statistical Abstract, 2008.* Washington, DC: US Government Printing Office.

Bureau of Labor Statistics. 2009. Labor Force Statistics from the Current Population Survey. http://www.bls.gov/cps/prev_yrs.htm.

Burger, Chester. 1964. *Survival in the Executive Jungle.* New York: Macmillan.

Burgess, Ernest W. 1925. "The Growth of the City." Pp. 47–62 in Robert E. Park and Ernest W. Burgess (eds.), *The City.* Chicago: University of Chicago Press.

Burgess, Giles H. 1989. *Industrial Organization.* Englewood Cliffs, NJ: Prentice Hall.

Burke, R. J., and C. A. McKeen. 1995. "Proportion of Men Employees in Organisations and the Experiences of Female Managers and Professionals." *Equal Opportunities International* 14(1,2): 27–36.

Burnham, L. 2001. "Welfare Reform, Family Hardship, and Women of Color." *Annals of the American Academy of Political and Social Science* 577: 38–48.

Burnham, Walter Dean. 1987. "The Turnout Problem." Pp. 97–133 in

A. James Reichley (ed.), *Elections American Style*. Washington, DC: Brookings Institution.

Burrowes, R., and B. Spector. 1973. "The Strength and Direction of Relationships Between Domestic and External Conflict and Cooperation: Syria, 1961–67." Pp. 294–324 in J. Wilkenfield (ed.), *Conflict Behavior and Linkage Politics*. New York: McKay.

Burstein, Paul. 1981. "The Sociology of Democratic Politics and Government." Pp. 291–319 in Ralph H. Turner and James F. Short, Jr. (eds.), *Annual Review of Sociology*, Vol. 7. Palo Alto, CA: Annual Reviews.

Burt, Martha. 1996. *Practical Methods for Counting Homeless People: A Manual for States and Local Jurisdictions*, 2nd ed. Washington, DC: The Urban Institute.

Burt, Martha, and Barbara Cohen. 1989. *America's Homeless: Numbers, Characteristics, and Programs that Serve Them*. Washington, DC: The Urban Institute.

Burt, Ronald. 1983. *Corporate Profits and Cooptation: Networks of Market Constraints and Directorate Ties in the American Economy*. New York: Academic Press.

Burtless, Gary. 1990. "Introduction and Summary." Pp. 1–30 in Gary Burtless (ed.), *A Future of Lousy Jobs?* Washington, DC: Brookings Institution.

———. 1986. "Public Spending for the Poor: Trends, Prospects, and Economic Limits." Pp. 18–49 in Sheldon H. Danziger and Daniel H. Weinberg (eds.), *Fighting Poverty: What Works and What Doesn't*. Cambridge, MA: Harvard University Press.

Business Week. 1999. "So Who Wants to Retire?" *Business Week* (November 8): 8.

Butler, Jon. 1990. *Awash in a Sea of Faith: Christianizing the American People*. Cambridge, MA: Harvard University Press.

Byrne, John A., with Lori Bongiomo. 1995. "CEO Pay: Ready for Takeoff." *Business Week* (April 24).

Caldwell, John. 1982. *Theory of Fertility Decline*. New York: Academic Press.

Calhoun, John C. 1962. "Population Density and Social Pathology." *Scientific American* 206: 139–48.

Callahan, Raymond E. 1962. *Education and the Cult of Efficiency: A Study of the Forces that Have Shaped the Administration of Public Schools*. Chicago: University of Chicago Press.

Callas, Dennis. 1993. "Differences in Mathematics Achievement Between Males and Females." *Community College Review* 21(3): 62–68.

Campbell, Angus, Philip E. Converse, and Willard L. Rogers. 1976. *The Quality of Life in America*. New York: Russell Sage Foundation.

Campbell, Angus, and Howard Schuman. 1968. "Racial Attitudes in Fifteen American Cities." Pp. 1–67 in *Supplemental Studies for the National Advisory Commission on Civil Disorders*. Washington, DC: U.S. Government Printing Office.

Campbell, Emily. 1990. "Television Violence: Social Science vs. the Law." *Loyola Entertainment Law Journal*.

Campbell, James R., and Jeffrey S. Beaudry. 1998. "Gender Gap Linked to Socialization for High-Achieving Senior Mathematics Students." *Journal of Educational Research* 91: 140–47.

Campbell, P. B. 1992. *Math, Science, and Your Daughter: What Can Parents Do?* Newton, MA: WEEA Publishing Center.

Campbell, Paul. 1997. Population Projections: States, 1995–2025. Current Population Reports: Population Projections. Report No. P25-1131. Washington, DC: U.S. Census Bureau. Also available on http://www.census.gov/prod/2/pop/p25/p25-1131.pdf.

Candland, Douglas Keith. 1995. *Feral Children and Clever Animals: Reflections on Human Nature*. New York and Oxford, England: Oxford University Press.

Canner, Glenn B., Stuart A. Gabriel, and J. Michael Woolley. 1991. "Race, Default Risk, and Mortgage Lending: A Study of the FHA and Conventional Loan Markets." *Southern Economic Journal* 58: 249–61.

Cantril, Hadley. 1940. *The Invasion from Mars*. Princeton, NJ: Princeton University Press.

Carden, M. L. 1978. "The Proliferation of a Social Movement." *Research in Social Movements, Conflict, and Change* 1: 179–96.

Carlson, Darren K. 2001. "Career Advice from Americans on 'Take Our Daughters to Work Day.'" The Gallup Organization: Poll Releases, April 26, 2001. http://www.gallup.com/poll/releases/pr010426.asp.

Carmichael, Stokeley, and Charles V. Hamilton. 1967. *Black Power: The Politics of Liberation in America*. New York: Vintage.

Carnevale, Dan. 1999. "Enrollment of Minority Freshmen Nears Pre-Hopwood Levels at U. of Texas at Austin." *Chronicle of Higher Education* (September 3).

Carpendale, Jeremy I., and Dennis L. Krebs. 1992. "Situational Variation in Moral Judgment: In a Stage or on a Stage?" *Journal of Youth and Adolescence* 21: 203–24.

Carpenter, Judi. 1987. Trends in Bachelor's and Higher Degrees, 1975–1985. *Center for Education Statistics Report*. Washington, DC: U.S. Government Printing Office.

Carter, Jason D., Judith A. Hall, Dana R. Carney, and Janelle C. Rosip. 2006. "Individual Differences in the Acceptance of Stereotyping." *Journal of Research in Personality* 40(6): 1103–1118.

Carter, Thomas P., and R. D. Segura. 1979. *Mexican Americans in School: A Decade of Change*. New York: College Entrance Examination Board.

Casper, Lynne, Sara S. McLanahan, and Irwin Garfinkel. 1994. "The Gender-Poverty Gap: What We Can Learn from Other Countries." *American Sociological Review* 59: 594–605.

Castells, Manuel. 1985. "High Technology, Economic Restructuring, and the Urban-Regional Process in the United States." Pp. 11–40 in Manuel Castells (ed.), *High Technology, Space, and Society*. Beverly Hills, CA: Sage.

———. 1977. *The Urban Question: A Marxist Approach* (Alan Sheridan, trans.). Cambridge, MA: MIT Press. (Originally published in Spanish, 1972.).

Castillo, Connie. 1996. Personal communication, American Sociological Association, Executive Office, November 7.

Catalyst. 2008. "2008 Catalyst Census of Women Board Directors of the Fortune 500." http://www.catalyst.org/publication/282/2008-catalyst-census-of-women-board-directors-of-the-fortune-500 (Downloaded October 22, 2009).

———. 2001. "Infobrief: Women CEOs." http://www.catalystwomen.org/press/infobriefs/infobrief2.html.

———. 1998. *The 1998 Catalyst Census of Women Board Directors of the Fortune 500*. New York: Catalyst.

Catania J. A., J. Canchola, D. Binson, M. M. Dolcini, J. P. Paul, L. Fisher, K. H. Choi, L. Pollack, J. Chang, W. L. Yarber, J. R. Heiman, and T. Coates. 2001. "National Trends in Condom Use Among At-Risk Heterosexuals in the United States." *Journal of Acquired Immune Deficiency Syndromes* 27(2): 176–82.

Catania, J., T. J. Coates, R. Stall, L. Bye, S. Kegeles, F. Capell, J. Henne, L. McKusick, S. Morin, H. Turner, and L. Pollack. 1991. "Changes in Condom Use Among Homosexual Men in San Francisco." *Health Psychology* 10: 190–99.

Cavender, Gray, Lisa Bond-Maupin, and Nancy C. Jurik. 1999. "The Construction of Gender in Reality Crime TV." *Gender & Society* 13 (5): 643–64.

Celingo, Jeffrey. 2000. "U. of California Sees Increase in Minority Applicants Admitted." *Chronicle of Higher Education*, April 14.

Celis, William, III. 1991. "Agony on Campus: What Is Rape? A Special Report: Students Trying to Draw Line Between Sex and an Assault." *The New York Times* (January 2): A1, B8.

Cell, John W. 1982. *The Highest Stage of White Supremacy: The Origins of Segregation in South Africa and the American South*. Cambridge, England: Cambridge University Press.

Center for the Analysis of Women in Politics. 2000. *CAWP Fact Sheet: Women in the U.S. Congress, 2000*. New Brunswick, NJ: Center for the Analysis of Women in Politics, Rutgers, The State University.

Centers for Disease Control. 2001a. Frequently Asked Questions (FAQs) About HIV and AIDS. http://www.cdcnpin.org/hiv/faq/virus.htm.

———. 2001b. Basic Statistics—Cumulative AIDS Cases. http://www.cdc.gov/hiv/stats/cumulati.htm.

———. 2001c. Basic Statistics—Exposure Categories. http://www.cdc.gov/hiv/stats/exposure.htm.

———. 2001d. HIV/AIDS Among Hispanics in the United States. http://www.cdc.gov/hiv/pubs/facts/hispanic.htm.

———. 2001e. U.S. HIV and AIDS cases reported through December 2000. Year-End edition, Vol. 12, No. 2. http://www.cdc.gov/hiv/stats/hasr1202.htm.

———. 2000a. U.S. HIV and AIDS cases reported through June 2000.

AIDS Surveillance Reports, Midyear edition, Vol. 12, No. 1. http://www.cdc.gov/hiv/stats/hasr1201.htm.

———. 2000b. HIV/AIDS Among African Americans. http://www.cdc.gov/hiv/pubs/facts/afam.htm.

———. 1996. AIDS Surveillance. http://www.cdc.gov.

———. 1992. HIV/AIDS Surveillance: U.S. AIDS Cases Reported Through February, 1992. Atlanta, GA: Centers for Disease Control.

———. 1991. HIV/AIDS Surveillance Report (January): 1–22.

Center on Education and the Workforce. 2010. "Help Wanted: Projections of Jobs and Education Requirements Through 2018." The Georgetown University Center on Education and the Workforce. http://www9.georgetown.edu/grad/gppi/hpi/cew/pdfs/FullReport.pdf.

Central Intelligence Agency. 2009. World Factbook: Country Comparisons. https://www.cia.gov/library/publications/the-world-factbook/rankorder/rankorderguide.html.

———. 2000. World Factbook 2000: Russia. http://www.cia.gov/cia/publications/factbook/geos/rs.html.

———. 1995. Russia Page. http://www.ic.gov/94/fact/country/200.html.

Century Foundation. 1995a. What's Wrong with Medicaid? http://www.tcf.org/Publications/Basics/medicaid/Whats_Wrong.html.

———. 1995b. What's Right with Medicaid? http://www.tcf.org/Publications/Basics/medicaid/Whats_Right.html.

Chafetz, Janet Saltzman. 1990. *Gender Equity: A Theory of Stability and Change.* Newbury Park, CA: Sage.

Chalfant, H. Paul, Robert E. Beckley, and C. Eddie Palmer. 1987. *Religion in Contemporary Society,* 2nd ed. Palo Alto, CA: Mayfield.

Chamberlain, Kerry, and Sheryl Zika. 1992. "Religiosity, Meaning in Life, and Psychological Well-Being." Pp. 138–48 in John F. Schumaker (ed.), *Religion and Mental Health.* New York: Oxford University Press.

Chambliss, William J. 1984. "The Saints and the Roughnecks." In William J. Chambliss (ed.), *Criminal Law in Action,* New York: Wiley.

———. 1969. *Crime and the Legal Process.* New York: McGraw Hill.

———. 1967. "Types of Deviance and the Effectiveness of Legal Sanctions." *Wisconsin Law Review* (Summer): 703–19.

———. 1964. "A Sociological Analysis of the Law of Vagrancy." *Social Problems* 12: 46–67.

Chambliss, William, and Milton Mankoff (eds.) 1976. *Whose Law What Order?: A Conflict Approach to Criminology.* New York: Wiley.

Chandler, Tertius, and Gerald Fox. 1974. *3000 Years of Urban Growth.* New York: Academic Press.

Charles, Camille Zubrinsky. 2003. "The Dynamics of Racial Segregation." *Annual Review of Sociology* 29: 167–207.

Charon, Joel. 2001. *Symbolic Interactionism: An Introduction, An Interpretation, An Integration,* 7th ed. Upper Saddle River, NJ: Prentice Hall.

———. 1992. *Ten Questions: A Sociological Perspective.* Belmont, CA: Wadsworth.

———. 1989. *Symbolic Interactionism: An Introduction, An Interpretation, An Integration,* 3rd ed. Englewood Cliffs, NJ: Prentice Hall.

Chase-Dunn, Christopher. 1989. *Global Formation; Structures of the World-Economy.* London: Basil Blackwell.

Chase-Dunn, Christopher, and Thomas D. Hall. 1997. *Rise and Demise: Comparing World Systems.* Boulder, CO: Westview Press.

Chase-Dunn, Christopher, Yukio Kawano, and Benjamin D. Brewer. 2000. "Trade Globalization Since 1795: Waves of Integration in the World-System." *American Sociological Review* 65: 77–95.

Chatters, Linda, and Robert Joseph Taylor. 1998. "Religious Involvement Among African Americans." *African American Research Perspectives* 4, 1. Also available on http://www.isr.umich.edu/rcgd/prba/persp/spring1998/lchatters.pdf.

Chaves, Mark. 1993. "Intra-Organizational Power and Internal Secularization in Protestant Denominations." *American Journal of Sociology* 99: 1–48.

Chaves, Mark. 2001. "Sexual Behavior of People Infected with HIV Alarms Researchers." Associated Press Report. http://www.drkoop.com/news/stories/2001/feb/ap/19_hivsex.html.

Chavez, Adolpho. 1991. "A Fair Share for All." *World Health* (July–August): 9–10.

Cherlin, Andrew. 1981. *Marriage, Divorce, Remarriage.* Cambridge. MA: Harvard University Press.

Chesler, Mark A., and William M. Cave. 1981. *A Sociology of Education: Access to Power and Privilege.* New York: Macmillan.

Chesney-Lind, Meda. 1996. "Girls' Crime and Woman's Place: Toward a Feminist Model of Female Delinquency." Pp. 166–80 in Henry N. Pontell (ed.), *Social Deviance: Readings in Theory and Research,* 2nd ed. Upper Saddle River, NJ: Prentice Hall.

Chicago Tribune. 1991. "Study Links Cancer in Kids, Electrical Appliances." *Chicago Tribune* (February 10): Sec. 1, 24.

Chiet, F. F. 1975. *The Useful Arts and the Liberal Tradition.* New York: McGraw-Hill.

Childe, V. Gordon. 1950. "The Urban Revolution." *Town Planning Review* 21: 3–17.

———. 1946. *What Happened in History.* London: Penguin.

China Daily. 2005. "China's Divorce Rate Up 21.4 Percent in 2004." http://www.chinadaily.com.cn/english/doc/2005-03/01/content_420456.htm (Downloaded October 29, 2009).

Chira, Susan. 1992. "Furor over 'Choice.'" *The New York Times* (October 28): 10.

———. 1991a. "The Big Test: How to Translate the Talk About School Reform into Action?" *The New York Times* (March 24): E1, 4.

———. 1991b. "Exams in Other Nations Studied in U.S. for Ideas." *The New York Times* (May 20): A12.

Chiricos, Theodore G., and Gordon P. Waldo. 1970. "Punishment and Crime: An Examination of Some Empirical Evidence." *Social Problems* XVIII: 1–18.

Chirot, Daniel. 1986. *Social Change in the Modern Era.* San Diego, CA: Harcourt Brace Jovanovich.

———. 1981. "Changing Fashions in the Study of the Social Causes of Economic and Political Change." Pp. 259–82 in James Short (ed.), *The State of Sociology.* Beverly Hills, CA: Sage.

Chirot, Daniel, and Thomas D. Hall. 1982. "World System Theory." *Annual Review of Sociology* 8: 81–106.

Choldin, Harvey M. 1985. *Cities and Suburbs: An Introduction to Urban Sociology.* New York. McGraw-Hill.

———. 1980. "Social Participation in Suburban Apartment Enclaves." Chapter 8 in Clare Underson and Valerie Karn (eds.), *The Consumer Experience of Housing.* West Mead, England: Gower.

———. 1978. "Urban Density and Pathology." Pp. 91–112 in Alex Inkeles et al. (eds.), *Annual Review of Sociology,* Vol 4. Palo Alto, CA: Annual Reviews.

Christensen, H. T. 1960. "Cultural Relativism and Premarital Sex Norms." *American Sociological Review* 25: 31–39.

Christiansen, Harold T., and C. F. Gregg. 1970. "Changing Sex Norms in America and Scandinavia." *Journal of Marriage and the Family* 32: 616–27.

Chronicle of Higher Education. 2009. "At Transfer Time, Thousands of California Students Hit a Dead End." October 5. http://chronicle.com/article/At-Transfer-Time-Thousands-of/48678/.

———. 2001a. "College Enrollment by Age of Students, 2001." http://www.chronicle.com/weekly/almanac/2001/nation/0102001.htm.

———. 2001b. Projections of College Enrollment, Degrees Conferred, and High-School Graduates, 2000 to 2011. http://chronicle.com/weekly/almanac/2001/nation/0102201.htm.

———. 1996. Academe Today: Almanac: The Nation. http://www.chronicle.com/.

———. 1995. "The French Wait to Consider University Reform." February 17: A41.

Church of Norway. 1996. Church of Norway: Basics and Statistics. http://nettvik.no/kirkebakken/kirken/Engelsk/statistics-eng.html.

Church of Sweden. 1996. The Church of Sweden in Brief. http://www.svkyrkan.se/svk/eng/liturgy.htm#statistik.

Cicirelli, Victor G. 1983. "Adult Children and Their Elderly Parents." pp. 31–46 in Timothy H. Brubaker (ed.), *Family Relationships in Late Life.* Beverly Hills, CA: Sage.

Cicirelli, Victor G., J. W. Evans, and J. S. Schiller. 1969. *The Impact of Head Start: An Evaluation of the Effects of Head Start on Children's Cognitive and Affective Development,* Vols. 1 and 2. Athens, OH: Westinghouse Learning Corporation and Ohio University.

Cicourel, Aaron. 1974. *Theory and Method in a Study of Argentine Fertility.* New York: Free Press.

Cicourel, Aaron, and J. Kitsuse. 1963. *Educational Decision Makers*. Indianapolis, IN: Bobbs-Merrill.

Cipolla, Carlo N. 1965. *The Economic History of World Population*. Sussex: Harvester Press.

Clark, Burton. 1978. "Academic Differentiation in National Systems of Higher Education." *Comparative Education Review* 22: 242–58.

Clark, Candace. 1988 "Sickness and Social Control." Pp. 471–91 in Candace Clark and Howard Robboy (eds.), *Social Interaction: Readings in Sociology*, 3rd ed. New York: St. Martin's Press.

Clark, Daniel. 1985. *Post-Industrial America: A Geographic Perspective*. New York: Methuen.

Clark, John, and Aaron Wildavsky. 1992. *The Moral Collapse of Communism: Poland as a Cautionary Tale*. San Francisco: Institute for Contemporary Studies Press.

Clark, Kenneth. 1965. *Dark Ghetto: Dilemmas of Social Power*. New York: Harper & Row.

Clark, Margaret. 1970. *Health in the Mexican-American Culture: A Community Study*, 2nd ed. Berkeley: University of California Press.

Clarke, Lee. 2002. "Panic: Myth or Reality?" *Contexts* 1(3): 21–26.

Clarke-Stewart, Alison. 1987. "Predicting Child Development from Care Forms and Features: The Chicago Study." Pp. 21–41 in Deborah A. Phillips (ed.), *Quality in Child Care: What Does Research Tell?* Washington, DC: National Association for the Education of Young Children.

———. 1985. Quoted and cited in *The New York Times* (May 29): Sec. 3, 15.

Clausen, Dan, and Alan Neustadtl. 1989. "Interlocks, PACs, and Corporate Conservatism." *American Journal of Sociology* 94: 749–73.

Clausen, John A. 1979. "Mental Disorder." Pp. 97–112 in Howard E. Freeman, Sol Levine, and Leo G. Reeder (eds.), *Handbook of Medical Sociology*, 3rd ed. Englewood Cliffs, NJ: Prentice Hall.

Clausen, John S. 1991. "Adolescent Competence and the Shaping of the Life Course." *American Journal of Sociology* 96: 805–42.

Clawson, Dan. 1995. "From the Editor's Desk." *Contemporary Sociology* 24: ix.

Clay, Phillip. 1980. "The Rediscovery of City Neighborhoods: Reinvestment by Long-Time Residents and Newcomers." Pp. 13–26 in Shirley B. Laska and Daphne Spain (eds.), *Back to the City: Issues in Neighborhood Renovation*. New York: Pergamon.

Cleary, Paul D., David Mechanic, and James R. Greenley. 1982. "Sex Differences in Medical Care Utilization: An Empirical Investigation." *Journal of Health and Social Behavior* 23: 106–19.

Cleckley, Hervey. 1976. *The Mark of Sanity*. St. Louis, MO: Mosby.

Clelland, Donald A., and Ian Robertson. 1974. "Social Stratification." Pp. 194–221 in Dushkin Publishing Group (ed.), *The Study of Society*. Guilford, CT: Dushkin Publishing Group.

Clements, John. 1991. *Taylor's Encyclopedia of Government Officials, Federal and State*. Dallas, TX: Political Research.

———. 1987. *Taylor's Encyclopedia of Government Officials: Federal and State*, Vol. XI, 1987–1988. Dallas, TX: Political Research.

Clinard, Marshall B. 1974. *Sociology of Deviant Behavior*, 4th ed. New York: Holt, Rinehart and Winston.

Clinard, Marshall B., and Peter C. Yeager. 1980. *Corporate Crime*. New York: Free Press.

Clines, Francis X. 1986. "Chernobyl Shakes Reindeer Culture of Lapps." *The New York Times* (September 14): 1, 20.

Cloward, Richard A., and Lloyd E. Ohlin. 1960. *Delinquency and Opportunity: A Theory of Delinquent Gangs*. New York: Free Press.

Clymer, Adam. 1991. "For Civil Rights Bill, the Name's the Game." *The New York Times* (May 5): Sect. 4, E, 115.

———. 1983. "Poll Finds Americans Don't Know U.S. Positions on Central America." *The New York Times* (July 1): 1, 2.

CNN. 2010. Crime Stats Test Rationale Behind Arizona Immigration Law. Posted: 10:42 p.m. EDT April 29. http://www.cnn.com/2010/CRIME/04/29/arizona.immigration.crime/.

———. 2001a. Bush Tax Cut Won't Be Big Deal for Some. Posted: 2:03 p.m. EDT May 27. http://www.cnn.com/2001/ALLPOLITICS/05/27/tax.cut/index.html.

———. 2001b. $1.35 Trillion Tax Cut Becomes Law. Web posted at: 12:19 p.m. EDT July 7. http://www.cnn.com/2001/ALLPOLITICS/06/07/bush.taxes/index.html.

———. 2001c. "Who Owns What in Russia's Media?" April 18, Web posted at: 1152 GMT http://europe.cnn.com/2001/WORLD/europe/04/17/russia.media.structure/.

———. 2001d. Ashcroft Won't Name Detainees. Web posted at 5:05 PM EST November 26. http://www.cnn.com/2001/LAW/11/26/inv.ashcroft.detainees/index.html.

Coakley, Joane. 1972. "Attitudes of Guidance Counselors." Appendix E in *Report of the Massachusetts Governor's Commission on the Status of Women*. Boston: Massachusetts Governor's Commission.

Coale, Ansley J. 1974. "The History of the Human Population." *Scientific American* 231(3): 40–51.

———. 1973. "The Demographic Transition." Pp. 53–72 in *Proceedings of the International Population Conference*, Liege, Vol. 1.

Coale, Ansley J., and Edgar Hoover. 1958. *Population Growth and Economic Development in Low-Income Countries*. Princeton, NJ: Princeton University Press.

Coale, Ansley J., and Melvin Zelnick. 1963. *New Estimates of Fertility and Population in the United States*. Princeton, NJ: Princeton University Press.

Cockburn, Alexander. 1991. "Left Alive." *New Statesman and Society* 168(4): 12–13.

Cockerham, William C. 2000. *Medical Sociology*, 8th ed. Upper Saddle River, NJ: Prentice Hall.

———. 1992. *Medical Sociology*, 5th ed. Englewood Cliffs, NJ: Prentice Hall.

———. 1989. *Medical Sociology*, 4th ed. Englewood Cliffs, NJ: Prentice Hall.

———. 1988. "Medical Sociology." Pp. 575–99 in Neil J. Smelser (ed.), *Handbook of Sociology*. Newbury Park, CA: Sage.

———. 1981. *Sociology of Mental Disorder*. Englewood Cliffs, NJ: Prentice Hall.

Cockerham, William C., Guenther Lueschen, Gerhard Kunz, and Joe L. Spaeth. 1986. "Social Stratification and Self-Management of Health." *Journal of Health and Social Behavior* 27: 1–14.

Coe, Rodney M. 1978. *Sociology of Medicine*, 2nd ed. New York: McGraw Hill.

Cohen, Albert K. 1955. *Delinquent Boys: The Culture of the Gang*. New York: Free Press.

Cohen, Albert K., and Harold M. Hodges, Jr. 1963. "Characteristics of the Lower Blue Collar Class." *Social Problems* 10: 303–33.

Cohen, Fredric. 1995. "Prom Pictures: Principals Look at Detracking." *Educational Leadership* 52: 85–86.

———. 1993. "Getting off the Tracks." *Executive Educator* 15: 29–31.

Cohen, Lawrence E., and Kenneth C. Land. 1987. "Age Structure and Crime: Symmetry Versus Asymmetry and the Projection of Crime Rates Through the 1990s." *American Sociological Review* 52: 170–83.

Cohen, Phillip N., and Matt L. Huffman. 2007. "Working for the Woman? Female Managers and the Gender Wage Gap." *American Sociological Review* 72(5): 681–704.

Colasanto, Diane, and J. Shriver. 1989. "Middle-Aged Face Marital Crisis." *Gallup Report* 284 (May): 34–38.

Colby, Anne, Lawrence Kohlberg, John Gibbs, and Marcus Lieberman. 1983. "A Longitudinal Study of Moral Development." *Monographs of the Society for Research in Child Development* 48: 200.

Cole, Robert E. 1989. *Strategies for Learning: Small-Group Activities in American, Japanese, and Swedish Industry*. Berkeley: University of California Press.

———. 1979. *Work Mobility and Participation: A Comparative Study of American and Japanese Industry*. Berkeley: University of California Press.

Cole, Stephen, and Robert Lejeune. 1972. "Illness and the Legitimation of Failure." *American Sociological Review* (June): 347–56.

Coleman, James S. 1995. "Comment on Kuran and Collins." *American Journal of Sociology* 100: 1616–19.

———. 1961. *The Adolescent Society*. New York: Free Press.

Coleman, James S., Ernest Q. Campbell, Carol J. Hobson, James

McPartland, Alexander Mood, Frederick D. Weinfield, and Robert L. York. 1966. *Equality of Educational Opportunity.* Washington, DC: U.S. Government Printing Office.

Coleman, James S., Thomas Hoffer, and Sally Kilgore. 1982. *High School Achievement: Public, Catholic, and Private Schools Compared.* New York: Basic Books.

College Board. 1998. "Financial Aid Is Not Enough: Improving the Odds of College Success." *College Board Review* 185 (summer). Evanston, IL: College Board. http://www.collegeboard.org/policy/html/glad.html.

———. 1983. *Academic Preparation for College: What Students Need to Know.* New York: College Board.

College Entrance Examination Board. 1974. *College-Bound Seniors, 1973–74.* Evanston, IL: College Entrance Examination Board.

Collier, John. 1947. *The Indians of the Americas.* New York: Norton.

Collins, Patricia Hill. 2000. *Black Feminist Thought: Knowledge, Consciousness, and the Politics of Empowerment,* rev. 10th anniversary ed. New York: Routledge.

———. 1991. *Black Feminist Thought: Knowledge, Consciousness, and the Politics of Empowerment.* New York: Routledge.

Collins, Randall. 1995. "Prediction in Macrosociology: The Case of the Soviet Collapse." *American Journal of Sociology* 100: 1552–93.

———. 1994. *Four Sociological Traditions.* New York: Oxford University Press.

———. 1988. *Theoretical Sociology.* San Diego, CA: Harcourt Brace Jovanovich.

———. 1987. "Looking Forward or Looking Back? Reply to Denzin." *American Journal of Sociology* 93: 180–84.

———. 1986. *Weberian Sociological Theory.* Cambridge and New York: Cambridge University Press.

———. 1985a. *Sociology of Marriage and the Family: Gender, Love and Property.* Chicago. Nelson-Hall.

———. 1985b. *Three Sociological Traditions.* New York: Oxford University Press.

———. 1981. "On the Microfoundations of Macrosociology." *American Journal of Sociology* 86: 984–1014.

———. 1979. *The Credential Society.* New York: Academic Press.

———. 1974. *Conflict Sociology: Toward an Explanatory Science.* New York: Academic Press.

———. 1971a. "A Conflict Theory of Sexual Stratification." *Social Problems* 19: 3–12.

———. 1971b. "Functional and Conflict Theories of Educational Stratification." *American Sociological Review* 36: 1002–19.

Coltrane, Scott. 2000. "Research on Household Labor: Modeling and Measuring the Social Embeddedness of Routine Family Work." *Social Forces* 62(4): 1208–34.

Coltrane, Scott, and Michele Adams. 2008. *Gender and Families* (Gender Lens Series, 2nd Edition). Lanham, MD: Rowman & Littlefield.

Comhaire, Jean, and Werner J. Cahnman. 1959. *How Cities Grew: The Historical Sociology of Cities.* Madison, NJ: Florham Park Press.

Committee on the Budget, U.S. House of Representatives. 1976. *Working Papers on Major Budget and Program Issues in Selected Health Programs.* Washington, DC: U.S. Government Printing Office.

Commoner, Barry. 1982. "The Economic Meaning of Ecology." Pp. 290–96 in Jerome H. Skolnick and Elliott Currie (eds.), *Crisis in American Institutions,* 5th ed. Boston: Little, Brown.

Comstock, George, and Victor C. Strasburger. 1990. "Deceptive Appearances: Television Violence and Aggressive Behavior." *Journal of Adolescent Health Care* 11: 31–44.

Conant, James B. 1952. *Modern Science and Modern Man.* Garden City, NY: Doubleday.

Conforti, Joseph M. 1972. "Newark: Ghetto or City?" *Society* 9: 20–32.

Congressional Quarterly. 2008. "Profile of the 111th Congress." *Congressional Quarterly Today,* November 6th.

Conley, Dalton. 1999. *Being Black, Living in the Red: Race, Wealth, and Social Policy in America.* Berkeley: University of California Press.

Conot, Robert. 1967. *Rivers of Blood, Years of Darkness.* New York: Bantam Books.

Conrad, Joseph W., and Joseph W. Schneider. 1980. *Deviance and Medicalization: From Badness to Sickness.* St. Louis, MO: Mosby.

Conrad, Peter. 1975. "The Discovery of Hyperkinesis: Notes on the Medicalization of Deviant Behavior." *Social Problems* 23: 12–21.

Consortium for Longitudinal Studies. 1983. *As the Twig Is Bent: Lasting Effects of Preschool Programs.* Hillsdale, NJ: Erlbaum.

———. 1979. *Lasting Effects After Preschool Summary Report.* Washington, DC: U.S. Department of Health, Education, and Welfare, Human Services Administration for Children, Youth, and Families.

Consumers Union. 1999. "Eating More, Eating Out More." *Consumer Reports on Health* 11(10): 2.

Cook, Rhodes. 1993. "House Republicans Scored a Quiet Victory in '92." *Congressional Quarterly Weekly Report* 51(16) (April 17): 965–68.

Cooley, Charles Horton. 1964. *Human Nature and the Social Order.* New York: Schocken. (Originally published in 1902.).

———. 1929. *Social Organization.* New York: Scribner's. (Originally published in 1909.).

Coontz, Stephanie. 2000. "Historical Perspectives on Family Studies." *Journal of Marriage and the Family* 62: 283–98.

Cooper, J., and J. C. McGaugh. 1969. "Leadership: Integrating Principles of Social Psychology." In C. A. Gibb (ed.), *Leadership.* Baltimore, MD: Penguin.

Cooper, Judith, Jacqueline Holman, and Valerie Braithwaite. 1983. "Self-Esteem and Family Cohesion: The Child's Perspective and Adjustment." *Journal of Marriage and the Family* 45: 153–58.

Cooper, Robert. 1997. *Detracking in a Racially-Mixed Urban High School, Report 12.* Baltimore, MD: Center for Research on the Education of Students Placed at Risk.

Corsaro, William A., and Thomas A. Rizzo. 1990. "An Interpretive Approach to Childhood Socialization: Reply to Handel." *American Sociological Review* 55: 466–68.

———. 1988. "Discussione and Friendship: Socialization Processes in the Peer Culture of Italian Nursery School Children." *American Sociological Review* 53: 879–94.

Corzine, Jay, and Lin Huff-Corzine. 1989. "On Cultural Explanations of Southern Homicide: Comment on Dixon and Lizotte." *American Journal of Sociology* 95: 178–82.

Coser, Lewis A. 1977. *Masters of Sociological Thought: Ideas in Historical and Social Context,* 2nd ed. New York: Harcourt Brace Jovanovich.

———. 1956. *The Functions of Social Conflict.* Glencoe, IL: Free Press.

Coser, Rose Laub. 1986. "Cognitive Structure and the Use of Social Space." *Sociological Forum* 1: 1–26.

Coser, Rose Laub, and Lewis Coser. 1979. "Jonestown as a Perverse Utopia." *Dissent* (Spring): 158–63.

Council on Environmental Quality. 1984. *Environmental Quality, 1983. 14th Annual Report of the Council on Environmental Quality.* Washington, DC: Council on Environmental Quality.

———. 1980. *The Global Report to the President of the United States, Entering the 21st Century.* New York: Pergamon.

Cousins, Albert N., and Hans Nagpaul. 1979. *Urban Life: The Sociology of Cities and Urban Society.* New York: Wiley.

Cowell, Alan. 1986. "Three Blacks Reported Slain in South African Violence." *The New York Times* (July 29): Sect. 1, 2.

Cowgill, Donald O. 1974. "Aging of Populations and Societies." *Annals of the American Academy of Political and Social Science* 415: 1–18.

Cox, Brenda G., James T. Massey, Daniel J. O'Connor, and Kathryn Chandler. 1999. "Response Rates in RDD Telephone Surveys: Are They Increasing, Decreasing, or Remaining the Same?" Paper presented at International Conference on Survey Response, Portland, OR, October 28–31.

Cox, Harold G. 1993. *Later Life,* 3rd ed. Englewood Cliffs, NJ: Prentice Hall.

Cox, Oliver Cromwell. 1948. *Caste, Class, and Race.* Garden City, NY: Doubleday.

Crain, Robert L., and J. Strauss. 1985. *School Desegregation and Black Occupational Attainments: Results from a Long-Term Experiment* (Report 359). Baltimore, MD: Center for the Social Organization of Schools.

Crain, Robert L., and C. Weisman. 1972. *Discrimination, Personality, and Achievement: A Survey of Northern Blacks.* New York: Seminar.

Crane, Jonathan. 1991a. "Effects of Neighborhoods on Dropping Out of School and Teenage Childbearing." Pp. 299–320 in Christopher Jencks and Paul E. Peterson (eds.), *The Urban Underclass.* Washington, DC: Brookings Institution.

———. 1991b. "The Epidemic Theory of Ghettos and Neighborhood Effects on Dropping Out and Teenage Childbearing." *American Journal of Sociology* 96: 1226–59.

Crawford, R. 1981. "Individual Responsibility and Health Politics." Pp. 468–81 in Peter Conrad and Rochelle Kern (eds.), *The Sociology of Health and Illness: Critical Perspectives.* New York: St. Martin's Press.

Cressey, Donald R. 1969. *Theft of the Nation: The Structure and Operations of Organized Crime in America.* New York: Harper & Row.

Crews, Kimberly A., and Patricia Cancellier. 1988. *U.S. Population: Charting the Change.* Washington, DC: Population Reference Bureau.

Crites, Marsha S. 1989. "Child Development and Intergenerational Programming." *Journal of Children in Contemporary Society* 20(3–4): 33–43.

Crocker, Valery, and Diane Kalemba. 1999. The Incidence and Impact of Women's Experiences of Sexual Harassment in Canadian Workplaces. *Canadian Review of Sociology and Anthropology* 36(4): 541–59.

Croog, S. H. 1961. "Ethnic Origins, Education Level, and Responses to a Health Questionnaire." *Human Organization* 20(2): 65–69.

Crosby, Faye J. 1995. Remarks at Briefing for Congressional Staff Members and Journalists, Washington, DC, September.

Crouch, Julie L., and Joel S. Milner. 1993. "Effects of Child Neglect on Children. Special Issue: Child Neglect." *Criminal Justice and Behavior* 20: 49–65.

Crowley, Joan E. 1986. "Longitudinal Effects of Retirement on Men's Psychological and Physical Well-Being." Pp. 147–73 in Herbert S. Parnes et al. (eds.), *Retirement Among American Men.* Lexington, MA: Lexington Books, D. C. Heath.

Cuber, John F., and Peggy B. Harroff. 1965. *Sex and the Significant Americans.* New York: Penguin Books.

Culhane, Dennis et al. 1994. "Public Shelter Admission Rates in Philadelphia and New York City: Implications of Turnover for Sheltered Population Counts," *Housing Policy Debate* 5(2): 107–40.

Culp, Rex E., Ruth V. Watkins, Harriet Lawrence, Dana Letts et al. 1991. "Maltreated Children's Language and Speech Development: Abused, Neglected, and Abused and Neglected." *First Language* 11: 377–89.

Cumming, Elaine, and William F. Henry. 1961. *Growing Old: The Process of Disengagement.* New York: Basic Books.

Cummings, Milton C., and David Wise. 1981. *Democracy Under Pressure: An Introduction to the American Political System,* 4th ed. New York: Harcourt Brace Jovanovich.

Cummins, Jim. 1988. "Teachers Are Not Miracle Workers: Lloyd Dunn's Call for Hispanic Activism." *Hispanic Journal of Behavioral Sciences* 10: 263–72.

Cunningham, Frances C., and John W. Williamson. 1980. "How Does the Quality of Health Care in HMOs Compare to That in Other Settings?" *Group Health Journal* (Winter): 4–13.

Cunningham, Jean A., Stephen J. Dollinger, Madelyn Satz, and Nancy S. Rotter. 1991. "Personality Correlates of Prejudice Against AIDS Victims." *Bulletin of the Psychonomic Society* 29(2): 165–67.

Curran, Libby. 1980. "Science Education: Did She Drop Out or Was She Pushed?" Pp. 22–41 in Brighton Women and Science Group (eds.), *Alice Through the Microscope: The Power of Science over the Lives of Women.* London: Virago.

Currie, Elliott. 1997. "Market, Crime, and Community: Toward a Mid-Range Theory of Post-Industrial Violence." *Theoretical Criminology* 1(2): 147–72.

———. 1985. *Confronting Crime: An American Challenge.* New York: Pantheon.

Currie, Elliott, and Jerome H. Skolnick. 1988. *America's Problems: Social Issues and Public Policy,* 2nd ed. Glenview, IL: Scott, Foresman.

———. 1984. *America's Problems: Social Issues and Public Policy.* Glenview, IL: Scott, Foresman.

Curry, Timothy Jon. 1993. "A Little Pain Never Hurt Anyone: Athletic Career Socialization and the Normalization of Sports Injury." *Symbolic Interaction* 16: 273–90.

Curry, Timothy, and Lynn Shibut. 2000. "The Cost of the Savings and Loan Crisis: Truth and Consequences." *FDIC Banking Review* (December): 26–35. http://www.fdic.gov/bank/analytical/banking /2000dec/brv13n2_2.pdf (Downloaded October 27, 2009).

Curry, Timothy J., and Richard H. Strauss. 1994. "A Little Pain Never Hurt Anybody: A Photo-Essay on the Normalization of Sports Injuries." *Sociology of Sport Journal* 11: 195–208.

Curtiss, Susan. 1977. *Genie: A Linguistic Study of a Modern-Day "Wild Child."* New York: Academic Press.

Cutler, Blayne. 1988. "New-Victorian (Women's Attitudes Toward Sex)." *American Demographics* (June): 16–17.

Cuzzort, R. P. 1989. *Using Social Thought: The Nuclear Issue and Other Concerns.* Palo Alto, CA: Mayfield.

Dahl, Robert A. 1985. *A Preface to Economic Democracy.* Berkeley: University of California Press.

———. 1982. *Dilemmas of Pluralist Democracy: Autonomy vs. Control.* New Haven, CT: Yale University Press.

———. 1981. *Democracy in the United States,* 4th ed. Boston: Houghton Mifflin.

———. 1961. *Who Governs?* New Haven, CT: Yale University Press.

———. 1957. "The Concept of Power." *Behavioral Science* 2: 201–15.

Dahrendorf, Ralf. 1959. *Class and Class Conflict in Industrial Society.* Stanford, CA: Stanford University Press.

Dannefer, Dale. 1984. "Adult Development and Social Theory: A Reappraisal." *American Sociological Review* 49: 100–16.

Darden, Joe T. 1987. "Choosing Neighbors and Neighborhoods: The Role of Race in Housing Preference." Pp. 15–42 in Gary A. Tobin (ed.), *Divided Neighborhoods: Changing Patterns of Racial Segregation.* Sage Urban Affairs Annual Reviews, Vol. 32. Beverly Hills, CA: Sage.

Darling-Hammond, L. 1994. "National Standards and Assessments: Will They Improve Education?" *American Journal of Education* 102: 479–511.

———. 1990. "Instructional Policy into Practice: 'The Power of the Bottom Over the Top.'" *Educational Evaluation and Policy Analysis* 12: 339–47.

Dasgupta, Debjani. 1995. "Reframing Development: The Chipko Movement as a Postcolonial, Ecofeminist, Grassroots Social Movement." Masters thesis, Southern Illinois University at Edwardsville, Department of Sociology.

D'Augelli, Anthony R., and Scott L. Hershberger. 1993. "African American Undergraduates on a Predominantly White Campus: Academic Factors, Social Networks, and Campus Climate." *Journal of Negro Education* 62(1): 67–81.

Davies, James C. 1962. "Toward a Theory of Revolution." *American Sociological Review* 27: 5–19.

Davies, Mark, and Denise B. Kandel. 1981. "Parental and Peer Influences on Adolescents' Educational Plans: Some Further Evidence." *American Journal of Sociology* 87: 363–87.

Davies, Scott. 1995. "Leaps of Faith: Shifting Currents in the Critical Sociology of Education." *American Sociological Review* 100: 1448–78.

Davis, Angela Yvonne. 1981. *Women, Race, and Class.* New York: Random House.

Davis, David Brion. 1966. *The Problem of Slavery in Western Culture.* Ithaca, NY: Cornell University Press.

Davis, Gerald, Kristina A. Diekmann, and Catherine H. Tinsley. 1994. "The Decline and Fall of the Conglomerate Firm in the 1980s: The Deinstitutionalization of an Organizational Form." *American Sociological Review* 59: 547–70.

Davis, James A., and Tom W. Smith. 1994. *General Social Surveys, 1972–1994: Cumulative Codebook.* Chicago: National Opinion Research Center.

Davis, Karen, and Cathy Schoen. 1978. *Health and the War on Poverty.* Washington, DC: Brookings Institution.

Davis, Kingsley. 1955. "The Origin and Growth of Urbanization in the World." *American Journal of Sociology* 60: 429–37.

———. 1947. "Final Note on a Case of Extreme Isolation." *American Journal of Sociology* 52: 432–37.

———. 1940. "Extreme Social Isolation of a Child." *American Journal of Sociology* 45: 554–65.

Davis, Kingsley, and Wilbert E. Moore. 1945. "Some Principles of Stratification." *American Sociological Review* 10: 242–49.

Davis, Nancy S., and Robert Robinson. 1988. "Class Identification of Men and Women in the 1970s and 1980s." *American Sociological Review* 53: 103–12.

Dawkins, Marvin P., and Jomills Henry Braddock, II. 1994. "The Continuing Significance of Desegregation: School Racial Composition and African American Inclusion in American Society." *Journal of Negro Education* 63: 394–404.

Deane, Phyllis. 1969. *The First Industrial Revolution*. Cambridge, England: Cambridge University Press.

Deaux, K., and R. Hanna. 1984. "Courtship in the Personals Column: The Influence of Gender and Sexual Orientation." *Sex Roles* 11: 363–75.

Deaux, Kay, and L. Laurie Lewis. 1984. "Structure of Gender Stereotypes: Interrelations Among Components and Gender Label." *Journal of Personality and Social Psychology* 46: 991–1004.

———. 1983. "Components of Gender Stereotypes." *Psychological Monographs* 13: 25.

DeBuono, Barbara, Stephen H. Zinner, Maxim Daamen, and William M. McCormack. 1990. "Sexual Behavior of College Women in 1975, 1986, and 1989." *New England Journal of Medicine* 322: 821–25.

de Chauliac, Guy. 1890. *Great Surgery*. Latin-English Translation.

Deegan, Mary Jo. 1991. *Women in Sociology: A Bio-Bibliographical Sourcebook*. New York: Greenwood Press.

De Fleur, Melvin L., and F. R. Westie. 1958. "Verbal Attitudes and Overt Acts: An Experiment on the Salience of Attitudes." *American Sociological Review* 23: 667–73.

Degler, Carl N. 1980. *At Odds: Women and the Family in America from the Revolution to the Present*. New York: Oxford University Press.

Dela Porta, Donatella. 1999. *Social Movements: An Introduction*. Malden, MA: Blackwell Publishers.

Deloria, Vine, Jr. 1994. *God Is Red: A Native View of Religion*. Golden, CO: Fulcrum.

De Maris, A., and Gerald R. Leslie. 1984. "Cohabitation with the Future Spouse: Its Influence upon Marital Satisfaction and Communication." *Journal of Marriage and the Family* 46: 77–84.

De Mause, Lloyd. 1975. "Our Forebears Made Childhood a Nightmare." *Psychology Today* (April): 85–87.

D'Emillio, John. 1983. *Sexual Politics, Sexual Communities*. Chicago: University of Chicago Press.

DeMott, Benjamin. 1991. "In Hollywood, Class Doesn't Put Up Much of a Struggle." *The New York Times* (January 20): Sect. 2, 1, 22.

———. 1990. *The Imperial Middle: Why Americans Can't Think Straight About Class*. New York: William Morrow.

Demos, John. 1970. *A Little Commonwealth: Family Life in Plymouth Colony*. New York: Oxford University Press.

Denemark, Robert A. 1992. "Core-Periphery Trade: The Debate with Brenner over the Nature of the Link and Its Lessons." *Humboldt Journal of Social Relations* 18, 1: 119–45.

Denton, Nancy, and Douglas S. Massey. 1988. "Residential Segregation of Blacks, Hispanics, and Asians by Socioeconomic Status and Generation." *Social Science Quarterly* (December): 797–817.

Denzin, Norman K. 1989. *The Research Act: A Theoretical Introduction to Sociological Research Methods,* 3rd ed. Englewood Cliffs, NJ: Prentice Hall.

———. 1987. "The Death of Sociology in the 1980s: Comment on Collins." *American Journal of Sociology* 93: 175–80.

DePalma, Anthony. 1992. "Community Colleges Forced to Restrict Access, and Goals." *The New York Times* (November 11): A1, B11.

———. 1990. "The Culture Question." *The New York Times* (November 4): 22–23.

Depner, Charles E., and Bent Ingersoll-Dayton. 1985. "Conjugal Social Support and Patterns in Later Life." *Journal of Gerontology* 40: 761–66.

De Prete, Thomas A., and Whitman T. Soule. 1988. "Gender and Promotion in Segmented Job Ladder Systems." *American Sociological Review* 53: 26–40.

Derksen, Linda, and John Gartrell. 1993. "The Social Context of Recycling." *American Sociological Review* 58: 434–42.

Dervarics, Charles. 1998. "Is Welfare Reform Reforming Welfare?" *Population Today* 26 (October): 1–2.

Desai, Sonalde, and Linda J. Waite. 1991. "Women's Employment During Pregnancy and After the First Birth: Occupational Characteristics and Work Commitment." *American Sociological Review* 56: 551–66.

de Soysa, Indra, and John R. Oneal. 1999. "Boon Or Bane? Reassessing the Productivity of Foreign Direct Investment." *American Sociological Review* 64: 766–82.

Despelder, Lynne Anne, and Albert Lee Strickland. 1983. *The Last Dance. Encountering Death and Dying*. Palo Alto, CA: Mayfield.

de Tocqueville. Alexis. 1955. *The Old Regime and the French Revolution*. (Stuart Gilbert, Jr.) Garden City, NY: Doubleday Anchor. (Originally published in French in 1856.).

Deutsch, Connie J., and Lucia A. Gilbert. 1976. "Sex-Role Stereotypes: Effects on Self and Others and on Personal Adjustment." *Journal of Counseling Psychology* 23: 373–79.

Devine, Donald J. 1972. *The Political Culture of the United States: The Influence of Member Values on Regime Maintenance*. Boston: Little, Brown.

Dewar, Helen. 1996. "Clinton to Sign Terrorism Bill Despite Lack of Enforcement Provisions, Aides Say." *The Washington Post*. Politicsnow Web, http://politicsnow.com/WP/1996–04/19/156F-041996–idx.html.

DeWitt, Karen. 1991. "Ideas and Trends: The Push to Consider a Once Taboo Subject: National School Tests." *The New York Times* (February 5): E5.

Dicker, Marvin. 1983. "Health Care Coverage and Insurance Premiums of Families, United States, 1980." *National Medical Care Utilization and Expenditure Survey, Preliminary Report No. 3*. DHHS Publication No. 83-20000. Washington, DC: U.S. Government Printing Office.

Didham, Cheryl K. 1990. "Equal Opportunity in the Classroom: Making Teachers Aware." Paper presented at the annual meeting of the Association of Teacher Educators, Las Vegas, February 5–8.

Diegmueller, Karen, and Debra Viadero. 1995. "Playing Games With History." Education Week, November 15. Also available on the http://www.edweek.com/ew/ew_printstory.cfm?slug=11hist.h15.

Dill, Karen E., and Jody C. Dill. 1998. "Video Game Violence: A Review of the Empirical Literature." *Aggression and Violent Behavior* 3: 407–28.

DiMaggio, Paul, Ester Hargittai, W. Russell Newman, and John P. Robinson. 2001. "Social Implications of the Internet." *Annual Review of Sociology* 37: 307–36.

Dinitz, Simon, Russell R. Dynes, and Alfred C. Clarke (eds.) 1969. *Deviance*. New York: Oxford University Press.

Dionne, E. J. 1991. *Why Americans Hate Politics*. New York: Simon & Schuster.

DiPrete, Thomas A., and David B. Grusky. 1990. "Structure and Trend in the Process of Stratification for American Men and Women." *American Journal of Sociology* 96: 107–43.

DiPrete, Thomas A., and Patricia A. McManus. 2000. "Family Change, Employment Transitions, and the Welfare State: Household Income Dynamics in the US & Germany." *American Sociological Review* 65: 343–70.

Directors and Boards. 1992. "Spotlight on Women Directors." *Directors and Boards* 16(4): 66–68.

Dixon, Jo, and Alan J. Lizotte. 1989. "The Burden of Proof: Southern Subculture-of-Violence Explanations of Gun Ownership and Homicide." *American Journal of Sociology* 95: 182–87.

———. 1987. "Gun Ownership and the Southern 'Subculture of Violence.'" *American Journal of Sociology* 93: 383–405.

Dobash, Russell P., Rebecca E. Dobash, Margo Wilson, and Martin Daly. 1992. "The Myth of Sexual Symmetry in Marital Violence." *Social Problems* 39: 71–91.

Dobbin, Fred, John R. Sutton, John W. Meyer, and W. Richard Scott. 1993. "Equal Opportunity Law and the Construction of Internal Labor Markets." *American Journal of Sociology* 99: 396–427.

Doherty, J., M. Malek, and Elizabeth Forbes Graham. 1992. *Postmodernism and the Social Sciences*. London: Macmillan.

Doherty, W. J., and R. H. Needle. 1991. "Psychological Adjustment and Substance Use Among Adolescents Before and After a Parental Divorce." *Child Development* 62: 328–37.

Dohrenwend, Bruce P. 1975. "Subcultural and Social-Psychological Factors in the Genesis of Mental Disorders." *Journal of Health and Social Behavior* 16: 365–92.

Domhoff, G. William. 2009. *Who Rules America? Challenges to Corporate and Class Dominance,* 6th ed. New York: McGraw Hill.

———. 2001. *Who Rules America? Power and Politics,* 3rd ed. Mountain View, CA: Mayfield.

———. 1983. *Who Rules America Now? A View for the Eighties.* Englewood Cliffs, NJ: Prentice Hall.

———. 1978. *Who Really Rules? New Haven and Community Power Reexamined.* New Brunswick, NJ: Transaction Books.

———. 1967. *Who Rules America?* Englewood Cliffs, NJ: Prentice Hall.

Donahue, M. J. 1985. "Intrinsic and Extrinsic Religiousness: Review and Meta-Analysis." *Journal of Personality and Social Psychology* 48: 400–19.

Doran, Peter T., and Maggie Kendall Zimmerman. 2009. "Examining the Scientific Consensus on Climate Change." *EOS* 90(3) (January). http://tigger.uic.edu/~pdoran/012009_Doran_final.pdf (Downloaded August 3, 2010).

Doskoch, Peter, and Marian M. Jones. 1996. "Toy Story." *Psychology Today* 29, 6: 12.

Dowdall, George W. 1974. "White Gains from Black Subordination in 1960 and 1970," *Social Problems* 22: 162–83.

Downey, Liam. 1998. "Environmental Injustice: Is Race or Income a Better Predictor?" *Social Science Quarterly* 79: 766–78.

Downs, A. Chris, and Sheila K. Harrison. 1985. "Embarrassing Age Spots or Just Plain Ugly? Physical Attractiveness Stereotyping as an Instrument of Sexism on American Television Commercials." *Sex Roles* 13: 9–19.

Downs, Anthony. 1957. *An Economic Theory of Democracy.* New York: Harper.

Doyle, H., and D. M. Kelly. 1979. "Comparison of Trends in Ten Denominations 1950–75." In D. R. Hoge and D. A. Roozen (eds.), *Understanding Church Growth and Decline: 1950–1978.* New York: Pilgrim Press.

Dreitzel, Hans Peter. 1970. *Recent Sociology.* New York: Macmillan.

Dru, Vincent. 2007. "Authoritarianism, Social Dominance Orientation, and Prejudice: Effects of Various Self-Categorization Conditions." *Journal of Experimental Social Psychology* 6: 877–883.

Drucker, Peter. 2006. "Mobilizing Immigrants and Blacks." *New Politics* 10, no. 4. http://www.wpunj.edu/newpol/issue40/Drucker40.htm. (Downloaded January 14, 2009)

Du Bois, W. E. B. 1973. *The Philadelphia Negro.* Millwood, NY: Kraus-Thomson. (Originally published in 1899.).

———. 1903. *The Souls of Black Folk.* Chicago: A. C. McClurg.

Duckitt, J., C. Wagner, I. du Plessis, and I. Birum 2002. "The Psychological Bases of Ideology and Prejudice: Testing a Dual Process Model." *Journal of Personality and Social Psychology* 83: 75–93.

Duncan, Beverly, and Stanley Lieberson. 1970. *Metropolis and Region in Transition.* Beverly Hills, CA: Sage.

Duncan, Greg. 1996. "Slow Motion: Earnings Mobility of Young Workers in the 1970s and 1980s." Paper presented at the annual meeting of the Midwest Sociological Society, Chicago.

Duncan, Greg J., with Richard Coe, Mary E. Corcoran, Martha S. Hill, Saul D. Hoffman, and James N. Morgan. 1984. *Years of Poverty, Years of Plenty: The Changing Economic Fortunes of American Workers and Families.* Ann Arbor: University of Michigan, Institute for Social Research.

Duncan, Greg J., and Willard Rodgers. 1991. "Has Children's Poverty Become More Persistent?" *American Sociological Review* 56: 538–50.

———. 1989. "Has Poverty Become More Persistent?" Ann Arbor: Institute for Social Research, University of Michigan.

Duncan, Otis Dudley. 1968. "Ability and Achievement." *Eugenics Quarterly* 15: 1–11.

———. 1959. "Human Ecology and Population Studies." Pp. 678–716 in Philip M. Hauser and Otis Dudley Duncan (eds.), *The Study of Population.* Chicago: University of Chicago Press.

Dunier, Mitchell. 1992. *Slim's Table: Race, Respect, and Masculinity.* Chicago: University of Chicago Press.

Durkheim, Emile. 1965. *The Elementary Forms of the Religious Life.* New York: Free Press. (Originally published in 1915.).

———. 1964a. *Suicide, A Study in Sociology* (J. A. Spaulding and George Simpson, trans.). Glencoe, IL: Free Press. (Originally published in French, 1897.).

———. 1964b. *The Rules of the Sociological Method.* New York: Free Press. (Originally published in 1893.).

———. 1956. *Education and Society.* Glencoe, IL: Free Press. (Originally published in French in 1922.).

———. 1953. "Individual and Collective Representations." In D. F. Pocock (trans.), *Sociology and Philosophy.* Glencoe, IL: Free Press. (Originally published in French, 1898.).

———. 1947. *Division of Labor in Society* (George Simpson, trans.) Glencoe, IL: Free Press. (Originally published in French in 1893.).

Dush, Claire, M. Kamp, Catherine L. Cohan and Paul R. Amato. 2003. "The Relationship Between Cohabitation and Marital Quality and Stability: Change Across Cohorts?" *Journal of Marriage and Family* 65(3): 539–549.

Duster, Troy. 1995. "Review Symposium: The Bell Curve." *Contemporary Sociology* 24: 158–61.

———. 1988. "From Structural Analysis to Public Policy: Review of William Julius Wilson, The Truly Disadvantaged; The Inner City, the Underclass, and Public Policy." *Contemporary Sociology* 17: 287–90.

Dworkin, Ronald W. 2001. "The Medicalization of Unhappiness." *Public Interest* 144: 85–99.

Dye, T. 1983. *Who's Running America: The Reagan Years.* Englewood Cliffs, NJ: Prentice Hall.

Dykstra, Peter. 2008. "History of Environmental Movement Full of Twists, Turns." CNN (December 15). http://articles.cnn.com/2008-12-10/tech/history.environmental.movement_1_fierce-green-fire-american-environmental-movement-philip-shabecoff?_s=PM:TECH.

Dyson, Michael Eric. 2006. *Come Hell or High Water: Hurricane Katrina and the Color of Disaster.* New York: Basic Civitas.

Eagan, Andrea Boroff. 1988. "The Damage Done: The Endless Saga of the Dalkon Shield." *Village Voice* (July 5).

Eagleton, Thomas. 1990. "The Influence of PACs." Presentation to Leadership Missouri Program, September 27, St. Louis, MO.

Easterlin, Richard. 1978. "What Will 1984 Be Like? Socioeconomic Implications of Recent Trends in Family Structure." *Demography* 15: 397–432.

———. 1968. *Population, Labor Force, and Long Swings in Economic Growth.* New York: National Bureau of Economic Research.

Eaton, Joseph W., and Robert J. Weil. 1955. *Culture and Mental Disorders.* Glencoe, IL: Free Press of Glencoe.

Eaton, Susan E., and Elizabeth Crutcher. 1994. *Slipping Towards Segregation: Local Control and Eroding Desegregation in Montgomery County, Maryland.* Cambridge, MA: Harvard Project on School Desegregation.

Ebaugh, Helen Rose Fuchs. 1988. *Becoming an Ex: The Process of Role Exit.* Chicago: University of Chicago Press.

Eckholm, Erik. 1990. "What Makes the 2 Sexes So Vulnerable to Epidemic." *The New York Times* (September 16): AIS.

Economist. 1991a. "Segregation by Stealth." *Economist* (April 13): 31.

———. 1991b. "The Ebb Tide: A Survey of International Finance." *Economist* (April 27): Spec. Sect.

Edmonds, Duncan, and Allister Sparks. 1995. "South Africa: An Interim Report." Canadian Security Intelligence Service Commentary No. 54. http://www.csis~scrs.gc.ca/_eng/comment/com.54e.html.

Edmonds, Ronald. 1979. "Some Schools Work and More Can." *Social Policy* 9(5): 28–32.

Education Resources Institute and Institute of Higher Education Policy. 1995. *College Debt and the American Family.* Boston: Education Resources Institute.

Education Week. 1989. "Tax Hike Needed, Chief Tells Montana House." *Education Week* (March 15): 21.

Edwards, Richard. 1979. *Contested Terrain.* New York: Basic Books.

Edwards, Richard C., Michael Reich, and Thomas E. Weisskopf. 1986. "Introduction." Pp. 1–4 in Richard C. Edwards, Michael Reich, and Thomas E. Weisskopf (eds.). *The Capitalist System,* 3rd ed. Englewood Cliffs, NJ: Prentice Hall.

———. 1972. *The Capitalist System,* 1st ed. Englewood Cliffs, NJ: Prentice Hall.

Egeland, Byron, Deborah Jacovitz, and L. Alan Sroufe. 1989. "Breaking the Cycle of Abuse: Relationship Predictors." *Child Development* 59: 1080–88.

Eggebeen, David J., and Daniel T. Lichter. 1991. "Race, Family Structure, and Changing Poverty Among American Children." *American Sociological Review* 56: 801–17.

Ehrenreich, Barbara, and John Ehrenreich. 1979. "The Professional and Managerial Class." Pp. 5–45 in Pat Walker (ed.), *Between Labor and Capital*. Boston: South End Press.

———. 1975. "Medicine and Social Control." Pp. 138–67 in B. R. Mandell (ed.), *Welfare in America: Controlling the "Dangerous" Classes*. Englewood Cliffs, NJ: Prentice Hall.

Ehrlich, Elizabeth, and Susan B. Garland. 1988. "For American Business, A New World of Workers." *Business Week* 3070 (September 19): 112–20.

Ehrlich, Howard J. 1973. *The Social Psychology of Prejudice*. New York: Wiley Interscience.

Ehrlich, Isaac. 1975. "The Deterrent Effect of Capital Punishment: A Question of Life and Death." *American Economic Review* 65: 397–417.

Eisinger, Peter K. 1973. "Conditions of Protest Behavior in American Cities." *American Political Science Review* 67: 11–28.

Eisler, Peter. 2000. "Secret Program Left Toxic Legacy." *USA Today* Online, http://www.usatoday.com/news/poison/001.htm.

Eitzen, D. Stanley, and Maxine Baca Zinn (eds.). 1989. *The Reshaping of America. Social Consequences of the Changing Economy*. Englewood Cliffs, NJ: Prentice Hall.

Eitzen, D. Stanley, and Doug A. Timmer. 1985. *Criminology*. New York: Wiley.

Ekehammar, B., N. Akrami, M. Gylje, and I. Zakrisson. 2004. "What Matters Most to Prejudice: Big Five Personality, Social Dominance Orientation, or Right-Wing Authoritarianism?" *European Journal of Personality* 18: 463–482.

Ekerdt, D. J., and R. Bosse. 1982. "Change in Self-Reported Health with Retirement." *International Journal of Aging and Human Development* 15: 213–23.

Elasmar, Michael, Kazumi Hasegawa, and Mary Brain. 1999. "The Portrayal of Women in U.S. Prime Time Television." *Journal of Broadcasting and Electronic Media* 43(1): 20–35.

Elgie, Robert, and Alex Rees Clark. 1980. "The Metropolitan Structure of Southern Metropolitan Areas: A Comparative Analysis." *Urban Geography* 1: 317–34.

Elkin, Frederick, and Gerald Handel. 1988. *The Child and Society: The Process of Socialization*, 5th ed. New York: McGraw Hill.

Elkind, David. 2001. *The Hurried Child: Growing Up Too Fast Too Soon*, 3rd ed. Cambridge, MA: Perseus.

Elliott, Delbert S., and Suzanne S. Ageton. 1980. "Reconciling Race and Class Differences in Self-Reported and Official Estimates of Delinquency." *American Sociological Review* 45: 95–110.

Elliott, Dorinda. 1993. "Russia's Nouveaux Richeskis: A New Elite Fiddles as the Economy Burns." *Newsweek* (February 22): 40.

Elliott, Rogers. 1988. "Tests, Abilities, Race, and Conflict." *Intelligence* 12: 333–50.

Ellison, Christopher G., and Jeffrey S. Levin. 1998. "The Religion-Health Connection: Evidence, Theory, and Future Directions." *Health Education and Behavior* 25: 700–20.

Ellison, Christopher G., and Patricia L. McCall. 1989. "Region and Violent Attitudes Reconsidered: Comment on Dixon and Lizotte." *American Journal of Sociology* 95: 174–78.

Ellsworth, R. N. 1903. Tables and Charts Showing the Occupations of the Fathers of the Students in the University of Michigan, November, 1902. James Burrill Angell Papers. Ann Arbor: University of Michigan.

Ellwood, David T. 1996. "Welfare Reform as I Knew It: When Bad Things Happen to Good Policies." *American Prospect* 26: 22–29, also http://epn.org/prospect/26/26ellw.html.

———. 1987. Divide and Conquer: Responsible Security for America's Poor. Occasional Paper 1. Ford Foundation Project on Social Welfare and the American Future. New York: Ford Foundation.

Ellwood, David T., and Mary Jo Bane. 1984. "The Impact of AFDC on Family Structure and Living Arrangements." Working paper prepared for U.S. Department of Health and Human Services, Grant No. 92A-82.

Ellwood, Robert S., Jr. 1987. *Many Peoples, Many Faiths*. Englewood Cliffs, NJ: Prentice Hall.

Emerson, Richard M. 1972. "Exchange Theory. Part I: A Psychological Basis for Social Change, and Part II: Exchange Relations and Networks." Pp. 38–87 in J. Berger. M. Zeldich, and B. Anderson (eds.). *Sociological Theories in Progress*, Vol. 2. Boston: Houghton Mifflin.

Emery, Robert F. 1989. "Family Violence." *American Psychologist* 44: 321–28.

Emirbayer, Mustafa, and Jeff Goodwin. 1994. "Network Analysis, Culture, and the Problem of Agency." *American Journal of Sociology* 99: 1411–54.

England, Paula. 1999. "The Case For Comparable Worth." *Quarterly Review of Economics and Finance* 39: 743–56.

England, Paula, George Farkas, Barbara Stanek Kilbourne, and Thomas Dou. 1988. "Explaining Occupational Sex Segregation and Wages: Findings from a Model with Fixed Effects." *American Sociological Review* 53: 544–58.

England, Paula, M. S. Herbert, Barbara S. Kilbourne, L. L. Reid, and L. M. Megdal. 1994. "The Gendered Valuation of Occupations and Skills: Earnings in 1980 Census Occupations." *Social Forces* 73, 1: 65–101.

Ensminger, Margaret F. 1987. "Adolescent Sexual Behavior as It Relates to Other Transition Behaviors in Youth." Pp. 36–55 in Sandra L. Hofferth and Cheryl D. Hayes (eds.), *Risking the Future: Adolescent Sexuality and Childbearing*, Vol. 11: *Working Papers and Statistical Appendixes*. Washington. DC: National Academy Press.

Entwisle, Doris R., and Karl L. Alexander. 1994. "Winter Setback: The Racial Composition of Schools and Learning to Read." *American Sociological Review* 59: 446–60.

———. 1992. "Summer Setback: Race, Poverty, School Composition, and Achievement." *American Sociological Review* 57: 72–84.

Entwisle, Doris R., Karl L. Alexander, and Linda Steffel Olson. 1994. "The Gender Gap in Math: Its Possible Origins in Neighborhood Effects." *American Sociological Review* 59: 822–38.

Environmental Protection Agency. 2000. *1999 Acid Rain Program Compliance Report*. Document EPA-430-R-00-007, August 2000. http://www.epa.gov/acidrain/comprpt/1999/index.html#summary.

Epstein, Cynthia Fuchs. 1970. *Women's Place: Options and Limits on Professional Careers*. Berkeley: University of California Press.

Epstein, Elizabeth, and Ruth Guttman. 1984. "Mate Selection in Man: Evidence, Theory, and Outcome." *Social Biology* 31: 243–78.

Epstein, S. S. 1981. "The Political and Economic Basis of Cancer." Pp. 75–82 in Peter Conrad and Rochelle Kern (eds.), *The Sociology of Health and Illness: Critical Perspectives*. New York: St. Martin's Press.

Erickson, Eugene P. 1988. "Estimating the Concentration of Wealth in America." *Public Opinion Quarterly* 52: 243–53.

Erickson, F., and S. Schultz. 1982. *The Counselor as Gatekeeper*. New York: Academic Press.

Erikson, Erik H. 1982. *The Life Cycle Completed: A Review*. New York: Norton.

———. 1968. "Generativity and Ego Integrity." Pp. 75–87 in Bernice Neugarten (ed.), *Middle Age and Aging*. Chicago: University of Chicago Press.

———. 1950. *Childhood and Society*. New York: Norton.

Erikson, Kai T. 1987. "Notes on the Sociology of Deviance." Pp. 21–23 in Earl Rubington and Martin S. Weinberg (eds.), *Deviance: The Interactional Perspective*, 5th ed. New York: Macmillan.

———. 1966. *Wayward Puritans: A Study in the Sociology of Deviance*. New York: Wiley.

Ermann, M. David, and Richard J. Lundman (eds.). 1978. *Corporate and Governmental Deviance: Problems in Organizational Behavior in Contemporary Society*. New York: Oxford University Press.

Eron, Leonard D. 1995. "Media Violence." *Pediatric Annals* 24(2): 84.

Esping-Andersen, Gosta. 1990. *The Three Worlds of Welfare Capitalism*. Princeton, NJ: Princeton University Press.

Esposito, D. 1973. "Homogeneous and Heterogeneous Ability Grouping: Principal Findings and Implications for Evaluating and Designing More Effective School Environments." *Review of Educational Research* 43: 163–79.

Etzioni, Amitai. 1996. "The Responsive Community: A Communitarian Perspective." 1995 American Sociological Association Presidential Address. *American Sociological Review* 61: 1–11.

———. 1982. *An Immodest Agenda: Rebuilding America Before the Twenty-First Century*, New York: McGraw-Hill.

———. 1975. *A Comparative Analysis of Complex Organizations*, rev. and enlarged ed. Glencoe, IL: Free Press.

Evans, Peter, Dietrich Rueschmeyer, and Theda Skocpol (eds.). 1985. *Bringing the State Back In*. Cambridge, England: Cambridge University Press.

Evans, Peter, and James E. Rauch. 1999. "Bureaucracy and Growth: A Cross-National Analysis of the Effects of 'Weberian' State Structures on Economic Growth." *American Sociological Review* 64: 748–65.

Ewens, William L., and Howard J. Ehrlich. 1969. "Reference Other Support and Ethnic Attitudes as Predictors of Intergroup Behavior." Revised version of paper presented to the joint meetings of the Midwest Sociological Society and Ohio Valley Sociological Society, Indianapolis, May.

Eyler, Janet, Valerie J. Cook, and Leslie E. Ward. 1983. "Resegregation: Segregation Within Desegregated Schools." Pp. 126–62 in Christine H. Rossell and Willis D. Hawley (eds.), *The Consequences of School Desegregation*. Philadelphia: Temple University Press.

Fagan, Jeffrey A. 2006. "Capital Punishment: Deterrent Effects and Capital Costs." http://www.law.columbia.edu/law_school/communications/reports/summer06/capitalpunish (Downloaded October 27, 2009).

Fagan, Jeffrey, Ellen Slaughter, and Eliot Hartstone. 1987. "Blind Justice? The Impact of Race on the Juvenile Justice Process." *Crime and Delinquency* 33(2): 224–58.

Fairweather, Hugh. 1976. "Sex Differences in Cognitive Tests." *Cognition* 4: 231–75.

Faludi, Susan. 1991. *Backlash: The Undeclared War Against American Women*. New York: Crown Publishers.

Faris, Robert E. L. 1979. *Chicago Sociology: 1920–1932*. Chicago: University of Chicago Press.

Farkas, George. 2003. "Racial Disparities and Discrimination in Education: What Do We Know and How Do We Know It, and What Do We Need to Know?" *Teachers College Record* 105: 1119–46.

Farkas, George, Lyndsey Wilkinson, Chandra Muller, Kathryn Schiller, and Kenneth Frank. 2005. "Teacher Grading Practices with School Contexts: Do They Disadvantage Low-Income and Minority Students?" Paper Presented at the Annual Meeting of the American Sociological Association, Philadelphia.

Farley, John E. 2010. *Majority-Minority Relations*, 6th ed. Upper Saddle River, NJ: Prentice Hall.

———. 2005. "Race, Not Class: Explaining Racial Housing Separation in the St. Louis Metropolitan Area, 2000." *Sociological Focus* 38(2): 33–150.

———. 2002. "Interracial Exposure Indices: When 'Average' is Not 'Typical.'" Paper presented at 2002 Annual Meeting of the Midwest Sociological Society, Milwaukee, WI, April.

———. 2001a. "Contesting Our Everyday Work Lives: The Retention and Graduation of Minority and Working Class Students in Sociology." Presidential Address, 2001 Annual Meetings of the Midwest Sociological Society, St. Louis, April. Forthcoming in *Sociological Quarterly* 43(1) (Winter, 2002).

———. 2001b. "Housing Segregation in the St. Louis Metropolitan Area, 2000." Paper presented at the 2001 Joint Annual Meetings of the Illinois and Wisconsin Sociological Associations, Rockford, IL, October 11–12.

———. 2000. *Majority-Minority Relations*, 5th ed. Upper Saddle River, NJ: Prentice Hall.

———. 1998. *Earthquake Fears, Predictions, and Preparations in Mid-America*. Carbondale: Southern Illinois University Press.

———. 1995. "Race Still Matters: The Minimal Role of Income and Housing Cost as Causes of Housing Segregation in St. Louis, 1990." *Urban Affairs Review* (formerly *Urban Affairs Quarterly*) 31 (November): 244–54.

———. 1994. "Twentieth Century Wars: Some Short-Term Effects on Intergroup Relations in the United States." *Sociological Inquiry* 64(2): 214–37.

———. 1993. "Housing Segregation in the St. Louis Metropolitan Area, 1980–1990: Comparing Trends at the Block and Census Tract Level." *Journal of Urban Affairs* 15: 515–27.

———. 1992a. "Twentieth Century Wars: Some Effects on Intergroup Relations in the United States." Paper presented to the Thematic Session on the Reconstruction of Society in the Aftermath of War, 1992 annual meeting of the American Sociological Association, Pittsburgh, August 20–24.

———. 1992b. *American Social Problems: An Institutional Analysis*, 2nd ed. Englewood Cliffs, NJ: Prentice Hall.

———. 1991. "Racial Housing Segregation in the St. Louis Metropolitan Area, 1990." Paper presented at the annual meetings of the Illinois Sociological Association, Chicago. October 17–18.

———. 1988. *Majority-Minority Relations*, 2nd ed. Englewood Cliffs, NJ: Prentice Hall.

———. 1987a. "Segregation in 1980: How Segregated Are America's Metropolitan Areas?" Pp. 95–114 in Gary Tobin (ed.), *Divided Neighborhoods: Changing Patterns of Racial Segregation*. Urban Affairs Annual Reviews, Vol. 32. Newbury Park, CA: Sage.

———. 1987b. "Excessive Black and Hispanic Unemployment in U.S. Metropolitan Areas: The Roles of Racial Inequality, Segregation, and Discrimination in Male Joblessness." *American Journal of Economics and Sociology* 46: 129–50.

———. 1986. "Health Care." Pp. 43–47 in Ann R. Ruwitch (ed.), *St. Louis Currents: The Community and Its Resources*. St. Louis, MO: Leadership St. Louis.

———. 1985. "The Factorial Ecology and Social Areas of Metropolitan St. Louis, 1980." Paper presented at the annual meeting of the Midwest Sociological Society, St. Louis, MO. April.

———. 1984. "Characteristics of Movers to, from, and Within St. Louis City, 1975–1980." Paper presented at the annual meeting of the Illinois Sociological Association, Chicago, October.

———. 1982. "Effects of Higher-Density Living on Children." Pp. 50–60 in *Proceedings: The Impact of Energy Policy and Technology on the Family*. Knoxville: University of Tennessee.

Farley, John E., Hugh D. Barlow, Marvin S. Finkelstein, and Larry Riley. 1993. "Earthquake Hysteria, Before and After: A Survey and Follow-Up on Public Response to the Browning Forecast." *International Journal of Mass Emergencies and Disasters* 11: 305–21.

Farley, John E., Hugh D. Barlow, Lewis G. Bender, Marvin S. Finkelstein, and Larry Riley. 1991a. "Earthquake Hysteria: Public Response to a Pseudoscientific Forecast of Disaster." Paper presented at the annual meetings of the Midwest Sociological Society, Des Moines, IA, April 11.

Farley, John E., Hugh D. Barlow, Marvin S. Finkelstein, Larry Riley, and Lewis G. Bender. 1991b. "Earthquake Hysteria, Before and After: A Survey and Follow-Up on Public Response to the Browning Forecast." Paper presented at the Research Conference on Public and Media Response to Earthquake Forecasts, Edwardsville, IL, May 18.

———. 1991c. "1990 Midwest Earthquake Scare: Public Response to a Pseudoscientific Forecast of Disaster." Paper presented at the UCLA International Conference on the Impact of Natural Disasters: Agenda for Future Action, Los Angeles, July 10.

Farley, Reynolds. 1984. *Blacks and Whites: Narrowing the Gap?* Cambridge, MA: Harvard University Press.

———. 1980. "Homicide Trends in the United States." *Demography* 17: 177–88.

———. 1977. "Trends in Racial Inequalities: Have the Gains of the 1960s Disappeared in the 1970s?" *American Sociological Review* 42: 189–208.

Farley, Reynolds, and Walter Allen. 1987. *The Color Line and the Quality of Life in America*. New York: Russell Sage.

Farley, Reynolds, Suzanne Bianchi, and Diane Colasanto. 1979. "Barriers to the Racial Integration of Neighborhoods: The Detroit Case." *Annals of the American Academy of Political and Social Science* 441: 47–113.

Farley, Reynolds, and William H. Frey. 1994. "Changes in the Segregation of Blacks and Whites During the 1980s: Small Steps Toward a More Integrated Society." *American Sociological Review* 59: 23–45.

———. 1992. "The Residential Segregation of Blacks, Latinos, and Asians: 1980 and 1990." Paper presented at the annual meeting of the American Sociological Association, Pittsburgh, August 21.

Farley, Reynolds, Howard Schuman, Suzanne Bianchi, Diane Colasanto, and Shirley Hatchett. 1978. "Chocolate City, Vanilla Suburbs: Will the Trend Toward Racially Separate Communities Continue?" *Social Science Research* 7: 319–44.

Farley, Reynolds, Charlotte Steeh, Maria Krysan, Tara Jackson, and Keith Reeves. 1994. "Stereotypes and Segregation: Neighborhoods in the Detroit Area." *American Journal of Sociology* 100: 750–80.

References

Farnham, Christie Anne. 1994. *The Education of the Southern Belle: Higher Education and Student Socialization in the Antebellum South.* New York: New York University Press.

Farnsworth, Margaret, and Michael J. Leiber. 1989. "Strain Theory Revisited: Economic Goals, Educational Means, and Delinquency." *American Sociological Review* 54: 263–74.

Farrar, L. L. 1978. "The Causes of World War I." Pp. 171–80 in L. L. Farrar (ed.), *War: A Historical, Political, and Social Study.* Santa Barbara, CA: ABC-Clio.

Fausto-Sterling, Anne. 1985. *Myths of Gender: Biological Theories About Women and Men.* New York: Basic Books.

Fava, Sylvia F. 1959. "Contrasts in Neighboring: New York City and a Suburban County." Pp. 122–31 in W. M. Dobriner (ed.), *The Suburban Community.* New York: Putnam.

Feagin, Joe R. 2000. *Racist America: Roots, Current Realities, and Future Reparations.* New York: Routledge.

———. 1991. "The Continuing Significance of Race: Antiblack Discrimination in Public Places." *American Sociological Review* 56: 101–16.

———. 1985. "The Global Context of Metropolitan Growth: Houston and the Oil Industry." *American Journal of Sociology* 90: 1204–30.

———. 1983. *The Urban Real Estate Game.* Englewood Cliffs, NJ: Prentice Hall.

———. 1972. "Poverty: We Still Believe That God Helps Those That Help Themselves." *Psychology Today* 6: 101–10.

Feagin, Joe R., and Clarice Booher Feagin. 1986. *Discrimination American Style: Institutional Racism and Sexism.* Englewood Cliffs, NJ: Prentice Hall.

Feagin, Joe R., and Hernan Vera. 2001. *Liberation Sociology.* Boulder, CO: Westview Press.

Feagin, Joe R., Hernan Vera, and Nikitah Imani. 1996. *The Agony of Education: Black Students at White Colleges and Universities.* New York: Routledge.

Feagin, Joe R., and Melvin P. Sikes. 1994. *Living with Racism: The Black Middle-Class Experience.* Boston: Beacon Press.

Featherman, David L. 1979. "Opportunities Are Expanding." *Society* 13: 4–11.

Featherman, David L., and Robert M. Hauser. 1978. *Opportunity and Change.* New York: Academic Press.

Federal Bureau of Investigation. 2000. *Uniform Crime Reports—Crime in the United States, 1999.* Washington, DC: U.S. Government Printing Office. Also available online at http://www.fbi.gov/ucr/99cius.htm.

———. 1999. *Crime in the United States, 1998. Uniform Crime Reports.* Washington, DC: U.S. Government Printing Office. Also available on http://www.fbi.gov/ucr/98cius.htm.

———. 1996. Federal Bureau of Investigation Home Page, Uniform Crime Reports. Washington, DC: Federal Bureau of Investigation. http://www.fbi.gov/.

———. 1995a. Uniform Crime Reporting Program Press Release—11/19/95. Washington, DC: Federal Bureau of Investigation. http://www.fbi.gov/ucrpress.htm.

———. 1995b. *Crime in the United States, 1994: Uniform Crime Reports.* Washington, DC: U.S. Government Printing Office.

———. 1992. *Uniform Crime Reports: Crime in the United States, 1991.* Washington, DC: U.S. Government Printing Office.

———. 1990. *Uniform Crime Reports: Crime in the United States, 1989.* Washington, DC: U.S. Government Printing Office.

———. 1989. *Uniform Crime Reports: Crime in the United States, 1988.* Washington, DC: U.S. Government Printing Office.

———. 1983. *Uniform Crime Reports: Crime in the United States, 1983.* Washington, DC: U.S. Government Printing Office.

———. 1979. *Uniform Crime Reports: Crime in the United States, 1979.* Washington, DC: U.S. Government Printing Office.

Federal Election Commission. 1996a. "House Campaign Financial Activity Through March 31 of the Election Year." http://www.fec.gov/press/sen15lng.htm.

———. 1996b. "Senate Campaign Financial Activity Through March 31 of the Election Year." http://www.fec.gov/press/hse15lng.htm.

Federal Statistics Office Germany. 2001. Population, by sex and citizenship. http://www.statistik-bund.de/basis/e/bevoe/bev_tab4.htm.

Federbush, Marsha. 1974. "The Sex Problems of School Math Books." Pp. 178–84 in Judith Stacey, Susan Bereaud, and Joan Daniels (eds.), *And Jill Came Tumbling After: Sexism in American Education.* New York: Dell.

Fellner, Jamie. 2000. "Punishment and Prejudice: Racial Disparities in the War on Drugs." *Human Rights Watch: United States* 12(2) (May). http://www.hrw.org/reports/2000/usa/.

Felson, Richard B. 1996. "Mass Media Effects on Violent Behavior." *Annual Review of Sociology* 22: 103–28.

Fendrich, James M. 1967. "Perceived Reference Group Support: Racial Attitudes and Overt Behavior." *American Sociological Review* 32: 960–70.

Fennema, Elizabeth et al. 1990. "Teachers' Attributions and Beliefs About Girls, Boys, and Mathematics." *Educational Studies in Mathematics* 21(1): 55–69.

Feree, Myra Marx, and Elaine J. Hall. 1990. "Visual Images of American Society: Gender and Race in Introductory Sociology Textbooks." *Gender and Society* 4: 500–33.

Ferguson, Ronald E. 1998. "Teachers' Perceptions and Expectations and the Black-White Test Score Gap." Pp. 273–317 in Christopher Jencks and Meredith Phillips (eds.), *The Black-White Test Score Gap.* Washington, DC: Brookings Institution.

Fessenden, Ford. 2000. "Deadly Statistics: A Survey of Crime and Punishment." *The New York Times* (September 22). Also available on http://www.nytimes.com/2000/09/22/national/22STUD.html.

Festinger, Leon. 1957. *A Theory of Cognitive Dissonance.* Stanford, CA: Stanford University Press.

Festinger, Leon, and J. Merrill Carlsmith. 1959. "Cognitive Consequences of Forced Compliance." *Journal of Abnormal and Social Psychology* 58: 203–10.

Feuer, Lewis. 1969. *The Conflict of Generations: The Character and Significance of the Student Movement.* New York: Basic Books.

Fiedler, Fred F., and J. F. Garcia. 1987. *New Approaches to Leadership: Cognitive Resources and Organizational Performance.* New York: Wiley.

Filley, Alan C., and Robert J. House. 1969. *Managerial Processes and Organizational Behavior.* Glenview, IL: Scott, Foresman.

Findley, W. G., and M. M. Bryan. 1971. *Ability Grouping 1970: Status, Impact, and Alternatives.* Athens: University of Georgia, Center for Educational Improvement.

Fine, Gary Alan. 1992. "The Culture of Production: Aesthetic Choices and Constraints in Culinary Work." *American Journal of Sociology* 97: 1268–94.

———. 1984. "Negotiated Order and Organizational Cultures." Pp. 239–62 in Ralph H. Turner (ed.), *Annual Review of Sociology,* Vol. 10. Palo Alto, CA: Annual Reviews.

———. 1979. "Cokelore and Coke Law: Urban Belief of Tales and the Problem of Multiple Origins." *Journal of American Folklore* 92: 477–82.

Finke, Roger, and Rodney Stark. 1992. *The Churching of America: 1776–1990.* New Brunswick, NJ: Rutgers University Press.

Finkelhor, David, with Sharon Araji, Larry Baron, Angela Browne, Stefanie Doyle Peters, and Gail Elizabeth Wyatt. 1986. *Sourcebook on Child Sexual Abuse.* Beverly Hills, CA: Sage.

Finkelstein, Marvin. 2004. *Net-Works: Workplace Change in the Global Economy: A Critical and Practical Guide.* Lanham, MD: Rowman and Littlefield.

Finney, Martha I. 1988. "The Right to Be Tested." *Personnel Administrator* (March): 74–75.

Firebaugh, Glenn, and Frank D. Beck. 1994. "Does Economic Growth Benefit the Masses? Growth, Dependence, and Welfare in the Third World." *American Sociological Review* 59: 631–53.

Firebaugh, Glenn, and Kevin Chen. 1995. "Vote Turnout of Nineteenth Amendment Women: The Enduring Effect of Discrimination." *American Journal of Sociology* 100: 972–96.

Firebaugh, Glenn, and Kenneth E. Davis. 1988. "Trends in Antiblack Prejudice, 1972–1984: Region and Cohort Effects." *American Journal of Sociology* 94: 251–72.

Fischer, Claude S. 1984. *The Urban Experience.* 2nd ed. New York: Harcourt Brace Jovanovich.

———. 1982. *To Dwell Among Friends: Personal Networks in Town and City.* Chicago: University of Chicago Press.

———. 1975. "Toward a Subcultural Theory of Urbanism." *American Journal of Sociology* 80: 1319–41.

———. 1973. "Urban Malaise." *Social Problems* 52: 221–35.

———. 1971. "A Research Note on Urbanism and Tolerance." *American Journal of Sociology* 76: 847–56.

Fischer, Claude S., and Robert M. Jackson. 1976. "Suburbs, Networks, and Attitudes." Chapter 11 in Barry Schwartz (ed.), *The Changing Face of the Suburbs*. Chicago: University of Chicago Press.

Fisher, Anne. 1998. "After All This Time, Why Don't People Know What Sexual Harassment Means?" *Fortune* 137(1) (January 12): 156.

Fisher, Bradley J., and David J. Hartman. 1995. "The Impact of Race on the Social Experience of College Students at a Predominantly White University." *Journal of Black Studies* 26(2): 117–34.

Fisher, Joseph C. 1976. "Homicides in Detroit: The Role of Firearms." *Criminology* 14: 387–400.

Fiske, Edward B. 1991. "U.S. Says Most of Growth in 80s Was in Major Metropolitan Areas." *The New York Times* (February 21): A18.

Flacks, Richard. 1967. "The Liberated Generation: An Exploration of the Roots of Student Protest." *Journal of Social Issues* 23(3): 52–75.

Fleischman, Arnold. 1977. "Sunbelt Boosterism: The Politics of Postwar Growth and Annexation in San Antonio." Pp. 151–168 in David C. Perry and Alfred J. Watkins (eds.), *The Rise of the Sunbelt Cities*, Urban Affairs Annual Reviews, Vol. 14. Beverly Hills, CA: Sage.

Flexner, E. 1975. *Century of Struggle*. Cambridge, MA: Harvard University Press.

Floge, Liliane, and Deborah M. Merrill. 1986. "Tokenism Reconsidered: Male Nurses and Female Physicians in a Hospital Setting." *Social Forces* 64: 925–47.

Flota, Michael W. 2010. "Exiting Voice: The Financial Services Modernization Act as Degenerative Adaptation and the Collapse of the Global Economy." Paper presented at the *Center for Interdisciplinary Writing and Research*. Daytona Beach, Florida, November 12.

———2008. "Two Roads Converging: The Paths to Neoliberalism in Sweden and South Korea." Paper presented at the 2008 Annual Meetings of the Southern Sociological Society, Richmond, Virginia.

———. 2003. *Constructing Collapse: The Rise and Fall of Financial Liberalization in Sweden and South Korea*. Doctoral Dissertation. University of California, Davis.

Foner, Anne, and Karen Schwab. 1981. *Aging and Retirement*. Monterey, CA: Brooks-Cole.

Forbes. 1995. "The Forbes Four Hundred—Index by Name." *Forbes* (October 16): 345–60.

Forbes.com. 2009. The Forbes Four Hundred. http://www.forbes.com/lists/2009/54/rich-list-09_The-400-Richest-Americans_Rank.html.

Ford, B. A., and Festus E. Obiakor. 1995. "What's Next for African American Exceptional Learners?" *CEC Today* 1: 12.

Ford, Clellan S., and Frank A. Beach. 1951. *Patterns of Sexual Behavior*. New York: Harper & Row.

Forste, Renata, and Koray Tanfer. 1996. "Sexual Exclusivity Among Dating, Cohabiting, and Married Women." *Journal of Marriage and the Family* 58: 33–48.

Fortescue, Stephen. 1999. "Privatisation, Corporate Governance and Enterprise Performance in Russia." *Russian and Euro-Asian Bulletin*, Contemporary Europe Research Centre, University of Melbourne (May). http://www.cerc.unimelb.edu.au/bulletin/bulmay98.htm.

Foss, Brian M. 1974. *New Perspectives in Child Development*. Harmondsworth: Penguin Education.

Foster, William Z. 1920. *The Great Steel Strike and Its Lessons*. New York: Huebsch.

Fox, Daniel M., and Robert Crawford. 1979. "Health Politics in the United States." Pp. 392–411 in Howard E. Freeman, Sol Levine, and Leo G. Reeder (eds.), *Handbook of Medical Sociology*, 3rd ed. Englewood Cliffs, NJ: Prentice Hall.

Foy, Felican (ed.). 1985. *The Catholic Almanac*. Paterson, NJ: St. Anthony's Guild.

Fraker, Susan. 1984. "Why Women Aren't Getting to the Top." *Fortune* 109(8) (April 16): 40–45.

Frank, Andre Gunder. 1969. "The Development of Underdevelopment." Pp. 3–17 in *Latin America: Underdevelopment or Revolution?* New York: Monthly Review Press.

Frank, David John, John W. Meyer, and David Miyahara. 1995. "The Individualist Polity and the Prevalence of Professionalized Psychology: A Cross-National Study." *American Sociological Review* 60: 360–77.

Franklin, John Hope. 1969. *From Slavery to Freedom: A History of Negro Americans*, 3rd ed. New York: Vintage Books.

Frazier, Nancy, and Myrna Sadker. 1974. *Sexism in School and Society*. New York: Dell.

Freedman, A., A. Kaplan, and B. Sadock. 1975. *A Comprehensive Textbook of Psychiatry–II*, 2nd ed., Vol. I. Baltimore, MD: Williams and Wilkins.

Freedman, Ronald. 1995. "Asia's Recent Fertility Decline and Prospects for Future Demographic Change." *Asia-Pacific Population Research Reports* No. 1 (January), also, University of Michigan Population Studies Center Report No. 450.

Freeman, Jo. 1979. "The Women's Liberation Movement: Its Origins, Organization, Activities, and Ideas." In Jo Freeman (ed.), *Women: A Feminist Perspective*. Palo Alto, CA: Mayfield.

———. 1973. "The Origins of the Women's Liberation Movement." *American Journal of Sociology* 78: 792–811.

French, Dan, and Sheldon Rothman. 1990. *Structuring Schools for Student Success: A Focus on Ability Grouping*. Quincy, MA: Massachusetts State Department of Education, Research Division.

Freud, Sigmund. 1970. *Beyond the Pleasure Principle*. New York: Bantam. (Originally published 1920.).

———. 1962. *Society and Its Discontents*. New York: Norton. (Originally published in German, 1930.).

Freudenheim, Milt. 1988. "Prepaid Programs for Health Care Encounter Snag." *The New York Times* (September 25): Sect. 1, 1, 32.

Frey, R. Scott, Thomas Deitz, and Linda Kalof. 1992. "Characteristics of Successful American Protest Groups: Another Look at Gamson's Strategy of Social Protest." *American Journal of Sociology* 98: 368–87.

Frey, William H. 1987. "Migration and Depopulation of the Metropolis: Regional Restructuring or Rural Renaissance?" *American Sociological Review* 52: 240–57.

Fried, Morton. 1967. *The Evolution of Political Society*. New York: Random House.

Friedkin, Noah E. 1999. "Choice Shift and Group Polarization." *American Sociological Review* 64: 856–75.

———. 1993. "Structural Bases of Interpersonal Influence in Groups: A Longitudinal Case Study." *American Sociological Review* 58: 861–72.

Friedland, Robert B. 1987. "Introduction and Background: Private Initiatives to Contain Health Care Expenditures." In Frank B. McArdle (ed.), *The Changing Health Care Market*. Washington, DC: Employee Benefit Research Institute.

Friedmann, Eugene A., and Robert J. Havighurst. 1954. *The Meaning of Work and Retirement*. Chicago: University of Chicago Press.

Friedman, Eugene A. II, and L. Orbach. 1974. "Adjustment to Retirement." Pp. 609–45 in Silvane Arieti (ed.), *American Handbook of Psychiatry*, Vol. 1. New York: Basic Books.

Friedrich, Carl J. 1972. "In Defense of a Concept." In Leonard Schapiro (ed.), *Political Opposition in One-Party States*. London: Macmillan.

Frierson, Henry T. 1989. "The Impact of Testing Skills Intervention upon Black Nursing Students' Licensure Examination Performance." *Journal of Negro Education* 58: 82–91.

Frieze, I., Jacqueline Ecles Parsons, P. Johnson, D. Ruble, and G. Zellman. 1978. *Women and Sex Roles: A Social Psychological Perspective*. New York: Norton.

Frisbie, W. Parker, and John D. Kasarda. 1988. "Spatial Processes." Pp. 629–66 in Neil J. Smelser (ed.), *Handbook of Sociology*. Newbury Park, CA: Sage.

Froehlke. 1990. "Centers for Disease Control, Study on Black Homicide."

Froman, R. D. 1981. "Ability Grouping: Why Do We Persist and Should We?" Paper presented at the annual meeting of the American Educational Research Association. Los Angeles.

Frueh, Terry, and Paul E. McGhee. 1975. "Traditional Sex-Role Development and Amount of Time Spent Watching Television." *Developmental Psychology* 11: 109.

Frydman, Roman, Kenneth Murphy, and Andrzej Rapaczynski. 1996. "Capitalism with a Comrade's Face." *Transition* 2 (January), also available on http://www.omri.cz/Publications/Transition/Contents/Feature/V02N02.html.

Fuerst, J. S. 1981. "Report Card: Chicago's All-Black Public Schools." *The Public Interest* 64: 79–91.

Furstenberg, Frank F., Theodore Hershberg, and L. Modell. 1975. "The

Origins of the Female-Headed Black Family: The Impact of the Urban Experience." *Journal of Interdisciplinary History* 6: 211–33.

Furstenberg. Frank F., S. Philip Morgan, and Paul P. Allison. 1987. "Paternal Participation and Children's Well-Being After Marital Dissolution." *American Sociological Review* 52: 695–701.

Fusfeld, Daniel R. 1976. *Economics,* 2nd ed. Lexington. MA: Health.

Gaard, Greta (ed.). 1993. *Ecofeminism: Women, Animals, and Nature.* Philadelphia: Temple University Press.

Gabriel, Ralph. 1963. *Traditional Values in American Life.* New York: Harcourt Brace Jovanovich.

Gaines, Margie I., and Margaret Davis. 1990. "Accuracy of Teacher Prediction of Elementary Student Achievement." Paper presented at the annual meetings of the American Educational Research Association, Boston, April 16–20.

Galagan, Patricia. 1993. "Trading Places at Monsanto." *Training and Development* 47(4): 45–49.

Galanter, Marc. 1974. "Why the 'Haves' Come Out Ahead: Speculations on the Limits of Legal Change." *Law and Society Review* 9: 95–160.

Gale, Dennis F. 1980. "Neighborhood Resettlement: Washington. D.C." Pp 95–115 in Shirley B. Laska and Daphne Spain (eds.), *Back to the City: Issues in Neighborhood Renovation.* New York: Pergamon.

Galliher, John F., and John R. Cross. 1983. *Morals Legislation Without Morality.* New Brunswick, NJ: Rutgers University Press.

Gallup, George, Jr. 2003. "Current Views on Premarital, Extramarital Sex." http://www.gallup.com/poll/8704/current-views-premarital-extramarital-sex.aspx#.

———. 1990. *The Gallup Poll: Public Opinion, 1989.* Wilmington, DE: Scholarly Resources.

———. 1989. *The Gallup Poll, 1988.* Wilmington, DE: Scholarly Resources.

———. 1988. *The Gallup Poll: Public Opinion, 1987.* Wilmington, DE: Scholarly Resources.

———. 1987. *The Gallup Poll: Public Opinion, 1986.* Wilmington, DE: Scholarly Resources.

———. 1984. *The Gallup Poll: Public Opinion, 1983.* Wilmington, DE: Scholarly Resources.

Gallup, George, Jr., and Jim Castelli. 1989. *The People's Religion: American Faith in the '90s.* New York: Collier Macmillan.

Gallup, George, Jr., and Frank Newport. 1990. "Americans Shift Toward Pro-Choice Position." *The Gallup Poll Monthly* (April): 2–4.

Gallup Organization. 2010. "Verdict on Healthcare Reform Bill Still Divided." http://www.gallup.com/poll/140981/Verdict-Healthcare-Reform-Bill-Divided.aspx (Downloaded August 1, 2010).

———. 2009. "Churchgoing Among U.S. Catholics Slides to Tie Protestants." http://www.gallup.com/poll/117382/church-going-among-catholics-slides-tie-protestants.aspx (Downloaded July 30, 2010).

———. 2007. "Race and Marriage." August 16, 2007. http://www.gallup.com/video/28420/Race-Marriage.aspx.

———. 2001a. Special Reports: Black-White Relations in the United States, July 2001 Update. http://www.gallup.com/poll/reports/bwr2001/sr010711.asp.

———. 2001b. Gallup Poll Topics: A–Z: Homosexual Relations. http://www.gallup.com/poll/indicators/indhomosexual.asp.

———. 2001c. Gallup Poll Topics: A–Z: Religion. http://www.gallup.com/poll/indicators/indreligion.asp.

———. 2001d. Poll Analyses, April 13, 2001, Easter Season Finds a Religious Nation. http://www.gallup.com/poll/releases/pr010413.asp.

———. 2001e. Gallup Poll Topics: A–Z: Healthcare System. http://www.gallup.com/poll/indicators/indhealthcare.asp.

———. 2000a. Gallup Poll Topics: A–Z: Taxes. http://www.gallup.com/poll/indicators/indtaxes.asp.

———. 2000b. Poll Analysis: Candidate Support by Subgroup. http://www.gallup.com/poll/releases/pr001106b.asp.

———. 1998. Social Audit: Haves and Have Nots. http://www.gallup.com/poll/socialaudits/have_havenot.asp.

———. 1997b. The Gallup Poll: Religious Faith Is Widespread but Many Skip Church. http://www.gallup.com/poll/news/970329.html.

———. 1997c. Special Reports: Global Study of Family Values. http://www.gallup.com/poll/reports/family.asp.

Galster, George C. 1990a. "Racial Discrimination in Housing Markets During the 1980s: A Review of the Audit Evidence." *Journal of Planning Education and Research* 9: 165–75.

———. 1990b. "Racial Steering in Urban Housing Markets: A Review of the Audit Evidence." *Review of Black Political Economy* 18: 105–29.

Gamoran, Adam. 1989. *Instructional Organization and Educational Equity.* Madison, WI: National Center on Effective Secondary Schools.

———. 1987. "The Stratification of High School Learning Opportunities." *Sociology of Education* 60: 135–55.

Gamoran, Adam, and Robert D. Mare. 1989. "Secondary School Tracking and Educational Inequality: Compensation, Reinforcement, or Neutrality?" *American Journal of Sociology* 94: 1146–83.

Gamoran, Adam, and Matthew Weinstein. 1995. *Differentiation and Opportunity in Restructured Schools.* Madison, WI: Center on Organization and Restructuring of Schools.

Gamoran, Adam, et al. 1995. "An Organizational Analysis of the Effects of Ability Grouping." *American Educational Research Journal* (Winter).

Gamson, William A. 1991. "Commitment and Agency in Social Movements." *Sociological Forum* 6(1): 27–50.

———. 1990. "The Social Psychology of Collective Action." Paper presented at the Annual Meetings of the American Sociological Association.

———. 1975. *The Strategy of Social Protest.* Homewood, IL: Dorsey.

Gamson, William A., and Andre Modigliani. 1989. "Media Discourse and Public Opinion on Nuclear Power: A Constructionist Approach." *American Journal of Sociology* 95: 1–37.

Gamson, William A., and Gadi Wolfsfeld. 1993. "Movements and Media as Interacting Systems." *The Annals of the American Academy of Political and Social Science* 528: 114–25.

Gans, Herbert J. 1972. "The Positive Functions of Poverty." *American Journal of Sociology* 78: 275–89.

———. 1971. "The Uses of Poverty: The Poor Pay All." *Social Policy* (July/August): 20–24.

———. 1967a. *The Levittowners.* New York: Random House.

———. 1967b. "The Negro Family: Reflections on the Moynihan Report." Pp. 445–57 in Lee Rainwater (ed.), *The Moynihan Report and the Politics of Controversy.* Cambridge, MA: MIT Press.

———. 1962. *The Urban Villagers.* New York: Free Press.

Ganz, Marshall. 2000. "Resources and Resourcefulness: Strategic Capacity in the Unionization of California Agriculture," 1959–1966. *American Journal of Sociology* 105: 1003–62.

Garbarino, Merwin S. 1976. *American Indian Heritage.* Boston: Little, Brown.

Garcia-Coll, Cynthia T., and Heidie A. Vazquez-Garcia. 1995. "Developmental Processes and Their Influence on Interethnic and Intercultural Relations." In Willis D. Hawley and Anthony Jackson (eds.), *Toward a Common Destiny: Improving Race and Ethnic Relations.* San Francisco: Jossey-Bass.

Gardner, Howard. 1992. *Multiple Intelligences: The Theory in Practice.* New York: Basic Books.

———. 1991. *The Unschooled Mind: How Children Think and How Schools Should Teach.* New York: Basic Books.

———. 1983. *Frames of Mind.* New York: Basic Books.

Gardner, Howard, Mindy L. Kornhaber, and Warren K. Wake. 1996. *Intelligence: Multiple Perspectives.* Orlando, FL: Harcourt, Brace.

Garfinkel, Harold. 1967. *Studies in Ethnomethodology.* Englewood Cliffs, NJ: Prentice Hall.

Garnier, Maurice, Jerald Hage, and Bruce Fuller. 1989. "The Strong State, Social Class, and Controlled School Expansion in France, 1881–1975." *American Journal of Sociology* 95: 279–306.

Garrett, C. S., P. L. Ein, and L. Tremaine. 1977. "The Development of Gender Stereotyping of Adult Occupations in Elementary School Children." *Child Development* 48: 507–12.

Gartrell, John, and Stephanie Amadeo Marquez. 1995. "The Spurious Relationship Between IQ and Social Behavior: Ethnic Abuse, Gender Ignorance, and Confounded Education." *Alberta Journal of Educational Research* 41: 277–82.

Gebhard, Paul H., John H. Gagnon, Wardell B. Pomeroy, and Cornelia V. Christenson. 1965. *Sex Offenders.* New York: Harper & Row.

Gedicks, Al. 2001. *Resource Rebels: Native Challenges to Mining and Oil Corporations.* Cambridge, MA: South End Press.

Geiger, H. Jack. 1975. "The Causes of Dehumanization in Health

Care and Prospects for Humanization." Pp. 11–36 in J. Howard and Ansalem Strauss (eds.), *Humanizing Health Care*. New York: Wiley-Interscience.

Geis, F. L., Virginia Brown, Joyce J. Walstedt, and Natalie Porter. 1984. "TV Commercials as Achievement Scripts for Women." *Sex Roles* 10: 513–25.

Geis, Gilbert. 1974. "Upperworld Crime." Pp. 114–37 in Abraham S. Bluberg (ed.), *Current Perspectives on Criminal Behavior*. New York: Alfred A. Knopf.

Geiser, Saul, and Maria Veronica Santelices. 2007. "Validity of High School Grades in Predicting Student Success Beyond the First Year: High School Grades vs. Standardized Tests as Indicators of Four-Year College Outcomes." Research and Occasional Paper Series CSHE.6.07, Center for the Study of Higher Education, University of California, Berkeley. http://cshe.berkeley.edu/publications/docs/ROPS.GEISER._SAT_6.12.07.pdf (Downloaded October 19, 2009).

Gelles, Richard J. 1995. *Contemporary Families: A Sociological View*. Thousand Oaks, CA: Sage.

———. 1983. "The Myth of Battered Husbands and New Facts About Family Violence." In O. Pocs and R. H. Walsh (eds.), *Marriage and Family 83/84*. Guilford, CT: Dushkin Publishing Group.

Gelles, Richard J., and Claire Pedrick Cornell. 1985. *Intimate Violence in Families*. Beverly Hills, CA: Sage.

Gelles, Richard J., and Murray Straus. 1988. *Intimate Violence*. New York: Simon & Schuster.

———. 1987. "Is Violence Toward Children Increasing? A Comparison of 1975 and 1985 National Survey Rates." *Journal of Interpersonal Violence* 2: 212–22.

———. 1979. "Violence in the American Family." *Journal of Social Issues* 35: 15–39.

Gergen, David. 2000. "No Place Like Home." *U.S. News and World Report* 128(24): 64.

Gerhards, Jurgen, and Dieter Rucht. 1992. "Mesomobilization: Organizing and Framing in Two Protest Campaigns in West Germany." *American Journal of Sociology* 98: 555–95.

Geschwender, James A. 1964. "Social Structure and the Negro Revolt: An Examination of Hypotheses." *Social Forces* 43: 250–56.

Getis, Arthur, Judith Getis, and Jerome Fellman. 1981. *Geography*. New York: Macmillan.

Gibbs, Jack P. 1981. *Norms, Deviances, and Social Control*. New York: Elsevier.

Giddens, Anthony. 1985. *The Constitution of Societies*. London: Macmillan.

———. 1984. *The Constitution of Society: Outline of the Theory of Structuration*. Berkeley and Los Angeles: University of California Press.

———. 1978. *Central Problems in Social Theory*. Berkeley: University of California Press.

Giele, Janet Z. 1988. "Gender and Sex Roles." Pp. 291–323 in Neil J. Smelser (ed.), *Handbook of Sociology*. Newbury Park, CA: Sage.

Giese, William. 1995. "Retirement: How Boomers Can Avoid a Bust." *Kipplinger's Personal Finance Magazine* (October): 50–55.

Gilbert, Jess, and Carolyn Howe. 1991. "Beyond State vs. Society: Theories of the State and New Deal Agricultural Policies." *American Sociological Review* 56: 204–20.

Gilens, Martin. 1995. "Racial Attitudes and Opposition to Welfare." *Journal of Politics* 57: 994–1014.

Gill, Stephen, and David Law. 1988. *The Global Political Economy: Perspectives, Problems, and Policies*. Baltimore: Johns Hopkins University Press.

Gilligan, Carol. 1982. *In a Different Voice: Psychological Theory and Women's Development*. Cambridge, MA: Harvard University Press.

Gilpin, Robert. 1979. "Three Models of the Future." Pp. 353–72 in G. Modelski (ed.), *Transitional Corporations and World Order*. San Francisco: Freeman.

Gintis, Herbert. 1974. "Sociology of Economics." Unit 21 in Dushkin Publishing Group (ed.), *The Study of Society*. Guilford, CT: Dushkin Publishing Group.

Gitlin, Todd. 1995. *The Twilight of Common Dreams: Why America Is Wracked by Culture Wars*. New York: Metropolitan Books.

Glaab, Charles N. 1963. *The American City: A Documentary History*. Homewood, IL: Dorsey.

Glaab, Charles N., and A. Theodore Brown. 1967. *A History of Urban America*. New York: MacMillan.

Glaser, Barry G., and Anselm L. Strauss. 1971. *Status Passage*. Chicago: Aldine.

Glass, Jennifer, and Valerie Camarigg. 1992. "Gender Parenthood, and Job-Family Compatibility." *American Journal of Sociology* 98: 131–151.

Glazer, Nathan. 1981. "Black English and Reluctant Judges." *The Public Interest* 62: 40–54.

———. 1976. *Affirmative Discrimination*. New York: Basic Books.

Glenn, Evelyn Makano. 1980. "Dialects of Wage Work: Japanese-American Women and Domestic Service, 1905–1940." *Feminist Studies* 6: 432–71.

Glenn, Norvall. 1966. "White Gains from Negro Subordination." *Social Problems* 14: 159–78.

Glenn, Norvall, and C. N. Weaver. 1981. "The Contribution of Marital Happiness to Global Happiness." *Journal of Marriage and the Family* 43: 161–68.

Glick, Paul. 1984. "Marriage, Divorce, and Living Arrangements: Prospective Changes." *Journal of Family Issues* 5: 7–26.

Glick, Paul C., and L. Sung-Ling. 1986. "Recent Changes in Divorce and Remarriage." *Journal of Marriage and the Family* 48: 737–47.

Glik, Deborah. 1990. "The Redefinition of the Situation: The Social Construction of Spiritual Healing Experience." *Sociology of Health and Illness* 12: 151–68.

Glock, Charles Y. 1964. "The Role of Deprivation in the Origin and Evolution of Religious Groups." Pp. 24–36 in Robert Lee and Martin E. Marty (eds.), *Religion and Social Conflict*. New York: Oxford University Press.

Glock, Charles Y., and Rodney Stark. 1965. *Religion and Society in Tension*. Chicago: Rand McNally.

Glueck, Sheldon, and Eleanor Glueck. 1956. *Physique and Delinquency*. New York: Harper.

Goelman, H., and A. R. Pence. 1987. "Effects of Child Care, Family, and Individual Characteristics on Children's Language Development." Pp. 89–104 in Deborah A. Phillips (ed.), *Quality in Child Care: What Does Research Tell?* Washington, DC: National Association for the Education of Young Children.

Goering, John, and Ron Wienk. 1996. "An Overview," Pp. 16–19 in John Goering and Ron Wienk (eds.), *Mortgage Lending, Racial Discrimination, and Federal Policy*. Washington, DC: Urban Institute Press.

Goffman, Erving. 1971. *Relationship in Public*. New York: Basic Books.

———. 1967. *Interaction Ritual: Essays on Face-to-Face Behavior*. New York: Doubleday.

———. 1961. *Asylums: Essays on the Social Situation of Mental Patients and Other Inmates*. Chicago: Aldine de Gruyter.

———. 1959. *The Presentation of Self in Everyday Life*. Garden City, NY: Doubleday.

Golden, Hilda H. 1981. *Urbanization and Cities*. Lexington, MA: D.C. Heath.

Golden, Mark, and B. Birns. 1968. "Social Class and Cognitive Development in Infancy." *Merrill-Palmer Quarterly* 14: 139–49.

Goldfarb, William. 1945. "Psychological Privation in Infancy and Subsequent Development." *American Journal of Orthopsychiatry* 15: 247–53.

Goldscheider, Calvin, and Frances K. Goldscheider. 1987. "Moving Out and Marriage: What Do Young Adults Expect?" *American Sociological Review* 52: 278–85.

Goldstein, Joshua. 1988. *Long Cycles: Prosperity and War in the Modern Age*. New Haven, CT: Yale University Press.

Goldstone, Jack A. (ed.), 1986. *Revolutions: Theoretical, Comparative, and Historical Studies*. New York: Harcourt Brace Jovanovich.

Goleman, Daniel. 1991. "Mortality Study Lends Weight to Patient's Opinion." *The New York Times* (March 21): B13.

Good, Thomas L. et al. 1990. "Using Work-Groups in Mathematics Instruction." *Educational Leadership* 47(4): 56–62.

Goode, Erich. 1996. "The Ethics of Deception in Social Research: A Case Study." *Qualitative Sociology* 19: 11–33.

———. 1990. *Deviant Behavior*, 3rd ed. Englewood Cliffs, NJ: Prentice Hall.

Goodenough, Ward H. 1957. "Cultural Anthropology and Linguistics." In Paul Garvin (ed.), *Report of the Seventh Annual Round Table Meeting* on Linguistics and Language Study. Georgetown Monograph Series, 9. Washington, DC: Georgetown University Press.

Goodwin, A. Lin. 1991. "Problems, Process, and Promise: Reflections on a Collaborative Approach to the Solution of the Minority Teacher Shortage." *Journal of Teacher Education* 42: 28–36.

Gordon, David. 1978. "Capitalist Development and the History of American Cities." In William Tabb and Larry Sawers (eds.), *Marxism and the Metropolis*. New York: Oxford University Press.

———. 1977a. "Capitalism and the Roots of the Urban Crisis." Pp. 82–112 in Roger E. Alcaly and David Mermelstein (eds.), *The Fiscal Crisis of American Cities*. New York: Vintage.

———. 1977b. "Class Struggle and the Stages of American Urban Development." Pp. 55–82 in David C. Perry and Alfred J. Watkins (eds.), *The Rise of the Sunbelt Cities*. Urban Affairs Annual Reviews, Vol. 14. Beverly Hills, CA: Sage.

———. 1975. "Recession Is Capitalism as Usual." *The New York Times Magazine* (April 27), pp. 18, 49, 52, 55, 60, 63.

———. 1973. "Capitalism, Class and Crime in America." *Crime and Delinquency* 19: 163–86.

———. 1971. *Problems in Political Economy*. Lexington, MA: Lexington Books, D.C. Heath.

Gordon, Milton M. 1964. *Assimilation in American Life*. New York: Oxford University Press.

Gordon, Robert. 1976. "Prevalence: The Race Datum in Delinquency Measurement and Its Implications for the Theory of Delinquency." Pp. 201–84 in Malcolm Klein (ed.), *The Juvenile System*. Beverly Hills, CA: Sage.

Goren, Arthur A. 1980. "Jews." Pp. 571–98 in Stephan Thernstrom, Ann Orlov, and Oscar Handlin (eds.), *Harvard Encyclopedia of American Ethnic Groups*. Cambridge, MA: Harvard University Press.

Goring, Charles. 1913. *The English Convict*. London: His Majesty's Stationery Office (Reprinted by Patterson Smith, Montclair, NJ, 1972.).

Gorski, Philip S. 1993. "The Protestant Ethnic Revisited: Disciplinary Revolution and State Formation in Holland and Prussia." *American Journal of Sociology* 99: 265–316.

Gortmaker, Steven. 1979. "Poverty and Infant Mortality in the United States." *American Sociological Review* 44: 280–97.

Gose, Ben. 1996. "Undergraduate Tuition Rises by an Average of 5%." *Chronicle of Higher Education* (October 4): A38.

Goslin, David A. 1965. *The School in Contemporary Society*. Glenview, IL: Scott, Foresman.

Gossett, Barbara J., Michael J. Cuyjet, and Irv Cockriel. 1998. "African Americans' Perception of Marginality in the Campus Culture." *College Student Journal* 32(1): 22–32.

Gottdiener, Mark. 1985. *The Social Production of Urban Space*. Austin: University of Texas Press.

Gottfredson, Michael R., and Travis Hirschi. 1990. *A General Theory of Crime*. Stanford, CA: Stanford University Press.

Gottfried, Robert S. 1983. *The Black Death: Natural and Human Disaster in Medieval Europe*. New York: Free Press.

Gould, Stephen Jay. 1981. *The Mismeasure of Man*. New York: Norton.

Gouldner, Alvin W. 1979. *The Future of Intellectuals and the Rise of the New Class*. New York: Seabury.

———. 1976. *The Dialectic of Ideology and Technology: The Origins, Future, and Grammar of Ideology*. New York: Seabury.

———. 1968. "The Sociologist as Partisan: Sociology and the Welfare State." *American Sociologist* 3(2): 103–16.

Gouldner, Helen, with Mayr Symons Strong. 1978. *Teachers' Pets, Troublemakers, Nobodies: Black Children in Elementary School*. Westport, CT: Greenwood Press.

Gove, Walter R. 1985. "The Effect of Age and Gender on Deviant Behavior: A Biopsychological Perspective." Pp. 115–44 in Alice S. Rossi (ed.), *Gender and the Life Course*. Hawthorne, NY: Aldine de Gruyter.

Gove, Walter R., Michael Hughes, and Omer R. Galle. 1979. "Overcrowding in the Home: An Investigation of Its Possible Consequences." *American Sociological Review* 44: 59–80.

Gove, Walter R., Suzanne T. Ortega, and Carolyn Briggs Style. 1989. "The Maturational and Role Perspectives on Aging and Self Through the Adult Years: An Empirical Evaluation." *American Journal of Sociology* 4: 1117–45.

Gover, Robert. 1981. *One Hundred Dollar Misunderstanding*. New York: Grove.

Gowlett, John. 1984. *Ascent to Civilization*. New York: Knopf.

Graham, Elspeth, Joe Doherty, and Mo Malek. 1992. "Introduction: The Context and Language of Postmodernism." Pp. 1–23 in Joe Doherty, Elspeth Graham, and Mo Malek (eds.), *Postmodernism and the Social Sciences*. New York: St. Martin's Press.

Granovetter, Mark. 1986. "The Micro-Structure of School Desegregation." Pp. 81–100 in Jeffrey Prager, Douglas Longshore, and Melvin Seeman (eds.), *School Desegregation Research: New Directions in Situational Analysis*. New York: Plenum.

Grant, Evalyn N., Christopher S. Lyttle, and Kevin B. Weiss. 2000. "The Relation of Socioeconomic Factors and Racial/Ethnic Differences in US Asthma Mortality." *American Journal of Public Health* 90: 1923–25.

Grant, Linda. 1984. "Females' 'Place' in the Desegregated Classroom." *Sociology of Education* 57: 98–111.

Grauerholz, Elizabeth, and Bernice A. Pescosolido. 1989. "Gender Representation in Children's Literature: 1900–1984." *Gender and Society* 3: 113–25.

Greeley, Andrew M. 1999. "Religion After 2000." Paper presented at Conference at University of California, Santa Barbara. Also available on http://www.agreeley.com/articles/rel2000.html.

———. 1991. *Faithful Attraction: Discovering Intimacy, Love, and Fidelity in American Marriage*. New York: Doherty.

———. 1982. *Catholic High Schools and Minority Students*. New Brunswick, NJ: Transaction Books.

———. 1977. *The American Catholic: A Social Portrait*. New York: Basic Books.

———. 1972. *The Denominational Society*. Glenview, IL: Scott, Foresman.

Green, K. C. 1982. Integration and Educational Attainment: A Longitudinal Study of the Effects of Integration on Black Educational Attainment and Occupational Outcomes. Ph.D. dissertation, University of California at Los Angeles.

Greenberg, Mark. 2001. "Welfare Reform and Devolution." *Brookings Review* 19(3): 20–24.

Greene, Theodore P. 1970. *America's Heroes: The Changing Models of Success in American Magazines*. New York: Oxford University Press.

Greenstone, J. David. 1991. "Culture, Rationality, and the Underclass." Pp. 399–408 in Christopher Jencks and Paul E. Peterson (eds.), *The Urban Underclass*. Washington, DC: Brookings Institution.

Grier, Peter. 2010. "Health Care Reform Bill 101: What the Bill Means to You." *Christian Science Monitor*. March 22. http://www.csmonitor.com/USA/Politics/2010/0322/Health-care-reform-bill-101-what-the-bill-means-to-you.

Griffin, Laura. 1999. "Welfare Cuts Leaving More Families Homeless, Study Finds." *The Dallas Morning News* (July 1).

Griffith, Jeanne E., Mary J. Frase, and John H. Ralph. 1989. "American Education: The Challenge of Change." *Population Bulletin* 44(4).

Gronval, Karin. 1984. "The Physical and Psychological Environment of Children in Sweden." *Current Sweden* 33.

Gross, Jane. 1990. "Men and Women in Office: On Parity and Equality." *The New York Times* (August 21): A18.

Grossman, Michael. 1982. "Government and Health Outcomes." *American Economic Review* 72(2): 191–95.

Grusky, David B., and Robert M. Hauser. 1984. "Comparative Social Mobility Revisited: Models of Convergence and Divergence in 16 Countries." *American Sociological Review* 49: 19–38.

Gugler, Joseph. 1982. "Overurbanization Reconsidered." *Economic Development and Cultural Change* 31: 173–89.

Guilford, Joy P. 1982. "Cognitive Psychology's Ambiguities: Some Suggested Remedies." *Psychological Review* 89: 48–59.

Guilford, Joy P. 1967. *The Nature of Human Intelligence*. New York: McGraw-Hill.

Guillemin, Jeane. 1978. "The Politics of National Integration: A Comparison of United States and Canadian Indian Administrations." *Social Problems* 25: 319–32.

Guinzberg, Suzanne. 1983. "Education's Earning Power." *Psychology Today* 17(7): 20–21.

Gundlach, James H., and Steven J. Stack. 1988. "The Impact of Hyper Media Coverage of Suicide: New York City. 1910–1920." Paper presented at the annual meeting of the American Sociological Association, Atlanta, August.

Gurney, Joan N., and Kathleen T. Tierney. 1982. "Relative Deprivation and Social Movements: A Critical Look at Twenty Years of Theory and Research." *Sociological Quarterly* 23: 33–47.

Gusfield, Joseph R. 1986. *Symbolism Crusade,* 2nd ed. Urbana and Chicago: University of Illinois Press. [Originally published in 1963.].

Guthrie, Doug, and Louise Marie Roth. 1999. "The State, Courts, and Equal Opportunities for Female CEOs in U.S. Organizations: Specifying Institutional Mechanisms." *Social Forces* 78(2): 511–43.

Gutman, Amy. 1987. *Democratic Education.* Princeton, NJ: Princeton University Press.

Gutman, Herbert. 1976. *The Black Family in Slavery and Freedom, 1750–1925.* New York: Pantheon.

Guzzardi, Walter. 1988. "Can Big Still Be Beautiful?" *Fortune* 117: 50–64.

Gwartney-Gibbs, Patricia A. 1986. "The Institutionalization of Premarital Cohabitation: Estimates from Marriage License Applications, 1970 and 1980." *Journal of Marriage and the Family* 48: 423–34.

Haan, N., M. B. Smith, and J. Block. 1968. "Moral Reasoning of Young Adults: Political-Social Behavior, Family Background, and Personality Correlates." *Journal of Personality and Social Psychology* 10: 183–201.

Hadaway, C. Kirk, Penny Long Marler, and Mark Chaves. 1993. "What the Polls Don't Show: A Closer Look at U.S. Church Attendance." *American Sociological Review* 58: 741–52.

Hadden, Jeffrey K., and Charles E. Swann. 1981. *Prime Time Preachers.* Reading, MA: Addison-Wesley.

Hadley, Jack, E. P. Steinberg, and J. Feder. 1991. "Comparison of Uninsured and Privately Insured Hospital Patients: Condition on Admission, Resource Use, and Outcome." *JAMA, Journal of the American Medical Association* 265(3) (January 16): 374–79.

Haertel, Edward H. 1987. "Comparing Public and Private Schools Using Longitudinal Data from the HSB Study." Pp. 9–32 in Edward H. Haertel, Thomas James, and Henry M. Levin (eds.), *Comparing Public and Private Schools,* Vol. 2: *Student Achievement.* New York: Falmer Press.

Hagan, John. 1985. *Modern Criminology: Crime, Criminal Behavior, and Its Control.* New York: McGraw Hill.

Hagan, John, John Simpson, and A. R. Gillis. 1987. "Class in the Household: A Power-Control Theory of Gender and Delinquency." *American Journal of Sociology* 92: 788–816.

Hajnal, John. 1965. "European Marriage Patterns in Perspective." In D. V. Glass and D. E. C. Eversly (eds.), *Population in History.* London: Edward Arnold.

Hall, Edward T. 1966. *The Hidden Dimension.* Garden City, NY: Doubleday.

Hall, John R. 1979. "Apocalypse at Jonestown." *Society* 16: 52–61.

Hall, Richard H. 2002. *Organizations: Structures, Processes, and Outcomes,* 8th ed. Upper Saddle River, NJ: Prentice Hall.

———. 1996. *Organizations: Structures, Processes, and Outcomes,* 6th ed. Upper Saddle River, NJ: Prentice Hall.

———. 1991. *Organizations: Structures, Processes, and Outcomes.* Englewood Cliffs, NJ: Prentice Hall.

———. 1963–1964. "The Concept of Bureaucracy: An Empirical Assessment." *American Journal of Sociology* 69: 32–40.

Haller, Emil J., and Sharon A. Davis. 1980. "Does Socioeconomic Status Bias the Assignment of Elementary School Students to Reading Groups?" *American Educational Research Journal* 17: 409–18.

Hallinan, Maureen, and Aage B. Sorensen. 1985. "Ability Grouping and Student Friendships." *American Educational Research Journal* 22: 485–99.

Hallouda, A., S. Amin, and S. Farid. 1983. *The Egyptian Fertility Survey 1980.* Vol. 2: *Fertility and Family Planning.* Cairo: Central Agency for Public Mobilization and Statistics.

Halpern, Diane F. 1992. *Sex Differences in Cognitive Abilities,* 2nd ed. Hillsdale, NJ: Lawrence Erlbaum.

Halpern, Sydney A. 1992. "Dynamics of Professional Control. Internal Coalitions and Crossprofessional Boundaries." *American Journal of Sociology* 97: 994–1021.

Hamer, Jennifer. 2001. *What It Means to Be a Daddy: Fatherhood for Black Men Living Away from Their Children.* New York: Columbia University Press.

Hamer, Dean, and Peter Copeland. 1994. *The Science of Desire: The Search for the Gay Gene and the Biology of Behavior.* New York: Simon and Schuster.

Hamilton, C. Horace. 1965. "Continuity and Change in Southern Migration." Pp. 53–78 in John C. McKinney and Edgar T. Thompson (eds.), *The South in Continuity and Change.* Durham, NC: Duke University.

Hamilton, Richard F. 1972. *Class and Politics in the United States.* New York: Wiley.

Hamm, Mark S. 1993. *American Skinheads: The Criminology and Control of Hate Crime.* Westport, CT: Praeger.

Hammersley, Martin. 1989. *The Dilemma of Qualitative Method: Herbert Blumer and the Chicago Tradition.* New York: Routledge.

Hammond, Phillip E. 1985. *The Sacred in a Secular Age: Toward Revision in the Scientific Study of Religion.* Berkeley: University of California Press.

Hampel, Paul. 2001. "History of Anthrax: United States Has Had Its Share of Anthrax Scares." *St. Louis Post-Dispatch* (November 11): B5.

Han, Shin-Kap, and Phyllis Moen. 1999. "Clocking Out: Temporal Patterning of Retirement." *American Journal of Sociology* 105: 191–236.

Handel, Warren H. 1997. "Nativism in the Passage of the Marijuana Tax Act of 1937." Paper presented at the 1997 Annual Meetings of the Midwest Sociological Society.

———. 1993. *Contemporary Sociological Theory.* Englewood Cliffs, NJ: Prentice Hall.

———. 1988. "Legalizing Drugs Could Help the Economy." *St. Louis Suburban Journals* (June).

———. 1982. *Ethnomethodology: How People Make Sense.* Englewood Cliffs, NJ: Prentice Hall.

———. 1979. "Normative Expectations and the Emergence of Meaning as Solutions to Problems: Convergence of Structural and Interactionist Views." *American Journal of Sociology* 84: 855–81.

Haniff, Nesha Z. 1991. "Epilogue." Pp. 247–56 in Walter R. Allen, Edgar P. Epps, and Nesha Z. Haniff (eds.), *College in Black and White: African American Students in Predominantly White and Historically Black Public Universities.* Albany: State University of New York Press.

Hannon, Peter, and Joe McNally. 1986. "Children's Understanding and Cultural Factors in Reading Test Performance." *Educational Review* 38: 237–46.

Hanson, R. A. 1975. "Consistency and Stability of Home Environment Measures Related to IQ." *Child Development* 46: 470–80.

Hao, Lingxin, and Andrew J. Cherlin. 2004. "Welfare Reform and Teenage Pregnancy, Childbirth and School Dropout." *Journal of Marriage and Family* 66: 179–94.

Hardy, J. B., D. W. Welchem, E. D. Mellito, and J. Kagan. 1976. "Pitfalls in the Measurement of Intelligence: Are Standardized Intelligence Tests Valid for Measuring the Intellectual Potential for Urban Children?" *Journal of Psychology* 94: 43–51.

Hare, A. Paul. 1976. *Handbook of Small Group Research,* 2nd ed. New York: Free Press.

Hargrove, Barbara. 1979. *The Sociology of Religion: Classical and Contemporary Approaches.* Arlington Heights, IL: AHM Publishing Corporation.

Harlan, Anne, and Carol Weiss. 1981. *Moving Up: Women in Managerial Careers.* Wellesley, MA: Wellesley College Center for Research on Women.

Harlow, Harry F. 1958. "The Nature of Love." *American Psychologist* 13: 673–85.

Harlow, Harry F., and Margaret Kuenne Harlow. 1970. "The Young Monkeys." In P. Cramer (ed.), *Readings in Developmental Psychology Today.* Del Mar, CA: CRM Books.

———. 1962. "Social Deprivation in Monkeys." *Scientific American* 207: 137–46.

Harlow, Harry F., and R. R. Zimmerman. 1959. "Affectational Response in the Infant Monkey." *Science* 130: 421–23.

Harnischfeger, A., and D. E. Wiley. 1980. "A Merit Assessment of Vocational Education Programs in Secondary Schools." Statement of the Subcommittee on Elementary, Secondary, and Vocational

Education of the Committee on Education, U.S. House of Representatives, September.

Harpaz, Itzhak, and Ilan Meshoulam. 1997. "Intraorganizational Power in High Technology Organizations." *Journal of High Technology Management Research* 8(1): 107–29.

Harrington, Michael. 1984. *The New American Poverty*. New York: Holt, Rinehart, and Winston.

———. 1979. "The New Class and the Left." Pp. 123–138 in B. Bruce-Briggs (ed.), *The New Class?* New Brunswick, NJ: Transaction Books.

Harrell, David E., Jr. 1967. *Emergence of the "Church of Christ" Denomination*. Lufkin, TX: Gospel Guardian Company.

Harris, Anthony R. 1991. "Race, Class, and Crime." Pp. 94–119 in Joseph F. Sheley (ed.), *Criminology. A Contemporary Handbook*. Belmont, CA: Wadsworth.

Harris, Chauncy D., and Edward L. Ullman. 1945. "The Nature of Cities." *Annals of the American Academy of Political and Social Science* 242: 7–17.

Harris, Daniel M., and Sharon Guten. 1979. "Health-Protective Behavior: An Exploratory Study." *Journal of Health and Social Behavior* 20: 17–29.

Harris, John F. 1996. "Clinton Signs 'Mighty Blow' Against Terrorism." Washington Post, Politicsnow Web, http://politicsnow.com/WP/1996-04/25/106F-042596-idx.html.

Harris, Kathleen Mullan. 1996. "Life After Welfare: Women, Work, and Repeat Dependency." *American Sociological Review* 61: 407–26.

———. 1993. "Work and Welfare Among Single Mothers in Poverty." *American Journal of Sociology* 99: 317–52.

Harris, Marvin. 1964. *Patterns of Race in the Americas*. New York: Walker.

Harris-Warrick, Ronald M., and Eve Marder. 1991. "Modulation of Neural Networks for Behavior." *Annual Review of Neuroscience* 14: 39–57.

Harrison, Bennett, and Barry Bluestone. 1988. *The Great U-Turn:Corporate Restructuring and the Polarizing of America*. New York: Basic Books.

Harrison, Bennett, and Sandra Kantner. 1978. "The Political Economy of States' Job Creation Efforts." *Journal of the American Institute of Planners* 44: 424–35.

Harry, Joseph. 1982. "Decision Making and Age Differences Among Gay Couples." *Journal of Homosexuality* 8 (Winter): 9–21.

Hart, Jordana. 1991. "Homeless Population Up, City Census Data Indicate." *Boston Globe* (December 26): 27.

Hartle, Terry. 1994. "How People Pay for College: A Dramatic Shift." *Chronicle of Higher Education* (November 9): POV.

Hartley, Ruth E. 1974. "Sex-Role Pressures and the Socialization of the Male Child." Pp. 185–98 in Judith Stacey, Susan Bereaud, and Joan Daniels (eds.), *And Jill Came Tumbling After: Sexism in American Education*. New York: Dell. [Reprinted from *Psychological Reports* 5 (1959).].

———. 1970. "American Core Culture: Changes and Continuities." In Georgene H. Seward and Robert C. Williamson (eds.), *Sex Roles in a Changing Society*. New York: Random House.

Hartz, Louis. 1955. *The Liberal Tradition in America: An Interpretation of American Political Thought Since the Revolution*. New York: Harcourt, Brace.

Harvey, Dak G., and Gerald T. Slatin. 1975. "The Relationship as Hypothesis." *Social Forces* 54: 140–59.

Harvey, David. 1973. *Social Justice and the City*. Baltimore, MD: Johns Hopkins University Press.

Harvey, William B., and Lea E. Williams. 1989. "Historically Black Colleges: Models for Increasing Minority Representation." *Education and Urban Society* 21: 328–40.

Hatala, Mark Nicholas, Katherine Milewski, and Daniel W. Baack. 1999. "Downloading Love: A Content Analysis of Internet Personal Advertisements Placed by College Students." *College Student Journal* 33, 1: 124–29.

Haub, Carl. 1991. "Top 10 Findings from the 1990 Census So Far." *Population Today* 19(7/8) (July/August): 3–4.

Haug, Marie, and Bebe Lavin. 1983. *Consumerism in Medicine*. Beverly Hills, CA: Sage.

———. 1981. "Practitioner or Patient: Who's in Charge?" *Journal of Health and Social Behavior* 22: 212–29.

Haupt, Arthur. 1990. "S-Night: Counting the Homeless." *Population Today* 18(4) (May): 3–4.

Haury, David L., and Linda A. Milbourne. 1999. "Should Students Be Tracked in Math or Science?" *ERIC Digest* (May). Also available on http://www.ed.gov/databases/ERIC_Digests/ed433217.html.

Hauser, Robert M. 1995. "Review Symposium: *The Bell Curve*." *Contemporary Sociology* 24: 149–53.

Hauser, Robert M., and David B. Grusky. 1988. "Cross-National Variation in Occupational Distributions, Relative Mobility Chances, and Intergenerational Shifts in Occupational Distributions." *American Sociological Review* 53: 723–41.

Hauser, Robert M., William H. Sewell, and Duane F. Alwin. 1976. "High School Effects on Achievement." Pp. 309–41 in Williart H. Sewell, Robert M. Hauser, and David L. Featherman (eds.), *Schooling and Achievement in American Society*. New York: Academic Press.

Havighurst, Robert, and R. Albrecht. 1953. *Older People*. New York: Longmans Green.

Havighurst, Robert, Bernice L. Neugarten, and Sheldon S. Tobin. 1968. "Disengagement and Patterns of Aging." Pp. 161–72 in Bernice L. Neugarten (ed.), *Middle Age and Aging: A Reader in Social Psychology*. Chicago: University of Chicago Press.

Hawley, Amos H. 1981. *Urban Society*, 2nd ed. New York: Random House.

———. 1950. *Human Ecology: A Theory of Community Structure*. New York: Ronald Press.

Hayes, Cheryl D. (ed.). 1987a. *Risking the Future: Adolescent Sexuality, Pregnancy, and Childbearing*. Report of the Panel on Adolescent Pregnancy and Childbearing, National Research Council, Vol. I. Washington, DC: National Academy Press.

———. 1987b. "Adolescent Pregnancy and Childbearing: An Emerging Research Focus." Pp. 1–6 in Sandra Hofferth and Cheryl D. Hayes (eds.), *Risking the Future: Adolescent Sexuality, Pregnancy, and Childbearing*, Vol. II: *Working Papers and Statistical Appendixes*. Washington, D.C.: National Academy Press.

Hayes, Cheryl D., and Sheila Kamerman (eds.). 1983. *Children of Working Parents: Experiences and Outcomes*. Washington, DC: National Academy Press.

Hayes, Thomas C. 1990. "Sick Savings Units Riddled with Fraud, FF Head Asserts." *The New York Times* (April 15).

Healey, James R., and Chris Woodyard. 2000. "Concerns Go Back 1 1/2 Years Before Recall." *USA Today* online, http://www.usatoday.com/money/consumer/autos/mauto823.htm.

Healy, Kieran. 2000. "Embedded Altruism: Blood Collection Regimes and the European Union's Donor Population." *American Journal of Sociology* 105: 1633–57.

Heath, Iona. 1999. "Commentary: There Must Be Limits to the Medicalisation of Human Distress." *British Medical Journal* 318: 439–40.

Heaven, Patrick C. L., Lee-Anne Organ, Sunila Supavadeeprasit, and Peter Leeson. 2006. "War and Prejudice: A Study of Social Values, Right-Wing Authoritarianism, and Social Dominance Orientation." *Personality and Individual Differences* 40: 599–608.

Hechter, Michael. 1995. "Introduction: Reflections on Historical Prophecy in the Social Sciences." *American Journal of Sociology* 100: 1520–27.

Hecksher, Charles. 1980. "Worker Participation and Management Control." *Journal of Social Reconstruction* (January–March).

Hedstrom, Peter. 1994. "Contagious Collectivities: On the Spatial Diffusion of Swedish Trade Unions, 1890–1940." *American Journal of Sociology* 99: 1157–79.

Heider, Fritz. 1958. *The Psychology of Interpersonal Relations*. New York: Wiley.

———. 1946. "Attitudes and Cognitive Organization." *Journal of Psychology* 21: 107–12.

Heilbroner, Robert. 1978. *Beyond Boom and Crash*. New York: Norton.

Heimer, Karen, and Ross L. Matsueda. 1994. "Role-Taking, Role Commitment, and Delinquency: A Theory of Differential Social Control." *American Sociological Review* 59: 365–90.

Helgesen, Sally. 1990. *The Female Advantage—Women's Ways of Leadership*. New York: Doubleday.

Helsing, Knud, Moses Szklo, and Georg Comstock. 1981. "Factors Associated with Mortality After Widowhood." *American Journal of Public Health* (1981): 802–09.

Hennessy, Judith. 2005. "Welfare, Work, and Family Well-Being: A Comparative Analysis of Welfare and Employment Status for Single Female-Headed Families Post-TANF." *Sociological Perspectives* 48(1): 77–104.

Henslin, James M. 1990. "America's Homeless." Pp. 265–66 in James M. Henslin, *Social Problems,* 2nd ed. Englewood Cliffs, NJ: Prentice Hall.

———. 1975. *Introducing Sociology.* New York: Free Press.

Henson, Kevin. 1996. *The Temp.* Philadelphia: Temple University Press.

Hermalin, Albert I., and Reynolds Farley. 1973. "The Potential for Residential Integration in Cities and Suburbs: Implications for the Busing Controversy." *American Sociological Review* 38: 595–610.

Herman, Edward S. 1981. *Corporate Control, Corporate Power.* Cambridge: Cambridge University Press.

Hernandez, Donald J. 1993. *America's Children: Resources from Family, Government, and the Economy.* New York: Russell Sage Foundation.

Hernandez, Jesus. 2009. "Redlining Revisited: Mortgage Lending Patterns in Sacramento 1930–2004." *International Journal of Urban and Regional Research* 33(2): 291–313.

Herrnstein, Richard J., and Charles Murray. 1994. *The Bell Curve: Intelligence and Class Structure in American Life.* New York: Free Press.

Herring, Cedrick, Hayward Derrick Horton, Verna Kieth, and Melvin Thomas. 2000. "Race Traitors, Self Haters, or Equal Opportunists? Explaining Support for Unpopular Views on Affirmative Action." Paper presented at 2000 annual meeting of the American Sociological Association, Washington, DC, August 12–16.

Heskiaoff, Heskia. 1977. "Computers and Productivity in Production and Administrative Functions in Manufacturing Industries in the United States." Ph.D. dissertation, Columbia University, New York.

Hess, Beth B. 1985. "America's Elderly: A Demographic Overview." Pp. 3–21 in Beth B. Hess and Elizabeth Markson (eds.), *Growing Old in America: New Perspectives on Old Age.* New Brunswick, NJ: Transaction Books.

Hetherington, E. M. 1999. "Should We Stay Together for the Sake of the Children?" Pp. 93–116 in E. M. Hetherington (ed.), *Coping With Divorce, Single Parenting, and Remarriage: A Risk and Resiliency Perspective.* Mahwah NJ: Erlbaum.

Hey, Robert. 1990. "Tactics Change Even as Congressional Lobbyists Multiply." *Christian Science Monitor* (June 19): 1.

Hicks, Alexander, and Joya Misra. 1994. "Political Resources and the Growth of Welfare in Affluent Capitalist Democracies." *American Journal of Sociology* 99: 668–710.

Hicks, Alexander, Joya Misra, and Tang Nah Ng. 1995. "The Programmatic Emergence of the Social Security State." *American Sociological Review* 60: 329–49.

Higginbotham, Elizabeth. 1992. "We Were Never on a Pedestal: Women of Color Continue to Struggle with Poverty, Racism, and Sexism." Pp. 183–90 in Margaret L. Andersen and Patricia Hill Collins (eds.), *Race, Class, and Gender: An Anthology.* Belmont, CA: Wadsworth.

Higginbotham, Elizabeth L., and Lynn Weber. 1992. "Moving Up with Kin and Community: Upward Social White Women." *Gender and Society* 6(3): 416–40.

Higgins, G. M. et al. 1982. Potential Population-Supporting Capacities of Lands in the Developing World: Technical Report of Land Resources for Population of the Future Project. Rome: United Nations Food and Agriculture Organization.

Hill, Martha S., and James N. Morgan. 1979. "Dimensions of Occupation." Pp. 293–334 in Greg J. Duncan and James N. Morgan (eds.), *Five Thousand American Families: Patterns of Economic Progress.* Ann Arbor: University of Michigan, Institute for Social Research.

Hill, Robert B. 1978. *The Illusion of Progress.* Washington, DC: National Urban League.

Hill, Steven. 2010. *Europe's Promise: Why the European Way Is the Best Hope in an Insecure Age.* Berkeley: University of California Press.

Hillery, G. A. 1955. "Definitions of Community: Areas of Agreement." *Rural Sociology* 20: 111–23.

Hilts, Philip J. 1990. "Forecast of AIDS Cases Is Cut by 10%." *The New York Times* (January 4): Sect. D, 20.

Himmelstrand, Ulf, Goran Akrne, Leif Lundberg, and Lar Lundberg. 1981. *Beyond Welfare Capitalism: Issues, Actors, and Forces in Societal Change.* London: William Heinemann.

Hirakubo, Nakato. 1999. "The End of Lifetime Employment in Japan." *Business Horizons* (November). Also available on http://www.findarticles.com/cf_0/m1038/6_42/58381519/print.jhtml.

Hirschfeld, Lawrence. 1996. *Race in the Making: Cognition, Culture, and the Child's Construction of Human Kinds.* Cambridge, MA: MIT Press.

Hirschi, Travis. 1980. "Labelling Theory and Juvenile Delinquency: An Assessment of the Evidence." Pp. 271–302 in Walter R. Gove (ed.), *The Labelling of Deviance,* 2nd ed. Beverly Hills, CA: Sage.

Hirsh, Kim S. 1993. "Demoted Along with Her Boss, One Secretary Fought Back." *Ms.* 4(3) (November): 93.

Hirschman, Albert O. 1970. *Exit, Voice and Loyalty: Responses to Decline in Firms, Organizations, and States.* Cambridge, MA: Harvard University Press.

Hite, Shere. 1987. *Women and Love: A Cultural Revolution in Progress.* New York: Alfred A. Knopf.

———. 1975. "Disengagement Theory: A Critique and a Proposal." *American Sociological Review* 40: 553–69.

Hochschild, Arlie. 1989. *The Second Shift: Working Parents and the Revolution at Home.* New York: Viking Penguin.

Hodge, Robert W., Paul M. Siegel, and Peter H. Rossi. 1964. "Occupational Prestige in the United States, 1925–1963." *American Journal of Sociology* 70: 286–302.

Hodge, Robert W., and Donald J. Treiman. 1968. "Class Identification in the United States." *American Journal of Sociology* 73: 286–302.

Hodge, Robert W., Donald J. Treiman, and Peter H. Rossi. 1966. "A Comparative Study of Occupational Prestige." Pp. 309–21 in Reinhard Bendix and Seymour Martin Lipset (eds.), *Class, Status, and Power: Social Stratification in Comparative Perspective,* 2nd ed. New York: Free Press.

Hodge, Robert, and David Tripp. 1986. *Children and Television: A Semiotic Approach.* Stanford, CA: Stanford University Press.

Hodgkinson, Harold L. 1986. "Reform? Higher Education? Don't Be Absurd!" *Phi Delta Kappan* 68: 271–74.

Hodgson, Susana. 1979. "Childrearing Systems: The Influence of Shared Childrearing on the Development of Competence." Pp. 96–178 in William Michelson, Saul V. Levine, and Anna-Rose Spina (eds.), *The Child in the City: Changes and Challenges.* Toronto: University of Toronto Press.

Hodson, Randy, Sandy Welsh, Sabine Rieble, Charyl Sorenson Jamison, and Sean Creighton. 1993. "Is Worker Solidarity Undermined by Autonomy and Participation? Patterns from the Ethnographic Literature." *American Sociological Review* 58: 398–416.

Hodgson, Geoffrey M. 1988. *Economics and Institutions: A Manifesto for a Modern Institutional Economics.* Cambridge: Polity Press.

Hoffer, Thomas, Andrew M. Greeley, and James S. Coleman. 1987. "Catholic High School Effects on Achievement Growth." Pp. 67–88 in Edward H. Haertel, Thomas James, and Henry M. Levin (eds.), *Comparing Public and Private Schools.* Vol. 2: *Student Achievement.* New York: Falmer Press.

———. 1985. "Achievement Growth in Public and Catholic Schools." *Sociology of Education* 58: 74–97.

Hoffmann, Lois Wladis. 1989. "Effects of Maternal Employment in the Two-Parent Family." *American Psychologist* (February): 283–92.

Holden, Constance. 1987. "Is the Time Ripe for Welfare Reform?" *Science* 238: 607–609.

Hole, Frank, and Joy McCorriston. 1991. *American Anthropology.*

Hollingsworth, J. Rogers. 1981. "Inequality in Levels of Health in England and Wales, 1891–1971." *Journal of Health and Social Behavior* 22: 268–83.

Holub, Shayla C., Marie S. Tisak and David Mullins. 2008. "Gender Differences in Children's Hero Attributions: Personal Hero Choices and Evaluations of Typical Male and Female Heroes." *Sex Roles* 58: 567–578.

Holusha, John. 1991. "Grace Pastiak's 'Web of Inclusion.'" *The New York Times* (May 5): Sect. 3, 1, 6.

Holzer, Harry J., and Keith R. Ihlanfeldt. 1996. "Spatial Factors and the Employment of Blacks at the Firm Level." *New England Economic Review* (May/June): 65.

Homans, George C. 1984. *Coming to My Senses*. New Brunswick, NJ: Transaction Books.
———. 1961. *Social Behavior: The Elementary Forms*. New York: Harcourt Brace Jovanovich.
———. 1950. *The Human Group*. New York: Harcourt Brace Jovanovich.
hooks, bell. 1997. *Killing Rage: Ending Racism*. New York: Henry Holt.
———. 1991. "Black Women Intellectuals." Pp. 147–64 in bell hooks and Cornel West, *Breaking Bread: Insurgent Black Intellectual Life*. Boston: South End Press.
———. 1981. *Ain't I a Woman: Black Women and Feminism*. Boston: South End Press.
Hooks, Gregory. 1994. "Regional Processes in the Hegemonic Nation: Political, Economic, and Military Influences on the Use of Geographic Space." *American Sociological Review* 59: 746–72.
Hope, K. 1984. *As Others See Us: Schooling and Social Mobility in Scotland and the United States*. Cambridge. England: Cambridge University Press.
Hoschschild, Jennifer. 1995. *Facing Up to the American Dream: Race, Class, and the Soul of the Nation*. Princeton, NJ: Princeton University Press.
House, James S., J. M. Lepkowski, D. R. Williams, R. P. Mero, P. M. Lantz, S. A. Robert, and J. Chen. 2000. "Excess Mortality Among Urban Residents: How Much, for Whom, and Why?" *American Journal of Public Health* 90: 1898–1904.
Hout, Michael. 1988. "More Universalism, Less Structural Mobility: The American Occupational Structure in the 1980s." *American Journal of Sociology* 93: 1358–1400.
———. 1982. "The Association Between Husbands' and Wives' Occupations in Two-Earner Families." *American Journal of Sociology* 88: 397–409.
Hout, Michael, and Andrew Greeley. 1987. "The Center Doesn't Hold: Church Attendance in the United States. 1940–1984." *American Sociological Review* 52: 325–45.
Howell, David. 1994. "The Skills Myth." *The American Prospect* 18: 81–90, also http://epn.org/prospect/18/18howe.html.
Hoyenga, Katherine Blick, and Kermit T. Hoyenga. 1979. *The Question of Sex Differences: Psychological, Cultural, and Biological Issues*. Boston: Little, Brown.
Hoyt, Homer. 1939. *The Structure and Growth of Residential Neighborhoods in American Cities*. Washington, DC: Federal Housing Administration.
Huber, Joan. 1995. "Centennial Essay: Institutional Perspectives on Sociology." *American Journal of Sociology* 101: 194–216.
Huber, Joan, and Glenna Spitze. 1988. "Trends in Family Sociology." Pp. 425–48 in Neil Smelser (ed.), *Handbook of Sociology*. Newbury Park, CA: Sage.
———. 1983. *Sex Stratification. Children, Housework, Jobs*. New York: Academic Press.
Hudson, Elizabeth. 1991. "Only 6% Pass Texas 'Master Teacher' Exam." *The Washington Post* (March 19): A8.
Huffman, Matt L., and Phillip N. Cohen. 2004. "Occupational Segregation and the Gender Gap in Workplace Authority: National Versus Local Labor Markets." *Sociological Forum* 19: 1.
Hughes, Charles C. 1993. "Culture in Clinical Psychiatry." Pp. 3–41 in Albert C. Gaw (ed.), *Culture, Ethnicity, and Mental Illness*. Washington, DC: American Psychiatric Press.
Hughes, Holly. 1993. "Metropolitan Structure and the Suburban Hierarchy." *American Sociological Review* 58: 417–33.
Human Rights Campaign. 2010. State Laws Listing. http://www.hrc.org/laws_and_elections/state_law_listing.asp (Downloaded July 28, 2010).
———. 2001. States That Prohibit Discrimination Based on Sexual Orientation. http://www.hrc.org.
Hunt, Albert R. 1987. "The Media and Presidential Campaigns." Pp. 52–74 in A. James Reichley (ed.), *Elections American Style*. Washington, DC: Brookings Institution.
Hunt, Chester, and Lewis Walker. 1974. *Ethnic Dynamics: Patterns of Intergroup Relations in Various Societies*. Homewood, IL: Dorsey.
Hunt, Morton. 1974. *Sexual Behavior in the 1970s*. New York: Dell.
Hunter, Alfred A. 1988. "Formal Education and Initial Employment: Unraveling the Relationships Between Schooling and Skills over Time." *American Sociological Review* 53: 753–65.

Hunter, Floyd. 1980. *Community Power Success: Atlanta's Policy Makers Revisited*. Chapel Hill: University of North Carolina Press.
———. 1955. *Community Power Structure*. Chapel Hill: University of North Carolina Press.
Hurn, Christopher. 1978. *The Limits and Possibilities of Schooling: An Introduction to the Sociology of Education*. Boston: Allyn and Bacon.
Husserl, Edmund. 1969. *Ideals*. London: Collier-Macmillan.
———. 1965. *Phenomenology and the Crisis of Western Philosophy*. New York: Harper and Row.
Hyde, Janet Shibley, E. Fennema, and S. J. Lamon. 1990. "Gender Differences in Mathematical Performance: A Meta-Analysis." *Psychological Bulletin* 107: 139–155.
Hyde, Janet Shibley, and Marcia C. Linn. 1988. "Gender Differences in Verbal Ability: A Meta-Analysis." *Psychological Bulletin* 104: 53–69.
Hyman, Herbert H. 1983. *Of Time and Widowhood: Nationwide Studies of Enduring Effects*. Durham, NC: Duke University Press.
Hyman, Herbert H., and Paul B. Sheatsley. 1964. "Attitudes Toward Desegregation." *Scientific American* 211:2–9.
Hyman, Herbert H., and Charles Wright. 1979. *Education's Lasting Influence on Values*. Chicago: University of Chicago Press.
Hyman, Herbert, Charles Wright, and John Shelton Reed. 1975. *The Enduring Effects of Education*. Chicago: University of Chicago Press.
Iannaccone, Laurence R. 1994. "Why Strict Churches Are Strong." *American Journal of Sociology* 99: 1180–1211.
———. 1988. "A Formal Model of Church and Sect." *American Journal of Sociology* 94: S241–S268.
Ianni, Francis A. J. 1975. *Black Mafia: Ethnic Succession in Organized Crime*. New York: Pocket Books.
———. 1974. "New Mafia: Black, Hispanic, and Italian Styles." *Society* 11: 30–36.
Iceland, John, and Rima Wilkes. 2006. "Does Socioeconomic Status Matter? Race, Class, and Residential Segregation." *Social Problems* 53(2): 248–73.
Ickes, William J., and Richard D. Barnes. 1978. "Boys and Girls Together and Alienated: On Enacting Stereotypical Sex Roles in Mixed Sex Dyads." *Journal of Personality and Social Psychology* 36: 669–83.
Idler, Ellen L., and Ronald J. Angel. 1990. "Self-Rated Health and Mortality in the NHANES-1 Epidemiologic Follow-Up Study." *American Journal of Public Health* 80: 440–52.
Idler, Ellen L., and Stanislav Kasl. 1991. "Health Perceptions and Survival: Do Global Evaluations of Health Status Really Predict Mortality?" *Journal of Gerontology* 46 (March): S55–S65.
Illich, Ivan. 1976. *Medical Nemesis*. New York: Pantheon.
Illinois Board of Higher Education. 2001. Gateway to Success: Rethinking Access and Diversity for a New Century. Springfield: Illinois Board of Higher Education. Also available on http://www.ibhe.state.il.us/Board/Agendas/2001/August/access%20and%20diversity%20final%20report%208-21-01.pdf.
Illinois Capital Development Board. 1977. *The East St. Louis Area: An Overview of State Capital Projects and Policies*. Springfield: Illinois Capital Development Board.
Imershein, Allen, Philip C. Rond, III, and Mary P. Mathis. 1992. "Restructuring Patterns of Elite Dominance and the Formation of State Policy in Health Care." *American Journal of Sociology* 97: 970–93.
Immigration and Naturalization Service. 2001. Illegal Alien Resident Population. http://www.ins.usdoj.gov/graphics/aboutins/statistics/_illegalalien/.
———. 1999. Annual Report: Legal Immigration, Fiscal Year 1998. Washington, D.C.: Immigration and Naturalization Service, Department of Justice. Also available on http://www.ins.usdoj.gov/graphics/publicaffairs/newsrels/98Legal.pdf.
Inglehart, Ronald. 1997. *Modernization and Postmodernization: Cultural, Economic, and Political Change in 43 Societies*. Princeton, NJ: Princeton University Press.
Inglehart, Ronald, and Wayne E. Baker. 2000. "Modernization, Cultural Change, and the Persistence of Traditional Values." *American Sociological Review* 65: 19–51.
Insko, Chester A., and W. H. Melson. 1969. "Verbal Reinforcement of Attitude in Laboratory and Nonlaboratory Contexts." *Journal of Personality* 37: 25–40.
Institute for Social Research, The University of Michigan. 2000. Table

7, Changes in Attendance at Church Services. http://www.umich.edu/-newsinfo/Releases/2000/Jan00/chrelig.htm.

———. 1983. *The Impact of OBRA Policies on Welfare Women and Their Children, 1981–1982.* Ann Arbor: Institute for Social Research, University of Michigan.

Institute for Taxation and Public Policy. 2000. Tax Model. http://www.ctj.org/html/mp0700.htm.

Institute of Medicine. 1990. *Broadening the Base of Treatment for Alcohol Problems.* Washington, DC: National Academy Press.

Interagency Council on the Homeless, U.S. Department of Housing and Urban Development. 1994. *Priority: Home! The Federal Plan to Break the Cycle of Homelessness.* Washington, DC: U.S. Government Printing Office.

International Economic Review. 1995. "International Trade Developments: During the First NAFTA Year, U.S.–Mexican Bilateral Trade Was Virtually in Balance." *International Economic Review* (April): 11–14.

International Study Center, Boston College. 2000. International Study Finds Asian Countries Dominate Math and Science Achievement: Report Shows Student Achievement for 38 Countries at the Eighth Grade. (Press Release, December 5) http://timss.bc.edu/timss1999i/press/press12_5.html.

Irwin, John. 1977. *Scenes.* Beverly Hills, CA: Sage.

Irwin, Michael, and John D. Kasarda. 1991. "Air Passenger Linkages and Employment Growth in U.S. Metropolitan Areas." *American Sociological Review* 56: 524–37.

Ishida, Hiroshi, John H. Goldthorpe, and Robert Erikson. 1991. "Intergenerational Class Mobility in Postwar Japan." *American Journal of Sociology* 96: 954–92.

Ishida, Hiroshi, Walter Muller, and John M. Ridge. 1995. "Class Origin, Class Destination, and Education: A Cross-National Study of Ten Industrial Nations." *American Journal of Sociology* 101: 145–93.

Ishii-Kuntz, Masako. 1988. "Acquired Immune Deficiency Syndrome and Sexual Behavior Changes in a College Sample." *Sociology and Social Research* 73: 13–17.

Ishikawa, Kaoru. 1984. "Quality Control in Japan." Pp. 1–5 in Naoto Sasaki and David Hutchins (eds.), *The Japanese Approach to Product Quality: Its Applicability to the West.* Oxford: Pergamon.

Jabin, Norma. 1987. "Attitudes Toward Disability: Horney's Theory Applied." *American Journal of Psychoanalysis* 47: 143–53.

Jackman, Mary. 1994. *The Velvet Glove: Paternalism and Conflict in Gender, Class and Race Relations.* Berkeley: University of California Press.

Jackson, Phillip W. 1968. *Life in Classrooms.* New York: Holt, Rinehart, and Winston.

Jacob, Julie. 1998. "Income Data Spark Debate Among Delegates." *AMNews* Annual Meeting '98 coverage. http://www.ama-assn.org/sci-pubs/amnews/pick_98/anna0713.htm.

Jacobs, David, and Katherine Wood. 1999. "Interracial Conflict and Interracial Homicide: Do Political and Economic Rivalries Explain White Killings of Blacks or Black Killings of Whites?" *American Journal of Sociology* 105: 157–90.

Jacobs, Jane. 1961. *The Death and Life of Great American Cities.* New York: Vintage.

Jacobs, Jerry A. 1989. *Revolving Doors: Sex Segregation and Women's Careers.* Stanford, CA: Stanford University Press.

Jacobs, P. A., M. Brunton, and M. M. Melville. 1965. "Aggressive Behavior, Mental Subnormality, and the XYY Male." *Nature* 208 (December): 1351–52.

Jacobson, Linda. 2001. "Research: Sizing Up Small Classes." *Education Week* (February 28). Also available on http://www.edweek.com/ew/ew_printstory.cfm?slug=24classsize.h20.

Jaeger, Richard M., and John A. Hattie. 1995. "Detracking America's Schools: Should We Really Care?" *Phi Delta Kappan* 77: 218–19.

Jain, Anjali, Leigh A. Chamberlin, Yvette Carter, Scott W. Powers, and Robert C. Whitaker. 2001. "Why Don't Low-Income Mothers Worry About Their Preschoolers Being Overweight?" *Pediatrics* 107: 1138–46.

Jain, S. 1984. "Women and People's Ecological Movement: A Case Study of Women's Role in the Chipko Movement in Uttar Pradesh." *Economic and Political Weekly* 19: 1788–94.

Jakubs, John F. 1986. "Recent Racial Segregation in U.S. SMSAs." *Urban Geography* 7: 146–63.

Janis, Irving L. 1972. *Victims of Groupthink: A Psychological Study of Foreign Policy Decisions and Fiascos.* Boston: Houghton Mifflin.

Janis, Irving L., and Leon Mann. 1977. *Decision Making: A Psychological Analysis of Conflict, Choice, and Commitment.* New York: Free Press.

Jaret, Charles. 1983. "Recent Neo-Marxist Urban Analysis." Pp. 499–525 in Ralph H. Turner and James F. Short, Jr. (eds.), *Annual Review of Sociology,* Vol. 9. Palo Alto, CA: Annual Reviews.

Jargowsky, Paul A., and Mary Jo Bane. 1991. "Ghetto Poverty in the United States, 1970–1980." Pp. 235–73 in Christopher Jencks and Paul E. Peterson (eds.), *The Urban Underclass.* Washington, DC: Brookings Institution.

Jeffers, Frances C., and Claude R. Nichols. 1970. "The Effects of Aging on Activities and Attitudes to Physical Well-Being in Older People." Pp. 301–10 in Erdman Palmore (ed.), *Normal Aging.* Durham, NC: Duke University Press.

Jencks, Charles. 1992. "The Postmodern Agenda." Pp. 10–39 in Charles Jencks (ed.), *The Postmodern Reader.* New York: St. Martin's Press.

Jencks, Christopher. 1994. *The Homeless.* Cambridge, MA: Harvard University Press.

———. 1991. "Is the American Underclass Growing?" Pp. 28–100 in Christopher Jencks and Paul E. Peterson (eds.), *The Urban Underclass.* Washington, DC: Brookings Institution.

Jencks, Christopher, Lauri Perman, and Lee Rainwater. 1988. "What Is a Good Job? A New Measure of Labor-Market Success," *American Journal of Sociology* 93: 1322–57.

Jencks, Christopher, and Paul E. Peterson (eds.). 1991, *The Urban Underclass.* Washington, DC: Brookings Institution.

Jencks, Christopher, Marshall Smith, Henry Ackland, Mary Jo Bane, David Cohen, Herbert Gintis, Barbara Heyns, and Stephan Michelson. 1972. *Inequality: A Reassessment of the Effect of Family and Schooling in America.* New York: Basic Books.

Jenkins, Brian M. 1987. "Will Terrorists Go Nuclear?" Pp. 350–57 in Walter Laqueur and Yonah Alexander (eds.), *The Terrorism Reader,* rev. ed. New York: NAL Penguin.

———. 1982. "Statements About Terrorism." *Annals of the American Academy of Political and Social Science* 463:11–19.

———. 1980. "The Study of Terrorism: Definitional Problems." *Rand Paper Series,* No. P-6563.

Jenkins, J. Craig, and Barbara Brents. 1991. "Reply: Capitalists and Social Security: What Did They Really Want?" *American Sociological Review* 56:129–32.

———. 1989. "Social Protest, Hegemonic Competition, and Social Reform: A Political Struggle Interpretation of the Origins of the American Welfare State." *American Sociological Review* 54: 891–909.

Jenkins, J. Craig, and Craig M. Eckert. 1986. "Channeling Black Insurgency: Elite Patronage and Professional Social Movement Organizations in the Development of the Black Movement." *American Journal of Sociology* 51: 812–29.

Jenkins, J. Craig, and Charles Perrow. 1977. "Insurgency of the Powerless: Farm Workers' Movements (1946–1972)." *American Sociological Review* 42: 249–68.

Jennings, M. Kent, and Richard G. Niemi. 1981. *Generations and Politics.* Princeton, NJ: Princeton University Press.

———. 1974. *The Political Character of Adolescence; Influence of Families and Schools.* Princeton, NJ: Princeton University Press.

Jarrell, Stephen B. and T. D. Stanley. 2004. "Declining Bias and Gender Wage Discrimination? A Meta-Regression Analysis." *Journal of Human Resources* 39 (3) (Summer 2004): 828–838.

Jiobu, Robert. 1988. "Ethnic Hegemony and the Japanese of California." *American Sociological Review* 53: 353–67.

Johnson, Benton. 1963. "On Church and Sect." *American Sociological Review* 28: 539–49.

Johnson, Chalmers. 2000. *Blowback: The Costs and Consequences of American Empire.* New York: Henry Holt.

———. 1987. "Perspectives on Terrorism." Pp. 267–85 in Walter Laqueur and Yonah Alexander (eds.), *The Terrorism Reader,* rev. ed. New York: Meridian.

Johnson, Dirk. 1991. "Census Finds Many Claiming New Identity: Indian." *The New York Times* (March 5): A1, A16.

Johnson, J., and T. Davidson. 1981. *The Persistence of Effects: A Supplement to an Evaluation of "Freestyle": A Television Series to Reduce Sex*

Role Stereotypes. Ann Arbor: Institute for Social Research, University of Michigan.

Johnson, J., J. Ettema, and T. Davidson. 1980. *An Evaluation of "Freestyle": A Television Series to Reduce Sex Role Stereotypes*. Ann Arbor: Institute for Social Research, University of Michigan.

Johnson, James A., Harold W. Collins, Victor L. Dupuis, and John H. Johansen. 1982. *Introduction to the Foundations of American Education*. Boston: Allyn and Bacon.

Johnson, Miriam M. 1988. *Strong Mothers, Weak Wives: The Search for Gender Equality*. Berkeley: University of California Press.

Johnston, David. 1990. "100 Possible Cases of Savings Fraud Given U.S. Priority." *The New York Times* (July 7): 1, 33.

Johnstone, Ronald L. 2000. *Religion in Society: A Sociology of Religion*. Upper Saddle River, NJ: Prentice Hall.

———. 1992. *Religion in Society*, 4th ed. Englewood Cliffs, NJ: Prentice Hall.

Joint Center for Political and Economic Studies. 1998. Data Bank Fact Sheet: Number of Black Elected Officials in the United States, by State and Office, January 1998. http://www.jointctr.org/databank/BEO.htm.

Jones, Elise F., Jacqueline Darroch Forrest, Noreen Goldman, Stanley Henshaw, Richard Lincoln, Jeannie I. Rosoff, Charles F. Westoff, and Deirdre Wulf. 1986. *Teenage Pregnancy in Industrialized Countries: A Study Sponsored by the Alan Guttmacher Institute*. New Haven, CT: Yale University Press.

Jones, Jaqueline. 1985. *Labor of Love, Labor of Sorrow: Black Women, Work, and the Family from Slavery to the Present*. New York: Basic Books.

Jones, Jeffrey M. 2008. "Majority of Americans Say Racism Against Blacks Widespread." http://www.gallup.com/poll/109258/majority-americans-say-racism-against-blacks-widespread.aspx.

———. 2007. "Some Americans Reluctant to Vote for Mormon, 72-Year-Old Presidential Candidates." Gallup Organization. February 20. http://www.gallup.com/poll/26611/Some-Americans-Reluctant-Vote-Mormon-72YearOld-Presidential-Candidates.aspx.

Jordan, Mary. 1992. "Students Test Below Average: In World, U.S. Fares Poorly in Math, Science." *The Washington Post* (February 6): A1, A4.

Jordan, Winthrop D. 1968. *White over Black*. Chapel Hill: University of North Carolina Press.

Josephy, Alvin M., Jr. 1968. *The Indian Heritage of America*. New York: Alfred A. Knopf.

Kain, John F. 2004. "A Pioneer's Perspective on the Spatial Mismatch Literature." *Urban Studies* 41: 7–32.

———. 1987. "Housing Market Discrimination and Black Suburbanization in the 1980s." Pp. 68–94 in Gary A. Tobin (ed.), *Divided Neighborhoods: Changing Patterns of Racial Segregation*. Sage Urban Affairs Annual Reviews, Vol. 32. Beverly Hills, CA: Sage.

Kaiser Commission on the Future of Medicaid. 1995. *Access to Health Care: Is Health Insurance Enough?* Washington, D.C.: Kaiser Commission on the Future of Medicaid.

Kalisch, P. A., and B. J. Kalisch. 1984. "Sex Role Stereotyping of Nurses and Physicians on Prime-Time Television: A Dichotomy of Occupational Portrayals." *Sex Roles* 10: 533–53.

Kalish, R. A., and D. K. Reynolds. 1976. *Death and Ethnicity: A Psychocultural Study*. Los Angeles: University of Southern California Press.

Kalle, Aarne, and Mark E. Van Buren. 1996. "Is Bigger Better? Explaining the Relationship Between Organization Size and Job Rewards." *American Sociological Review* 61: 47–66.

Kalleberg, Arne L., Barbara F. Reskin, and Ken Hudson. 2000. "Bad Jobs in America: Standard and Nonstandard Employment Relations and Job Quality in the United States." *American Sociological Review* 65: 256–78.

Kalmijn, Matthijs. 1994a. "Mother's Occupational Status and Children's Schooling." *American Sociological Review* 59: 257–75.

———. 1994b. "Assortive Mating by Cultural and Economic Occupational Status." *American Journal of Sociology* 100: 422–52.

———. 1991a. "Shifting Boundaries: Trends in Religious and Educational Homogamy." *American Sociological Review* 56: 786–800.

———. 1991b. "Status Homogamy in the United States." *American Journal of Sociology* 97: 496–523.

Kalmijn, Matthijs, and Henk Flap. 2001. "Assortative Meeting and Mating: Unintended Consequences of Organized Settings for Partner Choices." *Social Forces* 79: 1289–1313.

Kane, Edward J. 1992. "The Savings and Loan Insurance Mess." *Society* 29(3) (March/April): 4–10.

Kane, John, and April D. Wall. 2006. *The 2005 National Public Survey on White Collar Crime*. Fairmount, WV: National White Collar Crime Center. http://www.nw3c.org/research/site_files.cfm?fileid=b3d1badb-51ca-4acf-bd34-fdeb6b7a4ef1&mode=p (Downloaded October 27, 2009).

Kanter, Rosabeth Moss. 1983. *The Change Masters: Innovation and Entrepreneurship in the American Corporation*. New York: Simon & Schuster.

———. 1979. "Communes in Cities." In J. Case and R. Taylor (eds.), *Co-ops, Communes, and Collectives*. New York: Pantheon.

———. 1977. *Men and Women of the Corporation*. New York: Basic Books.

———. 1972. *Commitment and Community: Communes and Utopias in Sociological Perspective*. Cambridge, MA: Harvard University Press.

Kantrowitz, B. 1986. "A Mother's Choice." *Newsweek* pp. 46–51.

Kaplan, Lawrence. 1992. "Introduction." Pp. 3–14 in Lawrence Kaplan (ed.), *Fundamentalism in Comparative Perspective*. Amherst: University of Massachusetts Press.

Karatsu, Hajime. 1984. "Quality Control: The Japanese Approach." Pp. 9–14 in Naoto Sasaki and David Hutchins (eds.), *The Japanese Approach to Product Quality: Its Applicability to the West*. Oxford: Pergamon.

Karnow, Stanley. 1983. *Vietnam: A History*. New York: Viking Press.

Karr, S., and J. V. Wright. 1995. "Assessment: Proper Use for Persons with Problem Behaviors." Pp. 63–95 in Festus E. Obiakor and B. Algozzine (eds.), *Managing Problem Behaviors: Perspectives for General and Special Educators*. Dubuque, IA: Kendall-Hunt.

Kart, Cary S. 1976. "Some Biological Aspects of Aging." Pp. 179–83 in Cary S. Kart and Barbara Manard (eds.), *Aging in America: Readings in Social Gerontology*. Port Washington, NY: Alfred A. Knopf.

Kasarda, John D. 1990. "Structural Factors Affecting the Location and Timing of Urban Underclass Growth." *Urban Geography* 11: 234–64.

———. 1989. "Urban Industrial Transition and the Underclass." *Annals of the American Academy of Political and Social Science* 501: 26–47.

———. 1985. "Urban Change and Minority Opportunities." In P. E. Peterson (ed.), *The New Urban Reality*. Washington, DC: Brookings Institution.

———. 1980. "The Implication of Contemporary Redistribution Trends for National Policy." *Social Science Quarterly* 61: 373–400.

Kasper, Judith A., Daniel C. Walden, and Gail Wilensky. 1980. *NCHSR National Health Care Expenditure Study. Data Preview I: Who Are the Uninsured?* Hyattsville, MD: National Center for Health Services Research.

Katz, Elihu. 1957. "The Two-Step Flow of Communication: An Up-to-Date Report on an Hypothesis." *Public Opinion Quarterly* 21: 61–78.

Katz, Jack. 1996. "Families and Funny Mirrors: A Study in the Social Construction and Personal Embodiment of Humor." *American Journal of Sociology* 101: 1194–1237.

Katz, Janet, and Willaim J. Chambliss. 1991. "Biology and Crime." Pp. 245–71 in Joseph F. Sheley (ed.), *Criminology: A Contemporary Handbook*. Belmont, CA: Wadsworth.

Kaufman, Leslie. 2010. "At 40, Earth Day Is Now Big Business." *New York Times* (April 21). http://www.nytimes.com/2010/04/22/business/energy-environment/22earth.html?_r=1&ref=business (Downloaded August 3, 2010).

Kauzlarich, David, and Ronald C. Kramer. 1998. *Crimes of the American Nuclear State: At Home and Abroad*. Boston, MA: Northeastern University Press.

Kee, Lorraine, and Ken Leiser. 2000. "Interstate 70 Sit-In Reaped Rewards for Minorities in Construction." *St Louis Post-Dispatch* (July 9): A1.

Keller, Bill. 1990. "From State Pricing to Stoop Labor, Soviet System Dooms a Bumper Crop." *The New York Times* (August 20): A9.

Kelley, Jonathan, and M. D. R. Evans. 1995. "Class and Conflict in Six Western Nations." *American Sociological Review* 60: 157–78.

———. 1993. "The Legitimation of Inequality: Occupational Earnings in Nine Nations." *American Journal of Sociology* 99: 75–125.

Kellner, Douglas. 2001. "September 11, Terror War, and Blowback." http://www.publiceye.org/frontpage/911/d~kellner~911.htm.

Kelly, Dean. 1977. *Why Conservative Churches Are Growing*, rev. ed. New York: Harper & Row.

Kemp, Alice Abel, and E. M. Beck. 1986. "Equal Work, Unequal Pay:

Gender Discrimination Within Work-Similar Occupations." *Work and Occupations* 13: 324–47.

Kemper, Theodore D., and Randall Collins. 1990. "Dimensions of Microinteraction." *American Journal of Sociology* 96: 32–68.

Kempf, Angela M., and Patrick L. Remington. 2007. "New Challenges for Telephone Survey Research in the Twenty-First Century." *Annual Review of Public Health* 28 (April): 113–126.

Kennedy, Margaret A. 1992. "Testing to Uncover Unfair Hiring." *Nation's Business* (February): 36–37.

Kenney, Brett V. 1992. "The British Media Ban: The Difference Between Terrorist-Related Speech and Terrorist Acts." *Notre Dame Journal of Law, Ethics, and Public Policy* 6(1): 245–81.

Kenney, Martin. 1987. *Biotechnology: The University-Industrial Complex*. New Haven, CT: Yale University Press.

Kennickell, Arthur B. 2000. An Examination of Changes in the Distribution of Wealth from 1989 to 1998: Evidence from the Survey of Consumer Finances. Washington, DC: Federal Reserve Board. http://www.bog.frb.fed.us/pubs/oss/oss2/98/bull0100.pdf.

Kenniston, Kenneth. 1971. *Youth and Dissent: The Rise of a New Opposition*. New York: Harcourt Brace Jovanovich.

Kerbo, Harold R. 1983. *Social Stratification and Inequality: Class Conflict in the United States*. New York: McGraw-Hill.

Kessler, Ronald, and Horst Stipp. 1984. "The Impact of Fictional Television Suicide Stories on U.S. Fatalities: A Replication." *American Journal of Sociology* 90: 151–67.

Key, Mary Ritchie. 1975. "The Roles of Males and Females in Children's Books: Dispelling All Doubt." Pp. 56–70 in Rhoda Kesler Unger and Florence L. Denmark (eds.), *Woman Dependent or Independent Variable?* New York: Psychological Dimensions.

Keyes, R. 1980. *The Height of Your Life*. Boston: Little, Brown.

Khator, R. 1989. "Public Participation: The Chipko Aandolan in India." *Journal of Developing Societies* 5: 58–63.

Kieschnick, Michael. 1981. *Taxes and Growth: Business Incentives and Economic Development*. Washington, DC: Council of State Planning Agencies.

Kilborn, Peter T. 1991. "'Race Norming' Tests Becomes a Fiery Issue." *The New York Times* (May 19): Sect. E, 5.

———. 1990. "A Company Recasts Itself to Erase Bias on the Job." *The New York Times* (October 4): A1, D21.

Kilbourne, Barbara Stanek, Paula England, George Farkas, Kurt Beron, and Deborah Weir. 1994. "Returns to Skill, Compensating Differentials, and Gender Bias: Effects of Occupational Characteristics on the Wages of White Women and Men." *American Journal of Sociology* 100: 689–719.

Killian, Lewis M. 1984. "Organization, Rationality, and Spontaneity in the Civil Rights Movement." *American Sociological Review* 49: 770–83.

Kindleberger, Charles. 1989. *Manias, Panics and Crashes: A History of Financial Crises*. New York: Basic Books.

Kinder, D. R., and D. O. Sears. 1981. "Symbolic Racism Versus Racial Threats to the Good Life." *Journal of Personality and Social Psychology* 40: 414–31.

King, Charles E. 1989. "Homelessness in America." *The Humanist* 4 (May–June): 8, 32.

King, Donna, and Carol E. MacKinnon. 1988. "Making Difficult Choices Easier: A Review of Research on Day Care and Children's Development." *Family Relations* 37: 394–95.

Kingston, Paul William, and Steven L. Nock. 1987. "Time Together Among Dual-Earner Couples." *American Sociological Review* 52: 391–400.

Kinloch, Graham C. 1974. *The Dynamics of Race Relations: A Sociological Analysis*. New York: McGraw-Hill.

Kinsey, Alfred C. et al. 1953. *Sexual Behavior in the Human Female*. Philadelphia: Saunders.

———. 1948. *Sexual Behavior in the Human Male*. Philadelphia: Saunders.

Kirby, Douglas. 1997. *No Easy Answers: Research Findings on Programs to Reduce Teen Pregnancy*. Washington, DC: The National Campaign to Prevent Teenage Pregnancy. Summary available online at http://www.teenpregnancy.org/fmnoeasy.htm.

Kirkland, M. C. 1971. "The Effects of Tests on Students and Schools." *Review of Educational Research* 41: 303–50.

Kirschenman, Jolene, and Kathryn M. Neckerman. 1991. "'We'd Love to Hire Them, But … ': The Meaning of Race for Employers." Pp. 203–32 in Christopher Jencks and Paul E. Peterson (eds.), *The Urban Underclass*. Washington, DC: Brookings Institution.

Kiser, Edgar. 1995. "What Can Sociological Theories Predict? Comment on Collins, Kuran, and Tilly." *American Journal of Sociology* 100: 1611–15.

Kitsuse, John I., and Aaron V. Cicourel. 1963. "A Note on Official Uses of Statistics." *Social Problems* 2: 131–39.

Klein, Joe. 1993. "Why China Does It Better." *Newsweek* (April 12): 23.

Klemesrud, Judy. 1981. "The Voice of Authority Is Still Male." *The New York Times* (February 2): 16.

Kline, Benjamin. 2007. *First Along the River: A Brief History of the U.S. Environmental Movement*. Lanham: Rowman & Littlefield Publishers.

Kloss, Robert Marsh, Ron E. Roberts, and Dean S. Dorn. 1976. *Sociology with a Human Face*. St. Louis, MO: Mosby.

Kluegel, James R. 1990. "Trends in Whites' Explanations of the Black-White Gap in Socioeconomic Status, 1977–1989." *American Sociological Review* 55: 512–25.

Kluegel, James R., and Eliot R. Smith. 1986. *Beliefs About Inequality: Americans' Views of What Is and What Ought to Be*. Hawthorne, NY: Aldine de Gruyter.

———. 1982. "Whites' Beliefs About Blacks' Opportunity." *American Sociological Review* 47: 518–32.

Kmitch, Janet, Pedro Laboy, and Sarah Van Damme. 1995. "International Comparisons of Manufacturing Compensation." *Monthly Labor Review* 118(10): 3–9.

Knocke, D. 1981. "Power Structures." Pp. 275–332 in S. Long (ed.), *Handbook of Political Behavior*. New York: Plenum.

Koch, Wendy. 2008. "Homeless Numbers 'Alarming.'" *USA Today*, October 21. http://www.usatoday.com/news/nation/2008-10-21-homeless_N.htm (Downloaded December 5, 2009).

Kochhar, Rakesh. 2006. Growth in the Foreign-Born Workforce and Employment of the Native-Born. Pew Hispanic Center Report. August 10. http://pewhispanic.org/files/reports/69.pdf.

Koenig, Robert L. 1993a. "Rage Fuels the Rise of German Neo-Nazi Groups." *St. Louis Post-Dispatch* (February 28): 1A, 8A.

———. 1993b. "Refugees in Germany Live in Fear." *St. Louis Post-Dispatch* (March 1): 1A, 7A.

Kogut, Bruce, and Udo Zander. 2000. "Did Socialism Fail to Innovate? A Natural Experiment of the Two Zeiss Companies." *American Sociological Review* 65: 169–90.

Kohlberg, Lawrence. 1986. "A Current Statement on Some Theoretical Issues." Pp. 485–546 in Sohan Modgil and Celia Modgil (eds.), *Lawrence Kohlberg: Consensus and Controversy*. Philadelphia: Falmer Press.

———. 1984. *The Psychology of Moral Development: Moral Stages and the Life Cycle*, Vol. 2. San Francisco: Harper & Row.

———. 1975. "Moral Education for a Society in Moral Transition." *Educational Leadership* 33: 46–54.

———. 1969. "Stage and Sequence: The Cognitive-Developmental Approach to Socialization." Pp. 347–80 in D. A. Goslin (ed.), *Handbook of Socialization: Theory and Research*. Chicago: Rand McNally.

Kohn, Melvin L. 1978. "The Benefits of Bureaucracy." *Human Nature* (August).

———. 1969. *Class and Conformity*. Homewood, IL: Dorsey.

Kolbe, R., and J. C. LaVoie. 1981. "Sex-Role Stereotyping in Pre-School Children's Picture Books." *Social Psychology Quarterly* 44: 369–74.

Kollock, Peter, Philip Blumstein, and Pepper Schwartz. 1985. "Sex and Power in Interaction: Conversational Privileges and Duties." *American Sociological Review* 50: 34–46.

Koos, Earl. 1954. *The Health of Regionville*. New York: Columbia University Press.

Koratz, Gene. 1988. "The Year the Rich Really Forked Over More Taxes." *Business Week* 3061 (July 18): 16.

Kornberg, W. 1975. "A Pre-Columbian Metropolis." *Mosaic* (September–October): 26–33.

Kornhauser, William. 1959. *The Politics of Mass Society*. Glencoe, IL: Free Press.

Kosals, Leonid Ya., Rozalina R. Ryvkina, and Michael D. Intriligator. 2000. "Russia's Defense Enterprises: Between the State and the Market."

In Vlad Genin (ed.), *The Anatomy of Russian Defense Conversion*. Also available on http://www.ecaar~russia.org/kosalsl_e.htm.

Kosmin Barry A., and Ariela Keysar. 2009. American Religious Identification Survey, 2008. ARIS 2008 Report, Part 1a—Belonging. http://b27.cc.trincoll.edu/weblogs/AmericanReligionSurvey-ARIS/reports/p1a_belong.html (Downloaded November 28, 2009).

Kotlowitz, Alex. 1992. *There Are No Children Here: The Story of Two Boys Growing Up in the Other America*. New York: Vintage Anchor.

Kourvetaris, George A., and Betty A. Dobratz. 1982. "Political Power and Conventional Political Participation." Pp. 289–317 in Ralph H. Turner and James F. Short, Jr. (eds.), *Annual Review of Sociology*, Vol. 8. Palo Alto, CA: Annual Reviews.

Kozol, Harry L., Richard J. Boucher, and Ralph T. Garofalo. 1972. "The Diagnosis and Treatment of Dangerousness." *Crime and Delinquency* 18: 371–92.

Kozol, Jonathan. 1991. *Savage Inequalities: Children in America's Schools*. New York: Crown.

———. 1986. *Illiterate America*. New York: Anchor-Doubleday.

Kramer, Ronald C. 1984. "Corporate Criminality: The Development of an Idea." In Ellen Hochstedler (ed.), *Corporations as Criminals*. Beverly Hills, CA: Sage.

Krause, Neal, Christopher G. Ellison, and Keith M. Wulff. 1998. "Church-Based Emotional Support, Negative Interaction, and Psychological Well-Being: Findings from a National Sample of Presbyterians." *Journal for the Scientific Study of Religion* 37: 725–41.

Kriesi, Hanspeter. 1989. "New Social Movements and the New Class in the Netherlands." *American Journal of Sociology* 94: 1078–1116.

Krisberg, Barry, Ira Schwartz, Gideon Fishman, Zvi Eisikovits, Edna Guttman, and Karen Joe. 1987. "The Incarceration of Minority Youth." *Crime and Delinquency* 33(2): 173–205.

Kristof, Nicholas D. 1991. "Affirmative Action, Chinese Style, Makes Some Progress." *The New York Times* (March 31): 2E.

Kristol, Irving. 1978. *Two Cheers for Capitalism*. New York: Basic Books.

Kroll, R. A. 1978. "A Meta Analysis of Comparative Research on the Effects of Desegregation on Academic Achievement." Ph.D. dissertation, Western Michigan University. Dissertation Abstracts International 39: 601 1A.

Krugman, Paul. 1990. *The Age of Diminished Expectations: U.S. Economic Policy in the 1990s*. Cambridge, MA: MIT Press.

Krymkowski, Daniel H. 1991. "The Process of Status Attainment Among Men in Poland, the U.S., and West Germany." *American Sociological Review* 56: 46–59.

Kübler-Ross, Elisabeth. 1981. *Living with Death and Dying*. New York: Macmillan.

———. 1969. *On Death and Dying*. New York: Macmillan.

Kuhn, Thomas. 1962. *The Structure of Scientific Revolutions*. Chicago: University of Chicago Press.

Kunen, James S. 1996. "The End of Integration." *Time* 147(18) (April 29).

Kunkel, Dale, Kirstie M. Cope, and Erica Biely. 1999. "Sexual Messages on Television: Comparing Findings from Three Studies." *Journal of Sex Research* 36: 230–36.

Kuran, Timur. 1995. "The Inevitability of Future Revolutionary Surprises." *American Journal of Sociology* 100: 1528–51.

Kurdek, L. A., and J. P. Schmitt. 1986. "Early Development of Relationship Quality in Heterosexual Married, Heterosexual Cohabiting, Gay and Lesbian Couples." *Developmental Psychology* 22: 305–09.

Kurtz, P. David, James M. Gaudlin, Jr., John S. Wodarski, and Phyllis T. Howing. 1993. "Maltreatment and the School-Aged Child: School Performance Consequences." *Child Abuse and Neglect* 17: 581–89.

Kurzman, Charles. 1999. "Liberal Islam: Prospects and Challenges." *Middle East Review of International Affairs* 3 (September). Also available on http://www.biu.ac.il/SOC/besa/meria/journal/1999/issue3/jv3n3a2.html.

———. 1996. "Structural Opportunity and Perceived Opportunity in Social-Movement Theory: The Iranian Revolution of 1979." *American Sociological Review* 61: 153–70.

Kutnick, Peter. 1986. "The Relationship of Moral Judgement and Moral Action: Kohlberg's Theory, Criticism, and Revision." Pp. 125–48 in Sohan Modgil and Celia Modgil (eds.), *Lawrence Kohlberg: Consensus and Controversy*. Philadelphia: Falmer Press.

Kuykendall, Jack L. 1970. "Police and Minority Groups: A Theory of Negative Contact." *Police* 15: 47–56.

Ladner, Joyce, and Ruby Morton Gourdine. 1984. "Intergenerational Teenage Motherhood: Some Preliminary Findings." *Sage: A Scholary Journal on Black Women* 1(2): 22–24.

LaFrance, Marianne, and Barbara Carmen. 1980. "The Nonverbal Display of Psychological Androgyny." *Journal of Personality and Social Psychology* 38: 36–49.

Lake, Robert. 1981. *The New Suburbanites: Race and Housing in the Suburbs*. New Brunswick, NJ: Center for Urban Policy Research, Rutgers University.

Lamb, H. H. 1982. *Climate History and the Modern World*. London: Methuen.

Lamb, Michael E., M. Ann Easterbrooks, and George W. Holden. 1980. "Reinforcement and Punishment Among Preschoolers: Characteristics, Effects, and Correlates." *Child Development* 51: 1230–36.

Lamke, Leanne. 1982. "The Impact of Sex-Role Orientation on Self-Esteem in Early Adolescence." *Child Development* 53: 1530–35.

Lamm, Helmut, and C. Sauer. 1974. "Discussion-Induced Shift Toward Higher Demands in Negotiation." *European Journal of Social Psychology*.

Lammermeier, P. J. 1973. "The Urban Black Family in the Nineteenth Century: A Study of Black Family Structure in the Ohio Valley, 1850–1880." *Journal of Marriage and the Family* 35: 440–56.

Lane, Hana Umlauf (ed.). 1983. *The 1984 World Almanac and Book of Facts*. New York: Newspaper Enterprise Association.

Lang, Kurt. 1972. *Military Institutions and the Sociology of War: A Review of the Literature with Annotated Bibliography*. Beverly Hills, CA: Sage.

Langley, Travis, Edgar Neal, and K. M. Craig. 1992. "Aggression-Consistent, -Inconsistent, and -Irrelevant Priming Effects on Selective Exposure to Media Violence." *Aggressive Behavior* 18: 349.

Laqueur, Walter. 1987. "Reflections on Terrorism." Pp. 378–92 in Walter Laqueur and Yonah Alexander (eds.), *The Terrorism Reader*, rev. ed. New York: NAL Penguin.

Larkins, G. A., and S. E. Oldham. 1976. "Patterns of Racial Segregation in a Desegregated High School." *Theory and Research in Social Education* 4(2): 23–28.

Larson, Robert I. 2006. "Russia's Energy Policy: Security Dimensions and Russia's Reliability as an Energy Supplier." *FOI: Swedish Defense Research Agency Scientific Report*, March 2006. http://www2.foi.se/rapp/foir1934.pdf (Downloaded July 27, 2010).

Lash, Scott. 1990. *The Sociology of Postmodernism*. New York: Routledge.

Latane, B., and J. M. Darley. 1970. *The Unresponsive Bystander: Why Doesn't He Help?* New York: Appleton, Century, Crofts.

Latane, B., S. A. Nida, and D. W. Wilson. 1981. "The Effects of Group Size and Helping Behavior." In J. P. Rushton and R. M. Sorrentino (eds.), *Altruism and Helping Behavior: Social, Personality, and Developmental Perspectives*. Hillsdale, NJ: Erlbaum.

Lauer, Robert H., and Warren H. Handel. 1983. *Social Psychology: The Theory and Application of Symbolic Interactionism*, 2nd ed. Englewood Cliffs, NJ: Prentice Hall.

Laughlin, Patrick R., and P. Christopher Early. 1982. "Social Combination Models, Persuasive Arguments Theory, Social Comparison Theory, and Choice Shift." *Journal of Personality and Social Psychology* 42: 273–80.

Laumann, Edward O., John H. Gagnon, Robert T. Michael, and S. Michaels. 1994. *The Social Organization of Sexuality: Sexual Practices in the United States*. Chicago: University of Chicago Press.

Lavely, W. 1984. "The Rural Chinese Fertility Transition: A Report from Shifang Xian Sichuan." *Population Studies* 38: 365–84.

Lavergne, Gary M., and Bruce Walker. 2002. "Academic Performance of Top 10 Percent and Non–Top 10 Percent Students (Revised), Academic Years 1996–2001." Implementation and Results of the Texas Automatic Admissions Law (HB 588) at University of Texas, Austin, Demographic Analysis. Fifth report. http://www.utexas.edu/student/admissions/research/HB588-Report5.pdf (Downloaded October 19, 2009).

Lawler, Edward J., and Jeongkoo Yoon. 1996. "Commitment in Exchange Relations: Test of a Theory of Relational Cohesion." *American Sociological Review* 61: 89–108.

Lawton, Leora, and Merril Silverstein. 1994. "Affection, Social Contact, and Geographic Distance Between Adult Children and Their Parents." *Journal of Marriage and the Family* 56: 57–68.

Laythe, Brian, Deborah Finkel, and Lee A. Kirkpatrick. 2001. "Predicting Prejudice from Religious Fundamentalism and Right-Wing Authoritarianism: A Multiple-Regression Approach." *Journal for the Scientific Study of Religion* 40(1): 1–10.

Lazar, Irving. 1981. "Early Childhood Education is Effective." *Educational Leadership* 38: 303–05.

Lazar, Irving, R. Darlington, H. Murray, J. Royce, and A. Snipper. 1982. "Lasting Effects of Early Childhood Education." *Monographs of the Society for Research in Child Development* 47(1, 2, Serial No. 194).

Lazar, Irving, V. R. Hubbel, H. Murray, M. Rosche, and J. Royce. 1977. *The Persistence of Pre-School Effects: A Long-Term Follow-Up of Fourteen Infant and Pre-School Experiments. Summary.* Washington, DC: U.S. Department of Health and Human Services, Administration for Children, Youth, and Families.

Lea, G. 1982. "Religion, Mental Health, and Clinical Issues." *Journal of Religion and Health* 21: 336–51.

Leacock, E. B. 1969. *Teaching and Learning in City Schools.* New York: Basic Books.

Leatherman, Courtney. 1991. "Western Illinois Fires Nude-Beach Scholar." *Chronicle of Higher Education* (July 3).

Le Boeuf, Michael. 1982. *The Productivity Challenge: How to Make It Work for America and You.* New York: McGraw-Hill.

Le Bon, Gustave. 1960. *The Crowd: A Study of the Popular Mind.* New York: Viking. (Originally published in 1895).

Lee, Richard B. 1984. *The Dobe !Kung.* New York: Holt, Rinehart, and Winston.

Lee, Richard B., and Irven DeVore. 1968. *Man the Hunter.* Chicago: Aldine.

Lefrancois, Guy R. 1996. *The Lifespan,* 5th ed. Belmont, CA: Wadsworth.

Lefton, Mark, J. K. Skipper, and C. H. McCaghy (eds.). 1968. *Approaches to Deviance.* New York: Appleton-Century-Crofts.

Lehman, Jeffrey, and Sheldon Danzinger. 1995. Ending Welfare as We Know It: Values, Economics, and Politics. Cambridge, MA: The Electronic Policy Network. http://epn.org/library/danz01.html.

Leiter, K. C. W. 1974. "Ad Hocing in the Schools: A Study of Placement Practices in the Kindergartens of Two Schools." Pp. 17–75 in Aaron Cicourel, K. Jennings, S. Jennings, K. Leiter, R. MacKay, H. Mehan, and D. Roth (eds.), *Language Use and School Performance.* New York: Academic Press.

Lekachman, Robert. 1982. "The Specter of Full Employment." Pp. 68–74 in Jerome H. Skolnick and Elliott Currie (eds.), *Crisis in American Institutions,* 5th ed. Boston: Little, Brown.

Lemann, Nicholas. 1991. *The Promised Land: The Great Black Migration and How It Changed America.* New York: Vintage.

Lemert, Edwin M. 1978. "Primary and Secondary Deviation." In Earl Rubington and Martin S. Weinberg (eds.), *Deviance,* 3rd ed. New York: Macmillan.

Lemon, Bruce W., Vern L. Bengston, and James A. Peterson. 1972. "Activity Types and Life Satisfaction in a Retirement Community." *Journal of Gerontology* 27: 511–12.

Lenin, V. I. 1916. *Imperialism, the Highest Stage of Capitalism.* (Written in 1916 and published in pamphlet form in 1917 by Parus publishers, Petrograd, Russia.).

Lenski, Gerhard. 1988. "Rethinking Macrosociological Theory." *American Sociological Review* 53: 163–71.

———. 1966. *Power and Privilege: A Theory of Social Stratification.* New York: McGraw-Hill.

Lenski, Gerhard, and Jean Lenski. 1987. *Human Societies: An Introduction to Macrosociology,* 5th ed. New York: McGraw-Hill.

———. 1982. *Human Societies,* 4th ed. New York: McGraw-Hill.

———. 1963. *The Religious Factor: A Sociological Study of Religion's Impact on Politics, Economics, and Family Life,* rev. ed. Garden City, NY: Anchor Books.

Lenski, Gerhard, and Patrick D. Nolan. 1986. "Trajectories of Development: A Further Test." *Social Forces* 64: 794–95.

———. 1984. "Trajectories of Development: A Test of Ecological-Evolutionary Theory." *Social Forces* 63: 1–23.

Leonard, Jonathan. 1987. "The Interaction of Residential Segregation and Employment Discrimination." *Journal of Urban Economics* 21: 323–46.

Lever, Janet. 1994. "The 1994 Advocate Survey of Sexuality and Relationships: The Men." *The Advocate,* August 23: 16–24.

Levin, Jack, and James Alan Fox. 1985. *Mass Murder: America's Growing Menace.* New York: Plenum Press.

Levin, Jack, and William C. Levin. 1982. *The Functions of Prejudice,* 2nd ed. New York: Harper & Row.

Levine, Marc V. 1987. "Downtown Redevelopment as an Urban Growth Strategy: A Critical Appraisal of the Baltimore Renaissance." *Journal of Urban Affairs* 9: 103–23.

Levitan, Sar A. 1985. *Programs in Aid of the Poor,* 5th ed. Baltimore, MD: Johns Hopkins University Press.

Levy, Maury Z. 1979. "The Powers That Be." *Philadelphia* (September): 159–72, 255.

Lewin, Jeffrey S., and Robert Joseph Taylor. 1998. "Panel Analyses of Religious Involvement and Well-being in African Americans: Contemporaneous vs. Longitudinal Effects." *Journal for the Scientific Study of Religion* 37: 695–709.

Lewin, Kurt. 1943. "Forces Behind Food Habits and Methods of Change." *Bulletin of the National Research Council* 108: 35–65.

Lewin, Kurt, Ronald Lippitt, and Ralph K. White. 1939. "Patterns of Aggressive Behavior in Experimentally Created 'Social Climates.'" *Journal of Social Psychology* 10: 271–99.

Lewin, Tamar. 1992. "Nude Pictures Are Ruled Sexual Harassment." Pp. 84–86 in Paula S. Rothenberg (ed.), *Race, Class, and Gender in the United States: An Integrated Study.* New York: St. Martin's Press.

———. 1991. "In Crime, Too, Some Gender-Related Inequities." *The New York Times* (January 20). Week in Review Sect. F, 9.

Lewis, Aubrey. 1953. "Health as a Social Concept." *British Journal of Sociology:* 100–24.

Lewis, Jerry M. 1972. "A Study of the Kent State Incident Using Smelser's Theory of Collective Behavior." *Sociological Inquiry* 42: 87–96.

Lewis Mumford Center. 2001. "Ethnic Diversity Grows, Neighborhood Integration Lags Behind." *American Communities Project: Brown University.*

Lewontin, R. C., Steven Rose, and Leon J. Kamin. 1984. *Not in Our Genes.* New York: Pantheon.

Liazos, Alexander. 1972. "The Poverty of the Sociology of Deviance: Nuts, Sluts, and Preverts." *Social Problems* 20(1) (Summer): 103–20.

Lichter, Daniel. 1988. "Racial Differences in Unemployment in American Cities." *American Journal of Sociology* 993: 772–92.

Lichter, Daniel, Felicia B. LeClere, and Diane K. McLaughlin. 1991. "Local Marriage Markets and the Marital Behavior of Black and White Women." *American Journal of Sociology* 96: 843–67.

Lieberson, Stanley. 1992. "Einstein, Renoir, and Greeley: Some Thoughts About Evidence in Sociology." 1991 Presidential Address, American Sociological Association. *American Sociological Review* 57: 1–15.

———. 1980. *A Piece of the Pie: Blacks and White Immigrants Since 1880.* Berkeley: University of California Press.

Light, Donald, Jr. 1989. "Social Control and the American Health Care System." Pp. 456–74 in Howard E. Freeman and Sol Levine (eds.), *Handbook of Medical Sociology,* 4th ed. Englewood Cliffs, NJ: Prentice Hall.

Lightbourne, Robert, Jr., Susheela Singh, and Cynthia P. Green. 1982. "The World Fertility Survey: Charting Global Childbearing." *Population Bulletin* 37(1).

Lillard, Lee A., and Linda J. Waite. 1995. "'Til Death Do Us Part: Marital Disruption and Mortality." *American Journal of Sociology* 100: 1131–56.

Lin, Carolyn A. 1998. "Uses of Sex Appeals in Prime-Time Television Commercials." *Sex Roles* 38: 461–75.

Lin, Nan, and Yanjie Bian. 1991. "Getting Ahead in Urban China." *American Journal of Sociology* 97: 657–88.

Lindquist, Diane. 2001. "Rules Changes for *Maquiladoras.*" *Industry Week* (January 15). Also available on http://www.findarticles.com/cf_0/m1121/1_250/69388643/print.jhtml.

Link, Bruce et al. 1994. "Lifetime and Five-Year Prevalence of Homeless in the United States." *American Journal of Public Health* (December).

Linn, Marcia C., and Janet Shibley Hyde. 1989. "Gender, Mathematics, and Science." *Educational Researcher* 18(8): 17–27.

Linton, Ralph. 1936. *The Study of Man.* New York: Appleton-Century-Crofts.

Linz, Susan J. 1988. "Managerial Autonomy in Soviet Firms." *Soviet Studies* 40: 175–95.

Lippa, R., and S. Arad. 1999. "Gender, Personality, and Prejudice: The Display of Authoritarianism and Social Dominance in Interviews with College Men and Women." *Journal of Research in Personality* 33: 463–493.

Lipari, Rachel N., Paul J. Cook, Lindsay M. Rock, and Kenneth Matos. 2008. "2006 Gender Relations Survey of Active Duty Members." Defense Manpower Data Center. http://www.sapr.mil/contents/references/WGRA_OverviewReport.pdf.

Lipset, Seymour Martin. 1959. *Political Man*. Garden City, NY: Doubleday/Anchor Books.

Lipset, Seymour Martin, and Reinhard Bendix. 1960. *Social Mobility in Industrial Society*. Berkeley: University of California Press.

Lipset, Seymour Martin, Martin A. Trow, and James S. Coleman. 1956. *Union Democracy*. Glencoe, IL: Free Press.

Lissy, William E. 1993. "At the Top." *Compensation and Benefits Review* 25: 13.

Little, Allan, and George Smith. 1971. *Strategies of Compensation: A Review of Educational Projects for the Disadvantaged in the United States*. Paris: Organization for Economic Cooperation and Development.

Lively, Kit, Yi Shun Lai, Lisa Levenson, and Dylan Rivera. 1995. "Academics Assess Effect of New Ban on Racial Preferences." *Chronicle of Higher Education* (August 4): A1.

Livingston, Abby. 1991. "What YOUR Department Can Do." *Working Woman* (January): 59–60.

Livingston, Ivor L. 1985. "The Importance of Socio-Psychological Stress in the Interpretation of the Race-Hypertension Association." *Humanity and Society* 9: 168–75.

Lizotte, Alan J. 1978. "Extra-Legal Factors in Chicago's Criminal Courts: Testing the Conflict Model of Criminal Justice." *Social Problems* 25(5): 564–80.

Lloyd, Janice. 2009. "Home Schooling Grows." *USA Today* (January 15). http://www.usatoday.com/news/education/2009-01-04-homeschooling_N.htm (Downloaded October 29, 2009).

Locker, David. 1981. *Symptoms and Illness: The Cognitive Organization of Disorder*. London: Tavistock.

Lockwood, Anne Turnbaugh. 1996. *Tracking: Conflicts and Resolutions*. Thousand Oaks, CA: Corwin Press.

Loewen, James W. 2005. *Sundown Towns: A Hidden Dimension of American Racism*. New York: Free Press.

Lofland, John. 1985. *Protest: Studies of Collective Behavior and Social Movements*. New Brunswick, NJ: Transaction Books.

———. 1969. *Deviance and Identity*. Englewood Cliffs, NJ: Prentice Hall.

Lofland, Lyn H. 1973. *A World of Strangers: Order and Action in Public Space*. New York: Basic Books.

Loft, John D., and Phillip R. Kletke. 1989. "Human Resource Trends in the Health Field." Pp. 419–36 in Howard F. Freeman and Sol Levine (eds.), *Handbook of Medical Sociology*, 4th ed. Englewood Cliffs, NJ: Prentice Hall.

Loftin, Colin, and R. H. Hill. 1974. "Regional Subculture and Homicide." *American Sociological Review* 39: 714–25.

Logan, John. 2001. Ethnic Diversity Grows, Neighborhood Integration Is at a Standstill. Report by the Lewis Mumford Center, State University of New York at Albany, April 3, 2001. http://mumford1.dyndns.org/cen2000/WholePop/WPreport/page1.html.

Logan, John R., and Harvey L. Molotch. 1987. *Urban Fortunes: The Political Economy of Place*. Berkeley: University of California Press.

Logan, John R., Brian J. Stults, and Farley Reynolds. 2004. "Segregation of Minorities in the Metropolis: Two Decades of Change." *Demography* 41: 1–22.

Logue, John, and Dan Bell. 1992. "Worker Ownership in Russia: A Possibility After the Command Economy." *Dissent* 39, 2 (Spring): 199–204.

Lohr, Steve. 1992. "Little of $100 Billion Loss Can Be Retrieved." *The New York Times* (February 20): D7.

Lombroso, Cesare. 1972 [orig. 1911]. *Crime, Its Causes and Remedies*. Boston: Little, Brown.

London, Bruce, and David A. Smith. 1988. "Urban Bias, Dependence, and Economic Stagnation in Noncore Nations." *American Sociological Review* 53: 454–63.

Long, Larry H. 1980. "What the Census Will Show About Gentrification." *American Demographics* 2: 18–21.

Lopata, Helena Z. 1980. "The Chicago Woman: A Study of Patterns of Mobility and Transportation." *Signs: Journal of Women in Culture and Society* 5(3): S161–S169.

López, C., L. Cedillo, A. Juárez, and A. Zehe. 2001. "Influence of Electromagnetic Microwave Radiation on Human Health: A Statistical Case Study of Cancer Patients." Puebla, Mexico: Universidad Autónoma de Puebla. http://www.ece.buap.mx/~cloptez/resumen.html.

Loprest, Pamela J. 1999. "Families Who Left Welfare: Who Are They and How Are They Doing? Assessing the New Federalism: Discussion Papers 99-02." Washington, DC: The Urban Institute. http://newfederalism.urban.org/pdf/discussion99-02.pdf.

Lorde, Audre. 1992. "Age, Race, Class, and Sex: Women Redefining Difference." Pp. 401–07 in Paula S. Rothenberg (ed.), *Race, Class, and Gender in the United States: An Integrated Study*. New York: St. Martin's Press.

Lorenz, Konrad. 1966. *On Aggression*. New York: Harcourt Brace Jovanovich.

Lorber, Judith. 1975. "Good Patients and Problem Patients: Conformity and Deviance in a General Hospital." *Journal of Health and Social Behavior* 16: 213–25.

Lotz, Roy, and John D. Hewitt. 1976. "The Influence of Legally Irrelevant Factors on Felony Sentencing." *Sociological Inquiry* 47(1): 39–48.

Lowen, Linda. 2009. "Female CEOs Earn Less than Men, but Inspire More." Linda's Women's Issues Blog, About.Com Guide Guide to Women's Issues. http://womensissues.about.com/b/2009/09/28/female-ceos-earn-less-than-men-but-inspire-more.htm (Downloaded October 22, 2009).

Lowie, Robert H. 1954. *Indians of the Plains*. Garden City, NY: Natural History Press.

Lueck, Marjorie, Ann Ore, and Martin O'Connell. 1982. "Trends in Child-Care Arrangements of Working Mothers." Current Population Reports. Series P-23, No.117. Washington, DC: U.S. Government Printing Office.

Luft, Harold. 1978. "How Do Health Maintenance Organizations Achieve Their Savings?" *New England Journal of Medicine* 298: 1336–43.

Lui, K. J., W. W. Darrow, and G. W. Rutherford, 3rd. 1988. "A Model-based Estimate of the Mean Incubation Period for AIDS in Homosexual Men." *Science* 1988 Jun 3; 240(4857): 1333–35.

Luker, Kristen. 1991. "Dubious Conceptions: The Controversy over Teen Pregnancy." *The American Prospect* 5 (Spring): 73–83.

Lundberg, Ferdinand. 1968. *The Rich and the Super-Rich*. New York: Lyle Stewart.

Lundberg, Olle. 1986. "Class and Health: Comparing Britain and Sweden." *Social Science and Medicine* 23: 511–17.

Lunde, Donald T. 1970. *Murder and Madness*. San Francisco: San Francisco Book Company.

Lunn, Joan C. 1970. *Streaming in the Primary School*. London: National Foundation for Educational Research in England and Wales.

Lurie, Nancy Oestreich. 1985. "The American Indian: Historical Background." Pp. 136–49 in Norman R. Yetman, *Majority and Minority*, 4th ed. Boston: Allyn and Bacon.

Lynch, Edith M. 1973. *The Executive Suite: Feminine Style*. New York: AMACOM.

Lynd, Robert, and Helen Lynd. 1937. *Middletown in Transition*. New York: Harcourt, Brace, and World.

Lynn-Jones, Sean M., and Steven E. Miller (eds.) 1995. *Global Dangers: Changing Dimensions of International Security*. Cambridge, MA: MIT Press.

Lyon, Larry, Lawrence Felice, and M. Ray Perryman. 1980. "Community Power and Population Increase: An Empirical Test of the Growth Machine Model." *American Journal of Sociology* 86: 1387–1400.

Lyons, Richard D. 1975. "Revision Seen in Lobbying Law." *The New York Times* (April 20).

Lyotard, Jean-Francois. 1984. *The Post-Modern Condition: A Report on Knowledge* (Geoff Benington and Brian Marsuni, trans.). Manchester, England: Manchester University Press.

Lytton, Hugh, and David Romney. 1991. "Parents' Differential Socialization of Boys and Girls: A Meta-Analysis." *Psychological Bulletin* 109: 267–96.

Maccoby, Eleanor. 1980. *Social Development: Psychological Growth and the Parent-Child Relationship*. New York: Harcourt Brace Jovanovich.

Maccoby, Eleanor, and Carol Nagy Jacklin. 1974. *The Psychology of Sex Differences*. Stanford, CA: Stanford University Press.

Macionis, John J., and Vincent N Parillo. 2001. *Cities and Urban Life*. 2nd ed. Upper Saddle River, NJ: Prentice Hall.

MacKay, K. A., and G. D. Kuh. 1994. "A Comparison of Student Effort and Educational Gains of Caucasian and African American Students at Predominantly White Colleges and Universities." *Journal of College Student Development* 35: 217–23.

MacLean, Nancy. 2009. *The American Women's Movement, 1945–2000: A Brief History with Documents*. Boston: Bedford/St. Martin's.

Macy, Michael W. 1991. "Chains of Cooperation: Threshold Effects in Collective Action." *American Sociological Review* 56: 730–47.

Madans, Jennifer, and Joel C. Kleinman. 1980. "Use of Ambulatory Care by the Poor and Non-Poor." Pp. 43–50 in National Center for Health Statistics, *Health, United States, 1980*. Washington, DC: U.S. Government Printing Office.

Maddox, George L., and Richard T. Campbell. 1985. "Scope, Concepts, and Methods of Study of Aging." Pp. 3–33 in Robert Binstock and Ethel Shanas (eds.), *Handbook of Aging and the Social Sciences*. New York: Van Nostrand Reinhold.

Magner, Denise K. 1990. "3 Black Scholars Find That University of Michigan Offers a Winning Formula." *Chronicle of Higher Education* 37(5) (October 3): A20.

Mahard, Rita E., and Robert L. Crain. 1983. "Research on Minority Achievement in Desegregated Schools." Pp. 103–25 in Christine H. Rossell and Willis D. Hawley (eds.), *The Consequences of School Desegregation*. Philadelphia: Temple University Press.

Maher, Lisa. 1997. *Sexed Work: Gender, Race, and Resistance in a Brooklyn Drug Market*. Oxford, England: Clarendon Press.

Maher, Timothy. 1998. "Environmental Oppression: Who Is Targeted for Toxic Exposure?" *Journal of Black Studies* 28: 357–67.

Major, Brenda, Kay Deaux, and Peter J. D. Carnevale. 1981. "A Different Perspective on Androgyny: Evaluations of Masculine and Feminine Personality Characteristics." *Journal of Personality and Social Psychology* 41: 988–1001.

Makepeace, J. M. 1981. "Courtship Violence Among College Students." *Family Relations* 30: 97–102.

Malinowski, Bronislaw. 1967. *A Diary in the Strict Sense of the Term*. London: Routledge and Kegan Paul.

———. 1962. *Sex, Culture, and Myth*. New York: Harcourt, Brace, and World.

———. 1948. *Magic, Science and Religion and Other Essays*. Glencoe, IL: Free Press.

———. 1939. "The Group and the Individual in Functional Analysis." *American Journal of Sociology* 44: 938–64.

———. 1926. *Crime and Custom in Savage Society*. New York: Harcourt, Brace.

———. 1922. *The Argonauts of the Western Pacific*. New York: Dutton.

Malowist, M. 1959. "The Economic and Social Development of the Baltic Countries from the Fifteenth to the Seventeenth Centuries." *The Economic History Review* (New Series) 12(2): 177–89.

Malthus, Thomas Robert. 1965. *An Essay on Population*. New York: Augustus Kelly. (Originally published in 1798.).

Mann, Kenneth. 1985. *Defending White-Collar Crime: A Portrait of Attorneys at Work*. New Haven, CT: Yale University Press.

Mann, R. D. 1959. "A Review of the Relationship Between Personality and Performance in Small Groups." *Psychological Bulletin* 56: 241–70.

Mann, Thomas E. 1987. "Is the House of Representatives Unresponsive to Political Change?" Pp. 261–82 in A. James Reichley (ed.), *Elections American Style*. Washington, DC: Brookings Institution.

Mannheim, Karl. 1936. *Ideology and Utopia*. New York: Harcourt. (Originally published in German in 1929.).

Maracek, J., S. E. Finn, and M. Cardell. 1982. "Gender Roles in the Relationships of Lesbians and Gay Men." *Journal of Homosexuality* 8: 45–49.

Marascuilo, Leonard A., and Maryellen McSweeney. 1972. "Tracking and Minority Student Attitudes and Performance." *Urban Education* 6: 303–19.

Mare, Robert D. 1991. "Five Decades of Educational Assortive Mating." *American Sociological Review* 56: 15–32.

———. 1982. "Socioeconomic Effects on Child Mortality in the United States." *American Journal of Public Health* 2(6): 539–47.

Mare, Robert D., and Christopher Winship. 1991. "Socioeconomic Change and the Decline of Marriage for Blacks and Whites." Pp. 175–202 in Christopher Jencks and Paul E. Peterson (eds.), *The Urban Underclass*. Washington, DC: Brookings Institution.

Margolin, Leslie. 1992. "Beyond Maternal Blame: Physical Child Abuse as a Phenomenon of Gender." *Journal of Family Issues* 13: 410–23.

Margolin, Leslie, Dale A. Blyth, and Dominic Carbone. 1988. "The Family as a Looking Glass: Interpreting Family Influences on Adolescent Self-Esteem from a Symbolic Interaction Perspective." *Journal of Early Adolescence* 8: 211.

Mariano, Ann. 1988. "Affluent Get Thousands in Subsidies." *The Washington Post* (October 15): E1.

Marjoribanks, Kevin. 1972. "Environment, Social Class, and Mental Abilities." *Journal of Educational Psychology* 63: 103–09.

Marler, Penny Long, C. Kirk Hadaway, and Mark Chaves. 1998. "Over-reporting Church Attendance in America: Evidence that Demands the Same Verdict." *American Sociological Review* (February).

Marmor, Theodore R., Jerry L. Mashaw, and Philip L. Harvey. 1990. *America's Misunderstood Welfare State: Persistent Myths, Enduring Realities*. New York: Basic Books.

Marmor, Theodore, and Edward Tenner. 1977. "National Health Insurance. Canada's Path, America's Choice." *Challenge* 20: 13–21.

Marshall, Victor W. 1986. "A Sociological Perspective on Aging and Dying." Pp. 125–46 in Victor W. Marshall (ed.), *Later Life: The Social Psychology of Dying*. Beverly Hills, CA: Sage.

Martin, Elmer P., and Joanne Mitchell Martin. 1978. *The Black Extended Family*. Chicago: University of Chicago Press.

Martin J.A., B.E. Hamilton, P.D. Sutton, S.J. Ventura, et al. 2009. "Births: Final Data for 2006." *National Vital Statistics Reports* 57, 7.

Martin, Laura. 1986. "Eskimo Words for Snow: A Case Study in the Genesis and Decay of an Anthropological Example." *American Anthropologist* 88: 418–22.

Martin, William. 1981. "The Birth of a Media Myth." *The Atlantic* 247(6): 7–16.

Maruyama, G., and N. Miller. 1979. "Reexamination of Normative Influence Processes in Desegregated Classrooms." *American Educational Research Journal* 16: 273–83.

Marx, Gary T. 1974. "Religion: Opiate or Inspiration of Civil Rights Militancy Among Negroes?" In William M. Newman (ed.), *The Social Meanings of Religion*. Chicago: Rand McNally College Publishing Co.

Marx, Gary T., and Sanford Sherizen. 1987. "Corporations That Spy on Their Employees." *Business and Society Review* (Winter): 32–37.

Marx, Karl. 1967. *Capital: A Critique of Political Economy*. (Friedrich Engels, ed., Samuel Moore and Edward Aveling, trans.). New York: International Publishers. (Originally published in German in 1867, 1885, and 1894.).

———. 1964. *Selected Writings in Sociology and Social Philosophy* (Thomas B. Bottomore and Maximilien Rubel, eds. and trans.). New York: McGraw-Hill.

Marx, Karl, and Friedrich Engels. 1969. *The Communist Manifesto*. Baltimore, MD: Penguin. (Originally published in German in 1848.).

Mashaw, Jerry L., and Theodore R. Marmor. 1996. "The Great Social Security Scare." *The American Prospect* 29: 30–37, also available on http://epn.org/prospect/29/29mash.html.

Mason, Philip. 1971. *Patterns of Dominance*. London: Oxford University Press.

Massey, Douglas S. 2005. *Strangers in a Strange Land: Humans in an Urbanizing World*. New York: W. W. Norton and Company.

———. 1995. "Review Essay: The Bell Curve: Intelligence and Class Structure in American Life." *American Journal of Sociology* 101: 747–53.

———. 1990. "American Apartheid: Segregation and the Making of the Underclass." *American Journal of Sociology* 96: 329–57.

Massey, Douglas S., and Nancy A. Denton. 1993. *American Apartheid: Segregation and the Making of the Underclass*. Cambridge, MA: Harvard University Press.

———. 1988. "Suburbanization and Segregation in U.S. Metropolitan Areas." *American Journal of Sociology* 94: 592–626.

———. 1987. "Trends in the Residential Segregation of Blacks, Hispanics, and Asians: 1970–1980." *American Sociological Review* 52: 802–25.

Massey, Douglas S., and Mitchell L. Eggers. 1993. "The Spatial

Concentration of Affluence and Poverty During the 1970s." *Urban Affairs Quarterly* (December).

———. 1990. "The Ecology of Inequality: Minorities and the Concentration of Poverty 1970–1980." *American Journal of Sociology* 95: 1153–88.

Massey, Douglas S., Andrew B. Gross, and Kumiko Shibuya. 1994. "Migration, Segregation, and the Geographic Concentration of Poverty." *American Sociological Review* 59: 425–45.

Masters, J. C., and A. Wilkinson. 1976. "Consensual and Discriminative Stereotypes of Sex-Type Judgments by Parents and Children." *Child Development* 47: 208–17.

Mathews, Jay. 1992. "Undercover Bias Busters." *Newsweek* (November 23): 88.

Matthews, Rick A., and David Kauzlarich. 2000. "The Crash of ValuJet Flight 592: A Case Study in State-Corporate Crime," *Sociological Focus* 3(3) (August): 281–98.

Matsueda, Ross L. 1992. "Reflected Appraisals, Parental Labelling, and Delinquency: Specifying a Symbolic Interactionist Theory." *American Journal of Sociology* 97: 1577–1611.

Mauldon, Jane, and Kristin Luker. 1996. "Does Liberalism Cause Sex?" *The American Prospect* 24 (Winter): 80–85, also see http://epn.org/prospect/24/24maul.html.

Mazon, Mauricio. 1984. *The Zoot Suit Riots: The Psychology of Symbolic Annihilation*. Austin: University of Texas Press.

McAdam, Doug. 1986. "Recruitment to High-Risk Activism: The Case of Freedom Summer." *American Journal of Sociology* 92: 64–90.

———. 1983. "Tactical Innovation and the Pace of Insurgency." *American Sociological Review* 48: 735–54.

———. 1982. *Political Process and the Development of Black Insurgency, 1930–1970*. Chicago: University of Chicago Press.

McAdam, Doug, John D. McCarthy, and Mayer N. Zald. 1988. "Social Movements." Pp. 695–737 in Neil J. Smelser (ed.), *Handbook of Sociology*. Newbury Park, CA: Sage.

McAdam, Doug, and Ronnelle Paulsen. 1994. "Specifying the Relationship Between Social Ties and Activism." *American Journal of Sociology* 99: 640–67.

McArthur, Leslie A., and Susan V. Eisen. 1976. "Achievements of Male and Female Storybook Characters as Determinants of Achievement Behavior in Boys and Girls." *Journal of Personality and Social Psychology* 33: 467–73.

McBrien, Richard P. 1983. "Roman Catholicism: E Pluribus Unum." Pp. 179–89 in M. Douglas and S. Tipton (eds.), *Religion and America: Spiritual Life in a Secular Age*. Boston: Beacon Press.

McCague, James. 1968. *The Second Rebellion: The Story of the New York City Draft Riots of 1863*. New York: Dial.

McCall, Leslie. 2000. "Gender and the New Inequality: Explaining the College/Non-College Wage Gap." *American Sociological Review* 65(2): 234–55.

McCandless, B. R., W. S. Persons, III, and A. Roberts. 1972. "Perceived Opportunity, Delinquency, Race, and Body Build Among Delinquent Youth." *Journal of Consulting and Clinical Psychology* 38: 281–87.

McCarthy, John D., Clark McPhail, and Jackie Smith. 1996. "Images of Protest: Dimensions of Selection Bias in Media Coverage of Washington Demonstrations, 1982 and 1991." *American Sociological Review* 61: 478–99.

McCarthy, John D., and Mayer N. Zald. 1977. "Resource Mobilization and Social Movements: A Partial Theory." *American Journal of Sociology* 82: 1212–41.

———. 1973. *The Trend of Social Movements in America: Professionalization and Resource Mobilization*. Morristown, NJ: General Learning Press.

McClelland, David C. 1961. *The Achieving Society*. New York: Van Nostrand.

McComb, Chris. 2001. "Few Say It's Ideal for Both Parents to Work Full Time Outside of Home." The Gallup Organization: Poll Releases, May 4, 2001. http://www.galup.com/poll/releases/pr010504.asp.

McConahay, J. B., B. B. Hardee, and V. Batts. 1981. "Has Racism Declined in America? It Depends on Who Is Asking and What Is Asked." *Journal of Conflict Resolution* 25: 563–79.

McCord, William, and Joan McCord. 1978. "The Psychopath." In R. Martin Hackell and Lewis Yablonsky, *Crime and Delinquency*, 3rd ed. Chicago: Rand McNally College Publishing Company. (Originally published in 1964.).

McCoy, E. 1986. "Your One and Only." *Parents* 118–21, 236.

McDermott, Peter, et al. 1995. "'Should We Do It the Same Way?' Teaching in Tracked and Untracked High School Classes." Paper presented at the Annual Meeting of the Northeast Educational Research Association, Portsmouth, New Hampshire, October 25–27.

McKenna, Wendy, and Florence Denmark. 1978. "Women and the University." *International Journal of Group Tensions* 5: 226–34.

McKinley, James C., Jr. 2010. "Texas Conservatives Win Curriculum Change." New York Times (March 12). http://www.nytimes.com/2010/03/13/education/13texas.html (Downloaded July 29, 2010).

McLanahan, Sara. 1988. "The Consequences of Single Parenthood for Subsequent Generations." *Focus* 11: 16–21.

McLanahan, Sara, and Larry Bumpass. 1988. "Intergenerational Consequences of Family Disruption." *American Journal of Sociology* 94: 130–52.

McLeod, Jane D., and Michael J. Shannahan. 1993. "Poverty, Parenting, and Children's Mental Health." *American Sociological Review* 58: 351–66.

McLoughlin, William. 1978. *Revivals, Awakenings, and Reform*. Chicago: University of Chicago Press.

McLuhan, Marshall. 1964. *Understanding Media: The Extension of Man*. New York: McGraw-Hill.

McManus, Patricia A., and Thomas A. DiPrete. 2001. "Losers and Winners: The Financial Consequences of Separation and Divorce for Men." *American Sociological Review* 66: 246–68.

McMillen, Liz. 1997. "Linguists Find Debate over 'Ebonics' Uninformed: They See Black English as a Language 'Variety' and Decry the Attacks on Oakland's School Board." *Chronicle of Higher Education* (January 17): A16.

McPartland, J., and J. Braddock. 1981. "Going to College and Getting a Good Job: The Impact of Desegregation." In Willis D. Hawley (ed.), *Effective School Desegregation*. Beverly Hills, CA: Sage.

McPhail, Clark. 1993. "The Dark Side of Purpose: Individual and Collective Violence in Riots." Presidential Address at the annual meetings of the Midwest Sociological Society, Chicago, April 7–10. *Sociological Quarterly* 31: 1–32.

———. 1971. "Civil Disorder Participation: A Critical Examination of Recent Research." *American Sociological Review* 36: 1058–73.

McPhail, Clark, and Ronald T. Wohlstein. 1983. "Individual and Collective Behaviors Within Gatherings, Demonstrations, and Riots." Pp. 579–600 in Ralph H. Turner and James F. Short, Jr. (eds.), *Annual Review of Sociology*, Vol. 9. Palo Alto, CA: Annual Reviews.

McWhirter, Norris. 1985. *Guinness Book of World Records*. New York: Bantam.

McWilliams, Carey. 1949. *North from Mexico*. Philadelphia: Lippincott.

Mead, George Herbert. 1934. *Mind, Self, and Society*. Chicago: University of Chicago Press.

———. 1925. "The Genesis of the Self and Self-Control." *International Journal of Ethics* 35: 251–77.

Mead, Margaret. 1935. *Sex and Temperament in Three Primitive Societies*. New York: Dell.

Meadows, Donnella H. et al. 1972. *The Limits to Growth*. New York: New American Library.

Mechanic, David. 1978. *Medical Sociology*, 2nd ed. New York: Free Press.

———. 1963. "Religion, Religiosity, and Illness Behavior." *Human Organization* 22(3): 202–08.

Meece, Darrell. 2000. "Early Child-Care Experiences: Associations with Social Information Processing and Academic Performance During Kindergarten." Paper presented at the Biennial Meeting of the Conference on Human Development (Memphis, TN, April.) http://www.eric.ed.gov/ERICDocs/data/ericdocs2sql/content_storage_01/0000019b/80/42/9e/57.pdf (Downloaded November 22, 2009).

Mehan, Hugh, et al. 1992. *Untracking and College Enrollment, Research Report: 4*. Santa Cruz, CA: National Center for Research on Cultural Diversity and Second Language Learning.

Mehl, Lewis E. 1977. "Options in Maternity Care." *Women and Health* 2: 11–23.

Mekosh-Rosenbaum, Victoria, Joan Z. Spade, and George P. White.

1996. "Effects of Homogeneous and Heterogeneous Grouping on Classroom Environment and Achievement in Middle Schools." Paper presented at the Annual Meetings of the American Sociological Association.

Mellor, Earl F. 1984. "Investigating the Differences in Weekly Earnings of Women and Men." *Monthly Labor Review* 107: 17–28.

Melman, Seymour. 1983. *Profits Without Production*. New York: Knopf.

Mendelson, Robert, and Michael Quinn. 1977. *The Demise of an Urban Real Estate Entrepreneur*. Edwardsville, IL: Center for Urban and Environmental Research and Services, Southern Illinois University at Edwardsville.

Menshikov, Stanley. 1997. "Indicators and Trends of Economic Globalisation." Paper presented at Round Table on "Prospects for Global Interdependence and Their Impact on National Economies" under the auspices of The Gorbachev Foundation, Boston, December 15–16. Also available on http://www.globalxs.nl/home/m/menschivok/fast7.htm.

Merchant, Carolyn. 1996. *Earthcare: Women and the Environment*. New York: Routledge.

———. 1992. *Radical Ecology: The Search for a Livable World*. New York: Routledge.

———. 1989. *The Death of Nature: Women, Ecology, and the Scientific Revolution*. New York: Harper.

Merrick, Thomas W. 1986. "World Population in Transition." *Population Bulletin* 41(2).

Merrick, Thomas W., and Stephen J. Tordella. 1988. "Demographics: People and Markets." *Population Bulletin* 43(1).

Merton, Robert. 1973. *The Sociology of Science: Theoretical and Empirical Investigations*. Chicago: University of Chicago Press.

———. 1968. *Social Theory and Social Structure*, 2nd ed. New York: Free Press.

———. 1967. *On Theoretical Sociology*. New York: Free Press.

———. 1949. *Social Theory and Social Structure*. New York: Free Press.

———. 1938. "Social Structure and Anomie." *American Sociological Review* 3: 672–82.

Mesmer, Marie. 1998. "Pink Collar Workers in a White Collar World: The Case of Secretaries in England." Paper presented at Annual Meeting of the American Sociological Association.

Messerschmidt, James. 2000. *Nine Lives: Adolescent Masculinities, the Body, and Violence*. Boulder, CO: Westview Press.

Messerschmidt, James S. 1986. *Capitalism, Patriarchy, and Crime*. Totowa, NJ: Rowman and Littlefield.

Meyer, David S., and Susanne Staggenborg. 1996. "Movements, Countermovements, and the Structure of Political Opportunity." *American Journal of Sociology* 101: 1628–60.

Meyer, John W., and Michael T. Hannan (eds.). 1979. *National Development and the World System: Educational, Economic, and Political Change, 1950–1979*. Chicago: University of Chicago Press.

Meyerowitz, Joshua. 1985. *No Sense of Place: The Impact of Electronic Media on Social Behavior*. New York: Oxford University Press.

Meyerson, Rebecca. 1988. "The Distribution of Cancer Incidence in Madison and St. Clair Counties in Southwestern Illinois." Master's thesis, Southern Illinois University at Edwardsville.

Michael, Robert T., John H. Gagnon, Edward O. Laumann, and Gina Kolata. 1994. *Sex in America: A Definitive Survey*. Boston: Little, Brown.

Michalowski, Ray. 1985. *Order, Law, and Crime*. New York: Random House.

Michalowski, Raymond, and Susan Carlson. 1999. "Unemployment, Imprisonment and Social Structures of Accumulation: Historical Contingency in the Ruschh-Kircheimer Hypothesis." *Criminology* 37(2): 217–50.

Michels, Robert. 1967. *Political Parties: A Sociological Study of the Oligarchical Tendencies in Modern Democracy*. New York: Free Press. (Originally published in 1911.).

Michelson, William. 1977. *Environmental Choice, Human Behavior, and Residential Satisfaction*. New York: Oxford University Press.

———. 1976. *Man and His Urban Environment: A Sociological Approach*, with revisions. Boston: Addison-Wesley.

Mickelson, Roslyn Arlin. 1980. "Social Stratification Processes in Secondary Schools: A Comparison of Beverly Hills High School and Morningside High School." *Journal of Education* 4: 83–112.

Mies, M., and Vandana Shiva. 1993. *Ecofeminism*. London: Zed Books.

Milgram, Stanley. 1970. "The Experience of Living in Cities." *Science* 167: 1461–68.

Milhorn, Misty, Megan Monaghan, Darrel Montero, Maria Reyes, Tony Roman, Roy Tollasken, and Becca Walls. 2009. "North Americans' Attitudes Toward Illegal Drugs." *Journal of Human Behavior in the Social Environment* 19: 125–141.

Milkman, Ruth. 1987. *Gender at Work: The Dynamics of Job Segregation by Sex During Wold War II*. Urbana: University of Illinois Press.

Miller, Jane E. 2000. "The Effects of Race/Ethnicity and Income on Early Childhood Asthma Prevalence and Health Care Use." *American Journal of Public Health* 90: 428–30.

Miller, Jody. 2000. *One of the Guys: Girls, Gangs, and Gender*. New York: Oxford University Press.

———. 1998. "Up It Up: Gender and the Accomplishment of Street Robbery." *Criminology* 36(1): 37–66.

Miller, Karen A., Melvin L. Kohn, and Carmi Schooler. 1986. "Educational Self-Direction and Personality." *American Sociological Review* 51: 372–90.

Miller, M. M., and B. Reeves. 1976. "Dramatic TV Content and Children's Sex-Role Stereotypes." *Journal of Broadcasting* 20: 35–50.

Miller, N. 1980. "Making School Desegregation Work." In W. Stephan and Joe R. Feagin (eds.), *School Desegregation: Past, Present, and Future*. New York: Plenum.

Miller, S. M. 1997. "Born on Third Base: The Sources of Wealth of the 1997 Forbes 400." http://www.faireconomy.org/press_room/1997/born_on_third_base_sources_of_wealth_of_1997_forbes_400.

Miller, Walter. 1958. "Lower-Class Culture as a Generating Milieu of Gang Delinquency." *Journal of Sociological Issues* 14: 5–19.

Miller-Jones, Dalton. 1989. "Culture and Testing." *American Psychologist* 44: 360–66.

Millman, Marcia, and Rosabeth Moss Kanter. 1975. *Another Voice*. New York: Doubleday, Sociological Inquiry.

Mills, C. Wright. 1959. *The Sociological Imagination*. New York: Oxford University Press.

———. 1956. *The Power Elite*. New York: Oxford University Press.

———. 1951. *White Collar: The American Middle Classes*. New York: Oxford University Press.

Milner, Laura M., and James M. Collins. 2000. "Sex-Role Portrayals and the Gender of Nations." *Journal of Advertising* 29(1): 67–80.

Minor, W. William. 1978. "Deterrence Research: Problems of Theory and Method." Pp. 21–45 in James A. Cramer (ed.), *Preventing Crime*. Beverly Hills, CA: Sage.

Mintz, A. 1951. "Non-adaptive Group Behavior." *Journal of Abnormal Social Psychology* 46:150–159.

Mintz, Beth. 1975. "The President's Cabinet, 1897–1972." *Insurgent Sociologist* (Spring): 131–48.

Mintz, Beth, and Michael Schwartz. 1985. *The Power Structure of American Business*. Chicago: University of Chicago Press.

———. 1981a. "Interlocking Directorates and Interest Group Formation." *American Journal of Sociology* 48: 851–69.

———. 1981b. "The Structure of Intercorporate Unity in American Business." *Social Problems* 29: 87–103.

Mintz, Morton, and Jerry F. Cohen. 1976. *Power, Inc.* New York: Viking Press.

Mirande, Alfredo. 1987. *Gringo Justice*. Notre Dame, IN: University of Notre Dame Press.

Mire, Joseph. 1974. "Improving Working Life—The Role of European Unions." *Monthly Labor Review* 97: 6.

Mishel, Lawrence. 1995. "Rising Tides, Sinking Wages." *The American Prospect* 23 (Fall): 60–64; also http://epn.org/prospect/23/23mish.html.

Misra, Joya, and Alexander Hicks. 1994. "Catholicism and Unionization in Affluent Postwar Democracies: Catholicism, Culture, Party, and Unionization." *American Sociological Review* 59: 304–26.

Moadde, Mansoor. 1994. "Political Conflict in the World Economy: A Cross-National Analysis of Modernization and World-System Theories." *American Sociological Review* 59: 276–303.

Moen, Phyllis, Donna Dempster McClain, and Robin M. Williams, Jr. 1992. "Successful Aging: A Life-Course Perspective on Women's Multiple Roles and Health." *American Journal of Sociology* 97: 1612–38.

Moffit, Robert. 1992. "Incentive Effects of the U.S. Welfare System." *Journal of Economic Literature*.

Mokdad, Ali H., James S. Marks, Donna F. Stroup, and Julie L. Gerberding. 2004. "Actual Causes of Death in the United States, 2000." *Journal of the American Medical Association* 291(10): 1238, 1241.

Molm, Linda D. 1991. "Affect and Social Exchange: Satisfaction in Power-Dominance Relationships." *American Sociological Review* 56: 475–93.

———. 1990. "Structure, Action, and Outcomes: The Dynamics of Power in Social Exchange." *American Sociological Review* 55: 427–47.

———. 1987. "Linking Power Structure and Power Use." Pp. 101–29 in Karen S. Cook (ed.), *Social Exchange Theory*. Newbury Park, CA: Sage Publications.

Molm, Linda D, Gretchen Peterson, and Nobuyuki Takahashi. 1999. "Power in Negotiated and Reciprocal Exchange." *American Sociological Review* 64: 876–90.

Molm, Linda, Theron M. Quist, and Philip A. Wiseley. 1994. "Imbalanced Structures, Unfair Strategies: Power and Justice in Social Exchange." *American Sociological Review* 99: 98–121.

Molnar, Alex, Philip Smith, and John Zahorik. 2000. 1999–2000 Results of the Student Achievement Guarantee in Education (SAGE) Program Evaluation. Report No. CERAI-00-34, Center for Education Research, Analysis, and Innovation, School of Education, University of Wisconsin–Milwaukee. Also available on http://www.uwm.edu/Dept/CERAI/documents/cerai-00-34.html.

Molotch, Harvey. 2006. "Death on the Roof: Race and Bureaucratic Failure." Social Science Research Council, Understanding Katrina: Perspectives from the Social Sciences. http://understandingkatrina.ssrc.org/Molotch/ (Downloaded May 6, 2008).

———. 1979. "Media and Movement." Pp. 71–93 in Mayer N. Zald and John B. McCarthy (eds.), *The Dynamics of Social Movements*. Cambridge, MA: Winthrop.

———. 1976. "The City as a Growth Machine: Toward a Political Economy of Place." *American Journal of Sociology* 82: 309–33.

Molotch, Harvey, and Marilyn Lester. 1973. "Accidents, Scandals, and Routines: Resources for Insurgent Methodology." *Insurgent Sociologist* (Summer): 1–11.

Momeni, Jamshid A. (ed.). 1986. *Race, Ethnicity, and Minority Housing in the United States*. Westport, CT: Greenwood Press.

Monahan, John, and Henry J. Steadman. 1983. "Crime and Mental Disorder: An Epidemiological Appraisal." In Michael Tonry and Norval Morris (eds.), *Crime and Justice*. Chicago: University of Chicago Press.

Monk-Turner, Elizabeth. 1990. "The Occupational Achievements of Community and Four-Year College Entrants." *American Sociological Review* 55: 719–25.

———. 1988. "Educational Differentiation and Status Attainment: The Community College Controversy." *Sociological Focus* 21: 141–52.

Mooney, Carolyn J. 1995. "Religious Revival Grips Students at Church Colleges." *Chronicle of Higher Education* (May 19): A39.

Moore, Joan, and Harry Pachon. 1985. *Hispanics in the United States*, 2nd ed. Englewood Cliffs, NJ: Prentice Hall.

Moore, Kristin A., and S. B. Caldwell. 1977. "The Effect of Government Policies on Out-of-Wedlock Sex and Pregnancy." *Family Planning Perspectives* 9: 164–69.

Moore, Robert. 1975. "Race Relations in the Six Counties: Colonialism, Industrialization, and Stratification in Ireland." Race 14, Reprinted in Norman R. Yetman and C. Hoy Steele (eds.), *Majority and Minority. The Dynamics of Racial and Ethnic Relations*, 2nd ed. Boston: Allyn and Bacon.

Morbidity and Mortality Weekly Report. 2000. "Prevalence of Intimate Partner Violence and Injuries—Washington, 1998." *Morbidity and Mortality Weekly Report* 49(26): 589–92.

Morgan, David J. 1976. *Patterns of Population Distribution in a Residential Preference Model and Its Dynamic*. Chicago: University of Chicago, Department of Geography.

Morgan, S. Philip, Diane N. Lye, and Gretchen A. Condran. 1988. "Sons, Daughters, and the Risk of Marital Disruption." *American Sociological Review* 52: 278–85.

Morgan, S. Philip, Antonion McDaniel, Andrew T. Miller, and Samuel H. Preston. 1993. "Racial Differences in Household and Family Structures at the Turn of the Century." *American Journal of Sociology* 98: 798–828.

Moroney, J. R. 1972. *The Structure of Production in American Manufacturing*. Chapel Hill: University of North Carolina Press.

Morris, Aldon D. 1993. "Birmingham Confrontation Reconsidered: An Analysis of the Tactics of Mobilization." *American Sociological Review* 58: 621–36.

———. 1984. *The Origins of the Civil Rights Movement: Black Communities Organizing for Change*. New York: Free Press.

Morris, Allison. 1987. *Women, Crime, and Criminal Justice*. Oxford: Basil Blackwell.

Morris, Martina, Annette D. Bernhardt, and Mark S. Handcock. 1994. "Economic Inequality: New Methods for New Trends." *American Sociological Review* 59: 205–19.

Morris, N., and G. Hawkins. 1970. *The Honest Politician's Guide to Crime Control*. Chicago: University of Chicago Press.

Morrow, Raymond Allan, and Carlos Alberto Torres. 1995. *Social Theory and Education: A Critique of Social and Cultural Reproduction*. Albany: State University of New York Press.

Mortensen, Dale T. 1988. "Matching: Finding a Partner for Life or Otherwise." *American Journal of Sociology* 94, Supplement.

Mortimer, Jeylan T., and Roberta G. Simmons. 1978. "Adult Socialization." Pp. 421–54 in Alex Inkeles et al. (eds.), *Annual Review of Sociology*, Vol. 4. Palo Alto, CA: Annual Reviews.

Mosca, Gaetano. 1939. *The Ruling Class*. Hannah D. Kahn (trans.). New York: McGraw-Hill. (Originally published in Italian in 1896.).

Moscovici, Serge, and Marisa Zavalloni. 1969. "The Group as a Polarizer of Attitudes." *Journal of Personality and Social Psychology* 12: 125–35.

Moses, Robert, Mieko Kamii, Susan McAllister Swap, and Jeffrey Howard. 1989. *The Algebra Project: Organizing in the Spirit of Ella*. Harvard Educational Review 59, 4 (November 1989): 423–43. Reprint available on http://www.cpn.org/sections/topics/youth/stories-studies/algebra_project.html.

Moss, Simon A., and Simon Ngu. 2006. "The Relationship Between Personality and Leadership Preferences." *Current Research In Social Psychology* 11(6): 70–91.

Mott, Frank, and David Shapiro. 1978. "Pregnancy, Motherhood, and Work Activity." In Frank Mott (ed.), *Women, Work, and Family*. Lexington, MA: Lexington Books.

Mouw, Ted. 2000. "Job Relocation and the Racial Gap in Unemployment in Detroit and Chicago, 1980 to 1990." *American Sociological Review* 65: 730–53.

Moxon-Browne, Edward. 1983. *Nation, Class, and Creed in Northern Ireland*. Aldershot, Hampshire: Gower.

Muehlenhard, C. L., and M. A. Linton. 1987. "Date Rape and Sexual Aggression in Dating Situations: Incidence and Risk Factors." *Journal of Counseling Psychology* 34: 186–96.

Mueller, Edward N. 1980. "The Psychology of Political Protest and Violence." Pp. 69–99 in Ted Robert Gurr (ed.), *Handbook of Political Conflict*. New York: Free Press.

Mulhauser, Dana. 2001. "Financial Assistance for Students Rose Sharply over the Past Four Years." *Chronicle of Higher Education* (August 10).

Muller, Ina V. S., John A. Dossey, Eugene H. Owen, and Gary W. Phillips. 1993. Executive Summary of the NAEP 1992 Mathematics Report Card for the Nation and the States. NAEP Report No. 23-ST03. Washington, DC: U.S. Government Printing Office, http://www.enc.org/online/ENC2139.html.

Mullis, I. V. S., et al. 1991. *The State of Mathematics Achievement: NAEP's 1990 Assessment of the Nation and the Trial Assessment of the States*. Washington, DC: United States Department of Education, Office of Educational Research and Improvement.

Mumford, Lewis. 1938. *The Culture of Cities*. New York: Harcourt, Brace.

Munnell, Alicia, Lynn E. Browne, James McEneaney, and Geoffrey M. B. Tootell. 1992. Mortgage Lending in Boston: Interpreting HMDA Data, Working Paper No. 92-7. Boston: Federal Reserve Bank of Boston.

Murdie, Robert A. 1976. "Spatial Form in the Residential Mosaic." Pp. 237–72 in D. T. Herbert and R. J. Johnson (eds.), *Social Areas in Cities*, Vol. 1: *Spatial Processes and Form*. London: Wiley.

Murdock, George Peter. 1945. "The Common Denominator of Cultures." Pp. 123–42 in Ralph Linton (ed.), *The Science of Man in the World Crisis*. New York: Columbia University Press.

———. 1935. "Comparative Data on the Division of Labor by Sex." *Social Forces* 15: 551–53.

Murphy, Jane M. 1976. "Psychiatric Labeling in Cross-Cultural Perspective." *Science* 191: 1019–27.

Murray, Charles. 1993. "The Coming White Underclass." *Wall Street Journal* (October 23).

———. 1984. *Losing Ground: American Social Policy, 1950–1980.* New York: Basic Books.

Murray, John P. 2008. "Media Violence: The Effects Are Both Real and Strong." *American Behavioral Scientist* 51(8): 1212–30.

Myers, David G., and G. D. Bishop. 1970. "Discussion Effects on Racial Attitudes." *Science* 169: 778–89.

Myers, David G., and M. F. Kaplan. 1976. "Group-Induced Polarization in Simulated Juries." *Personality and Social Psychology Bulletin* 2: 63–66.

Myrdal, Gunnar. 1944. *An American Dilemma: The Negro Problem and Modern Democracy.* New York: Harper & Row.

NAACP. 2000. NAACP Voting Irregularities Public Hearing. Summary of the Testimony. Miami, Florida, Saturday, November 11, 2000. http://www.naacp.org/communications/press_releases/florida_irregularities.asp.

Nader, Ralph, and Mark Green. 1972. "Coddling the Corporations: Crime in the Suites." *New Republic* 166: 18–24.

Nadler, Richard. 2008. *Immigration and the Wealth of States.* Overland Park, KS: America's Majority Foundation.

Nan, Lin, and Wen Xie. 1988. "Occupational Prestige in Urban China." *American Journal of Sociology* 93: 793–832.

Nash, Gary B., et al. (eds.). 1986. *The American People: Creating a Nation and a Society.* New York: Harper & Row.

Nash, Roy. 1976. *Teacher Expectations and Pupil Learning.* London: Routledge and Kegan Paul.

Nathanson, Stephen. 1991. "The Death Penalty Does Not Deter Murder." Pp. 119–26 in Carol Wekesser (ed.), *The Death Penalty: Opposing Viewpoints.* San Diego, CA: Greenhaven Press.

National Center for Education Statistics. 2009. Contexts of Elementary and Secondary Education. http://nces.ed.gov/programs/coe/2009/section4/table-pex-1.asp (Downloaded November 22, 2009).

———. 2008. Bachelor's degrees conferred by degree-granting institutions, by sex, race/ethnicity, and field of study: 2006–07, Table 285. http://nces.ed.gov/programs/digest/d08/tables/dt08_285.asp.

———. 2001a. *Digest of Education Statistics, 2000.* Washington, DC: U.S. Department of Education. Also available on http://nces.ed.gov/pubsearch/pubsinfo.asp?pubid=2001034.

———. 2001b. National Assessment of Educational Progress (NAEP)—The Nation's Report Card. http://nces.ed.gov/nationsreportcard/.

———. 2000a. *The Condition of Education, 2000.* Washington, DC: U.S. Government Printing Office. Also available on http://nces.ed.gov/pubs2000/coe2000/.

———. 2000b. *Digest of Education Statistics, 2000.* Washington, DC: U.S. Government Printing Office. Also available on http://nces.ed.gov/pubs2000/digest/.

———. 1996a. Results from the NAEP 1994 U.S. History Assessment. http://www.ed.gov/NCES/naep/y25flk/hbro.shtml.

———. 1996b. NAEP 1994 Reading: A First Look. Findings from the National Assessment of Educational Progress. http://www.ed.gov/NCES/pubs/Rea94FL/Rea94FL.html.

———. 1995. High School Students Ten Years After "A Nation at Risk." Washington, DC: U.S. Department of Education, National Center for Education Statistics. Adobe file can be downloaded from National Center for Education Statistics Web, http://www.ed.gov/NCES/.

———. 1993. "AIDS Knowledge and Attitudes for 1991." *Advance Data* 225. Washington, DC: U.S. Government Printing Office.

———. 1991. *Projections of Educational Statistics to 2002.* Washington, DC: U.S. Government Printing Office.

———. 1990a. *Projections of Education Statistics to 2000: An Update.* Washington, DC: U.S. Department of Education.

———. 1990b. *The Condition of Education, 1991.* Vol. 2: Postsecondary Education. Washington, DC: U.S. Department of Education.

———. 1989. *Integrated Post-Secondary Data System (IPEDS), "Completions" Survey.* Washington. DC: U.S. Department of Education.

———. 1987. *Trends in Bachelors and Higher Degrees. 1975–1985.* Washington, DC: U.S. Government Printing Office.

National Center for Health Statistics. 2009. Health, United States: 2008. Updated Tables. http://www.cdc.gov/nchs/hus/updatedtables.htm (Downloaded November 30, 2009).

———. 2001a. Births: Final Data for 1999. *National Vital Statistics Report* 49, 1. Washington, DC: U.S. Government Printing Office. Also available on http://www.cdc.gov/nchs/data/nvsr/nvsr49/nvsr49_01.pdf.

———. 2001b. Deaths: Preliminary Data for 1999. *National Vital Statistics Report* 49, 3. http://www.cdc.gov/nchs/data/nvsr/nvsr49/nvsr49_03.pdf.

———. 2001c. *Health, United States, 2001, with Urban and Rural Health Chartbook.* Hyattsville, MD: National Center for Health Statistics. http://www.cdc.gov/nchs/products/pubs/pubd/hus/01tables.htm#NEW.

———. 2001d. Births: Preliminary Data for 2000. *National Vital Statistics Report* 49, 5. http://www.cdc.gov/nchs/releases/01news/newbirth.htm.

———. 2000. *Health, United States, 2000, With Adolescent Health Chartbook.* Hyattsville, Maryland: National Center for Health Statistics. http://www.cdc.gov/nchs/data/hus00.pdf.

———. 1999. Current Estimates from the National Health Interview Survey, 1996. *Vital and Health Statistics* 10, 200. http://www.cdc.gov/nchs/data/series/sr_10/sr10_200.pdf.

———. 1996a. "Births, Marriages, Divorces, and Deaths, November, 1995." Monthly Vital Statistics Report 44 (May): 11.

———. 1996b. "Births and Deaths, United States: 1995." Monthly Vital Statistics Report 45(3) (October 4): Supplement 2.

———. 1996c. Health, United States: 1995. Washington, DC: U.S. Government Printing Office, also available through http://www.cdc.gov.

———. 1996d. AIDS Surveillance. Washington, DC: U.S. Government Printing Office; also available through http://www.cdc.gov.

———. 1996e. "Advance Report of Final Natality Statistics, 1994." Monthly Vital Statistics Report 44(11) (June 24): Supplement; also can be downloaded from http://www.cdc.gov.

———. 1992a. "Advance Report of Final Mortality Statistics, 1989." Monthly Vital Statistics Report 40, p. 8. Hyattsville. MD: Public Health Service.

———. 1992b. *Health, United States, 1991.* Hyattsville, MD: Public Health Service.

———. 1991a. "Births, Marriages, Divorces, and Deaths for 1990," Monthly Vital Statistics Report 39, p. 12. Hyattsville, MD: Public Health Service.

———. 1991b. *Health, United States, 1990.* Hyattsville, MD: Public Health Service.

———. 1991c. "Advance Report of Final Natality Statistics, 1989," Monthly Vital Statistics Report 40, p. 8, Supplement. Hyattsville, MD: Public Health Service.

———. 1990. "Advance Report of Final Natality Statistics, 1988," Monthly Vital Statistics Report 39, p. 4, Supplement. Hyattsville, MD: Public Health Service.

———. 1988. *Health, United States, 1988.* DHHS Publication No. (PHS) 88–1232. Washington. DC: U.S. Government Printing Office.

———. 1987. Monthly Vital Statistics Report: Births, Marriages, Divorces, and Deaths for 1987. Washington. DC: U.S. Government Printing Office.

———. 1986. Current Estimates from the Health Interview Survey, United States, 1985, Series 10, No. 160. Washington, DC: U.S. Government Printing Office.

———. 1984. *Health, United States, 1984.* Washington, DC: U.S. Government Printing Office.

———. 1980. "Basic Data on Depressive Symptomatology, 1974–75." U.S. National Health Survey. Hyattsville, MD: Public Health Service.

National Center for Public Policy and Higher Education. 2008. *Measuring Up, 2008: The National Report Card on Higher Education.* San Jose, CA: National Center for Public Policy and Higher Education. http://measuringup2008.highereducation.org/print/NCPPHEMUNationalRpt.pdf (Downloaded July 29, 2010).

National Coalition for the Homeless. 1996. "NCH Fact Sheet: Homeless Families with Children." http://www2.ari.net/home/nch/families.html.

National Commission on Excellence in Education. 1983. *A Nation at Risk: The Imperative for Educational Reform.* Washington, DC: U.S. Government Printing Office.

National Criminal Justice Reference Service. 1996. "Criminal

Victimization 1994: National Crime Victimization Survey." http://www.ncjrs.org/txtfiles/cv94.txt.

———. 1994. "Violent Crime." http://www.ncjrs.org/txtfiles/violncvs.txt.

National Hospice Organization. 1997. Hospice Fact Sheet. http://www.nho.org/facts.htm.

National Institute of Education. 1985. *College Test Scores Declining: Research in Brief.* Washington, DC: U.S. Government Printing Office.

National Institute of Justice. 1988a. *International Crime Rates.* Washington, DC: U.S. Government Printing Office.

———. 1988b. *Report to the Nation on Crime and Justice,* 2nd ed. Washington, DC: U.S. Government Printing Office.

———. 1987. *Sourcebook of Criminal Statistics.* Washington, DC: U.S. Government Printing Office.

National Institute of Mental Health. 1982. *Television and Behavior: Ten Years of Scientific Progress and Implications for the Eighties.* Washington, DC: U.S. Government Printing Office.

National Institute on Drug Abuse. 1999. *Drug Abuse and Addiction Research: 25 Years of Discovery to Advance the Health of the Public.* The Sixth Triennial Report to Congress from the Secretary of Health and Human Services. Washington, DC: U.S. Government Printing Office. Also available on http://165.112.78.61/STRC/STRCIndex.html.

National Opinion Research Center. 1991. General Social Surveys, 1990. Press release issued January 8. Chicago: National Opinion Research Center.

———. 1983. General Social Survey, 1972–1983. *Cumulative Codebook.* Chicago: National Opinion Research Center.

National Research Council. 1989. *A Common Destiny: Blacks and American Society.* Washington, DC: National Academy Press.

National Science Foundation. 1996. Women, Minorities, and Persons with Disabilities in Science and Engineering: 1996 (NSF 96-311). Arlington, VA: Author. Also available online at http://www.nsf.gov/sbe/srs/nsf96311/start.htm.

Nation's Health. 1997. "Child Abuse and Neglect Still a Widespread Problem in America." *Nation's Health* 27, 5.

NEA Today. 1996. "A Bridge from Math to Algebra." *NEA Today* 15(4) (November): 19–22.

Nee, Victor. 1996. "The Emergence of a Market Society: Changing Mechanisms of Stratification in China." *American Journal of Sociology* 101: 908–949.

Nee, Victor, Jimy M. Sanders, and Scott Sernau. 1994. "Job Transitions in an Immigrant Metropolis: Ethnic Boundaries and the Mixed Economy." *American Sociological Review* 59: 849–72.

Neier, Arych. 1985. "No One Is Safe." Pp. 11–16 in Gary E. McCuen (ed.), *Political Murder in Central America: Death Squads and U.S. Policies.* Hudson, WI: Gary E. McCuen Publications.

Nelkin, Dorothy, and Michael Pollack. 1981. *The Atom Besieged.* Cambridge, MA: MIT Press.

Nettles, Michael T. 1991. "Racial Similarities and Differences in the Predictors of College Student Achievement." Pp. 75–91 in Walter R. Allen, Edgar P. Epps, and Nesha Z. Haniff (eds.), *College in Black and White: African American Students in Predominantly White and Historically Black Public Universities.* Albany: State University of New York Press.

Neustadtl, Alan, and Dan Clawson. 1988. "Corporate Political Groupings: Does Ideology Unify Business Political Behavior?" *American Sociological Review* 53: 172–90.

Newcomb, Michael, and P. M. Bentler. 1980. "Assessment of Personality and Demographic Effects of Cohabitation and Marital Success." *Journal of Personality Assessment* 44(1): 11–24.

Newcombe, Nora, Mary M. Bandura, and Dawn C. Taylor. 1983. "Sex Differences in Spatial Abilities and Spatial Activities." *Sex Roles* 9: 377–86.

Newport, Frank. 2009. "This Easter, Smaller Percentage of Americans Are Christian." The Gallup Organization: Poll Releases, April 10, 2009. http://www.gallup.com/poll/117409/Easter-Smaller-Percentage-Americans-Christian.aspx.

———. 2001. "Americans See Women as Emotional and Affectionate, Men as More Aggressive." The Gallup Organization: Poll Releases, February 21, 2001. http://www.galup.com/poll/releases/pr010221.asp.

———. 1999. "Americans Today Much More Accepting of a Woman, Black, Catholic, or Jew As President." Poll Analysis, Gallup Poll, March 29. http://www.galup.com/poll/releases/pr990329.asp.

Newport, Frank, David W. Moore, and Lydia Saad. 1999. "Long-Term Gallup Poll Trends: A Portrait of American Public Opinion Through the Century." The Gallup Organization: Poll Releases, December 20, 1999. http://www.galup.com/poll/releases/pr991220.asp.

Newport, Frank, and Maura Strausberg. 2001. "Americans' Belief in Psychic and Paranormal Phenomena Is Up over Last Decade." Poll Analysis, Gallup Poll, June 8. http://www.galup.com/poll/releases/pr010608.asp.

Newsweek. 1988a. "Seven Minutes to Death." *Newsweek* (July 18): 18–24.

———. 1988b. "More Deadly Than Poison." *Newsweek* (August 1): 28–31.

———. 1988c. "Lost on the Planet Earth: American Adults Know Shockingly Little Geography." *Newsweek* (August 8): 31.

———. 1988d. "The Threat of a Global Grain Drain." *Newsweek* (August 15): 36.

Newton, George D., and Franklin E. Zimring. 1969. *Firearms and Violence in American Life.* Consultant report to the National Commission on the Causes and Prevention of Violence. Washington, DC: U.S. Government Printing Office.

New York Times. 2009. "Your Senator is (Probably) a Millionaire" (November 25). http://economix.blogs.nytimes.com/2009/11/25/your-senator-is-probably-a-millionaire/ (Downloaded July 28, 2010).

———. 1992. "Ex-Chief of Columbia Savings Is Indicted." *The New York Times* (June 25): D6.

———. 1991a. "U.S. Has Highest Rate of Imprisonment in World." *The New York Times* (January 7): A17.

———. 1991b. "Texas Judge Backs Law on School Aid. *The New York Times* (April 16): A17.

———. 1991c. "Poverty Blamed for Blacks' High Cancer Rate." *The New York Times* (April 17): A18.

———. 1982. "Librarians Say 'Go Ask Alice' Censored Most in Schools." *The New York Times* (November 28): Sect. 1, 73.

———. 1977. "Assembly Draws Bill to Regulate 'Medicaid Mills' and Limit Abuse." *The New York Times* (February 15): 35.

Nichols, Andrea. 2001. "Veiling Practices of Muslim Immigrant Women in the US." Paper presented at annual meeting of the Illinois Sociological Association, October 11–12, Rockford, IL.

Niebuhr, H. Richard. 1929. *The Social Sources of Denominationalism.* New York: Holt.

Nielsen, Niels C., Jr. 1993. *Fundamentalism, Mythos, and World Religions.* Albany: State University of New York Press.

Nielson, François, and Arthur S. Alderson. 1995. "Income Inequality, Development, and Dualism: Results from an Unbalanced Cross-National Panel." *American Sociological Review* 60: 674–701.

Noah, Timothy. 1991. "Census Bureau's Count of Homeless Fails to End Debate." *Wall Street Journal* (April 15): B5C.

Nock, S. L., and P. W. Kingston. 1988. "Time with Children: The Impact of Couples' Work-time Commitments." *Social Forces* 67: 59–85.

Noel, Donald L. 1972. "Slavery and the Rise of Racism." Pp. 153–74 in Donald L. Noel (ed.), *The Origins of American Slavery and Racism.* Columbus, OH: Charles E. Merrill.

———. 1968. "A Theory of the Origins of Ethnic Stratification." *Social Problems* 16:157–72.

Nolan, Patrick D. 1987. "World System Status, Income Inequality and Economic Growth: A Criticism of Recent Criticism." *International Journal of Comparative Sociology* 28(1–2): 69–75.

Nolen, Susan Bobbit, and Thomas M. Haladyna. 1990. "Personal and Environmental Influences on Students' Beliefs About Effective Study Strategies." *Contemporary Educational Psychology* 15(2):116–30.

Nordstrom, Bruce. 1992. "Lessons About Gender from Native American Traditions: Gender Roles, Puberty Rites, Gender Identity and Homosexuality in Native American Cultures." Paper presented at the annual meeting of the Midwest Sociological Society, Kansas City, MO, April 4.

Noss, John B. 1980. *Man's Religions,* 6th ed. New York: Macmillan.

Novak, Michael. 1971. *The Rise of the Unmeltable Ethnics.* New York: Macmillan.

Noyelle, Thierry J., and Thomas N. Stanback, Jr. 1983. *The Economic Transformation of American Cities.* Totowa, NJ: Rowman and Allanheld.

Nye, F. Ivan. 1974. "Emerging and Declining Family Roles." *Journal of Marriage and the Family* 36: 238–44.

Oakes, Jeannie. 1995. "Two Cities' Tracking and Within-School Segregation." *Teachers College Record* 96: 681–90.

Oakes, Jeannie, and The RAND Corporation. 1990. "Opportunities, Achievement, and Choice: Women and Minority Students in Science and Mathematics." In Cozden (ed.), *Review of Research in Education* (pp. 153–222). Washington, DC: American Educational Research Association.

Oakley, Robert. 1987. "International Terrorism." *Foreign Affairs* 65: 611–29.

Obiakor, Festus E. 1998. "Teacher Expectations of Multicultural Exceptional Learners: Impact on 'Accuracy' of Self-Concepts." Paper presented at the International Convention of the Council for Exceptional Children, Minneapolis, MN, April 16. Also available through ERIC Document Reproduction Service.

O'Brien, J. E. 1971. "Violence in Divorce-Prone Families." *Journal of Marriage and the Family* 33: 692–98.

O'Brien, Patrick. 1982. "European Economic Development: The Contribution of the Periphery." *Economic History Review* 35(1): 1–18.

O'Brien, Robert M. 1985. *Crime and Victimization Data.* Beverly Hills, CA: Sage.

O'Connor, Brian P. 1993. "Appraisals of Musical Ability in Bar Bands: Identifying the Weak Link in the Looking Glass Self Chain. *Basic and Applied Social Psychology* 14: 69.

O'Dea, Thomas, and Janet O'Dea Aviada. 1983. *Sociology of Religion,* 2nd ed. Englewood Cliffs, NJ: Prentice Hall.

Oden, S., L. J. Schweinhart, and D. P. Weikart. 2000. *Into Adulthood: A Study of the Effects of Head Start.* High/Scope Educational Research Foundation Report No. N-R1059. Ypsilanti, MI: High/Scope Educational Research Foundation.

Oegema, Dirk, and Bert Klandermans. 1994. "Why Social Movement Supporters Don't Participate: Erosion and Nonconversion of Support." *American Sociological Review* 59: 703–22.

Ogbu, John U. 1986. "Structural Constraints in School Desegregation." Pp. 21–45 in Jeffrey Prager, Douglas Longshore, and Melvin Seeman (eds.), *School Desegregation Research: New Directions in Situational Analysis.* New York: Plenum.

———. 1978. *Minority Education and Caste: The American System in Cross-Cultural Perspective.* New York: Academic Press.

Ogburn, William F. 1966. *Social Change with Respect to Culture and Original Nature.* New York: Dell. (Originally published in 1922.).

———. 1933. "The Family and Its Functions." *Recent Trends in the U.S. Report of the President's Research Committee on Social Trends.*

O'Hare, William P., Kelvin M. Pollard, Taynia L. Mann, and Mary M. Kent. 1991. "African Americans in the 1990s." *Population Bulletin* 46, 1.

O'Hare, William P., and Margaret L. Usdansky. 1992. "What the 1990 Census Tells Us About Segregation in 25 Large Metros." *Population Today* 20(9): 6–7.

O'Keeffe, Dennis. 2000. The Waltzing Matilda Story. http://waltzingmatilda.com/wmhome.html.

O'Neill, Brian, and Deborah Balk. 2001. "World Population Futures." *Population Bulletin* 56, 3 (September). Also available on http://www.prb.org/Template.cfm?Section=PRB&template=/ContentManagement/ContentDisplay.cfm&ContentID=3897.

Okamoto, Dina, and Paula England. 1999. "Is There a Supply Side to Occupational Sex Segregation?" *Sociological Perspectives* 42(4): 557–83.

Olday, David E. 1981. "Premarital Cohabitation: An Assessment of the Consequences for Marriage." Paper presented at the annual meeting of the Midwest Sociological Society, Minneapolis, MN.

Oldendick, Robert W., and Michael W. Link. 1999. "Call-Screening: What Problems Does It Pose for Survey Researchers?" Paper presented at International Conference on Survey Response, Portland, OR, October 28–31.

Oliver, Melvin L., and Thomas M. Shapiro. 1995. *Black Wealth, White Wealth: A New Perspective on Racial Inequality.* New York: Routledge.

———. 1990. "Wealth of a Nation: A Reassessment of Asset Inequality in America Shows at Least One-Third of Households Are Asset-Poor." *American Journal of Economics and Sociology* 49: 129–51.

Oliver, Melvin L., A. Wade Smith, and Karen Rose Wilson. 1989. "Supporting Successful Black Students: Personal, Organizational, and Institutional Factors." *National Journal of Sociology* 3: 199–221.

Ollenberger, Jane C., and Helen A. Moore. 1992. *A Sociology of Women: The Intersection of Patriarchy, Capitalism, and Colonization.* Englewood Cliffs, NJ: Prentice Hall.

Olneck, Michael R., and David B. Bills. 1980. "What Makes Sammy Run? An Empirical Assessment of the Bowles-Gintis Correspondence Theory." *American Journal of Education* 89: 27–61.

Olsen, Lance. 1992. "Cyberpunk and the Crisis of Postmodernity." Pp. 142–52 in George Slusser and Tom Shippey (eds.), *Fiction 2000: Cyberpunk and the Future of Narrative.* Athens: University of Georgia Press.

Olsen, Marvin E. 1990. "The Affluent Prosper While Everyone Else Struggles." Presidential address delivered at the 1990 annual meetings of the North Central Sociological Association, Louisville, KY; reprinted in *Sociological Focus* 23: 73–87.

Olzak, Susan. 1989. "Labor Unrest, Immigration, and Ethnic Conflict in Urban America, 1880–1914." *American Journal of Sociology* 94: 1303–33.

Ono, Hiroshi. "Lifetime Employment in Japan: Concepts and Measurements." Paper presented at the annual meeting of the American Sociological Association, Montreal Convention Center, Montreal, Quebec, Canada, Aug 11, 2006. http://www.allacademic.com/meta/p_mla_apa_research_citation/1/0/4/1/3/p104138_index.html (Downloaded October 23, 2009).

OpenEducation.net. 2008. College Graduation Rates—Statistics Tell a Sad Tale. http://www.openeducation.net/2008/11/20/college-graduation-rates-statistics-tell-a-sad-tale/ (Downloaded July 29, 2010).

Opp, Karl-Dieter, and Christiane Gern. 1993. "Dissident Groups, Personal Networks, and Spontaneous Cooperation: The East German Revolution of 1989." *American Sociological Review* 58: 659–80.

Opp, R. D. 1989. "Freshman Interest in Teaching: Recent Trends." *Journal of Teacher Education* 40: 43–48.

Oppenheimer, Valerie Kincaide. 1988. "A Theory of Marriage Timing." *American Journal of Sociology* 94: 563–91.

Orfield, Gary. 1997. "Does Desegregation Help Close the Gap?" (Testimony of Gary Orfield, March 22, 1996). *Journal of Negro Education* 66: 241–254.

Orfield, Gary, and Susan E. Eaton. 1996. *Dismantling Desegregation: The Quiet Reversal of Brown v. Board of Education.* New York: The New Press.

Orfield, Gary and Chungmei Lee. 2007. *Historical Reversals, Accelerating Resegregation, and the Need for New Integration Strategies.* A Report of the Civil Rights Project, UCLA. http://civilrightsproject.ucla.edu/research/k-12-education/integration-and-diversity/historic-reversals-accelerating-resegregation-and-the-need-for-new-integration-strategies-1.

Orfield, Gary, and John T. Yun. 1999. *Resegregation in American Schools.* Cambridge, MA: The Civil Rights Project, Harvard University.

Organization for Economic Cooperation and Development. 2010. "OECD Health Data, Selected Data." http://stats.oecd.org/Index.aspx?DataSetCode=HEALTH.

———. 1979. *The State of the Environment in OECD Countries.* Paris: Organization for Economic Cooperation and Development.

Orlovsky, Jacob. 1977. "Sex-Role Orientation, Identity Formation, and Self-Esteem in College Men and Women." *Sex Roles* 3: 561–75.

Orr, Deborah, and Susan Kitchens. 2001. "I'll Pay Yours if You'll Pay Mine." *Forbes Global* (September 3). http://www.forbes.com/global/2001/0903/036.html.

Orr, J. Edwin. 1994. *Campus Aflame: A History of Evangelical Awakenings in Collegiate Campuses.* Edited by Richard Owen Roberts. Wheaton, IL: International Awakening Press.

Orum, Anthony. 1988. "Political Sociology." Pp. 393–423 in Neil Smelser (ed.), *Handbook of Sociology.* Newbury Park, CA: Sage.

———. 1972. *Black Students in Protest.* Washington, DC: American Sociological Association.

Oskamp, Stuart, Karen Kaufman, and Lianna Atchison Wolterbeek. 1996. "Gender Role Portrayals in Preschool Picture Books." *Journal of Social Behavior and Personality* 11(5): 27–40.

Ouchi, William G., and Alan L. Wilkins. 1985. "Organizational Culture." Pp. 457–83 in Ralph H. Turner and James F. Short (eds.), *Annual Review of Sociology*, Vol. 11. Palo Alto, CA: Annual Reviews.

Ovando, Martha N., and Betty J. Alford. 1997. "Creating a Culture of Detracking in a Learner-Centered School: Issues, Problems, and Possibilities." Paper presented at the Annual Meeting of the American Association of School Administrators.

Owen, Carolyn, Howard C. Eisner, and Thomas R. McFaul. 1981. "A Half-Century of Social Distance Research: National Replication of the Bogardus Studies." *Sociology and Social Research* 66: 80–98.

Owen, David. 1985. *None of the Above: Behind the Myth of Scholastic Aptitude*. Boston: Houghton Mifflin.

Packard, Vance. 1983. *Our Endangered Children: Growing Up in a Changing World*. Boston: Little, Brown.

Page, Susan. 2008. "Poll: Young Voters Hint at Electorate Shift." *USA Today* (October 16). http://www.usatoday.com/news/politics/election2008/2008-10-05-poll-youth_N.htm#data.

Pager, Devah. 2003a. "The Mark of a Criminal Record." *American Journal of Sociology* 108(5): 937–975.

———. 2003b. "Blacks and Ex-Cons Need Not Apply." *Contexts* 2: 4.

———. 2007. *MARKED: Race, Crime, and Finding Work in an Era of Mass Incarceration*. Chicago: University of Chicago Press.

Pager Devah, and Hana Shepherd, 2008. "The Sociology of Discrimination: Racial Discrimination in Employment, Housing, Credit, and Consumer Markets." *Annual Review of Sociology* 34: 9.1–9.29.

Pagnini, Deanna L., and S. Philip Morgan. 1990. "Intermarriage and Social Distance Among U.S. Immigrants at the Turn of the Century." *American Journal of Sociology* 96: 405–32.

Paik, Haejung, and George Comstock. 1994. "The Effects of Television Violence on Antisocial Behavior: A Meta-Analysis." *Communication Research* 21: 516–46.

Paine, Robert. 1987. "Accidents, Ideologies, and Routines: Chernobyl over Norway." *Anthropology Today* 30(4): 7–10.

Palen, J. John. 1987. *The Urban World*, 3rd ed. New York: McGraw-Hill.

Palmer, Francis H. 1970. "Socioeconomic Status and Intellective Performance Among Negro Preschool Boys." *Developmental Psychology* 3: 1–9.

Palmore, Erdman. 1970. "Predictors of Successful Aging." *The Gerontologist* 19(5): 427–31.

Pampel, Fred, and John B. Williamson. 1988. "Welfare Spending in Advanced Industrial Democracies, 1950–1980." *American Journal of Sociology* 93: 1424–56.

Panel on Population Projections. 2000. *Beyond Six Billion: Forecasting the World's Population*. Washington: National Academy Press.

Parcel, Toby, and Elizabeth G. Menaghan. 1994. "Early Parental Work, Family Social Capital, and Early Childhood Outcomes." *American Journal of Sociology* 99: 972–1009.

Parenti, Michael. 1986. *Inventing Reality: The Politics of the Mass Media*. New York: St. Martin's Press.

Pareto, Vilfredo. 1935. *The Mind and Society*, Vols. I–IV. London: Jonathan Cape. (Originally published in Italian in 1915–1919.).

Parillo, Vincent N. 1994. *Strangers to These Shores: Race and Ethnic Relations in the United States*. New York: MacMillan.

Park, Robert E. 1967. *On Social Control and Collective Behavior* (Ralph H. Turner, ed.). Chicago: University of Chicago Press.

———. 1927. "Human Nature and Collective Behavior." *American Journal of Sociology* 32: 733–41.

Park, Robert E., and Ernest W. Burgess. 1921. *Introduction to the Science of Sociology*. Chicago: University of Chicago Press.

Parkinson, C. Northcote. 1957. *Parkinson's Law*. New York: Houghton Mifflin.

Parnes, Herbert S., and Lawrence J. Less. 1985. "Introduction and Overview." Pp. 1–29 in Herbert S. Parnes et al. (eds.), *Retirement Among American Men*. Lexington, MA: Lexington Books, D. C. Heath.

Parsons, Jacquelynne Ecles, Terry F. Adler, and Caroline M. Kaczala. 1982. "Socialization of Achievement Attitudes and Beliefs: Parental Influences." *Child Development* 53: 310–21.

Parsons, Talcott. 1978. *Action Theory and the Human Condition*. New York: Free Press.

———. 1977. *Social Systems and the Evolution of Action Theory*. New York: Free Press.

———. 1971. *The System of Modern Societies*. Englewood Cliffs, NJ: Prentice Hall.

———. 1966. *Societies: Evolutionary and Comparative Perspectives*. Englewood Cliffs, NJ: Prentice Hall.

———. 1962. "The Law and Social Control." Pp. 56–72 in William M. Evans (ed.), *Law and Sociology: Exploratory Essays*. New York: Free Press.

———. 1959. "The School Class as a Social System: Some of Its Functions in American Society." *Harvard Educational Review* 29: 297–318.

———. 1951. *The Social System*. Glencoe, IL: Free Press.

———. 1947. "Introduction." In Max Weber, *The Theory of Social and Economic Organization*, A. M. Henderson and Talcott Parsons (trans.). New York: Oxford University Press.

———. 1937. *The Structure of Social Action*. New York: McGraw-Hill.

Parsons, Talcott, and Robert F. Bales. 1955. *Family, Socialization, and Interaction Process*. Glencoe, IL: Free Press.

Pascarella, Ernest T., and Patrick T. Terenzini. 1991. *How College Affects Students: Findings and Insights from Twenty Years of Research*. San Francisco: Jossey-Bass.

Passel, Jeffrey S. 2006. *The Size and Characteristics of the Unauthorized Immigrant Population in the United States: Estimates Based on the March, 2005 Current Population Survey*. Pew Hispanic Center Research Report, March 6. http://pewhispanic.org/files/reports/61.pdf (Downloaded July 3, 2008).

———. 1986. "Immigration to the United States." *Presentation at Census Table*, Honolulu, HI, August.

Patchen, Martin. 1982. *Black-White Contact in the Schools: Its Social and Academic Effects*. West Lafayette, IN: Purdue University Press.

Patchen, Martin, G. Hofmann, and W. R. Brown. 1980. "Academic Performance of Black High School Students Under Different Conditions of Contact with White Peers." *Sociology of Education* 53: 33–50.

Paternoster, Raymond. 1991. *Capital Punishment in America*. New York: Lexington Books.

Paternoster, Raymond, Linda Saltzman, Gordon Waldo, and Theodore Chiricos. 1983. "Perceived Risk and Social Control: Do Sanctions Really Deter?" *Law and Society Review* 17(3): 478.

Paterson, Sharyl Bender, and Mary Alyce Lach. 1990. "Gender Stereotypes in Children's Books: Their Prevalence and Influence on Cognitive and Affective Development." *Gender and Education* 2(2): 185–98.

Patterson, Thomas E. 1980. *The Mass Media Election: How Americans Choose Their President*. New York: Praeger.

Pattison, Joseph E. 1990. *Acquiring the Future: America's Survival and Success in a Global Economy*. Homewood, IL: Dow Jones-Irwin.

Payer, Lynn. 1988. *Medicine and Culture*. New York: Holt.

Pear, Robert. 1991. "Low Medicaid Fees Seen as Depriving the Poor of Care." *The New York Times* (April 2): A1.

———. 1983. "Disability Reviews Spur Legal 'Crisis.'" *The New York Times* (September 8): p.1.

Pearce, Diana. 1982. "Women in Poverty." Pp. 7–32 in Arthur I. Blaustein (ed.), *The American Promise: Equal Justice and Economic Opportunity*. New Brunswick, NJ: Transaction Books.

———. 1976. "Black, White, and Many Shades of Gray: Real Estate Brokers and Their Racial Practices." Ph.D. dissertation, University of Michigan, Ann Arbor.

Pearson, Rick. 1997. "House Oks School Funding Special Session Sends Bill To Edgar, 83-31" *Chicago Tribune* (December 2, evening) 1:3.

Penrod, Steven. 1986. *Social Psychology*, 2nd ed. Englewood Cliffs, NJ: Prentice Hall.

Peplau, L.A. 1981. "What Homosexuals Want in Relationships." *Psychology Today* 15: 28–38.

Perle, Eugene D. 1981. "Perspectives on the Changing Ecological Structure of Suburbia." *Urban Geography* 2: 237–54.

Perrow, Charles. 1986. *Normal Accidents: Living with High-Risk Technologies*. New York: Basic Books.

———. 1979. *Complex Organizations: A Critical Essay*, 2nd ed. Glencoe, IL: Free Press.

Pescosolido, Bernice A., and Beth A. Rubin. 2000. "The Web of Group Affiliations Revisited: Social Life, PostModernism, and Sociology." *American Sociological Review* 65: 52–76.

Peskin, Janice. 1982. "Measuring Household Production for the GNP." *Family Economics Review* (Summer): 16–25.

Petersen, Trond, and Laurie A. Morgan. 1995. "Separate and Unequal: Occupation-Establishment Sex Segregation and the Gender Wage Gap." *American Journal of Sociology* 101: 329–365.

Peterson, Bill. 1997. "The Undercount Problem in the 1990 Census." http://www.geom.umn.edu/docs/education/chance/teaching_aids/census/census.html.

Peterson, John M. 1989. "Tracking Students by Their Supposed Abilities Can Derail Learning." *American School Board Journal* 176(5): 38.

Peterson, L. R., and A. Roy. 1985. "Religiosity, Anxiety, and Meaning and Purpose: Religion's Consequences for Psychological Well-Being." *Review of Religious Research* 27: 49–62.

Peterson, Paul E. 1991. "The Urban Underclass and the Poverty Paradox." Pp. 3–27 in Christopher Jencks and Paul F. Peterson (eds.), *The Urban Underclass*. Washington, DC: Brookings Institution.

Peterson, Richard R. 1996. "A Re-Evaluation of the Economic Consequences of Divorce." *American Sociological Review* 61: 528–36.

Peterson, Ruth D., and William C. Bailey. 1988. "Murder and Capital Punishment in the Evolving Context of the Post-Furman Era." *Social Forces* 66: 774–807.

Pettigrew, Thomas F. 1971. *Racially Separate or Together*. New York: McGraw-Hill.

———. 1969a. "Race and Equal Educational Opportunity." Pp. 69–79 in Harvard Educational Review Editors (eds.), *Equality of Educational Opportunity*. Cambridge, MA: Harvard University Press.

———. 1969b. "The Negro and Education: Problems and Proposals." Pp. 49–112 in Irwin Katz and Patricia Gurin (eds.), *Race and the Social Sciences*. New York: Basic Books.

Pew Research Center for the People and the Press. 2009. Majority Continues to Support Civil Unions: Most Still Oppose Same-Sex Marriage. October 9. http://people-press.org/report/553/same-sex-marriage.

———. 2006. "The Cell Phone Challenge to Survey Research." Press release, May 15. Wolrd Wide Web, http://people-press.org/reports/pdf/276.pdf (Downloaded July 20, 2010).

———. 2001. Military Action a Higher Priority Than Homeland Defense, But Guarded Confidence in Military Success. http://www.people-press.org/sept01rpt2.htm.

Phalen, Patricia F. 2000. "Pioneers, Girlfriends and Wives: An Agenda for Research on Women and the Organizational Culture of Broadcasting." *Journal of Broadcasting & Electronic Media* 44(2): 230–37.

Phelan, Jo, Bruce G. Link, Ann Stueve, and Robert E. Moore. 1995. "Education, Social Liberalism, and Economic Conservatism: Attitudes Toward Homeless People." *American Sociological Review* 60: 126–40.

Philipp, Thomas. 1980. "Muslims." Pp. 732–33 in Stephan Thernstrom, Ann Orlov, and Oscar Handlin (eds.), *The Harvard Encyclopedia of American Ethnic Groups*. Cambridge, MA: Harvard University Press.

Phillips, David P., and Daniel J. Paight. 1987. "The Impact of Televised Movies About Suicide: A Replication." *New England Journal of Medicine* 317(13): 809–11.

Phillips, Deborah, Kathleen McCartney, and Sandra Scarr. 1987. "Child-Care Quality and Children's Social Development." *Developmental Psychology* 23: 537–43.

Physicians' Task Force on Hunger. 1985. Report of the Physicians' Task Force on Hunger in America.

Piaget, Jean. 1952. *The Origins of Intelligence in Children*. New York: Norton.

———. 1932. *The Moral Judgment of the Child*. London: Routledge and Kegan Paul.

———. 1926. *The Language and Thought of the Child*. New York: Harcourt, Brace.

Piaget, Jean, and Barbel Inhelder. 1969. *The Psychology of the Child*. New York: Basic Books.

Pierson, Donald. 1942. *Negroes in Brazil*. Chicago: University of Chicago Press.

Piliavin, Irving, Rosemary Gartner, Craig Thornton, and Ross L. Matsueda. 1986. "Crime Deterrence and Rational Choice." *American Sociological Review* 51: 101–19.

Pincus, Fred L. 1980. "The False Promises of Community Colleges: Class Conflict and Vocational Education." *Harvard Educational Review* 50: 332–61.

Pines, Maya. 1982. "Behavior and Heredity: Links for Specific Traits Are Growing Stronger." *The New York Times* (June 29): 19, 22.

———. 1981. "The Civilizing of Genie." *Psychology Today* (September): 28–34.

Pinker, Steven. 1994. *The Language Instinct*. New York: HarperCollins.

———. 2002. *The Blank Slate: The Modern Denial of Human Nature*. New York: Penguin Books.

Pisko, Valena White, and Joyce D. Stern (eds.). 1985. *The Condition of Education*, 1985 Edition. Statistical Report, National Center for Education Statistics. Washington, DC: U.S. Government Printing Office.

Pitt, Leonard. 1966. *The Decline of the Calfornios: A Social History of the Spanish-Speaking, 1846–1890*. Berkeley: University of California Press.

Piven, Frances Fox, and Richard A. Cloward. 1988. *Why Americans Don't Vote*. New York: Pantheon.

Plomin, R. 1986. *Development, Genetics, and Psychology*. Hillsdale, NJ: Erlbaum.

Plutchik, Robert. 1962. *The Emotions*. New York: Random House.

Plutzer, Eric. 1988. "Work Life, Family Life, and Women's Support of Feminism." *American Sociological Review* 53: 640–49.

Polanyi, Karl. [1944] 2001. *The Great Transformation*. Boston: Beacon Press.

———. 1963. "Ports of Trade in Early Societies." *The Journal of Economic History* 23: 30–45.

Polermo, George B. 1995. "Adolescent Criminal Behavior: Is TV Violence One of the Culprits?" *International Journal of Offender Therapy and Comparative Criminology* 39: 11–22.

Polsby, Nelson W. 1980. *Community Power and Political Theory*. New Haven, CT: Yale University Press.

———. 1959. "Three Problems in the Analysis of Community Power." *American Sociological Review* 24: 796–803.

Pontusson, Jonas. 2005. *Inequality and Prosperity: Social Europe vs. Liberal America*. Ithaca: Cornell University Press.

Pope, Liston. 1942. *Millhands and Preachers*. New Haven, CT: Yale University Press.

Popenoe, David. 1996. *Life Without Father*. New York: Free Press.

———. 1988. *Disturbing the Nest: Family Change and Decline in Modern Societies*. New York: Aldine de Gruyter.

Popkin, Susan J., James E. Rosenbaum, and Patricia M. Meaden. 1993. "Labor Market Experiences of Low-Income Black Women in Middle-Class Suburbs: Evidence from a Survey of Gautreaux Program Participants." *Journal of Policy Analysis and Management* 12: 556–74.

Population Reference Bureau. 2010. 2010 World Population Data Sheet. http://www.prb.org/pdf10/10wpds_eng.pdf (Downloaded August 1, 2010).

———. 2009. 2009 World Population Data Sheet. http://www.prb.org/pdf09/09wpds_eng.pdf.

———. 2001 World Population Data Sheet. http://www.prb.org/pubs/wpds2001/.

———. 1996a. 1996 World Population Data Sheet. Washington, D.C.: Population Reference Bureau.

———. 1996b. *The United States at Mid-Decade*. Washington, DC: Population Reference Bureau.

———. 1993. 1993 World Population Data Sheet. Washington, DC: Population Reference Bureau.

———. 1990. 1990 World Population Data Sheet. Washington, DC: Population Reference Bureau.

———. 1988a. 1988 World Population Data Sheet. Washington, DC: Population Reference Bureau.

———. 1988b. The United States Population Data Sheet of the Population Reference Bureau, Inc., 7th ed. Washington. DC: Population Reference Bureau.

Porter, John. 1972. "Dilemmas and Contradictions of a Multiethnic Society." *Royal Society of Canada, Transactions* 10:193–205.

———. 1965. *The Vertical Mosaic*. Toronto: University of Toronto Press.

Porterfield, Austin. 1946. *Youth in Trouble*. Fort Worth, TX: Leo Pottisham Foundation.

Portes, Alejandro. 2000. "The Hidden Abode: Sociology as Analysis of the Unexpected." (1999 American Sociological Association Presidential Address.) *American Sociological Review* 65: 1–18.

———. 1977. "Urban Latin America: The Political Condition from Above and Below." Pp. 59–70 in Janet Abu-Lughod and Richard Hay, Jr. (eds.), *Third World Urbanization*. Chicago: Maaroufa.

Post, Tom. 1993. "Airdrop America: Clinton's New Relief Plan for Bosnia Pushes Washington into an Aggressive Role in the Conflict." *Newsweek* (March 8): 30–31.

Postman, Neil. 1992. *Technopoly: The Surrender of Culture to Technology*. New York: Alfred A. Knopf.

———. 1985. *Amusing Ourselves to Death: Public Discourse in the Age of Show Business*. New York: Elisabeth Sifton/Viking Penguin.

Power, F. Clark, Ann Higgins, and Lawrence Kohlberg. 1989. *Lawrence Kohlberg's Approach to Moral Education*. New York: Columbia University Press.

Prechel, Richard. 1994. "Economic Crisis and the Centralization of Control over the Managerial Process: Corporate Restructuring and Neo-Fordist Decision-Making." *American Sociological Review* 59: 723–45.

Presser, Stanley, and Linda Stinson. 1998. "Data Collection Mode and Social Desirability Bias in Self-Reported Religious Attendance," *American Sociological Review* 63: 137–45.

Princeton Religion Research Center. 1990. *Religion in America: 1990*. Princeton, NJ: American Institute of Public Opinion.

———. 1984. *Religion in America: 1984*. Princeton, NJ: American Institute of Public Opinion.

Prior, Lindsay. 1993. *The Social Organization of Mental Illness*. London: Sage.

Project on Ethnic Relations. 1994. Managing Ethnic Conflict: The Kona Statement. Princeton, NJ: Project on Ethnic Relations; also see http://www.netcom.com/~ethnic/konal.html.

Project Vote Smart. 1996. "Vote Smart Web: Soft Money Contributions Breakdown for 1995." http://www.vote-smart.org/softmoney.html#combined.

Prothro, E. Terry. 1952. "Ethnocentrism and Anti-Negro Attitudes in the Deep South." *Journal of Abnormal and Social Psychology* 47: 105–08.

Public Citizen, Global Trade Watch. 1995. *NAFTA's Broken Promises: Corporate Promises of U.S. Job Creation Under NAFTA*. Washington: Public Citizen.

Pugh, D. S., D. J. Hickson, and C. R. Hinings. 1985. *Writers on Organizations*. Beverly Hills, CA: Sage.

Pullum, Geoffrey K. 1991. *The Great Eskimo Vocabulary Hoax*. Chicago: University of Chicago Press.

Purpel, David, and Kevin Ryan. 1976. "It Comes with the Territory: The Inevitability of Moral Education in the Schools." Pp. 44–54 in David Purpel and Kevin Ryan (eds.), *Moral Education... It Comes with the Territory*. Berkeley, CA: McCutchan.

Quillian, Lincoln. 1999. "Migration Patterns and the Growth of High-Poverty Neighborhoods, 1970–1990." *American Journal of Sociology* 105: 1–37.

———. 1995. "Prejudice as a Response to Perceived Group Threat: Population Composition and Anti-Immigrant and Racial Prejudice in Europe." *American Sociological Review* 60: 586–611.

Quinn, Joseph F., and Olivia S. Mitchell. 1996. "Social Security on the Table." *The American Prospect* 26: 76–81; also available on http://wpn.org/prospect/26/26quine.html.

Quinn, Michael. 1984. Housing Quality Trends in Metro East. Center for Urban and Environmental Research and Services Report No.20. Edwardsville, IL: Southern Illinois University.

Quinney, Richard. 1979. *Capitalist Society: Readings for a Critical Sociology*. Homewood, IL: Dorsey.

Quinton, Wendy J., Gloria Cowan, and Brett D. Watson. 1996. "Personality and Attitudinal Predictors of Support for Proposition 187—California's Anti–Illegal Immigrant Initiative." *Journal of Applied Social Psychology* 26: 2204–23.

Radcliffe-Brown, A. R. 1952. *Structure and Function in Primitive Society*. Glencoe, IL: Free Press.

———. 1950. "Introduction." Pp. 1–85 in A. R. Radcliffe-Brown and D. Forde (eds.), *African Systems of Kinship and Marriage*. London: Oxford University Press.

———. 1935. "On the Concept of Functionalism in the Social Sciences." *American Anthropologist* 37: 394–402.

Radin, Norma. 1972. "Three Degrees of Maternal Involvement in a Preschool Program: Impact on Mothers and Children." *Child Development* 43: 1355–64.

Radu, Michael S. 1987. "Terror, Terrorism, and Insurgency in Latin America." Pp. 298–302 in Walter Laqueur and Yonah Alexander (eds.), *The Terrorism Reader*, rev. ed. New York: NAL Penguin.

Rae, Bob. 1991. "A Socialist Credo." *Dissent* 38 (Winter 1991): 42–45.

Rainwater, Lee. 1966. "Fear and the House-as-Haven in the Lower Class." *Journal of the American Institute of Planners* 32: 23–31.

Rainwater, Lee, and William L. Yancey (eds.). 1967. *The Moynihan Report and the Politics of Controversy*. Cambridge, MA: MIT Press.

Rand Corporation. 1994. "Student Performance and the Changing American Family." http://www.rand.org/publications/RB/RB8009/.

Rank, Mark R. 1989. "Fertility Among Women on Welfare: Incidence and Determinants." *American Sociological Review* 54: 296–304.

Raper, Arthur. 1933. *The Tragedy of Lynching*. Chapel Hill: University of North Carolina Press.

Rapping, Elayne. 2000. "You've Come Which Way, Baby?" *Women's Review of Books*, 17(10/11): 20–23.

Rassmussen, Howard. 1975. "Medical Education—Revolution or Reaction?" *Pharos* 38: 53–59.

Ravitch, Diane. 2010a. Address to 2010 National Education Association Representative Assembly, July 6. http://www.nea.org/grants/40246.htm (Downloaded July 29, 2010).

———. 2010b. *The Death and Life of the Great American School System: How Testing and Choice are Undermining Education*. New York: Basic Books.

———. 2009. "Obama Gives Bush a 3rd Term in Education." *Huffington Post*, June 13.

———. 1983. *The Troubled Crusade: American Education, 1945–1980*. New York: Basic Books.

Ravitz, Mel. 1988. "Community Development: Salvation or Suicide?" *Social Policy* 19(2): 17–21.

Raymond, Jack. 1971. "Free Enterprise and National Defense." Pp. 71–76 in Seymour Melman (ed.), *The War Economy of the United States*. New York: St. Martin's Press.

Reed, Charles B. 2010. "It Still Doesn't Add Up: Cal State's Proposed Budget Boost Isn't Big Enough to Secure California's Future." *Los Angeles Times*, May 27.

Reed, John Shelton. 1972. *The Enduring South: Subcultural Persistence in Mass Society*. Lexington. MA: Heath.

Rees, Philip H. 1979. Residential Patterns in American Cities: 1960. Research Paper No. 189, Department of Geography, University of Chicago.

———. 1970. "Concepts of Social Space: Toward an Urban Social Geography." Pp. 306–94 in Brian J. L. Berry and Frank Horton (eds.), *Geographic Perspectives on Urban Systems*. Englewood Cliffs, NJ: Prentice Hall.

Regional Research and Development Services. 1988. Report to KTVI, Channel 2, St. Louis. Edwardsville: Regional Research and Development Services, Southern Illinois University at Edwardsville.

Rehberg, Richard A., and Evelyn R. Rosenthal. 1978. *Class and Merit in the American High School*. New York: Longman.

Reich, Michael. 1986a. "The Proletarianization of the Labor Force." Pp. 122–31 in Richard C. Edwards, Michael Reich, and Thomas E. Weisskopf (eds.), *The Capitalist System: A Radical Analysis of American Society*, 3rd ed. Englewood Cliffs, NJ: Prentice Hall.

———. 1986b. "The Political-Economic Effects of Racism." Pp. 304–11 in Richard C. Edwards, Michael Reich, and Thomas E. Weisskopf (eds.), *The Capitalist System: A Radical Analysis of American Society*, 3rd ed. Englewood Cliffs, NJ: Prentice Hall.

———. 1981. *Racial Inequality: A Political-Economic Analysis*. Princeton, NJ: Princeton University Press.

Reimer, Rita Ann. 1986. "Work and Family Life in Sweden." *Social Change in Sweden*, Vol. 34. New York: Swedish Information Service.

Reimers, Cordella W. 1984. "Sources of the Family Income Differential Between Hispanics, Blacks, and White Non-Hispanics." *American Journal of Sociology* 89: 889–903.

Reis, H. T., and S. Wright. 1982. "Knowledge of Sex-Role Stereotypes in Children Aged 3 to 5." *Sex Roles* 8: 1049–56.

Reiss, Albert J. 1959. "Rural-Urban and Status Differences in Interpersonal Contact." *American Journal of Sociology* 65: 182–95.

Reiss, Ira L. 1960. "Toward a Sociology of the Heterosexual Love Relationship." *Marriage and Family Living* 22(2): 139–45.

Reiss, Ira L., and G. R. Lee. 1988. *Family Systems in America*, 4th ed. New York: Holt, Rinehart, and Winston.

Reskin, Barbara F. 1988. "Bringing the Men Back In: Sex Differentiation and the Devaluation of Women's Work." *Gender and Society* 2: 58–81.

Reskin, Barbara F., and Debra Branch McBrier. 2000. "Why Not Ascription? Organizations' Employment or Male and Female Managers." *American Sociological Review* 65: 210–33.

Reskin, Barbara F., and Patricia A. Roos. 1990. *Job Queues, Gender Queues. Explaining Women's Inroads into Male Occupations*. Philadelphia: Temple University Press.

Reuters. 2009. "FACTBOX: How Many Lobbyists Are There in Washington?" (September 13). http://www.reuters.com/article/idUSN1348032520090913 (Downloaded July 28, 2010).

Reynolds, Anne. 1992. "Charting the Changes in Junior Faculty Relationships: Socialization, Acculturation, and Gender." *Journal of Higher Education* 15: 637.

Reynolds, Arthur J., Judy A. Temple, Dylan L. Robertson, and Emily A. Mann. 2001. "Long-Term Effects of an Early Childhood Intervention on Educational Achievement and Juvenile Arrest: A 15-Year Follow-up of Low-Income Children in Public Schools." *JAMA: The Journal of the American Medical Association* 285(18) (May 9): 2339–46.

Rheingold, H. L., and K. V. Cook. 1975. "The Contrasts of Boys' and Girls' Rooms as an Index of Parents' Behavior." *Child Development* 46: 459–63.

Richardson, Joanna. 1996. "Voluntary Busing Plan is Unveiled in Denver." *Education Week* 15(18): 6.

Riddell, Tom, Steve Ramos, and Jean Shackelford. 1979. *Economics: A Tool for Understanding Society*. Reading, MA: Addison-Wesley.

Riesman, David. 1961. *The Lonely Crowd*. New Haven, CT: Yale University Press.

Riesman, David, with Nathan Glazer and Reuel Denney. 1969. *The Lonely Crowd*, abridged edition with a 1969 preface. New Haven, CT: Yale University Press.

Rigby, Ken. 1988. "Sexist Attitudes and Authoritarian Personality Characteristics Among Australian Adolescents." *Journal of Research in Personality* 22: 465–73.

Riley, John W. 1983. "Dying and the Meanings of Death: Sociological Inquiries." Pp. 194–216 in Ralph H. Turner and James F. Short (eds.), *Annual Review of Sociology*, Vol. 9. Palo Alto, CA: Annual Reviews.

Riley, Matilda White, and Kathleen Bond. 1983. "Beyond Ageism: Postponing the Onset of Disability." Pp. 243–52 in Matilda White Riley, Beth B. Hess, and Kathleen Bond (eds.), *Aging in Society: Selected Reviews of Recent Research*. Hillsdale, NJ: Erlbaum.

Riley, Matilda White, and Anne Foner, with Mary E. Morre, Beth B. Hess, and Barbara K. Roth. 1968. *Aging and Society: An Inventory of Research Findings*, Vol. I. New York: Russell Sage Foundation.

Riley, Matilda White, Anne Foner, and Joan Waring. 1988. "Sociology of Age." Pp. 243–90 in Neil J. Smelser (ed.), *Handbook of Sociology*. Newbury Park, CA: Sage.

Riley, Matilda White, Marilyn Johnson, and Anne Foner. 1972. *Aging and Society, Vol. III: A Sociology of Age Stratification*. New York: Russell Sage Foundation.

RISMEDIA. 2000. "Poll: Sexes Not Equal Yet." http://www.rismedia.com/news.page/24/10883.

Rist, Ray C. 1970. "Student Social Class and Teacher Expectations: The Self-Fulfilling Prophecy in Ghetto Education." *Harvard Educational Review* 40: 411–51.

Ritchey, Ferris J., Mark LaGory, and Jeffrey Mullis. 1991. "Gender Differences in Health Risks and Physical Symptoms Among the Homeless." *Journal of Health and Social Behavior* 32: 33–48.

Ritzer, George. 2008. *The McDonaldization of Society*, 5th ed. Los Angeles: Pine Forge Press.

———. 1989. "The Permanently New Economy: The Case for Reviving Economic Sociology." *Work and Occupations* 16: 243–72.

———. 1975. *Sociology: A Multiple Paradigm Science*. Boston: Allyn and Bacon.

Ritzer, George, and David Walczak. 1986. *Working: Conflict and Change*. Englewood Cliffs, NJ: Prentice Hall.

Rivet, Paul. 1960. *Mayan Cities* (Miriam Kochan and Lionel Kochan, trans.). New York: Putnam.

Robb, Barbara, and Michael Raven. 1982. "Working Mothers and Children's Perceptions." *Research in Education* 27: 75–83.

Robert Wood Johnson Foundation. 1983. *Special Report: Updated Report on Access to Health Care for the American People*. Princeton, NJ: Robert Wood Johnson Foundation.

Robinson, B.A. 2009. Religions of the World: Numbers of Adherents. http://www.religioustolerance.org/worldrel.htm (Downloaded November 28, 2009).

———. 2001. Religions of the World: Numbers of Adherents; Rates of Growth. http://www.religioustolerance.org/worldrel.htm.

Robinson, John. 1977. *How Americans Use Their Time: A Social Psychological Analysis of Everyday Behavior*. New York: Praeger.

Robinson, Pauline K., Sally Coberly, and Carolyn S. Paul. 1985. "Work and Retirement." Pp. 503–27 in Robert H. Binstock and Ethel Shanas (eds.), *Handbook of Aging and the Social Sciences*. New York: Van Nostrand Reinhold.

Robnett, Belinda. 2000. *How Long? How Long?: African-American Women in the Struggle for Civil Rights*. Oxford: Oxford University Press.

Rodgers, H. R. 1978. "Hiding Versus Ending Poverty." *Political Sociology* 8: 253–66.

Roest, Annette M.C., Judith Semon Dubas, and Jan R.M. Gerris. 2010. "Value Transmissions Between Parents and Children: Gender and Developmental Phase as Transmission Belts." *Journal of Adolescence* 33: 21–31.

Roethlisberger, Fritz J., and William J. Dickson. 1939. *Management and the Worker*. Cambridge. MA: Harvard University Press.

Rogers, Stacy J., and Danelle D. Deboer. 2001. "Changes in Wives' Income: Effects on Marital Happiness, Psychological Well-Being, and the Risk of Divorce." *Journal of Marriage and the Family* 63: 458–72.

Rogoff, B. 1982. "Integrating Context and Cognitive Development." Pp. 125–70 in M. E. Lamb and A. L. Brown (eds.), *Advances in Developmental Psychology*, Vol. 2. Hillsdale, NJ: Erlbaum.

———. 1981. "Schooling and the Development of Cognitive Skills." Pp. 233–94 in H. C. Triandis and A. Heron (eds.), *Handbook of Cross-Cultural Psychology*. Rockleigh, NJ: Allyn and Bacon.

Rohan, Thomas H. 1989. "Mexican Border Boom: Salvation or Slavery?" *Industry Week* 237: 46–49.

Rohlen, T. P. 1983. *Japan's High Schools*. Berkeley: University of California Press.

Roman, Tsilia. 1986. "Role Conflict in the Portrayal of Female Heroes of Television Crime Dramas: A Theoretical Conceptualization." *Interchange* 17: 23–32.

Rona-Tas, Akos. 1994. "The First Shall Be bLast? Entrepreneurship and Communist Cadres in the Transition from Socialism." *American Journal of Sociology* 100: 40–69.

Roof, Wade Clark. 1979. "Socioeconomic Differentials Among White Socio-Religious Groups in the United States." *Social Forces* 58(1): 280–89.

Roozen, David A., and Jackson W. Carroll. 1979. "Recent Trends in Church Membership and Participation: An Introduction." In D. R. Hoge and D. A. Roozen (eds.), *Understanding Church Growth and Decline: 1950–1978*. New York: Pilgrim Press.

Roper Organization. 1985. *Virginia Slims Poll*. New York: Richard Weiner.

———. 1980. *The Virginia Slims American Women's Poll*. New York: Richard Weiner.

Roscoe, Bruce, and Nancy Bernaske. 1985. "Courtship Violence Experienced by Abused Wives: Similarities in Patterns of Abuse." *Family Relations* 34: 419–24.

Rose, Jerry D. 1982. *Outbreaks: The Sociology of Collective Behavior*. New York: Free Press.

Rose, Ellen Cronan. 1993. "The Good Mother: From Gaia to Gilead." Pp. 149–67 in Carol J. Adams (ed.), *Ecofeminism and the Sacred*. New York: Continuum.

Rose, Susan D. 1988. *Keeping Them Out of the Hands of Satan. Evangelical Schooling in America*. New York: Routledge.

Rosenbaum, David E. 1990. "Big Shortfall in Corporate Taxes Thwarts Key Goal of 1986 Law." *The New York Times* (May 6): Al.

Rosenbaum, James E. 1976. *Making Inequality: The Hidden Curriculum of High School Tracking*. New York: Wiley.

Rosenbaum, James E., and Takehiko Kariya. 1991. "Do School Achievements Affect the Early Jobs of High School Graduates in the United States and Japan?" *Sociology of Education* 64: 78–95.

Rosenbaum, James E., and Susan J. Popkin. 1991. "Employment and Earnings of Low-Income Blacks Who Move to Middle-Class

Suburbs." Pp. 342–46 in Christopher Jencks and Paul E. Peterson (eds.), *The Urban Underclass*. Washington, DC: Brookings Institution.

Rosenberg, Charles E. 1987. *The Case of Strangers*. New York: Basic Books.

Rosenberg, Morris, Carmi Schooler, and Carrie Schoenbach. 1989. "Self-Esteem and Adolescent Problems: Modelling Reciprocal Effects." *American Sociological Review* 54: 1004–18.

Rosenberg, Morris, Carmi Schooler, Carrie Schoenbach, and Florence Rosenberg. 1995. "Global Self-Esteem and Specific Self-Esteem: Different Concepts, Different Outcomes." *American Sociological Review* 60: 141–56.

Rosener, Judy B. 1990. "Ways Women Lead." Harvard Business Review (December).

Rosenfield, Rachel, and Arne L. Kalleberg. 1990. "A Cross-National Comparison of the Gender Gap in Income." *American Journal of Sociology* 96: 69–106.

Rosengren, Karl, P. Arvidson, and D. Sturesson. 1975. "The Barseback 'Panic.'" *Acta Sociologica* 18: 303–21.

Rosenthal, R., and D. B. Rubin. 1982. "Further Meta-Analytic Procedures for Assessing Cognitive Gender Differences." *Journal of Educational Psychology* 74: 708–12.

Rosenthal, Robert. 1989. "Experimenter Expectancy, Covert Communication, and Meta-Analysis Methods." Paper presented at the annual meetings of the American Psychological Association, New Orleans, August 11–15.

Rosenthal, Robert, and Lenore Jacobson. 1968. *Pygmalion in the Classroom: Teacher Expectation and Pupils' Intellectual Development*. New York: Holt, Rinehart and Winston.

Rosnow, Ralph L., and Gary Allen Fine. 1976. *Rumor and Gossip: The Social Psychology of Hearsay*. New York: Elsevier.

Ross, Catherine, John Mirowsky, and William C. Cockerham. 1983. "Social Class, Mexican Culture, and Fatalism: Their Effects on Psychological Distress." *American Journal of Community Psychology* 11: 383–99.

Ross, Catherine E., and Chi-ling Wu. 1995. "The Links Between Education and Health." *American Sociological Review* 60: 719–45.

Rossi, Alice S. 1985. "Gender and Parenthood." Pp. 161–91 in Alice S. Rossi (ed.), *Gender and the Life Course*. Hawthorne, NY: Aldine.

Rossi, Peter H., James D. Wright, Gene A. Fisher, and Georgianne Willis. 1987. "The Urban Homeless: Estimating Their Composition and Size." *Science* 235 (March 13): 1336–42.

Rossides, Daniel W. 1997. *Social Stratification: The Interplay of Class, Race, and Gender*. Upper Saddle River, NJ: Prentice Hall.

Rostow, Walter W. 1965. *The Stages of Economic Growth*. London: Cambridge University Press.

———. 1960. *The Stages of Economic Growth: A Non-Communist Manifesto*. Cambridge, England: Cambridge University Press.

Roszak, Theodore. 1969. *The Making of a Counter-Culture: Reflections on the Technocratic Society and Its Youthful Opposition*. New York: Doubleday.

Rothenberg, Julia Johnson, et al. 1997. "Changes in Pedagogy: A Qualitative Result of Teaching Heterogenous Classes." Paper presented at the Annual Meeting of the American Educational Research Association, March 24–28, Chicago.

Rothman, Robert. 1991. "S.A.T. Verbal Results Hit All-Time Low; Math Scores Down for First Time Since '80." *Education Week* 11(1): 5.

Rothschild, Joyce, and J. Allen Whitt. 1986. *The Cooperative Workplace: Potentials and Dilemmas of Organizational Democracy and Participation*. New York: Cambridge University Press.

Rothschild-Whitt, Joyce. 1979. "The Collectivist Organization: An Alternative to Rational-Bureaucratic Models." *American Sociological Review* 44: 500–27.

Roy, William G. 1983. "The Unfolding of the Interlocking Directorate Structure of the United States." *American Sociological Review* 48: 248–57.

Rubin, Beth, and Pedro A. Noguera. 2004. "Tracking Detracking: Sorting Through the Dilemmas and Possibilities of Detracking in Practice." *Equity and Excellence in Education* 37: 92–101.

Rubin, I. 1966. "The New Kinsey Report." *Sexology* (February): 443–46.

Rudwick, Elliott M. 1964. *Race Riot at East St. Louis, July 2, 1917*. Carbondale: Southern Illinois University Press.

Ruggles, Steven. 1994. "The Origins of African-American Family Structure." *American Sociological Review* 59: 136–51.

Rushing, William A. (ed.). 1969. *Deviant Behavior and Social Processes*. Chicago: Rand McNally.

Rushton, J. Philippe. 1975. "Generosity in Children: Immediate and Long-Term Effects of Modeling, Preaching, and Moral Judgment." *Journal of Personality and Social Psychology* 31: 459–66.

Russell, Christina H., and Charles L. Glenn. 1988. "The Cambridge Controlled Choice Plan." *Urban Review* 20(2): 75–94.

Russell, J. C. 1958. *Late Ancient and Medival Population*. Philadelphia: American Philosophical Society.

Rutter, Michael et al. 1979. *Fifteen Thousand Hours*. Cambridge. MA: Harvard University Press.

Ruzek, Cheryl Burt. 1980. "Medical Response to Women's Health Activities: Conflict, Accommodation, and Cooptation." Pp. 335–54 in Julius A. Roth (ed.). *Research in the Sociology of Health Care: A Research Annual*. Vol. I: *1980: Professional Control of Health Services and Challenges to Such Control*. Greenwich. CT: JAI Press.

Ryan, William. 1971. *Blaming the Victim*. New York: Vintage.

———. 1967. "Savage Discovery: The Moynihan Report." Pp. 445–57 in Lee Rainwater (ed.), *The Moynihan Report and the Politics of Controversy*. Cambridge. MA: MIT Press.

Ryff, Carol. 1985. "The Subjective Experience of Life-Span Transitions." Pp. 97–113 in Alice Rossi (ed.), *Gender and the Life Course*. Hawthorne. NY: Aldine de Gruyter.

Rytina, Steve L. 1992. "Sealing the Intergenerational Continuity of Occupation: Is Occupational Inheritance Ascriptive After All?" *American Journal of Sociology* 97: 1658–88.

———. 1989. "Life Chances and the Continuity of Rank: An Alternative Interpretation of Mobility Magnitudes Over the Life Cycle." *American Sociological Review* 54: 910–28.

Rytina, Steve L., Peter M. Blau, Terry Blum, and Joseph Schwartz. 1988. "Inequality and Intermarriage: A Paradox of Motive and Constraint." *Social Forces* 66: 645–75.

Saad, Lydia. 2001. Majority Considers Sex Before Marriage Morally Okay. Gallup News Service, May 24. Also available Saad, Lydia. 2000. "Most Working Women Deny Gender Discrimination in Their Pay." The Gallup Organization: Poll Releases, February 7, 2000. http://www.galup.com/poll/releases/pr000207.asp.

Sabato, Larry. 1987. "Real and Imagined Corruption in Campaign Financing." In A. James Reichley (ed.), *Elections American Style*. Washington, DC: Brookings Institution.

Sacks, Oliver. 1989. *Seeing Voices: A Journey into the World of the Deaf*. Berkeley: University of California Press.

Saez, Emmanuel. 2009a. Striking It Richer: The Evolution of Top Incomes in the United States (Updated with 2007 estimates). http://elsa.berkeley.edu/~saez/saez-UStopincomes-2007.pdf (Downloaded October 14, 2009).

———. 2009b. Income Inequality in the United States, 1913–1998. Tables and Figures Updated to 2007 in Excel Format. http://elsa.berkeley.edu/~saez/TabFig2007.xls (Downloaded October 23, 2009).

Safran, Claire. 1988. "Hidden Lessons: Do Little Boys Get a Better Education Than Little Girls?" Pp. 35–37 in Paula S. Rothenberg (ed.), *Racism and Sexism: An Integrated Study*. New York: St. Martin's Press.

Sagor, Stanley E., and Archie Brodsky. 1984. "The Issue of Safety." Pp. 17–49 in Stanley E. Sagor. Richard I. Fembloom, Peggy Spindel, and Archie Brodsky (eds.), *Home Birth: A Practitioner's Guide to Birth Outside the Hospital*. Rockville, MD: Aspen Systems.

St. John, Nancy H. 1975. *School Desegregation: Outcomes for Children*. New York: Wiley.

St. Louis Post-Dispatch. 1992a. "Despite Recession, CEOs Got Richer, Forbes Says." *St. Louis Post-Dispatch* (May 11): 8A.

———. 1992b. "55% of Eligible Adults Voted—Most Since 1960." *St. Louis Post-Dispatch* (November 5): 13A.

———. 1992c. "The Congressional Surprise." *St. Louis Post-Dispatch* (November 5): 2C.

———. 1992d. "New Congress Prepared to Push Clinton Agenda." *St. Louis Post-Dispatch* (November 5): 8C.

———. 1991. "Life Span Gap Narrows for Blacks, Whites." *St. Louis Post-Dispatch* (August 29): SA.

———. 1988a. "Court Rules Against School Paper: Censoring Allowed at Hazelwood." *St. Louis Post-Dispatch* (January 14): 1.

———. 1988b. "Deficit Leads List of Concerns in Poll." *St. Louis Post-Dispatch* (September 25): 7a.

———. 1987. "Homelessness Rocks Families, Mayors Report." *St. Louis Post-Dispatch* (December 17): 1, 10.

———. 1985a. "Hunger Reported Epidemic in U.S., Hitting 20 Million." *St. Louis Post-Dispatch* (February 27): 1, 10.

———. 1985b. "Baby Bust: Middle Class Caught in Squeeze, Study Says." *St. Louis Post-Dispatch* (December 8): 1.

Sale, Kirkpatrick. 1993. *The Green Revolution: The American Environmental Movement, 1962–1992.* New York: Will and Change Publishers.

———. 1975. *Power Shift: The Rise of the Southern Rim and Its Challenge to the Eastern Establishment.* New York: Random House.

Salleh, A. 1991. Review of "Staying Alive: Women, the Ecology, and Development." *Hypatia* 6(1): 206–14.

Salpukas, Agis. 1988. "Company News: Unions Wary of Icahn on Eastern." *New York Times* (September 15): D6.

Saltman, Juliet. 1990. *A Fragile Movement: The Struggle for Neighborhood Stabilization.* New York: Greenwood/Praeger.

———. 1978. *Open Housing: Dynamics of a Social Movement.* New York: Praeger.

Sampson, Robert J. 1987. "Urban Black Violence: The Effect of Male Joblessness and Family Disruption." *American Journal of Sociology* 93: 348–82.

Sampson, Robert J, Jeffrey D. Morenoff, and Felton Earls. 1999. "Beyond Social Capital: Spatial Dynamics of Collective Efficacy for Children." *American Sociological Review* 64: 633–60.

Samuelson, Kurt. 1961. *Religion and Economic Action: A Critique of Max Weber* (E. Geoffrey French, trans.) New York: Harper & Row.

San Francisco Chronicle. 1995a. "Registrations Soar with Motor Voter Law; Despite GOP Qualms, Republicans Doing Well." *San Francisco Chronicle* (March 27): A3.

———. 1995b. "Editorial—'Motor Voter' Revs Up." *San Francisco Chronicle* (August 20): A16.

Sanacore, Joseph. 1990. Intra-Class Grouping with a Whole Language Thrust. Teacher Classroom Guide.

Sandier, Simone. 1983. "Comparison of Health Expenditures in France and the United States, 1950–1978." Vital and Health Statistics, Series No.21, DHHS Publication No. (PHS) 83–1405. Washington, DC: U.S. Government Printing Office.

San Giovanni, Lucinda. 1978. *Ex-nuns: A Study of Emergent Role Passages.* Norwood, NJ: Ablex.

Sapir, Edward. 1921. *Language: An Introduction to the Study of Speech.* New York: Harvest Books.

Sasaki, Masamichi, and Tatsuzo Suzuki. 1987. "Changes in Religious Commitment in the United States, Holland, and Japan." *American Journal of Sociology* 92: 1055–76.

Sattel, Jack W. 1989. "The Inexpressive Male: Tragedy or Sexual Politics?" Pp. 174–82 in Michael S. Kimmel and Michael A. Messner (eds.), *Men's Lives.* New York: Macmillan.

Sattler, Jerome M. 1988. *Assessment of Children,* 3rd ed. San Diego, CA: Jerome M. Sattler.

Savage, Wendy. 1986. *A Savage Enquiry.* London: Virago.

Savelsberg, Joachim J. 1994. "Knowledge, Domination, and Criminal Punishment." *American Journal of Sociology* 99: 911–43.

Savoye, Craig. 2001. "Diplomas, Hugs, and a Mountain of Debt." *Christian Science Monitor* (May 29): 3.

Sawers, Larry, and William K. Tabb (eds.). 1984. *Sunbelt/Snowbelt.* New York: Oxford University Press.

Sayers, Janet. 1980. "Psychological Sex Differences." Pp. 42–62 in The Brighton Women and Science Group (eds.), *Alice Through the Microscope: The Power of Science over Women's Lives.* London: Virago.

Scarr, S., and Richard A. Weinberg. 1976. "IQ Test Performance of Black Children Adopted by White Families." *American Psychologist* 31: 726–39.

Schafer, Walter E., Carol Olexa, and Kenneth Polk. 1972. "Programmed for Social Class: Tracking in High School." Pp. 34–54 in Kenneth Polk and Walter B. Schafer (eds.), *Schools and Delinquency.* Englewood Cliffs, NJ: Prentice Hall.

Scheff, Thomas J. 1975. *Labeling Madness.* Englewood Cliffs, NJ: Prentice Hall.

Schein, Edgar H. 1957. "Reaction Patterns to Severe Chronic Stress in American Army Prisoners of War of the Chinese." *Journal of Social Issues* 13(3): 21–30.

Schein, Edgar H., with Inge Schneier and Curtis H. Barker. 1961. *Coercive Persuasion: A Socio-psychological Analysis of the "Brainwashing" of American Civilian Prisoners by the Chinese Communists.* New York: Norton.

Schender, Andy. 1997. "Reducing the Number of Uninsured Children: Building upon Medicaid Coverage is a Better Approach than Creating a New Block Grant to the States." Center on Budget and Policy Priorities (June 5). http://www.igc.apc.org/medicaid/cbpp-1.htm.

Schmidt, William F. 1990. "White Men Get Better Deals on Cars, Study Finds." *The New York Times* (December 13): A26.

Schneider, Jeffrey M. 1989. "Tracking: A National Perspective." *Equity and Choice* 6: 11–17.

Schneider, Joseph W., and Peter Conrad. 1980. "The Medical Control of Deviance: Conquests and Consequences." Pp. 1–53 in Julius A. Roth (ed.), *Research in the Sociology of Health Care: A Research Annual,* Vol. 1: 1980: Professional Control of Health Services and Challenges to Such Control. Greenwich, CT: JAI Press.

Schnittker, Jason, Jeremy Freese, and Brian Powell. 2003. "Who Are Feminists and What Do They Believe? The Role of Generations." *American Sociological Review* 68: 1–17.

Schoen, Robert, and James R. Kluegel. 1988. "The Widening Gap in Black and White Marriage Rates: The Impact of Population Composition and Differential Marriage Propensities." *American Sociological Review* 53: 895–907.

Schoen, Robert, Karen Woodrow, and John Baj. 1985. "Marriage and Divorce in Twentieth Century American Cohorts." *Demography* 22: 101–14.

Schoenberg, Tom. 1995. "Student Borrowing Increases After Changes in U.S. Policy." *Chronicle of Higher Education* (September 29): A6.

School Boys of Barbiana. 1970. *Letter to a Teacher.* (Nora Rossi and Tom Cole, tr.). New York: Random House.

Schooler, Carmi, and Atushi Naoi. 1988. "The Psychological Effects of Traditional and Economically Peripheral Job Settings in Japan." *American Journal of Sociology* 94: 335–55.

Schor, Juliet B. 1997. "Civic Engagement and Working Hours: Do Americans Really Have More Free Time Than Ever Before?" Paper prepared for presentation at Conference on Civic Engagement in American Democracy, September 26–28, 1997, Portland Maine. http://www.silcom.com/~rdb/swt/putok.htm.

Schorr, Lisbeth B., with Daniel Schorr. 1988. *Within Our Reach: Breaking the Cycle of Disadvantage.* New York: Anchor-Doubleday.

Schrag, C. 1984. Crime and Justice: American Style. Rockwell, MD: National Institute of Mental Health, 1971. Pp. 90–92 quoted in William J. Chambliss (ed.), *Criminal Law in Action,* 2nd ed. New York: Wiley.

Schultz, Theodore W. 1961. "Investment in Human Capital." *American Economic Review* 51: 1–17.

Schumaker, John E. 1998. "Can Religion Make You Happier?" *Free Inquiry* 18: 28–31.

Schumaker, John F. 1992. "Mental Health Consequences of Irreligion." Pp. 54–69 in John F. Schumaker (ed.), *Religion and Mental Health.* New York: Oxford University Press.

Schuman, Howard. 1975. "Free Will and Determinism in Public Beliefs About Race." Pp. 375–80 in Norman R. Yetman and C. Hoy Steele (eds.), *Majority and Minority: The Dynamics of Race and Ethnic Relations,* 2nd ed. Boston: Allyn and Bacon. Earlier version appeared in TransAction 7(2): 44–48.1 (1969).

Schuman, Howard, and Lawrence Bobo. 1988. "Survey-Based Experiments on White Racial Attitudes Toward Residential Segregation." *American Journal of Sociology* 94: 273–99.

Schuman, Howard, and Maria Krysan. 1999. "A Historical Note on Whites' Beliefs About Racial Inequality." *American Sociological Review* 64: 847–55.

Schuman, Howard, and Cheryl Reiger. 1992. "Historical Analogies, Generational Effects, and Attitudes Toward War." *American Sociological Review* 57: 315–26.

Schuman, Howard, and Jaqueline Scott. 1989. "Generations and Collective Memories." *American Sociological Review* 54: 359–81.

Schur, Edwin M. 1980. *The Politics of Deviance.* Englewood Cliffs, NJ: Prentice Hall.

Schwab, Gustav. 1974. *Gods and Heroes: Myths and Epics of Ancient Greece.* New York: Pantheon.

Schwab, William A. 1992. *The Sociology of Cities.* Englewood Cliffs, NJ: Prentice Hall.

Schwartz, Charles. 1975. "The Corporate Connection." *Bulletin of the Atomic Scientist* (October).

Schwitzer, Alan M.; Oris T. Griffin, Julie R. Ancis, and Celeste R. Thomas. 1999. "Social Adjustment Experiences of African American College Students." *Journal of Counseling and Development* 77(2): 189–98.

Scott, Christopher F., and Susan Sprecher. 2000. "Sexuality in Marriage, Dating, and Other Relationships: A Decade Review." *Journal of Marriage and the Family* 62: 999–1018.

Scott, W. Richard. 1992. *Organizations: Rational, Natural, and Open Systems.* Englewood Cliffs, NJ: Prentice Hall.

Seager, Joni. 1993. *Earth Follies: Coming to Feminist Terms with the Global Environmental Crisis.* New York: Routledge.

Sears, David O., and Harris M. Allen. 1984. "The Trajectory of Local Desegregation Controversies and Whites' Opposition to Busing." Pp. 123–51 in Norman Miller and Marilyn Brewer (eds.), *Groups in Contact: The Psychology of Desegregation.* New York: Academic Press.

Sears, Robert K., F. F. Maccoby, and H. Lewin. 1957. *Patterns of Child Rearing.* Evanston, IL: Row, Peterson.

Sedlack, M., and S. Schlossman. 1986. *Who Will Teach? Historical Perspectives on the Changing Appeal of Teaching as a Profession.* Santa Monica, CA: Rand Corporation.

See, Katherine O'Sullivan. 1986. *First World Nationalisms: Class and Ethnic Politics in Northern Ireland and Quebec.* Chicago: University of Chicago Press.

Seeborg, Michael C., and Kristin Jaeger. 1993. "The Impact of Local Labor Markets on Black and White Family Structure." *Journal of Socio-Economics* 22: 115–30.

Seeman, Melvin, and J. W. Evans. 1962. "Alienation and Learning in a Hospital Setting." *American Sociological Review* 22: 772–83.

Seeman, Melvin, and Teresa E. Seeman. 1983. "Health Behavior and Personal Autonomy: A Longitudinal Study of the Sense of Control in Illness." *Journal of Health and Social Behavior* 24: 144–60.

Seifer, Nancy. 1973. *Absent from the Majority: Working-Class Women in America.* New York: American Jewish Committee.

Sellers, Nancy; Jamie Satcher, and Robert Comas. 1999. "Children's Occupational Aspirations: Comparisons by Gender, Gender Role Identity, and Socioeconomic Status." *Professional School Counseling* 2(4): 314–18.

Sellin, Thorsten. 1980. *The Penalty of Death.* Beverly Hills, CA: Sage.

———. (ed.), 1967. *Capital Punishment.* New York: Harper & Row.

———. 1959. *The Death Penalty.* Philadelphia: American Law Institute.

Selznick, Philip. 1957. *Leadership in Organizations.* Evanston, IL: Row, Peterson.

———. 1952. *The Organizational Weapon.* New York: McGraw Hill.

Semyonov, Moshe. 1988. "Bi-Ethnic Labor Markets, Mono-Ethnic Labor Markets, and Socioeconomic Inequality." *American Sociological Review* 53: 256–66.

Semyonov, Moshe, and Yinon Cohen. 1990. "Ethnic Discrimination and the Income of Majority-Group Workers." *American Sociological Review* 55: 107–14.

Sen, Gita, and Caren Grown. 1987. *Development, Crises, and Alternative Visions: Third World Women's Perspectives.* New York: Monthly Review Press.

Serrill, Michael S. 1987. "In the Grip of the Scourge." *Time* (February 16): 58–59.

Service, Elman R. 1975. *Origins of the State and Civilization.* New York: Norton.

Sewell, William H. 1992. "A Theory of Structure: Duality, Agency, and Transformation." *American Journal of Sociology* 98: 1–29.

Sewell, William H., and Vimal P. Shah. 1968. "Parents' Education and Children's Educational Aspirations and Achievements." *American Sociological Review* 33: 191–209.

Sexton, Patricia Cayo. 1991. *The War on Labor and the Left: Understanding America's Unique Conservatism.* Boulder, CO: Westview Press.

Shaheen, Jack G. 2001. *Reel Bad Arabs: How Hollywood Vilifies a People.* Northampton, MA: Interlink Publishing.

Shanas, Ethel. 1979. "Social Myths as Hypothesis: The Case of Family Relations of Old People." *Gerontologist* 19: 2–9.

Shanas, Ethel, Peter Townsend, Dorothy Wedderburn, Hennig Friis, P. Milhj, and Jan Stehouwer. 1968. *Old People in Three Industrial Societies.* New York: Atherton Press.

Shapiro, Susan P. 1990. "Collaring the Crime, Not the Criminal: Reconsidering the Concept of White Collar Crime." *American Sociological Review* 55: 346–65.

Sharma, Sarla. 1986. "Assessment Strategies for Minority Groups." *Journal of Black Studies* 17: 111–24.

Sharp, David. 1996. "Preliminary Results of Latest US Child Abuse Survey Released." *Lancet* 384(9027) (August 31): 606.

Sharp, Rachel, and Anthony Green. 1975. *Education and Social Control.* London: Routledge and Kegan Paul.

Shea, Christopher. 1996. "Who Wars with Whom?" *Chronicle of Higher Education* 42(43) (Jul 5, 1996):A6–A7.

Sheldon, Randall L. 1982. *Criminal Justice in America: A Sociological Approach.* Boston: Little, Brown.

Sheldon, William. 1949. *Varieties of Delinquent Youth: An Introduction to Constitutional Psychiatry.* New York: Harper.

Sheley, Joseph (ed.). 1991. *Criminology: A Contemporary Handbook.* Belmont, CA: Wadsworth.

Shevky, Eshref, and Wendell Bell. 1955. *Social Area Analysis: Theory, Illustrative Application, and Computational Procedures.* Stanford, CA: Stanford University Press.

Shevky, Eshref, and Marilyn Williams. 1949. *The Social Areas of Los Angeles.* Berkeley: University of California Press.

Shibutani, Tamatsu. 1986. *Social Processes: An Introduction to Sociology.* Berkeley: University of California Press.

Shields, Peter G., and Curtis C. Harris. 1991. "Molecular Epidemiology and the Genetics of Environmental Cancer." *JAMA, Journal of the American Medical Association* 266(5): 681–87.

Shirk, Martha. 1992. "Where They Stand on Welfare/Family: Candidates Reflect Prevailing View that Welfare Serves the Poor Poorly." *St. Louis Post-Dispatch* (October 25): BI.

Shiva, Vandana. 1990. In Irene Diamond and Gloria Orenstein (eds.), *Reweaving the World: The Emergence of Ecofeminism.* San Francisco: Sierra Club Books.

Shonk, James H. 1992. *Team-Based Organization: Developing a Successful Team Environment.* Homewood, IL: Business One Irwin.

Short, James F., Jr., and Ivan F. Nye. 1958. "Extent of Unrecorded Delinquency: Tentative Conclusions." *Journal of Criminal Law, Criminology and Police Science* 49: 296–302.

Shroyer, M. Gail, Carol A. Borchers, Nancy J. Smith, and Emmett L. Wright. 1994. "Science and Mathematics Equity Issues at a Local School District Level." *School Science & Mathematics* 94(2): 65–79.

Shultz, T. R., D. Wells, and M. Sarda. 1980. "Development of the Ability to Distinguish Intended Actions from Mistakes, Reflexes, and Passive Movements." *British Journal of Clinical and Social Psychology* 19: 301–10.

Simmel, Georg. 1964. "The Metropolis and Mental Life." Pp. 409–24 in Kurt Wolf (ed. and trans.), *The Sociology of Georg Simmel.* New York: Free Press. (Originally published in 1905.).

Simmons, J. L. 1969. *Deviants.* Berkeley, CA: Glendessary.

Simmons, James W. 1978. "The Organization of the Urban System." Chapter 1.4 in Larry S. Bourne and James W. Simmons (eds.), *Systems of Cities.* New York: Oxford University Press.

Simmons, Rosa, and Susan G. Broyler. 1983. *Fall Enrollment in Colleges and Universities, 1980.* Washington, DC: National Center for Education Statistics.

Simmons, Wendy W. 2001. "Majority of Americans Say More Women in Political Office Would Be Positive for the Country." The Gallup Organization: Poll Releases, January 4, 2001. http://www.gallup.com/poll/releases/pr010104.asp.

Simon, David R., and D. Stanley Eitzen. 1993. *Elite Deviance,* 4th ed. Boston: Allyn and Bacon.

———. 1986. *Elite Deviance,* 2nd ed. Boston: Allyn and Bacon.

Simon, Julian L. 1981. *The Ultimate Resource.* Princeton, NJ: Princeton University Press.

Simon, Julian L., and Herman Kahn. 1984. *The Resourceful Earth: A Response to Global 2000.* New York: Basil Blackwell.

Simpson, George Eaton, and J. Milton Yinger. 1985. *Racial and Cultural Minorities: An Analysis of Prejudice and Discrimination,* 5th ed. New York: Plenum.

Simpson, Ida Harper, David Stark, and Robert A. Jackson. 1988. "Class Identification Processes of Married, Working Men and Women." *American Sociological Review* 53: 284–93.

Simpson, John H. 1981. "Is There a Moral Majority?" Paper presented at the joint annual meeting of the Society for the Scientific Study of Religion and the Religious Research Association, Baltimore, October 30.

Simpson, Miles. 1990. "Political Rights and Income Inequality: A Cross-National Test." *American Sociological Review* 55: 682–93.

Sindler, Allan P. 1978. *Bakke, DeFunis, and Minority Admissions: The Quest for Equal Opportunity.* New York: Longman.

Singer, Joel David, and Melvin Small. 1972. *The Wages of War. 1816–1965: A Statistical Handbook.* New York: Wiley.

Sivard, Ruth Leger. 1987. *World, Military and Social Expenditures 1987–1988,* 12th ed. Washington, DC: World Priorities.

Sjoberg, Gideon. 1960. *The Preindustrial City.* Glencoe, IL: Free Press.

———. 1955. "The Preindustrial City." *American Journal of Sociology* 60: 438–45.

Skinner, B. F. 1968. *The Technology of Teaching.* New York: Appleton-Century-Crofts.

———. 1938. *The Behavior of Organisms.* New York: Appleton-Century-Crofts.

Skocpol, Theda. 1979. *States and Social Revolutions: A Comparative Analysis of France, Russia, and China.* Cambridge, England: Cambridge University Press.

Skolnick, Arlene, and Stacey Rosenkrantz. 1994. "The New Crusade for the Old Family." *The American Prospect* 18 (Summer): 59–65; also, http://epn.org/prospect/_18/18skol.html.

Skolnick, Jerome H. 1969. *The Politics of Protest.* New York: Simon & Schuster.

Slack, W. V., and Douglas Porter. 1980. "The Scholastic Aptitude Test: A Critical Appraisal." *Harvard Educational Review* 50: 154–175.

Slater, Philip F. 1970. *The Pursuit of Loneliness.* Boston: Beacon Press.

———. 1955. "Role Differentiation in Small Groups." Pp. 498–515 in A. Paul Hare (ed.), *Small Groups: Studies in Social Interaction.* New York: Alfred A. Knopf.

Slavin, Robert E. 1995. "Detracking and Its Detractors: Flawed Evidence, Flawed Values." *Phi Delta Kappan* 77: 220–21.

Sloan, John Henry, Arthur L. Kellerman, and Donald T. Reay. 1988. "Handgun Regulations, Crime, Assaults, and Homicide." *New England Journal of Medicine* 319: 1256–62.

Slomczynski, Kazimierz M., and Tadeusz K. Krauze. 1987. "Cross-National Similarity in Social Mobility Patterns: A Direct Test of the Featherman-Jones-Hauser Hypothesis." *American Sociological Review* 52: 598–611.

Smallwood, Scott. 2001. "Success and New Hurdles for T.A. Unions." *Chronicle of Higher Education* (July 6).

Smeeding, Timothy, Barbara Boyle Torrey, and Martin Rein. 1988. "Patterns of Income and Poverty: The Economic Status of Children and the Elderly in Eight Countries." In John L. Palmer, Timothy Smeeding, and Barbara Boyle Torrey (eds.), *The Vulnerable.* Washington, DC: Urban Institute.

Smelser, Neil J. 1988. "Social Structure." Pp. 103–29 in Neil J. Smelser (ed.), *Handbook of Sociology.* Newbury Park, CA: Sage.

———. 1968. "Sociological History: The Industrial Revolution and the British Working Class Family." Pp. 76–91 in Neil J. Smelser (ed.), *Essays in Sociological Explanation.* Englewood Cliffs, NJ: Prentice Hall.

———. 1963. *Theory of Collective Behavior.* New York: Free Press.

Smith, Adam. 1910. *The Wealth of Nations.* London: J. M. Dent. (Originally published in 1776.)

Smith, Bradley A. 1995. "Campaign Finance Regulation: Faulty Assumptions and Undemocratic Consequences." *Policy Analysis* (September 13): 238; also available on http://www.cato.org/po238.html.

Smith, Jack. 1976. "The Great Los Angeles Air Raid." In John Caughey and La Rue Caughey (eds.), *Los Angeles: Biography of a City.* Los Angeles: Los Angeles Times.

Smith, Lauren A., Paul H. Wise, Wendy Chavkin, Diana Romero, and Barry Zuckerman. 2000. "Implications of Welfare Reform for Child Health: Emerging Challenges for Clinical Practice and Policy." *Pediatrics* 106: 1117–25.

Smith, Richard A., Richard B. Alexander, and M. Gordon Wolman. 1987. "Water-Quality Trends in the Nation's Rivers." *Science* 235: 1607–15.

Smith, Shanna L., and Cathy Clous. 1997. "Documenting Discrimination by Homeowners' Insurance Companies Through Testing." Pp. 106–17 in Gregory D. Squires (ed.), *Insurance Redlining: Disinvestment, Reinvestment, and the Evolving Role of Financial Institutions.* Washington, DC: Urban Institute Press.

Smith, Stacy L., and Edward Donnerstein. 1998. "Harmful Effects of Exposure to Media Violence: Learning of Agression, Demotional Desensitization, and Fear." Pp. 167–202 in Russel G. Green and Edward Donnerstein (eds.), *Human Aggression: Theories, Research, and Implications for Social Policy.* San Diego, CA: Academic Press.

Smits, Jeroen, and Wout Ultee. 1999. "Occupational Homogamy in Eight Countries of the European Union, 1975–89." *Acta Sociologica* 42: 55–69.

Smock, Pamela J., Wendy D. Manning, and Sanjiv Gupta. 1999. "The Effect of Marriage and Divorce on Women's Economic Well-Being." *American Sociological Review* 64: 794–812.

Sniderman, Paul M., and Thomas Piazza. 1993. *The Scar of Race.* Cambridge, MA: Harvard University Press.

Snow, David A., F. Burke Rochford, Jr., Steven K. Worden, and Robert D. Benford. 1986. "Frame Alignment Processes, Micromobilization, and Movement Participation." *American Sociological Review* 51: 464–81.

Snow, David A., Louis A. Zurcher, Jr., and Sheldon Eckand-Olson. 1980. "Social Networks and Social Movements: A Microstructural Approach to Differential Recruitment." *American Sociological Review* 45: 787–801.

Snowdon, David. 2001. *Aging with Grace: What the Nun Study Teaches Us about Leading Longer, Healthier, and More Meaningful Lives.* New York: Bantam Books.

Snyder, David, and Edward L. Kick. 1979. "Structural Position in the World System and Economic Growth, 1955–1970: A Multiple-Network Analysis of Transnational Intersections." *American Journal of Sociology* 84: 1096–1126.

Snyder, Jim. 1995. "Aid Reduces Dropout Rate More than Loans, Study Finds." *Chronicle of Higher Education* (April 28): A56.

Soldo, Beth J., and Emily M. Agree. 1988. "America's Elderly." *Population Bulletin* 43(3).

Sorauf, Frank. 1992. *Inside Campaign Finance.* New Haven, CT: Yale University Press.

Sorensen, Annemette, and Sara McLanahan. 1987. "Married Women's Economic Opportunity, 1940–1980." *American Journal of Sociology* 93: 659–87.

Sorensen, Annemette, and Heike Trappe. 1995. "The Persistence of Gender Inequality in Earnings in the German Democratic Republic." *American Sociological Review* 60: 398–406.

Sorokin, Pitirim A. 1941. *The Crisis of Our Age.* New York: E. P. Dutton.

———. 1937. *Social and Cultural Dynamics.* New York: American Book.

Sotirin, Patty, and Heidi Gottfried. 1999. "The Ambivalent Dynamics of Secretarial 'Bitching:' Control, Resistance, and the Construction of Identity." *Organization* 6(1): 57–80.

Soukhanov, Anne H. 1994. "Word Watch: Rug-Ranking." *Atlantic Monthly* 274(4): 136.

South, Scott J., and Kim M. Lloyd. 1995. "Spousal Alternatives and Marital Dissolution." *American Sociological Review* 60: 21–35.

South, Scott J., and Glenna Spitze. 1994. "Housework in Marital and Nonmarital Households." *American Sociological Review* 59: 327–47.

Southard, E. E. 1917. "Alienists and Psychiatrists." *Mental Hygiene* 1: 567–71.

Southern Poverty Law Center. 1998. "Millenium 'Y2Kaos': Fear of Computer Bug Fueling Far Right." *SPLC Intelligence Report,* Fall. Also available online at http://www.splcenter.org/intelligenceproject/ip-4h1.html.

Sovani, N. V. 1964. "The Analysis of Over-Urbanization." *Economic Development and Cultural Change* 12: 113–22.

Sowell, Thomas. 1990. *Preferential Policies.* New York: Morrow.

Spain, Daphne. 1980. "Black-to-White Successions in Central City Housing: Limited Evidence of Urban Revitalization." *Urban Affairs Quarterly* 15: 381–96.

Sparks, Allister. 1995. *Tomorrow Is Another Country: The Inside Story of a Negotiated Revolution.* London: William Heinemann.

Spates, James L., and John J. Macionis. 1987. *The Sociology of Cities,* 2nd ed. Belmont, CA: Wadsworth.

Special Committee on Aging. U.S. Senate. 1980. *Developments in Aging, 1980.* Washington, DC: U.S. Government Printing Office.

Spector, Malcolm, and John I. Kitsuse. 1977. *Constructing Social Problems.* Menlo Park, CA: Cummings.

Spence, Janet T., Kay Deaux, and Robert L. Helmreich. 1985. "Sex Roles in Contemporary American Society." Pp. 149–78 in Gardner Lindzey and Elliot Aronson (eds.). *Handbook of Social Psychology,* Vol. 1. New York: Random House.

Spence, Janet T., Robert L Helmreich, and Joy Stapp. 1975. "Ratings of Self and Peers on Sex Role Attributes and Their Relations to Self-Esteem and Conceptions of Masculinity and Feminity." *Journal of Personality and Social Psychology* 32: 29–39.

Spencer, Gregory, U.S. Bureau of the Census. 1986. Current Population Reports, Population Estimates and Projections. Series P-25, No. 995. Projections of the Hispanic Population: 1983 to 2080. Washington, DC: U.S. Government Printing Office.

Spicer, Edward H. 1980a. "American Indians." Pp. 58–114 in Stephan Thernstrom, Ann Orlov, and Oscar Handlin (eds.), *Harvard Encyclopedia of American Ethnic Groups.* Cambridge. MA: Harvard University Press.

———. 1980b. "American Indians, Federal Policy Toward." Pp. 114–22 in Stephan Thernstrom, Ann Orlov, and Oscar Handlin (eds.), *Harvard Encyclopedia of American Ethnic Groups.* Cambridge, MA: Harvard University Press.

Spitz, Rene A. 1945. "Hospitalism: An Inquiry into the Genesis of Psychiatric Conditions in Early Childhood." In Anna Freund et al. (eds.), *The Psychoanalytic Study of the Child.* New York: International Universities Press.

Spitzer, R. L., and Wilson, P. T. 1975. "Classification in Psychiatry." Pp. 826–845 in A. M. Freedman, H. I. Kaplan, and B. J. Sadock, *Comprehensive Textbook of Psychiatry-II,* Vol. 1, 2nd ed. Baltimore: Williams & Wilkins.

Squires, Gregory D. 1998. New Hope for Urban Borrowers. *Washington Post,* December 30, Page A19. Also available on http://washingtonpost.com:80/wp-srv/WPlate/1998-12/30/0071-123098-idx.html.

———. 1989a. "Runaway Factories Are Also a Civil Rights Issue." Pp. 179–81 in D. Stanley Eitzen and Maxine Baca Zinn (eds.), *The Reshaping of America: Social Consequences of a Changing Economy.* Englewood Cliffs, NJ: Prentice Hall.

———. (ed.) 1989b. *Unequal Partnerships: The Political Economy of Urban Redevelopment in Post-War America.* New Brunswick, NJ: Rutgers University Press.

Srole, Leo. 1980. "Mental Health in New York." *The Sciences* 20(10): 16–29.

———. 1972. "Urbanization and Mental Health: Some Reformulations." *American Scientist* 60: 576–83.

Srole, Leo, Thomas Langer, Stanley Michael, Marvin Opler, and Thomas Rennie. 1962. *Mental Health in the Metropolis: The Midtown Manhattan Study.* New York: McGraw-Hill.

Stack, Carol B. 1974. *All Our Kin: Strategies for Survival in a Black Community.* New York: Harper & Row.

Stack, Steven. 1994. "Divorce." Pp. 153–63 in *Encyclopedia of Human Behavior,* Vol. 2. New York: Academic Press.

Stacy, J., S. Bereaud, and J. Daniels. 1974. *Sexism in American Education.* New York: Dell.

Stammer, Larry. 1999. "Commitment to Church Wanes, Survey Reports." *Seattle Times,* February 26. http://seattletimes.nwsource.com/news/nation-world/html98/cath_012699.html.

Stampp, Kenneth. 1956. *The Peculiar Institution.* New York: Alfred A. Knopf.

Stander, Valerie, and Larry Jensen. 1993. "The Relationship of Value Orientation to Moral Cognition: Gender and Cultural Differences in the United States and China Explored." *Journal of Cross Cultural Psychology* 24: 42–52.

Stanley, Julian C, (ed.) 1973. *Compensatory Education for Children Ages 2 to 8, Recent Studies of Environmental Intervention.* Baltimore, MD: Johns Hopkins University Press.

Star, Jack. 1984. "Putting a Clamp on Your Medical Costs." *Chicago* (June): 166–71, 192–93.

Stark, Rodney. 2001. *One True God: The Historical Consequences of Monotheism.* Princeton, NJ: Princeton University Press.

———. 1987. "Estimating Church Membership Rates, 1971–1980." *Review of Religious Research* 29: 69–77.

———. 1985. "Church and Sect." In P. Hammond, ed., *The Sacred in a Secular Age.* Berkeley: University of California Press.

Stark, Rodney, and William S. Bainbridge. 1985. *The Future of Religion.* Berkeley: University of California Press.

———. 1981. "American-Born Sects: Initial Findings." *Journal for the Scientific Study of Religion* 20: 130–49.

———. 1979. "Of Churches, Sects, and Cults: Preliminary Concepts for a Theory of Religious Movements." *Journal for the Scientific Study of Religion* 18: 117–33.

Starr, Paul. 1982. *The Social Transformation of American Medicine.* New York: Basic Books.

Statistics Norway. 2000. Average Yearly Earnings for Women as Per Cent of Men's in Certain Industries and Industry Groups, Full-time Wage and Salary Earners. 1980, 1990, and 1996. http://www.ssb.no/english/subjects/00/02/10/wmnorway/gifs/side52b.shtml.

Steeh, Charlotte, Nicole Kirgis, Brian Cannon, and Jeff DeWitt. 1999. "Are They as Bad as They Seem? Nonresponse Rates at the End of the Twentieth Century." Paper presented at International Conference on Survey Response, Portland, OR, October 28–31.

Steele, Claude M. 1999. "Thin Ice: 'Stereotype Threat' and Black College Students." *Atlantic Online* (*Atlantic Monthly* digital edition) (August, 1999) http://www.theatlantic.com/issues/99aug/9908stereotype.htm.

———. 1995. Paper presented at the annual meeting of the American Psychological Association.

Steele, Claude M., and Joshua Aronson. 1995. "Stereotype Threat and the Intellectual Test Performance of African Americans." *Journal of Personality and Social Psychology* 69: 797–811.

Steele, Shelby. 1990. *The Content of Our Character: A New Vision of Race in America.* New York: St. Martin's Press.

Steelman, Linda Carr, and Brian Powell. 1991. "Sponsoring the Next Generation: Parental Willingness to Pay for Higher Education." *American Journal of Sociology* 96: 1505–29.

Steffensmeier, Darrell J., Emilie Anderson Allan, Miles D. Harer, and Cathy Streifel. 1989. "Age and the Distribution of Crime." *American Journal of Sociology* 94: 803–31.

Stein, Leonard I. 1967. "The Doctor-Nurse Game." *Archives of General Psychiatry* 16: 699–703.

Steinberg, Laurence, Susie D. Lamborn, Nancy Darling, Nina Mounts, and Sanford Dornbusch. 1994. "Over-Time Changes in Adjustment and Competence Among Adolescents from Authoritative, Authoritarian, Indulgent, and Neglectful Families." *Child Development* 65: 754–70.

Steinberg, Marc W. 1999. "The Talk and Back Talk of Collective Action: A Dialogic Analysis of Repertoires of Discourse Among Nineteenth-Century English Cotton Spinners." *American Journal of Sociology* 105: 736–80.

Steinhauser, Paul. 2009. "Poll: Did Obama's Reaction to Gates Arrest Hurt Him?" http://www.cnn.com/2009/POLITICS/08/04/obama.gates.poll/.

Stenson, Jacqueline. 2001. "Dietitians Lament Loss of Family Meals." http://www.msnbc.com/news/477797.asp?cp1=1.

Sternbach, R. A., and B. Tursky. 1965. "Ethnic Differences Among Housewives in Psychophysical and Skin Potential Responses to Electric Shock." *Psychophysiology* 1(3): 241–46.

Sternberg, Robert J. 1994. "Commentary: Reforming School Reform: Comments on 'Multiple Intelligences: The Theory in Practice.'" *Teachers College Record* 95: 561–69.

———. 1988. *The Triangle of Love.* New York: Basic Books.

Sternlieb, George. 1977. "The City as Sandbox." In J. John Palen (ed.), *City Scenes.* Boston: Little, Brown.

Sternlieb, George, and James W. Hughes. 1983. "The Uncertain Future of the Central City." *Urban Affairs Quarterly* 18: 455–72.

———. 1975. *Post-Industrial America: Metropolitan Decline and Interregional Job Shifts.* New Brunswick, NJ: Rutgers University, Center for Urban Policy Research.

Stevenson, Harold W., Shin-Ying Lee, and James W. Stigler. 1986. "Mathematics Achievement of Chinese, Japanese, and American Children." *Science* 231: 693–99.

Stinchcomb, Arthur. 1994. "Freedom and Oppression of Slaves in the

Eighteenth-Century Carribean." *American Sociological Review* 59: 911–29.

Stockard, Jean, and Miriam M. Johnson. 1992. *Sex and Gender in Society*, 2nd ed. Englewood Cliffs, NJ: Prentice Hall.

Stogdill, Ralph M. 1974. *Handbook of Leadership: A Survey of Theory and Research*. New York: Free Press.

Stokes, Randall, and Albert Chevan. 1996. "Female-Headed Families: Social and Economic Context of Racial Differences." *Journal of Urban Affairs* 18: 245–68.

Stoner, J. A. F. 1961. "A Comparison of Individual and Group Decisions Involving Risk." Master's thesis, Massachusetts Institute of Technology, School of Industrial Management, Cambridge, MA.

Stouffer, Samuel A., A. A. Lumsdaine, M. H. Lumsdaine, M. R. Williams, M. B. Smith, Irving L. Janis, S. A. Star, and L. S. Cottrell. 1949. *The American Soldier*. Vol. II: *Combat and its Aftermath*. Princeton, NJ: Princeton University Press.

Stout, Hilary. 1990. "Senate Panel Finds a Simple Answer to Question of Corporate Tax Receipts." *The Wall Street Journal* (May 4): A6.

Strang, David, and James N. Baron. 1990. "Categorical Imperatives: The Structure of Job Titles in California State Agencies." *American Sociological Review* 55: 479–95.

Straus, Murray A. 1980. "A Sociological Perspective on the Causes of Family Violence." In Maurice R. Green (ed.), *Violence and the Family*. Boulder, CO: Westview Press.

Straus, Murray A., and R. J. Gelles. 1986. "Societal Change and Change in Family Violence from 1975 to 1985 as Revealed by Two National Surveys." *Journal of Marriage and the Family* 48: 465–79.

Strauss, Anselm, Leonard Schatzman, Rue Bucher, Danuta Ehrlich, and Melvin Sabslim. 1964. *Psychiatric Ideologies and Institutions*. New York: Free Press.

Stryker, Robin. 1990. "Science, Class, and the Welfare State: A Class-Centered Functional Account." *American Journal of Sociology* 96: 684–726.

Stubbs, Jonathan K. 1993. "Lawyer Competence: Perceptual Prisms, Self-Scrutiny, and the Looking Glass." *Journal of the Legal Profession* 18: 233.

Substance Abuse and Mental Health Services Administration. 2008. National Survey on Drug Use and Health, Illicit Drug Use, by Race/Ethnicity, in Metropolitan and Non-Metropolitan Counties, 2004 and 2005. http://www.drugabusestatistics.samhsa.gov/2k7/popDensity/popDensity.htm (Downloaded October 26, 2009).

Sullivan, Amy. 2010. "Young Evangelicals: Expanding Their Mission." *Time* (June 1). http://www.time.com/time/nation/article/0,8599,1992463,00.html (Downloaded July 30, 2010).

Sullivan, Joseph F. 1990. "New Jersey Ruling to Lift School Aid for Poor Districts." *The New York Times* (June 6): A1.

Sumner, William Graham. 1906. *Folkways*. Boston: Ginn.

Sundquist, James L. 1982. *Dynamics of the Party System: Alignment and Realignment of Political Parties in the United States*, rev. ed. Washington, DC: Brookings Institution.

Suplee, C. 1991. "Brain May Determine Sexuality." *The Washington Post* (August 30): A1, A13.

Suro, Roberto. 1991. "Where America Is Growing: The Suburban Cities." *The New York Times* (February 22): A1, A10.

Susser, Mervyn W., Kim Hopper, and Judith Richman. 1983. "Society, Culture, and Health." Pp. 23–49 in David Mechanic (ed.), *Handbook of Health, Health Care, and the Health Professions*. New York: Oxford University Press.

Susser, Mervyn W., William Watson, and Kim Hopper. 1985. *Sociology in Medicine*, 3rd ed. New York: Oxford University Press.

Sutherland, Edwin H. 1983. *White-Collar Crime*. New Haven, CT: Yale University Press. (Originally published in 1949.)

———. 1947. *Criminology*, 4th ed. Philadelphia: Lippincott.

———. 1940. "White Collar Criminality." *American Sociological Review* 5: 1–12.

Swanson, Guy. 1960. *The Birth of the Gods*. Ann Arbor: University of Michigan Press.

Swatos, William H. 1983. "Enchantment and Disenchantment in Modernity: The Significance of 'Religion' as a Sociological Category." *Sociological Analysis* 44: 321–38.

Swedish Institute. 2001. Fact Sheets on Sweden, Social Insurance in Sweden (Published April, 2001). Stockholm: The Swediesh Institute. Also available on http://www.si.se/docs/infosweden/engelska/fs5z.pdf.

———. 2000. Fact Sheets on Sweden, The Financial Circumstances of Swedish Households. (Published May 2000) Stockholm: The Swedish Institute.

———. 1999. Fact Sheets on Sweden: The Swedish Population. http://www.si.se/docs/infosweden/engelska/fs67.pdf.

———. 1988. "Fact Sheets on Sweden: General Facts on Sweden." Stockholm: Swedish Institute.

Sweetser, D. A. 1985. "Broken Homes, Stable Risk, Changing Reasons, Changing Forms." *Journal of Marriage and the Family* 47: 709–15.

Swenson, Peter. 2002. *Capitalists Against Markets: The Making of Labor Markets and Welfare States in the United States and Sweden*. Oxford: Oxford University Press.

Sykes, Gresham M. 1978. *Criminology*. New York: Harcourt, Brace, Jovanovich.

Szinovacz, Maximiliane. 1996. *Women's Retirement: Policy Implications of Recent Research*. Thousand Oaks, CA: Sage.

Szymanski, Albert. 1976. "Racial Discrimination and White Gain." *American Sociological Review* 41: 403–14.

Tabah, Leon. 1980. "World Population Trends: A Stocktaking." *Population and Development Review* 6: 355–90.

Tabb, William, and Larry Sawers (eds.). 1978. *Marxism and the Metropolis*. New York: Oxford University Press.

Tach, Laura Marie, and George Farkas. 2006. "Learning Related Behaviors, Cognitive Skills, and Ability Grouping When School Begins." *Social Science Research* 35: 1048–79.

Taeuber, Karl, and Alma F. Taeuber. 1965. *Negroes in Cities*. Chicago: Aldine.

Tagliabue, John. 1987. "A Nuclear Taint in Milk Sets Off German Dispute." *The New York Times* (January 31): 1, 4.

Taira, Koji, and Solomon B. Levine. 1996. "Employment Flexibility and Joblessness in Low-Growth, Restructured Japan." *Annals of the American Academy of Political and Social Research* 544: 140–53.

Tan, Alexis S. 1979. "TV Beauty Ads and Role Expectations of Adolescent Female Viewers." *Journalism Quarterly* 56: 283–88.

Tarrow, Sidney. 1989. *Struggle, Politics, and Reform: Collective Action, Social Movements, and Cycles of Protest*. Ithaca, NY: Cornell University Press.

———. 1982. Social Movements, Resource Mobilization, and Reform During Cycles of Protest. Western Studies Program Project, Social Protest and Policy Innovative Work, Paper 1. Ithaca, NY: Cornell University Press.

Task Force on Education for Economic Growth, Educational Commission of the States. 1983. *Action for Excellence: A Comprehensive Plan to Improve Our Nation's Schools*. Denver, CO: A. B. Hirschfield Press.

Taylor's World of Politics. 1987. "Changes Across the Nation Resulting from the 1986 Elections." *Taylor's World of Politics* (April): 5.

Taylor, Howard F. 1995. "Review Symposium: The Bell Curve." *Contemporary Sociology* 24: 153–58.

Taylor, Marylee C. 1995. "White Backlash to Workplace Affirmative Action: Peril or Myth?" *Social Forces* (73: 1385–1413).

Teachman, Jay D. 1987. "Family Background, Educational Resources, and Educational Attainment." *American Sociological Review* 52: 548–57.

———. 1983. "Early Marriage, Premarital Fertility, and Marital Dissolution." *Journal of Family Issues* 4: 105–26.

Telles, Edward E. 1994. "Industrialization and Racial Inequality in Employment: The Brazilian Example." *American Sociological Review* 59: 46–63.

Terkel, Studs. 1967. *Division Street, America*. New York: Pantheon Books.

The Pluralism Project, Harvard University. 2001. Statistics. http://www.pluralism.org/resources/statistics/index.php.

The Sociology Writing Group. 2001. *A Guide to Writing Sociology Papers*. New York: Worth Publishers.

Thernstrom, Abigail. 1980. "E Pluribus Plura: Congress and Bilingual Education." *The Public Interest* 60: 3–22.

Thernstrom, Stephan, Ann Orlov, and Oscar Handlin (eds.). 1980. *Harvard Encyclopedia of American Ethnic Groups*. Cambridge, MA: Harvard University Press.

Thomas, L. Eugene, Robert C. Deguilo, and Nancy W. Sheehan. 1988.

"Identity Loss and Psychological Crisis in Widowhood: A Reevaluation." *International Journal of Aging and Human Development* 26: 225–39.

Thomas, Marlo. 1987. *Free to Be... a Family*. New York: Bantam.

Thomas, Rich, and Larry Reibstein. 1991. "The Pay Police." *Newsweek* (June 17): 44–45.

Thomas, W. I. 1966. *W. I. Thomas on Social Organization and Personality*. (Morris Janowitz, ed.). Chicago: University of Chicago Press.

Thomas, William L. (ed.). 1956. *Man's Role in Changing the Face of the Earth,* Vol.1. Chicago: University of Chicago Press.

Thomlinson, Ralph. 1976. *Population Dynamics: Causes and Consequences of World Population Change,* 2nd ed. New York: Random House.

Thompson, E. P. 1963. *The Making of the English Working Class*. New York: Vintage.

Thompson, Linda, and Alexis J. Walker. 1989. "Gender in Families: Women and Men in Marriage, Work, and Parenthood." *Journal of Marriage and the Family* 51: 845–71.

Thorndike, Robert B. 1969. "Review of Pygmalion in the Classroom." *Teachers College Record* 70: 805–07.

Thorne, Barrie. 1993. *Gender Play*. New Brunswick, NJ: Rutgers University Press.

Thornton, Arland. 1991. "Influence of the Marital History of Parents on the Marital and Cohabitational Influences of Children." *American Journal of Sociology* 96: 868–94.

Thornton, Arland, William G. Axinn, and Daniel H. Hill. 1992. "Reciprocal Effects of Religiosity, Cohabitation, and Marriage." *American Journal of Sociology* 98: 628–51.

Thornton, Arland, and Dehorah Freedman. 1984. "The Changing American Family." *Population Bulletin* 38(4).

Thornton, Russell. 1987. *American Indian Holocaust and Survival: A Population History Since 1492*. Norman: University of Oklahoma Press.

Thurow, Lester C. 1977. "The Myth of the American Economy." *Newsweek* (February 14): 11.

Tice, Dianne M. 1992. "Self-Concept Change and Self-Presentation: The Looking Glass Self is Also a Magnifying Glass." *Journal of Personality and Social Psychology* 63: 435.

Tienda, Marta, and Haya Stier. 1991. "Joblessness and Shiftlessness: Labor Force Activity in Chicago's Inner City." Pp. 135–54 in Christopher Jencks and Paul E. Peterson (eds.), *The Urban Underclass*. Washington, DC: Brookings Institution.

Tierney, Kathleen. 2006. "The Red Pill." Social Science Research Council, *Understanding Katrina: Perspectives from the Social Sciences.* http://understandingkatrina.ssrc.org/Tierney/ (downloaded May 6, 2008).

Tilly, Charles. 1995. "To Explain Political Processes." *American Journal of Sociology* 100: 1594–1610.

———. 1978. *From Mobilization to Revolution*. Reading, MA: Addison-Wesley.

———. 1974. "The Chaos of the Living City." Pp. 86–108 in Charles Tilly (ed.), *An Urban World*. Boston: Little, Brown.

Time. 1989. "A Blow to Affirmative Action." *Time* (February 6): 60.

Tittle, Charles R. 1980. "Labelling and Crime: An Empirical Evaluation." Pp. 241–70 in Walter R. Gove (ed.), *The Labelling of Deviance,* 2nd ed. Beverly Hills, CA: Sage.

Tobias, Sheila. 1978. *Overcoming Math Anxiety*. New York: Norton.

Tobin, Gary (ed.). 1987. *Divided Neighborhoods*. Urban Affairs Annual Reviews, Vol. 32. Newbury Park, CA: Sage.

Toennies, Ferdinand. 1963. *Community and Society*. New York: Harper & Row. (Originally published in German as Gemeinschaft und Gesellschaft in 1887.).

Toffler, Alvin. 1970. *Future Shock*. New York: Random House.

Tolbert, Caroline J. and Ramona S. McNeal. 2003. "Unraveling the Effects of the Internet on Political Participation." *Political Research Quarterly* 56: 175-85.

Tolchin, Martin. 1988. "House Backs Conference Bill on Major Illness." *The New York Times* (June 3): 32.

Tolnay, Stewart E. 1995. "The Spatial Diffusion of Fertility: A Cross-Sectional Analysis of Counties in the American South." *American Sociological Review* 60: 299–308.

Tolnay, Stewart, and E. M. Beck. 1992. "Racial Violence and Black Migration in the American South, 1910 to 1930." *American Sociological Review* 57: 103–16.

Toner, Robin. 1991. "Women in Politics Gain, But Road Is a Long One." *The New York Times* (February 25): A6.

———. 1990a. "Nonvoters: Turned Off by Campaigns, or Just Too Busy to Vote." *The New York Times* (November 7): BI, B6.

———. 1990b. "Voters Oust Governing Party in 14 States; Congress Is Shaken but Few Are Unseated." *The New York Times* (November 8): A1, B6.

Tonry, Michael H. 1996. *Malign Neglect—Race, Crime, and Punishment in America*. New York: Oxford University Press.

Toth, Jennifer. 1991. "Number of Children Living on America's Streets Swells." *Los Angeles Times* (October 31): A6.

Touraine, Alain. 1971. *The Post-Industrial Society*. (Leonard F. X. Mayhew, trans.). New York: Random House. (Originally published in French in 1969.).

Townsend, John Marshall. 1978. *Cultural Comparisons and Mental Illness: A Comparison of Germany and America*. Chicago: University of Chicago Press.

Townsend, Linda, and Alexis J. Walker. 1990. "American Women Get Mad: Women's Attitudes Are Changing. Here's What You Can Expect in the 1990s." *American Demographics* (August): 26–32.

Townsend, Patrick, with Joan E. Gebhardt. 1990. *Commit to Quality*. New York: Wiley.

Toynbee, Arnold. 1946. *A Study of History*. New York: Oxford University Press.

Trebelicock, Michael J., and Matthew Sudak. 2006. "The Political Economy of Emigration and Immigration." *New York University Law Review* 81: 234–293. http://www.law.nyu.edu/journals/lawreview/issues/vol81/no1/NYU108.pdf.

Treisman, Daniel. 1985. "Terror Error." *The New Republic* 193(16): 16–18.

Trevino, Roberto A. and Alan J. Richard. 2002. "Attitudes Towards Drug Legalization Among Drug Users." *American Journal of Drug and Alcohol Abuse* 28 (1): 91–108.

Tribe, Laurence. 1989. Quoted in *Time,* "A Blow to Affirmative Action" (February 6): 60.

Troeltsch, Ernst. 1932. *The Social Teaching of the Christian Churches*. (Olive Wyon, trans.). New York: Macmillan.

Tsui, A. O., and Donald J. Bogue. 1979. "Declining World Fertility: Trends, Causes, Implications." *Population Bulletin* 33(4).

Tuch, Steven A. 1987. "Urbanism, Region, and Tolerance Revisited: The Case of Racial Prejudice." *American Sociological Review* 52: 504–10.

Tumin, Melvin M. (ed.). 1970. *Readings on Social Stratification*. Englewood Cliffs, NJ: Prentice Hall.

———. 1953. "Some Principles of Stratification: A Critical Analysis." *American Sociological Review* 18: 378–94.

Turner, Margery Austin, Stephen L. Ross, George C. Galster, and John Yinger. 2002. "Discrimination in Metropolitan Housing Markets: National Results from Phase I HDS 2000." Final Report. Washington, DC: U.S. Department of Housing and Urban Development. http://www. huduser.org/Publications/pdf/Phase1_Report.pdf (downloaded November 13, 2003).

Turner, J. Ray, Blair Wheaton, and Donald A. Lloyd. 1995. "The Epidemiology of Social Stress." *American Sociological Review* 60: 104–25.

Turner, Ralph H., and Lewis M. Killian. 1987. *Collective Behavior,* 3rd ed. Englewood Cliffs, NJ: Prentice Hall.

Turner, Ralph H., Joanne M. Nigg, and Denise H. Paz. 1986. *Waiting for Disaster: Earthquake Watch in California*. Berkeley and Los Angeles: University of California Press.

Twaddle, Andrew C. 1979. *Sickness Behavior and the Sick Role*. Cambridge. MA: Schenkman.

Twaddle, Andrew C., and Richard Hessler. 1977. *A Sociology of Health*. St. Louis, MO: Mosby.

Twentieth Century Fund. 1983. *Report of the Twentieth Century Fund Task Force on Federal Elementary and Secondary Education* Policy. New York: Twentieth Century Fund.

Tyree, Andrea, Moshe Semyonov, and Robert W. Hodge. 1979. "Gaps and Glissandos: Inequality, Economic Development, and Social Mobility in 24 Countries." *American Sociological Review* 44: 410–24.

Uchitelle, Louis. 1991a. "Insurance as a Job Benefit Shows Signs of Over-work." *The New York Times* (May 1): A1, D23.

———. 1991b. "2 Health Plans With Payments Tied to Income." *The New York Times* (May 1): D23.

Udry, J. Richard. 2000. "Biological Limits of Gender Construction." *American Sociological Review* 65: 443–57.

———. 1988. "Biological Predispositions and Social Control in Adolescent Sexual Behavior." *American Sociological Review* 53: 709–722.

Udry, J. Richard, and John O. G. Billy. 1987. "Initiation of Coitus in Early Adolescence." *American Sociological Review* 52: 841–55.

Udy, Stanley H., Jr. 1959. "Bureaucracy and 'Rationality' in Weber's Organizational Theory: An Empirical Study." *American Sociological Review* 24: 791–95.

Uhara, Edwina. 1990. "Dual Exchange Theory, Social Networks, and Informed Social Support." *American Journal of Sociology* 96: 521–57.

Unger, Irwin. 1989. *These United States: The Questions of Our Past,* 4th ed. Englewood Cliffs, NJ: Prentice Hall.

United Nations. 2007. *Human Development Report, 2007/2008.* New York: United Nations Development Program.

———. 2001. World Population Prospects: The 2000 Revision—Highlights. New York: Population Division, Department of Economic and Social Affairs, United Nations. http://www.un.org/esa/population/wpp2000.htm.

———. 1997. World Population, 1996—Tables. http://www.undp.org/popin/wdtrends/pop/fpop.html.

———. 1988. *1986 Energy Statistics Yearbook.* New York: United Nations.

———. 1985. *Demographic Yearbook 1983.* New York: United Nations.

United Nations Crime and Justice Information Network. 1996. "World Crime Survey." http://www.ifs.univie.ac/~uncjin/wcs.html.

United Nations, Department of Economic and Social Affairs, Population Division. 2010. *World Urbanization Prospects, The 2009 Revision.* New York: United Nations.

United Nations Population Division. 2009. World Population Prospects: The 2008 Revision Population Database. http://esa.un.org/unpp/ (Downloaded December 2, 2009).

USA Today. 1991. "By the Numbers, Tracking Segregation in 219 Metropolitan Areas." (November 11): 3A.

———. 2009. "Women CEOs Slowly Gain on Corporate America." (January 2). http://www.usatoday.com/money/companies/management/2009-01-01-women-ceos-increase_N.htm (Downloaded October 22, 2009).

U.S. Bureau of the Census. 2009. *Statistical Abstract of the United States: 2009.* Washington, DC: U.S. Government Printing Office.

———. 2008. U.S. Population Projections. National Population Projections (based on Census 2000): Summary Tables. http://www.census.gov/population/www/projections/summarytables.html.

———. 2004. Ancestry: 2000. http://www.census.gov/prod/2004pubs/c2kbr-35.pdf.

———. 1996a. "Income and Poverty: 1994 Graphs. Median Household Income by Race and Hispanic Origin: 1967–1994." http://www.census.gov/hhes/income.

———. 1996b. "Table H-1. Share of Aggregate Income Received by Each Fifth and Top 5 Percent of Households, by Race and Hispanic Origin of Householder, 1967–1994." http://www.census.gov/income/hol.prn.

———. 1996c. Economics, Income, Detailed Historical Tables, Table P-12. http://www.census.gov/ftp/pub/hhes/income/histinc/p12.prn.

———. 1996d. "Income and Poverty: 1994 Poverty Summary." http://www.census.gov/hhes/income/povsum.html.

———. 1996e. "Historical Poverty Tables—Persons, Table 18." http://www.census.gov/hhes/poverty/histpov/povperdet.html.

———. 1996f. *Statistical Abstract of the United States, 1995.* Washington, DC: U.S. Government Printing Office. (Also available in CD-ROM format, CD-SA-95.).

———. 1996g. "Income Table F-2. Race and Hispanic Origin of Householder—Families by Median and Mean Income: 1947–1994." http://www.census.gov/hhes/income/histinc/f2.prn.

———. 1996h. "Percent of Persons 25 Years and Over Who Have Completed High School and College, by Race, Hispanic Origin, and Sex: Selected Years, 1940–1993." http://www.census.gov/population/socdemo/education/table18.txt.

———. 1996i. 1992 Census of Manufactures. Concentration Ratios in Manufacturing. http://www.census.gov/ftp/pub/mcd/mancen/download/mc92cr.sum.

———. 1996j. Current Population Reports: Population Characteristics, Report P20–489, Educational Attainment in the United States: March, 1995. Washington, DC: U.S. Government Printing Office. Internet version available in Adobe Acrobat format through Census Bureau site, http://www.census.gov.

———. 1996k. Current Population Reports: Consumer Income, Report P60–194, Poverty in the United States, 1995. Washington, DC: U.S. Government Printing Office. Internet version available in Adobe Acrobat format through Census Bureau http://www.census.gov.

———. 1996l. "Population Projections for the United States." http://www.census.gov/pub/population/projections.

———. 1996m. "Annual Projections of Total U.S. Population." http://www.census.gov/population/projections/proj1/html.

———. 1996n. "State Population Estimates and Components of Change, 1990–1995." http://www.census.gov/population/estimates/states.

———. 1996o. "Resident Population of the United States, Middle Series Projections." http://www.census.gov/population/www/projections/respop/html.

———. 1996p. "Income 1995." http://www.census.gov/hhes/income/income95/in95sum.html.

———. 1996q. "Urban and Rural Population, 1900 to 1990." http://www.census.gov/population/censusdata/urpop0090.dat.

———. 1996r. "Metropolitan Area Population Estimates, 1990–95." http://www.census.gov/population/www/estimates/metropop.html.

———. 1996s. Current Population Reports: Consumer Income, Report P60-193, Money Income in the United States, 1995. Washington, DC: U.S. Government Printing Office. Internet version available in Adobe Acrobat format through Census Bureau site, http://www.census.gov.

———. 1996t. "Top 25 American Indian Tribes for the United States: 1990 and 1980." http://www.census.gov/population/socdemo/race/indian/ailang1.txt.

———. 1996. FT900—U.S. International Trade in Goods and Services: 1991, final revisions. http://www.census.gov/foreign-trade/Press-Release/91_press_releases/Final_Revisions_1991/ft900_91.txt.

———. 1995a. *Statistical Abstract of the United States,* 1995. Washington, DC: U.S. Government Printing Office.

———. 1995b. "Asset Ownership of Households." http://www.census.gov/pub/hhes/www.wealth.html.

———. 1992a. Press release, September 3, 1992. Washington, DC: U.S. Department of the Interior, Bureau of the Census.

———. 1992b. Current Population Reports, Population Characteristics. Series P-20; No. 458, Household and Family Characteristics: March, 1991. Washington, DC: U.S. Government Printing Office.

———. 1992c. Current Population Reports. Population Characteristics. Series P-20, No. 461, Marital Status and Living Arrangements, March, 1991. Washington, DC: U.S. Government Printing Office.

———. 1992d. Current Population Reports, Population Characteristics. Series P-20, No. 462, Educational Attainment in the United States: March 1991 and 1990. Washington, DC: U.S. Government Printing Office.

———. 1992e. Current Population Reports, Population Characteristics. Series P-20, No. 458, Household and Family Characteristics: March, 1991. Washington, DC: U.S. Government Printing Office.

———. 1992f. Current Population Reports, Consumer Income. Series P-60, No. 181, Poverty in the United States, 1991. Washington, DC: U.S. Government Printing Office.

———. 1992g. *Statistical Abstract of the United States,* 1992. Washington, DC: U.S. Government Printing Office.

———. 1992h. 1987 Census of Manufactures. Concentration Ratios in Manufacturing. Washington, DC: U.S. Government Printing Office.

———. 1991a. Current Population Reports; Population Characteristics. Series P-20, No. 450, Marital Status and Living Arrangements, March 1990. Washington, DC: U.S. Government Printing Office.

———. 1991b. 1990 Census of Population: Public Law Counts. Washington, DC: U.S. Bureau of the Census.

———. 1991c. Current Population Reports: The Hispanic Population of the United States, 1990. Washington, DC: U.S. Government Printing Office.

———. 1991d. Current Population Reports, Population Characteristics. Series P-20, No. 455, The Hispanic Population of the United States: March, 1991. Washington, DC: U.S. Government Printing Office.

———. 1991e. Current Population Reports, Consumer Income. Series P-60, No. 174, Money Income of Households, Families, and Persons in the United States: 1990. Washington, DC: U.S. Government Printing Office.

———. 1991f. Current Population Reports, Consumer Income. Series P-60, No. 175, Poverty in the United States, 1990. Washington, DC: U.S. Government Printing Office.

———. 1991g. "Asian and Pacific Islander Population Doubled." Census and You 26, 12 (December): 3.

———. 1990a. Current Population Reports: Consumer Income, Series P-60, No. 168. Money Income and Poverty Status in the United States, 1989. Washington, DC: U.S. Government Printing Office.

———. 1990b. *Statistical Abstract of the United States, 1990.* Washington, DC: U.S. Government Printing Office.

———. 1990c. Current Population Reports: Population Characteristics, Series P-20, No. 443, School Enrollment: Social and Economic Characteristics of Students, October, 1988 and 1987. Washington, DC: U.S. Government Printing Office.

———. 1990d. Current Population Reports: Population Characteristics, Series P-20, No. 447, Household and Family Characteristics: March, 1990 and 1989. Washington, DC: U.S. Government Printing Office.

———. 1989. Current Population Reports: Population Characteristics, Series P-20, No. 433, Marital Status and Living Arrangements, March, 1988. Washington, DC: U.S. Government Printing Office.

———. 1988a. Current Population Reports: Population Estimates and Projections, Series P-25, No. 1022, United States Population Estimates by Age, Sex, and Race, 1980 to 1987. Washington, DC: U.S. Government Printing Office.

———. 1988b. Current Population Reports: Population Characteristics, Series P-20, No. 423, Marital Status and Living Arrangements: March, 1987. Washington, DC: U.S. Government Printing Office.

———. 1988c. Current Population Reports: Population Characteristics, Series P-20, No. 431, The Hispanic Population in the United States: March, 1988 (Advance Report). Washington, DC: U.S. Government Printing Office.

———. 1988d. Current Population Reports: Consumer Income, Series P-60, No. 180, Poverty in the United States, 1986. Washington, DC: U.S. Government Printing Office.

———. 1987a. Current Population Reports: Consumer Income, Series P-60, No. 157, Money Income and Poverty Status of Families and Persons in the United States: 1986. (Advance Data from the March, 1987, Current Population Survey.) Washington, DC: U.S. Government Printing Office.

———. 1987b. *Statistical Abstract of the United States, 1988.* Washington, DC: U.S. Government Printing Office.

———. 1986a. Current Population Reports: Population Characteristics, Series P-20, No. 411, Household and Family Characteristics: March, 1985. Washington, DC: U.S. Government Printing Office.

———. 1986b. Current Population Reports: Population Estimates and Projections, Series P-25, No. 995. Washington, DC: U.S. Government Printing Office.

———. 1986c. 1982 Census of Manufactures. Concentration Ratios in Manufacturing, Report No. MC82–S-7. Washington, DC: U.S. Government Printing Office.

———. 1985. Current Population Reports: Consumer Income. Money Income and Poverty Status of Persons and Families in the United States: 1984. Advance Data from the March, 1985, Current Population Survey, Series P-60, No. 149. Washington, DC: U.S. Government Printing Office.

———. 1984a. Current Population Reports: Population Estimates and Projections, Series P-25, No. 952. Washington, DC: U.S. Government Printing Office.

———. 1984b. Current Population Reports, Series P-20, No. 395, Fertility of American Women, June, 1983. Washington, DC: U.S. Government Printing Office.

———. 1983a. 1980 Census of the Population: Ancestry of the Population by State: 1980, Supplementary Report No. PC80-S1–10. Washington, DC: U.S. Government Printing Office.

———. 1983b. Current Population Reports: Population Characteristics: School Enrollment: Social and Economic Characteristics of Students (Advance Report). Washington, DC: U.S. Government Printing Office.

———. 1983c. 1980 Census of Population: Characteristics of the Population, General Population Characteristics, United States Summary, Report No. PC80-1–B1. Washington, DC: U.S. Government Printing Office.

———. 1981. 1980 Census of the Population, Age: Sex, Race, and Spanish Origin of the Population by Regions, Divisions, and States: 1980, Report No. PC80-S1–1. Washington, DC: U.S. Government Printing Office.

———. 1976. *Statistical Abstract of the United States, 1976.* Washington, DC: U.S. Government Printing Office.

———. 1975. *Historical Statistics of the United States, Colonial Times to 1970.* Washington, DC: U.S. Government Printing Office.

———. 1963. 1960 Census of Population. Part C, General Social and Economic Characteristics, United States Summary. Washington, DC: U.S. Government Printing Office.

U.S. Bureau of Labor Statistics. 2001. Most Requested Series: Labor Force Statistics from the Current Population Survey. http://146.142.4.24/cgi-bin/surveymost?lf.

———. 1995. Press release, December 1. http://www.bls.gov/pub/news.release/ecopro.txt.

———. 1988. U.S. Dept. of Labor, USDL88-369: Usual Weekly Earnings of Wage and Salary Workers: Second Quarter, 1988. Washington, DC: U.S. Government Printing Office.

U.S. Census Bureau. 2010. 2010 Statistical Abstract, Births, Deaths, Marriages, and Divorces. http://www.census.gov/compendia/statab/cats/births_deaths_marriages_divorces.html (Downloaded July 28, 2010).

———. 2009a. Income, Poverty, and Health Insurance Coverage in the United States: 2008. Table 1. Income and Earnings Summary Measures by Selected Characteristics: 2007 and 2008. http://www.census.gov/prod/2009pubs/p60-236.pdf.

———. 2009b. People Without Health Insurance Coverage by Race and Hispanic Origin Using 2- and 3-Year Averages: 2005–2006 and 2007–2008. Table 8. http://www.census.gov/prod/2009pubs/p60-236.pdf.

———. 2009c. Historical Income Tables-Families. http://www.census.gov/hhes/www/income/histinc/incfamdet.html.

———. 2009d Detailed Income Tablauation from CPS. Tabe HINC01. http://www.census.gov/hhes/www/income/dinctabs.html (Downloaded October 13, 2009).

———. 2009e. Income, Poverty, and health Insurance Coverage in 2008. Current Population Reports, Consumer Income. P-60, No. 236(RV). http://www.census.gov/prod/2009pubs/p60-236.pdf (Downloaded October 13, 2009).

———. 2009f. "Men's and Women's Earnings by State: 2008 American Community Survey." http://www.census.gov/prod/2009pubs/acsbr08-3.pdf (Downloaded October 22, 2009).

———. 2009g American Community Survey, Table POV03. "People in Families with Related Children Under 18 by Family Structure, Age, Sex, Iterated by Income-to-Poverty Ratio and Race." U.S. Census Fact Finder. http://www.census.gov/hhes/www/cpstables/032009/pov/new03_100.htm (Downloaded December 2, 2009).

———. 2009h Health Insurance: 2008, Highlights. http://www.census.gov/hhes/www/hlthins/hlthin08/hlth08asc.html (Downloaded October 30, 2009).

———. 2009i. Educational Attainment in the United States, 2008. Table 1. http://www.census.gov/population/www/socdemo/education/cps2008.html (Downloaded November 22, 2009).

———. 2009j. School Enrollment—Social and Economic Characteristics of Students. http://www.census.gov/population/www/socdemo/school/cps2008.html (Downloaded November 22, 2009).

———. 2009k. Income, Poverty, and Health Insurance Coverage in the United States, 2008. *Current Population Reports* p-60-236(RV). http://www.census.gov/prod/2009pubs/p60-236.pdf (Downloaded July 22, 2010).

———. 2008 American Community Survey, Table GCT1205. Median Age at First Marriage for Women. U.S. Census Fact Finder. http://factfinder.census.gov/servlet/GCTSubjectShowTablesServlet.

———. 2008b. "Net Worth and the Assets of Households, 2002." *Current Population Reports, Household Economic Studies* 115: 70.

———. 2008c. U.S. Population Projections, National Population Projections, Released 2008 (Based on Census 2000). http://www.census.gov/population/www/projections/summarytables.html (Downloaded August 1, 2010).

———. 2007. Custodial Mothers and Fathers and Their Child Support. *Current Population Survey, Consumer Income Report* P60-234. http://www.census.gov/prod/2007pubs/p60-234.pdf (Downloaded October 30, 2009).

———. 2004. Income 2002. Cross-Reference of Income Tables by Detailed Socioeconomic Characteristicsfor Households, Families, People, and Unrelated Indivduals. Table U1. http://www.census.gov/hhes/www/income/income02/crsref.html (Downloaded October 13, 2009).

———. 2001a. Current Population Reports: Population Characteristics. Report No. P60-213. Money Income in the United States, 2000. http://www.census.gov/prod/2001pubs/p60-213.pdf.

———. 2001b. Current Population Reports, Household Economic Studies, Series P70-71, *Household Net Worth and Asset Ownership: 1995*. Washington, DC: U.S. Government Printing Office. Also available on http://www.census.gov/prod/2001pubs/p70-71.pdf.

———. 2001c. Current Population Reports: Population Characteristics. Report No. P60-214. Poverty in the United States, 2000. http://www.census.gov/prod/2001pubs/p60-214.pdf.

———. 2001d. Current Population Reports, Household Economic Studies, Series P70-76, *Reasons People Do Not Work: 1996*. Washington, DC: U.S. Government Printing Office. Also available on http://www.census.gov/prod/2001pubs/p70-76.pdf.

———. 2001e. 2000 Census of Population and Housing, Population by Race, Including All Specific Combinations of Two Races, for the United States: 2000. http://www.census.gov/population/cen2000/phc-t1/tab02.txt.

———. 2001f. Income 2000. http://www.census.gov/hhes/www/income00.html.

———. 2001g. Current Population Reports, Report No. P20-536, Educational Attainment in the United States: March 2000 (Update, Detailed Tables) http://www.census.gov/population/www/socdemo/education/p20-536.html.

———. 2001h. FT900—U.S. International Trade in Goods and Services, Exhibit 14, Exports, Imports, and Balance of Goods by Selected Countries and Geographic Areas, 2000. http://www.census.gov/foreign-trade/Press-Release/2000pr/12/exh14.txt.

———. 2001i. *Statistical Abstract of the United States, 2000*. Washington, DC: U.S. Government Printing Office. Also available on http://www.census.gov/prod/www/statistical-abstract-us.html.

———. 2001j. 1997 Economic Census—Manufacturing. Concentration Ratios in Manufacturing. http://www.census.gov/prod/ec97/m31s-cr.pdf.

———. 2001k. Profiles of General Demographic Characteristics, 2000 Census of Population and Housing, United States. Washington, DC: U.S. Government Printing Office. Also available on http://www2.census.gov/census_2000/datasets/demographic_profile/0_National Summary/.

———. 2001l. Current Population Reports, Population Characteristics. Report No. P20-537, America's Family and Living Arrangements, 2000. Washington, DC: U.S. Government Printing Office. Also available on http://www.census.gov/prod/2001pubs/p20-537.pdf.

———. 2001m. PCT14. Unmarried-Partner Households By Sex of Partners [7]—Universe: Households. Data Set: Census 2000 Summary File 1 (SF 1) 100-Percent Data. (All states available as of June 21, 2001). http://factfinder.census.gov/servlet/DTTable?_ts=11179836830.

———. 2001n. Enrollment Status of the Population 3 Years Old and Over, by Age, Sex, Race, Hispanic Origin, Nativity, and Selected Educational Characteristics: October 2000. http://www.census.gov/population/socdemo/school/ppl-148/tab01.txt.

———. 2001o. Statistical Tables: Public Elementary-Secondary Education Finances, 1998–99. http://www.census.gov/govs/school/99tables.pdf.

———. 2001p. Inmigrants, Outmigrants, and Net Migration for Regions, by Race and Hispanic Origin, Income in 1999, Occupation, and Industry. http://www.census.gov/population/socdemo/migration/p20-538/tab19.txt.

———. 2001q. Ranking Tables for States: Population in 2000 and Population Change from 1990 to 2000 (PHC-T-2). http://www.census.gov/population/www/cen2000/phc-t2.html.

———. 2001r. Population by Sex, Age, and Citizenship Status: March 2000. http://www.census.gov/population/socdemo/foreign/p20-534/tab0101.txt.

———. 2001s. Difference in Population by Race and Hispanic or Latino Origin, for the United States: 1990 to 2000. http://www.census.gov/population/cen2000/phc-tl/tab04.txt.

———. 2001t. Census 2000 PHC-T-5. Ranking Tables for Incorporated Places of 100,000 or More: 1990 and 2000, Table 3. Incorporated Places of 100,000 or More, Ranked by Numeric Population Change: 1990 to 2000. http://www.census.gov/population/cen2000/phc-t5/tab03.xls.

———. 2001u. 2000 Census of Population and Housing. QT-03. Profile of Selected Economic Characteristics: 2000. Census 2000 Supplementary Survey Summary Tables. http://factfinder.census.gov/home/en/c2ss.html.

———. Census 2000, Summary File 3. Selected Occupational Groups and Subgroups by Sex for the United States: 2000. Washington, DC: U.S. Government Printing Office. Also available on http://www.census.gov/prod/2003pubs/c2kbr-25.pdf.

———. 2000a. Current Population Reports. Report no. P-60, No. 209, Money Income in the United States, 1999. Washington, DC: U.S. Government Printing Office. Also available on http://www.census.gov/prod/2000pubs/p60-209.pdf.

———. 2000b. Current Population Reports: Consumer Income. Report No. P-60, No. 210, Poverty in the United States, 1999. Washington, DC: U.S. Government Printing Office. Also available through Census Bureau Web site, http://www.census.gov.

———. 2000c. Current Population Reports. Report No. P-60, No. 211. Health Insurance Coverage: 1999. Also available on http://www.census.gov/prod/2000pubs/p60-211.pdf.

———. 2000d. *Statistical Abstract of the United States, 2000*. Washington, DC: U.S. Government Printing Office. Also available on http://www.census.gov/prod/www/statistical-abstract-us.html.

———. 2000e. Current Population Reports. Report No. P-20, No. 536. Educational Attainment in the United States, March, 2000. Washington, DC: U.S. Government Printing Office. Data also available on http://www.census.gov/population/www/socdemo/education/p20-536.html.

———. 2000f. Components of Change for the Total Resident Population: Middle Series, 1999 to 2100. http://www.census.gov/population/projections/nation/summary/np-t6-a.txt.

———. 2000g. Projections of the Total Resident Population by 5-Year Age Groups, Race, and Hispanic Origin with Special Age Categories: Middle Series, 2025 to 2045. http://www.census.gov/population/projections/nation/summary/np-t4-f.txt.

———. 2000h. Total Midyear Population for the World: 1950–2050. http://www.census.gov/ipc/www/worldpop.html.

———. 1999. *Statistical Abstract of the United States, 1999*. Washington, DC: U.S. Government Printing Office. Available via at http://www.census.gov/statab/www/.

———. 1998a. Interracial Tables, Table 1, Race of Wife by Race of Husband: 1960, 1970, 1980, 1991, and 1992. http://www.census.gov/population/socdemo/race/interractab1.txt.

———. 1998b. Current Population Reports: Population Characteristics. Report No. P-20, No. 515, Household and Family Characteristics: March 1998 (Update). Washington, DC: U.S. Government Printing Office. Also available through Census Bureau Web site, http://www.census.gov.

———. 1998c. Current Population Reports: Population Characteristics. Report No. P-20, No. 514, Marital Status and Living Arrangements: March 1998 (Update). Washington, DC: U.S. Government Printing Office. Also available through Census Bureau Web site, http://www.census.gov.

———. 1998d. Marital Status and Living Arrangements: March, 1998 (Update). Current Population Reports: Population Characteristics. Report No. P20-514.

U.S. Citizenship and Immigration Service. 2009. *Yearbook of Immigration Statistics, 2008.* http://www.dhs.gov/files/statistics/publications/LPR08.shtm (Downloaded December 2, 2009).

———. 2003. *Estimates of the Unauthorized Immigrant Population Residing in the United States: 1990 to 2000.* http://uscis.gov/graphics/shared/aboutus/statistics/2000ExecSumm.pdf (downloaded December 11, 2003).

U.S. Commission on Civil Rights. 1976. *Fulfilling the Letter and Spirit of the Law: Desegregation of the Nation's Schools.* Washington, DC: U.S. Government Printing Office.

———. 1974. *Toward Quality Education for Mexican Americans, Mexican American Study Report No. 4.* Washington, DC: U.S. Government Printing Office.

U.S. Commission on Child and Family Welfare. 1996. Parenting Our Children: In the Best Interest of the Nation. Report of the U.S. Commission on Child and Family Welfare. http://www.acfc.org/study/usccwma1.htm.

U.S. Department of Agriculture. 2001. Food Security in the United States: Conditions and Trends. http://www.ers.usda.gov/briefing/foodsecurity/trends/index.htm.

U.S. Department of Defense. 1996. DOD News Briefing. The Honorable Edwin Dorn, USD, Personnel and Readiness. July 2. http://www.defenselink.mil/news/Jul1996/t070396_t0702dor.html.

U.S. Department of Education. 1989. *Digest of Educational Statistics.* Washington, DC: U.S. Government Printing Office.

———. 1987a. *Schools That Work: Educating Disadvantaged Children.* Washington, DC: U.S. Government Printing Office.

———. 1987b. *Elementary and Secondary Education Indicators in Brief.* Washington, DC: U.S. Government Printing Office.

U.S. Department of Health and Human Services. 2001a. "HHS Reports New Child Abuse and Neglect Statistics." Press Release, April 2, 2001.

———. 2001b. Building Their Futures: How Early Head Start Programs Are Enhancing the Lives of Infants and Toddlers in Low-Income Families: Summary Report. Washington, DC: U.S. Department of Health and Human Services. Also available on http://www2.acf.dhhs.gov/programs/hsb/EHS/(Sum-Rpt-new-1-10-2001.pdf.

U.S. Department of Health, Education, and Welfare, National Cancer Institute, National Institute of Environmental Health Sciences, and National Institute of Occupational Safety and Health. 1978. Estimates of the Fraction of Cancer in the United States Related to Occupational Factors. Washington. DC: U.S. Government Printing Office.

U.S. Department of Housing and Urban Development. 2008. HUD Reports Drop in the Number of Chronically Homeless Persons. http://www.hud.gov/news/release.cfm?content=pr08-113.cfm (Downloaded December 5, 2009).

———. 2005. Discrimination in Metropolitan Housing Markets. National Results from Phase 1, Phase 2, and Phase 3 of the Housing Discrimination Study (HDS). http://www.huduser.org/publications/hsgfin/hds.html.

———. 1991. *1989 Housing Discrimination Study.* Washington, DC: U.S. Government Printing Office.

———. 1979. *Experimental Housing Allowance Program: A 1979 Report of Findings.* Washington, DC: U.S. Department of Housing and Urban Development.

U.S. Department of Labor. 1987. *Workforce 2000: Work and Workers for the 21st Century.* Washington, DC: U.S. Government Printing Office.

———. 1965. *The Negro Family: The Case for National Action* (The "Moynihan Report"). Washington, DC: U.S. Government Printing Office.

U.S. Environmental Protection Agency. 1990. *National Air Pollution Emission Estimates, 1940–1988.* Research Triangle Park, NC: U.S. Environmental Protection Agency.

———. 1984. *Draft National Environmental Report.* Washington, DC: U.S. Government Printing Office.

U.S. Food and Drug Administration. 2001. Consumer Update on Wireless Phones. http://www.fda.gov/cdrh/ocd/mobilphone.html.

U.S. National Advisory Commission on Civil Disorders. 1968. *Report of the National Advisory Commission on Civil Disorders.* New York: New York Times Company, Bantam Books.

U.S. National Center for Health Statistics. 2006. *National Vital Statistics Reports (NVSR), Births: Final Data for 2006* 57(7): Tables 79, 80.

U.S. National Commission on the Causes and Prevention of Violence. 1968. *Report to the National Commission on the Causes and Prevention of Violence.* New York: Bantam Books.

U.S. News Online. 1996. "Crime." http://www.usnews.com/usnews/issue/crime.htm.

U.S. Strategic Bombing Survey. 1947. *The Effects of Strategic Bombing on German Morale.* Washington, DC: U.S. Government Printing Office.

Upchurch, Dawn M., Carol S. Aneshensel, Clea A. Sucoff, and Lene Levy-Storms. 1999. "Neighborhood and Family Contexts of Adolescent Sexual Activity." *Journal of Marriage and the Family* 61: 920–33.

Urban Institute. 2001. "Characteristics of Recent Welfare Population Dispel Some but Not All Concerns as Time Limits Approach." Press Release, April 27. Also available on at http://www.urban.org/news/pressrel/pr010427.html.

Useem, Elizabeth L. 1990. "Social Class and Ability Group Placement in Mathematics in the Transition to Seventh Grade: The Role of Parental Involvement." Paper presented at the annual meeting of the American Educational Research Association, Boston, April 16–20.

Useem, Michael. 1984. *The Inner Circle: Large Corporations and the Rise of Business Political Activity in the U.S. and U.K.* New York: Oxford University Press.

Uttal, Lynet. 1999. "Using Kin for Child Care: Embedment in the Socioeconomic Networks of Extended Families." *Journal of Marriage and the Family* 61: 845–58.

Vago, Steven. 1988. *Law and Society,* 2nd ed. Englewood Cliffs, NJ: Prentice Hall.

Valentino, Nicholas, and David O. Sears. 2005. "Old Times There Are not Forgotten: Race and Partisan Realignment in the Contemporary South." *American Journal of Political Science* 49: 672–88.

Van Arsdol, Maurice, Santo F. Camilleri, and Calvin F. Schmid. 1958. "The Generality of Urban Social Area Indices." *American Sociological Review* 23: 277–84.

Van de Kaa, Dirk J. 1987. "Europe's Second Demographic Transition." *Population Bulletin* 42(1).

Van den Berghe, Pierre L. 1978. *Race and Racism: A Comparative Perspective,* 2nd ed. New York: Wiley.

VanderHart, Peter G. 2006. "Why Do Some Schools Group by Ability?" *American Journal of Economics and Sociology* 65: 435–62.

Van der Werf, Martin. 2001. "Anti-Sweatshop Groups Find It Hard to Turn Campus Idealism into Real Change." *Chronicle of Higher Education* (January 5).

Vanek, Joann. 1973. "Keeping Busy: Time Spent in Housework, U.S., 1920–1970." Ph.D. dissertation, University of Michigan, Ann Arbor.

Vanfossen, Beth E., James D. Jones, and Joan Z. Spade. 1987. "Curriculum Tracking and Status Maintenance." *Sociology of Education* 60: 104–22.

Van Rossem, Ronan. 1996. "The World System Paradigm as General Theory of Development: A Cross-National Test." *American Sociological Review* 61: 508–27.

Vaughan, Diane. 1996. *The Challenger Launch Decision: Risky Technology, Culture, and Deviance at NASA.* Chicago: University of Chicago Press. (Paperback edition, 1997).

———. 1990. *Uncoupling: Turning Points in Intimate Relationships.* New York: Vintage Books.

Vaughn-Roberson, Courtney, et. al. 1989. "Sexism in Basal Readers: An Analysis of Male Main Characters." *Journal of Research in Childhood Education* 4(1): 62–68.

Veblen, Thorstein. 1921. *Engineers and the Price System.* New York: Viking.

Verbrugge, Lois M. 1985. "Gender and Health: An Update on Hypotheses and Evidence." *Journal of Health and Social Behavior* 26: 156–182.

Vernacchio, Louis. 1995. "Depersonalizing the Medical Student." *America* 25: 16–18.

Vernon, Raymond, Debora L. Spar, and Glenn Tobin. 1991. *Iron Triangles and Revolving Doors: Cases in U.S. Foreign Economic Policymaking.* New York: Praeger.

Vester, Heinz Gunter. 1990. "Collective Behavior and Social Movements Under Postmodern Conditions." Paper presented at meetings of the International Sociological Association.

Veves, Michael. 1989. "Beyond Tracking: A Teacher's View." *Equity and Choice* 6, 1: 18–22.

Veysey, Laurence R. 1965. *The Emergence of the American University*. Chicago: University of Chicago Press.

Vogelstein, Bert, and Kenneth W. Kinzler. 1992. "Carcinogens Leave Fingerprints." *Nature* 355: 209–10.

Vold, George B., and Thomas L. Bernard. 1986. *Theoretical Criminology*, 3rd ed. New York: Oxford University Press.

Voss, Laurie Scarboro. 1997. "Teasing, Disputing, and Playing: Cross-Gender Interactions and Space Utilization Among First and Third Graders." *Gender and Society* 11(2): 238–57.

Waber, D. P. 1979. "Cognitive Abilities and Sex-Related Variations in the Maturation of Cerebral Cortical Functions." In M.A. Wittig and A. C. Peterson (eds.), *Sex-Related Differences in Cognitive Functioning*. New York: Academic Press.

———. 1977. "Sex Differences in Mental Abilities, Hemispheric Lateralization, and Rate of Physical Growth at Adolescence." *Developmental Psychology* 12: 278–282; 13: 29–38.

Wadsworth, Tim. 2010. "Is Immigration Responsible for the Crime Drop? An Assessment of the Influence of Immigration on Changes in Violent Crime Between 1990 and 2000." *Social Science Quarterly* 91: 531–553. http://www3.interscience.wiley.com/journal/123341598/abstract?CRETRY=1&SRETRY=0.

Wahlsten, Douglas. 1995. "Increasing the Raw Intelligence of a Nation Is Constrained by Ignorance, Not Its Citizens' Genes." *Alberta Journal of Educational Research* 41: 257–264.

Waite, Linda J., and Lee A. Lillard. 1991. "Children and Marital Disruption." *American Journal of Sociology* 96: 930–53.

Walder, Andrew. 1995. "Local Governments as Industrial Firms: An Organizational Analysis of China's Transitional Economy." *American Journal of Sociology* 101: 263–301.

Waldholz, Michael. 1991. "Research Shows How Sunlight Disables Gene, Resulting in Form of Skin Cancer." *The Wall Street Journal* (November 15): B3.

Walker, Mary. 2001. "A World Where Womanhood Reigns Supreme (The Seeds of My Own Re-evaluations)." http://www.islamfortoday.com/mary_walker.htm. Originally published in *Impact Magazine*.

Wallace, Ruth A., and Alison Wolf. 1991. *Contemporary Sociological Theory: Continuing the Classical Tradition*. Englewood Cliffs, NJ: Prentice Hall.

Wallach, Lori, and Michelle Sforza. 1999. "NAFTA at 5." *Nation* 268(3): 7–12.

Wallach, Michael A., Nathan Kogan, and Daryl J. Bem. 1962. "Group Influence on Individual Risk Taking." *Journal of Abnormal and Social Psychology* 65: 75–86.

Wallerstein, Immanuel. 1989. *The Modern World-System III: The Second Era of Great Expansion of the Capitalist World-Economy, 1730–1840*. New York: Academic Press.

———. 1980. *The Modern World-System II: Mercantilism and the Consolidation of the European World Economy, 1600–1750*. New York: Academic Press.

———. 1979. *The Capitalist World-Economy*. Cambridge, England: Cambridge University Press.

———. 1976. "Modernization: Requiescat in Pace." Pp. 131–35 in Lewis Coser and Otto Larsen (eds.), *The Uses of Controversy in Sociology*. New York: Free Press (reprinted as Chapter 7 in Wallerstein 1979).

———. 1974a. "The Rise and Future Demise of the World Capitalist System: Concepts for Comparative Analysis." *Comparative Studies in Society and History* 16(4): 387–415.

———. 1974b. *The Modern World-System: Capitalist Agriculture and the Origins of European World Economy in the Sixteenth Century*. New York: Academic Press.

Wallerstein, James S., and Clement J. Wyle. 1947. "Our Law-Abiding Law Breakers." *Probation* (April): 107–18.

Wallerstein, Judith S., and Sandra Blakeslee. 1989. *Second Chances: Men, Women, and Children a Decade After Divorce*. New York: Ticknor and Fields.

Wallerstein, Judith S., and Joan B. Kelly. 1990. *Surviving the Breakup: How Children and Parents Cope with Divorce*. New York: Basic Books.

———. 1980. "California's Children of Divorce." *Psychology Today* 13(8): 67–76.

Wallis, T. J. 2000. "Sexual Harassment on the Job." *Career World* 28(5): 16–20.

Walsh, Andrew. 1998. "Church, Lies, and Polling Data." *Religion in the News* 1, 2 (Fall). Also available on http://www.trincoll.edu/depts/csrpl/RIN%20Vol.1No.2/Church_lies_polling.htm.

Walsh, Bryan. 2010. "With Oil Spill (and Blame) Spreading, Obama Will Visit Gulf." *Time* (Saturday, May 1). http://www.time.com/time/health/article/0,8599,1986323,00.html#ixzz0vJw5DVei.

Walster, E., E. Berscheid, and G. W. Walster. 1973. "New Directions in Equity Research." *Journal of Personality and Social Psychology* 25: 151–76.

Walster, E., and G. W. Walster. 1969. "The Matching Hypothesis." *Journal of Personality and Social Psychology* 6: 248–53.

Walters, Joseph, and Howard Gardner. 1984. The Crystallizing Experience: Discovering an Intellectual Gift. Harvard Univ., Cambridge, MA. Harvard Project Zero. ERIC Accession No. ED254544.

Walton, John. 1977. "The Bearing of Social Science Research on Public Issues: Floyd Hunter and the Study of Power." Pp. 263–72 in John Walton and Donald E. Carns (eds.), *Cities in Change: Studies on the Urban Condition*, 2nd ed. Boston: Allyn and Bacon.

———. 1966. "Substance and Artifact: The Current State of Research on Community Power Structure." *American Journal of Sociology* 71: 430–38.

Waquant, Loic J. D., and William Julius Wilson. 1989. "The Cost of Racial and Class Exclusion in the Inner City." *Annals of the American Academy of Political and Social Science* 501: 8–25.

Ward, Kathryn B. 1988. "Women in the Global Economy." Pp. 17–48 in B. Gutek, Ann Strassberg, and Laurie Harwood (eds.), *Women and Work*. Beverly Hills, CA: Sage.

———. 1984. *Women in the World-System: Its Impact on Status and Fertility*. New York: Praeger.

Warheit, G. J., C. E. Holzer, III, and J. J. Schwab. 1973. "An Analysis of the Social Class and Racial Differences in Depressive Symptomatology: A Community Study." *Journal of Health and Social Behavior* 14: 291–99.

Warner, W. Lloyd, Paul S. Hunt, Marchia Meeker, and Kenneth Eels. 1949. *Social Class in America*. New York: Harper.

Warren, Karen J. 1993. "A Feminist Philosophical Perspective on Ecofeminist Spiritualities." Pp. 119–32 in Carol J. Adams (ed.), *Ecofeminism and the Sacred*. New York: Continuum.

Washington Post. 1992. "Shantytowns Becoming Commonplace in New York." *The Washington Post* (January 4): E6.

Wasserman, Ira. 1984. "Imitation and Suicide: A Reexamination of the Werther Effect." *American Sociological Review* 49: 427–36.

Wasserman, Miriam. 1970. *The School Fix: NYC, USA*. New York: Outerbridge and Dienstfrey.

Watkins, Alfred J., and David W. Perry. 1977. "Regional Change and the Impact of Uneven Urban Development." Pp. 19–54 in David W. Perry and Alfred J. Watkins (eds.), *The Rise of the Sunbelt Cities*, Urban Affairs Annual Reviews, Vol. 14. Beverly Hills, CA: Sage.

Watson, Andrew. 1988. "The Reform of Agricultural Marketing in China Since 1978." *China Quarterly* 113: 1–28.

Watson, Bruce. 1996. "A Freedom Summer Activist Becomes a Math Revolutionary." *Smithsonian* 26(11) (February): 114–25.

Watson, L. W., and G. D. Kuh. 1996. "The Influence of Dominant-Race Environments on Student Involvement, Perceptions, and Educational Gains: A Look at Historically Black and Predominantly White Liberal Arts Institutions." *Journal of College Development* 37: 415–24.

Watson, Russel. 1993. "They're Bearish on Russia." *Newsweek* (April 12): 22.

Watson, Warren, Kamalesh Kumar, and Larry Michaelsen. 1993. "Cultural Diversity's Impact on Interation Process and Performance: Comparing Homogeneous and Diverse Task Groups." *Academy of Management Journal* 36: 590–602.

Wattleton, Faye. 1988. "America's Teens: Sexually Active, Sexually Illiterate." *Education Digest* 53: 51–53.

Wax, Murray L., and Joan Cassell. 1990. "The Looking Glass Self: Introductory Notes on Anorexia Nervosa." *Mid-American Review of Sociology* 14: 135.

Wayne, Leslie. 1984. "The Irony and the Impact of Auto Quotas." *The New York Times* (April 8): Sect. 3, 1.

Weaver, Ross Lee. 1990. "Separate Is Not Equal." *Principal* 69(5): 40, 42.

Weber, C. U., P. W. Foster, and D. P. Weichert. 1978. "An Economic Analysis of the Ypsilanti Perry Preschool Project." *Monographs of the High/Scope Educational Research Foundation* 5.

Weber, Eugen. 1999. *Prophecies, Cults, and Millennial Beliefs through the Ages.* Cambridge, Massachusetts: Harvard University Press.

Weber, Max. 1968. *Economy and Society.* (Ephriam Fischoff et al., trans.). New York: Bedminster Press. (Originally published in German, 1922.).

———. 1963. *The Sociology of Religion.* (Ephraim Fischoff, trans.). Boston: Beacon. (Originally published in German, 1920.).

———. 1962. *Basic Concepts in Sociology.* London: Peter Owen.

———. 1958a. *The Protestant Ethic and the Spirit of Capitalism.* (Talcott Parsons, trans.) New York: Scribner's Sons. (Originally published in German 1904–1905.).

———. 1958b. *The Religion of India.* (Hans Gerth and Don Martindale, trans.). New York: Free Press. (Originally published in German, 1920.).

———. 1952. *Ancient Judaism.* (Hans Gerth and Don Martindale, eds. and trans.). New York: Free Press. (Originally published in German in 1920.).

———. 1951. *The Religion of China.* (Hans Gerth, trans.). New York: Free Press. (Originally published in German, 1920.).

———. 1946. *From Max Weber: Essays in Sociology.* (Hans H. Gerth and C. Wright Mills, eds. and trans.). New York: Oxford University Press.

Webster, David S. 1986. *Academic Quality Rankings of American Colleges and Universities.* Springfield, IL: Thomas.

Webster, David S., Clifton F. Conrad, and Eric L. Jensen. 1988. "Objective and Reputational Rankings of Ph.D.-Granting Departments of Sociology, 1965–1982." *Sociological Focus* 21: 113–26.

Webster, Pamela, Terri L. Orbuch, and James S. House. 1995. "Effects of Childhood Family Background on Adult Marital Quality and Perceived Stability." *American Journal of Sociology* 101: 404–32.

Wector, Dixon. 1941. *The Hero in America.* New York: Charles Scribner's Sons.

Weeks, John R. 1999. *Population: An Introduction to Concepts and Issues,* 7th ed. Belmont, CA: Wadsworth.

———. 1992. *Population: An Introduction to Concepts and Issues,* 5th ed. Belmont, CA: Wadsworth.

———. 1989. *Population: An Introduction to Concepts and Issues,* 4th ed. Belmont, CA: Wadsworth.

———. 1986. *Population: An Introduction to Concepts and Issues,* 3rd ed. Belmont, CA: Wadsworth.

Weg, Ruth B. 1985. "Beyond Babies and Orgasm." Pp. 206–22 in Beth B. Hess and Elizabeth W. Markson (eds.), *Growing Old in America,* 3rd ed. New Brunswick, NJ: Transaction Books.

Weinberg, M. 1977. *Minority Students: A Research Appraisal.* Report to the Department of Health, Education, and Welfare, Office of Education. Washington, DC: System Development Corporation.

Weinberg, Richard A. 1989. "Intelligence and IQ: Landmark Issues and Great Debates." *American Psychologist* 44: 98–104.

Weinstein, Bernard L., Harold T. Gross, and John Rees. 1985. *Regional Growth and Decline in the United States,* 2nd ed. New York: Praeger.

Weiss, R. S. 1984. "The Impact of Marital Dissolution on Income and Consumption in Single-Parent Households." *Journal of Marriage and the Family* 46: 115–27.

Weiss, Robert J. 1985. "Affirmative Action: A Brief History." *Journal of Intergroup Relations* 15(2): 40–53.

Weitz, Rose, and Deborah A. Sullivan. 1986. "The Politics of Childbirth: The Re-emergence of Midwifery in Arizona." *Social Problems* 33.

Weitzman, Lenore. 1985. *Divorce Revolution: The Unexpected Social and Economic Consequences for Women and Children in America.* New York: Free Press.

Wekerle, Gerda. 1980. "Women in the Urban Environment." *Signs: Journal of Women in Culture and Society* 5(3): S188–S214.

Welch, W. P. 1982. "Campaign Contributions and Legislative Voting: Milk Money and Dairy Price Supports." *Western Political Quarterly* 35: 478–79.

Wellington, Allison. 1994. "Accounting for the Male-Female Wage Gap Among Whites: 1976–1985." *American Sociological Review* 59: 839–48.

Wellisz, Slaneslaw H. 1971. "Economic Redevelopment and Urbanization." Pp. 39–58 in Leo Jacobson and Ved Prakash (eds.), *Urbanization and National Development.* Beverly Hills, CA: Sage.

Wellman, Barry. 1979. "The Community Question: The Intimate Networks of East Yorkers." *American Journal of Sociology* 84: 1201–31.

Wells, Amy Stewart. 1995. "Reexamining Social Science Research on School Desegregation: Long- Versus Short-Term Effects." *Teachers College Record* 96: 691–706.

Wells, Amy Stuart, Bianca J. Baldridge, Jacquelyn Duran, Courtney Grzesikowski, Richard Lofton, and Allison Roda. 2009. *Boundary Crossing for Diversity, Equity and Achievement: Interdistrict School Desegregation and Educational Opportunity.* Charles Hamilton Houston Institute for Race and Justice Report. http://www.tc.columbia.edu/i/a/document/11666_Wells_Final_wBleeds.pdf (Downloaded November 22, 2009).

Wells, Amy Stewart, and Robert L. Crain. 1997. *Stepping over the Color Line: African-American Students in White Suburban Schools.* New Haven, CT: Yale University Press.

———. 1994. "Perpetuation Theory and the Long-Term Effects of School Desegregation." *Review of Educational Research* 64: 531–55.

Wennberg, John E. 1983. *A Study of the Nature, Costs, and Cost Implications of Hospital Market Variations in the Use of Inpatient Services, Final Report.* (Research Project Supported by Health Care Finance Administration).

Wennberg, John E., Klim McPherson, and Philip Caper. 1984. "Will Payment Based on Diagnostic-Related Groups Reduce Hospital Costs?" *New England Journal of Medicine* 311: 295–300.

Westby, David L. 1991. *The Growth of Sociological Theory: Human Nature, Knowledge, and Social Change.* Englewood Cliffs, NJ: Prentice Hall.

Western, Bruce. 1995. "A Comparative Study of Working-Class Disorganization: Union Decline in Eighteen Advanced Capitalist Countries." *American Sociological Review* 60: 179–201.

Western, Bruce, and Eric Olin Wright. 1994. "The Permeability of Class Boundaries to Intergenerational Mobility Among Men in the United States, Canada, Norway, and Sweden." *American Sociological Review* 59: 606–29.

Wheaton, Blair. 1990. "Life Transitions, Role Histories, and Mental Health." *American Sociological Review* 55: 209–23.

Wheeler, D. L. 1992. "Studies Linking Homosexuality to Genes Draw Criticism from Researchers." *Chronicle of Higher Education* (February 5): A7–A9.

Wheeler, Ladd. 1966. "Toward a Theory of Behavioral Contagion." *Psychological Review* 73: 179–92.

Wheeler, Stanton, Kenneth Mann, and Austin Sarat. 1988. *Sitting in Judgment: The Sentencing of White Collar Criminals.* New Haven, CT: Yale University Press.

Wheelock, Anne. 1992. *How "Untracking" Can Save America's Schools* :New Press.

Whitaker, Mark. 1985. "Ten Ways to Fight Terrorism." *Newsweek* (July 1): 26–29.

White, Betsy. 1992. "Blacks' Fail Rate Exceeds Whites' on Teacher Test." *Atlanta Journal* (April 4): C2.

White, L. K., and Alan Booth. 1985. "The Quality and Stability of Remarriages: The Role of Stepchildren." *American Sociological Review* 50: 689–98.

White, Lynn, and John N. Edwards. 1990. "Emptying the Nest and Parental Well-Being: An Analysis of National Panel Data." *American Sociological Review* 55: 235–42.

White, Ralph K., and Ronald Lippitt. 1960. *Autocracy and Democracy.* New York: Harper & Row.

White, Sheldon. 1970. "The National Impact of Head Start." *Disadvantaged Child* 3: 163–84.

Whiting, Beatrice Blyth, and Carolyn Pope Edwards. 1988. *Children of Different Worlds: The Formation of Social Behavior.* Cambridge, MA: Harvard University Press.

———. 1976. "A Cross-Cultural Analysis of Sex Differences in the Behavior of Children Aged Three Through Eleven." In S. Cox (ed.), *The Emerging Self.* Chicago: Science Research Associates.

Whitley, B. E. 1999. "Right-wing authoritarianism, social dominance orientation, and prejudice." *Journal of Personality and Social Psychology* 77: 126–134.

Whitney, Craig R. 1997. "Jeanne Calmet, World's Elder, Dies at 122"

New York Times (August 5). http://www.nytimes.com/1997/08/05/world/jeanne-calment-world-s-elder-dies-at-122.html (Downloaded August 1, 2010).
Whitt, Allen. 1982. *Urban Elites and Mass Transportation.* Princeton, NJ: Princeton University Press.
Whorf, Benjamin Lee. 1956. *Thought and Reality: Selected Writings of Benjamin Lee Whorf.* (John B. Caroll, ed.). Cambridge, MA: Technology Press of the Massachusetts Institute of Technology.
Whyte, William Foote. 1981. *Street Corner Society,* 3rd ed. Chicago: University of Chicago Press. (Originally published in 1943.).
Wiegman, O., M. Kuttschreuter, and B. Baarda. 1992. "A Longitudinal Study of the Effects of Television Viewing on Aggressive and Prosocial Behaviours." *British Journal of Social Psychology* 31: 147–64.
Wilensky, Harold L. 1967. *Organizational Intelligence: Knowledge and Policy in Government and Industry.* New York: Basic Books.
———. 1964. *Complex Organizations: A Critical Essay,* 2nd ed. Glenview, IL: Scott, Foresman.
Wilkes, Rima, and John Iceland. "Hypersegregation in the Twenty-First Century." *Demography* 41: 23–36.
Wilkinson, David. 1987. "Central Civilization." *Comparative Civilization Review* 17: 31–59.
Wilkinson, Richard. 1997. *Unhealthy Societies: The Afflictions of Inequality.* New York: Routledge.
Willard, W. 1972. *Curanderismo and Health Care.* Tucson: University of Arizona, College of Medicine, Division of Social Perspectives in Medicine (mimeograph).
Willems, Helmut. 1995. "Right-Wing Extremism, Racism, or Youth Violence? Explaining Violence Against Foreigners in Germany." *New Community: Journal of the European Research Centre on Migration and Ethnic Relations* 21(4).
Williams, David R. 1986. "Socioeconomic Differentials in Health: The Role of Psychosocial Factors." Ph.D. dissertation, University of Michigan. Dissertation Abstracts International Abstract No. 3878a.
Williams, J. Allen, JoEtta A. Vernon, Martha C. Williams, and Karen Maleca. 1987. "Sex Role Socialization in Picture Books: An Update." *Social Science Quarterly* 68: 148–56.
Williams, John E., and John R. Stabler. 1973. "If White Means Good, Then Black..." *Psychology Today* (July): 51–54.
Williams, Lena. 1991. "When Blacks Shop, Bias Often Accompanies Sale." *The New York Times* (April 30): A1, A14.
Williams, Robert L. 1997. "Ebonics as a Bridge to Standard English..." Commentary. *St. Louis Post-Dispatch,* January 28: 13b.
Williams, Robin. 1977. "Competing Models of Multiethnic and Multiracial Societies: An Appraisal of Possibilities and Performances." Paper presented at the annual meeting of the plenary session of the American Sociological Association, Chicago.
———. 1970. *American Society: A Sociological Interpretation.* 3rd ed. New York: Alfred A. Knopf.
Williamson, John B., Anne Munley, and Linda Evans, with Barbara H. Vinick and Sharlene Hesse. 1980. *Aging and Society.* New York: Holt, Rinehart, and Winston.
Willie, Charles Vert. 1979. *The Caste and Class Controversy.* Bayside, NY: General Hall.
Willis, Paul E. 1977. *Learning to Labor: How Working Class Kids Get Working Class Jobs.* New York: Columbia University Press.
Willits, F. K., and D. M. Crider. 1988. "Religion and Well-Being: Men and Women in the Middle Years." *Review of Religious Research* 26: 332–42.
Willms, J. Douglas. 1987. "Patterns of Academic Achievement in Public and Private Schools: Implications for Public Policy and Future Research." Pp. 113–34 in Edward H. Haertel, Thomas James, and Henry M. Levin (eds.), *Comparing Public and Private Schools.* Vol. 2, Student Achievement. New York: Falmer Press.
Wilson, Barbara Foley, and Sally Cunningham Clarke. 1992. "Remarriages: A Demographic Profile." *Journal of Family Issues* 13: 123–41.
Wilson, Bryan R. 1985. "Secularization: The Inherited Model." In P. Hammond (ed.), *The Sacred in a Secular Age.* Berkeley: University of California Press.
———. 1961. *Sects and Society.* Berkeley: University of California Press.
———. 1959. "An Analysis of Sect Development." *American Sociological Review* 24: 2–15.
Wilson, Edward O. 1978. *On Human Nature.* Cambridge, MA: Harvard University Press.
Wilson, Franklin D. 1988. "Aspects of Migration in Advanced Industrial Society." *American Sociological Review* 53: 113–26.
Wilson, James Q. 1980. *American Government: Institutions and Policies.* Lexington, MA: D.C. Heath.
Wilson, James Q., and Richard J. Herrnstein. 1985. *Crime and Human Nature.* New York: Simon & Schuster.
Wilson, John. 1978. *Religion in American Society: The Effective Presence.* Englewood Cliffs, NJ: Prentice Hall.
Wilson, Kenneth L., and Anthony M. Orum. 1976. "Mobilizing People for Collective Action." *Journal of Political and Military Sociology* 4: 187–02.
Wilson, Susan. 1982. "A New Decade: The Gifted and Career Choice." *Vocational Guidance Quarterly* 31(1): 53–59.
Wilson, Thomas C. 1991. "Urbanism, Migration, and Tolerance: A Reassessment." *American Sociological Review* 56: 117–23.
Wilson, William Julius. 1996. *When Work Disappears: The World of the New Urban Poor.* New York: Alfred A. Knopf.
———. 1991a. "Public Policy Research and The Truly Disadvantaged." Pp. 460–81 in Christopher Jencks and Paul E. Peterson (eds)., *The Urban Underclass.* Washington. DC: Brookings Institution.
———. 1991b. "Studying Inner City Social Dislocations: The Challenge of Public Agenda Research." 1990 American Sociological Association Presidential Address. Reprinted in *American Sociological Review* 56: 1–14.
———. 1989. "The Underclass: Issues, Perspectives, and Public Policy." *The Annals of the American Academy of Political and Social Science* 501: 182–92.
———. 1987. *The Truly Disadvantaged: The Inner City, the Underclass, and Public Policy,* Chicago: University of Chicago Press.
———. 1980. *The Declining Significance of Race: Blacks and Changing American Institutions,* 2nd ed. Chicago: University of Chicago Press.
———. 1978. *The Declining Significance of Race: Blacks and Changing American Institutions.* Chicago: University of Chicago Press.
———. 1973. *Power, Racism, and Privilege.* New York: Free Press.
Wilson, William Julius, and Katherine O'Sullivan See. 1988. "Race and Ethnicity." Pp. 223–42 in Neil Smelser (ed.), *Handbook of Sociology.* Newbury Park, CA: Sage.
Wimberley, Dale W. 1990. "Investment Dependence and Alternative Explanations of Third World Mortality: A Cross National Study." *American Sociological Review* 55: 75–91.
Winch, Robert F. 1958. *Mate Selection.* New York: Harper & Row.
Wingert, Pat. 1996. "The Sum of Mediocrity: In Math, Americans Finish Way Out of the Money." *Newsweek* (December 2): 98.
Wirth, Louis. 1964. *On Cities and Social Life.* Chicago: University of Chicago Press.
———. 1938. "Urbanism as a Way of Life." *American Journal of Sociology* 44: 1–24.
Witt, Susan D. 1997. "Parental Influence on Children's Socialization to Gender Roles." *Adolescence* 32, 126: 253–60.
Witter, R. A., W. A. Stock, M. A. Okun, and M. J. Haring. 1985. "Religion and Subjective Well-Being in Adulthood: A Quantitative Synthesis." *Review of Religious Research* 26: 332–42.
Wolf, Eric R. 1982. *Europe and the People Without History.* Berkeley: University of California Press.
Wolf, Richard. 1966. "The Measurement of Environments." In Anne Anastasi (ed.), *Testing Problems in Perspective.* Washington, DC: American Council on Education.
Wolff, Edward N. 1995. *Top Heavy: A Study of the Increasing Inequality of Wealth in America.* New York: Twentieth Century Fund.
———. 1992. *The Rich Get Increasingly Richer.* Washington, DC: Economic Policy Institute.
Wolfgang, Marvin E., and Frances Ferracuti. 1981. *The Subculture of Violence.* Beverly Hills, CA: Sage.
Wolfner, Glenn D., and Richard J. Gelles. 1993. "A Profile of Violence Toward Children." *Child Abuse and Neglect: The International Journal* 17: 197–212.
Wolitski, Richard J., Ronald O. Valdiserri, Paul H. Denning, and William C. Levine. 2001. "Are We Headed for a Resurgence of the HIV Epidemic Among Men Who Have Sex With Men?" *American Journal of Public Health* 91: 883–88.

Wolkoff, Michael J. 1983. "The Nature and Property Tax Abatement Awards." *Journal of the American Planning Association* 49: 77–84.

———. 1982. "Chasing a Dream: The Use of Tax Abatements to Spur Urban Economic Development." Discussion Paper No. 8206. Public Policy Analysis Program. Rochester, NY: University of Rochester.

Women on Words and Images. 1974. "Look Jane Look. See Sex Stereotypes." Pp. 159–77 in Judith Stacey, Susan Bereaud, and Joan Daniek (eds.), *And Jill Came Tumbling After: Sexism in American Education*. New York: Dell.

Wong, Raymond Sin-Kwok. 1990. "Understanding Cross-National Variation in Occupational Mobility." *American Sociological Review* 55: 560–73.

Woodward, Kenneth L. 1989. "Religion: Searching for New Meaning about Heaven." *Newsweek* (March 27): 52–55.

Woodward, Kenneth L., E. Salholz, and J. Buckley. 1981. "The Church Versus the State." *Newsweek* (February 23): 78–79.

World Almanac. 1988. *World Almanac and Book of Facts*, 1988 ed.

World Bank. 2010. World Development Indicators. "Gross National Income Per Capita 2009, Atlas Method and PPP Purchasing." New York: Oxford University Press. http://siteresources.worldbank.org/DATASTATISTICS/Resources/GNIPC.pdf.

———. 2008. *World Development Indicators*. New York: Oxford University Press. Also available on http://www.worldbank.org.

———. 2000. *World Development Indicators*. New York: Oxford University Press. Also available on http://www.worldbank.org.

———. 1992. *World Development Report, 1992*. New York: Oxford University Press.

———. 1991. *World Development Report, 1991*. New York: Oxford University Press.

———. 1990. *World Development Report, 1990*. New York: Oxford University Press.

———. 1988. *World Development Report, 1988*. New York: Oxford University Press.

———. 1986. *World Development Report, 1986*. New York: Oxford University Press.

———. 1984. *World Development Report, 1984*. New York: Oxford University Press.

World Health Organization. 1973. *International Pilot Project in Schizophrenia*. Geneva, Switzerland: World Health Organization.

———. 1946. Constitution of the World Health Organization. New York: World Health Organization, Interim Commission.

World Resources Institute. 1996. A Guide to the Global Environment: The Urban Environment. 1. Cities and the Environment: Urban Growth Patterns. http://www.wri.org/wri/wr_96–97ud_txt2.html.

World Values Study Group. 1994. 1994 World Values Survey, 1981–1984 and 1990–1993 (Computer file). ICPSR version. Ann Arbor, MI: Institute for Social Research, Inter-university Consortium for Political and Social Research (distributor).

Worsley, Peter. 1984. *The Three Worlds: Culture & World Development*. Chicago: University of Chicago Press.

Wortman, Paul M., and Fred B. Bryant. 1985. "School Desegregation and Black Achievement; An Integrative Review." *Sociological Methods and Research* 13: 289–324.

Wright, Eric Olin. 2000. "Working-Class Power, Capitalist-Class Class Interests, and Class Compromise." *American Journal of Sociology* 105: 957–1002.

Wright, Erik Olin, and Janeen Baxter, with Gunn Elisabeth Birkelund. 1995. "The Gender Gap in Workplace Authority: A Cross-National Study." *American Sociological Review* 60: 407–35.

Wright, Richard. 1937. "The Ethics of Living Jim Crow." In Richard Wright, *Uncle Tom's Children*. New York: Harper & Row.

Wright, Sam. 1978. *Crowds and Riots: A Study in Social Organization*. Beverly Hills, CA: Sage.

Wrigley, E. A. 1969. *Population and History*. New York: McGraw-Hill.

Wu, Lawrence. 1996. "Effects of Family Instability, Income, and Income Instability on the Risk of a Premarital Birth." *American Sociological Review* 61: 386–406.

Wylie, Jeanie. 1989. *Poletown: Community Betrayed*. Urbana: University of Illinois Press.

Yabiku, Scott T., William G. Axinn, and Arland Thornton. 1999. "Family Integration and Children's Self-Esteem." *American Journal of Sociology* 104: 1494–1524.

Yamagishi, Toshio, Mary R. Gilmore, and Karen S. Cook. 1988. "Network Connections and the Distribution of Power in Exchange Networks." *American Journal of Sociology* 93: 833–51.

Yamaguchi, Kazuo. 1986. "Models for Comparing Mobility Tables: Toward Parsimony and Substance." *American Sociological Review* 52: 482–94.

Yandle, Tracy, and Dudley Burton. 1996. "Reexamining Environmental Justice: A Statistical Analysis of Historical Hazardous Waste Landfill Siting Patterns in Metropolitan Texas." *Social Science Quarterly* 77: 477–92.

Yankelovich, Daniel. 1981. *New Rules: Searching for Self-Fulfillment in a World Turned Upside Down*. New York: Random House.

———. 1974. The New Morality: A Profile of American Youth in the '70s. New York; McGraw-Hill.

Yarber, William L., and Mohammad R. Torabi. 1999. "Public Opinion From a Rural State About Condoms for HIV Protection" 1993 and 1998." *Journal of Sex Education and Therapy* 24: 56–62.

Yinger, J. Milton. 1986. "Afterword. The Research Agenda: New Directions for Desegregation Studies." Pp. 229–54 in Jeffrey Prager, Douglas Longshore, and Melvin Seeman (eds.), *School Desegregation Research: New Directions in Situational Analysis*. New York: Plenum.

———. 1982. *Countercultures: The Promise and Peril of a World Turned Upside Down*. New York; Free Press.

Yinger, John. 1995. *Closed Doors, Opportunities Lost: The Continuing Costs of Housing Segregation*. New York: Russell Sage Foundation.

Yllo, K. 1983. "Sexual Equality and Violence Against Wives in American States." *Journal of Comparative Family Studies* 14: 67–86.

Yoder, Janice D., and Patricia Aniakudo. 1997. "Outsider Within the Firehouse: Subordination and Difference in the Social Interactions of African American Women Firefighters." *Gender and Society* 11(3): 324–42.

Youniss, James. 1980. *Parents and Peers in Social Development*. Chicago: University of Chicago Press.

Yukl, G. 1981. *Leadership in Organizations*. Englewood Cliffs. NJ: Prentice Hall.

Zabin, Laurie S., Marilyn B. Hirsch, Edward A. Smith, Rosalie Streett, and Janet B. Hardy. 1986. "Adolescent Pregnancy Prevention Program: A Model for Research and Evaluation." *Journal of Adolescent Health Care* 7: 77–87.

ZAGAT. 2009. "Hard Times for Restaurants, Good Times for Diners." http://www.zagat.com/About/Index.aspx?menu=PR166 (Downloaded October 28, 2009).

Zajonc, Robert B. 1960. "The Concepts of Balance, Congruity, and Dissonance." *Public Opinion Quarterly* 24: 280–96.

Zald, Mayer N., and Robert Ash. 1966. "Social Movement Organizations: Growth, Decay, and Change." *Social Forces* 44: 321–40.

Zald, Mayer N., and John D. McCarthy (eds.). 1979. *The Dynamics of Social Movements: Resource Mobilization, Social Control, and Tactics*. Cambridge, MA: Winthrop.

———. 1975. "Organizational Intellectuals and the Criticism of Society." *Social Service Research* 49: 344–62.

Zald, Mayer N., and Burt Useem. 1987. "Movement and Countermovement Interaction: Mobilization, Tactics, and State Involvement." Pp. 247–72 in Mayer N. Zald and John D. McCarthy (eds.), *Social Movements in an Organizational Society*. New Brunswick, NJ: Transaction Books.

Zaret, David. 1996. "Petitions and the 'Invention' of Public Opinion in the English Revolution." *American Journal of Sociology* 101: 1487–1555.

Zborowski, Mark. 1969. *People in Pain*. San Francisco: Jossey-Bass.

Zedlewski, Sheila R., and Sarah Brauner. 1999. "Declines in Food Stamp and Welfare Participation: Is There a Connection? Assessing the New Federalism: Discussion Papers 99–13." Washington, DC: The Urban Institute. http://newfederalism.urban.org/pdf/discussion99-13.pdf.

Zeisel, Hans. 1976. "The Deterrent Effects of the Death Penalty: Facts v. Faith." Pp. 317–40 in P.E. Kurland (ed.) *The Supreme Court Review*. Chicago: University of Chicago Press.

Zeitlin, Irving M. 1987. *Ideology and the Development of Sociological Theory*, 3rd ed. Englewood Cliffs, NJ: Prentice Hall.

Zeitlin, Maurice. 1984. *The Civil Wars in Chile (or the bourgeois revolutions that never were)*. Princeton, NJ: Princeton University Press.

———. 1974. "Corporate Ownership and Control: The Large Corporation and the Capitalist Class." *American Journal of Sociology* 79: 1073–1119.

Zetterberg, H. 1966. "The Secret Ranking." *Journal of Marriage and the Family* 28: 136–142.

Zhang, Cui-xia. 1991. "The Relationship Between Family Life and Academic Career: A Comparison of American and Chinese College Married Women Faculty." Master's thesis, Southern Illinois University at Edwardsville.

Zhang, Cui-xia, and John E. Farley. 1995. "Gender and the Distribution of Household Work: A Comparison of Self-Reports by Female College Faculty in the United States and China." *Journal of Comparative Family Studies* 25: 195–205.

Zhao, Dingxin. 2000. "State-Society Relations and the Discourses and Activities of the 1989 Beijing Student Movement. *American Journal of Sociology* 105: 1592–1632.

Zick, A., C. Wolf, B. Küpper, E. Davidov, P. Schmidt, and W. Heitmeyer. 2008. "The Syndrome of Group-Focused Enmity: The Interrelation of Prejudices Tested with Multiple Cross-Sectional and Panel Data." *Journal of Social Issues* 64: 363–383.

Zigler, Edward, E. F. Abelson, and V. Seitz. 1973. "Motivational Factors in the Performance of Economically Disadvantaged Children on the Peabody Picture Vocabulary Test." *Child Development* 44: 294–303.

Zill, Nicholas. 1984. National survey conducted by Child Trends, Inc. Washington, DC: 1984, reported by Marilyn Adams, "Kids Aren't Broken by the Break Up." *USA Today*, p. SD.

Zillman, Dolf,, and James B. Weaver. 1999. "Effects of Prolonged Exposure to Gratuitous Media Violence on Provoked and Unprovoked Hostile Behavior." *Journal of Applied Social Psychology* 29: 145–65.

Zimbardo, Philip G. 1972. "The Pathology of Imprisonment." *Society* 9: 4–8.

Zimmerman, Don H., and Candace West. 1975. "Sex Roles, Interruptions, and Silences in Conversation." In Barrie Thorne and Nancy Henley (eds.), *Language and Sex*. New York: Newbury House.

Zimring, Franklin E., and Gordon Hawkins. 1986. *Capital Punishment and the American Agenda*. New York: Cambridge University Press.

Zola, Irving. 1972. "Medicine as an Institution of Social Control." *Sociological Review* 20: 487–504.

———. 1966. "Culture and Symptoms: An Analysis of Patients' Presenting Complaints." *American Sociological Review* 31: 615–30.

Zweigenhaft, Richard L., and G. William Domhoff. 1991. *Blacks in the White Establishment? A Study of Race and Class in America*. New Haven, CT: Yale University Press.

Zwerdling, Daniel. 1978. *Workplace Democracy*. New York: Harper & Row.

Zysman, John. 1983. *Governments, Markets and Growth: Financial Systems and the Politics of Industrial Change*. Ithaca, NY: Cornell University Press.

Index

Abdul-Rauf, Mahmoud, 52, 61
Abolitionism, 300, 489–490
Abortion debate, 387, 482
Absolute poverty, 168–169
Abstract reasoning skills, 130
Achieved status, 87, 158–159
Acting crowds, 457
Activism, 18–19, 108–109
Adaptation: trained incapacity, 277–278
Addams, Jane, 17
Adorno, Theodor, 31, 45, 189–190
Adulthood: life cycle roles, 140–142
Advertising: gender portrayal on television, 229; sexual behavior in, 136–137
Affectional role of family, 409
Affirmative action, 192, 212–217
Afghanistan, 388, 394
African Americans: attacks on culture, 203; Black churches and social change, 139–140, 145–146; decriminalizing drug use, 301; deindustrialization, 174–175; drug imprisonment, 295; Ebonics, 82; exploitation and the origins of intergroup inequality, 201–202; extended family and kinships, 400; Gates arrest, 4–5; gender roles, 222–223; gender roles and, 228; hip hop, 100, 102–105; institutional discrimination, 189; internal colonialism, 193; interracial marriage, 33, 401–402; jazz origins, 334; Jim Crow laws, 158; Los Angeles riots, 450; minorities in the U.S., 200–201; popular music as a threat, 194(box); poverty groups, 169–170; poverty rate and number of people living below poverty level in the U.S., 171(table); race and ethnicity, 187; race and wealth ownership, 159–160; racial segregation, 465, 467–468; redlining, 467–468; response to 9/11, 101(box); Slim's table survey, 43(box); sociology of sport, 112–115(box); victims of street crime, 299; voting patterns, 9–10; wealth distribution, 156; Wilson, William Julius, 210–211; women's movement, 489–490. *See also* Race
African National Congress (ANC), 198
Age: gender portrayal on television, 229
Agents of socialization, 133–140, 145–146
Agnew, Spiro, 303
Agriculture: class structure, 161; economic systems, 329; gender inequality, 242; industrialization and urbanization, 440; mechanical solidarity, 16–17; primary economic sector, 327; redistribution, 360; vagrancy laws, 294
A.H. Robins Company, 302
AIDS, 411, 418–419
Aiken, Henry, 36(box)

"Ain't I a Woman" speech, 489
Air travel, terrorism and, 292–293, 390
Airplane crash, ValuJet, 302, 304
Alaska natives, 200–201
Alienation of workers, 279–280
Alimony, 423–424
Allotment, 203
Al-Qaeda, 293, 387, 394
Alton, Illinois, 450
Altruism, 26
Amala, 120
Amalgamation, 199
American Community Survey (Census Bureau publication), 45
American culture and beliefs: gender roles, 110–111; ideal versus real culture, 108; rights of racial and ethnic groups, 110; self-fulfillment, 111–112; sexuality, 111; values and beliefs, 108
American Dental Association (ADA), 369
American Indians: internal colonialism, 193; minorities in the U.S., 200–201. *See also* Native Americans
American Medical Association (AMA), 369
American Sociological Association (ASA), 17, 19, 63
American Sociological Review, 19, 63
America's Most Wanted (television program), 229
Ancient civilizations: agricultural economies, 329; estimated populations of major world cities, A.D. 800–1600, 441(table); hunter and gatherer societies, 242, 328–329; preindustrial city, 439(box); urbanization, 439–440
Androgynous individuals: gender roles, 244
Androgynous societies, 223–225; Costs of the Male Gender Role to Men and (Women?), 246(box)
Anglo-conformity, 196
Anomie, 17, 102, 496; deviant behavior theory, 308–311, 310(table)
Anthony, Susan B., 489
Anthrax, 390(box)
Anthropology, 13
Antifeminist movement, 482
Antinuclear movements, 484
Antitrust laws, 312, 316
Antiwar movements, 249
Apartheid, 157–158, 197–198
Apathetic voters, 381
Applied sociology, 21
Arapesh people, 223
Archaeology, 13
Arena of conflict, city as, 451–452
Arranged marriages, 403
Asch, Solomon, 264
Ascribed status, 87, 89, 158–159

I-1

Asian Americans: intermediate status, 205–206; population of selected groups, 208(table); poverty rate and number of people living below poverty level in the U.S., 171(table)
Asian culture: cultural diffusion, 99–100
Assault, 298–299
Assimilation, 107; functionalist/assimilationist theories about race and ethnic relations, 195–196; Latin America, 198–199
Attitudes: critical attitude towards statistics, 46(box); family as agent of socialization, 134; interracial marriage, 33; prejudice and discrimination, 191–192; social prestige, 154. *See also* Socialization
Attractiveness: standards of, 80
Attractiveness, standards of: gender portrayal on television, 229
Australia: class systems, 158; liberal welfare states, 378
Authoritarianism, 272, 391
Authority, 366; in marriage, 405–406; organizational, 270; structured sexual inequality, 231–232
Automobile manufacturing: concentrated economy, 345–346; globalization and, 348; growth of American cities, 442–443; Korea and Taiwan, 326
Automobile sales: discrimination against minority groups, 204
Automobile workers, 271(box)
Autonomous work groups, 288
Autonomy of the secretary, 282
Aviation safety laws, 304

Baby boomers, 174
Bales, Robert, 243
Baltzell, E. Digby, 372(box)
Bangkok, Thailand, 444–445
Barber, Benjamin, 388–389(box)
Barnett, Ross, 486
Bay of Pigs invasion, 266–267
Bears, 186
Beccaria, Cesare, 296
Beer, Samuel, 498(box)
Behavior. *See* Group behavior; Human behavior; individual behavior
Belgium: economic inequality and productivity, 178(table)
Beliefs: countercultures, 105; family as agent of socialization, 134; oral traditions shaping cultural beliefs, 83; recent changes in America's, 108; resocialization, 142. *See also* Ideology; Values
Bell, Daniel, 331
Best, Joel, 46(box)
Bhopal, India, 488
Bias: social construction of reality, 66–67; telephone interviews, 38–39
Bilineal systems, 408
Bilingualism, 82
Bin Laden, Osama, 394
Binder, Amy, 194(box)
Biological basis: deviant behavior, 307–308; gender role socialization, 225–226
Bioterrorism, 390(box)
Birth control: birth control movement, 490; Dalkon Shield scandal, 302
Birth rates, 330
Birth records, 44

Black bears, 186
Black churches, 145–146
Black Panthers, 305
Black table, 206–207(box)
Blaming the victim, 170
Blasé attitude, 447
Block, Fred, 357, 361
Blood drives, 26
Blowback, 293, 394
Blumer, Herbert, 69(box)
Boas, Franz, 83
Body-type theory of deviant behavior, 307
Boom periods, 352
Bosnia, 61
Boundaries, organizational, 269
Boundary maintenance, 102, 316
Bourgeoisie, 15–16, 161, 441
BP oil disaster, 302, 312, 334–335, 489
Branch Davidians, 483
Brayer, Menachem M., 253(box)
Brazil: socioeconomic mobility, 160
Bretton Woods system, 355–357
Britain: combating terrorism, 293; socioeconomic mobility, 160. *See also* United Kingdom
Browning, Iben, 461(box)
Buffet, Warren, 166(box)
Bureaucracy: characteristics of the ideal type, 272–273; democracy and, 274; dysfunctions of, 277–280; evaluating, 276–277; globalization and work organization, 283–289; interactionist view of, 280–283; large-scale tasks, 273–274; lone minority, 283; Marx on, 274–276; middle manager, 282–283; organizational democracy versus bureaucracy, 286–287(box); Organizational Practices and Opportunities for Female Managers, 275(box); pervasiveness of, 276; professionals, 281–282; rationalization, 273; ritualism, 309; secretary, 282; state, 375
Burgess, Ernest W., 17–18
Burning river (Ohio), 487
Bus boycotts, 198
Busch Stadium, St. Louis, 449–450
Bush, George H.W., 487–488; Afghanistan, 394; comparable worth legislation, 239
Bush, George W., 489; affirmative action, 216; corporate wealth and government power, 370; increasing income gap under, 152; inheritance tax, 97; 911 response, 101(box); young voters, 109
Bust periods, 352

Calcutta, India, 444
California: imprisonment rate for drug activity, 292
Cambridge-Somerville, Youth Study, 36–37(box)
Canada: class systems, 158; collective bargaining, 165; comparable worth legislation, 239; economic inequality and productivity, 178(table); ethnic conflict, 388–389(box); homicide rate, 298; language as cultural symbol, 81–82; liberal welfare, 377–378; recycling practices, 20–21; socioeconomic mobility, 160
Cap and trade legislation, 489
Capital punishment, 296–298
Capitalist economic system, 335–337; class structure,

161; concentrated economies, 343–346; Durkheim's solidarity theory, 17; economic cycle and, 352–353; globalization and, 347–348; greed and, 340–341; how capitalist markets work, 354(fig.); individual and corporate capitalism, 336; key functions, 91(table); leading to higher crime rates, 317; Marxian thought, 15; multinational corporations, 346–347; power of the state, 373, 375; Soviet introduction of, 337; Weberian thought, 16

Carbon fuel use, 489

Careers: bureaucracies, 273

Carson, Rachel, 487

Carter, Jimmy, 270–271

Caste systems, 157–158, 197–198

Castro, Fidel, 266–267

Catholic Church: assimilation in Latin America, 199; sexual abuse, 310(box)

Cause and effect: control variables, 33; correlation of variables, 32–33; independent variables, 31; McCord's study of, 36(box); quantitative research methods, 33; single-parent homes and teen parenthood, 34–35; sociology's interest in, 27

Cement truck (urban legend), 459

Census, U.S., 45; categorizing race, 32; gay couples, 417; poverty in America, 168; U.S. metropolitan areas, 440; wealth distribution, 155–156; work experience of the poor, 170

Central American Indians, 439–440

Central Intelligence Agency (CIA), 394

CEO compensation, 152–153

Chamber of Commerce, 369

Change, forces for, 13–15

Characteristics of sociology, 4–5

Charismatic authority, 366

Charismatic cults, 482–483

Cheating, culture of, 310(box)

Chernobyl nuclear disaster, 99, 488

Cherokee tribe, 201

Chesney-Lind, Meda, 318–320(box)

Chicago School, 17–18

Chicago School sociologists, 70, 448

Chicanos, 193. *See also* Hispanic population

Child abuse, 11, 412–413

Child care: gender roles and family cohesion, 244; tax revenues funding, 176; urban underclass, 471; welfare reform, 376–377

Child support, 424

Childhood: projection, 190; social learning and prejudice, 191

Childhood and Society (Erikson), 127

Children: adults' socialization through changing roles, 142; adults' socialization through parenthood, 141; coercive organizations, 263; conflicting messages from agents of socialization, 138–139; *Damned Lies and Statistics*, 46(box); effects of divorce on, 423–424; Erikson's eight stages of life, 127; family as agent of socialization, 133–135; family of procreation, 400; feral, 120–121; fewer and none, 420–421; financial effects of divorce, 257(box); gender roles and family cohesion, 244; gender roles in schools, 227–228; gender roles in the home, 226–227; gender roles on television, 228–229; gendered power in the home, 234; human trafficking, 181(box); industrialization and child labor, 441–442; intergenerational mobility, 159; modeling behaviors, 137–138; modeling gender roles, 231; nature versus nurture, 122–123; out-of-wedlock births and poverty, 171–173; peers and gender roles, 229–230; Piaget's theory of cognitive development, 129–130; reward and punishment, 138; Sears, Maccoby, and Levin study, 36(box); selective exposure to attitudes and behaviors, 137; staying in a marriage for the sake of, 424–426; victims of street crime, 299; What the Deaf Teach the Hearing about Language and Thought, 86(box). *See also* Family; Socialization

Chile: socialist revolutions, 385–386

China: agricultural economy, 329; androgynous society, 224; capitalist shift, 338; college women faculty and household work in the United States and China, 14; foot binding, 80; gender roles, 223; global stratification, 181(box); industrialization, 339; industrialization and overurbanization, 445; Korean War resocialization of American P.O.W.s, 142–143; male dominance, 225; marriage and divorce, 404–405(box); marriage for love, 403(fig.); mixed economy, 339; modernization theory, 381–382; social revolution, 385, 484–485; socialism resulting from the overthrow of feudalism, 341–342

Chipko movement (India), 250

Chippewa tribe, 201

Choctaw tribe, 201

Choice: conflicting agents and, 139

Christianity: Western and Islamic treatment of women, 252–253(box). *See also* Religion

Chrysler Corporation, 285

Cities: suburbs as, 470–471. *See also* Urban life and society; Urbanization

Civil disobedience, 455–456

Civil Rights Act (1964), 486, 491; employment discrimination legislation, 251; gender discrimination, 52; sexual harassment, 241

Civil Rights movement, 19; conflicting agents and social change, 140; desegregation, 198; life course of, 485–487; protest movements, 480; social origins of new feminism, 249; Wilson and, 210; women's movement and, 491

Civil War, 134(box); industrialization and urbanization, 442; lynch mobs, 457

Class. *See* Socioeconomic class

Class conflict: Marxist thought, 15–16; poverty and, 177; single-parent homes and teen parenthood, 34–35

Class consciousness, 103, 165, 366

Class structure, 161

Classless communist society, 493

Clean Air Act (1990), 59–60, 488

Clean Water Act, 488

Cleavages, overlapping and cross-cutting, 105

Climate change, 334–335, 489

Clinton, Bill, 488; affirmative action, 216; gender-wage inequality legislation, 255; impeachment, 303; increasing income gap under, 152; NAFTA, 349; young voters, 109

Clubs: exchange relationships, 72; informal segregation, 206–207(box); normative organizations, 263; risky shift, 267; women's participation, 126(box)

Coalitions, 263; interest groups, 369
Cocaine use, 295
Coercive force, 367
Coercive organizations, 263
Cognitive development: Kohlberg's moral development stages, 131–132; Piaget's theory of, 129–130; social and cultural influences on, 130–131
Cognitive processes, 127, 129
Cognitive reasoning, 129–130
Cognitive-developmental theories of socialization, 127–133
Cognitive-dissonance theory, 191
Cohabitation, 416–417, 427
Cohesion: family, 242–244, 266; group, 264–266
Collective bargaining, 165
Collective behavior, 476; breakdown of social control, 453; causes of, 452–453; crowd dynamics, 453–456; earthquake hoax, 461(box); precipitating incident, 453; structural conduciveness, 453; types of, 454(table). *See also* Crowd behavior
Collective identity: relative-deprivation theory of social movements, 483–484
Collectives, household, 482
Collins, Randall, 19, 56, 73(box)
Colonialism: internal, 193
Colors, 83–84
Common sense, 5–6, 46(box)
Communal movements, 482
Communication: feral children, 120; married couples, 255–256; media as one-way method, 137; organizational flexibility, 280–281; rumors, 458–459; universal social tasks, 93
Communications technology, 484
Communism, 338–339, 342
Community: decline of, 448–449; sociology of sport, 112(box)
Comparable worth legislation, 238–239, 255
Competition: concentrated economy, 345–346; conflict theory of race relations, 192–193; culture of cheating, 310(box)
Complexity of human behavior, 9–10
Composite definition of social class, 162
Computer geeks, 100–102
Computer technology: organizational expansion, 279
Comte, Auguste, 13, 15
Concentrated economy, 343–346
Concentric zones model of population distribution, 463, 464(fig.)
Concrete operations stage, 129
Conflict: Canada's ethnic and linguistic differences, 82; conflict theory and functionalism, 60(table); former Yugoslavia, 55–56; id and superego, 126–127; Jihad versus McWorld, 388–389(box); Rocky Mountain states population growth, 492; role conflict, 88; theories and values, 27–28; unhappy marriages, 422; universal ethnic inequality and conflict, 197; urban life, 451–452; violence and, 57–58; war and revolution in industrialized economies, 330–331
Conflict theory, 52; assimilation of oppressed groups, 107; Collins, Randall, 73(box); cooperation and conflict, 61–63; culture against structure, 103–106; defined, 56–60; deviant behavior, 313, 316–318; economic cycle, 352; false consciousness, 96–98; functionalist perspective and, 60(table); gender inequality, 242(fig.); gender roles, 245; ideology, 84; key thinkers, 58–59(box), 62–63(box); Mills, C. Wright, 10, 18–19, 56; race relations, 192–195; roles of conflict, 59–60; social arrangements, 61; social change, 492–493; social structure and culture, 95–96; socialization, 144–147; sources of male power, 245; stratification, 177–178; uneven development among cities, 474–475; values debate, 63–64; yard sales, 74–75. *See also* Marx, Karl
Conflicts: outside threats to group cohesion, 265–266
Conformity, group, 264, 277–278
Congress, U.S.: affirmative action, 216; comparable worth legislation, 239; corruption in multinational corporations, 347; criminalization of marijuana, 293; NAFTA, 349; party unity, 380–381; percentage of women among U.S. senators and representatives, 232(fig.); representing corporate wealth, 369–370
Congress of Industrial Organizations (CIO), 195
Conley, Frances, 241
Consensus: assimilation, 107; cooperation and, 54–56; functionalist and conflict perspectives, 60(table); hunting and gathering societies, 328
Constitutional monarchies, 375
Constraint, morality of, 130–131
Contagion (crowd behavior), 454–455
Contagion (financial behavior), 356(fig.)
Content analysis, 45
Content of messages, 125
Control groups, 35–36, 38
Control variables, 33–35
Conventional level of moral development, 131–132
Convergence (crowd dynamic), 454–455
Cooley, Charles Horton, 18, 67, 69(box), 230
Cooperation, 54–56; functionalism and conflict theory, 61–63; Korea and Taiwan's global economy niches, 326; Piaget's morality of, 130–131
Cooperatives, worker, 286–287(box)
Co-optation of social movements, 486–487
Corporal punishment, 11
Corporate capitalism, 336
Corporate crime, 301–302, 304, 306–307, 312
Corporate elite, 166(box)
Corporate group: benefiting from policy decisions, 371–372
Corporate management, 336–337
Corporate sector: as bureaucracy, 273; CEO compensation, 152–153; congressional representation, 369–370; defining class, 161–162; structured sexual inequality, 233–234; utilitarian organizations, 263; women's underrepresentation, 231–232
Corporatist-statist welfare states, 378
Correlation: McCord's studies, 36(box); single-parent homes and teen parenthood, 34–35; of variables, 32–33
Corruption: corporate crime, 302; multinational corporations, 347; Russia, 337–338
Coser, Lewis, 62–63(box), 63
Cosmopolites, 450
Costs of the Male Gender Role to Men and (Women?), 246(box)
Countercultures, 105–106
Countermovements, 387, 482
Coup attempts: Afghanistan, 394; former Soviet Union, 480
Courtship, 403, 414

Crack cocaine, 295
Credentials, 366–367
Crime, 298–307; characteristics of criminals, 306–307; corporate, 301–302, 312; feminist criminology, 318–320(box); legalization and decriminalization of drugs, 300–301; organized, 303; policy creation, 292; political, 303, 305; poverty and, 176; state-corporate crime, 304; statistics on, 306–307; street crime, 298–299; urban underclass, 472; victimless, 299–300; white-collar, 292, 301. *See also* Deviance
Criminals, characteristics of, 306–307
Cronkite, Walter, 120
Cross-cutting cleavages, 105
Crowd behavior: cultural norms, 85; expressive crowds, 456–457; mass behavior, 458–462; panics, 458; protest behavior, 456; riots, 457–458
Crowd dynamics, 453–456
Crowding, urban, 449
Crystal, Graef, 152
Cuba: Bay of Pigs invasion, 266–267; socialism resulting from the overthrow of feudalism, 342; socialist system, 337; Spanish-American War, 202
Cuban Americans, 200, 303
Cults, 142
Cultural capital, 135
Cultural diffusion, 99–100, 109–110
Cultural influences on cognitive development, 130
Cultural integration, 93–94
Cultural lag, 99, 243
Cultural relativism, 94–95
Cultural values: blood donation, 26
Culture: arranged marriages, 403; conflict theory of culture against structure, 103–106; cultural variation in gender roles, 223–225; defining, 80–81; functionalist perspective, 90–92; ideology, 84; influencing cognitive development, 130; institutions, 90; language, 81–84; male dominance, 225; Marx on, 95–96; multiculturalism, 106–108; oral traditions shaping cultural beliefs, 83; postmodernist notion of, 334; romantic love, 403; segregation and attacks on, 202–203; shared values, 84; social anthropology, 13; social norms, 84–85; socialization, 143; standards of attractiveness, 80; structure and, 98–106; subcultural explanations of deviance, 311–313; traditional American gender roles, 221–223; universals, 92–95, 223; Western and Islamic treatment of women, 252–253(box); world-systems theory, 386–387. *See also* American culture
Current Population Survey (Census Bureau publication), 45
Cuyahoga River, 487
Cyclical change, social change and, 493–494

Dahrendorf, Ralf, 56, 58(box)
Dalkon Shield, 302
Damned Lies and Statistics (Best), 46(box)
Data archives, 44
Data sources, 44–47
Date rape, 414
Dating, 404
Davis, Kingsley, 177
Day care. *See* Child care
DDT, 487

Deaf individuals, 86(box)
Death: civil rights workers, 486; Ford Explorer tire failure, 312; panics, 458; terrorist activities, 387; ValuJet crash, 302, 304
Death records, 44
Debt, national, 354–355
Decision avoidance, 277
Decline of social movements, 487–489
The Declining Significance of Race (Wilson), 209–212
Deegan, Mary Jo, 63
Deindustrialization, 174–175, 331
Delayed gratification, 309
Delayed marriage, 415–416
Delinquency study, 37(box)
Democracy, 375; bureaucracy and, 274; globalization threatening, 351, 388–389(box); industrialization and, 330; informal organizations, 269–270; organizational democracy versus bureaucracy, 286–287(box); social movements, 480; terrorism threatening, 293; What Makes a Union Democratic?, 271(box)
Democratic National Convention: police riot, 458
Democrats: employment discrimination legislation, 251; environmental movement, 488; ideology, 379–380
Demographic transition, 441–442
Demographic transition theory, 493
Dempster-McClain, Donna, 126(box)
Denmark: blood donation, 26; economic inequality and productivity, 178(table); social inequality and productivity, 179
Denny, Reginald, 450
Dependency theory, 181(box), 351–352, 383
Dependent variables, 31, 35
Deprived groups, 451
Derived phase of panic, 458
Desegregation, 191
Deterrence, 296
Detroit, Michigan, 387, 474
Development, economic: dependency theory, 383; division of labor, 88–89; hunting and gathering economies, 328–329; modernization theory, 381–382; politics of Third World development, 381–387; postindustrial economy, 331; primate cities hindering, 445; sustainable, 351–352; uneven, 381, 473–475; world-system theory, 383–387
Development, human: nature versus nurture, 121–123. *See also* Socialization
Deviance, 292; an argument against studying, 317(box); anomie theory of, 308–311; biological and psychological theories of deviant behavior, 307–308; conflict theory of, 316–318; deterrence, 296; dysfunctions of, 316; functionalist perspective, 315–316; labeling tradition, 313–315; normalization of, 278; organizational deviance contributing to ValuJet crash, 304; rule making and, 293–295; sanctions as response to, 296; similarities between deviants and nondeviants, 313–314; sociological view of, 293–298; subcultural explanations of, 311–313. *See also* Crime
Devil worship symbol, 459
Dictatorship, 375
Differential association, 311
Diffused responsibility, 449–450

Diller, Barry, 152
Discrimination, 188; affirmative action, 213–217; caste systems, 158; employment discrimination legislation, 251; feminist movement, 247; hiring the underclass, 212; individual, 188; institutional, 188–189, 205, 214; prejudice and, 191–192; race versus class, 209; racial segregation, 465, 467–468; racial steering, 467; sexism, 221; status of American minority groups, 203–205; What Makes a Fair Footrace?, 213(box); against whites, 192
Disease: AIDS, 411; bioterrorism, 390(box); Costs of the Male Gender Role to Men and (Women?), 246(box)
Dispersed collective behavior, 454(table)
Dissent: sociology giving voice to, 22; state crime as prevention of, 305
Distress, 356(fig.)
Diversity programs, 106–108
Divine right of kings, 96–97
Division of labor, 88–89; bureaucracies, 272; China, 14; domestic, 74–75; gendered power in the home, 234–235; modern married couples, 418–419(box); roles and statuses, 89; world-system theory, 384
Divorce: black underclass, 212; causes of, 422–423; China, 404–405(box); data archives, 44; gender and the financial effects of, 257(box); gender roles and family cohesion, 244; percentage of women in the paid labor force, by marital status and presence and age of children, 234–235; predicting, 8–9; remarriage, 426–427; socialization through singlehood, 141–142; sociological imagination and, 12–13; uncoupling, 144–145(box); unemployment and, 27; in the United States, 421–422
Domestic violence, 245
Domhoff, G. William, 369–372
Dominant group: conflict theory of uneven development, 474; gender roles and, 221; segregation and attacks on culture, 202–203; terrorism by, 390(box)
Dominican Republic, 11
Downsizing, 284–285
Downwardly mobile, 451
Dramaturgical perspective of impression management, 70–71, 73(box)
Dreams, 372(box)
Drift fishing, 104(box)
Dropouts, societal, 309
Drug use and trafficking: imprisonment rate, 292; legalization and decriminalization of drugs, 300–301; organized crime, 303; victimless-crime laws, 299–300; youth gangs, 310
Du Bois, W.E.B., 18, 58(box)
Duality of structure theory, 98
Dunier, Mitchell, 43(box)
Durkheim, Emile, 16–17, 53, 55(box); anomie, 308; functionalist perspective of deviance, 315–316; market efficiency, 358–359; Parsons and, 18; society as biological organism, 92; on suicide, 30
Dyads, 263
Dysfunctions, 56; of bureaucracy, 277–280; deviance, 316; ethnocentrism, 94; gender roles, 244–245; group processes, 266–267; of inequality, 180–182

Early America: gender roles, 222

Earth Day, 488–489
Earth in the Balance (Gore), 488
Earthquakes, 461(box)
Eating disorders: looking-glass self, 125
Ebonics, 82
Ecofeminism, 250–251
Ecology, human, 462–463
Economic change: social change, 328
Economic crisis, 286, 353, 355–356
Economic cycle, 352–353
Economic dimension: cultural and social context of economic activity, 358–359; economics of urban growth, 442–443; functional specialization, 443–444; gender role dysfunctions, 244–245; influencing social arrangements, 326–327; of stratification, 153; structured sexual inequality, 233–234; uneven development among American cities, 473
Economic growth: conflict during, 62–63; primate cities, 444–445
Economic independence and divorce, 422–423
Economic sectors, 327–328
Economic sociology, 358–361
Economic structure, 95, 96(fig.)
Economic success, deviant behavior and, 308–309
Economic systems, 327–328; agricultural, 329; communism, 338–339; concentrated economy, 343–346; embedded economy, 360–361; evolutionary stages, 339(fig.); financial systems, 353–357; hunter and gatherer, 328–329; industrial economies, 329–331; mixed, 339–340; multinational corporations, 346–347; postindustrial, 331–335; social consequences of modern systems, 340–343; socialism, 337–338; socialism and capitalism, 341. *See also* Capitalist economic system
Economics, 13; Marxist thought, 15–16; Weberian thought, 16
Education: achieved status, 87; affirmative action, 213–217; college women faculty and household work in the United States and China, 14; composite definition of social class, 162; diversification of sociology, 19; family function, 408–409; functionalist perspective of stratification, 179; gender inequality, 220, 237–238; gendered income inequality, 235–236; How Emigration Created a Private School Boom, 11; institutional discrimination, 189; key functions, 91(table); latent functions, 54; median income by sex and level of education, 236(table); occupational prestige, 163; percentage of bachelor's degrees awarded to women by discipline, 228(table); percentage of women among degree recipients in selected professions, 255(fig.); postindustrial economy, 332; predictability in love and sex, 42(box); role in a postindustrial economy, 333–334; social prestige, 154; sociology in Hitler's Germany, 21–22; sociology of sport, 112–115(box); welfare reform, 376. *See also* Higher education; Schools
Edwards, Richard, 340
Efficiency: Japanese workplace innovations, 287
Ego, 126–127
Eight stages of life, 127
Eisenhower, Dwight D., 486
El Salvador, 388
Elections: American culture, 109; apathetic voters, 381; false

consciousness, 97–98; telephone polls, 38–39; voting patterns of major social groups, 381. *See also* Voting rights
Electronic media, 332–333
Elite interests: rule making, 294
Ellison, Larry, 152–153, 166(box)
Embedded economy, 360–361
Emergence of social movements, 485, 487, 489
Emergency situations: pluralistic ignorance, 450; trained incapacity, 277–278
Emergent norms, 455–456
Emigration, 11
Emotional behavior: collective behavior, 453, 454(table); Costs of the Male Gender Role to Men and (Women?), 246(box); expressive crowds, 456–457; gender roles, 221–222; terrorism as emotionally charges term, 389
Emotional support of family, 409
Employee-owned businesses, 342
Employment: affirmative action, 213–217; deindustrialization, 174–175; discrimination against minority groups, 204; gender discrimination legislation, 251; government policy and poverty, 175–176; labor force participation rates of men and women in the United States, 224(fig.); low wages and poverty, 175; percentage of women among degree recipients in selected professions, 255(fig.); poverty and, 168–169; public opinion and gender equality, 254; socialization through, 141; work experience of the poor, 170–171; work status of poor people age 16 and over, 172(fig.). *See also* Occupations; Work force
Endangered Species Act, 488
Endogamy, 401–402
Engels, Friedrich, 276
Engineering: sexual harassment, 240
Entertainment media, 332–333
Environment, social: aspects of, 92; cultural adaptation, 92; cultural lag, 99; culture against structure, 99–103; functionalist perspective, 53; socialization theories and, 128(table)
Environmental concerns: BP oil disaster, 302, 312, 334–335, 489, 489; changes in American values, 110; conflict and social change, 492; conflict theory, 59–60; ecofeminism, 250; recycling practices, 20–21
Environmental movement, 487–489
Environmental Protection Agency (EPA), 488–489
Equal Employment Opportunity Commission, U.S. (EEOC), 240–241
Equal Rights Amendment (ERA), 490
Equilibrium, 56, 60(table)
Equity markets, 355
Erie Canal, 442
Erikson, Erik, 127, 128(table)
Errors, statistical, 46(box)
Eskimos, 82–83
Esping-Anderson, Gosta, 378
Estate systems, 157–158
Ethics: moral development stages, 132
Ethnic conflict, 388–389(box)
Ethnic villagers, 450–451
Ethnicity: Americans' rights, 110; Canada's ethnic and linguistic differences, 82; functionalist/assimilationist theories, 195–196; race and, 186–187; racial and ethnic groups in the U.S., 199–200; social-area analysis and factorial ecology, 465; voting patterns, 381
Ethnocentrism, 94, 195; drift fishing, 104(box); ecofeminism, 251
Ethnomethodology, 65–67
Evaluations: of professionals, 281–282
Evolutionary change theory of social change, 493–494
Exchange mobility, 159
Exchange theory, 71–73, 73(box)
Exclusive relationships, 404–405
Executive branch, 370
Executive salaries, 152–153
Existing data sources, 44–47
Exit, 355
Exogamy, 401–402
Expansion, bureaucratic tendency toward, 279
Expedia, 152
Experimental groups, 35–36
Experiments, 35–38; conformity within groups, 264; McCord's classroom experiments, 36; quantitative research methods, 33
Expertise, 366–367
Explanation, 29, 29(fig.)
Exploitation, 112; ideological racism, 188; origins of intergroup inequality, 201–202
Expressive crowds, 456–457
Expressive leader, 270–271
Expressive occupations, 335
Extended family, 399–400

Factionalism of social movements, 487
Factorial ecology, 465
Fads, 462
Fair footrace, 213(box)
Fair Housing Act (1968), 486
Fair trade, 349
False consciousness, 96–98
Family: concerns over changes in, 398; defined, 398–399; economic function, 408; extended, 399–400; female roles, 222–223; feral children, 120; functionalist perspective of gender inequality, 243; functions of, 408–411; the future of, 431–432; gender roles and family cohesion, 242–244; gender roles and family specialization, 243; gendered power in the home, 234–235; individual capitalism, 336; as institution, 90; intergenerational mobility, 159; key functions, 91(table); linguistic relativity, 84; median income and net worth, 154, 156(fig.); memberships in, 400; natural and social experiments in housing, 36–38; nonworking poor, 170; nuclear, 400; outside threats to group cohesion, 266; preindustrial cities, 439(box); primary groups, 265(fig.); religious norms, 94; role inequality, 411–412; Sears, Maccoby, and Levin study, 36(box); single parents, 427–431; single-parent homes and poverty, 170; single-parent homes and teen parenthood, 32–34; Slim's table survey, 43(box); social-area analysis and factorial ecology, 465; socialization through, 133–135, 141; sports-career aspirations, 113; status transferral, 408; teaching gender roles, 226–227; violence within, 412–414; violent crime against, 298–299; yard sale, 74–75

Family of orientation, 400
Family of procreation, 400
Family-based organizations, Korean, 326
Farm Bureau, 369
Farnham, Christie, 134(box)
Farrakhan, Louis, 366
Fascism: A Case Study (Adorno), 31
Fashion, 453, 462
Faubus, Orval, 486
Federal Aviation Administration (FAA), 304
Federal Bureau of Investigation (FBI), 305
Federal Emergency Management Agency (FEMA), 277
Federal Housing Administration (FHA), 469
Female genital mutilation, 225
Female role, 222
The Feminine Mystique (Friedan), 490
Feminism: antifeminist movement, 482; challenging male power, 245–249; contemporary, 247–248; ecofeminism, 250–251; origins of American, 246–247; protest movements, 480; social origins, 249; social theory, 249
Feminist criminology, 318–320(box)
Feral children, 120–121
Ferraro, Geraldine, 231
Feudal systems, 158; agricultural economies, 329; defining class, 161; power and, 296; social mobility, 157; socialism resulting from the overthrow of, 341–342
Fictitious commodities, 361
Financial assets, 156
Financial crisis, 355–356
Financial systems, 353–357
Finland: economic inequality and productivity, 178(table)
Firestone-Bridgestone tires, 312
Fishing, 104(box)
Fixed-response survey questions, 39
Flexibility, bureaucratic, 280–281
Food: cultural lag, 99; ethnocentrism, 94; urban legends and rumors, 460
Food and beverage industry, gendered inequality in, 238
Food stamps, 376–377
Foot binding, 80
Force, 367
Ford Motors, 285, 312
Foreign aid, 386
Foreign investment, 386
Formal operations stage, 130
Formal organizations, 262–264, 268–269, 272–283
Formal sanctions, 296
France: antinuclear movement, 484; blood donation, 26; corporatist-statist welfare states, 378; economic inequality and productivity, 178(table); French Revolution, 498–499(box); mixed economy, 339
Fraud, 302
Free Speech Movement, 132–133
Free trade, 349–352
Freeh, Louis, 305
French and Indian War, 390(box)
French Revolution, 498–499(box)
Freud, Sigmund: key theorists on socialization and development, 128(table); nature and nurture, 125–127
Friedan, Betty, 490
Friends: socialization through, 135–136. *See also* Peers

Front-stage/back-stage behavior, 70–71
Frost Belt cities, 473
Functional specialization, 443–444
Functionalist perspective, 52; bureaucracies, 274, 276; conflict theory and, 60(table); consensus and cooperation, 54–56, 61–63; culture and social structure, 90–92, 99–103; defined, 53; deviance, 315–316; dysfunctions, 56; economic cycle, 352; equilibrium, 56; functions, 54; gender roles, 243–245; ideology, 84; interdependency, 53–54; key thinkers, 55(box), 62–63(box); modernization theory, 381–382; race and ethnic relations, 195–196; social arrangements, 61; social change, 492–493; socialization, 143–144; stratification, 177–179, 180(box); subcultures in group conflict, 105; values debate, 63–64; yard sales, 74–75. *See also* Durkheim, Emile; Merton, Robert; Parsons, Talcott
Functionalist/assimilationist theories about race and ethnic relations, 195–196
Functions, 54, 71
Funhouse mirrors, 66(box)

Game stage, 124, 128(table)
Gang activity: anomie and, 309–311; deviant labeling, 315; urban underclass, 472
Gans, Herbert, 41, 180(box)
Garage sale, 74–75
Garfinkel, Harold, 65, 67
Gates, Bill, 166(box), 331
Gates, Henry Louis, 4–5, 205
Gay marriage, 417–420
Gay population, urban, 450
Gay rights: civil union, 111; protest movements, 480
Gemeinschaft (community), 445, 447, 449
Gender: androgynous societies, 223–225; comparable worth, 238–239; conflict over American roles, 108–111; conflict theory of uneven development, 474; Durkheim's study of suicide, 30; family attitudes towards, 134–135; feminism challenging male power, 245–249; gender-role socialization, 225–230; inequality in income and job situation, 220; lone minority, 283; median income by sex and level of education, 236(table); origins of inequality, 242–243; percentage of women among statewide office holders and legislators, 232(fig.); percentage of women among U.S. senators and representatives, 232(fig.); sex and gender roles, 220–221; sexual assault, 251–252; single-parent homes and teen parenthood, 34–35; Slim's table survey, 43(box); social channeling, 146–147; socioeconomic mobility, 159–160; sources of male power, 245; structured inequality, 231–240; subcultural adaptation, 103; traditional American gender roles, 221–223; urbanization and feminist social theory, 249; victims of street crime, 299; voting patterns, 381; War on Drugs, 294–295; world-systems theory, 386–387. *See also* Feminism; Women
Gender roles, 220–221; conflict perspective, 245; Costs of the Male Gender Role to Men and (Women?), 246(box); dysfunction of, 244–245; ecofeminism, 250–251; employment discrimination legislation, 251; family specialization and cohesion, 243–244; functionalist perspective, 243–245; gay and lesbian couples,

417–418; gendered power in the home, 234–235; limitations of change for, 253; looking-glass self, 230; sexual assault, 251–252; sexual double standard, 251; sexual orientation and, 256; teaching in the home, 226–227; on television, 228–229
General Electric, 312
General Motors, 474
Generalization, 7–8
Generosity, 26
"Genie" (feral child), 120
Germ warfare, 390(box)
Germany: antinuclear movement, 484; corporatist-statist welfare states, 378; crime policy, 292; economic inequality and productivity, 178(table); market socialism, 343; terrorist activity, 388–389; totalitarianism of the Nazi state, 375; unification and capitalist system, 337–338; World War II, 21–22, 31, 375
Gesellschaft (association), 447
Glass ceiling, 223, 233
Global self-esteem, 125
Global stratification, 181
Global warming, 334–335, 489
Globalization: consequences of, 347–349, 351–352; free trade and protectionism, 349–352; postindustrial economies, 331; state socialism and, 342; work organization, 283–289; world-system theory, 383
Goal displacement, 278–279
Gold, 357
Gold Rush, 457
Google, 336(fig.)
Gorbachev, Mikhail, 337, 480
Gore, Al, 109, 488–489
Gore, Tipper, 194(box)
Governance: blood collection, 26; male dominance, 225; oligarchy in organizations, 269—270; power elite concept, 18–19; real-life application of sociology, 20–22
Government: capitalist systems, 335–336; comparable worth legislation, 239; conflict theory of uneven urban development, 474; interest group coalitions, 369; key functions, 91(table); locally owned enterprises, 342–343; medical experimentation, 367; mixed economies, 339–340; percentage of women among statewide office holders and legislators, 232(fig.); percentage of women among U.S. senators and representatives, 232(fig.); policy beneficiaries, 370–371; protest crowds, 456; protest movements, 480; South Africa's end of apartheid, 198; state crime, 303, 305; suburbanization, 468–469; Taiwanese business cooperation, 326; terrorism and, 387–389; universal social tasks, 93; utilitarian organizations, 263; women's underrepresentation, 232–233
Graham, Otis, 206–207(box)
Great Depression, 356, 361
Great Lakes, 442
Greece: blood donation, 26
Greed, capitalism and, 340–341, 360
Group behavior, 4–5; blood donation, 26; characteristics of leaders, 271–272; corporate crime, 301–302; crowds, 85; Durkheim's study of suicide, 30; exchange theory, 72; exogamy and endogamy, 401–402; funhouse mirrors, 66(box); group interests and rule making, 293; instrumental and expressive leadership, 270–271; oligarchy and democracy, 269–270; organizations, characteristics of, 268–269; social construction of reality, 66–67; Sub-Arctic survival exercise, 262; subcultures, 103, 105; terrorism, 387; Wirth on urban life, 448. *See also* Bureaucracy; Collective behavior; Conflict theory; Human behavior; Social movements; Urban life and society; individual behavior
Group conformity, 264, 277–278
Group dynamics: Coser, Lewis, 62–63(box); dysfunctional processes, 266–267; group conformity, 264; group size, 263–264; outside threats and group cohesion, 264–266; primary and secondary groups, 264; risky shift, 267
Group polarization, 267
Groupthink, 266–267
Guilds, 378
Gulf of Mexico: BP disaster, 302, 312, 489
Gun control, 381
Gun use, 298–299
Gunn, David, 387

Harlow, Harry, 121
Hart, H.L.A., 36(box)
Harvard University, 36(box), 498(box)
Hazardous substances, 367
Health and medicine: blood donation, 26; consequences of poverty, 176–177; corporate sector benefiting from policy, 371; Dalkon Shield, 302; gendered wage inequality, 237–239; government experimentation, 367; health insurance benefits, 375; key functions of health care, 91(table); male dominance, 225; marijuana laws, 294; occupational importance, 178; sexual harassment, 240–241; social change, 491; sociological application, 20; tax revenues funding, 176; women's participation in clubs, 126(box). *See also* Disease
Heterogeneity, urban, 448
Hierarchy: bureaucracies, 272; Marx on bureaucracy, 274–276; urban, 444
Higher education: career choice, 372–374(box); collective behavior, 453; courtship violence, 414; to fill empty marriage, 144(box); Free Speech Movement, 132–133; functionalist perspective of stratification, 179; sexual harassment in, 241–242; socialization through employment, 141; sociology of sport, 112–115(box); Title IX, 491; women's gender roles, 223. *See also* Education
Hill, Anita, 241
Hill, Julia "Butterfly," 488
Hinterland, 444
Hip hop, 100–102, 105
Hiring discrimination, 212, 237–238
Hirschfeld, Lawrence, 186
Hispanic population: attacks on culture, 203; bilingualism, 82; contemporary feminism, 247; deindustrialization, 174–175; discrimination against whites, 192; institutional discrimination, 189; minorities in the U.S., 200–201; poverty groups, 169–170; poverty rate and number of people living below poverty level in the U.S., 171(table); race and wealth ownership, 159–160; status of American minority groups, 203–205; suburbanization, 469–470; wealth distribution, 156

Historical development of sociology, 13–19
Historical explanations of racism, 196–197
HIV/AIDS, 411
Hobos, 309
Hochschild, Arlie, 418–419(box)
Homans, George C., 73(box), 498(box)
Homeland defense, 101(box)
Homeland Security, Office of, 277
Homelessness, 176–177, 472
Homicide rates, 298
Homogamy, 402
Homosexuals: gay and lesbian couples, 417–420; politics of, 256; social-psychological theories of discrimination, 190
Honolulu, Hawaii, 319–320(box)
Hopwood ruling, 216
Horatio Alger myth, 160–161, 165
Hormonal variations and gender roles, 225–226
Hostile takeovers, 336–337
Household collectives, 482
Household work, 234–235
Households by type, 399(fig.)
Housewife role, 222–223, 234–235
Housing, 20; American minority groups, 204; government policy and suburbanization, 469; homelessness, 472; natural and social experiments, 36–38; poverty and, 176; racial steering, 467; redlining, 467–468; urban crowding, 449
Hull-House, 17
Human behavior, 4; cognitive-dissonance theory, 191; complicating factors, 9–10; deviance and, 293; economic sociology, 358; effects of urban living, 475; feral children, 120–122; gender roles, 221; microsociology and macrosociology, 72(box); moral reasoning, 132–133; nature versus nurture, 121–123; reflexivity, 360; scientific study of, 8–9; self-study, 10; socialization through, 121; various social sciences, 12–13. *See also* Group behavior; Mass behavior; Socialization; individual behavior
Human development: gender, 225–226
Human ecology, 462–463
Human trafficking, 181(box)
Humor, 66(box)
Hungary: socioeconomic mobility, 160
Hunter and gatherer societies, 328–329; gender inequality, 242; primitive communism, 338; reciprocity, 360
Hurricane Andrew, 277
Hurricane Katrina, 277, 447(box), 489
Hypothesis, 29–30, 33
Hysteria, mass, 460, 462

Iacocca, Lee, 285
Id, 125–126
Ideal culture, 108
Ideal type bureaucracy, 272–273
Ideas: Weberian thought, 16
Ideational superstructure, 95, 96(fig.)
Identification, 138
Identity: play stage teaching, 123–124; relative-deprivation theory of social movements, 483–484; subcultures providing, 102

Ideological racism, 187–188
Ideological sexism, 221
Ideology: conflict theory, 57; cultural structures, 84; feminism as, 246; Iran-Contra case, 303, 305; liberals and conservatives, 379–380; Marx on, 95–96; shaping political systems, 395; social movements, 480; sociology of sport, 113; terrorists, 387. *See also* Values
Ignorance, pluralistic, 450
Illegitimate power, 367
Illinois: imprisonment rate for drug activity, 292
Image. *See* Self-image
Imagination. *See* Sociological imagination
Immigrants/immigration: How Emigration Created a Private School Boom, 11; immigration reform, 6; organized crime, 303; racial and ethnic groups in the U.S., 199–200; white ethnics, 206
Imperialism, 384, 386
Impersonality of bureaucracies, 273
Impression management, 70–71
Incapacity, trained, 277–278
Income, 153; achieved status, 87; composite definition of social class, 162; downsizing and outsourcing, 284; gender inequality, 225; gender roles and, 221; government policy beneficiaries, 370–371; high income as power, 367; low wages and poverty, 175; Marxist theory, 161–162; median income by sex and level of education, 236(table); median women's income as a percentage of median men's income, 235(fig.); occupational prestige, 163; poverty in America, 169; status of American minority groups, 203–204; structured sexual inequality, 234–240
Income distribution, 154–155, 215, 220
Income gap, 52; CEO compensation, 152–153
Income inequality: causes of, 236–237; contemporary feminism, 247; financial effects of divorce, 257(box); gender role dysfunctions, 245; occupational segregation, 239–240; urban underclass, 472
An Inconvenient Truth (film), 489
Independent variables, 31
India: caste systems, 157–158; dietary norms, 94; ecofeminism, 250; global stratification, 181(box)
Indian territory, 202
Indians of Central and South America, 439–440
Indigenous populations: ecofeminism, 250; preindustrial cities, 439–440
Individual behavior: blood donation, 26; exchange theory, 72; white-collar crime, 301. *See also* Group behavior
Individual capitalism, 336
Individual discrimination, 188
Individual-society interaction: microsociology and macrosociology, 72(box)
Industrial economies, 329–331
Industrialization and industrialized countries, 13; bureaucracy and, 276; capitalist systems, 336; deindustrialization, 174–175; demographic transition, 441–442; Durkheim's solidarity theory, 16–17; economics influencing social arrangements, 326–327; European and American development of sociology, 17; gender inequality, 242; income distribution, 154–155; Marxist thought, 15–16; secondary groups, 264; social movements, 480; Third World cities, 386, 445; urbanization and, 440; war and

revolution, 330–331; Weberian thought, 16; worker alienation, 279–280
Inequality, social and economic: Americans' and racial inequality, 110; an argument against studying deviance, 317(box); bureaucracy and, 276; class and socioeconomic mobility, 160; class conflict, 177; class consciousness, 165; concentrated economies, 346; conflict theory of uneven development, 474; downsizing and outsourcing, 284–285; dysfunctions of, 180–182; economic inequality and productivity, 178(table); effects of a postindustrial economy, 332–333; exploitation and the origins of intergroup inequality, 201–202; family role inequality, 411–412; family violence, 412; financial effects of divorce, 257(box); income distribution, 154–155; internal colonialism, 193; leading to higher crime rates, 317; marriage roles, 415; origins of gender inequality, 242–243; public opinion and gender inequality, 254–256; race and wealth ownership, 159–160; relative-deprivation theory of social movements, 483–484; resurgence of the women's movement, 490–491; status of American minority groups, 203–205; stratification, 89; structured sexual inequality, 231–240; theories and values, 27; universal ethnic inequality, 197; wealth distribution, 155–156. *See also* Poverty; Socioeconomic class; Stratification
Infidelity, 42(box)
Informal groups, 268–269
Informal sanctions, 296
Informal segregation, 206–207(box)
Informal structure, 280–281
Information flow: financial systems and, 353–354; as source of power, 367
Information technology: corporate capitalism, 336; tertiary economic sector, 327
Infrastructure: uneven development, 473; urban fiscal crisis leading to inadequacy of, 472
Ingroup, 264–265
Inheritance laws, 97–98; Taiwanese, 326
Inheritance patterns, 407–408
Inherited wealth, 178–179
Inland ports, 442–443
Inner city populations: escaping from the underclass, 209, 212. *See also* Urban life and society; Urbanization
Innovation, deviant behavior and, 308–309, 310(table)
Institutional discrimination, 188–189, 205, 214
Institutional sexism, 221
Institutionalization of social movements, 486–488
Institutions, 90; American institutions and their key functions, 91(table); sport as, 113
Instrumental leader, 270–271
Insurance companies: redlining, 467–468
Insurgent groups, 388–389, 391
Integration, cultural and social, 93–94. *See also* Civil Rights movement
Interaction ritual chain theory, 73(box)
Interactionism. *See* Symbolic-interactionism
Interdependency, 53–54
Interest group coalitions, 369
Intergenerational mobility, 159
Interlocking directorates, 344–345
Intermediate status groups, 205–208

Internal colonialism theory, 193
International comparisons of mobility, 160–161
International loans, 386
International Monetary Fund (IMF), 386
Internet, 406–407(box), 491–492
Internship of Japanese Americans, 207
Interpersonal relationships: urban life and, 449
Interpretation of messages, 125
Interracial marriage, 33, 110, 401–402
Intersexuality, 256–257
Interstate highway system, 469
Inter-University Consortium for Political and Social Research (ICPSR), 44
Interviews, 38–39, 41–43
Intimidation: sexual harassment as, 241
Invisible wall, 206–207(box)
Iran, 137; modernization and social change, 495–496; social revolution, 484
Iran-Contra case, 303, 305
Iraq, sanctions against, 293
Ireland, 378
Irish Catholics, 208–209
Iron law of oligarchy, 269, 286(box)
Islam: dietary norms, 94; Western and Islamic treatment of, 252–253(box)
Islamist movements, 482
Israel, 158, 389
Italian Americans: organized crime, 303
Italy: economic inequality and productivity, 178(table)

Jackson, Jesse, 366, 487
Jackson, Michael, 456–457
Japan: automobile industry, 438; economic inequality and productivity, 178(table); executive salaries, 152; gender roles, 223; homicide rate, 298; social inequality and productivity, 179–180; socioeconomic mobility, 160; stock markets, 355; work organization, 285–286
Japanese Americans: WWII internship, 207
Jargon, 102
Jazz, 334
Jewish Americans, 205–208, 207(box)
Jihad, 388–389(box)
Jim Crow system, 158, 198, 315–316, 457
Jobs: downsizing and outsourcing, 284–285; escaping from the underclass, 209, 212; gender inequality, 220; impact of social and economic change, 327; institutional discrimination, 189; postindustrial shift in, 331–332; split labor-market theory, 193–194. *See also* Employment; Work force
Johnson, Lyndon B., 19, 216
Jones, Jim, 483
Judaism: dietary norms, 94; Western and Islamic treatment of women, 252–253(box). *See also* Religion
Juvenile delinquents. *See* Youth

Kamala, 120
Kanter, Rosabeth Moss, 281
Keating, Charles, 303
Kellner, Douglas, 394
Kennedy, John F., 486
Kennedy, Ted, 370

Kennedy administration: Bay of Pigs invasion, 266–267
Kindleberger, Charles, 356
Kindleberger's simplified model of financial crises, 356(fig.)
King, Martin Luther, Jr., 132, 487
King, Rodney, 450, 453
Kinsey report, 42(box)
Kinship, 398–399
Kohlberg, Lawrence, 128(table), 131–132
Korea: automobile industry, 326, 348
Korean War, 142–143
Koresh, David, 483
Kosovo, 55–56
Ku Klux Klan, 387, 482, 487

Labeling tradition, 313–315
Labor force. *See* Globalization; Work force
Labor movement, 165, 194–195. *See also* Marx, Karl
Labor unions: class consciousness, 366; downsizing and outsourcing jobs, 284–285; gendered inequality in the workplace, 238; utilitarian organizations, 263; What Makes a Union Democratic?, 271(box)
Labor/liberal coalition, 369, 371–372
Land: agricultural economies, 329; American Indian, 202; gender inequality in ownership, 224–225; urban land use policies, 474–475
Language: computer geeks, 100; cultural diffusion, 99; culture structures, 81–84; fashions and fads in, 462; feral children, 120; jargon in subcultures, 102; linguistic relativity, 82–84; oral traditions shaping cultural beliefs, 83; segregation and attacks on culture, 203; socialization, 121; What the Deaf Teach the Hearing about Language and Thought, 86(box)
Large-scale tasks of bureaucracies, 273–274
Latent functions, 54
Latin America: assimilation, 198–199
Latino Americans. *See* Hispanic population
Laughter, 66(box)
Law: divorce, 423–424; hostility to labor, 165; moral development stages, 132; rule making, 293; sanctions as response to deviance, 296; ValuJet violation of, 304
Lawrence v. Texas, 313
Leadership: characteristics of leaders, 271–272; instrumental and expressive, 270–271; oligarchy in informal organizations, 269–270; resource-mobilization theory of social movements, 484. *See also* Governance
League of Women Voters, 490
Lebanon: insurgency, 388
Legal system: affirmative action, 216–217; black youths, 113; key functions, 91(table)
Legal-rational authority, 366
Legitimate power, 366–367
Lenders: redlining, 467–468
Lenience policy, Chinese, 143
Lenin, V.I., 384
Lenski, Gerhard, 62(box), 63
Liazos, Alexander, 317(box)
Liberal Welfare States, 377–378
Liberation theology, 482
Libya, 292, 388
Lieberman, Joseph, 208
Life expectancy, poverty and, 176–177

Life stages, Erikson's, 127
Lifestyles: American values and beliefs, 109–110; countercultures, 105; suburban, 470; urban social segregation, 463, 465, 467–468
Lifetime employment, 285–286
Lilly Ledbetter Fair Pay Act (2009), 239
Linguist-relativity theory, 83–84
Literary Digest presidential election poll (1936), 39
Lobbyists, 380–381
Localized collective behavior, 454(table)
Locally owned enterprises, 342–343
Logging industry, 488
Logos, rumors about, 459
Lone minority, 283
Long sixteenth century, 383
Longevity of marriage leading to divorce, 422
Looking-glass self, 67–68, 124–125, 230
Los Angeles riots, 450, 453
Los Angeles Times, 390(box)
Lower class, 167(box), 311–312
Lower-middle class, 167(box)
Lower-upper class, 166(box)
Lunch counter sit-ins, 486
Luxembourg: blood donation, 26
Lynch mob, 457

Maccoby, Eleanor, 36(box)
Macrosociology, 52–53; exchange theory, 71–72; functionalist-conflict overlap, 63–64; key thinkers, 62–63(box); microsociology and, 71–76. *See also* Conflict theory; Functionalist perspective
Madoff, Bernard, 292, 310(box)
Magic, 91–92
Majority groups, 205–209
Male dominance, 14, 225, 250
Male role, 221–222
Malinowski, Bronislaw, 91
Malnutrition, 176
Managerial staff: bureaucracies, 273; Japanese work organization, 285; Organizational Practices and Opportunities for Female Managers, 275(box); professionals, 282
Mandela, Nelson, 198
Mania, 356(fig.)
Manifest Destiny, 250
Manufacturing: corporate crime, 302; deindustrialization, 174–175; impact of social and economic change, 326–327; industrial economies, 329–331; mixed economies, 339–340; postindustrial decline in, 331–333; secondary economic sector, 327; worker alienation, 279–280
Mao Zedong, 483
Maquiladoras (foreign-owned factories), 348
Marijuana, 293, 300, 314
Marijuana Tax Act, 293
Marital sex, 411
Market socialism, 342–343
Marriage, 8–9; black underclass, 212; changing roles within, 415; children and, 420–421; China, 404–405(box); civil unions for gays, 111; cohabitation instead of, 416–417; college women faculty and household work in the United States and China, 14; culture of cheating,

310(box); data archives, 44; defined, 399; delayed, 415–416; division of labor, 418–419(box); Durkheim's study of suicide, 30; exogamy and endogamy, 401–402; family of procreation, 400; the future of, 431–432; gay and lesbian couples, 417–420; how couples stay together, 424(box); inheritance patterns, 407–408; interracial, 33, 110, 401–402; lack of communication, 255–256; the making of the Southern Belle, 134(box); mate selection, 401–405; meeting partners, 406–407(box); patterns of, 400–401; percentage of women in the paid labor force, by marital status and presence and age of children, 248(fig.); power and authority, 405–406; residency patterns, 406–407; Sex in America survey, 42(box); similarities in partners, 402; socialization through, 141; spouse abuse, 413–414; staying in an unhappy marriage, 422; uncoupling, 144–145(box). *See also* Divorce; Family

Marx, Karl, 15–16, 18, 58(box); on bureaucracy, 274–276; communism, 338–339; conflict perspective, 56; defining social class, 161–162; economic evolution stages, 339(fig.); ideology, 84; market efficiency, 358–359; postmodernist and, 334; power and wealth, 367; reserve army of the unemployed, 352–353; social change, 493; social structure and culture, 95–96; socialist revolutions, 385; theory of racism, 194–195; uneven development, 474–475; worker alienation, 279–280

Mass behavior, 458–462; fashions and fads, 462; mass hysteria, 460, 462; rumors, 459; urban legends, 459–460

Masses, 452

Master status, 87, 314

Masturbation, 42(box)

Material culture, 80–81

Mathematics and science education, 227–228

Matriarchy, 405–406

Matrilineal systems, 408

Matrilocality, 407

May Queen, 134(box)

McCord, Joan, 36–37(box)

McDonnell Douglas, 304

McGovern, George, 97

McWorld, 388–389(box)

Mead, George Herbert, 69; Chicago school, 18; key theorists on socialization and development, 128(table); socialization, 123–124; symbolic-interactionist theory, 69(box)

Mead, Margaret, 223, 242

Meaning, postmodernist notion of, 334

Media: conflict theory on money and power, 57; criminalization of marijuana, 293; false consciousness, 97; one-way communication, 137; oral traditions shaping cultural beliefs, 83; personal ads, 406–407(box); romantic love, 402–403; selective exposure, 142–143; sexual and violent behavior, 136–137; socialization through, 136–137; teaching gender roles, 226; terrorism and, 390; two-step flow of communications, 461(box). *See also* Television

Median family income, 154

Medieval Europe: false consciousness, 97; mass hysteria over plague, 460

Mentally ill individuals, 307–308, 472

Mercantilism, 378

Merton, Robert, 53, 55(box); anomie, 308–309

Mesomorphs, 307

Messages: conflicting, 138–140; content and interpretation, 125; sending, 69–71

Meteorology, 9

Metropolitan area, 440; which ones are growing, 446–447(box). *See also* Urban life and society; Urbanization

Metropolitan statistical area (MSA), 468

Mexican Americans, 200, 202

Mexico: assimilation, 199; globalization, 438; NAFTA, 349

Mexico City, 444

Michels, Robert, 269, 286(box)

Microsociology, 52–53; exchange theory, 71–72; macrosociology and, 71–76. *See also* Symbolic-interactionism

Microsociology-macrosociology links, 71–75, 73(box)

Middle class: Black, 113; child abuse, 413; marijuana laws, 294; shrinking of, 169; subjective class, 162–163; voting patterns, 381

Middle manager, 282–283

Military: authoritarian leadership, 272; Bay of Pigs invasion, 266–267; coercive organizations, 263; response to 9/11, 101(box); sexual harassment, 240; total institutions, 142

Miller, Walter B., 311–312

Million Man March, 366

Mills, C. Wright, 10, 18–19, 56, 368, 372(box)

Mind, Self, and Society (Mead et. al.), 18

Minoan Crete society, 242

Minority groups: affirmative action, 213–217; ideological racism, 188; intermediate status groups, 205–208; status of American groups, 203–205; United States, 200–205. *See also* African Americans; Asian Americans; Hispanic population

Missouri earthquake, 461(box)

Mixed economy, 339–340

Mobility, socioeconomic. *See* Socioeconomic mobility

Mobs: crowd dynamics, 457

Model society, 482

Modeling, 137–138

Modeling behavior: gender-role socialization, 230–231; teaching gender roles, 226

Modernization, 17; androgynous society, 224; consequences of rapid social change, 495–496; escalating social change, 495–496; Weber on, 62(box)

Modernization theory, 181(box), 381–382, 493–494

Moen, Phyllis, 126(box)

Monarchy, 375

Money and power, 57

Monkey studies, 121

Monogamy, 400

Monopolies, 344

Monopolistic capitalism, 341

Montreal, Canada, 451(fig.)

Moore, Barrington, Jr., 498(box)

Moore, Wilbert, 177

Moral behavior, 132–133; gender role development, 226; socialization theories and, 128(table)

Moral crusades, 293

Moral reasoning, 130, 132–133

Mores, 84–85

Mormons, 401
Mott, Lucretia, 489
Movies: class consciousness, 165
Moynihan, Daniel Patrick, 428–430
Moynihan Report, 428–430
Multiculturalism, 106–108, 196
Multinational corporations, 346–347, 351, 369, 384
Multiple nuclei pattern of population distribution, 463, 464(fig.)
Mundugumor people, 223
Murdock, George Peter, 93(table), 223
Music, popular, 194(box)
Mysticism, 99–100

Nader, Ralph, 110
NASA, 278
Nation of Islam, 482
National American Woman Suffrage Association, 490
National Association for the Advancement of Colored People (NAACP), 18
National Organization for Women (NOW), 491
National Rifle Association (NRA), 381
Nationalist movements, 387
Nation-states, weakening of, 351
Native Americans, 201; attacks on culture, 203; cultural pluralism, 196(fig.); disease, 390(box); gender roles, 223–224; poverty groups, 169–170. *See also* American Indians
Native people: autonomy, 82
NATO troops, 55–56
Natural disasters: earthquakes, 461(box); environmental movement and, 489; trained incapacity, 277
Natural experiments, 36–37
Natural resources: imperialism, 384; primary economic sector, 327
Natural sciences, 10
Nature versus nurture, 121–123, 128(table)
Navajo tribe, 201
Navy, U.S.: sexual harassment, 240
Nazi Germany, 31
Negotiated order, 281
Neolocality, 406
Neo-Nazis, 387
Netherlands: economic inequality and productivity, 178(table)
New Deal legislation, 375
New Guinea: androgynous society, 223
New rich, 166(box)
New York City, 442, 445, 471
New Zealand: class systems, 158; liberal welfare states, 378
Nicaraguan contras, 303, 305
Nixon, Richard, 97, 270–271, 305, 357, 488
Nomadic societies, 328
Nonmarital sex, 410–411
Nonmaterial culture, 80
Nonworking poor, 170
Norm of maximization, 340–341
Normalization of deviance, 278
Normative organizations, 262–263
Norms: collectivities developing, 469(fig.); crime and, 292; emergent, 455; informal bureaucratic structures, 280; job and career, 141; learning through socialization, 121; religious, 94; response to 9/11, 101(box); of science, 8; of subcultures, 100–102
North American Free Trade Agreement (NAFTA), 349–350
North Korea, 337
Northern Ireland: overlapping cleavages, 105
Norway: blood donation, 26; economic inequality and productivity, 178(table); empowering workers, 287–288; socioeconomic mobility, 160; urban legends, 459
Nuclear family, 400
Nuclear materials, government processing of, 305
Nuclear power, 488
Nurturance and identification, 138, 143
Nurture, 121–123

Obama, Barack: comparable worth legislation, 239; employment discrimination legislation, 251; environmental stance, 489; labor unions, 165; racial attitudes, 204; young voters, 110
Observation, 6–8; cycle of scientific inquiry, 29(fig.); field observation, 41–44; qualitative research methods, 33; theory testing, 29–30
Occupational segregation, 238–240
Occupations: achieved status, 87; bureaucracies, 273; effects of a postindustrial economy, 332–333; expressive, 335; gender roles, 220–221, 223; gender roles on television, 229; gendered wage inequality, 237; importance to society, 178; modeling gender roles, 231; occupational prestige, 163–164; percentage of women among degree recipients in selected professions, 255(fig.); public opinion and gender equality, 254; sexual harassment, 240; social prestige, 154; socioeconomic mobility, 160; stratification, 89; structured sexual inequality, 233–234; teaching gender roles, 226–227; teaching gender roles in the schools, 227. *See also* Employment; Work force
Ohio: burning river, 487
Oil industry: BP disaster, 302, 312, 334–335, 489
Oklahoma City bombing, 292, 387, 451–452
Old rich, 166(box)
Oligarchy, 269—270, 286–287(box)
Oligopolistic capitalism, 341, 345
Olympic Project for Human Rights, 112(box)
Open stratification system, 157
Open-ended survey questions, 39–40
Operational definitions of variables, 31–32
Oppressed groups: assimilation, 107
Oracle, Inc., 152
Order, negotiated, 281
Order perspective, 53
Oregon: imprisonment rate for drug activity, 292
Organization of social movements, 485–490
Organizations: characteristics of, 268–269; formal, 262–263; oligarchy, 269—270. *See also* Bureaucracy
Organized crime, 303
Origins of Crime (McCord and McCord), 37(box)
Outgroups, 264–265
Out-migration, urban, 471
Out-of-wedlock births, 171–173
Outside threats, 264–266
Outsourcing, 284–285
Overlapping cleavages, 105
Overstimulation, 447–448

Overurbanization, 444–445
Ownership of the means of production, 161
Ozone layer degradation, 488

Palestine, 389
Palfrey House, Harvard University, 36(box)
Palin, Sarah, 231
Panic (financial behavior), 356(fig.)
Panics, 458, 460
Parents: socialization through parenthood, 141; teaching gender roles, 226–227. *See also* Children; Family
Park, Robert E., 17–18, 70
Parks, Rosa, 485
Parsons, Talcott, 18, 53, 55(box), 243, 316
Participant observation, 41–44, 43(box)
Part-time employment: downsize and outsourcing jobs, 284–285; gender inequality and, 237–238
Patriarchy, 405–406
Patrilineal systems, 407–408
Patrilocality, 407
Paul, Alice, 490
Peers: causes of collective behavior, 452–453; primary groups, 265(fig.); reward and punishment, 138; socialization through, 135–136; teaching gender roles, 226, 229–230
People's Temple, 483
Peripheral countries, 385–386
Persian Gulf War, 394
Personal ads, 406–407(box)
Personal cults, 482–483
Personal dilemmas, 125–127, 128(table)
Personal interviews, 39, 42(box)
Personal space, 85
Personality: causes of social movements, 483
Peso devaluation, 349–350
Pesticides, 487
Petit bourgeoisie, 161–162
Philippines: gender roles, 223
Physical anthropology, 13
Physical environment, 92–93, 99, 130
Piaget, Jean, 128(table), 129–131
Pittsburgh, Pennsylvania, 327
Place, importance of, 136–137
Plague, 460
Play stage, 123–124, 128(table)
Pluralism, 196
Pluralistic ignorance, 450
Pluralists, 367–368
Poland: capitalist shift, 337; socioeconomic mobility, 160; Solidarity movement, 480
Polanyi, Karl, 359, 360–361
Polarization, group, 267
Police: Democratic National Convention riot, 458; formal sanctions, 296; organizational characteristics, 269; urban panic, 449–450
Political action committees (PACs), 380–381
Political crime, 303, 305
Political goals: protest crowds, 456
Political parties, 380–381; social democrats, 165; women's underrepresentation, 232–233. *See also* Democrats; Republicans
Political representation: lack of diversity, 369–370; percentage of women among statewide office holders and legislators, 232(fig.); percentage of women among U.S. senators and representatives, 232(fig.); structured sexual inequality, 231–232
Political science and thought, 13; Marxist thought, 15–16; Weberian thought, 16
Political-process theory of social movements, 484–485
Politics: affirmative action, 216–217; of being sexually different, 256–257; changes in American values, 109–110; characteristics of elected officials, 369–370; countercultures, 105; male dominance, 225; political power, 367; religious movements, 482; social movements and, 484–485; of stratification, 153–154; of Third World development, 381–387; uneven urban development, 474–475; What Makes a Union Democratic?, 271(box); world-systems theory, 386–387
Pollution. *See* Environmental concerns
Polyandry, 401
Polygamy, 401
Polygyny, 401
Ponzi scheme, Madoff's, 292, 310(box)
Popay (Native American leader), 196(fig.)
Popular culture, 165, 194(box)
Population, organization, environment, and technology (P.O.E.T) complex, 463
Population density and distribution: crowding, 449; escalating social change, 495; estimated populations of major world cities, A.D. 800–1600, 441(table); human ecology, 462–463; metro areas in the United States, 446–447(box); models of, 463, 464(fig.); percent of population in central cities, suburban areas, and outside metropolitan areas, 469(table); preindustrial cities, 439(box); prisons, 292; shantytowns, 444; urban decline, 471; western states growth, 491–492; world's largest cities, 2009, 442(table)
Port cities, 442–443
Portugal: assimilation in Latin America, 199; blood donation, 26
Positivism, 15, 65–66
Postconventional level of moral development, 132
Postindustrial economy, 132, 331–335, 362; rise of professions, 333; science and education, 333–334; technological challenges, 334–335
Postindustrialism, 468, 473
Postmodernism: terrorism and, 292
Postmodernism, ethnomethodology and, 66
Postpartum sex taboo, 54
Posttest, 35, 37–38
Poverty: absolute, 168–169; affirmative action, 214; American situation, 168–169; black and Hispanic underclass, 212; blaming the victims, 160–161; causes of, 170–176; consequences of, 176–177; defining, 167–168; drug use and, 300–301; gang activity, 310; government policy and jobs, 175–176; Herbert Gans and the functions of poverty, 180(box); homelessness, 472; innovation and deviant behavior, 308–309; low wages, 175; out-of-wedlock births and, 171–173; poverty rate and number of people living below poverty level in the U.S., 171(table); relative and absolute concepts of, 168; single-parent homes, 427–428; single-parent homes and teen parenthood, 34–35; social channeling, 146–147;

Poverty (continued): social characteristics of, 169–170; unemployment and, 174–175; urban underclass, 471–472; welfare reform, 375–377; What Makes a Fair Footrace?, 213(box); Wilson's analysis, 19. *See also* Welfare

Powder cocaine, 295

Power: agricultural economies, 329; an argument against studying deviance, 317(box); characteristics of elected officials, 369–370; concentrated economies, 346; conflict theory on money and power, 57; Costs of the Male Gender Role to Men and (Women?), 246(box); defined, 366; distribution in the U.S., 368–369; Domhoff's career path, 372(box); ecofeminism, 250; feminism challenging male power, 245–249; formal and informal sanctions against deviance, 296; gender roles and, 221; gendered occupational segregation, 238; gendered power in the home, 234–235; of group dynamics and behavior, 262; interest group coalitions, 369; legitimate, 366; male dominance, 225; in marriage, 405–406; measuring, 368; pluralist and power elite theorists, 367–368; political dimension of stratification, 153–154; public policy controversy, 371–372; rule making and deviance, 294; sexual harassment, 241; social exchange, 72–74; sources of male power, 245, 367; the state, 373, 375; structured sexual inequality, 231–235; victimless crime, 299; War on Drugs, 294–295. *See also* Politics

Power elite concept, 18–19, 166(box), 367–368

Precipitating incident, 453

Preconventional level of moral development, 131

Predatory crime, 298–299

Predictability of human behavior, 8–9, 42(box)

Prediction, 29, 29(fig.)

Preindustrial city, 439(box)

Preindustrial societies: polygamy, 401

Prejudice: discrimination and, 191–192; projection, 190; racial and ethnic, 188; scapegoats, 190; social learning, 190–191; white ethnics, 208–209

Preoperational stage, 129

Presentation of self, 70–71

Presidential elections: bureaucracy and democracy, 274; discrimination against minority groups, 205; false consciousness, 97–98; race and gender attitudes, 111; women candidates, 231

President's Science Advisory Commission, 370

Prestige. *See* Social prestige

Pretest, 35, 37–38

Primary deviance, 314

Primary economic sector, 327, 385

Primary groups, 264; informal structure and, 281

Primate cities, 444–445

Primitive communism, 338

Prisoners of war, 142–143

Prisons: coercive organizations, 263; racial bias, 295; total institutions, 142. *See also* Crime; Deviance

Private school, 11

Privatization, 335–337

Procter and Gamble corporation, 459

Production, ownership of the means of, 161

Productivity: industrial economies, 330; social inequality, 179–180

Professional occupations, 163; gendered inequality in, 238; percentage of women among degree recipients in selected professions, 255(fig.); postindustrial economy, 333; small business coalition, 369; workplace roles, 281–282

Prohibition, 294, 300, 303, 313

Projection, 190

Proletariat, 15–16, 161

Property, wives as, 245

Property crime, 298–299

Property taxes, 474

Prostitution, 299, 314

Protection, family role in, 409

Protectionism, 349–352

Protest behavior, 456; exercising power through, 367; state crime as control of, 305

Protest crowds, 457–458

Protest movements, 480; regressive movements and, 482

Protestant Reformation, 16

Protestant work ethic, 381–382

Providence (television program), 229

Psychology, 4, 12–13; deviant behavior, 307–308; nature versus nurture, 121–123

Public opinion: crime policy, 292; gender equality, 254–256

Puerto Ricans, 193, 202. *See also* Hispanic population

Punishment and reward, 138

Punishment-avoidance stage of moral development, 131

Qualitative methods, 33–35, 41–43, 45

Quality control (QC) circles, 285, 287–288

Quantitative methods, 33–35, 41, 45

Questionnaires, 38

Race: an argument against studying deviance, 317(box); ascribed status, 87; assimilation in Latin America, 198–199; census categories, 32; characteristics of criminals, 306–307; contemporary feminism, 247; criminalization of marijuana, 293–294; ethnicity and, 186–187; functionalist/assimilationist theories, 195–196; gender roles and, 228; internal colonialism theory, 193; linguistic relativity, 84; majority and minority groups, 187, 208–209; modeling gender roles, 231; popular music as a threat, 194(box); predictability in love and sex, 42(box); racial and ethnic groups in the U.S., 199–200; racial composition of census tracts, St. Louis, 466(fig.); racial segregation, 465, 467–468; redlining, 467–468; single-parent homes and poverty, 427–429; single-parent homes and teen parenthood, 34–35; Slim's table survey, 43(box); as social construction, 186; social-area analysis and factorial ecology, 465; social-psychological theories of race relations, 189–191; social-structural theories of race relations, 192–197; split labor-market theory, 193–194; suburbanization, 469–470; universal ethnic inequality, 197; voting patterns, 381; War on Drugs, 294–295; welfare reform, 377. *See also* Discrimination; Prejudice

Race mobility, 159–160

Race relations: race versus class, 209, 212; social change theories, 493

Racial caste system, 157–158

Racial groups: Americans' rights, 110

Racial steering, 467
Racism, 108; historical explanations of, 196–197; ideological, 187–188; Marxist theory, 194–195; regressive movements, 482; sociological applications, 20; symbolic, 191–192
Radcliffe-Brown, A.R., 92
Rap music, 194(box)
Rape, 251–252, 414
Rational expectations theory, 292
Rational maximizers, 360
Rationalization, 16; bureaucratic development, 273
Raw meat vendor, 358
Reactivity, 9; unobtrusive observation, 44
Reagan, Ronald, 270
Reagan administration, 487–488; comparable worth legislation, 239; Space Shuttle program, 278
Real culture, 108
Real estate: racial steering, 467
Real wages, 168–169
Reality: Sewell's duality of structure theory, 98; social construction of, 65–69
Reality television, 263
Real-life applications, 19–22
Reasoning: socialization theories, 128(table)
Reasoning skills, 130
Rebellion: deviant behavior and, 309
Rebellion, deviant behavior and, 310(table)
Recession, economic, 168, 352–353, 355–356
Reciprocity, 360
Recycling, 20
Red Cross, 26
Redistribution, 360
Redlining, 467–468
Reflexivity of human behavior, 360
Reform: Chicago School, 17; protest movements, 480; welfare, 375–377
Regents of the University of California v. Bakke, 216
Regressive movements, 480–481; temperance movement, 294
Reindeer herding, 99
Relative poverty, 168–169
Relative-deprivation theory of social movements, 483–484
Reliability: sampling procedures, 40; of variables, 32
Religion: ascribed status, 87; assimilation in Latin America, 199; Black churches, 145–146; blood collection, 26; capitalism and greed, 340–341; as coercive organization, 263; countercultures, 105; cults, 142; cultural integration, 94; divine right of kings, 96–97; Durkheim's study of suicide, 30; family as agent of socialization, 134; family function, 408–409; freedom of, 52; fundamentalism resulting from rapid social change, 495–496; Jihad versus McWorld, 388–389(box); key functions, 91(table); overlapping cleavages, 105; personal cults, 482–483; predictability in love and sex, 42(box); preindustrial city, 439(box); primary groups, 265(fig.); redistribution, 360; social movements, 482; socialization through, 135; as variable, 31; Western and Islamic treatment of women, 252–253(box)
Remarriage, 426–427
Repression: social movement emergence, 484
Reproduction, 93; birth control movement, 490

Republicans: employment discrimination legislation, 251; environmental movement, 488; ideology, 379–380
Reputational approach to measuring power, 368
Research: change over time and place, 9–10; data source use, 44–47; Domhoff's, 372–374(box); Durkheim's study of suicide, 30; experiments, 35–38; explanation versus prediction, 29; field observation, 41–44; limitations of, 6–8; quantitative and qualitative methods, 33–35; reactivity, 9; Slim's table survey, 43(box); statistical errors, 46(box); surveys, 38–40; theories and values affecting, 27–31; theory generation, 30–31; theory testing, 29–30; using and measuring variables, 31–33
Reserve army of the unemployed, 352–353
Resocialization, 142
Resource competition: conflict theory of race relations, 192–195; resource-mobilization theory of social movements, 484
Resource flow, 353–354
Resource-mobilization theory of social movements, 484
Respectability: Slim's table survey, 43(box)
Responsibility, self-fulfillment and, 112
Resurgence of social movements, 489–490
Retreatism, deviant behavior and, 309, 310(table)
Revolt of the Black Athlete, 112(box)
Revolutionary movements, 480
Reward and punishment, 138, 142–143
Rio de Janeiro, Brazil, 309(fig.)
Riots: cities and social conflict, 451–452; crowd dynamics, 457–458
Risk factors: divorce, 12–13; predictability of human behavior, 8–9
Risk-taking behavior, 357; group and individual behavior, 262
Risky shift, 267
Ritualism, 279; deviant behavior and, 309, 310(table)
A.H. Robins Company, 302
Rock music, 99
Rocky Mountain region, 491–492
Role assignment, 93
Role change, 142
Role conflict, 88, 138–140
Role strain, 88
Roles: of conflict, 59–60; conflict over American gender roles, 110–111; marriage, 415; sex and gender roles, 220–221; social, 87–88; statuses and, 89–90; subcultural adaptation, 103; traditional American gender roles, 221–223. *See also* Gender roles
Roman Empire, 329, 439–440
Romantic love, 402–403, 404–405(box)
Rome, ancient, 120
Romulus and Remus, 120
Roosevelt, Franklin, 270
Roughnecks (gang), 315
Ruby Ridge, Idaho, 305
Rule making, 293–296
Rules and regulations: bureaucracies, 273; normalization of deviance, 278; Organizational Practices and Opportunities for Female Managers, 275(box); ritualism, 279
Ruling class: divine right of kings, 97; economic structure and ideational superstructure, 96(fig.); Marxist class system, 161

Rumors, 452, 458–460
Rural life, 445, 447
Russia: capitalist shift, 337–338; industrialization, 339; male dominance, 225; modernization theory, 381–382; socialist revolution, 385–386; terrorism, 391

SabreTech, 304
Sacks, Oliver, 86(box)
St. Louis, Missouri, 367, 449–450, 466(fig.), 467, 471
Saints (gang), 315
Sami population (Lapland), 82–83
Sampling, statistical, 40; Sex in America survey, 42(box)
Sanctions, 84; formal and informal, 296; "promiscuity" of Hawaiian girls, 319–320(box)
Sanger, Margaret, 490
Sanitation systems, 178
São Paulo, Brazil, 444
Saudi Arabia, 375
Savelsberg, Joachim, 292
Savings-and-loan fraud, 302–303
Scandinavia: male dominance, 225; Social Democratic welfare states, 378–379; workplace innovations, 287–288
Scapegoats, 190
Schemas, 98, 129
Schools: information segregation, 206–207(box); the making of the Southern Belle, 134(box); primary groups, 265(fig.); segregation and attacks on culture, 203; socialization through, 135; teaching gender roles, 227–228. *See also* Education; Higher education
Science: human behavior study, 8–9; postmodernist challenges, 334–335; President's Science Advisory Commission, 370; role in a postindustrial economy, 333–334; sociology as, 6–8
Scientific method: cycle of scientific inquiry, 29(fig.); Durkheim's application to human social behavior, 16–17; positivism, 15. *See also* Research
Search and seizure, 299
Sears, Maccoby, and Levin study, 36(box)
Seattle, battle in, 109, 349, 456
The Second Shift (Hochschild), 418–419(box)
Secondary deviance, 314
Secondary economic sector, 327
Secondary groups, 264, 448
Secretary, 282
Sectoral model of population distribution, 463, 464(fig.)
Sects, religious, 482
Seeing Voices (Sacks), 86(box)
Segregation, 189; attacks on culture, 202–203; concentrating the urban underclass, 471; functionalist/assimilationist theories, 195–196; informal, 206–207(box); occupational, 238–240; racial, 465, 467–468; social change, 480; social-area analysis and factorial ecology, 465; urban social segregation, 463, 465, 467–468; U.S. and South Africa, 197–198. *See also* Civil Rights movement
Selective exposure, 137, 142–143
Self, construction of: achieved and ascribed statuses, 87(fig.); Kohlberg's moral development stages, 131–132; looking-glass self, 67–68; sending messages as presentation of, 69–71; subjective class, 162–163
Self-esteem, 125

Self-fulfilling prophecy, 68, 314
Self-fulfillment, 111–112
Self-image: deviant status and, 309(fig.); gender portrayal on television, 229; looking-glass self, 67–68, 230; out-of-wedlock births and poverty, 171–172; socialization, 123
Self-interest, 56–57, 358, 402
Self-perpetuation, 278–279
Self-regulating market, 359–360
Self-study, 10
Senate subcommittees, 278–279
Sending messages, 69–71
Seneca Falls, New York convention, 246–247, 489
Sensorimotor stage, 129
Separatist movements, 387
September 11, 2001, 394, 459; response to, 101(box); subculture emerging from, 100
Serial monogamy, 400
Service economy, 331, 332(fig.)
Service-sector jobs, 163–164, 171; deindustrialization, 174–175; gendered inequality, 238–239; value of, 178
Sewell, William, 98
Sex in America survey research, 42(box)
Sexism, 221, 480, 491; China's androgynous society, 224; social-psychological theories of, 190
Sexual abuse of children, 413
Sexual assault, 251–252
Sexual behavior, family role in regulating, 409–410
Sexual double standard, 251
Sexual harassment, 240–241
Sexual orientation: intersexuality and the politics of being different, 256–257. *See also Entries beginning with Gay*; Homosexuals
Sexuality: American beliefs and values, 111; female genital mutilation, 225; feminist criminology, 319–320(box); marital sex, 411; media socialization, 136–137; out-of-wedlock births and poverty, 171–173; postpartum sex taboo, 54; sexual double standard, 251; universal rules governing reproduction and interaction, 93
Shantytowns, 309(fig.), 444
Shared values, 84
Shipping, 442
Siblings, 134
Sign language, 86(box), 120
Significant others, 123–125
Silent Spring (Carson), 487
Silicon Valley, California, 326
Simmel, Georg, 447–448, 475
Simpson, O.J., 205
Singh, J.A.L., 120
Single parents, 376, 427–431
Singlehood, 141–142, 415–416
Single-person households, 416
Singles life, 450
Sioux tribe, 201
Sit-ins, 455, 486
Skepticism, organized, 8
Ski clubs, 267
Skin color, 186
Skinhead groups, 387
Slavery, 181(box), 199, 201–202
Slim's Table, 43(box)

Small business coalition, 369, 371
Small businesses: Taiwan, 326
Smallpox, 390(box)
Smith, Adam, 378
Snow, 83–84
Social anthropology, 13, 91
Social arrangements: conflict theory and functionalism, 60(table), 61; Taiwan and Korea, 326
Social bonds: Slim's table survey, 43(box)
Social change, 491–492; agents of, 145–146; conflict and, 60; economic change and, 328; equilibrium and conflict theories of, 492–493; evolutionary change theory, 493–494; social movements, 480; theories of, 494(fig.); Tilly's research, 498–499(box); urbanization and, 440–441
Social channeling, 146–147
Social class. *See* Socioeconomic class
Social construction: gender roles, 242; race, 186
Social contracts, 132
Social control, 295–296; breakdown of, 453; deviance and, 316
Social Democratic welfare states, 378–379
Social dynamics, 15
Social environment, 92
Social equality in industrial economies, 330
Social expectations, 125–127
Social experiments, 37–38
Social group, 262. *See also* Group behavior
Social influences: on cognitive development, 130
Social institutions: protest movements, 480
Social learning, 190–191
Social movements: causes of, 483–484; communal movements, 482; environmental movement, 487–489; Free Speech Movement, 132–133; life course of, 485–491; necessary conditions for, 485; personal cults, 482–483; protest movements, 480; regressive movements, 480–481; religious movements, 482; temperance movement, 294; women's movement, 489–491. *See also* Civil Rights movement
Social networking: communication, 137
Social norms, 84–85
Social prestige, 154; composite definition of social class, 162; occupational prestige, 163–164
Social psychology, 13, 18, 53
Social reality: microsociology and macrosociology, 72(box)
Social roles, 68–69; adult socialization through changing, 142; game stage of socialization, 124; learning through socialization, 121; life cycle roles, 140–142; multiple, 126(box); Piaget's concrete operations stage, 129
Social sciences, 4; economics, 13; political science, 13; psychology, 12–13; self-study, 10; sociology as, 8–9; value neutrality, 16; values influencing research, 28
Social segregation, 463, 465, 467–468. *See also* Segregation
Social services: urban fiscal crisis, 472
Social statics, 13, 15
Social status, 86–87; achieved, 87, 158–159; ascribed, 87, 158–159; roles and, 89–90; social-area analysis and factorial ecology, 465; stratification, 153. *See also* Socioeconomic class
Social structure: cultural relativism, 94–95; culture, 90–92, 98–106; defined, 85–86; division of labor, 88–89;
ethnocentrism, 94; false consciousness, 97; institutions, 90; Marx on, 95–96; roles, 87–88; social status, 86–87; stratification, 89; universal social tasks, 92–95; universals, 92–95; women's subordinate position, 80
Social theory, feminist, 249
Social upheaval, feminism and, 249
Social-area analysis, 465
Social-democratic parties, 165
Socialist bureaucracy, 286–287(box)
Socialist economy, 337–338, 341, 394
Socialist revolution, 385–386
Socialization, 93; agents of, 133–140; becoming human, 121; cognitive-developmental theories, 127–133; conflict theory, 144–147; conflicting agents and choice, 139; conflicting agents and social change, 139–140; conflicting messages, 138–140; family, 133–135, 409; feral children, 120–122; functionalist perspective, 143–144; gender roles, 222(fig.), 225–230; interactionist theories, 123–125; key theorists, 128(table); life cycle roles, 140–142; looking-glass self, 124–125; the making of the Southern Belle, 134(box); marriage and family, 141; Mead on, 123–124; media, 136–137; nature versus nurture, 121–123; nurturance and identification, 138; ordinary and total institutions, 143; peers, 135–136; Piaget's theory of cognitive development, 129–130; processes, 137–138; religion, 135; resocialization in total institutions, 142–143; reward and punishment, 138; schools, 135; self-esteem and significant others, 125; social control, 295–296; through singlehood, 141–142; uncoupling, 144–145(box)
Social-psychological theories of race relations, 189–191
Social-structural theories of race relations, 192–197
Societal factors/individual factors: blood collection, 26
Societal organization, race and, 210–211
Socioeconomic class: American social classes today, 166–167(box); class consciousness in the United States, 165; class systems, 158–160; composite definition, 162; crime statistics, 306–307; cultural capital, 135; exchange mobility, 159; Kohlberg's bias in moral development, 132; low-income neighborhood studies, 41; Marxian definition of, 161–162; media socialization, 136–137; overlapping cleavages, 105; race versus, 209, 212; Slim's table survey, 43(box); socioeconomic mobility, 159–160; status transferral, 408; subcultural explanations of deviance, 311–313; subjective definition, 162–163; tax legislation, 370–371; victims of street crime, 299; voting patterns, 381; world-systems theory, 386–387. *See also* Class conflict
Socioeconomic mobility, 156–161; black and Hispanic underclass, 212; international comparisons of, 160–161; urban underclass, 472
Sociological imagination, 10–12, 19; college women faculty and household work in the United States and China, 14; importance of, 21–22
Sociology: characteristics of, 4–5; common sense and, 5–6; emergence and development, 13–19; as a science, 6–8
Sodomy laws, 313
Solidarity: functionalist perspective of socialization, 143–144; mechanical and organic, 16–17
Solidarity movement, 480
Sorokin, Pitirim, 498(box)

Sorting Out Cause-Effect Relationships: Single-Parent Homes and Teenage Parenthood, 32–34
South Africa, 157–158, 195–198
South American Indians, 439–440
Southern Belle, making of the, 134(box)
Soviet Union, former: bureaucracy and the collapse of, 276; communism, 338–339; lack of consensus, 54–56; male dominance, 225; social movements, 480; socialism resulting from the overthrow of feudalism, 341–342; socialist economy, 337; structural strain, 483; terrorism, 391
Space Shuttle program, 278
Spanish-American War, 202
Special interest groups, 380–381
Specialization: family, 243; functional, 443–444; hunter and gatherer societies, 328; Marx on bureaucracy, 276; organizational, 270
Speculation, 356
Split labor-market theory, 193–194
Sport: religious freedom, 52; sociology of, 112–115(box)
Spouse abuse, 413–414
Squatter settlements, 444
Stability, forces for, 13–15
Standard of living, 177–178, 330, 341, 350, 381, 423–424
Standardized tests, 215
Stanford University: sexual harassment, 241
Stanton, Elizabeth Cady, 489
State, the, 373, 375
State crime, 303, 305
State-corporate crime, 304
Status. *See* Social status; Socioeconomic mobility
Status group, 262
Status transferral, 408
Stealing, 295, 314
Steering, racial, 467
Stereotypes, 188, 191; drug policy, 292; gender roles on television, 229; intermediate status groups, 208; urban heterogeneity, 448
Stewart, Martha, 310(box)
Stock markets, 355
Stockholders, 336–337
Stone, Lucy, 489–490
Strain, structural, 483, 485
Stratification, 89; caste systems, 157–158; class systems, 158–160; conflict perspective, 177–178; dimensions of, 153; economic dimension, 153; feudal systems, 158; functionalist perspective, 177–179; global, 181; Herbert Gans and the functions of poverty, 180(box); hunter and gatherer life, 242; income distribution, 154–155; open stratification system, 157; political dimension, 153–154; postindustrial economy, 332–333; poverty, 167–177; preindustrial city, 439(box); social prestige, 154; socioeconomic mobility, 156–161; wealth distribution, 155–156; world-system theory of development, 384–385. *See also* Gender
Streaking fad, 458
Street crime, 298–300, 306
Stress: adult socialization through changing social roles, 142; conflicting agents, 138–140
Structural conduciveness, 453
Structural mobility, 159, 166

Structural strain, 483, 485
Structure: conflict theory of culture against structure, 103–106; culture against, 99–103
Student Nonviolent Coordinating Committee (SNCC), 486
Student protest, 249, 286(box); collective crowd behavior, 454; conflicting agents and social change, 139; crowd dynamics, 455
Sub-Arctic Survival exercise, 262
Subcultures, 100–102; as adaptation, 102–103; countercultures, 105–106; drift fishing, 104(box); explanations of deviance, 311–313; group conflict, 103, 105; hip hop, 100–102; jargon, 102; providing identity in mass society, 102; in the workplace, 141
Subject channeling in the schools, 227–228
Subjective class, 162–163
Subjectivity: sexual harassment, 241
Subordinate class: economic structure and ideational superstructure, 96(fig.); false consciousness, 96–98; Marxist theory, 161–162
Subsistence level production, 328–329
Suburban communities, 451, 468–471; American minority groups, 204; population shifts, 476
Suburbanites, 451
Suffrage: black, 486; women's, 490
Suicide: Durkheim's study of, 30; personal cults, 483
Sun Belt cities, 473
Superego, 125–126
Superstructures, 95
Supreme Court, U.S.: affirmative action, 219; comparable worth legislation, 239; desegregation, 198; forbidding racial discrimination and segregation, 486; search and seizure, 299; sexual harassment case, 241; sodomy laws, 313
Surplus, 328–329
Survey of Consumer Finance (SCF), 156
Surveys: quantitative research methods, 33; research methods, 38–40; Sex in America, 42(box)
Survival exercise, 262
Sustainable development, 351–352
Sutherland, Edwin, 311
Sweden: economic inequality and productivity, 178(table); empowering workers, 287–288; mixed economy, 339; Social Democratic welfare states, 379; social norms, 85; socioeconomic mobility, 160
Switzerland: economic inequality and productivity, 178(table)
Symbolic racism, 191–192
Symbolic-interactionism, 18, 52; bureaucracy, 280–283; class consciousness, 103; defined, 64; ethnomethodology, 65–67; gender-role socialization, 225–230; interpreting situations and messages, 65; key thinkers, 69(box); looking-glass self, 67; self-fulfilling prophecy, 68; sending messages, 69–71; social construction of reality, 65–69; social roles, 68–69; socialization theories, 123–125; yard sales, 74–75
Symbols: language as cultural symbol, 81–82
Systems theory, 53

Tables, data, 45–47
Tabula rasa (blank slate), 123
Tailhook Convention, 240
Taiwan, 326
Taliban regime, 252(box), 293, 389(box)

Tax revenue and legislation: beneficiaries of, 370–371; conflict theory of uneven urban development, 474; income and wealth gaps, 152; social services, 176

Tea Party movement, 456, 482

Technological environment, 92, 99

Technology: computer geeks, 100–102; economic systems and social arrangements, 326; escalating social change, 494–495; functionalist perspective, 53; globalization and, 347–348; industrial economies, 329–331; modernization theory, 383; occupational prestige, 163; organizational expansion, 279; postindustrial economy, 334–335; resource-mobilization theory of social movements, 484; survey research, 38–40; tertiary economic sector, 327; western states growth, 491–492

Teen pregnancy/teen parents, 34–35, 141, 171–173, 376

Telephone interviews, 38–39

Television: reality television, 263; sexual and violent behavior in, 136–137; teaching gender roles, 228–229

Temperance movement, 294, 313

10 percent solution, 216

Teotihuacan, 440(fig.)

Terrorism, 387–395; blowback, 394; causes of, 292; combating, 292–293; historical context, 390(box); against intermediate Muslim and Middle Eastern Americans, 208; Jihad versus McWorld, 388–389(box); response to 9/11, 101(box); vulnerable groups, 391

Tertiary economic sector, 327, 331

Thailand: gender roles, 223

"The Social Context of Recycling," 20–21

"The War of the Worlds," 460, 462

Theories, 8; explanation versus prediction, 29; quantitative research methods, 33; research and, 28–31; values and, 27–28

Theory generation, 30–31; field observation, 40–41

Theory testing, 29–30

Therapeutic technique, 67

Third World: conflict theory of uneven development, 474; economic systems, 330–331; politics of development, 381–387; socialist revolutions, 385–386; urbanization, 444–445

Thomas, Clarence, 241

Thought, 86(box)

Tiananmen Square, 385, 485

Tilly, Charles, 498–500(box)

Title IX, 491

Toennies, Ferdinand, 445, 447, 475

Tokyo, Japan, 445

Tolerance in the city, 451

Total institutions, 142–143

Totem pole, 497(fig.)

Touraine, Alain, 331

Tourism, 390

Toys and play: teaching gender roles, 226–227

Traditional authority, 366

Trained incapacity, 277–278

Triads, 263

Tribalism, 388–389(box)

Trobriand Islanders, 91–92

The Truly Disadvantaged (Wilson), 211

Truth, Sojourner, 489–490

Tuberculosis, 278–279

Tucker, Jim Guy, 302

2 Live Crew, 194(box)

Two-step flow of communications, 461(box)

Typographers' union, 271(box)

Uncoupling, 144–145(box)

Underclass, 209; urban groups, 451, 471–472; Wilson's view of, 210–211

Unemployment: cause and effect, 27; deindustrialization, 174–175; economic cycle, 352–353; feminist criminology, 318; poverty and, 174–175; status of American minority groups, 204; underclass, 212; urban underclass, 471–472

Uneven development, 381, 473–475

Union Carbide chemical explosion, 488

Unions. *See* Labor unions

United Kingdom: economic inequality and productivity, 178(table); mixed economy, 339; monarchy, 375; overlapping cleavages, 105

Universal ethical principles, 132

Universal ethnic inequality and conflict, 197

Universalism: bureaucracies, 273

Universals, cultural and structural, 92–95; gender roles, 223

University of California at Berkeley, 132–133, 216

University of Chicago, 17–18

Unobtrusive observation, 44

Upper-middle class, 166(box)

Urban legends, 459–460

Urban life and society, 438; causes of collective behavior, 452–453; conflict theory of uneven development, 474–475; cosmopolites, 450; crowding, 449; decline of community, 448–449; deprived, trapped, and downwardly mobile, 451; diffused responsibility, 449–450; ethnic villagers, 450–451; fiscal crisis, 472; gang activity, 310–311; human ecology, 462–463; interpersonal relationships, 449; models of population distribution, 463; pluralistic ignorance, 450; population decline, 471; preindustrial city, 439(box); racial segregation, 465, 467–468; rural life and, 445, 447; social segregation, 463, 465, 467–468; social-area analysis and factorial ecology, 465; suburbanization, 451, 468–471; tolerance, 451; underclass, 471–472; uneven development, 473–475; Wirth on, 448

Urban social ecology, 462–463

Urban social segregation, 463, 465, 467–468

Urban villages, 450–451

Urbanization, 13, 438–439; Chicago School, 17; class structure, 161; criminalization of marijuana, 293–294; demographic transition, 441–442; economics of urban growth, 442–443; emergence of the Civil Rights movement, 485; estimated populations of major world cities, A.D. 800–1600, 441(table); feminist social theory, 249; functional specialization, 443–444; large-scale, 438–440; period of emergence of major U.S. urban centers, 443(table); social change and, 440–441; in the Third World, 444–445; urban hierarchy, 444

Uruk, 439(box)

USA Today, 305

Utilitarian organizations, 263

Vagrancy laws, 294

Validity: of variables, 32
Valois Cafeteria, Chicago, Illinois, 43(box)
Values: conflict theory and functionalism, 57, 60(table), 63–64; countercultures, 105; cultural and social context of economic activity, 358–359; fashions and fads reflecting, 462; group cohesion and, 264–265; recent changes in America's, 108; resocialization, 142; shared, 84; of subcultures, 100–102; theories and, 27–28; value neutrality, 16, 18; Weberian thought, 16
ValuJet crash, 302, 304
Variables, using and measuring, 31–33
Vaughan, Diane, 144–145(box), 278
Veil, wearing the, 252–253(box)
Veterans Administration (VA), 469
Victimless crime, 299–300
Victorian era: sexual double standard, 251
Vietnam: socialist revolution, 385; socialist system, 337
Vietnam War, 19, 108, 139, 367, 455–456
Vincennes warship, 262
Violence: an argument against studying deviance, 317(box); collective behavior in crowds, 454; conflict and, 57–58; Costs of the Male Gender Role to Men and (Women?), 246(box); courtship, 414; domestic, 245, 412–414; informal sanctions, 296; against intermediate status groups, 208; media socialization, 136–137; popular music as a threat, 194(box); riots, 457–458; sexual assault, 251–252; sexual orientation and, 257; South Africa, 198; subculture of, 312; theories and values in research, 28; universal social tasks, 93; urban conflict, 451–452
Violent crime, 298–299
Visual language, 86(box)
Voluntary immigration, 206–207
Voluntary organizations, 262–263
Voluntary social roles, 126(box)
Voter turnout, 9–10
Voting patterns of major social groups, 381
Voting rights, 147; for Blacks, 486; discrimination against minority groups, 205; institutional discrimination, 189; traditional American gender roles, 222; voting as power, 367; for women, 490
Voting Rights Act (1965), 486

Wages: concentrated economies, 346; downsizing and outsourcing, 284; Japanese, 285. *See also* Income
War on Drugs, 294–295
War on Poverty, 19
Warner, W. Lloyd, 162
Watergate burglary, 305
Wealth, 153; composite definition of social class, 162; corporate elite, 166(box); distribution in the United States, 155–156; government policy beneficiaries, 370–371; income distribution in the United States, 154–155; inheritance patterns, 407–408; inherited, 178–179; Marxist theory, 161–162; as power, 367
Weapons, 330
Weather, study of, 9
Weaver, Randy, 305
Weber, Max, 16, 62(box); capitalism and greed, 340–341; conflict theory and functionalism, 63; ideal-type bureaucracy, 272–273; market efficiency, 358–359; postmodernist and, 334; power and politics, 366; power and wealth, 367; the state, 373; stratification dimensions, 162; worker alienation, 279–280
Welfare: corporatist-statist welfare states, 378; evaluating different approaches, 378–379; liberal welfare states, 377–378; reforms, 375–377; social democratic welfare states, 378–379
Welfare hotels, 472
Welles, Orson, 460, 462
Wells, H.G., 460, 462
What Makes a Fair Footrace?, 213(box)
What the Deaf Teach the Hearing about Language and Thought, 86(box)
When Work Disappears: The World of the New Urban Poor (Wilson), 211
Whistleblowers, 287(box)
White ethnics, 206, 208–209
White-collar crime, 292, 301, 306–307
Whites: discrimination against, 192; South African caste system, 198; split labor-market theory, 193–194
Whyte, William F., 41–42
Widows, 427
Will, George, 194(box)
Williams, Robin, 126(box)
Wilmington, Delaware, 498–499(box)
Wilson, William Julius, 19, 209–212
Wing County, Washington, 306
Wiretapping, 305
Wirth, Louis, 17–18, 448, 475
Wolves, children raised by, 120
Women: adults' socialization through parenthood, 141; affirmative action, 213–217; blood donation, 26; causes of income inequality, 236–237; college women faculty and household work in the United States and China, 14; economic independence and divorce, 422–423; effects of divorce on, 423–424; feminist criminology, 318–320(box); financial effects of divorce, 257(box); Kohlberg's bias in moral development, 132; the making of the Southern Belle, 134(box); median women's income as a percentage of median men's income, 235(fig.); multiple social roles, 126(box); nonmarital sex, 410–411; nonworking poor, 170; Organizational Practices and Opportunities for Female Managers, 275(box); out-of-wedlock births and poverty, 171–173; percentage of bachelor's degrees awarded to women by discipline, 228(table); percentage of women in the paid labor force, by marital status and presence and age of children, 248(fig.); polyandry, 401; postpartum sex taboo, 54; response to 9/11, 101(box); sexual harassment, 240–241; single-parent homes and poverty, 170; standards of attractiveness, 80; Western and Islamic treatment of, 252–253(box); women of color and contemporary feminism, 247, 249. *See also* Feminism; Gender
Women's movement: Civil Rights movement and, 491; life cycle of, 489–491
Work force: alienation of, 279–280; contemporary feminism, 247; effects of postindustrial economy, 332–333; gender roles and family cohesion, 244; gendered hiring patterns, 237–238; gendered power in the home, 234–235; globalization and, 283–289; Marxist thought,

15–16; Organizational Practices and Opportunities for Female Managers, 275(box); percentage of women in the paid labor force, by marital status and presence and age of children, 248(fig.); sexual harassment, 240–241; structured sexual inequality, 233–234; welfare reform, 376–377. *See also* Bureaucracy; Employment; Income; Occupations

Work organization: globalization and, 283–289; Japanese, 285–286

Work teams, 288

Worker cooperatives, 286–287(box)

Working class: American class system, 167(box); contemporary feminism, 247; ethnic villagers, 450–451; gender roles, 222–223; income inequality, 152–153; inheritance tax, 97–98; occupational prestige, 163–164; subjective class, 162–163

Working Women's Institute, 240–241

Workplace roles: organizational democracy versus bureaucracy, 286–287(box); preindustrial cities, 439(box); professionals, 281–282; Scandinavian innovations, 287–288; United States, 288. *See also* Bureaucracy

World systems theory, 181(box), 351–352, 383–387

World Trade Center, 452, 459

World Trade Organization (WTO), 109, 349, 456

World War II, 207, 330, 388–389

Yankee City, 162

Yard sale, 74–75

Y2K scare, 460

Youth: changes in American values, 109–110; countercultures, 105–106; feminist criminology, 318; lower-class culture and crime, 311–312

Yugoslavia, former, 54–56

Zhang, Cui-xia, 14

Zimbabwe: mixed economy, 339